D0169834

Argentina

Danny Palmerlee

Sandra Bao, Andrew Dean Nystrom, Lucas Vidgen

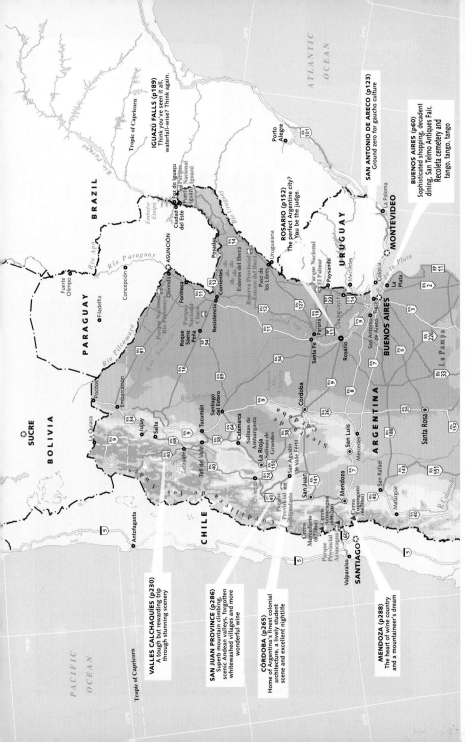

IGUAZÚ FALLS (p189)
Think you've seen it all,
waterfall-wise? Think again.

SAN ANTONIO DE ARECO (p123)
Ground zero for gaucho culture

ROSARIO (p152)
The perfect Argentine city?
You be the judge.

BUENOS AIRES (p60)
Sophisticated shopping, decadent
dining, San Telmo Antiques Fair,
Recoleta cemetery and
tango, tango, tango

VALLES CALCHAQUÍES (p230)
A tough but rewarding trip
through stunning scenery

SAN JUAN PROVINCE (p286)
Superb mountain climbing,
scenic Andean valleys, forgotten
whitewashed villages and more
wonderful wine

CÓRDOBA (p265)
Home of Argentina's finest colonial
architecture, a lively student
scene and excellent nightlife

MENDOZA (p288)
The heart of wine country
and a mountaineer's dream

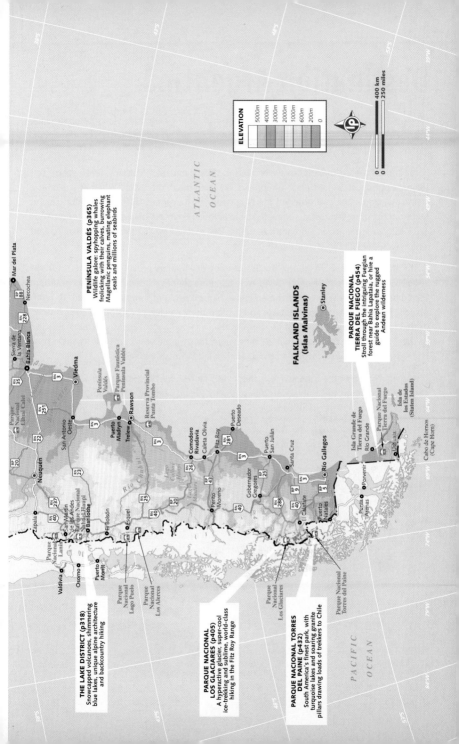

PENINSULA VALDÉS (p365)
Wildlife galore: spyhopping whales frolicking with their calves, burrowing Magellanic penguins, mating elephant seals and millions of seabirds

PARQUE NACIONAL TIERRA DEL FUEGO (p454)
Stroll through the intriguing Fuegian forest near Bahía Lapataia or hire a guide to explore the rugged Andean wilderness

FALKLAND ISLANDS (Islas Malvinas)

THE LAKE DISTRICT (p318)
Snowcapped volcanoes, shimmering blue lakes, unique alpine architecture and backcountry hiking

PARQUE NACIONAL LOS GLACIARES (p405)
A hyperactive glacier, super-cool ice-trekking and sublime, world-class hiking in the Fitz Roy Range

PARQUE NACIONAL TORRES DEL PAINE (p432)
South America's finest park, with turquoise lakes and soaring granite pillars drawing loads of trekkers to Chile

ATLANTIC OCEAN

PACIFIC OCEAN

ELEVATION

5000m
4000m
3000m
2000m
1000m
600m
200m
0

0   400 km
0   250 miles

Mar del Plata
Necochea
Sierra de la Ventana
Bahía Blanca
Viedma
San Antonio Oeste
Península Valdés
Parque Faunística Península Valdés
Puerto Madryn
Trelew
Rawson
Reserva Provincial Punta Tombo
Comodoro Rivadavia
Caleta Olivia
Fitz Roy
Puerto Deseado
Puerto San Julián
Santa Cruz
Gobernador Gregores
Perito Moreno
Río Gallegos
El Calafate
Puerto Natales
Parque Nacional Los Glaciares
Parque Nacional Torres del Paine
Punta Arenas
Porvenir
Isla Grande de Tierra del Fuego
Río Grande
Ushuaia
Parque Nacional Tierra del Fuego
Isla de los Estados (Staten Island)
Cabo de Hornos (Cape Horn)
Stanley
Neuquén
Zapala
San Martín de los Andes
Bariloche
Parque Nacional Nahuel Huapi
Parque Nacional Lanín
El Bolsón
Esquel
Parque Nacional Los Alerces
Parque Nacional Lago Puelo
Puerto Montt
Osorno
Valdivia
Parque Nacional Lihué Calel

RN 228
RN 88
RN 35
RP 251
RN 3
RP 20
RN 22
RN 23
RP 20
RP 25
RN 40
RN 25
RP 43
RN 26
RN 281
RP 25
RN 3
RN 288
RP 9
RP 5
RN 40
RN 237
RN 40

Río Chubut
Lago Colhué Huapí
Lago Buenos Aires

Destination Argentina

Let's set aside momentarily the sultry tango bars of Buenos Aires, Mendoza's fabulous wine, the glaciers of Patagonia and all that eye-popping Andean scenery and talk about Argentines. They're gonna make your trip.

Argentines are so friendly, so welcoming in their demeanor, that any sense you're tip-toeing around a stranger's place disappears like wine down the gullet. Whether you're in a stylish Palermo restaurant ordering the best steak you'll ever eat, or following your gaucho guide on horseback across a surreal volcanic landscape, your experiences with Argentines will excite your memories more than anything. Rest assured, you'll roam in good hands. And what you'll see will blow your mind.

The thundering falls of Iguazú, the Jesuit ruins of Misiones province, and the sunburnt adobe villages of the Andean northwest are all, quite simply, astounding. Further south, in the Central Andes, you can climb the Americas' highest peaks in summer and board through powder in winter. Lower your latitude and explore the Valdivian forests of the Lake District, or trek beneath the fantastic granite spires of the Fitz Roy Range. Finally, you reach the end of the world, Tierra del Fuego, where windswept fjords draw you into their mystical spell and Magellanic penguins wobble across lonely windswept shorelines.

And the city life? It's superb. From the stylish stores, old-time cafés and smoky tango bars of Buenos Aires to colonial Córdoba to the tree-lined sidewalks of Mendoza, Argentina boasts cities you'll never want to leave.

So take your pick, enjoy the wine, and do it while it's cheap. You'll wonder why every loose-footed traveler on the planet isn't here. Yet.

JANE SWEENEY

People of Argentina

Beautifully dressed tango dancers will place you under their spell (p44)

KRZYSZTOF DYDYNSKI

OTHER HIGHLIGHTS

- Absorb Argentina's indigenous heritage at a Mapuche reservation in the Lake District (p324)
- Enjoy afternoon tea with Welsh-speaking old-timers in Gaiman, Patagonia (p372)

© REUTERS/ENRIQUE MARCARIAN/PICTURE MEDIA

Admire the fancy footwork of Argentine soccer players (p38)

Gauchos keep the cowboy faith in towns like San Antonio de Areco (p123)

MICHAEL COYNE

Cities & Towns

Bars, wine and plazas make Mendoza (p295) a must-see

The well-preserved buildings of Salta (p223) are a visual delight

OTHER HIGHLIGHTS

- Photograph Argentina's finest colonial architecture in Córdoba (p265)
- Hit Rosario (p152) for French Renaissance architecture, neon and an edgy buzz
- Relax in leafy San Martín de los Andes (p327)
- Wander the adobe-lined streets of lovely Tilcara (p221)

Track down a treasure at San Telmo's antiques fair (p106) in Buenos Aires

PHILIP & KAREN SMITH

Journey to Ushuaia (p445), the southernmost city in the world

KRZYSZTOF DYDYNSKI

Enjoy the intense sensuality of a Buenos Aires tango show (p98)

Buenos Aires' revamped Puerto Madero district (p75) is a popular place for a stroll

KRZYSZTOF DYDYNSKI

Natural Wonders

View bizarrely shaped La Olla cave at Parque Nacional Monte León (p385), Patagonia

CHRIS BARTON

KERRY LORIMER

Marvel at the sheer power of Iguazú Falls (p189)

OTHER HIGHLIGHTS

- Count the shades of brown in the northwest's Quebrada de Humahuaca (p219)
- Watch wildlife in the wetlands of Esteros del Iberá (p173), northeast Argentina
- Journey to the clouds on Salta's Tren a las Nubes (Train to the Clouds; p230)
- Spot the southern right whales of Reserva Faunística Península Valdés (p365), Patagonia

Shudder at the awesome iciness of the Perito Moreno Glacier (p410), Patagonia

JANICE MARIE SHELDON

JOHN HAY

Explore the baffling rock formations of Parque Provincial Ischigualasto (p317), San Juan province

CHRIS BARTON

Cabo Dos Bahías (p376), Patagonia, is a penguin playground

Sunset is spectacular at Parque Nacional Nahuel Huapi (p345), Lake District

JANICE MARIE SHELDON

Action & Adventure

ALFREDO MAIQUEZ

A brandy-toting Saint Bernard poses, poised to warm up skiiers at Cerro Catedral (p346)

Fly-fishing (p460) is world class in the Lake District, Patagonia and in Esteros del Iberá

CHRIS BARTON

OTHER HIGHLIGHTS

- Climb 6962m Cerro Aconcagua (p301), the highest mountain in the western hemisphere
- Hike beneath the granite spires of the Fitz Roy Range (p405)
- Snowbirds, get a serious powder fix – in July! – at Las Leñas ski resort (p308)
- Get a bird's-eye view paragliding in La Cumbre (p276), Central Sierras

Trek to 2076m Cerro López, above the glacial waters of Lago Nahuel Huapi (p345), Lake District

NICK TAPP

MARK NEWMAN

Drench yourself in the mist of Iguazú Falls (p189)

JOHN HAY

Drive through the Valley of the Moon at Parque Provincial Ischigualasto (p317)

Sleep among stunning scenery at Parque Nacional Torres del Paine (p432), Patagonia

BRENT WINEBRENNER

Epicurean Delights

KRZYSZTOF DYDYNSKI

Feast on the biggest and best steaks on the planet in a Buenos Aires *parrilla* (p91)

KRZYSZTOF DYDYNSKI

Suck down a gourd full of strong *mate*, (p55) the bitter national beverage

Enjoy wine tasting in Mendoza (p297)

KRZYSZTOF DYDYNSKI

OTHER HIGHLIGHTS

■ Devour *alfajores* (a sweet national treat) by the dozen, and buy a jar of *dulce de leche* (milk caramel) to smear on *everything* (p54)

■ Warm up to tea and cookies in Patagonia's Welsh teahouses (p373 and 398)

■ Slurp down all the delicious ice cream (p95) you can

Contents

Lonely Planet books provide independent advice. Lonely Planet does not accept advertising in guidebooks, nor do we accept payment in exchange for listing or endorsing any place or business. Lonely Planet writers do not accept discounts or payments in exchange for positive coverage of any sort.

Los libros de Lonely Planet ofrecen información independiente. La editorial no acepta ningún tipo de propaganda en las guías, así como tampoco endorsa ninguna entidad comercial o destino. Los escritores de Lonely Planet no aceptan descuentos o pagos de ningun tipo a cambio de comentarios favorables.

Regional Map Contents

THE ANDEAN NORTHWEST p211

NORTHEAST ARGENTINA p151

CÓRDOBA & THE CENTRAL SIERRAS p264

MENDOZA & THE CENTRAL ANDES p287

BUENOS AIRES pp62–3

THE PAMPAS & THE ATLANTIC COAST p117

THE LAKE DISTRICT p319

PATAGONIA p354

TIERRA DEL FUEGO p439

16

The Authors

DANNY PALMERLEE
Coordinating Author

Danny has spent nearly every waking moment of the past six years studying, traveling in and writing about Latin America, a region he's been no less than infatuated with since he first backpacked through Mexico and Central America in 1991. He works as a freelance writer based in Buenos Aires, and has written about South America and Mexico for the *Miami Herald*, the *Dallas Morning News*, the *San Francisco Chronicle*, the *Houston Chronicle* and several other US publications. Along with other Lonely Planet titles, Danny was the coordinating author of *South America on a Shoestring*.

Danny wrote the following chapters: Destination Argentina, Getting Started, Itineraries, Snapshot, History, Environment, Córdoba & the Central Sierras, Mendoza & the Central Andes, The Lake District, Directory, Transportation and Glossary. He also cowrote the Culture chapter.

The Coordinating Author's Favorite Trips

Of all my mad-dash road trips, two stand out. The drive to the magical village of Cachi (p230) in Valles Calchaquíes was tops. I rented a car in Tucumán (p239) and made groovy Cafayate (p233) in two easy days. It was the next day's drive up the spectacular Quebrada de Cafayate (p232) that really blew me away. Then the high, dusty RP 33 is all hairpins and cliffs to Cachi.

The second was entirely dirt, from Villa La Angostura (p334) to Villa Traful (p334), over the spectacular Paso Córdoba to San Martín de los Andes (p327) and back to Angostura via RN 234, the amazing Siete Lagos (Seven Lakes) route (p329). Do your best to rent a car (always get the CD player) and do them both.

SANDRA BAO

Sandra's relationship with Buenos Aires started at birth. After she turned nine, her family left Argentina for greener pastures in the US. She picked up a psychology degree from the University of California, Santa Cruz, but quickly realized she enjoyed traveling more than studying people's neuroses, and so spent much of her young adulthood backpacking through dozens of countries. Her 'Buenos Aires Querido' has drawn Sandra back many times over the years, as have the gargantuan steaks, sugary *alfajores* and spontaneous street tango.

Sandra wrote the Buenos Aires chapter, and would like to dedicate her work to her *porteño* godfather, Norberto Mallarini, a wonderful man who passed away during the production process of this book. He and Sandra's godmother, Elsa, were always there in Buenos Aires to provide a warm bed and home-cooked dinner. Norberto will be greatly missed.

ANDREW DEAN NYSTROM

Born a mile high in Colorado, Andrew has always gravitated toward geographic extremes. Since earning his BA in Conservation Geography and Education from the University of California, Berkeley, he has contributed to a dozen guidebooks (including Lonely Planet's *Bolivia*, *South America on a Shoestring* and *Mexico*) and has been translated in a dozen languages. He has surveyed South America's surreal landscapes for the *Dallas Morning News*, *Denver Post*, *Houston Chronicle*, *Miami Herald*, the *Oregonian*, *San Francisco Chronicle* and Yahoo! Travel.

When not out rambling, Andrew runs an adventure travel planning consultancy from his garden cottage straddling a major earthquake fault in Alta California. Andrew wrote the Patagonia and Tierra del Fuego chapters.

LUCAS VIDGEN

Still trying to figure out a way to eat steak, drink espresso and tango at the same time, Lucas first fell in love with Argentina while researching Lonely Planet's *South America on a Shoestring*.

He now lives in downtown Buenos Aires, where friends, family and other freeloaders are pleased to find that his sofa folds out to become a bed.

Lucas wrote The Pampas & the Atlantic Coast, Northeast Argentina and The Andean Northwest chapters.

CONTRIBUTING AUTHORS

Dereck Foster wrote the Food & Drink chapter. Born in Buenos Aires, Dereck has written about food and wine for the *Buenos Aires Herald* for more than 30 years. He has written three books – *Food & Drink in Argentina*, *El Gaucho Gourmet* and *The Argentines: How They Live and Work* – and lectures frequently in both Spanish and English.

David Goldberg MD wrote the Health chapter. Dr Goldberg completed his training in internal medicine and infectious diseases at Columbia-Presbyterian Medical Center in New York City, where he has also served as voluntary faculty. At present, he is an infectious diseases specialist in Scarsdale NY and the editor-in-chief of the website mdtravelhealth.com.

Thomas Kohnstamm cowrote the Culture chapter. Thomas is a New York–based writer who frequently covers South American politics, history and culture. His first memory of Argentina was watching Diego Maradona single-handedly embarrass the English team in the 1986 World Cup – Falklands War payback, perhaps. He went on to study history and politics at university in Buenos Aires and taught in the Pampas, then watched Argentina's economic decline as an MA student in Latin American Studies at Stanford University.

Getting Started

Argentina is cheap, and more and more people are realizing it's one of the most exciting destinations in the world. Traveling in Argentina is so easy that you could throw your bags together in half a day and be off. Of course, there are ways to make it even easier.

This section will help you know when to go, how much you might spend and where to go for more information. The Internet resources here are intended to help you waste as much of the boss's time as possible, surfing the Internet and daydreaming when you should be working.

WHEN TO GO

See Climate Charts (p462) for more information.

Argentina's seasons are reversed from the northern hemisphere's. Spring and autumn/fall are the best times to visit Buenos Aires (the summer is hot and humid). Mendoza, Córdoba and the Lake District are all spectacular in autumn/fall, when the leaves are fiery reds and yellows, the temperatures are comfortable and the crowds are thin.

Summer (again, we're talking Argentina's summer) is the best time to hit Patagonia, when the weather's milder and more services are available. Outside this time, public transport becomes trickier as services thin out. Northern Argentina can be brutally hot in summer and is best visited in spring, when the greens are greenest. Winter and autumn/fall are also pleasant.

Ski season runs mid-June through mid-October, and the resorts are most expensive and most crowded in July and August when every *porteño* (person from Buenos Aires) seems to be on the slopes.

The most expensive times to travel are the Argentine vacation months of January, February and July.

COSTS & MONEY

Argentina's cheap. Since the economic collapse in 2001 and the subsequent devaluation of the peso, travel in Argentina has become extremely affordable. You'll be constantly amazed at how far you can stretch your cash. If you're on a budget, you can get by on US$20 to US$25 per day – outside Buenos Aires – by sleeping in hostels or cheap hotels and eating at non-touristy restaurants. Things get pricier when you add tours and entertainment, however.

Buenos Aires is more expensive than the rest of Argentina and good hotel rooms here *start* at around US$20 to US$25 per double. In the provinces you can land a good hotel for US$15 per double, while an

---

SEASONS SOUTH OF THE EQUATOR

Aussies and Kiwis know this already. You 'top-siders' have some figuring to do (and we're not talking about which way the water swirls when you flush the toilet). Most importantly, you need to know the seasons in the southern hemisphere:

- **Winter**: June, July, August
- **Spring**: September, October, November
- **Summer**: December, January, February
- **Autumn/Fall**: March, April, May

Once you've got this, then start flushing toilets and staring into the bowl.

DON'T LEAVE HOME WITHOUT...

- Hat, sunglasses and sunblock
- Tampons – they're tough to find in smaller towns
- Ziplock bags – to waterproof your gizmos and much, much more
- Duct tape – make your own mini-roll around a pencil stub or lighter
- Handy wipes – great for those overnight bus rides
- Swiss Army knife – be sure it has a corkscrew!
- Ear plugs – essential for hostels and streetside hotel rooms
- Universal sink plug – a must for hand washing your clothes
- Dental floss – sews your clothes, laces your shoes and more!
- Peanut butter – you can't get it in Argentina
- ATM card – handiest way to get cash
- Hunger for steak

---

extra US$5 to US$10 will get you something very comfortable. Dinners can be as cheap as US$2 per person and as much as US$20 per person for a gourmet meal, with a great bottle of wine and dessert, at a top-end restaurant.

TRAVEL LITERATURE

One of the hottest travelogues to hit the shelves of late is none other than Ernesto 'Che' Guevara's *The Motorcycle Diaries* (2003), in which the young medical student recounts his eye-opening journey in 1951–52 through Argentina, Chile, Brazil, Venezuela, Peru and Colombia by motorcycle. Although only part of it takes place in Argentina, it's a must-read.

In *Bad Times in Buenos Aires* (1999), Miranda France touches on everything from the quality of Argentine condoms to the country's obsession with psychoanalysis, in a wry account of her stay in the capital while working as a journalist in the 1990s.

If you're going to be wandering down to Patagonia (and even if you're not), pick up Bruce Chatwin's *In Patagonia* (1977), which is one of the most informed syntheses of life and landscape for any part of South America. For a glimpse into some gripping Patagonian mountaineering, read Gregory Crouch's *Enduring Patagonia* (2001), in which the author details his ascents of Cerro Torre's brutal west face and several other wild climbs.

Nick Reding's *The Last Cowboys at the End of the Earth: The Story of the Gauchos of Patagonia* (2001) takes place mostly in Chile, but is equally pertinent to the conditions and changes in neighboring Argentine Patagonia. It's part travelogue and part history and filled with memorable characters.

Frequently reprinted, William Henry Hudson's *Idle Days in Patagonia* (1893) is a romantic account of the 19th-century naturalist's adventures in search of migratory birds. Also check out his *The Purple Land* (1885) and *Far Away and Long Ago* (1918).

Make a special effort to locate Lucas Bridges' *The Uttermost Part of the Earth* (1947), which describes his life among the indigenous peoples of Tierra del Fuego.

HOW MUCH?

Great bottle of store-bought wine US$5

Bife de chorizo (sirloin steak) US$4

Espresso US$0.60

Double scoop of ice cream US$0.50

Four-hour bus ride US$5

LONELY PLANET INDEX

Liter of gas/petrol US$0.65

Liter of bottled water US$0.65

Liter of Quilmes beer US$0.60 (store), US$1 (bar)

Souvenir T-shirt US$4

Hot dog on the street US$0.35

TOP FIVES

Festivals & Events

From beer and wine fests to gaucho and horse festivals, Argentina's fiestas truly run the gamut of celebrations. The following are just our favorites; for more, see p466 and the Festivals & Events section under most regional destinations.

- **Festival Nacional del Folklore** (National Folk Music Festival), Cosquín; January (p274)
- **Fiesta Nacional de la Vendimia** (National Wine Harvest Festival), Mendoza; February/March (p293)
- **Buenos Aires Tango** (Tango Festival), Buenos Aires; March (p85)
- **Fiesta Nacional de la Cerveza** (Oktoberfest), Villa General Belgrano; October (p280)
- **Día de la Tradición** (Day of Tradition), San Antonio de Areco; November (p124)

Movies & Books

Argentina has both inspired and produced numerous outstanding books and movies. The following were chosen for their psych-you-up value.

- *The Motorcycle Diaries (Diarios de motocicleta)*, 2004 movie directed by Walter Salles
- *In Patagonia*, 1977 book by Bruce Chatwin
- *La Ciénaga*, 2001 movie directed by Lucrecia Martel
- *The Uttermost Part of the Earth*, 1947 book by Lucas Bridges
- *Historias Minimas* (Minimal Stories), 2002 movie directed by Carlos Sorin

Weird & Wacky Places

After all, everywhere has its oddities. The following offbeat places will get you thinking just how, well, diverse this planet is.

- Museo Rocsen (p282)
- Difunta Correa shrine (p312)
- Interpretive Center at San Ignacio Miní (p188)
- Gaucho Antonio Gil shrines (p172)
- Parque El Desafío, Gaiman (p372)

Parks

Argentina is a nature-lover's dream, and its parks are truly one of the best reasons to be here. For a complete list, see p50, but don't miss the following:

- Parque Nacional Los Glaciares (p405)
- Parque Nacional Iguazú (p191)
- Parque Nacional Tierra del Fuego (p454)
- Parque Nacional Lanín (p331)
- Parque Provincial Ischigualasto (p317)

INTERNET RESOURCES

The Web is a great place to plan your trip. For websites about specific topics (such as hostels or gay and lesbian resources), see the appropriate section in the Directory (p458). The following should get you started:

Argentina Turistica (www.argentinaturistica.com) Packed with information in English and Spanish, this is one of the best all around sites on the Web.

Buenos Aires Herald (www.buenosairesherald.com) An international view of the country and world can be found at the website of BA's excellent English-language newspaper.

Latin American Network Information Center (www1.lanic.utexas.edu/la/argentina) This site has a massive list of Argentine websites. If you can't find it here…well, never mind, 'cause you'll find it here.

Lonely Planet (www.lonelyplanet.com) Succinct summaries on traveling to most places on earth; postcards from other travelers; and the Thorn Tree bulletin board, where you can ask questions before you go or dispense advice when you get back.

Sectur (www.turismo.gov.ar) The official Argentine state tourist board's website offers a decent dose of information in English and Spanish.

Itineraries
CLASSIC ROUTES

GRAND LOOP
Six to 12 Weeks / Humahuaca to Tierra del Fuego

From **Buenos Aires** (p60), head to **Reserva Faunística Península Valdés** (p365) for whale watching before journeying to **Ushuaia** (p445), the world's southernmost city. From here, follow the Southern National Parks Circuit (p25) before winding your way up to the **Lake District** (p318), with a chocolate stop in **Bariloche** (p336). Bump down the lake-studded **Ruta de los Siete Lagos** (Seven Lakes Route; p329) to the leafy resort of **San Martín de los Andes** (p327) before exploring the Valdivian forests of **Parque Nacional Lanín** (p331).

Pop over to **Neuquén** (p323) for some dinosaur appreciation and continue north to the volcanic landscapes near **Malargüe** (p306). Then go to **Mendoza** (p288) for wine tasting and the Andean scenery around **Parque Provincial Aconcagua** (p301). Head north to **Barreal** (p313) and downhill to bustling **San Juan** (p308) and the desert rocks of **Parque Provincial Ischigualasto** (p317).

From **La Rioja** (p255), go north to **Tucumán** (p239) and on to the canyons of **Quebrada de Cafayate** (p232). Then head to **Salta** (p223) to journey through **Quebrada de Humahuaca** (p219). Travel across the endless Chaco, visiting **Reserva Provincial Esteros del Iberá** (p173) en route. Continue east to the Jesuit missions and finish beneath the massive falls of **Parque Nacional Iguazú** (p191). Fly back to Buenos Aires and party till your plane leaves.

Budget a minimum six to eight weeks (and plenty of film!) for the Grand Loop, which traverses over 8800km, from Tierra del Fuego and Los Glaciares in the south, through the beautiful Lake District, to the traditional villages and Andean scenery of northwest Argentina. From the wine country to wildlife, you'll have seen it all.

NORTHERN LOOP

**Three to Five Weeks /
Iguazú Falls, Mendoza & the Andean Northwest**

After a couple of days in **Buenos Aires** (p60), head for the heart of wine country – **Mendoza** (p288). Be sure to take a trip up RN 7 to **Parque Provincial Aconcagua** (p301), home of the Americas' highest peak. Journey north to San Juan and see the wild rock formations and dinosaur exhibits of **Parque Provincial Ischigualasto** (p317). Cut east and spend a day exploring **Córdoba** (p265), the finest colonial center in Argentina (gotta love those Jesuits!).

Take an overnight bus to **Tucumán** (p239), where you'll find some seriously odd 1960s architecture, a beautiful central plaza and one of the liveliest street scenes in Argentina. Take the scenic route to Salta, stopping in mellow lakeside **Tafí del Valle** (p244) and overnighting in beautiful **Cafayate** (p233). Suck down plenty of the town's dry *torrontés* white wine before heading up the spectacularly eroded valley **Quebrada de Cafayate** (p232) to **Salta** (p223), whose central plaza is one of Argentina's finest.

From Salta, venture up RN 9 for beautiful whitewashed adobe villages, traditional Andean culture, fabulous crafts and rugged high-mountain scenery. Don't miss the wee village of **Purmamarca** (p223) and its famous Cerro de los Siete Colores (Hill of Seven Colors).

Further north, the otherworldly Andean valley **Quebrada de Humahuaca** (p219) is a must; after you explore it, overnight in lively little **Tilcara** (p221) before heading back to Salta to kick off the final leg: the wondrous **Parque Nacional Iguazú** (p191). Whether you make the arduous overland journey across the Chaco or fly via Buenos Aires, you'll want at least two days marveling at the mammoth falls and hiking through the park's subtropical forests. Close things off with a little silence at the Jesuit ruins of **San Ignacio Miní** (p188) before your return to Buenos Aires.

Covering nearly 4700km, the Northern Loop takes you to four of Argentina's finest cities – Buenos Aires, Mendoza, Córdoba and Salta – and through some of its most spectacular parks, including Parque Provincial Aconcagua and Parque Nacional Iguazú, home of the thundering Iguazú falls.

ROADS LESS TRAVELED

FORGOTTEN ANDES & PARKS

Two to three weeks /
San Luis to Corrientes

Venturing off the beaten track in Argentina will turn up tiny villages, empty roads and rarely visited provincial parks that you'll have almost entirely to yourself. Begin in the wee provincial capital of **San Luis** (p283), from where you can visit the spectacular **Parque Nacional Sierra de las Quijadas** (p284), similar to San Juan's Ischigualasto, sans the people. Bus over to **San Juan** (p308), rent a car and head for the hills: drive up to **Barreal** (p313) in the breathtaking Valle de Calingasta for hiking, rafting, climbing and land sailing beneath the country's highest peaks. Head up RP 412 to the traditional towns of **Rodeo** (p315), **San José de Jáchal** (p315) and **Huaco** (p315), and stop en route for a dip in the thermal baths of **Pismanta** (p316). Take RN 40 back to San Juan and bus out to the fascinating **Difunta Correa Shrine** (p312).

From San Juan, take an overnight bus to **Córdoba** (p265), a colonial city that foreigners often skip. After a day or two exploring the city and the Jesuit *estancias* of the **Central Sierras** (p274), grab an overnighter to **Resistencia** (p201), an odd city of sculptures and the nearest hub to **Parque Nacional Chaco** (p205). From **Corrientes** (p166), catch some live *chamamé* (folk music of northeast Argentina), and head to **Reserva Provincial Esteros del Iberá** (p173), a wetlands preserve and wildlife sanctuary comparable to Brazil's Pantanal.

By now you'll be aching for human contact: either join the crowds at **Iguazú Falls** (p191), a full day's travel away, or head back to Buenos Aires, flying from Corrientes or journeying overland.

> Just because the crowds head elsewhere doesn't mean this 2850km trip lacks sights. In fact, the forgotten back roads and little-visited villages and parks make this a very special trip through an Argentina that most foreigners never see.

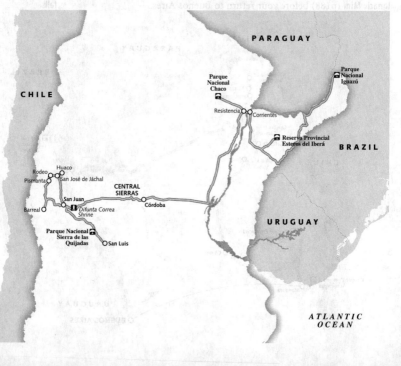

TAILORED TRIPS

SOUTHERN NATIONAL PARKS CIRCUIT   Patagonia, Tierra del Fuego & the Lake District

Though the sadistic manage this circuit in 10 days, two weeks is really the minimum to appreciate the mystical landscapes of Patagonia and Tierra del Fuego. It's the end of the world, after all, so don't sell yourself short. After allowing for a couple of days in Buenos Aires, fly to **Ushuaia** (p445), the southernmost city in the world, and visit nearby **Parque Nacional Tierra del Fuego** (p454). Take a quick flight to **El Calafate** (p412) and visit spectacular Perito Moreno Glacier from the southern access point of **Parque Nacional Los Glaciares** (p410). Bus down to **Puerto Natales** (p427) and trek the famous **Parque Nacional Torres del Paine** (p432). Head north again to **El Chaltén** (p405) for mind-altering hikes in the **Fitz Roy area** (p406) of Los Glaciares. Then back to El Calafate for your return flight to Buenos Aires. *Chau!*

With an extra two weeks, begin the trip by heading south by bus (rather than plane) and stop in **Puerto Madryn** (p359) on your way down for whale watching at **Reserva Faunística Península Valdés** (p365). After exploring the national parks of Patagonia and Tierra del Fuego, fly from El Calafate up to **Bariloche** (p336). From here you can explore the Lake District national parks of **Nahuel Huapi** (p345) and **Lanín** (p331). Before your flight back to Buenos Aires, you may even be able to squeeze in trips to nearby **Parque Nacional Lago Puelo** (p351) and **Parque Nacional Los Alerces** (p398). By then, you'll deserve a night on the town in Buenos Aires.

WINE TOUR   Mendoza, San Juan & the Andean Northwest

Prime your palate for Argentina's world-class wine. Following the grape juice trail will not only give you a serious sampling of the country's finest libation, you'll be introduced to many of its most interesting regions. Uncork your trip by starting in beautiful **Mendoza** (p288), Argentina's Andes-flanked wine capital. Be certain to stop at **Bodega La Rural** (p297), home of South America's largest (and best) wine museum. Squeeze in a day trip to **Puente del Inca** (p301) and the lung-busting heights of the **Cristo Redentor** (p303) on the Chilean border.

Take a crack-of-dawn bus to **San Rafael** (p303), rent a bike and ride out to the city's wineries, making **Bianchi Champañera** (p304) your last stop for a bit of bubbly. The next day, head to **San Juan** (p308) to try the excellent Syrah and regional whites produced near this leafy provincial capital. Squeeze in a day trip to **Parque Provincial Ischigualasto** (p317) or up RN 40 to **San José de Jáchal** (p315) if you can. From San Juan, take an overnight bus to **Tucumán** (p239), and head the next day to lovely little **Cafayate** (p233) to hit a few wineries and dazzle your tastebuds with the regional *torrontés* white wine. Return to Tucumán for your flight back to Buenos Aires.

Snapshot

The big news for most Argentina-bound travelers is that the country is suddenly cheap. Before the economy crashed in December 2001, the Argentine peso was pegged to the US dollar, making Argentina one of South America's most expensive countries to visit. After the crash, the peso plummeted to four to the dollar, and savvy European and North American travelers began pouring in to gobble down giant Argentine steaks at US$3 a pop and travel an exciting country that had long been too costly. The peso has since leveled off at about three to the dollar, and Argentina remains one of the best-value countries in South America.

Of course, a tanking economy means different things for Argentines. For the country's middle and lower classes, it's been hell. In 2001, those with bank accounts saw caps placed on their withdrawals (see p34), and the country's poor faced limits on what they could eat.

Perhaps the most tightly wound moment of all was the protest known as the *cacerolazo* (from the word *cacerola* or pan). It began on December 20, 2001, when people began taking to their balconies in Buenos Aires banging pots and pans. The banging moved to the streets, then to cities throughout Argentina, and finally culminated in the resignation of President de la Rua (see p35). The *cacerolazo* has become symbolic of discontent, and as a form of social protest has spread throughout Latin America and even the world. With Argentina's economy still on the skids, you may become familiar with the sound of the *cacerolazo*. Just listen for the pans.

Speaking of toppling the big boys, Argentina beat the US in the battle for the 2004 Olympic gold in basketball – no small feat. Sports, of course, are always a hot topic in Argentina, none more so than soccer (p38). The country's disgraced golden boy Diego Maradona continues to rear his head entering and reentering drug rehab and, not surprisingly, the Argentine press.

Transvestites have also been getting their share of press, appearing on everything from talk shows to news hours. You'll surely get to know Florencia de la V, the beloved transvestite star of *Los Roldán*, Argentina's most popular TV sitcom. De la V appeared naked and sporting a photo-enhanced pregnant belly on the cover of *Rolling Stone* in 2004, and continues to dazzle the Argentine public.

On December 30, 2004, an overcrowded Buenos Aires nightclub caught fire, killing 188 people and wounding hundreds more. City mayor Arribal Ibarra closed the city's nightclubs for two weeks of mourning, two city officials resigned, and thousands of protesters demanded the mayor's resignation for not enforcing safety standards. Ibarra did not resign, but the club owner was later charged with involuntary manslaughter.

In January 2005, after a year of self-imposed exile in Chile, ex-president Carlos Menem (p34) returned to Argentina after federal judges dropped two international warrants for his arrest. Although he still faced charges of embezzlement and tax fraud, and despite the fact most Argentines blame his corruption for the country's economic collapse, Menem vowed to run again for president in 2007. Keep your eyes peeled.

FAST FACTS

Population: 39,144,750 (12 million live in greater Buenos Aires)

Population growth rate: 1.02%

Adult literacy rate: 97.1%

Inflation rate (2004): 13.4%

Population below poverty line: 51.7%

Unemployment rate: 17-23%

Area: 2,766,890 sq km or about one-third the size of the contiguous US

Number of psychologists: about one per 900 inhabitants (the highest ratio in the world)

Percentage of Argentine households consuming *yerba mate*: 92%

Approximate national annual consumption of *yerba mate*: 200,000 tons

History

Argentina's fascinating history is visible everywhere, from the pre-Inca hill fortresses of the northwest, to stunning colonial architecture of cities like Salta and Córdoba. You can travel back in time by visiting a myriad of places, like San Antonio de Areco, where gaucho traditions still hold strong, or even as far south as Patagonia, where cave paintings leave you wondering about the past. The Italian heritage dating to the immigration boom of the late 19th century manifests itself through production of wine and olive oil in Mendoza province, language in Buenos Aires and pizza and pasta throughout the country.

NATIVE PEOPLES

It's generally accepted that human settlement of the Americas began nearly 30,000 years ago when the ancestors of Amerindians, taking advantage of lowered sea levels during the Pleistocene Epoch, walked from Siberia to Alaska via a land bridge across the Bering Strait. Not exactly speedy about moving south, they reached what is now Argentina sometime around 10,000 BC. One of the oldest and most impressive archaeological sites in Argentina is Cueva de las Manos (Cave of the Hands; p403) in Patagonia, where mysterious cave paintings, mostly of left hands, date from 7370 BC.

When the Spanish hit the scene, much of current-day Argentina was inhabited by highly mobile peoples who hunted the guanaco (a wild relative of the llama) and the rhea (a large bird resembling an emu) with bow and arrow or *boleadoras* (heavily weighted thongs that could be thrown up to 90m to ensnare the hunted animal).

The Pampas were inhabited by the Querandí, hunters and gatherers who are legendary for their spirited resistance to the Spanish. The Guaraní, indigenous to the area from northern Entre Ríos through Corrientes and into Paraguay and Brazil, were semi-sedentary agriculturalists, raising sweet potatoes, maize, manioc and beans, and fishing the Río Paraná.

Of all of Argentina, the northwest was the most developed. Several indigenous groups, most notably the Diaguita, practiced irrigated agriculture in the valleys of the eastern Andean foothills. The region's inhabitants were influenced heavily by the Tiahanaco empire of Bolivia and by the great Inca empire which expanded south from Peru into current-day Argentina beginning in the early 1480s. In Salta province, the ruined stoned city of Quilmes (p235) is one of the best preserved pre-Incan indigenous sites, where some 5000 Quilmes, part of the Diaguita civilization, lived and withstood the Inca invasion. Further north in Tilcara (p221), you can see a completely restored *pucará* (walled city) about which little is known.

In the Lake District and Patagonia, the Pehuenches and Puelches were hunter-gatherers, and the pine nuts of the araucaria, or *pehuén* tree, formed a staple of their diet. The names were given to them by the Mapuche, who entered the region from the west as the Spanish pushed south. Today there are many Mapuche reservations, especially in the area around Junín de los Andes (p325), where you can still sample foods made from pine nuts.

Argentina's national beer, Quilmes, is named after an indigenous group of northwest Argentina.

TIMELINE

1480s	1536
Inca of Peru begin movement into Andean northwest of current-day Argentina	Pedro de Mendoza establishes Puerto Nuestra Señora Santa María del Buen Aires on the Río de la Plata

Journey back in time to the epoch of Patagonia's first human inhabitants and see how their world changed in the centuries to come in *Patagonia: Natural History, Prehistory and Ethnography at the Uttermost End of the Earth*, by Colin McEwen et al.

Until they were wiped out by Europeans, there were indigenous inhabitants as far south as Tierra del Fuego, where the Selk'nam, Haush, Yahgan and Alacaluf peoples lived as mobile hunters and gatherers. Despite frequently inclement weather they wore little or no clothing, but constant fires (even in their bark canoes) kept them warm and gave the region its Spanish name, Tierra del Fuego (Land of Fire).

ENTER THE SPANISH

Just over a decade after Spaniard Christopher Colombus (Cristóbal Colón) accidentally encountered the Americas, other Spanish explorers began probing the Río de la Plata estuary. Most early explorations of the area were motivated by rumors of vast quantities of silver. Spaniard Sebastian Cabot optimistically named the river the Río de la Plata (River of Silver), and to drive the rumors home, part of the new territory was even given the Latin word for silver *(argentum)*. But the mineral riches that the Spanish found in the Inca Empire of Peru never panned out in this misnamed land.

The first real attempt at establishing a permanent settlement on the estuary was made by Spanish aristocrat Pedro de Mendoza in 1536. He landed at present-day Buenos Aires and, not one to mince words, named the outpost Puerto Nuestra Señora Santa María del Buen Aire (Port Our Lady Saint Mary of the Good Wind). After the colonists tried pilfering food from the indigenous Querandí, the natives turned on them violently. Within four years, Mendoza fled back to Spain without a lick of silver, and the detachment of troops he left behind beat it up river to the gentler environs of Asunción, present-day capital of Paraguay.

NORTHWEST SUPREMACY

The most comprehensive, though not necessarily most readable, book on Argentine history is David Rock's *Argentina 1516-1987: From Spanish Colonization to Alfonsín*. It's worth the grunt.

Although Spanish forces reestablished Buenos Aires by 1580, it remained a backwater in comparison to Andean settlements founded by a separate and more successful Spanish contingency moving south from Alto Perú (now Bolivia). With ties to the colonial stronghold of Lima, capital of the Viceroyalty of Peru, and financed by the bonanza silver mine at Potosí, the Spanish founded some two dozen cities as far south as Mendoza (1561), all during the latter half of the 16th century. Santiago del Estero, founded in 1551, is the country's oldest permanent settlement.

The two most important population centers at the time were Tucumán (founded in 1571) and Córdoba (founded 1573). Tucumán lay in the heart of a rich agricultural region and supplied Alto Perú with grains, cotton and livestock. Córdoba became an important educational center, and Jesuit missionaries established *estancias* in the surrounding sierras to supply Alto Perú with mules, foodstuffs and wine. Córdoba's Manzana Jesuítica (Jesuit Block; p267) is now the finest preserved group of colonial buildings in the country, and several Jesuit *estancias* (p278) in the Central Sierras are also exquisitely preserved. These sites, along with the central plazas of Salta (founded 1582; p223) and Tucumán (p239), boast the country's finest colonial architecture.

The greatest culprit in this northward orientation was the protectionist King of Spain, whose mercantile policy decreed that commerce between Spain and the colonies had to be routed through Lima.

THE JESUITS

Northeast Argentina, along the upper regions of the Uruguay and Paraná rivers, was colonized later with the help of Jesuit missionaries who concentrated the indigenous Guaraní in settlements. Starting around 1607, the Jesuits established 30 missions, including the marvelously preserved San Ignacio Miní (p188) which should be on every architecture-lover's hit list.

Perhaps as many as 100,000 indigenous peoples lived in the Jesuit settlements, which resembled other Spanish municipalities but operated with a political and economic autonomy that did not apply to other Iberian settlers. Weary of their accumulating wealth and power, the Spanish crown expelled the Jesuits in 1767, and the mission communities disintegrated rapidly, almost fading into the wilderness.

South America's oldest university is Córdoba's Universidad Nacional de Córdoba, founded in 1613 and elevated to university status in 1622.

BUENOS AIRES: BOOTLEGGER TO BOOMTOWN

As the northwest prospered, Buenos Aires suffered the Crown's harsh restrictions on trade for nearly two centuries. But because the port was ideal for trade, frustrated merchants turned to smuggling, and contraband trade with Portuguese Brazil and nonpeninsular European powers flourished. The increasing amount of wealth passing through the city fueled much of its initial growth.

With the decline of silver mining at Potosí in the late 18th century, the Spanish crown was forced to recognize Buenos Aires' importance for direct transatlantic trade. Finally forced to relax its restrictions, Spain made Buenos Aires the capital of the new Viceroyalty of the Río de la Plata – which included Paraguay, Uruguay and the mines at Potosí – in 1776.

Although the new Viceroyalty had internal squabbles over trade and control issues, when the British raided the city in 1806 and again in 1807, the response was unified. Locals rallied against the invaders without Spanish help and chased them out of town.

The late 18th century also saw the emergence of the legendary gaucho of the Pampas (see p122). The South American counterpart to North America's cowboys, they hunted wild cattle and broke in wild horses that had multiplied after being left behind by previous expeditions on the Río de la Plata.

For an interpretation of the gaucho's role in Argentine history, check out Richard W Slatta's Gauchos and the Vanishing Frontier (1983).

INDEPENDENCE & INFIGHTING

Toward the end of the 18th century, *criollos* (Argentine-born colonists) became increasingly dissatisfied and impatient with Spanish authority. The expulsion of British troops from Buenos Aires gave the people of the Río de la Plata new confidence in their ability to stand alone. After Napoleon invaded Spain in 1808, Buenos Aires finally declared its independence on May 25, 1810. To commemorate the occasion, the city's main square was renamed Plaza de Mayo (p73).

Independence movements throughout South America soon united to expel Spain from the continent by the 1820s. Under the leadership of General José de San Martín and others, the United Provinces of the Río de la Plata (the direct forerunner of the Argentine Republic) declared formal independence at Tucumán on July 9, 1816.

Despite achieving independence, the provinces were united in name only. Lacking any effective central authority, the regional disparities within

One of the best-known contemporary accounts of post-independence Argentina is Domingo Faustino Sarmiento's Life in the Argentine Republic in the Days of the Tyrants.

1776	1810
Spain names Buenos Aires the capital of the new Viceroyalty of the Río de la Plata	Buenos Aires declares its independence from Spain on May 25

Argentina – formerly obscured by Spanish rule – became more obvious. This resulted in the rise of the caudillos (local strongmen), who resisted Buenos Aires as strongly as Buenos Aires had resisted Spain.

Argentine politics was thus divided between the Federalists of the interior, who advocated provincial autonomy, and the Unitarists of Buenos Aires, who upheld the city's central authority. For nearly two decades, bloody and vindictive conflicts between the two factions left the country nearly exhausted.

THE REIGN OF ROSAS

Juan Manuel de Rosas came to prominence as a caudillo in Buenos Aires province and represented the interests of rural elites and land owners. While he championed the Federalist cause, he also helped centralize political power in Buenos Aires and required that all international trade be funneled through the capital. His reign lasted over 20 years, and he set ominous precedents in Argentine political life, creating the *mazorca* (his ruthless political police force) and institutionalizing torture.

Under Rosas, Buenos Aires continued to dominate the new country, but his extremism turned many against him, including some of his strongest allies. Finally, in 1852, a rival caudillo named Justo José de Urquiza (once a staunch supporter of Rosas) organized a powerful army and forced Rosas from power. Urquiza's first task was to draw up a constitution, which was formalized by a convention in Santa Fe on May 1, 1853. Urquiza became the country's first president. The Constitution (still in force today despite its frequent suspension) pointed to the triumph of Unitarism, and subsequent economic developments confirmed Buenos Aires' power in the coming decades. In 1862, Buenos Aires was declared the capital of the Argentine Republic.

THE FLEETING GOLDEN AGE

Argentina's second president, Bartolomé Mitre, was concerned with building the nation and establishing infrastructure, but his goals were subsumed by the Paraguayan War which lasted from 1865 to 1870. Not until Domingo Faustino Sarmiento, an educator and journalist from San Juan, became president did progress in Argentina really kick in. Sarmiento is still revered for his promotion of education, and his childhood home in San Juan is now a lovely museum (p309), both honoring the man and displaying his colonial-style home.

Buenos Aires' economy boomed and immigrants poured in from Spain, Italy, Germany and eastern Europe. The city's population grew nearly sevenfold from 1869 to 1895. The new residents worked in the port, lived tightly in the tenement buildings and developed the famous tango (p44) in the brothels and nightspots. Basque and Irish refugees became the first shepherds, as both sheep numbers and wool exports increased nearly tenfold between 1850 and 1880.

Still, much of the southern Pampas and Patagonia were inaccessible for settlers because of fierce resistance from indigenous Mapuche and Tehuelche. Argentina's next president, Nicolás Avellaneda, took care of that. In 1879, Avellaneda's minister of war, General Julio Argentino Roca, carried out a ruthless campaign of extermination against the indigenous

Take a more personalized look into Argentina's past with Monica Szurmuk's *Women in Argentina*, a collection of travel narratives by women – both Argentine and foreign – who traveled here between 1850 and 1930.

In 1901, tired of robbing trains and running from the US law, Butch Cassidy and the Sundance Kid packed it up and moved to Cholila, Argentina. They gave ranching a shot before abandoning it again for the gun.

A fascinating, fictionalized version of ex-president Juan Perón's life, culminating in his return to Buenos Aires in 1973, is Tomás Eloy Martínez's *The Peron Novel*.

1816	1862
Formal independence from Spain is declared at Tucumán on July 9	Buenos Aires is declared capital of the Argentine Republic

people in what is known as the 'Conquista del Desierto' (Conquest of the Desert). The campaign doubled the area under state control and opened up Patagonia to settlement and sheep. Junín de los Andes' Vía Cristi memorial (p325) is likely the region's most impressive and moving tribute to the Mapuche lives lost in this 'war.'

By the turn of the 20th century, Argentina had a highly developed rail network (financed largely by British capital), fanning out from Buenos Aires in all directions. Still, the dark cloud of a vulnerable economy loomed. Because of inequities in land distribution, the prosperity of the late 19th century was far from broad. Industry could not absorb all the immigration. Labor unrest grew. As imports surpassed exports, the economy showed signs of stress. Finally, with the onset of the Great Depression, the military took power under conditions of considerable social unrest. An obscure but oddly visionary colonel, Juan Domingo Perón, was the first leader to try to come to grips with the country's economic crisis.

> Although Argentines criticize the casting of Madonna as Eva Perón, Hollywood's *Evita* (1996), based on the musical by Andrew Lloyd Webber, is still worth a watch.

THE PERÓN DECADE

Lieutenant General Juan Perón emerged in the 1940s to become Argentina's most revered, as well as most despised, political figure. He first came to national prominence as head of the National Department of Labor, after a 1943 military coup toppled civilian rule. In this post, he organized relief efforts after a major earthquake in San Juan, which earned praise throughout the country. In the process he also met Eva (Evita) Duarte (see p32), the radio actress who would become his second wife and make her own major contribution to Argentine history. With the help of Evita, Perón ran for and won the presidency in 1946.

> Eva Perón speaks for herself, to some degree, in her ghostwritten autobiography *La Razón de Mi Vida* (My Mission in Life), well worth a read for Evitaphiles.

During previous sojourns in Fascist Italy and Nazi Germany, Perón had grasped the importance of spectacle in public life and also developed his own brand of watered-down Mussolini-style fascism. He held massive rallies from the balcony of the Casa Rosada, with the equally charismatic 'Evita' at his side. Although they ruled by decree rather than consent, the Peróns legitimized the trade union movement, extended political rights to working-class people, secured voting rights for women and made university education available to any capable individual.

Economic difficulties and rising inflation undermined Juan Perón's second presidency in 1952, and Evita's death the same year dealt a blow to both the country and the president's popularity. In late 1955, a military coup sent him into exile in Spain and initiated nearly three decades of catastrophic military rule.

> For a glimpse into the life of Argentina's beloved Eva Perón, check out Julie M Taylor's *Eva Perón: The Myths of a Woman*.

PERÓN'S EXILE & RETURN

During exile, Perón and his associates constantly plotted their return to Argentina. In the late 1960s, increasing economic problems, strikes, political kidnappings and guerrilla warfare marked Argentine political life. In the midst of these events, Perón's opportunity to return finally arrived in 1973, when the beleaguered military relaxed their objections to Perón's Justicialist party (popularly known as the Peronistas) and loyal Peronista Hector Cámpora was elected president. Cámpora resigned

1869–95	1946
Economy booms, immigration skyrockets and Buenos Aires' population grows from 90,000 to 670,000	With Eva Perón at his side, Juan Perón takes power and makes sweeping changes to the political structure

EVITA, LADY OF HOPE

'I will come again, and I will be millions.'

Eva Perón, 1952

From her humble origins in the Pampas, to her rise to power beside President Juan Perón, Eva María Duarte de Perón is one of the most revered political figures on the planet. Known affectionately to all as Evita, she is Argentina's beloved First Lady, in some ways even eclipsing the legacy of her husband, who governed Argentina from 1946 to 1955.

At age 15, Eva Duarte left her hometown of Junín for Buenos Aires, looking for work as an actor. After stints in theater and film she landed a job in radio. In 1944, Duarte attended a benefit at Buenos Aires' Luna Park for victims of an earthquake in San Juan. Here she met General Juan Perón, head of the National Department of Labor, who was entranced by her intensity and vision. They were married by 1945.

Shortly after Perón won the presidency in 1946, Evita went to work in the office of the Department of Labor and Welfare. During Perón's two terms, Evita empowered her husband both through her charisma and by reaching out to the nation's poor who came to love her dearly. She created the Fundación Eva Perón through which she built housing for the poor, created programs for children, and extended subsidies and distributed clothing and food items directly to needy families. She fervently campaigned for the aged, urging her husband to add elderly rights to the constitution and successfully pushing through a law granting pensions to elderly people in need. The foundation created medical trains and buses that traveled the country, offering health services directly to the poor. She created the Partido Peronista Femenino (Peronista Feminist Party), and, in 1947, successfully pushed through a law extending suffrage to women.

When Perón ran for his second term, thousands gathered in the streets of Buenos Aires demanding she be his running mate. She accepted publicly, but declined in a radio announcement the following day, due to opposition within the military government. The same year, at age 33, Evita died of cancer on July 26.

Although Evita is remembered for extending social justice to those she called the country's *descamisados* (shirtless ones), her rule with Perón was hardly free from controversy. Together they ruled the country with an iron fist, jailing opposition leaders and closing opposition newspapers. When *Time Magazine* referred to her as an 'illegitimate child' she banned the publication, and when she traveled to Europe in 1947 she was refused entrance to Buckingham Palace. However, there is no denying the extent to which she empowered women at all levels of Argentine society and helped the country's poor.

When she said she'd return to 'be millions' in a speech shortly before her death, she probably had no idea of its prophetic truth. Evita today enjoys near-saint status (many have petitioned the Vatican unsuccessfully) and has practically become a pop icon after the release of the Hollywood musical *Evita*, starring Madonna (a serious bone of contention in Argentina). She is loved throughout the world. In Argentina she was, for many, 'our Lady of Hope.'

To get a little closer to Evita, stop by the Museo Evita (p80), or visit her tomb in the Recoleta Cemetery (p78).

upon Perón's return, paving the way for new elections easily won by Perón.

After an 18-year exile, Perón once again symbolized Argentine unity, but there was no substance to his rule. Chronically ill, Perón died in mid-1974, leaving a fragmented country to his ill-qualified third wife – and vice president – Isabelita.

1952	1955
Eva Perón dies of cancer on July 26 at age 33	Juan Perón is exiled to Spain after another military coup

THE DIRTY WAR & THE DISAPPEARED

In the late 1960s and early '70s, antigovernment feeling was rife, and street protests often exploded into all-out riots. Armed guerrilla organizations like the Ejército Revolucionario del Pueblo (ERP) and the Montoneros emerged as radical opponents of the military, oligarchies and US influence in Latin America. Perón's bumbling widow, Isabelita, along with her adviser, José López Rega, created the Triple A (Alianza Argentina Anticomunista), a death squad to take on the revolutionary groups. With increasing official corruption exacerbating Isabelita's incompetence, Argentina found itself plunged into chaos.

On March 24, 1976, a bloodless military coup, led by army general Jorge Rafael Videla, took control of the Argentine state apparatus and ushered in a period of terror and brutality. Videla's sworn aim was to crush the guerrilla movements and restore social order, and much of the Argentine press and public gave their support. During what the regime euphemistically labeled the Process of National Reorganization (known as El Proceso), security forces went about the country arresting, torturing, raping and killing anyone on their hit list of suspected leftists.

During the period between 1976 and 1983, often referred to as the Guerra Sucia or Dirty War, human rights groups estimate that some 30,000 people were 'disappeared.' To disappear meant to be abducted, detained, tortured and probably killed with no hope of legal process. Ironically, the Dirty War ended only when the Argentine military attempted a real military operation.

FALKLANDS/MALVINAS WAR

Argentina's economy continued to decline during military rule and eventually collapsed in chaos. El Proceso was coming undone.

In late 1981, General Leopoldo Galtieri assumed the role of president. To stay in power amid a faltering economy and mass social unrest, Galtieri played the nationalist card and launched an invasion in April 1982 to dislodge the British from the Falkland Islands (p424), which had been claimed by Argentina as the Islas Malvinas for nearly a century and a half.

Overnight, the move unleashed a wave of nationalist euphoria that then subsided almost as fast. Galtieri underestimated the determined response of British Prime Minister Margaret Thatcher, and after only 74 days, Argentina's ill-trained, poorly motivated and mostly teenaged forces surrendered ignominiously. In 1983, Argentines elected civilian Raúl Alfonsín to the presidency.

AFTERMATH OF THE DIRTY WAR

In his successful 1983 presidential campaign, Alfonsín pledged to prosecute military officers responsible for human rights violations during the Dirty War. He convicted high-ranking junta for kidnapping, torture and homicide, but when the government attempted to also try junior officers, these officers responded with uprisings in several different parts of the country. The timid administration succumbed to military demands and produced a Ley de la Obediencia Debida (Law of Due Obedience), allowing lower-ranking officers to use the defense that they

Hectór Olivera's 1983 film *Funny Dirty Little War*, available on DVD, is an unsettling but excellent black comedy set in a fictitious town just before the 1976 military coup.

Set in the 1970s during Argentina's Dirty War, *Imagining Argentina* is an enthralling novel about a Buenos Aires playwright who acquires the ability to see *desaparecidos*, people who 'disappeared' at the hands of generals.

Nunca Más, the official report of the National Commission on the Disappeared, systematically details military abuses from 1976 to 1983.

1976–83	1982
Military juntas control Argentina and kill an estimated 30,000 during the 'Dirty War'	The Falkland Islands War

Patricia Sagastizabal's award-winning *A Secret for Julia* is a gripping novel about a Dirty War survivor living in London years later when one of her former torturers tracks her down.

were following orders, as well as a Punto Final (Stopping Point), beyond which no criminal or civil prosecutions could take place. These measures eliminated prosecutions of notorious individuals such as Navy Captain Alfredo Astiz (the Angel of Death), who was implicated in the disappearance of a Swedish-Argentine teenager and the highly publicized deaths of two French nuns.

In December 1990, president Carlos Menem pardoned Videla and his cohorts even though the Argentine public overwhelmingly opposed it. During the 1995 presidential campaign, Dirty War issues resurfaced spectacularly when journalist Horacio Verbitsky wrote *The Flight* (1996), a book based on interviews with former Navy Captain Adolfo Scilingo, in which Scilingo acknowledges throwing political prisoners, alive but drugged, into the Atlantic. In January 2005, Scilingo went to trial in Spain facing numerous counts of human rights abuses and a prison sentence of 6000 years.

Demand for a complete list of the disappeared is still strong within Argentina. Human rights organizations like the Madres de la Plaza de Mayo (mothers of Dirty War victims, who still march around the Plaza de Mayo every Thursday) keep up their protests, campaigning for justice and information about the Disappeared (*desaparecidos*) and their children. Most of the criminals of El Proceso, however, still walk the streets.

RECENT DEVELOPMENTS

Most Argentines feel an atrocity such as the Dirty War could never happen again, and visiting the country after more than 20 years of civilian rule leaves one amazed that it did happen.

Carlos Menem's tenure as president (1989–99) ushered in a period of false economic stability through a combination of radical free market reform and pegging the peso to the US dollar. It was a period of both upward mobility for the Argentine middle-class and rampant government corruption, during which Menem sold off state-owned enterprises including YPF (the national oil company), the national telephone company, the postal service and Aerolíneas Argentinas. Menem changed the constitution to allow himself to run for a second term (which he won), and unsuccessfully tried again so he could run for a third term in 1999. Amid accusations of corruption, Menem stepped down. Adding to his scandals, Menem married Chilean Cecilia Bolocco, former Miss Universe and 35 years his junior. In 2001, he was placed under house arrest and fled to Chile where he remained under self-imposed exile until returning to Argentina in January 2005 (after warrants were dropped), pledging to run again for president.

Many blame Menem for the economic crisis that began near the end of his term and plunged the country into dire economic straits by 2001. Fernando de la Rua succeeded Menem in the 1999 elections, inheriting an unstable economy and US$114 billion in foreign debt. With the peso pegged to the US dollar, Argentina was unable to compete on the international market and exports slumped. A further decline in international prices of agricultural products pummeled the Argentine economy, which depended heavily on farm product exports.

By 2001, the economy teetered on the brink of collapse, and the administration, with Finance Minister Domingo Cavallo at the wheel, took

1983	2001
Raúl Alfonsín becomes the first civilian leader of the country since 1976	Argentine economy goes into tailspin; President de la Rua places caps on bank withdrawals and later resigns amid violent protests

measures to end deficit spending and slash state spending, including employee salaries and pensions. After attempted debt swaps and talk of devaluing the peso, middle-class Argentines began emptying their bank accounts. De la Rua responded to the bank run by placing a cap of US$250 per week on withdrawals. It was the beginning of the end.

By mid December, unemployment hit 18.3% and unions began a nationwide strike. Things came to a head on December 21 when middle-class Argentines took to the streets banging pots and pans in what became known as the *cacerolazo* (from the word *cacerola*, meaning pan) in protest against de la Rua's handling of the economic situation. Rioting spread throughout the country, leaving over 25 dead, and President de la Rua finally resigned. Three interim presidents resigned by the time Eduardo Duhalde took office in January 2002, becoming the fifth president in two weeks. Duhalde devalued the peso in January 2002 and announced Argentina would default on US$140 billion in foreign debt, the biggest default in world history.

Since then, with the peso hovering around three to the US dollar, things have settled down, and there's even a positive mood. Argentine exports are up, giving the country currency to repay its debt, yet investor confidence is still slim. Nestor Kirchner became president in 2003 after opponent Carlos Menem stepped out of the race. In January 2005, Kirchner put forth a take-it-or-leave-it offer to foreign investors, offering to swap the country's debt for new bonds which Argentina would be more likely to pay back. For investors, it's a better offer than Argentina's previous offer to pay back a quarter of its debt. For Argentines, the standard of living is still one of Latin America's highest, and while times are still tough, there's a palpable optimism throughout most of the country.

2002	2004
Argentina defaults on international debt, the largest default in world history	Argentina wins two Olympic gold medals, beating the US in basketball and Paraguay in soccer

The Culture

THE NATIONAL PSYCHE

Throughout Latin America and much of the world, Argentines endure a reputation for being snobbish European wanna-bes who regard themselves as superior to the rest of Latin Americans. They think that they're economically superior (they once were), that they play the best soccer (they often do), that they have the most beautiful women (depends on your taste), and that they dance the most sophisticated dance in the world (no contest). Indeed, the classic Argentine stereotype is grounded, at least partially, in truth. But anyone who spends some time in Argentina – especially outside Buenos Aires – finds the stereotype immediately challenged by warmth, friendliness and the gregarious social nature that more accurately defines the Argentine psyche.

To understand the contrasts, one must delve deeper into the stereotype. There are two basic Argentines: *porteños* (people from Buenos Aires) and folks from the rest of the country. *Porteños* suffer the same reputation outside of Buenos Aires that Argentines suffer outside of Argentina. They're the snobby urbanites who romp around the country in their fashionable clothes, who can dance a tango but know nothing about the *chacarera*, the *samba* or the *carnavalito* (traditional folk dances), and are friendly with the locals only when their 2005 Peugeot breaks down on a bumpy dirt road more suitable for pickups. Truth is, *porteños* inhabit one of the world's most fashionable and cosmopolitan and coolest cities, but when they hit the provinces and their urban smarts fail to serve them, the rest of Argentina winks and gets its digs.

Stereotypes aside, there's no denying the fact that Argentines are some of the most welcoming, sociable, endearing folks on the planet. Talk to anyone who has traveled in the country and they'll inevitably remark on the friendliness of the people. Opinionated, brash and passionate, Argentines are quick to engage in conversation and will talk after dinner or over coffee until the wee hours of the morning. Argentina's most visible customs are entirely social in nature. The tradition of drinking *mate* is more about

Argentines almost always exchange a kiss on the cheek in greeting – even among men. In formal and business situations, though, it is better to go with a handshake.

SOCIAL DOS & DON'TS

■ Remember to preface any request with the appropriate salutation – *buenos días* (good morning), *buenas tardes* (good afternoon) or *buenas noches* (good evening) – and use *usted* (the formal term for 'you') unless you are certain that informality is appropriate. However, people in Buenos Aires can be considerably more to the point.

■ When dealing with official bureaucracy, try to be polite no matter what. Even if they appear to flaunt the power of their position, it is often best to play along and be respectful.

■ *Porteños* tend to dress up for business, nicer restaurants, casinos and nightclubs. Be aware that some places that are informal by day may become formal in the evening. Athletic shoes are not appropriate for a number of night spots.

■ Some sensitive subjects to avoid in conversation with Argentines (at least until you know them better) are the Dirty War, Argentina's international debt and the Falklands (call them Las Islas Malvinas). Brits should avoid discussions about the Falkland Islands War.

■ Some fans are very serious about *fútbol* (soccer). Cheering for the wrong team in the wrong bar could result in more than just a verbal rebuke.

sharing among friends than about the tea's stimulating properties, and the famous *asado* (barbecue) is equal parts beef and buddies, where family and friends turn a meal into an all-day social event.

While Argentines are friendly and passionate they, especially *porteños*, also have a subtle broodiness to their nature. This stems from a pessimism Argentines have acquired as they have watched their country, one of the world's economic powerhouses during the late 19th and early 20th centuries, descend into a morass of immense international debt. They've endured military coups, severe government repression (such as that of the Dirty War of 1976–83), and year after year they've seen their beloved Argentina, rich in resources, people and beauty, plundered by corrupt politicians.

But this is just a part of the picture. Add everything together and you get a people who are fun, fiery, opinionated and proud. And you'll come to love them for it.

Argentines tend to not shy away from stereotypes. Fair-complexioned people are called *Rusos* (Russians), Asians are called *Chinos* (Chinese) and if anyone is overweight, they may get a *gordo* (fatty).

LIFESTYLE

Although Buenos Aires holds more than one-third of the country's population, it's surprisingly unlike the rest of Argentina or, for that matter, much of Latin America. The city's core neighborhoods, especially the Microcentro, are more akin to Paris or New York than Caracas or Lima. As it is throughout the country, one's lifestyle in the capital depends mostly on money. A modern flat rented by a young advertising creative in Buenos Aires' Las Cañitas neighborhood differs greatly from a family home in one of the city's impoverished *villas* (poor neighborhoods), where electricity and clean water are luxuries and street crime comes in daily doses.

Argentina's 97.1% literacy rate is approximately the same as in the United States.

Geography and ethnicity also play an important role. Both of these Buenos Aires homes have little in common with that of an indigenous family living in an adobe house in a desolate valley of the Andean Northwest, where life is eked out through subsistence agriculture and earth goddess Pachamama outshines Evita as a cultural icon. In regions such as the Pampas, Mendoza province and Patagonia, a provincial friendliness surrounds a robust, outdoor lifestyle. This is cattle, wine and mountain country, with strong gaucho (Argentine cowboy) traditions, *asados* and *estancias* (ranches).

By Latin American standards, Argentina has a large middle class, though it has struggled greatly since the recession that began in 1999. Still, middle-class neighborhoods throughout the country are often quiet and tree-lined, with at least one fairly new car in the driveway. Buying new furniture, however, is a luxury, and middle-class homes are often decorated with the pleasant furnishings that have been in the family for years, and the requisite photos of family members vacationing in places like Bariloche or Villa Carlos Paz adorn the walls.

Three Argentines have won the Nobel Prize for Science, while two have won the Nobel Prize for Peace: Carlos Saavedra Lamas (1936) and Adolfo Perez Esquivel (1980).

The devotion to family is something all Argentines have in common. The Buenos Aires ad exec joins her family for weekend dinners, and the café owner in San Juan meets cousins and friends out at the family *estancia* for a Sunday among the alamos (poplars) and grapevines. Especially within the country's poorer households, children commonly live with their parents until they're married. Many kids live at home while attending university or, if there's enough money in the bank, go off to school somewhere like Córdoba to live with roommates in modern student high-rises.

Argentine culture has long been known for its machismo and the accompanying dose of misogyny and homophobia. But things are changing. Women occupy 30% of Argentina's congressional seats (compared with about 12% in the US and France), while the workforce is nearly 40% female.

ARGENTINE JOKES

Here are some classic jokes that make light of the famous Argentine pride and bravado.

- How does an Argentine commit suicide?
  He jumps off his ego.

- How do you recognize an Argentine spy?
  From the sign on his back that says, 'I am the greatest spy in the world.'

- A man meets an Argentine on the street and asks him for a light. The Argentine starts patting his pants, chest and back pockets. 'Sorry,' he says, 'I can't find my lighter – but man, do I have a great body!'

Especially among the country's youth, women are breaking out of their traditional roles and men are becoming more accepting of that fact.

In 2002, Buenos Aires passed Latin America's first ordinance allowing gay civil unions, and organizations are fighting to extend the law throughout the province. Openly gay restaurants, bars and hotels are found throughout the capital, and the city's gay tango scene is growing. Outside the capital and the Atlantic's beach resorts, however, tolerance is less apparent (see p466).

Argentines frequently honor national, religious and cultural icons on the anniversary of their death, not on their birthday.

POPULATION

The great majority of Argentines live in cities. Of the country's nearly 40 million people, 12 million live in greater Buenos Aires alone. The country's second biggest city is Córdoba (1,300,000), followed by Rosario (1,095,000), Mendoza (with the inclusion of greater Mendoza), Tucumán and La Plata. What's left is a country with *lots* of open space (which you'll have to cross any time you want to go somewhere).

The birth rate is 2.24 children per woman, which is higher than Brazil and Chile, but lower than most of Latin America.

Compared to countries like Bolivia, Peru and Ecuador, Argentina has a small indigenous population. Historically, native populations were relatively thin along the coast and in the Pampas, and those who did not die from hard labor and disease were eradicated during the Conquista del Desierto (Conquest of the Desert; see p30). Unlike other Latin American countries, Argentina was built more on the backs of imported European labor – primarily Italian and Spanish – than indigenous or African slavery. The most visible indigenous cultures in Argentina today are found in the Lake District and the Andean Northwest.

SPORTS

Fútbol (soccer) is Argentina's passion and is far and away the most popular sport in the country. The national team has been to the World Cup final game four times and has triumphed twice, in 1978 and 1986. Argentines (and the media) devote a great deal of time following the Boca Juniors, River Plate and other club teams, and the fanatical behavior of the country's *hinchas* or *barra brava* (hooligans) rival that of their European counterparts.

Uruguayan writer and famous Latin American social/political critic Eduardo Galeano published Soccer in Sun & Shadow *in 1998, which has many observations on Argentine soccer.*

Horse racing, polo and boxing are also popular, followed by tennis, rugby, golf, cricket, basketball and Formula One automobile racing. Among the best-known national sports figures are soccer legends Diego Maradona and Gabriel Batistuta, tennis stars Guillermo Vilas and Gabriela Sabatini, the late boxers Oscar Bonavena and Carlos Monzón, ex-Formula One standouts Juan Manuel Fangio (see p143) and Carlos Reutemann and basketball phenomenon Emanuel Ginobili, who holds a championship ring with the NBA's San Antonio Spurs.

For well over a century, the Campeonato Argentino Abierto de Polo (Argentine Open Polo Championship) has been held in the Palermo section of Buenos Aires. Most polo events are open to the public and are often free of charge. Argentina is recognized as having some of the best polo horses and players in the world. The players are also known as relentless playboys who make cameo appearances at parties in New York City and nightclubs in Monaco.

Like soccer, rugby traces its origins to the English influence on Argentine culture. The national team, the Pumas, plays world-class international competition, but rugby is still primarily popular as a school sport. Even the asthmatic Ernesto 'Che' Guevara was a famously enthusiastic rugby player during his youth.

MULTICULTURALISM

About 97% of the Argentine population claims European descent (mainly Spanish and Italian). If this statistic is in fact true, Argentina is the least racially diverse country in the Americas. However, on a closer look, Argentina is a country that has been influenced by numerous cultures and never fails to surprise, with seemingly random enclaves of Syrians, Welsh, Bavarians, Croatians and others who offer their own unique cultural twists.

From the mid-19th century on, Italians, Basques, English, Ukrainians and other European immigrants flooded into Argentina. Italian surnames became more common than Spanish names. These days, some of the distinctive ethnic groups include the Anglo-Argentines throughout the country, the Welsh-Argentines in Chubut province, the Germans of Eldorado in Misiones province, the Bulgarians and Yugoslavs of Roque Sáenz Peña in the Chaco and the Ukrainians of La Pampa. Argentina also has a substantial Jewish population of about 300,000 (see p128). Middle Eastern immigrants, though not numerous, have attained great political influence – the most obvious case being former president Carlos Menem, who was of Syrian ancestry.

Immigrants from Asia are a visible presence in Buenos Aires and increasingly in the interior. The first Japanese Argentines arrived during the late 19th century immigration boom. Today they are a well-established community and there are even Japanese-Argentine sumo wrestlers. Koreans, who number in the tens of thousands, are a more recent immigrant group and are only now starting to be welcomed into Argentine society. The Chinese-Argentine population is not particularly well integrated into the country, but there is a miniature Chinatown around Calle Arribeños beside the Belgrano train station in Buenos Aires.

There is still a reasonably large indigenous population in the northern highlands and sprinkled throughout other regions of the country. The largest groups are the Quechua of the northwest and the Mapuche of northern Patagonia, but there are important populations of Guaraní, Tobas and others in the Chaco and in northeastern cities such as Resistencia and Santa Fe.

RELIGION

Roman Catholicism is the official state religion, though only a relatively small percentage of Argentines attend mass regularly. Even so, the church still holds much sway over the culture; up until recently, the president of Argentina had to be Catholic. As in the rest of Latin America, the religion sometimes morphs into fascinating blends of indigenous tradition or local belief and official church doctrine. Shrines adorned with water bottles and

Although Gabriel Batistuta will forever live in Diego Maradona's shadow, he scored a record 56 goals for the Argentine national soccer team, while Maradona scored 34.

Buenos Aires' Jewish community of a third of a million people is the largest of its kind in Latin America.

María Luisa Bemberg's historically based films illuminate the relationship between Argentine women and the church. The Oscar-nominated *Camila* recounts the tale of a Catholic socialite who fell in love with a young Jesuit priest in 1847, and was later executed by the government.

car parts and devoted to the female saint Difunta Correa (see p314) add color to roads throughout the country. You are also likely to see shrines decorated with red flags honoring the saintlike Gaucho Antonio Gil (p172), a sort of gaucho Robin Hood worshipped by many.

There is a good-sized Jewish community in Buenos Aires, which has been in the city for a number of generations. Evangelical Protestantism is gaining followers in Argentina as are the Jehovah's Witnesses, Hare Krishnas and Mormons – it is almost impossible to miss the enormous Mormon tabernacle near the Buenos Aires airport.

Visitors to Recoleta and Chacarita cemeteries in Buenos Aires will see pilgrims going to the resting places of Juan and Eva Perón, psychic Madre María and tango singer Carlos Gardel. Followers come to communicate and to ask for favors by praying at the tombs, and they leave offerings.

> Under the old Argentine constitution, Carlos Menem had to convert from Islam to Catholicism to become president.

WOMEN IN ARGENTINA

Argentine women are making progress in their struggle for social and economic independence and equality. More and more educated women are excelling in the job market, but glass ceilings exist and the core of most businesses is a boys' club. Catholicism holds less sway over the country than it once did, but the Church – under a conservative political agenda – played a major role in the evolution of the society and its current mores.Only recently have women started to push beyond the roles of mother and homemaker. On the flip side, women such as Las Madres de la Plaza de Mayo (below) have been able to exert a unique power from that role.

The rights of women continue to improve as Argentina moves away from its insular mind-set – thanks to greater outside influence and the effects of the international tourism boom – but Argentina's famous machismo does not die easily.

ARTS
Literature

Despite its rich history, Argentine writing only reached an international audience during the Latin American literary explosion of the 1960s and 1970s, when the stories of Jorge Luis Borges, Luisa Valenzuela, Julio Cortázar, Adolfo Bioy Casares and Silvina Ocampo, among many others, were widely translated for the first time.

The two writers most responsible for creating international interest in Argentine literature are Jorge Luis Borges and Julio Cortázar (opposite). The pair's recognition as great Argentine writers is somewhat ironic, as

> Doris Meyer's biography *Victoria Ocampo: Against the Wind and the Tide* (1990) is one of the few opportunities that English readers will have to read Victoria Ocampo's essays.

LAS MADRES DE LA PLAZA DE MAYO

In 1977, a year after a military coup trampled human rights in all domains, 14 mothers marched into the Plaza de Mayo in Buenos Aires, in spite of a ban on public gatherings ordered by the military government. They demanded information about their missing children, who had 'disappeared' as part of the government's efforts to quash political opposition. The group, which took on the name Las Madres de la Plaza de Mayo (The Mothers of Plaza de Mayo), developed into a powerful social movement and were the only political organization who overtly challenged the military government. They were particularly effective as they carried out their struggle under the banner of motherhood, which made them relatively unassailable in Argentine culture. Their movement showed the power of women – at least in a traditional role – in Argentine culture and they are generally credited as helping to kick start the reestablishment of the country's civil society.

JORGE LUIS BORGES & JULIO CORTÁZAR

As a half-Jewish, half-English Argentine who was educated in Europe, Borges (1899–1986) was influenced by everything from Jewish Cabalists to HG Wells, Cervantes and Kafka. His tight, precise, paradoxical *ficciones* are part essay and part story, blurring the line between myth and truth, underscoring the idea that reality is a matter of perception and that an infinite number of realities can exist simultaneously. His early stories like 'Death and the Compass' and 'Streetcorner Man' offer a metaphysical twist on Argentine themes, and his later works, such as 'The Lottery in Babylon,' 'The Circular Ruins' and 'Garden of the Forking Paths,' are works of fantasy. His short-story collections published in English include *Labyrinths, The Aleph, A Universal History of Iniquity* and *Collected Fictions,* a complete collection of his stories.

Julio Cortázar (1914–84) was also greatly influenced by Europe; he was born in Belgium and died a French citizen. Despite being discovered and influenced by Borges in the 1940s, Cortázar's writing was considerably different. His short stories and novels are more anthropological and concern people living seemingly normal lives in a world where the surreal becomes common-place. This gave Cortázar the opportunity to address the idea of the absurd and farce in modern life. Cortázar's most famous book is *Hopscotch,* a novel influenced by Borges' 'The Garden of the Forking Paths.' *Hopscotch* requires the reader to first read the book straight through, then read it a second time, 'hopscotching' through the chapters in a prescribed but nonlinear pattern for a different take on the story.

neither considered themselves to be part of an Argentine national literary tradition. Both were interested in universal human themes and were greatly influenced by European writers and philosophers.

The contemporary, post-boom generation of Argentine writers is more reality-based, often reflecting the influence of popular culture and directly confronting the political realities of the authoritarian Argentina of the 1970s. One of the most famous post-boom Argentine writers is Manuel Puig, who studied film in Italy and took up screenwriting before beginning his career as a short-story writer and novelist. In the Argentine tradition, Puig did much of his writing in exile, fleeing Argentina during the Perón years and ultimately settling in Mexico.

The late Osvaldo Soriano (1943–97), perhaps Argentina's most popular contemporary novelist, wrote *A Funny Dirty Little War,* later adapted into a film, and *Winter Quarters* (1989). In Soriano's *Shadows* (1993), the protagonist is lost in an Argentina where the names are the same, but all the familiar landmarks and points of reference have lost their meaning.

The youngster of the post-boom generation is Rodrigo Fresán, whose novel *The History of Argentina* was an international bestseller. Both his short stories and two more recent works, *Jardines de Kensington* and *Mantra,* deal with the uncertainty of life in modern Argentina.

Cinema

Argentine cinema has achieved international stature, especially since the end of the military dictatorship in 1983. Many Argentine films, both before and after the Dirty War, are available abroad and new films are reaching the international market all the time.

On of the best places to start is Luis Puenzo's *The Official Story* (1985). This movie, which is standard viewing in any history of Argentina class, deals with a controversial theme of the Dirty War: the adoption of the children of missing or murdered parents by those responsible for their disappearance or death. Some critics, however, challenged Puenzo for apparently implying that Argentines were innocently ignorant of the atrocities of the time. The film won an Oscar for best foreign language film.

Borges was famous for his dry ironic wit and once described the British-Argentine Falkland Islands War as 'two bald men fighting over a comb.'

Federico Andahazi's sexually explicit but unquestionably literary *The Anatomist* (1998) caused an uproar when the wealthy sponsor of a national literary prize tried to overturn the award her committee had given the author.

Perhaps the best internationally known film to deal with Argentina is Héctor Babenco's English-language *Kiss of the Spider Woman* (1985), starring William Hurt and the late Raúl Julia. Based on Manuel Puig's novel, this Oscar-winning film portrays the intricate way in which the police and military abused political prisoners and exploited informers. It tells the story of two prisoners, a middle-aged gay man and a young revolutionary, who explore ideas of sexuality and suffering while acting out scenes from old movies.

Want to learn more about the history and beginnings of Argentine cinema? Check out www .surdelsur.com/cine/cinein /indexingles.html

Madonna's *Evita* (1996), directed by Alan Parker, caused controversy in the country as many resented the choice of a sex symbol to play a national cultural icon. Madonna also made a couple of disparaging remarks about Argentine food and how difficult it was to find a good gym in Buenos Aires, which led to protests and a domestic remake of the movie in the same year, cast with a more chaste – and more Argentine – Evita. It was called *Eva Perón: the True Story,* starring Esther Gori.

The film *Seven Years in Tibet,* starring Brad Pitt, was mostly filmed in Patagonia.

Today's cutting-edge Argentine cinema includes director Lucrecia Martel, whose 2001 *La Ciénaga* (The Swamp) tells the story of the crises of two families in Salta, with almost a documentary-style realism. In 2004, she released the acclaimed *la Niña Santa* (The Holy Girl), which deals with conflicts of religion and desire. Pablo Trapero's gritty *El Bonaerense* (2002) received considerable international attention. This story of a young rural locksmith who is forced to leave his family to join the Buenos Aires police force is an indictment of the corruption and wastefulness of the entire Buenos Aires police culture. Mariano Llinás is another popular director, whose 2002 film *Balnearios* shows how the influx of outsiders shapes and changes people's existence in little tourist towns. For film buffs, the Museu del Arte Latinoamericano de Buenos Aires (MALBA: The Buenos Aires Museum of Latin American Art, p79) has a weekly film series which touches on various cultural, political and historical topics.

Popular Argentine actor Rodrigo de la Serna played Alberto Granado, Che Guevara's humorous and often lecherous travel partner in the 2004 movie version of Guevara's *The Motorcycle Diaries*. De la Serna arguably stole the film.

Music & Dance

Music and dance are unavoidable in Argentina and none is more famous than the beautiful and complex tango (see the boxed text, p44). There is, of course, more to music and dance in Argentina than just the tango: from the Buenos Aires Opera to the burgeoning DJ dance scene to venerated Argentine rock bands.

Traditional music is generally known as *folklórico*. The late Atahualpa Yupanqui was a giant of this genre, which takes much of its inspiration from classic Andean highlands music. Los Chalchaleros are a northern *folklórico* institution who have turned out more than 40 albums over a 50-year career. Crooner Mercedes Sosa of Tucumán, with her huge international following, is the reigning diva of this music. *Folklórico* is sort of an umbrella genre that captures a lot of styles and there are many contemporary branches (*chamamé, chacarera, carnavalito* and *copla*) that are popular throughout the countryside, claiming fans of all ages.

Born in Córdoba in the early 1940s, *cuarteto* is Argentina's original pop music: despised by the middle and upper classes for its arresting rhythm and off-beat musical pattern (called the '*tunga-tunga'*), as well as its working-class lyrics, it is definitely music from the margins. Although definitively *cordobés* (from Córdoba), it's played in working-class bars, dance halls and stadiums throughout the country.

Buenos Aires' Teatro Colón is one of the world's premier opera houses and hosts top world talent. Tickets are unfortunately hard to come by, as many of the theater's 3500 seats are held by season ticketholders. However, it is sometimes possible to watch touring ensembles rehearse (see p75).

Rock musicians such as Charly García (formerly a member of the pioneering group Sui Generis) and Fito Páez are national icons and have been around for years – although they are no longer exactly hip with the younger generation. Los Fabulosos Cadillacs (winners of a Grammy in 1998 for best alternative Latin rock group) popularized ska and reggae mixed with rock and they still tour the world. Bersuit Vergarabat, who put out their first album in 1992, is still going strong as one of the most popular, and populous (eight members), bands in the country. Their classic Argentine rock sound, mixed with a variety of Latin rhythms, is woven with numerous cultural and political references. Other popular national rock acts include the off-beat Babasónicos, Divididos, Catupecu Machu and Natas.

Cumbia Villera is a relatively recent musical phenomenon: a fusion of *cumbia* (originally a Colombian dance music) and gangsta posturing with a punk edge and reggae overtones. This spawn of Buenos Aires shantytowns has aggressive lyrics that deal with marginalization, poverty and the Argentine economic crisis. Gauchin and Los Pibes Chorros are a couple of the many young Cumbia Villera groups.

Charly García's version of the Argentine national anthem does what Jimi Hendrix did for 'The Star-Spangled Banner,' but it earned García a court appearance for 'lacking respect for national symbols.'

Electronic music has made its way into Argentina and takes on various forms in popular music. Hybrid *bandas electrónicas* (electronic bands) are led by the likes of Intima, Mujik and Adicta, who consider British groups like Massive Attack their influences. Pop music groups disappear as quickly as they come onto the scene, but Rosal and Miranda are bands of the moment. DJ-based club and dance music is increasingly popular, particularly in the cities. Some of the heavyweights to look out for are Bad Boy Orange (the reigning king of Argentine drum 'n' bass), DiegoRo-K (who has been around since the mid-1980s, and is known as the Maradona of Argentine DJs), Fabian Dellamonica and Zucker.

Architecture

As the indigenous population was relatively nomadic in central and southern Argentina, the country does not have the great pre-Columbian architecture of Andean South America, though a few significant archaeological sites do exist in the Andean Northwest (see p235). This region has notable, if not abundant, Spanish colonial architecture in cities such as Salta and Tucumán, and in villages in isolated areas like the Quebrada de Humahuaca. Other areas for colonial architecture, or at least atmosphere, include Córdoba and Carmen de Patagones. Buenos Aires itself has scattered colonial examples, but is essentially a turn-of-the-century city whose architectural influences are predominantly French. The neighborhoods of San Telmo, Recoleta and La Boca all offer different and intriguing domestic architecture.

The palatial Teatro Colón opera house was built in France and then shipped part and parcel to Buenos Aires, where it was reassembled in 1908.

Catholicism has provided Argentina with some of its finest monuments, from the lonely, picturesque churches of the Andean Northwest to the colonial cathedral in Córdoba and the neo-Gothic basilicas of Luján and La Plata. Recent architecture tends to the large and impersonal, with a substantial number of modernistic glassy buildings in the downtown area.

Theater

Theater is important in Argentina, not only in cosmopolitan Buenos Aires, but even in the most remote of provinces. The country's legendary performers include Luis Sandrini and Lola Membrives, and foreign writers like Federico García Lorca and Jean Cocteau have explored the Buenos Aires theater scene. Argentina's most famous contemporary playwrights and directors include Juan Carlos Gené, Ciro Zorzoli, Lorena Vega, José Muscari and Daniel Veronese.

THE TANGO   Sandra Bao

The air hangs heavy, smoky and dark. Streams of diffused light illuminate a large, open space. A lone woman, dressed in slit skirt and high heels, sits with legs crossed at one of the small tables surrounding a wooden dance floor. Her eyes dart at the figures all around her, casually looking here and there, in search of the subtle signal. Her gaze sweeps over several tables and suddenly locks onto a stranger's eyes, and there it is: the *cabezazo*, the signal, a quick tilt of his head. She briefly considers the offer, then nods with a slight smile. His smile is broader, and he gets up to approach her table. As he nears she rises to meet him, and the new pair head out toward the dance floor, reaching it just as the sultry music begins to play.

The tango hasn't always been quite so mysterious, but it does have a long and somewhat complex history. Though the exact origins can't be pinpointed, the dance is thought to have started in Buenos Aires in the 1880s. Legions of European immigrants, mostly lower-class men, arrived in the great village of Buenos Aires to seek their fortunes in the new country. They settled on the capital's *arrabales* (fringes), but missing their motherlands and the women they left behind, they sought out cafés and bordellos to ease the loneliness. Here the men mingled and danced with waitresses and prostitutes. It was a strong blend of machismo, passion and longing, with an almost fighting edge to it.

Small musical ensembles were soon brought in to accompany early tangos, playing tunes influenced by Pampas *milonga* verse, Spanish and Italian melodies and African *candombe* drums. (The *bandoneón*, a type of small accordion, was brought into these sessions and has since become an inextricable part of the tango orchestra.) Here the tango song was also born. It summarized the new urban experience for the immigrants and was permeated with nostalgia for a disappearing way of life. Themes ranged from profound feelings about changing neighborhoods to the figure of the mother, male friendship and betrayal by women. Sometimes, raunchy lyrics were added.

The perceived vulgarity of the dance was deeply frowned upon by the reigning elites, but it did manage to influence some brash young members of the upper classes. These rebel jet-setters took the new novelty to Paris and created a craze – a dance that became an acceptable outlet for human desires, expressed on the dance floors of elegant cabarets. The trend spread around Europe and even to the USA, and 1913 was considered by some 'the year of the tango.' When the evolved dance returned to Buenos Aires, now refined and famous, the tango finally earned the respectability it deserved. The golden years of tango were just beginning.

Gardel & the Tango

In June 1935, a Cuban woman committed suicide in Havana; meanwhile, in New York and in Puerto Rico two other women tried to poison themselves. And it was all over the same man – a man none of them had ever met. The man was tango singer Carlos Gardel, El Zorzal Criollo, the songbird of Buenos Aires, and he had just died in a plane crash in Colombia.

Though born in France, Gardel was the epitome of the immigrant *porteño*. When he was three, his destitute single mother brought him to Buenos Aires. In his youth, he worked at a variety of menial jobs, but he also managed to entertain his neighbors with his rapturous singing. A performing career began after he befriended Uruguayan-born José Razzano, and the two of them sang together in a popular duo until Razzano lost his voice. From 1917 onward, Gardel performed solo.

Carlos Gardel played an enormous role in creating the tango *canción* (song). Almost single-handedly, he took the style out of Buenos Aires' tenements and brought it to Paris and New York. His crooning voice, suaveness and overall charisma made him an immediate success in

The official theater season is June to August, but there are always performances on Buenos Aires' version of Broadway, Avenida Corrientes, and at smaller theater companies in the city. Espacio Callejón and Teatro del Abasto are two recommended theatre spaces. In summer, some of the best shows are seen in the provincial beach resort of Mar del Plata.

Latin American countries, and for a while his timing was perfect. His star rose in tango's golden years of the 1920s and 1930s and Gardel became a recording star. Unfortunately, his later film career was tragically cut short by that fatal plane crash.

Every day a steady procession of pilgrims visits Carlos Gardel's sarcophagus in the Cementerio de la Chacarita in Buenos Aires, where a lit cigarette often smolders between the metal fingers of his life-size statue. The large, devoted community of his followers, known as *gardelianos,* cannot pass a day without listening to his songs or watching his films. Another measure of his ongoing influence is the common saying that 'Gardel sings better every day.' Elvis should be so lucky.

Tango at a Milonga Today

Tango is not an easy dance to describe; it needs to be seen and experienced. Despite a long evolution from its origins, it's still sensual and erotic. The upper bodies are held upright and close, with faces almost touching. The man's hand is pressed against the woman's back, guiding her, with their other hands held together and out. The lower body does most of the work. The woman's hips swivel, her legs alternating in short or wide sweeps and quick kicks, sometimes between the man's legs. The man guides, a complicated job since he must flow with the music, direct the woman, meld with her steps and avoid other dancers. He'll add his own fancy pivoting moves, and together the couple flows in a communion with the music. Pauses and abrupt directional changes punctuate the dance. It's a serious business, which takes a good amount of concentration, and while dancing the pair wear hard expressions. Smiling and chatting are reserved for between songs.

At an established *milonga* (tango dance hall), choosing an adequate partner involves many levels of hidden codes, rules and signals that dancers must follow. After all, no serious *milonguera* (female regular at a *milonga;* the male equivalent is *milonguero*) wants to be caught dancing with someone stepping on her toes (and expensive tango heels). In fact, some men will only ask an unknown woman to dance after the second song, so as not to be stuck for the four tango songs that make a session. It's also considered polite to dance at least two songs with any partner; if you are given a curt *'gracias'* after just one, consider that partner unavailable to you for the rest of the night.

Your position in the area surrounding the dance floor can be critical. At some of the older *milongas,* the more-established dancers have reserved tables. Ideally, you should sit where you have easy access to the floor and to other dancers' line of sight. You may notice couples sitting further back (they often dance just with each other), while singles sit right at the front. And if a man comes into the room with a woman at his side, she is considered 'his' for the night. For couples to dance with others, they either enter the room separately, or the man may signal his intent by asking another woman to the floor. Then 'his' woman becomes open for asking.

The *cabezazo* – the quick tilt of the head, eye contact and uplifted eyebrows – can happen from way across the room. The woman to whom the *cabezazo* is directed either nods yes and smiles, or pretends not to have noticed. If she says yes, the man gets up and escorts her to floor. If you're at a *milonga* and don't want to dance with anyone, don't look around too much; you could be breaking some hearts.

So what is the appeal of the tango? Experienced *milongueros* will tell you that the adrenaline rush you get from an excellent performance is like a successful conquest: it can lift you up to exhilarating heights. But watch out – the dance can become as addictive as an insidious drug. Once you have fallen for the passion and beauty of the tango's movements you may spend your life trying to attain a physical perfection that can never be fully realized. The true *milonguero* attempts to make the journey as graceful and passionate as possible.

Environment

THE LAND

With a total land area of about 2.8 million sq km, excluding the South Atlantic islands and the Antarctic quadrant claimed as national territory, Argentina is the world's eighth-largest country, only slightly smaller than India. It stretches from La Quiaca on the Bolivian border to Ushuaia in Tierra del Fuego (a distance of nearly 3500km) and encompasses a vast array of environments and terrain.

The Andes

The Andean chain runs the length of Argentina, from the Bolivian border in the north to the South Atlantic, where the chain disappears.

At a lung-popping 6962m, Mendoza province's Cerro Aconcagua is the highest peak in the western hemisphere.

In the extreme north lies the southern extension of the Bolivian *altiplano*, a thinly populated high plain between 3000m and 4000m in altitude and punctuated by even higher volcanic peaks. Although days can be surprisingly hot (sunburn is a serious hazard at high altitude), frosts occur almost nightly. Rainfall throughout the Andes can be erratic, although rain-fed agriculture is feasible from Tucumán northward. South of Tucumán, where rainfall is inadequate for crops, perennial streams descending from the Andes provide irrigation water, which has brought prosperity to the wine-producing Cuyo region (the provinces of Mendoza, San Juan and San Luis). You'll see the evidence everywhere: *asequias* (irrigation channels) line every street in nearly every town, bringing water to the shade trees.

On the region's far western edge is the massive Andean crest, featuring 6960m Aconcagua, the western hemisphere's highest peak. Hot in summer, the area is pleasant the rest of the year despite cool winter nights. Often in winter, the zonda, a hot, dry wind descending from the Andes, causes dramatic temperature increases (see p309).

The Chaco & Mesopotamia

East of the Andes and their foothills, much of northern Argentina consists of subtropical lowlands. The arid western area, known as the Argentine Chaco, is part of the much larger Gran Chaco region, which extends into Bolivia, Paraguay and Brazil. Summers are brutally hot here in the provinces of Santiago del Estero, Chaco, Formosa, and northern Santa Fe and Córdoba. (See the Northeast Argentina (p150) and Córdoba & the Central Sierras (p263) chapters for more information on these provinces.)

At its mouth, the Río de la Plata is an amazing 190km wide, making it the widest river in the world.

Between the Río Paraná and Río Uruguay, the climate is mild, and rainfall is heavy in the provinces of Entre Ríos and Corrientes, which make up most of Mesopotamia. Hot and humid Misiones, a politically important province surrounded on three sides by Brazil and Paraguay, contains part of Iguazú Falls, which descend from southern Brazil's Paraná Plateau.

Rainfall decreases from east to west; shallow summer flooding is common throughout Mesopotamia and the eastern Chaco, while only the immediate river floodplains become inundated in the west. The Chaco has a well-defined winter dry season, while Mesopotamia's rainfall is evenly distributed throughout the year.

The Pampas

Bordered by the Atlantic Ocean and Patagonia and stretching nearly to Córdoba and the Central Sierras, the Pampas are Argentina's agricultural heartland. Geographically, this region covers the provinces of

Buenos Aires and La Pampa, as well as southern chunks of Santa Fe and Córdoba.

This area can be subdivided into the Humid Pampas, along the littoral, and the Arid Pampas of the western interior and the south. More than a third of the country's population lives in and around Buenos Aires, where the humid climate resembles New York City's in the spring, summer and autumn. Annual rainfall exceeds 900mm, but several hundred kilometers westward it's less than half that. Buenos Aires' winters are relatively mild.

The Pampas are an almost completely level plain of wind-borne loess (a fine-grained silt or clay) and river-deposited sediments. The absence of relief makes the area vulnerable to flooding from the relatively few, small rivers that cross it. Only the granitic Sierra de Tandil (484m; p126) and the Sierra de la Ventana (1273m; p131), in southwestern Buenos Aires province, and the Sierra de Lihué Calel (p135) disrupt the otherwise monotonous terrain. The coast of Buenos Aires province features attractive, sandy beaches at resorts like Mar del Plata and Necochea, which *porteños* (inhabitants of the capital) overrun in January and February.

Patagonia & the Lake District

Patagonia, of which the Lake District is a subregion, is the region south of the Río Colorado, consisting of the provinces of Neuquén, Río Negro, Chubut and Santa Cruz. It's separated from Chilean Patagonia by the Andes.

The cordillera is high enough that Pacific storms drop most of their rain and snow on the Chilean side. In the extreme southern reaches of Patagonia, however, enough snow and ice still accumulate to form the largest southern hemisphere glaciers outside of Antarctica.

East of the Andean foothills, the cool, arid Patagonian steppes support huge flocks of sheep, whose wool is almost all exported to Europe. For such a southerly location, temperatures are relatively mild, even in winter, when more uniform atmospheric pressure moderates the strong gales that blow most of the year.

Except for urban clusters like Comodoro Rivadavia (center of the petroleum industry) and Río Gallegos (wool and meatpacking), Patagonia is thinly populated. Tidal ranges along the Atlantic coast are too great for major port facilities. In the valley of the Río Negro and at the outlet of the Río Chubut, there's farming and cultivation of fruit orchards.

Tierra del Fuego

The world's southernmost permanently inhabited territory, Tierra del Fuego (Land of Fire) consists of one large island (Isla Grande), unequally divided between Chile and Argentina, and many smaller ones, some of which have been the source of longtime contention between the two countries. When Europeans first passed through the Strait of Magellan (which separates Isla Grande from the Patagonian mainland), the fires stemmed from the activities of the now endangered Yahgan people; nowadays, the fires result from the flaring of natural gas in the region's oil fields.

The northern half of Isla Grande, resembling the Patagonian steppes, is devoted to sheep grazing, while its southern half is mountainous and partly covered by forests and glaciers. As in Patagonia, winter conditions are rarely extreme, although trekking and outdoor camping are not advisable except for experienced mountaineers. For most visitors, though, the brief daylight hours during this season may be a greater deterrent than the weather.

With a special focus on Latin America, Ron Mader's Planeta (www .planeta.com) is the most comprehensible online resource for exploring ecotourism and environmental reporting; check out the Argentina pages.

Join *National Geographic* photographer David McLain behind the shutter as he shoots Patagonia with writer Tim Cahill and shares his photo secrets with you. It's tucked away online at www.nationalgeographic .com/adventure/0305 /photo_index.html.

Between 1995 and 2000, the Patagonian ice fields melted twice as fast as they had over the previous two decades.

WILDLIFE

Because Argentina is so large and varied, it supports a wide range of flora and fauna. The country's subtropical rainforests, palm savannas, high-altitude deserts, high-latitude steppes, humid temperate grasslands, alpine and sub-Antarctic forests and coastal areas all support distinctive biota that will be unfamiliar to most visitors, or at least to those from the northern hemisphere. To protect these environments, Argentina has created an extensive system of national parks (opposite). More detailed descriptions of the parks and their species can be found in the relevant regional chapters.

The spotted suede sold throughout Argentina is carpincho, made from capybara, the largest rodent in the world. Females weigh up to 66kg and reach 130cm in length.

Plants

In the high northern Andes, vegetation consists of sparse bunch grasses (ichu) and low, widely spaced shrubs, known collectively as tola. In a few favored sites at lower elevations, most notably in Salta and Tucumán provinces, the summertime rains create geographical islands of dense subtropical forest.

In the Chaco, open savannas alternate with nearly impenetrable thorn forests, while Mesopotamian rainfall is sufficient to support swampy lowland forests as well as upland savanna. Misiones' native vegetation is mostly dense subtropical forest, though its upper elevations are studded with araucaria pines.

The once lush native grasses of the Argentine Pampas have suffered under grazing pressure from introduced European livestock and the proliferation of grain farms, so much so that very little native vegetation remains, except along watercourses like the Río Paraná.

Most of Patagonia lies in the rain shadow of the Chilean Andes, so the vast steppes of southeastern Argentina resemble the sparse grasslands of the arid Andean highlands. Closer to the border there are pockets of dense *Nothofagus* (southern beech) and coniferous woodlands that owe their existence to the winter storms that sneak over the cordillera. Northern Tierra del Fuego is a grassy extension of the Patagonian steppe, but the heavy rainfall of the mountainous southern half supports verdant southern beech forests.

Animals

Northeast Argentina boasts the country's most diverse animal life. One of the best areas on the entire continent to enjoy wildlife is the swampy Esteros del Iberá (p173), in Corrientes province, where animals such as swamp deer, capybara and caiman, along with many large migratory birds, are commonly seen. It's comparable – arguably even better – than Brazil's more famous Pantanal.

The largest dinosaur ever discovered was the *Argentinosaurus huinculensis*, uncovered in Neuquén province; the herbivore measured a massive 40m long and 18m high.

In the drier northwest, the most conspicuous animal is the domestic llama, but its wild cousins, the guanaco and vicuña, can also be seen. Your odds of seeing them, their yellow fur a puff of color against the cactus-studded backdrop, are excellent if you travel by road through Parque Nacional Los Cardones (p237) to Salta. Many migratory birds, including flamingos, inhabit the high saline lakes of the Andean northwest.

In less densely settled areas, including the arid Pampas of La Pampa province, guanacos, foxes and even pumas are not unusual sights. Many bodies of water, both permanent and seasonal, provide migratory bird habitats.

Most notable in Patagonia and Tierra del Fuego is the wealth of coastal wildlife, ranging from Magellanic penguins, cormorants and gulls to sea lions, fur seals, elephant seals and whales. Several coastal reserves, from

---

UNESCO WORLD HERITAGE SITES

The UN Educational, Scientific and Cultural Organization (Unesco) has designated the following sites in Argentina World Heritage Sites. The first was Parque Nacional Los Glaciares (1981), and the most recent was the magnificent Quebrada de Humahuaca (2003).

- Cueva de las Manos (p403)
- *Estancias* of Córdoba Province (p278)
- Jesuit Missions of the Guaraní: San Ignacio Miní (p188), Santa Ana (p187), Loreto (p188)
- Manzana Jesuítica (Jesuit Block), Córdoba (p267)
- Parque Nacional Iguazú (p191)
- Parque Nacional Los Glaciares (p405 and p410)
- Parque Nacional Talampaya (p261)
- Parque Provincial Ischigualasto (p317)
- Quebrada de Humahuaca (p219)
- Reserva Faunística Península Valdés (p365)

Río Negro province south to Tierra del Fuego, are home to enormous concentrations of wildlife that are one of the region's greatest visitor attractions. Inland on the Patagonian steppe, as in the northwest, the guanaco is the most conspicuous mammal, but the flightless rhea, resembling the Old World ostrich, runs in flocks across the plains. For more on Patagonia's wildlife, see p374.

Magellanic penguins, native to Patagonia and Tierra del Fuego, have approximately 27 feathers per sq centimeter!

NATIONAL & PROVINCIAL PARKS

Argentina's national parks lure visitors from around the world. One of Latin America's first national park systems, Argentina's dates from the turn of the 20th century, when explorer and surveyor Francisco P Moreno donated 7500 hectares near Bariloche to the state in return for guarantees that the parcel would be preserved for the enjoyment of all Argentines. This area is now part of Parque Nacional Nahuel Huapi (p345) in the Andean Lake District.

Since then, the country has established many other parks and reserves, mostly but not exclusively in the Andean region. There are also important provincial parks and reserves, such as Reserva Faunística Península Valdés (p365), that do not fall within the national park system but deserve attention. In general, the national parks are more visitor-oriented than the provincial parks, but there are exceptions: Parque Nacional Perito Moreno has few visitor services, for example, while Península Valdés has many.

Note that some Argentine park personnel, including rangers, can be very cautious and patronizing with respect to activities beyond the most conventional and may sometimes exaggerate the difficulty of hikes and climbs.

Before seeing the parks, visitors to Buenos Aires should stop at the **national parks administration** (Administración de Parques Nacionales; ☎ 011-4312-0783; www.parquesnacionales.gov.ar; Santa Fe 690) for maps and brochures, which are often in short supply in the parks; there may be a charge for some. Admission to most national parks is US$4 (US$2 for Argentines) for adults; free for children under 12. Admission to provincial parks varies, but usually hovers around US$3; one exception is Parque Provincial Aconcagua, where trekking permits cost US$20 to US$50 and climbing permits US$100 to US$300.

Founded by the former CEO of Patagonia clothing company, Conservación Patagónica (www.pata gonialandtrust.org) has controversially purchased thousands of acres in Patagonia and Esteros del Iberá in order to preserve them. The website is excellent.

Park *	Features	Page Ref
Monumento Natural Laguna de los Pozuelos	High-altitude lake in Jujuy province: abundant bird life, including three species of flamingos	p219
Parque Nacional Baritú	On the Bolivian border in Salta province: nearly virgin subtropical montane forest	p238
Parque Nacional Calilegua	Transitional lowland forest, subtropical montane forest and subalpine grassland	p236
Parque Nacional Los Cardones	Montane desert park west of Salta: striking cardon cacti, wandering guanacos	p237
Parque Nacional Finca El Rey	Mountainous park in eastern Salta province: lush subtropical forest and coniferous Andean forest	p238
Parque Nacional Río Pilcomayo	Subtropical marshlands and palm savannas: colorful birds, caiman and nocturnal mammals	p209
Parque Nacional Chaco	Dense, subtropical thorn forests, marshes, palm savannas and colorful birds; very accessible but rarely visited	p205
Parque Nacional Iguazú	Home of the awesome Iguazú Falls. Also subtropical rainforest and abundant birds, mammals and reptiles	p191
Parque Nacional Mburucuyá	Quebracho and palm forests, estuaries and islands: capybaras, foxes, gazunchos, river wolves and swamp deer (swamp deer?!). Off the beaten track	p171
Reserva Provincial Esteros del Iberá	Tranquil wetland reserve in Corrientes province: arguably a better wildlife site than Brazil's famous Pantanal	p173
Parque Nacional El Palmar	On the Río Uruguay, see the last extensive stands of yatay-palm savanna and bird watch your brains out	p179
Parque Nacional Talampaya	Rich desert scenery and extraordinary geological, paleontological and archaeological resources	p261
Parque Provincial Ischigualasto	Known as Valley of the Moon: surreally scenic paleontological preserve with wild rock formations	p317
Parque Nacional Quebrada del Condorito	Stunning rocky grasslands across the Pampa de Achala in the Sierras Grandes: condors, condors, condors	p281
Parque Nacional Sierra de las Quijadas	Polychrome desert canyons and the site of major dinosaur discoveries. Wonderfully quiet	p284
Parque Provincial Aconcagua	Home of the western hemisphere's highest peak, 6960m Aconcagua	p301

ENVIRONMENTAL ISSUES

Argentina's diverse environments have spawned challenges ranging from pollution to deforestation to overgrazing. One highly visible example of an industrial problem is the contamination of the Río Riachuelo in Buenos Aires' La Boca neighborhood. The capital's dense traffic – thanks to diesel-spewing buses, countless private vehicles and fleets of taxis – has the usual impact on air quality, though rain clears the air with some regularity.

Maria Julia Alsogaray, secretary of the environment under president Carlos Menem, once appeared for a photo shoot clad in a fur coat.

Despite Argentina's self-sufficiency in petroleum and abundant (if sometimes remote) hydroelectric capacity, the Argentine government has promoted nuclear power since 1950. The 357-megawatt Atucha I reactor, near Buenos Aires, has supplied energy to the capital since 1974. There is also a functioning reactor at Río Tercero, in Córdoba province. Although Argentina's constitution prohibits the importation of nuclear waste, the federal government is considering accepting and treating nuclear spent nuclear rods from Australia, a possibility that has been met with fierce opposition from anti-nuclear groups within Argentina.

Park *	Features	Page Ref
Parque Provincial Volcán Tupungato	Centerpiece: 6650m summit of Tupungato, a more challenging climb than nearby Aconcagua	p303
Parque Nacional Lihué Calel	Pinkish peaks, isolated valleys, petroglyphs and a surprising range of fauna and flora	p135
Parque Provincial Payunia	Boasts a higher concentration of volcanic cones (over 800 of them) than anywhere else in the world	p307
Parque Nacional Laguna Blanca	Desolate lake, lots of nothingness: ancient volcanoes and lava flows, nesting colonies of black-necked swans, Andean flamingos	p324
Parque Nacional Lanín	Lake District park: extensive forests of monkey puzzle trees (Araucaria) and southern beech capped by the perfect cone of Volcán Lanín	p331
Parque Nacional Nahuel Huapi	758,000 hectares around the exquisite Lago Nahuel Huapi: lakes, views, snowboarding, hikes, trees, fun – and lots of people	p345
Parque Nacional Los Arrayanes	Tiny park inside Parque Nacional Nahuel Huapi: protects stands of the unique arrayán tree	p335
Parque Nacional Lago Puelo	Lago Puelo, an aquamarine, low-altitude lake set among High Andean peaks	p351
Parque Nacional Los Alerces	Unique Valdivian forest, which includes impressive specimens of the redwood-like alerce tree	p398
Reserva Faunística Península Valdés	Wildlife enthusiast's dream: whales, sea lions, Magellanic penguins	p365
Reserva Provincial Punta Tombo	Known for its enormous nesting colony of burrowing Magellanic penguins	p373
Parque Nacional Perito Moreno	Awesome glacial lakes, alpine peaks, Andean-Patagonian forest and guanaco; way off the beaten track	p404
Monumento Natural Bosques Petrificados	Isolated park featuring immense specimens of petrified Proaraucaria trees	p383
Parque Nacional Monte León	Argentina's first coastal national park outside Tierra del Fuego	p385
Parque Nacional Los Glaciares	Home to Argentina's must-sees: the famous Moreno Glacier and the awesome pinnacles of the Fitz Roy Range	p405 & p410
Parque Nacional Tierra del Fuego	Argentina's first shoreline national park: alpine glaciers and peaks, marine mammals, seabirds, shorebirds and extensive southern beech forests	p454

* Parks are listed generally north to south, west to east.

The Canadian company Barrick Gold currently operates a massive gold-mine in San Juan province which is having dramatic effects on both the landscape and the people. Locals and environmentalists in and around the town of San José de Jáchal (p315) have fervently protested Barrick's use of highly toxic cyanide which is contaminating both soil and groundwater.

With Argentina's economic collapse and the country's subsequent ability to compete on the international market, production of soy has skyrocketed and become Argentina's single most important cash crop. Farmers throughout the Pampas now plant mono-crops of genetically modified, herbicide-resistant soy, which is rapidly depleting the ground of its minerals, and contributing to high levels of herbicide in soils throughout the region.

Deforestation is a major issue in the eastern Chaco, the Yungas and the subtropical rainforests of Misiones, where commercial tea plantations and timber companies continue to destroy the biologically diverse forests.

Problems in Patagonia include oil pollution from tankers emptying their ballasts offshore, climate change and overfishing, all of which have contributed to the deaths of Magellanic penguins and other marine mammals.

For a close and outstanding look at Argentina's environmental problems, and to learn how to help, check out Fundación Vida Silvestre Argentina (www.vidasilvestre.org.ar), in Spanish and English.

Food & Drink Dereck Foster

Argentines love eating. A great deal of their social and political life involves a table, be it for a leisurely coffee, an informal meal or an elegant banquet. The food must meet two criteria: abundance and a good price/quality relationship. Sophistication is not a national feature, and beef and pasta are the two pillars upon which the national menu is based. Shortly after you arrive, you might find yourself saying 'Oh, no! Not another barbecue!' Argentines will likely press upon you the national passion of *parrillada* (mixed grill). Take heart. There are also a number of interesting (mostly regional) dishes that deserve more than passing attention.

El Gaucho Gourmet (2001), by Dereck Foster, offers a bilingual, brief history of eating in Argentina.

STAPLES & SPECIALTIES

When it comes to national cuisine, beef is the operative word in Argentina, but it is only one part of a varied national menu. Besides the obvious Spanish influence, there is a strong Italian flavor provided by pizza and pasta, and in more recent times the US has added its touch via widespread McDonald's and Burger King restaurants (and some local imitators). The Middle East is also strongly represented, mostly in the large cities and the northwest.

Per-head beef consumption in Argentina has gone down by about 50% over the past 15 years.

In the southernmost, Patagonia area, lamb and seafood (including delicious king crab and oysters) almost wipe beef off the map. The central Pampas are where the best beef in the world is available, although pork and chicken are increasingly important. In the west, Mendoza, San Juan and La Rioja pride themselves on chivito (goat). In the northwest, with roots dating back to pre-Columbian times, the food is spicy and frequently hot (thanks to the liberal use of chilies) and is hard to find elsewhere. The northeast also offers food dating far back, but it is milder and more bland. River fish, such as the dorado and pacú, are especially sought after.

Meals

Argentines are not great breakfast eaters. A typical breakfast consists of *café con leche y medialunas* (coffee with milk and croissants), although hotels catering to tourists offer American-style breakfasts. The croissants come sweetish *(dulce)* or plain *(salada)*. Toast *(tostadas)*, with butter *(manteca)* and/or jam *(mermelada)* is an alternative. Sweet pastries *(facturas)* which can be seen and bought at any *confitería* and most bars, are a common snack. Bacon-and-eggs people may have trouble finding their bacon. Ask for *panceta* (pork belly), the usual cut used for bacon, or *tocino,* the also-popular back fat.

Mollejas (the thymus glands of cows) are so popular in Argentine asado that they are imported from places like the USA, where it is less of a delicacy.

Argentines make up for breakfast at lunch and dinner, although the three-course lunch is now far less common. While most places begin service around noon, the popular time to lunch is between 1 and 1:30pm. Dinners can begin at 8pm, but an Argentine will seldom eat before 9pm, and meals can draw out long after midnight on weekends.

Snacks

In big cities, it's easy to snack at any time on almost anything you desire. *Kioscos* (kiosks) are all over town and provide sweets, cookies, ice cream and well-packaged sandwiches. On many streets, hot dog *(pancho)* sellers patrol and peanut brittle sellers prepare their wares in copper kettles over gas flames. A more substantial snack is the empanada, a tasty turnover

HERE'S THE BEEF   *Sandra Bao*

You walk into a traditional *parrilla* (steak house), breezing past the stuffed bull and sizzling *asado* (barbecue grill) at the entrance, and sit down hungry, knife and fork in hand. You don't know a word of Spanish, you've never had to choose between more than two or three cuts of steak in your life and the menu has at least 10 different choices. What do you do? Don't fret. We'll give you a better idea of what will show up on your plate.

But first, you should have an idea of where Argentina's famous beef comes from. When the first Spaniards came over to Argentina from Europe, with the intention of colonizing the area, they brought some cows. Because stubborn locals were unwilling to let themselves be dominated, the Spaniards' first efforts at a colony proved unfruitful. They ended up abandoning the cattle in the Pampas and moving away, and here the herds found the bovine equivalent of heaven: plenty of lush, fertile grasses on which to feed, with few natural predators to limit their numbers. Things were great until the Europeans decided to start recolonizing the Pampas and capturing the cattle for their own use. (The gauchos, however, had been taking advantage of these free-roaming meals-on-the-hoof all along.)

Today, intermixing with other European bovine breeds has produced a pretty tasty beef. Why is it so good? Any Argentine will say it's because free-range Argentine cows eat nutritious Pampas grass, lacking in the massive quantities of corn, antibiotics and growth hormones that American or European stocks are given in feedlots. This makes for a leaner, more natural-tasting meat. (Though these days it's not entirely organic: efforts to reduce *aftosa,* or foot-and-mouth disease, have resulted in Argentina's need to inoculate its herds.)

The average intake of beef is around 60kg per person per year, though in the past Argentines ate even more. Most of this consuming takes place at the family *asado,* often held on Sunday in the backyards of houses all over the country. (If you are lucky enough to be invited to one, make sure you attend.) Here the art of grilling beef has been perfected. This usually involves cooking with coals and using only salt to prepare the meat. On the grill itself, which is often waist-high and made of bricks, slanted runners funnel the excess fat to the sides to avoid flare-ups, and an adjustable height system directs the perfect amount of heat to the meat.

Emerging from this family tradition, the commercial steak house offers a little bit of everything. The *parrillada* might have an assortment of *chorizo* (spicy sausage), *pollo* (chicken), *costillas* (ribs) and *carne* (beef). It can also come with more exotic items such as *chinchulines* (small intestines), *tripa gorda* (large intestine), *molleja* (thymus gland or sweetbreads), *ubre* (udder), *riñones* (kidneys) and *morcilla* (blood sausage). You can order a *parrillada* for as many people as you want; they adjust their servings according to the party's size.

You could skip the mixed grill and dive right into the beef cuts. Here's a guide:

bife de chorizo	sirloin; a thick, juicy and popular cut
bife de costilla	T-bone; a cut close to the bone; also called *chuleta*
bife de lomo	tenderloin; a thinly cut, more tender piece
cuadril	rump steak; often a thin cut
ojo de bife	eye of round steak; a choice smaller morsel
tira de asado	a narrow strip of rib roast
vacío	flank steak; textured and chewy, but tasty

If you don't specify, your steak will be overcooked. Ask for it *a punto* (medium). To get it pink on the inside ask for *jugoso* (rare), and if you want it well-done, say *bien hecho.* Be sure not to miss *chimichurri,* a tasty marinade often made of olive oil, garlic and parsley. Also try the *salsa criolla,* a condiment made of diced tomato, onion and parsley – it's harder to find.

stuffed with ground beef or ham and cheese, chicken, or other fillings. Cheap and filling, they come either baked (*al horno*), which is the best way, or fried (*frito*).

Pizza, whole or by the slice, is another popular snack available everywhere. The best pizzas are often in the scruffier, less elegant pizzerias.

Sandwiches de miga are a great buy, although hardly hearty, made with thin slices of white bread. The most usual are made with *jamón y queso* (ham and cheese) and can be toasted *(tostado)*. *Alfajores,* cookie-type sandwiches that come with *dulce de leche* (creamy caramel) filling or fruit jams and jellies, are also good snacks.

Desserts

In restaurants, fruit salad and ice cream are almost always on the menu. *Flan* is a baked custard that comes with a choice of either cream or *dulce de leche* topping. *Queso y dulce* consists of slices of fresh cheese with quince *(membrillo)* or sweet potato *(batata)* preserve.

Ice cream *(helado)* is particularly good in Argentina. Based on the Italian tradition, there are three basic types: the large-scale, such as Frigor (Nestle); the semi-artisanal, produced by chains like Freddo; and the artisanal, made by small ice-creameries *(heladerías)*. *Helados* are eaten all year long and flavors are extremely varied. Jauja in Bariloche (p350) arguably makes the country's best ice cream.

Torta galesa (Welsh cake) is a delicious fruitcake unknown in Wales. Welsh settlers in Argentina created it to tide them over during the harsh Patagonian winters, when food was scarce.

DRINKS

Alcoholic Drinks

Wine, beer and distilled drinks are the top-ranking alcoholic drinks. Unusual beverages, more popular in the country than in cities, are *caña*, distilled from sugar cane, and a local gin made by Bols and Llave.

The most popular beer is Quilmes, followed by Isenbeck (made by Germany's Warsteiner), Andes and the Brazilian Brahma. Beers come in liter bottles, half-liter bottles known as *porrones*, and draft, ordered as *chopp*. Beer usually comes served with a snack, such as peanuts or potato chips (except when ordered to go with a meal).

The oldest functioning winery in Argentina is Gonzales Videla, founded in 1840.

Argentine wines are now distributed worldwide and many are world class. They scale the entire price range from very cheap (less than a soft drink) to very expensive. Mendoza is the premier wine region, with just over 70% of wine production. Malbec is the definitive Argentine wine, though San Juan is rightly famous for its Syrah and the area around Cafayate for its *torrontés* white.

Nonalcoholic Drinks

Argentines are great coffee drinkers, and they like it strong. They drink coffee and milk in the morning and innumerable cups of espresso *(café express)* during the day. An espresso with a drop of milk is *café cortado,* while a *lágrima* is mostly milk with a drop or two of coffee. *Cafe de filtro* is regular, nonespresso, coffee, but it's generally not served in cafés.

To learn more about *mate,* check out www .soygaucho.com/english /mate/index.html; for supplies, try www .gauchogourmet.com.

Black and herbal teas are also available, such as *manzanilla* (chamomile) and *peperina* (an Argentine mint). In the cooler and cold seasons, try a *submarino:* a bar of chocolate is placed in a glass of very hot milk and allowed to melt slowly.

Although fresh fruit is plentiful in the markets, fruit juices in bars and *confiterías* are usually limited to orange *(exprimido de naranja)* and grapefruit *(pomelo)*. A *licuado* is fruit liquefied in a blender with milk or water, such as apple *(manzana)* with water, and banana with milk.

Soft drinks *(gaseosas)* are big business in Argentina, from Coke to *amargos Serrano* (a herbal infusion) and flavored mineral waters. Mineral waters come *con gas* (carbonated) and *sin gas* (plain). Tap water in the cities is drinkable, but if you have doubts, ask for *agua mineral* (mineral water) or *un sifón de soda* (carbonated water in a spritzer bottle), used for mixing with whisky, juices and the like.

MATE & ITS RITUAL   *Sandra Bao & Danny Palmerlee*

Nothing captures the essence of *argentinidad* (Argentinity) as well as the preparation and consumption of *mate* (pronounced **mah**-tay), perhaps the only cultural practice that truly transcends the barriers of ethnicity, class and occupation in Argentina. More than a simple drink, *mate* is an elaborate ritual, shared among family, friends and coworkers. In many ways, sharing is the whole point.

Yerba mate is the dried, chopped leaf of *Ilex paraguayensis*, a relative of the common holly. Also known as Paraguayan tea, it became commercially important during the colonial era on the Jesuit missions' plantations in the upper Río Paraná. Europeans quickly took to the beverage, crediting it with many admirable qualities. The Austrian Jesuit Martin Dobrizhoffer wrote that *mate* 'provokes a gentle perspiration, improves the appetite, speedily counteracts the languor arising from the burning climate and assuages both hunger and thirst.' After the Jesuits' expulsion in 1767, production declined, but since the early 20th century, production has increased dramatically.

Argentina is the world's largest producer and consumer of *yerba mate*. Argentines consume an average of 5kg per person per year, more than four times their average intake of coffee. It's also popular in parts of Chile, southern Brazil, Paraguay and, in particular, Uruguay, which consumes twice as much per capita as Argentina.

Preparing *mate* is a ritual in itself. In the past, upper-class families even maintained a slave or servant whose sole responsibility was preparing and serving it. Nowadays, one person, the *cebador* (server) fills the *mate* gourd almost to the top with yerba, heating but not boiling the water in a *pava* (kettle) and pouring it into the vessel. Drinkers then sip the liquid through a *bombilla*, a silver straw with a bulbous filter at its lower end that prevents the yerba leaves from entering the tube.

Gourds can range from simple calabashes to carved wooden vessels to the ornate silver museum pieces of the 19th century. *Bombillas* also differ considerably, ranging in materials from inexpensive aluminum to silver and gold with intricate markings, and in design from long straight tubes to short, curved models.

There is an informal etiquette for drinking *mate*. The *cebador* pours water slowly as he or she fills the gourd. The gourd then passes clockwise, and this order, once established, continues. A good *cebador* will keep the *mate* going without changing the yerba for some time. Each participant drinks the gourd dry each time. A simple *'gracias'* will tell the server to pass you by. Don't hold the *mate* too long before passing it on.

There are marked regional differences in drinking *mate*. From the Pampas southwards, Argentines take it *amargo* (without sugar), while to the north they drink it *dulce* (sweet) with sugar and *yuyos* (aromatic herbs). Purists, who argue that sugar ruins the gourd, will keep separate gourds rather than alternate the two usages.

An invitation to *mate* is a cultural treat and not to be missed, although the drink is an acquired taste and novices may find it bitter and very hot at first. (On the second or third round, both the heat and bitterness will diminish.) Because drinking *mate* is a fairly complex process, it is rarely served in restaurants or cafés, except in teabag form. As a foreigner, it is therefore easy to spend an entire holiday in Argentina without ever experiencing it. The simple solution is to do what traveling Argentines do: buy a thermos (stores rarely lack a thermos shelf), a *mate* gourd, a *bombilla* and a bag of herb. The entire set-up will cost you US$7 to US$15, depending on the thermos you choose.

Before drinking from your gourd, you must first cure it by filling it with hot water and yerba and letting it soak for 24 hours. When it's ready, you have to fill your thermos; nearly all restaurants, cafés and hotels are used to filling thermoses, sometimes charging a small amount. Simply whip out your thermos and ask: *'¿Podía calentar agua para mate?'* ('Would you mind heating water for *mate*?'). Even gas stations are equipped with giant tanks of precisely heated water for drinkers on the road. Once you have your water, you're off to the park to join the rest of the locals drinking *mate* in the shade.

CELEBRATIONS

Food during the holidays in Argentina is similar to that in Europe and the US. At Christmas, stores begin to fill up with many of the items typical in the northern hemisphere, although here in the south it's hot, hot, hot this time of year. During Holy Week *(Semana Santa)*, fish and seafood hold sway, but whatever the occasion it is the *asado* in the limelight at most celebrations. You may need to make restaurant reservations during holiday periods.

Buenos Aires consumes more sweets per capita than any city outside London.

WHERE TO EAT & DRINK

Argentines love to eat out, and there is no lack of places, from simple pubs to elegant restaurants. The simplest places and usually the most economical are cafés and bars, where simple snacks are available all day. Pubs, which are cafés with a pseudo-British touch, offer a few more choices. Café life is typical of Buenos Aires, and much financial, romantic, social and political business is conducted there.

Supermarkets are open seven days a week in the large cities.

Confiterías, open all day, offer a restricted menu, while restaurants, open only at meal times, have a more complete menu. When you tire of beef and *parrillas,* you can try one of Argentina's Chinese or Japanese restaurants (sushi is becoming very popular). Or dine at a Middle Eastern restaurant (widespread in Buenos Aires and usually excellent); many are *tenedor libre* (all you can eat for a set price).

Recently, health foods and organic products have become accessible in Argentine cities, but vegetarian restaurants are scarce. Most menus do include a few vegetarian choices to help out, and pastas are good. Just make sure it doesn't come with a beef sauce like *salsa boloñesa. Sin carne* means 'without meat,' and the words *soy vegetariano/a* ('I'm a vegetarian') will come in handy when explaining to an Argentine why you don't eat their delicious steaks.

With very few exceptions, Argentine restaurants are less formal than in the US or Europe. Reservations are taken but are necessary only on weekends at better restaurants, especially during peak travel times in hotspots like Mar del Plata or Bariloche. If in doubt, call ahead. Expect to linger over your meal and chat over coffee or drinks afterward. Your bill will rarely be presented until you ask for it *('la cuenta, por favor').* A waiter is a *mozo* and a waitress *señorita* (or *moza*). Standard opening hours are 1pm to 3:30pm and 9pm to midnight, but many places are open earlier (the tourist influence).

Menus come in two types: a regular menu and *menú fijo* or *menú del día,* which refer to fixed-price meals, sometimes including a drink. Many menus are 'translated' into English (and sometimes French) with results ranging from useful to hilarious to incomprehensible.

Smoking and nonsmoking areas are common, but cigars are discouraged. The wine list is *la carta de vinos* and readily available, but sommeliers

---

BUENOS AIRES' TOP FIVE

- **Sabot** Argentine eatery popular with everyone from CEOs to porters (p92)
- **Bar Uriarte** Some of the best food and wine in hip Palermo Viejo (p95)
- **Filo** Trendy place with great food and an artsy atmosphere (p93)
- **Broccolino** Italian restaurant popular with both locals and tourists (p91)
- **Río Alba** *Parrilla* serving some of the tastiest grilled meat in the city (p95)

are scarce. When your bill arrives you may note an item called *cubierto* (cover charge). This is not a tip, which is up to you to pay, usually around 10%. Free drinks such as a glass of sparkling wine or sherry are frequently offered at the start of a meal.

EATING WITH KIDS

Argentines adore children (sometimes to extremes, which can spoil your meal), and eating out with the kids is common. A number of restaurants incorporate special menus for the junior brigade, but all (save perhaps the five-star outfits) will cater to your reasonable demands – from serving half portions to preparing something special in the kitchen.

EAT YOUR WORDS

Want to make sure you don't order cow brains or testicles? Get behind the cuisine scene by getting to know the language. For pronunciation guidelines, see p489.

One of the best restaurant guides available comes with brief English translations: *Los Recomendados 2005*, by Alicia Delgado and Maria Esther Perez.

Useful Phrases

I'd like to make a reservation.
    Quisiera hacer una reserve.   kee-see-*air*-a a-*ser oo*-na re-*ser*-va
Do you accept credit cards?
    ¿Aceptan tarjetas de crédito?   a-*sep*-tan tar-*khe*-tas de *kre*-dee-to
When do you serve (meals/breakfast/ lunch/dinner)?
    ¿A qué hora sirven (comidas/desayuno/   a ke *o*-ra *seer*-ven (ko-*mee*-das/
    almuerzo/cena)?   de-sa-*shu*-no/al-*mwair*-zo/*se*-na)
Table for ..., please.
    Una mesa para ..., por favor.   *oo*-na *me*-sa *pa*-ra ... por fa-*vor*
Can I see the menu please?
    ¿Puedo ver el menú, por favor?   *pwe*-do ver el me-*noo*, por fa-*vor*
What do you recommend?
    ¿Qué me aconseja?   ke me a-con-*se*-kha
What's today's special?
    ¿Cuál es el plato del día?   kwal es el *pla*-to del *dee*-a
What's the soup of the day?
    ¿Cuál es la sopa del día?   kwal es la *so*-pa del *dee*-a
I'll try what she/he's having.
    Probaré lo que ella/él está comiendo.   pro-ba-*ray* lo ke *e*-sha/el es-*ta*
        ko-*myen*-do
We'd like to share the salad.
    Quisiéramos compartir la ensalada.   kee-*syair*-a-mos kom-par-*teer* la
        en-sa-*la*-da
What's in this dish?
    ¿Qué ingredientes tiene este plato?   ke een-gre-*dyen*-tes *tye*-ne es-te *pla*-to
Can I have a (beer) please?
    ¿Una (cerveza) por favor?   *oo*-na (ser-*ve*-sa) por fa-*vor*
Is service/cover charge included in the bill?
    ¿El precio en el menú incluye el servicio de cubierto?   el *pre*-syo en el me-*noo* in-*cloo*-she el
        sair-*vee*-syo de coo-*byair*-to
Thank you, that was delicious.
    Muchas gracias, estaba buenísimo.   *moo*-chas *gra*-syas es-*ta*-ba bwe-*nee*-see-mo
The bill, please.
    La cuenta, por favor.   la *kwen*-ta por fa-*vor*
I'm a vegetarian.
    Soy vegetariana/o.   soy ve-khe-tair-*ya*-na/o

I'd like ...
Quiero ...   kyair-o ...

Food and Drink in
Argentina, by Dereck
Foster and Richard Tripp,
is a color guide for visitors
and expats (in English).

a knife
un cuchillo   oon koo-*chee*-sho
a fork
un tenedor   oon te-ne-*dor*
a spoon
una cuchara   oo-na koo-*cha*-ra
a nonsmoking area
el área de no fumadores   el *a*-re-a de no foo-ma-*do*-res

Food Glossary

achuras	a-*choo*-ras	organ meats
alfajor	al-fa-*khor*	a sandwich biscuit (cookie) usually filled with *dulce de leche*
anchi	*an*-chee	a popular sweet dessert with cornflour and citrus fruit
arroz	a-*ros*	rice
bife	*bee*-fe	general name for steak (*bife de chorizo* is thick and boneless, similar to New York strip)
bifes a la criolla	*bee*-fes a la kree-*o*-sha	steaks slowly cooked in a casserole
boga	*bo*-ga	delicious freshwater fish
budin de choclo	boo-*deen* de *chok*-lo	a corn souffle
buseca	boo-*se*-ka	a tripe and vegetable soup
cabrito	ka-*bree*-to	goat (kid)
carbonada	kar-bo-*na*-da	typical beef, corn, pumpkin and vegetable stew, with peaches in season
carre ahumado	*ka*-re a-oo-*ma*-do	smoked pork loin
cayote	ka-*sho*-te	fig leaf gourd, eaten usually as jam or in syrup
centolla	sen-*to*-sha	southern king crab
cerdo	*sair*-do	pork
chanfaina	chan-*fai*-na	a stew with tomatoes, onions, peppers and (usually) lamb and liver; a Patagonian version is made with fish
charqui	*char*-kee	air-dried beef, similar to South African biltong
chimichurri	chee-mee-*choo*-ri	an Argentine herb marinade, also used as a dressing
chinchulines	cheen-choo-*lee*-nes	small intestine
chirimoya	chee-ree-*mo*-sha	apple custard
chivito	chee-*vee*-to	young goat (kid)
choripán	cho-ree-*pan*	Argentina's answer to the hot dog, made with spicy chorizo
chorizo	cho-*ree*-zo	sausage (also *salchicha* and *morcilla*)
churrasco	choo-*ras*-ko	grilled beef
ciervo	*syair*-vo	venison
cochinillo	ko-chee-*nee*-sho	suckling pig, younger than a lechón
cordero patagónico	kor-*dair*-o pa-ta-*go*-nee-ko	Patagonian lamb, celebrated for its lean, herb-flavored meat
corvina	kor-*vee*-na	sea fish, similar to a perch
criadillas	kree-a-*dee*-shas	testicles
dorado	do-*ra*-do	celebrated river fish, dear to anglers and gourmets alike
dulce de batata	*dool*-se de ba-*ta*-ta	sweet potato (yam) preserve, frequently eaten with cheese
dulce de leche	*dool*-se de *le*-che	caramelized milk, Argentina's most popular sweet
dulce de membrillo	*dool*-se de mem-*bree*-sho	quince preserve, frequently eaten with cheese

empanada	em-pa-*na*-da	pastry similar to a turnover, usually filled with beef and fried or baked
escabeche	as-ka-*be*-che	an oil, vinegar and herb marinade
garrapiñada	ga-ra-pee-*nya*-da	caramelized peanuts or almonds
gaznate	gaz-*na*-te	brandy-flavored pastry cone usually filled with *dulce de leche*
helado	el-*a*-do	ice cream
hígado	*ee*-ga-do	liver
jamón	kha-*mon*	ham
langostino	lan-gos-*tee*-no	prawn
lechón	le-*chon*	suckling pig
lengua	*len*-gwa	tongue
mantecol	man-te-*kol*	sweet made with ground peanuts and sugar
martineta	mar-tee-*ne*-ta	type of quail, found on the Pampas and Patagonia
matambre	ma-*tam*-bre	flank or skirt steak, usually stuffed, rolled up and eaten cold
medialuna	me-dya-*loo*-na	croissant
mollejas	mo-*she*-khas	either the thymus or pancreas, a popular part of an *asado*
morcilla	mor-*see*-sha	black pudding (blood sausage)
morron	mo-*ron*	red pepper
palta	*pal*-ta	avocado
pan dulce	pan *dool*-se	a sweet bread containing dried fruit, nuts and some brandy, similar to panettone
pavo	*pa*-vo	turkey
pejerrey	pe-khe-*ray*	a very fine river fish
pionono	pyo-*no*-no	a version of a Swiss roll with a savory filling
pollo	*po*-sho	chicken
puchero	poo-*chair*-o	local version of a French *pot au feu* or the Spanish *cocido*
salpicón	sal-pi-*kon*	a vegetable and meat (usually chicken, tuna or beef) salad eaten cold
surubi	soo-*roo*-bi	large, delicate river fish
sesos	*se*-sos	brains
ternera	tair-*nair*-a	veal
tocino del cielo	to-*see*-no de *sye*-lo	a rich, creamy egg and sugar dessert (also *yemas quemadas*)
torta galesa	*tor*-ta ga-*le*-sa	a rich fruit cake, created by the Welsh colony in Patagonia
ubre	*oo*-bre	udder
vizcacha	veez-*ka*-cha	a member of the chinchilla family, almost always eaten in a pickled form

Buenos Aires

Buenos Aires is buzzing with newfound energy. The crash of Argentina's peso has turned one of the world's most expensive cities into one of the cheapest, and from a traveler's perspective this place feels like Prague – *before* it took off. BA is getting hotter by the second and the secret's just coming out, so cash in your chips while you can; there's no better time to visit.

The city means something different to everyone you ask. It means watching the amazingly orchestrated kicks of a tango dancer's feet at a smoky *milonga* (dance salon). It means screaming and jumping at a classic Boca versus River *fútbol* (soccer) match, along with thousands of other excited fans. It means wolfing down tender, juicy steaks the size of your head for US$5. It means wandering BA's downtown under the grand facades of elaborate European-style buildings – you'd think you were in the heart of London or Paris, not South America! It means stopping at an old-time café and imagining life a hundred years ago, then popping back out into the mad rush of pedestrianized Florida and realizing you're very much in the 21st century. BA is old-world languor with a twist of modern infusion, shaken together and mixed wildly with Argentina's own effusive personality.

This elegant yet rough-edged city welcomes intrepid travelers looking for something different but strangely familiar; it looks forward to meeting those keen to experience the unpredictable passions of a faraway destination slowly being discovered by more and more lucky souls. Come to Buenos Aires – you'll come to know and love this city as much as we do.

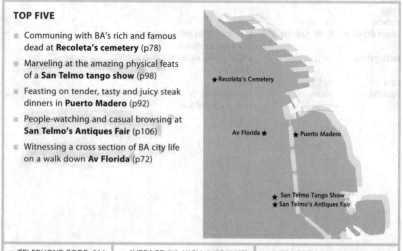

TOP FIVE

- Communing with BA's rich and famous dead at **Recoleta's cemetery** (p78)
- Marveling at the amazing physical feats of a **San Telmo tango show** (p98)
- Feasting on tender, tasty and juicy steak dinners in **Puerto Madero** (p92)
- People-watching and casual browsing at **San Telmo's Antiques Fair** (p106)
- Witnessing a cross section of BA city life on a walk down **Av Florida** (p72)

★ Recoleta's Cemetery

Av Florida ★   ★ Puerto Madero

★ San Telmo Tango Show
★ San Telmo's Antiques Fair

■ TELEPHONE CODE: 011   ■ AVERAGE JUL HIGH: 14°C (58°F)   ■ AVERAGE DEC HIGH: 28°C (82°F)

HISTORY

El Puerto de Nuestra Señora Santa María del Buen Aire was founded in 1536 by Pedro de Mendoza, who arrived from Spain with an expedition he personally financed. Food shortages and Indian attacks prompted Mendoza's departure in 1537 – he died at sea on the way home. Meanwhile, other expedition members left the settlement, sailed 1600km upriver and founded Asunción (now capital of Paraguay).

Others followed later, and by 1541 the original settlement was completely abandoned. In 1580 a new group of settlers moved downriver from Asunción under Juan de Garay's command and repopulated Mendoza's abandoned outpost.

For the next 196 years Buenos Aires (as it came to be called) was a backwater and a smuggler's paradise due to trade restrictions imposed by Spain. All the same, its population had grown to around 20,000 by 1776, the year Spain decreed it capital of the enormous new Viceroyalty of the Río de la Plata. Suddenly BA was a very important place. Many *porteños* (inhabitants of BA) have had a notoriously high opinion of themselves and their town ever since.

After repelling British invasions in 1806 and 1807, *porteños* reckoned they could handle themselves without Spain's help (or interference). Napoleon's 1808 conquest of Spain led to BA's *cabildo* (town council) cutting ties with the mother country in May 1810. Decades of power struggles between BA and the other former viceregal provinces ensued, escalating more than once into civil war.

Finally in 1880 the city was declared the federal territory of BA, a separate entity from the surrounding province of the same name, and the nation's capital forevermore.

BA's population by then was nearly half a million, and waves of immigrants (chiefly Spanish and Italian) continued to roll in. Many of them settled on the southern edge of town, to work in the booming meat-processing industries and port. An 1871 yellow-fever epidemic had already driven the wealthy northward, and now the middle class abandoned La Boca and San Telmo to the throngs of newcomers.

The nation's agricultural exports soared from 1880 to 1914, which resulted in great wealth accumulating in BA. Well-heeled *porteños* flaunted it by building opulent French-style mansions, and the government spent lavishly on public works, including parks, ornate offices and a subway line. Much of the unique look BA dates from this period, although Av 9 de Julio's transformation into a block-wide mega-boulevard didn't occur until the late 1930s.

By 1900 South America's largest city had more than a million inhabitants, and it has kept growing. Since 1930 the majority of new arrivals have been mestizos (a person of mixed Indian and Spanish descent) from Argentina's interior or neighboring countries, many of whom live in shantytowns.

BA has been overtaken in population by Mexico City and São Paulo, and shares their problems of pollution, poverty, decaying infrastructure and unemployment. Some hopeful signs include the as-yet shaky comeback of Argentina's economy, an influx of foreign tourism that is helping to revitalize neighborhoods like San Telmo, an expansion of the subway system, and the conversion of the once-abandoned Puerto Madero area into a complex of apartments, offices and restaurants.

ORIENTATION

Buenos Aires (population three million, stretching to 13 million in greater Buenos Aires) is a huge city, but most places of interest to travelers are concentrated in just a few easily accessible neighborhoods. At the heart of the city is Microcentro, the downtown business center. Just south is San Telmo, known for its tango and Sunday antiques market. La Boca is further south still and famous for its colorful houses clad in corrugated metal.

West of the Microcentro is Congreso, the seat of BA's politics. North of both are Retiro and Recoleta, upscale areas of fancy stores and museums. North of these are Palermo and Belgrano, upper-middle-class suburbs with plenty of shopping and spacious parks.

From Ezeiza, the international airport, the quickest way into town is via taxi (US$15). If you're alone there are good and frequent airport shuttles (US$7.50). Cheapest is public bus (US$0.50), but these take a long time and aren't very comfortable. For details, see p108.

(Continued on page 70)

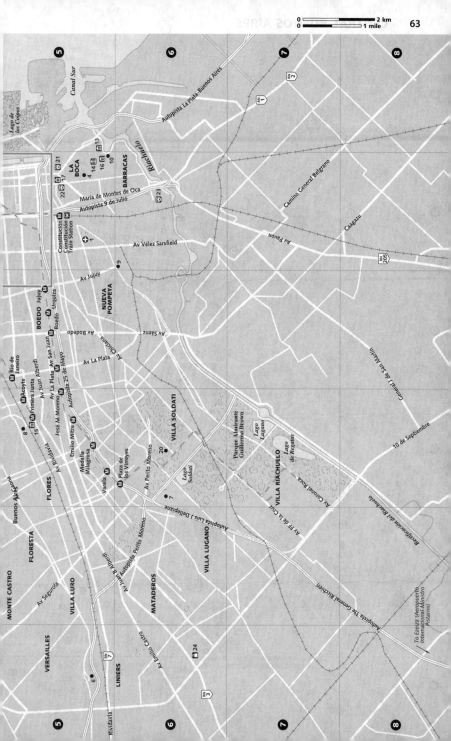

0 ⸻ 2 km
0 ⸻ 1 mile

5 **6** **7** **8**

Canal Sur

Lago de
los Coipos

Autopista La Plata-Buenos Aires

Riachuelo

RN 2

RN 1

13

21
17
LA BOCA
14 16 10
4
22
23
BARRACAS

María de Montes de Oca
Autopista 9 de Julio

Camino General Belgrano

Caagazú

Constitución
Constitución
Train Station

Av Pavón

RN 205

1

Av Vélez Sarsfield

9

Av Jujuy

Jujuy

NUEVA
POMPEYA

BOEDO

Urquiza

Boedo

Av Bodedo

Av Sáenz

General J de San Martín

Río de
Janeiro

Acoyte

Primera Junta

José M. Moreno

8
15

Av Rivadavia

Av Juan Alberdi

Av La Plata
Av San Juan
Autopista 25 de Mayo

Av La Plata

Av Chiclana

Emilio Mitre

10 de Septiembre

Medalla
Milagrosa

Varela

Plaza de
los Virreyes

Av Perito Moreno

VILLA SOLDATI

20

Parque Almirante
Guillermo Brown

Lago
Laguna

Lago
de Regatas

Rectificación del Riachuelo

FLORES

Buenos Aires

FLORESTA

MONTE CASTRO

Av Segurola

VILLA LURO

VERSAILLES

Av Juan B Alberdi
Autopista Perito Moreno

Lago
Soldati

Autopista Luis J Dellepiane

7

VILLA RIÁCHUELO

Av Coronel Roca

AV FF de la Cruz

VILLA LUGANO

MATADEROS

Av Emilio Castro

24

Autopista Tte. General Richieri

To Ezeiza (Aeropuerto
Internacional Ministro
Pistarini)

RN 7

6

LINIERS

Rivadavia

RN 3

5 **6** **7** **8**

0
0
1 km
0.5 miles

Dique No 3
Dique No 2
Dique No 1

Olga Cosentini
Dealezzi
R. Vera Peñaloza

Av Alicia Moreau de Justo
Av Ing Huergo
Azopardo

Av Eduardo Madero
Av Alicia Moreau de Justo
Av Ing Huergo

Puente de la Mujer
Av Paseo Colón

Av Leandro N Alem
Plaza AP Justo
Av Paseo Colón

Av Roseti
Av de la Rábida
Parque Colón

LA CITY
Juan D Perón
Sarmiento
Plaza de Mayo
Balcarce
Adolfo Alsina
Defensa
Av Belgrano
Bolívar
Venezuela

MICROCENTRO
Florida
Maipú

Diagonal Norte
Diagonal Roque Sáenz Peña
Catedral
Bolívar
Perú
Moreno

Av Julio Roca
Chacabuco
Belgrano
México
Chile
Estados Unidos
Carlos Calvo

SAN TELMO
Balcarce
Defensa
Plaza Dorrego
Bolívar
Av San Juan
Autopista 25 de Mayo
To La Boca border (600m)

Florida
9 de Julio
Cerrito
Libertad
Talcahuano
Rivarola
Uruguay
Paraná
Montevideo
Rodríguez Peña
Av Callao
Riobamba
Ayacucho

Bartolomé Mitre
Av de Mayo
Hipólito Yrigoyen
Piedras
Tacuarí
Lima
Salta
Santiago del Estero
San José
Luis Sáenz Peña
Virrey Cevallos
Solís
Av Entre Ríos
Combate de los Pozos

MONTSERRAT
Av Belgrano
Bernardo de Irigoyen

Independencia

CONSTITUCION
Humberto Primo
San José
San Juan
Entre Ríos
Humberto Primo
Carlos Calvo
Estados Unidos
México
Chile
Venezuela
Pichincha
Av San Juan

Plaza Lavalle
Plaza de la República
Plaza del Congreso
Plaza 1 de Mayo

BALVANERA
Junín
Pasco
Pichincha
Rincón
Adolfo Alsina
Moreno
Sarandí

Av Rivadavia
Hipólito Yrigoyen
Av Callao
Congreso
Pasco

Departamento Central de la Policía Federal Argentina

Pasteur
Uriburu
Pasteur
Av Corrientes
Juan D Perón
Sarmiento
Av Callao
To Once Train Station (800m)

Basílica de San Francisco
Edificio MOP

See Central Buenos Aires Map (pp64–7)

PALERMO SOHO

PALERMO HOLLYWOOD

ENTERTAINMENT 🎭	(pp98–104)
Amerika	64 C8
Café Homero	65 B6
Club del Vino	66 C7
El Camarín de las Musas	67 D7
Esquina Carlos Gardel	68 E8
Glam	69 E7
La Catedral	70 D8
La Peña del Colorado	71 D6
La Salsera	72 C8
La Viruta/La Estrella	73 B7
Mint	74 F3
Niceto Club	75 B6
Pachá	76 C1
Podestá	77 C6
Salon Canning	78 C7
Thelonius Bar	79 D6
Tiempo de Gitanos	80 B5

SHOPPING 🛍	(pp104–7)
Atípica	81 C6
El Cid	82 C6
Feria de Pulgas	83 A5
Feria Plaza Serrano	(see 26)
La Mercería	84 C6
Mercado de Abasto	85 E8
Objeto	86 C6
Oda	87 C6
Paseo Alcorta	88 F4
Rapsodia	89 C6

BUENOS AIRES IN...

Two Days

Start with a stroll in **San Telmo** (p76) and duck into some antiques stores. Walk to **Plaza de Mayo** (p73) for historical perspective, then wander the **Microcentro** (p72), perhaps veering east to **Puerto Madero** (p75) – a great spot for a break.

Keep heading northward into **Retiro** (p77) and **Recoleta** (p78), stopping off at the **Museo Nacional de Bellas Artes** (p78) to admire some impressionism. Be sure to also visit the **Cementerio de la Recoleta** (p78) to commune with the elite dead. For dinner, **Palermo Viejo** (p95) can't be beat.

On day two take a quick side trip to **La Boca** (p77) and watch a soccer game if your timing is right. Shop on **Av Santa Fe** (p104) or **Palermo Viejo** (p104), and at night catch a **tango show** (p98) or performance at the **Teatro Colón** (p75).

Four Days

Follow the two-day itinerary, then on your third day add a trip to **Tigre** (p110). On the fourth day think about taking a **tango lesson** (p100), going to the **Mataderos fair** (p106) if it's a weekend, seeing more museums, walking around the **Congreso area** (p75) and checking out **Palermo's parks** (p79). Be sure to find yourself a good steak restaurant for your last meal.

(Continued from page 61)

INFORMATION
Bookstores

El Ateneo (Map pp64–7; ☎ 4325-6801; Florida 340) Limited number of books in English, but has some travel guides. Other branches at Florida 629 and Av Santa Fe 1860 (Map pp64–7).

Librería ABC (Map pp64–7; ☎ 4314-8106; www .libreriasabc.com.ar; Córdoba 685) The best in town for English and German books, including Lonely Planet guides.

Cultural Centers

Centro Cultural Borges (Map pp64–7; ☎ 4319-5359; www.ccborges.org.ar in Spanish; cnr Viamonte & San Martín) One of BA's best, offering cheap art exhibits, music, classes and workshops.

Centro Cultural Konex (Map pp64–7; ☎ 4816-0500; www.centroculturalkonex.org.ar in Spanish; Av Córdoba 1235) Innovative theater and music.

Centro Cultural Recoleta (Map pp64–7; ☎ 4803-1041; www.centroculturalrecoleta.org in Spanish; Junín 1930) Art exhibits, a kids' science museum and outdoor films in summer.

Centro Cultural Ricardo Rojas (Map pp64–7; ☎ 4954-5523; www.rojas.uba.ar in Spanish; Corrientes 2038) Exceptionally good, offering a very wide range of quality, inexpensive classes.

Centro Cultural San Martín (Map pp64–7; ☎ 4374-1251; www.ccgsm.gov.ar in Spanish; Sarmiento 1551) An excellent cultural resource, with many free or inexpensive offerings.

There are also several foreign cultural centers located in the Microcentro (p72):

Alianza Francesa (Map pp64–7; ☎ 4322-0068; www .alianzafrancesa.org.ar; Av Córdoba 946)

British Arts Centre (Map pp64–7; ☎ 4393-6941; www .britishartscentre.org.ar in Spanish; Suipacha 1333; ☺ 3-9pm Tue-Fri, 6-9pm Sat)

Instituto Goethe (Map pp64–7; ☎ 4311-8964; www .goethe.de/hs/bue; Av Corrientes 319)

Emergency

Ambulance (☎ 107)

Fire (☎ 100)

Police (☎ 101)

Tourist police (Comisaría del Turista; Map pp64–7; ☎ 4346-5748, 0800-999-5000; turista@policiafederal .gov.ar; Av Corrientes 436; ☺ 24hr) Provides interpreters and helps victims of robberies and rip-offs.

Internet Access

Internet cafés and *locutorios* (telephone offices) with Internet access are very common everywhere in the center; you can often find one by just walking two blocks in any direction. Rates are very cheap at about US$0.50 per hour, and connections are quick.

Libraries

Biblioteca Lincoln (Map pp64–7; ☎ 5382-1536; www.bcl.edu.ar in Spanish; Maipú 672) Located inside the Instituto Cultural Argentino-Norteamericano, this library is good for English newspapers, magazines and books.

Biblioteca Nacional (Map pp68-9; ☎ 4806-9764; Agüero 2502) BA's main library and downright ugly.

The Alianza Francesa (French) and Instituto Goethe (German) have foreign libraries also.

Media

BA's most popular newspapers are the entertaining *Clarín* and the more moderate *La Nación*. The English-language daily *Buenos Aires Herald* covers Argentina and the world from an international perspective, and German speakers have *Argentinisches Tageblatt*. International newspapers like the *New York Times*, *USA Today*, the *Guardian* and *Le Monde* are available at kiosks on Florida. Magazines like *Time*, *Newsweek* and the *Economist* are also fairly easy to obtain.

Eighty cable channels offer TV viewers plenty of choice, including CNN, BBC and ESPN plus many European channels. Channels are overrun with reality shows, bimboled dance parties and *telenovelas* (soap operas). There are five regular channels:

Canal 2 (América TV; www.america2.com.ar in Spanish) Heavy on the sports, news and entertainment; check out Roberto Pettinato's personality show *Indomables*.

Canal 7 State-run channel and thus claims the lowest ratings; known for its general interest and cultural programming.

Canal 9 Smut at its best and expresses no shame in using sex to sell; imports trashy shows like *Top Model* and *Living with My Ex*.

Canal 11 (Telefé; www.telefe.com.ar in Spanish) Boasts Marcelo Tinelli's long-running *Videomatch* along with popular transvestite Lisa Florencia de la Vega.

Canal 13 (www.canal13.com.ar in Spanish) Grupo Clarín's high-quality channel, offering the satire *Caiga quien caiga* along with popular news show *Telenoche*.

Dozens of FM stations serve BA. FM 92.7 has tango, 92.3 has Argentine folk, 97.4 has classical music, 95.9 has national/international rock and pop, 98.3 has Argentine rock and pop only and 97.1 has the BBC in English (from noon to 5pm).

Medical Services

Hospital Alemán (Map pp68-9; ☎ 4821-1700; Pueyrredón 1640)

Hospital Británico Marcelo T de Alvear (Map pp64-7; ☎ 4812-0040; Marcelo T de Alvear 1573); Perdriel (Map pp62-3; ☎ 4304-1081; Perdriel 74)

Hospital Municipal Juan Fernández (Map pp68-9; ☎ 4808-2600; Cerviño 3356)

Money

Banks and *cambios* (money-exchange offices) are common in the city center; banks have longer lines and more limited opening hours but may offer better rates. A good *cambio* to try is **Alhec** (Map pp64-7; ☎ 4316-5000; Paraguay 641; ⏰ 10am-4:30pm Mon-Fri).

Even in Buenos Aires it's hard to change traveler's checks. Only a few fancy hotels and banks will take them, and you won't get a favorable rate. One exception is American Express (see following), but you'll have to line up.

ATMs are everywhere in BA and dispense pesos only. The following local representatives can help you replace lost or stolen cards:

American Express (Map pp64-7; ☎ 4312-1661; Arenales 707) Also changes traveler's checks 10am to 3pm Monday to Friday.

MasterCard (Map pp64-7; ☎ 4348-7070; Perú 151)

Visa (Map pp64-7; ☎ 4379-3400; basement fl, Corrientes 1437)

Post

Correo Central (Map pp64-7; ☎ 4894-9191; www .correoargentino.com.ar; Sarmiento 151; ⏰ 8am-8pm Mon-Fri, 9am-1pm Sat)

Correo Internacional (Map pp64-7; ☎ 4316-1777; Av Antártida Argentina; ⏰ 10am-5pm Mon-Fri) For international parcels over 2kg. A 5kg package to North America costs US$70, to Europe US$85 and to Australia US$105.

DHL Internacional (Map pp64-7; ☎ 0810-222-2345; www.dhl.com.ar; Av Córdoba 783)

Federal Express (Map pp64-7; ☎ 0810-333-3339; www.fedex.com; Maipú 753)

OCA (Map pp64-7; ☎ 0810-999-7700; www.oca.com.ar; Viamonte 526) For domestic packages.

Telephone

The easiest way to make a phone call in BA is at a *locutorio* (small telephone office). Street phones require coins or *tarjetas telefónicas* (magnetic phone cards available at many kiosks). Faxes are cheap and widely available at most *locutorios* and Internet cafés. For more information on telephone and cell phones, see p470.

Tourist Information

Automóvil Club Argentino (ACA; Map pp68-9; ☎ 4802-6061; www.aca.org.ar; Av del Libertador 1850) National auto club which sells excellent maps and provides road information; also see p479.

Secretaría de Turismo de la Nación (Map pp64-7; ☎ 4312-2232; www.turismo.gov.ar; Santa Fe 883; ⏰ 9am-5pm Mon-Fri) Dispenses information on Buenos Aires and Argentina.

There are many tourist kiosks in BA; hours vary slightly throughout the year.

Aeroparque airport tourist kiosk (☎ 4773-9805; ⏱ 8am-8pm) For flight info call ☎ 5480-6111.

Ezeiza airport tourist kiosk (☎ 4480-0224; ⏱ 8am-8pm) For flight info call ☎ 5480-6111.

Florida & Diagonal Roque Sáenz Peña tourist kiosk (Map pp64-7; ⏱ 9am-6pm Mon-Sat)

Florida & Marcelo T de Alvear tourist kiosk (Map pp64-7; ⏱ 10am-7pm)

Puerto Madero tourist kiosk (Map pp64-7; ☎ 4313-0187; Dique 4; ⏱ 11am-6pm Mon-Fri, 11am-7pm Sat)

Recoleta tourist kiosk (Map pp64-7; Quintana 596; ⏱ 10:30am-6:30pm Mon-Fri, 10am-7pm Sat & Sun)

Retiro bus station tourist kiosk (Map pp64-7; ☎ 4311-0528; ⏱ 7:30am-1pm Mon-Sat) Located on 2nd floor, perpendicular to bus slot No 34, at Local 83.

San Telmo tourist kiosk (Map pp64-7; Defensa 1250; ⏱ 11am-5pm Mon-Fri, 11am-7pm Sat & Sun)

Travel Agencies

The following agencies all arrange tours in BA and Argentina, and staff speak English.

Argentinago (Map pp64-7; ☎ 4372-7268, in USA ☎ 786-245-0513; www.argentinago.com; Tucumán 1427, 2nd fl, Room 201) American-run, with Western-style service; also helps foreigners with buying/managing property in BA.

Asatej (Map pp64–7; ☎ 4114-7500; www.asatej.net in Spanish; Florida 835, 3rd fl, Room 320) Argentina's nonprofit student and discount travel agency. Excellent service.

Pride Travel (Map pp64-7; ☎ 5218-6556; www.pride -travel.com; Room 2E, Paraguay 523) Gay-oriented; also helps arrange short- or long-term stays in BA.

Say Hueque (Map pp64-7; ☎ 5199-2517; www.say hueque.com; Viamonte 749, 6th fl) Backpacker-oriented and offers packages around Argentina (especially Patagonia).

Tangol (Map pp64-7; ☎ 4312-7276; www.tangol.com; Florida 971, Local 59) Backpacker-oriented and offers regular and more unusual tours around BA.

Wow Argentina (Map pp64-7; ☎ 15-5603-2926; www .wowargentina.com.ar; Room 2F, Av Santa Fe 882) Small agency catering to an upper-class clientele.

DANGERS & ANNOYANCES

Buenos Aires has been getting a bad rap these past few years. A city in hard times makes some people desperate, and you may hear of store robberies or *secuestros exprés* ('express' kidnappings) – but do realize that these activities are generally not aimed at foreigners.

In general, BA is as safe as many other big cities in the world. You can comfortably walk around at all hours of the night in many places, even as a lone woman. People stay out very late, and there's almost always somebody else walking on any one street at any hour of the night. Some neighborhoods where you should be careful at night, however, are Constitución (around the train station), the eastern border of San Telmo, and La Boca (where, outside tourist streets, you should be careful even during the day).

Crime against tourists is almost always of the petty sort, such as pickpockets in crowded markets or buses – things smart travelers easily guard themselves against. Minor nuisances include lack of respect shown by cars toward pedestrians, lax pollution controls and cigarette smoke everywhere. For dealing with taxis, see p109.

Remember that using your head is good advice anywhere: don't stagger around drunk, always be aware of your surroundings and look like you know exactly where you're going, with the attitude that you could kick the ass of anyone who gives you grief. And realize that if you're reasonably careful, the closest thing to annoyance you'll experience is being shortchanged, tripping on loose sidewalk tiles, stepping on the ubiquitous dog pile or getting flattened by a crazy bus driver. Watch your step.

SIGHTS
Microcentro & Plaza De Mayo   Map pp64–7

BA's Microcentro is where the big city hustles: here you'll see endless crowds of business suits and power skirts speaking into cell phones as they hasten about the narrow streets in the shadows of skyscrapers and old European buildings.

Pedestrianized Florida is in some ways the main artery of this region, always jammed during the day with businesspeople, shoppers and tourists seeking vehicle-free access from north to south without the ubiquitous bus fumes and honking taxis. Buskers, beggars and street vendors thrive here as well, adding color and noise. The recent renovation of buildings such as beautiful Galerías Pacífico, near Florida and Av Córdoba, adds elegance to the area.

Further south is BA's busy financial district, which offers several museums to investigate. After that comes Plaza de Mayo, often filled with people resting on benches or taking photos of historic buildings.

East of the Microcentro and Plaza de Mayo you'll find the city's newest barrio, Puerto Madero, a renovated waterfront area that stretches south toward the neighborhood of San Telmo. This project has renovated once-abandoned brick warehouses into upscale restaurants, offices and loft apartments, and has become one the trendiest places to eat in the city.

GALERÍAS PACÍFICO

Covering an entire city block, this beautiful French-style **shopping center** (☎ 5555-5110; ⊗ 10am-9pm Sun-Thu, 10am-12:30am Fri & Sat) dates from 1889 and boasts vaulted ceilings with paintings done in 1954 by muralists Antonio Berni, Juan Carlos Castagnino, Manuel Colmeiro, Lino Spilimbergo and Demetrio Urruchúa. All were adherents of the *nuevo realismo* (new realism) school of Argentine art. For many years the building went semi-abandoned, but a joint Argentine–Mexican team repaired and restored the murals in 1992.

The beautiful structure, which is dotted with fairy lights at night, is now a central meeting place sporting upscale stores and a large food court. Tourist-oriented tango shows take place here at 8pm on weekends, and the excellent Centro Cultural Borges takes up the 3rd floor. Guided tours are on tap twice per day.

MUSEO MITRE

Bartolomé Mitre, who became Argentina's president in 1862, resided at this colonial house, now a **museum** (☎ 4394-8240; San Martín 336; admission free; ⊗ 1-6pm Mon-Fri). After leaving office, he founded the influential daily *La Nación*, still a *porteño* institution. The museum provides a good reflection of 19th-century upper-class life. It's full of Mitre's personal effects, such as home decorations and furniture.

MUSEO DE LA POLICÍA FEDERAL

In the heart of the financial district, this **museum** (☎ 4394-6857; San Martín 353, 7th fl; admission free, children under 15 not permitted; ⊗ 1-6pm Tue-Fri) proudly displays a whole slew of uniforms and medals. There's also the skeleton of a police dog who died on duty, plus cockfighting and gambling exhibits. Grisly forensic photos, along with dummies of murder victims, are for pre-appetizer viewing only.

MUSEO HISTÓRICO DR ARTURO JÁURETCHE

This **museum** (☎ 4331-6600; Sarmiento 362; admission free; ⊗ 10am-6pm Mon-Fri, tours by appointment) makes some sense of Argentina's chaotic economic history. Well-lit displays on paper money and counterfeiting are no doubt scrutinized by BA's current money forgers. The million-peso bill from 1981 gives an idea of the hyperinflation *porteños* had to deal with.

CORREO CENTRAL

The massive **main post office** (☎ 4316-3000; Sarmiento 151; ⊗ 8am-8pm Mon-Fri, 9am-1pm Sat) fills an entire city block. It took 20 years to complete the impressive beaux arts structure, originally modeled on New York City's main post office. Inside is a small post and telegraph museum, but hours are unpredictable.

PLAZA DE MAYO

Planted between the Casa Rosada, the Cabildo and the city's main cathedral is grassy Plaza de Mayo, BA's ground zero for the city's most vehement protests. On Thursdays at 3:30pm, the Madres de la Plaza de Mayo (the Mothers of Plaza de Mayo) still march around the square in their unrelenting campaign for a full account of Dirty War atrocities (see p33).

In the plaza's center is the **Pirámide de Mayo**, a small obelisk built to mark the first anniversary of BA's independence from Spain. Looming on the plaza's north side is the **Banco de la Nación** (1939), the work of famed architect Alejandro Bustillo. Most other public buildings in this area belong to the late 19th century and are the main photo subjects for the many tourists that visit this spot.

CABILDO

The mid-18th-century **Cabildo** (town council; Map pp64-7; ☎ 4342-6729; Bolívar 65; admission US$0.35, Fri free; ⊗ 10:30am-5pm Tue-Fri, 11:30am-6pm Sun & holidays, tours in Spanish 4pm daily) is not the size it once was, due to the building of surrounding avenues, but still has a section of the *recova* (colonnade) that once spanned Plaza de Mayo. The museum inside offers scanty exhibits, but a lively crafts market sets up in the patio on Thursdays and Fridays.

CASA ROSADA

Taking up the whole east side of the Plaza de Mayo is the unmistakable pink facade of the Casa Rosada (Pink House). Though the offices of top dog Néstor Kirchner are here, the presidential residence is in the calm suburbs of Olivos, north of the center.

The side of the palace facing Plaza de Mayo is actually the back of the building. It's from these balconies, however, that Juan and Eva Perón, General Leopoldo Galtieri, Raúl Alfonsín and other politicians have preached to throngs of impassioned Argentines. Pop celebrity Madonna also crooned from here for her movie *Evita*.

The salmon pink color of the Casa Rosada, which positively glows at sunset, could have come from President Sarmiento's attempt at making peace during his 1868–74 term (blending the red of the Federalists with the white of the Unitarists). Another theory, however, is that the color comes from painting the palace with bovine blood, which was a common practice in the late 19th century. During the Menem years another coat was painted on the front of the building, but funds ran out and today it remains a two-toned symbol of Argentina's volatile economy.

Free guided tours of the Casa Rosada take place at 4pm Monday to Friday (English tours on Fridays at 4pm only). Show up one hour in advance to reserve a spot.

The **Museo de la Casa Rosada** (☎ 4344-3802; admission free; ☼ 10am-6pm Mon-Fri, 2-6pm Sun, tours 3pm & 4:30pm Sun) provides displays of Perón memorabilia and a truncated chronology of Argentine presidents. Entrance to both tour and museum are at Hipólito Yrigoyen 219; bring your passport.

CATEDRAL METROPOLITANA
The solemn baroque **cathedral** (☎ 4331-2845; www.horariosdemisa.com.ar; cnr Rivadavia & San Martín; admission free; ☼ 8am-7pm Mon-Fri, 9am-7:30pm Sat & Sun) is a significant religious and architectural landmark, but more importantly, it contains the tomb of General José de San Martín, Argentina's most revered hero. Outside the cathedral you'll see a flame keeping his spirit alive.

Tours of the church are given at 11:30am Monday to Friday; tours of the crypt are given at 1:15pm Monday to Friday; tours of both are given at 4pm daily. All tours are in Spanish. Occasional free choir concerts are also on the docket.

MANZANA DE LAS LUCES
The Manzana de las Luces (Block of Enlightenment) includes the city's oldest colonial church, the Jesuit Iglesia San Ignacio. During colonial times this was BA's center of learning, and still symbolizes high culture in the capital. The first to occupy this block were the Jesuits, and two of the five original buildings of the Jesuit Procuraduría still remain. Dating from 1730, these buildings include defensive tunnels discovered in 1912. The Universidad de Buenos Aires has occupied the site since independence in 1810 .

Historical tours (☎ 4331-9534; Perú 272; tours US$1; ☼ 3pm Mon-Fri, 3pm, 4:30pm & 6pm Sat & Sun) in Spanish provide the only regular public access to the block's interior.

MUSEO DE LA CIUDAD
Wander among the permanent and temporary exhibitions on *porteño* life and history, including historical photographs and old furniture, in the **city museum** (☎ 4331-9855; Adolfo Alsina 412; local/foreigner US$0.35/1, Wed free; ☼ 11am-7pm Mon-Fri, 3-7pm Sat & Sun). Salvaged doors and ancient hardware found a home next door at the museum's annex. Nearby, at the corner of Defensa, is the **Farmacia de la Estrella**, a functioning homeopathic pharmacy with gorgeous woodwork and elaborate turn-of-the-19th-century ceiling murals.

MUSEO ETNOGRÁFICO JUAN B AMBROSETTI
This small but attractive **anthropological museum** (☎ 4331-7788; www.museos.buenosaires.gov.ar in Spanish; Moreno 350; admission US$0.35; ☼ 3-7pm Wed-Sun) displays collections from the Andean northwest, Patagonia and elsewhere in South America. Beautiful indigenous artifacts, including intricate jewelry and Mapuche ponchos, are presented, while an African and Asian room showcases priceless items. Guided tours in Spanish are given on weekends from 3pm to 5pm.

BASÍLICA DE SANTO DOMINGO
Further south, at Defensa and Av Belgrano, the 18th-century Dominican Basílica de Santo Domingo has a colorful history. On its left tower are the replicated scars of shrapnel launched against British troops who holed up here during the 1806 invasion. The **Museo de la Basílica del Rosario** (☎ 4331-1668; admission US$0.75; ☼ by appointment

only) displays the flags that were captured from the British.

Puerto Madero

The newest and least conventional of the capital's 48 official barrios is Puerto Madero, located east of the Microcentro and Plaza de Mayo. It's a wonderful place to stroll, boasting cobbled paths and a long line of attractive brick warehouses that have been converted into ritzy new lofts, business offices and upscale restaurants. It carries a bumpy history, however.

In the mid-19th century competing commercial interests began to fight over the location of a modernized port for Argentina's burgeoning international commerce. Puerto Madero was finally chosen, and the city's mudflats were transformed into a series of modern basins and harbors consistent with the aspirations and ambitions of a cosmopolitan elite. It was completed in 1898, but Puerto Madero had exceeded its budget and was tarnished by scandal – suspicions arose from the sale of surrounding lands likely to increase in value. The practical side of the scheme didn't go so well either: by 1910, the amount of cargo was already too great for the new port, and poor access to the rail terminus at Plaza Once made things even worse. Only the 1926 completion of Retiro's Puerto Nuevo solved these hassles.

Today you'll find some of BA's most expensive real estate in Puerto Madero. Much has been done already, but many of the buildings envisioned by planners are still works in progress. BA's newest neighborhood has some of its oldest history, and continues to evolve.

FRAGATA SARMIENTO

Over 23,000 Argentine naval cadets and officers have trained aboard this 85m **sailing ship** (Map pp64-7; ☎ 4334-9386; Dique No 3; admission US$0.75; 🕑 9am-6pm), which sailed around the world 40 times between 1899 and 1938 but never actually participated in combat. On board are records of its voyages, plenty of nautical items and even the stuffed remains of Lampazo (the ship's pet dog).

MUSEO DE LA INMIGRACIÓN

Located in the historic Hotel de Inmigrantes, this **museum** (Map pp64-7; ☎ 4317-0285; Av Antártida Argentina 1355; admission free; 🕑 10am-5pm Mon-Fri, 11am-6pm Sat & Sun) tells the story of the thousands of European immigrants who landed in BA beginning in the late 1880s. Old photos, videos and memorabilia show how the new settlers were treated, as well as the progress of their new lives.

RESERVA ECOLÓGICA COSTANERA SUR

The beautifully marshy land of this **nature preserve** (Map pp62-3; ☎ 4315-1320; Av Tristán Achával Rodríguez 1550; 🕑 8am-7pm Nov-Mar, 8am-6pm Apr-Oct) makes it a popular site for weekend outings, when hundreds of picnickers, cyclists and families come for fresh air and natural views. Bird-watchers will adore the 200-plus bird species that pause to rest here, and a few lucky folks might spot a river turtle or nutria. You can rent bikes just outside on the weekends (daily in summer).

Congreso & Avenida Corrientes

Map pp64–7

Congreso is an interesting neighborhood mix of old-time cinemas and theaters, bustling commerce and hard-core political flavor all in one. The buildings still hold that European aura, but there's more grittiness here than in the Microcentro: it's more local-city feel and worn-out atmosphere, and lacks the well-dressed crowds.

Separating Congreso from the Microcentro is Av 9 de Julio, 'the widest street in the world!' as proud *porteños* love to boast. While this may be true – it's 16 lanes at its widest – the nearby side streets Cerrito and Carlos Pellegrini make it look even broader. At Avs 9 de Julio and Corrientes lies the city's famous **Obelisco**, which soars above the oval Plaza de la República.

Plaza Lavalle is surrounded by the austere neoclassical **Escuela Presidente Roca** (1902), the French-style **Palacio de Justicia** (1904) and the landmark **Teatro Colón.** Nearby is also the **Templo de la Congregación Israelita**, Argentina's largest synagogue.

Finally, head around 10 blocks south of Plaza Lavalle to the **Palacio del Congreso**, together with its plaza and obligatory monument. This site is also another locus for the nation's *piqueteros* (picketers) and their many grievances.

TEATRO COLÓN

The **Colón** (tours ☎ 4378-7132, shows ☎ 4378-7344; www.teatrocolon.org.ar; Libertad 621; tours US$2.50;

English tours 11am, 1pm & 3pm) is one of the city's major landmarks, a gorgeous world-class facility for opera, ballet and classical music. It was the southern hemisphere's largest theater until the Sydney Opera House was built in 1973. Opening night was in 1908 with a presentation of Verdi's *Aïda*, and visitors have been wowed ever since. Even through times of economic hardship, the elaborate Colón remains a high national priority – essentially, this place rocks.

Excellent guided visits are very worthwhile and are available in many languages (call ahead), but only Spanish and English tours have regular schedules.

PALACIO DEL CONGRESO

Colossal and topped with a green dome, the Palacio del Congreso cost more than twice its projected budget and set a precedent for contemporary Argentine public-works projects. It was modeled on the Capitol Building in Washington, DC, and was completed in 1906. Across the way, the **Monumento a los Dos Congresos** honors the congresses of 1810 in BA and 1816 in Tucumán, both of which led to Argentine independence.

Inside the Congreso, free guided tours are given of the **Senado** (☎ 4010-3000, ext 3885) on weekdays at 11am (English, Spanish and French), 4pm (English) and 5pm and 6pm (Spanish); go to the entrance at Hipólito Yrigoyen 1849.

PALACIO DE LAS AGUAS CORRIENTES

About six blocks west of Plaza Lavalle, this gorgeous and eclectic Swedish-designed water-works building (1894) is topped by French-style mansard roofs and covered in 170,000 glazed tiles and 130,000 enameled bricks. If you like quirky museums, check out the small **Museo del Patrimonio Aguas Argentinas** (☎ 6319-1104; museo_patrimonio@aguasargentinas.com.ar; admission free; 9am-1pm Mon-Fri) on the 1st floor; bring ID and enter via Riobamba.

San Telmo

Full of charm and personality, San Telmo is one of BA's most attractive and historically rich barrios. Narrow cobbled streets and low-story colonial housing retain an old-time feel, though the tourist dollar is bringing about a few changes.

Historically, San Telmo is famous for the violent street fighting that took place when British troops, at war with Spain, invaded the city in 1806. British forces advanced up narrow Defensa, but an impromptu militia drove the British back to their ships. The victory gave *porteños* confidence in their ability to stand apart from Spain, even though the city's independence had to wait another three years.

After this San Telmo became a fashionable, classy neighborhood, but in the late 19th century a yellow-fever epidemic hit and drove the rich into present-day Recoleta. Many older mansions were subdivided and became *conventillos* (tenements) to house poor families. Today, these *conventillos* attract artists, bohemians and expatriates looking for large spaces at low rents.

The heart of San Telmo is **Plaza Dorrego**, which hosts its famous Sunday antiques market (see the boxed text, p106). Nearby, the neocolonial and baroque **Iglesia Nuestra Señora de Belén** (Map pp64-7; Humberto Primo 340) was a Jesuit school until 1767, when the Bethlemite order took it over.

MUSEO HISTÓRICO NACIONAL

This **national historical museum** (Map pp62-3; ☎ 4307-1182; Defensa 1600; admission US$0.75; 11am-5pm Tue-Fri, 11am-7pm Sun) is located at the supposed site of Pedro de Mendoza's original foundation of the city in 1536. Inside, a panorama of artifacts, paintings, weapons and period furniture relives the Argentine experience, from its shaky beginnings and independence to the present. Major figures of Argentine historical periods, such as San Martín, Rosas and Sarmiento, are represented. In addition, there are portrayals of the British invasions of 1806 and 1807, along with period knickknacks from late-19th-century *porteño* life. Opening times may vary throughout the year, so call ahead.

MUSEO PENITENCIARIO

Just off the plaza, this **penal museum** (Map pp64-7; ☎ 4362-0099; Humberto Primo 378; admission US$0.35; 2-5pm Tue & Fri, noon-7pm Sat & Sun) occupies a building that was first a convent and later a women's prison. Check out the photograph of famous anarchist Simón Radowitzky's release from prison, and a wooden desk carved by inmates at Ushuaia for president Roberto M Ortiz. Reconstructed old jail cells give an idea of the prisoners' conditions.

MUSEO DE ARTE MODERNO
Housed in a recycled tobacco warehouse, this roomy **museum** (Map pp64-7; ☎ 4361-1121; Av San Juan 350; local/foreigner US$0.35/1, Wed free; 🕐 10am-8pm Tue-Fri, 11am-8pm Sat & Sun) exhibits the figurative works of contemporary Argentine artists, as well as temporary exhibitions. Only hard-core modern-art lovers need visit.

MUSEO DEL TRAJE
This small **clothing museum** (Map pp64-7; ☎ 4343-8427; Chile 832; admission free; 🕐 3-7pm Tue-Sat) is always changing its wardrobe. You can hit upon civilian and military clothing from colonial times to the present, or '60s vintage hippie wear. Come by and see what hot fashions the dummies are wearing when you're in town.

La Boca   Map pp62–3
Blue collar and raffish to the core, La Boca is very much a locals' neighborhood. In the mid-19th century, La Boca became home to Spanish and Italian immigrants who settled along the Riachuelo, the sinuous river that divides the city from the surrounding province of Buenos Aires. Many came during the booming 1880s and ended up working in the many meat-packing plants and warehouses here, processing and shipping out much of Argentina's vital beef. After sprucing up the shipping barges, the port dwellers splashed leftover paint on the corrugated-metal siding of their own houses – unwittingly giving La Boca what would become one of its claims to fame. Unfortunately, some of the neighborhood's color also comes from the rainbow slick of industrial wastes on the river.

Caminito is the barrio's most famous street, and on weekends busloads of camera-laden tourists come here for photographs and to browse the small weekend crafts fair while watching tango dancers perform for spare change. A riverside pedestrian walkway offers a close-up sniff of the Riachuelo, while a few museums provide mental stimulation. Four blocks inland is **La Bombonera** stadium, home of the Boca Juniors soccer team – the former club of disgraced superstar Diego Maradona.

FUNDACIÓN PROA
This elegant **art foundation** (☎ 4303-0909; www .proa.org in Spanish; Pedro de Mendoza 1929; admission US$1;

BOCA WARNING

La Boca is not the kind of neighborhood for casual strolls – it can be downright rough in spots. Don't stray from the riverside walk or the tourist sections of Caminito, Del Valle Iberlucea and Magallanes, especially alone or toting expensive cameras. There's nothing you'd really want to see outside these areas anyway.

🕐 11am-7pm Tue-Sun) exhibits works by only the most cutting-edge national and international artists in both traditional and more unusual mediums. Visit the rooftop terrace – views are excellent and you can grab a drink, too.

MUSEO DE BELLAS ARTES DE LA BOCA
On display here are the works of Benito Quinquela Martín, which center on La Boca's port history, as well as those of more contemporary Argentine artists. The **museum** (☎ 4301-1080; Pedro de Mendoza 1835; admission US$0.35; 🕐 10am-5:30pm Tue-Fri, 11am-6pm Sat & Sun) also holds a small but excellent collection of painted wood bowsprits (carved statues decorating the front of ships) that's definitely worth a peep.

MUSEO DE LA PASIÓN BOQUENSE
High-tech and spiffy, this funky **fútbol museum** (☎ 4362-1100; www.museoboquense.com in Spanish; Brandsen 805; adult/student with ISIC card US$3/US$2; 🕐 10am-7pm) chronicles the rough-and-tumble neighborhood, La Bombonera stadium, some soccer idols' histories, past highlights on many videos, the championships, the trophies and, of course, the gooooals. It's located right under the stadium.

MUSEO HISTÓRICO DE CERA
Reconstructions of historical figureheads (literally just their heads!) and dioramas of scenes in Argentine history are the specialty of this small and very tacky **wax museum** (☎ 4301-1497; www.museodecera.com.ar; Del Valle Iberlucea 1261; local/foreigner US$1.25/2; 🕐 10am-6pm Mon-Fri, 11am-8pm Sat & Sun). Also see stuffed snakes and creepy wax limbs depicting bite wounds – all barely worth the price of admission.

Retiro   Map pp64–7
Well-located Retiro is one of the ritziest neighborhoods in BA – but it hasn't always

been this way. The area was the site of a monastery during the 17th century, and later became the country retreat *(retiro)* of Agustín de Robles, a Spanish governor. Since then, Retiro's current **Plaza Libertador General San Martín** – which sits on a bluff – has played host to a slave market, military fort and even a bullring. Things are more quiet and exclusive these days.

French landscape architect Charles Thays designed the leafy Plaza San Martín, whose prominent monument is the obligatory equestrian statue of José de San Martín. Surrounding the plaza are several landmark public buildings, such as the **Palacio San Martín**, an art nouveau mansion originally built for the elite Anchorena family; the neo-Gothic **Palacio Haedo**; and the 120m-high **Edificio Kavanagh** (1935), once South America's tallest building.

The 76m **Torre de los Ingleses** (☾ noon-7pm Thu-Sun), across Av del Libertador from Plaza San Martín, was a donation by the city's British community in 1916. Opposite the plaza is the impressive **Retiro train station** (Estación Retiro), built in 1915 when the British controlled the country's railroads. Don't wander behind the station – it's a shantytown.

MUSEO DE ARMAS

Outside George W Bush's imagination, you will never see so many weapons of mass destruction. Check out the excellent **collection** (☎ 4311-1071; Santa Fe 702; admission US$0.75; ☾ noon-7pm Mon-Fri) of bazookas, grenade launchers, machine guns, muskets, pistols, lances and swords – even the gas mask for a combat horse is on display.

MUSEO DE ARTE HISPANOAMERICANO ISAAC FERNÁNDEZ BLANCO

This neocolonial-era mansion turned **museum** (☎ 4327-0228; Suipacha 1422; local/foreigner US$0.35/1; ☾ 2-7pm Tue-Sun) holds some gorgeous pieces of silverwork, religious paintings, Jesuit statuary and antiques. There's been no effort to place items in any historical context, but everything is in great condition and an attractive garden provides peaceful sanctuary.

TEATRO CERVANTES

Six blocks west of Plaza San Martín, you can't help but notice the lavishly ornamented **Teatro Cervantes** (☎ 4816-4224; www.teatrocervantes.gov.ar; Libertad 815; ☾ tours in Spanish 2pm Fri).

The landmark building dates from 1921 and holds a historical theater with grand tiled lobby and plush red velvet chairs. Enjoy the elegance – however faded – with a tour.

MUSEO NACIONAL DEL TEATRO

Exhibits at this tiny, low-key **museum** (☎ 4815-8883, ext 156; Av Córdoba 1199; admission free; ☾ 10am-6pm Mon-Fri) trace the history of Argentine theater from its colonial beginnings. Check out the gaucho suit worn by Gardel and the *bandoneón* that once belonged to Paquita Bernardo, Argentina's first musician to play the accordion-like instrument.

Recoleta & Barrio Norte

BA's wealthiest citizens live and breathe in Recoleta, the city's most exclusive and fashionable neighborhood. In the 1870s many upper-class *porteños* originally lived in southerly San Telmo, but during the yellow-fever epidemic they relocated north to here. Today you can best see much of the wealth of this sumptuous quarter on **Av Alvear**, where many of the old mansions (and newer international boutiques) are located.

Full of lush parks, classy museums and French architecture, Recoleta is best known for its **Cementerio de la Recoleta**. Next door to the cemetery, the 1732 **Iglesia de Nuestra Señora del Pilar** (Map pp64–7) is a baroque colonial church, while just in front the **Plaza Intendente Alvear** hosts the city's most popular crafts fair (see the boxed text, p106). A little further north is the sinuous sculptural flower **Floralis Genérica**, whose giant metal petals close up at night.

CEMENTERIO DE LA RECOLETA

Walk for hours in this **city of the dead** (Map pp64-7; ☎ 4803-1594; cnr Junín & Guido; admission free; ☾ 7am-6pm), wandering among impressive statues and marble sarcophagi. Crypts hold the remains of the city's most elite: past presidents, military heroes, influential politicians and the just plain well-connected rich and famous. Hunt down Evita's grave, and bring your camera – there are some great photo ops here.

MUSEO NACIONAL DE BELLAS ARTES

Argentina's top **fine-arts museum** (☎ 4803-0802; www.aamnba.com.ar; Av del Libertador 1473; admission free; ☾ 12:30-7:30pm Tue-Fri, 9:30am-7:30pm Sat, Sun & holidays), showcases works by Renoir, Monet,

Gauguin, Rembrandt and van Gogh, along with classic Argentine artists. Other offerings include temporary exhibits and a cinema.

CENTRO CULTURAL RECOLETA

This renovated **cultural center** (☎ 4803-1041; www.centroculturalrecoleta.org in Spanish; Junín 1930; donation US$0.35; ⊙ 2-9pm Tue-Fri, 10am-9pm Sat & Sun) houses a variety of facilities, including museums, galleries, exhibition halls and a cinema. There's a hands-on science museum for children, along with free outdoor films in summer and frequent movies in the Microcine.

MUSEO XUL SOLAR

Xul Solar was a painter, inventor and poet, and this **museum** (Map pp68-9; ☎ 4824-3302; www.xulsolar.org.ar in Spanish; Laprida 1212; admission US$1; ⊙ noon-8pm Mon-Fri, 2-7pm Sat, closed Jan) highlights over 80 of his unique, bizarre and surreal paintings; the guy was in a class by himself.

Palermo   Map pp68–9

Palermo is heaven on earth for BA's middle class. Its large, grassy parks – regally punctuated with grand monuments – are popular destinations on weekends, when families fill the shady lanes, cycle the bike paths and paddle on the peaceful lakes. Many important museums and elegant embassies are also located here, and Palermo Viejo (see the boxed text, below) has become one of the city's hottest destinations.

Palermo's green spaces haven't always been for the masses. The area around **Parque 3 de Febrero** was originally the 19th-century

dictator Juan Manuel de Rosas' private retreat and became public parkland after his fall from power. Within these green spaces you'll find the **Jardín Japonés** (☎ 4804-4922; www.jardinjapones.com; cnr Avs Casares & Berro; admission US$1.50; ⊙ 10am-6pm), a peaceful retreat with koi ponds, teahouse and cultural offerings; the surprisingly decent Jardín Zoológico (p80), BA's main zoo; and the nearby **Jardín Botánico Carlos Thays**, which will appeal to botanists and cat-lovers (it's full of feral felines). There's also the **Planetario Galileo Galilei** (☎ 4771-9393; www.planetario.gov.ar in Spanish; cnr Avs Sarmiento & Belisario Roldán; ⊙ 2-8pm Sat & Sun), a planetarium with weekend shows at 6pm and 7:15pm. Just south of the zoo and a major landmark is **Plaza Italia**, Palermo's main transport hub.

A small but popular neighborhood in Palermo is further north at **Las Cañitas**. Many restaurants and other nightspots attract hordes of hip folk at night, when Av Baéz clogs with traffic. Southeast of Las Cañitas is the landmark **Centro Islámico Rey Fahd** (☎ 4899-0201; Av Int Bullrich 55; tours available), built by Saudis on land donated by ex-president Carlos Menem.

MUSEO DE ARTE LATINOAMERICANO DE BUENOS AIRES (MALBA)

Sparkling inside its glass-and-cement walls, this airy **modern-arts museum** (☎ 4808-6500; www.malba.org.ar; Av Figueroa Alcorta 3415; adult/student with ISIC card US$2/1; ⊙ noon-8pm Thu-Mon, noon-9pm Wed, closed Tue) is one of BA's newest and finest. Art patron Eduardo Constantini displays his collection, which includes work by Argentines Xul Solar and Antonio Berni, plus some pieces by Mexicans Diego Rivera and Frida Kahlo. A cinema screens art-house films.

HIP OLD PALERMO

Palermo Viejo, full of low buildings, leafy sidewalks and the occasional cobbled street, is one of the capital's most trendsetting spots – just come to Plaza Serrano on any Saturday night to see why. Roughly bounded by Santa Fe, Scalabrini Ortiz, Córdoba and Dorrego, Palermo Viejo is further divided into Palermo Hollywood (north of the train tracks) and Palermo Soho (south of the tracks).

This neighborhood has attracted dozens of ethnic, ultramodern restaurants; anyone yearning for Japanese, Vietnamese, Brazilian, Greek or even Norwegian food can satisfy their craving. Modern international cuisine tops the list, however, and the quality is high. But Palermo Viejo also offers many designer clothing shops and small theme boutiques. These restaurants and shops are spread throughout Palermo Viejo, which takes up a huge area; it's fun to just walk around and explore.

Be aware that, at night, Godoy Cruz mutates into the capital's transvestite red-light district. This doesn't necessarily make it *very* dangerous, but it attracts iffy characters, so watch your step.

JARDÍN ZOOLÓGICO

Artificial lakes, pleasant walking paths and frolicking lions, tigers and bears (oh my!) entertain the crowds on sunny weekends. Over 350 species are represented at this **zoo** (☎ 4806-7411; cnr Las Heras & Sarmiento; admission US$2-3.50, under 13 free; ☻ 10am-6pm Dec-Feb, 10am-6pm Tue-Sun Mar-Nov), and some buildings are impressive in themselves; be sure to check out the elephant house. An aquarium, monkey island, petting zoo and large aviary are other highlights; white tigers have been bred here.

MUSEO NACIONAL DE ARTE DECORATIVO

Located in the stunning beaux arts mansion called Palacio Errázuriz (1911), this **museum** (☎ 4802-6606; Av del Libertador 1902; admission from US$0.75; ☻ 2-7pm Tue-Sun) now displays the posh belongings of Chilean aristocrat Matías Errázuriz. Everything from Renaissance religious paintings to porcelain dishes to Italian sculptures to artwork by El Greco and Rodin can be admired. On the 1st floor is a smaller museum showcasing exquisite pieces of Asian art.

MUSEO EVITA

Everybody who is anybody in Argentina has their own museum, and Eva Perón is no exception. See her immortalized in **Museo Evita** (☎ 4807-9433; Lafinur 2988; local/foreigner US$0.75/1.75;

☻ 2-7:30pm Tue-Sun) through videos, historical photos, books, old posters and newspaper headlines – even her fingerprints are recorded. The prize memorabilia, however, has to be her wardrobe: dresses, shoes, handbags, hats and blouses stand proudly behind shining glass, forever pressed and pristine.

MUSEO DE MOTIVOS ARGENTINOS JOSÉ HERNÁNDEZ

This modest-sized **museum** (☎ 4803-2384; www .museohernandez.org.ar; Av del Libertador 2373; local/ foreigner US$0.35/1, Sun free; ☻ 1-7pm Wed-Sun, Spanish tours 4:30pm Sat & Sun) has permanent exhibitions on Mapuche crafts, such as exquisite ponchos, and other indigenous items; the diverse changing exhibitions range from gaucho accoutrements to modern toys to chess photography. Gaudy Carnaval costumes are also incongruously on display.

Belgrano   Map pp62–3

Bustling Av Cabildo, the racing heartbeat of Belgrano, is an overwhelming jumble of noise and neon; it's a two-way street of clothing, shoe and housewares shops that does its part in supporting the mass consumerism of *porteños*. For a bit more peace and quiet step away from the avenue, where Belgrano becomes a leafy barrio of museums, parks and good eateries.

Only a block east of Av Cabildo, **Plaza Belgrano** is the site of a modest but fun weekend market (see the boxed text, p106). On a sunny day it's full of shoppers, families with strollers and a few buskers. Near the plaza stands the Italianate **Iglesia de la Inmaculada Concepción**, a church popularly known as 'La Redonda' because of its impressive dome.

Just a few steps from the plaza is the **Museo Histórico Sarmiento** (☎ 4782-2354; www.mu seosarmiento.gov.ar; Juramento 2180; admission US$0.35, Thu free; ☻ 2-7pm Tue-Fri, 3-7pm Sun, Spanish tours 4pm Sun), which highlights the memorabilia of Domingo F Sarmiento, one of Argentina's most famous forward-thinking presidents, diplomats and educators. The classically educated Sarmiento was an eloquent writer who analyzed 19th-century Argentina from a cosmopolitan, clearly Eurocentric point of view.

Also close by is the **Museo Enrique Larreta** (☎ 4784-4040; Juramento 2291; admission US$0.35, Thu free; ☻ 2-8pm Mon & Wed-Fri, 3-8pm Sat & Sun, Spanish tours 4pm & 6pm Sun), which has on display the

---

PRAYING FOR KITSCH

The quirky will find heaven at **Tierra Santa** (Map pp68-9; ☎ 4784-9551; www.tierra santa-bsas.com.ar; Av Costanera R Obligado 5790; ☻ 9am-9pm Fri, noon-11pm Sat, Sun & holidays Apr-Nov, 4pm-12:30am Fri-Sun Dec-Mar; adult/ 3-11 yrs US$3.50/1.50), 'the world's first religious theme park,' according to literature. Roughly based on Jerusalem, this tacky destination covers the creation of the world, the manger scene at Bethlehem, the Wailing Wall, the Last Supper and the Resurrection (every half hour!). Locals are visibly moved by the spectacle, and when emotions overwhelm are happy to sit drinking coffee at the Baghdad Café being served by employees dolled up in Middle Eastern garb. You won't find a place like this anywhere else on earth – and especially not in Jerusalem.

To get to Tierra Santa, take bus No 28, 33, 37, 42, 45, 107 or 160.

well-known novelist's gorgeous art collection. The house and gardens are also beautiful.

About five blocks north, the **Museo Casa de Yrurtia** (☎ 4781-0385; O'Higgins 2390; admission US$0.35; ♥ 1-7pm Tue-Fri, 3-7pm Sun, tours 4pm Sun) honors the well-known Argentine sculptor Rogelio Yrurtia. His old house, complete with attractive garden, is full of his and other artists' works; look for Picasso's *Rue Cortot, Paris*.

Four blocks northeast of Plaza Belgrano, French landscape architect Charles Thays took advantage of the contours of **Barrancas de Belgrano** to create an attractive, wooded public space on one of the few natural hillocks in the city. Retirees spend the afternoon at the chess tables beneath its ombú tree, while children skate around the band shell.

Across Juramento from the Barrancas, Belgrano's growing **Chinatown** fills the 2100 block of Arribeños, with more Chinese businesses spilling over to side streets.

Once & Caballito

BA's most ethnically colorful neighborhood is Once, with sizable groups of Jews, Peruvians and Koreans. The cheap market around Once train station always bustles and is fun to wander around, while the nearby **Museo Casa Carlos Gardel** (Map pp68-9; ☎ 4964-2071; www .museosbuenosaires.gov.ar; Jean Jaurés 735; local/foreigner US$0.35/1, Wed free; ♥ 11am-6pm Mon & Wed-Fri, 11am-7pm Sat & Sun, closed Tue) offers tango fans some insight into the dance's most famous singer.

West of Once is Caballito, a calm and pleasant neighborhood where locals go about their daily routines. Here you'll find the **Museo Argentino de Ciencias Naturales** (Map pp62-3; ☎ 4982-6595; Ángel Gallardo 470; admission US$0.75; ♥ 2-7pm), a good natural-science museum that's definitely worth a peek for its taxidermy and skeletons. Further south of that is a storefront that holds the one-man show and very unofficial **Museo Ernesto Che Guevara** (Map pp62-3; ☎ 4903-3285; museocheguevara@yahoo .com.ar; Rojas 129; admission free; ♥ 9am-7pm Mon-Fri). Eccentric Eladio 'Toto' González has few actual Che items, but he's full of stories and Cuba-related papers and photos.

ACTIVITIES

Extensive greenery in Recoleta and Palermo provides good areas for recreation, especially on weekends when some areas are closed to cars. You can also head to the Reserva Ecológica Costanera Sur (p75), an ecological paradise just east of Puerto Madero; it's excellent for walks, runs and bike rides.

Cycling

Bike paths interlace Parque 3 de Febrero, where rental bikes are available in good weather; look for them on Av de la Infanta Isabel near Av Libertador (Map pp68–9). The Reserva Ecológica Costanera Sur (p75) also has bike rentals on weekends and daily in summer.

For more serious cycling head to Nuevo Circuito KDT in Palermo (Map pp68–9), where **Sprint Haupt** (☎ 4807-6141; Salguero 3450; ♥ 9am-7pm Wed & Fri-Sun, 9am-8:30pm Tue & Thu) rents bicycles for use inside the banked velodrome. Rates are US$1 to US$2 per hour; park entry is US$0.75.

For information on bike tours, see p84.

Swimming

Some upscale hotels, such as the Crowne Plaza Panamericano (p87; from US$27 per day) and the **Hilton** (Map pp64-7; ☎ 4891-0000; Güemes 351; Mon-Fri/Sat & Sun US$22/30) have swimming pools open to nonguests. A few of the larger health clubs have indoor pools (see p82). Otherwise try Palermo's **Club de Amigos** (Map pp68-9; ☎ 4801-1213; Figueroa Alcorta 3885), which has a covered pool open December to February only; **Punta Carrasco** (Map pp68-9; ☎ 4807-1010; cnr Costanera Norte & Sarmiento) has an outdoor pool open December to March. Both charge around US$5 to US$7 per day.

Golf & Tennis

BA's most convenient golf course is the 18-hole **Campo Municipal de Golf** (Map pp68-9; ☎ 4772-7261; Av Tornquist 1426). It's open during daylight hours every day except Monday; greens fees are US$20 on weekdays and US$30 on weekends. Practice your long shots at the **Asociación Argentina de Golf's driving range** (Map pp68-9; ☎ 4804-8649; Av Costanera 1835) and at the **Costa Salguero Driving Range** (Map pp68-9; ☎ 4805-4732; cnr Avs Costanera & Salguero). Both are open from around 8am daily and charge US$2 for 50 balls.

There are both cement and clay tennis courts at **Punta Carrasco** (Map pp68-9; ☎ 4807-1010; www.puntacarrasco.com.ar in Spanish; cnr Av Costanera Norte & Sarmiento; ♥ 8am-midnight). Rates are US$4 to US$8 per hour. You can buy balls here, and racquets are occasionally available to rent, but don't count on it. Nearby is **Parque General**

Manuel Belgrano (Map pp68-9; ☎ 4807-7879; Salguero 3450; ☷ 8am-10pm Mon-Fri, 8am-8pm Sat & Sun), with eight clay courts; rates are US$3 to US$5 per hour. You'll need your own equipment.

Climbing Walls

Boulder (Map pp68-9; ☎ 4802-4113; Arce 730; ☷ 3-11pm Mon-Fri, 3-9pm Sat & Sun) is the city's only decent indoor climbing wall. They'll set up a rope if you don't lead climb; the US$3 day-use fee includes belays. They rent harnesses; shoe use is free (they don't stock all sizes).

Health Clubs

The king of BA's gyms is **Megatlon** (Map pp64-7; ☎ 4322-7884; www.megatlon.com in Spanish; Reconquista 335), with about a dozen branches throughout the city. Expect most or all gym services, including a wide variety of classes; some have indoor pool. Day rates start at US$5. Other decent gyms include **Le Parc** (Map pp64-7; ☎ 4311-9191; www.leparc.com in Spanish; San Martín 645) and **Sport Club Cecchina** (Map pp64-7; ☎ 5199-1212; www.sportclub.com.ar in Spanish; Bartolomé Mitre 1625); both cost US$7 per day.

Yoga & Pilates

Most gyms and some cultural centers also offer yoga and Pilates classes.

Centro GREYG (Map pp68-9; ☎ 4832-3559; centrogreyg@hotmail.com; Jorge Luis Borges 2295) This Palermo Viejo studio has Hatha and Sai yoga classes three times weekly for US$3.50 per class.

Tamara Di Tella Pilates (Map pp68-9; ☎ 4833-0603; www.cuerpodiet.com in Spanish; cnr Aráoz & Juncal; ☷ 8am-9pm Mon-Fri, 9am-2pm Sat) The 'Pilates Queen' has over a dozen branches; facilities are modern and four sessions cost US$25.

Vida Natural (Map pp68-9; ☎ 4826-1695; www.yogacentro.com.ar in Spanish; Charcas 2852; ☷ 8:30am-12:30pm & 2-8:30pm Mon-Fri, 8:30am-12:30pm Sat) This naturalistic center in Palermo offers Ashtanga, Hatha and Iyengar yoga. Therapeutic massage and chakra balancing also available.

WALKING TOUR

Start at the leafy **Plaza San Martín** (**1**; p78), designed by French landscape architect Carlos Thays. If you like guns, swords and cannons, stop in at the **Museo de Armas** (**2**; p78). Otherwise, head down pedestrianized Florida to the elegant **Galerías Pacífico** (**3**; p73), one of the capital's most beautiful malls. Take a peek inside at the ceiling murals; there's often free tango shows just outside (donation suggested).

From here you'll head west on Córdoba, crossing the impressive **Av 9 de Julio** (**4**; p75). Soon you'll come to **Teatro Cervantes** (**5**; p78) and the notable **Templo de la Congregación Israelita** (**6**; p75). Walk south along Libertad to the **Teatro Colón** (**7**; p75), one of BA's most impressive buildings; take a tour if you've got time. Then keep going south and turn left at Av Corrientes. You'll soon bisect Av 9 de Julio again, but under the shadow of the BA's famous **Obelisco** (**8**; p75). Just after you cross, turn left at Carlos Pellegrini and then right at pedestrian Lavalle; keep going until the junction at Florida.

If you need a break, stop at the classic café **Richmond** (**9**; p96) – the old atmosphere can't be beat. After your *café con leche* (coffee with milk), keep heading south on Florida and then down Diagonal Roque Sáenz Peña to **Plaza de Mayo** (**10**; p73). Tour the surrounding buildings, then head west on Av de Mayo past **Café Tortoni** (**11**; p96), arguably the city's most famous historic café, to the far-off **Plaza del Congreso** (**12**) and Palacio del Congreso (p76). Note the rococo **Confitería del Molino** (**13**), a now-defunct café that presently molders in BA's air. If you're aching for another *open* coffee shop, however, backtrack to Café Tortoni.

COURSES

Visitors have many opportunities to study almost anything in BA, from tango (see p100) to cooking to languages. Most cultural centers offer classes in Spanish, including the excellent Centro Cultural Ricardo Rojas (p70), which also teaches tango, flamenco, tai chi, capoeira, Hebrew, photography and even intensive mime.

Those proficient in Spanish and seeking cooking classes can try **Mausi Sebess** (☎ 4791-4355; www.mausisebess.com; Av Maipú 594, Vicente López) or **Gato Dumas** (☎ 4783-3357; www.gatodumas.com.ar; Olazabal 2836, Belgrano). Mausi may offer English-speaking teachers in the future. Both schools offer degrees and are located outside the center, in BA's suburbs.

WALK FACTS

Start: Plaza San Martín
End: Plaza del Congreso
Distance: 4km
Duration: three to four hours

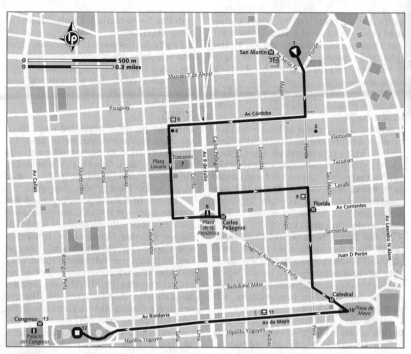

Language

BA has become a major destination for students of Spanish, and more good institutes are opening up all the time. All the following institutes organize social activities and offer home-stay programs.

AADE (Map pp64-7; ☎ 4953-2883; www.espanol.org.ar; Bartolomé Mitre 2062, 2nd fl, Room 8) One-off group/private classes cost US$6/7; group/private classes of 10 hours per week US$57/67; group/private classes of 20 hours per week US$107/127.

BAESP (Map pp64-7; ☎ 4381-2076; www.baesp.com; Av Rivadavia 1559 2C) One-time registration fee US$40. Group/private classes of 10 hours per week US$70/120; group/private classes of 20 hours per week US$100/200.

Etorno Lingüístico (Map pp64-7; ☎ 4343-1495; www .entorling.com.ar; Carlos Pellegrini 27, 4E) Group/private classes US$7/9 per hour.

University de Buenos Aires (UBA; Map pp64-7; ☎ 4343-5981; www.idiomas.filo.uba.ar; 25 de Mayo 221) One of three campuses that offer Spanish classes; this is Philosophy and Letters. Long-term classes only, for two/four months at eight/four hours per week (both US$525). In July and August one-month classes available. Italian, German, French, Portuguese and Japanese also taught.

Vía Hispana (Map pp64-7; ☎ 4893-2765; www.via hispana.com; Av Córdoba 435, 3B) Twenty classes per week US$150; for one/two months price drops to US$540/800. More intensive classes also available. Private classes US$9 per hour.

There are many private tutors within the city, charging in the range of US$7 to US$10 per hour.

Bruna Monserrat (☎ 4772-3902; bruna espanol@yahoo.com.ar)

Gabriela López (☎ 4361-9843, 15-5455-3176; gabitazz@yahoo.com)

Gisela Giunti (☎ 4371-5122, 15-5626-0162; giseela@yahoo.com)

Jose Serebrenik (☎ 4951-3393; www.jose serebrenik.com.ar)

BUENOS AIRES FOR CHILDREN

Those with children have it good in BA. On weekends Palermo's parks bustle with families taking walks or picnicking. Shopping malls fill with strollers, while zoos, museums and theme parks are also popular.

Good green spots in the city include Palermo's **3 de Febrero park**, where on weekends traffic isn't allowed on the lakeside ring road (and you can rent bikes). Other good stops here include a planetarium (p79), zoo (p80) and Japanese garden (p79). If you're downtown and need a nature break, think about the Reserva Ecológica Costanera Sur (p75), a large nature preserve with good bird watching, pleasant gravel paths and no vehicular traffic.

Some shopping malls make safe destinations for families, and most come with playground, video arcade and cineplex. Paseo Alcorta (p106) is particularly good, while the Abasto (p106) boasts a full-blown **Museo de los Niños** (Children's Museum; ☎ 4861-2325; www .museoabasto.org.ar in Spanish; Av Corrientes 3247; 2 adults & 1/2 children US$5/7; ☒ 1-8pm Tue-Sun) where kids enter a miniature play city.

In San Telmo check out the **Museo Argentino del Títere** (Argentine Puppet Museum; Map pp64-7; ☎ 4304-4376; www.museoargdeltitere.com.ar in Spanish; Piedras 905; admission free; ☒ 3-6pm Tue-Sun), which has inexpensive shows (weekends and holidays at 4pm, daily in summer) that will amuse the little urchins.

In Recoleta visit the **Museo Participativo de Ciencias** (Map pp64-7; ☎ 4807-3456; www.mpc.org .ar; Junín 1930; admission US$2; ☒ 3:30-7:30pm summer, 12:30-7:30pm Mon-Fri, 3:30-7:30pm Sat & Sun winter), in the Centro Cultural Recoleta. This hands-on science museum has interactive displays that focus on fun learning. Hours vary depending on school schedules.

A bit outside the center, in Caballito, is the good Museo Argentino de Ciencias Naturales (natural science museum; p81).

Heading to Tigre (p110), just north of center, makes a great day excursion. Get there via the Tren de la Costa; it ends right at Parque de la Costa (p110), a typical amusement park with fun rides and activities. Boat trips and a fruit/housewares market are on tap nearby.

Outside the city is the exceptional zoo, **Parque Temaikén** (☎ 03488-436-900; www.temaiken .com.ar in Spanish; RP 1, Km 25, Escobar; adult/child under 10 US$5/3.50; ☒ 10am-7pm summer, 10am-6pm Tue-Sun winter). Only the most charming animal species are on display (think meerkats, pygmy hippos and white tigers), roaming freely around spacious, clean and natural enclosures. An excellent aquarium comes with touch pools, and plenty of interactive areas provide mental stimulation. Taxis from the center cost US$20 and take 40 minutes, or

grab Bus No 60 marked 'Escobar' from the center (US$0.50).

Finally, BA has dozens of ice-cream shops that help calm down temper tantrums; see the boxed text, p95 for suggestions.

For more particulars on traveling with children in Argentina, see p462.

TOURS

There are plenty of organized tours, from the large tourist-bus variety to more intimate car trips to guided bike rides to straight-up walks. Other than the following listings, see Travel Agencies (p72), most of which broker tours or offer their own.

The city of Buenos Aires organizes **free monthly tours** (☎ 4114-5791; equitur@buenosaires .gov.ar) that follow the footsteps of Jorge Luis Borges, Federico García Lorca, Eva Perón and Carlos Gardel. Check availability of English guides; reservations are crucial. They may also have regular city tours for free but contact the **office** (☎ 4313-0187; www.buenosaires .gov.ar) ahead of time for schedules. The free newsletter *Ciudad Abierta* (available at the Secretaría de Turismo; p71) often has information on all these tours on its back page.

Bike Tours (Map pp64-7; ☎ 4311-5199; www.bike tours.com.ar; Florida 868 14H) Offers bike tours around the city; tours cost US$25 to US$30 and include bike, helmet and guide. Bike rentals available (US$15 per 24 hours).

Bob Frassinetti (☎ 15-4475-3983; bob@artdealer .com.ar) Friendly collector Bob speaks excellent English and offers shopping trips for antique-lovers. Full-day tours start at US$40.

Buenos Aires Visión (Map pp64-7; ☎ 4394-2986; www.buenosaires-vision.com.ar; Esmeralda 356, 28th fl) Large groups and comfy buses (tours from US$7); gaucho fiesta is US$34.

Cicerones (☎ 4330-0880; www.cicerones.org.ar) Nonprofit company offers free tours by volunteers; cultural exchanges are emphasized. Donations gladly accepted.

Eternautas (☎ 4384-7874, 15-4173-1078; www .eternautas.com) General city tours cost US$15 and walking tours US$2. More cerebral tours center on history, economy and cultural themes; cost depends on group size. Guides are all historians.

Urban Biking (☎ 4855-5103; www.urbanbiking.com) Offers similar services to Bike Tours.

Wow Argentina Small travel agency offers private, custom three- to four-hour tours for US$95. See p72.

FESTIVALS & EVENTS

Most of BA's traditional festivities are oriented toward its culture of horses, gauchos and tango, but recently many contemporary offerings focusing on the arts have cropped up around the city. During much of the year you'll find these special events celebrating everything from fashion to dance to theater to wine to music of all kinds, though springtime is when the lion's share of these events occur. Check with tourist offices for exact dates as they vary from year to year. Palermo's Predio Ferial (Map pp68–9) is the venue for many of the city's bigger events.

January & February

Carnaval Get sprayed with foam while enjoying Afro-Latin *murga* rhythms around Plaza de Mayo. BA's Carnaval is relatively tame, but the recent lifting of a long-running ban on tossing water balloons may liven things up.

Chinese New Year Head to Belgrano's tiny Chinatown for firecrackers and festivities (date depends on the lunar calendar).

March

Buenos Aires Tango (www.festivaldetango.com.ar) Masterful performances shown at different venues all over the city.

Exposición de Caballos Criollos (www.caballoscriollos .com in Spanish; Predio Ferial) Horse-lovers shouldn't miss this event showcasing the hardy Argentine-bred equines in their full glory.

April

Feria del Libro (www.el-libro.com.ar in Spanish; Predio Ferial) International festival which attracts over a million book-lovers for three weeks.

Festival International de Cine Independiente (www.bafilmfest.com) Another biggie, and highlights both national and international independent films, many are screened at the Abasto shopping mall.

May

Arte BA (www.arteba.com; Predio Ferial) Exhibitions from hundreds of art galleries, dealers and institutions, with both national and international contemporary art on display.

June

Anniversary of Gardel's death (June 24) Numerous tango events during the week culminate in a pilgrimage to the singer's tomb in the Cementerio de la Chacarita. Gardel's birthday on December 11 sees similar festivities.

July

La Rural (www.ruralarg.org.ar in Spanish; Predio Ferial) A mecca for livestock-lovers. Gaucho shows and agricultural machinery are other attractions at this quirky event.

August

Fashion BA Four days that spotlight the city's latest designer threads and hot models on the catwalk. A fall collection shows in March; both events are at Palermo's Predio Ferial.

GAY & LOVING IT IN BUENOS AIRES

There is a live-and-kicking gay scene in BA, and it's become even livelier since December 2002, when Argentina became Latin America's first country to accept civil unions between same-sex couples. Tolerance is good news for everyone, and BA is benefiting by having outstripped Rio as South America's number-one gay destination. Perhaps this will also widen the scope of BA's November Marcha del Orgullo Gay (gay pride parade; www.marchadelorgullo.org.ar), but for now it's downright tame compared to other international cities like San Francisco or Sydney.

Look up current sweetheart spots in free booklets such as *La Otra Guía*, *Queer X* and *Latino*, available at gay bars, cafés and discos. Free gay maps have also become widely available, even at tourist offices. And heftier gay magazines such as *NX* and *Imperio* can be bought at newsstands. The main nighttime cruising area is around Avs Santa Fe and Pueyrredón, where discount admission coupons are handed out on street corners.

For daylight romps, head to San Telmo's Sunday antiques fair (p106) and take a break at Pride Café (p93). Or head east to Puerto Madero for a walk at the lovely Reserva Costanera Ecológica Sur (p75), another notable cruising spot.

For general gay information, there's Lugar Gay (p88) in San Telmo; it's also a B&B. Other resources include **Grupo Nexo** (Map pp64-7; ☎ 4375-0359; www.nexo.org in Spanish; Callao 339, 5th fl) and **Comunidad Homosexual Argentina** (CHA; ☎ 4361-6382; www.cha.org.ar in Spanish; Tomás Liberti 1080). For travel details there's **Pride Travel** (p72). The website www.friendlyapartments.com .ar specializes in renting to gay visitors, and if you want to check online activities try **www.the gayguide.com.ar** (☎ 4833-1332). In November 2004 there was even a **gay and lesbian cinefest** (www.diversafilms.com.ar). Gay pride has arrived in BA, and it's definitely here to stay.

September
Feria de Anticuarios (www.feriadeanticuarios.org) Antique-lovers must attend this event, where BA's ritziest and most expensive antiques are exhibited and sold. It's at Recoleta's Palais de Glace.

La Semana del Arte en Buenos Aires (www.lasemana delarte.com.ar in Spanish) Dozens of venues open their doors for this artistic mega-event that highlights some of the country's best contemporary artists.

Vinos y Bodegas (☎ 4382-2001; Predio Ferial) Great for fine food and wine-tasting.

October
Guitarras del Mundo (www.festivaldeguitarras .com.ar) Dozens of Argentine and international guitarists strum their stuff. Performances occur at venues throughout the city.

November
Maratón de Buenos Aires (www.maratondebuenos aires.com)

Marcha del Orgullo Gay (www.marchadelorgullo.org.ar in Spanish) Thousands of BA's gay, lesbian and transgender citizens march from Plaza de Mayo to the Congreso. It's usually the first Saturday in November.

December
Campeonato Abierto de Pato (☎ 4331-0222; www .fedpato.com.ar in Spanish) A quirky championship which showcases Argentina's traditional sport involving horseback riders wrestling over a leather-encased ball.

Campeonato Abierto de Polo (☎ 4343-0972; www .aapolo.com in Spanish) Pretend to be aristocracy and watch from the stands at Palermo's polo fields.

Festival Buenos Aires Danza Contemporánea (www.buenosairesdanza.com.ar in Spanish) The city's major contemporary dance party that occurs every two years (the next one's in 2006). Performances, seminars and workshops take place in the city's cultural centers and theaters.

SLEEPING
BA's tourist boom has exploded the accommodations front, and many places to stay are opening up or upgrading their facilities. Generally you won't have trouble finding the type of place you're looking for, but make a reservation if traveling during any holidays or the busier months like July, August, and November through January.

Many places will help you with transport to and from the airport if you reserve ahead of time. Breakfast (which ranges from continental to buffet) is included almost everywhere, even at hostels; exceptions are noted in the reviews.

Microcentro & Plaza de Mayo
Map pp64–7

BA's Microcentro, along with being very central, has the widest variety of accommodations in the city. Toward the north you'll be closer to the busy pedestrian streets of Florida and Lavalle, as well as the upscale neighborhoods of Retiro and Recoleta. The Plaza de Mayo area, however, contains more historical government buildings, as well as the bustling banking district, and it's within walking distance of San Telmo. Nights tend to be a bit calmer, as most businesspeople who work here flee the center after the day is done.

BUDGET
Portal del Sur Hostel (☎ 4342-8788; www.portaldel surba.com.ar; Hipólito Yrigoyen 855; dm US$7-9, s/d US$20/26; ✷ 🖳) A great new hostel in a charming old building, nicely remodeled into beautiful dorms and sumptuous, hotel-quality private rooms. The highlight here is the sunny rooftop deck and attached airy common lounge. Some rooms have air-con, and free tango and salsa classes are available.

V & S Youth Hostel (☎ 4322-0994; www.hostelclub .com; Viamonte 887; dm/s US$7/20, d US$22-24; 🖳) This modern and comfortable hostel has good vibes and a good location. A large-screen TV shows movies daily, and a pleasant kitchen/dining/lobby area makes socializing easy. Dorms are a good size, clean and carpeted. Free salsa, tango and Spanish classes.

Milhouse Youth Hostel (☎ 4345-9604; www.mil househostel.com; Hipólito Yrigoyen 959; dm US$6-7, d US$21-23; 🖳) Located in a beautiful old mansion, this popular hostel offers a plethora of activities and services, and a party atmosphere. Dorms and private rooms are well kept, and most surround a pleasant open patio. Common spaces are boisterous, and there's a pool table and rooftop terrace.

Hotel Alcázar (☎ 4345-0926; Av de Mayo 935; s/d US$12/15) Long popular with budget travelers, these old digs have basic but somewhat charming fan-cooled rooms of all different sizes. Some sport balconies, so you can have it noisy but bright. There's no breakfast but you should reserve in advance anyway – the location is good and prices even better.

MIDRANGE
Hotel Frossard (☎ 4322-1811; www.hotelfrossard.com .ar; Tucumán 686; s/d US$20/27; 🅿 ✷) Here's a little

gem in the Microcentro: an intimate hotel with 18 high-ceilinged rooms in a charming older building. Doubles are small and cozy, but triples have more breathing room. The location is excellent; the pedestrian streets of Florida and Lavalle are just a block away.

Hotel Goya (☎ 4322-9311; www.goyahotel.com.ar; Suipacha 748; s/d US$19/27; P ⚹) This intimate, friendly, spotless, central, quiet and comfortable hotel is an excellent deal. 'Classic' rooms have showers that open to the sink area, while 'superior' rooms are more luxurious and have bigger bathrooms.

Gran Hotel Hispano (☎ 4345-2020; www.hhispano .com.ar; Av de Mayo 861; s/d US$27/33; ⚹ 🖳) Don't be put off by the tiny lobby; upstairs, the patio atrium and halls are spacious and pleasant. Rooms are cute, squeaky clean and come with fridges; look at a few as they vary in size. The hordes claim rooms here quickly, so reserve in advance.

Howard Johnson (☎ 4326-6607; www.davincihotel .com.ar; Tucumán 857; s/d US$51/57; P ⚹ 🖳 ⚹) This is a branch of the popular American chain, well-situated near the pedestrian streets of Florida and Lavalle. The 48 rooms are clean and modern, and come with king-size beds for couples. Services include pool, gym and sauna.

Hotel Facón Grande (☎ 4312-6360; www.hotelfacon grande.com; Reconquista 645; s/d US$34/44; P ⚹ 🖳) The pleasant gaucho-themed lobby is amusing, as are the dressed-up staff. Rooms aren't quite up to gaucho standard, but they're comfortable enough. Guests receive a welcome drink, and there's a small playroom for the kids.

TOP END

Crowne Plaza Panamericano (☎ 4348-5000; www .buenosaires.crowneplaza.com; Carlos Pellegrini 551; d US$188; P ⚹ ⚹ 🖳 ⚹) You won't be staying at this five-star hotel for the rooms or services; it's the 23rd-floor pool you're after – it comes with atrium, small bar and awesome views. Spa services and a gorgeous lobby full of businessmen and fancy tourists complete the picture.

Hotel NH Jousten (☎ 4321-6750; www.nh-hotels .com; Corrientes 280; d US$129; P ⚹ 🖳) This very cool hotel chain (there are four NH hotels in BA) does great minimalist things with wood, tile, glass and fabrics. Rooms are gorgeous and simple, but tastefully designed. Part of the roof has a wonderful terrace

with views, and looming above that is the luxurious presidential suite.

Hotel Nogaró (☎ 4331-0091; www.hotelnogaro.com; Av Julio Roca 562; d US$88; P ⚹ 🖳) Elegant and sophisticated earth-tone designs make this four-star hotel a good upscale choice in the Plaza de Mayo area. Bathrooms are small, but the atmospherically lit rooms are modern, clean, comfortable and come with hardwood floors. Ask for a tub with jets – it shouldn't cost much more.

Congreso & Avenida
Corrientes   Map pp64–7

This region contains many of the city's theater and cultural centers. Lively Corrientes has many modest shops, services and bookstores along with some of BA's older movie theaters. The Plaza de Congreso area is always moving, sometimes with mostly peaceful public demonstrations. It's not quite as packed as the Microcentro and is less touristy, but still bustles hard day and night.

BUDGET

Hotel Nuevo Reina (☎ 4381-2496; Av de Mayo 1120; s/d US$10/14, without bathroom US$7/10) This once-elegant building still has some charm that's apparent in the grand old halls, high ceilings and original light fixtures. Prices will probably go up after the remodel (beautiful new rooms cost US$20/30 per single/double). Tango classes are given in the airy breakfast room (but not during breakfast).

BA Stop (☎ 4382-7406; www.bastop.com; Av Rivadavia 1194; dm/s/d US$6/12/18; 🖳) Here's a pleasant and intimate hostel located in the heart of Little Spain, BA's Spanish district. There are just 32 beds (and three bathrooms for them all!), good common areas, artsy decor, high ceilings and Ping-Pong and pool tables. It's small and congenial, and a good place to meet other travelers.

Hotel Chile (☎ 4383-7877; hotelchile@argentina .com; Av de Mayo 1297; s/d US$14/20; ⚹) This popular old standby continues to offer an art nouveau facade outside and 70 decent budget rooms inside. Corner rooms have the best balconies and views, but are noisy and have only fans. Inside rooms come with air-con and are darker and more peaceful.

MIDRANGE

Fiamingo Apart Hotel (☎ 4374-4400; www.fiamingo apart.com.ar; Talcahuano 120; s/d US$27/34; P ⚹ 🖳)

Families should make a beeline to this place; the good suites are very spacious and come with kitchenette (no stove, just microwave and sink). Staff are friendly and windows are double-paned for peace and quiet. It's a great deal for the price, but call first to confirm and reserve.

Ibis Hotel (☎ 5300-5555; www.hotelibis.com; Hipólito Yrigoyen 1592; s & d US$27; P ⊠ ⚡ ⌨) This place is popular, and it's no wonder: prices are low and the location is great, right on Plaza del Congreso. The minuses include showers only (no bathtubs), but snag a room with view to the front and you can soak in the views.

Hotel Lyon (☎ 4372-0100; www.hotel-lyon.com.ar; Riobamba 251; s/d US$34/57) If you're a traveling family or group, this place is for you. Old apartments have been converted to very spacious, simple rooms with entry halls, large bathrooms and separate dining areas with fridges (but no kitchens). Furniture is outdated but slightly charming.

Hotel Molino (☎ 4374-9112; www.molinohotel.com.ar; Av Callao 164; s/d US$20/24; ⚡) Singles are small and have open showers that get everything wet, but rooms in general are neat and come with tasteful decor. Staff are friendly and the lobby sparkles; this is a good choice in Congreso.

TOP END

Broadway All-Suites (☎ 4378-9300; www.broadway-suites.com.ar; Av Corrientes 1173; s & d US$85; P ⚡ ⌨) The fancy lobby emulates a hip lounge, and they're also doing wonderful things with leather, glass, wood and tile. All are integrated into the beautifully modern suites with little perks like CD players, microwaves and safety boxes. Gay men will love this place and the attractive staff running it.

Castelar Hotel & Spa (☎ 4383-5000; www.castelar hotel.com.ar; Av de Mayo 1152; s/d from US$55/82; ⊠ ⚡ ⌨) The high-ceilinged lobby is grand, and while the standard rooms are just good enough the superiors are bigger and more luxurious. Spa services, including a Turkish bath, are available. It's good value for the location and charm.

San Telmo   Map pp64–7
San Telmo has some of the most atmospheric flavor in BA. Buildings are more charming, historical, and less modernized than in the center, and tend to have fewer

stories. More and more nightclubs and restaurants are popping up here, though it still calms way down when the night curtain drops. Most of your accommodations options here will be in the more modest hostel and guesthouse categories rather than high-class hotels.

BUDGET

Che Lagarto Hostel (☎ 4343-4845; www.chelagarto .com; Venezuela 857; dm US$8, s/d/tw US$15/24/30; ⚡ ⌨) Looking nothing like its previous incarnation, the new Che Lagarto sparkles with large, open common spaces, lovely artwork and modern services. A pleasant bar/dining area offers nourishment, while dorms and rooms are comfortable (most come with private bathroom). There's a kitchen and patio area, and the hostel is well located between San Telmo and Microcentro.

Garden House (☎ 4305-0517; www.gardenhouseba .com.ar; Av San Juan 1271; dm US$6, d US$18-20; ⌨) World travelers Anna and Javier, along with their friendly staff, offer six doubles and two dorms (all with shared bathroom) along with some comfortable common spaces. It's a bit far from the center, but the good vibes are worth it. Cheap but excellent weekly *asados* (barbecues) take place on the terrace.

Sandanzas Hostel (☎ 4300-7375; www.sandanzas .com.ar; Balcarce 1351; dm US$6-7, d US$17-20; ⌨) This small 'cultural' hostel has just 26 beds and is enthusiastically run. It's a colorful place with good-sized dorms, five doubles (only one with private bathroom) and occasional music concerts in the common area. The location is in a gritty blue-collar neighborhood near Plaza Lezama.

Via Via Hostel (☎ 4300-7259; Chile 324; dm/d US$4.50/10; ⌨) This intimate hostel, in a remodeled 1850s house with modern decor and indoor/outdoor hallways, offers five private rooms and one six-bed dorm (all share bathrooms). It tends to be tranquil despite the café and all its cultural activities out front. Breakfast is extra.

MIDRANGE

Lugar Gay (☎ 4300-4747; www.lugargay.org; Defensa 1120; s US$25-35, d US$35-50; ⌨) First: it's for gay men only. Second: the rooftop terrace is for nude sunbathing, so don't be offended (as if). The eight rooms are hip and elegant, and on the premises are a tango salon, tiny café, hot tub, solarium and kitchenette. Information on BA's gay scene is available whether you are staying here or not.

El Sol de San Telmo (☎ 4300-4394; www.elsolde santelmo.com; Chacabuco 1181; s/d US$15/30; ✂ ▣) Here's a fine budget guesthouse in an old and faded, but charming, house. There are 12 modest rooms with high ceilings, wood floors and the occasional private bathroom. Guests have use of the kitchen and leafy rooftop patio, along with the salon for tango classes. Breakfast is extra.

TOP END

Boquitas Pintadas (☎ 4381-6064; www.boquitas -pintadas.com.ar; Estados Unidos 1399; d US$45-94) With six themed rooms sporting different decor every two months, this self-proclaimed 'pop' hotel lands in a class by itself. Enjoy the small but gorgeous terraces, hot tub and snazzy bar downstairs. The only drawback is its location, which is west of San Telmo, in Constitución.

Mansion Dandi Royal (☎ 4307-7623; www.hotel mansiondandiroyal.com; Piedras 922; d US$69-140; ℗ ✂ ▣) For upscale tango lovers only. An early-1900s family mansion has been lovingly renovated into a luxurious hotel complete with tango murals on walls, glass chandeliers, curved wood staircase and more. Rooms are gorgeous. There's a small rooftop pool, sunny patios and tango salons.

Retiro
Map pp64–7

Retiro is a great place to be, *if* you can afford it: many of BA's most expensive hotels, along with some of its richest inhabitants, have planted roots here. Close by are leafy Plaza San Martín, Retiro bus terminal and many upscale stores and business services. Recoleta and the Microcentro are just a short stroll away.

BUDGET

Recoleta Hostel (☎ 4812-4419; www.trhostel.com.ar; Libertad 1216; dm/s/d US$8/17/19; ▣) The best thing about this HI-affiliated hostel remains its location, both in an old mansion and in trendy Retiro. Ceilings are high, the courtyard pleasant and common spaces adequate, but dorms are small. Four doubles are available, one with private bathroom.

Hotel Central Córdoba (☎ 4311-1175; www.hotel centralcordoba.com.ar; San Martín 1021; s/d US$17/20; ℗ ✂) The snazzy lobby starts things out right, and the rooms (despite being a bit

small) are comfortable, neat and clean. The Retiro location is spot on – the Kilkenny bar (p98) is within easy staggering distance – so book well ahead.

MIDRANGE

Suipacha y Arroyo Suites (☎ 4325-8200; www.sya suites.com; Suipacha 1359; ste US$59-67; ℗ ✂ ▣) They're remodeling, but until they finish this is an interesting combination of modern hipness and a rough-around-the-edges look. All 78 suites are pleasant, comfortable and spacious, and come with kitchenette. Perks include sauna, business center, outdoor pool and paddle-tennis court.

Hotel Principado (☎ 4313-3022; www.principado .com.ar; Paraguay 481; s/d US$45/50; ℗ ✂ ▣) There's nothing too surprising at this place, other than it having good rooms at great prices in a central location. Most of the typical hotel and room services are available, including minibar, hairdryer and a business center.

TOP END

Hotel Bel Air (☎ 4816-0016; www.hotelbelair.com.ar in Spanish; Arenales 1462; s US$80-90, d US$85-125; ℗ ✂ ✂ ▣) The lobby bar here is downright sensuous, and the nearby café has upscale tourists sitting pretty. Upstairs, rooms are beautifully modern and styled with simple yet functional furniture. Robes in the

---

THE AUTHOR'S CHOICE

Art Hotel (Map pp64-7; ☎ 4821-4744; www .arthotel.com.ar; Azcuénaga 1268; d US$65-90; ✂ ▣) A stunningly gorgeous addition to the Recoleta scene, this boutique hotel is located in a town house over 100 years old and doubles as an art gallery. Walk into the intimate lobby and just around the corner is a small exhibition room displaying contemporary Argentine paintings, murals or photographs. Upstairs, the 36 unique rooms have been artfully designed into tranquil spaces with materials such as wood, glass, metal and textiles. Thoughtful touches such as curved doors, canopied beds, romantic drapes and dark wood floors take advantage of architectural details and add to the charm, while more art hangs on the walls. It's a romantic place to stay, so bring your significant other and enjoy the fluffy pillows and atmospheric lighting.

bathrooms are a nice touch, and those here for work will appreciate the business center and meeting rooms.

Howard Johnson Plaza (☎ 4891-9200; www.hj florida.com.ar in Spanish; Florida 944; s & d US$139; ✗ ✗ ▣) Right smack at the start of pedestrian Florida is this modern hotel, part of the popular HoJo chain. An elevator takes you from the shopping arcade to the attractive atrium lobby and restaurant. The 77 rooms are large, beautiful and quiet; services include a conference room and access to a gym.

Recoleta & Barrio Norte   Map pp64–7

Most of the accommodations in Recoleta (Barrio Norte is more of a subneighborhood) are expensive, and what cheap hotels there are tend to be full much of the time. Buildings here are grand and beautiful, befitting the city's richest barrio, but if you stay in this area you'll only see how a very small percentage of BA's inhabitants live. Still, Recoleta's fabulous cemetery is nearby, along with some lovely parks, museums and boutiques.

BUDGET

Juncal Palace Hotel (☎ 4821-2770; www.juncalpalace hotel.com.ar; Juncal 2282; s/d US$14/19; ✗) There are just 26 pleasant and comfortable rooms at this intimate hotel. The comfy rooms have flowery bedspreads and some sport small balconies. This is a great deal for Recoleta, so it's often booked; be sure to reserve in advance.

Hotel Lion D'or (☎ 4803-8992; www.hotel-liondor .com.ar; Pacheco de Melo 2019; s/d US$15-22, without bathroom US$8/9) Some rooms at these charming old digs are small, basic and dark; some are absolutely grand. All are clean and good value, and while a few are a bit rough around the edges most have been modernized. There's a great old marble staircase, and the elevator is just fabulous.

MIDRANGE

Ayacucho Palace Hotel (☎ 4806-1815; www.ayacucho hotel.com.ar; Ayacucho 1408; s/d US$30/40; ✗ ▣) The 64 clean and fairly modern wood-floored rooms here are comfortable yet nondescript, while the services are acceptable. It's a fair deal for the Recoleta area, and you'll only be a few blocks away from the barrio's famous cemetery and weekend crafts fair.

Hotel El Castillo (☎ 4815-4561; www.hotel-elcast illo.com.ar; Marcelo T de Alvear 1893; s/d US$20/24; ✗)

This hotel is a mix of old and new styles, which include a grand stairway and nice, comfortable and spacious wood-floored rooms overlooking the street. Despite not serving breakfast (unlike almost every other hotel in BA) it's very popular, so reserve in advance.

Prince Hotel (☎ 4811-8004; www.princehotel .ar in Spanish; Arenales 1627; s/d US$25/30; ℗ ✗) The clean and neat little rooms are good value here; some come with balconies. Blemishes include carpet stains and limited services, but at this price you can't complain too much. Be sure to check out the ancient metal elevator.

TOP END

Alvear Palace Hotel (☎ 4808-2100; www.alvearpalace .com; Av Alvear 1891; d US$358; ℗ ✗ ✗ ▣ ✗) Old-world sophistication and superior service will help erase the trials of that long 1st-class flight, while the bathtub Jacuzzi, Hermès toiletries and Egyptian-cotton bedsheets aid your trip into dreamland. Fine restaurants, an elegant tearoom and heated indoor pool await your presence the next day.

Art Suites (☎ 4821-6800; www.artsuites.com.ar; Azcuénaga 1465; d US$109-165; ℗ ✗ ▣) Fifteen excellent, very modern and spacious apartment suites have minimalist decor, full kitchens, sunny balconies and slick hip furniture. Windows are double-paned, security is excellent, staff speak English and long-term discounts are available. Advance reservations required.

Palermo   Map pp68–9

Despite being a bit northwest from the center, Palermo has much to offer the traveler. Not only is it full of extensive parklands – which are great for weekend jaunts and sporting activities – but you can't get more choice in cutting-edge restaurants, designer boutiques and hip dance clubs. Many of these places are located in the extensive subneighborhood of Palermo Viejo, which is further subdivided into Palermo Soho and Palermo Hollywood. If you like trendy entertainment, Palermo is your hood.

BUDGET

Casa Jardín (☎ 4774-8783; www.casajardinba.com.ar; Charcas 4416; dm/s/d US$8.50/14/24) This isn't your typical hostel; it's a tranquil little place that sleeps only 13 guests and doubles as a casual art gallery that occasionally puts on an open house. There's a great leafy rooftop patio for hanging out, and charm abounds. Keep an eye out for the resident pet tortoise.

Giramondo Hostel (☎ 4772-6740; www.hostelgiramondo.com.ar; Güemes 4802; dm US$8-10, s & d US$20-35; 🖳) This spacious new hostel is located in a remodeled old house. It's a nice place, with high ceilings, charming details and a superhip bar (with great music) in the basement. Rooms surround an open staircase on three floors, and there's a rooftop patio and bar for *asados*.

MIDRANGE

Como en Casa (☎ 4831-0517; www.bandb.com.ar; Gurruchaga 2155; s US$30-45, d US$40-55; 🖳) This pleasant guesthouse has a homey atmosphere and mazelike hallways that lead to 11 simple rooms of all sizes; the cheapest have shared bathrooms. A two-bedroom apartment (no kitchen) is available for groups. Plenty of common spaces and a nice garden add to this intimate place to stay.

Malabia House (☎ 4832-3345; www.malabiahouse.com.ar; Malabia 1555; s US$65-80, d US$90-115; ✂ 🔀 🖳) Fifteen luxurious bedrooms – all stocked with modern furnishings, terry-cloth robes and slippers – line this beautifully renovated old house. Common spaces are gracious, charming and include tiny courtyard gardens. Candles, soft music and a comfortable homey feel add peace and romance.

Lulu Guesthouse (☎ 4772-0289; www.luluguesthouse.com; Emilio Zolá 5185; dm/d US$15/30; 🔀 🖳) Each of the eight wonderfully artistic rooms here sports a different size and theme, while decor is comfortably rustic and cute patios abound. Rooms with shared bathroom are US$20 to US$25; the cozy attic dorm (the only room with air-con) sleeps four. It's located in BA's transvestite red-light district.

La Otra Orilla (☎ 4867-4070; www.otraorilla.com.ar; Julián Álvarez 1779; s US$20-65, d US$25-70; 🖳) Just five beautiful rooms – four upstairs – greet you at this small but pleasant guesthouse. All are different in size, shape and color. The large suite has a great view of the leafy back garden, while two of the rooms share bathrooms. The only flaw: a large dog that barks at strangers.

Long-Term Rentals

Any establishment listed above will significantly discount a long-term stay, so negoti-

ate a deal in advance. You can also check the **Buenos Aires Herald** (www.buenosairesherald.com /classifieds) or **La Nación** (http://clasificados.lanacion.com.ar/Indexinmuebles.asp in Spanish) for apartment rentals.

Traditionally you need an Argentine 'guarantor' to cover your rent, but so many long-term foreigners are now pouring into BA that a plethora of rental agencies and websites are popping up to help them find furnished apartments without this requirement. Expect to pay a much higher monthly rate for this service, however; locals usually commit to at least one or two years when obtaining a lease for unfurnished apartments, and consequently pay less. Sites to check:

www.argentinago.com
www.apartmentsba.com
www.bytargentina.com
www.midtownba.com.ar

EATING

Since the devaluation of the peso, BA has become a ridiculously affordable place to eat out. While the variety of cuisine is limited in many areas, this certainly isn't the case in Palermo Viejo (a subneighborhood of Palermo). Here, dozens of surprisingly good, upscale restaurants serving international cuisine – much of it with an ethnic bent – have popped up in the past few years. Reservations are usually unnecessary, except for weekend dinners at popular restaurants. Most restaurants here serve both lunch and dinner; exceptions are noted in reviews.

Microcentro & Plaza de Mayo
Map pp64–7

La Sortija (☎ 4328-0824; Lavalle 663; mains US$2-5) Here's a steal of a place, where you can fill up on a chunk of grilled meat, salad and a drink for US$3.50 all told. The *vacío* (a chewy but tasty flank cut) is only US$2 per half-portion, and a *choripán* (sausage sandwich) goes for just US$0.50. It's very popular so go after the lunch rush.

Broccolino (☎ 4322-7754; Esmeralda 776; mains US$3-7) Pick from over 25 varieties of toppings for your rigatoni, fusilli or spaghetti. If you can't decide, try the delicious vegetarian ravioli with Sicilian sauce (spicy red peppers, tomato and garlic). Portions are large and service is quick; this joint hops with locals and tourists alike.

Sabot (☎ 4313-6587; 25 de Mayo 756; mains US$4-7; ⊙ lunch Mon-Fri) Reflecting what BA's food is all about, this *porteño* eatery draws everyone from CEOs and bank managers to secretaries and porters. The capital's best roasted goat and pepper steak are on the menu, but vegetarians have some options also. Service is efficient. Reservations are a must after 1:30pm.

Granix (☎ 4343-4020; Florida 165, 1st fl; tenedor libre US$4; ⊙ lunch Mon-Fri) One of the best vegetarian choices in BA, this place is modern and clean. Choices are all good, from the attractive salad bar to hot mains, and you can be sure none of Argentina's meat culture has landed here.

La Estancia (☎ 4326-0330; Lavalle 941; mains US$3-13) Tourists gawk and take photos of meat roasting on the grill – the smell filling the air is enough of an appetizer. This steak house has been serving up the barbecued goods since 1962, along with substantial salads and plenty of wines. On weekends enjoy tango and folk shows.

Rey Castro (☎ 4342-9998; Perú 342; mains US$4-6.50) Rustic brick arches surround smoky atmosphere, and Castro's music plays while trendy diners sample Cuban dishes like *ropa vieja* (shredded meat stew). On weekends there's live music, dancing and a raucous drag show.

Puerto Madero   Map pp64–7

There's plenty of restaurants in this upscale waterfront area, popular for power business lunches on weekdays. Almost all places have views of the attractive nearby dikes, and many sport outdoor covered terraces.

La Caballeriza (☎ 4514-4444; Av Alicia Moreau de Justo 580; mains US$5-9) This popular restaurant is designed to look like a fancy renovated barn. It works, though, and as you nibble your juicy *bife de chorizo* (sirloin steak) you can imagine hearing some neeeiighs. Good prices and better food keep the back patio packed with businessfolk at lunch, so consider making reservations.

Bice (☎ 4315-6216; Av Alicia Moreau de Justo 192; mains US$7-16) The pasta is outrageously good here: try the black fettucini with shrimp or the spinach-and-ricotta ravioli with four-cheese sauce. Risotto, meats and fish like trout, salmon and tuna will also tickle your taste buds. Order the mousse with pears for dessert, and snag a table near the water.

Siga la Vaca (☎ 4315-6801; Av Alicia Moreau de Justo 1714; lunch US$6-9, dinner US$8-9) Only the truly hungry should set foot in this *tenedor libre parrilla*, where mountains of food are available for consumption. Work your way from the appetizer/salad bar to the grill, where the good stuff hangs out. Prices vary depending on the meal and day.

Congreso & Avenida Corrientes   Map pp64–7

Chiquilín (☎ 4373-5163; Sarmiento 1599; mains US$3.50-8) This traditional *parrilla* is packed at midnight on a Saturday night. Wait staff are efficient and the hanging hams and wine bottles add a congenial atmosphere. Specials like paella on Monday and *puchero* (a meat and vegetable stew) on Wednesday add welcome detours to the regular menu.

Biwon (☎ 4372-1146; Junín 548; mains US$4-8) The best Korean food in BA; go for the *bulgogi*

PASS THE BEEF…ERRR, MAKE THAT THE TOFU

Argentine cuisine is internationally famous for its succulent grilled meats, but this doesn't mean vegetarians – or even vegans – are completely out of luck.

Most restaurants, including *parrillas* (steak restaurants), serve a few items acceptable to most vegetarians, such as green salads, omelettes, mashed potatoes, pizza and pasta dishes. *Sin carne* means 'without meat,' and the words *soy vegetariano/a* – 'I'm a vegetarian' – will come in handy when explaining to an Argentine why in the world you don't eat their delicious steaks.

There are some surprisingly good vegetarian restaurants in BA. The ones we review are Granix (above), La Esquina de las Flores (p94), Lotos (p94), Artemesia (p96), Bio (p96) and Krishna (p96), but there are others. The last two we just mentioned have small but good health-food shops, or you can try **Dietética Viamonte** (Map pp64–7; ☎ 4322-4364; Viamonte 859; ⊙ 8:30am-7:30pm Mon-Fri, 8am-1pm Sat), which offers an extensive selection of health foods, including bulk grains, cereals, dried fruit and bakery goods.

Best of luck to all vegetarians visiting BA, and may the Argentine beef gods forgive you.

(grill the meat yourself at the table), *bibimbap* (rice bowl with meat, vegies, egg and hot sauce – mix it all up) or *kim chee chigue* (kim chee soup with pork – for adventurous, spice-loving tongues only!). The English on the menu really helps.

Cervantes II (☎ 4372-5227; Juan D Perón 1883; mains US$2-5) This local *parrilla* simply bustles with the lunchtime crowd taking advantage of the large portions and efficient service. Order the *agua de sifón* (soda water) to go along with your *bife de chorizo*, or savor some inexpensive *ravioles con tuco* (ravioli with sauce).

Laurak Bat (☎ 4381-0682; Av Belgrano 1144; mains US$5-7) Popular with homesick Basques, this traditional restaurant is set around an old Guérnica tree brought from the home country. Seafood specialties include *abadejo al pil pil* (a traditional fish dish), *cazuela de kokotxas* (fish-cheek stew) and mussels a la Provence. For dessert there's *leche frita* (fried milk) and *tarta vasca* (a type of Basque tart).

Pippo (☎ 4375-5887; Paraná 356; mains US$1.50-4) Dishing up large servings of *parrilla* and pasta for small prices, it's no wonder Pippo's still going strong after 66 years. Service is fast and efficient, the tablecloths are paper and there's a no-smoking section in back. There's another **Pippo** (☎ 4375-2709; Montevideo 341) on the other side of the same block.

Pizzería Güerrín (☎ 4371-8141; Corrientes 1368; slices US$0.50; ⏰ 7am-2am) After watching a movie on Corrientes it's late, you're hungry and have only a few pesos left – what do you do? Stop here, point at a prebaked slice behind the glass counter and eat standing up, for really cheap. Empanadas and plenty of desserts are also available.

San Telmo & Constitución   Map pp64–7

Pappa Deus (☎ 4361-2110; Bethlem 423; mains US$3-8; ⏰ 9am-2am) Come by on a weekday, and a strategic spot on the plaza – right under a shady umbrella – will double the enjoyment of your pumpkin- and spinach-filled black ravioli. Other creative dishes, all thoughtfully presented, include lamb with roasted peppers and a crisp prosciutto salad.

Abril (☎ 4342-8000; Balcarce 722; lunch US$3-4, dinner US$7) Probably San Telmo's best bistro, offering limited but excellent three-course prix-fixe meals that arrive beautifully presented. Abril's small, intimate dining room is softly illuminated by candlelight, and the neighborhood's tango atmosphere adds to the romance – bring your date.

Desnivel (☎ 4300-9081; Defensa 855; mains US$1.50-3; ⏰ lunch & dinner Tue-Sun, dinner Mon) This famous local joint is packed like a rock concert at lunch, serving up the traditional *chorizo* (sausage) sandwich and a super tasty *bife de lomo* (tenderloin steak). Add salad and a double espresso, and you can walk away happy and buzzing for US$5.

Bar Plaza Dorrego (☎ 4361-0141; Defensa 1098; mains US$3-8; ⏰ 8am-2am Sun-Thu, till 6am Fri & Sat) You can't beat the atmosphere at this old joint; sip your *café cortado* (coffee with milk) or *submarino* (hot milk with chocolate) by the sunny picture window and watch the world pass by. Tango music, antique bottles and scribbled graffiti might take you back in time – at least until your hamburger lands on the table.

La Farmacia (☎ 4300-6151; Bolívar 898; mains US$4-6) Head up to the 2nd floor for an intimate table or a sofa to lounge on, or to the slightly slanted rooftop patio for some fresh air. Order innovative dishes like lamb ratatouille, salmon ravioli and spinach *ñoquis* (gnocchi); apple crepes and lemon pie are for dessert.

Pride Café (☎ 4300-6435; Balcarce 869; mains US$1.50-3; ⏰ 10am-10pm Sun-Fri) This cute little modern corner café is set out in black and white and attracts gay men on Sundays during San Telmo's antiques fair. Good music complements the homemade pastries and 'queer coffee,' while salads, sandwiches and sushi nights add interest.

Retiro   Map pp64–7

Filo (☎ 4311-0312; San Martín 975; mains US$4-8; ⏰ noon-2am) It's hard to figure out what's best at this excellent, highly creative place, especially when you look at the dizzying menu. Twenty varieties of pizza and 15 kinds of salads are on offer. Other choices include *panini*, pasta and meats, along with a whirlwind of desserts. Don't forget to check out the art gallery downstairs.

Gran Bar Danzón (☎ 4811-1108; Libertad 1161; mains US$4-8; ⏰ dinner) It's hard to be hipper than this ultimate lounge-bar-restaurant. Food couldn't be tastier: the menu is graced with dishes like duck confit with taleggio cheese, risotto with king crab and portabello, and pear and *arugula* (rocket) salad.

A special conservation system makes it possible to order many wines by the glass.

La Chacra (☎ 4322-1409; Av Córdoba 941; mains US$4-10; ☺ noon-2am) Resist the urge to ride the stuffed cow in the entryway and check out the *asado* roasting in the window instead. Inside, order the succulent grilled meats – including seven kinds of *lomo* – while deer and boar heads high on the walls watch you munch on their bovine cousins.

La Esquina de las Flores (☎ 4813-3630; Av Córdoba 1587; mains US$1.50-3; ☺ 8:30am-8:30pm Mon-Fri, 8:30am-3pm Sat) This clean and modern vegetarian restaurant also has a small health-food store (buy soy flour, whole-wheat breads and organic *mate*, the traditional Argentine drink). There's a tiny fast-food section here as well, but if you prefer to sit down go upstairs. They've even got a dish for macrobiotics.

Nucha (☎ 4813-9507; Paraná 1343; coffee & snacks US$2-3; ☺ 8am-9pm Mon-Thu, 9am-2am Fri & Sat, 9am-9pm Sun) Modern, trendy and very popular is this little café, which attracts everyone from little old ladies to slick young hipsters. There's plenty in the tempting pastry counter – cheesecake, *medialunas* (croissants) or lightly layered afternoon cake – to go with your imported tea, iced coffee with ice cream or *mate*.

Lotos (☎ 4814-4552; Av Córdoba 1577; mains US$1-2; ☺ 11:30am-6pm Mon-Fri, 11:30am-4pm Sat) Right next door to La Esquina de las Flores is this equally renowned vegetarian spot. It's cafeteria-style, so just point at what looks good. Choices include delicious healthy soups, extensive salad ingredients and filling mains, while in the basement is a good health-food store.

Empire Bar (☎ 4312-5706; Tres Sargentos 427; mains US$5-12; ☺ lunch & dinner Mon-Fri, dinner Sat) This popular spot is filled with both tourists and locals for its almost authentic Thai cuisine. Go for the crispy wrapped prawns, *panang* chicken in red curry or *tom ka gai* (a soup of chicken and coconut milk) for lunch; for dessert, there's banana fritters or mango (if it's in season) with sweet rice. Surroundings are modern and snazzy.

Mumbai (☎ 4315-0075; Paraguay 436; mains US$4-7.50; ☺ lunch & dinner Mon-Fri, dinner Sat) This new restaurant serving the business district is Indian-run and fairly authentic. Good dishes include the chicken tikka masala (tandoori-cooked chicken in a curry sauce) and *gosht saag* (lamb served with spinach).

Biryani rice dishes are also tasty, and vegetarians have decent choices too.

Recoleta & Barrio Norte

Cumaná (Map pp64-7; ☎ 4813-9507; Paraná 1343; mains US$2-5) If you've never tried *cazuela*, this is the place to do it. These deliciously homey, stick-to-your-ribs pot stews are filled with squash, corn, eggplant, potatoes and/or meats. Also popular are the pizzas, empanadas, pastas and calzones. Come early, though – it's ridiculously crowded here.

Arte Sano (Map pp68-9; ☎ 4963-1513; Lucio N Mansilla 2740; mains US$1.50-3.50; ☺ 8am-10pm Mon-Fri, 9am-8pm Sat) This health-food eatery cooks up excellent dishes like *budín tricolor* (chard, carrot and squash tart), *milanesa de soja* (breaded soybean 'steak') or whole-wheat pizza. An attached store sells brown rice, powdered ginger and baked goods, and services include yoga classes and natural-food workshops.

Grant's (Map pp64-7; ☎ 4823-5894; Junín 1155; lunch US$3-6, dinner US$4.50-6) This *tenedor libre* is one of the best in town: the buffet tables overflow with a fantastic assortment of foods, including plenty of *parrilla* and desserts. Be aware that drinks are mandatory and cost extra. There's another **Grant's** (Map pp64-7; ☎ 4801-9099; Av General Las Heras 1925) near Ayacucho.

El Sanjuanino (Map pp64-7; ☎ 4805-2683; Posadas 1515; mains US$2.50-5.50) This friendly little place probably has the cheapest food in Recoleta. Sit at one of the eight tables and order spicy empanadas, tamales or *locro* (a traditional meat-and-corn stew). The curved brick ceiling adds to the local atmosphere, but take your food to go – Recoleta's lovely parks are close by.

Munich Recoleta (Map pp64-7; ☎ 4804-3981; RM Ortiz 1871; mains US$5-8) This traditional old place hasn't changed much since Jorge Luis Borges was a regular; even the waiters seem to be the same. The food is consistently good; try the omelettes, brochettes, grilled salmon or vegie soup, and finish off with the tasty *flan casera* (homemade flan).

Palermo
Map pp68–9

Palermo, especially the extensive subneighborhood of Palermo Viejo, is ground zero for innovative cuisine in BA. Hundreds of restaurants, many of them serving wonderfully creative and very good food, have popped up here in the past few years. Another neighborhood in Palermo with exceptional restaurants is Las Cañitas; there's a separate listing for these after the Palermo Viejo section.

Río Alba (☎ 4773-5748; Av Cerviño 4499; mains US$4-10) This well-regarded *parrilla* serves some of the tastiest grilled meat in town. Try the house specialty, *ojo de bife* (rib eye); it's steak at its best, and at US$5 the half-portion is plenty. If you're lucky, you'll get a waiter who will remember your party of 12's order without having to write a single thing down.

Bella Italia (☎ 4802-4253; República Árabe Siria 3285; mains US$5-7; ☿ dinner Mon-Sat) Some of BA's best Italian food is cooked up at this fancy little place. Try the delicate tagliatelle (a thin ribbon pasta, served with bacon), the lemon ravioli with salmon and *arugula* or the braised rabbit. There's a sister café on the next block, which serves similar but lighter fare.

Mykonos (☎ 4779-9000; Olleros 1752; mains US$4.50-10; ☿ dinner) At the edge of Belgrano is this peaceful Greek restaurant…at least until they start breaking plates during the nightly traditional dance show. Food is fairly good; try the *tzatziki* (a cucumber-and-yogurt sauce), spanakopita (spinach pastry) and *musaka* (eggplant with spicy meat).

LICKING YOUR WAY THROUGH BA

Because of Argentina's Italian heritage, its *helado* (ice cream) is some of the best ice cream in the world. Amble into an *heladería*, order a cone and a creamy concoction will be artistically swept into a mountainous peak. Important: *granizado* means with chocolate flakes.

Some of the tastiest *heladerías* in town:
Freddo (Map pp64-7; ☎ 0800-3337-3336; www.freddo.com.ar; cnr Ayacucho & Av Quintana, Recoleta) See the website for other branches.
Heladería Cadore (Map pp64-7; ☎ 4374-3688, Av Corrientes 1695, Congreso)
Munchi's (Map pp64-7; ☎ 0800-555-5050; www.munchis.com.ar; cnr MT de Alvear & Florida, Retiro) See the website for other branches.
Persicco (Map pp68-9; ☎ 0810-333-7377; cnr Salguero & Cabello, Palermo)
Una Altra Volta (Map pp68-9; ☎ 4805-1818; Av del Libertador 3060, Palermo)
Vía Flaminia (Map pp64-7; ☎ 4342-7737; Florida 121, Microcentro)

Anastasia (☎ 4802-8640; cnr Bulnes & Cabello; mains US$3-7) The *pastas caseras* (homemade pastas) are mighty fine, but most folks come here for the succulent grilled meats. The atmosphere exudes richness and sophistication, attracting an older, well-dressed clientele. *Mate* helps wash down those tasty ribs.

Palermo Viejo   Map pp68–9

Sudestada (☎ 4776-3777; Guatemala 5602; mains US$5-8.50; ☿ lunch & dinner Mon-Sat) Fusion is the game here, and the players are Thailand, Vietnam, Malaysia and Singapore. Check out Sudestada's spicy curries, tender stir-fries and delicious noodle dishes; the grilled rabbit is fantastic. Alcoholic drinks come with exotic Asian flavor – or sip an equally intoxicating Thai iced tea.

Bar Uriarte (☎ 4834-6004; Uriarte 1572; mains US$6-8) This ultratrendy and mighty good-looking eatery has high noise levels, but the food makes up for it: sample the rabbit ravioli, risotto with creamed corn, marinated zucchini with ricotta or lamb carpaccio. For dessert, the chocolate mousse with raspberries is unforgettable.

Central (☎ 4776-7374; Costa Rica 5644; mains US$6-8) The minimalist decor and cool young things perched on high stools are right out of a fashion magazine, but Central also offers an excellent menu that ranges from trout with Mediterranean vegetables to baked squash tarts. Tasty appetizers and luscious desserts deliver the goods equally well.

Cluny (☎ 4831-7176; El Salvador 4618; mains US$6-8) You can't get more attractive, hip and elegant than Cluny, which features an interior patio and simply gorgeous ambience. The food's top-notch, with a good selection of steaks, salmon and pastas – don't miss the black ravioli stuffed with lamb.

Dashi (☎ 4776-3500; Fitz Roy 13; mains US$6-11) BA's sweetest sushi is rolled up at sleek and minimalist Dashi, though it's heavy on the salmon. The boat platters are still bedazzling, however, especially after lovely appetizers like *gyoza* (dumplings), miso soup and yakitori skewers. Other Japanese delicacies include tempura, teriyaki and *teppan* (table grills).

Mark's Deli & Coffeehouse (☎ 4832-6244; El Salvador 4701; mains US$2.50-3; ☿ 8:30am-9:30pm Mon-Sat, 10:30am-9pm Sun) Sandwiches, salads and soup are fresh, tasty and well prepared, though authenticity is off – the sandwich bread's a little pasty and the Caesar salad lettuce isn't romaine. However, supercool patio seating and sidewalk tables keep this place buzzing, as do the iced coffees and double mochas.

Artemesia (☎ 4863-4242; José Antonio Cabrera 3877; mains US$4-6; ☺ dinner, lunch Tue-Sat) This artsy eatery focuses on mostly vegetarian healthy fare. Choose from the carrot-cilantro dip or quinoa salad for an appetizer, and follow it with a main like broccoli ravioli, squash tart, vegie stir-fry or salmon in Thai coconut sauce. The sweet ginger lemonade is excellent.

Bar 6 (☎ 4833-6807; Armenia 1676; mains US$5-8.50; ☺ breakfast, lunch & dinner Mon-Sat) The long bar, velvet sofas, curved wood ceiling and reggae music are pleasant enough, as is the food: try the excellent grilled salmon, vegie stir-fry or Mediterranean linguini and white fish with citrus, ginger and corn.

Bio (☎ 4774-3880; Humboldt 2199; mains US$4-5; ☺ 9am-midnight Tue-Sun, 9am-noon Mon) Organic fare like soy burgers, seitan *milanesas*, tofu with steamed vegies and whole-wheat pastas will feed both your body and soul, along with mushroom salads and the Mediterranean couscous with dried tomatoes. Fresh juices are also available.

Krishna (☎ 4833-4618; Malabia 1833; mains US$2.50-3.50; ☺ lunch Tue-Sun, dinner Wed-Sun) Colorful thematic decor and low tables offer a slice of hippiness. This tiny and casual vegetarian spot is popular for its *thalis*, soy burgers, *koftas* (balls of ground vegetables) and cheese/chutney crepes. Drinks are equally exotic: sample the ginger lemonade or mango *lassi*.

THE AUTHOR'S CHOICE

Olsen (Map pp68-9; ☎ 4776-7677; Gorriti 5870; mains US$5.50-11; ☺ lunch & dinner Tue-Sat, 10:30am-8pm Sun) Olsen is famous for its Sunday brunch, but chef Germán Martitegui cooks up other meals with equal aplomb. Arrive for dinner and you might order lamb ravioli with blackcurrant compote, venison with roasted quince or grilled tuna in yogurt dressing. Lunches are prix-fixe, generously sized and excellent as well. The spacious ambience here – complete with high ceilings, a central fire stove and peaceful garden out front – is stunningly Scandinavian, and you'll enjoy it even more after downing a shot of vodka, assiduously kept at exactly 18° below zero.

Las Cañitas   Map pp68-9

Las Cholas (☎ 4899-0094; Arce 306; mains US$2.50-4) Las Cholas has found the golden rule of many successful restaurants: quality food, trendy design and bargain prices. Eat up traditional Argentine food like *locro*, empanadas, tamales, *puchero* and *cazuelas* (meat and vegie stews). You can also try *mate*. Come early 'cause it fills by 9pm.

Morelia (☎ 4772-0329; Báez 260; mains US$4-9; ☺ dinner) Choose from 24 kinds of pizza: the Napolitana (with tomatoes and garlic) is wonderfully simple, though the Montecattini (prosciutto and *arugula*) beats most pies too. Ask for it *a la parrilla* and it'll arrive thin and crisp. For dessert, the *frambuesas* (raspberries) with ice cream are heaven.

Soul Café (☎ 4778-3115; Báez 246; mains US$3.50-8; ☺ dinner Tue-Sun) This self-proclaimed 'boogie restaurant' is just that, with '60s posters on the tables and soul music on the speakers, all in a red-tinted atmosphere. Creative dishes include sushi, 'funk salad' and *langostinos paranoicos* (shrimp with garlic). Try the 'James Brownie' for dessert.

DRINKING
Cafés

BA's café tradition is strong, and *porteños* will spend hours solving the world's problems over a cheap *cortado*. Many of the city's classic cafés are a step back in time, rich with tradition and history, with some the previous haunts of writers like Jorge Luis Borges and Julio Cortázar.

Most cafés serve alcohol as well as caffeine, and also have a surprisingly good range of food and snacks. They're usually open from early morning to late at night.

Café Tortoni (Map pp64-7; ☎ 4342-4328; www .cafetortoni.com.ar in Spanish; Av de Mayo 829) The classic Tortoni is arguably BA's most well-known and traditional café. Both locals and tourists mix here, taking in the grand old surroundings while sipping coffee, nibbling snacks or playing pool in the back. Good tango shows are offered nightly, with jazz on weekends.

Richmond (Map pp64-7; ☎ 4322-1341; Florida 468) Looking for a billiards game or chess match? Head to the basement at this very traditional café, or sink into a leather chair and admire the Dutch chandeliers and English-style surroundings while sipping hot chocolate – just like Jorge Luis Borges did.

El Gato Negro (Map pp64-7; ☎ 4374-1730; Av Corrientes 1669) Tea-lined wooden cabinets and a spicy aroma welcome you to this pleasant little sipping paradise. Enjoy imported cups of coffee or tea along with breakfast and dainty *sandwiches de miga* (thinly sliced white-bread sandwiches). Tea is sold by weight, and exotic herbs and spices are also on offer.

La Biela (Map pp64-7; ☎ 4804-0449; Av Quintana 600) Before or after dining, the older *porteño* elite while away the hours here, high on caffeine. It's a classic Recoleta landmark, and its pleasant front terrace is wonderful on a sunny afternoon – especially when the weekend *feria* is in full swing. The 'special coffees' are laced with alcohol.

Café de la Paix (Map pp64-7; ☎ 4804-6820; Av Quintana 595) This modern yet traditional café is across from Recoleta's famous cemetery. It has a patio for warm days and the menu is full of basic lunch fare like sandwiches, salads and pizzas, so order up; you'll be styling with the best.

Clásica y Moderna (Map pp64-7; ☎ 4812-8707; Av Callao 892) Serving up coffee since 1938, this cozy, intimate bookstore/café continues to ooze history and atmosphere from its brick walls. It's nicely lit and serves upscale meals, while regular live performances of folk music, jazz, blues and tango liven things up.

Petit Paris Café (Map pp64-7; ☎ 4312-5885; Av Santa Fe 774) This well-situated and elegant café is a great stop for your daily java jolt. The large picture windows do much to help you enjoy views of Plaza San Martín, while the busy street traffic offers a good sense of this bustling city. It's a popular place with businessmen and little old ladies.

Bars

BA has some great drinking holes. Most of them offer a wide range of beverages and open around 8pm or 9pm and stay open until 4am to 6am; those in the center (which cater to businesspeople) are open from lunchtime and close earlier (say midnight), since many serve food also. For the hippest scene in town, head to Plaza Serrano (in Palermo Viejo) at 2am on a weekend night; settle in at one of the many trendy bars surrounding the plaza.

Gibraltar (Map pp64-7; ☎ 4362-5310; Perú 895) Good comfortable spaces and decent at-

---

THE AUTHOR'S CHOICE

Milión (Map pp64-7; ☎ 4815-9925; Paraná 1048) This richly elegant, dimly lit and very sexy bar takes up three floors of a renovated old mansion. The garden out back is a pleasant leafy paradise, but up the grand marble staircase is the solid tiled balcony, which holds the best seats in the house. There are elegant tapas to accompany the wide range of cocktails; try the special slushy *mojito*, mint julep or Long Island iced tea. Downstairs a small restaurant serves international dishes; electronic music plays in the background and art films are projected onto the high ceilings.

---

tempts at foreign cuisine make for a generally happy vibe, and the bar's a good spot to hang out for those who are alone. Homesick Brits can watch English football, play darts and eat roast on Sunday, while the pool tables in back occasionally host competitions.

Mundo Bizarro (Map pp68-9; ☎ 4773-1967; Guatemala 4802) Red lights and a definite lounge feel give this Palermo Viejo bar a very young, sensuous touch. Mondays there's sushi, Tuesday and Wednesdays are two-for-one nights and Sundays see cheap burgers and beer. Rockabilly, hip-hop and rock music are standard offerings.

Janio (Map pp68-9; ☎ 4833-6540; Malabia 1805) By day you can lounge at a sidewalk table and take in the sunshine, while at night the airy rooftop terrace is an excellent choice. Pink Floyd and a burgundy color scheme hang in the air, while frozen margaritas or cool whiskey shots appease the trendy masses.

Shamrock (Map pp64-7; ☎ 4812-3584; Rodríguez Peña 1220) Rockin' during the 'longest' happy hour in town, which runs from 6pm to midnight daily, this contemporary Irish joint in Barrio Norte has become a classic meeting place for the expat drinking community. DJs rule from Thursdays to Saturdays, when the Basement Club disco revs into gear.

Le Cigale (Map pp64-7; ☎ 4312-8275; 25 de Mayo 722) A dark and moody atmosphere, filled with electronic music and smoky air, characterizes this sultry downtown watering hole. It's packed with black-clad youth and grungy foreigners on weekends, when there's often live music, and the fairy lights really shine on Tuesday's 'French' nights.

Dadá (Map pp64-7; ☎ 4314-4787; San Martín 941) An intimate and cool atmosphere, along with moody art, sets this downtown bistro-bar apart. The funky tiled countertop serves as a base for the mixed potions coming from behind, while jazz turns to bossa nova as night falls – this is when fresh tourists replace the worn-out businessmen heading home.

Van Koning (Map pp68-9; ☎ 4772-9909; Báez 325) Great rustic spaces make this intimate Las Cañitas pub feel like the inside of a boat; after all, it's a 17th-century-style seafaring theme complete with dark wood beams, flickering candles and blocky furniture. The bars on two floors serve 40 brews, with Heineken, Guinness and Quilmes on tap.

Druid In (Map pp64-7; ☎ 4312-3688; Reconquista 1040) There's live Scottish bagpipes on Thursdays, Celtic music on Fridays and jazz on Saturdays at this modest Irish pub. A wide range of aged whiskeys, imported liquors, blended cocktails and more than 30 beers temper the pizza, sandwiches and British food they serve.

Kilkenny (Map pp64-7; ☎ 4312-7291; Marcelo T de Alvear 399) BA's most popular Irish bar has become, well, just too damn popular. Weekends are a crush, and hefty doormen keep the nondrinking riffraff out. The dark woodsy atmosphere is congenial enough and harbors deep booths, tall counters and a wrap-around bar.

Seddon Bar (Map pp64-7; ☎ 4342-3700; Defensa 695) Antique train mirrors decorate this popular and historical San Telmo nightspot, and the live entertainment covers all: jazz, blues, rock, tango, Cuban or even funk bands play almost nightly. Come before midnight on Saturday night or you may not find a seat in the house.

Deep Blue (Map pp64-7; ☎ 4827-4415; Ayacucho 1240) There's plenty of blue around, including pool table surfaces (though upstairs they're orange). Corrugated metal ceilings and rowdy DJs contribute to the feisty atmosphere, where drinks reach the US$5 mark, smoke pervades the neon sheen, and Tex-Mex and burgers satisfy the hungry.

Unico (Map pp68-9; ☎ 4775-6693; Honduras 5604) If you like your bars loud and crowded, you'll love this Palermo Viejo corner magnet. It's not overly large, so on weekends people spill out the door onto the sidewalk tables. Plenty of tapas, salads and sandwiches, along with the ultracool music, make for long nights here.

ENTERTAINMENT

BA is like a runaway Mack truck when it comes to delivering the goods on entertainment. Dozens of venues offer first-rate theatrical productions, independent or contemporary movies, sultry tango shows, raging dance parties and exciting sports matches.

Most newspapers publish entertainment supplements on Friday; the *Buenos Aires Herald* does one in English called *Get Out*. Free publications in Spanish include *Llegás* and *Ciudad Abierta*. The Internet is handy too; try www.whatsupbuenosaires.com in English, and www.xsalir.com and www.adondevamos.com in Spanish.

At *carteleras* (discount ticket offices), you can buy tickets at cut-rate prices for many entertainment events such as live theater, movies and tango shows.

Cartelera Baires (Map pp64-7; ☎ 4372-5058; www.entradascondescuento.com; Corrientes 1382; ☿ 10am-10pm Mon-Thu, 10am-11pm Fri, 10am-midnight Sat, 2-10pm Sun) In Cine Lorange.

Cartelera Espectáculos (Map pp64-7; ☎ 4322-1559; www.123info.com.ar; Lavalle 742; ☿ noon-10pm Mon-Fri, noon-11pm Sat, noon-9pm Sun) Right in the middle of the movie district.

Cartelera Vea Más (Map pp64-7; ☎ 4370-5319; ☿ 10am-10pm) In the Paseo La Plaza complex, Local 2.

Tango

Tango is experiencing a renaissance, both at the amateur and professional levels and among all ages. Classes, *milongas* and shows are everywhere; for a wealth of information grab the free booklets *el tangauta* and *BA Tango*; they're often available from tango venues or tourist offices.

Sensationalized tango shows are common, but purists don't consider them authentic – though this doesn't make them necessarily bad. These shows cost around US$35 (more with dinner included). Modest shows are more intimate and cost far less, say around US$8.

For free (or donation) tango, head to San Telmo on a Sunday afternoon; dancers do their thing right in Plaza Dorrego. Another sure bet is weekends on Caminito in La Boca, and there are often dancers in front of Galerías Pacíficos, too (the mall itself has free tango shows at 8pm from Friday to Sunday). All of these buskers are of quite good standard, so remember to toss some change into their hats.

The following listings offer different types of tango shows; for classes and *milongas*, see the boxed text, p100. Spanish-language website www.tangodata.com.ar has information on the city's *milongas*, classes and shows.

Café Tortoni (Map pp64–7; ☎ 4342-4328; www.cafetortoni.com.ar in Spanish; Av de Mayo 829; show US$6) This most classic of BA's cafés puts on excellent shows twice nightly, starting at 8pm Monday, 9pm Tuesday to Thursday and 8:30pm Friday to Sunday. A second show takes place about two hours later on those same nights.

Café Homero (Map pp68–9; ☎ 4775-6763; José Antonio Cabrera 4946; show US$3.50–8.50) This cozy neighborhood *tanguería* in Palermo Viejo offers intimate tango shows, folkloric music and boleros. It has great local flavor and good seats, and tapas are available.

Centro Cultural Torquato Tasso (Map pp62–3; ☎ 4307-6506; Defensa 1575; shows US$3.50–7) This colorful, spacious venue offers good, cheap tango shows featuring well-known artists. Sometimes dinner/show combinations are available. Rock and folk music also plays.

Chiquilín Tango (Map pp64–7; ☎ 4373-5163; www.chiquilin-tango.com.ar; Montevideo 310; show & dinner US$30, show only US$15) Chiquilín has yet to become established but looks great, and if the show's quality is anything like the traditional restaurant's food this place should take off.

El Balcón (Map pp64–7; ☎ 4362-2354; Humberto Primo 461, 1st fl) Grab a balcony spot on a Sunday afternoon and watch both the tango show and the antiques fair on Plaza Dorrego at the same time. The show's free, but your meal is not – order something. Tango shows run Fridays to Sundays only.

Bar Sur (Map pp64–7; ☎ 4362-6086; www.bar-sur.com.ar; Estados Unidos 299; show US$30) For a very intimate tango show this is your place – there are only a dozen tables in the dim atmosphere. Dancers do a good job of not knocking over your drink with their high leg kicks.

Señor Tango (Map pp62–3; ☎ 4303-0231; www.senortango.com.ar in Spanish; Vietes 1655; show & dinner US$54, show only US$34) Señor Tango is the closest you'll get to Las Vegas in BA. Some might think it the best show in town, and it's cer-

---

LUNA PARK

If unique large-scale spectacles like the Beijing Circus, Tom Jones or the Pope come to town, Luna Park's dressing rooms are probably their destination. Originally a boxing stadium, **Luna Park** (Map pp64–7; ☎ 4324-1010; www.lunapark.com.ar in Spanish; cnr Bouchard & Corrientes) has a capacity of 15,000 and hosted such historical moments as Carlos Gardel's wake (1935), Eva Duarte's meeting with Juan Perón (1944) and Diego Maradona's wedding (1989).

Other productions held here include fashion shows, ice-skating spectacles and mass religious baptisms, but Luna Park hasn't forgotten its roots; 25 boxing titles have been fought within the walls of this historic place, and even Ricky Martin can't match that record.

---

tainly the most outrageous (live horses are involved). Dish out the bucks and you can be the judge.

El Viejo Almacén (Map pp64–7; ☎ 4307-7388; www.viejoalmacen.com; cnr Balcarce & Independencia; show & dinner US$50, show only US$35) This long-running (since 1969) and highly regarded tango show features exceptional professional singers, dancers and musicians. Note that the restaurant is across the street from the tango show.

Esquina Carlos Gardel (Map pp68–9; ☎ 4867-6363; www.esquinacarlosgardel.com.ar; Carlos Gardel 3200; show & dinner US$60, show only US$40) One of the newest and priciest shows in town. Perhaps the fact that Gardel sang at this old cabaret adds to the novelty. It's been refurbished since then, of course, and seats 450. The balcony costs double.

Caminito Tango Show (Map pp62–3; ☎ 4301-1520; Del Valle Iberlucea 1151) The show's free, and you only get it with your inexpensive lunch (the very limited dishes cost US$2 to US$3.50). The dinner show is only on Friday nights, when you should reserve ahead.

Nightclubs

BA's *boliches* (discos) are the throbbing heart of its world-famous nightlife. To be cool, don't arrive before 2am or even 3am and dress as stylishly as you can. Admission ranges from US$3 to US$7 and often includes a drink; some clubs offer dinners

MILONGAS & TANGO CLASSES

Tango classes are available just about everywhere, from youth hostels to cultural centers to all the *milongas* (dance halls, also used to refer to the dance itself). With so many foreigners flooding BA to learn the dance, many instructors now teach in English (group classes cost around US$3). For general information, contact the **Academia Nacional del Tango** (Map pp64-7; ☎ 4345-6967; www.anacdeltango.org.ar in Spanish; Av de Mayo 833) above Café Tortoni.

Confitería Ideal (Map pp64-7; ☎ 5265-8069; www.confiteriaideal.unlugar.com in Spanish; Suipacha 384) The mother of all tango halls, with *milongas* and tango classes offered practically every day. The atmosphere is classic and the history rich.

El Beso (Map pp68-9; ☎ 4953-2794; Riobamba 416) Here's another traditional place popular for its good *milongas* (Tuesday, Saturday and Sunday nights) and daily classes. The space upstairs has a good feel, and there's a convenient bar as you enter.

La Catedral (Map pp68-9; ☎ 15-5325-1630; Sarmiento 4006) Hip, trendy and casual tango in a rough-and-tumble warehouse space. A hazy air and funky art on the walls makes it more of a party, and there are plenty of wallflowers, tourists and socialites. The best *milonga* is Tuesday.

La Viruta/La Estrella (Map pp68-9; ☎ 4774-6357; www.lavirutatango.com; Armenia 1366) Still going strong after 10 years, this Palermo Viejo venue has *milongas* on Wednesday and Friday through Sunday, while classes are given Wednesday through Sunday.

Niño Bien (Map pp64-7; ☎ 4147-8687; Humberto Primo 1462) Takes place on Thursdays and attracts a large variety of aficionados – some consider it the best *milonga* in town. Great atmosphere, a large ballroom and good (but crowded) dance floor. It's far from the center; take a taxi here.

Salon Canning (Map pp68-9; ☎ 4832-6753; Scalabrini Ortíz 1332) An excellent dance floor and some of BA's finest dancers grace this traditional venue. Tango company **Parakultural** (www.parakultural.com.ar) stages good events here; *milongas* and classes every day.

Torquato Tasso (Map pp62-3; ☎ 4307-6506; Defensa 1575) Classes are offered daily at this popular venue in San Telmo. It's a well-known, lively and artsy place that also puts on good weekend shows with famous musicians. *Milongas* happen on Sundays.

and shows before the dancing starts. Check out the website www.brandongayday.com.ar for current raves; there are many such last-minute parties happening in BA at any one time, so ask around.

Asia de Cuba (Map pp64-7; ☎ 4894-1328; Dealessi 750, Puerto Madero Este; ☽ nightly) Try not to let the pair of women in tiny leather outfits dancing on stage distract you from the delightfully eclectic mix of music. This is one of BA's best clubs; the music and the even mix of tourists and Argentines make it worth checking out. Avoid the US$8 cover charge by grabbing dinner here beforehand.

Niceto Club (Map pp68-9; ☎ 4779-9396; Niceto Vega 5510; ☽ Thu-Sat) The most popular drag shows in town are here on Thursday nights, when theater company Club 69 takes over. Fifteen actors jump on stage about 3am, riling up the crowd with wonderfully skimpy outfits and fun theatrical antics, then join in to dance the night away. Fridays through Sundays see different shows, music, DJs and bands.

Cocoliche (Map pp64-7; ☎ 4331-6413; Av Rivadavia 878; ☽ Fri & Sat) This electronic-music paradise

is based in a modest yet slightly glamorous old mansion. It's the downstairs basement that holds the main attractions, which include cutting-edge bands and some of the best DJs in town. When you need a break, head to the 2nd-floor 'chill out' room, but make sure to grab a drink (and perhaps a date) first.

Pachá (Map pp68-9; ☎ 4788-4280; near cnr Av Costanera R Obligado Norte & La Pampa; ☽ Fri & Sat) Famous guest DJs spin tunes for the spruced-up clientele attracted to this 'temple of electronic music' and its good sound system. Pachá's lost some of its original luster (as all clubs do after time) but still holds a spot near the top. Take bus No 45 from the city center.

Glam (Map pp68-9; ☎ 4963-2521; José Antonio Cabrera 3046; ☽ Thu-Sat) Housed on three floors in an old mansion with tall brick hallways, this maze-like gay club really rocks out. The guys are very good-looking and there are no shows to distract, just casual lounges, pretty bars and free condoms at the door. Thursdays and Saturdays are the biggest nights here.

Museum (Map pp64-7; ☎ 4543-3894; Perú 535; ☾ Wed & Sat) This chic disco features a Wednesday night 'after-office' party where fun-loving *porteños* cast aside their cubicles, throw down two-for-one drinks and dance their way over the midweek hump. Saturday night features rotating shows and renderings of Latin music and American chart-toppers from the '80s and '90s.

Podestá (Map pp68-9; ☎ 4832-2276; Armenia 1740; ☾ Thu-Sat) Located in residential Palermo Viejo, this dark two-level club is full of loud thumping beats and denim-clad local youths. On Thursday there's live rock upstairs, while the rest of the time electronic, house and '80s music is pumped out by invited DJs.

La Salsera (Map pp68-9; ☎ 4864-1733; Yatay 961; ☾ Fri-Sun) Despite its slightly odd location, this place rocks and offers a great scene; just about everyone seems to be dancing and having fun. Upstairs it's much darker and more sedate, and the place to go after you've developed a thirst from all that moving around. Salsa classes are available earlier on.

Maluco Beleza (Map pp64-7; ☎ 4372-1737; Sarmiento 1728; ☾ Wed-Sun) This popular Brazilian *boliche* gets really packed, with crowds swaying to samba music and live bands on Saturdays. Lithe professional dancers hop on stage and further stir the excitement, but if you like it more sedate head upstairs, where it's darker and more laid-back (but still loud).

Palacio BA (Map pp64-7; ☎ 4331-3231; Adolfo Alsina 940; ☾ Fri & Sat) Fridays are *canilla libre* (all you can drink), while on Sundays the venue changes to the 'Big One' – both nights are popular with cute and slightly snobby gays. Three floors come with open balconies, chandeliers and thick drapes – a palace indeed, but with colored lights and thick disco beats.

Mint (Map pp68-9; ☎ 4771-5870; cnr Avs Costanera R Obligado & Sarmiento ☾ Wed-Sat) One of the cooler clubs in BA, where folks concentrate on having a good time on the dance floor rather than looking like movie stars off of it. Guest DJs offer an entertaining mix of US and Latin hits, and a kick-ass riverside patio is best for chilling out. Mint opens early on Wednesday for 'after office' night.

Amerika (Map pp68-9; ☎ 4865-4416; Gascón 1040; ☾ Fri-Sun) This huge club attracts all types, but Fridays are especially popular with gays,

while Saturdays have a good mixed crowd. The music's techno, dance, '90s and Latin, and despite the *canilla libre* (all you can drink, except on Sunday), it's not completely insane – but the floors do get sticky.

Contramano (Map pp64-7; Rodríguez Peña 1082; ☾ Wed-Sun) This Recoleta venue is still packing them in after 20 years. It's for more mature gay clientele, with mostly a bunch of older *locas* ('crazy girls') checking each other out. Fridays are best here, though drag and stripper shows, along with a raffle, run on Sundays. Our prediction: they'll be playing bingo within a year.

UNNA (Map pp64-7; Suipacha 927; ☾ Sat night only) Too bad no guys are allowed here – UNNA's a lesbian club full of hot young things either dancing to the beats, smooching in dark corners or ogling out their next date. Music ranges from pop to electronica to salsa to *cumbia* (originally a Columbian dance music), and the occasional show and free beer manages to entertain the girls well enough (again, sorry guys).

Opera Bay (Map pp64-7; ☎ 4315-8666; Grierson 225; ☾ Wed-Sat) So it looks like a flattened Sydney Opera House – it's still got a dramatic setting, with a back deck and pool that look over pretty Puerto Madero at night. Wednesday nights see 'after office' parties that go from 7pm to 2am; men outnumber women three to one these nights and are especially aggressive after a hard day's work.

Classical Music & Opera

Teatro Colón (Map pp64-7; ☎ 4378-7344; www.teatrocolon.org.ar; Libertad 621) BA's premier venue for the arts, Teatro Colón has hosted some very prominent figures such as Placido Domingo, Luciano Pavarotti and Arturo Toscanini. Ticket prices vary widely, usually from US$3.50 to US$75. Occasional free concerts are given; scan the website for current events.

Teatro San Martín (Map pp64-7; ☎ 0800-333-5254; www.teatrosanmartin.com.ar in Spanish; Av Corrientes 1530) Along with art exhibitions, ballet, photography, cinema and theater, this large complex hosts classical ensembles.

Teatro Avenida (Map pp64-7; ☎ 4381-0662; www.balirica.org.ar in Spanish; Av de Mayo 1222) This 1906 venue highlights Argentine productions, mostly opera, classical and flamenco.

La Scala de San Telmo (Map pp64-7; ☎ 4362-1187; www.lascala.org.ar in Spanish; Pasaje Giuffra 371)

This San Telmo venue puts on tango, classical groups, piano, musical comedies and other music-related shows and workshops.

Live Music
ROCK & BLUES
The following are smaller venues that showcase mostly local groups; international stars tend to play at large venues like soccer stadiums or Luna Park (p99). Blues isn't as popular as rock, but still has its own loyal following.

La Trastienda (Map pp64-7; ☎ 4342-7650; www .latrastienda.com in Spanish; Balcarce 460; ⌚ open daily, shows only Fri & Sat) This restaurant, theater and CD store multitasks even further by showcasing live groups from rock to latin pop to tango, plus dance and theatrical productions. The Wailers played here in 2004.

Mitos Argentinos (Map pp64-7; ☎ 4362-7810; www.mitosargentinos.com.ar in Spanish; Humberto Primo 489; ⌚ Fri-Sun) This cozy old brick-walled house in San Telmo has hosted rock, blues and tango groups for over 10 years. Rock music plays nightly during the week, while tango rules on Sunday .

Blues Special Club (Map pp62-3; ☎ 4854-2338; Almirante Brown 102; ⌚ Wed-Sun) Fridays at this good-sized, semi-artsy venue are great for jam sessions; on Saturday at midnight the shows really start rockin'. Blues folk like Dave Meyers, Phil Guy, Eddie King and Aaron Burton have all added to the dark and smoky atmosphere.

Cemento (Map pp64-7; ☎ 4304-6228; Estados Unidos 1234; ⌚ Thu-Sat, sometimes Sun) This hole-in-the-wall is mighty unimpressive on the outside, but the cavernous space inside has played host to such well-known Argentine rock groups as Babasonicos, Los Gardelitos and Attaque 77. It's mostly *rock nacional* (Argentine rock), with occasional punk and heavy-metal gigs.

El Samovar de Rasputín (Map pp62-3; ☎ 4302-3190; Del Valle Iberlucea 1251; ⌚ Fri & Sat) Check out the photos of Napo, the hippyish owner, with Keith Richards, Eric Clapton and Pavarotti. Blues biggies Taj Mahal and James Cotton have also played this club in La Boca, though the bands are usually Argentine. Bus No 29 gets you here from the city center.

JAZZ
Jazz is on the move in BA, and you may see more and more bars, cafés or other venues inviting jazz artists to entertain their crowds. Café Tortoni (p96) has jazz on Fridays at 9pm and Saturdays at 11pm, while Clásica y Moderna (p97) occasionally hosts jazz groups.

Club del Vino (Map pp68-9; ☎ 4833-0048; José Antonio Cabrera 4737; ⌚ Fri-Sun) This elegant spot, reminiscent of a small winery, is prettily lit up with fairy lights from the outside. Inside there's a good restaurant, pleasant fountain courtyard, intimate theater and a tiny 'wine museum.' There's live jazz (along with tango, folk, blues and even flamenco) for US$5 to US$10.

Thelonious Bar (Map pp68-9; ☎ 4829-1562; Salguero 1884; ⌚ Fri & Sat) Cozily ensconced on the 2nd floor of an old mansion, this intimate, dimly lit and artsy jazz bar has high brick ceilings and a good sound system. Thelonious is traditionally known for its great jazz lineups, but these days you can occasionally hit a wailing DJ night instead; call ahead to make sure.

Notorious (Map pp64-7; ☎ 4815-8473; www.notorious.com.ar in Spanish; Av Callao 966; ⌚ nightly) This slick joint is one of BA's premier jazz venues. In back, the café hosts live jazz shows every night. There's another **branch** (☎ 4371-0370) in the Foro Gandhi bookstore on Corrientes 1743. Log on to the website for schedules.

FLAMENCO & FOLK
For more information on flamenco venues and classes check out *Contratiempo*, a free monthly newsletter available at some tourist offices, cultural centers and the Spanish embassy.

Música folklórica definitely has its place in BA. There are several *peñas* (folk-music clubs) in the city, but other venues occasionally host folk music.

Cantares (Map pp64-7; ☎ 4381-6965; www.cantar establao.com.ar in Spanish; Av Rivadavia 1180; ⌚ Wed-Sun) This flamenco venue is in a small space but the dances are authentic and the tapas tasty. On Wednesdays, Thursdays and Sundays you can opt for the show only (US$5), but Fridays and Saturdays the only option includes dinner (US$10). Reservations are highly recommended.

Tiempo de Gitanos (Map pp68-9; ☎ 4776-6143; www.tiempodegitanos.com.ar; El Salvador 5575; ⌚ Wed-Sun) This Palermo Hollywood venue offers live flamenco shows in an intimate and comfortable restaurant setting. Nibble on tapas and sip from the extensive wine list while tapping (or clapping) along to the beat. Dinner/shows start at 9pm/10pm and cost US$12 to US$17; reserve in advance.

Guayana (Map pp64-9; ☎ 4381-4350; Lima 27; ☺ open daily, shows Fri & Sat only) For great local working-class flavor, try this nondescript *confitería* near Av 9 de Julio. It's not fancy at all, just a local spot offering cheap food and surprisingly good music. Live tango and folk tunes play from 12:30am to 5am on Friday and Saturday nights.

La Peña del Colorado (Map pp68-9; ☎ 4822-1038; www.lapeniadelcolorado.com.ar in Spanish; Güemes 3657; ☺ closed Mon) Itching to pick up a guitar and strum along with singing *porteños*? La Peña will provide the guitar, or you can bring your own. Almost-nightly folk shows entertain the lively crowds, and northern specialties like *humitas de Chala* (similar to tamales) and spicy empanadas are excellent.

Theater

Av Corrientes, between Avs 9 de Julio and Callao, has traditionally been the capital's center for theater, but there are now dozens of venues throughout the city. The *Buenos Aires Herald* and other local newspapers are a good source for listings. The following venues, both large and small, offer productions like theater, opera, dance, music and art exhibits.

El Camarín de las Musas (Map pp68-9; ☎ 4862-0655; www.elcamarindelasmusas.com.ar in Spanish; Mario Bravo 960) This trendy newish venue offers contemporary dance, plays and theatrical workshops. There's a good café in front.

Teatro Avenida (Map pp64-7; ☎ 4381-0662; www.balirica.org.ar in Spanish; Av de Mayo 1222) Dates from 1906; shows only Argentine productions, mostly opera, with occasional flamenco.

Teatro Cervantes Architecturally gorgeous but faded, with three halls, grand lobby and red velvet chairs. Presents theater, comedy, musicals and dance at affordable prices. See also p78.

Teatro Colón BA's premier venue for the arts, including theater; everyone who's anyone has played, acted, sung or danced here. See also p75.

Teatro El Vitral (Map pp64-7; ☎ 4371-0948; Rodríguez Peña 344) Intimate, with three halls seating from 36 to 165 people; has comedy, drama, music and theater productions.

Teatro Presidente Alvear (Map pp64-7; ☎ 4374-6076; www.teatrosanmartin.com.ar in Spanish; Av Corrientes 1659) Inaugurated in 1942 and named after an Argentine president whose wife sang opera. Holds over 700 and shows many musical productions, including tango.

Teatro San Martín (Map pp64-7; ☎ 0800-333-5254; www.teatrosanmartin.com.ar in Spanish; Av Corrientes 1530) This major venue showcases international cinema, theater, dance and music, covering both conventional and more unusual events. It also has impressive art galleries.

Cinemas

BA is full of cinemas, both historical neon classics and slick modern multiscreens. The traditional cinema districts are along pedestrian Lavalle (west of Florida) and on Av Corrientes, but newer cineplexes are spread throughout the city; most large shopping malls have one. Tickets cost US$3 to US$4.

Check out the *Buenos Aires Herald* for original titles of English-language films. Spanish-language newspapers list movies also but titles have often been changed. Except for kids' films, most movies remain in their original language (with Spanish subtitles).

Sports

Fútbol (soccer) is a national obsession, and witnessing this passion at a live game is part of the BA experience.

Tickets for *entradas populares* (bleachers) and *plateas* (fixed seats) cost anywhere from US$3.50 to US$15, but can skyrocket if a team is doing well. Especially popular games, such as the *súper clásico* between River and Boca, also command higher rates. As a traveler and tourist, you should always sit in the *platea;* the *popular* section is a real experience, but can get far too rowdy with ceaseless standing, singing, drinking, jumping, pot smoking, and even occasional fighting. It's also where the *barra brava* (the Argentine equivalent of England's hooligans) sit.

Tickets are available at stadiums, or try www.ticketek.com.ar, which sells tickets to certain games. Some companies can make it easy for you by providing ticket, transport and a guide to a match. **Tangol** (Map pp64-7; ☎ 4312-7276; www.tangol.com; Florida 971, Local 59) is a recommended company that charges from US$35 for this privilege.

When going to a game, don't carry anything that makes you stand out as a tourist. Keep pricey cameras hidden (or leave them at home), avoid wearing jewelry and don't carry more money than you'll need that day. Games are usually safe, but passion heightens emotions and sometimes things get carried away. For more information on Argentine *fútbol* see www.afa.org.ar and www.futbolargentino.com.ar (in Spanish).

The following are some of the clubs based in BA.

Argentinos Juniors (Map pp62-3; ☎ 4551-6887; Punta Arenas 1271)

Boca Juniors (Map pp62–3; ☎ 4362-2260; www.bocajuniors.com.ar; Brandsen 805)

Club Atlético Vélez Sársfield (Map pp62-3; ☎ 4641-5663; www.velezsarsfield.com in Spanish; Juan B Justo 9200)

Club Deportivo Español (Map pp62-3; ☎ 4612-8111; www.almargen.com.ar in Spanish; Santiago de Compostela 3801)

Club Ferrocarril Oeste (Map pp62-3; ☎ 4431-8282; www.ferroweb.com.ar in Spanish; Avellaneda 1240)

Club Huracán (Map pp62-3; ☎ 4942-1965; www.clubhuracan.com; Almancio Alcorta 2570)

River Plate (Map pp62-3; ☎ 4788-1200; www.cariverplate.com.ar in Spanish; Presidente Figueroa Alcorta 7597)

San Lorenzo de Almagro (Map pp62-3; ☎ 4918-8192; www.sanlorenzo.com.ar in Spanish; Varela 2680)

SHOPPING

For those with hard currency there's some good shopping to be had in BA. Florida is a multipurpose pedestrian strip that buzzes with shoppers, while Santa Fe is a bit less pedestrian-friendly but equally prominent as the city's main shopping artery. San Telmo is ground zero for antiques, and Av Pueyrredón near Once train station is *the* place for cheap (though not the highest quality) clothing. Jewelry shops are found on Libertad south of Corrientes. Palermo Viejo has become a great neighborhood to browse in, with dozens of designers setting up shop alongside trendy houseware stores and kitschy boutiques (not to mention excellent restaurants). Shopping malls are where many *porteños* go to spend money, and they stock pretty much anything you could want.

Store hours in BA are generally from 9am or 10am to 8pm or 9pm weekdays, with many open at least a few hours on Saturday. Most stores close on Sunday. Almost all shopping malls are open from 10am to 9pm daily, with a few closing at 10pm.

Antiques & Art

Gabriel del Campo (Map pp64-7; ☎ 4361-2061; gabrieldelcampo@hotmail.com; Defensa 990; ☒ 10am-7pm) At this exceptional shop you'll find wonder-fully unique things, from Asian tapestries to shelves made from rowboats to Eiffel sculptures to carousel animals to old doors. Religious objects and lighthouse models also take up space here.

Imhotep (Map pp64-7; ☎ 4862-9298; Defensa 916; ☒ 11am-6pm Sun-Fri) Come find amazing old knickknacks at this eccentric shop. Small oddities like Indian statuettes, ceramic skulls, Chinese snuff boxes, precious stone figurines and gargoyles make up some of the bizarre collectibles here. The boar's head is a nice touch as well.

Silvia Pettrocia (Map pp64-7; ☎ 4362-0156; spantiques@velocom.com.ar; Defensa 1002; ☒ 10:30am-7:30pm) Some of San Telmo's most gorgeous antiques can be found at this store, which is chock-full of Italian statuary, old furniture, giant urns, fancy light fixtures and grand picture frames – great fodder for your mansion on the Riviera.

Feria de Pulgas (Map pp68-9; cnr Álvarez Thomas & Dorrego; ☒ 10am-8pm) This dusty, dim covered flea market in Palermo Viejo sells antiques: precious things like ancient wood beds, glass soda bottles, ceramic vases, paintings, clocks, chandeliers and even old cars. It's a pile-up, so you'll have to sift through to find your treasure.

Galería Aguilar (Map pp64-7; ☎ 4393-1852; www.galeriamuseoaguilar.com.ar; Suipacha 1176; ☒ 8am-9pm) It's wall-to-wall, floor-to-ceiling abstract, geometric, landscape and portrait paintings in this gallery-museum, which claims to stock 1500 paintings. There are black-and-white etchings by Antonio Berni, along with works by Argentine artists Xul Solar, Benito Quinquela Martín and Emilio Pettoruti.

Galería Rubbers (Map pp64-7; ☎ 4816-1864; www.rubbers.com.ar; Av Alvear 1595; ☒ 11am-8pm Mon-Fri, 11am-1:30pm Sat) This contemporary and very upscale art gallery, on the edge of Recoleta and Retiro, exhibits only established Argentine painters and sculptors. The beautiful Barrio Norte location is on the 3rd floor of the El Ateneo bookstore (p70).

Camping Equipment

Camping Center (Map pp64-7; ☎ 4314-0305; www.camping-center.com.ar in Spanish; Esmeralda 945; ☒ 10am-8pm Mon-Fri, 10am-5pm Sat) High-quality camping, mountaineering and rock-climbing equipment, as well as general backpacking products (including name-brand clothing from the US) are available at this modern store.

Montagne (Map pp64-7; ☎ 4312-9041; www
.montagneoutdoors.com.ar in Spanish; Florida 719; ☺ 10am-
8:30pm Mon-Sat, noon-8pm Sun) This shop sells
outdoor clothing that is stylish, good quality and made in Argentina. Choose from
a small selection of tents, backpacks and
camping gear upstairs. There are several
other Montagne branches, including one
in Barrio Norte at Santa Fe 1780 (Map
pp64-7).

Clothing & Accessories

Cat Ballou (Map pp64-7; ☎ 4811-9792; Av Alvear 1702;
☺ 11am-8pm Mon-Fri, 10:30am-2pm Sat) Alicia Goñi
designs the delicate clothing, while Florencia Pieres creates much of the jewelry and
decorations at this cool corner boutique.
Fabrics are silky, frilly, satiny, velvety and
wispy – just the sort of things that feel good
on your skin.

Gabriela Capucci (Map pp64-7; ☎ 4815-3636;
Av Alvear 1477; ☺ 10:30am-8pm Mon-Sat) Bright
patchwork dresses, creative handbags,
wispy scarves, vintage tops, velvet pillows
and eclectic accessories fill this small space.
Colors are bright, textile patterns are all
over the map and costume jewelry is wild.

El Cid (Map pp68-9; ☎ 4832-3339; www.el-cid
.com.ar in Spanish; Gurruchaga 1732; ☺ 1-8:30pm Mon,
10am-8:30pm Tue-Sat, 4-8pm Sun) Some of the
classiest men's threads can be found at this
Palermo Viejo boutique. Come shop for
Nestor Goldberg's designer shirts, pants,
jackets, accessories and jeans.

La Mercería (Map pp68-9; ☎ 4831-8558; Armenia
1609; ☺ 9am-8pm Mon-Thu, 9:30am-8:30pm Fri & Sat,
1-8pm Sun) Bright and colorful accessories like
scarves, hats, jewelry, pillows and lots of
handbags line the shelves at this luscious
place. Fabrics and materials offering a wonderful tactile experience include lace, knits,
wool yarns, beads and buttons; this boutique doubles as a crafts store.

Objeto (Map pp68-9; ☎ 4834-6866; Gurruchaga 1649;
☺ 11am-8pm Mon-Sat) The designers here have
displayed some of the wackiest, most outra-
geously fun clothes; dresses hang with crazy
details like leather and plastic cutouts, doll
eyes and Japanese *anime* themes. Creativ-
ity and unconventionality dominate – these
aren't your regular street duds.

Rapsodia (Map pp68-9; ☎ 4833-5814; www.rap
sodia.com.ar; El Salvador 4757; ☺ 11am-8pm Mon-Sat)
This trendy boutique carrying a large selection of wearable fashions is a must for styl-

ish travelers. Old and new are blended with
exotic twists into creative feminine styles
that will please most shoppers. It's fancy
and cool, and will make you feel wonderfully fashionable.

Crafts & Souvenirs

Kelly's Regionales (Map pp64-7; ☎ 4311-5712; Paraguay 431; ☺ 9:30am-7:30pm Mon-Fri, 9:30am-4pm Sat)
If you're looking for that perfect cowhide
to throw over your sofa, or cutting-edge
Mapuche poncho to wear with your mini-
skirt, you'll probably find it here. There are
fine animal masks from Salta and gaucho
paraphernalia like *boleadoras* (weighted,
leather-covered balls attached to a length
of thin rope, historically used as a hunting weapon by gauchos and some of Argentina's indigenous peoples) and *mates*, along
with cheap souvenir knickknacks.

Atípica (Map pp68-9; ☎ 4833-3344; El Salvador 4510;
☺ 2-8pm Mon-Fri, 11am-8pm Sat) This tiny shop,
on the edge of Palermo Viejo, stocks local
artists' crafts, along with those of northern
artists who use indigenous techniques for
their works. All are unique pieces; items include picture frames, wall hangings, ceramics, glass, textiles, jewelry and even furniture.
Quality is high and prices fair.

Oda (Map pp68-9; ☎ 4831-7403; Costa Rica 4670;
☺ 11am-8pm Mon-Sat) Over a dozen crafts
artists are represented at this simple boutique. Offerings include unusual costume
jewelry, knit hats, creative wooden toys,
painted trays, glass ashtrays and small metal
sculptures. All are handmade creations and
would make good original gifts.

Music

El Ateneo (Map pp64-7; ☎ 4325-6801; Florida 340;
☺ 9am-10pm Mon-Thu, to midnight Fri & Sat, noon-
10pm Sun) BA's landmark bookseller stocks
a limited number of books in English and
also has a decent selection of music CDs.
There are several branches within the city.
The gorgeous Gran Splendid branch (Map
pp64-7), located in an old renovated cinema, is at Santa Fe 1860.

Musimundo (Map pp64-7; ☎ 4322-9298; www.musi
mundo.com in Spanish; Corrientes 1753; ☺ 9:30am-9:30pm
Mon-Sat, 11am-9pm Sun) With over 50 branches
throughout the city, this is BA's largest
music retailer; listening stations make select-
ing the hippest CDs a snap. There are many
branches throughout the city.

BUENOS AIRES STREET MARKETS

Some of BA's best crafts and souvenirs are sold at its many street markets, often by the artists themselves. You may have to sort through some tacky kitsch, but you'll find creative and original art also.

Feria Artesanal (Map pp64-7; Plaza Intendente Alvear; ☿ 10am-7pm) A hugely popular fair, with hundreds of booths and dozens of creative goods. Hippies, mimes and tourists abound here in Recoleta, just outside the cemetery.

Feria Plaza Serrano (Map pp68-9; Plaza Serrano; ☿ noon-7pm Sat & Sun) Costume jewelry, hand-knit tops, funky clothes, hippie bags and leather accessories fill the crafts booths at this small but lively fair on fashionable Plaza Serrano in Palermo Viejo.

Feria de San Telmo (Map pp64-7; Plaza Dorrego; ☿ 10am-5pm Sun) Everybody comes to this wonderful feria; you'll find antique seltzer bottles, jewelry, artwork, vintage clothing, collectibles and tango shows. Stretches down Defensa to Parque Lezama. It's occasionally open on Saturday afternoons.

Feria Artesanal La Boca (Map pp62-3; cnr Caminito & Mendoza; ☿ 10am-6pm Thu-Sun) Tango themes dominate the goods at this small and lively crafts fair, giving La Boca even more color than usual. Tango dancers entertain, while along Caminito itself are many pictures to buy.

Feria Plaza Belgrano (Map pp62-3; cnr Juramento & Cuba; ☿ 10am-8pm Sat, Sun & holidays) Belgrano's pleasant market is great on a sunny weekend. You'll find high-quality imaginative crafts, as well as some kitschy junk. The performers and tarot readers draw a crowd, too.

Feria De Mataderos (Map pp62-3; ☎ 4687-5602; www.feriademataderos.com.ar; cnr Avs Lisandro de la Torre & de los Corrales; ☿ 11am-9pm Sun & holidays Apr-Nov, 6pm-midnight Sat Dec-March) This unique market is far off in the southwestern barrio of Mataderos. There are shows of horsemanship, folk dancing and cheap authentic treats to be had. From downtown, take bus No 155 (also marked 180) or 126; it's about an hour's ride away, but worth it.

Zival's (Map pp64-7; ☎ 5128-7500; www.tangostore.com; Av Callao 395; ☿ 9:30am-10pm Mon-Sat) One of the better music stores here, especially when it comes to tango, jazz and classical music. Listening stations and a big sale rack are pluses, and they'll ship tango CDs, VHS tapes, books and sheet music abroad, too (check the website).

Shoes & Leather Goods

Casa López (Map pp64-7; ☎ 4311-3044; www.casalopez.com.ar; Marcelo T de Alvear 640/658; ☿ 9am-8pm Mon-Fri, 9:30am-7pm Sat, 10am-6pm Sun) Bring your limousine; some of BA's finest-quality leather jackets, luggage, bags and accessories live here. Service is overly attentive; there are two shops almost next to each other here, and other branches at Galerías Pacífico and Patio Bullrich.

Guido Mocasines (Map pp64-7; ☎ 4813-4095; www.guidomocasines.com.ar in Spanish; Rodríguez Peña 1290; ☿ 9:30am-8pm Mon-Fri) Men come here for sleek, smooth leathers to place on their feet; expect fine service, upscale prices and some of the best quality in BA. There are a few conservatively styled women's shoes as well. There is another branch on Av Quintana 333.

Rossi y Carusso (Map pp64-7; ☎ 4811-1965; www.rossicaruso.com; Santa Fe 1601; ☿ 9:30am-8pm Mon-Fri, 10am-7pm Sat) Choose from fancy boots, belts, bags, saddles, gaucho knives and silver *mates*. It's expensive and the service is professional; don't come dressed scruffily. There is two other branches, one on Santa Fe and the other in Galerías Pacífico.

Shopping Malls

Paseo Alcorta (Map pp68-9; ☎ 5777-6500; www.altopalermo.com.ar in Spanish; Salguero 3172; ☿ 10am-10pm) Large and upscale, with international boutiques like YSL, Lacroix and Dior. Other stores sell leather goods, clothing, sportswear and accessories. There's a large food court, cinema complex and children's play area.

Mercado de Abasto (Map pp68-9; ☎ 4959-3400; www.altopalermo.com.ar; cnr Corrientes & Anchorena; ☿ 10am-10pm) One of the most beautiful malls in BA, this remodeled old market holds more than 200 shops, a large cinema, a covered plaza, a kosher McDonald's and a good children's museum. It's in Once, Carlos Gardel's old neighborhood.

Unicenter (☎ 4733-1166; www.unicenter.com.ar; cnr Paraná & Panamericana, Martínez; ☿ 10am-10pm) With around 300 shops, Unicenter claims to be the biggest shopping center in South America. There are 14 movie screens, a bowling alley, a small amusement park and parking for 6500 cars. It's located in the northern suburb of Martínez.

Galerías Pacífico (Map pp64–7; ☎ 5555-5110; www .galeriaspacifico.com.ar; cnr Florida & Av Córdoba; ☒ 10am-9pm Mon-Sat, noon-9pm Sun) Centrally located right on pedestrian Florida, this gorgeous mall is always full of shoppers and tourists. Murals on the ceiling were painted by famous artists; for more information, see p73. Free tango shows at 8pm Friday to Sunday.

Patio Bullrich (Map pp64–7; ☎ 4814-7412; www .altopalermo.com.ar; Av del Libertador 750; ☒ 10am-9pm) BA's most exclusive shopping center once hosted livestock auctions, but these days it tends toward sales of Persian rugs, double-breasted tweed suits and Dior's latest designs. Other boutiques include Lacoste, Lacroix and Versace; also on offer are coffee shops, cinemas and a food court.

Wine

El Fenix (Map pp64–7; ☎ 4811-0363; Av Santa Fe 1199; ☒ 8am-8pm Mon-Sat) This large corner store offers a wide selection of fine Argentine wines, imported liquor (such as whisky), deli items and even Habano cigars. They'll deliver anywhere in BA.

Winery (Map pp64–7; ☎ 4311-6607; Av Leandro N Alem 880; www.winery.com.ar in Spanish; ☒ 9am-11pm Mon-Sat) This is an attractive chain store that offers a large selection of Argentine wines. This location offers tasting of 35 wines by the glass; sample five for US$3 to US$8.50. The café and wineshop are located upstairs, the modern lounge-restaurant downstairs. There's a smaller branch at Corrientes 302 with just a café.

GETTING THERE & AWAY
Air

BA is Argentina's international gateway and easily accessible from North America, Europe and Australasia, as well as other capital cities in South America.

Almost all international flights arrive at BA's Ezeiza airport (officially Aeropuerto Internacional Ministro Pistarini), about 35km south of center. Most domestic flights use Aeroparque airport (officially Aeroparque Jorge Newbery), a short distance from downtown BA. Flight information for both airports, in English and Spanish, is available at ☎ 5480-6111 (www.aa2000.com.ar). For a list of airline offices located in BA, see p473.

Boat

BA has a regular ferry service to and from Colonia (p113) and Montevideo (p114), both in Uruguay. Ferries leave from the **Buquebus terminal** (Map pp64–7; cnr Avs Antártida Argentina & Córdoba). There are many more launches in the busy summer season. For more information, see p476.

Bus

If you're heading out of town, you'll probably have to visit BA's modern Retiro bus station (Map pp64–7). It's 400m long, three floors high and has slots for 75 buses. The bottom floor is for cargo shipments and luggage storage, the top for purchasing tickets and the middle for everything else. There's an **information booth** (☎ 4310-0700) that provides general bus information and schedules; they'll also help you with the local bus system. Other services include a **tourist office** (☎ 4311-0528; ☒ 7:30am-1pm Mon-Sat), located on the 2nd floor on the other side of station from bus slot No 34, telephone offices (some with Internet access), restaurants, cafés and dozens of small stores.

You can buy a ticket to practically anywhere in Argentina and departures are fairly

---

EZEIZA ARRIVAL & DEPARTURE TIPS

When you arrive at Ezeiza and want to change money, don't go to the first *cambio* (exchange house) you see. For better rates, go past the row of transport booths and veer to the right to find Banco de la Nación's small office; the rates here are identical to downtown offices and they're open 24 hours.

For shuttles and taxis to the center, see p108. There's a **tourist information booth** (☎ 4480-0024) just beyond the city's taxi stand.

When you leave BA on an international flight you'll have to pay a departure tax of US$18 (payable in Argentine pesos or US dollars). If you're heading to Montevideo or Punta del Este this tax will be US$8.

frequent to the most popular destinations. Reservations are not necessary except during peak summer and winter holiday seasons (January, February and July).

Here are some sample destinations; be aware your final ticket price varies according to bus company, class and season.

Destination	Cost (US$)	Duration (hr)
Asunción (Paraguay)	25–36	18
Bariloche	40	22
Comodoro Rivadavia	39	28
Córdoba	12	9½
Foz do Iguaçu (Brazil)	40	18
Mar del Plata	15	5½
Mendoza	35	15
Montevideo (Uruguay)	26	8
Puerto Iguazú	32	18
Puerto Madryn	39	20
Punta del Este	30	9
Rio de Janeiro (Brazil)	67	42
Rosario	10	4
Santiago (Chile)	34	21
São Paulo (Brazil)	63	38

Train

Trains serve BA's suburbs and nearby provinces. Here are the most useful train stations (all served by Subte) and their destinations:

Constitución Train Station   Map pp62–3
Roca line (☎ 4304-0028) To the southern suburbs, Rosario, La Plata, Bahía Blanca, Atlantic beach towns.

Lacroze Train Station   Map pp62–3
Urquiza line (☎ 0800-777-3377) From the terminus of Subte Línea B to the northwestern suburbs.

Once Train Station   Map pp62–3
Sarmiento line (☎ 0800-333-3822) To the southwestern suburbs, Luján, Santa Rosa.

Retiro Train Station   Map pp64–7
Belgrano line (☎ 0800-777-3377) To the northern suburbs.
Mitre line (☎ 4317-4445) To Tigre, Rosario.
San Martín (☎ 4959-0800) To the northern suburbs.

GETTING AROUND
To/From the Airport

The best, most affordable way to and from Ezeiza is to take a shuttle with **Manuel Tienda León** (MTL; Map pp64-7; ☎ 4314-3636; www.tiendaleon .com; cnr Av Madero & San Martín). You'll see its stand immediately as you exit customs. Shuttles cost US$7.50 one way, run every half hour from 6am to 12:45am and take about 40 minutes. Avoid its taxi service, overpriced at US$20; if you want to take a taxi, just go around the counter to the nearby freestanding city taxi service, which charges US$15 to the center including tolls (avoid taxi touts!). MTL also does transfers from Ezeiza to Aeroparque for US$8.

Real shoestringers can take public bus No 86 into town, which costs US$0.50 and can take up to 1½ hours. Catch it outside the Aerolíneas Argentinas terminal, a short walk from the international terminal.

To get from Aeroparque to the center you can take public buses No 33 or 45 (don't cross the street; take them going south). MTL has shuttles to the center for US$2.75; taxis cost US$3.50.

Bicycle

BA is not a great city for cycling. Traffic is dangerous and hardly respectful toward bicycles; the biggest vehicle wins the right of way, and bikes are low on the totem pole. Still, some spots call out for two-wheeled exploration, such as Palermo's parks and the Reserva Ecológica Costanera Sur; on weekends and some weekdays you can rent bikes at these places (see p81). You can also join city bike tours (p84).

Bus

BA has a huge and complex bus system. If you want to get to know it better, you'll have to buy a *Guia T* (bus guidebook); they're sold at any newsstand, but try to find the pocket version for US$1. Just look at the grids to find out where you are and where you're going, and find a matching bus number. Most routes (but not all) run 24 hours.

Route	Bus No
Microcentro to Palermo Viejo	111
Microcentro to Plaza Italia (in Palermo)	64
Microcentro to Congreso	24
Microcentro to San Telmo	29
Retiro to San Telmo via Plaza de Mayo	22
Retiro to Palermo Viejo	106
Recoleta to La Boca via Congreso & San Telmo	39
Plaza Italia to La Boca via Retiro & Plaza de Mayo	152, 29
Plaza Italia to Constitución via Retiro	59
Once to La Boca via Plaza de Mayo	64

Car

Anyone considering driving in BA should know that most local drivers are reckless, aggressive and even willfully dangerous. They'll ignore speed limits, road signs, road lines and traffic signals. They'll tailgate you mercilessly and honk even before signals turn green. Buses are a nightmare to deal with, and parking can be a bitch. Reconsider your need to have a car in this city; public transport will often get you anywhere cheaper and with much less stress.

If, however, you still want to rent a car, expect to pay around US$35 to US$50 per day. You'll need to be at least 21 years of age and have a valid driver's license; having an international driver's license isn't crucial. You'll need to present a credit card and your passport, though. The following agencies are all in Retiro:

Avis (Map pp64-7; ☎ 4326-5542; www.avis.com.ar in Spanish; Cerrito 1527)

Hertz (Map pp64-7; ☎ 4816-8001; www.hertz.com.ar; Paraguay 1138)

New Way (Map pp64-7; ☎ 4515-0331; www.new-way rentacar.com.ar; Marcelo T de Alvear 773)

Subte (Underground)

BA's Subte opened in 1913 and is the quickest way to get around the city, though it can get mighty hot and crowded during rush hour. It consists of lines (Líneas) A, B, C, D and E, and at time of research a new H line was due to open in 2005. Four parallel lines run from downtown to the capital's western and northern outskirts, while the Línea C runs north–south and connects the two major train stations of Retiro and Constitución.

One-ride magnetic cards for the Subte cost US$0.70. To save time and hassle buy several rides, since queues can get backed up. At some stations platforms are on opposite sides, so make sure of your direction *before* passing through the turnstiles. Trains operate 5am to 10pm Monday to Saturday and 8am to 10pm on Sundays, so don't rely on the Subte to get you home after dinner. Service is frequent on weekdays, but on weekends you'll wait longer.

Taxi & Remise

BA's numerous and cheap taxis are conspicuous by their black-and-yellow paint jobs. Meters start at US$1.44 day or night. Drivers do not expect a big tip, but it's cus-

tomary to let them keep small change. Most rides within the center cost around US$2 to US$4.

Almost all taxi drivers are honest people making a living, but there are a few bad apples in the bunch. Try not to give taxi drivers large bills; not only will they usually not have change, but there have been cases where a driver quickly and deftly replaced a larger bill with a smaller one. One strategy is to state how much you are giving them and ask if they have change for it ('*¿Tienes cambio de un veinte?*' is 'Do you have change for a twenty?').

Be very wary of receiving counterfeit bills; at night have the driver turn on the *luz* (light) so you can carefully check your change (look for a watermark on bills). And make sure you get the right change. Also, if you are obviously a tourist going to or from a touristy spot, don't ask how much the fare is; this makes quoting an upped price tempting, rather than using the meter. And finally, try to have an idea of where you're going, or you might be taking the 'scenic' route (keeping in mind there are many one-way streets). A good way to imply you know where you're going is to give the taxi an intersection rather than a specific address.

Remises look like regular cars and don't have meters. They cost about the same as street taxis but are considered more secure, since an established company sends them out. Most hotels and restaurants will call a *remise* for you.

AROUND BUENOS AIRES

So you've spent days tramping on noisy and busy streets, visiting all the sights and smells of BA. You're ready to get away from the capital and experience something different and more peaceful. Where do you go?

Luckily for you, there are many trips that take you a world away from BA's concrete jungle. Most can be done in a day, but a few are better if you have more time to spare. For something a little different, head across the Rio de la Plata into neighboring Uruguay. Montevideo is a laid-back capital city with a definite change of pace, while the ritzy resort of Punta del Este provides sun, sand and some of the continent's best people-watching.

BUENOS AIRES

TIGRE & THE DELTA

When *porteños* look for a quick weekend getaway from the cement of BA, they beeline to the tranquil riverside suburb of Tigre. The city itself is a pleasant enough place, but it's really the delta just beyond Tigre they're after. Latté-colored waters – rich with iron from the jungle streams flowing from inland Argentina – along with reedy shores are far from any stereotypical paradise, but there are many hidden gems in this marshy region. Boat rides into the delta offer peeks at local stilt houses and colonial mansions, or you can just get off and explore along some peaceful trails. All along the shores are signs of water-related activity, from sailing to kayaking, canoeing to sculling.

Information

Bonanza Deltaventura (☎ 4798-2254; www.delta ventura.com) Offers marshy adventures that include transport from your hotel, breakfast, a two-hour hike, canoe trip and *asado* (barbecue) for US$45.

Ente Municipal de Turismo (☎ 4512-4497; www.tigre .gov.ar; ☼ 9am-5pm) Tigre's top-notch tourist office, located behind McDonald's, will help you sort out the confusing delta region. There's a smaller booth (☎ 4512-4497; ☼ 9am-5pm Fri-Sun) at the train station itself .

Sights & Activities

Tigre itself is very walkable and holds some attractions. Be sure to check out the **Puerto de Frutos** (Sarmiento 160; ☼ 11am-7pm), where vendors sell mostly housewares, wicker baskets and

dried flowers, along with a modest selection of fruits. Weekends are best, when a large crafts fair sets up. Nearby is Tigre's tacky amusement park, **Parque de la Costa** (☎ 4002-6000; www.parquedelacosta.com.ar; adult/child US$7/5; ☼ 11am-midnight Dec-Feb, 11am-7pm Sat, Sun & holidays rest of year).

The **Museo Naval de la Nación** (☎ 4749-0608; Paseo Victorica 602; admission US$0.75; ☼ 8:30am-5:30pm Mon-Fri, 10:30am-6:30pm Sat & Sun) traces the history of the Argentine navy with an eclectic mix of historical photos, model boats and airplanes, artillery displays and pickled sea critters. The **Museo Histórico Prefectura Naval Argentina** (☎ 4749-6161; Liniers 1264; admission free; ☼ 10am-noon & 2-6pm Wed-Sun) has small exhibits on the Argentine coast guard's diving and nautical equipment, WWII radios and model boats, among other things.

The waterways of the delta region offer a glimpse into how locals live along the peaceful canals, with boats as their only transportation. Frequent commuter launches leave from Estación Fluvial (located behind the tourist office) for various destinations in the delta for US$2.25 to US$3.50 round-trip. A popular destination is the **Tres Bocas neighborhood**, a half-hour boat ride from Tigre where you can take residential walks on narrow paths connected by bridges over narrow channels.

A few companies offer guided tours of the delta region; these all cost US$2 to US$5 and take one to two hours.

Sleeping

Reservations are highly recommended on weekends; breakfast is included at most places. The following places are in Tigre itself.

B&B Escariza (☎ 4749-2499; www.casonalaruchi.com.ar) Lavalle 557; s/d US$20/28) This homey, family-run B&B is in an 1893 mansion. Most of the five romantic bedrooms have balconies; all have shared bathrooms with original tiled floors. There's a pool and large garden out back.

Villa Julia (☎ 4749-0242; www.newage-hotels.com; Paseo Victoria 800; s/d US$47/94;) The seven rooms are all different at this gorgeous mansion, where original tilework, large balconies and thick robes make for a very special stay. The atmosphere is lovely, and there's a swimming pool and restaurant.

Things are much more peaceful in the delta. Prices listed following are for weekends; weekday stays can be half-off. Meals are usually included. Check with the tourist office for many more choices (including houses to rent).

Alpenhaus (☎ 4731-4526; www.alpenhaus.com.ar; d from US$97;) A 60-minute boat ride from Tigre. This German-themed *hostería* (lodging house) offers three large, modern alpine-style *cabañas* (US$140) along with more modest but still pleasant rooms. There's a great pool and grassy lounging areas; the food is Eastern-European inspired.

Atelier (☎ 4731-3532; www.cabaniasatelier.com.ar in Spanish; d from US$60;) An 80-minute boat ride from Tigre. The cute stilted *cabañas* are fully stocked, while the grassy grounds (which include a swimming pool) are quite pleasant enough. It's a good place for families, with games available for the kids.

Los Pecanes (☎ 4728-1932; www.hosterialospecanes.com; d from US$40) A 90-minute boat ride from Tigre. You'll feel right at home at this friendly family-run B&B with just three simple but comfortable guest rooms. The homemade meals are healthy, the garden is lovely and there are activities to keep you entertained.

Getting There & Away

Tigre, 28km from BA, has two train stations. Either take the Mitre train line from Retiro train station (US$0.35) or take the Mitre train line to Mitre station, which is right at Tren de la Costa's Maipú station; this is a very pleasant train ride that ends near Tigre's Puerto de Frutos (US$0.50 Monday to Friday and US$1 Saturday and Sunday).

Bus No 59, 152 and 60 also go to Maipú station. The No 60 should be marked Panamericana, Alto, Bajo or Escobar. The Panamericana is the fastest. It costs US$0.50 and takes one to 1½ hours.

COLONIA (URUGUAY)

☎ 52 / pop 29,000

Charming and quaint are words often used to describe this idyllic little getaway from BA. On summer weekends, hundreds of Argentines descend upon Colonia to escape the searing city heat, walk the tranquil cobbled streets and enjoy the spectacular sunsets. And despite the fact that Colonia is located in neighboring Uruguay, frequent ferries make it easy to access from Argentina – even if you only have a day.

Information

All of Colonia's museums are open from 11am to 5pm daily; one US$0.50 ticket gives you admission to all. The main **tourist office** (☎ 26141; General Flores 499; 8am-7pm Mon-Fri, 9am-7pm Sat & Sun) has a hotel reservation office next door (same contact information) that will help travelers find accommodation. There's also a tourist office at the **ferry port** (☎ 24897; 9am-9pm but varies) and another at **Manuel de Lobos and San Miguel** (☎ 28506; 9am-6pm), near the Puerta de Campo.

CROSSING INTO URUGUAY

Traveling from BA into Uruguay is fairly easy and straightforward, but you'll need a valid passport. Nationals of Western Europe, the USA, Canada, Australia and New Zealand will receive a tourist card on entry, which is valid for 90 days. Other nationals require visas. It's wise to check the current visa situation during your tenure, however, as this information can change in the blink of an eye.

Uruguay's unit of currency is the peso, but US dollars and Argentine pesos are widely accepted for tourist services.

Uruguay's telephone country code is ☎ 598. The country is one hour ahead of Argentina, but daylight saving may affect time differences.

Sights

The city's heart – and main tourist attraction – is the Barrio Histórico, a historical neighborhood that doubles as a Unesco world cultural heritage site. It's full of colonial architecture and worthy sights, starting with the **Puerta de Campo** (1745) on Calle Manuel de Lobos, the restored entrance to the old city. A short distance west is **Plaza Mayor 25 de Mayo**, off which the narrow and roughly cobbled Calle de los Suspiros (Street of Sighs), lined with tile-and-stucco colonial houses, runs south almost to the water. Just beyond this street is the **Museo Portugués** (Plaza Mayor 25 de Mayo 180), which has good exhibits on the Portuguese period, including Lusitanian and colonial dress.

Off the southwestern corner of the Plaza Mayor are the ruins of the 17th-century **Convento de San Francisco**, within which stands the 19th-century **faro** (lighthouse). At the western end of the Plaza Mayor, on Calle del Comercio, is the **Museo Municipal** (Plaza Mayor 25 de Mayo 77). Kitty-corner to the museum, on the northwestern edge of the plaza, is the **Archivo Regional** (Calle de las Misiones de los Tapes 115), which contains a small museum and bookshop.

Head to the western end of Misiones de los Tapes to the dinky **Museo del Azulejo** (tile museum), a 17th-century house with a sampling of colonial tilework. From there, the riverfront Paseo de San Gabriel leads north to **Plazoleta San Martín**. Turn east and you will reach Av General Flores; continue east a block and turn south on Calle Vasconcellos to reach the landmark **Iglesia Matriz** on the shady **Plaza de Armas**, also known as Plaza Manuel Lobo. The church, begun in 1680, is Uruguay's oldest, though it has been completely rebuilt twice. The plaza holds the foundations of a house dating from Portuguese times.

Heading back north to Av General Flores and then beyond it a block further north brings you near the **Museo Español** (San José 164), which has exhibitions of replica colonial pottery, clothing and maps. At the northern end of nearby Calle España is the **Puerto Viejo** (old port), now a yacht harbor. One block east, at Calle del Virrey Cevallos and Rivadavia, the **Teatro Bastión del Carmen** is a theater and gallery complex that incorporates part of the city's ancient fortifications. The huge chimney is newer, dating from the 1880s.

Sleeping

Rates skyrocket and reservations are crucial on summer weekends and during Argentine holidays. If you're stuck, the hotel reservation office next to the main tourist office can help. Most places include breakfast.

Posada Manuel de Lobo (☎ 22463; www.colonianet.com/posadamdelobo; Ituzaingó 160; US$35/45; **P** 🛇) Gorgeous, well-appointed rooms with modern bathrooms, wood floors and old-time charm are available at this well-located spot. Superiors are huge and include Jacuzzi tub (US$50 to US$65).

La Posada del Gobernador (☎ 22918; www.hotelleoncia.com in Spanish; 18 de Julio 205; s/d US$35/45; **P** 🛇) Its colonial architecture and location in the Barrio Histórico make for a decent stay. Rooms have charm, and most open to a patio or balcony. There's a peaceful garden and swimming pool in back.

Posada del Río (☎ 23002; www.colonianet.com/delrio in Spanish; Washington Barbot 258; s/d US$12/17; 🛇) This serene and friendly place, on a tree-lined street close to a pleasant sandy beach, offers 11 small, modest and intimate rooms (get one inside around the courtyard).

Hostal Colonial (☎ 30347; hostelling_colonial@hotmail.com; Av General Flores 440; dm US$6; d US$12-16; 🖳) Good courtyard rooms line this old building; out of five doubles, two have private bathroom. There is kitchen use and free bike rentals, and horse rides can be organized.

Eating

El Drugstore (☎ 25241; Vasconcellos 179; mains US$4-10) Vivid colors and funky modern-art reproductions decorate this creative eatery. Tasty food includes grilled salmon, ñoquis with mussel sauce and abundant salads. There's live music almost nightly.

Pulpería de los Faroles (☎ 30271; Misiones de los Tapes 101; mains US$3-7) Set in the Barrio Histórico, this upscale spot has brick walls, colorful chairs and cartwheel chandeliers. Food ranges from seafood to pastas to meats, but the menu is limited.

Viejo Barrio (☎ 25399; Vasconcellos 169; mains US$3-7) This pleasant restaurant on Plaza de Armas is popular for its exceptional homemade pasta dishes. The menu is small but effective, and service is good.

Getting There & Away

Colonia is 60km from BA and it takes one to two hours to get there by ferry.

Buquebus (in Colonia ☎ 22919, in Buenos Aires ☎ 011-4316-6500; www.buquebus.com) has both fast (US$30 one way) and slow (US$13 to US$17 one way) ferries to Colonia. Ferryturismo is part of Buquebus and has identical prices.

MONTEVIDEO (URUGUAY)
☎ 2 / pop 1.3 million

Montevideo is probably South America's most laid-back capital. Population is only 1.3 million, but many of these folks are students and young workers, and they give the city a lively buzz. It also has a decidedly European feel, thanks to a large influx of Spanish and Italian immigrants who arrived during the late 19th and early 20th centuries.

Information
Alliance Française (☎ 408-6012; www.alianzafrancesa .edu.uy; 18 de Julio 1772; ☽ 8am-7:30pm) A well-stocked library with books, magazines and CDs. Short-term visitors can avoid membership fees by paying a US$50 refundable deposit.
Municipal tourist office (☎ 903-0649; Palacio Municipal; ☽ 10am-6pm Mon-Fri, 11am-6pm Sat & Sun) Small but well informed.
Oficina de Informes (☎ 409-7399; ☽ 9am-9pm) Well-equipped; located at the bus terminal.

Sights
Montevideo lies on the east bank of the Río de la Plata. Its key commercial and entertainment area is Av 18 de Julio, but its functional center is **Plaza Independencia**. It's here that you'll find the somber yet dramatic **Mausoleo de Artigas** (admission free; ☽ 9am-5pm), which celebrates the achievements of Uruguay's independence hero; look for stairs underneath the statue of Artigas on horseback.

Just a block west of the plaza is the **Museo Torres García** (☎ 916-2663; Sarandí 683; admission free; ☽ 9am-8pm Mon-Fri), a gallery devoted to Joaquín Torres García (1874–1949). One of Uruguay's most famous artists, García progressed from a fairly conventional landscape painter to a more abstract artist.

Three blocks east of the plaza is the **Museo del Gaucho y de la Moneda** (☎ 900-8764; 18 de Julio 998; admission free; ☽ 10am-5pm Mon-Fri), located in the Banco de la República. This is a split-personality museum; half economy-related and half gaucho frenzy.

Most of Montevideo's grand 19th-century neoclassical buildings – legacies of the beef boom – have all but crumbled, but vestiges of a colonial past still exist in the **Ciudad**

SECURITY IN MONTEVIDEO

Montevideo is sedate by most standards, but street crime is on the rise. Take the usual precautions, especially in the Ciudad Vieja, which can be dangerous at night. If you want to report a crime, contact the **tourist police** (☎ 908-9015; Plaza Entrevero).

Vieja, the city's picturesque historic center. Museums here include the **Museo de Arte Decorativo** (☎ 915-1101; 25 de Mayo 376; admission free; ☽ 12:15-6pm Tue-Sat, 2-6pm Sun), which was once the home of a wealthy merchant. It's full of baroque knickknacks like gilded housewares, tapestries, sculptures, ornate pianos and fancy chandeliers.

Toward the ferry terminal, at the corner of Castellano and Piedras, is the **Mercado del Puerto**. This 1868 wrought-iron superstructure shelters a gaggle of reasonably priced *parrillas* and upmarket seafood restaurants. It's a lively, colorful spot where artists, craftspeople and street musicians hang out, especially on Saturday afternoons.

East of Montevideo's downtown, the riverfront **Rambla** leads past residential suburbs and sandy **beaches** frequented by Montevideanos in summer and on weekends; catch bus No 64, which goes from 18 de Julio along the coast road – the beaches get better the further out of town you go.

Sleeping
Hotel NH Columbia (☎ 916-0001; www.nh-hotels.com; Rambla Gran Bretaña 473; d US$90; P ✷ ▣ ▨) This minimally decorated (think chrome and abstract art) hotel sits right on the Rambla and the front rooms have great views over the water. Rooms are comfortable and spacious with all the mod cons you'd expect for the price. Rates can almost halve during the off-season and midweek; be sure to ask for discounts.

Hotel Lafayette (☎ 902-4646; www.lafayette.com .uy; Soriano 1170; s/d US$28/36; P ✷ ▨) The Lafayette's rooms are a good deal, but the location is the real winner. If you can get a room with a view of the river you'll be more than happy. Facilities include a gym, sauna, Jacuzzi and babysitting service.

Hotel Solís (☎ 915-0279; Bartolomé Mitre 1314; s & d US$16, s/d with shared bathroom US$7/12) A longstanding budget choice in the old town, the Solís offers ageing but neat rooms, all with balconies overlooking the street. Rooms with private bathroom also have cable TV, and are one of the better budget deals in town.

Red Hostel (☎ 908-8514; www.redhostel.com; San José 1406; dm/s/d US$7/15/18; 🖳) This cool new hostel is located in an old mansion with many of the walls painted in red hues. Dorms are clean and spacious and there's a pleasant rooftop patio. Kitchen access, and fireplace in common room.

Hotel London Palace (☎ 902-0024; www.lphotel .com; Rio Negro 1278; s/d US$30/35; 🅿 😵) With its antique furniture, hall runners and modern rooms that manage to retain a vestige of style, the London Palace is a step above the rest in this price range.

Pensión Nuevo Ideal (☎ 908-2913; Soriano 1073; d with shared/private bathroom US$3.50/7) The lobby of this attractive little hotel is a good indication of what's in store: there's plenty of light, the place is spotless and the decor is tasteful yet restrained. Blasting hot showers are an added bonus.

Eating

For good local atmosphere check out the Mercado del Puerto (p113).

Arcadia Restaurant (☎ 902-0111; Radisson Hotel, Plaza Independencia; mains US$7-12) The views are reason enough to eat here, though it's also great for some of the most imaginative food in town, mixing Uruguayan, Italian and Japanese influences. Cheap burgers are also available.

Café Sucré Salé (☎ 408-6012; 18 de Julio 1772; mains US$2-4) Run by a real live French chef, this place in the Alliance Française has excellent breakfasts (brioche!) and a shady courtyard area with tinkling fountain.

El Rincón de las Poetas (cnr Aquiles Lanza & San José; set meals US$3-5) Classic Uruguayan dishes are on offer at this spot in the Mercado de la Abundancia, which can make for an atmospheric meal with its wrought iron and old-time feel.

La Vegetariana (☎ 901-6418; Rio Negro 1311; mains US$2-3.50) Pay at the front, grab a plate and help yourself from the vegetarian steam trays, which include polenta, noodles, ravioli, rice, squash and more. Browse the salad bar as well, then hit the desserts.

Restaurante de los Vascos (☎ 902-3519; San José 1168; mains US$2-5) An excellent selection of Basque and Spanish dishes are on offer here,

as is the best paella in town. Cheap *jarras* (jugs) of red wine are bound to keep you hanging around.

Getting There & Away

Montevideo is 220km from BA. There are daily 35-minute flights with Pluna/Varig, LAPA and Aerolíneas (p473); note the US$8 departure tax from BA. Buses to or from Montevideo airport cost US$0.70 and take 40 minutes; taxis are US$7.

To get to Montevideo by boat, **Buquebus** (cnr Dársena Norte & Av Córdoba 879) has *buqueaviones* (high-speed ferries) with daily departures (US$52, 2½ to three hours). Ferryturismo has bus-ferry combinations via Colonia (US$32, four hours).

There are also buses daily from BA's Retiro bus terminal (US$20 to US$26, eight hours).

PUNTA DEL ESTE (URUGUAY)

☎ 42 / pop 1200

'Punta' – with its many beaches, elegant seaside homes, yacht harbor, high-rise apartments and upscale hotels and restaurants – is one of South America's most glamorous resorts. In summer – when prices skyrocket and rooms are hard to find – the well-heeled hordes of BA overrun the hot sands and concrete. Famous celebrities and models come for photo shoots, while beach bunnies sun themselves from sunrise to sunset.

Punta has a main **tourist office** (☎ 46519; cnr Rambla Artigas & Calle 31; ☽ 8am-midnight) along with one at the **bus terminal** (☎ 494042; ☽ 8am-9pm) and another at Av Gorlero 942 (☎ 441218; ☽ 9am-10pm).

Sights & Activities

Punta's center is very walkable: you can casually stroll from one end to the other in less than a half hour. Close to the center on the Río de la Plata side of the peninsula is Playa Mansa, whose calm sands attract more families and low-key beachgoers. Playa Brava is on the east side but less than a five-minute walk away; it has a more active crowd and boasts fierce waves that claim a few lives each year, so be careful when swimming here.

The best beaches are a short bus ride away. Stretching up the northeast is a run of sand that ends 10km away at **La Barra** and **Bikini Beach**, where discos and hip shops attract the trendy crowds and the people-watching can't be beat. Heading up the northwest are more beaches that end 15km away at **Punta Ballena**, whose main tourist attraction is **Casapueblo** (☎ 578041; admission US$3; ☼ 9am-sunset). This free-form, neo-Mediterranean structure (a luxury hotel/restaurant/art gallery) was inspired by Uruguayan artist Carlos Páez Vilaró and boasts unforgettable views; buses drop you at a junction 2km away.

Sleeping

Budget accommodations in Punta are limited; reservations are crucial in summer. All prices below are for the summer high season; low-season prices drop by 25% to 50%. Breakfast is included at all hotels.

Hotel Remanso (☎ 447412; www.hotelremanso.com.uy in Spanish; cnr Calle 20 & Esq 28; d US$125-140; ⓟ ⌘ 🖳 🐾) Good, comfortable, modern rooms are on offer at this upscale hotel (superiors come with Jacuzzi tub). Facilities include attractive lobby, gym, conference room and rooftop swimming pool.

Palace Hotel (☎ 441919; palacepunta@hotmail.com; cnr Gorlero & Esq 11; s/d US$50/75; ⓟ 🖳 🐾) This three-star hotel has acceptable rooms, but is probably best for its colonial-style interior grassy garden, complete with pool. There's an Italian restaurant on the premises, the lobby is pleasant and pets are accepted.

1949 Hostel (☎ 440719; www.1949hostel.com; cnr Calles 18 & 30; dm US$15; 🖳) A new kid on the block, this hostel is close to the bus terminal and offers good dorm rooms that include locker use, breakfast and sea views. There's a kitchen for guest use, a common room with videos, and surfboards for rent. One double with private bathroom is available (US$50, reserve in advance).

Hotel Azul (☎ 441117; hotelzul@adinet.com.uy; Av Gorlero 540; s/d US$80/90; ⓟ ⌘) Big, comfortable rooms with nonoffensive decor are available at this modern hotel toward the end of the peninsula. Bathrooms are a decent size, but don't expect good views.

Hotel Marbella (☎ 441814; www.hotelmarbella.8m.com; Calle 31, No 615; s/d US$39/55; ⌘ 🖳) Close to the terminal, this decent hotel has clean, quiet and good-sized rooms, some with ocean peeks. Fridges are included, and rooms Nos 105 and 106 have small patios where pets can stay.

Residencial 32 (☎ 493506; Calle 32, No 640; s/d US$20/35) Twenty-two basic but tidy budget rooms await at this no-nonsense place. Halls

are hard-edged and there's no carpet anywhere to soften the edges, but it's cheap and right next to the bus terminal.

El Hostal (☎ 441632; albergues@hostellinguruguay.org; Calle 25, No 544; dm US$10) This small hostel has good four- to six-bed dorms and a small common room up front. There's a side patio for warm-weather days and a tiny kitchen for heating water only (no cooking).

Eating

Restaurant hours are more limited outside summer, with some places opening only on weekends.

Lo de Tere (☎ 440492; cnr Rambla Artigas & Calle 21; mains US$9-20) The surroundings aren't too impressive at this upscale restaurant, but the emotionally expressive menu has international flair. Dishes run the well-trod gamut of chicken, lamb, seafood and beef, but there's mushroom risotto and pasta for the vegetarians.

Blue Cheese (☎ 446633; Calle 20, No 717; mains US$7-9.50) Pastas, seafood and meats dominate the menu at this very popular waterside restaurant (be prepared to wait). The salad bar is an added plus and there's a nice patio out front.

El Mejillón (☎ 445895; cnr Rambla Artigas & Calle 11; mains US$5.50-13) This large, modern restaurant is surrounded by an extensive outdoor patio and water views. Seven types of *chivito*, the national dish, are available; this is a steak topped with healthy things like lettuce, bacon, fried egg and potato salad. Lots of seafood, meats and pasta are also on the menu.

El Pobre Marino (☎ 443306; Calle 11, No 694; mains US$5-7.50) The menu is short and uncomplicated, but the seafood is excellent. Order the mussels a la provençal for starters, then head to the grilled fish with garlic. Paella, homemade pasta and seafood stew are other choices, while a seafaring theme puts it all in perspective.

Getting There & Away

Punta del Este is 360km from BA. There are daily flights (45 minutes) with Pluna, LAPA and Aerolíneas (p473); note the US$8 departure tax from BA. Daily buses leave from BA's Retiro bus terminal (US$30, 10 hours); many buses connect with Montevideo (US$5, two hours). Punta's bus station is right near the center. Bus-boat combinations are available with Buquebus via Colonia or Montevideo.

The Pampas & the Atlantic Coast

Some of Argentina's classic imagery comes from this relatively small but geographically diverse region. In the eyes of many, Argentina outside of Buenos Aires *is* the Pampas, and while this is far from the truth, there's no doubt that the rolling green grasslands have played a major part in both the history and culture of the country.

This is where the gaucho came into being, that romantic, independent cowboy figure whose legend lives on in the Argentine national psyche. It's also, of course, cattle country, and you'll see enough of them dotted around the countryside, munching on the lush grass, fattening themselves up for the trip to a *parrilla* (mixed grill) near you.

The coastline is where *porteños* (inhabitants of Buenos Aires) come to play in the summer months, when the city empties out and resort towns like Mar del Plata, Necochea and Pinamar shake off their off-season tranquillity and spring to life.

There's more here than just beef and beaches, though. Out west are rolling hills covered in caldén forests, deserts which are home to flamingo-dotted salt lakes, and extensive native grasslands. Those looking to cool off can hit the mountains in Tandil or the peaceful (except for absolute peak season) hamlet of Sierra de la Ventana. Parque Nacional Lihué Calel is hard (but not impossible) to get to, which adds to its appeal – some days you might have it to yourself. It's worth a stop to see the amazing biodiversity that can exist in a near-desert environment.

Culture vultures shouldn't miss the mellow town of San Antonio de Areco, which is ground zero for gaucho culture, and maintains many traditions rarely seen in the rest of the country. Also worth a look-in is colonial Luján, one of South America's most important religious centers.

TOP FIVE

- Cooling it in leafy **Sierra de la Ventana** (p131)
- Hitting the beach and bars in **Mar del Plata** (p136)
- Getting away from it all in **Villa Gesell** (p143)
- Going gaucho in **San Antonio de Areco** (p123)
- Hanging with the armadillos in **Parque Nacional Lihué Calel** (p135)

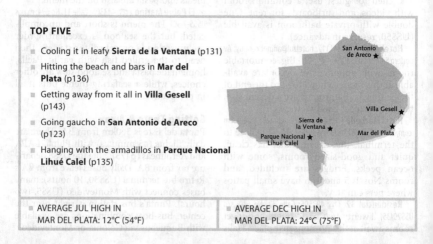

San Antonio de Areco ★

Villa Gesell ★

Sierra de la Ventana ★

Mar del Plata ★

Parque Nacional Lihué Calel ★

- AVERAGE JUL HIGH IN MAR DEL PLATA: 12°C (54°F)
- AVERAGE DEC HIGH IN MAR DEL PLATA: 24°C (75°F)

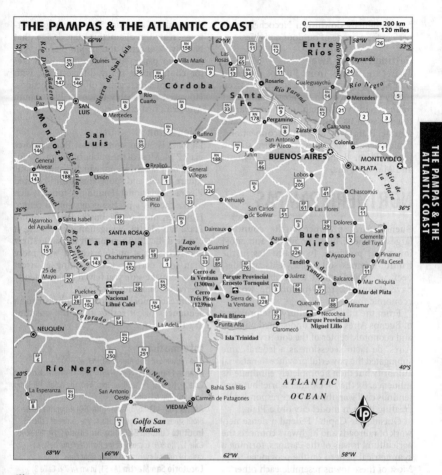

Climate

Temperatures on the Pampas fluctuate wildly through the year, with lows as low as 6°C below zero and highs as high as 38°C, although such extremes are rare and the temperature is generally comfortable. Summer is great for the beach, of course, while spring sees wildflowers blooming and fall is characterized by the yellows and ochres of falling leaves.

The region is divided into two main climactic zones: the Wet (or Humid) Pampas along the coast, where much of the rain falls, and the Dry Pampas, which is out toward the west. There can be as much as 1000mm of rainfall per year (mostly falling heavily on a few days, as opposed to being spread out through the year), although drought is the largest single problem for farmers in the region.

National & Provincial Parks

The Pampas and coast are home to a small but excellent selection of protected areas. The Parque Provincial Ernesto Tornquist (p133) is a hikers' paradise, where you can scale the peaks of Cerro de la Ventana (1136m) or check out the stunning Garganta del Diablo (Devil's Throat) gorge. Parque Nacional Lihué Calel (p135) is set in a near-desert landscape with surreal granite rock formations and is home to nearly half the province's animal species. More modest Parque Provincial Miguel Lillo (p148) is a leafy haven right by downtown Necochea that's perfect for a range of outdoor activities.

Getting There & Away

There are flights from Buenos Aires to Bahía Blanca and Mar del Plata. Buses from nearly every town run to most destinations in the country although, of course, larger towns (such as Santa Rosa, La Plata and Mar del Plata) will have better connections. Trains depart Buenos Aires' Retiro station for La Plata, Bahía Blanca, Villa Ventana and Mar del Plata.

NORTHERN PAMPAS

Buenos Aires province is the country's largest, richest, most populous and most important province. Its wealth lies in the fruitful Pampas soil; high yields of hides, beef, wool and wheat for global markets have stamped Argentina on the world's economic map.

From the mid-19th century, the province of Buenos Aires was the undisputed political and economic center of the country. Buenos Aires' de facto secession as a federal zone subjugated the powerful province to national authority but didn't completely eliminate its influence. By the 1880s, after a brief but contentious civil war, the province responded by creating its own model city of La Plata.

Outside the Capital Federal a dense network of railroads and highways connects the agricultural towns of the Pampas, forming a symmetrical pattern on the provincial map. Most of these towns resemble each other as much as any part of the endlessly flat Pampas resembles another.

LA PLATA

☎ 0221 / pop 857,800

An easy day trip from Buenos Aires, this bustling university city offers visitors a gorgeous cathedral and one of Argentina's best natural-history museums. There's also an interesting history to its perfect grid layout.

When Buenos Aires became Argentina's new capital, Governor Dardo Rocha founded La Plata in 1882 to give the province of Buenos Aires its own top city. After detailed study, Rocha chose engineer Pedro Benoit's elaborate city plan, which was based upon balance and logic. The superposition of

diagonals on a regular 5km-square grid pattern created a distinctive star design that handily connected the major plazas. Very pretty on paper, this blueprint now makes for confusion at many intersections, with up to eight streets going off in all directions. However, it probably made La Plata South America's first completely planned city.

Orientation

La Plata is 56km southeast of Buenos Aires via RP 14. Most of the public buildings are located on Plaza Moreno, which occupies four square blocks and sports the graffiti-covered Piedra Fundacional (Founding Stone), which marks the city's precise geographical center. However, most of the bustle occurs around Plaza San Martín. Navigation is confusing: it can be difficult to remain on the same street after crossing at an intersection with more than four corners; keep looking at street signs to make sure you haven't inadvertently veered off onto another street.

On each block, address numbers run in sequences of 50 rather than the customary 100.

Information

ACA (Automóvil Club Argentina; ☎ 482-9040)

Alianza Francesa (☎ 483-1616; alianzaf@netverk.com.ar; Calle 59, No 626; ☼ 8:30am-1pm Wed, Thu & Sat, 2-8:30pm Mon-Fri) Cultural center.

Asatej (☎ 483-8673; Calle 5, No 990) Argentina's non-profit student travel agency. It's at the corner of Calle 53.

Instituto Cultural Británico-Argentino (☎ 489-9690; Calle 12, No 869) Located off the Plaza Moreno; hosts occasional cultural events and Friday night films.

Locutorio San Martín (Av 51, btwn Av 7 & Calle 8) Serves as a telephone office. Is also a *cartelera*, offering discount tickets to local entertainment events.

Municipal tourist office (Entidad Municipal de Turismo; ☎ 427-1535; www.laplata.gov.ar; ☼ 10am-1pm, 2-5pm Mon-Fri, 10am-6pm Sat & Sun) Just off Plaza San Martín.

Post office (cnr Calle 4 & Av 51)

Sights

La Plata's main sights are all within walking distance. Near Plaza Moreno is the beautiful neo-Gothic **cathedral** (☎ 427-3504), which was begun in 1885 but not inaugurated until 1932. The cathedral was inspired by medieval predecessors in Cologne and Amiens, and has fine stained glass and polished granite floors; tours are US$1.50 and include an elevator ride to the top.

LA PLATA

THE PAMPAS & THE ATLANTIC COAST

Opposite the cathedral is the **Palacio Municipal**, designed in German Renaissance style by Hanoverian architect Hubert Stiers. On the west side of the plaza, the **Museo y Archivo Dardo Rocha** (☎ 427-5591; Calle 50, No 933; admission free; ⏰ 9am-6pm Mon-Fri) was the vacation house of the city's creator and contains period furniture and many of his personal knickknacks.

Three blocks northeast, the monstrous **Teatro Argentino** (☎ 0800-666-5151) looms in a strange architectural form, but boasts great acoustics for opera, ballet and symphonies. Two blocks further northeast, in front of Plaza San Martín, is the ornate **Palacio de la Legislatura** (☎ 422-0081), also in German Renaissance style. Nearby, catch the French

Classic **Pasaje Dardo Rocha**, once La Plata's main railroad station and now the city's major cultural center, containing four museums. Also close by is the Flemish Renaissance **Casa de Gobierno**, housing the provincial governor and his retinue. And over to the northwest a few blocks are the original buildings of the **Rectorado de la Universidad Nacional** (1905), which was once a bank but is now the university administrative offices. On Sundays, have a look at the crafts fair **Feria Artesanal** on Plaza Italia.

Plantations of eucalyptus, gingko, palm and subtropical hardwoods cover **Paseo del Bosque**, parkland which was expropriated from an *estancia* (ranch) at the time of the city's founding. It attracts a collection of strolling families, sports-playing fanatics, smooching lovers and sweaty joggers. You'll find various interesting sights strewn within, such as the **Anfiteatro Martín Fierro** (marked Teatro de Aire Libre), an open-air facility that hosts music and drama performances; the **Observatorio Astronómico** (☎ 423-6593; ☼ 9am-4:30pm Mon-Fri); the modest **Jardín Zoológico** (☎ 427-3925; admission US$0.75; ☼ 9am-6pm); and the **Museo de Ciencias Naturales** (☎ 425-7744; admission US$1; ☼ 10am-6pm). Hugely popular with school groups, this notable museum has paleontological, zoological, archaeological and anthropological collections of lifetime director Francisco P Moreno, the famous Patagonian explorer. Four stories and countless display rooms offer something for everyone: Egyptian tomb relics, Jesuit art, amusing taxidermy, amazing skeletons, dried-out mummies, ancient pottery, scary insects and reconstructed dinosaurs (find the milodón stool). Its exterior mixes Corinthian columns, Ionic posterior walls and Hellenic windows with Aztec- and Inca-style embellishments. Free tours in Spanish are given at 2pm and 4pm from Tuesday to Friday, and on Saturdays and Sundays there are seven daily. Call a week or two in advance for an English tour (these cost US$3 per person).

Sleeping

Howard Johnson Corregidor (☎ 425-6800; www .hotelcorregidor.com.ar; Calle 6, No 1026; s/d from US$42; P ▣) Modern rooms here hold no surprises: they're pleasant and comfortable and what you'd expect from a HoJos. Some have patios, and the presidential suite is something special (US$85). There's a tiny gym for working out.

Hotel García (Calle 2, No 525; s/d US$8/12) Friendly and clean, this budget place offers 15 small, basic rooms, some of which face an outdoor hallway. Showers are open so everything in the bathroom gets wet – but the cable TV makes up for it. There's no telephone, but it's close to the bus and train stations.

Benevento Hotel (☎ 423-7721; www.hotelbene vento.com.ar in Spanish; Calle 2, No 645; s/d US$18/28; ▨ ▣) This wonderfully renovated old-style hotel offers high ceilings, wood-floored rooms and tasteful decor. Singles are tiny, but doubles are fairly comfortable. All outside rooms have balconies, though they overlook a busy intersection.

Eating & Drinking

La Trattoría (☎ 422-6135; cnr Calles 10 & 47; mains US$3-5) Over by Diagonal 74, this hip and modern eatery is a popular place for pizza, pasta and sandwiches. Watch sports on the two large, but not overbearing, video screens, or head outside and have a seat at a sidewalk table – very pleasant in warm weather.

Confitería París (☎ 482-8840; cnr Av 7 & Calle 49; mains US$2-4; ☼ 7:30am-10pm; ✗) Popular with tea-sipping locals, this large, modern café also offers plenty of breakfast and lunch items like omelettes, sandwiches, salads, burgers and pizza; desserts are elaborate. A massive pastry counter serves those looking for take-out.

Cervicería Modelo (☎ 421-1321; cnr Calles 5 & 54; mains US$3-5; ☼ 8am-2:30am) An excellent old-time atmosphere makes the peanut-shell-strewn floor fit right in with the hanging hams, while sidewalk tables filled with happy patrons makes enjoying your drink or meal a genuine local experience. The only bow to modern times is a large TV screen for sports fans.

Wilkenny (☎ 483-1772; cnr Calles 11 & 50; US$3-7; ☼ 9am-2am Sun-Wed, 9am-6am Thu-Sat) With such treats as Irish stew and wild boar or rabbit, washed down with a Sam Smith or Guinness, this pub makes a great stop for either drinking or eating. Dark wood booths and good music are other pluses.

Entertainment

There are a few movie theaters, such as **Cine Ocho** (☎ 482-5554; Calle 8, No 981) and **Cine San Martín** (☎ 483-9947; Av 7, No 923).

Getting There & Away

Vía Sur's bus No 129 leaves every 20 minutes from Buenos Aires (US$1.50, 1½ hours). Catch them in front of Retiro train station on Martín Zuviría; the bus makes stops along Av 9 de Julio and at Constitución train station (which has frequent trains to La Plata for US$0.50, 1¼ hours). La Plata's bus terminal has plenty of connections to other parts of Argentina.

LUJÁN

☎ 0232 / pop 78,200

Luján is a peaceful, religious tourist town with a large number of stores and rolling carts selling devotional souvenirs. The streets are lined with orange and palm trees and are very walkable, there's a leafy, elevated riverside area full of restaurants and more shops, and paddleboats are available for a leisurely cruise on the river.

According to legend, in 1630 an ox-drawn wagon containing a small terracotta statue of the Virgin Mary suddenly got stuck on the road and would not budge until the image was removed. The wagon was heading to Santiago del Estero, but the devoted owner took this pause as a sign and built a chapel on the site. 'La Virgencita' soon became Argentina's patron saint, and she's since upgraded her quarters into Luján's striking French Gothic Basilica Nuestra Señora de Luján.

In early October a massive pilgrimage originates in Buenos Aires' barrio of Liniers. Thousands of pilgrims *walk* the 65km stretch, which can take 18 hours – it can be an incredible sight. Other large gatherings occur on April 21, May 8 (the Virgin's day), the third week of November and December 8 (Immaculate Conception Day).

Orientation & Information

Luján is around 65km west of Buenos Aires on RN 7. Most places of interest are near the basilica, though Plaza Colón, five blocks southeast via Calle San Martín, is another center of activity.

Post office (Mitre 575)

Tourist kiosk (cnr Lavalle & 9 de Julio; ☾ 10am-6pm Mon-Fri, 9am-8pm Sat & Sun)

Tourist office (☎ 420453; ☾ 8am-6pm Mon-Fri, 9am-7pm Sat & Sun) Near the river at the west end of Lavalle, down from La Recova restaurant.

Sights

BASÍLICA NUESTRA SEÑORA DE LUJÁN

Every year five million pilgrims from throughout Argentina visit Luján to honor the Virgin for her intercession in affairs of peace, health, forgiveness and consolation. The terminus of their journeys is this imposing **basilica** (☎ 420058; tours US$0.35; ☾ every 30 min from 10am-5pm Mon-Fri, 10am-6pm Sat & Sun), whose hallowed halls are lined with confession boxes just before you reach the 'Virgencita,' who occupies a high chamber behind the main altar. Devotees have lined the stairs with plaques acknowledging her favors. Under the basilica you can tour a **crypt** (US$1; every 30 min) that harbors virgin statues from all over the world. Masses take place in the basilica several times a day, mostly morning and evening.

Within the basilica, Irish visitors in particular will be interested to find Gaelic inscriptions, Irish surnames and a window dedicated to St Patrick.

COMPLEJO MUSEOGRÁFICO ENRIQUE UDAONDO

This gorgeous colonial-era **museum complex** (☎ 420245; admission US$0.65; ☾ noon-6pm Wed-Fri, 10am-6pm Sat & Sun & holidays) rambles with display rooms, pretty patios, gardens and tiled outdoor walkways. The Sala General Jose de San Martín showcases Argentina's battles for independence with historic etchings, presidential bios and period items. The Sala de Gaucho contains some beautiful *mate* ware, ponchos, horse gear, guitars and other gaucho paraphernalia, as well as a reconstruction of Ricardo Güiraldes' (author of *Don Segundo Sombra*; 1886–1927) study. There's a Federal-era room, outlining Juan Manuel de Rosas' exploits (and some major anti-unitarian sentiment), the 'conquest' of the desert (essentially the conquest of Patagonia's indigenous people) and more period items including huge and nifty hair combs. Near the entry to the complex you'll also see a room portraying an old prison chamber, as the *cabildo* (town council) building used to be a prison.

The nearby **Museo de Transporte** (☎ 420245; admission US$0.35; ☾ noon-6pm Wed-Fri, 10am-6pm Sat, Sun & holidays) has a remarkable collection of horse-pulled carriages from the late 1800s, including some truly fit for Cinderella. Also on display are a 'popemobile,' the first steam locomotive to serve the city from Buenos Aires and a monster of a hydroplane that was used to cross the Atlantic in 1926. The peaceful garden outside harbors some old wooden wagons and a brick windmill. The most offbeat exhibits, however, are the stuffed and scruffy remains of Gato and Mancha, the hardy Argentine criollo horses ridden by adventurer AF Tschiffely from Buenos Aires to Washington DC. This trip took 2½ years, from 1925–28.

Sleeping

Rates rise on weekends and holidays, when reservations are in order. All hotels include breakfast.

Hotel de la Paz (☎ 424034; hoteldelapaz@hotmail.com; 9 de Julio 1054; s/d US$12/17; ℗) Well located and with friendly staff, Hotel de la Paz hints at old-time charm. The homey rooms are small and bathrooms have open showers.

Hotel del Virrey (☎ 420797; San Martín 129; s/d US$13/17; P ⓟ) Right near the basilica is this modern hotel offering 18 decent rooms. There's pool access.

Hotel Hoxón (☎ 429970; www.hotelhoxon.com.ar in Spanish; 9 de Julio 760; s/d US$13/20; P ⓟ) Rooms at this semiclassy hotel are modern, clean

and comfortable. The swimming pool and gym make it a good deal.

Eating

Carnivorous pilgrims won't go hungry in Luján; just don't expect much beyond traditional Argentine fare. The central parts of San Martín, 9 de Julio and the riverfront are all lined with restaurants ready to serve.

THE PAMPAS & THE ATLANTIC COAST

THE RISE & ROMANCE OF THE GAUCHO

No one could have predicted the rise to respectability of that accidental icon, the Argentine gaucho. Dressed in *bombachas* (baggy trousers), the modern gaucho, with his leather *rastra* (silver-studded belt) around his waist and a sharp *facón* (long-bladed knife) in his belt, is the idealized version of a complex historical figure. To many Argentines and foreigners he is a latter-day version of the romantic characters portrayed in José Hernández' epic poem *Martín Fierro* and Ricardo Güiraldes' novel *Don Segundo Sombra*. Like his counterpart, the North American cowboy, he has received elaborate cinematic treatment. Ironically, only when he became a sanitized anachronism did he achieve celebrity.

Without the rich pastures of the Pampas and the cattle and horses that multiplied on them, the gaucho could never have flourished. In a sense, he replaced the Pampas Indian; usually a mestizo (a person of mixed Indian and Spanish descent), he hunted burgeoning herds of cattle just as the Querandí Indians did the guanaco and rhea. As long as cattle were many, people few, and beef, hides and tallow of some commercial value, his subsistence and independence were assured. This achieved, he could amuse himself gambling and drinking in the *pulpería* (tavern).

Just as the gauchos had replaced the Pampas Indians, so large landowners squeezed out the gauchos. The primitive livestock economy gave way to *saladeros* (salting factories), which made use of a wider variety of products: processed hides, tallow and salted or jerked beef.

For their *saladeros*, landowners needed labor; the gaucho, with his horseback skills, was a desirable if unwilling source of manpower, and landowners used their influence to coerce him. Classifying the gaucho as a 'lawless' element, discriminatory laws soon prevented men without jobs from traveling freely over the Pampas. Punishment for 'vagrancy' was often military conscription. As sheep replaced cattle on the Pampas, land was fenced and marked, forcing the gaucho to the fringes or onto the *estancias* (ranches).

Unlike the frontier, the *estancia* was not a democracy, and the gaucho was no longer his own master. He became instead a hired hand for an institution whose physical aspects bespoke hierarchy. As European immigrants came to occupy many *saladero* jobs, which often were detested by real gauchos, friction arose between gaucho 'natives' and Italian 'gringos.' Despite resistance, the day of the free-roaming gaucho was over by the late 19th century.

Ironically, about this time Argentina discovered the gaucho's virtues in what has become known as *literatura gauchescha* (literature about the usually illiterate gauchos). *Martín Fierro* romanticized the life of the independent gaucho as he was disappearing, much as the open-range cowboy of the American West was romanticized.

Hernández deplored both opportunistic strongmen like Juan Manuel de Rosas, who claimed to speak for the gaucho, and 'civilizers' like Sarmiento, who had no scruples about discarding the people of the countryside. The gaucho's fierce independence, so often depicted as lawlessness, became admirable, and Hernández almost single-handedly rehabilitated the gaucho's image as Argentines sought an identity in a country rapidly being transformed by immigration and economic modernization. Having fought alongside the gaucho, Hernández eloquently championed him in the public forums of his country, noting the positive gaucho values that even Sarmiento admired: courtesy, independence and generosity. By the time the gaucho's fate was decided, urban Argentines had elevated him to a mythical status, incorporating these values into their own ideology.

Berlín (☎ 426767; San Martín 151; mains US$3-5; ⏰ 8am-2am) German specialties here include smoked meats, sausage with sauerkraut and apple strudel. Sunny sidewalk seating is a plus, but the attached ice-cream shop isn't up to standard.

La Recova (☎ 422280; San Martín 1; mains US$2-5; ⏰ 9am-5pm) This lunchtime *parrilla* has some pleasant outdoor seating. On weekends they fire up the picture-window grill for a full *asado* (barbecue) experience.

L'Eau Vive (☎ 421774; Constitución 2112; mains US$5.50-6.50; ⏰ lunch & dinner Tue-Sun; ✗) Two kilometers from the center you'll find this friendly French restaurant run by Carmelite nuns from around the world. Taxis here cost US$1 or take bus No 501 from the center.

Getting There & Away

Lujan's **bus terminal** (☎ 420040; Av de Nuestra Señora de Luján & Almirante Brown) is just three blocks north of the basilica. From Buenos Aires' Plaza Italia in Palermo take Transportes Atlántida (No 57), which leaves every half hour (US$1.50, 1½ to two hours). There are also daily departures from Estación Once in Buenos Aires, but you need to change trains in Moreno (US$1).

SAN ANTONIO DE ARECO

☎ 02326 / pop 21,300

Nestled in the verdant Pampas of northern Buenos Aires province, San Antonio de Areco is a peaceful and serene town that dates from the early-18th-century construction of a chapel in honor of San Antonio de Padua. The locals are friendly, with many men around town wearing traditional gaucho berets. It's the kind of place where a hearty *'buenos dias'* or *'buenas tardes'* is in order every time you greet someone, and there are more bicycles than cars (with no one locking them either). The town is also well known for its silverwork, and many craftspeople have set up shop here.

San Antonio de Areco's compact center and nontrafficked streets are very walkable. At the beginning of the 18th century, Plaza Ruiz de Arellano was the site of the corrals belonging to the town's founding *estanciero* (ranch owner). In its center, the Monumento a Vieytes honors locally born Juan Hipólito Vieytes, a figure in the early independence movement. Around the plaza are several historic buildings, including the

iglesia parroquial (parish church) and the Casa de los Martínez (site of the main house of the original Ruiz de Arellano *estancia*).

The *puente viejo* (old bridge; 1857), across the Río Areco, follows the original cart road to northern Argentina. Once a toll crossing, it's now a pedestrian bridge leading to San Antonio de Areco's main attraction, the Museo Gauchesco Ricardo Güiraldes.

Orientation

San Antonio de Areco is 113km west of Buenos Aires via RN 8. V Alsina is the main drag, though the town's numerous sites of interest and shops are scattered throughout the surrounding streets.

Information

There are a few banks with ATMs around the Plaza Ruiz de Arellano.

Areco Online (☎ 455698; Ruiz de Arellano 285; per hr US$2-3) Internet access.

Post office (cnr Alvear & Av Del Valle)

Tourist office (☎ 453165; cnr E Zerboni & Ruiz de Arellano; ⏰ 8:30am-10pm Mon-Fri, 8am-8pm Sat & Sun) In a white, stand-alone building in the park.

Sights

MUSEO GAUCHESCO RICARDO GÜIRALDES

Inaugurated by the provincial government in 1938, a decade after Güiraldes' death, this **museum** (☎ 454780; cnr R Güiraldes & Sosa; admission US$0.75; ⏰ 11am-5pm Wed-Mon) in Parque Criollo is a sort of gaucholand of restored or fabricated buildings, including an old flour mill, a re-created tavern and a colonial-style chapel. The main deal is a 20th-century reproduction of an 18th-century *casco* (ranch house), which holds a wooden bed belonging to Juan Manuel de Rosas (perhaps the ultimate rural landowner), lots of gorgeous horse gear and various works of gauchesco art. Two rooms are dedicated to Güiraldes himself.

MUSEO Y TALLER DRAGHI

This small **museum and workshop** (☎ 454219; Lavalle 387; admission US$1.75; ⏰ 10:30am-1pm, 3:30-7:30pm) highlights an exceptional collection of silver *facónes* (gaucho knives), beautiful horse gear and intricate *mate* paraphernalia. It's mainly the workshop of Juan José Draghi and family, however, and guided tours are given.

SAN ANTONIO DE ARECO

INFORMATION
Areco Online...................................1 C3
Post Office.......................................2 B4
Tourist Office...................................3 B2

SIGHTS & ACTIVITIES
Casa de los Martínez......................4 B3
Centro Cultural Usina Vieja.........5 B2
Iglesia Parroquial...........................6 B3
Museo Gauchesco Ricardo
Güiraldes.....................................7 A1
Museo y Taller Draghi..................8 B2

SLEEPING
Estancia La Cinacina....................9 A3
Hospedaje Balcón Colonial.......10 C2
Hostal de Areco.........................11 B2
Hostal Draghi.........................(see 8)
Residencial El Hornero..............12 B3

EATING
Don Seguno Café.................(see 22)
La Costa.....................................13 B2
Ramos Generales.....................14 C3

SHOPPING
Alvaro Ignacio Caldera.............15 B3
Cristina Giordano de Bincaz....16 C2
Dulces del Pago.........................17 A2
El Tonel Kiosko..........................18 A2
La Olla de Cobre.......................19 B2
Raúl Horacio Draghi..................20 C4
Sogas Areco...............................21 A3

TRANSPORT
Bus Terminal.............................22 D3

CENTRO CULTURAL USINA VIEJA

Dating from 1901, the **Centro Cultural Usina Vieja** (V Alsina 660; admission free; ☼ 11am-5pm Tue-Sun) is an eclectic museum in an old power plant dating from 1901. Check out the funky collection of ancient radios, typewriters, sewing machines and record players. Farm equipment, sculptures, an old-time grocery store and even a small airplane are also on display, as are rotating exhibits of local artists' work and some examples of Florencio Molina Campos' amusing caricatures of gaucho life.

Festivals & Events

San Antonio de Areco is the symbolic center of Argentina's vestigial cowboy culture, and puts on the country's biggest gaucho celebra-tion on **Día de la Tradición** (in mid-November). If you're in the area, don't miss it; attractions include displays of horsemanship, folk dancing, craft exhibitions and guided tours of historic sites.

Sleeping

Prices listed are for weekends, when rates rise and singles are nearly impossible to find.

Hostal Draghi (☎ 454219; reception at Lavalle 387; draghi@lq.com.ar; r US$22;) Just five large, gorgeous rooms (some with kitchenette) are available at this tranquil place. A grassy garden with fountain soothes the spirit, and free bike rentals are available.

Hospedaje Balcón Colonial (☎ 456376; www.balconcolonial.com.ar in Spanish; Lavalle 536; s/d US$10/17)

HISTORIC ESTANCIAS

Surrounding San Antonio de Areco are a number of *estancias* (ranches), offering overnight accommodations with all meals included. These *estancias* were originally built by rich European immigrants for farming and cattle, but due to financial considerations many have been turned into dude-type ranches with activities that include horse riding, swimming, *asados* (barbecues) and gaucho shows and folk dances. Prices below include meals and many of these activities. San Antonio's tourist office can give you more information on accommodations and tours. In Buenos Aires the **Secretaría de Turismo de la Nación** (Map pp64-7; ☎ 011-4312-2232; Av Santa Fe 883) can supply a full list of *estancias* around Buenos Aires.

Estancia La Bamba (☎ 02326-456392; www.la-bamba.com.ar) One of the oldest, about 15km east of Areco; it dates from 1830, has spa services and once hosted Carlos Gardel.

Estancia La Cinacina (☎ 02326-452045; www.lacinacina.com.ar in Spanish; Mitre 9) This is closest to Areco and US$13 buys an all-you-can-eat *asado*, entertainment in the form of folk music and dance, along with a tour of the *estancia's* museum. Ring ahead for reservations and schedules.

Estancia La Porteña (☎ 02326-453770, in Buenos Aires ☎ 011-4822-1325; www.estancialaportenia.com.ar; r per person US$135) Unquestionably the most historic of *estancias* near Areco, this one belongs to the Güiraldes family. It dates from 1850 and has a garden designed by the renowned French architect Charles Thays, responsible for Buenos Aires' major public parks.

Estancia El Ombú (☎ 02326-92080, in Buenos Aires ☎ 011-4710-2795; r 1/2 people US$111/160) Belonged to General Pablo Ricchieri, who first inflicted universal military conscription on the country. Stays here include unlimited drinks and bike rental.

Three small but clean rooms are on offer at this homey place.

Hostal de Areco (☎ 456118; Zapiola 25; d US$17) Clustered with two other hotels, which aren't as personable, but do have pools. The rooms here are on the smaller side, but clean and comfortable.

Residencial El Hornero (☎ 452733; Moreno 250; s/d US$7/12) Here's a little heaven for garden-lovers, with lush greenery surrounded by pleasant patio halls and sitting areas; rooms are casual and modest.

Eating

San Antonio de Areco has fewer places to eat than you might expect, but there are some good ones.

El Almacén (☎ 15-683233; Bolívar 66; mains US$3-7) Decorated as an early-20th-century general store, this cozy and quaint place cooks mostly basic Argentine dishes. Check out the old gas pump outside.

La Costa (☎ 452481; cnr M Belgrano & E Zerboni; mains US$1.50-4) Except for an omelette or salad, there's little for the vegetarian at this modest *parrilla*.

Ramos Generales (☎ 456376; Zapiola 143; mains US$2.50-6) This upscale restaurant offers traditional *parrilla* and pasta, though a few oddities like rabbit and *jabalí* (wild boar) are thrown in.

Shopping

San Antonio de Areco's artisans are known throughout the country, with many of their disciples practicing their trades in other cities and provinces. *Mate* paraphernalia, *rastras* (silver-studded belts) and *facónes*, produced by skilled silversmiths, are among the most typical.

Raúl Horacio Draghi (☎ 454207; Guido 391) Internationally known Raúl Horacio Draghi works in leather as well as silver.

Alvaro Ignacio Caldera (☎ 455861; M Belgrano 213) Alvaro is a top silversmith who claims to have made a belt buckle for ex-president and tabloid fodder Carlos Menem. Custom-made items here take weeks to make and cost hundreds to thousands of pesos.

Sogas Areco (☎ 453797; General Paz near Italia) Check out this place for horse gear and gaucho clothing.

Cristina Giordano de Bincaz (☎ 452829; Sarmiento 112) There's a working loom here, plus some beautiful ponchos and *fajas* (intricate woven bands).

La Olla de Cobre (☎ 453105; Matheu near Zapiola) If looking for a gift of artisanal chocolates and tinned confections, come on over.

Dulces del Pago (☎ 454751; Zerboni 280) This store offers a good variety of fruit preserves, as well as homemade *dulce de leche* (Argentina's national sweet).

El Tonel Kiosko (cnr Güiraldes & Puente Viejo) For a funky good time, check out the second-largest wine barrel in Argentina; it's at the kiosk just across the Puente Viejo. Take a gander at the goods inside, or sit down for coffee or *mate*, but don't expect a traditional café or many tables; it's a very eclectic place run by an odd couple.

Getting There & Away

Buses run frequently from Buenos Aires to Areco (US$8, two hours). General Belgrano, which leaves from the **Don Seguno café** (☎ 15-680868), and Chevallier, which leaves from its small **bus terminal** (☎ 453904), are located almost next to each other on Ruta 8. Both serve as the town's bus terminal. A few long-distance services are available.

SOUTHERN PAMPAS

The fertile flats of Argentina's Pampas lands are only occasionally disrupted by the dimples of low mountain ranges. The easterly Sierras de Tandil are rounded hills whose peaks – none higher than 500m – take their names from the counties they cross: Olavarría, Azul, Tandil and Balcarce. Also in La Pampa are the modest granite boulders of Parque Nacional Lihué Calel. Almost 300km east in Buenos Aires province, the scenic Sierra de la Ventana – its jagged peaks rising to 1300m – attracts adventurous hikers and climbers.

Travelers looking for peaceful, laid-back towns will find Tandil and Sierra de la Ventana (both named for their nearby hills) excellent for relaxed exploration and activity. While the larger cities like Bahía Blanca and Santa Rosa aren't destinations in their own right, they do have some interesting surrounding highlights, and provide decent resting points while traveling to more popular destinations to the west and south of the country.

TANDIL

☎ 02293 / pop 110,000

Perhaps the most scenically diverse city in the Pampas, Tandil manages to have the charm of a small town while offering the services of a city. It sits leisurely at the northern edge of the Sierras de Tandil, a 2.5-million-year-old mountain range worn down to gentle, grassy peaks and rocky out-

croppings. It's a hub of rock climbing and mountain biking, and traditionally attracts masses of visitors at Easter to see Calvario, a hill ostensibly resembling the site of Christ's crucifixion at Golgotha (so book ahead).

Today Tandil is an important dairy zone, the heart of a rich cheese-producing region and home to esteemed schools of agronomy and lactose production. The hundreds of cheeses produced in the numerous *queserías* (cheese factories) around Tandil are sold in specialty stores throughout town. Downtown is relaxed, and there are numerous high-quality artisan shops along its cobblestone streets.

The city of Tandil arose from Fuerte Independencia, a military outpost established in 1823 by Martín Rodríguez. One of the most notorious incidents in provincial history began here in the early 1870s when a group of renegade gauchos, followers of the eccentric healer Gerónimo de Solané (popularly known as Tata Dios), gathered at nearby Cerro La Movediza to distribute weapons before going on a murderous rampage against European settlers and recent immigrants.

Orientation

Tandil is 384km south of Buenos Aires via RN 3 and RN 226, and 170km northwest of Mar del Plata via RN 226. The main commercial streets are Rodríguez and 9 de Julio, while the center of social activity is Plaza Independencia, a two-block area bounded by Rodríguez, Belgrano, Chacabuco and Pinto.

Information

ACA (☎ 425463; Rodríguez 399)

Bank Boston (Pinto 745) Has ATM.

Cyber World (☎ 433975; Rodríguez 827; per hr US$0.30; ⏱ 10:30am-late) Internet access.

Hospital Municipal Ramón Santamarina (☎ 422010; Paz 406)

Post office (9 de Julio 455)

Tourist kiosk (bus terminal; ⏱ 8am-6pm Mon-Sat)

Tourist office (Dirección de Turismo; ☎ 432073; www .tandil.gov.ar; Espora 1120; ⏱ 8am-8pm Mon-Fri, 9am-8pm Sat, 9am-1pm Sun) Way out of the center and vaguely close to the bus terminal. Bus No 505 (US$0.30) passes here, or a *remise* (taxi without a meter) from the plaza will cost US$1. Distributes a good city map and useful brochures.

Sights

Tandil's museums include the historic **Museo Tradiciónalista Fuerte Independencia** (4 de Abril 845;

admission free; 4-8pm Tue-Sun) and the **Museo de Bellas Artes** (☎ 432067; Chacabuco 353; admission US$0.60; 5-8pm Tue-Sun).

Activities

The easy walk to **Parque Independencia** from the southwestern edge of downtown offers good views of the city, particularly at night. The **Dique del Fuerte**, only 12 blocks south of Plaza Independencia, is a huge reservoir where the Balneario Municipal runs three **swimming** pools. The Centro Nautico del Fuerte rents **canoes** and **kayaks** in summer.

At the north edge of town, where Tata Dios gathered his supporters over a century ago, the **Piedra Movediza** (a 300-ton 'rocking stone') once teetered precariously atop **Cerro La Movediza** for many years before falling. The site still attracts visitors – go figure. Take bus No 503 (blue).

To go horse riding in the Reserva Natural Sierra del Tigre, contact **Gabriel Barletta** (☎ 427725, 15-584833; Avellaneda 673; half-day tours per person US$12). For all other outdoor activities, contact **Chao Tandil** (☎ 432542; www.chaotandil .com.ar in Spanish), an organization run by highly trained guides who offer trekking (US$7, three hours), mountain biking (US$10, three hours) and rock climbing (US$7).

Sleeping

Reservations are a must during summer, Easter week and on holiday weekends.

Hotel Libertador (☎ 422127; www.hotel-libertador .com.ar in Spanish; Mitre 545; s/d US$30/43; P 🍴) The smartest hotel in town is this modern four star, a couple of blocks from the plaza. Rooms are spacious and the restaurant isn't bad either.

Plaza Hotel (☎ 427160; plazah@speedy.com.ar; General Pinto 438; s/d US$30/40; P 🍴 🖳) This hotel's been at it for a while now, but it has been well maintained. Rooms are decent sized, the breakfast buffet is a well-rounded affair and there are plaza views.

Hotel Crillon (☎ 424159; crillontandil@ciudad.com.ar; San Martín 449; s/d US$20/27) A pleasant older-style hotel with modern bathrooms. Rooms are spacious, if a bit on the bare side, and have cable TV.

Hotel Kaikú (☎ 423114; Mitre 902; s/d US$7/11) With friendly staff, large bathrooms and a cheap restaurant attached, this modest and tidy hotel is good value and by far the best budget bet in the center.

THE AUTHOR'S CHOICE

Epoca de Quesos (☎ 448750; cnr San Martín & 9 de Julio; mains US$5-7) In one of Tandil's oldest buildings, Epoca de Quesos sells over 130 different local cheeses and dozens of locally cured meats. You can taste and buy at the counter or sit in the cavernous back rooms and split a huge sampler plate over a beer.

Camping Municipal Pinar de la Sierra (☎ 425370; Av San Gabriel & M de San Martín; per site for up to 4 people US$5) Just beyond the Dique del Fuerte, this clean, shady facility has a grocery and hot showers. Some No 500 (yellow) buses go there; ask the driver.

Eating

Benvenuto (☎ 447001; cnr San Martín & Alem; mains US$2-4; dinner) One of the few restaurants in the country doing only pasta, and they do it very well – it's all homemade and deliciously fresh. The putanesca sauce may have you hanging around town for a few unscheduled days.

Restaurant Maxim (☎ 442444; cnr Pinto & Rodríguez; meals US$2-5; breakfast, lunch & dinner) Breakfast on the plaza? The Maxim is your spot: light and sunny, with heaps of sidewalk seating, but get there before the old guys grab all the tables.

Tandil has a couple of legendary *parrillas:*

La Giralda (☎ 424830; Constitución y Rodríguez; all you can eat US$4)

El Viejo Trebol (☎ 442333; cnr 14 de Julio & Mitre; mains US$3-8)

Drinking

For such a small town, Tandil has several good bars.

Bar Tolomé (☎ 422951; Mitre 602; 7:30am-late) Dead midweek and lively on weekends, this relaxed bar serves pizzas and sandwiches when a beer's not enough.

Liver Pool (cnr 9 de Julio & San Martín) The British pub atmosphere and dedicated regulars make this spot a town favorite.

Gloria (9 de Julio 975) This two-floor disco plays pop hits and feels more like a big bar.

Shopping

La Cuchillería (☎ 494937; San Martín 786) From 8cm whittlers to 36cm *facónes,* this high-end

THE GAUCHO JUDÍO

The image of the gaucho is one that defines the Argentine character. But a little known fact is that many of the gauchos were of Jewish origin.

The first recorded instance of mass Jewish immigration to Argentina was in the late 19th century, when 800 Russian Jews arrived in Buenos Aires, fleeing persecution from Czar Alexander III in their homeland.

The Jewish Colonization Association, set up with funds from a wealthy German philanthropist, began to distribute 100-hectare parcels of land to immigrant families in the provinces of Entre Ríos, Santa Fe, Santiago del Estero, La Pampa and Buenos Aires.

The first major colony was in Moíses Ville in Santa Fe province, which became known at the time as Jerusalem Argentina. Today there are only about 300 Jewish residents left in town (or 15% of the population), but many Jewish traditions prevail: the tiny town boasts four synagogues, the bakery sells Sabbath bread and kids in the street use Yiddish slang like 'schlep' and 'schlock.'

The Jews quickly got involved in farming and agriculture, and, after some initial language and cultural difficulties, began to assimilate into Argentine society. Although they maintained their old customs, they took on some of their adopted country's as well; thus it was not an unusual sight to see a figure on horseback in baggy pants, canvas shoes and skullcap, on his way to throw a lump of cow on the *asado* (barbecue).

Many of their descendants have since left the land, in search of education and opportunities in the cities, but the Argentine population still includes about 300,000 Jews, the highest number of any country in Latin America.

knife shop sells a wide array of quality handmade blades.

Talabartería Carlos A Berruti (☎ 425787; Rodríguez 787) Especially good for leather, this store also stocks an assortment of *mates*, knives, silverwork and ponchos.

Getting There & Away

Several bus companies go to Buenos Aires daily from Tandil's **bus terminal** (☎ 432092; Av Buzón 650 at Portugal). There are buses every two hours to Mar del Plata and frequent services to other destinations along the coast. The following table shows approximate travel times and midseason fares for some popular destinations.

Destination	Cost (US$)	Duration (hr)
Buenos Aires	13	5¼
Córdoba	30	13
General Alvear	26	12
Mar del Plata	6	3
Mendoza	35	15
Necochea	6	2¾
Rosario	27	9
San Juan	35	18
San Luis	30	12
Santiago del Estero	37	17
Tucumán	39	18

Getting Around

Tandil's excellent public transportation system reaches every important sight. Bus No 500 (yellow) goes to Dique del Fuerte and the municipal campground, No 501 (red) goes to the bus terminal, and No 503 (blue) goes to Cerro La Movediza, the university and the bus terminal.

Localiza auto rentals (☎ 424140; Av Avellaneda 1012) is the most reliable rental-car company in town.

BAHÍA BLANCA

☎ 0291 / pop 314,500

Grandiose buildings, an attractive plaza and boulevards lined with shade trees and palms give oft-overlooked Bahía Blanca the essence of a cosmopolitan city in miniature. With South America's largest naval base just down the road, the city has a lively feel with some excellent eating and entertainment options. Add to this a few intriguing museums and a very convenient location, and Bahía Blanca is a worthwhile stop.

In an early effort to establish military control on the periphery of the Pampas, Colonel Ramón Estomba situated the pompously named Fortaleza Protectora Argentina at the natural harbor of Bahía Blanca in 1828. In 1884 the railway connected the

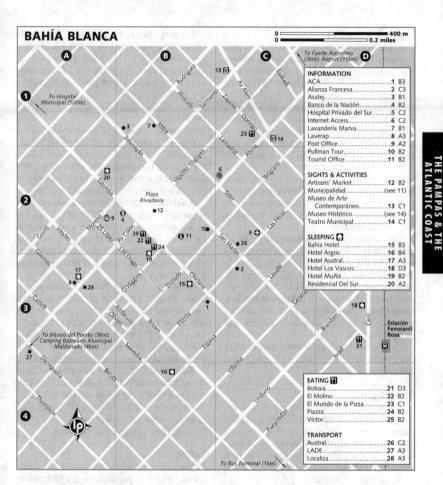

BAHÍA BLANCA

THE PAMPAS & THE ATLANTIC COAST

area with Buenos Aires, but another 11 years passed before Bahía Blanca officially became a city. Only recently has this port city's commerce and industry flourished, primarily through agriculture and petrochemicals.

Orientation

Bahía Blanca is located 654km southwest of Buenos Aires via RN 3, 530km east of Neuquén via RN 22, and 278km north of Viedma via RN 3.

Information

ACA (☎ 455-0076; Chiclana 305)
Alianza Francesa (☎ 455-1986; afbahiab@infovia.com.ar; Fitzroy 49; ⊙ 9:30am-12:30pm & 4-8:30pm Mon-Fri)

Asatej (☎ 456-0666; www.asatej.net in Spanish; Zelerrayan 267, Local 7) Sells discount international flights, issues student ID cards and is the STA representative.
Banco de la Nación (Estomba 52) May also change traveler's checks.
Hospital Municipal (☎ 456-8484; Estomba 968)
Hospital Privado del Sur (☎ 455-0270; Las Heras 164)
Internet access (Alsina 108; per hr US$0.50) Also has *locutorio* (private telephone office).
Lavandería Marva (Mitre 186) Laundry.
Laverap (Av Colón 197) Laundry.
Post office (Moreno 34)
Pullman Tour (☎ 455-4950; San Martín 171) Change money and traveler's checks here.
Tourist office (☎ 459-4007; Alsina 65; ⊙ 8am-7pm Mon-Sat) In the basement of the Municipalidad.

Sights & Activities

On the outskirts of town, in the former customs building hardly noticeable among the massive grain elevators and fortresslike power plant of Puerto Ingeniero White, the **Museo del Puerto** (☎ 457-3006; Guillermo Torres 4131; admission by donation; ☷ 9am-noon Tue-Fri, 3-7pm Sat & Sun, closed Jan) is an iconoclastic tribute to immigrants and their heritage, and includes an archive with documents, photographs and recorded oral histories. The best time to visit is for a weekend afternoon tea, when local groups prepare regional delicacies, each week representing a different immigrant group. Live music often accompanies the refreshments. Bus No 504 from the plaza goes to the museum.

The neoclassical **Teatro Municipal** (cnr Alsina & Zapaiola Dorrego), is the main performing-arts center in the city. In the same building is **Museo Histórico** (☎ 456-3117; Zapiola Dorrego 116; admission free; ☷ 9am-noon Tue-Fri, 3-7pm Sat & Sun). Also worth checking out is **Museo de Arte Contemporáneo** (☎ 459-4006; Sarmiento 454; admission free; ☷ 2-8pm Tue-Sun), showcasing local and national artists.

On the weekends an **artisans' market** takes over Plaza Rivadavia, situated opposite the Municipalidad.

Sleeping

Catering mainly to the business set, accommodations in Bahía Blanca are generally more expensive than in other Argentine towns of a similar size; however, good deals can be found. The budget area is across from the train station. There is no lodging near the bus terminal.

BUDGET

Hotel Los Vascos (☎ 452-0977; Cerri 747; s/d with shared bathroom US$5/10) Across from the train station, Los Vascos is without doubt the best of the budget bunch in the area. Rooms are pleasant and basic, and the wooden floors and spotless shared bathrooms add to the appeal, as does the friendly family who run the place.

Residencial del Sur (☎ 452-2452; Rodriguez 80; s/d US$8/12; P ☷) Cute and central, the Sur really stands out in this town. Rooms are small but comfortable, with spotless modern bathrooms. They don't take phone reservations, but you can call first to see if they have a room before racing over.

Camping Balneario Municipal Maldonado (☎ 452-9511; Parque Marítimo Almirante Brown; sites US$2; ☷ year-round; ☷) This basic campground, 4km southwest of downtown, has saltwater swimming pools. Hot water and electricity are available in summer only.

MIDRANGE

Hotel Austral (☎ 456-1700; www.hoteles-austral.com.ar in Spanish; Av Colón 159; s/d US$26/30; P ☷) With its grand piano and wood-paneled lobby, the Austral is definitely the class act in this town's hotel scene. Rooms have been recently remodeled and are pleasant and spacious.

Hotel Muñiz (☎ 456-0060; www.hotelmuniz.com.ar in Spanish; O'Higgins 23; s/d US$21/28; P ☷ ☐) Set in a beautiful old building in a very central location, the Muñiz's rooms are nothing particularly special, but the whole place has an irresistible old-timey feel that makes the place a bargain.

Hotel Argos (☎ 455-0404; www.hotelargos.com; España 149; s/d US$34/41; P ☷ ☐) Posh both outside and in, Argos offers top-of-the-line service in a sparkling hotel with plush, fully carpeted and very quiet rooms. Breakfast is filling, the gym modern and the service professional without being pretentious.

Bahia Hotel (☎ 455-3050; www.bahia-hotel.com.ar in Spanish; Chiclana 251; s/d US$17/26; P ☷ ☐) More spacious than most hotels around this price, the Bahia is functional if a little bland. The minibalconies (standing room only) overlooking the main street are a bonus.

Eating

Piazza (cnr O'Higgins & Chiclana; mains US$3-5; ☷ breakfast, lunch & dinner) A popular lunch spot right on the plaza, with an imaginative menu and a fully stocked bar. Chocoholics should not miss the chocolate mousse (US$1.50).

Bizkaia (☎ 452-0191; Soler 769; mains US$3-6) Basque colors and cuisine dominate this small informal restaurant, favored by locals for fish and seafood. Expect a bit of a wait for the well-prepared dishes.

El Mundo de la Pizza (☎ 454-5054; Zapiola Dorrego 55; mains US$4-7) This large diner with posters of silver-screen stars and old advertisements is the venue for excellent pizzas and empanadas. It's considered by many locals to be the best pizzeria in town.

Víctor (☎ 452-3814; Chiclana 83; mains US$3-8) Choose from a variety of daily specials, including *sorrentinos* (large raviolis), barbecued chicken or, of course, *parrilla*. Service is attentive, but the atmosphere is friendly and informal.

El Molino (☎ 451-2756; Chiclana 83) El Molino is set in a clutch of fairly similar restaurants right on the plaza. What sets this one apart is the excellent US$3 *tenedor libre* (all you can eat) which includes a *parrillada* (mixed grill including steak) platter.

Drinking

For a night on the town, head to **Fuerte Argentino**, about nine blocks northeast from Plaza Rivadavia, where *boliches* (nightclubs) and bars are clustered in a convenient cul-de-sac. There's a pleasant sculpture garden nearby where you can catch your breath.

Getting There & Away

AIR

Austral (☎ 456-0561; San Martín 298) hops to Buenos Aires (US$75). **Líneas Aéreas del Estado** (LADE; ☎ 452-1063; Darragueira 21) does the same trip for about US$54.

BUS

A key transport hub for southern Buenos Aires province and points south, Bahía Blanca's **bus terminal** (☎ 481-9615; Brown 1700) is about 2km east of Plaza Rivadavia. All of the bus companies are represented and there's a decent snack bar. For transport to Sierra de la Ventana, La Estrella leaves daily, except Saturday, at 6am and 8:40pm; Expreso Cabildo leaves at 8:20pm weekdays and at 1:30pm Saturday; and Cerri Bus leaves at 7am, 1pm and 7pm.

Destination	Cost (US$)	Duration (hr)
Bariloche	16-20	14
Buenos Aires	12-16	7-10
Comodoro Rivadavia	23	15
Córdoba	24	12½
La Plata	13-16	9
Mar del Plata	10	7
Mendoza	25	16
Neuquén	16	10
Río Gallegos	40	26
Sierra de la Ventana	2	2
Trelew	14-20	12

TRAIN

Trains leave from the once-grand but now run-down **Estación Ferrocarril Roca** (☎ 452-9196;

Av Cerri 750) for Buenos Aires daily at around 7pm. Fares range from US$5 *turista* (2nd class) to US$12 *coche cama* (sleeper carriage).

Getting Around

Austral provides its own transport to the **airport** (☎ 452-1665), 15km east of town on the naval base, RN 3 Norte, Km 674. Local buses cost US$0.30, but take only Tarjebus cards, available from kiosks. Bus Nos 505, 512, 514, 516 and 517 serve the terminal from downtown. Bus No 505 goes out Av Colón to Balneario Maldonado. For rental cars, try **Localiza** (☎ 456-2526; Av Colón 194).

SIERRA DE LA VENTANA

☎ 0291 / pop 2000

When things really start to heat up in the summer down on the lowlands, Argentines in the know head for the hills, and in particular this charming, slow-paced town, 125km north of Bahía Blanca.

The town's laid-back front masks the wealth of things to do here: hikers, climbers, horse riders, mountain bikers, kayakers and fishers won't be twiddling their thumbs for too long.

A couple of hotels have swimming pools to help you cool off, or you can always take a short stroll down to the river, which has shady sitting areas, perfect for picnicking and whiling the day away, Argentine style.

To reach the town from Bahía Blanca, take RN 33 to Tornquist, then RP 76. Sierra de la Ventana is divided into two sectors by Río Sauce Grande: Villa Tivoli has all of the businesses and services, while Villa Arcadia is a more residential area and also the locale for many hotels.

Information

There are several Internet cafés on San Martín, charging around US$1 per hour.

Banco de la Provincia (San Martín 260) Has an ATM.
Laverap (Güemes, near San Martín) Laundry.
Locutorio Televentana (Av San Martín 2910)
Post office (cnr Av Roca & Alberdi)
Tourist office (☎ 491-5303; www.comarcaturistica .com.ar in Spanish; Roca 17; ☽ 8:30am-1:30pm & 3:30-8:30pm) Near the train station. Distributes a useful packet of maps and flyers and can help find accommodations.

Sleeping

Hotel Atero (☎ 491-5002; fax 491-5344; cnr Av San Martín & Güemes; s/d US$8/16) This lovely old building

THE AUTHOR'S CHOICE

Hotel Provincial (☎ 491-5024; Drago 130; s/d US$16/20; P ☒) Fans of crumbling grandeur won't want to miss this big old place overlooking town. Dating from 1945, it's not in such a bad way, and the curving hallways and huge dining/ballroom add some real touches of class.

has thoroughly remodeled rooms with balconies overlooking the street. It's long been a favorite (and rightly so), so if you're coming in summer, it's wise to book ahead.

Residencial Carlitos (☎ 491-5285; Coronel Suárez 80; r per person US$7; ☒) Over the bridge in quiet, leafy Villa Arcadia, the owner-run Carlitos offers foam mattresses, small bathrooms and a good-sized swimming pool across the road, all located in a large garden environment.

Hospedaje La Perlita (☎ 491-5020; Calle E Morón; s/d US$6/8) Basic, clean rooms cluster around an overgrown garden at this very friendly and secure hostel, but there's no breakfast or kitchen use.

Camping El Paraíso (☎ 491-5299; Los Paraísos & Diego Meyer; adult/child US$2/1) This is a well-shaded, full-facility campground on the river.

Eating

Restaurant Atero (☎ 491-5316; cnr Av San Martín & Güemes; mains US$3-6; ☺ breakfast, lunch & dinner) For fresh-made pastas, big salads, a decent wine list and (just possibly) a game of football on TV, this restaurant in the Hotel Atero is the place to come.

Eneas (☎ 491-5144; cnr San Martín & Los Tilos; mains US$2-5) A casual yet refined eatery specializing in pizzas and calzones. There's a couple of pool tables out the back and a big-screen TV for the inevitable football game.

Sol y Luna (☎ 15-573-4565; Av San Martín 393; mains US$2-6) Pastas and pizzas are the way to go here, but don't overlook the soy burgers and other vegie specials, all served in an attractive dining room by the witty, friendly owners.

Hotel Provincial (☎ 491-5024; Drago 130; meals US$3-6; ☺ breakfast, lunch & dinner) Within this large hotel, the attractive bar/restaurant is a worthwhile spot to enjoy a drink or snack while gazing over the rolling green hills. See also above.

Getting There & Away

Buses leave from Av San Martín, just next to the *locutorio*. Buy tickets in the small kiosk behind the ice-cream shop. La Estrella goes to Buenos Aires (US$12, eight hours), La Plata (US$12, 12 hours) and Bahía Blanca (US$2, two hours). **GeoTur** (☎ 491-5355) runs a door-to-door service between Sierra de la Ventana and Tornquist (US$1, one hour), stopping at Saldungaray and Villa Ventana (US$0.60), three times daily.

From the **train station** (☎ 491-5164; cnr Av San Martín & Roca), trains leave at 11pm Tuesday, Thursday and Sunday for Buenos Aires (US$5 to US$7, 11 hours) and at 7am for Bahía Blanca (US$2, two hours).

AROUND SIERRA DE LA VENTANA
☎ 0291

Lots of trekking and climbing options are on offer in this region. Well-recommended **GeoTur** (☎ 491-5355; Av San Martín 193, Sierra de la Ventana) organizes a wide range of such activities, including hikes in Cerro Tres Picos.

Villa Ventana

Oddly enough, there *is* a place more laid-back than Sierra de la Ventana, and it's just down the road. Out of the peak season Villa Ventana has the feel of a place yet undiscovered, which may make it more attractive than the more established Sierra de la Ventana, 17km to the southeast.

Dirt roads named after birds cut through town in the pattern of an armadillo shell, each lane gorgeously shaded in a green circus of tall trees and curling ivy. Birdsongs and the clip-clop of horses' hooves may be the only sounds. However, as more people seeking serenity descend, the less serene it becomes: avoid weekends and Easter holidays.

SLEEPING

If you're visiting during the peak season, book accommodations in advance; in the off-season, call to confirm what is open.

Hostería La Peninsula (☎ 491-0012; cnr Golondrina & Cruz del Sur; s/d with half pension US$15/30; ☒) Right at the entrance to town, this is definitely the most sophisticated lodging in Villa Ventana. Rooms are good and comfortable, and the pool (when it's operating) is a welcome addition.

Residencial La Colina (☎ 491-0063; cnr Pillahuinco & Carpintero; r US$13) If La Peninsula is full, you could give this, one of the few other full-time hotels in town, a go. Tiny concrete rooms with even tinier bathrooms don't sound like much, but the owner's friendly enough and knows plenty about the area.

Camping Pablito (☎ 491-0019; sites US$4; ☾ year-round) About three blocks from the entrance to town, Pablito is a large, full-service (hot water, showers and firepots) campground.

There are lots of cabins with kitchens to rent; ask the tourist office for a list and help with vacancies. Prices start around US$30 for a double.

La Ponderosa (☎ 491-0078)
Pablito (☎ 491-0019)
Rancho Villa (☎ 491-0052)

EATING

Rancho Villa (☎ 491-0052; cnr Cruz del Sur & Zorzal; meals US$2-4; ☾ breakfast, lunch & dinner) Fine dining hasn't really made it to Villa Ventana yet, but you could try here for burgers and fast food.

Las Golondrinas (☎ 491-0047; cnr Cruz del Sur & Hornero; meals US$5-9) This is the place for 'high-mountain' cuisine. It's a good place, if only for drinks in a deluxe, relaxed environment.

GETTING THERE & AWAY

Shuttles connect Sierra de la Ventana with Villa Ventana (US$0.60, 20 minutes) at 6:40am, 10:40am and 7pm daily, leaving from the GeoTur office. To go to Sierra de la Ventana, take the GeoTur micro from the main plaza at 8am, 12:30pm and 7pm. Weekend times vary. A *remise* will cost from US$4 to US$6. From Bahía Blanca, just ask to be dropped off at the entrance to town along RP 76.

Cerro Tres Picos

The 1239m Cerro Tres Picos, southwest of Villa Ventana but accessed from RP 76, is a worthwhile backpack trip. Since this is the private property of Estancia Funke, there is a US$3 admission charge. Contact **Monica Silva** (☎ 494-0058) for permission to hike and camp. Those making a day hike must begin by 9am; overnighters can start as late as 2pm.

Parque Provincial Ernesto Tornquist

An imposing set of wrought-iron gates mark the entrance to the scenic 6700-hectare **Parque Provincial Ernesto Tornquist** (☎ 494-0039; admission US$1.50; ☾ hikes 9am-3pm), 5km from Villa Ven-

tana. The informative **Centro de Visitantes** has a well-organized display on local ecology, enhanced by audiovisuals. The park's high point is the two-hour hike to 1136m **Cerro Ventana**, which offers dramatic views of surrounding hills and the distant Pampas. At the Cerro Ventana trailhead, rangers and volunteer guides collect the entry fee and guide groups along a short, well-marked and otherwise easy hike. Insistent hikers may be able to get permission to go solo by signing a waiver, although the guides are supposedly supplied for safety reasons. A later start is better to have the view to yourself instead of sharing it with dozens of *porteños* huffing and puffing their way to the crest of what is probably the country's most-climbed peak. In summer there are five-hour ranger-guided walks to the gorge at **Garganta del Diablo** (Devil's Throat).

SLEEPING

Hotel El Mirador (☎ 494-1338; RP 76, Km 226; s/d US$15/20; 4-person cabin US$45; P ✖ ☙) Pleasant A-frame cabins and an ample hotel offer all the amenities of a three-star place at the foot of Cerro Ventana.

Campamento Base (☎ 491-0067; RP 76, Km 224; sites per person US$2) This friendly campground at Cerro Ventana has shaded campsites with clean bathrooms and excellent hot showers.

SANTA ROSA

☎ 02954 / pop 82,000

About 600km from Buenos Aires and very much a midway point for the whole country (you can catch a bus here from pretty much anywhere), Santa Rosa's main drawcard is that it's the base for exploring Parque Nacional Lihué Calel, an isolated but pretty park that's home to a surprising assortment of vegetation and wildlife.

The city was founded in 1892 by French, Spanish and Italian immigrants who arrived with the expansion of the railroads at the turn of the 19th century. But one measure of Santa Rosa's continuing isolation and insignificance is that until 1951 the surrounding area remained a territory rather than a province.

Orientation

North of Av España, the city consists of a standard grid centered on the spotless but nearly shadeless Plaza San Martín, the site of a rather ugly modernistic cathedral. Most businesses are on the plaza and its surrounding streets, though a more recent focus of activity is the modern Centro Cívico, seven blocks east on Av Pedro Luro.

Information

You'll find several ATMs in the center.

ACA (☎ 422435; Av San Martín 102) At the corner of Coronel Gil.

Alianza Francesa (☎ 423947; Lagos 67; ☽ 2-10pm Mon-Fri)

Post office (Hilario Lagos 258)

Tourist Information Center (☎ 436555; Luro 365; ☽ 24hr) In the bus terminal.

Tourist office (☎ 424404; www.turismolapampa.gov.ar in Spanish; cnr Luro & San Martín; ☽ 7am-8:30pm Mon-Fri, 9:30am-1pm & 2-8:30pm Sat & Sun) Across the road from the bus terminal. Helpful staff speak some English.

Sights & Activities

The **Museo de Ciencias Naturales y Antropológicas** (☎ 422693; Pellegrini 180; admission free; ☽ 8am-5pm Mon-Fri, 5-9pm Sat & Sun), like so many natural-science museums, is heavy on the stuffed-animal collection, particularly featuring birds of the Pampas. It also features a good little live snake exhibit and a bit about dinosaur fossil discoveries in the area.

The **Museo de Bellas Artes** (☎ 427332; cnr 9 de Julio & Villegas; admission free; ☽ 7am-1:30pm & 2-8pm Tue-Fri, 6:30-9:30pm Sat & Sun) is an unexpectedly modern gallery and contains works by local and national artists. There are five rooms of rotating exhibitions and a little sculpture garden out the back. The emphasis on contemporary/abstract is surprisingly strong – on the day of research they were showing a series of installations composed of rotting fruit.

The **Teatro Español** (☎ 455325; Hilario Lagos 54; admission free; ☽ 10am-noon & 4-6:30pm Mon-Fri, weekend hr vary) is Santa Rosa's major performing-arts venue and dates from 1927.

Laguna Don Tomás, 1km west of center, is the place for locals to boat, swim, play sports or just stroll.

Sleeping

Hotel Calfucurá (☎ 433303; calfuar@cpenet.com.ar; San Martín 695; s/d US$21/28; P ⊠ ⊠) The sedate atmosphere and handy location around the corner from the bus terminal make this a winner. It's the best hotel in town by far, and rooms are comfy, if nothing special.

Hotel San Martín (☎ 422549; www.hsanmartin.com .ar in Spanish; cnr Alsini & Pelligrini; s/d US$25/30; P ⊠) Opposite the sadly defunct train station, the San Martín offers clean and quiet rooms in a reasonably central location. Breakfast is a standard affair, but the coffee is excellent.

Centro Recreativo Municipal Don Tomás (☎ 455 358; west end of Av Uruguay; sites US$1; ⊠) From the bus terminal, take the local Transporte El Indio bus. Camping facilities are excellent and include picnic tables, *parrillas*, a swimming pool, hot showers, a fitness course for joggers and shade trees. Bring repellent for the ferocious mosquitoes.

Eating

Camelot (☎ 435566; Pueyrredón 25; meals US$4-6; ☽ dinner Mon-Sat) Here's some geographical confusion for you – an Irish pub in the middle of Argentina named after an English castle. Still…the food's good and the Guinness is cold, so who cares?

Club Español (☎ 423935; Hilario Lagos 237; meals US$3-8) There's good Argentine and Spanish food here, as well as outstanding service, and the Spanish tiled courtyard (replete with tinkling fountain) is as good a place as any in town to while away a few hours.

La Recova (☎ 424444; cnr Hipólito Yrigoyen & Avellaneda; meals US$1.50-4; ☽ breakfast, lunch & dinner) Good for breakfast or their set-meal lunches (US$3), this sunny little place right on Plaza San Martín does the whole *confitería* (café) thing to perfection.

Getting There & Away

Austral (☎ 433076; cnr Lagos & Moreno) flies to Buenos Aires. Taxis to the airport, which is 3km from town, cost about US$1.50.

The **bus terminal** (☎ 422952, 422249; Luro 365) has departures for Bahía Blanca (US$6, five hours), Buenos Aires (US$15, eight hours), Puerto Madryn (US$11, 10 hours), Mendoza (US$17, 12 hours), Neuquén (US$11, 15 hours) and Bariloche (US$18, 21 hours).

AROUND SANTA ROSA
☎ 02954

Doctor Pedro Luro, an influential early resident, imported exotic game species such as Carpathian deer and European boar into the pastures and native caldén forests of **Reserva Provincial Parque Luro** (☎ 499000; admission US$0.30; ☽ 9am-7:30pm), a 7500-hectare park that was formerly a hunting preserve. Luro also built an enormous French-style mansion (now a museum) to accommodate foreign hunters.

With the decline of sport hunting by the European aristocracy during and after WWI, followed by the Great Depression, Luro went bankrupt. His heirs had to sell the preserve, which fell into disrepair; animals escaped through holes in the fences, and some suffered depredation by poachers (which continues to this day). During and after WWII, Luro's successor Antonio Maura exploited the forests for firewood and charcoal, grazed cattle and sheep, and bred polo ponies.

Since its acquisition by the province in 1965, Parque Luro has served as a recreational and historical resource for the people of La Pampa, offering paths for **biking** and short **hiking** trails. Its **Centro de Interpretación** contains good material on local ecology and early forest exploitation, as well as on Luro and Maura.

Guided tours of the **Castillo Luro**, as the museum is known, were suspended at time of research as the place was getting renovated, but should have started again by the time you read this. Wandering around the place gives a good insight into the personal indulgences that Argentine landowners could afford in the first half of the 20th century, even for places where they spent only a month or two each year. Note, for instance, the walnut fireplace, an obsession that Luro was able to satisfy only by purchasing an entire Parisian restaurant.

Parque Luro is about 35km south of Santa Rosa via RN 35. Besides the museum, there are picnic areas, a small zoo, a restaurant and the **Sala de Caruajes**, a collection of turn-of-the-century carriages. There's a daily bus service from Santa Rosa which drops you about 3km from the park entrance. Ask at the main tourist office in Santa Rosa about getting a ride with park staff.

PARQUE NACIONAL LIHUÉ CALEL
☎ 02952

Like the Sierras de Tandil, and the Sierra de la Ventana in Buenos Aires province, Parque Nacional Lihué Calel (a Pehuenche phrase meaning Sierra de la Vida or Range of Life) is a series of small, isolated mountain ranges and valleys in the nearly featureless landscape of the Pampas. Located 226km southwest of Santa Rosa, its salmon-colored, exfoliating granite peaks do not exceed 600m, but still manage to offer a variety of subtle environments that change with the seasons.

Though desertlike Lihué Calel receives only about 400mm of rainfall per year, water is an important factor in the landscape. Sudden storms can bring flash floods and create brief but impressive waterfalls over granite boulders near the visitor center. Even when the sky is cloudless, the subterranean streams in the valleys nourish the *monte* (a scrub forest with a surprising variety of plant species). Within the park's 10,000 hectares exist 345 species of plants, nearly half the total found in the entire province.

In this thinly populated area survives wildlife that is now extinct in the Humid Pampas further east. Large felines including puma, yagouaroundi and Geoffroy's cat have been glimpsed, but the most common predator is the Patagonian fox. Also in residence are other large mammals such as the guanaco (more common on the Patagonian steppe) and smaller species like the mara (Patagonian hare), vizcacha (a wild relative of the chinchilla) and armadillo.

The varied birdlife includes the rhea-like ñandú and many birds of prey, such as the carancho (crested caracara). Although you're not likely to encounter them unless you like to overturn rocks, be aware of the highly poisonous pit vipers commonly known as yarará.

Until General Roca's so-called Conquista del Desierto (Conquest of the Desert, 1879), Araucanian Indians successfully defended the area against European invasion. Archaeological evidence, including petroglyphs, recalls their presence and that of their ancestors. Lihué Calel was the last refuge of the Araucanian leader Namuncurá, who eluded Argentine forces for several years before finally surrendering.

More information is available at the tiny **visitor center** (☎ 436595).

Sights & Activities
From the park campground, an excellent signed nature trail follows an intermittent stream through a dense thorn forest of caldén and other typical trees. The trail leads to a petroglyph site, unfortunately vandalized. The friendly and knowledgeable rangers accompany visitors if their schedule permits.

THE PAMPAS & THE ATLANTIC COAST

There's a marked trail to the 589m peak, which bears the charming name **Cerro de la Sociedad Científica Argentina**. Fortunately, this climb is fairly gradual. Watch for flowering cacti such as *Trichocereus candicans* between the boulders, but remember that the granite is very slippery when wet. From the summit, there are outstanding views of the entire sierra and its surrounding marshes and salt lakes, such as Laguna Urre Lauquen to the southwest.

If you have a vehicle, visit **Viejo Casco**, the big house of former Estancia Santa María before the provincial government expropriated the land; it was later transferred to the national park system. It's possible to make a circuit via the **Valle de las Pinturas**, where there are some undamaged petroglyphs. Ask rangers for directions.

Sleeping

Near the visitor center is a comfortable and free **campground** with shade trees, firepits, picnic tables, clean toilets, cold showers (great in the baking-hot summer) and electricity until 11pm (bring a flashlight). Nearby you're likely to see foxes, vizcachas and many, many birds. Stock up on food before arriving; the nearest decent supplies are at the town of Puelches, 35km south.

ACA Hostería (☎ 436101; s/d US$7/10) If you don't want to camp, you have one choice: this basic but functional place on the highway. There is a restaurant (which is nothing to get excited about) and the park entrance is a short walk away.

Getting There & Away

From Santa Rosa, Edu Bus, Tus and El Valle go to the park daily (US$2, 3¾ hours). These companies change regularly, so check what's available when you're there.

If you can afford it, driving is the best way to visit Parque Nacional Lihué Calel. To rent a car in Santa Rosa, try **Rent Auto** (☎ 435770; cnr Luro & P Harris).

ATLANTIC COAST

For *porteños* and others from Buenos Aires province, summer means the beach, and the beach means the Atlantic coast in general, and Mar del Plata in particular. Every summer millions of Argentines take a holiday from their friends, families and coworkers, only to run into them on the beaches. Those who can't make it in person participate vicariously in the beach scene every afternoon via nationwide TV.

Beach access is unrestricted, but *balnearios* (bathing resorts) are privately run, so access to toilets and showers is limited to those who rent tents. Legally, *balnearios* must have lifeguards, medical services, toilets and showers. Most also have *confiterías* and even shops.

Even by Argentine standards, prices are hard to pin down, since they rise every two weeks between December 15 and February 15, and then decline slowly until the end of March, when most hotels and *residenciales* (short-stay accommodations) close. Those that stay open year-round lower their prices considerably, though Semana Santa (Holy Week) is an excuse to raise them briefly.

North of Mar del Plata to Cabo San Antonio, gentle dunes rise behind the generally narrow beaches of the province. Southwest from Mar del Plata to Miramar, steep bluffs highlight the changing coastline, although access is still good for bathing. Beyond Miramar, toward Necochea, the broad sandy beaches delight bathers, fishing enthusiasts and windsurfers.

MAR DEL PLATA

☎ 0223 / pop 700,000

It's worth going to Mar del Plata on a summer weekend if only so you'll never again be tempted to say 'gee this beach is crowded.' There's a couple of places where you could get a few strokes in without taking somebody's eye out, but mostly it's shoulder-to-shoulder sun-frazzled *porteños*. During the week, and especially in the nonsummer months, the crowds disperse, hotel prices drop and the place takes on a much more relaxed feel.

First impressions of the extremes to which this resort town has taken itself can be abhorrent. But, after spending a few days on its comically packed beaches, watching street performers on the beachside Plaza Colón or exploring the wonders of the port, it's hard not to give in to the adoration the country feels for the place. If summer crowds aren't your bottle of lotion, visit in spring or autumn, when prices are lower and the area's natural attractions are easier to enjoy.

MAR DEL PLATA

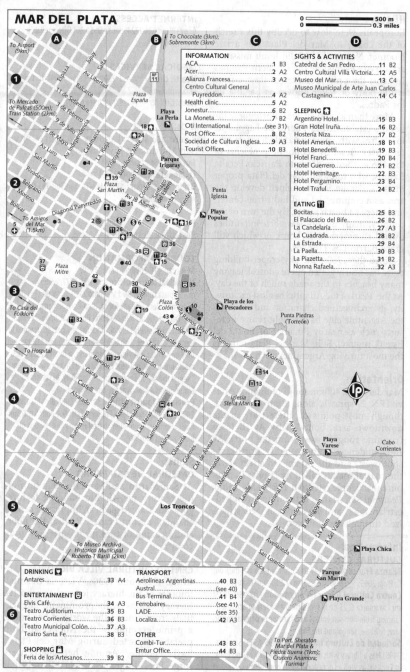

0 ——————— 500 m
0 ——————— 0.3 miles

INFORMATION
ACA..1 B3
Acer..2 A2
Alianza Francesa.......................3 A2
Centro Cultural General
  Puyreddon.............................4 A2
Health clinic..............................5 A2
Jonestur....................................6 B2
La Moneta.................................7 B2
Oti International..................(see 31)
Post Office................................8 B2
Sociedad de Cultura Inglesa.....9 A3
Tourist Offices.........................10 B3

SIGHTS & ACTIVITIES
Catedral de San Pedro............11 B2
Centro Cultural Villa Victoria...12 A5
Museo del Mar.......................13 C4
Museo Municipal de Arte Juan Carlos
  Castagnino...........................14 C4

SLEEPING 🏠
Argentino Hotel.......................15 B3
Gran Hotel Iruña.....................16 B2
Hostería Niza...........................17 B2
Hotel Amerian.........................18 B1
Hotel Benedetti.......................19 B3
Hotel Franci.............................20 B4
Hotel Guerrero........................21 B2
Hotel Hermitage......................22 B3
Hotel Pergamino......................23 B4
Hotel Traful.............................24 B2

EATING 🍴
Bocitas....................................25 B3
El Palacacio del Bife................26 B2
La Candelaria..........................27 A3
La Cuadrada...........................28 B2
La Estrada...............................29 B4
La Paella..................................30 B3
La Piazetta..............................31 B2
Nonna Rafaela........................32 A3

DRINKING 🍷
Antares...................................33 A4

ENTERTAINMENT 🎭
Elvis Café................................34 A3
Teatro Auditorium...................35 B3
Teatro Corrientes....................36 B3
Teatro Municipal Colón...........37 A3
Teatro Santa Fe......................38 B3

SHOPPING 🛍️
Feria de los Artesanos.............39 B2

TRANSPORT
Aerolíneas Argentinas.............40 B3
Austral..............................(see 40)
Bus Terminal...........................41 B4
Ferrobaires.......................(see 41)
LADE................................(see 35)
Localiza..................................42 A3

OTHER
Combi-Tur...............................43 B3
Emtur Office............................44 B3

THE PAMPAS & THE
ATLANTIC COAST

History

Europeans were slow to occupy this stretch of the coast, so Mar del Plata was a late bloomer. Not until 1747 did Jesuit missionaries try to evangelize the southern Pampas Indians; the only reminder of their efforts is the body of water known as Laguna de los Padres.

More than a century later, Portuguese investors established El Puerto de Laguna de los Padres, with a pier and a *saladero* (slaughterhouse). Beset by economic problems in the 1860s, they sold out to Patricio Peralta Ramos, who founded Mar del Plata proper in 1874. Peralta Ramos helped develop the area as a commercial and industrial center, and later as a beach resort. By the turn of the century, many upper-class *porteño* families owned summerhouses, some of which still grace Barrio Los Troncos.

Since the 1960s, the skyscraper-building craze has nearly gotten out of control, leaving many beaches in the shade much of the day. As the 'Pearl of the Atlantic' has lost exclusivity, its architectural character and its calm, the Argentine elite have sought refuge in resorts such as nearby Pinamar or Punta del Este (Uruguay). Still, Mar del Plata remains the most thriving Argentine beach town.

Orientation

Mar del Plata, 400km south of Buenos Aires via RN 2, sprawls along 8km of beaches, though most points of interest are in the downtown area, bounded by Av JB Justo (running roughly west from the port), Av Independencia (runs roughly northeast–southwest) and the ocean. On street signs, the coastal road is called Av Peralta Ramos, but most people refer to it as Blvd Marítimo. *Peatonal* San Martín is the downtown pedestrian mall, and Rivadavia is pedestrianized through the summer.

Information

CULTURAL CENTERS

Alianza Francesa (☎ 494-0120; afmardeldir@af-mdp.org; La Rioja 2065; ⏰ 8:30am-1:30pm & 2:30-8pm Mon-Fri)
Centro Cultural General Pueyrredón (☎ 499-7878; cnr Catamarca & 25 de Mayo) Offers a variety of activities ranging from film screenings and theater to popular music, jazz, folklore, tango and the like.
Sociedad de Cultura Inglesa (☎ 495-6513; San Luis 2498) Has a library with newspapers, magazines and books in English, as well as occasional films and lectures.

INTERNET ACCESS

Acer (Rivadavia 2724; per hr US$0.30) Offers reliable Internet service.

MEDICAL SERVICES

Health clinic (☎ 493-2309; Av Colón 3294) Northwest of downtown.
Hospital (☎ 477-0262; JB Justo 6700)

MONEY

There are several money exchanges along San Martín and Rivadavia.
Jonestur (San Martín 2574)
La Moneta (Rivadavia 2623)
Oti International (☎ 494-5414; San Luis 1632) The Amex representative.

POST

Post office (Av Luro 2460)

TOURIST INFORMATION

ACA (☎ 491-2096; Av Colón 1450)
Municipal tourist office (☎ 495-1777; emtur@ mardelplata.com.ar; Blvd Marítimo 2400, Local 60; ⏰ 8am-10pm mid-Dec–Semana Santa, 8am-8pm Semana Santa–mid-Dec) In the old Rambla Hotel Provincial, opposite Plaza Colón. Exceptionally helpful. Since the city gets so crowded in summer, staff cope with tourists in assembly-line fashion, but they have maps, informative brochures, a monthly activities magazine and an efficient computerized information system. There is usually an English-speaker on duty. In summer, Emtur opens a branch at the bus terminal.
Provincial tourist office (☎ 495-5340; Blvd Marítimo 2400; ⏰ 9am-8pm Mon-Fri, 9am-1pm & 4-8pm Sat & Sun) Basic information on other coastal resorts and the rest of Buenos Aires province.

Sights

CATEDRAL DE SAN PEDRO

At San Martín and San Luis, this turn-of-the-century neo-Gothic building features gorgeous stained glass, an impressive central chandelier from France, English-tile floors and a ceiling of tiles from other European countries.

CENTRO CULTURAL VILLA VICTORIA

In the 1920s and 1930s, Victoria Ocampo, founder of the literary journal *Sur*, hosted literary salons with prominent intellectuals from around the world at her home, a prime example of the Norwegian-built prefabs imported during Mar del Plata's 'belle epoque.' Among her guests were Jorge Luis Borges, Gabriela Mistral, Igor

Stravinsky and Rabindranath Tagore. It is now a **museum and cultural center** (☎ 492-0569; Matheu 1851; admission US$1; ☽ 6-9pm summer, 1-7pm Mon-Fri, 1-8pm Sat & Sun other times).

MUSEUMS

Built in 1909 as the summer residence of a prominent Argentine family, the Villa Ortiz Basualdo is now the **Museo Municipal de Arte Juan Carlos Castagnino** (☎ 486-1636; Av Colón 1189; adult/student US$1/0.50, Tue free; ☽ 5-10pm Fri-Wed). Resembling a Loire Valley castle, its Belgian interior exhibits paintings, drawings, photographs and sculptures by Argentine artists. Take bus No 221, 581 or 592.

In the Villa Emilio Mitre (1930), yet another former summer residence of the Argentine oligarchy, the **Museo Archivo Histórico Municipal Roberto T Barili** (☎ 495-1200; Lamadrid 3870; admission US$1; ☽ noon-10pm) houses a superb collection of turn-of-the-century photographs, along with other exhibits, recalling Mar del Plata's colorful past. Catch bus No 523, 524 or 591.

Housing the most extensive seashell collection you're ever likely to see, the **Museo del Mar** (☎ 451-3553; Av Colón 1114; admission US$3; ☽ 9am-2am Dec-Mar, 8am-9pm Mon-Thu, 8am-midnight Fri & Sat, 9am-9pm Sun Apr-Nov) exhibits more than 30,000 shells, representing 6000 species from around the world. In a sleek new building, the museum also contains a small tide pool, an aquarium and a delightful café, complete with Internet service.

THE PORT

Mar del Plata is one of the country's most important fishing ports and seafood-processing centers. At **Baquina de Pescadores** – the picturesque wharf hidden behind the ugly YPF fuel tanks – fisherfolk and stevedores follow their routine on and around kaleidoscopically colored wooden boats, monitored by sea lions who have established a large colony – mostly male – along one side of the pier.

In the early morning, unfazed by the chilly sea breeze, the fishermen load their nets and crates before spending the day at sea, escorted by the sea lions. At about 5pm, the pier gets noisy and hectic as the returning fishermen sort and box the fish, bargain for the best price and tidy up their boats and tools. The sea lions return to seek or fight over a resting spot. Braving their horrendous

stench affords excellent opportunities for photography: separated by a fence, you can approach within a meter of the sea lions.

Just past the colony is the port's fantastic graveyard of **ruined ships**, half-sunken and rusting in the sun. Here the **Escollera Sur** (southern jetty) begins its long stretch some 2km out to sea, with panoramic views of the city from its tip. Climb the yellow ladders and walk on top of the sea wall for the best views. You can walk back to the **Centro Comercial Puerto** (the port's commercial center) and close the day in one of its great restaurants.

Local bus Nos 221, 511, 522, 551, 561, 562 and 593 go to the wharf from downtown. A taxi costs US$2.

Tours

Combi-Tur (☎ 493-0732) Combi-Tur has more extensive, less specialized excursions leaving daily at 3:30pm from Plaza Colón, at Colón and Arenales.

Crucero Anamora (☎ 489-0310; www.anamoracrucero .com.ar in Spanish) The 30m boat offers one-hour harbor tours (US$5) several times daily in summer and twice daily on weekends in winter from Dársena B at the port.

Emtur office (Blvd Marítimo) Emtur conducts free organized tours of various city sights; register one day in advance at the office.

Ocean Flyers (☎ 15-682-5911; www.vuelopanoramico .com.ar in Spanish) Offers half-hour scenic flights over town for a bargain US$11. Call and they'll pick you up from your hotel.

Turimar (☎ 489-7775) Offers similar tours as well as six-hour fishing excursions (US$22) which leave weekends and holidays at 7am. They also depart from Dársena B.

Festivals & Events

Mar del Plata's elaborate tourist infrastructure guarantees a wide variety of special events throughout the year. On February 10 Mar del Plata celebrates **Fundación de la Ciudad**.

Started in 1950, though interrupted for decades by Argentina's political and economic woes, Mar del Plata's **International Film Festival** takes place in mid-March. Participants come from around the world.

Sleeping

It's worth reiterating that prices climb considerably from month to month during summer and drop in the off-season, when many of Mar del Plata's 700 hotels and *residenciales* close their doors. The least expensive accommodations are near the bus terminal.

BUDGET

Hotel Pergamino (☎ 495-7927; hotelpergamino@ciu dad.com.ar; Tucumán 2728; dm/s/d US$ 4.50/8/13) Good value, clean and comfortable budget rooms. If you've got a few spare pesos, it's definitely worth getting a room, although the dorms will do in a pinch.

Hostería Niza (☎ 495-1695; hotelniza@mail.com; Santiago del Estero 1843; s/d US$6/12) This centrally located *hostería* (lodging house), run by three delightful sisters, is excellent value, though cold in the winter. It's a homelike place, definitely the cheapest in the center and an old backpackers favorite.

Rates at Mar del Plata's crowded camp-grounds, mostly south of town, are around US$2 per person; the tourist office prints out information about their facilities.

MIDRANGE

Argentino Hotel (☎ 493-0091; www.argentinohotel -mdp.com.ar in Spanish; Belgrano 2225; s/d US$30/47; P ⊠) This four-star property offers spacious, good-value rooms right in the center of the action.

Hotel Guerrero (☎ 491-8200; www.hotelguerrero .com.ar; Av JB Alberdi 2258; s/d US$38/48; P ⊠ ⌑) Rooms are cozily decorated and have mini-fridges in this hotel just a block off the ocean.

Hotel Traful (☎ 493-6650; fax 495-7084; Yrigoyen 1190; r US$30; P ⊠ ⌑ ☏) This nondescript three-star hotel near the ocean has modest rooms with cable TV and reasonable-sized baths.

Gran Hotel Iruña (☎ 491-1060; www.granhotel iruna.com in Spanish; Av JB Alberdi 2270; s/d from US$26/33; P ⊠) Recently remodeled, this four-star hotel offers plush rooms with air-con and excellent baths, a staggering breakfast buffet, a games room and assistance with tours and excursions.

Hotel Benedetti (☎ /fax 493-0031/2/3; Av Colón 2198; s/d US$30/40) This comfortable hotel has

---

good, plain rooms with TVs and substantial baths. The best part is the games room with pool, Ping-Pong and table soccer.

Hotel Franci (☎ 486-3740; francihmdp@speedy.com .ar; Sarmiento 2742; r US$16) Across the road from the bus terminal, the Franci has tidy little rooms with cable TV. The sun+ny breakfast area and friendly owner are bonuses.

TOP END

Hotel Amerian (☎ 491-2000; www.amerian.com; Libertad 2936; r US$65; P ⊠ ⌑) A thoroughly modern business hotel right on the seafront, the Amerian offers all the style you'd expect for the price. Slightly cheaper 'city view' rooms are available, but being that the view is largely car park, it's worth paying a bit more for the stunning sea views.

Sheraton Mar del Plata (☎ 414-0000; www.shera ton.com/mardelplata; Alem 4221; r with city/sea views US$104/116; P ⊠ ⌑ ☏) The Sheraton once again blows the competition out of the water with its facilities and modern styling. It's a bit out of town, but if you've got the bickies (*alfajores?*) to stay here, you won't be complaining about the US$1.50 cab ride back and forth.

Eating

Although Mar del Plata's numerous restaurants, pizzerias and snack bars usually hire extra help between December and March, they often struggle to keep up with impatient crowds, and there are always long lines. Around the bus terminal you can find very cheap *minutas* (snacks).

La Estrada (☎ 495-8992; Entre Ríos 2642; mains US$6-11; ☽ dinner Mon-Thu, lunch & dinner Sat & Sun) The best deal at this family-style *parrilla* is the US$3.50 *parrillada*, which includes salad and dessert. Drinks are extra.

La Candelaria (☎ 492-5533; Santa Fe 2633; mains US$4-6; ☽ dinner daily, lunch Sat & Sun) The friendly owners take excellent care of everything from decor to dinner at this cozy place with an imaginative menu. The paella for two (US$11) is a winner, as is the small but tasty wine list and bumper crop of dessert options.

Nonna Raffaela (☎ 493-5861; Alberti 2583; meals US$3-6) Formerly a pasta-only joint, Nonna Raffaela has now branched out to serve excellent Italian-style seafood dishes, including lobster and octopus. The decor may remind you of your grandmother's house.

THE AUTHOR'S CHOICE

Hotel Hermitage (☎ 451-9633; hermitage@ lcnet.com.ar; Blvd Marítimo 2657; r with city/sea views US$80/100; P ⊠ ⌑ ☏) Built in 1942, this is by far the classiest hotel in town, with a majestic lobby that has sweeping ocean views, a casino, Turkish bath and slightly worn but comfortably refined rooms.

La Paella (☎ 493-9628; Entre Ríos 2025; dishes US$5-9) The name may imply just paella, but this highly recommended place actually does a wide range of dishes, including frogs' legs, and it has an English menu.

Bocitas (Rivadavia 2262; mains US$3-4; ❤ 24hr) This place can't be topped when it comes to cheap thin-crust pizza; it's low on atmosphere, but you can't beat the opening hours.

La Cuadrada (☎ 494-2288; 9 de Julio 2737; mains US$2-4) One of the most often recommended *parrillas*, La Cuadrada also serves good-value set lunches (US$4).

La Piazzetta (☎ 494-5113; San Luis 1652; mains US$3-8) This Italian restaurant, a member of the International Slow Food Association, offers fine homemade pastas and a range of other dishes. A cheesy keyboard soloist is on hand to accompany your lunch.

El Palacio del Bife (☎ 494-7727; Córdoba 1857; meals US$3-8) A highly recommended *parrilla* with a massive menu (that's also available in English). Come hungry and come wanting meat, although the homemade pastas are also worth a try.

Piedra Buena (☎ 480-0147; Centro Comercial Puerto; meals US$6-10) Of the bunch of seafood restaurants down at the port, this is reputedly the best, and is certainly the most atmospheric. There's a huge range of seafood on offer, a good atmosphere and a seafood bisque (US$7) that comes highly recommended.

Drinking

The area southwest of Plaza Mitre is particularly conducive to barhopping.

Antares (☎ 492-4455; Córdoba 3025; ❤ 8pm-late) The six homebrews on tap at Mar del Plata's only microbrewery include imperial stout, pale ale and barley wine – excellent cures for the Quilmes blues. Food is available and there is live music most weekends. Come early if you want a table out the front.

La Cuadrada (☎ 494-2288; 9 de Julio 2737) In an eccentrically remodeled colonial building, this café-cum-bar is truly a work of art worth stepping into. Check out the bizarre central fountain and the basement with furniture sculpted from the ground. See above.

Entertainment

NIGHTCLUBS

After tanning on the beach all day, Argentines take their hot, bronzed bodies to

THE PAMPAS & THE ATLANTIC COAST

THE AUTHOR'S CHOICE

Amigos del Mar (☎ 491-6054; Guido 2056; mains US$5-9) Apart from the hearty *'buenas noches'* greeting you get on arrival, this Japanese restaurant is the real deal. Bamboo screens, jangly background music and a sushi sashimi platter that's worth the trek 1.5km west (or US$1 taxi ride) on its own.

the nightclubs and dance until the morning hours. The most popular clubs are along Av Constitución, about 3km from downtown. Bus No 551 from downtown runs along the entire avenue. Keep your eyes peeled during the day for discount flyers handed out along San Martín and Rivadavia.

Sobremonte (☎ 479-2600; Constitución 6690; admission US$4-6; ❤ midnight-dawn Dec-Mar, midnight-dawn Thu-Sat off-season) Ground zero for the city's most fashionable summertime clubbers, Sobremonte is three throbbing discos, a Mexican restaurant and a lounge all under one roof.

Chocolate (☎ 479-4848; Constitución 4451; admission US$3-5; ❤ midnight-dawn Dec-Mar, midnight-dawn Thu-Sat off-season) This is another long-time favorite, with two floors, a patio and a standard soundtrack covering everything from techno to *rock nacional* (Argentine rock).

LIVE MUSIC

Casa del Folklore (☎ 472-3955; San Juan 2543; ❤ from 9pm summer, from 9pm Fri & Sat winter) Music usually gets under way after 11pm at this lively *peña* (folk music club) northwest of downtown, where there's plenty of food, drink and dancing.

Elvis Café (☎ 492-4529; Almirante Brown 2639; ❤ 9pm-late Fri & Sat) This small venue features everything from Rolling Stones cover bands to live tango performances.

THEATER

When Buenos Aires shuts down in January, many shows come from the capital to Mar del Plata. Theaters mostly cater to vacationers by showing comedies that range from café concert (stand-up comedy) to vulgar but popular burlesque. As in Buenos Aires, there are *carteleras* that offer half-price tickets to movies and theater presentations.

The local branch of Cartelera Baires is at Santa Fe 1844, Local 33.

Teatro Auditorium (☎ 493-6001; Blvd Marítimo 2280) Part of the casino complex, this place offers quality musical theater.

Other venues include **Teatro Municipal Colón** (☎ 499-6210; Yrigoyen 1665), **Teatro Corrientes** (☎ 493-7918; Corrientes 1766) and **Teatro Santa Fe** (☎ 491-9728; Santa Fe 1854).

Shopping

Mar del Plata is famous for sweaters and jackets. Shops along Av JB Justo, nicknamed 'Avenida del Pullover,' have competitive, near-wholesale prices. To get there, take bus No 561 or 562.

Feria de los Artesanos (Plaza San Martín) Every afternoon vendors set up their stalls on Plaza San Martín to offer for sale everything from *mate* gourds and knives to sweaters and silverwork.

Mercado de Pulgas (Plaza Rocha) This relaxed flea market, selling everything including the kitchen sink, is at 20 de Septiembre between San Martín and Av Luro, seven blocks northwest of Plaza San Martín.

Getting There & Away

AIR

Aerolíneas Argentinas and Austral share **offices** (☎ 496-0101; Moreno 2442) and have several daily flights to Buenos Aires (from US$65).

LADE (☎ 493-8211; Blvd Marítimo 2300, Local 5) has flights to various parts of the country. It's in the casino.

Destination	Cost (US$)
Bahía Blanca	45
Bariloche	85
Buenos Aires	45
Puerto Madryn	55
Trelew	65
Viedma	47

BUS

Mar del Plata's busy **bus terminal** (☎ 451-5406; Alberti 1602) is very central. Dozens of companies serve most major destinations throughout the country. There are generally two departures per week to Patagonian destinations south of Bariloche. Rapido del Sud departs hourly for nearby coastal resorts.

Destination	Cost (US$)	Duration (hr)
Bahía Blanca	10	7
Bariloche	25	19
Buenos Aires	8.5	5½
Comodoro Rivadavia	32	24
Córdoba	17	18
Jujuy	25	27
La Plata	9	5
Mendoza	20	18
Miramar	1	1
Necochea	3	2
Neuquén	12	12
Paraná	20	12½
Pinamar	3	2½
Posadas	20	19
Puerto Madryn	24	16½
Rosario	7	7½
Salta	25	26
San Juan	20	20
Santa Fe	19	12
Santiago del Estero	17	20
Trelew	24	18
Tucumán	20	24
Villa Gesell	2.50	1½

TRAIN

The **train station** (☎ 475-6076; Av Luro 4700 at Italia; 🕓 6am-midnight) is about 2km from the beach. Tickets can also be purchased at the **Ferrobaires office** (☎ 451-2501; Alberti 1602; 🕓 8am-9pm) which is located at the bus terminal.

During summer, the tourist train El Marplatense travels seven times daily (eight on Sunday) to Buenos Aires. Reservations should be made far in advance, since it's usually booked solid through the season. One-way fares cost US$7 *(turista)* to US$16 (super Pullman). There are daily departures through the slower seasons as well.

Getting Around

Despite Mar del Plata's sprawl, frequent buses reach just about every place in town. For information on local destinations, the tourist office can help.

Aeropuerto Félix U Camet (☎ 479-0194, 479-2787; RN 2 Km 396) is 10km north of the city. To get there by bus, take No 542 from the corner of Blvd Marítimo and Belgrano. **Aerolíneas Argentinas** (☎ 478-3314) has a minibus service for US$2. Otherwise, a taxi or *remise* costs about US$4 per person.

Car rentals are available at **Localiza** (☎ 493-3461; Córdoba 2270).

AROUND MAR DEL PLATA
☎ 02266

Mar Chiquita
Along RP 11, 34km north of Mar del Plata, the peaceful resort of Mar Chiquita is a paradise for swimming, fishing and windsurfing (there's a December windsurf regatta). Fed by creeks from the Sierras de Tandil and sheltered by a chain of sand dunes, its namesake estuary – Laguna Mar Chiquita – alternately drains into the ocean or absorbs seawater, depending on the tides. There are several campgrounds and hotels, including **Camping Playa Dorada** (☎ 0223-493-9607).

Rápido del Sud goes eight times daily to Mar Chiquita from Mar del Plata's bus terminal and from the casino. The cheaper local bus No 221 (US$0.70) leaves hourly from stops along Blvd Marítimo. Ask the driver; some 221 buses stop short.

Museo del Automovilismo Juan Manuel Fangio
Named for Argentina's most famous race car driver, this **museum** (☎ 425540; www.museo fangio.com; cnr Dardo Rocha & Mitre, Balcarce; adult/child US$2.50/1; ☯ 10am-5pm Mon-Fri, 10am-6pm Sat), one of the country's finest, preserves a multi-million-dollar collection of classic and racing cars in his birthplace of Balcarce, 60km northwest of Mar del Plata via RN 226. Occupying an early-20th-century building, the museum stresses the worldwide exploits of Fangio and his contemporaries, but also makes an effort to put automotive history into a global context.

Fangio, who died in 1995 at the age of 84, is the subject of Stirling Moss and Doug Nye's biographical tribute *Fangio: a Pirelli Album*. El Rápido runs frequent buses from Mar del Plata (US$1.50).

VILLA GESELL
☎ 02255 / pop 24,300

This little beachside town goes a fair way to countering the Atlantic coast blues. Despite the recent wave of high-rise mania, the place retains the feel of a summer getaway village even in the peak season.

In the 1930s, merchant, inventor and nature-lover Carlos Gesell designed this resort of zigzag streets, planting acacias, poplars, oaks and pines to stabilize the shifting dunes. Though he envisioned a town merging with the forest he had created, it wasn't long before high-rise vacation shares began their malignant growth.

Still, Villa Gesell maintains a mellow, woodsy feel. The town is known for its summer choral performances and rock and folk concerts, and its funky downtown lacks the slick elitism that graces its counterpart, Pinamar, just up the coast.

Orientation
Villa Gesell is 100km northeast of Mar del Plata via RP 11 and about 360km south of Buenos Aires via RP 11.

Av 3, Gesell's only paved road, parallels the beach and runs from Av Buenos Aires, north of town, south to the bus terminal and most of the campgrounds. Gesell's restaurant, shopping and entertainment center is along this thoroughfare between Paseos 102 and 110. Everything is within walking distance, including the beach, three blocks to the south.

With few exceptions, streets are numbered rather than named. Avenidas (all 11 of them) run east–west, parallel to the beach. Paseos, numbered 100 through 152, run north–south.

Information
There are many banks with ATMs on Av 3.
ACA (☎ 462273; Av 3 btwn Paseos 112 & 113)
Hospital Municipal Arturo Illía (☎ 462618; cnr Calle 123 & Av 8)
Gesell.net (Paseo 105, No 289; per hr US$0.30) Internet access.
Post office (Av 3 btwn Paseos 105 & 106)
Secretaría de Turismo (☎ 458596; www.gesell.com.ar in Spanish; Av Buenos Aires at Camino de los Pioneros, btwn RP 11 & Circunvalación; ☯ 8am-8pm Mon-Fri, 10am-6pm Sat & Sun) Has friendly staff and reliable maps.
Tourist office (☎ 478042; Av 3, No 820; ☯ 8am-8pm summer only) The more conveniently located office in the municipality.

Sights & Activities
The **Muelle de Pesca** (Playa & Paseo 129), Gesell's 15m fishing pier, offers year-round fishing for mackerel, rays, shark and other varieties of marine life.

Horse riding is a popular activity at places like **Nazareno Cruz** (☎ 457015; cnr Calle 313 & Alameda 201), where you can rent horses independently or take guided excursions (US$5 per hour) daily in summer and on weekends in winter.

For bicycle rentals, try **Casa Macca** (per day US$15; Av Buenos Aires ☎ 468013; Av Buenos Aires at Paseo 101; Av 3 ☎ 466030; cnr Av 3 & Paseo 126) or **Rodados Lucky** (☎ 462965; cnr Av 3 & Paseo 121).

You can rent surf gear from **Windy** (Paseo 104) down on the beachfront.

Tours

Turismo Aventura Edy (☎ 463118, 466797; cnr Av 3 & Paseo 111, Plaza Gesell; US$6 per person; ☺ Dec-Apr, Sat & Sun May-Nov) runs trips to **Faro Querandí**, the local lighthouse, carrying up to 10 passengers in 4WD jeeps on a 30km trip over dunes, with stops along the way for photography, swimming and exploring. The lighthouse itself, one of the highest and most inaccessible in the country, soars impressively above the surrounding dense forest. Four-hour trips leave daily in summer at 9am and 3pm.

Sleeping

Villa Gesell has 200-plus hotels, *hosterías*, *hospedajes* (usually a large family home with a few extra bedrooms; the bathroom is shared), *aparthoteles* and the like: a lot close outside of summer; those listed here are open all year.

BUDGET

Los Medanos (☎ 463205; Av 5, No 549; per person US$8) One of the better budget options in town, with decent-sized rooms and modern bathrooms. Try to get a room upstairs for better light and ventilation.

Hospedaje Villa Gesell (☎ 466368; Av 3, No 812; per person US$7) The best part about this place is its centrality. The rooms are comfortable, though windowless, and the doors all open onto an interior patio.

Villa Gesell's dozen campgrounds usually charge from US$2 to US$4 per person with a four-person minimum. Most close at the end of March, but three clustered at the southern end of town on Av 3 are open all year. They are **Camping Casablanca** (☎ 470771), **Camping Mar Dorado** (☎ 470963) and **Camping Monte Bubi** (☎ 470732).

MIDRANGE

Hotel Merimar (☎ 462243; hotelmerimar@hotmail.com; cnr Paseo 107 & Playa; s/d US$40/47; P 🖭) The Merimar's small but comfortable rooms are in an excellent location – literally spitting distance from the beach (not that we would ever condone such antisocial behavior). Rooms at the

front have good balconies overlooking the whole scene.

Hotel Tamanacos (☎ 468753; tamanacos@gesell .com.ar; cnr Paseo 103 & Av 1; s/d US$16/32; P 🖭 🖭) A mere 100m away from the beach, this cute little hotel has some great common sitting areas, particularly the front balcony, and a good breakfast buffet. Rooms are on the small side, but good value for the price.

Hotel Bella Vista (☎ 462293; www.gesell.com.ar /bellavista in Spanish; cnr Av 4 & Paseo 114; s/d US$27/33; 🖭 🖭) One of the town's older hotels, the Bella Vista has an expansive back lawn, an inviting bar and clean, midsize rooms.

Residencial Viya (☎ 462757; residencialviya@gesell .com.ar; Av 5, No 582, btwn Paseos 105 & 106; s/d US$8/16) Rooms are smallish, but pleasant, and open onto a small patio at this friendly, owner-operated *residencial* on a quiet street.

Hotel Walkirias (☎ 468862; www.gesell.com.ar /walkirias in Spanish; Paseo 102 btwn Av 2 & Buenos Aires; s/d US$20/40) Rampantly ugly from the outside, the Walkirias has a good cozy feel to it on the inside. There's a pool table in the sitting area and rooms are spacious, with good beds and huge showers.

Hosteria Casablanca (☎ 464083; cnr Av 1 & Paseo 103 bis; s/d US$25/40; P 🖭) A cute chalet-style building located a short walk from the beach. There's a good balcony out front to hang out on, and the spotless rooms come with modern bathrooms.

TOP END

Hotel ACA Spa (☎ 462960; www.gesell.com.ar/hotelaca in Spanish; Av 1 btwn Paseos 112 & 113; s/d US$46/96; P 🖭 🖭) One of the more stylish of the ACA hotels, this one has good-sized rooms with ample balconies, a lovely breakfast area and, inexplicably, a whole load of Indian decorations on the walls.

Hotel Bahia (☎ 462838; www.hotelbahia-gesell .com.ar in Spanish; Av 1, No 855 btwn Paseos 108 & 109; r US$85; P 🖭 🖭) One of the better four-star high-rises down on the beachfront, the Bahia has spacious rooms with little sitting areas and good views. Plenty of extras, like the gym, sauna, breakfast buffet and heated pool make this place good value.

Eating

Villa Gesell has a wide variety of restaurants, mostly along Av 3, catering to all tastes and budgets.

El Estribo (☎ 460234; cnr Av 3 & Paseo 109; mains US$2-5) You won't get very far in this town without somebody recommending that you eat at El Estribo. A *bife de chorizo* will set you back US$3 and the *parrilla* for two (which actually has enough meat for three) costs US$7.

Lo de Pepe (☎ 460236; Av 3, No 852; mains US$3-6) If El Estribo is booked out (and it may well be), this friendly little *parrilla* is a perfectly acceptable alternative. The steaks are juicy, the decorations are boxing posters and the wine list is just fine.

La Delfina (☎ 465859; cnr Paseo 104 & Av 2; mains US$3-6) The wide menu, good wine list and relaxed atmosphere make this a popular choice for locals and tourists alike.

Cartagena de las Indies (☎ 462858; Av 3, No 215 at Paseo 102; set meals US$4) Gesell's most upscale eatery, the mains here sometimes aren't worth the price tag, but the set meals are always good value, and the sidewalk seating is a winner, too.

Entertainment

For such a small town, Villa Gesell comes alive with music in the summer months, when venues book everything from rock to choral music. Gesell is famous for its Encuentros Corales, an annual gathering of the country's best choirs.

Cine Teatro Atlas (☎ 462969; Paseo 108, btwn Avs 3 & 4) Such rock-and-roll greats as Charly García and Los Pericos have played this small theater, which doubles as a cinema during off-season months.

Playa Hotel (☎ 458027; cnr Alameda 205 & Calle 303, Barrio Norte) This European country–style hotel established Villa Gesell as a vacation resort, and every summer the Sociedad Camping Musical organizes chamber music concerts in its auditorium.

Anfiteatro del Pinar (☎ 467123; cnr Av 10 & Paseo 102) There are performances in January, February and Semana Santa. Gesell's Encuentros Corales takes place annually in this lovely amphitheater.

Pueblo Límite (☎ 452845; www.pueblolimite.com in Spanish; Av Buenos Aires 2600; admission US$3-8) A sort of small town megadisco, this complex, across from the Secretaría de Turismo, has two dance clubs (one for Latino music, one for electronica), four restaurants, a bar and cheap food booths in the front.

Shopping

Feria Artesanal, Regional y Artística (Av 3, btwn Paseos 112 & 113; nightly mid-Dec–mid-Mar, Sat & Sun mid-Mar–mid-Dec) This is an excellent arts and crafts fair.

Getting There & Away

The **main bus terminal** (☎ 477253; cnr Av 3 & Paseo 140) is on the south side of town. Most buses stop here first and then at the **Parada Los Pinos Mini Terminal** (☎ 458059; cnr Blvd Silvio Gesell & Av Buenos Aires), closer to the center of town. Get off here if you're walking.

Empresa Río de la Plata has several direct buses daily to Buenos Aires (US$11, six hours) in summer and offers combination tickets to Rosario, Córdoba and La Rioja. There are also daily runs to La Plata (US$8, 6½ hours) and Mar del Plata (US$2.50, 1½ hours). Rápido del Sud leaves regularly to other coastal resorts.

PINAMAR

☎ 02254 / pop 25,000

There's no doubt that Pinamar is *the* place to be in terms of upmarket beach towns. Smaller than Mar del Plata, it also has a more exclusive feel, probably because it's more family oriented. If you're looking for nightlife, you'll be far happier in Mar del Plata.

Bathed by a tropical current from Brazil, Pinamar's waters are pleasantly warm, and its clean beaches slope gradually into a sea abundant with fish. Its extensive forests, sandy streets, luxury homes and hotels, chic shops and posh restaurants give it a very different feel to other towns along the coast.

Pinamar was founded and designed in 1944 by architect Jorge Bunge, who figured out how to stabilize the shifting dunes by planting pines, acacias and pampas grass. It was the refuge for the country's upper echelons and remained so until relatively recently. Punta del Este, Uruguay, has lately gained popularity over Pinamar as a seaside getaway close to Buenos Aires. The place seems to have more adventure sports and hip *balnearios* than any other resort along the coast.

Orientation

Pinamar sits 120km north of Mar del Plata via RP 11, and 320km southeast of Buenos Aires via RN 2. It was planned around an axis formed by Av Libertador, which runs parallel to the beach, and Av Bunge, which is perpendicular to the beach. On either side of Bunge, the streets form two large fans, making orientation tricky at first. The easiest way to keep track of your hotel is by picking and memorizing the nearest high-rise. The newer parts of town follow a conventional grid.

Most shops, restaurants and hotels are on or within a few blocks of Av Bunge, the main thoroughfare.

Information

There are plenty of Internet cafés on Av Bunge, charging around US$0.30 per hour.

ACA (☎ 482744; Del Cazón 1365)

Community Hospital (☎ 491710; Shaw 250)

Municipal tourist office (☎ 491680; Av Bunge 654 at Libertador; ☺ 8am-10pm summer, 8am-8pm rest of year) Busy. Has a good pocket-size map with useful descriptions of Pinamar, Valería, Ostende and Cariló.

Post office (Jasón 524)

Telephone office (cnr Jasón & Shaw)

Activities

Through summer, Pinamar is a haven for every outdoor activity from windsurfing and waterskiing to horse riding and hiking.

Several shops in town offer rental for biking, including **Leo** (☎ 488855; Bunge 1111; per hr US$2-3) and **Macca** (☎ 494183; Bunge 1075; per hr US$2-3).

The tourist office provides a list of folks who rent horses for riding in the summer. **Ismael** (☎ 497700, cnr Bunge & Av Intermedanos; per hr US$3) is the only one open year-round, but call ahead of time if it's a winter weekday.

Boards for **surfing** can be rented (US$2 per hour) during summer from the pier, a few blocks south of Av Bunge. **Sky surfing** (that strange hybrid of surfing and paragliding) is the latest craze to hit Pinamar, and if you want to learn how to do it (or just watch someone else), go to Sport Beach, the last *balneario* located about 5km north of Av Bunge.

Here's a good one: sand boarding. To give it a shot, follow jeep tours to nearby dunes or contact **Wenner Explorer** (☎ 02267-15-636131; cnr Laurel & Playa; US$10-15; ☺ Sat & Sun).

Fishing, especially for shark and bass, is popular year-round, both from the pier and by boat. Cantina Tulumei (right) offers four-hour fishing excursions (US$13 per person) and will cook up the catch back at the cantina that evening.

Sleeping

Pinamar lacks real budget accommodations – prices are notably higher than in Gesell – but there is a youth hostel in nearby Ostende. Reservations are a must in the high season. Prices below are for summer, but off-season rates are up to 40% lower.

BUDGET

Albergue Bruno Valente (☎ 482908; cnr Mitre & Nuestras Malvinas, Ostende; HI members/nonmembers US$6/7) About eight blocks south of Pinamar's center, this large youth hostel gets packed in summer and cold and empty in winter. The kitchen is huge and the bathrooms are institutional. The building itself is a decaying historic hotel built in 1926.

Hospedaje Acacias (☎ 485175; Del Cangrejo 1358; d US$15) Cheerful, airy rooms open onto a small grassy area and the entire place has a welcoming feel.

Camping Saint Tropez (☎ 482498; cnr Quintana & Nuestras Malvinas, Ostende; 2 people in summer US$5) Due to its choice beachfront location, this small site fills up quickly in summer.

MIDRANGE & TOP END

Hotel Soleado (☎ 490340; cnr Sarmiento & Nuestras Malvinas; r US$48; P) Right on the beach, but a fair way out of town, the Soleado is a modern, good-looking hotel with a full bar and spacious pleasant rooms.

Hotel Arenas (☎ 482480; www.hotelarenaspinamar.com; Av Bunge 700; r US$100; P ⊠ ⚛) Right in the middle of the main street, this not-too-ugly four-star hotel has pretty much everything, including games rooms, a spa, sauna and Jacuzzi. Rooms are good sized and comfortable, and most have roomy balconies.

Hotel del Bosque (☎ 482480; www.hotel-delbosque.com; Av Bunge 1550; d US$100; P ⊠ ⚛) Named for the 1.6-hectare eucalyptus grove it sits on, this ultramodern four-star property is one of the finest in town. Its many amenities include tennis courts and a driving range. Unfortunately it's a long tramp to the beach.

Hotel Algeciras (☎ 485550; www.algecirashotel.com.ar in Spanish; Av Libertador 75; r US$95; P ⊠ ⚛) This tasteful four-star hotel is an expansive brick chalet-style structure with a lovely pool, a Jacuzzi, a sauna and luxurious rooms.

Eating

Cantina Tulumei (☎ 488696; Bunge 64; mains US$5) This is the place for reasonably priced, quality seafood. In summer, get here early or make a reservation because the place fills up fast and people tend to linger.

Con Estilo Criollo (☎ 490818; cnr Av Bunge & Marco Polo; mains US$6-13) Ask anybody in town for a good *parrilla*, and they'll probably send you straight here; they serve superb pork and *chivito a la parrilla* (grilled kid).

Ojalá (☎ 480626; cnr Bunge & Marco Polo; set meals US$4; ⏰ breakfast, lunch & dinner) A happening little *confitería* on the main street, Ojalá has a good selection of cakes and sidewalk seating.

Freddo (cnr Av Bunge & Simbad El Marino; ⏰ 9am-11pm) Freddo scoops excellent ice cream; it's closed in the dead of winter, though.

Getting There & Away

Pinamar has a slick new **bus terminal** (☎ 403500; cnr Jasón & Av Intermedanos). Rapido del Sud runs up and down the coast in both directions several times a day, stopping at all coastal destinations between Mar del Plata (US$4.50, 2½ hours) and San Clemente del Tuyú (US$3, two hours). There are also daily buses to Buenos Aires.

Trains run to Pinamar's **Estación Divisadero** (☎ 497973) in January and February only. Get tickets to Constitución (Buenos Aires) at the bus terminal.

SAN CLEMENTE DEL TUYÚ

☎ 02252 / pop 11,050

With absolutely none of the glitz or glamour of the resorts down the coast, San Clemente is a favorite for low-key beachgoers. It's also the closest beach town to the capital, and while eating and sleeping options are slim, they're good enough to keep you happy if you're on a short break from the big smoke.

It's only a few kilometers from Punta Rasa, the southern tip of Bahía Samborombón, and its location near Cabo San Antonio puts it on the flyway for migratory birds from as far away as Alaska and Canada.

Sleeping & Eating

Gran Hotel Fontainbleau (☎ 421187; www.fontaine bleau.com.ar; Calle 3 2290; s/d US$35/40; P ✕ ✓) The pick of the beachfront high-rises, the Fontainebleau has comfy if slightly dated rooms whose best features are undoubtedly the big balconies overlooking the sea.

Hotel Sun Shine (☎ 430316; www.rpm-net.com.ar /sunshine; Av Talas del Tuyú 3025; s/d US$13/20) A bit of a walk from the center, and a couple of blocks from the beach, the Sun Shine is still the best budget deal in town, offering big, clean rooms with cable TV.

There are several campgrounds (US$2 per person) at the entrance to town.

La Querencia (☎ 423081; Calle 1, No 2453; mains US$3-6) In summer, there are plenty of eating options, but this frequently recommended *parrilla* stays open year-round. They also do a great line in seafood and some excellent homemade pastas.

Pizzería Tropicana (☎ 421176; cnr Calle 1 & Calle 2; mains US$2-6) In a wedge-shaped building a block from the beach, the Tropicana is another year-round place which serves good pizza and tasty empanadas.

Getting There & Away

Frequent buses connect San Clemente with Buenos Aires from the **bus terminal** (☎ 421340; cnr Calle 10 & Av San Martín). There are also buses down the coast toward Pinamar, Villa Gesell and Mar del Plata (US$5, five hours) and to Buenos Aires (US$6, six hours).

NECOCHEA

☎ 02262 / pop 88,200

Totally pumping in summer and near dead in winter, Necochea's beach-town feel is undisturbed by the high-rises that keep springing up. With 74km of beachfront, it's fairly certain that you'll be able to find a spot to lay your towel. The foresty Parque Lillo is a great bonus here, as are the walking and horse-riding opportunities out to the west of town.

Necochea lacks the woodsy allure (as well as the elitism) of the smaller resorts of Pinamar and Villa Gesell, but it has some of the best-value lodging on the coast.

Orientation

Necochea is 128km southwest of Mar del Plata via RP 88, the direct inland route. Car-clogged RN 11 is the coastal route from Cabo Corrientes in Mar del Plata. It takes you past dramatic headlands as far south as the family resort of Miramar, and then heads inland to RP 88.

The south-flowing Río Quequén Grande separates Neuquén, on its western bank, from the village of Quequén on the eastern side.

Though streets have both names and numbers, everyone just uses the numbers.

THE PAMPAS & THE
ATLANTIC COAST

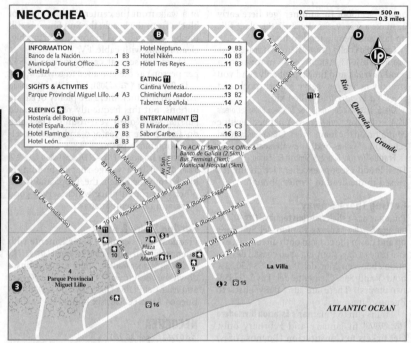

NECOCHEA

INFORMATION	
Banco de la Nación	...1 B3
Municipal Tourist Office	...2 C3
Satelital	...3 B3

SIGHTS & ACTIVITIES	
Parque Provincial Miguel Lillo	...4 A3

SLEEPING	
Hostería del Bosque	...5 A3
Hotel España	...6 B3
Hotel Flamingo	...7 B3
Hotel León	...8 B3

Hotel Neptuno	...9 B3
Hotel Nikén	...10 B3
Hotel Tres Reyes	...11 B3

EATING	
Cantina Venezia	...12 D1
Chimichurri Asador	...13 B2
Taberna Española	...14 A2

ENTERTAINMENT	
El Mirador	...15 C3
Sabor Caribe	...16 B3

To ACA (1.5km); Post Office & Banco de Galicia (2.5km); Bus Terminal (3km); Municipal Hospital (5km)

La Villa

ATLANTIC OCEAN

0   500 m
0   0.3 miles

Even-numbered streets run parallel to the sea; odd numbers run perpendicular.

The focus of tourist activity is in 'La Villa,' the newer part of town between Av 10 and the beach. Calle 83 (Alfredo Butti) is its main commercial street. The area is dead in winter. Banks and other year-round businesses are near Plaza Dardo Rocha in the old town (Centro); most of the shops and restaurants line the streets just northwest of the plaza.

Information

ACA (☎ 422106; Av 59, No 2073)
Banco de Galicia (Calle 60, No 3164) Has ATM.
Banco de la Nación (cnr Calle 6 & Calle 83) Has ATM.
Municipal hospital (☎ 422405; Av 59, btwn Calles 100 & 104)
Municipal tourist office (☎ 430158; www.necochea net .com.ar; Av 2 & Calle 79; 9am-10pm, closes 5pm winter) On the beach.
Post office (Av 58 & Calle 63)
Satelital (Calle 4, No 4063; per hr US$0.30) Internet access.

Sights & Activities

The dense pine woods of **Parque Provincial Miguel Lillo**, a large greenbelt along the beach,

are widely used for bicycling, horse riding, hiking and picnicking.

The Río Quequén Grande, rich in rainbow trout and mackerel, also allows for adventurous canoeing, particularly around the falls at Saltos del Quequén. At the village of **Quequén** at the river's mouth, several stranded shipwrecks offer good opportunities for exploration and photography below sculpted cliffs. The **faro** (lighthouse) is another local attraction.

Sleeping

Prices given here are for the January peak period; they can almost halve during the rest of the year.

Hotel España (☎ 422896; www.hotel-espana.com .ar in Spanish; Calle 89, No 215; s/d US$27/33; P) A small hotel with wonderfully comfortable rooms; some at the front have balconies overlooking the street, but all have good natural light.

Hotel Tres Reyes (☎ 422011; hoteltresreyes@telpin .com.ar; Calle 4 bis, No 4123; s/d US$25/30; P) The 'Three Kings' has some excellent rooms overlooking the plaza and some reasonable

THE PAMPAS & THE ATLANTIC COAST

THE AUTHOR'S CHOICE

Hostería del Bosque (☎ 420002; jfrigerio@telpin.com.ar; Calle 89, No 350; s/d US$23/27; P) Once home to a Russian princess, this is by far the most atmospheric place to stay in town. Rooms are quaint and comfortable, bathrooms modern and the beautiful Parque Lillo is right outside the front door.

ones out back. The decor is fairly business-like and functional, but it's a good deal for the price.

Hotel León (☎ 424800; www.hotel-leon.com.ar in Spanish; Av 79, No 229; s/d US$20/26; P 🔀) This place shines just a little brighter than the standard midrange Argentine hotel. It has a touch (no more) of elegance, the rooms are well kept and it's a short stroll to the beach.

Hotel Nikén (☎ 432323; www.hotelniken.com.ar in Spanish; Calle 87, No 335; s/d US$33/43; P 🔀 🖵 🖳) Outstandingly ugly from the outside, the Nikén's charms are fortunately all interior, with modern, spacious rooms and a ripping breakfast buffet.

Hotel Neptuno (☎ 422653; Calle 81, No 212; s/d US$7/14) An excellent little budget hotel a couple of hundred meters from the beach. Rooms are small but comfortable and come with TV and good firm beds.

Hotel Flamingo (☎ 420049; hotflamingo@mixmail.com; Calle 83, No 333; s/d US$10/15) The Flamingo's rooms are surprisingly well decked out for a budget joint, with minibars and (relatively) large bathrooms.

Eating

Chimichurri Asador (☎ 420642; Calle 83, No 345; all you can eat US$4.50) Well liked for its delicious meats, Chimichurri offers a special that includes *asado*, *parrillada*, empanadas, salad and dessert.

Taberna Española (☎ 525126; Calle 89, No 360; mains US$4-7) For the Spanish take on the whole seafood thing, this is the place to come, and come hungry. The *picada de mariscos* (series of small seafood dishes; US$6) is a gut buster – delicious fishy dishes just keep on coming.

Entertainment

There are several dance clubs located on the beach, which are impossible to miss on a weekend night.

El Mirador (☎ 15-505746; cnr Av 2 & Calle 79, Playa; admission US$2-6; ☾ Fri & Sat) Where Av 2 hits the beach, this tropically flavored club beats out the usual mix of *rock nacional*, house and international dance pop. There's an older crowd on Saturday.

Sabor Caribe (cnr Av 2 & Calle 87, Playa; mains US$2-4; ☾ Fri & Sat) For salsa, merengue and an overall good vibe try this disco at the end of Calle 87.

Getting There & Away

The **bus terminal** (☎ 422470; Av 58, btwn Calle 47 & Av 45) is near the river. Several companies run daily buses to Buenos Aires ($15, seven hours). Empresa Córdoba Mar del Plata serves the interior, and there are often special services by other carriers in summer. El Rápido connects Necochea with Mar del Plata (US$3, two hours), Bariloche, Tandil (US$6, 2¾ hours) and Santa Rosa. Rapido del Sud connects Necochea with other coastal destinations.

THE AUTHOR'S CHOICE

Cantina Venezia (☎ 424014; Av 59, No 259; mains US$4-6; ☾ dinner daily summer, dinner Wed-Sun winter) Still going strong after 40 years, this Italian/seafood restaurant is the pick of the seafood joints near the port. Prices are a little higher than the rest, but more than justified by the quality and size of the meals. It's not a great area, so you might want to get a taxi (US$1) home.

Northeast Argentina

Encompassing natural wonders, lusty carnival celebrations and a couple of lively cities, the northeast of Argentina offers a lot more than its most famous landmark, the Iguazú Falls. Which is not to say that Iguazú shouldn't be on every traveler's 'don't miss' list. Measuring more than 2km across, the falls certainly earn their place on the Unesco World Heritage list. Many people hop straight from Buenos Aires to the falls and back again, but doing so means missing out on a whole lot in between.

Misiones province, home to Iguazú, also hosts the region's second-most visited attraction, the magical 17th-century Jesuit missions from which Misiones takes its name. Rosario, on the Paraná river delta, is worth visiting for its excellent galleries and museums, jumping nightlife, striking architecture and well-developed riverfront. As Argentina's third-largest city, it holds many of the attractions of Buenos Aires without being so overwhelming, and many travelers rate it their favorite city. Santa Fe, while slightly more humble, is another drawcard with its well-preserved historical landmarks and a large university.

Possibly because of the proximity to Brazil, Carnaval is celebrated with particular fervor in this part of Argentina, most notably in the stately provincial capital of Corrientes, but also in the otherwise-mellow resort town of Gualeguaychú. The region also holds some of the country's best national parks and protected areas. Nature enthusiasts are well catered for, both in terms of biodiversity and relative ease of access to these wild and beautiful areas.

NORTHEAST ARGENTINA

TOP FIVE

- Gaping in wonder at the force of **Iguazú Falls** (p189)
- Exploring **Rosario** (p152), many visitors' favorite city
- Checking out the birdlife in **Reserva Provincial Esteros del Iberá** (p173)
- Chilling out on the riverside in **Gualeguaychú** (p174)
- Getting snap happy at the historic **Jesuit Missions** (p183)

- AVERAGE JUL HIGH IN ROSARIO: 15°C (59°F)
- AVERAGE DEC HIGH IN ROSARIO: 28°C (82°F)

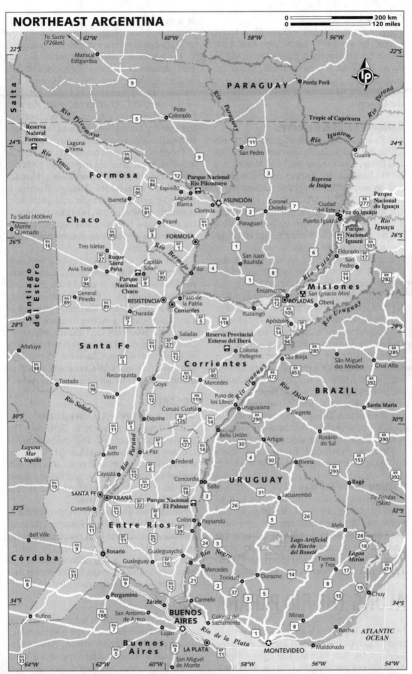

NORTHEAST ARGENTINA

NORTHEAST ARGENTINA

Climate

Temperatures recorded in the northeast have ranged between 5°C below zero and 43°C above, but an average temperature would be about 23°C. As you move north, things get a lot more tropical and humid, but out west there's not a whole lot of rain, especially in the Chaco.

National Parks & Reserves

There are some excellent national parks within the region, holding a variety of wildlife and fauna. The Parque Nacional Mburucuyá (p171) boasts three distinct natural regions, and an abundance of wildlife packed into a small area.

Parque Nacional El Palmar (p179) is home to an array of birds, mammals and reptiles, but most notably, is the last refuge of extensive stands of yatay palms.

Parque Nacional do Iguaçu (p192) and Parque Nacional Iguazú (p191) are access points for viewing the incredible Iguazú Falls, and also provide habitat for orchids, big cats, birdlife and other flora and fauna.

Parque Nacional Chaco (p205) has a variety of ecosystems, including marshes, open grasslands, palm savannas, scrub forest and denser gallery forests, and a corresponding diversity of wildlife, especially birds, including the rhea, jabirú stork, roseate spoonbill, cormorants and common caracaras.

Parque Nacional Río Pilcomayo (p209) has a similar makeup to Parque Nacional Chaco, but with the added bonus of lagoons where alligators are frequently spotted.

Reserva Provincial Esteros del Iberá (p173) is a bird-watchers' wonderland.

Getting There & Away

There are flights from Buenos Aires to Rosario, Santa Fe, Posadas, Resistencia and Formosa. Bus connections are available from most towns to destinations all over the country, but of course, services will be more frequent (and more direct) from larger cities. Trains run from Buenos Aires to Rosario.

ALONG THE RÍO PARANÁ

Northeast Argentina's largest and most interesting cities sit baking in the sun along the banks of the Río Paraná. The river – South America's second longest, after the Amazon –

is a central feature for those cities on its shores, and has become an important tourist attraction and primary means for cooling off in the summer. Sportfishing for sábalo, surubí, dorado and other river species attracts visitors from around the world, especially outside the oppressively hot summer. East of the river, in Corrientes province, the wetland wilderness of Esteros del Iberá, one of the country's most beautiful and least visited national parks, also draws many visitors.

Oceangoing vessels travel as far upriver as Rosario, home to some impressive architecture, excellent nightlife and a long, pleasant *costanera* (waterfront). Though Rosario is Santa Fe province's largest and most economically powerful city, the title of administrative capital goes to Santa Fe, a somewhat dull modern city with some impressive colonial architecture.

Corrientes, one of the region's first permanent Spanish settlements and capital of its namesake province, is a laid-back and sweltering city with one of the best-preserved city centers in the country. The entire province of Corrientes shows a strong indigenous presence, especially from the Guaraní, whose vocabulary graces everything from street signs to local expressions. *Chamamé*, the nationally loved folk music of Corrientes, is heavily influenced by Guaraní language and music.

ROSARIO

☎ 0341 / pop 1,095,900 / elevation 25m

Che Guevara was born in Rosario. The buildings are beautiful and the nightlife is rocking (but only on weekends). There are also plenty of artists and musicians around, the galleries are good, the beaches are close, and the riverside is happening – we should all be there right now, basically.

Situated on the upper Paraná river delta, 320km from Buenos Aires, Rosario has a long, accessible waterfront with restaurants, parks and *balnearios* (river beaches). The nearby river islands have a rich cultural history and are now popular hangouts for the hordes that brave the scorching summer sun.

History

Rosario's first European inhabitants settled here informally around 1720 without sanction from the Spanish crown. After independence, Rosario quickly superseded Santa Fe as the province's economic powerhouse,

ROSARIO

0 _____ 1 km
0 _____ 0.5 miles

INFORMATION		
ACA	**1**	A4
Alianza Francesa	**2**	C3
Asatej	**3**	C3
Centro Cultural Rivadavia	**4**	C3
Centro de Expresiones		
Contemporáneos	**5**	C3
Exprinter	**6**	C3
Grupo 3 de Turismo	**7**	C3
Hacker Cybercafé	**8**	C4
Librería Ross	**9**	C3
Municipal Tourist Office	**10**	D3
Rosario Central	**11**	C3

SIGHTS & ACTIVITIES		
Ernesto 'Che' Guevara's First		
Home	**12**	C3
Estación Fluvial	(see 14)	
Monumento Nacional a la		
Bandera	**13**	D3
Museo del Paraná y las Islas	**14**	D3
Museo Histórico Provincial Dr Julio		
Marc	**15**	A4
Museo Municipal de Bellas Artes Juan B		
Castagnino	**16**	A4
Museo Provincial de Ciencias Naturales		
Dr Ángel Gallardo	**17**	B3

SLEEPING		
Benidorm Hotel	**18**	C4
Hotel Imperio	**19**	C3
Hotel La Paz	(see 24)	
Hotel La Viña	**20**	C4
Hotel Libertador	**21**	C3
Hotel Litoral	**22**	C3
Hotel Majestic	**23**	C3
Hotel Plaza	**24**	C4
Hotel Plaza del Sol	**25**	C4
Hotel Plaza Real	**26**	B3
Hotel Republica	**27**	C3
Nuevo Hotel Europa	**28**	C3
Romijor Hotel	**29**	C4

EATING		
Amarra 702	**30**	D3
Bajo Cero	**31**	B3
La Rosario	**32**	C4
Las Tinajas	**33**	B4
Rich	**34**	C4
Rincón Vegetariano	**35**	C3
Victoria	**36**	B3

DRINKING		
Bara Bajo	(see 37)	
Fénix Bar	**37**	C3
Mi Refugio	**38**	B3

ENTERTAINMENT		
La Traición de Rita Hayworth	**39**	B3
Teatro del Rayo	**40**	C3
Teatro El Círculo	**41**	C4

SHOPPING		
Mercado de Pulgas del Bajo	**42**	D3

TRANSPORT		
Aerolíneas Argentinas	**43**	C3
Austral	(see 43)	
Dollar Rent-a-Car	**44**	C3
Local Bus Terminal	**45**	C3
Localiza	**46**	C3
Pluna	(see 9)	

NORTHEAST ARGENTINA

though, to the irritation of *rosarinos* (inhabitants of Rosario), the provincial capital retained political primacy.

The Central Argentine Land Company, an adjunct of the railroad, was responsible for bringing in agricultural colonists from Europe, for whom Rosario was a port of entry. From 1869 to 1914, Rosario's population grew nearly tenfold to 223,000, easily overtaking the capital in numbers. Rosario's industrial importance in the first half of the 20th century – its role in agricultural exports and its economic ties to the beef market of the Chicago Mercantile Exchange – earned Rosario the nickname 'Chicago Argentino.'

Though the decline of economic and shipping activity during the 1960s led to a drop in the city's population and power, Rosario's importance as a port was rivaled only by Buenos Aires. Its title as Argentina's second city, however, was usurped by Córdoba – a status still hotly contested by *rosarinos*.

Nationalistic Argentines cherish Rosario, home of a monument to the nation's flag, as 'Cuna de la Bandera' (Cradle of the Flag). There is a brashness about it that you won't see in other major cities such as Córdoba or Mendoza. A slogan gracing many a tourist brochure reads, 'Rosario, to know you is to love you.' In fact, the city demands a little time, but exploration will surely be rewarded. Another slogan across some T-shirts puts things more precisely: *'Rosario, me mata'* (Rosario, you kill me).

Orientation

RN 9, the main route to Córdoba, is also the major freeway connecting Rosario with Buenos Aires. Heading north to Santa Fe are RN 11 and its parallel freeway, A 008. Motorists are able to bypass the city on Av Circunvalación.

Rosario displays a very regular grid pattern, except where the curvature of the bluffs above the river channel dictates otherwise. Traditionally, the focus of urban activities is Plaza 25 de Mayo, but the pedestrian streets of San Martín and Córdoba mark the commercial center. There are some 70 square blocks of open space in Parque Independencia, southwest of downtown.

Information

BOOKSTORES

Librería Ross (☎ 440-4820; Córdoba 1347) Has a small selection of classics in English.

CULTURAL CENTERS

Alianza Francesa (☎ 424-8461; afrosario@ciudad.com.ar; San Luis 846; ⏰ 8am-noon & 4-10pm Mon-Fri)

Centro Cultural Rivadavia (☎ 480-2401; Av San Martín 1080) A good place to find out what's happening in town. It shows free or inexpensive films and hosts dance and theater events. Its galleries provide a showcase for the local arts community.

Centro de Expresiones Contemporáneas
(☎ 480-2243; cnr Av del Huerto & Bajada Sargento Cabral) Consists of recycled historical buildings now providing space for special exhibitions; there is sometimes an admission charge.

EMERGENCY

Medical (☎ 435-1111)
Police (☎ 448-6666)

INTERNET ACCESS

Hacker Cybercafé (3 de Febrero 1280; per hr US$0.30; ⏰ 9:30am-3am Mon-Fri, 1:30pm-3am Sat & Sun)

MEDICAL SERVICES

Hospital Clemente Alvarez (☎ 480-2111; Rueda 1110) Southwest of the city center.

MONEY

Money exchanges along San Martín and Córdoba change cash and traveler's checks, the latter with the usual commission. There are numerous ATMs.

Exprinter (Córdoba 960)

POST

Post office (Córdoba 721) There are many *locutorios* (private long-distance telephone offices) on Córdoba and San Martín.

TOURIST INFORMATION

ACA (Automóvil Club Argentina; ☎ 440-1278; Blvd Oroño 1302 at 3 de Febrero)

Municipal tourist office (☎ 480-2230; Av del Huerto; ⏰ 7am-7pm) On the waterfront. It has a computerized information system and slick bilingual brochures, and offers weekend walking tours of the city.

TRAVEL AGENCIES

Asatej (☎ 425-3798; Av Corrientes 653, 6th fl) The nonprofit student travel agency.

Grupo 3 de Turismo (☎ 449-1783; Córdoba 1147) The Amex representative.

Sights & Activities

MUSEO DEL PARANÁ Y LAS ISLAS

Thanks to the romantic, engaging murals of local painter Raúl Domínguez, this **museum** (☎ 440-0751; cnr Av Belgrano & Rioja; admission US$0.30; ⏰ 10:30am-noon Tue, 2:30-4pm Wed & Thu, 4-7pm Sun), on the 1st floor of the waterfront Estación Fluvial, is a worthwhile sight. Life on the islands of the Paraná river so enchanted Domínguez that he created this small museum, filling it with photographs, artifacts, historical documents and his own paintings. It's an interesting glimpse beyond the city grid, especially worth a visit if you plan to visit the islands. The museum is now run by Domínguez' wife Clemencia and their grandchildren, who will gladly answer any questions about the islands or the painter.

MONUMENTO NACIONAL A LA BANDERA

Manuel Belgrano, who designed the eloquently simple Argentine flag, rests in a crypt beneath a colossal 78m tower in architect Angel Guido's boat-shaped monument *Santa Fe 581*, a conspicuously overbearing manifestation of patriotic hubris, even by the standards of a country known for its nationalism. The monument's redeeming attributes are its location near the Paraná waterfront and the dizzying views of the river and surrounds from its tower, accessed by elevator. Its **museum** (☎ 480-2238; admission incl tower elevator US$0.30; ⏰ 9am-7pm) contains the original flag embroidered by Catalina de Vidal. For information about Rosario's yearly Flag Week celebrations, see p156.

NORTHEAST ARGENTINA

MUSEO HISTÓRICO PROVINCIAL DOCTOR JULIO MARC

One of the more modern museums in the country, the **Museo Histórico Provincial Doctor Julio Marc** (☎ 472-1457; Parque Independencia; admission free; ◷ 9am-5pm Tue-Fri, 4-7pm Sat & Sun) features plenty of post-Independence exhibits plus excellent displays on indigenous cultures from all over Latin America. There's also colonial and religious artifacts and the most ornate collection of *mate* paraphernalia you're ever likely to see.

MUSEO MUNICIPAL DE BELLAS ARTES JUAN B CASTAGNINO

This **museum** (☎ 480-2542; cnr Av Pellegrini & Blvd Oroño; admission US$0.30; ◷ noon-7pm Tue-Fri, 10am-7pm Sat & Sun) is definitely one of the best funded of the fine arts. It houses a permanent collection of European and Argentine fine art, with occasional contemporary exhibitions.

MUSEO PROVINCIAL DE CIENCIAS NATURALES DR ÁNGEL GALLARDO

This **museum** (☎ 4941-3777; Moreno 750; ◷ 3-6pm) is a huge collection of stuffed animals and other grisly items. The crumbling mansion that it's housed in nearly steals the show and the spider and insect exhibits will make you want to rush out and buy a mosquito net immediately.

LA COSTANERA

One of Rosario's most attractive features is its waterfront. It stretches some 15km from its southern end at Parque Urquiza to the Embarcadero Costa Alta, near the city's northern edge. The grassy, tree-filled **Costanera Sur**, just below downtown, stays busy year-round with family picnics, Sunday soccer matches, evening joggers and lip-hungry couples.

In summer, however, it's the **Costanera Norte** that attracts the crowds. The stretch along the busy Av E Carrasco, north of Av Puccio, has the most to offer. Here begins the **Rambla Cataluña**, a tree-lined riverfront with small sandy beaches, shoreline cafés, bars, volleyball nets and tanning bodies.

The widest beach is further north at **Balneario La Florida** (admission US$1; ◷ late Sep-May 1), with services including umbrellas, showers, clothing check and outdoor bars. The sidewalk stops at La Florida and picks up again at its northern edge at **Costa Alta**, where there

are more beaches and a pier with boats to the islands.

To get to Rambla Cataluña take bus No 153 from the center of town north 6km to Av Puccio (here the bus turns inland). Stroll up the *rambla* (boardwalk) along Cataluña beach and look for a spot to lay your towel.

RIVER ISLANDS

Rosario sits on the banks of the Río Paraná upper delta, an area characterized by largely uninhabited, subtropical islands and winding *riachos* (streams). **Isla Invernada** and **Isla del Espinillo**, the two main islands visible from Rosario's shore (though part of neighboring Entre Ríos province), are accessible by boat year-round from Costa Alta (see left) and from the **Estación Fluvial** (Ferry Station; ☎ 447-3838, 448-1888), just southeast of the Monumento Nacional a la Bandera.

Boats from Costa Alta leave every 20 minutes (US$1 roundtrip), from 9am to 8pm in summer (less frequently in winter) for the various *balnearios* along the western shore of Isla Invernada. The *balnearios* are all pretty similar, with sandy beaches, gregarious summer crowds, cafés, ice-cream stands, umbrella rentals, music, billboards and boats from the mainland. Bring plenty of sunblock.

From the Estación Fluvial there are regular boats to the southern *balnearios* of Costa Esperanza (which offers everything from quad-runners to boat trips), Vladimir and Oasis for US$2 roundtrip. You can also visit the island and settlement of **Charigüe**. Boats leave the Estación Fluvial at 9am, 12:30pm and 5pm on weekends only and cost US$3 roundtrip. The island has few restaurants, so pack a lunch.

The **Ciudad de Rosario I** (☎ 449-8688) offers two-hour cruises on the Paraná for US$3; it leaves from Estación Fluvial weekends and holidays at 2:30pm and 5pm.

COMPLEJO MUNICIPAL ASTRONÓMICO EDUCATIVO ROSARIO

Those interested in more distant environments can visit the planetarium at the **municipal observatory** (☎ 480-2554; Parque Urquiza; admission free), which has shows (US$1) from 5pm to 6pm Saturday and Sunday. From 9pm to 10pm Friday through Sunday, visitors can view the austral skies through its 2250mm refractor telescope and 4500mm reflecting telescope. Parque Urquiza borders the river, about seven blocks southwest of the Estación Fluvial on Belgrano.

ERNESTO 'CHE' GUEVARA'S FIRST HOME

Though not on the formal tourist circuits, the apartment building at Entre Ríos 480, designed by Alejandro Bustillo, was where Ernesto Guevara Lynch and Celia de la Serna lived in 1928 after the birth of their son, Ernesto Guevara de la Serna, popularly known as 'Che.' According to biographer Jon Anderson, young Ernesto's birth certificate was falsified (he was born more than a month before the official date of June 14), but this was certainly Che's first home, however briefly.

Festivals & Events

Every June, Rosario celebrates **La Semana de la Bandera** (Flag Week), climaxed by ceremonies on June 20, the anniversary of the death of Manuel Belgrano, the flag's designer. Additionally, the town has its own **Semana de Rosario** in the first week of October, as well as the national **Encuentro de las Colectividades**, a tribute to the country's immigrants, in November.

Sleeping

BUDGET

Romijor Hotel (☎/fax 421-7276; Laprida 1050; s/d with TV US$7/14) Airless but spacious rooms in this comfy, old-style hotel which is close enough to the center. Bathrooms are surprisingly large, with bathtubs.

Hotel Litoral (☎ 421-1426; Entre Ríos 1045; s/d US$7/11) This modernish hotel, across from noisy Plaza Sarmiento, has attractive balconies in many of its spotless rooms (which come with TV and fan); otherwise they're small and dark.

Hotel La Viña (☎ 421-4549; 3 de Febrero 1244; s/d US$7/10; ✖) This centrally located but faceless hotel is good value for small rooms with TV. However, some carpeted rooms have a very musty smell.

The best and most natural camping sites are on **Isla Invernada** (sites per person US$1); see p155 for details on how to get there. On the mainland, **Camping Municipal** (☎ 471-4381; sites per person US$1) is about 9km north of the city; take bus No 35 from the center to Barra 9.

MIDRANGE

Though exceptions certainly exist, Rosario's midrange accommodations are generally run-of-the-mill establishments.

Hotel Plaza del Sol (☎ 421-9899; www.hotelesplaza .com in Spanish; San Juan 1055; r US$40; P ✖ ▯ ✉) This four-star property offers excellent-value doubles right in the center of town. The breakfast buffet is huge and the swimming pool and sundeck area on the 11th floor have great views of the city.

Hotel Plaza (☎ 421-8666; www.hotelesplaza.com in Spanish; Barón de Maua 26; r US$29; P ✖) There's some serious 70s action going on in the lobby here, but it fades rapidly as you approach the rooms. They're comfortable enough, if a little heavy on the pastels, with smallish, modern bathrooms.

Hotel La Paz (☎ 421-0905; Barón de Maua 36; s/d US$14/17; P ✖) Still looking good after more than 50 years, the La Paz has simple but elegant rooms. Get one out front for a balcony overlooking Plaza Montenegro.

Hotel Majestic (☎ 440-5872; www.hotelmajestic .com.ar; San Lorenzo 980; s/d US$25/30; ✖) Slightly cramped but otherwise stylish rooms. The location is quiet but central.

Hotel Imperio (☎ 448-0091; www.hotelimperio.com .ar; Urquiza 1264; s/d US$24/27; ✖ ✉) The Imperio's rooms are functional but slightly on the small side. The restaurant is good, and the swimming pool and sundeck are definite pluses.

Hotel Libertador (☎ 424-1005; www.solans.com; Av Corrientes 752; s/d US$30/40; P ✖ ▯) Tall people beware: the Libertador has some seriously low ceilings, and anybody topping 6'2" will be acquiring a serious stoop. Apart from that, the rooms are fine, if a bit sterile.

Hotel Republica (☎ 424-8580; www.solans.com; San Lorenzo 955; s/d US$30/36; ✖) Apart from those annoying fake wood floors, the Republica has good-value rooms, some with city views, others that look out over the river.

Hotel Plaza Real (☎ 440-8800; www.plazarealhotel .com in Spanish; Santa Fe 1632; ste US$60; P ✖ ▯ ✉) Rosario's finest hotel offers luxurious suites in a modern building. Designed more for the business crowd than the average traveler, this is nonetheless a very comfortable place to stay.

Nuevo Hotel Europa (☎ 424-0382; San Luis 1364; s/d US$17/20; ✖) Shabby on the outside, stylish on the inside, this hotel near Plaza Sarmiento is good value. Rooms are big enough and beds are firm.

Benidorm Hotel (☎ 421-9368; San Juan 1049; s/d US$13/20) Most of the rooms at this friendly no-frills hotel have windows and firm beds.

THE AUTHOR'S CHOICE

Rich (☎ 440-8657; San Juan 1031; meals US$6-10) Specializing in exquisite Italian-influenced cuisine in a beautiful old building, Rich is one of the finest and most atmospheric restaurants in town. Budget-watchers shouldn't overlook the tasty *rotisería* (take-out shop) alongside.

Eating

Rincón Vegetariano (☎ 411-0833; Mitre 720; all you can eat US$3; ☽ Mon-Sat) With over 50 meat-free hot and cold dishes in a *tenedor-libre*-style setting, this place is ground zero for *parrilla* (mixed grill) dodgers.

Amarra 702 (☎ 447-7750; cnr Buenos Aires & Av Belgrano; mains US$3-5) Tastefully decorated and with a refined atmosphere, this restaurant down near the river serves up some imaginative fish, chicken and meat dishes. The paella for two (US$7) would easily feed three.

Victoria (☎ 425-7665; cnr San Lorenzo & Roca; mains US$2-5; ☽ 7:30am-late Mon-Sat, 8pm-late Sun) This atmospheric café-cum-bar in an old brick building offers a US$3 lunch special and delicious salads. It's a great place for a beer, too.

Las Tinajas (☎ 481-7332; Av Carlos Pellegrini 1455; all-you-can-eat Mon-Fri lunch US$4, Mon-Thu dinner US$6, Fri-Sun dinner US$7) This branch of the well-liked Las Tinajas chain puts even Las Vegas buffets to shame. More than 300 dishes, including seafood, fresh pastas, *parrillada* (mixed grill including steak), salty Chinese food and loads of desserts.

La Rosario (☎ 440-7985; Laprida 1220; meals US$4-6, with music extra US$1; ☽ dinner) This small ultrachic restaurant serves creative house specialties that are best enjoyed Thursday through Saturday nights when there's live music. Reservations are recommended.

The spot for excellent ice cream is **Bajo Cero** (☎ 425-1538; cnr Santa Fe & Roca; ☽ 9am-11pm). There are also several good, cheap cafés and riverside restaurants along the Rambla Cataluña.

Drinking & Dancing

Fénix Bar (Tucumán 1002; ☽ Thu-Sat) The Bara Bajo crowd (see right) often starts out at the lively (and loud) Fénix Bar.

Mi Refugio (☎ 440-6186; España 445; ☽ 8pm-late Sat) The best place to go to listen (or dance) to tango music. They often have a live orchestra. Meals (US$2 to US$3) are available.

Entertainment

NIGHTCLUBS

Clubs generally open their doors shortly after midnight, but the dance floors often remain deserted until after 2am, when the lines begin to form. There are several clubs northwest of downtown along Rivadavia. A cab from the center should cost around US$3.

Bara Bajo (San Martín 370; admission US$3; ☽ 2am-dawn Fri & Sat) This barlike dance club plays house, techno and *rock nacional* (Argentine rock) and usually gets packed.

Moebius (Rivadavia 2459; admission US$3-5) The line at the door gets frighteningly large after about 2:30am but the thugs in front keep it orderly. Expect dance music.

THEATER

Teatro El Círculo (☎ 448-3784, 448-1089; Laprida 1235) The city's main performing-arts venue.

Teatro del Rayo (☎ 424-6075; San Martín 473; ☽ 8:30pm Wed, Thu, Sat & Sun, 5pm Fri) This cozy theater and bar with wooden tables shows art films and cult classics on a small screen. It also has occasional theater performances.

La Traición de Rita Hayworth (☎ 15-616-2868; Dorrego 1170) A small performing-arts venue, bar and café, this intimate place is well worth visiting. Reservations are recommended.

SPORTS

Rosario has two first-division soccer teams. **Newell's Old Boys** (☎ 421-1180) has offices and plays at **Estadio Parque Independencia** (☎ 424-4169). **Rosario Central** (☎ 421-0000, 421-4169; Mitre 857) has a **stadium** (☎ 438-9595; cnr Blvd Avellaneda & Av Génova); tickets are also sold here. Always call to check on game times.

Shopping

Mercado de Pulgas del Bajo (cnr Av Belgrano & Buenos Aires) This picturesque flea market, where dealers sell everything from silverwork to leather goods, takes place weekend and holiday afternoons.

THE AUTHOR'S CHOICE

Soho Club (☎ 430-7421; Salta 2298; ☽ Wed-Sat) A combination restaurant/wine bar/dance club, the Soho spins cool grooves, has regular happy hours and features a Friday night 'glamor night' (so get yourself snazzed up).

NORTHEAST ARGENTINA

NORTHEAST ARGENTINA

Getting There & Away

AIR

Aerolíneas Argentinas/Austral (☎ 424-9517; Santa Fe 1412) have several daily flights to Buenos Aires (US$45). International services are with Varig and **Pluna** (☎ 425-6262; Córdoba 1015, 2nd fl); they go to Brazil (US$410) and Uruguay (US$88).

BUS

Long-distance buses use the **Estación Mariano Moreno** (☎ 437-2384/5/6; www.terminalrosario.com.ar in Spanish; Cafferata 702), near Santa Fe. From downtown Calle San Juan, take bus No 101.

Rosario is a major transport hub and there are direct daily services to nearly all major destinations, from Puerto Iguazú in the north to Comodoro Rivadavia down south.

There is international service to Asunción (US$22, 17 hours) and Ciudad del Este in Paraguay; Porto Alegre and Rio de Janeiro in Brazil; and Montevideo (US$27, 10 hours), Piriápolis and Punta del Este in Uruguay.

The following table shows midseason fares, which may rise or fall depending on demand. All destinations are served daily and most several times a day. Travel times are approximate.

Destination	Cost (US$)	Duration (hr)
Bariloche	52	24
Buenos Aires	7	4
Córdoba	9	6
Corrientes	15	12
Jujuy	25	16
La Plata	9	6
Mar del Plata	7	7½
Mendoza	15	12
Neuquén	42	16
Paraná	6	3
Resistencia	15	10
Salta	25	16
Santa Fe	5	2
Santiago del Estero	15	10
Tucumán	17	12

TRAIN

From Rosario's **train station** (☎ 430-7272; Av del Valle 2700), southbound services to Retiro, Buenos Aires (US$4, five hours) leave at 6am Monday through Saturday. Take bus No 138 from San Juan and Mitre to the station.

Getting Around

Aerolíneas Argentinas runs its own buses to **Aeropuerto Fisherton** (☎ 451-2997, 451-1226), 8km west of town. Public buses to Fisherton travel only within about 1km of the airport. A taxi or *remise* (taxi without a meter) costs about US$5.

From the local bus terminal on Plaza Sarmiento, the city's extensive system services virtually everywhere. To get to the city center from the long-distance terminal, take a bus marked 'Centro' or 'Plaza Sarmiento,' but buy a *tarjeta magnética* (magnetic bus card) from a terminal kiosk first; buses do not accept coins.

To rent a car, try **Dollar Rent-a-Car** (☎ 426-1700; Paraguay 892) or **Localiza** (San Lorenzo ☎ 439-1336; San Lorenzo 1286; Córdoba ☎ 435-1234; Córdoba 4199).

SANTA FE

☎ 0242 / pop 524,300

Santa Fe is a sassy little town, perfect for the late riser; the locals eat late, go out late and – you guessed it – go home late. The university ensures a young population, out and about on the lively riverfront or in the happening bar district, La Recoleta.

The original Santa Fe de la Veracruz, as Juan de Garay called it upon its foundation in 1573 while on expedition from Asunción (Paraguay), was nearly 80km northeast of present-day Santa Fe. By the mid-17th century, the location proved intolerable for the original Spanish settlers who, wearied of constant Indian raids, floods and isolation, packed the place up and moved it to its current location on a tributary of the Río Paraná. Although the city was rebuilt on the exact urban plan of abandoned Santa Fe La Vieja (Old Santa Fe), a neo-Parisian building boom in the 19th century and more recent construction have left only isolated colonial buildings. Those that remain, however, are well worth seeing.

Orientation

Santa Fe's remaining colonial buildings are within a short walk of Plaza 25 de Mayo, the town's functional center. Av San Martín, north of the plaza, is the major commercial street; between Juan de Garay and Eva Perón, it's an attractive *peatonal* (pedestrian mall).

RN 11 links Santa Fe with Rosario (167km) and Buenos Aires (475km) to the south and

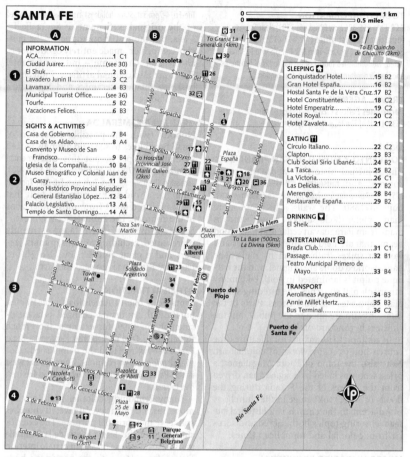

SANTA FE

0 — 1 km
0 — 0.5 miles

INFORMATION
ACA...1 C1
Ciudad Juarez.....................(see 30)
El Shuk...................................2 B3
Lavadero Junín II....................3 C2
Lavamax.................................4 B3
Municipal Tourist Office.......(see 36)
Tourfe....................................5 B2
Vacaciones Felices..................6 B3

SIGHTS & ACTIVITIES
Casa de Gobierno....................7 B4
Casa de los Aldao....................8 A4
Convento y Museo de San
Francisco.............................9 B4
Iglesia de la Compañía..........10 B4
Museo Etnográfico y Colonial Juan de
Garay.................................11 B4
Museo Histórico Provincial Brigadier
General Estanislao López.....12 B4
Palacio Legislativo..................13 A4
Templo de Santo Domingo.....14 A4

SLEEPING
Conquistador Hotel................15 B2
Gran Hotel España..................16 B2
Hostal Santa Fe de la Vera Cruz..17 B2
Hotel Constituentes................18 C2
Hotel Emperatriz.....................19 C2
Hotel Royal............................20 C2
Hotel Zavaleta........................21 C2

EATING
Círculo Italiano.......................22 C2
Clapton..................................23 B3
Club Social Sirio Libanés..........24 B2
La Tasca.................................25 B2
La Victoria..............................26 C1
Las Delicias............................27 B2
Merengo.................................28 B2
Restaurante España.................29 B2

DRINKING
El Sheik..................................30 C1

ENTERTAINMENT
Brada Club.............................31 C1
Passage..................................32 B1
Teatro Municipal Primero de
Mayo..................................33 B4

TRANSPORT
Aerolíneas Argentinas.............34 B3
Annie Millet Hertz...................35 B3
Bus Terminal..........................36 C2

NORTHEAST ARGENTINA

---

with Resistencia (544km) and Asunción to the north. Between Rosario and Santa Fe, the faster *autopista* (freeway) A 008 parallels the ordinary route. To the east, the Uranga Sylvestre Begnis tunnel (RN 168), beneath the Paraná, connects Santa Fe with its twin city of Paraná (25km) in Entre Ríos province.

Information
Telecom long-distance telephone services are in the bus terminal and at *locutorios* downtown.

CULTURAL CENTERS
Alianza Francesa (☎ 455-8575; info@alianzafrancesasf .com.ar; Blvd Galvez 2147; ☺ 8am-10pm Mon-Fri, 9am-1pm Sat)

INTERNET ACCESS
El Shuk (cnr San Martín & Av Corrientes; per hr US$0.30)

LAUNDRY
Lavadero Junín II (Av Rivadavia 2834)
Lavamax (9 de Julio, btwn Salta & Lisandro de la Torre)

MEDICAL SERVICES
Hospital Provincial José María Cullen (☎ 459-9719, 459-8337; Irigoyen Freyre) West of downtown.

MONEY
Tourfe (San Martín 2500) Collects 3% commission on traveler's checks. Several ATMs are along the San Martín *peatonal*.

POST
Post office (Av 27 de Febrero 2331) Near Mendoza.

TOURIST INFORMATION

ACA (☎ 455-3862; Av Rivadavia 3101) Near Suipacha.
Municipal tourist office (☎ 457-4123; bus terminal, Belgrano 2910; ☽ 7am-1pm & 3-8pm) Santa Fe's motivated, well-informed tourist office has loads of brochures and detailed information in loose-leaf binders.

TRAVEL AGENCIES

Vacaciones Felices (☎ 456-1608; Lisandro de la Torre 2632, Local 4) The local Amex representative.

Sights

CONVENTO Y MUSEO DE SAN FRANCISCO

The principal historical landmark is this convent and **museum** (☎ 459-3303; Amenábar 2257; ☽ 8am-noon & 4-7pm summer, to 6:30pm winter), built in 1680. The walls, which are more than a meter thick, support a roof which is made from Paraguayan cedar and hardwood beams that are held together by fittings and wooden spikes, rather than by nails. The hand-worked doors are original, and the baroque pulpit is laminated in gold. Like many other colonial churches, the building's floor plan duplicates the Holy Cross. Parts of the interior patio are open to the public, but the cloisters beyond are off limits.

In addition to its architectural features, the church houses many works of colonial art. Note also the tomb of Padre Magallanes, a priest who was killed by a jaguar that, driven from the shores of the Paraná during the floods of 1825, took refuge in the church.

Adjacent to the church is a **historical museum** covering topics both sacred and secular from colonial and republican times.

MUSEO HISTÓRICO PROVINCIAL BRIGADIER GENERAL ESTANISLAO LÓPEZ

In a moist but well-preserved late-17th-century building, this **museum** (☎ 459-3760; San Martín 1490; ☽ 8:30am-noon & 4-7pm Mon-Fri, 5:30-8:30pm Sat & Sun) contains permanent exhibits on the 19th-century civil wars, provincial governors and caudillos (provincial strongmen), period furnishings and religious art, plus a room with temporary displays on more contemporary themes. The collection of antique pistols and solid silver horse gear alone make it worth a visit.

MUSEO ETNOGRÁFICO Y COLONIAL JUAN DE GARAY

This **museum** (☎ 459-5857; 25 de Mayo 1470; admission free, donation requested; ☽ 8:30am-noon & 2:30-7pm Tue-Fri, 4-7pm Sat, Sun & holidays) has a scale model of the original settlement of Santa Fe La Vieja, but the real showstopper is the gaucho 'campchair', made entirely of cow bones and leather. Gruesome – but comfortable! There are also colonial artifacts, indigenous basketry, Spanish ceramics and a gaucho's stuffed horse.

GRANJA LA ESMERALDA

Nobody (with the possible exception of small boys) likes to see wild animals locked in confined spaces, but this **experimental farm/zoo** (☎ 457-9202; Av Aristóbulo del Valle 8700; admission US$0.50; ☽ 9am-7pm Mon-Fri, 8am-7pm Sat & Sun) has a wild and woodsy feel to it that makes it stand apart from most other zoos in the country. The animals seem almost… happy. Provincial native fauna is mainly represented, including toucans, pumas, jaguars and a giant anteater. Bus No 10 bis, from Av Rivadavia, goes to the farm.

OTHER ATTRACTIONS

Santa Fe is one of Argentina's oldest cities, but the 20th century has changed its face considerably: in 1909, for example, the French Renaissance **Casa de Gobierno** (Government House; Plaza 25 de Mayo) replaced the demolished colonial *cabildo* (town council). Four blocks west is the **Palacio Legislativo** (3 de Febrero, btwn 4 de Enero & Av Urquiza).

Many remaining colonial buildings are museums, although several revered churches still serve their original purpose. The exterior simplicity of the Jesuit **Iglesia de la Compañía** (east side Plaza 25 de Mayo) masks an ornate interior. Dating from 1696, it's the province's best-preserved colonial church.

The **Templo de Santo Domingo** (cnr 3 de Febrero & 9 de Julio) dates from the mid-17th century but has undergone several modifications. Its interior is Ionian, while the exterior is a combination of Ionian and Roman styles.

The **Casa de los Aldao** (☎ 459-3222; Monseñor Zaspe 2845; admission free; ☽ 8am-1pm Mon-Fri) is a restored two-story, early-18th-century house. Like others of its time, it has a tiled roof, balconies and meter-thick walls.

Sleeping

The seedy area around the bus terminal is the budget hotel zone. It's not dangerous – just the town center for various unsavory transactions.

Hostal Santa Fe de la Vera Cruz (☎ 455-1740; hostal_santafe@ciudad.com.ar; Av San Martín 2954; s/d standard US$25/33; P ✗) The standard rooms here are just fine, but for an extra US$10 or so, you can go for the superior, which are some of the nicest rooms in town.

Hotel Constituentes (☎ 452-1586; San Luis 2862; s/d US$10/13) A few steps above most of the hotels around the bus terminal, this place has big rooms with cable TV and blasting hot showers. Rooms at the front can suffer from street noise.

Conquistador Hotel (☎ 400-1195; linverde@gigared .com; 25 de Mayo 2676; s/d US$33/37; P ✗ ✉) The most modern hotel in town, the Conquistador lays out the charms, with sauna, hydromassage, fluffy bathrobes, gymnasium and a huge buffet breakfast.

Gran Hotel España (☎ 455-2264; linverde@gigared .com.ar; 25 de Mayo 2647; s/d US$13/20; P ✗ ✉) Nothing too fancy about the rooms here, but they're definitely good value, even more so when you consider that you can use the facilities at the Conquistador across the road free of charge.

Hotel Zavaleta (☎ 455-1841; hzavaleta@infovia .com.ar; Irigoyen Freyre 2349; s/d US$15/18; P ✗) The Zavaleta's getting a bit weary these days, but the rooms are comfortable, the beds are firm, and the location, right on the plaza and near the bus terminal, is hard to beat.

Hotel Emperatriz (☎ 453-0061; emperatrizhotelsf@ hotmail.com; Irigoyen Freyre 2440; s/d US$9/13; P ✗) The best of the budget picks in town, this place is set in a beautifully remodeled old house. The lobby is a lot more impressive than the rooms are, but they're still light and spacious.

Hotel Royal (☎ 452-7359; Irigoyen Freyre 2256; s/d with shared bathroom US$5/7) Cheap and basic, the gloominess of the rooms here is offset by the friendly management and the proximity to the bus terminal…it'll do for a night.

Eating

On Belgrano, across from the bus terminal, several very good, inexpensive places serve Argentine staples, such as empanadas, pizza and *parrillada,* and for a half-decent feed at any time, the café inside the terminal is open 24 hours. Otherwise, around the *peatonal* is the best bet.

Clapton (☎ 453-2236; Av San Martín 2300; meals US$3-5; ✓ breakfast, lunch & dinner) This modern café right on the *peatonal* serves good pizzas, sandwiches and salads at relatively cheap prices, and good-value set meals.

Las Delicias (☎ 453-2126; Av San Martín 2882; breakfast US$2-3, lunch & dinner US$3-5; ✓ breakfast, lunch & dinner) If you ever had any doubts that croissants are made of butter, get down to Las Delicias. Are these things buttery! You nearly need special gloves to eat them to stop them flying across the room. Otherwise, a huge range of fine pastries are on offer in this pleasantly traditional place.

El Quincho de Chiquito (☎ 460-2608; cnr Brown & Obispo Vieytes; all you can eat US$4-6) Tourists and locals both flock to this riverside eatery, some distance north of downtown. Because of its size, service is pretty impersonal, but it still serves outstanding grilled river fish, such as boga and sábalo, and exceptional hors d'oeuvres, such as fish empanadas. Drinks are extra. Take bus No 16 on Av Gálvez, which parallels Suipacha four blocks to the north.

La Tasca (San Martín 2846; breakfast US$1.50, lunch & dinner US$3-4; ✓ breakfast, lunch & dinner) Nothing mind-blowing on the menu here, but it's got a great old-time feel with tiled walls and hardwood furniture. Breakfast and snacks are good and cheap, and there are occasional exhibitions featuring local artisans.

Club Social Sirio Libanés (cnr 25 de Mayo & Eva Perón; meals US$4-8) In a rather aristocratic dining room, attentive waiters serve well-prepared Middle Eastern–style dishes; it's a unique place to eat.

Círculo Italiano (☎ 452-0628; Hipólito Yrigoyen 2457; meals US$3-6) Part of the Italian social club, Círculo Italiano prepares good, moderately priced lunch specials and tasty pastas. Come for the ritzy atmosphere, the waiters in linen jackets, the complimentary pâté or the extensive wine list. Stay for the classic rock on the sound system.

La Victoria (cnr San Martín & Santiago del Estero; pizza US$2) Right in the middle of Recoleta (see the next section) and still pumping at 3am, the Victoria is the place to come before, after or in between laps to have a few drinks and load up on good pizza and snacks.

Restaurante España (San Martín 2644; meals US$3-5) A huge menu covers the range of seafood, steaks, pasta, chicken and crepes, with a few Spanish dishes thrown in to justify the name. The wine list is a winner, too, as is the classy but unpretentious atmosphere.

NORTHEAST ARGENTINA

Merengo (☎ 459-3458; General López 2634; alfajores from US$0.30; ⏰ 9am-6pm) Since 1851 little Merengo has been making some of the town's best *merengo alfajores* (Santa Fe's sugar-crusted version of the country's favorite snack).

Drinking

Santa Fe's nightlife centers around the intersection of Av San Martín and Santiago del Estero, which is the heart of the area known as La Recoleta. Barhopping around here is easily done on foot, and there are plenty of people out and about on weekend nights.

El Sheik (25 de Mayo 3452) Laid-back without being tranquil, this place attracts a young crowd with its cheap drinks and good music.

Ciudad Juarez (☎ 452-7383; 25 de Mayo 3424) Another Recoleta stronghold, this Tex-Mex bar has a devoted crowd and loud music.

Entertainment

Passage (☎ 453-3435; Av San Martín 3243; admission US$1) Passage has been dishing out rock, electronica and Latin grooves for years, and it is still a good place to cut loose, if only for its small size, central location and cheap cover.

Brada Club (25 de Mayo 3328; admission US$1) A hip…very hip (ie wear your best, or go out and buy some) club that plays ambient electronica early on before breaking out the big beats in the wee hours.

Teatro Municipal Primero de Mayo (☎ 459-7777; Av San Martín 2020) Designed in the French Renaissance style which was so common in Argentina at the turn of the 20th century, this theater presents both drama and dance performances.

Getting There & Away

AIR

Aerolíneas Argentinas (☎ 452-5959; 25 de Mayo 2287) has 45 weekly nonstop flights to Buenos Aires (US$41).

BUS

The **bus terminal** (☎ 457-2490; Belgrano 2940) has a tourist office that posts all fares for destinations throughout the country, so you don't have to run from window to window for comparison. Here are some sample fares:

Destination	Cost (US$)	Duration (hr)
Asunción (Paraguay)	18	13
Bahía Blanca	20	14
Buenos Aires	12	6
Córdoba	9	5
Corrientes	14	10
Formosa	15	8
Lima (Peru)	100	60
Mar del Plata	19	12
Montevideo (Uruguay)	23	12
Neuquén	38	16
Paraná	1	40min
Resistencia	13	9½
Rosario	5	2
Tucumán	18	12

Getting Around

For US$0.50, city bus A goes to **Aeropuerto Sauce Viejo** (☎ 457-0642), which is 7km south of town on RN 11. To rent a car, try the **Annie Millet Hertz office** (☎ 456-4480/1; Lisandro de la Torre 2548).

AROUND SANTA FE
Alto Verde

Beyond Santa Fe, the Río Paraná has fostered a little known but intriguing way of life among the people of 'suburban' villages, such as Alto Verde. When the river rises, these fisherfolk evacuate their houses for temporary refuge in the city, but when the floods recede they rebuild their houses on the same spot.

Shaded by enormous willows and other trees, Alto Verde is a picturesque fishing village on Isla Sirgadero. To reach the village, catch a launch from Puerto del Piojo, in the port complex at the eastern end of Mendoza in Santa Fe, or take bus No 15 from Obispo Gelabert.

Cayastá

The Río San Javier has eroded away part of the **Cayastá ruins** (⏰ 8:30am-noon & 3:30-7pm Mon-Fri, 4-7pm Sat & Sun summer, 8am-1pm & 2-6pm Mon-Fri, 10am-1pm & 3-6pm Sat & Sun winter), which is the original site of Santa Fe La Vieja, including half of the Plaza de Armas. However, excavations have revealed the sites of the *cabildo* and the Santo Domingo, San Francisco and Merced churches. Authorities have erected protective structures to guard the remains of these buildings. For educational purposes, they have also reconstructed a

NORTHEAST ARGENTINA

typical period house with furnishings. You can usually talk your way onto the grounds even when it's closed.

Cayastá is 76km northeast of Santa Fe on RP 1. Paraná Medio bus company goes regularly from Santa Fe's bus terminal (US$2.50). Buy tickets at window number 14.

PARANÁ

☎ 0343 / pop 275,000

On the hilly banks of its namesake river, Paraná rolls out with a relaxed and stately assurance, a fitting counterpart to hectic Santa Fe across the river. If you arrive in Paraná on a Sunday, you could be forgiven for thinking that the town has been evacuated – in a way it has. This is the day when

everybody heads down to the *costanera*, and the grassy riverside strip transforms into a sea of folding lawn chairs and a flurry of *mate*-sipping activity. It's a good place for strolling at any time, especially around sundown when the promenaders come out.

Though it's the capital of Entre Ríos province, Paraná retains a relaxed, small-town feel. With low buildings and 19th-century architecture, its city center is compact and manageable.

Paraná's accommodations are comfortable, but its nightlife is slim. Beyond the few downtown sights, Paraná has little to offer aside from staring at the cathedral from a bench in the plaza or hanging out on the river with everyone else.

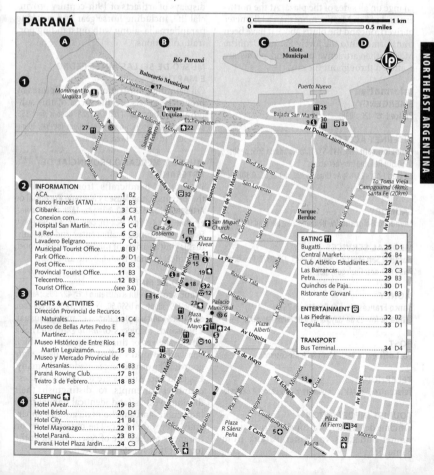

PARANÁ

0   1 km
0   0.5 miles

Río Paraná

Islote Municipal

Balneario Municipal

Monument to Urquiza

Puerto Nuevo

Bajada San Martín

Parque Urquiza

Av Laurencena

Blvd Bartolomé Mitre

Etchevehere

Av Doctor Laurencena

To Toma Vieja Campgo
und (4km); Santa Fe (20km)

Malvinas

Blvd Moreno

Garay

San Lorenzo

Parque Berduc

Casa de Gobierno

San Miguel Church

Plaza Alvear

Colón

La Paz

Rosario Tala

Palacio Municipal

Plaza 1 de Mayo

Plaza Alberti

Av Urquiza

25 de Mayo

LN Alem

Plaza R Sáenz Peña

Plaza M Fierro

Moreno

Alsina

NORTHEAST ARGENTINA

Orientation

Paraná sits on a high bluff on the east bank of the Río Paraná, 500km north of Buenos Aires via RN 9 and RN 11, which passes through Santa Fe; routes through southern Entre Ríos are shorter but slower because of substandard roads. The Uranga Silvestre Begnis tunnel, beneath the main channel of the Paraná, connects the city to Santa Fe.

The city plan is more irregular than most Argentine cities, with numerous diagonals, curving boulevards and complex intersections. Plaza 1 de Mayo is the town center; on Saturday mornings virtually the entire town congregates for a *paseo* (outing) down the *peatonal* José de San Martín.

Except for José de San Martín, street names change on all sides of the plaza. At the northern end of San Martín, more than a kilometer of riverfront and the bluffs above it have been transformed into the lovely Parque Urquiza. Many other attractive parks and plazas are scattered throughout the city.

Information

EMERGENCY
Police (☎ 420-9038)

INTERNET ACCESS
Conexion.com (☎ 431-5125; Av Rivadavia 665; per hr US$0.30) Reliable Internet access.
La Red (☎ 423709; Av Urquiza 790; per hr US$0.30) Good Internet access.

LAUNDRY
Lavadero Belgrano (Av Belgrano 306; per load US$2)

MEDICAL SERVICES
Hospital San Martín (☎ 423-4545, 421-8378; Presidente Perón 450, near Gualeguaychú)

MONEY
Banco Francés (José de San Martín 763) Has ATM.
Citibank (cnr 25 de Mayo & Av 9 de Julio) Has ATM.

POST
Post office (cnr 25 de Mayo & Monte Caseros)

TELEPHONE
Telecentro (San Martín, btwn Uruguay & Pazos) A *locutorio*.

TOURIST INFORMATION
Oficina del Túnel is a tourist office at the tunnel outlet, as you enter Paraná from Santa Fe.

ACA (☎ 431-1319; Buenos Aires 333)
Municipal tourist office (☎ 423-0183; Italia s/n; ☼ 8am-8pm)
Park office (☎ 420-1837; ☼ 8am-8pm) This tourist office is on the riverfront between Bajada San Martín and Av Doctor Laurencena.
Provincial tourist office (☎ 422-3384; Laprida 5; ☼ 8am-9pm)
Tourist office (☎ 422-4282) At the bus terminal.

Sights & Activities

MUSEO HISTÓRICO DE ENTRE RÍOS MARTÍN LEGUIZAMÓN
Flaunting local pride, this modern **museum** (☎ 420-7869; Buenos Aires 286; admission US$1; ☼ 7:30am-12:30pm & 3-7:30pm Tue-Fri, 10am-noon Sat & Sun) on Plaza Alvear contains well-arranged displays of artifacts of 19th-century provincial life, including horse gear and smoking paraphernalia, along with outstanding portrait collections.

MUSEO DE BELLAS ARTES PEDRO E MARTÍNEZ
Oil paintings, illustrations and sculptures by provincial artists are the focus of this subterranean **museum** (☎ 420-7868; Buenos Aires 355; admission free; ☼ 9am-noon & 4-7:30pm Tue-Sat, 10am-noon Sun), just off Plaza Alvear.

MUSEO Y MERCADO PROVINCIAL DE ARTESANÍAS
Promoting handicrafts from throughout the province, the **Museo y Mercado Provincial de Artesanías** (☎ 422-4540; Av Urquiza 1239; admission free; ☼ 8am-1pm & 4-7pm Mon-Fri, 8am-1pm Sat, 9am-noon Sun) is a combined crafts center and museum displaying a variety of media including wood, ceramics, leather, metal, bone and iron.

MUSEO DE MATE
Francisco Scutellá's **museum** (☎ 422-0995; Antonio Crespo 159; admission US$0.50; ☼ 7am-12:30pm & 4-8pm, closed Sat & Sun if sunny) is Paraná's most unusual. Thousands of pieces of *mate* paraphernalia fill the shelves of this small museum, which boasts the world's tallest and smallest *mate* gourds. The ornate pieces made in Germany, England and Austria are testimony to these countries' attempts to distinguish their drinking vessels (and identical habits) from indigenous and gaucho *mate* gourds; apparently they didn't take. The museum was on the move at the time of research; ask at the tourist office for its new location.

RIVER ACTIVITIES

From the northern edge of downtown, Parque Urquiza slopes steeply downward to the banks of the Río Paraná and the **Balneario Municipal**. During the summer months the waterfront fills with people strolling, fishing, swimming and practicing other languorous methods of staying cool. Beware of *jejenes* (annoying biting insects) along the river in summer.

River fishing is a popular local pastime, and tasty local game species like boga, sábalo, dorado and surubí reach considerable size. For licenses, contact the **Dirección Provincial de Recursos Naturales** (☎ 431-6773; 25 de Mayo 565).

The **Paraná Rowing Club** (☎ 431-2048) conducts hour-long river excursions for US$3; these depart at 3:30pm and 5pm Friday to Sunday from the Puerto Nuevo at Costanera and Vélez Sarsfield. Located on the riverfront, the rowing club has a café, and you can use its facilities, including a private beach, a swimming pool and showers, for US$2 per day.

Festivals & Events

Every February Paraná hosts the **Fiesta Nacional de Música y Artesanía Entrerriana**, featuring regional folk music and crafts.

At Diamante, 44km south of Paraná, the January **Fiesta Nacional de Jineteada y Folklore** celebrates gaucho culture and music. Diamante is also the site of February's **Fiesta Provincial del Pescador** (Provincial Fisherman's Festival).

Sleeping

Hotel Mayorazgo (☎ 423-0333; www.mayorazgohotel .com; Etchevehere near Blvd Moreno, Parque Urquiza; s/d US$30/50; P ✕ ⊇) Every room in this expansive five-star hotel faces the river; only those on the 1st floor, however, have huge balconies. A casino, a pool, a travel agency and tanning booths are a few of the amenities available.

Paraná Hotel Plaza Jardín (☎ 423-1700; www .hotelesparana.com.ar; 9 de Julio 60; s/d US$17/24) Set in a lovely old colonial building, this hotel has a peaceful patio that's great for a break from the midday heat. Rooms are OK: modern enough and clean, but none too large.

Gran Hotel Paraná (☎ 422-3900; www.hotelesparana .com.ar; Av Urquiza 976; s US$20-37, d US$26-47) The standard rooms here probably aren't worth the price, but the superior ones definitely are: they're tastefully decorated and luxurious. The breakfast buffet is rocking.

Hotel City (☎ 431-0086; Racedo 231; s/d with TV US$7/11; P) Directly opposite the train station, this simple hotel has a delightful patio garden and cool rooms with high ceilings. The price drops if you share a bathroom.

Hotel Bristol (☎ 431-3961; Alsina 221; r US$12) Well kept and quiet, this clean and attractive hotel is the best place near the bus terminal.

Gran Hotel Alvear (☎ 422-0000; paranacity@yahoo .com; San Martin 637; s/d US$15/20; P ✕) Some hotels look great from the outside, but are a big letdown once you get to the rooms. The Alvear works the other way – looks like a shocker, but rooms are comfortable and stylish, in a fading-glory kind of way.

Toma Vieja Campground (☎ 424-7721; end of Av Blas Parera; sites US$3) On the scenic site of the old waterworks overlooking the river, Toma Vieja is Paraná's only official (and only decent) campsite. Services include hot showers and electricity, and there's a store nearby. Bus No 5 leaves hourly from the terminal.

Eating

The central market at the corner of Carlos Pellegrini and Bavio is a great place to stock up on food.

Las Barrancas (☎ 432-0939; Av Urquiza 843; mains US$2-4) With its leafy tiled patios set in a lovely old colonial-style building, this is one of the more atmospheric choices in town. The menu is simple, specializing in meat and pasta, and they have live music on weekends.

Ristorante Giovani (☎ 423-0527; Av Urquiza 1045; meals US$2-3 ⊙ lunch & dinner) Though the fish can be hit or miss, this highly esteemed, upscale *parrilla* serves excellent meats and delectable pastas and features a very impressive wine list.

Petra (☎ 423-0608; 25 de Mayo 32; all-you-can-eat lunch/dinner US$2/3; ⊙ lunch & dinner) With a huge range of mostly Chinese food on offer, some claim that this is the best deal north of Ushuaia – and the food is surprisingly good. Drinks not included.

Club Atlético Estudiantes (☎ 422-2484; cnr Los Vascos & Bertozzi; meals US$4-6) Inside the athletic club on the western end of Parque Urquiza, this is one of the best seafood restaurants in town, and you can check out the club trophies while you eat.

NORTHEAST ARGENTINA

NORTHEAST ARGENTINA

THE AUTHOR'S CHOICE

Bugatti (☎ 15-504-0770; Portside; meals US$4-5; ☺ dinner, lunch Sun only) No surprises on the menu – meat, chicken, pasta and fish – but the elegance of the dining room in this renovated post office is worth making the trip for. Even if you're not hungry, the balcony bar is a great place to have a few drinks as the sun goes down.

Quinchos de Paja (☎ 423-1845; Av Doctor Laurencena at Salta; mains US$4-7) Locals and tourists alike flock to this seafood institution for delicious river fish. Also on offer are the standard pasta and *parrilla* offerings.

Entertainment

Teatro 3 de Febrero (☎ 420-1657/8; 25 de Junio 60) This municipal theater puts on exhibitions of local art, inexpensive films and other activities.

Tequila (☎ 421-9286; Linieres 334; ☺ midnight-dawn Thu-Sat) This Tex-Mex-flavored dance club on the river plays the usual mix of mainstream *marcha*, house and salsa.

Las Piedras (☎ 422-9665; cnr Av Rivadavia & Libertad Córdoba; ☺ 9am-1pm & 6pm-late) This bar-cum-sandwich shop has live music on Friday and Saturday nights, usually followed by dancing. It's a small, fun place.

Getting There & Away

BUS

The **bus terminal** (☎ 422-1282; Av Ramírez btwn Posadas & Moreno) is opposite Plaza Martín Fierro. Paraná is a center for provincial bus services, but Santa Fe is more convenient for long-distance trips. Buses leave every 20 minutes for Santa Fe (US$1, 40 minutes). Some other destinations:

Destination	Cost (US$)	Duration (hr)
Buenos Aires	12	6½
Córdoba	10	6
Corrientes	14	10
Mar del Plata	20	12½
Mendoza	17	15
Resistencia	13	9½
Rosario	5	2½
Tucumán	18	12
Salta	28	17
Santa Fe	1	40min

CAR

Motorists should be aware of irritating document checks from the provincial police at each end of the Uranga Silvestre Begnis tunnel between Paraná and Santa Fe. The passenger vehicle toll is US$1.

Getting Around

Bus Nos 1, 4, 5 and 9 run between the terminal and the center for US$0.30. You can hire a car at **Localiza** (☎ 423-1707; cnr 25 de Mayo & Arturo Illía).

LA PAZ
☎ 03437

There's not a whole lot to do in La Paz, and the town seems fairly content to keep it that way. Located on the east bank of the Paraná, about 160km northeast of Entre Ríos' provincial capital, La Paz is known for excellent fishing and good camping.

There's a **tourist office** (☎ 423501) at Vieytes 1143. In February the town springs to life with the **Fiesta Nacional de Pesca Variada de Río** (National River Fishing Festival). **Hotel Milton** (☎ 422232; www.miltonhotel.com.ar in Spanish; Italia 1029; s/d US$12/18; ⓟ ☒) is comfortable and by the plaza. For more modest accommodations, try the basic, rather cramped **Residencial Las Dos M** (☎ 421303; Urquiza 825; s/d US$8/10). **La Veredera** (cnr Moreno & San Martin; dishes US$3-4; ☺ breakfast, lunch & dinner) is an above-average *confitería* (café) on the plaza with a good selection of fish dishes. The central **bus terminal** (☎ 422365) has departures to Mercedes (US$9, four hours), Paraná (US$3, four hours) and Buenos Aires (US$13, five hours), among others.

CORRIENTES
☎ 03783 / pop 364,500

Just below the confluence of the Ríos Paraná and Paraguay, Corrientes is one of Argentina's oldest cities. The city's colorful streets and early-20th-century balconied buildings rising up from the muddy waters of the Río Paraná were the setting for Graham Greene's novel *The Honorary Consul*. The previously moribund Carnaval Correntino (p168) has experienced a revival and is now attracting crowds of up to 80,000.

Well-preserved Plaza 25 de Mayo is surrounded by a combination of Italianate and 19th-century French architecture, and by older, slightly decrepit colonial buildings that betray the city's age and add to its charm.

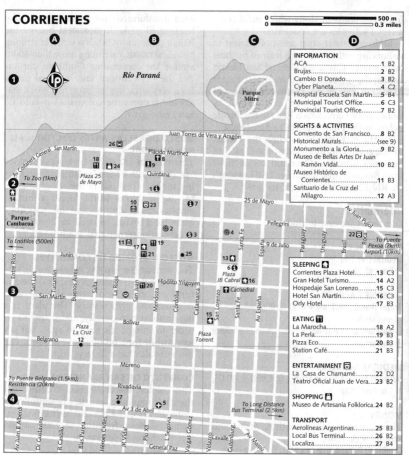

CORRIENTES

INFORMATION	
ACA	1 B2
Brujas	2 B2
Cambio El Dorado	3 B2
Cyber Planeta	4 C2
Hospital Escuela San Martín	5 B4
Municipal Tourist Office	6 C3
Provincial Tourist Office	7 B2

SIGHTS & ACTIVITIES	
Convento de San Francisco	8 B2
Historical Murals	(see 9)
Monumento a la Gloria	9 B2
Museo de Bellas Artes Dr Juan Ramón Vidal	10 B2
Museo Histórico de Corrientes	11 B3
Santuario de la Cruz del Milagro	12 A3

SLEEPING	
Corrientes Plaza Hotel	13 C3
Gran Hotel Turismo	14 A2
Hospedaje San Lorenzo	15 B3
Hotel San Martín	16 C3
Orly Hotel	17 B3

EATING	
La Marocha	18 A2
La Perla	19 B3
Pizza Eco	20 B3
Station Café	21 B3

ENTERTAINMENT	
La Casa de Chamamé	22 D2
Teatro Oficial Juan de Vera	23 B2

SHOPPING	
Museo de Artesanía Folklórica	24 B2

TRANSPORT	
Aerolíneas Argentinas	25 B3
Local Bus Terminal	26 B2
Localiza	27 B4

NORTHEAST ARGENTINA

Much of its *costanera* is wide, tree-lined, perfectly landscaped and full of people throughout the evening. Corrientes is a magnet for regional indigenous crafts, which artisans sell in the evening on the plaza JB Cabral and in the Museo de las Artesania Folklórica and its neighboring shops. Guaraní culture has a strong presence.

Perhaps as a reply to nearby Resistencia's claim as the City of Sculpture, Corrientes is setting itself up as the City of Murals, and there are indeed quite a few to be seen as you wander the streets. The tourist offices have maps detailing their locations.

If you're wondering where everybody is in the late afternoon, check the riverbank, a favorite spot for *mate* drinking and fishing.

Sunset across the Río Paraná is particularly spectacular.

Corrientes was originally called Vera de los Siete Corrientes, after its founder Juan Torres de Vera y Aragón and the shifting *corrientes* (currents) of the Paraná. Corrientes suffered repeated Indian uprisings before establishing itself as the first Spanish settlement in the region.

Orientation

Corrientes' regular grid centers on Plaza 25 de Mayo, though the major public buildings are more spread out than in most Argentine cities. There are several other important plazas, including Plaza La Cruz and Plaza JB Cabral. Between Salta and San Lorenzo,

Junín is a *peatonal* along which most commercial activities are concentrated.

Junín and most other areas of interest to visitors are within a triangle formed by three main streets: Costanera General San Martín (which changes names to Plácido Martínez at its eastern end), north–south Av España, and Av 3 de Abril, a westward extension of Av Gobernador Ferré, which leads to the Puente Belgrano (Belgrano Bridge) to Resistencia.

To the east, RN 12 parallels the Paraná to Ituzaingó and to Posadas, the capital of Misiones province. Overland connections from Buenos Aires, which lies 1025km south via RN 12 and other roads, are good.

Information

Locutorios are easy to find.

EMERGENCY
Medical (☎ 107)
Police (☎ 101)

INTERNET ACCESS
Brujas (Mendoza 787; per hr US$0.30) Offers reliable Internet service.
Cyber Planeta (☎ 15-684261; San Lorenzo 735) Reliable Internet service.

MEDICAL SERVICES
Hospital Escuela San Martín (☎ 420697/8, 421371; Av 3 de Abril 1251)

MONEY
There are several banks with ATMs on and around 9 de Julio.
Cambio El Dorado (9 de Julio 1341) You can change money here.

POST
Post office (cnr San Juan & San Martín)

TOURIST INFORMATION
ACA (☎ 422844; cnr 25 de Mayo & Mendoza)
Municipal tourist office (☎ 423779; Plaza JB Cabral; ☼ 7am-1pm & 3-8pm)
Provincial tourist office (☎ 427200, 424565; 25 de Mayo 1330; ☼ 7am-1pm & 3-9pm Mon-Fri, 8am-noon & 4-8pm Sat & Sun) Friendly and helpful.

Sights
MONUMENTO A LA GLORIA & HISTORICAL MURALS
In recent years, the east side of San Juan, between Plácido Martínez and Quintana, has been transformed into a shady, beautifully landscaped park. A **monument** honors the Italian community, while a series of striking historical **murals**, extending more than 100m around the corner onto Quintana, chronicles the city's history since colonial times. It's a very attractive addition to a block that already features the colonial Convento de San Francisco.

MUSEO DE BELLAS ARTES DOCTOR JUAN RAMÓN VIDAL
This **museum** (☎ 436722; San Juan 634; admission free; ☼ 9am-noon & 6-9pm Tue-Sat) is as interesting for the great old house it occupies as for the jumble of works found within. It emphasizes sculpture and oil paintings from local artists, as well as hosting the occasional international exhibitions.

MUSEO HISTÓRICO DE CORRIENTES
This **museum** (9 de Julio 1044; admission free; ☼ 8am-noon & 4-8pm Mon-Fri) exhibits weapons, antique furniture, coins and items dealing with religious and civil history. The place is a big jumbled mess, really, and if there's an order to things, it's hard to spot, but it's worthwhile for a bit of a poke around. The museum also has a library.

CONVENTO DE SAN FRANCISCO
This colonial **church** (Mendoza 450) dates from the city's founding, and was beautifully restored in 1939. The convent has its own museum, the **Museo Francisco** (☎ 422936; admission free; ☼ 8am-noon & 5-9pm Mon-Fri).

OTHER SIGHTS
Out on the tree-lined Av Costanera is a small but interesting **zoo** (☎ 427626; Av Costanera at Junin; admission free; ☼ 10am-6pm), beyond which are excellent views of the **Puente Belgrano**, the bridge crossing the Paraná river to Resistencia.

On the south side of Plaza La Cruz is the **Santuario de la Cruz del Milagro**, which contains a 16th-century cross that, according to legend, defied all efforts of rebellious Indians to burn it.

Festivals & Events
Inspired by immigrants from the provincial town of Paso de los Libres on the Brazilian border, Corrientes' traditionally riotous **Carnaval Correntino** nearly disappeared until a

THE AUTHOR'S CHOICE

Gran Hotel Turismo (☎ 433174; Entre Ríos 650; s/d US$10/15; P ✗ ⚑) Built in 1948, this stately old hotel has an attractive restaurant, a large pool, a bar and an excellent riverside location. The rooms are slightly worn, but it's a charming old place, and a lot more atmospheric than other hotels in town.

recent revival, and it's once again an event worth attending. Celebrated Friday through Sunday the last three weekends in February and the first weekend of March, Carnaval attracts participants from neighboring provinces and countries to the parades along Av Ferré; crowds have reached 80,000.

Sleeping

During Carnaval, the provincial tourist office maintains a list of *casas de familia* (family accommodations) where lodging generally ranges from US$4 to US$12 per person. Most hotels offer substantial discounts for cash payment.

Corrientes Plaza Hotel (☎ /fax 466500; www .hotelplazactes.com.ar in Spanish; Junín 1549; s/d US$23/28; P ✗ 🖥 ⚑) The finest hotel in the true center, the Plaza's generous rooms are a little heavy on the pastel paintwork, but otherwise an excellent deal.

Hospedaje San Lorenzo (☎ 421740; San Lorenzo 1136; r US$7) The San Lorenzo is small, and many rooms lack proper ventilation, but budget accommodations are a problem in this city, and this is about the best there is on offer.

Orly Hotel (☎ 420280; hotelorly@arnet.com.ar; San Juan 867; s/d US$17/21; P ✗) This compact hotel offers small but well-presented rooms overlooking the plaza. Facilities include room safes and minibars.

Hotel San Martín (☎ 421061; hsanmartin@impsat .com.ar; Santa Fe 955; s/d standard US$34/52, superior US$54/67, ste US$15/20; P ✗) A reasonable deal right on the plaza. Rooms are clean, if aging, but for some reason none of them face the front, where the views are best.

Eating

The Junín *peatonal* has cafés and *confiterías* (pastry shops), but shuts down during the midday heat.

Corrientes Plaza Hotel (US$2; ☯ breakfast) Big breakfasters should check out the breakfast buffet. Excellent coffee is served, and you can cram yourself with all the toast, cereal, croissants and cake that you can manage. See left.

La Perla (☎ 423008; cnr 9 de Julio & Mendoza; pastries from US$1; ☯ 8am-1pm & 4-11pm Mon-Sat) An old-fashioned, Italian-style bakery and café that serves mind-altering pastries and excellent coffee; each cup comes with *chipasitos* (small cheese pastries). Everything is warm when the doors open at 4pm.

Pizza Eco (☎ 425900; Hipólito Yrigoyen 1108; large pizzas US$4; ☯ 7am-1pm & 5pm-3am) Both the atmosphere and the pizza rate well at this friendly spot. A dozen empanadas cost US$2 to US$4.

La Marocha (☎ 438699; cnr Salta & Quintana; meals US$3-5; ☯ breakfast, lunch & dinner) A cute little restaurant/bar with a wider-than-normal selection of salads, meat dishes and some good breakfasts. Also a good range of wines and cocktails.

Station Cafe (☎ 420280; San Juan 867; meals US$2-3; ☯ breakfast, lunch & dinner) Good sandwiches, salads and homemade pastas at this tastefully decorated, modern café. Try the *ñoquis parisienne* (gnocchi with chicken, ham and cheese; US$2) or a primavera sandwich (US$2).

Entertainment

Puente Pexoa (☎ 451687; RN 12 at La Retonda Virgen de Itatí roundabout; ☯ opens 8:30pm, 1st band at 11:30pm Fri & Sat) Corrientes is the heartland of the lively music and dance known as *chamamé* (see the boxed text, p170), and seeing a

THE AUTHOR'S CHOICE

Enófilos (☎ 439271; Junín 172; dishes US$4-7) This modern yet rustically decorated little bar/restaurant overlooks the plaza, just a 10-minute walk from the center. Serving some of the most creative dishes available outside of Buenos Aires, it's a great place to get off the pizza, pasta, *parrilla* treadmill. As well, they are wine specialists, selling bottles from a climate-controlled wine room, and also by the glass with meals. Wine appreciation courses are occasionally on offer and a small deli sells imported meats and cheeses.

CHAMAMÉ

While the rest of the country is doing the tango, northeast Argentina is dancing the *chamamé*. One of the country's most intoxicating musical forms, *chamamé* is rooted in the polka, which was brought to the littoral region by European immigrants in the early 19th century, and is heavily influenced by the music and language of the indigenous Guaraní. Its definitive sound is the accordion, which is traditionally accompanied by the guitar, the *guitarrón* (an oversized guitar used for playing bass lines), the larger *bandoneón* (accordion) and the *contrabajo* (double bass). Of course, a *conjunto* (band) is hardly complete without a singer or two.

Chamamé is as much a dance as it is a musical genre, and it's a lively one. It is a dance for a couple, except when the man takes his solo *zapateo* (folkloric tap dance). Corrientes province is the heart of *chamamé* and is therefore the easiest place to find a live performance. Sitting in on an evening of music and dancing, or taking to the floor if you're brave, is one of the joys unique to the province.

live performance is difficult outside the provinces of northeastern Argentina. This relaxed restaurant features dances every weekend and it can be outrageous fun when the dancing starts. Men and women show up in full gaucho regalia, and up to four *conjuntos* (bands) may play each night. From downtown, take bus No 102 marked '17 de Agosto' 7km east of town to the Virgen de Itatí roundabout. It's just off the roundabout; the driver will point it out. A taxi back will cost US$4 to US$6.

Teatro Oficial Juan de Vera (☎ 427743; San Juan 637) This theater honoring the city's colonial founder offers classical-music concerts and other cultural events.

NORTHEAST ARGENTINA

Shopping

Museo de Artesanía Folklórica (Quintana 905; ⏰ 8am-8pm Mon-Fri, 8am-noon & 4-8pm Sat) In a converted colonial house with an interior courtyard, this museum sells local crafts including palm weavings, silver- and leatherwork and wood carvings. Fine antique crafts are on exhibit. Other rooms around the courtyard are occupied by working artisans who will sell to you directly.

La Casa de Chamamé (Pellegrini 1790) This CD shop specializes in Corrientes' roots music, and the friendly staff will let you listen before you buy.

Getting There & Away

AIR

Aerolíneas Argentinas/Austral (☎ 423918; Junín 1301) flies to Buenos Aires daily (US$80). There are also flights to Buenos Aires from nearby Resistencia with both Austral and Aerolíneas Argentinas.

BUS

Resistencia, northwest of Corrientes in El Chaco province, has better long-distance bus connections, especially to the west and northwest (see p204). Buses to Resistencia (US$0.50, 40 minutes) leave regularly throughout the day from the **local bus terminal** (Av Costanera General San Martín at La Rioja). Buses to provincial destinations like Goya and Esquina also leave from here.

Corrientes has a **long-distance bus terminal** (Av Maipú, btwn Manatiales & Nicaragua). At least four buses daily head to Buenos Aires (US$18 to US$28, 12 hours), some via Paraná, Santa Fe and Rosario, and others via Entre Ríos. There are regular runs to Posadas (US$7, 4½ hours), capital of Misiones province, where there are connections to the former Jesuit missions and to Puerto Iguazú (US$12, 10 hours). Transportes El Zonda crosses the Chaco to Tucumán, and Puerto Tirol serves the western bank of the Paraná, with routes running from Formosa south to Buenos Aires.

Tata/El Rápido goes to Paso de los Libres (US$6, six hours), on the Brazilian border, via the interior city of Mercedes, which is the place to access the Esteros del Iberá preserve. Empresa Tala goes to Uruguaiana, Brazil and Asunción, Paraguay, and Co-Bra offers direct service to Brazil.

Getting Around

Local bus No 105 (US$0.40) goes to the **airport** (☎ 458684), about 10km east of town on RN 12. Austral/Aerolineas Argentinas runs a minibus to Resistencia to coincide with flight schedules.

Bus No 6 runs between the local bus terminal and the long-distance terminal on

Av Maipú. Bus No 103 connects the long-distance terminal with downtown.

For car rental, try **Localiza** (☎ 426270; Av 3 de Abril 1047).

PASO DE LA PATRIA

☎ 03783

If you need some down time, Paso de la Patria may well be the place for you: wandering the sandy streets and gazing at the river are two major entertainment options in this flood-prone little village, 30km northeast of Corrientes.

Sitting at the confluence of the Ríos Paraguay and Paraná, this is really a fishing town and, hard as it is to believe, the place is heaving in August, when it hosts the Fiesta Internacional del Dorado.

High season is July to September; early October to early March is the closed (no fishing) season.

There is a **tourist office** (☎ 494493, ext 23; ✆ 7am-1pm & 3-8pm) at 25 de Mayo 425.

Festivals & Events

The highlight of the annual **Fiesta Internacional del Dorado**, which is held in mid-August, is a four-day competition for the largest specimens of the carnivorous dorado, known as the 'tiger of the Paraná' for its fighting nature. The dorado weighs up to 25kg, and the minimum allowable catch size is 75cm. Entry costs around US$50 for a three-person team. In addition to the dorado, other local sport species include the surubí (weighing up to 70kg), the tasty boga, sábalo, pejerrey, pacú, patí, manduví, mangrullo, chafalote and armado. Methods include trolling, spinning and fly casting. Night fishing is possible.

Sleeping & Eating

Several campgrounds charge about US$2 per tent per day, plus US$1 per vehicle, with all facilities. Many *correntinos* (inhabitants of Corriento) have weekend houses here and often rent them to visitors. Prices for a two-bedroom house start at around US$35 per day for up to six people. For more information, contact the tourist office.

Hotel Costa del Sol (☎ 494337; Belgrano s/n; s/d US$10/15; P ⊗ ⊾) This is an efficiently run brick place about 1km out of town. Rooms are comfortable and spotless and they offer a range of (mainly fishing-based) tours and activities.

La Barra (La Rioja 262; meals US$2-3) This place has a good airy dining area and shady sidewalk tables. While you're here, you have to try the local favorite: *surubí milanesa* (a river fish covered in breadcrumbs and fried).

Getting There & Away

There is frequent bus service to and from Corrientes (US$1, one hour). Ask at the tourist office in Plaza Cabral (p168) about the regular combi service, which is faster and will save you the trek to the bus terminal.

PARQUE NACIONAL MBURUCUYÁ

Way off the beaten track, this 176-sq-km **national park** (☎ 498022; mburucuya@apn.gov.ar; admission free) lies about 180km southeast of Corrientes. It belongs to the same ecoregion as the Reserva Provincial Esteros del Iberá (p173) and, while visitor services are nowhere near as advanced, it offers a much greater biodiversity.

The land was donated by Danish botanist Troels Pederson, whose work in the area identified around 1300 species of plants, including some previously undiscovered ones. The park holds three natural regions: the Chaco, characterized by palm, carob and quebracho forests, pastures and riverine estuaries; the Paraná Forest, with magote islands, pindó palms and tacuarazú cane; and the Spinal Zone, with its xerófilo forests, yatay palms and grasslands. There is an abundance of fauna: 150 species of birds have been spotted, as well as capybaras, yacarés, foxes, gazunchos and the near-extinct aguará guazú, river wolf and swamp deer.

At present there are only two walking trails within the park. The Sendero Yatay passes through 2.5km of forests and grassland dotted with yatay palms to a lookout point on the Estero Santa Lucia. The Sendero Aguará Popé has explanatory signs along its 1.2km length as it winds through a variety of environments and crosses a small creek where alligators are often spotted.

The **visitor center** (✆ 9am-5pm) is 9km into the park.

Sleeping & Eating

Camping is the only option within the park itself, at a small, rustic campground (free; with toilets and drinking water) next to the visitor center.

NORTHEAST ARGENTINA

The reasonable **Residencial Verón** (☎ 498006; Rivadavia 662; r US$5; **P**) – in the small and friendly town of Mburucuyá, 12km west of the park – has basic rooms with shared bathroom and kitchen facilities for guests' use.

There are a couple of pizzerias, burger joints and a supermarket on the main plaza in the town of Mburucuyá, but if you're camping, you'd be better off buying supplies in Corrientes, where there is a wider choice at better prices.

Getting There & Away

There are twice-daily buses from Corrientes to the town of Mburucuyá (US$3, three hours). From there, **Remises El Minuto** (☎ 498199; Belgrano 749) do the half-hour trip to the visitor center for around US$8. Take note that the access road to the park is unpaved, sandy and often impassable, even in a four-wheel drive, after heavy rains. Call the visitor center first to check on conditions.

MERCEDES
☎ 03773 / pop 20,750

Although most people who pass through here are on their way to the spectacular Reserva Provincial Esteros del Iberá (opposite), it could be worth your while hanging around a day or so: the downtown is a photogenic hopscotch of crumbling old buildings on cobblestoned streets and, being that this is cattle country, you're likely to see a few real-life gauchos out and about.

Mercedes' other satellite attraction is the utterly surreal roadside shrine to the gaucho Antonio Gil, an enormously popular religious phenomenon (see the boxed text, below), 9km west of town. There is a small, irregularly attended tourist office in the bus terminal and a post office on the corner of Rivadavia and Martínez.

Sleeping & Eating

Mercedes Gran Hotel (☎ 421820; Guazú 750; s/d US$12/20; **P** **⊠** **⊛**) Not as Gran as it used to

---

GAUCHO ANTONIO GIL

Spend any time on the road in northern Argentina and you're bound to see at least one roadside shrine surrounded by red flags and votive offerings. These shrines pay homage to gaucho Antonio Gil, a Robin Hood–like figure whose shrine and burial place just out of Mercedes attracts tens (some say hundreds) of thousands of pilgrims every year.

Little is known for sure about El Gauchito, as he is affectionately known, but many romantic tales have sprung up to fill the gaps. What is known is that he was born in 1847 and joined the army – some versions say to escape the wrath of a local policeman whose fiancée had fallen in love with Gil – to fight in the War of the Triple Alliance.

Once the war ended, Gil was called up to join the Federalist Army but, unwilling to do so, he went on the run with a couple of other deserters. The trio roamed the countryside, stealing cattle from rich landowners and sharing it with poor villagers, who in turn gave them shelter and protection.

The law finally caught up with the gang, and Gil was summarily hung by the feet from the espinillo tree, that still stands near his grave, and beheaded.

So how is it that this freeloading, cattle-rustling army deserter attained saintlike status? Moments before his death, Gil informed his executioner that the executioner's son was gravely ill. Gil told the soldier that if he were buried – not the custom with army deserters in those days – the man's son would recover.

After lopping off Gil's head, the executioner carried it back to the town of Goya where, of course, a judicial pardon awaited Gil. On finding that his son was indeed seriously ill, the soldier returned to the site and buried the body. His son recovered quickly, word spread and a legend was born.

Antonio Gil's last resting place is now the site of numerous chapels and storehouses holding thousands of votive offerings – including T-shirts, bicycles, pistols, knives, license plates, photographs, cigarettes, hair clippings and entire racks of wedding gowns – brought by those who believe in the gaucho's miracles. January 8, the date of Gil's death, attracts the most pilgrims to the Mercedes site.

If you are driving and you pass one of the roadside shrines, the story goes that you must sound your horn, or else suffer long delays on the road or, more ominously, never arrive at all.

be, this sprawling complex is nonetheless the best in town. Smallish rooms are redeemed by big balconies and leafy, quiet grounds.

Hotel Ita Pucú (☎ 421015; Batalla de Salta 645; s/d US$6/12; ☒) With a sort of spaghetti-western feel, this friendly low-roofed hotel has plenty of character and decent rooms that open onto a grassy garden. Breakfast is extra.

At the Antonio Gil shrine, you'll find inexpensive camping in what is an otherwise desolate area.

Delicias del Iberá (☎ 422508; Pujol 1162; breakfast US$2-4; ☒ breakfast) One of the few places in town open for an early breakfast, the Delicias puts out a good buffet spread in a comfortable and sunny dining room.

La Casa de Chirola (☎ 422308; cnr Sarmiento & Pujol; meals US$3-5) This family-run place on the Plaza 25 de Mayo serves good pastas, sandwiches and weekend *parrillada*.

Getting There & Away

The **bus terminal** (☎ 420165; cnr San Martín & Alfredo Perreyra) has daily departures to Buenos Aires (US$13, nine hours), La Plata (US$16, 12 hours), Resistencia (US$6, four hours) and Corrientes (US$5, 3½ hours).

Due to the deteriorating condition of the road, the only transport to Colonia Pellegrini (US$4, four hours) is currently in combis, with one departure early morning and one at midday (departing when they're full). Ask at the information booth at the bus terminal for the latest departure details.

RESERVA PROVINCIAL ESTEROS DEL IBERÁ

☎ 03773

This wetlands wilderness, covering 13,000 sq km in the north-central part of the province (14% of its entire territory), is a wildlife cornucopia comparable with – if not superior to – Brazil's Pantanal. Aquatic plants and grasses, including 'floating islands,' dominate the marsh vegetation, while trees are relatively few. Notable wildlife species include reptiles such as the caiman, mammals such as the maned wolf, howler monkey, neotropical otter, capybara, pampas and swamp deer, and more than 350 bird species. Much (but not all) of the wildlife is nocturnal.

For independent travelers, the settlement of Colonia Pellegrini, 120km northwest of Mercedes on Laguna Iberá, is the easiest place from which to organize trips into the marshes. Though some groceries are available in Pellegrini itself, the best place to purchase most supplies is Mercedes, 107km southwest of Colonia Pellegrini. The park is most enjoyable in winter and spring when the heat is far less oppressive. There is a **visitor center** (☒ 7:30-noon & 2-6pm) across the causeway from Colonia Pellegrini, with information on the reserve. They can also help arrange tours.

Tours

Since the logistics of visiting the Esteros are awkward, organized tours can be a good alternative. Three-hour launch tours, which cost about US$8 per hour for up to five people, are a bargain.

Estancia Capi-Vari (☎ /fax 420180; Beltrán 190, Mercedes) arranges stays on an estancia at the southwestern corner of the reserve. Both Posada Aguapé and Hostería Ñandé Retá also offer excursions into the wetlands (see below).

Sleeping

Hostería Ñandé Retá (☎ 499411; www.nandereta .com; s/d with full board US$27/36) This peaceful, rustic and comfortable *hostería* (lodging house) in Colonia Pellegrini is a bargain. They also arrange transport from Mercedes and offer tours of the wetlands.

Posada Aguapé (☎ 499412, in Buenos Aires ☎ 011-4742-3015; www.iberaesteros.com.ar; s/d US$62/78; ☒) This luxurious colonial-style posada is in a beautiful setting above the lake in Colonia Pellegrini. It has a swimming pool and bar. Numerous excursions, including an excellent bird-watching tour, can be arranged on site. Spanish, English, French, German and Italian are all spoken.

A number of *hospedajes* (family homes) offer rooms with private bathroom for around US$5 per person, the best of which is probably **Hospedaje los Amigos** (☎ 15-49375), in Colonia Pellegrini, which also has a decent *comedor* (basic cafeteria) out front serving meals for US$2 to US$4.

Camping is possible at Colonia Pellegrini for about US$1 per person.

Getting There & Away

Colonia Pellegrini, 107km northeast of Mercedes via RP 40, is the best center for visiting the Esteros (see left for details about getting there).

ALONG THE RÍO URUGUAY

Lively Carnaval celebrations, a 19th-century palace, hot-spring spas and a national park preserving palm groves teeming with wild-life are among the attractions along the Uruguay. As with the Paraná, aquatic recreation, especially sportfishing, draws many visitors to the region. The river also constitutes Argentina's northern border with Uruguay and, further north, Brazil. Four bridges and a dam provide easy access to these neighbors, whose influences have blended with those of indigenous and immigrant groups to produce interesting and sometimes surprising results.

The Uruguay and Paraná converge just north of Buenos Aires to flow into the Río de la Plata. In Gualeguaychú, the first major town along the Uruguay, you begin to see shops and stands selling *feijoada* (Brazil's national dish) and *chipa* (manioc-flour rolls, a Guaraní staple omnipresent in Paraguay). RN 14 runs north from Gualeguaychú roughly paralleling the Uruguay as far as Santo Tomé in Corrientes province, the last town covered in this section. It passes densely forested riverside areas and runs through grasslands where cattle graze alongside rheas.

GUALEGUAYCHÚ

☎ 03446 / pop 81,400

Gualeguaychú is the first substantial town encountered by travelers arriving in Entre Ríos province from Buenos Aires. It's a mellow little riverside place, and the pace of life creeps along for most of the year. A couple of good museums and the lush Parque Unzué make it a good place for chilling out for a few days, and it's a popular destination for Argentine holidaymakers during the summer months.

All this tranquillity disappears in January and February, however, when the town blasts into action, hosting some of Argentina's flashiest Carnaval celebrations.

Orientation

Some 220km north of Buenos Aires and 13km east of RN 14, Gualeguaychú sits on the east bank of its namesake river, a tributary of the Uruguay. Plaza San Martín, occu-pying four square blocks, is the center of its very regular grid pattern. RN 136 bypasses the city center en route to the Puente Internacional General Libertador San Martín, a toll bridge leading to the Uruguayan city of Fray Bentos.

Information

There are several banks, mostly with ATMs, along Av 25 de Mayo.

ACA (☎ 426088; cnr Urquiza & Chacabuco)

Alianza Francesa (afgualeguaychu@hotmail.com; 25 de Mayo 502)

Hospital Centenario (☎ 427831; cnr 25 de Mayo & Pasteur) At the western approach to town.

Post office (cnr Urquiza & Ángel Elías)

Telecentro (25 de Mayo 562; per hr US$0.30) Offers Internet access; also located at bus terminal.

Tourist office (☎ 423688; www.gualeguaychuturismo .com in Spanish; Tiscornia s/n; ⏰ 8am-10pm summer, 8am-8pm winter) Near the intersection with the Av Costanera, south of Plaza Colón. Has good brochures and maps and a list of accommodations. There is also a branch at the bus terminal which keeps the same hours.

Sights & Activities

A handful of colonial buildings remain in Gualeguaychú, in addition to more recent ones important in Argentine political and literary history. The **Museo Haedo** (San José 105; admission free; ⏰ 9am-noon & 4-7pm), just off Plaza San Martín, is the municipal museum, occupying the oldest house in town (1800). It features mostly antique furniture and weaponry. A free guided tour in rapid-fire Spanish is available on request.

In the mid-19th century, the colonial **Casa de Andrade** (cnr Andrade & Canonigo JJ Borques) belonged to *entrerriano* (from the province of Entre Ríos) poet, journalist, diplomat and politician Olegario Andrade. **Casa de Fray Mocho** (Fray Mocho 135), was the birthplace of José S Álvarez, founder of the influential satirical magazine *Caras y Caretas* at the turn of the 20th century; Fray Mocho was his pen name. Dating from the early 20th century, the unusual **Casa de la Cultura** (☎ 427989; 25 de Mayo, near Montevideo) has occasional public exhibitions, and is the place to contact for entrance to the houses listed above.

The **Teatro Gualeguaychú** (☎ 431757; Urquiza 705; ⏰ 7am-9pm Mon-Fri) was inaugurated in 1914 with a performance of *Aïda*, and still hosts symphonies, ballet and theater. Check at the Casa de la Cultura for tours.

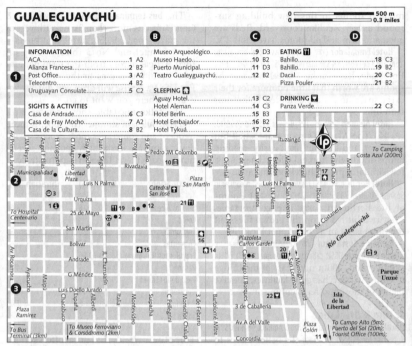

GUALEGUAYCHÚ

0 — 500 m
0 — 0.3 miles

INFORMATION	
ACA	1 A2
Alianza Francesa	2 B2
Post Office	3 A2
Telecentro	4 B2
Uruguayan Consulate	5 C2

SIGHTS & ACTIVITIES	
Casa de Andrade	6 C3
Casa de Fray Mocho	7 A2
Casa de la Cultura	8 B2
Museo Arqueológico	9 D3
Museo Haedo	10 B2
Puerto Municipal	11 B2
Teatro Gualeyguaychú	12 B2

SLEEPING	
Aguay Hotel	13 C2
Hotel Aleman	14 C3
Hotel Berlín	15 B3
Hotel Embajador	16 B2
Hotel Tykuá	17 D2

EATING	
Bahillo	18 C3
Bahillo	19 B2
Dacal	20 C3
Pizza Pouler	21 B2

DRINKING	
Panza Verde	22 C3

At the former train station, at the south end of Maipú, the **Museo Ferroviario** (cnr Maestra Piccini & Maipú) is an open-air exhibit of steam locomotives, dining cars and other hardware from provincial rail history. Alongside the museum, the new **Corsódromo** (Blvd Irazusta) is the main site for Gualeguaychú's lively Carnaval (see below).

Parque Unzué is a spacious greenbelt across the river, and it is good for swimming, picnicking, camping, fishing and relaxing. It also contains the city's **Museo Arqueológico** (☎ 428820; Parque Unzué; ⏰ 6-9pm Mon-Sat).

A stroll along Av Costanera yields views across the river to the park and various inlets and landscapes. Guided tours of the river are offered on the launch **Ciudad de Gualeguaychú** (☎ 423248). Call or contact the tourist office. Tours cost US$2 to US$3 and leave from the **Puerto Municipal**.

Festivals & Events

Gualeguaychú's summer **Carnaval** has a national and even international reputation, so if you can't go to Rio or Bahía, make a stop here any weekend from mid-January to late February. Admission to the Corsódromo costs about US$5, plus another US$2 to US$3 to guarantee a seat.

Every October for more than 30 years, on the Día de la Raza weekend, high-school students have built and paraded floats through the city during the **Fiesta Provincial de Carrozas Estudiantiles**. Other local celebrations include numerous *jineteadas* (rodeos) throughout the year.

Sleeping

Aguaý Hotel (☎ 422099; www.hotelaguay.com.ar; Av Costanera 130; s/d US$25/35; ❄ ◪) All rooms in this modern hotel have balconies (most with great views over the river), excellent bathrooms, air-con and heating. There's a small gym, a rooftop pool and spa – great value.

Puerto Sol (☎ 434017; San Lorenzo 477; s/d US$13/22; ❄) With its pastel paint job and matching bedspreads, the Puerto Sol feels more like a youth hostel, but it's actually a pretty decent place. It's central and clean, with a pleasant outdoor sitting area.

Hotel Tykuá (☎ 422625; www.tykuahotel.com.ar in Spanish; Luis N Palma 150; s/d US$12/23) Bright and

NORTHEAST ARGENTINA

modern rooms in this new building surround a very Zenlike courtyard. Beds are good and firm and all rooms have cable TV.

Hotel Embajador (☎ 424414; www.hotel-embajador .com; cnr 3 de Febrero & San Martín; s/d US$13/25; ☒) The Embajador has a funky '70s feel to it, and the rooms are worth that little bit more for their extra space and marble-floored bathrooms with tub.

Hotel Aleman (☎ 426153; Bolivar 535; s/d US$8/13; ⓟ ☒) The Aleman's rooms are small but well kept, and touches like bedside reading lamps add to the homelike feel. There are a few similarly priced hotels in this area.

Hotel Berlín (☎ 425111; www.hotelberlin.com.ar in Spanish; Bolívar 733; s/d US$21/33; ⓟ ☒) Rooms at the Berlín are large and comfortable. They're a bit heavy on the brown tiles, but the hotel is set in a good, quiet location.

Camping Costa Azul (☎ 422662; Av Costanera s/n; sites up to 4 people US$8, cabanas for 4 people US$13) This campground, 200m northeast of the bridge to Parque Unzué, has good facilities, but take plenty of mosquito repellent in summer.

Eating & Drinking

Dacal (☎ 427602; cnr San Lorenzo & Andrade; mains US$2-3, parrilla for 2 US$5) One of the better places to eat in town, Dacal looks right across the *costanera* to the river and serves good fish, pasta and meat. It fills up quickly in summer, so it might be worth making a reservation.

Campo Alto (☎ 429593; cnr San Lorenzo & Concordia; all you can eat US$5, meals US$3) Thatched-roof bungalows, occasional live music and shady outdoor seating make this *asador libre* (all-you-can-eat barbecue) one of the most enjoyable eating options in town.

Pizza Pouler (☎ 433109; cnr 25 de Mayo & 3 de Febrero; mains US$5-13) This upscale restaurant serves good pizza as well as meat, fish and pasta.

Panza Verde (cnr LN Alem & Luis Doello Jurado; ☺ from 6pm) A happening little neighborhood bar which also serves *picadas* (snacks). On a clear, balmy night, the rooftop terrace is the place to be.

Bahillo (ice-cream cones from US$0.80; ☺ 10am-9pm) Head to one of their two branches (corner of Costanera and San Lorenzo, and corner of Díaz and 25 de Mayo) for ice cream.

Getting There & Around

Gualeguaychú's new airport is up and running, but at the time of research, commercial flights had been cancelled.

The **bus terminal** (☎ 440688; Bulevar Jurado & General Artigas) is more than 3km southwest of the plaza. For US$0.50, infrequent buses – No 2 (white) and No 3 (blue) – stop on Blvd Artigas across from the terminal and take circuitous routes to the town center. For US$1 a *remise* will drop you downtown exactly where you want to go.

The following table shows winter fares and schedules; in summer transport is more frequent and sometimes more expensive. All destinations are served daily and most several times a day. Travel times are approximate.

Destination	Cost (US$)	Duration (hr)
Buenos Aires	8	3½
Colón	3	1½
Concordia	4.50	3
Corrientes	12	6½
Fray Bentos (Uruguay)	2.50	1
Paraná	5	4½
Paso de los Libres	8	7
Resistencia	14	10
Rosario	8	7½
Santa Fe	7	5½

Three times weekly, El Litoral offers service to Córdoba (US$18, 11 hours) by way of Santa Fe.

CONCEPCIÓN

☎ 03442 / pop 68,400

More accurately (but less commonly) known as Concepcíon del Uruguay, this little town has an enchanting plaza, a couple of good hotels and a surprisingly hip shopping precinct. Its tourist services make it a suitable stopover for travelers on long trips north, and it has some interesting architecture in its own right. Concepción is on the Río Uruguay east of the junction of RN 14 from Buenos Aires and RP 39 to Paraná, and midway between Gualeguaychú and Parque Nacional El Palmar.

Orientation

The bus terminal is between Rocamora and Galarza. Calle 9 de Julio is one block south of Galarza, and all three streets lead east to the river. On the way, Rocamora passes one block north of the central Plaza General Francisco Ramírez, Galarza runs along the north edge and 9 de Julio hits the middle.

Information

An ATM that accepts most cards is in the bus terminal. Concepción has a lively street press scene; pick up a copy of *¿Adónde ir?* or *¿Que haces hoy?* for a wealth of cultural and entertainment options.

Main tourist office (☎ 440812; Elías 50; ⏰ 8am-8pm) On the edge of town, eight blocks west of the terminal.

Tourist office (☎ 425820; 9 de Julio 844; ⏰ 7am-1pm) This is a more conveniently located office, a short walk from the main plaza.

Sights

Concepción has some great architecture, particularly around the plaza. Don't miss the **casino**, **police headquarters** or the **basilica**. The basilica's left wing holds former president Justo José de Urquiza's remains in a replica of Napoleon's mausoleum.

The region's primary attraction, however, is **Palácio San José** (right), which was General Urquiza's enormous residence, 30km west of town. Here, Urquiza was assassinated by the forces of his rival, Ricardo López Jordán.

Sleeping & Eating

Grand Hotel (☎ 425586; www.turismoentrerios.com/grand hotel in Spanish; cnr Eva Perón & Rocamora; s US$20-38, d US$30-55; Ⓟ 🐾) By far the best hotel in town, the Grand's gleaming brass banisters and softly spoken staff will have you entranced from the moment you walk in the door.

Residencial Centro (☎ 427429; Mariano Moreno 130; s/d US$7/10; 🐾) The best budget deal in town. Downstairs rooms are older and have a bit more style, but upstairs you get more light, as well as air-con.

Hotel Carlos 1 (☎ 426776; www.turismoentrerios .com/hotelcarlos1 in Spanish; Eva Peron 115; s/d $20/26; Ⓟ 🐾) If the Grand is full, you could try this place across the road. The rooms (while serviceable) aren't nearly as nice, but they do have some of the largest shower stalls in the country.

Apart Hotel Bonato (☎ 427621; www.turismoentre rios.com/aparthotelbonato in Spanish; Eva Peron 115; r per person US$5, apt $20-26; Ⓟ 🐾) If you don't feel like engaging with the whole Concepción scene (ie you're just here to see the palace), there's no shame in staying at this place across from the bus terminal. None at all. The apartments are a great deal, with fully equipped kitchens and the rooms aren't a bad deal, either.

Balneario Municipal Itapé (☎ 427852; Av 3 de Febrero s/n; sites for 2 people US$3; ⏰ closed winter)

This basic campground is 15 blocks south of the plaza.

El Remanso (cnr Eva Perón & Rocamora; parrilla US$3) Right on the pedestrian walkway, this is the finest *parrilla* in town. Linen tablecloths and candlelight help make a very agreeable mood.

Getting There & Around

The **bus terminal** (☎ 422352; cnr General Galarza & Chiloteguy) is 10 blocks west of the plaza. Bus No 1 (US$0.50) runs between it and the plaza, and other *colectivos* (local buses) serve the campgrounds for the same price. A *remise* to the plaza costs US$0.50. There are frequent departures for destinations all over the country.

Destination	Cost (US$)	Duration (hr)
Buenos Aires	9	4½
Gualeguaychú	3	1¼
Colón	1	¾
Concordia	2.50	2½
Paraná	4.50	5
Paso de los Libres	12	8
Corrientes	15	14
Paysandú (Uruguay)	2.50	1½

PALACIO SAN JOSÉ

☎ 03442

Topped by twin towers and surrounded by elegant gardens, Justo José Urquiza's ostentatious pink **palace** (☎ 432620; RN 39, Km 30; adult/child US$0.30/free; ⏰ 8am-7pm Mon-Fri, 9am-6pm Sat & Sun) is 33km west of Concepción via RP 39. It was built in part to show up Urquiza's arch rival Juan Manuel de Rosas in Buenos Aires, and in part to show the power and wealth of Entre Ríos. Local caudillo (provincial strongman) Urquiza, commanding an army of provincial loyalists, Unitarists, Brazilians and Uruguayans, was largely responsible for Rosas' downfall in 1852 and the eventual adoption of Argentina's modern constitution.

Allies like Sarmiento and Mitre supped at Urquiza's 8.5m dining-room table and slept in the palatial bedrooms. Urquiza's wife, 25 years his junior, turned the bedroom where López Jordán murdered her husband into a permanent shrine.

There are buses from Concepción to Caseros (at 5:15am, 11:30am and 1:15pm), from where you can take a *remise* (US$2) to the palace.

COLÓN

☎ 03447 / pop 19,200

This town has an attractive waterfront lined with many impressive older buildings, and a new geothermal spa. One of three main Entre Ríos border crossings, Colón sits on the west bank of the Río Uruguay and is connected to the Uruguayan city of Paysandú by the Puente Internacional General Artigas.

The shady, tree-lined streets make it a good place to walk around. It's definitely one of the more picturesque riverside towns, and a great place to base yourself for spa soaking and trips to Parque Nacional El Palmar (opposite).

Plaza San Martín is the main square, but is far outshone by the charms of nearby Parque Quirós.

Information

Post office (cnr Artigas & 12 de Abril)

Tourist office (☎ 421996; cnr Gouchon & Av Costanera; ☻ 7am-9pm Mon-Sun) Occupies the former Aduana (Customs Building), built by Urquiza. There is also a small office, keeping odd hours, in the bus terminal.

Sights & Activities

The **Termas de Colón** (☎ 424717; www.vivitermas colon.com.ar in Spanish; cnr Lavalle & Sabatier; admission US$2; ☻ 8am-10pm), at the northern edge of town, is a thermal spa with 10 pools, both indoor and outdoor, ranging from 33°C to 40°C. The source is a 1500m-deep well drilled to tap the region's abundant geothermal aquifers.

Some 4km northwest of Colón is the **Molino Forclaz**, the area's first flour mill. It's also worth visiting the nearby village of **Colonia San José**, 8km west, where in 1857 European pioneers established the country's second agricultural colony. An interesting regional **museum** (☎ 15-644091; admission US$0.50; ☻ 10am-noon & 4-6pm Tue-Sun) displays period tools and memorabilia.

In mid-February the city hosts the **Fiesta Nacional de la Artesanía**, a crafts fair held in Parque Quirós that features live folkloric entertainment by nationally known artists.

Sleeping

Hotel Palmar (☎ 421952; www.hotelpalmar.com.ar in Spanish; Ferrari 295; s/d US$17/30; P ✗ ♨) The Palmar's rustic yet modern lobby leads on to some ordinary, but functional, motel-style rooms. Try to get one at the front for views of the lovely Parque Quirós.

Hotel Quirinale Internacional (☎ 421133; cnr Herminio J Quirós y Noalles; s/d US$50/65; P ✗ ♨) The Quirinale feels a bit out of place here – a hulking 15-story five-star hotel. It offers a range of day-spa treatments and the hotel is fully equipped. Rooms are slightly worn, but views out over the river and surrounds are superb.

Hotel EMI (☎ 423615; Noalles 570; s/d US$7/10) A reasonable budget deal about a 10-minute walk from the river. Rooms downstairs have cable TV, but upstairs you get more air and light.

Camping Municipal Norte (☎ 421917; cnr Alejo Peyret & Paysandú; sites for 2 people US$5; ☻ closed winter, except long weekends) This campground is almost at the water's edge, and stretches north from the foot of Paysandú almost to the Termas de Colón complex. There is also more camping for the same price near the river on the south side of town.

Eating

La Pava Dorada (☎ 422124; cnr Peyret & Alberdi; meals from US$3; ☻ lunch & dinner) Fish (mostly boga and surubí) here is excellent, but the standout item is the fondue, which comes with 16 (count 'em) different sauces. River views and candlelight create great atmosphere.

La Cosquilla del Ángel (☎ 423711; Alejo Peyret 180; mains US$5-8) A block from the water, this is a classy joint in every respect – except for the names of the dishes. Don't let the sobriquet 'Mr Ed' keep you from ordering the delightful salad of mixed greens topped with walnuts and surrounded by *aceto verde* (a purée of greens and vinegar). Preparation, presentation and service are all top-notch, with a very good and reasonably priced wine list, as well.

Getting There & Around

Colón's **bus terminal** (☎ 421716; cnr Rocamora & 9 de Julio) is seven blocks inland (roughly west) of the river and eight blocks north of the main shopping and entertainment street, 12 de Abril. The many north–south buses that stop here also pass the entrance to Parque Nacional El Palmar.

Paccot and Copay go to Paysandú, Uruguay (US$2, 45 minutes) five times daily Monday to Saturday, and once (at 8:30pm) on Sunday.

PARQUE NACIONAL EL PALMAR

☎ 03447

On the west bank of the Río Uruguay, midway between Colón and Concordia, 8500-hectare **Parque Nacional El Palmar** (☎ 493053; RN 14, Km 199; adult/child US$4/2) preserves the last extensive stands of yatay palm on the Argentine littoral. In the 19th century, the native yatay covered large parts of Entre Ríos, Uruguay and southern Brazil, but the intensification of agriculture, ranching and forestry throughout the region destroyed much of the palm savannas and inhibited the reproduction of the species.

Most of the remaining palms in El Palmar are relics, some more than two centuries old, but under protection from grazing and fire they have once again begun to reproduce. Reaching a maximum height of about 18m, with a trunk diameter of 40cm, the larger specimens clustered throughout the park accentuate a striking and soothing subtropical landscape that lends itself to photography. The grasslands and the gallery forests along the river and creeks shelter much wildlife, including birds, mammals and reptiles.

Most activities are oriented toward the park's natural attractions. Park admission is collected at the entrance on RN 14 from 7am to 7pm, but the gate is open 24 hours.

Information

All the park's main facilities are 12km down the dirt road leading from the entrance. The **visitor center** (☒ 9am-6:30pm) has displays on natural history, including a small herpetarium (reptile house), and offers video shows throughout the day. The park administration was once the *casco* (main house) of the *estancia* (ranch). Guided bicycle tours (US$2, one hour) of the park leave from a concession near the center.

Sights & Activities

WILDLIFE-WATCHING

To view the wildlife, go for walks along the watercourses or through the palm savannas, preferably in early morning or just before sunset. The most conspicuous bird is the ñandú or rhea, but there are also numerous parakeets, cormorants, egrets, herons, storks, caracaras, woodpeckers and kingfishers. Among the mammals, the carpincho or capybara, a semiaquatic rodent weighing up to 60kg, and the vizcacha, a relative of the

chinchilla, are common sights, but there are also foxes, raccoons and wild boar.

Vizcachas inhabit the campground; their nocturnal squeaks and reflective eyes sometimes disturb campers, but they are harmless (as are the enormous toads that invade the showers and toilets at night). The same is not true of the yarará, a deadly pit viper that inhabits the savannas. Bites are rare, but watch your step and wear high boots and long trousers when hiking.

RÍO URUGUAY

There is excellent access to the river for swimming and boating from the campground (which is across the parking lot from the visitor center), as well as a series of short hiking trails that make up El Paseo de la Glorieta.

ARROYO LOS LOROS & ARROYO EL PALMAR

Arroyo Los Loros, a short distance north of the campground by gravel road, is a good place to observe wildlife. Five kilometers south of the visitor center is Arroyo El Palmar, a pleasant stream with a beautiful swimming hole, accessible by a good gravel road. It's a fine place to see birds and, crossing the ruined bridge, visitors can walk for several kilometers along a palm-lined road now being reclaimed by savanna grasses.

Sleeping & Eating

Los Loros (☎ 493031; sites per tent US$1.50, plus per person US$1.50) This campground across the parking lot from the visitor center is the only place to stay in the park. It has shady, level sites, hot showers, electricity and a small store. Rates vary with the season; 'family plans,' for two adults and one to three children, can bring prices down.

The nearest hotels are in the cities of Concordia, about 65km north of the park entrance on RN 14, and Colón, roughly the same distance south.

La Cosquilla (☎ 493031; mains US$2-6; ☒ breakfast, lunch & dinner) Opened by the owner of La Cosquilla del Ángel in Colón (see opposite), but now under new management, this restaurant next to the visitor center has a similar menu, plus tasty sandwiches starting at US$1.20.

Getting There & Away

El Palmar is 360km northwest of Buenos Aires on RN 14, a major national highway,

NORTHEAST ARGENTINA

so there are frequent north–south bus services. Any bus running between Buenos Aires and Concordia, or between Concordia and Gualeguaychú, Concepción or Colón, will drop you at the park entrance. There is no public transport to the visitor center and camping area, but hitching should not be difficult in summer. A *remise* between Colón or Concordia and the visitor center should cost about US$10. Some drivers will throw in a brief car tour of the park at the same price. A *remise* to town from the park entrance can run as low as US$8.

CONCORDIA

☎ 0345 / pop 151,700

Visitors come to this attractive agricultural and livestock center on the Río Uruguay mostly for its riverside beaches and fishing, but the city holds some other attractions. It also offers a border crossing, via the Salto Grande hydroelectric project, to the Uruguayan city of Salto.

Concordia, 431km north of Buenos Aires and 65km north of Parque Nacional El Palmar via RN 14, has been hit hard by the country's recent financial crisis. The flour mill has closed, and the citrus industry (a mainstay of the local economy) is suffering, leading to a protracted cancellation of the annual citrus festival.

Information

There are several banks with ATMs in the vicinity of Plaza 25 de Mayo.

ACA (☎ 421-6544; cnr Pellegrini & Corrientes)

Cibercentro Colón (Pellegrini at Plaza 25 de Mayo; per hr US$0.30) For phone calls and Internet access.

Hospital Felipe Heras (☎ 421-2580; Entre Ríos 135)

La Mulatona (☎ 421-1517; Estrada 43) Wash your clothes here.

Municipal tourist office (☎ 421-2137; ⏱ 7am-8pm) Next to the cathedral.

Post office (Hipólito Yrigoyen, btwn 1 de Mayo & Buenos Aires)

Sights & Activities

On the west side of Plaza 25 de Mayo, the 19th-century **Catedral San Antonio de Padua** is the city's signature landmark. Facing Plaza Urquiza, at the corner of Entre Ríos and Ramírez, the **Palacio Arruabarrena** (1919) is a French-style building with some wild statuary on its elaborate exterior. The *palacio* contains the **Museo Regional de Concordia**

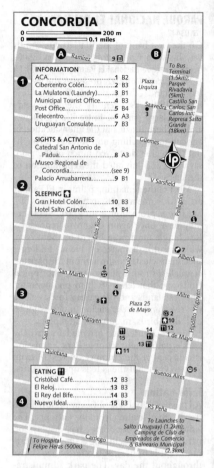

CONCORDIA

0 — 200 m
0 — 0.1 miles

INFORMATION	
ACA	1 B2
Cibercentro Colón	2 B3
La Mulatona (Laundry)	3 B1
Municipal Tourist Office	4 B3
Post Office	5 B4
Telecentro	6 A3
Uruguayan Consulate	7 B3

SIGHTS & ACTIVITIES	
Catedral San Antonio de Padua	8 A3
Museo Regional de Concordia	(see 9)
Palacio Arruabarrena	9 B1

SLEEPING	
Gran Hotel Colón	10 B3
Hotel Salto Grande	11 B4

EATING	
Cristóbal Café	12 B3
El Reloj	13 B3
El Rey del Bife	14 B3
Nuevo Ideal	15 B3

To Bus Terminal (1.5km); Parque Rivadavia (5km); Castillo San Carlos; San Carlos Inn; Represa Salto Grande (18km)

To Hospital Felipe Heras (500m)

To Launches to Salto (Uruguay) (1.2km); Camping de Club de Empleados de Comercio & Balneario Municipal (2.3km)

(☎ 421-1883; admission free; ⏱ 7am-7pm Mon-Fri, 9am-1pm & 4-9pm long weekends only). The falling plaster in the museum adds to the charm of the displays of photos and objects from earlier times. Other interesting buildings ring the plaza.

In the riverside Parque Rivadavia, at the northeastern edge of town, are the ruins of **Castillo San Carlos** (1888), built by a French industrialist who mysteriously abandoned the property years later. French writer Antoine de Saint-Exupéry briefly lived in the building; there's a monument to the *Little Prince* nearby.

Some 18km north of town, the 39m-high **Represa Salto Grande** (☎ 421-2600 for tours; ⏱ tours 8am-1:30pm Mon-Sat) and its 80,000-hectare reservoir is a joint Argentine–Uruguayan dam project that also supports a road and railway bridge linking the two countries. Don't expect dramatic vistas; the area is very flat. Unlike at Yacyretá and Itaipú, however, the general public does get to go inside for a look at the dam's turbines.

Festivals & Events
Fishing enthusiasts crowd Concordia during January's **Fiesta Nacional de la Boga**, in search of the region's tastiest river fish. In better times, the city holds its **Fiesta Nacional de Citricultura** (National Citrus Festival) the first week in December. Check with the tourist office to see if the festival has started up again.

Sleeping
Hotel Salto Grande (☎ 421-0034; www.hotelsalto grande.com.ar in Spanish; Urquiza 581; s/d standard US$24/26, deluxe US$36/42; ✂ ▨) Concordia's fanciest hotel is another example of the Mysterious Pricing Structure: rooms get more expensive the higher you go in the building, but the top rooms seem to differ from those on the 1st floor only in that you get a quilted bedspread and a slightly larger TV.

San Carlos Inn (☎ 431-0725; Parque Rivadavia; s/d US$27/30; ℗ ✂ ▢ ▨) Set in the lush grounds of the Parque Rivadavia, the San Carlos Inn's rooms are nothing special, but it's an excellent quiet spot to rest up for a few days. Rooms have sweeping river views, as does the grassy sundeck.

Gran Hotel Colón (☎ 15-508-3121; Pellegrini 611; s/d US$8/12) While it's obviously seen better days, the Gran Colón still has that special something – it could be the sweeping staircase or the balconies overlooking the park, or the antique room furniture. Or it could just be that it's the cheapest, most central option. Street noise makes the front rooms a bad choice for light sleepers.

Camping de Club de Empleados de Comercio (☎ 422-0080; Costanera s/n; sites US$5) The most convenient camping place is at the Balneario Municipal at the foot of San Juan, close to the port for crossings to Salto. It has showers and toilets, but like so many campgrounds along the river, it sometimes floods.

Eating
El Reloj (☎ 422-2822; Pellegrini 580; pizzas from US$4) This spacious brick-walled pizzeria has good

ambience and a staggering selection of pizza options. A haven for the indecisive, they don't grumble about doing half and halfs, either.

Cristóbal Café (☎ 421-5736; cnr Pellegrini & 1 de Mayo; set meals US$3; ◷ breakfast, lunch & dinner) A hip restaurant with a fairly standard menu and a well-stocked bar. The set meals are a bargain and it has live music on weekends.

Nuevo Ideal (☎ 421-2668; cnr 1 de Mayo & Urquiza; dishes US$2-3; ◷ breakfast, lunch & dinner) When they open up the big glass doors at this plaza-side café, the temptation to linger grows even stronger. Good snacks and light meals don't help, either. Live music on weekends.

El Rey del Bife (☎ 421-2644; Pellegrini 590; mains US$2-7) Despite its name, 'The King of Beef,' this popular place has the town's best selection of local fish – surubí, boga and dorado – and seafood. They sometimes have *vizcacha en escabeche* (vizcacha in marinade).

Getting There & Away
At the time of research, flights to and from Concordia's airport had been cancelled.

The **bus terminal** (☎ 421-7235; cnr Justo & Hipólito Yrigoyen) is 13 blocks north of Plaza 25 de Mayo.

Two Flecha Bus and two Chadre buses go to Salto, Uruguay (US$2, 1¼ hour), between 11:30am and 6:30pm Monday to Saturday.

The long-distance bus services between Buenos Aires and the provinces of Corrientes and Misiones resemble those passing through Gualeguaychú, Concepción and Colón. Three Expreso Singer buses stop en route to Puerto Iguazú (12 hours) between 6:30pm and 10:45pm. Many buses serve Buenos Aires (US$11, 6¼ hours), and Flecha Bus has direct service to La Plata.

From the port beyond the east end of Carriego, launches cross the river to Salto (US$2, 15 minutes) four times a day in winter, five in summer, between 9am and 6pm Monday to Saturday. At the time of research, Sunday service had been cancelled, but it may resume.

Getting Around
Micro No 2 (US$0.30) takes Yrigoyen south from the terminal to the center. On its northward run No 2 stops at the entrance to Parque Rivadavia; catch it on Pellegrini in front of Banco de la Nación. A *remise* to

the terminal from the center should cost about US$1.

PASO DE LOS LIBRES

☎ 03772 / pop 43,800

About 700km north of Buenos Aires and 370km south of Posadas on RN 14, Paso de los Libres is a stopover and border-crossing town. It offers Corrientes province's easiest access to Brazil, to the much larger city of Uruguaiana on the opposite bank of the river. There's not much reason to linger here.

Orientation

On the west bank of the Uruguay, Paso de los Libres has a standard rectangular grid, centered on Plaza Independencia. The principal commercial street is Av Colón, one block west. The international bridge to Uruguaiana is about 10 blocks southwest.

Information

There's no tourist office, but try the ACA office near the border complex before the bridge.

Hospital San José (☎ 421404; Calle T Alisio) On the east side of Plaza España.

Libres Cambio (Av Colón 901) Changes money.

Telecentro Mercosur (Colón 975; per hr US$0.30) Internet.

Sleeping & Eating

Hotel Alejandro Primero (☎ 421100; Pago Largo 1156; s/d US$17/27; P ✕) This is the best hotel in town (which isn't really saying much). River views and spacious rooms are redeeming features, as is the good 1st-floor restaurant.

Hotel Las Vegas (☎ 423490; Sarmiento 554; s/d US$10/15; P ✕) The Las Vegas is like an experiment in time travel – a new hotel constructed to replicate the exact feel of a '70s motel. Well done, guys! Rooms are comfortable and the showers rock.

Hotel Capri (☎ 421260; M Llanes s/n; s/d US$7/10) Across the dirt lot from the bus terminal, the Capri is the place to be if you need a lie down and an early breakfast between bus treks.

In addition to the Alejandro's restaurant, there are a couple of restaurants around Plaza Independencia, as well as food stalls outside the bus terminal.

Getting There & Away

Flights to and from Paso de los Libres had been cancelled at time of research.

The **bus terminal** (☎ 425600) is at the corner of Av San Martín and Santiago del Estero. Crucero del Norte passes through Paso de los Libres daily en route between Buenos Aires (US$9, 9½ hours) and Posadas (US$7, six hours). Flecha Bus has a Saturday bus that serves Colón, Concepción and Gualeguaychú on the way to Buenos Aires. More buses bypass the town, but can drop you off at the Esso station on RN 14, from which a taxi can take you the 16km downtown.

Tata/El Rápido serves Corrientes (US$6, six hours) via the interior city of Mercedes, from where it is possible to visit the Esteros del Iberá (p173). There are also daily buses to Paraná (US$6.50, 5½ hours) and Santa Fe, and service to Rosario Friday to Wednesday. Paso de los Libres is also a stopover between Córdoba and Puerto Iguazú from Friday to Wednesday.

Vans to Uruguaiana, Brazil (US$0.50), leave frequently from 7am onwards, stopping on Av San Martín at Av Colón and across from the bus terminal, among other places.

Getting Around

A *remise* from the airport to town costs around US$2. The area between the bus terminal and downtown is dodgy; walk through it at your own risk. Minibuses between the terminal and downtown (a minimum of 13 blocks) cost US$0.30 to US$0.50 depending on the distance. Taxi rates are posted outside the terminal.

YAPEYÚ

☎ 03772 / pop 2120

This placid village on the west bank of the Río Uruguay, 55km north of Paso de los Libres and 6km southeast of RN 14, was founded in 1626 as the southernmost of the Jesuit missions. With dirt streets and a slow pace, Yapeyú is a good place to relax and spend a lazy day or three. You're more likely to smell baking bread here than the various noxious fumes common in many Argentine population centers, but the nocturnal tranquillity is sometimes shattered by dogs barking throughout the town. Tiny Yapeyú is trying its hardest. What few sights there are around town are well signposted in Spanish, English, Portuguese and Guaraní. For a map, ask at the Museo de Cultura Jesuítica.

Under the Jesuits the *reducción* (Indian settlement) had a population of more than

8000 Guaraní Indians tending as many as 80,000 cattle. After the order was expelled in 1767, the Indians dispersed and the mission fell into ruins. Many houses in the area are built of red sandstone blocks salvaged from mission buildings. Another historical note: José de San Martín, Argentina's greatest national hero and known as 'the Liberator', was born here in 1778, in a modest dwelling whose ruins still exist in a protected site.

Sights & Activities

Everything in town is within easy walking distance of the central Plaza San Martín. On its south side is the **Museo de Cultura Jesuítica** (admission free; ☺ 8am-noon & 3-6pm Tue-Sun), with a carved image of the Vírgen Morena (the Virgin Mary in indigenous form) and several small stylized Guaraní dwellings set among the foundations of mission buildings. The photographic displays are a good introduction to the mission zone. A sundial and a few other mission relics are also on display.

It's a measure of the esteem that Argentines hold for the Liberator that they have built **Casa de San Martín** (☺ 8am-noon & 2:30-6pm), a building to protect the house where he was born, even though it's mostly been reduced to its foundations. Bronze plaques from associations and groups from all over the country line the walls. Horses sometimes graze on the grounds at night.

On the west side of the plaza, the Gothic-spired parish **church** dates from 1899, but contains some important images from the Jesuit period.

Sleeping & Eating

Yapeyú has limited accommodations.

El Paraíso Yapeyú (☎ 493056; cnr Paso de los Patos & San Martín; s/d US$10/15; P ✗ ✵) Modern two-bedroom bungalows down on the waterfront. They're definitely a bargain, and the *parrilla* on the grounds is open for dinner. They can also arrange river activities, such as tours and pedal-boat hire.

Hotel San Martín (☎ 493120; Sargento Cabral 712; s/d with fan $7/10) This cheerful hotel is on the plaza. Rooms have TVs and face an inner courtyard; there's not much natural light if you want privacy.

Camping Paraíso (Maipo s/n; per site US$3; ☺ summer & long weekends only) This campground near the river has hot showers, but insects can be abundant and the most low-lying areas

can flood in heavy rain – choose your site carefully.

Restaurant El Paraíso (☎ 493053; Gregoria Matorras s/n; mains US$2-3; ☺ 7am-midnight) The menu is simple but there are views of the river here, two doors south of the Casa de San Martín. Out front is a large, 300-year-old palo borracho tree, in which, they say, a young San Martín used to play. With a grand, bulbous and thorny trunk, this is a particularly fine example of this species, which is seen throughout Central and South America.

Getting There & Away

The small bus terminal is at Av del Libertador and Sargento Cabral, two blocks west of the plaza. Crucero del Norte stops twice a day en route between Paso de los Libres (US$2, one hour) and Posadas (US$7, five hours). Tata serves Buenos Aires. More buses stop on the highway at the edge of the town.

Buses sometimes arrive early, and you may have to stand for a few hours once you board.

SANTO TOMÉ
☎ 03756 / pop 21,000

Santo Tomé is 140km north of Yapeyú via RN 14. It's possible to cross to the Brazilian town of São Borja, which also has Jesuit ruins, via a bridge across the Río Uruguay.

The **Hotel Pucara** (☎ 420340; San Martín 557; s/d US$5/8; P) offers good rooms and there are several campgrounds along Av San Martín.

Crucero del Norte and Singer run four to five buses daily to Posadas (US$4, 2½ hours) and Paso de los Libres (US$4, 3½ hours). The latter also exchanges pesos for Brazilian reals.

POSADAS & THE JESUIT MISSIONS

The ruins of 17th-century Jesuit missions are the major attraction in this region. Beginning in 1607 in the upper Paraná region of Argentina and Paraguay, the Jesuits established 30 missions, the principle behind which was *reducción* or *congregación*: concentrating the Guaraní, breaking their nomadic habits and reorganizing their political structure. Sixteen of the missions were in

NORTHEAST ARGENTINA

Argentina, mostly in Misiones with a few in Corrientes. Today San Ignacio Mini, near Posadas, is the best restored, while between San Ignacio and Posadas are two more large ruins, Santa Ana and Loreto.

As well as being a possible base for exploration of the missions (including those across the Paraná in Paraguay), Posadas, the capital of Misiones province, is also a gateway to Iguazú Falls, as well as to Brazil and Paraguay. The region around Posadas also offers a fleeting glimpse of a major and controversial hydroelectric project, the Yacyretá dam.

The landscape here is an attraction. Approaching Posadas from the south you will see a change to gently rolling low hills, stands of bamboo, and papaya and manioc plantations. The highway passes tea and *mate* plantations growing from the region's trademark red soil.

Misiones' Sierra Central separates the watersheds of the Paraná and Uruguay. The range reaches as high as 800m, though it rarely exceeds 500m. The natural vegetation is mostly subtropical forest, as well as some large remaining stands of native araucaria, which resemble pine trees. The province is the country's largest producer of *yerba mate*, the staple drink of Argentines and of many Uruguayans, Paraguayans and Brazilians. In recent years plantation forestry has become an important industry, with northern-hemisphere pines and Australian eucalyptus replacing the native araucarias.

POSADAS
☎ 03752 / pop 305,000

Posadas, a modern riverside city with an abundance of shade trees, leafy parks and plazas, is a brief stopover en route to Paraguay or Iguazú for most travelers. It's within striking distance of several Jesuit missions, including San Ignacio Miní, about 50km east, and, across the river on the Paraguayan side, Trinidad and Jesús. The city has lost some of its low-lying areas to flooding from the Yacyretá hydroelectric project, another possible side trip.

Posadas was originally part of Corrientes province, but in the 1880s became the capital of the newly created territory of Misiones. It served as the gateway to the pioneering agricultural communities of interior Misiones

and in 1912 was linked with Buenos Aires by the Urquiza railway. Today Posadas is the province's commercial center.

Orientation
Posadas is on the south bank of the upper Río Paraná, 1310km north of Buenos Aires by RN 14, 310km east of Corrientes via RN 12 and 300km southwest of Puerto Iguazú, also via RN 12. A handsome, modern international bridge links Posadas with the Paraguayan city of Encarnación.

Plaza 9 de Julio is the center of Posadas' standard grid and of the city center, and the impressive 19th-century facade of the Casa de Gobierno stretches along almost its entire east side. Av Bartolomé Mitre is the southern boundary of the center and leads east to the international bridge.

Theoretically, all downtown streets have been renumbered, but new and old systems continue to exist side by side, creating great confusion for nonresidents, since many locals use the old system. In this text the newer, four-digit street numbers are given as much as possible; some places, such as the Paraguayan consulate, still cling to their old three-digit addresses.

Information
BOOKSTORES
Liverpool Libros (☎ 434170; Av Corrientes 2074) At the foot of Entre Ríos; has English-language books.

CULTURAL CENTERS
Alianza Francesa (☎ 423519; Rivadavia 1470; ⏱ 3-9:30pm Mon-Fri)

INTERNET ACCESS
Many of the numerous *locutorios* in town offer Internet access.
WEBe.ar (Junín 2168; per hr US$0.30) Has good connections, air-con and tons of ergonomic stations.

MEDICAL SERVICES
Hospital General R Madariaga (☎ 447775; Av López Torres 1177) About 1km south of downtown.

MONEY
Banca Nazionale del Lavoro (Bolívar, southeastern cnr of Plaza 9 de Julio) Has an ATM. There are several other banks and ATMs downtown.
Cambios Mazza (Bolívar, btwn San Lorenzo & Colón) Changes traveler's checks for a 1% commission plus US$0.25 per check.

POSADAS

0 — 400 m
0 — 0.2 miles

INFORMATION	
Abra Misiones	1 B2
ACA	2 B2
Alianza Francesa	3 B1
Banco Nacionale de Lavaro	4 B2
Cambios Mazza	5 B2
German Consulate	6 A2
Liverpool Libros	7 A2
Paraguayan Consulate	8 B2
Provincial Tourist Office	9 B2
WEBe-ar	10 A2

SIGHTS & ACTIVITIES	
Museo de Ciencias Naturales e Historia	11 A2

SLEEPING	
Hotel Canciller	12 A2
Hotel Colonial	13 A3
Hotel Continental	14 B2
Hotel de Turismo Posadas	15 A2
Hotel Julio César	16 B2
Le Petit Hotel	17 B3
Posadas Hotel	18 B2
Residencial Misiones	19 B2

EATING	
Diletto	20 B2
Espeto del Rey	21 A3
Ipanema	22 B2

La Querencia	23 B2
Los Pinos Pizzeria	24 B2

ENTERTAINMENT	
Teatro El Desván	25 B2

TRANSPORT	
Aerolíneas Argentinas	26 B2
Launches to Paraguay	27 C1
Localiza	28 B2

NORTHEAST ARGENTINA

POST
Post office (cnr Bolívar & Ayacucho)

TOURIST INFORMATION
ACA (☎ 436955; cnr Córdoba & Colón)
Provincial tourist office (☎ 447540; turismo@misiones
.gov.ar; Colón 1985; ☼ 8am-8pm Mon-Fri, 8am-noon &
4-8pm Sat & Sun) Well-organized, well-informed staff. Offers
numerous maps and brochures.

TRAVEL AGENCIES
Abra Misiones (☎ 422085; abramisiones@arnet.com.ar;
Colón 1975) Offers half-day tours to the Jesuit missions
(US$22) and many other tour options.

Sights
The natural-history section of the **Museo de
Ciencias Naturales e Historia** (☎ 423893; San Luis 384;
admission free; ☼ 7am-noon & 2-8pm Mon-Fri, 9am-noon
Sat & Sun) focuses on fauna and the geology
and mineralogy of the province. The museum also has an excellent serpentarium
(with demonstrations of venom extraction),
an aviary and an aquarium. Its historical section stresses prehistory, the Jesuit missions
and modern colonization.

Festivals & Events
Posadas celebrates **Carnaval** (in February or
March, depending on the year) with great
gusto, and seems to try to outdo other
northern cities in the skimpiness of dancers'
costumes.

Sleeping
BUDGET
Hotel de Turismo Posadas (☎ 437401; Bolívar 2176;
s/d US$9/13; ☢) The rooms at this very friendly
high-rise have a nautical theme and the
bathroom doors resemble hatches. Rooms
have TV and balconies; upper floors have
good river views.

　　Residencial Misiones (☎ 430133; Av Azara 1960;
s/d US$6/9) It's casual, clean and quiet here,
and a well-equipped kitchen and clothes-
washing facilities are at guests' disposal.
Rooms (and beds) vary in quality, so have
a look at a few.

MIDRANGE
Posadas Hotel (☎ 440888; www.hotelposadas.com.ar
in Spanish; Bolívar 1949; s/d standard US$25/30, deluxe
US$32/37; P ☢) With by far the best-looking

interiors of any hotel in town, the Posadas has that somber ambience missing from many modern hotels. Rooms are spacious, comfortable and well decorated.

Hotel Continental (☎ 440990; www.hoteleramis iones.com.ar; Bolívar 1879; s/d standard US$22/30, especial US$30/38; 🖳) Don't write off the standard rooms at this 13-floor hotel right on the plaza. The *especiales* may be a bit more modern, but the standards have more character, and excellent views of the plaza and river.

Le Petit Hotel (☎ 436031; lepetit@hotmail.com; Santiago del Estero 1635; s/d US$15/21; P 😤) Le Petit just has a great feel to it. The rooms are nothing special (although they are clean and light), but the leafy patio and friendly husband-and-wife team who run the place make it a memorable option.

Hotel Canciller (☎ 440599; Junín 1710; s/d US$14/20; P 😤) This semimodern five-story hotel is pretty good value – rooms are spacious, but you'll need a high tolerance for pastel color schemes.

Hotel Colonial (☎ 436149; Barrufaldi 2419; s/d US$12/18; 😤) The Colonial is a bit of a walk from the center, but a warm atmosphere and tastefully decorated (if slightly cramped) rooms make up for that. Definitely a quiet location.

Hotel Julio César (☎ 427930; www.juliocesarhotel .com.ar in Spanish; Entre Ríos 1951; s/d US$18/25; P 😤 😤) The marble lobby and leather lounge suites in the lobby make this place look like the best in town, but some heavy handed tilework in the rooms means it loses points in the end.

Eating

Espeto del Rey (☎ 436798; cnr Tucumán & Ayacucho; all you can eat US$4) It's a sign of hard economic times that the del Rey has become a *tenedor libre*. Mandioca salad is part of the spread and there's an impressive wine list.

THE AUTHOR'S CHOICE

Diletto (☎ 449784; Bolívar 1729; mains US$3-9) Set in a grand old dining room with linen tablecloths and fine glassware, Diletto is probably the fanciest restaurant in town. It's also a good place to try the region's enormous frogs: their *ranas a la provenzal* is the whole body, not just the legs. The extensive fish menu includes trout.

La Querencia (☎ 437117; Bolívar 322; mains US$3-7) This is Posadas' spiffiest *parrilla*, on the south side of Plaza 9 de Julio. They have a wide menu, a good wine list and a battery of overhead fans to keep the place from getting stuffy.

Los Pinos Pizzeria (☎ 427252; cnr Buenos Aires & Sarmiento; mains US$3-4) The place to go for pizza, draft beer or empanadas. There's a well-stocked bar, and classical music on the sound system during the week. Weekends things get a bit livelier. The lovely old building began as a pharmacy.

Ipanema (Av Azara 1629; breakfast US$1-2, lunch & dinner US$3-5; 🕒 breakfast, lunch & dinner) Set in an arcade a few steps from the plaza, the Ipanema has good-value breakfasts and plenty of outdoor seating. A full bar and *minutas* (short orders) are also on offer.

Entertainment

Teatro El Desván (Sarmiento, btwn Colón & San Lorenzo) This theater company offers works by major Spanish-language playwrights such as Federico García Lorca, and also has a children's theater.

Getting There & Away

AIR

Aerolíneas Argentinas (☎ 422036; cnr Ayacucho & San Martín) flies 13 times weekly to Aeroparque in Buenos Aires (US$86).

BUS

Micros to Encarnación, Paraguay (US$1), leave every 20 minutes from the corner of San Lorenzo and Entre Rios. With border formalities, the trip can take more than an hour, but is often quicker.

To get your Argentine exit stamp, you'll need to get off the bus on the Posadas side of the bridge and cross the road to the immigration counter. Locals usually stay on the bus; hold on to your ticket to catch the next one when you're done. On the Paraguayan side, everyone gets off for passport checks but buses don't wait.

Although US$1 launches cross the Paraná to Encarnación from the dock at the east end of Av Guacurarí, they are pretty much for locals only. Foreigners' passports are not stamped at the docks; you must make the long trek to the foot of the bridge for this – getting caught without a stamp in Paraguay can result in a hefty fine.

Posadas' **bus terminal** (☎ 425800; Quaranta, RN 12 & Av Santa Catalina) is reachable from downtown by bus No 8, 15, 21 or 24 (US$0.70). If you're coming from the south, don't get off at the first terminal (at the *'cruce'* or crossroads); be sure you're as far into town as possible.

The following table shows winter fares; summer service will be more frequent and sometimes more expensive. All of the following destinations are served daily and most several times a day. Travel times are approximate.

Destination	Cost (US$)	Duration (hr)
Asunción (Paraguay)	8	6
Buenos Aires	22	14
Córdoba	25	18
Corrientes	7	4½
Ituzaingó	3	1
Paso de los Libres	6	7
Porto Alegre (Brazil)	25	12
Puerto Iguazú	8	5½
Resistencia	7	5
Rosario	20	16
San Ignacio	1	1
São Paulo (Brazil)	48	24
Tucumán	20	18
Yapeyú	5	7

Horianski and Águila Dorada buses to San Ignacio Miní (US$1, one hour) begin at 5:15am and continue roughly half-hourly.

Getting Around

Aerolíneas Argentinas runs its own minibus to the airport, 12km southwest of town via RN 12. The No 8 bus (US$0.40) also goes there from San Lorenzo (between La Rioja and Entre Ríos), as does the No 24 from Junín, south of Córdoba. A *remise* costs about US$4.

Localiza (☎ 432322; Colón 1935, btwn Bolívar & Córdoba) is a very straightforward and honest rental agency. A toll of US$2.30 is charged on RN 12 shortly out of town on the way north to the missions, and again on the way back.

AROUND POSADAS
Yacyretá Dam
☎ 03786

This gigantic hydroelectric project is in Corrientes province near the town of Ituzaingó, 1½ hours west of Posadas by bus.

Completed in 1997, it formed a monstrous reservoir of 1800 sq km, inundated low-lying areas of Posadas and Encarnación, and forced the relocation of nearly 40,000 people. Multibillion-dollar cost overruns on the corruption-riddled project added greatly to Argentina's foreign debt.

The **Argentine-Paraguayan Entidad Binacional Yacyretá** (☎ 420050) runs free guided tours (leaving at 10am, 11am, 3pm, 4pm and 5pm). Guides are well rehearsed, but the bus rarely slows and never stops for photographs.

A museum displays artifacts unearthed in the process of construction and a scale model of the project, and you can also see the city built to house the dam workers.

Visitors opting to stay overnight in Ituzaingó might try **Hotel Géminis** (☎ 420324; Corrientes 943; s/d US$7/15). Águila Dorada (among others) links Ituzaingó with Posadas (US$2, one hour) and Corrientes.

Santa Ana & Loreto

These are two of the former Jesuit *reducciones* that gave Misiones province its name. They are both off of RN 12 heading east and north toward San Ignacio (the site of a third and better-restored mission, p188) and Puerto Iguazú.

At **Santa Ana** (admission US$1; ☯ 7am-6pm), which was founded 43km northeast of Posadas in 1633, dense forest has been partially removed to reveal a settlement that once housed 2000 Guaraní neophytes. A 1994 deal between the Argentine and Italian governments saw work started to excavate the site, but so far the only things uncovered and still standing are the walls of the main church and the cemetery. The rest lies in wait, 1.5m underground.

The church's walls have been propped up with interior scaffolding and a few photogenic strangler figs grow atop them, lending a dramatic effect to what must have been a magnificent building in its time, though none of its decorative embellishments remain.

To the right side of the church is the cemetery, used by villagers into the latter half of the 20th century but now neglected. Here are overgrown graves and crypts with doors agape, revealing coffins fallen from their shelves and burst open; if this place doesn't give you the willies, you haven't watched enough horror movies. Some of the markers toward the back bear Japanese writing.

Loreto (admission US$1; 7am-6:30pm), founded in 1632, has even fewer visible remains than Santa Ana, and may not be worth the effort to visit via public transport. The old stone latrine and a chapel are partially restored. A wander along the path through the forest reveals many low stretches of wall and big moss-covered building stones. It's a wild and jungly place – not so instructive for mission life, but it has an undeniable atmosphere.

Both sites have very modest museums at their entrances, and just outside Loreto is a kiosk, selling chips and drinks. Apart from that, there is no food, and there is nowhere to stay in either of these places.

GETTING THERE & AWAY
Buses heading north from Posadas stop at the turnoffs on RN 12 for both sites. Santa Ana's is at Km 43, from where it's a 1km walk to the ruins. Loreto's is at Km 48, with a 3km walk.

SAN IGNACIO
☎ 03752 / pop 10,550
The big attraction here are the ruins of San Ignacio Miní, the most impressive remnants of all the former *reducciones* in the region, including those in Paraguay. While you could conceivably belt out here on a day trip from Posadas, a better idea is to stay the night; the hotels are comfortable enough, and you'll have a chance to check out the sound and light show at the ruins as well as Quiroga's house, both of which are worth hanging around for.

Everything in town is within walking distance, but don't believe any of the signs that say that this hotel or that is 500m away: by some curious physical phenomenon it seems that everything in San Ignacio is 500m away from any given point – except that it isn't.

San Ignacio is 56km northeast of Posadas via RN 12. From the highway junction, the broad Av Sarmiento leads about 1km to Calle Rivadavia, which leads six blocks north to the ruins.

Sights
SAN IGNACIO MINÍ
These **mission ruins** (entrance on Calle Alberdi s/n; admission US$4; 7am-7pm) are impressive for the quantity of carved ornamentation still visible and for the amount of restoration done. No

roofs remain, but many of the living quarters and workshops have been re-erected.

First founded in 1611 in the state of Paraná, Brazil, but abandoned after repeated attacks by Brazilian slavers, San Ignacio was established at its present site in 1696 and functioned until the Jesuits finally gave in to the order of expulsion in 1768. The ruins, rediscovered in 1897 and restored between 1940 and 1948, belong to a style known as 'Guaraní baroque.' At its peak, in 1733, the *reducción* had a Guaraní population of nearly 4000.

The entrance is on the north side on Calle Alberdi, where visitors pass through the **interpretive center**. Fans of truly bizarre museums cannot afford to miss this one. In between the quite sensible exhibits on Guaraní and Jesuit history are three rooms whose interiors sit somewhere between modern-art installation and amusement-park haunted house. Stuffed animals, fluorescent paint, black light – they've pulled out all the stops… then, as you emerge blinking into the sunlight thinking it's all over, you're greeted by half a miniature pirate ship, crammed into the central patio.

San Ignacio Miní's centerpiece is the enormous red sandstone church. At 74m long and 24m wide with walls 2m thick at the base, it is the focal point of the settlement. Scaffolding keeps some of the walls from collapsing, but the weathered wood blends well with the surroundings. For photography, focus on the details, especially the elaborately carved doorways.

Just west of the *cabildo* (on the church's west side) is a row of columns. A strangler fig has grown around one of them, leaving the column barely visible; it is billed as the 'tree with the heart of stone.'

Just before the exit is another museum containing some excellent carved paving stones and another model.

Every night there is a Luz y Sonido (light and sound show) at the ruins; it costs US$2.

CASA DE HORACIO QUIROGA
Uruguay-born of Argentine parents, Quiroga was a poet and novelist who also dabbled in other activities, including snapping some of the earliest photographs of the rediscovered ruins at San Ignacio Miní and farming cotton (unsuccessfully) in the Chaco. He lived in San Ignacio from 1910 to

1917, when his first wife committed suicide (as did Quiroga himself, terminally ill, 20 years later). Quiroga's regionally based stories transcend both time and place without abandoning their setting. Some of his short fiction is available in English translation in *The Exiles and Other Stories.*

Quiroga's house (☎ 470124; Av Quiroga s/n; admission US$1; ✆ 8am-7pm winter, 8am-8pm summer) is at the southern end of town, offering grand views of the Río Paraná. A small museum contains photos and some of the writer's possessions and first editions.

Quiroga's permanent **Casa de Piedra** is one of those simple but lovely houses that artists seem to inhabit, and holds various memorabilia, including butterfly specimens, an enormous snakeskin and the writer's rusted motorcycle (without sidecar). A replica of his initial wooden house, built for Nemesio Juárez's 1996 biographical film *Historias de Amor, de Locura y de Muerte* (Stories of Love, Madness and Death), stands nearby.

Sleeping & Eating

Hotel San Ignacio (☎ 470422; cnr Sarmiento & San Martín; s/d US$8/15, cabanas for 4/5 people US$22/25; ✗) For a place that's a combination hotel/bar/ restaurant/Internet café/pool hall/teen hangout, the San Ignacio's actually pretty mellow. Rooms in the main building are spotless and quiet and the funky A-frame bungalows out the back are great value for larger groups.

Residencial Doka (☎ 470131; residoka@yahoo.com .ar; Alberdi 518; r per person US$5; P ✗) Located just a few steps from the ruins, the Doka has fairly nondescript rooms that sleep up to five people. It is set well back from the road and is therefore quiet. Kitchen facilities are available.

There are several places to eat near the exit to the ruins.

Don Valentín (☎ 15-647961; Alberdi 444; mains US$2-5, set menu US$3-6) Just across from the entrance to the ruins, Don Valentín is a step up from the production-line operations serving tour groups along here.

La Aldea (Los Jesuitas s/n; dishes US$3-7; ✆ breakfast, lunch & dinner) Five hundred meters (no, really) from the entrance to the ruins, this barn of a place has tables at the front, inside and on the rear deck. Serves excellent pizzas and *minutas* and is one of the only eating options open late at night.

Getting There & Away

The bus terminal is at the western end of Av Sarmiento, the main road into town. Services between Posadas (US$1, one hour) and Puerto Iguazú (US$7, four hours) are frequent with several companies, but buses along RN 12 also stop readily en route in either direction.

IGUAZÚ FALLS

Even the most hardened of waterfall yawners will be taken aback by the Iguazú Falls. This is more than your average gee-isn't-gravity-neat type of experience. The power, size and sheer noise of the falls are truly spectacular. The falls lie split between Brazil and Argentina within 2100 sq km of national park, much of it rainforest teeming with unique flora and fauna: there are thousands of species of insects, hundreds of species of birds and many mammals and reptiles.

The falls are easily reached from either side of the Argentine–Brazilian border, as well as from nearby Paraguay. A good selection of inexpensive food and lodging can be found in both Puerto Iguazú, Argentina, and Foz do Iguaçu, Brazil.

History & Environment

Álvar Núñez Cabeza de Vaca and his expedition were the first Europeans to view the falls, in 1542. According to Guaraní tradition, the falls originated when an Indian

NORTHEAST ARGENTINA

warrior named Caroba incurred the wrath of a forest god by escaping downriver in a canoe with a young girl named Naipur, with whom the god had become infatuated. Enraged, the god caused the riverbed to collapse in front of the lovers, producing a line of precipitous falls over which Naipur fell and, at their base, turned into a rock. Caroba survived as a tree overlooking his fallen lover.

The geological origins of the falls are more prosaic. In southern Brazil, the Río Iguaçú passes over a basaltic plateau that ends abruptly just east of the confluence with the Paraná. Where the lava flow stopped, thousands of cubic meters of water per second now plunge down as much as 80m into sedimentary terrain below. Before reaching the falls, the river divides into many channels with hidden reefs, rocks and islands separating the many visually distinctive cascades that together form the famous *cataratas* (waterfalls). In total, the falls are more than 2km across.

Seeing the Falls

Opinion is divided as to which side – the Brazilian or the Argentine – offers the best views of the falls. Try to see both, and if at all possible, visit on clear days. The difference between a clear and an overcast day at the falls is vast, only in part because of the rainbows and butterflies that emerge when the sun is shining. Ideally you should allow for a multiple-day stay to have a better shot at optimal conditions.

While the Argentine side – with its variety of trails and two free boat rides – offers many more opportunities to see individual falls close up, the Brazilian side yields the more panoramic views, allowing visitors to get a better idea of the immensity of the entire falls. And the Brazilian side has one extreme close-up from a catwalk at the bottom of the falls that is not to be missed. One intriguing option is the full-moon tours of the Argentine side of the falls; see opposite for details.

You can base yourself on either side and easily see everything there is to see.

NATIONAL PARKS

Brazil's Parque Nacional do Iguaçu is the larger of the two, at 1500 sq km, but Argentina's 550-sq-km Parque Nacional Iguazú is far more pristine. High temperatures, rainfall and humidity encourage a diverse habitat, and the parks' subtropical rainforest contains more than 2000 identified plant species, countless insects, 400 species of birds and many mammals and reptiles.

Resembling the tropical Amazonian rainforest to the north, the forests of the falls region consist of multiple levels, the highest a closed canopy more than 30m tall. Beneath the canopy are several additional levels of trees, plus a dense ground-level growth of shrubs and herbaceous plants. One of the most interesting species is the guapoy (strangler fig), an epiphyte that uses a large tree for support until it finally asphyxiates its host. This species covers the ruins of many abandoned Jesuit mission buildings elsewhere in the province.

Other epiphytes exploit their hosts without harming them. Orchids use the limbs of large trees like the lapacho or palo rosa for support only, absorbing essential nutrients from rainfall or the atmosphere. At lower levels in the forest, you will find wild specimens of *yerba mate,* which Argentines and other residents of the Río de la Plata region use for tea.

Mammals and other wildlife are not easily seen in the parks, because many are either nocturnal or avoid humans – which is not difficult in the dense undergrowth. This is the case, for instance, with large cats such as the puma and jaguar. The largest mammal is the tapir, which is a distant relative of the horse, but the most commonly seen is the coati, a relative of the raccoon. It is not unusual to see iguanas, and do watch out for snakes.

Birds deserve special mention. Many birds that you might see in zoos or pet shops are found in the wild here, including toucans, parrots, parakeets and other colorful species. The best time to see them is early morning along watercourses or in the forest, although the trees around the visitor center do not lack flocks.

Dangers & Annoyances

The Río Iguaçu's currents are strong and swift; more than one tourist has been swept downriver and drowned in the area of Isla San Martín. It should go without saying that no one should get too close to the falls proper.

Park wildlife is potentially dangerous: in 1997 a jaguar killed the infant son of a park ranger. While this is not cause for hysteria, visitors should respect the big cats. In the unlikely event that you encounter one, don't panic. Speak calmly but loudly, do not run or turn your back on the animal, and do everything possible to appear bigger than you are, by waving your arms or clothing for example.

A much more likely encounter (almost a certain one on the Argentine side's Paseo Inferior) is with the bands of begging coatis that have become accustomed to the human presence. Though these clownish omnivores seem tame, they can become aggressive if fed (or teased with food), and they will bite. You've heard the spiel: they're wild animals, and feeding them harms them and can be dangerous for you as well. Be content with taking photos, and hold on to your lens cap.

Humans may abscond with your personal belongings, so watch your things while hiking. Though not epidemic, it happens.

You are likely to get soaked, or at least very damp, from the spray at the falls. Keeping your cash, documents and camera in plastic bags is not a bad idea.

Parque Nacional Iguazú

☎ 03757

The **park** (☎ 491445; admission US$10; ⏱ 9am-6pm) has a new visitor center with lockers and other amenities, including a small train to take visitors from the park entrance to the falls. A gift shop, restaurants and snack bars are among the park's many other facilities.

On the three nights around the full moon, rangers lead **tours** (☎ 491469; incl dinner & park admission US$10) of the falls. Weather permitting, these leave at 8:30pm and 9:15pm. Buses leave the terminal at 7:25pm and 8:20pm on these nights.

SIGHTS

The tower near the old visitor center offers a good overall view, but walking around is the best way to see the **falls**. Plan your hikes before or after the midmorning influx of tour buses. At midday you can take a break from the heat at the restaurant and *confitería* (café offering light meals) here.

Signs point the way to the two circuits, the Paseo Superior and Paseo Inferior, which provide most of the viewing opportunities

---

THE RIDE OF A LIFETIME

If you think that the constructed walkways give you a close-up view of Iguazú Falls, think again – you have actually missed out on a once-in-a-lifetime photo opportunity.

In the early days of Iguazú's popularity as a tourist attraction, it was possible to hire a local with a rowboat who would take you right out to the edge of the falls and keep the boat there by rowing madly against the current while you and your friends took photos, spat and did all that other stuff you do at the edge of a waterfall.

But the inevitable has a way of happening, and so it was that one day in 1938 the rower found himself overpowered by the current, and the boat – with seven German tourists on board – went sliding over the edge. There were no survivors and these boat trips were immediately prohibited.

And so ends the history of yet another foolish but exhilarating sightseeing option.

---

via a series of trails, bridges and *pasarelas* (catwalks). The Paseo Superior is entirely level and gives good views of the tops of several cascades and across to more. The Paseo Inferior descends to the river, passing delightfully close to more falls on the way. This is prime coati country, but remember, no matter how cute they look, don't feed them. At the bottom of the path a free launch makes the short crossing to **Isla Grande San Martín**, an island with a trail of its own that gives the closest look at several falls, including **Salto San Martín**, a huge, furious cauldron of water whose violence is second only to the Garganta del Diablo. It's possible to picnic and swim on the lee side of the island, but don't venture too far off the beach.

A train from the visitor center operates regularly to shuttle visitors from site to site. At the last stop, follow the trail to the lookout point perched right on the edge of the mighty falls. Of all the sights on earth, the **Garganta del Diablo** (Devil's Throat) must come closest to the experience of sailing off the edge of a flat earth imagined by early European sailors. On three sides, the deafening cascade plunges to a murky destination; the vapors soaking the viewer blur the base of the falls and rise in a smokelike plume that can often be seen from several kilometers away.

ACTIVITIES

Relatively few visitors venture beyond the immediate area of the falls to appreciate the park's forest scenery and wildlife. Because the forest is so dense, there are few trails, but walks along the road beyond Puerto Canoas will usually reward you with wildlife sightings.

Along the road about 400m east and south of the big Sheraton hotel is the entrance to the **Sendero Macuco** interpretive nature trail, which leads through dense forest to a nearly hidden waterfall, **Salto Arrechea**. The first 3km of the trail, to the top of the waterfall, is almost completely level, but a steep lateral drops to the base of the falls and beyond to the Río Iguaçu, about 650m in all. This part of the trail is muddy and slippery – watch your step and figure about an hour each way from the trailhead. Early morning is the best time for the trip, with better opportunities to see wildlife, which may include bands of caí monkeys. Take mosquito repellent.

To get elsewhere in the forest, hitch or hire a car to go out on RN 101 toward the village of **Bernardo de Irigoyen**. Few visitors explore this part of the park, but it is still nearly pristine forest.

Iguazú Jungle Explorer (☎ 421600; www.iguazu junglexplorer.com), at the visitor center, offers various excursions: by speedy inflatable boats to the bottom of several of the waterfalls, including the Garganta del Diablo, of course (US$10, 15 minutes); by large 4WD flatbed trucks along the Sendero Yacaratiá (US$9, one hour); rafting down the upper Iguazú (US$5, 30 minutes); various combinations of these and other trips as well.

SLEEPING

Sheraton Internacional Iguazú (☎ 491800; fax 491 841; Parque Nacional Iguazú; r US$185-237; P X □ ■) The only place to stay within the park itself, this luxury hotel, as seen from outside, couldn't be much uglier, but inside it's first rate. All rooms have balconies and tiled floors, and facilities include restaurants, tennis courts, a gym and a pool.

GETTING THERE & AWAY

The park is 20km northeast of Puerto Iguazú by paved highway. From Puerto Iguazú's terminal, buses leave hourly for the park (US$1, 30 minutes) between 7:30am and 7:30pm, with return trips between 8:45am and 8:15pm; catch an early one to avoid the heat and the tour buses that swarm around the falls about 11am, when noisy Brazilian helicopters also begin their flights. The buses make flag stops at points along the highway. A cab from town to the park entrance is about US$8.

If you're based in Foz do Iguaçu, inexpensive tours to the Argentine park give you more time to spend at the falls, without the hassle of waiting for bus connections (see p198). For details on bus services to Puerto Iguazú, see p199.

Parque Nacional do Iguaçu (Brazil)

The **Brazilian park** (admission US$3.50, payable in Brazilian, Argentine or US currency; ☼ 1-5pm Mon, 8am-6pm Tue-Sun summer, 1-5pm Mon, 8am-5pm Tue-Sun winter) sports an enormous new visitor center with very little in it other than a ticket booth, exchange window and ATM, big lockers (US$1.25 for 24 hours), fabulous bathrooms and a gift shop. The parking lot adjacent to the center charges US$3 per car.

When buying tickets visitors are asked their nationality (which is then printed on the ticket!). Double-decker buses leave about every 15 minutes from the back of the visitor center for the pleasant, forested ride into the falls part of the park. Keep your eyes peeled for animals. Recorded messages in different languages warn and inform you about various things, including the various stops the bus makes.

The first stop is the **Poço Preto Trail** (US$45), a 9km guided trek through the jungle on foot or by bike. The trail ends at Taquara island, where you can kayak or take a boat cruise to Porto Canoas.

The second stop is the **Macuco Safari** (US$36), where you can ride through the jungle in a trailer pulled by a jeep.

The bus then stops at the **Bananeiras Trail** (US$20), a 2km walk passing lagoons and observing aquatic wildlife which ends with a boat ride to Porto Canoas.

Next is the **Campo de Desafios** (☎ 45-529-6040; www.campodedesafios.com.br in Spanish), an activity center offering rafting (US$23), abseiling (US$23), rock climbing (US$10) and a canopy tour (US$29).

The last stop is lovely Hotel Tropical das Cataratas (see p199), the best place to get off. From here you walk 1.5km down a paved **trail** with brilliant views of the falls on the Argentine side, the jungle and the river below. The views build up to the grand finale at the end of the trail: a metal catwalk jutting out into the river at the foot of the falls, getting you within shouting distance of the Garganta del Diablo and nearly spitting distance of the Brazilian falls. But don't spit – the constant wind created by the dropping water will just blow it back in your face. You'll get wet here one way or the other. On a clear day in the afternoon you should be able to see a circular rainbow in the spray.

Also at the end of the trail is an elevator up to a viewing platform at the top of the falls at Porto Canoas, the last stop of the double-decker buses.

Porto Canoas has a gift shop, a fast-food restaurant (burgers US$3) and an excellent buffet restaurant with hot and cold dishes and an outstanding salad bar featuring arugula, watercress and much more for US$9. Whether you opt to eat or just down a cold one, you should sit out on the deck for a million-dollar view of the river and the top of the falls before catching the bus back.

Though Argentina has banned helicopter flights over its side of the falls because they disturb wildlife, including nesting birds, Brazilian helicopters still make the flights on their side. A 10-minute ride costs US$60 per person.

GETTING THERE & AWAY

On weekdays 'Parque Nacional' buses run from Foz do Iguaçu's urban bus terminal to the park entrance (US$0.50, 40 minutes) between 6am and midnight (every 20 minutes until 8pm and every 30 minutes thereafter), making stops along Av Juscelino Kubitschek and Av das Cataratas. On weekends and holidays, buses run roughly every 40 minutes between 8am and 6pm. Don't forget the park's curtailed Monday hours.

A taxi from downtown Foz to the park entrance costs around US$14.

To access the Brazilian park from Puerto Iguazú you can take a bus all the way to Foz do Iguaçu's terminal and catch the 'Parque Nacional' bus (also see p196). To save time and avoid backtracking, get off instead at Av das Cataratas, just beyond immigration on the Brazilian side of the bridge, and flag down the Parque Nacional bus there. If you're only

planning to spend a day visiting the park, border formalities are usually minimal, but it's wise to check ahead of time (see the boxed text, p198).

PUERTO IGUAZÚ

☎ 03757 / pop 32,000

Woodsy little Puerto Iguazú would be a fun place to hang out in its own right: it's big enough to provide some good eating and sleeping options, but small enough to retain a relaxed, intimate atmosphere. Truth is, though, that everybody is here to see the star of the show – the thundering Iguazú Falls, just down the road.

Puerto Iguazú sits at the confluence of the Río Paraná and the Río Iguazú and is far less hazardous, in terms of street crime, than Foz do Iguaçu (Brazil) and Ciudad del Este (Paraguay). By staying here and making day trips to the Brazilian side, most travelers can avoid purchasing a Brazilian visa.

Orientation

Some 300km northeast of Posadas via paved RN 12 (which passes through a corner of the national park), Puerto Iguazú has an irregular city plan, but is small enough that you will find your way around easily. The main drag is the diagonal Av Victoria Aguirre, but most services are just north of this in a rabbit warren of streets that cross each other at odd angles.

The Hito Argentino, a small obelisk at the confluence of the Ríos Paraná and Iguazú (at the western end of Av Tres Fronteras), marks the beginning of Argentine territory. From here you can see Brazil and Paraguay, both of which have similar markers on their sides of the confluence.

Information

ACA (☎ 420165) On the highway to the park, at Km 4.
Banco de Misiones (Av Victoria Aguirre 330) Has an ATM.
Hospital Marta Teodora Shwartz (☎ 420288; cnr Av Victoria Aguirre & Ushuaia)
Lavadero Liuba (cnr Bompland & Av Misiones)
Post office (Av San Martín 780)
Telecentro Internet (cnr Av Victoria Aguirre & Eppens)
Tourist office (☎ 420800; Av Victoria Aguirre 311; ☽ 8am-noon & 4-8pm Mon-Fri, 4-8pm Sat & Sun) Depending on staffing, service ranges from indifferent to very friendly and informative. There is also a small office which keeps irregular hours at the bus terminal.

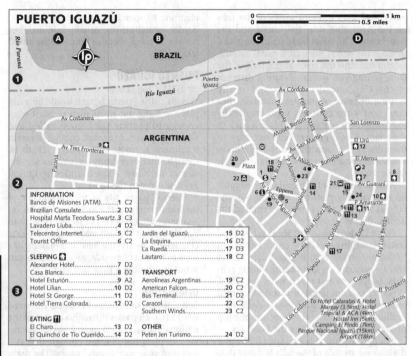

PUERTO IGUAZÚ

INFORMATION	
Banco de Misiones (ATM)..........1	C2
Brazilian Consulate...................2	D2
Hospital Marta Teodora Swartz..3	C3
Lavadero Liuba........................4	C3
Telecentro Internet..................5	C2
Tourist Office.........................6	C2

SLEEPING	
Alexander Hotel......................7	D2
Casa Blanca...........................8	D2
Hotel Esturión........................9	A2
Hotel Lilian...........................10	D2
Hotel St George......................11	D2
Hotel Tierra Colorada...............12	D2

EATING	
El Charo...............................13	D2
El Quincho de Tío Querido......14	D2

Jardín del Iguazú....................15	D2
La Esquina............................16	D2
La Rueda..............................17	D3
Lautaro................................18	C2

TRANSPORT	
Aerolíneas Argentinas..............19	C2
American Falcon.....................20	C2
Bus Terminal.........................21	D2
Caracol................................22	C2
Southern Winds......................23	C2

OTHER	
Peten Jen Turismo...................24	D2

Dangers & Annoyances

Motorists should be aware that car theft is quite common in the triple-border area, though carjacking is unusual on the Argentine side of the border. It's a good idea to engage antitheft devices in your car and use secure parking at night.

Tours

Many local operators offer day tours to the Brazilian side of the falls. For about US$17, these include a meal and a trip to Itaipú dam. One company offering such trips is **Peten Jen Turismo** (☎ 422577; petenjenturismo@iguazunet.com; Córdoba 170), opposite the bus terminal.

Sleeping

The 'tropical breakfast' offered by some hotels is a buffet with fresh fruit included.

BUDGET

Hostel Inn (☎ /fax 420649; www.hostel-inn.com; RN 12, Km 5; dm US$6; P 🅿 💻 🌐) Set on three hectares of land, this ex-casino is part of a chain of excellent hostels around the country. Offering free Internet, a bar, restaurant and a huge pool, among other things, it's as great place to stay, relax and meet people.

Hotel Tierra Colorada (☎ /fax 420649; hoteltierra colorada@iguazunet.com; El Urú 265; s/d US$12/15; P 🅿 💻) A modern brick building with basic but comfortable rooms, this is a better deal than it appears at first sight. Plenty of light and space make this a good choice.

Camping El Pindo (☎ 421795; per tent US$2.50 plus per person US$2.20; 🌐) At Km 3.5 of RN 12 on the southern edge of town, very convenient to the *rotonda* (traffic circle) bus stop. It has clean bathrooms, and hot water after 6pm.

MIDRANGE

Alexander Hotel (☎ 420429; Av Córdoba 222; www .hotelguia.com/hoteles/alexander in Spanish; s/d US$23/30; P 🅿 🌐) There's plenty of orange going on in the color scheme here, but if a semiluxurious hotel near the bus terminal is what you're after, the Alexander hits the spot.

Hotel Margay (☎ 421340; www.hotelmargay.com .ar in Spanish; RN 12, Km 3.5; s/d US$31/42; P 🅿 🌐) The Margay's low-slung hacienda vibe stops at the lobby, but the rooms are modern, spacious and comfortable. Big firm beds, minifridges and a separate room for toilet and shower are added bonuses.

Casa Blanca (☎ 421320; www.casablancaiguazu.com .ar in Spanish; Av Guarani 121; s/d US$18/20; P X) Simple but spotless rooms and a welcoming atmosphere are the key points for this little hotel just a short walk from the bus terminal.

Hotel Lilian (☎ 420968; Fray Luis Beltran 183; s/d US$13/20; X) Bright and cheerful, the Lilian offers good-value, air-con rooms on the top floor and slightly cheaper ones with fan downstairs. Bonuses are a shady balcony and superclean, massive bathrooms.

Hotel Tropical (☎ 420650; RN 12, Km 4; s/d US$20/30; P X ⏛) There's a pleasing motel-like laid-back feel to the Tropical. Rooms are service-able, although nothing fancy, but the pace here seems to guarantee a tranquil stay.

Hotel Saint George (☎ 420633; www.hotelsaint george.com in Spanish; Av Córdoba 148; s/d US$38/45; P X ⏛) This is a comfortable, low-key option near the bus terminal. Rooms are well appointed and some have great views.

TOP END

Hotel Cataratas (☎ 421823; www.hotelcataratas.com.ar in Spanish; RN 12, Km 3.5; s/d US$80/100, ste with Jacuzzi US$175; P X ⏛ ⏛) Iguazú's only five-star hotel lays it all on: the somber atmosphere, two double beds to a room, a business center and a decent restaurant. There aren't a whole lot of surprises here, but it's all definitely very deluxe.

Eating

For the cheapest eats, stroll around the triangle formed by Av Brasil, Perito Moreno and Ingeniero Eppens. One reader recommends the Saturday fruit market at Córdoba and Félix de Azara.

La Esquina (☎ 420633; cnr Córdoba & Amarante; mains US$5-7) With its soft classical music, extensive wine list and imaginative Italian menu, La Esquina is a great dinner option. Outdoor seating is perfect for balmy Iguazú nights.

El Charo (☎ 421529; Av Córdoba 106; set meals US$4) Another great place to sit and watch the world go by, El Charo has the usual range of *parrillada* offerings, with outdoor seating and some good-value set meals.

La Rueda (☎ 422531; Córdoba 28; mains US$3-6) Spanish and French dishes dominate the menu at this upscale restaurant, but there's also plenty of steak and a huge range of homemade pastas.

THE AUTHOR'S CHOICE

Hotel Esturión (☎ 420100; www.hotelesturion .com; Av Tres Fronteras 650; s/d US$35/40; P X ⏛ ⏛) Since the economic crash, hotels like the Esturión have become ab-solute bargains. But let's not gloat about this. A Zenlike lobby, beautifully sculptured grounds, tennis courts, restaurant, an ex-cellent pool area and some great views – this place has it all.

El Quincho de Tío Querido (☎ 420027; Bompland s/n; meals US$3-6; ⏱ dinner) A fairly standard *parrilla* menu is on offer here, but the large patio dining area set back from the road scores big points, as does the lengthy wine list and well-stocked bar.

Lautaro (☎ 422142; Brasil 7; mains US$3-6; ⏱ break-fast, lunch & dinner) Well-presented meals and great pizzas are on offer at this ultramodern café/restaurant/bar (the waiting staff wear headsets). There's live music most nights, and breezy sidewalk seating for people-watching.

Jardín del Iguazú (☎ 420850; Av Misiones; meals US$3-5; ⏱ breakfast, lunch & dinner) Tables here are arranged in a leafy outdoor setting. The menu pretty much sticks to *parrillada* and an impressive salad bar. Live music (no guar-antees on quality) is sometimes on offer.

Getting There & Away

Aerolíneas Argentinas (☎ 420168; Av Victoria Aguirre 295), **Southern Winds** (☎ 420390; Perito Moreno 184) and **American Falcon** (☎ 422655; Av Victoria Aguirre 564) all fly daily to Buenos Aires (US$100).

The **bus terminal** (☎ 420854; cnr Avs Córdoba & Misiones) has departures for all over the country. **Agencia Noelia** (☎ 422722; Local 2) sells tickets for most lines. The following are a sample of fares available:

Destination	Cost (US$)	Duration (hr)
Buenos Aires	27-35	20
Córdoba	34	23
Corrientes	12	10
La Plata	25	22
Paraná	25	15
Posadas	8	5½
Resistencia	14	10
San Ignacio	7	4
Santa Fe	28	13

There are international services, as well as Brazilian domestic services, across the border in Foz do Iguaçu.

Getting Around

Caracol (☎ 420064; Av Victoria Aguirre 563) charges US$2 to the airport and makes hotel pick ups; phone for reservations. *Remises* cost about US$9.

Frequent buses with three different lines cross to Foz do Iguaçu, Brazil (US$1, 35 minutes), and to Ciudad del Este, Paraguay (US$1, one hour), from Platform 1 at the bus terminal. All of these buses will stop near the *rotonda* at the edge of town.

Groups of three or more people hoping to see both sides of the falls as well as Ciudad del Este and the Itaipú hydroelectric project may find a shared cab or *remise* a good idea; figure on it costing up to US$45 for a full day of sightseeing. The tourist office on Av Victoria Aguirre may be able to arrange such trips for less. Strictly as transport to Foz do Iguaçu, a taxi costs around US$20.

For information on immigration procedures, see the boxed text, p198.

FOZ DO IGUAÇU (BRAZIL)

☎ 045 / pop 281,000

Much more of a city than little Puerto Iguazú across the border, Foz makes a good base from which to see both sides of the falls. The nightlife is definitely better, the eating options a tad more sophisticated, and you get the added bonus of checking out what is a fairly representative Brazilian town.

On the down side, Foz's high-rise buildings and relatively sparse greenery make its streets hotter than those of woodsy Puerto Iguazú, Argentina, and there is more street crime here. Another factor to consider is the cost of a Brazilian visa (recommended for anything more than a day trip for those who require visas); if you're not pushing on into Brazil, you may want to avoid that expense. For more details, see the boxed text, p198.

With the 1970 construction of the Itaipú hydroelectric project, the city's population exploded from a modest 34,000, and commercial opportunities across the river in Ciudad del Este attracted many other new ethnic communities. Today Foz is home to several thousand Muslims, many of them of Lebanese origin, and smaller communities of Japanese and Koreans.

Orientation

Foz do Iguaçu is at the confluence of Río Iguaçu and Río Paraná, 630km south of Curitiba by BR 277. The Ponte Presidente Tancredo Neves is a bridge that links the city to Puerto Iguazú, Argentina, across the Rio Iguaçu, while the Ponte da Amizade connects it to Ciudad del Este, Paraguay, across the Paraná. Fifteen kilometers upstream is Itaipú, the largest operating hydroelectric project in the world.

Foz do Iguaçu has a compact center with a fairly regular grid. Av das Cataratas, at the southwest edge of town, becomes Rodovia das Cataratas and leads 20km to the world-famous falls via BR 469, passing the turnoff for the Argentine border on the way. Westbound BR 277 leads to Ciudad del Este. The main downtown street is Av Juscelino Kubitschek, often referred to simply as 'JK' (zho-ta-*ka*).

Information

Most hotels and restaurants in town accept dollars, Paraguayan guaraníes and Argentine pesos. Calculate rates as it's often cheaper to pay in Brazilian reals.

INTERNET ACCESS

Locutorio Café Internet (Café Pizza Net; Rua Rebouças; per hr US$1) Just east of Rua Almirante Barroso. Decent Internet access. Phone calls can also be made from here.

LAUNDRY

Guiga Mara Lavanderia (Rua Tarobá 834) Washes clothes.

MONEY

BBV (Av Brasil) At the east end of Rio Branco; has an ATM.
Safir Turismo (Av Brasil at Bartolomeu de Gusmão) Changes both cash and traveler's checks, the latter with a 6% commission.

POST

Post office (Praça Getúlio Vargas; cnr Av Juscelino Kubitschek & Rio Branco)

TOURIST INFORMATION

The bimonthly publication *Folha da Amizade*, available at many hotels, contains some useful information, mostly in Portuguese but also in English and Spanish.

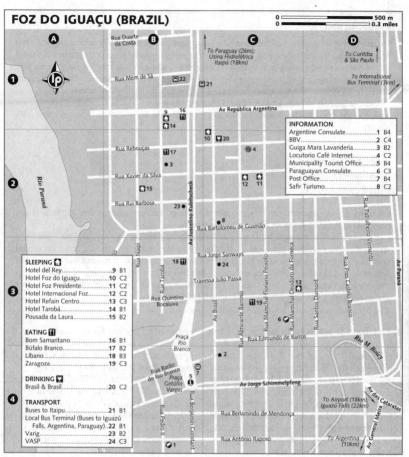

FOZ DO IGUAÇU (BRAZIL)

0   500 m
0   0.3 miles

To Paraguay (2km);
Usina Hidrelétrica
Itaipú (18km)

To Curitiba
& São Paulo

To International
Bus Terminal (3km)

INFORMATION
Argentine Consulate	1 B4
BBV	2 C4
Guiga Mara Lavandería	3 B2
Locutorio Café Internet	4 C2
Municipality Tourist Office	5 B4
Paraguayan Consulate	6 C3
Post Office	7 B4
Safir Turismo	8 C2

SLEEPING
Hotel del Rey	9 B1
Hotel Foz do Iguaçu	10 C2
Hotel Foz Presidente	11 C2
Hotel Internacional Foz	12 C2
Hotel Refain Centro	13 C3
Hotel Tarobá	14 B1
Pousada da Laura	15 B2

EATING
Bom Samaritano	16 B1
Búfalo Branco	17 B2
Líbano	18 B3
Zaragoza	19 C3

DRINKING
Brasil & Brasil	20 C2

TRANSPORT
Buses to Itaipu	21 B1
Local Bus Terminal (Buses to Iguazú Falls, Argentina, Paraguay)	22 B1
Varig	23 B2
VASP	24 C3

Rua Duarte da Costa

Rua Mem de Sá

Av República Argentina

Rua Rebouças

Rua Xavier da Silva

Rua Rui Barbosa

Rua Bartolomeu de Gusmão

Rua Jorge Sanways

Travessa Julio Passa

Rua Quintino Bocaiuva

Rua Edmundo de Barros

Praça Rio Branco

Rua Barão do Rio Branco

Praça Getúlio Vargas

Av Jorge Schimmelpfeng

Rua Berlamindo de Mendonça

Rua Antônio Raposo

Rio Paraná

Rua Juscelino Kubitscheck

Rua Naipi

Rua Tarobá

Rua Almirante Barroso

Av Brasil

Rua Marechal Floriano Peixoto

Rua Marechal Deodoro da Fonseca

Rua Santos Dumont

Rua Pres Castelo Branco

Rua Patuthcho Vemaldo

Av Paraná

Rio M Boicy

Av das Cataratas

Av General Meira

Rua Benjamin Constant

Rua Pedro II

To Airport (18km);
Iguazú Falls (22km)

To Argentina (10km)

NORTHEAST ARGENTINA

Municipal tourist office (☎ 523-8581; Praça Getúlio Vargas; 🕐 8am-8pm) Has maps, lists of hotels (one star and above only) and tourist newspapers with English-language descriptions of attractions. Most of the staffers speak English, and some also speak Italian, Spanish or German. Quality of information can range from awful to good.

Teletur (☎ 0800-451516; 🕐 7am-11pm) Maintains an information service with English-speaking operators.

Tourist booths airport (🕐 9am until the last plane); long-distance bus terminal (☎ 522-2590; 🕐 7:30am-6pm)

Dangers & Annoyances

Don't try to make your way down to the Rio Paraná; there is no path on the steep hillside and the shantytown on the city's eastern edge is not a salubrious neighborhood. Beware of taxi drivers and of touts wearing official-looking badges, caps, T-shirts or vests who try to direct new arrivals to accommodations. They will tell you the hotel you want no longer exists or is located in a dangerous part of town, then try to extract commissions from you and/or the place they steer you to.

Sights

With an installed capacity of 12.6 million kilowatts, the binational **Usina Hidrelétrica Itaipú** (Itaipú dam) is the largest hydroelectric project in the world. It's also an illustration of the ways in which massive development projects have plunged countries like Brazil many billions of dollars into debt without hope of repayment. The **Centro de Recepção**

ENTERING BRAZIL

For day-trippers border formalities are minimal; you need your passport, but neither Argentine nor Brazilian authorities usually stamp it. If you need to 'renew' your visa, you can get an exit stamp on the Argentine side, sneak past Brazilian immigration and pick up another 90 days on the way back in. From time to time, however, readers have reported that Australian, New Zealand, French, British or US citizens needed a visa to cross to Foz do Iguaçu, so check in advance.

Entry to Brazil is definitely tighter for US citizens than it once was, but most North Americans have few problems at the border. Technically, the following need visas (which can come with a cost):

■ Australians (US$35)

■ Canadians (US$40)

■ Japanese (US$50)

■ US citizens (US$100)

If getting a visa, organize it before you get the border. You can arrange one at the Brazilian consulate in Puerto Iguazú, or before you leave home.

It doesn't hurt to travel light, ie with as little gear as possible, to establish your temporary status. If you're spending the night or continuing on into Brazil, let the bus driver know you need to clear immigration, and try to get a ticket from the conductor if the bus won't wait. Both Argentine and Brazilian formalities are usually handled on the Argentine side of the bridge on the way out. Those just passing through Foz on the way to Ciudad del Este in Paraguay must get an Argentine exit stamp but not a Brazilian entrance stamp.

---

de Visitantes (☎ 524-2533; www.itaipu.gov.br; Av Tancredo Neves 6702) is located 10km north of Foz. Free guided tours of the Brazilian side of the Itaipú hydroelectric project are at 8am, 9am, 10am, 2pm, 3pm and 3:30pm Monday to Saturday, with night visits at 8:30pm on Friday and Saturday nights. The bus stops 600m short of the visitors center, outside the **Ecomuseu** (☎ 520-5817; Av Tancredo Neves 600; ☺ 2-5pm Mon, 9-11am & 2-5pm Tue-Sat), which is worth a quick look if you have time.

Across Av Juscelino Kubitschek from Foz's downtown local bus terminal, Conjunto C buses (US$0.50) run north every 10 minutes from 5:30am until 11pm. It's better to catch the bus on the street rather than from inside the terminal as the bus makes a long circuit of the city after leaving the terminal before passing by it again.

Tours

The Hotel del Rey (below) offers economical all-day trips to the Argentine side of the falls for US$10 per person, plus park admission.

Sleeping

BUDGET

Hotel Del Rey (☎ 523-2027; Rua Tarobá 1020; s/d standard US$7/10, deluxe US$17/23; ⊠ ☐ ⧉) The standard rooms here are fairly standard, but the deluxes are a steal – more like two-bedroom apartments. The whole place is spotless and the breakfast buffet is huge.

Pousada da Laura (☎ 572-3374; Rua Naipi 671; s/d with fan US$7/12) A laid-back and down-to-earth place, Laura's doesn't push any of the luxury buttons that other places in town do, but it has a modest appeal. There are some fine hammocking opportunities around the central patio.

MIDRANGE

Hotel Tarobá (☎ 523-9722; taroba@foznet.com.br; Rua Tarobá 1048; s/d US$11/16; Ⓟ ⊠ ☐ ⧉) Another spotless place close to the bus terminal, the Tarobá also offers a rocking breakfast buffet. The tiled rooms are bright and spacious and all have minifridges and cable TV.

Hotel Rafain Centro (☎ 521-3500; www.rafaincentro .com.br; Rua Marechal Deodoro da Fonseca 984; s/d US$45/49; Ⓟ ⊠ ⧉) The Rafain is a surprisingly good deal for these prices. It's a four-star hotel, but rooms are decorated in style and have large balconies. Prices may vary with demand – try bargaining a little.

Hotel Foz do Iguaçu (☎ 5232-4455; www.hotelfoz doiguacu.com.br; Av Brasil 97; s/d US$25/33; Ⓟ ⊠ ☐ ⧉) Judging by the look of the lobby, the Foz has pretensions of being something much grander than it actually is. Rooms are OK, but the standout is the pool deck area, where you can while away the hours, while ordering from the nearby bar.

Hotel Foz Presidente (☎ 727450; www.fozpresidentehoteis.com.br; Rua Xavier da Silva 1000; s/d US$20/27; P ⚡ ☒ ☎) Central but showing its age, the President offers a range of rooms (ask to see a few). The great advantage of this place is that if it's full, they have a sister hotel around the corner, so you're pretty much guaranteed a bed.

TOP END

Hotel Internacional Foz (☎ 521-4100; www.internacionalfoz.com.br; Rua Almirante Barosso 2006; s/d from US$67/82; P ☒ ☒ ☎ ☎) Without doubt the finest hotel in the center, the Internacional has all the five-star comforts. Rooms are spacious, if somewhat somber, and there is a nightclub, beauty parlor, gym, business center and sauna on the premises.

Hotel Tropical das Cataratas (☎ 521-7000; ggrctr@tropicalhotel.com.br; Parque Nacional do Iguaçu; s/d from US$150/174; ☎) A grand old hotel right in the park and near the falls, the Cataratas has elegant common areas, a pool, tennis courts, a restaurant and more. The rooms themselves are not so luxe, but the setting and overall ambience may make it all worth it.

Eating

As in Uruguay and Argentina, many establishments in Foz have gone 'all you can eat' to attract bargain-conscious clientele in these tough economic times.

Búfalo Branco (☎ 523-9744; cnr Ruas Tarobá & Rebouças; all you can eat US$10) It's huge, they offer meat done every way possible and there's a live 'show' twice a night, but this place still somehow retains a touch of class. Besides – where else in town are you going to eat bulls' testicles? If you don't want the full spread you may be able to negotiate a price.

Zaragoza (☎ 574-3084; Rua Quintino Bocaluva 882; dishes US$8-30) This upmarket restaurant has a fine ambience and an excellent wine selection. Spanish and seafood dishes dominate the menu and comfortable seating is available inside or out on the pleasant patio.

Bom Samaritano (☎ 523-2311; cnr Avs República Argentina & Juscelino Kubitschek; all you can eat US$3) This friendly restaurant is the centerpiece

of the Praça de Alimentação (food court), and has meat, pasta, salads and such traditional Brazilian dishes as *feijoada* (meat stew with rice and beans).

Líbano (Av Juscelino Kubitschek 185; kebabs US$1) Sure, the lights may be fluorescent and the seats may be plastic, but the falafels and *schwarmas* hit the spot in this very basic open-front Lebanese fast-food joint.

Entertainment

Brasil & Brasil (☎ 523-1013; cnr Av Brasil & Rua Rebouças) Frequent live music is the draw at this popular open-air bar, where you can dance from 8pm or 9pm to the wee hours. Drinks are cheap but be sure to keep track or pay as you go. B-girls operate here also, so if a pretty local miss starts to chat you up, it's best to determine exactly what's what before jumping into action.

Shopping

The Feira Iguaçu is a line of stalls selling handicrafts and other items. It extends along Rebouças for about half a block either side of Av Brasil.

Getting There & Away

Most flights are domestic services to Rio de Janeiro (US$110) or São Paulo (US$140), in addition to intermediate points, with **VASP** (☎ 523-2212; Av Brasil 845) and **Varig** (☎ 523-2111; Av Juscelino Kubitschek 463).

Long-distance bus services from Foz do Iguaçu include Curitiba (US$20, 9½ hours, 10 daily) via BR 277, São Paulo (US$31, 17 hours, six daily) and Rio (US$40, 21 hours, two daily).

Getting Around

To get to/from the airport, catch the 'Aeropuerto/Parque Nacional' bus from the local bus terminal or one of the stops along Av Juscelino Kubitschek; the trip takes 30 minutes and costs US$0.50. A taxi costs about US$9.

All long-distance buses arrive and depart from the **international bus terminal** (rodoviária internacional; ☎ 522-2950; Av Costa e Silva), 6km northeast of downtown. To get downtown, walk downhill to the bus stop and catch any 'Centro' bus. They start at 5:30am and run roughly every 15 minutes until 1am.

Buses to Puerto Iguazú (US$1) start from the terminal at 8am and run roughly every 15 minutes daily (every half hour on Sunday and holidays) until 8pm; they make a few stops along Av Juscelino Kubitschek. Buses for Ciudad del Este, Paraguay (US$1), begin running at 7am and leave every 10 minutes (every half hour on Sunday and holidays); catch them on JK across from the local bus terminal. The bridge can back up badly as early as 7:30am due to Paraguayan customs checks, so if you need to be somewhere, catch the first bus or allow yourself extra time. Avoid sitting opposite the rear doors, as ne'er-do-wells along the bridge make a sport of tossing things through the doors at passengers.

THE GRAN CHACO

The Gran Chaco is a vast alluvial lowland, stretching north from the northern edges of Santa Fe and Córdoba provinces, across the entire provinces of Chaco and Formosa, and into western Paraguay, eastern Bolivia and along the southwestern edge of Brazil. It reaches west through most of Santiago del Estero province, drying up as it goes, and skirts the southeastern edge of Salta province. The western side, known as the Chaco Seco (Dry Chaco), has been deemed the Impenetrable, due to its severe lack of water across an endless plain of nearly impassable thorn scrub.

The Chaco Húmedo (Wet Chaco), to the east, offers more to see, especially – almost solely – to nature enthusiasts and bird-lovers. The gallery forests, marshes and palm savannas of Parque Nacional Chaco, as well as the subtropical marshlands of Parque Nacional Río Pilcomayo, on the Paraguayan border, offer excellent birding opportunities and the rare chance of spotting such mammals as howler monkeys or giant anteaters. These areas are best visited in the cooler, drier months of April through November.

Resistencia, capital of Chaco province, is really the only city that stands out up here, and it does so primarily because of a unique artistic tradition and cultural commitment that has led to hundreds of public sculptures throughout the city.

Crossing the Chaco from Formosa to Salta along the northern RN 81 is brutal and can take nearly two days; RN 16 from Resistencia is much faster.

History

In colonial times, Europeans avoided the hot, desolate Chaco, whose few hunter-gatherer peoples resisted colonization and were not numerous enough to justify their pacification for *encomiendas* (the colonial labor system). Today, about 20,000 Guaycurú (Toba, Mocoví) and Mataco peoples remain in both the region's interior and urban areas.

The earliest Spanish settlement was probably Concepción del Bermejo (75km north of present-day Roque Sáenz Peña), which was founded in 1585 but abandoned in 1632 due to Indian resistance; its remains were rediscovered only recently. After the mid-18th century, Jesuit missionaries had some success among the Abipone people, but the religious order's expulsion from the Americas in 1767 again delayed European settlement.

Permanent settlement came much later. Oppressive summer heat, Indian resistance and poisonous snakes discouraged exploration of the dense thorn forests until the mid-19th century, when woodcutters from Corrientes entered the region's forests to exploit the valuable hardwood quebracho tree, whose name literally means 'axe breaker.' This eventually opened the region to agricultural expansion, which has primarily taken the form of cotton and cattle production.

Colonization proceeded from the province and city of Corrientes but was not really permanent until 1872. Resistencia, founded in 1750 as the Jesuit *reducción* of San Fernando del Río Negro, was the jumping-off point for woodcutters. The two railroads built across the Chaco have made it easier to get logs to Resistencia and Formosa, where there is sufficient water to process the tannins from the quebracho, which are then used for tanning leather.

Most of the region's agricultural development took place after 1930, when cotton production increased rapidly. New settlers of mostly central European origin – Austrians, Bulgarians, Czechs, Russians, Yugoslavs and some Spaniards – came via the Humid Pampas (along the coast). The region is currently suffering accelerated forest clearance for rain-fed agriculture, as cotton and oil crops, especially sunflowers, become more important. Petroleum exploration is also proceeding in the area north of Castelli, along the border between the two provinces.

RESISTENCIA

☎ 03722 / pop 422,400

Resistencia is Fat City for sculpture-lovers. There are over 300 of them dotted around the streets for anyone to see and ponder. A good range of styles are represented, too (not just the who's-that-guy-on-horseback school): figurative, abstract, religious, even a few funky '70s numbers.

The town also has some interesting cultural centers and museums, including the unusual Fogón de los Arrieros – an eclectic museum, cultural center and bar all in one – whose founder, Aldo Boglietti, later initiated Resistencia's growth into northeast Argentina's 'open-air museum.' The city has little in the way of notable architecture, but its interesting artistic tradition makes it a worthwhile stopover.

First settled in 1750, Resistencia grew rapidly with the development of the tannin industry and subsequent agricultural progress. It acquired its name after successful resistance against numerous indigenous attacks throughout the 19th century.

Orientation

Plaza 25 de Mayo is the focus of the city center. Occupying four square blocks, the plaza is one of South America's largest public squares. It has eight fountains and numerous

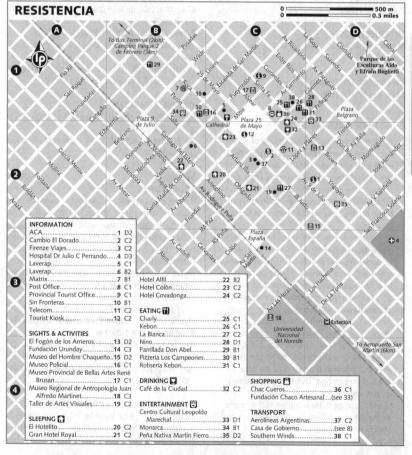

RESISTENCIA

0 — 500 m
0 — 0.3 miles

NORTHEAST ARGENTINA

INFORMATION	
ACA	1 D2
Cambio El Dorado	2 C2
Firenze Viajes	3 C2
Hospital Dr Julio C Perrando	4 D3
Laverap	5 C1
Laverap	6 B2
Matrix	7 B1
Post Office	8 C1
Provincial Tourist Office	9 C1
Sin Fronteras	10 B1
Telecom	11 C2
Tourist Kiosk	12 C2

SIGHTS & ACTIVITIES	
El Fogón de los Arrieros	13 D2
Fundación Urunday	14 C3
Museo del Hombre Chaqueño	15 D2
Museo Policial	16 C1
Museo Provincial de Bellas Artes René Brusan	17 C1
Museo Regional de Antropología Juan Alfredo Martinet	18 C4
Taller de Artes Visuales	19 C2

SLEEPING	
El Hotelito	20 C2
Gran Hotel Royal	21 C2
Hotel Alfil	22 B2
Hotel Colón	23 C2
Hotel Covadonga	24 C2

EATING	
Chaily	25 C1
Kebon	26 C1
La Bianca	27 C2
Nino	28 D1
Parrillada Don Abel	29 B1
Pizzería Los Campeones	30 B1
Rotisería Kebon	31 C1

DRINKING	
Café de la Ciudad	32 C2

ENTERTAINMENT	
Centro Cultural Leopoldo Marechal	33 D1
Monarca	34 B1
Peña Nativa Martín Fierro	35 D2

SHOPPING	
Chac Cueros	36 C1
Fundación Chaco Artesanal	(see 33)

TRANSPORT	
Aerolíneas Argentinas	37 C2
Casa de Gobierno	(see 8)
Southern Winds	38 C1

NORTHEAST ARGENTINA

sculptures, and is planted with quebracho, ceibo, lapacho and other native trees.

Street names change at the plaza. Av Sarmiento is the main access route from RN 16, which leads east to Corrientes, and west to Roque Sáenz Peña and across the Chaco to Salta and Santiago del Estero. Av 25 de Mayo leads northwest from the plaza to RN 11, which also goes north to Formosa and the Paraguayan border at Clorinda.

Information

CULTURAL CENTERS
Alianza Francesa (☎ 424480; alianza.francesa@ ecomchaco.com.ar; Roque Sáenz Peña 453; ✆ 8am-noon & 4:30-8:30pm Mon-Fri, 8am-noon Sat)

EMERGENCY
Police (☎ 432002)

INTERNET ACCESS
Matrix (☎ 449666; Roca 401; per hr US$0.30)

LAUNDRY
Laverap (☎ 424223; Vedia 23)
Laverap (☎ 445833; Vedia 319)

A TOWN'S BEST FRIEND

Stray dogs wandering the streets of South American towns sometimes inspire fear, even outright panic. Not in Resistencia. In the late 1950s and early '60s, a stray dog inspired the love of the entire town, and Víctor Marchese's statue on Calle Mitre, in front of the Casa de Gobierno, immortalizes him.

His name was Fernando. As the story goes, he wandered the streets and slept in doorways and finally befriended a bank manager, who allowed Fernando to join him for breakfast every morning in his office. Before long, Fernando was the delight of downtown, inspiring people's daydreams with his daily, carefree adventures in the Plaza 25 de Mayo. In a town devoted to the arts, Fernando was bohemianism in fur, and was a welcome regular at the Fogón de los Arrieros. When Fernando died on May 19, 1963, the municipal band played a funeral march and people across town shut their shades in respect. He is buried at the Fogón de los Arrieros, where another sculpture by Marchese marks his grave.

MEDICAL SERVICES
Hospital Dr Julio C Perrando (☎ 425050; Av 9 de Julio 1101) Near Mena.

MONEY
There are several ATMs in and around Plaza 25 de Mayo.
Cambio El Dorado (Jose María Paz 36) Changes traveler's checks at reasonable rates.

POST
Post office (Plaza 25 de Mayo at Av Sarmiento & Yrigoyen)

TELEPHONE
Telecom (cnr Av 9 de Julio & Pellegrini) *Locutorios* are easy to find; try this one.

TOURIST INFORMATION
ACA (☎ 470507; cnr Avs 9 de Julio & Italia) Three blocks from Plaza 25 de Mayo.
Provincial tourist office (☎ 423547; direccion .turismo@ecomchaco.com.ar; Santa Fe 178; ✆ 7am-8pm Mon-Fri)
Tourist kiosk (☎ 458289; Roca, on Plaza 25 de Mayo; ✆ 7am-1pm & 2-8pm Mon-Fri, 7am-noon Sat)

TRAVEL AGENCIES
Firenze Viajes (☎ 433333; www.firenzeviajes.com in Spanish; JB Justo 148)
Sin Fronteras (☎ 431055; sinfronterasevt@infovia.com .ar; Necochea 70)

Sights
SCULPTURES
There's insufficient space to provide details for the more than 300 sculptures in city parks and on sidewalks, but the tourist office, when it has funds, distributes a list with their locations, offering a purposeful introduction to the city. The best starting point is the **Parque de las Esculturas Aldo y Efraín Boglietti** (cnr Avs Laprida & Sarmiento), alongside the old French railroad.

If you prefer your sculptures under a roof, check out the **Museo Provincial de Bellas Artes René Brusan** (☎ 448000, ext 2511; Mitre 150; admission free; ✆ 8am-noon & 6-8pm Tue-Fri). Another center for the local arts community that is worth popping into is the **Taller de Artes Visuales** (☎ 422695; Arturo Illía 353; ✆ 9am-1pm Mon-Fri).

EL FOGÓN DE LOS ARRIEROS
Founded in 1942 by Aldo Boglietti, this is a cultural center, art gallery and bar that for decades has been the driving force be-

hind Resistencia's artistic commitment and progressive displays of public art. Still the keystone of the region's art community, it is now famous for its eclectic collection of art objects from around the Chaco, Argentina, and the region's arts community. The **museum** (☎ 426428; Brown 350; admission US$2; 9am-noon & 9:30pm-11pm Mon-Fri, 9am-noon Sat) also features the wood carvings of local artist and cultural activist Juan de Dios Mena.

OTHER MUSEUMS

The odd **Museo Policial** (☎ 421551; Roca 233; admission US$1; 8am-noon & 5-9pm Mon-Fri summer, 8am-noon & 4-8pm Mon-Fri winter), the provincial police museum, features grisly photos of auto accidents, tales of crimes of passion, and tedious drug-war rhetoric. It redeems itself with absorbing accounts of *cuatrerismo* (cattle rustling, still widespread in the province) and social banditry, including the remarkable tale of two 1960s outlaws who, after killing a policeman, lived for five years on the run, helped by the poor rural people of the province. Police officers accompany visitors on guided tours.

Archaeology, rather than the considerably broader field of anthropology, is the focus of the **Museo Regional de Antropología Juan Alfredo Martinet** (☎ 422257; Av Las Heras 727; admission free; 8am-noon & 4-8pm Mon-Fri) at the Universidad Nacional del Noreste.

The **Museo del Hombre Chaqueño** (Museum of Chaco Man; ☎ 426112; Arturo Illía 655; admission free; 9am-noon Mon-Sat) focuses on the colonization of the Chaco and provides information and exhibits on the Guaraní, Mocoví, Komlek and Mataco provincial indigenous cultures.

Festivals & Events

During the third week of July, Resistencia's Plaza 25 de Mayo hosts the **Concurso Nacional e Internacional de Escultura y Madera**, a competition in which the participants have seven days to carve a trunk of urunday (a native tree) into a work of art. (Local sculptors are nothing if not adaptable: contestants from this sweltering city won a prize for the best ice sculpture at the 1998 Winter Olympics in Sapporo, Japan.) For more information, contact the **Fundación Urunday** (☎ 436694; Av San Martín 465).

In August the **Exposición de Ganadería** showcases the region's best livestock.

Sleeping

BUDGET

Resistencia's choices for budget accommodations are slim.

El Hotelito (☎ 459699; Av Alberdi 311; s/d US$5/8) Airy, whitewashed rooms with huge, clean shared bathrooms. The owners speak some English.

Hotel Alfil (☎ 420882; Santa María de Oro 495; s/d US$8/12; P) A bit out of the center, but in a quiet location, the Alfil is a reasonable deal for the price. Rooms are slightly dark, but the amiable owner makes up for that.

Camping Parque 2 de Febrero (☎ 458323; Av Avalos 1100; sites US$2) This well-staffed campground has good facilities, including shade, but can get crowded and noisy in high season – not least because of the dance clubs across the road.

MIDRANGE

Gran Hotel Royal (☎ 443666; José M Paz 297; s/d US$15/19; P) Comfortable, if somewhat uninspired, rooms with big TVs and small shower stalls. The central location and spotless presentation make this one a good deal.

Hotel Covadonga (☎ 444444; www.hotelcovadonga.com.ar in Spanish; Güemes 200; s/d from US$23/28; P) Resistencia must have been experiencing a freak cold snap when they designed this, the city's finest hotel – the amenities include a Jacuzzi and sauna. It's a fairly solid affair – rooms are bright and well equipped – but the real draw here is the open-air 2nd-story pool.

Hotel Colón (☎ 422861; hotelcolon@gigared.com.ar; Santa María de Oro 143; s/d US$15/25; P) An older hotel with some lovely touches, such as dark wood paneling and multiple light wells. Rooms are neat, but unrenovated and showing their age a bit.

Eating

Eating well in Resistencia is easily done, and there's no need to break the bank to do it. Restaurants with wholesome, affordable food are plentiful.

Nino (☎ 449977; Don Bosco 133; meals US$2-3; breakfast, lunch & dinner) Wooden floorboards and muted lighting give this little place great atmosphere. The menu runs the usual gamut of pizza, meats and pastas, but food is well presented and the wine selection excellent.

Charly (☎ 439304; Güemes 213; meals around US$4; lunch & dinner Mon-Sat) You know times are tough when the snobbiest restaurant in town can only bring itself to charge US$4 for a meal. Carefully prepared meat and fish dishes are the winners here, but there's also a wide range of salads and almost too many wine choices. If you want to save money, you can eat pretty much the same dishes in a more humble environment in the restaurant's *rotisería* around the corner at Brown 71.

Kebon (☎ 422385; cnr Güemes & Don Bosco; meals US$5; ☯ lunch & dinner Mon-Sat) The real debate is whether this place or Charly is the best in town, but the truth is, they're pretty similar. Try them both! Once again, for budget-watchers, the take-out *rotisería* of the same name next door is a bargain.

La Bianca (☎ 443600; Colón 102; dishes US$2-4) The exposed brick walls lined with good art make this one of the more charming options in town. Pasta and steak feature heavily on the menu, but there are some good fish dishes as well.

Parrillada Don Abel (☎ 449252; cnr Cangallo & Perón; meals US$4-7; ☯ lunch & dinner, closed Sun night) This *parrilla* is inside a homey *quincho* (thatched-roof building) and serves substantial portions of pasta and grilled surubí, in addition to the usual grilled beef. *Parrilla* items go for US$2 to US$3.

Pizzería Los Campeones (☎ 424285; Perón 300; pizzas US$3-5) This down-home pizzeria, with sidewalk seating on a very busy street, also serves unbeatable slices at US$0.60 a pop.

Drinking

El Fogón de los Arrieros (☎ 426418; Brown 350). Stopping into El Fogón's friendly bar – a local institution for decades – is almost mandatory. The attached cultural center presents occasional live music and small-scale theatrical events. Call for information (also see p202).

Café de la Ciudad (☎ 420214; Pellegrini 109; ☯ 7-2am Sun-Thu, 1pm-dawn Fri & Sat) With an eclectic publike atmosphere, this bar-café gets lively on weekend nights. It's also good for morning coffee and afternoon sandwiches (US$1 to US$4).

Entertainment

Peña Nativa Martín Fierro (☎ 423167; Av 9 de Julio 695) Try this place on Friday or Saturday night after 10pm for live folk music and tango. It also has a *parrilla* restaurant.

Centro Cultural Leopoldo Marechal (☎ 422649; Pellegrini 272; ☯ 9am-noon & 7-9pm Mon-Fri) This cultural center has regular art exhibitions and performances.

Monarca (☎ 15-668088; Perón 393; admission with drink US$2) The kids go Friday and the older crowd Saturday. The street out front gets nearly as lively as the dance floor and the music requires plenty of drinks.

Shopping

Chac Cueros (☎ /fax 433604; Güemes 163) Chac Cueros specializes in high-quality leather goods made from the hide of carpinchos, the animals valued for the suede produced from their tan, naturally dimpled skin.

Fundación Chaco Artesanal (☎ 459372; Pellegrini 272; ☯ 9am-noon & 4-8pm Mon-Sat) This association, in the Centro Cultural Leopoldo Marechal, sells an outstanding selection of indigenous crafts.

Getting There & Away
AIR
Aerolíneas Argentinas (☎ 445550; JB Justo 184) and **Southern Winds** (☎ 443300; Güemes 251) fly to Buenos Aires' Aeroparque (from US$80).

BUS
Resistencia's **bus terminal** (☎ 461098; cnr Av MacLean & Islas Malvinas) is an important hub for destinations in all directions. Godoy Resistencia buses make the rounds between Corrientes and Resistencia (US$0.50, 40 minutes) at frequent intervals throughout the day.

There are frequent daily services to the destinations listed below.

Destination	Cost (US$)	Duration (hr)
Buenos Aires	13	13
Córdoba	22	12
Formosa	3	2
Gualeguaychú	14	10
Laguna Blanca	6	5½
La Plata	18	15½
Mendoza	28	24
Mercedes	6	4
Paraná	13	9½
Posadas	7	5
Puerto Iguazú	14	10
Roque Sáenz Peña	4	2
Rosario	11	9½
Salta	18	12
San Luis	22	20
Santa Fe	13	9½
Tucumán	16	12

Godoy SRL, El Tala and Empresa Yacyretá have early-morning buses to Asunción, Paraguay (US$7, five hours).

Getting Around

Aeropuerto San Martín is 6km south of town on RN 11; take bus No 3 (black letters) from the post office on Plaza 25 de Mayo.

The bus terminal is a US$2 taxi ride from the center, or you can take bus No 3 (a minibus), 4, 8 or 10 from the **Casa de Gobierno** (Plaza 25 de Mayo) near the post office.

City buses cost US$0.30; pay on board.

PARQUE NACIONAL CHACO

Preserving several diverse ecosystems that reflect subtle differences in relief, soils and rainfall, this very accessible but little-known **park** (☎ 03725-496166; park entrance free; visitor center ☯ 9am-7pm) protects 15,000 hectares of the humid eastern Chaco. It is 115km northwest of Resistencia via RN 16 and RP 9.

Ecologically, Parque Nacional Chaco falls within the 'estuarine and gallery forest' sub-region of the Gran Chaco, but the park encompasses a variety of marshes, open grasslands, palm savannas, scrub forest and denser gallery forests. The most widespread ecosystem is the *monte fuerte* (literally 'strong mount'), where mature specimens of quebracho, algarrobo and lapacho reach above 20m, while lower stories of immature trees and shrubs provide a variety of habitats at distinct elevations.

Scrub forests form a transitional environment to seasonally inundated savanna grasslands, punctuated by caranday and pindó palms. More open grasslands have traditionally been maintained by human activities, including grazing and associated fires, but these are disappearing. Marshes and gallery forests cover the smallest areas, but they are biologically the most productive. The meandering Río Negro has left several shallow oxbow lakes where dense aquatic vegetation flourishes.

Mammals are few and rarely seen, but birds are abundant, including the rhea, jabirú stork, roseate spoonbill, cormorants, common caracaras and other less conspicuous species. The most abundant insect species is the mosquito, so plan your trip during the relatively dry, cool winter and bring insect repellent.

Park service personnel are extremely hospitable and will accompany visitors if their duties permit.

Activities

Hiking and bird-watching are the principal activities, best done in the early morning or around sunset. Some areas are accessible only while horse riding; inquire about horses and guides (US$1.50 per hour) in Capitán Solari, 6km east of the park.

Sleeping & Eating

The *municipalidad* (city hall) in Capitán Solari provides information on *casas de familia* in town. Several families open their doors, at fair prices, to travelers.

Camping is the only alternative at the park itself. Fortunately, there are numerous shaded sites with clean showers (cold water only) and toilets, despite many ants and other harmless *bichos* (critters). A tent or other shelter is essential. There are fire pits, picnic tables, plenty of wood lying around for fuel, and no fees.

Weekends can be crowded with visitors from Resistencia, but at other times you may have the park to yourself. Sometimes on weekends a *concessionaire* (traveling food vendor) from Resistencia sells meals, but it's better to bring everything you need from Resistencia or Capitán Solari.

Getting There & Away

Capitán Solari is 2½ hours from Resistencia by bus (US$2). La Estrella has four buses daily, at 6:30am, 12:30pm, 5:30pm and 8pm; return buses from Capitán Solari to Resistencia leave at 5:30am, 11:30am and 5pm.

From Capitán Solari, you will have to walk the 5km or catch a lift to the park entrance. A *remise* costs about US$1. The road may be impassable for motor vehicles in wet weather. If possible, avoid walking in the midday heat.

ROQUE SÁENZ PEÑA

☎ 03732 / pop 83,700

Way out in the Chaco, 168km west of Resistencia, this city has become an attraction for its thermal baths, fortuitously discovered by drillers seeking potable water in 1937. Those baths closed for some years, but have now been renovated and reopened, and they offer some of the best day-spa deals in the country. The city also boasts one of the country's better zoos, and is the gateway to the 'Impenetrable' of the central Chaco.

Roque is primarily a service center for cotton and sunflower growers and, as the Chaco province grows nearly two-thirds of the country's total cotton crop, in May it hosts the **Fiesta Nacional del Algodón** (National Cotton Festival).

Properly speaking, the city goes by the cumbersome name of Presidencia Roque Sáenz Peña, after the Argentine leader responsible for the adoption of electoral reform and universal male suffrage in 1912.

Orientation

Roque Sáenz Peña straddles RN 16, which connects Resistencia with Salta. Its regular grid plan centers on willow-shaded Plaza San Martín; Av San Martín is the principal commercial street.

Information

ACA (☎ 420471; cnr Rivadavia & 25 de Mayo)

Banco de la Nación (Av San Martín 301) Currency exchange. Also has an ATM.

Hospital 4 de Junio (☎ 421404; Las Malvinas 1350)

Municipal tourist office (Brown 541; ☺ 6am-noon & 2:30-8:30pm) In the thermal bath complex.

Post office (Belgrano 602, at Mitre)

Telefónica locutorio (Av San Martín 692)

Sights

THERMAL BATHS COMPLEX

Roque's **Complejo Termal Municipal** (☎ 430030; www.elchacotermal.com.ar in Spanish; Brown 545; ☺ 6am-noon & 2:30-8:30pm) has been around since the '30s, and draws its water (said to have 50% more salinity than sea water) from 150m below ground. The center has been newly renovated and is now a top-class facility, offering thermal baths, saunas and Turkish baths (all US$2). There are also a variety of treatments on offer, including kinesiology, massage and aromatherapy.

PARQUE ZOOLÓGICO Y COMPLEJO ECOLÓGICO

At the junction of RN 16 and RN 95, 3km east of downtown, this spacious and nationally renowned **zoo** (☎ 422145; adult US$1, plus per vehicle US$1, kids free; ☺ 8am-6pm) and botanical garden emphasizes regionally important birds and mammals, not ecological exotics. Featured species are tapir and jaguar, but there are also crocodiles, llamas, monkeys, a bafflingly large chicken pen, snakes (including a boa constrictor), condors and vultures.

The zoo has two large artificial lakes frequented by migratory waterfowl. A small snack bar operates, but you may find the heady aroma from nearby enclosures to be a bit of an appetite killer. Bus No 2 goes from 14th Calle to the zoo (US$0.30), but it's also within reasonable walking distance, if it's not too hot.

Sleeping

Hotel Gualok (☎ 420715; Av San Martín 1198; s/d US$18/25; P ✷ ▯) There's something about the fading elegance of this place that the tarnished mirrors and chipped paintwork just can't take away. Additionally, it's the best-equipped hotel in town, with spacious and light rooms.

Hotel Presidente (☎ 424498; Av San Martín 771; s/d US$13/26; P ✷) The Presidente must have got a bulk deal on mirrors from some place – they're everywhere! Rooms are large, beds are comfy and a single is half the price of a double, a refreshing change of pace.

Orel Hotel (☎ 424139; ifmalina@yahoo.com.ar; cnr Saavedra & San Martín; s/d US$8/12) The rooms are simple, clean and colorful, and have cable TV. Some have windows looking out on to the street (noisy), others face the hallway (and lack privacy). Still…the price is right.

Camping El Descanso (sites free) Two kilometers along the eastern approach to town just north of RN 16, this campground has good, shady facilities, and sporadic hot water, but can be noisy on weekends. Take bus No 2 from downtown.

Eating

Sarava (cnr San Martín & 25 de Mayo; dishes US$2-4; ☺ breakfast, lunch & dinner) A better-than-average *confitería* serving the regular range of steak, chicken, burgers and sandwiches, with a full bar. The outdoor tables are a good place to while away a few hours between your spa treatments.

Sky Blue (cnr Mitre & Mariano Moreno; pizzas from US$2.50; ☺ 8pm-late) At the corner of Calles 14 and 23, Sky Blue is an outdoor *choppería* that is good for evening pizza and *chopp* (beer).

Getting There & Away

The **bus terminal** (☎ 420280; Petris or Calle 19, btwn Avellaneda & López y Planes) is about seven blocks east of downtown; take bus No 1 from Av Mitre. Some sample fares:

Destination	Cost (US$)	Duration (hr)
Buenos Aires	16	17
Córdoba	20	15
Posadas	11	7
Resistencia	4	2
Rosario	15	11
Salta	16	9
Santa Fe	30	9½
Tucumán	13	10

FORMOSA

☎ 03717 / pop 231,900

Located on a horseshoe bend of the Río Paraguay, Formosa is primarily a stop on the way to Paraguay or the nearby Parque Nacional Río Pilcomayo. It's a fine place to spend a day or two wandering the streets, and the riverfront *costanera* has been carefully restored, making it a great venue for strolling as the sun goes down on a balmy evening.

This far north, with its Paraguayan street market, cheap *licuados* (blended fruit drinks) and evening platoons of adolescent motorscooter racers, Argentina begins to paint a different picture. It's a good place to get a feel for the country across the river, and a much better place to stay than Clorinda, where you cross the border.

Orientation

Formosa is 169km north of Resistencia and 113km south of Clorinda (on the border with Paraguay) via RN 11. It is also possible, though still not easy, to cross the northern Chaco via RN 81 and continue to Bolivia.

Av Doctor Luis Gutñiski, as RN 11 is called as it passes through town, heads eastward to Plaza San Martín, a four-block public park beyond which Av 25 de Mayo, the heart of the city, continues to the shores of the Río Paraguay.

From the north side of Plaza San Martín, Av Independencia is RN 11, heading north. Av Circunvalación allows motorists to avoid the downtown area.

Unlike in many Argentine towns, street names do not change on either side of the plaza but rather along either side of Av Gonzales Lelong, seven blocks north of the plaza.

Information

Alianza Francesa (☎ 420162; Tucumán 745)

Banco de Galicia (Av 25 de Mayo 160) Has an ATM.

Hospital Central (☎ 426194; Salta 545)

Police (☎ 429000)

Post office (Plaza San Martín at Av 9 de Julio 930)

Provincial tourist office (☎ 425192; Uriburu 820; ☉ 7am-12:30pm & 4-8pm Mon-Fri) Near Fontana.

Telecom locutorio (25 de Mayo, btwn Moreno & Rivadavia; per hr US$0.30) Has Internet access.

Turismo de Castro (☎ 434777; 25 de Mayo 275) Travel agency.

Sights

In the Casa Fotheringham, a pioneer residence that was the province's first Casa de Gobierno, the **Museo Histórico** (municipal historical museum; cnr Belgrano & Av 25 de Mayo; admission free; ☉ 8am-1pm & 4-8pm Mon-Sat) focuses on the foundation and development of Formosa. It's a small, well-organized museum, thankfully light on the stuffed-animal collections (ranking only two display cases full). The province was part of the Paraguayan Chaco until the 19th-century War of the Triple Alliance, and the museum also houses uniforms, weapons and relics from the period. There are a few old indigenous weavings as well.

Festivals & Events

Formosa's annual **Fiesta del Río**, lasting a week in mid-November, features an impressive nocturnal religious procession in which 150 boats from Corrientes sail up the Río Paraguay.

In February Formosa celebrates **Carnaval** on weekends, while **Día de la Fundación de Formosa** celebrates the city's founding on April 8. The **Fiesta de la Virgen de la Catedral** honors the Virgen del Carmen, Formosa's patron saint, on July 16.

Sleeping

Hotel de Turismo (☎ 437333; hoteldeturismoformosa@ arnet.com.ar; cnr Av 25 de Mayo & San Martín; s/d US$30/37; P ❄ ⚊) Without doubt the finest hotel in town, most of the Turismo's rooms have great river views. Big balconies and an excellent swimming pool and sundeck are also on offer.

Hotel Río (☎ 431555; Rivadavia 1102; s/d US$12/16; P ❄) With a curvy reception counter and the green velvet sofa adorning the lobby, this place promises to be a '70s funk-fest. The excitement dies pretty quickly once you get to the rooms, though, which are spacious, comfortable and modern.

Hotel San Martín (☎ 426769; Av 25 de Mayo 380; s/d US$9/19; ⊠) Good for the price, but otherwise uninteresting, the San Martín is surprisingly quiet for its central location. Some rooms are definitely better than others, so have a look around if you can.

Hotel Plaza (☎ 426767; hotelplaza@elpajarito.com .ar; Uriburu 920; s/d US$15/19; P ⊠ ⏸ ⏻ ⊠) So there are some weird stains on the carpet... The rooms in this aging hotel have a good feel, nonetheless, and many overlook the plaza.

Hotel Colón (☎ 426547; Belgrano 1068; s/d US$11/15; ⊠) Although their slogan 'the most like your home' may be stretching it a bit, the Colón's rooms are clean and comfortable. Downstairs is a travel agent.

Camping Banco Provincial (☎ 429877; RN 11 at El Cruce; sites per person US$3; ⊠) About 4km south of Formosa on RN 11, this decent campground has well-kept facilities, including a swimming pool and tennis courts.

In town, **ACA** (Av Gutñiski 3025) will sometimes permit people to park or pitch a tent overnight on its spacious grounds.

Eating

Raíces (☎ 427058; Av 25 de Mayo 65; mains US$3-8) This refined, locally esteemed restaurant has more than 13 surubí dishes on the menu, as well as plenty of tasty meat, chicken and pasta dishes.

El Tano Marino (☎ 420628; Av 25 de Mayo 55; mains US$3-9) Similar in price and menu items to Raíces next door, with slightly more serious decor. Both places have wonderful wine lists.

Copetín Yayita (☎ 431322; Belgrano 926; mains US$1-2; ⏰ breakfast, lunch & dinner) Gnocchi, ravioli, *lomitos* (thin steak sandwiches) and burgers all cost less than US$3 at this funky eatery. *Licuados* are cheap, and the *sopa de bagre* (catfish soup) is very popular.

Il Viale (☎ 430974; Av 25 de Mayo 287; mains US$3-5; ⏰ breakfast, lunch & dinner) In addition to coffee, this *confitería* serves good, though pricey, sandwiches and burgers.

Shopping

Instituto de Communidades Aborigenes 'Casa de las Artesanias' (San Martín 82; ⏰ 8am-1pm & 4-8pm Mon-Sat) In a historic building near the river, this artisan cooperative sells string bags, palo santo wood carvings, weavings and other items. The goods range from shoddy to

beautiful. All proceeds go to the indigenous communities – the Mataco, Toba and Pilaga – who make the crafts.

Getting There & Away

AIR
Austral (☎ 429314; Av 25 de Mayo 601) flies daily to Buenos Aires.

BUS
Formosa's modern **bus terminal** (☎ 451766; cnr Av Gutñiski & Antártida Argentina) is 15 blocks west of Plaza San Martín. Some of the destinations served:

Destination	Cost (US$)	Duration (hr)
Asunción (Paraguay)	6	3
Buenos Aires	22	16
Córdoba	30	15
Clorinda	2	1¾
Laguna Blanca	5	3
La Plata	24	17½
Rosario	13	12
Santa Fe	15	8
Salta	17	15
Tucumán	22	14

Getting Around

Aeropuerto El Pucú is only 4km south of town along RN 11, so cabs are an inexpensive option.

The bus marked 'Tejon' passes by the bus terminal on its way to the airport.

For car rental, try **Auto-Rent** (☎ 431721; España 557).

CLORINDA
☎ 03718 / pop 47,240

Little Clorinda is a town of dirt roads and street markets; most visitors are here to cross to Asunción, Paraguay (where customs checks are thorough to say the least), via the Puente Internacional San Ignacio de Loyola (bridge between Argentina and Paraguay), or to visit nearby Parque Nacional Rió Pilcomayo. If you *are* here to visit the park, staying in nearby Laguna Blanca is better: it's a smaller town, but much prettier, and access to the park from there is just as simple, if not easier. Otherwise stay in agreeable Formosa.

If you're stuck and have to stay in Clorinda, there's inexpensive lodging at the **Hotel San Martín** (☎ 421211; 12 de Octubre 1150; s/d US$8/11; P ⊠), which, with its exposed brick walls and understated decor, manages to scrape together a bit of style. **La Pupuruchi** (☎ 425291; 548 San Martín; meals US$1-2; 😊 lunch & dinner) is a hugely popular lunch spot with an excellent salad bar (US$1 extra).

Godoy Cruz buses cross the border at regular intervals from Clorinda's bus terminal at San Martín and Paraguay, where Navarro buses to Parque Nacional Río Pilcomayo also depart.

PARQUE NACIONAL RÍO PILCOMAYO

West of Clorinda, the wildlife-rich marshlands of 60,000-hectare Parque Nacional Río Pilcomayo (resembling Parque Nacional Chaco in its ecology and environments), hug the Paraguayan border. Its outstanding feature is shallow, shimmering **Laguna Blanca**, where, at sunset, yacarés (alligators) lurk on the lake's surface. Other wildlife (except for birds) is likelier to be heard than seen among the dense aquatic vegetation.

From the park's campground, a wooden *pasarela* leads to the lakeshore, where there is a platform overlook about 5m high, plus three lake-level platforms for swimming and sunbathing (the water is barely a meter deep). It's especially tranquil and appealing late in the day, after picnickers and day-trippers have returned to Clorinda and Formosa, but carry plenty of mosquito repellent. The 9km dirt access road from the highway is impassable after heavy rains; ask at the **ranger station and information center** (☎ 03718-470045; RN 86, Laguna Blanca; 😊 9am-5pm Mon-Fri) about conditions before you set out.

Sleeping & Eating

The free camping facilities are seldom used except on weekends; automobiles cannot enter the campground proper, but must park nearby. Barbecues with wood are provided and there are bathrooms. The shower water is saline and most people prefer the lake, which offers relief from the heat. A small shop sells basic food and cold drinks, including beer, just outside the park entrance.

Residencial Guaraní (☎ 03718-470024, cnr San Martín & Sargento Cabral; s/d US$7/8; P ✗) In the town of Laguna Blanca, 11km beyond the turnoff, this hotel has basic rooms set around a leafy courtyard and a restaurant (😊 breakfast, lunch & dinner) which serves standard fare for US$2 to US$3.

Getting There & Away

Godoy Cruz and Navarro run buses from Formosa and Clorinda along RN 86 to Naick-Neck and Laguna Blanca. The three-hour trip from Formosa costs US$3. *Traffics* (informal share taxis) congregate near the plaza in Laguna Blanca offering rides to Clorinda; they leave when they are full (US$2, one hour).

You will have to hike, hitch or take a *remise* to get the 9km from the turnoff on RN 86 to the park entrance. Just past the turnoff are a group of houses where locals offer horse transport to the park (look for the sign '*alquilo caballos*'): a group of three to the park entrance costs US$17 and whole-day tours of the park on horseback cost US$5 per person, plus US$8 for a guide).

The Andean Northwest

Argentina's most 'traditional' region, the Noroeste Andino (Andean Northwest) consists of the provinces of Jujuy, Salta, Tucumán, La Rioja, Catamarca and Santiago del Estero; all of which had thriving cities when Buenos Aires was still an insignificant hinterland. Today, these cities vary from the brash and energetic Tucumán to the gracious tourist headquarters of Salta.

Travelers with an urge to get off the beaten track also have plenty of opportunities to do so in this region, most notably on the tough but rewarding trip through the Valles Calchaquíes from Cafayate to Cachi.

The mellow little town of Cafayate is becoming a hot destination for foreigners and Argentines alike, as much for its wine-tasting possibilities as for access to the surreal landscape of the Quebrada de Cafayate. The Tren a las Nubes (Train to the Clouds) out of Salta is a must-see, both for train enthusiasts and anyone wishing to get out into the wild, desertlike Andean region.

The region's tangible pre-Columbian and colonial past makes the trip south from Peru and Bolivia to the Argentine heartland a journey through time as well as space. Even now, the northern provinces resemble the Andean countries much more than they do the cultural core of the Argentine Pampas. Substantial Quechua communities exist as far south as Santiago del Estero. The Quebrada de Humahuaca offers more stunning scenery, with towns like Tilcara offering accommodations as comfortable as any in the country.

TOP FIVE

- Taking in the breathtaking **Quebrada de Humahuaca** (p219)
- Going rough and rugged in the **Valles Calchaquíes** (p230)
- Taking to the rails on the **Tren a las Nubes** (p230)
- Sharing some Incan ruins with a couple of llamas at **Quilmes** (p235)
- Living it up in sophisticated **Tucumán** (p239)

Quebrada de Humahuaca ★

Valles Calchaquíes ★

★ Tren a las Nubes

Quilmes ★ ★ Tucumán

■ AVERAGE JUL HIGH IN TUCUMÁN: 12°C (54°F)   ■ AVERAGE DEC HIGH IN TUCUMÁN: 23°C (73°F)

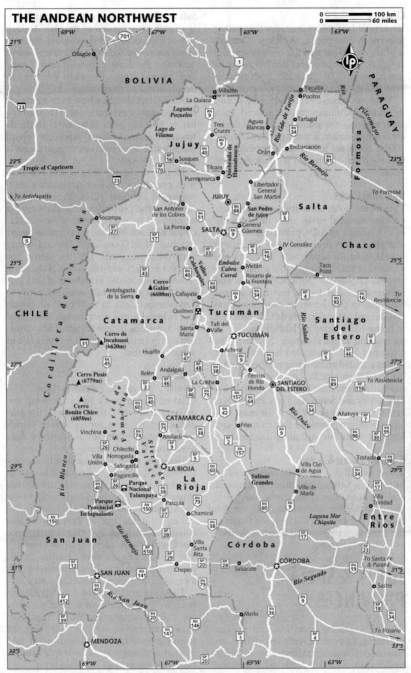

THE ANDEAN NORTHWEST

Climate

Dryness and the cold characterize the weather patterns in the extreme northwest. Drought is often a problem here (as is staying warm at night). Many zones are classified as virtual desert, receiving less than 250mm of rain per year, in a good year.

Although closest to the equator – and therefore technically more tropical than other regions – the altitudes here keep things chilly (Humahuaca, for example, sits at a cool 3000m above sea level). Further south there is enough sun and rain to produce excellent wines.

National Parks

This region holds some important and fascinating national parks, most of which are in the Jujuy and Salta provinces, with the exception of Parque Nacional Talampaya (p261) in La Rioja province. This park has something for everyone: aboriginal petroglyphs, photogenic rock formations and unique flora and fauna. Parque Nacional Calilegua (p236) preserves the subtropical cloud forest of the Serranía de Calilegua and is home to an array of birdlife, as well as pumas and jaguars. Parque Nacional Los Cardones (p237) is 65,000 hectares full of cactus-studded photo opportunities. Parque Nacional Baritú (p238) contains subtropical montane forest, itself home to monkeys, big cats, otters and forest squirrels. Parque Nacional Finca El Rey (p238) is the most biologically diverse park in the country, and teems with birdlife, including toucans.

Getting There & Away

There are flights from Buenos Aires to Jujuy, Salta, Santiago del Estero, Catamarca and La Rioja. Bus connections are generally available for destinations all over the country, but services will be more frequent (and more direct) from larger towns, such as those listed above.

JUJUY & SALTA PROVINCES

One of Argentina's smallest and poorest provinces, Jujuy is nevertheless rich in archaeological and cultural resources. Bounded by Bolivia to the north, Chile to the west and

Salta province to the south and east, Jujuy is a southern extension of the high Andean steppe (altiplano), where soaring volcanic peaks tower over *salares* (saline lakes), above 4000m in the thinly populated west. To the east, a lower range of foothills gives way to deeply dissected river valleys – like the Quebrada de Humahuaca, whose Río Grande has exposed some spectacular desert landforms – before opening onto subtropical lowlands toward the Gran Chaco. Jujuy has several wildlife and fauna reserves, though access is generally not easy.

In the Noroeste, Salta is the province with everything. One of Argentina's best-preserved colonial cities, the provincial capital is the center for excursions to the subtropical montane forests of Parque Nacional El Finca Rey, the polychrome desert canyons of El Toro and Cafayate, along with their vineyards, and the sterile but scenic salt lakes and volcanoes of the puna (Andean highlands). Hundreds of archaeological sites and colonial buildings testify to Salta's importance in both pre-Columbian and colonial times, even though it declined with Argentine independence. Today tourism serves an increasingly important role in Salta's fortunes.

JUJUY

☎ 0388 / pop 267,400 / elevation 1240m

A lot of people knock Jujuy for being unexciting, and really, stuck between the gorgeous scenery to the north and Salta's lively sophistication to the south, the town does have a battle on its hands.

However, there are some beautifully preserved old buildings, a couple of museums are worth stopping in at, and the climate is perpetually springlike, due mainly to the city's distinction of being the highest provincial capital in the country. Travelers can also entertain themselves by trying to pronounce the town's name correctly (huoy-huoyy!). You are likely to see more Quechua in this city than any other in the northwest, lending a particularly Andean feel to the place.

The Spaniards founded San Salvador de Jujuy in 1592 as the most northerly of their colonial cities in present-day Argentina. Now commonly known as simply Jujuy, the town's proper name distinguished it as a Spanish settlement and also avoided confusion with nearby San Pedro de Jujuy.

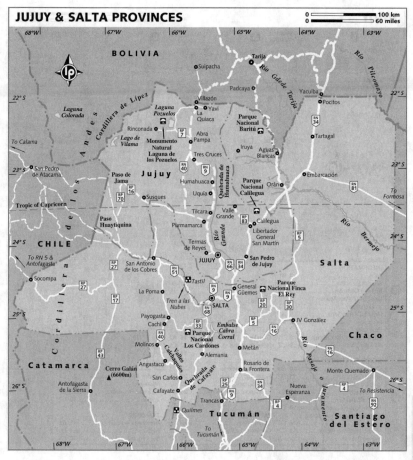

JUJUY & SALTA PROVINCES

0   100 km
0   60 miles

THE ANDEAN NORTHWEST

On August 23, 1812, during the wars of independence, General Belgrano ordered the evacuation of Jujuy. Its citizens complied and the city was razed to prevent advancing royalist forces, loyal to the Spanish crown, from capturing the strategic site. The province of Jujuy bore the brunt of conflict during these wars, with Spain launching repeated invasions down the Quebrada de Humahuaca from Bolivia; the city of Jujuy was sacked by royalists twice in later years.

Orientation

Jujuy sits above the floodplain of the Río Grande at its confluence with the smaller Río Xibi Xibi. Jujuy consists of two main parts: the old city, with a fairly regular grid pattern between the Río Grande and the Río Xibi Xibi, and a newer area south of the Xibi Xibi that sprawls up the nearby hills. Shantytowns crowd the floodplain of the Río Grande beneath the San Martín bridge.

Information

ACA (Automóvil Club Argentina; ☎ 422-2568; cnr Senador Pérez & Alvear)

Alianza Francesa (☎ 422-8013; Gorriti 370; ☒ 3:30-9pm Mon-Fri) Cultural center.

Graffiti Turismo (☎ 423-4033; cnr Belgrano & Otero) Changes cash, but commissions can be substantial.

Hospital Pablo Soria (☎ 422-1298; cnr Argentinas & Córdoba)

Locutorio (cnr Belgrano & Lavalle; per hr US$0.30) Private telephone office offering Internet access.

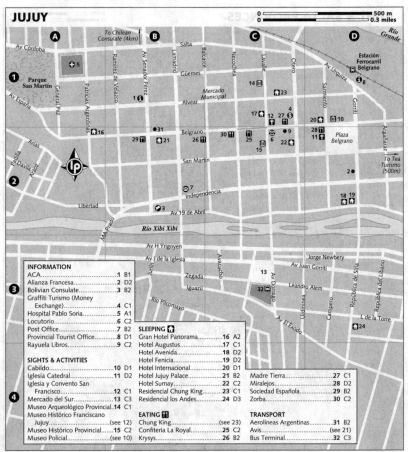

Post office (cnr Independencia & LaMadrid)

Provincial tourist office (☎ 422-1343; www.jujuy
.gov.ar in Spanish; Urquiza 354; ⏱ 8am-9pm Mon-Fri)
Located in the old train station. The staff are some of
the best that a traveler might come across in northwest
Argentina; they are unusually well organized and keen to
offer assistance.

Rayuela Libros (☎ 423-0658; Belgrano 638) Good
bookstore.

Tea Turismo (☎ 423-6270; teajujuy@imagine.com.ar;
San Martín 128) Travel agent; good for excursions.

Sights

IGLESIA CATEDRAL

On the west side of Plaza Belgrano, Jujuy's
1763 **cathedral** (⏱ 8am-12:30pm & 5pm-8:30pm) replaced a 17th-century predecessor destroyed

by Calchaquí Indians. The outstanding feature, salvaged from the original church, is
the gold-laminated Spanish-baroque pulpit, probably built by local artisans under
the direction of a European master. On the
plaza, directly across the street, a lively artisans' market sells some excellent pottery.

MUSEO ARQUEOLÓGICO PROVINCIAL

If you have even a basic grasp of Spanish,
this **museum** (☎ 422-1315; Lavalle 434; admission free;
⏱ 7:30am-1pm & 2-9pm Sun-Fri, 7:30am-1pm Sat) is
well worth your while: the guided tour is
excellent and the strong emphasis on sha-
manism in the area fascinating. If not, the
poorly labeled exhibits will probably leave
you a bit cold.

CABILDO & MUSEO POLICIAL

On the north side of Plaza Belgrano is the **cabildo** (colonial town-council building) and **police museum** (☎ 423-7715; admission free; ☽ 8am-noon & 4-8pm Mon-Fri). The building and its attractive colonnade deserve more attention than the museum housed within, which pays indiscriminate homage to authority, and glories in grisly photographs of crimes and accidents – partially lightened by the surprisingly camp poses of mannequins in uniform.

MUSEO HISTÓRICO PROVINCIAL

During Argentina's civil wars, a bullet pierced through the imposing wooden door of this colonial house, killing General Juan Lavalle, a hero of the wars of independence. The story of Lavalle and other provincial events unfolds in this **museum** (☎ 422-1355; Lavalle 256; admission US$1; ☽ 8am-12:30pm & 4-8pm Mon-Sun). There is also a collection of religious and colonial art, and exhibits on the independence era, the evacuation of Jujuy, provincial governors and 19th-century fashion. A bit of effort has been made with labels in English, but mostly you're on your own here.

IGLESIA Y CONVENTO SAN FRANCISCO & MUSEO HISTÓRICO FRANCISCANO JUJUY

While the Franciscan order has been in Jujuy since 1599, the current **church and convent** (cnr Belgrano & Lavalle), the third at this address, dates only from 1912. Nevertheless, its **museum** (☽ 8am-noon & 5-9pm) retains diverse relics from the early Franciscan presence, as well as a strong selection of colonial art from the Cuzco school, a world-renowned style of painting that came about in the 17th century. Indigenous Peruvians were taught to paint by Spanish conquerors in the style of the great Spanish and Flemish masters. It all started in the city of Cuzco, in Peru, and still exists today.

MERCADO DEL SUR

Jujuy's lively southern market, opposite the bus terminal at Av Dorrego and Leandro Alem, is a genuine trading post where Quechua men and women swig *mazamorra* (a pasty maize soup served cold) and surreptitiously peddle coca leaves (unofficially tolerated for native people, despite Argentine drug laws; see the boxed text, p223).

Festivals & Events

In August, Jujuy's biggest event, the weeklong **Semana de Jujuy**, commemorates Belgrano's evacuation of the city during the wars of independence. The next largest gathering is the religious pilgrimage known as the **Peregrinaje a la Virgen del Río Blanco y Paypaya** on October 7. The March harvest festival is the **Festival de la Humita y El Folclor**, while May's **Fiesta de la Minería** honors the mining industry. September's **Fiesta Nacional de los Estudiantes** is a student festival featuring elaborate floats. The **Festival de la Humita y El Folclor** (harvest festival) is in March; May's **Fiesta de la Minería** honors the mining industry. In August, Jujuy's biggest event, the weeklong **Semana de Jujuy**, commemorates Belgrano's evacuation of the city during the wars of independence. September's **Fiesta Nacional de los Estudiantes** is a student festival featuring elaborate floats. The second-largest event is the religious pilgrimage known as the **Peregrinaje a la Virgen del Río Blanco y Paypaya** on October 7.

Sleeping

BUDGET

Jujuy's budget accommodations are mostly near the old train and bus terminals.

Residencial Chung King (☎ 422-8142; Alvear 627; s/d US$3/5, with bathroom US$5/7) Good rooms, but make sure you're at the back away from the noisy restaurant downstairs. This is probably the best budget option near the city center; it's a poky little place and some rooms are better than others, so have a look at a few.

Residencial los Andes (☎ 422-4315; residencallos andes@infovia.com.ar; República de Siria 456; s/d US$6/10) This *residencial* (short-stay accommodations), a few blocks east of the bus terminal, is better value than some midrange hotels. Hardwood floors and spacious bathrooms definitely make it the top pick in this area. Rooms upstairs have much better light.

Hotel Sumay (☎ /fax 423-5065; www.imagine.com .ar/sumay; Otero 232; s/d US$12/22; ☒) Rooms here have TV, telephones and some of the lowest beds you're ever likely to see. It's a notch up in luxury, is fairly central and has a cozy little bar-*confitería* (café serving light meals). Staff can also help organize excursions.

Hotel Avenida (☎ 423-6136; Av 19 de Abril 469; s/d US$13/20; ☒ ☒) The Avenida was probably quite stylish once upon a time, but the luster has definitely started to fade. Still, it's well positioned between the city and the

THE ANDEAN NORTHWEST

THE AUTHOR'S CHOICE

Zorba (☎ 424-3048; cnr Necochea & Belgrano; mains US$3-5; ☽ breakfast, lunch & dinner) Seriously good Greek food (yes, you read that right) in the middle of Jujuy! It's all here: the salads, the dolmades, the *koftas* (balls of grounds vegetables). Fans of the big breakfast will want to check out the Americano – it has one of pretty much everything you could hope for to start the day.

---

bus terminal, with smallish but acceptable rooms featuring hectic wallpaper patterns.

MIDRANGE

Hotel Jujuy Palace (☎ 423-0433; jpalace@imagine.com.ar; Belgrano 1060; s/d US$33/40) If you've got a bit extra to spend, it's well worth your while to get a room at the Palace. The large rooms are spacious and modern, tastefully decorated with terrific views and the bathrooms feature good-sized tubs.

Gran Hotel Panorama (☎ /fax 423-2533; hotelpanorama@mail.cooptel.com.ar; Belgrano 1295; s/d US$25/32; ☒) The Panorama is a four-star property with plain but spacious rooms that could be better presented. This is partly redeemed by the huge windows giving great views of the city skyline.

Hotel Augustus (☎ 423-0203; Belgrano 715; s/d US$24/32; ℗ ☒) Offers good value for money and features some classy touches, such as parquetry floors and individual reading lamps. Some of the rooms have excellent city views.

Hotel Internacional (☎ 423-1599; interjuy@imagine.com.ar; Belgrano 501; s/d US$23/30) Close to the center, Hotel Internacional is a high-rise property with all the trimmings. Rooms are pleasant, if somewhat dated, and some have spectacular views out over the plaza.

Hotel Fenicia (☎ 423-1800; www.quintar.com.ar; Av 19 de Abril 427; s/d US$23/35) This hotel overlooks the Xibi Xibi; its rooms are a bit run-down, but worth the price for the views from their great balconies.

Eating & Drinking

Miralejos (☎ 422-4911; Sarmiento 368; meals US$3-5; ☽ breakfast, lunch & dinner) Plazaside dining at its finest. Miralejos offers the full gamut of steaks and pastas, with a few fish dishes thrown in. The outside tables are a great

place for breakfast and the eclectic music selection is interesting, to say the least.

Krysys (☎ 423-1126; Balcarce 272; mains US$3-5; ☽ closed Sun) The best *parrilla* (mixed-grill restaurant) option is this central, upscale place offering all your barbecued favorites in a relaxed atmosphere. The *bife de chorizo* (sirloin; US$3) is particularly large, and you could get away with ordering a half, unless you're ravenous.

Sociedad Española (☎ 423-5065; Belgrano 1102; mains US$3-6) It's always worth seeking out the Spanish Club for fine food, including paella, in a pleasant atmosphere, and Jujuy's branch is no exception.

Chung King (☎ 422-8142; Alvear 627; mains $3-12) This is actually three restaurants in one. There is a pizzeria, a restaurant with an extensive Argentine menu and fine service, and a *peña* (folk club) with regional artists providing entertainment while you have dinner.

Madre Tierra (☎ 422-9578; Belgrano 619; 4-course lunch US$3.50; ☽ lunch Mon-Sat) Madre Tierra is an Argentine standout. The vegetarian food is excellent and the salads, crepes and soups can be washed down with either carrot or apple juice. It's an earthy place where the simple, wholesome, home-cooked food makes a welcome change to the standard Argentine fare.

Confitería La Royal (☎ 422-6202; Belgrano 766; breakfast US$1.50, meals US$3-4; ☽ breakfast, lunch & dinner) Slap-bang in the middle of town, La Royal is a good spot for people-watching, a steaming mug of coffee and a read of the morning newspaper.

Upstairs at the Mercado del Sur (p214), several eateries serve inexpensive regional specialties, which are generally spicier than elsewhere in Argentina; try *chicharrón con mote* (stir-fried pork with boiled maize) or a spicy *sopa de maní* (peanut soup).

Getting There & Away

AIR

Aerolíneas Argentinas (☎ 422-1288; Senador Pérez 322) flies to Buenos Aires' Aeroparque airport (US$120) daily and offers complementary shuttle service to the airport.

BUS

The **bus terminal** (☎ 422-1375; cnr Av Dorrego & Iguazú) has provincial and long-distance services, but Salta has more alternatives.

Chile-bound buses from Salta to Calama (US$23 to US$40; prices depend on whether it's a day or night bus) pick up passengers in Jujuy on Tuesday and at 8:45am Friday; make reservations in advance if possible at the Géminis office at the terminal.

There are frequent services south to Salta and north to destinations in the Quebrada de Humahuaca as far as the Bolivian border at La Quiaca. For Parque Nacional Calilegua, there are services every half hour throughout the day to San Pedro and Libertador San Martín. Sample fares include the following:

Destination	Cost (US$)	Duration (hr)
Buenos Aires	30	23
Catamarca	13	10
Córdoba	16	2½
Humahuaca	3	2½
La Quiaca	6	4
La Rioja	8	8
Libertador San Martín	2	2
Mendoza	18	14
Pocitos	6	6
Purmamarca	2	1¼
Resistencia	20	18
Salta	3	2
San Juan	16	10
San Pedro	2	1
Tilcara	3	1¾
Tucumán	6	5
Uquía	3	2½
Yuto	4	3

Getting Around

If you're after a rental car, Avis (☎ 423-0433; Belgrano 1060) is at Hotel Jujuy Palace.

LA QUIACA & VILLAZÓN (BOLIVIA)

☎ 0388 La Quiaca / pop 12,400 / elevation 3442m
Truly the end of the line, La Quiaca is the Argentine border town and, while it has decent enough places to stay and eat, there's really nothing (apart from a missed bus connection) that would prompt you to hang around. With the closure of the railroad, La Quiaca has become a ghost town. It's one of few Argentine towns that lacks a lively street life, especially at night.

If you do find yourself stuck here, a trip to Yavi (p218) is the best option. Some people like it so much that they end up staying for a few days.

Across the bridge in Villazón, the story is much the same: there are far more interest-

ing places down the road, and if you can move on, it's a good plan.

This used to be a buzzing commercial center, back when prices were so radically different that Argentines crossed the border to go shopping. Now that things have evened out, Villazón looks like reverting to just another obscure little border town.

Near Abra Pampa, a forlornly windy town 90km north of Humahuaca, RN 9 becomes a mostly paved road that climbs abruptly to the altiplano typical of southern Bolivia. Except in the summer rainy season, nightly frosts make agriculture precarious, so people focus subsistence efforts on livestock (such as llamas, sheep, goats and cows) that can survive on the sparse ichu grass. Off the main highway, look for flocks of the endangered vicuña, a wild relative of the llama and alpaca.

Orientation

La Quiaca consists of two discrete sections, separated by the tracks of the defunct train station; most services are west of the tracks. At the north end of town, a bridge across the Río Villazón (also called Río La Quiaca) links La Quiaca with Villazón. To get to Argentine and Bolivian customs you have to walk or take a taxi *colectivo* (local bus) to the bridge, on the east side of the tracks, then cross on foot.

Information

ACA station (cnr RN 9 & Sánchez de Bustamante) For maps or motorist services.

Banco de la Nación (cnr RN 9 & Pellegrini) Will not cash traveler's checks, so you may have to cross to Villazón to change at Universo Tours.

Banco Jujuy (Árabe Siria 445) If you need an ATM, try this bank.

Locutorio (cnr Av España & 25 de Mayo) Note that phone calls are expensive here (double Salta prices), and no collect calls of any sort are possible.

Post office (cnr San Juan & Sarmiento)

TIME DIFFERENCE

From October to April, there is a one-hour time difference between Bolivia and Argentina (noon in Villazón is 1pm in La Quiaca). From May to September, the Argentine province of Jujuy, where La Quiaca is located, operates on Bolivian time (only more efficiently).

Dangers & Annoyances

You need to be more on your guard in Villazón than in other parts of Bolivia. Like many frontier towns, fake police scams, baggage theft, pickpocketing and counterfeit US banknotes are big business. There have been reports of hefty price gouging for Bolivian visas at this border, so if you need one, it's best to get one elsewhere. For more on visas, see p472.

Sleeping

LA QUIACA

Hosteria Munay (☎ 423924; Belgrano 51; s/d US$10/13) For its clean and comfortable rooms and handy location between the bus terminal and the border, it's hard to beat the Munay.

Hotel Frontera (☎ 422269; cnr Belgrano & Árabe Siria; s/d with shared bathroom US$4/6) You can tell from the prices that there's nothing fancy going on here, but it's OK for a night and the restaurant out front is good, cheap and popular.

VILLAZÓN

Palace Hotel (☎ 0596-5302; s/d US$7/12) Although it looks more like a shopping mall than a hotel, the Palace is the best place to stay in town. Rooms are decent-sized, bathrooms are modern and (a real bonus here) there are functioning windows.

Grand Palace Hotel (☎ 0596-5333; 25 de Mayo s/n; r per person US$5) Showing some definite signs of wear, this not-so-grand palace is nonetheless the pick of the budget bunch around the bus terminal.

Eating

Parrillada La Cabaña (☎ 422624; Av España 550; 4-course set lunch US$2; ☉ breakfast, lunch & dinner) This diner, between 9 de Julio and Belgrano, serves regional specialties and is very popular with locals. The set lunch is an absolute bargain.

La Coyita (☎ 422226; Av España & Belgrano; mains US$3-4) This is a *parrilla* just across the road from the bus terminal. It's cleaner and friendlier than most options in town and has a large menu including such tasty items as pizza, *milanesa* (breaded steak) and pastas.

Ragu (cnr 9 de Julio & Árabe Siria; mains US$2-5) Ragu is a bar serving simple meals, such as chicken, *milanesa* and *lomito* (thin steak), and is endowed with a terrific pot-bellied stove for those frosty nights. Check out the stylish cash register.

Chifa Jardin (☎ 0596-5058; cnr Junin & Argentina, Villazón; meals US$1.50-2; ☉ breakfast, lunch & dinner) Food choices are rather limited on the Bolivian side. This little place opposite the plaza has decent Chinese food and roast chicken and does good-value breakfasts.

Getting There & Away

From the La Quiaca **bus terminal** (cnr Belgrano & Av España), several companies have frequent connections to Jujuy (US$6, four hours) and less frequently to Salta (US$10, eight hours) and intermediate points. There is no transport to Bolivia leaving from here.

There are plenty of touts at the bus terminal all vying for your business. They'll tell you anything, including 'all buses are direct to Salta and take just six hours!' Be firm and find out the real deal from the bus company ticket offices.

In Villazón, all northbound buses depart from around the central terminal. Note that some companies charge different prices depending on demand for tickets, so if you have time it could be worthwhile asking when the cheapest departure is. Buses leave for Tupiza daily (US$1.25, three hours). Some continue or make connections to Potosí (US$3.75 to US$10, nine to 13 hours) with further connections to Sucre, Oruro, Cochabamba and La Paz. There are also daily departures along the amazing route to Tarija, continuing to Bermejo and Yacuiba (US$2.50, eight hours).

AROUND LA QUIACA

☎ 03887

Yavi

While there's not much to do in La Quiaca, the colonial village of **Yavi**, 16km east via paved RP 5, more than justifies a detour; if waiting for a southbound bus, check your bags and spend a morning or afternoon in the milder climate of the sheltered valley of the Río Yavi.

The altar, paintings, and woodcarvings of its patron and several other saints has brought much renown to Yavi's **Iglesia de San Francisco** (☉ 9am-noon & 3-6pm Tue-Fri, 9am-noon Sat). This church is in remarkable condition for a late-17th-century building. It's presumably open the hours listed above, but you may still have to track down the caretaker to get in; alternatively ask at the nearby museum. Two blocks south of the church are the ruins of the **molino**, a small flour mill.

Across the street from the church, in less than splendid condition, the **Casa del Marqués Campero** belonged to a Spanish noble whose marriage to the holder of the original *encomienda* (farm using indentured indigenous labor) created a family that dominated the regional economy in the 18th century. Now a **museum** (admission free; 9am–noon & 3–6pm Mon–Sat), it contains nothing of the marqués' possessions, which are scattered around Jujuy, Hornillos and Salta, but the eclectic contents (like an old Victrola) lend it a certain charm and there's an interesting antiquarian library. A small artisan's market is also here and you can purchase locally made woolen goods.

Near Yavi there are several short hikes in the Cerros Colorados, including one to rock paintings and petroglyphs at **Las Cuevas** and another to springs at **Agua de Castilla**. The Hostal de Yavi organizes good-value tours of these and other local attractions.

The **Hostal de Yavi** (490508; hostaldeyavi@hotmail.com; Güemes 222; dm/s/d US$5/15/23) offers beautiful, simple rooms that, combined with a lovely sitting area out front, make it the best place to stay in town. Five-hour tours (in English, French or Spanish) can be arranged to explore the surrounding countryside from around US$13 per person.

Flota La Quinqueña provides regular public transport from La Quiaca to Yavi (US$5), but shared cabs (US$5 roundtrip, including waiting time) are another alternative. Every half hour or so, there's a pickup truck (US$1) that runs from La Quiaca's Mercado Municipal on Av Hipólito Yrigoyen.

Monumento Natural Laguna de los Pozuelos

Three species of flamingos plus coots, geese, ducks and many other birds breed along the barren shores of this 16,000-hectare lake, at an altitude of nearly 4000m. You may also see the endangered vicuña. The lake has been declared a Ramsar site (an international conservation designation for wetland habitats and associated wildlife) because of its importance to waterbirds. There are archaeological sites here, as well.

Because the park is so isolated, a car is the best transportation option, but carry extra fuel; there is no gasoline available beyond Abra Pampa, midway between Humahuaca and La Quiaca. Make sure you also take plenty of drinking water. Be aware that heavy summer rains can make the unpaved routes off the main highway impassable.

From Abra Pampa it is possible to take a local bus on a roundtrip through the park (there are two services a week) or there are mid-morning buses to Rinconada, west of the lake, where there are simple accommodations. Empresa Mendoza goes daily (US$4) and on request, the bus will drop you off at the Río Cincel ranger station, where it's a 7km walk over level puna to the lake.

Camping is possible on very exposed sites, with basic infrastructure, at the ranger station. For the latest information, ask at the tourist office in Jujuy (see p213) or at the Centro Cultural in Abra Pampa.

QUEBRADA DE HUMAHUACA

The long, narrow World Heritage–listed Quebrada de Humahuaca, north of Jujuy, is an artist's palette of color splashed on barren hillsides. The canyon dwarfs the hamlets where Quechua peasants scratch a living from irrigated agriculture and scrawny livestock.

Because the Spaniards colonized this area from Peru in the late 16th century, it has many cultural features that recall the Andean countries, particularly the numerous historic adobe churches. Earthquakes leveled many of the originals, which were often rebuilt in the 17th and 18th centuries with thick walls, simple bell towers and striking doors and paneling hewn from the wood of the unusual cardón cactus. Whether you come south from La Quiaca or head north from Jujuy, there's something interesting every few miles on this colonial post route between Potosí and Buenos Aires.

The valley's main settlement is the village of Humahuaca, 130km from Jujuy, but there are so many worthwhile sights that the convenience of a car would be a big plus. Otherwise, buses are frequent enough that you should be able to do the canyon on a 'whistle-stop' basis, flagging down a bus when you need one. It is best to visit the Quebrada de Humahuaca in the morning, when there's little wind and before the afternoon heat. Northbound travelers recommend the right side of the bus for better views (southbound, the left side).

HUMAHUACA

☎ 03887 / pop 6140 / elevation 3000m

The cobblestoned streets, adobe houses and quaint plaza here make Humahuaca a photographer's dream. The largest settlement between Jujuy and the Bolivian border, it's also a good place to base yourself while exploring the Quebrada de Humahuaca. There's a large Quechua population, and there's some good handicrafts shops and peñas scattered around town.

Orientation

Straddling the Río Grande east of RN 9, Humahuaca is very compact so everything is within easy walking distance. The town center is between the highway and the river, but there are important archaeological sites across the bridge.

Information

Banco de Jujuy (Jujuy 337) Has an ATM that accepts credit cards.

Hospital Belgrano (Santa Fe 34; ☒ 8am-1pm & 2-6pm) There's always someone on duty for any emergency that might arise.

Locutorio (Jujuy 399) Behind the municipalidad (city hall).

Post office (Buenos Aires) Across from the plaza.

Tourist office (Cabildo at Tucumán & Jujuy; ☒ 7am-12:30pm Mon-Fri)

Sights

Built in 1641, Humahuaca's **Iglesia de la Candelaria** (Calle Buenos Aires) faces the plaza. It contains an image of the town's patron saint, as well as 18th-century oils by Marcos Sapaca, a painter of the Cuzco school.

Across from the church, municipal offices occupy the **Cabildo**, famous for its clock tower, where a life-size figure of San Francisco Solano emerges daily at noon to deliver a benediction. Tourists and locals alike gather in the plaza to watch the spectacle, but be sure to arrive early because the clock is erratic and the figure appears only briefly.

From the plaza, a staircase climbs to the **Monumento a la Independencia**, a chauvinistic travesty that is not the best work of Tilcara sculptor Ernesto Soto Avendaño. The Indian statue is a textbook example of indigenismo, a twisted nationalist tendency in Latin American art and literature that romantically extols the virtues of native cultures overwhelmed by European expansion.

Festivals & Events

Besides the **Carnaval Norteño**, which is celebrated throughout the Quebrada de Humahuaca in February, Humahuaca observes February 2 as the day of its patron saint, the **Virgen de Candelaria**.

Sleeping

Hostal Azul (☎ 421596; www.hostalazulhumahuaca.com.ar in Spanish; Barrio Milagrosa s/n; s/d US$20/37; ☒) Set around a peaceful courtyard, the Azul's rooms are beautiful and simple, with big firm beds and modern bathrooms.

Posada del Sol (☎ 421466; elsolposada@imagine.com.ar; Barrio Milagrosa s/n; dm/s/d US$4/5/11) Just 400m across the bridge, Posada del Sol is a funky adobe place with beautifully designed rooms, all with shared bathroom. There is a well-stocked kitchen, and you can call to get them to pick you up from the bus terminal.

Hotel de Turismo (☎ 421154; Buenos Aires 630; s/d US$10/15; ☒ ☒) Offering huge rooms with balconies, and a massive swimming pool, wooden floors and touches like writing desks in the rooms, this hulking old place is seriously falling apart, but it's one of the best budget bets in town.

Eating

El Fortín (☎ 421126; Buenos Aires 200; mains US$2-6) El Fortín is worth a look, and is particularly good for groups. Specialties of the region are served, so you'll be able to tuck into a steaming bowl of locro (a spicy stew of maize, beans, beef, pork and sausage).

El Portillo (☎ 421288; Tucumán 69; mains US$3-5; ☒ breakfast, lunch & dinner) A simple but good menu in rustic surrounds. If you've got a hankering for llama stew, this is probably the place to try it. Live music is on offer every night from 8pm.

La Cacharpaya (☎ 421016; Jujuy 317; mains US$2-6) For regional dishes including tamales, empanadas and chicken, try this spot on Jujuy, between Santiago del Estero and Tucumán.

There's an acceptable confitería at the bus terminal, but on Belgrano, very close to the bus terminal, is El Rancho Confitería, which is a better alternative for coffee and a light meal.

Shopping

Visit the handicrafts market, near the train station, for woolen goods, souvenirs and the atmosphere. The quality is excellent,

THE ANDEAN NORTHWEST

but northbound travelers will probably find similar items at lower prices in Bolivia.

Getting There & Away

The **bus terminal** (cnr Belgrano & Entre Ríos) is about three blocks south of the plaza. There are numerous southbound buses to Salta and Jujuy, and northbound buses to La Quiaca (US$3, three hours).

Transportes Mendoza (☎ 421016; cnr Belgrano & Salta) offers service to the Andean village of Iruya (US$2, three hours) daily, except Thursday, at 10:15am and return from Iruya at 3pm; buses may not leave at all in summer when it rains. Tickets are available from the bus terminal.

AROUND HUMAHUACA
☎ 03887

Coctaca

Covering about 40 hectares, Coctaca contains northwestern Argentina's most extensive pre-Columbian ruins. Although they have not yet been excavated, many of the ruins appear to have been broad agricultural terraces on an alluvial fan, though there are also obvious outlines of clusters of buildings. The nearby school trains guides to the site. Even if you aren't an archaeology buff, the ruins are still interesting.

The road may be impassable after rain. It's possible to hike the 10km to the ruins, but leave before the heat of the day and take water. After crossing the bridge across the Río Grande in Humahuaca, follow the dirt road north and bear left until you see the village of Coctaca.

Uquía

The 17th-century **Iglesia de San Francisco de Paula** in this roadside village displays a restored collection of paintings from the Cuzco school, featuring the famous *ángeles arcabuceros,* which are angels armed with Spanish colonial weapons. The church is normally closed except during mass. Intending visitors should ask at the house of Adriana Valdivieso, two blocks south of the plaza; she keeps the 17th-century key and will accompany visitors to the church.

Hostal de Uquía (☎ 490523; hostaluquia@hotmail .com; s/d/t US$15/23/35) is a neat little place next to the church with decent rooms, a good restaurant and plenty of tourist information about the area.

Iruya

The beautiful village of Iruya is a speck of white in a valley with startling splashes of colored rocks, in the northwest of Salta province. Cobbled streets, a well-preserved church and whitewashed buildings give Iruya an ageless feel and it's a great spot to kick back from the road for a couple of days. There are also excellent walks in the surrounding countryside.

Buses leave most days from Humahuaca. If you're driving, there is 50km of dirt track to negotiate off RN 9, between Humahuaca and Abra Pampa.

TILCARA
☎ 0388 / pop 3300 / elevation 2461m

Orientation

Tilcara, on the east bank of the Río Grande, is connected by a bridge to RN 9, which leads south to Jujuy and north to Humahuaca and La Quiaca. Its central grid is irregular beyond the village nucleus, focused on Plaza Prado. As in many small Argentine villages, people pay scant attention to street names and numbers.

Information

Locutorio (cnr Bolívar & Lavalle) On the north side of Plaza Prado.

Post office (Plaza Prado, cnr Belgrano & Rivadavia)

Provincial tourist office (☎ 495-5002; Belgrano) A makeshift office next to Hotel de Turismo. It has plenty of information about accommodations.

Sights

EL PUCARÁ

Rising above the sediments of the Río Grande valley, an isolated hill provides the site for this reconstructed **pre-Columbian fortification** (☎ 495-5073; admission US$1; ⏰ 9am-6pm), situated 1km south of the village center. It was discovered in 1903 and reconstructed in the 1950s. It was built from stone by indigenous people and is one of the biggest in the region. It's basically a fortified town with restored houses and an old church. Very little is known about the site but it is quite large and there are terrific views.

There are even better views from the hill on the road leading to the fort; from the south end of the bridge across the Río Huasamayo, it's an easy 15-minute climb to the top.

THE ANDEAN NORTHWEST

MUSEO ARQUEOLÓGICO DR EDUARDO CASANOVA

The Universidad de Buenos Aires runs this outstanding, well-presented **museum** (☎ 495-5006; Belgrano 445; admission US$1, free Tue; ☼ 9am-12:30pm & 2-6pm) of regional artifacts. There are some artifacts from the site of the *pucará*, and exhibits give an insight into the life of people living around that time. The room dedicated to ceremonial masks and their manufacture is particularly impressive. The museum is located in a striking colonial house on the south side of Plaza Prado. Admission is also good for El Pucará.

MUSEO JOSÉ ANTONIO TERRY

Also located in a colonial building on the east side of Plaza Prado is this **art museum** (☎ 495-5005; Rivadavia 459; admission US$2, Thu free; ☼ 9am-7pm Tue-Sat, 9am-6pm Sun). It features the work of a Buenos Aires–born painter whose themes were largely rural and indigenous; his oils depict native weavers, market and street scenes, and portraits. Also featured is work from local artists, as well as the occasional traveling exhibition of contemporary art.

Festivals & Events

Tilcara celebrates several festivals during the year, the most notable of which is January's **Enero Tilcareño**, with sports, music and cultural activities. February's **Carnaval** is equally important in other Quebrada de Humahuaca villages, as is April's **Semana Santa** (Holy Week). August's indigenous **Pachamama** (Mother Earth) festival is worthwhile.

Sleeping & Eating

Rincon de Fuego (☎ 495-5130; www.rincondefuego.com in Spanish; Ambrosetti 445; s/d US$50/60; P ▣) Set in a stone cottage up the hill from town, the rooms here are lovely, cool and quiet. Beds

---

THE AUTHOR'S CHOICE

Posada de Luz (☎ 495-5017; www.posadade luz.com.ar in Spanish; cnr Ambrosetti & Alverro; r US$27-37; P ▣) With a nouveau-rustic charm, this little place is spectacular. More expensive rooms have sitting areas, but all feature pot-bellied stoves and individual terraces with great views out over the valley. This is a fantastic place to unwind for a few days.

---

are some of the comfiest in the region and the sitting areas absolutely seductive. It's not the best value in town, but it's still a pretty good deal.

Hotel de Turismo (☎ /fax 495-5720; tilcahot@imagine .com.ar; Belgrano 590; s/d US$16/22; P ▣ ▣) The rooms here are a bit cramped and definitely in need of a face-lift, but the mountain views and good-sized pool (which only gets filled in the middle of summer) make up for a lot.

Hostel Malka (☎ 495-5197; www.malkahostel.com .ar in Spanish; San Martín s/n, Barrio Malka; s/d US$17/20, dm/s/d with shared bathroom US$6/12/15, 15% discount for HI cardholders) Relocated *porteños* Juan and Teresa Brambati offer guests excellent Hostelling International accommodations at this secluded hilltop hostel, four blocks from Plaza Prado at the east end of San Martín. Breakfast and dinner are extra. They can also hook you up with local tour operators for a 10% discount.

Los Puestos (☎ 495-5100; cnr Belgrano & Padilla; meals US$4-7) A charming little place on the main street done out in the rustic/modern style that is popular here. Regional specialties feature heavily on the menu, and the adventurous may go for a barbecued llama (US$3).

El Cafecito (cnr Belgrano & Rivadavia; ☼ 8am-10pm) Opposite the post office, El Cafecito wouldn't be out of place in downtown Madrid, but it's an agreeable spot for coffee (US$0.80) and croissants, and the homemade cakes (US$1) are worth keeping an eye out for.

La Peñalta is a *peña*, with live music, on the north side of Plaza Prado.

Getting There & Away

The bus terminal is about 500m west of the town center. All the bus companies have kiosks at the bus terminal. There are 26 buses daily to Jujuy (US$3, 1¾ hours), six of which continue to Salta. The 24 daily northbound services to Humahuaca (US$1, 45 minutes) and La Quiaca also stop in Tilcara, and there are several buses daily to Purmamarca.

AROUND TILCARA

From an overlook on RN 9, only a few kilometers south of Tilcara, the astounding hillside cemetery of **Maimará**, a picturesque valley settlement beneath the hill known as La Paleta del Pintor (the Painter's Palette), is a can't-miss photo opportunity. The town also has a worthwhile anthropological and historical museum.

THE ANDEAN NORTHWEST

WHAT'S THE DEAL WITH THE COCA?

Once you start getting seriously north, you'll probably start seeing signs outside shops advertising Coca and Bica. The first refers to those notorious leaves, mainly grown in Peru and Bolivia, which are used to produce cocaine. Bica refers to bicarbonate of soda, an alkaline that, when chewed along with the leaves (as is customary among Andean peoples) releases their mild stimulant effect and combats fatigue and hunger.

Such open commerce may be slightly confusing, especially since Argentina's drug laws prohibit the use, sale and possession of coca leaves, and since it seems that every time you're about to nod off on a bus in this part of the world, it gets pulled over by police looking for those exact same leaves.

The deal is this: small amounts of coca leaves are unofficially tolerated by police, particularly in the Andean north, for use by locals. These bus searches are generally looking for big hauls (or the powdered derivative, known as *blanco* to avoid confusion).

Although there are no reported cases of foreigners being busted with coca leaves, you should bear in mind that they are definitely illegal and, as a foreigner, you would be running a great risk by possessing or using them.

And as for trying to take them out of the country? Let's just say that there are better budget accommodations than the prison system.

Part of a chain that ran from Lima to Buenos Aires during viceregal times, **La Posta de Hornillos** (admission free; ☺ 9am-6pm Wed-Mon) is a beautifully restored way station 11km north of the Purmamarca turnoff. It was the scene of several important battles during the wars of independence. The informal but informative guided tours make this an obligatory stop on the way through the Quebrada de Humahuaca.

For information about Parque Nacional Calilegua, see p236.

PURMAMARCA

☎ 0388

Beneath the polychrome Cerro de los Siete Colores (Hill of Seven Colors), a few kilometers west of RN 9 via RP 52, this tiny village's outstanding asset is its 17th-century **Iglesia Santa Rosa de Lima**.

There are simple accommodations in town around the plaza, including **Hostería La Posta** (☎ 490-8079; s/d US$10/12), which has good rooms and a decent restaurant; and **Hostería Bebo Ville** (☎ 490-8038; dm US$4), behind the church, which is basic but comfortable.

There are many buses to Jujuy (US$2, 1¼ hours) and others to Tilcara and Humahuaca. Tilcara is about 30km away.

SALTA

☎ 0387 / pop 531,400 / elevation 1214m

By far the most happening city in the north of the country, Salta's attractions are varied. The nightlife here pumps, there are a few good galleries and a museum or two to keep you informed. There's also some wonderfully well-preserved colonial architecture.

The city's young population – combined with a steady stream of travelers heading to and from Bolivia – gives the streets a lively feel that is lacking in many towns in the region.

Plaza 9 de Julio is a visual delight, and if you're at all at a loss for something to do here, grab a table plazaside and watch the world go by.

If you need to arrange anything through a travel agent, you'll find this is a convenient place to do it, as the town is crawling with them.

History

Founded in 1582 by Hernando de Lerma, Salta lies in a basin surrounded by verdant peaks. This valley's perpetual spring attracted the Spaniards, who could pasture their animals in the surrounding countryside and produce crops that it was not possible to grow in the frigid Bolivian highlands, where the mining industry created enormous demand for hides, mules and food. When the extension of the Belgrano railroad made it feasible to market sugar to the immigrant cities of the Pampas, the city managed to recovered slightly from its 19th-century decline.

THE ANDEAN NORTHWEST

THE ANDEAN NORTHWEST

SALTA

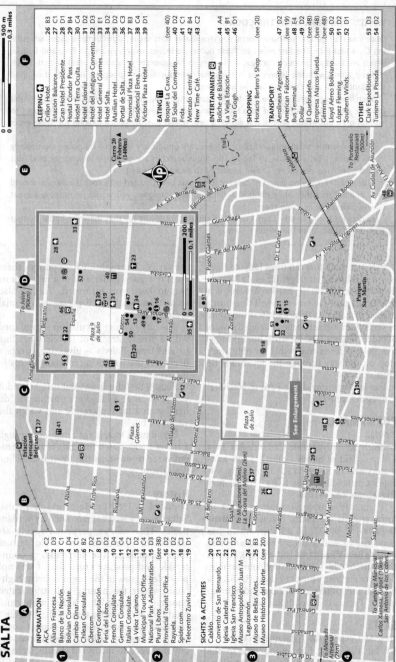

INFORMATION
ACA..	1 C2
Alianza Francesa..............................	2 D3
Banco de la Nación..........................	3 C1
Bolivian Consulate..........................	4 D4
Cambio Dinar...................................	5 C1
Chilean Consulate............................	6 B2
Cibercom...	7 D2
Every Computación........................	8 D1
Feria del Libro.................................	9 D1
French Consulate.............................	10 D4
German Consulate............................	11 C4
Italian Consulate..............................	12 C2
La Veloz Turismo.............................	13 D2
Municipal Tourist Office...................	14 C4
National Park Administration............	15 D3
Plural Libros....................................	(see 38)
Provincial Tourist Office...................	16 D2
Rayuela...	17 D2
Spider.com......................................	18 C3
Telecentro Zuviría...........................	19 D1

SIGHTS & ACTIVITIES
Cabildo..	20 C2
Convento de San Bernardo..............	21 D3
Iglesia Catedral................................	22 C1
Iglesia San Francisco.......................	23 D2
Museo Antropológico Juan M	
Leguizamón.................................	24 E2
Museo de Bellas Artes.....................	25 B3
Museo Histórico del Norte...............	(see 20)

SLEEPING
Crillon Hotel....................................	26 B3
Estación Balcarce.............................	27 C1
Gran Hotel Presidente......................	28 D1
Hostal Condor Pass..........................	29 B4
Hostel Terra Oculta..........................	30 C4
Hotel Colonial.................................	31 D2
Hotel del Antiguo Convento............	32 D3
Hotel General Güemes......................	33 E1
Hotel Salta......................................	34 D2
Marilian Hotel..................................	35 D2
Portal de Salta.................................	36 C3
Provincial Plaza Hotel.......................	37 B3
Residencial Elena.............................	38 C4
Victoria Plaza Hotel.........................	39 D1

EATING
Bosque La Cava...............................	(see 40)
El Solar del Convento.......................	40 D2
Frida..	41 C1
Mercado Central..............................	42 B4
New Time Café.................................	43 C2

ENTERTAINMENT
Boliche de Balderama.......................	44 A4
La Vieja Estación.............................	45 B1
Van Gogh..	46 D1

SHOPPING
Horacio Bertero's Shop....................	(see 20)

TRANSPORT
Aerolíneas Argentinas......................	47 D2
American Falcon...............................	(see 19)
Bus Terminal...................................	48 E4
Dollar..	49 D2
El Quebradeño................................	(see 48)
Empresa Marcos Rueda....................	(see 48)
Geminis...	(see 48)
Lloyd Aéreo Boliviano......................	50 D2
López Fleming.................................	51 D2
Southern Winds...............................	52 D1

OTHER
Clark Expeditions.............................	53 D3
Turismo La Posada...........................	54 D2

Orientation

From the central Plaza 9 de Julio, Salta's conventional grid extends in all directions until it ascends the eastern overlooks of Cerro 20 de Febrero and Cerro San Bernardo, whose streets hug their contours. Although Salta has sprawled considerably, most points of interest are within a few blocks of Plaza 9 de Julio. North–south streets change their names on either side of the plaza, but the names of east–west streets are continuous.

Information

BOOKSTORES

There are three good downtown bookstores:
Feria del Libro (Buenos Aires 83)
Plural Libros (Buenos Aires 220)
Rayuela (Buenos Aires 94)

CULTURAL CENTERS

Alianza Francesa (☎ 431-2403; afsalta@sinectis.com.ar; Santa Fe 20; ☽ 5-10pm Mon-Fri)

IMMIGRATION

Migraciones (☎ 422-0438; Maipú 35) Around 11 blocks west of Plaza 9 de Julio.

INTERNET ACCESS

There are plenty of Internet cafés dotted around town and many *locutorios* also offer Internet access. Some of the cheaper cafés with good connections:
Cibercom (Buenos Aires 97; per hr US$0.30; ☽ until 2am most days) Next to the provincial tourist office
Every Computacion (Deán Funes 141; per hr US$0.30) Opposite the post office.
Spider.com (Caseros 316; per hr US$0.30) Two blocks east of the plaza.

MEDICAL SERVICES

Hospital San Bernardo (☎ 431-7472; Tobías 69)

MONEY

Banco de la Nación (cnr B Mitre & Belgrano) Cashes traveler's checks; it and several other banks around Plaza 9 de Julio have ATMs.
Cambio Dinar (B Mitre 101) Changes cash and traveler's checks, the latter at a high commission.

POST

Post office (Deán Funes 140)

TELEPHONE

Telecentro Zuviria (Plaza 9 de Julio)

TOURIST INFORMATION

ACA (☎ 431-0551; cnr Rivadavia & Mitre)
Municipal tourist office (☎ 437-3341; cnr Av San Martín & Buenos Aires; ☽ 9am-8pm) In high season it maintains a smaller office at the bus terminal, which closes from 1pm to 4pm.
National Park Administration (Administración de Parques Nacionales; ☎ 431-0255; Santa Fe 23; ☽ Mon-Fri mornings) Has information and reasonable maps on the province's several national parks. If it's closed, try knocking – someone may be there.
Provincial tourist office (☎ 431-0950; Buenos Aires 93; ☽ 9am-9pm) Has some English-speaking staff, brochures and maps, and is helpful in locating accommodations in private houses.

TRAVEL AGENCIES

For city tours and excursions in the Salta area, try any of the travel agencies on Buenos Aires, between Caseros and Alvarado. Also see p226.
Los Veloz Turismo (☎ 401-2000; Buenos Aires 44) Sells tickets for the Tren a las Nubes (p230).

Sights

MUSEO HISTÓRICO DEL NORTE

This **museum** (☎ 421-5340; Caseros 549, Plaza 9 de Julio; admission US$1.50; ☽ 9:30am-1:30pm & 3:30-8:30pm Tue-Fri, 9:30am-1:30pm & 4:30-8pm Sat, 9:30am-1pm Sun) holds collections of religious and modern art, period furniture, and historic coins and paper money, plus horse-drawn and ox-drawn vehicles, including an old postal wagon and a hearse. Worthwhile in its own right is the 18th-century *cabildo* housing the museum, as is taking a breather on the balcony out front which overlooks the plaza.

MUSEO DE BELLAS ARTES

Salta's **fine-arts museum** (☎ 421-4714; Florida 20; admission US$1; ☽ 8:30am-1pm & 4:30-8:00pm Mon-Sat) is lodged in the Arias Rengel family's two-story colonial mansion, with its 2m-thick adobe walls. It displays both modern painting and sculpture and has far more interesting work than the contemporary arts museum. The interior patio features a sculpture garden and a wooden staircase that leads to a hanging balcony.

MUSEO DE ARTE CONTEMPORÁNEO

This new **gallery** (☎ 437-0498; Zuviría 90; admission US$0.30; ☽ 9am-1pm & 4:30-8:30pm Mon-Fri, 10:30am-1pm & 5-8:30pm Sat) has on display the work of

THE ANDEAN NORTHWEST

contemporary artists from the city, as well as Argentine and international artists. The space itself is world class, well lit and expertly curated. Exhibitions change rapidly, so it's always worthwhile popping in to see what's on offer, but plans are afoot to establish a permanent exhibition of *salteño* (natives of Salta) work.

IGLESIA CATEDRAL

Salta's 19th-century **cathedral** (cnr España & Mitre; ✆ 7am-noon & 4-8pm) harbors the ashes of General Martín Miguel de Güemes, a *salteño* and independence hero, as well as those of other important historical figures; even today, the gauchos of Salta province proudly flaunt their red-striped *ponchos de güemes*.

CONVENTO DE SAN BERNARDO

Only Carmelite nuns may enter this 16th-century **convent** (cnr Caseros & Santa Fe), but visitors can approach the blindingly whitewashed adobe building (consider sunglasses) to admire the carved, 18th-century algarrobo door. At Caseros and Santa Fe, the building was originally a hermitage, later a hospital and, later still, a convent proper.

CERRO SAN BERNARDO

For outstanding views of Salta and its surroundings, take the **teleférico** (gondola; ✆ 431-0641; roundtrip US$3; ✆ 10am-7:45pm) from Parque San Martín to the top and back. A trail that takes you up the hill begins at the Güemes monument at the top of Paseo Güemes.

On the lower slopes of Cerro San Bernardo is the **Museo Antropológico Juan M Leguizamón** (✆ 422-2960; cnr Ejército del Norte & Polo Sur; admission US$1; ✆ 1-6pm Mon, 8:30am-6pm Mon-Fri, 8am-noon & 3-6pm Sat). It has good representations of local ceramics, especially from the

Tastil ruins (the region's largest pre-Inca town), and some interesting attempts at the whole interactive museum thing – check out the cave of the Shamans, surely one of the more bizarre exhibits you're ever likely to see.

Tours

Salta is also the base for a range of innovative tours, offered by many companies around town. For city tours (US$12) and excursions in the Salta area, try any of the travel agencies on Buenos Aires, between Caseros and Alvarado. A guided bicycle tour is a good way to see the city on a sunny day; they usually take in the major sights and include bike rental. Or arrange a trip to such destinations as Cachi and Molinos, San Antonio de los Cobres (US$62), Cuesta del Obispo and Valles Calchaquíes. Consider a full-day tour to Parque Nacional El Rey; it leaves very early in the morning to give visitors the best possible opportunity to spot native birds and animals, and supplies guides to explain life in this remote forest. A leisurely two-day trip can be organized to difficult-to-reach Iruya, located among some magical landscape at an altitude of 2700m.

Clark Expediciones (✆ /fax 421-5390; www.clark expediciones.com; Caseros 121) Specializes in bird-watching trips to the province's national parks and more remote areas. It also doubles as a bookstore; English-speaking owner Ricardo Clark has authored several books on Argentine birds.

Turismo la Posada (✆ 421-6544; www.turismola posada.com.ar in Spanish; Buenos Aires 94) This company has staff that speak English and French; it has a good variety of trips, and offers horse riding, trekking and rafting.

Sleeping
BUDGET

Hostal Condor Pass (✆ 422-1050; Urquiza 675; dm/d US$4/12; 🖳) About as accommodating as accommodations get, with rooms for two to five people, laundry, kitchen, good bathrooms – even a babysitter! All smack in the middle of town.

Hostel Terra Oculta (✆ /fax 421-8769; www.terra oculta.com in Spanish; Cordoba 361; dm US$4; 🖳) Well set up and offering a range of services, from free Internet to Spanish classes, this place has a good, fun atmosphere and is walking distance from the bus terminal. The rooftop bar/restaurant is a great place to get a posse together before hitting the town.

THE AUTHOR'S CHOICE

Hotel Colonial (✆ 431-0805; www.hotelcolonial salta.com.ar in Spanish; Zuviría 6; s/d US$20/27) This classic building on the plaza is aging, but loaded with character. The furniture has obviously been there since day one (check the sponge factor on your mattress, for that matter), the balconies have plaza views, there's a delightfully bright and cheery breakfast area and even a saloon/piano bar (with piano). In short, a bargain.

Estación Balcarce (☎ 431-7191; Balcarce 980; dm/r US$4/12; 🖳) Smack in the middle of Salta's *zona viva*, and offering discounts and 'excursions' to local pubs and clubs, this one's definitely the party animal's choice. Rooms are surprisingly quiet for the location, although they lack decent ventilation.

Residencial Elena (☎ 421-1529; Buenos Aires 256; s/d US$10/15) This attractive option is in a neocolonial building with a charming interior patio. Family-run, it's a solid budget choice midway between the center of town and the bus terminal.

Camping Municipal Carlos Xamena (☎ 423-1341; Av Libano; sites per person/tent US$1/1; 🏊) One of Argentina's best campgrounds, Carlos Xamena has 500 tent sites and a huge swimming pool (it takes a week to fill in the spring). From downtown, take southbound bus No 13 ('Balneario'), which also connects with the train station. The major drawback is that in summer, when *salteños* flock here to catch some rays, they play outrageously loud music for the swimmers and sunbathers. Mercifully, they switch off the sound system by early evening. You can purchase food and drinks at the nearby supermarket.

MIDRANGE
Victoria Plaza Hotel (☎ 431-8500; www.hotelvic toriaplaza.com.ar; Zuviría 16; s/d US$28/37) The cheerful and bright rooms here have added touches of comfort, like minibars and sofas. The bathrooms have good-sized tubs (finally!) and, depending on which room you get, there are fine city/mountain/plaza views.

Provincial Plaza Hotel (☎ 432-2003; reservas@ hotelprovincial.com.ar; Caseros 786; r US$40; P 🚫 🖳 🏊) The rooms aren't all that huge, but they're big enough – it's a good deal for the price. The service is excellent and the sauna is a bonus, as is the truly *grande* breakfast buffet.

Hotel General Güemes (☎ 431-4800; hotel guemes@hotmail.com; España 446; s/d US$18/23; 🚫) In a central but quiet location, the Güemes has aging but well-maintained rooms. Bathrooms are spotless, but feature ridiculously small shower stalls.

Marilian Hotel (☎ 421-6700; Buenos Aires 176; hotel marilian@arnet.com.ar; s/d US$26/33; P 🚫) One of the newest hotels in town. What the Marilian lacks in character it more than makes up for in spaciousness and modernity. Rooms are bright and service is excellent.

Portal de Salta (☎ 431-7019; www.portaldesalta hotel.com.ar in Spanish; Alvarado 341; s/d US$28/36) A delightfully presented hotel done out in dark woods, gleaming brass and somber colors. Rooms are a bit cramped, but modern and comfortable nonetheless.

Hotel del Antiguo Convento (☎ 422-7267; www .hoteldelconvento.com.ar; Caseros 113; s/d US$23/30; P 🚫 🏊) There really is nothing *antiguo* or conventlike about this place: rooms are modern and sunny and there's a great little pool area out the back.

Crillon Hotel (☎ 422-0400; Ituzaingó 30; s/d US$14/ 28; P 🚫 🏊) The Crillon is another central hotel that doesn't offer a whole lot more than its neat and tidy rooms. It is good for the price, though.

TOP END
Gran Hotel Presidente (☎ 431-1022; www.granhotel presidente.com; Belgrano 353; s/d US$40/60; P 🚫 🖳 🏊) By far the most 'serious' hotel in the center, the Gran Presidente is modern, with spacious rooms and newly renovated bathrooms. There's an excellent indoor pool, sauna, gym and sundeck, as well as the inevitably huge breakfast buffet.

Hotel Salta (☎ 431-0740; hotelsalta@arnet.com.ar; Buenos Aires 1; s/d US$40/60; P 🚫 🏊) This is an attractive, centrally located property, but several readers have found it to be less-than-outstanding value. In its defense, some of the small rooms have magnificent views; if you're paying these rates make sure you get a view.

Eating
New Time Café (cnr Mitre & Caseros; breakfast US$1-2, snacks US$2-4; ☮ breakfast, lunch & dinner) In the running for the ultimate plazaside café: shady tables, great views of the *cabildo*, Cerro San

---

THE AUTHOR'S CHOICE

Portazuelo Restaurant (☎ 431-0104; Av de Turista 1; dishes US$3-5; ☮ breakfast, lunch & dinner) On a sunny day there's no better place to be than on the balcony of this restaurant in the Portazuelo Hotel, enjoying some of the best views in Salta. The food is well prepared, with welcome Mediterranean touches like sun-dried tomatoes and calamari salad, and the service here is excellent.

THE ANDEAN NORTHWEST

Bernado and cathedral, a leafy plaza across the way…they also serve coffee and food.

El Solar del Convento (☎ 421-5124; Caseros 444; meals US$3-7) Don't let the prices fool you – this is some of Salta's best eating. Excellent service, a varied menu and softly tinkling classical background music make this a good choice for a special night out.

Bosque la Cava (☎ 422-4198; cnr Caseros & Dean Funes; meals US$4) Plenty of French influence at this refined restaurant near the plaza. The wine list is excellent and the surrounds simple, but pleasing (with the occasional animal skin thrown in).

Frida (☎ 432-0771; Balcarce 935; meals US$5-7) A good selection of red and white meats (try the rabbit in mustard sauce – yum!), eclectic decor and a good wine list make this place one of the finer dining options available in the area.

Mercado Central (cnr Florida & San Martín) This large, lively market is very interesting as well as one of the cheapest places in town. You can supplement inexpensive pizza, empanadas and *humitas* (stuffed corn dough, resembling Mexican tamales) with fresh fruit and vegetables.

Entertainment

A lot of cafés around the plaza, such as Van Gogh and New Time Café (p227) have live music late at night on weekends.

La Casona del Molino (☎ 434-2835; Luis Burela 1; mains US$7-17) For impromptu entertainment, don't miss this former mansion, about 20 blocks west of Plaza 9 de Julio. A real Salta experience, it also serves great empanadas and *humitas* in several spacious rooms, each with different performers (though the distinction between audience and performer is dubious in this participatory milieu).

Boliche de Balderrama (☎ 421-1542; Av San Martín 1126) This former bohemian haunt is now a popular *peña*. It's a big, solid place and the walls are adorned with photos and paintings of Argentina. A cover charge for the music will sometimes be added to your dinner bill.

Shopping

A large artisan's market sets up every Sunday on Balcarce, south of the station.

Mercado Artesanal (☎ 439-2808; west end of Av San Martín; ☉ 8am-8:30pm) For souvenirs, this provincially sponsored market is the most noteworthy place. Articles for sale include native handicrafts like hammocks, string bags, ceramics, basketry, leather work and the region's distinctive ponchos. To get here, take bus No 2, 3 or 7 from downtown.

In the Cabildo, opposite Hotel Salta, is Horacio Bertero's shop. Horacio Bertero is a protégé of silversmith Raúl Horacio Draghi, San Antonio de Areco's best-known artisan.

Getting There & Away

AIR

Aerolíneas Argentinas (☎ 431-1331; Caseros 475), **Southern Winds** (☎ 421-0808; España 421) and **American Falcon** (☎ 422-3100; Zuviría 20) fly daily to Buenos Aires' Aeroparque (US$120).

Lloyd Aéreo Boliviano (LAB; ☎ 431-0320; Caseros 529) flies Tuesday, Thursday and Sunday to Santa Cruz (Bolivia).

BUS

Salta's **bus terminal** (☎ 431-5227; Av Hipólito Yrigoyen), southeast of downtown, has frequent services to all parts of the country. Most companies are located in the terminal, but a few have offices nearby or elsewhere in town. There are plans for a fancy new terminal to be built on the same site, replacing the current aging facility, but when this is due to take place is anyone's guess.

Géminis (☎ 431-7979) goes to destinations in neighboring Chile and it has an office at the terminal. **Tur Bus** (☎ 431-9719; Syria 638) also makes the trip across the Andes to various Chilean towns.

El Quebradeño (☎ 431-4068) goes daily to San Antonio de los Cobres and **Empresa Marcos Rueda** (☎ 421-4447) serves the altiplano village of Cachi, departing daily at 7am; it also has a second service departing in the afternoon at 1pm on Tuesday, Thursday and Saturday.

THE AUTHOR'S CHOICE

La Vieja Estación (☎ 421-7722; Balcarce 885; cover charge US$1, dinner & show US$8) With a jumping *peña* (folk music) scene every night, this is one of the best places to come for live folk music and a warm, intimate atmosphere. If you're lucky, you'll catch some regional dance as well, with the dancers decked out in full gaucho regalia.

Sample fares to destinations in Argentina and neighboring countries:

Destination	Cost (US$)	Duration (hr)
Angastaco	7	6
Antofagasta (Chile)	22	15
Arica (Chile)	27	24
Buenos Aires	37	22
Cachi	6	4¼
Cafayate	5	3½
Calama (Chile)	20	13
Catamarca	11	6
Córdoba	22	14
Iquique (Chile)	25	23
Jujuy	3	2
La Quiaca	10	8
La Rioja	18	14
Mar del Plata	25	26
Mendoza	26	18
Molinos	8	6½
Resistencia	19	13
Rosario	25	16
San Antonio de los Cobres	4	5
San Juan	21	16
San Pedro de Atacama (Chile)	15	12
Santiago (Chile)	50	24
Santiago del Estero	12	7
Tucumán	8	4½

TRAIN

The **Ferrocarril Belgrano** (☎ 421-3161; Ameghino 690) no longer offers regular passenger services. One of Salta's popular attractions, though, is the scenic ride to and beyond the mining town of San Antonio de los Cobres on the famous Tren a las Nubes (p230).

Getting Around

Aeropuerto Internacional El Aybal (☎ 437-5113) is 9km southwest of town on RP 51; buses to and from the airport cost US$1. **Shuttles** (☎ 423-1648) leave from the airline offices about 1½ hours before the flight (US$2).

Local bus No 5 connects the train station and downtown with the bus terminal on Av Hipólito Yrigoyen, which is southeast of downtown. Bus No 13 connects the station with the municipal campground.

Renting a car is a good way to see Salta's countryside. Among the agencies are **López Fleming** (☎ 421-4143; Paseo Güemes 92) and **Dollar** (☎ 432-1616; dollarsalta@arnet.com.ar; Buenos Aires 88). There are other car-rental agencies next to Dollar if you want to compare prices.

SAN ANTONIO DE LOS COBRES

☎ 0387 / pop 3500 / elevation 3750m

This dusty little mining town is more or less the destination for the Tren a las Nubes (p230). It's also fairly representative of hundreds of little puna towns, which truly feel like they're another world away from the cultural and political influences of Buenos Aires. It's a largely Quechua town, but the posters and political graffiti scribbled on its adobe walls serve as reminders that it's still part of Argentina.

In colonial times, transportation from northwestern Argentina depended on pack trains, most of which passed through the Quebrada de Humahuaca on the way to Potosí, but an alternative route crossed the rugged elevations of the Puna de Atacama to the Pacific and then continued to Lima. It was a rugged journey, indeed – taking 20 days to cover the 800km if you were lucky.

Sleeping & Eating

Until recent times, San Antonio had only the most basic accommodations and food, and still, for the most part, what you see is what you get.

Hostería de las Nubes (☎ 490-9059; Caseros 441; s/d US$15/20) This hotel goes a long way to filling the accommodations gap with 12 rooms with private bathrooms, double-glazed windows, and a total of 30 beds. It also has a restaurant, central heating and a TV lounge. Rates can rise by 20% in the July to August peak season.

El Palenque (☎ 490-9019; Belgrano s/n; r per person with shared bathroom US$4) The most comfortable of the very basic budget accommodations here. Make sure you stock up on blankets, as nights can get very chilly.

Huari Huasi (Belgrano s/n; meals US$2.50-4; ☾ breakfast, lunch & dinner) One of the few actual restaurants in town, this one is pretty good. They offer filling meals in a cozy, simple environment.

Getting There & Away

There are daily buses from Salta to San Antonio de los Cobres (US$4, five hours) with El Quebradeño. Or catch the scenic Tren a las Nubes from Salta to San Antonio de los Cobres and beyond.

Do not waste time trying to hitch across the Andes because there are almost no vehicles; even the summer (December to

February) buses operated by Géminis from Salta now go via the Paso de Jama.

TREN A LAS NUBES

From Salta, the Tren a las Nubes (Train to the Clouds) leaves the Lerma Valley to ascend the multicolored Quebrada del Toro, continuing past the important ruins of Tastil, as it parallels RN 51. To reach the heights of the puna on the Chilean border, 571km west (though the Tren a las Nubes travels less than half this distance), the track makes countless switchbacks and even spirals, passes through 21 tunnels more than 3000m in total length, and crosses 31 iron bridges and 13 viaducts. The trip's highlight – a stunning viaduct 64m high and 224m long, weighing 1600 tons, and spanning an enormous desert canyon at La Polvorilla – is a magnificent engineering achievement unjustified on any reasonable economic grounds. At Abra Chorillos, an altitude of 4575m makes this the fourth-highest operating line in the world.

From March to November, **Los Veloz Turismo** (☎ 401-2000; www.trenalasnubes.com.ar; Buenos Aires 44, Salta) operates the Tren a las Nubes service as far as La Polvorilla; most trips depart on Saturdays only. The train leaves at 7am and returns to Salta at 10pm. The fare is US$70 for the 438km roundtrip, which reaches a maximum altitude of 4200m. Meals are additional, ranging from a US$7 fixed-price lunch in the dining car to sandwiches and hamburgers for US$2 to US$4. Departures vary depending on interest in the service, with two in March but 13 in July.

VALLES CALCHAQUÍES

Definitely one of Argentina's most appealing off-the-beaten-track areas, the Valles Calchaquíes combine striking natural landscapes with unique cultural and historical resources. The vernacular architecture here merits special attention – even modest adobe houses might have neoclassical columns and/or Moorish arches. The town of Cachi is the most accessible and pleasant to wander around, and the bus trip there is well worth it (see the boxed text, opposite).

In these valleys, north and south of Cafayate and one of the main routes across the Andes to Chile and Peru, Calchaquí Indians put up some of the stiffest resistance to Spanish rule. In the 17th century, plagued with labor shortages, the Spaniards twice tried to impose forced labor obligations on the Calchaquíes, but found themselves having to maintain armed forces to prevent the Indians from sowing their own crops and attacking pack trains.

Military domination did not solve Spanish labor problems, since their only solution was to relocate the Indians as far away as Buenos Aires, whose suburb of Quilmes bears the name of one group of these displaced people. The last descendants of the 270 families transported to the viceregal capital had died or had dispersed by the time of Argentine independence.

When their resistance failed, the Calchaquíes lost the productive land that had sustained them for centuries and would have done so much longer. Those riches found their way into the hands of Spaniards who formed large rural estates, the haciendas of the Andes.

Bus runs are scarce along the valley, but if you find yourself stuck, you can usually get a ride in a pickup truck, whose frequent (but irregular) departures are the way the locals get around. To organize a ride, start asking around as soon as possible, and ask everywhere, literally – shops, hotels, restaurants and hospitals. Eventually somebody will know someone who's just about to leave (in a strictly Argentine sense), and you'll be on your way.

Cachi

☎ 03868 / pop 1800 / elevation 2280m
Whichever way you're coming from, Cachi is a breath of fresh air. Better developed and more picturesque than the villages to the south, but far more quaint and endearing than the bustle of Salta, the cobblestone streets, adobe houses and stunning surrounds captivate many travelers, inspiring them to stay for an extra couple of days just to soak it all in.

On the west side of Plaza 9 de Julio, the **Mercado Artesanal** (☎ 491053; www.salnet.com.ar /cachi; ☼ 9am-2pm & 3-8pm Mon-Fri, 10am-3pm & 5-8pm Sat, 10am-3pm Sun) is both a crafts market and the tourist office.

On the east side of the plaza, the simple but attractive **Iglesia San José** (1796) features a three-bell tower, graceful arches and a tightly fitted ceiling of cardón wood. The confessional and other features are also made of cardón.

Directly south of the church, Cachi's **Museo Arqueológico Pío Pablo Díaz** (admission US$1; 8:30am-7:30pm Mon-Fri, 8:30am-6:30pm Sat, 10am-1pm Sun) presents a professionally arranged account of the surrounding area's cultural evolution, with good sections on pre-Calchaquí cultures. The museum is a welcome contrast to many provincial institutions that make little effort to interpret their materials in a regional context.

SLEEPING & EATING

Hospedaje El Cortijo de María Luisa (491034; s/d US$28/41) This charming, recycled colonial-style building is truly one of the best in the country. It's a cozy little nook-and-cranny place. You get your own small sitting room, use of the kitchen and there's a good chance you'll have the whole place to yourself.

Hostería Cachi (491105; www.soldelvalle.com.ar in Spanish; s/d US$30/40; P) With its hilltop position, this modern hotel has the best views in town (as well as the best restaurant), and there are worse ways to spend your day than relaxing poolside checking them out. Rooms are spacious and well designed, with ultrahip bathrooms, and there's even a little zoo out the back.

Hotel Nevado de Cachi (491004; s/d US$7/10, with shared bathroom US$4/8) A modest, good-value and central hotel, it's just off the plaza next to the bus stop. The shared bathrooms are in a lot better condition than the private ones, and the upstairs rooms are much more cheerful than the downstairs ones.

Camping Municipal (sites US$3) On a hilltop about 1km southwest of the plaza, Camping Municipal has shaded sites surrounded by hedges; sites without hedges are slightly cheaper. The **Albergue Municipal** (dm US$2) is on the same grounds, offering very basic 10- to 15-bed dorms. Reservations must be made at the tourist office.

Confitería Cachi (meals US$3; breakfast, lunch & dinner) On the north side of plaza, this simple *confitería* is a good place for a coffee after your bus ride into town. It also does a range of excellent meals including *milanesas* and set lunches.

GETTING THERE & AWAY

You can reach Cachi by the Marcos Rueda (in Salta 0387-421-4447) bus from Salta. There is a daily bus to Salta (US$6, 4¼ hours) at 7:15am; there is also a second bus at 1pm on

KIDS ACTING UP? PUT 'EM ON THE BUS TO CACHI!

The bus ride from Salta to Cachi is one of the most spectacular you are ever likely to undertake. The bus grinds its way up narrow, winding roads that twist and curl around the imposing Cuesta de Obispo, giving passengers sweeping views of valley floors and peaks that seem to mirror endlessly into the distance. It's tempting to stick your nose out the window as you career up and down the winding roads. Certainly locals know the real value of the scenery – they hold wailing kids up to the windows and the result is nearly always silence. Now, that's impressive!

Just before Cachi, as you enter Parque Nacional Los Cardones, the landscape levels out to plains of cardón cacti standing sentry in terrain reminiscent of a lunar landscape.

Cachi may be time consuming to reach by public transport, but it's definitely worth the detour. The journey is the best part of the trip.

Tuesday, Wednesday and Saturday. There are also departures to Molinos (US$2, three hours) and Angostaca (US$4, five hours).

From Cachi, buses continue to La Poma, an old hacienda town that, for all practical purposes, is the end of the line. The road beyond, to San Antonio de los Cobres, is impassable except for 4WD vehicles; it's much easier to approach San Antonio from Salta via the Quebrada del Toro.

Molinos & Around

03868 / pop 500 / elevation 2000m

One of the most attractive of the little towns along the valley, Molinos' laid-back pace is augmented by its treelined streets and good accommodations options.

Dating from 17th-century *encomiendas,* the town of Molinos takes its name from the still-operative grain mill on the Río Calchaquí; the town's restored 18th-century **Iglesia de San Pedro de Nolasco**, in the Cuzco style, features twin bell towers and a traditional tiled roof. Like Angastaco, Molinos was a way station on the trans-Andean route to Chile and Peru. Well into the 20th century, pack trains passed here with skins, wool, blankets and wood for sale in Salta and subsequent shipment to Buenos Aires.

About 1.5km west of Molinos is the **Criadero Coquera**, where INTA, Argentina's agricultural extension service, raises vicuñas; alongside it is the **Casa de Entre Ríos**, part of the former Estancia Luracatao, where there's a very fine artisans' market with spectacular alpaca *ponchos de güemes* for sale.

Across from the church, the beautifully restored 18th-century **Hostal Provincial de Molinos** (☎ 494002; s/d US$37/50) has simple but comfortable rooms and a good restaurant. It's also known as the Casa de Isasmendi, after *encomendero* (Spaniard) Nicolás Severo de Isasmendi (1753–1857). Isasmendi, Salta's last colonial governor, was born, lived and died in this sprawling residence in a town that was a stronghold of royalist resistance. Restored in 1988, it features a small but worthwhile archaeology museum and an artisans' shop.

There are a few little *hospedajes* (family homes) scattered around town, which are more like homestays than anything, and **Cordones de Molinos** (☎ 464061; per person with shared bathroom r US$5) is one of the better ones, featuring firm beds and a blasting hot shower.

Daily, except Tuesday and Thursday, at 6:45am a Marcos Rueda bus goes to Salta (US$8, 6½ hours) via RN 40 through Cachi and RP 33 through Parque Nacional Los Cardones.

Angastaco

☎ 03868 / pop 2561 / elevation 1900m

From Cafayate, paved RN 40 continues north to San Carlos, beyond which it becomes a bumpy, dusty gravel surface passing among wildly tilted sedimentary beds even more interesting than the Quebrada de Cafayate. Angastaco, 74km north of Cafayate and 51km beyond San Carlos, resembles other oasis settlements placed at regular intervals in the Valles Calchaquíes, with vineyards, fields of peppers and ruins of an ancient *pucará*. You'll also find an **archaeological museum** in the municipal building. Its opening hours are erratic; if it's closed ask in the *municipalidad*.

Pensión Cardón (per person with/without private bathroom US$3.50/2.50) is cheap, clean, basic and good value for the price. Breakfast is also available here . **Hostería Angastaco** (☎ 491123, 15-639016; s/d US$25/35; P ☎) offers slightly more comfort, and dinners cost about US$3.

The manager's daughter can also organize horse rides for about US$5 per hour.

Marcos Rueda has a bus to Molinos, Cachi and Salta (US$7, six hours). There's also a daily bus to Cafayate.

QUEBRADA DE CAFAYATE

Salta's Lerma valley receives abundant rainfall from summer storms that drop their load on the slopes surrounding the city, but higher ranges to the south and west inhibit the penetration of subtropical storms. In several areas, the rivers that descend from the Andes have carved deep *quebradas* (canyons) through these arid zones, exposing the multicolored sedimentary strata under the surface soils.

Many of these layers have eroded to strange, sometimes unearthly formations, which southbound travelers from Salta can appreciate from paved RN 68, but which are even more intriguing when explored up close. The canyon deserves national or provincial park status for its extraordinary scenery.

Properly speaking, the Quebrada de Cafayate is the Quebrada del Río de las Conchas, after the river that eroded the canyon. Beyond the tiny village of Alemanía, about 100km south of Salta, the scenery changes suddenly and dramatically from verdant hillsides to barren, reddish sandstones. To the east, the Sierra de Carahuasi is the backdrop for distinctive landforms bearing evocative names like Garganta del Diablo (Devil's Throat), El Anfiteatro (The Amphitheater), El Sapo (The Toad), El Fraile (The Friar; a nearby farm sells empanadas and cold drinks), El Obelisco (The Obelisk) and Los Castillos (The Castles). Just north of Cafayate, Los Médanos is an extensive dune field.

Getting There & Away

There are several ways to explore or at least see the canyon. The ideal option is renting a car (which is possible in Salta but not in Cafayate) or renting a bicycle (which is possible in Cafayate); you could also take the bus, hitch or walk. Tours from Salta are brief and regimented.

Here is the lowdown for those without a private vehicle: you can disembark from any El Indio bus (with your rental bike or by foot), tour around for awhile and then flag another bus later on. Be aware of the schedules between Salta and Cafayate, as you probably don't want to get stuck in the canyon after dark (although if you have a tent, there are worse places to camp). Also carry food and plenty of water in this hot, dry environment. Alternatively you could hitch between the most interesting sites, but you may want to catch one of the buses if it gets late.

A good place to start your exploration is the impressive box canyon of Garganta del Diablo. Remember that the most interesting portion of the Quebrada is much too far to walk in a single day, so see as much as you can before continuing to Cafayate; you can always double back the next day.

CAFAYATE
☎ 03868 / pop 11,800 / elevation 1700m
The most important town in extreme southwestern Salta province, Cafayate is a popular tourist destination, but rarely overrun with visitors except on weekends. It is small and slow paced and a great base from which to explore the surrounding countryside of the Quebrada de Cafayate. Everything is within walking distance – including the wineries, where you can taste a local drop

or two – but why not do as the locals do and get around on a bicycle. Cafayate also has many young artists and craftspeople, so check out the local handicrafts.

Orientation
Cafayate sits at the foot of the Calchaquí Valley, near the junction between RN 40, which goes northwest to Molinos and Cachi, and RN 68, which goes to Salta through the Quebrada de Cafayate. Through town, RN 40 is Av General Güemes. As in many provincial towns, few people bother with street names.

Information
Banco de la Nación (Plaza San Martín) It's better to change money elsewhere, but you could try this bank or the larger shops or hotels.
La Satamanca Cyber Café (Av General Güemes, btwn Belgrano & Hurtado; per hr US$0.30)
Locutorio (cnr Av General Güemes & Belgrano)
Locutorio Cafayete (cnr Av General Güemes & Alvarado)
Post office (cnr Av General Güemes & Córdoba)
Tourist information kiosk (northeast cnr of Plaza San Martín; ☼ 8am-10pm)

CAFAYATE

0	200 m
0	0.1 miles

INFORMATION
Banco de la Nación..................1 C3
La Satamanca Cyber Cafe.......2 D3
Lavandería..............................3 C3
Locutorio...............................4 D2
Locutorio Cafayate.................5 D3
Post Office.............................6 D2
Tourist Information Kiosk........7 D2

SIGHTS & ACTIVITIES
Museo Arqueológico...............8 C3
Museo de Vitivinicultura.........9 D3

SLEEPING
El Portal de los Viñas.............10 D3
Hostal del Valle.....................11 C3
Hostal Killa...........................12 D3
Hotel Asturias.......................13 D3
Hotel Tinkunaku....................14 D2
Villa Vicuña..........................15 D2

EATING
Baco.....................................16 D2
El Cafayateño.......................17 C2
El Rancho.............................18 D3
Heladería Miranda................19 D2
La Carreta de Don Olegario...20 D2

SHOPPING
Mercado Artesanal................21 D2

TRANSPORT
El Aconquija Buses................22 C2
El Cafayeño Buses................23 C2
El Indio Buses.......................24 D2

OTHER
Turismo Cordillerano.............25 D2

To Bodega La Banda (1km);
Bodega La Rosa (1.5km)

Sevilla
Brachieri
Córdoba
Salta
Jujuy
Alvarado
Mitre
Diego de Almagro
Buenos Aires
Calchaquí
Rivadavia
Quintana de Niño
Plaza San Martín
General Güemes
Belgrano
San Martín
9 de Julio
Sebastián Arias
Iglesia Nuestra Señora del Rosario
Nuestra Señora del Rosario
V Toscano
Calchaquí
M Hurtado
Colón
Peñalva

To Huayra Sanipy (1km)

To Camping Lorohuasi (1km);
Bodega Etchart (3km)

THE ANDEAN NORTHWEST

Sights & Activities

MUSEO ARQUEOLÓGICO

In this private **museum** (☎ 421054; cnr Colón & Calchaquí; admission by donation), the late Rodolfo Bravo, a dedicated aficionado of and expert on the region, left an astounding personal collection of Calchaquí ceramics, as well as colonial and more recent artifacts, such as elaborate horse gear and wine casks. While there's not much explanation, the material itself is worth seeing. Drop in at any reasonable hour.

WINERIES

The **Museo de Vitivinicultura** (Av General Güemes; admission US$0.30; ☼ 10am-1pm & 5-8pm Mon-Fri), near Colón, details the history of local wine production and displays a range of antiquated winemaking equipment.

Three nearby wineries offer tours and tastings; these are free but it's good manners to buy a bottle of wine after the tastings. The 3000-hectare **Bodega Etchart** (☎ 421529; RN 40; ☼ 7:30am-noon & 3-6:30pm Mon-Fri, 8am-noon Sat) is at the southern approach to town.

At the north end of town, the smaller 800-hectare **Bodega La Banda** (Vasija Secreta; ☎ 421850; RN 40; ☼ 9am-1pm & 2-7pm) offers cheerful tours, which are recommended and can be done in English. The whole place is classified as a national museum.

Bodega La Rosa (☎ 421201; RN 40; ☼ 8am-5pm Mon-Thu, 8am-4pm Fri, 9am-1pm Sat & Sun), belonging to Michel Torino, is near the RP 68 junction to the Quebrada de Cafayate, north of town. The imposing Casa de Alto, an Italian-style villa at the junction, is no longer part of the Torino properties and is not open to the public.

Tours

Turismo Cordillerano (☎ 422137; www.turismocordillerano.com.ar in Spanish; Quintana de Niño 59) offers a range of local tour options, such as three-hour treks in the Quebrada de Cafayate (US$12 per person), four-hour car tours in the Quebrada (US$8 per person) and bicycle hire for US$5 per day. It can also arrange horse trekking.

Festivals & Events

La Semana de Cafayate, at the end of February or beginning of March, is a three-day folklore festival. The annual **Fiesta de la Virgen**, in early October, is worthwhile if you're in the area.

Sleeping

Cafayate's accommodations are a bargain out of season but go up significantly in summer. Many places close off-season, but those listed below stay open all year.

BUDGET

Huayra Sanipy (☎ 422311; Nuestra Señora del Rosario 285; dm US$3.50) A cheerful little hostel offering dorms with two, six and eight beds. Lockers in rooms are a welcome sight, as is the small but well-stocked library and comfy hangout area. Kitchen facilities are available.

El Portal de los Viñas (☎ 421098; Nuestra Señora del Rosario 153; s/d US$7/14) Here you will find comfortable, good-sized rooms with terra-cotta tiled floors set around a cheerful, vine-shaded courtyard. Bathrooms are spacious and clean, if somewhat aging.

Camping Lorohuasi (☎ 421051; per car, person & tent US$1; 🚗) This municipal campground at the south end of town can get dusty when the wind blows. Facilities are decent and include dependably hot showers, though some of the toilets are a bit of a disgrace. There's a small grocery, but you can also buy food in town, which is just a 10-minute walk away.

MIDRANGE

Villa Vicuña (☎ 422145; Belgrano 76; s/d US$20/40) Set in a converted house, the Vicuña is part of a new wave of accommodations in Cafayate. Featuring beautiful, spotless rooms with reproduction antique furniture, this is a very comfortable and intimate place to stay.

Hostal Killa (☎ 422254; hostalkillacafayate@hotmail.com; Colón 47; s/d US$20/27) Another new, upmarket option are the sunny, spacious rooms in this converted colonial house. The place has been beautifully restored and there's a stylishly rustic breakfast/sitting area out back.

Hostal del Valle (☎ 421039; hostaldelvalle@norte virtual.com; San Martín 243; s/d US$13/17) With its bright and cheery rooms and almost jungle-like interior courtyard, this place is definitely one of the bargains in this price range.

Hotel Tinkunaku (☎ 421148; Diego de Almagro 12; s/d US$13/22; 🅿 ☒ 🚗) Clean and modern rooms in a quiet but central location. The place has a relaxed, family atmosphere and a huge swimming pool out back.

Hotel Asturias (☎ 421328; asturias@infonoa.com.ar; Av General Güemes 154; s/d US$17/27) Right by the plaza in a great old building, the Asturias is one of those weird places with cramped rooms and massive bathrooms. Still, it's not a bad deal, particularly for the awesome swimming pool and lawn area out back.

Eating

El Rancho (☎ 421256; cnr Av General Güemes & Belgrano; mains US$4-10) Also serving regional specialties, El Rancho is a bit more intimate, despite the name, with a large fireplace surrounded by tables, perfect for warming the tush on chilly winter nights.

El Cafayateño (cnr Quintana de Niño & Nuestra Señora del Rosario; mains US$2-5; ☺ breakfast & lunch) A good spot for breakfast in the sun or a light meal, this café is a popular little place.

La Carreta de Don Olegario (☎ 421004; Av General Güemes 2; mains US$2-6) The wide menu here, with many regional dishes (such as *locro*), is definitely an attraction, but not everything is always available.

Heladería Miranda (Av General Güemes btwn Córdoba & Diego de Almagro; ☺ 10am-10pm) This *heladería* (ice-cream shop) is Cafayate's pride and joy, serving imaginative wine-flavored ice creams such as *torrontés* (dry white wine from Cafayate) and cabernet.

Shopping

Mercado Artesanal (Av General Güemes; ☺ 9am-10pm) Check out the handicrafts here, across from the tourist office.

Getting There & Away

El Indio (Belgrano, btwn Av General Güemes & Salta) has four buses daily to Salta (US$5, 3½ hours), except Sunday when there are three. There are also four daily to San Carlos (up the Valle Calchaquí; US$0.70, 40 minutes), except Sunday (three), and one to Angastaco (US$2, two hours). **El Cafayateño** (cnr San Martín & Buenos Aires) goes twice daily to Salta except Sunday (once). **El Aconquija** (Mitre 77) leaves three times per day for Tucumán (US$8, 5½ hours) passing through Tafí del Valle; one goes via Santa María (US$6, two hours).

Getting Around

Plenty of places hire bikes for about US$5 per day. Try Turismo Cordillerano (opposite).

AROUND CAFAYATE
Quilmes

☎ 03892

Dating from about AD 1000, **Quilmes** (admission US$2; ☺ 8am-6pm) was a complex urban

THE AUTHOR'S CHOICE

Baco (☎ 15-402-8366; cnr Av General Güemes & Rivadavia; meals US$2-3) Crammed full of rustic decorations, this is the most frequently recommended restaurant in town. It serves up interesting variations on Argentine standards and a good selection of local wines for around US$6 per bottle.

settlement that occupied about 30 hectares and housed as many as 5000 people. The Quilmes Indians survived contact with the Incas, which occurred from about AD 1480 onwards, but could not outlast the siege of the Spaniards who, in 1667, deported the last 2000 inhabitants to Buenos Aires.

Quilmes' thick walls underscore its defensive purpose, but clearly this was more than just a *pucará*. Dense construction sprawls both north and south from the central nucleus, where the outlines of buildings, in a variety of shapes, are obvious even to the casual observer. For revealing views of the extent of the ruins, climb the trails up either flank of the nucleus, which offer vistas of the valley once only glimpsed by the city's defenders. Give yourself at least half a day, preferably more, to explore the nucleus and the surrounding area.

There is a small **museum** at the entrance, which is well presented but poorly labeled. The admission charge also entitles you to explore the ruins (which feature llamas for tourists to hire). The museum shop features a good selection of handicrafts.

SLEEPING & EATING

Posada Quilmes (☎ 421075; s/d US$24/33; P ☺) This hotel blends so well into its surroundings that it's surprisingly inconspicuous from outside, but its high ceilings and skylights manage to convey the expansiveness of the desert. It's beautifully decorated with Incan motifs and slate floors.

A large but stylish **bar/confitería** (meals US$3-4; ☺ breakfast, lunch & dinner) offers *parrilla*, pasta and great views of the ruins.

GETTING THERE & AWAY

Buses from Cafayate to Santa María or Tafí del Valle will drop passengers at the junction, but from there you'll have to walk or hitch (there is little traffic) 5km to the ruins.

THE ANDEAN NORTHWEST

It will probably be easier to get a lift back to the highway, since you can approach any vehicle visiting the ruins.

Another option is to hire a taxi in Cafayate or Santa Maria. You should be able to bargain a driver down to about US$20 for the roundtrip.

Santa María

☎ 03838 / pop 11,000

The northernmost settlement along RN 40 in Catamarca province, the crossroads town of Santa María de Yokavil lies in the midst of a richly endowed archaeological zone. It's home to the **Museo Arqueológico Provincial Eric Boman** (cnr Belgrano & Sarmiento; ☯ 9am-8pm), in the Centro Cultural Yokavil, which also houses the **tourist office** (☎ 421083; ☯ 8am-10pm) and a well-stocked handicrafts store. This museum is named for the Swedish archaeologist who did extensive pioneering research here in the early 20th century. This tidy oasis is just 35km south of Quilmes, and 80km northwest of Tafí del Valle in Tucumán province, and it is a good stopover or base for visits to Quilmes.

Places to stay in town include **El Algarroba** (☎ 422222; Sarmiento 410; s/d US$7/15), with modern, spacious rooms that include full kitchens, and **Residencial Inti Huasi** (☎ 420476; Belgrano 156; s/d US$5/7), which is basic but comfortable. Some, but not all, buses en route between Tucumán, Tafí del Valle and Cafayate stop here.

NATIONAL PARKS OF JUJUY & SALTA PROVINCES

Jujuy and Salta provinces have four important national parks, but only Los Cardones and Calilegua are easily accessible. El Rey is increasingly accessible thanks to road improvements, while Baritú must be approached through Bolivia. If you're in Buenos Aires, it's a good idea to contact the very helpful **national parks administration** (☎ 011-4312-0820; Av Santa Fe 690; ☯ 10am-5pm Mon-Fri) for information. Alternatively you could drop into the **Salta office** (☎ 0387-431-0255; Santa Fe 23).

Parque Nacional Calilegua

☎ 03886

On the eastern border of Jujuy province the arid altiplano gives way to the dense subtropical cloud forest of the Serranía de Calilegua, whose preservation is the goal of this accessible 75,000-hectare park. At the park's highest elevations, about 3600m, verdant Cerro Hermoso reaches above the forest and offers boundless views of the Gran Chaco to the east. Birdlife is abundant and colorful, but the tracks of rare mammals, such as pumas and jaguars, are easier to see than the animals themselves.

In 2000 both the Argentine branch of Greenpeace and the local Aymará (Kolla) organization Tinkunaku lost their battle to halt construction of a gas pipeline that now runs through Calilegua and nearby Baritú, and across the Andes to Antofagasta in Chile. There is concern that this pipeline will threaten regional ecosystems in the national parks.

INFORMATION

The **park headquarters** (☎ 422046) is in the village of Calilegua, just off RN 34, north of the town of Libertador General San Martín. Donated by the Ledesma sugar mill, the building includes a visitor center with exhibits on the region's national parks and monuments, including Calilegua, Baritú, El Rey and Laguna de los Pozuelos. The staff can also provide the latest information on road conditions, since many areas are inaccessible during the summer rainy season.

At the **park entrance** (admission free; ☯ 9am-6pm), just north of Libertador General San Martín on RP 83 heading toward Valle Grande, there is an **Intendencia** (☎ 422046; pncalilegua@cooperlib .com.ar) where you may be able to pick up maps and any last-minute information you're after, but if you can't, don't worry – trails are well marked.

WILDLIFE

Receiving 2000mm of precipitation a year, but with a defined winter dry season, Calilegua comprises a variety of ecosystems correlated with altitude. The transitional *selva*, from 350m to 500m above sea level, consists of tree species common in the Gran Chaco, such as lapacho and palo amarillo, which drop their leaves in winter. Between 550m and 1600m, the cloud forest forms a dense canopy of trees more than 30m tall, punctuated by ferns, epiphytes and lianas, covered by a thick fog in summer and autumn. Above 1200m, the montane forest is composed of pines (a general term for almost any conifer, such as cedar), aliso and queñoa. Above 2600m this grades into moist puna grasslands, which become drier as one proceeds west toward the Quebrada de Humahuaca.

The 230 bird species include the condor, brown eagle, torrent duck and the colorful toucan. Important mammals, rarely seen in the dense forest, include tapir, puma, jaguar, collared peccary and otter.

SIGHTS & ACTIVITIES

Nature-oriented activities will be the focus of any visit to Calilegua. The best places to view birds and mammals are near the stream courses in the early morning or very late afternoon, just before dark. From the ranger station at Mesada de las Colmenas, follow the steep, rugged and badly overgrown trail down to a beautiful creek usually marked with numerous animal tracks, including those of large cats. The descent takes perhaps an hour, the ascent twice that.

There are seven different trails in the park ranging from a few hundred meters to a couple of kilometers. Generally the trails range in difficulty; you should ask the rangers for advice. Local guides are available at about US$3 per hour, but unless you need explanations, aren't really necessary as you can't leave the trails. Recommendations have been given for **Patricia** (☎ 421501; Libertador General San Martín).

There are excellent views from 3600m Cerro Hermoso, although there are no detailed maps; ask rangers for directions. Ordinary vehicles cannot go far past the Mesada de las Colmenas, but the road itself offers outstanding views of Cerro Hermoso and the nearly impenetrable forests of its steep ravines.

From Valle Grande, beyond the park boundaries to the west, it's possible to hike to Humahuaca along the Sierra de Zenta, or to Tilcara, but the treks take at least a week.

SLEEPING & EATING

There are several places to stay in nearby Libertador General San Martín including **Hotel Los Lapachos** (☎ 25798; Entre Ríos 400; s/d US$15/18; P 🗙), with comfortable and spacious rooms, and **Hotel Chosen** (☎ 425798; Ovejero 435; s/d US$7/10), which offers basic rooms near the plaza. There are a few *confiterías*

around the plaza, serving standard dishes and snacks.

Camping is the only option in the park itself. The developed **campsite** (Aguas Negras) is on a short lateral road near the ranger station at the entrance. It is free and has balky bathrooms and water shortages. Beware of mosquitoes, which are a lesser problem at higher elevations. Although there are no other developed campsites, you can camp on a level area at the ranger station at Mesada de las Colmenas, which has great open views to the east.

GETTING THERE & AWAY

La Veloz del Norte buses between Salta and Orán stop at the excellent and reasonable restaurant belonging to the Club Social San Lorenzo, next door to the park headquarters. There are many buses to Ledesma, only a couple of kilometers south of Calilegua.

There are local buses every day from Libertador General San Martín to Valle Grande (two hours) that go through the park; buses generally leave early in the morning and return late in the evening. Inquire at the park headquarters' visitor center for the most current information.

If you're in a group, a taxi is a good option. It costs US$0.30 per person from Libertador General San Martín to Parque Nacional Calilegua (four people to a taxi). You should arrange the price before you get in the taxi.

Otherwise, it should be possible to hitch to the park and Valle Grande with the logging trucks that pass through the park on RP 83. Start from the bridge at the north end of Libertador General San Martín, where there is a good dirt road through mostly shady terrain to Aguas Negras, 8km west.

Parque Nacional Los Cardones

Occupying some 65,000 hectares on both sides of the winding highway from Salta to Cachi across the Cuesta del Obispo, Parque Nacional Los Cardones takes its name from the candelabra cactus known as the cardón, the park's most striking plant species. Only 100km from Salta, the park finally obtained official national park status in 1997.

In the absence of forests in the Andean foothills and the puna, the cardón has long been an important source of timber for rafters, doors, window frames and similar uses. As such, it is commonly found in native construction and in the region's colonial churches. According to Argentine writer Federico Kirbus, clusters of cardones can be indicators of archaeological sites; the indigenous people of the puna ate its sweet black seed, which, after passing through the intestinal tract, readily sprouted around their latrines.

Los Cardones is free to enter and still has no visitor services, but there is a ranger in Payogasta, 11km north of Cachi. Make sure you take plenty of water and protection from the sun. Buses between Salta and Cachi will drop you off or pick you up, but verify times. Most people disembark at Valle Encantada, which is generally recognized as the most accessible, picturesque part of the park.

Parque Nacional Baritú

Hugging the Bolivian border in Salta province, Baritú is the northernmost of the three Argentine parks conserving subtropical montane forest. Like Parque Nacional Calilegua and Parque Nacional Finca El Rey, it protects diverse flora and harbors a large number of endangered or threatened mammals, including black howler and capuchin monkeys, the southern river otter, Geoffroy's cat, the jaguar and the Brazilian tapir. The park's emblem is the ardilla roja (yungas forest squirrel), which inhabits the moist montane forest above 1300m. Admission to the park is free and information can be obtained from Parque Nacional Calilegua's headquarters (p236).

It was here, in 1963, that Che Guevara's psychopathic disciple Jorge Ricardo Masetti tried to start the Argentine revolution by infiltrating from Bolivia. At present, the only road access to Baritú is through Bolivia, where southbound travelers from Tarija may inquire about entry via a lateral off the highway that goes to the border station at Bermejo/Aguas Blancas. There are currently no facilities for visitors.

The national parks administration recently accepted the offer of an extra 3200 hectares of land north of the current Baritú border from Techint and Gasoducto Norandino, the companies responsible for the gas pipeline through Calilegua and Baritú parks (see p236).

Parque Nacional Finca El Rey

Confined to a narrow strip no wider than about 50km, Argentina's subtropical humid forests extend from the Bolivian frontier south of Tarija almost to the border between Tucumán and Catamarca provinces. Parque Nacional Finca El Rey, comprising 44,000 hectares almost directly east of Salta, is the southernmost Argentine park protecting this unusual habitat, the most biologically diverse in the country. The park takes its name from the *estancia* (extensive ranch for cattle or sheep) that formerly occupied the area and whose expropriation led to the park's creation.

The park's emblem is the giant toucan, appropriate because of the abundant birdlife, but the mosquito might be just as appropriate (check yourself for ticks, for that matter). Most of the same mammals found in Baritú and Calilegua are also present here. The staff maintain a vehicular nature trail along the Río Popayán and there's a foot trail (actually an abandoned road) to moss-covered **Pozo Verde**, a 2½-hour climb to an area teeming with birdlife. There are also six shorter trails. All trails involve river crossings, so bring some waterproof shoes, or expect to get your feet wet.

Entry to the park is free and the best time to visit is between April and October.

There is free camping at the park's headquarters, in a grassy area with water and pit toilets, but no other infrastructure; there is also a campground at Popayán. The park's comfortable *hostería* (lodging house) has been closed for some time now, but contact the park's **office** (in Salta ☎ 0387-431-2683; España 366, 3rd fl; ☺ 9am-2pm Mon-Fri) for up-to-date information.

As the crow flies, El Rey is only about 100km from Salta, but via paved RN 9, paved but rutted RP 5, and RP 20 it's more than 200km from the provincial capital. There is public transport as far as the junction of RN 9 and RP 5, but even if you can hitch to the second junction, there is little traffic for the last 46km before the park headquarters. The latter road is much improved, but even 4WD vehicles are no sure bet in heavy summer rains. Contact park administration to see about the possibility of getting a ride with park staff, from the first junction, usually on a Friday or Sunday.

THE ANDEAN NORTHWEST

TUCUMÁN & AROUND

Tucumán is Argentina's smallest province, but its size belies its importance. From colonial times, when it was an important way station en route to Potosí, through the early independence period and into the present, Tucumán has played a critical role in the country's political and economic history. In contemporary Argentina, Tucumán means sugar, and while this monoculture has enabled the province to develop secondary industry, it has also created tremendous inequities in wealth and land distribution, as well as ecological problems.

TUCUMÁN

☎ 0381 / pop 833,100 / elevation 420m

Tucumán (formally known as San Miguel de Tucumán), unlike its provincial cousins to the south, is brash, energetic and seductive; it has a real buzz on the streets, particularly in the evening. The impression of this sophisticated city is that it is on the brink of urban greatness. We're not talking Buenos Aires here, but Tucumán is the cradle of Argentine independence and the city proudly wears that label. It has flourished in the past, and given an economic boost, it will probably do so again in the future. Tucumán has a character all of its own with its colonial and 19th-century historical sites, lots of cultural attractions, and the din of the city's many hip café-bars.

History

Founded in 1565, Tucumán and its hinterland were oriented toward Salta and Bolivia for most of the colonial period. Only during and after Argentine independence did Tucumán distinguish itself from the rest of the region. In the culmination of the ferment of the early 19th century, Tucumán hosted the congress that declared Argentine independence in 1816. Dominated by Unitarist merchants, lawyers, soldiers and clergy, the congress accomplished little else; despite a virtual boycott by Federalist factions, it failed to agree on a constitution that would have institutionalized a constitutional monarchy in hopes of attracting European support.

Unlike other colonial cities of the Noroeste, Tucumán successfully reoriented its economy after independence. Modern Tucumán dates from the late 19th century and owes its importance to location; at the southern end of the frost-free zone of sugarcane production, it was just close enough to Buenos Aires to take advantage of access to the federal capital's growing market. By 1874 a railroad connected Tucumán with Córdoba, permitting easy transport of sugar, and local and British capital contributed to the industry's growth.

Orientation

Tucumán's geographical focus is the rectangular Plaza Independencia, site of major public buildings like the Casa de Gobierno; street names change north and south of Av 24 de Setiembre, west of Av Alem/Mitre and east of Av Avellaneda/Sáenz Peña.

Information

BOOKSTORES

El Ateneo (25 de Mayo 182) A good example of Tucumán's sophistication. It's a combination of a bookstore and a café – you won't find many cities up this way hosting such a creation. El Ateneo has books in English and Spanish, and plenty of maps of the region.

CULTURAL CENTERS

Alianza Francesa (☎ 421-9651; aftucuman@arnet .com.ar; Mendoza 257; ⊙ 5-9:30pm Mon-Fri) **Centro Cultural Dr Alberto Rougués** (☎ 422-7976; Laprida 31; entry US$1; ⊙ 8:30am-12:30pm & 4:30-9pm Mon-Fri, 10:30am-12:30pm & 6:30-8:30pm Sat) Has rotating exhibits of provincial painters.
Centro Cultural Eugenio Flavio Virela (Universidad Nacional de Tucumán) (☎ 421-6024; 25 de Mayo 265) To learn what's happening in town, visit this center, a respite from the noisy downtown streets. It has exhibitions, an auditorium and a small café. There are also crafts for sale.

INTERNET ACCESS

There are plenty of Internet cafés dotted around town, all varying in connection speed and price. Two of the cheapest (US$0.30 per hour) with good connections:
Tucumán Cybercenter (San Juan 612; ⊙ 9am-11pm Mon-Sat, 6-11pm Sun)
Web City (Mendoza 383)

MONEY

There are several exchange houses on San Martín between Maipú and Junín.
Maguitur (San Martín 765; ⊙ 8:30am-2pm & 4-6:30pm Mon-Fri, 10am-noon Sat) Cashes traveler's checks for a 1.25%

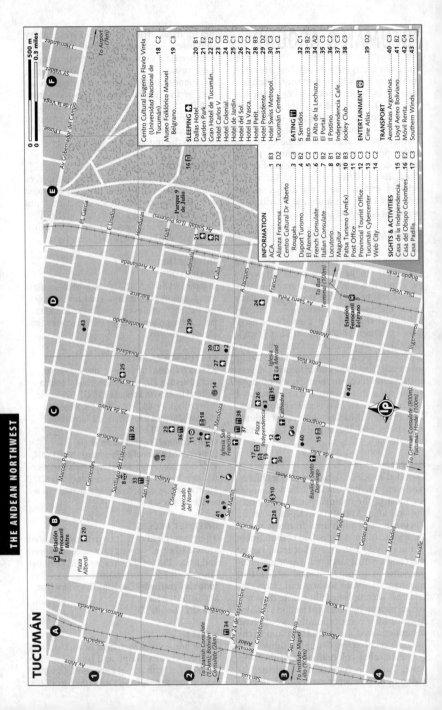

TUCUMÁN

THE ANDEAN NORTHWEST

INFORMATION	
ACA.................................	1 B3
Alianza Francesca..............	2 D2
Centro Cultural Dr Alberto	
Rougués............................	3 C3
Duport Turismo..................	4 B2
El Ateneo...........................	5 C3
French Consulate................	6 C3
Italian Consulate................	7 B2
Locutorio...........................	8 B1
Maguitur............................	9 B2
Patsa Turismo (AmEx)........	10 B3
Post Office.........................	11 C3
Provincial Tourist Office.....	12 C3
Tucumán Cybercenter.........	13 C2
Web City............................	14 C2

SIGHTS & ACTIVITIES	
Casa de la Independencia....	15 C3
Casa del Obispo Colombres..	16 E2
Casa Padilla......................	17 C3

Centro Cultural Eugenio Flavio Virela	
(Universidad Nacional de	
Tucumán)...........................	18 C2
Museo Folklórico Manuel	
Belgrano............................	19 C3

SLEEPING 🏠	
Dallas Hotel.......................	20 B1
Garden Park.......................	21 E2
Gran Hotel de Tucumán.......	22 E2
Hotel Carlos V....................	23 C2
Hotel Colonial....................	24 D3
Hotel de Jardin...................	25 C1
Hotel del Sol......................	26 C3
Hotel la Vasca....................	27 C2
Hotel Petit.........................	28 B3
Hotel Presidente.................	29 C3
Hotel Swiss Metropol..........	30 C3
Tucumán Center..................	31 C2

EATING 🍴	
5 Sentidos.........................	32 C1
Baco..................................	33 B2
El Alto de la Lechuza..........	34 A2
El Portal............................	35 C2
Il Postino...........................	36 C3
Independencia Cafe............	37 C3
Jockey Club.......................	38 C3

ENTERTAINMENT 🎭	
Cine Atlas..........................	39 D2

TRANSPORT	
Aerolíneas Argentinas........	40 C3
Lloyd Aereo Boliviano........	41 B2
Móvil Renta.......................	42 C4
Southern Winds..................	43 C3

commission with a US$5 minimum exchange. Many downtown banks have ATMs.

POST
Post office (cnr Córdoba & 25 de Mayo)

TELEPHONE
Locutoria (Maipú 360; ☸ 24hr)

TOURIST INFORMATION
ACA (☎ 431-1522; Crisóstomo Álvarez 901)
Information office (Brígido Terán 350) At the bus terminal.
Provincial tourist office (☎ 430-3644; 24 de Setiembre 484, on Plaza Independencia; ☸ 8am-10pm Mon-Fri, 9am-9:30pm Sat & Sun)

TRAVEL AGENCIES
Duport Turismo (☎ 422-0000; duporttur@tucbbs.com.ar; Mendoza 720, Local 3) Offers city tours (US$20) and excursions to Tafí del Valle (US$20); for another US$10, the Tafí trip can include the ruins at Quilmes.
Patsa Turismo (☎ 421-6806; Chacabuco 38) The Amex representative, but does not exchange currency.

Sights

CASA PADILLA
Alongside the Casa de Gobierno, this partly restored mid-19th-century house first belonged to provincial governor José Frías (1792–1874), then to his mayor son-in-law Ángel Padilla and to the latter's son. A display of European art and period furniture make up the collection housed by the **museum** (25 de Mayo 36; admission US$1; ☸ 9:30am-12:30pm & 4:30-7:30pm Mon-Fri, 9am-noon Sat).

CASA DE LA INDEPENDENCIA
(CASA HISTORICAL)
Unitarist lawyers and clerics (Federalists boycotted the meeting) declared Argentina's independence from Spain on July 9, 1816, in this dazzlingly whitewashed late-colonial **house** (☎ 431-0826; Congreso 151; admission US$2; ☸ 9am-1pm & 4-6pm Mon-Fri, 9am-1pm Sat & Sun). Portraits of the signatories line the walls of the room where the declaration was signed.

The interior patio is a pleasant refuge from Tucumán's bustle. The house is 1½ blocks south of Plaza Independencia. There's a light-and-sound show nightly except Thursday at 8:30pm; entry is US$2.60/1 per adult/child.

MUSEO FOLKLÓRICO MANUEL BELGRANO
Occupying a colonial house that once belonged to the family of Bishop José Eusebio

Colombres, a major figure in the independence movement who also fostered local sugar cultivation, is this pleasant and interesting **museum** (☎ 421-8250; 24 de Setiembre 565). It has been closed for renovation for some time, though the items are stored in the provincial tourist office and can be seen there. The collection features a good collection of Río de la Plata horse gear, indigenous musical instruments and weavings, Toba wood carvings, Quilmes pottery and samples of *randa* (an intricate lace resembling Paraguayan *ñanduti*) from the village of Monteros, 53km south of Tucumán. Some items are for sale.

CASA DEL OBISPO COLOMBRES
In the center of Parque 9 de Julio (formerly Bishop Colombres' El Bajo plantation), this 18th-century **house** (admission free; ☸ 8am-noon & 4-8pm) has the first ox-powered *trapiche* (sugar mill) of Tucumán's post-independence industry. Guided tours, in Spanish, explain the operation of the mill, some of whose equipment is still in working order.

INSTITUTO MIGUEL LILLO
Life-size replicas of dinosaurs and other fossils from San Juan's Parque Provincial Ischigualasto populate the garden of this **natural history museum** (☎ 423-4127; Miguel Lillo 251; admission free; ☸ 9am-noon & 3-6pm Mon-Fri).

Activities
The staff at the provincial tourist office have information on a variety of outdoor activities. Trekking and hiking are popular in the Sierra de Aconquija; one well-liked excursion is the four-day hike to Tafí del Valle. Readers have enthusiastically recommended **Héctor Heredia** (☎ 422-6205; fax 430-2222; Balcarce 1067) as a mountain guide for the Sierra, Tafí del Valle and surrounding areas. Héctor (also known as 'El Oso' or 'the Bear') can arrange extended treks in the provinces of Tucumán and Catamarca, and gives a good explanation of what to expect in advance.

Festivals & Events
Celebrations of **Día de la Independencia** (Argentina's Independence Day) on July 9 are especially vigorous in Tucumán, the cradle of the country's independence. *Tucumanos* also celebrate the **Batalla de Tucumán** (Battle of Tucumán) on September 24.

Sleeping

The cheapest places to stay are near the old bus terminal, but are pretty shabby. The area around Plaza Alberdi and the Ferrocarril Mitre has experienced something of a revival in recent years, with upgraded but still reasonably priced accommodations and restaurants.

BUDGET

Hotel Petit (☎ 421-3902; Crisóstomo Álvarez 765; s/d US$4/7) With a maze of leafy patios, this place is definitely the best budget hotel in town. Rooms with shared bathroom are cheaper, but paying a bit more will get you cable TV as well.

Hotel La Vasca (☎ 421-1288; Mendoza 289; s/d US$6/8) Another good budget choice, the La Vasca's rooms have classy hardwood furniture and face a pretty courtyard. Bathrooms are aging, but well maintained.

MIDRANGE

Hotel Presidente (☎ 431-1414; www.tucuman /hotelpresidente in Spanish; Monteguado 249; s/d US$27/34; P ❌ ❷) A modern, comfortable hotel near the center, the Presidente is perhaps the best hotel in this price range. Some would say that two swimming pools are excessive, but that's just the way they do things in this town.

Hotel de Jardin (☎ 431-0500; www.hoteljar din.com.ar in Spanish; Las Piedras 463; s/d US$24/33; P ❌ ❷ ❷) In a central location and with all the amenities, the Jardin offers very good value. Rooms here are unrenovated, but pleasant, with plenty of dark wood paneling.

Garden Park (☎ 431-0700; www.gardenparkhotel .com.ar; Av Soldati 330; s/d US$33/40; P ❌ ❷) With spacious rooms and great views overlooking the park, this place is a bargain if you've got the pesos to spend. Mostly set

---

THE AUTHOR'S CHOICE

Tucumán Hostel (☎ 420-1584; www.tucuman hostel.com.ar; Buenos Aires 669; dm with/without HI card US$3.50/4.50; P ❷) By far the best of Tucumán's hostels. Set in a beautifully redone old building with a fully equipped kitchen, good common areas and bar. Guests are eligible for discounts at restaurants and bars around town.

---

up for businesspeople, it also makes a very comfortable place to stay for your average Joe or Joanne.

Grand Hotel de Tucumán (☎ 450-2250; www .grandhotel.com.ar; Av Soldati 380; s/d US$35/43; P ❌ ❷ ❷) Once Tucumán's finest, the Grand is slipping a bit with the arrival of the newcomers. Still, it offers all the comforts, great park views and an excellent buffet breakfast.

Hotel del Sol (☎ 431-1755; www.hoteldelsol.com.ar; Las Piedras 35; s/d US$30/40; P ❌) The Sol offers comfortable rooms right on the plaza. The place has been pretty much untouched since the '70s, and is looking a bit frayed, but you can't beat the location.

Hotel Colonial (☎ 422-2738; San Martín 35; s/d US$15/22; P ❌) Got a hankering for that 70s hacienda meets Burt Reynolds porn palace vibe? The Colonial's the place for you. Rooms are spacious enough, but the bathrooms are a bit cramped.

Dallas Hotel (☎ 421-8500; dallashotel@arnet.com.ar; Corrientes 980; s/d US$19/25; P ❌) Good-sized rooms and a relaxed, comfortable atmosphere make the Dallas a good choice in this price range. Discounts are available if you pay cash or stay for a few days.

Hotel Carlos V (☎ 431-1666; 25 de Mayo 330; s/d US$22/27; P ❌) A classic ambience, good restaurant and central location are this hotel's big drawcards. Otherwise, rooms can be a bit cramped. Ask to see a few.

TOP END

Tucumán Center (☎ 452-5555; www.tucumancenter hotel.com.ar; 25 de Mayo 230; s/d US$50/60; P ❌ ❷) By far the finest hotel in the center, the Tucumán is modern and well appointed. It offers big discounts in the off-season and when you pay in cash.

Swiss Hotel Metropol (☎ 431-1180; www.swiss hotelmetropol.com.ar; 24 de Setiembre 524; s/d US$40/50; P ❌ ❷ ❷) The modern rooms and spacious bathrooms on offer here are perhaps slightly offset by the tiny balconies (standing room only). The fantastic rooftop pool makes up for a lot, though.

Eating

Independencia Café (☎ 430-3588; cnr 25 de Mayo & San Martín; breakfast US$1.70, meals US$3-4; ❤ breakfast, lunch & dinner) Try this busy little place, with its rushed service, for good breakfasts or a midday snack.

THE AUTHOR'S CHOICE

5 Sentidos (☎ 431-2569; Muñecas 491; ☺ 9am-1pm & 4-9pm) One of the surprisingly few '*mate* bars' operating in the country, the 5 Senses gives you a chance to sample the national obsession with the tea-like beverage without having to invest in the necessary hardware yourself. Also on offer are local arts and crafts and a range of tempting homemade pastries.

El Portal (☎ 422-6024; 24 de Setiembre; mains US$3-10) Half a block east of Plaza Independencia, this rustic indoor/outdoor eatery has a tiny (like six items) menu, but is an excellent place to try regional specialties like *locro* and *humitas*.

Jockey Club (☎ 4251038; San Martín 451; set lunch US$4) Don't let the old-time elegance, marble staircases and huge gilt-edged mirrors fool you – the set lunches here are a real bargain.

Il Postino (☎ 421-0440; cnr 25 de Mayo & Córdoba; mains US$4-6) Pizza and pasta are served with panache in this old atmospheric warehouse eatery. Get here early on weekends because it's very popular. Possibly the best pizzas in this part of Argentina.

Baco (☎ 15-572-0091; Catamarca 605; tapas $1-2, mains $3-5; ☺ dinner Tue-Sun) Part of Tucumán's tapas bar explosion, Baco has an intimate atmosphere, a fine wine list and live entertainment on Saturdays.

El Alto de la Lechuza (☎ 400-7171; 24 de Setiembre 1199; dishes US$2-5; ☺ dinner Wed-Sun) Founded in 1939 and billing itself as Argentina's oldest *peña*, this place offers the standard *parrilla* and pasta fare as well as a few regional specialties. The real reason to come here, though, is the music; the venue has hosted such greats as Mercedes Sosa and Tito Segura.

Getting There & Away

AIR

Aerolíneas Argentinas (☎ 431-1030; 9 de Julio 110) and **Southern Winds** (☎ 421-1410; Marcos Paz 194) both have daily flights to Buenos Aires' Aeroparque airport (US$110). **Lloyd Aéreo Boliviano** (LAB; ☎ 422-3030; San Martín 667, 4th fl) flies on Wednesday, Friday and Saturday to Santa Cruz, Bolivia (US$185), from Salta.

BUS

Tucumán's sparkling **bus terminal** (☎ 422-2221; Brígido Terán 350) is a major public-works project with 60 platforms, a post office, telephone services, a supermarket, bars and restaurants. Inside the complex, Shopping del Jardín's **information booth** (☎ 430-6400, 430-2060; ☺ 6:30am-11:30pm) provides information on the bus station and the shopping center only.

The following table lists sample destinations and fares from Tucumán.

Destination	Cost	Duration (hr)
Amaichá del Valle	6	4
Buenos Aires	30	16
Cafayate	26	5½
Catamarca	8.50	4
Córdoba	10	8
Jujuy	7	4
La Rioja	7	6
Mar del Plata	20	24
Mendoza	20	13
Neuquén	37	18
Pocitos	11	8
Posadas	20	18
Resistencia	16	2
Río Gallegos	77	40
Salta	8	4½
San Juan	15	12
San Martín	45	30
Santiago (Chile)	30	23
Santiago del Estero	3	2
Tafí del Valle	5	3
Termas de Río Hondo	2	1
Trelew	47	21

Getting Around

Aeropuerto Internacional Benjamín Matienzo (☎ 426-4906) is situated 8km east of downtown via Av Gobernador del Campo, which is the northern boundary of Parque 9 de Julio. Empresa 120 Alderete operates airport minibuses (US$0.50) that leave from the bus terminal every 20 minutes during the day.

For getting around the city, keep in mind that the buses here do not accept cash, so you will need to purchase *cospeles* (tokens; US$0.30) from the downtown kiosks; *cospeles* are less readily available elsewhere in the city.

If you want to rent a car, try **Móvil Renta** (☎ 431-0550; San Lorenzo 370).

THE ANDEAN NORTHWEST

AROUND TUCUMÁN

Until 1767 the ruins of **San José de Lules**, 20km south of Tucumán, was a Jesuit *reducción* (Indian settlement created by Spanish missionaries) among the region's Lule Indians. After the Jesuits' expulsion, the Dominicans assumed control of the complex, whose present ruins date from the 1880s and once served as a school. The small museum has replicas of colonial documents and a plethora of busts of various Argentine independence heroes. There are numerous ghost stories about the place, and legends of buried Jesuit treasure.

To get to Lules, a pleasant site for an afternoon outing, take the El Provincial bus from downtown Tucumán.

TAFÍ DEL VALLE

☎ 03867 / pop 3070 / elevation 2100m
About 100km northeast of Tucumán the narrow gorge of the Río de los Sosas, with its dense, verdant subtropical forest on all sides, opens onto a misty valley beneath the snowy peaks of the Sierra del Aconquija. The precipitous mountain road (RN 38 to RP 307) from Tucumán to Tafí del Valle is a spectacular trip and well worth staying awake for on the bus.

When the summer heat drives *tucumanos* out of the provincial capital, they seek refuge in the cool heights around the hill station of Tafí del Valle, whose population can swell to 15,000 or more at this time of year. The town makes a pleasant stopover with some good hiking opportunities, although it's probably best avoided at the height of summer.

Orientation

Av Miguel Critto is the main street running east to west. If you turn left out of the bus terminal, onto Av Miguel Critto, walk about 200m and turn left again, you will be heading into the center of town. Juan de Perón runs south off Critto just before the plaza; most places to eat are along here, as well as souvenir shops and a couple of places to stay. Most public services are on or near the Centro Cívico, which features an unusual semicircular plaza.

Information

Banco de la Provincia (Centro Cívico) Changes US dollars cash. Long-distance telephones are also here.

Casa del Turista (Av Miguel Critto; ⏱ 8am-6pm) Tourist information near the plaza.

Sights & Activities

CAPILLA LA BANDA

This 18th-century **Jesuit chapel** (☎ 421685; Av José Frías Silva; admission US$1; ⏱ 8am-10pm summer, 8am-6pm winter), acquired by the Frías Silva family of Tucumán on the Jesuits' expulsion and then expanded in the 1830s, was restored to its original configuration in the 1970s. Note the escape tunnel in the chapel. A small archaeological collection consisting mostly of funerary urns, but also religious art of the Cuzco school, ecclesiastical vestments and period furniture that once belonged to the Frías Silvas is on display in the **museum** next door.

The chapel is a short distance south of downtown. Cross the bridge over the Río Tafí del Valle then follow the road around to the right onto José Silva. Turn left onto the third dirt road along the left-hand side of José Silva. The chapel is a little way along.

HIKING

Several nearby peaks and destinations make hiking in the mountains around Tafí del Valle an attractive prospect; try 3000m **Cerro El Matadero**, a four- to five-hour climb; 3800m **Cerro Pabellón** (six hours); and 4600m **Cerro El Negrito**, reached from the statue of Cristo Redentor on RN 307 to Acheral. The village of La Ciénaga is about seven hours away. The trails are badly marked, and no trail maps are available. You can hire a guide for about US$3 an hour. Ask for more information at Casa del Turista.

Guaypo Excursiones (☎ 421477; Peatonal los Faroles s/n) offers guided walks to nearby waterfalls and other scenic locations. They charge US$20 for a half-day trip, regardless of group size, so you might want to get a gang together.

Sleeping

Hotel Tafí (☎ 421007; www.hoteltafi.com.ar in Spanish; Belgrano 177; s/d US$18/22; P ⏼) With a slick alpine ski-lodge feel, the Tafí is a very good deal at these prices. Rooms are medium-sized, and the huge fireplace makes the comfortable lounge area the place to be on a chilly night.

Hostel la Cumbre (☎ 421768; Perón 120; www .turismoentucuman.com/lacumbrehostel in Spanish; s/d with shared bathroom US$4/8) These basic rooms set around a cheery courtyard are the pick of the bunch of Tafí's budget places. The owner has loads of information on tours and hikes in the area and there's a cozy TV room.

Hostería Huayra Puca (☎ 421190; www.huayrapuca.com.ar in Spanish; Menhires 71; s/d US$20/23; ☐) Set in a light and airy building of interesting design, this place offers comfortable, good-sized rooms. Multilingual staff, loads of local information and transfers to and from Tucumán are other bonuses.

La Rosada Hostería (☎ 421323; cnr Belgrano & Peatonal los Faroles; s/d US$22/25) Peaceful and simple but well decorated, the Rosada offers good value. Rooms are huge, with terracotta tiled floors, and the breakfast buffet is enough to keep you going all day.

Hostería del ACA (☎ /fax 421027; cnr Gobernador Campero & San Martín; s/d ACA members US$27/34, nonmembers US$34/40) The biggest hotel in town offers clean, modern (if slightly soulless) rooms with huge bathrooms. Those at the front have excellent views out over town and down the valley.

Autocamping del Sauce (☎ 421084; sites/cabañas per person US$2/3) Tafí's campground, to the west of the town center, is acceptable at this price, but toilets and showers are very run-down, although the grounds are well kept. Shade is limited (a lesser problem in overcast Tafí than elsewhere in the country). Bunks in small *cabañas* are available, but these would be claustrophobic at their maximum capacity of four people.

Eating & Drinking

El Rancho de Félix (☎ 421022; cnr Belgrano & Juan de Perón; mains US$3-5) A big warm barn of a place that's incredibly popular for lunch. Regional specialties like *locro* and *humitas* feature heavily on the menu, but *parrilla* and pasta are also on offer.

Don Pepino (Juan de Perón; mains US$3-5) The coziest of the *parrilla* options, usually featuring live entertainment at most mealtimes. If you've been hanging out to try *chivo a la parrilla* (barbecued goat), this is probably the place to do it.

Bar El Paraíso (☎ 1558-75179; Juan de Perón 176; sandwiches US$1-2.50, mains US$2-4) This bar is where locals congregate to dine cheaply and watch Seagal or Stallone videos. There is a pleasant patio overlooking Juan de Perón.

THE AUTHOR'S CHOICE

Hostería Lunahuana (☎ /fax 421330; www.lunahuana.com.ar; Av Miguel Critto 540; s/d US$30/40; ℗ ⊠) The best hotel in town and one of the most attractive in the region. Rooms sleep three comfortably, with mezzanines accessed by spiral staircases. The whole place is decked out with interesting and tasteful decorations. A bargain.

There's a cozy bar at the bus terminal, good for whiling away a few hours before your next bus.

Getting There & Away

Tafí's new **bus terminal** (☎ 421031; Miguel Critto), near the corner of Av Juan Calchaquí, is about 600m east of the town center. Empresa Aconquija has eight buses a day to Tucumán (US$3, three hours). Buses heading the other way, direct to Cafayate, leave twice a day (US$6, four hours). Buses to Amaichá del Valle and Quilmes are US$2.50 and US$4, respectively.

Beyond Tafí the paved road zigzags over the 3050m pass known as Abra del Infiernillo (Little Hell Pass), an alternative route to Cafayate and Salta, passing the impressive Diaguita ruins at Quilmes.

Getting Around

Hourly in summer (every three hours in winter), local Aconquija buses do most of the circuit around Cerro El Pelado, in the middle of the valley. One goes on the north side, another on the south side, so it's possible to make a circuit of the valley by walking the link between them.

TERMAS DE RÍO HONDO

☎ 03858 / pop 27,700 / elevation 270m

Termas de Río Hondo's main attraction is its thermal springs, and even the most basic accommodations have hot mineral baths. Very much a destination for Argentine tourists, Río Hondo is not as interesting for international visitors. That being said, at least out of season you'll be comfortable at bargain-basement prices, as competition between hotels is hot, making it a decent spot to overnight.

The restaurant scene in Río Hondo is also pretty good, and if you're partial to sweet substances the many shops selling excellent chocolates around town will not disappoint. If you're getting truly desperate you could consider the small tourist train that does two-hour laps of the town for US$2.

The town has two unusual features: it has a triangular Plaza San Martín as well as one of the country's few public monuments to Juan and Evita Perón.

Outside town, the 30,000-hectare Dique Frontal is a reservoir used for water sports such as swimming, boating, fishing and windsurfing (see Getting Around, opposite).

Information

El Frontal de Río Hondo, the town's weekly newspaper, publishes a 24-page supplement (US$1) full of information about thermal baths.

Banco de la Nación (Caseros) Does foreign exchange, but don't expect to change traveler's checks.

Hospital Rural (☎ 421578; cnr Antonio Taboada & Buenos Aires) West of downtown.

Locutorios (Rivadavaria) There are several *locutorios*, including this one, which have Internet access for US$0.30.

Municipal tourist office (☎ 422143; Caseros 132, btwn Rivadavia & Sarmiento; ☺ 6:30am-12:30pm & 3-9pm) Helpful tourist office.

Post office (Av Alberdi, btwn 9 de Julio & Maipú)

Sleeping

Most of Río Hondo's hotels close in summer, but a few remain open. Prices nearly halve in the off-season.

Hotel Los Pinos (☎ 421043; www.lospinoshotel.com .ar in Spanish; Maipú 201; d colonial/Americano US$68/89; ☒ ☒ ☒) This four-star property is in the most attractive building in town. The pool is huge, and you can also count on a sauna, gymnasium and tennis courts.

Grand City Hotel (☎ 421028; Belgrano 245; s/d US$10/20; ☒) A traditional hotel overlooking the park, the Grand has comfortable rooms with spacious bathrooms and a relaxed pool area shaded by a big old palm tree.

El Hostal del Abuelo (☎ 421489; www.elhostaldel abuelo.com.ar in Spanish; San Francisco Solano 168; s/d US$53/80; ☒) Terma's snootiest hotel packs it all in: gym, shopping center and two restaurants. Rooms are as luxurious and spacious as you'd expect, but the smallish swimming pool can get a bit crowded when they have a full house.

Casino Center Hotel (☎/fax 421346; www.spa .hoteltermalcasinocenter.com in Spanish; Caseros 126; s/d US$23/37) Friendly and exhibiting a warm '70s decor, this hotel is very handy if you want to have a flutter at the casino across the road. There's an indoor pool, but the outdoor one is definitely one of the biggest and best in town.

Hotel Semi Ramus (☎ 421416; Caserois 303; s/d US$10/20; ☒ ☒) A short walk from the center, the Ramis offers reasonable value for the price and changes the water in its pool regularly, which is a plus in this town.

Along the river, several campgrounds near downtown charge around US$2 for a site: **Camping Mirador** (☎ 421392), **Camping del Río** (☎ 421985) and **Camping La Olla** (☎ 423157).

Eating

A short stroll around town will reveal a plethora of eateries; here are a few favorites.

S'kala (cnr Sarmiento & Caseros; meals $US3-4; ☺ breakfast, lunch & dinner) A restaurant-cum-café-cum-bar, S'kala has modern decor and is a good sunny spot for breakfast in the morning – coffee and *medialunas* (croissant) US$1 – or cocktails in the evening.

La Casa de Ruben (☎ 421265; Sarmiento 69; mains US$4-5; ☺ breakfast, lunch & dinner) Ruben's House gets no points whatsoever for atmosphere, but the quality of the food, size of the servings and reasonable prices make this a popular option any time of the year.

Express (☎ 423323; Rivadavia 170; mains $2-5) A pleasantly cool and dark place with an army of overhead fans working overtime to keep the air circulating. The menu runs the gamut of meats, pastas and excellent pizzas, and the place packs out later at night when it converts into a bar.

Giovanni Cremas Heladas has a couple of outlets around town, including one located on Rivadavia. Head here to sample Río Hondo's best ice cream. For those with an even sweeter tooth, head for La Bombonerie; if you get out of this place without a bag of chocolates, then you did better than most.

Getting There & Away

The **bus terminal** (☎ 421513; Las Heras btwn España & 12 de Octubre) is half-a-dozen blocks west of the plaza and two blocks north of Av Alberdi. The following is a list of sample destinations and fares.

Destination	Cost (US$)	Duration (hr)
Buenos Aires	17	15
Córdoba	8	7
Jujuy	7	5
La Plata	17	16½
La Rioja	5	6
Mar del Plata	30	21
Mendoza	18	10
Paraná	19	9
Rosario	13	10
Salta	8	5
San Juan	15	9
Santa Fe	18	11
Santiago del Estero	1.50	1
Tucumán	2	1

Getting Around

Empresa 4 de Junio (☎ 421826) goes to the Dique Frontal for US$0.40. Catch it downtown along RN 9 or Av Juan de Perón.

SANTIAGO DEL ESTERO

☎ 0385 / pop 420,600 / elevation 200m

In many respects Santiago del Estero is a stopover place, receiving visitors looking to break their journey between Buenos Aires and Salta. The city itself, however, is pleasant with some good cafés and interesting colonial buildings and museums. It holds an important place in Argentine history as the 'Madre de Ciudades' (Mother of Cities). Founded in 1553, it was Spain's first urban settlement in what is now Argentina, and for centuries it was an important stopover between the Pampas and the mines of Bolivia.

If you're looking to just relax for a few days or take a longer break, Catamarca is probably a bit more attractive, while nearby Tucumán is far more exciting.

Orientation

Reflecting its early settlement, Santiago's urban plan is fairly irregular. The town center is Plaza Libertad, from which Av Libertad, trending southwest to northeast, bisects the city. North and south of the plaza, Av Independencia and the pedestrian mall Av Tucumán are important commercial areas, but Av Belgrano, which crosses Av Libertad and parallels Tucumán/Independencia, is the main thoroughfare. Belgrano divides into Norte (North) and Sur (South) on either side of Av Rivadavia. Street names change either side of Avs Libertad and Belgrano.

Information

Several downtown banks have ATMs.

ACA (☎ 421-2270; cnr Av Sáenz Peña & Belgrano)

Alianza Francesa (☎ 4228865; Independencia 341)

Banco Galicia (Avellaneda) The best place to try changing traveler's checks (and cash) is this place opposite Plaza Liberta.

Cybernauta (Independencia; per hr US$0.50; ⏰ 24hr) Internet access; Close to the corner of Mitre.

Intijet (☎ 422-7534; 24 de Setiembre 249) Should be able to help with travel arrangements in the province.

Provincial tourist office (☎ 421-4243, 0800-450016; Av Libertad 417; ⏰ 7:30am-1:30pm & 3-8pm Mon-Fri, 9:30am-12:30pm & 3:30-8:30pm Sat & Sun) Besides providing visitor information, this helpful office displays work by local artists. It's opposite Plaza Libertad.

Sights & Activities

MUSEO WAGNER DE CIENCIAS ANTROPOLÓGICAS Y NATURALES

The city's natural-history and archaeological **museum** (☎ 421-1380; Avellaneda 355; admission free; ⏰ 7:30am-1:30pm & 2-8pm Mon-Fri, 10am-noon Sat) was founded by two French archaeologist brothers. The exhibits are chronologically arranged and splendidly displayed, focusing on fossils, funerary urns (owls and snakes are recurring motifs) and Chaco ethnography. A new section has been added, detailing dinosaur fossil discoveries in the region. A friendly staff offers free guided tours when they have time.

PARQUE AGUIRRE

Named for the city's founder and only 10 blocks from Plaza Libertad, this enormous park has a small **zoo**, camping areas, a swimming pool (when the erratic Río Dulce provides sufficient water) and – be alert! – a drivers' training center operated by ACA.

Festivals & Events

Santiago's chaotic **Carnaval**, in February, resembles celebrations in the Quebrada de Humahuaca. During the entire last week of July, *santiaguinos* (people who live in Santiago del Estero) celebrate the **founding of the city**.

Sleeping

BUDGET

Residencial Emaus (☎ 421-5893; Av Moreno Sur 675; s/d US$7/10) With its light and airy rooms with TV, the Emaus is definitely the pick of the budget bunch located around the bus terminal.

THE ANDEAN NORTHWEST

Hotel Palace (☎ 421-2701; palacehotel@volsinsectis .com.ar; Tucumán 19; s/d US$10/15) A semimodern hotel that's starting to fray around the edges, the Palace is still a reasonable deal. Interior rooms could be better ventilated, but the ones at the front are noisier.

Campamento las Casuarinas (☎ 421-1390; Parque Aguirre; sites per person US$1) This municipal campground is normally a pleasant, shady and secure area, less than 1km from Plaza Libertad, but it can be oppressively crowded and deafeningly noisy on weekends.

MIDRANGE

Nuevo Hotel Bristol (☎ 421-8387; Av Moreno Sur 677; s/d US$15/25; 🗙 🖵 🔊) For a little more com-

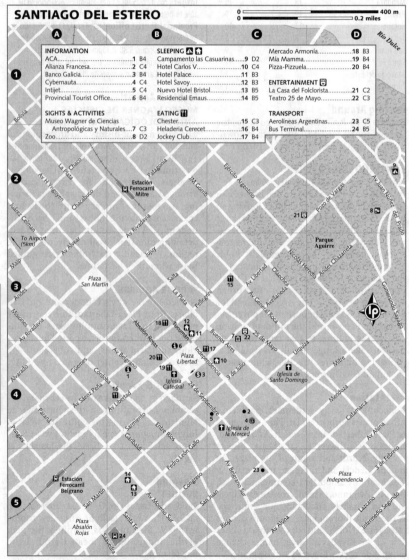

SANTIAGO DEL ESTERO

INFORMATION		SLEEPING			Mercado Armonía	18	B3
ACA	1 B4	Campamento las Casuarinas	9	D2	Mía Mamma	19	B4
Alianza Francesa	2 C4	Hotel Carlos V	10	C4	Pizza-Pizzuela	20	B4
Banco Galicia	3 B4	Hotel Palace	11	B3			
Cybernauta	4 C4	Hotel Savoy	12	B3	ENTERTAINMENT		
Intijet	5 C4	Nuevo Hotel Bristol	13	B5	La Casa del Folclorista	21	C2
Provincial Tourist Office	6 B4	Residencial Emaus	14	B5	Teatro 25 de Mayo	22	C3
SIGHTS & ACTIVITIES		EATING			TRANSPORT		
Museo Wagner de Ciencias		Chester	15	C3	Aerolíneas Argentinas	23	C5
Antropológicas y Naturales	7 C3	Heladeria Cerecet	16	B4	Bus Terminal	24	B5
Zoo	8 D2	Jockey Club	17	B4			

fort close to the bus terminal, you could try this place; rooms are spacious and modern with generously sized bathrooms. Try to get one with an exterior window – the inside ones can get stuffy.

Hotel Savoy (☎ 421-1234; fax 421-1235; www.savoy santiago.com.ar in Spanish; Tucumán 39; s/d US$10/17; P 🔀) The eye-popping grandeur of the facade and lobby of this place make up for the fairly ordinary rooms. Still, this is good value, smack in the middle of town.

TOP END

Hotel Carlos V (☎ 424-0303; hotelcarlosv@arnet.com .ar; Independencia 110; s/d US$33/38; junior ste US$67; presidential ste US$83; P 🔀 🖭) By far the most luxurious option in town, the regular rooms here are plush, but go for the upgrade if you really want to spoil yourself. Rooms with a balcony have great city and plaza views.

Eating

Mía Mamma (☎ 429-9715; 24 de Setiembre 15; mains US$3-6) Tastefully decorated and with service that's almost overly attentive, this Italian/ Argentine restaurant right on the plaza is one of the best places to eat in town.

Chester (☎ 422-4972; cnr Pelligrini & Av General Roca; mains US$3-5) With decor like that of a British pub, the Chester offers good-quality, filling serves of all the Argentine standards. After midnight, the place turns into a bar, fills up with drinkers and the party really starts.

Pizza-Pizzuela (☎ 424-1392; Absalón Rojas 78; pizzas US$3-5) This central pizzeria serves up no-fuss food that is quick and hot. If you're not that hungry, it does *pizzetas* (minipizzas) for about US$1.50.

Jockey Club (☎ 421-7518; Independencia 68; mains US$3-5) For fine dining right on the square, check this place out. You don't even have to be short to get in. A fairly standard range of dishes, but set meals (US$4) are a bargain.

Heladería Cerecet (cnr Av Libertad & Córdoba) This *heladería* has some of the best ice cream in Santiago del Estero, served in drab, no-nonsense surroundings. A double cone will cost you US$1.

Mercado Armonía (Tucumán, btwn Pelligrini & Salta) Santiago's market is cheap, but less appealing than some Argentine markets.

Entertainment

La Casa del Folclorista (Pozo de Vargas, Parque Aguirre; entry US$2) To the east of town, this is a big barn

of a place that has live folk bands some evenings, and a bargain *parrilla libre* for US$2. The music tends to kick off around 11pm.

Teatro 25 de Mayo (☎ 421-4141) In the same building as the Palacio Legislativo is Teatro 25 de Mayo, Santiago's prime theater venue.

Getting There & Away

AIR

Aerolíneas Argentinas (☎ 422-4335; 24 de Septiembre 547) flies daily to Buenos Aires (US$100).

BUS

Santiago's aging **bus terminal** (☎ 421-3746; cnr Pedro León Gallo & Saavedra) is eight blocks southwest of Plaza Libertad. Below are sample destinations and fares to all parts of the country.

Destination	Cost (US$)	Duration (hr)
Bahía Blanca	35	20
Bariloche	61	31
Buenos Aires	20	13
Catamarca	6	4½
Córdoba	8	6
Corrientes	13	9
Jujuy	9	7
La Rioja	9	12
Mar del Plata	23	19
Mendoza	23	17
Neuquén	49	22
Paraná	27	9½
Pocitos	13	13
Resistencia	13	8
Río Gallegos	74	44
Roque Sáenz Peña	10	6
Rosario	15	10
Salta	12	7
San Juan	20	16
Santa Fe	16	7½
Santa Rosa	24	15
Termas de Río Hondo	1.50	1
Tucumán	3	2

Getting Around

Bus No 15 goes to **Aeropuerto Mal Paso** (☎ 434-0337; Av Madre de Ciudades), situated 6km southwest of downtown. A taxi from the city center costs US$2.

Central Santiago del Estero is compact and walking suffices for almost everything except connections to the train station and the airport. If you're weary, a taxi just about anywhere around town should cost less than US$1.

CATAMARCA & LA RIOJA

Among modern Argentina's provinces, remote La Rioja and Catamarca are poor relations, but they are rich in scenery, folklore and tradition. Both were home to several important pre-Columbian cultures, mostly maize cultivators, who developed unique pottery techniques and styles, and the region has many important archaeological sites.

Offering great beauty to visitors with a car and time to explore, these provinces require a little patience and a desire to get off the beaten track; those who make the effort will be rewarded with wonderful scenery, friendly locals and open spaces all to themselves.

CATAMARCA

☎ 03833 / pop 187,300 / elevation 530m

When the seemingly endless renovations of Plaza 25 de Mayo are finally done, Catamarca will be an impressive town. There's an energy to the streets here that's almost inexplicable given that, really, this place is an economic backwater and destination for pilgrims on their way to pay homage to Nuestra Señora del Valle. Some beautiful old buildings dot the streets, and the magnificent cathedral, opposite Plaza 25 de Mayo, is also well worth a visit after dark.

Orientation

Nearly everything is in walking distance in the city center, an area 12 blocks square circumscribed by four wide avenues: Av Belgrano to the north, Av Alem to the east, Güemes to the south and Virgen del Valle to the west. The focus of downtown is the beautiful Plaza 25 de Mayo (the work of Carlos Thays, who also designed Mendoza's Parque San Martín and Tucumán's Parque 9 de Julio), a shady refuge from summer heat. South of the plaza, Rivadavia is a permanent pedestrian mall between San Martín and Mota Botello.

Information

ACA (☎ 424513; Av República 102)

BBVA Francés (Rivadavia 520) Cashes traveler's checks and has an ATM.

Internet kiosk (Esquiú; per hr US$0.30) The cheapest option to get online.

Locutorio (Rivadavia; per hr US$0.30) Has Internet facilities.

Central tourist office (☎ 437743; turismocatamarca@cedeconet.com.ar; Av República 446; ☑ 7am-9pm) Well stocked and with staff ready to answer questions about the town and province.

Post office (San Martín 753)

Yokavil Turismo (☎ 430066; www.yokavilturismo.com.ar in Spanish; Galería Paseo del Centro, Rivadavia 916) Arranges tours to area attractions, including Gruta de la Virgen del Valle (US$10).

Sights & Activities

CATEDRAL BASÍLICA DE NUESTRA SEÑORA DEL VALLE

Opposite Plaza 25 de Mayo, and dating from 1859, the cathedral shelters the Virgen del Valle, who is the patron of Catamarca and one of northern Argentina's most venerated images since the 17th century. Her diamond-studded crown can be seen in early April and on December 8, when multitudes of pilgrims converge on Catamarca to pay her homage. (She is also, in a curious juxtaposition of the sacred and profane, the Patrona Nacional de Turismo.)

The cathedral also contains an elaborately carved altar to St Joseph, an ornate baroque pulpit and an exhibition of paintings of the Virgin.

MUSEO ARQUEOLÓGICO ADÁN QUIROGA

A rambling collection of precolonial pottery, mummies, skulls, metalwork, and colonial and religious artifacts, this **museum** (☎ 437413; Sarmiento 450; admission US$1; ☑ 7am-1pm & 2:30-8:30pm Mon-Fri, 10am-7pm Sat & Sun) isn't for those who like their collections orderly and sophisticated, but there is something charming about the chaos. The first display hall contains assorted tools, ceramics, funerary pots and mummies from 3000 BC to the 18th century. The colonial-history room mixes disparate objects like rifles and musical instruments with fossils. The third room, also historical, presents ecclesiastical material and the personal effects of Fray Mamerto Esquiú. Spanish-speaking guides for large groups are available on request.

MUSEO DE BELLAS ARTES LAUREANO BRIZUELA

Named for a prominent *catamarqueño* (a person who lives in Catamarca) painter, the **fine-arts museum** (☎ 437563; Sarmiento 347; admission free; ☑ 8am-noon & 3-8pm Mon-Fri) exhibits his own

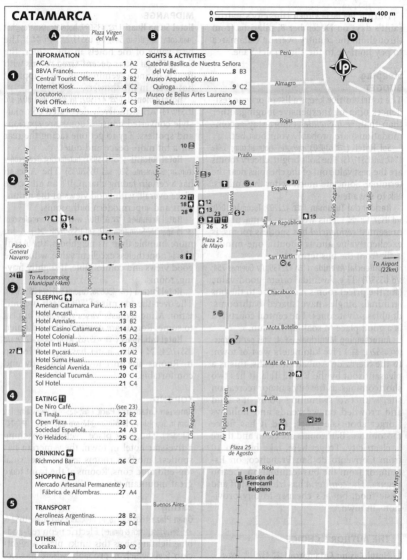

CATAMARCA

0　　　　　　400 m
0　　　　　0.2 miles

INFORMATION
ACA..1 A2
BBVA Francés........................2 C2
Central Tourist Office............3 B2
Internet Kiosk.......................4 C2
Locutorio..............................5 C3
Post Office............................6 C3
Yokavil Turismo....................7 C3

SIGHTS & ACTIVITIES
Catedral Basílica de Nuestra Señora
　del Valle...........................8 B3
Museo Arqueológico Adán
　Quiroga............................9 C2
Museo de Bellas Artes Laureano
　Brizuela...........................10 B2

SLEEPING
Amerian Catamarca Park........11 B3
Hotel Ancasti........................12 B2
Hotel Arenales......................13 B2
Hotel Casino Catamarca.........14 A2
Hotel Colonial.......................15 D2
Hotel Inti Huasi.....................16 A3
Hotel Pucará.........................17 A2
Hotel Suma Huasi..................18 B2
Residencial Avenida...............19 C4
Residencial Tucumán.............20 C4
Sol Hotel..............................21 C4

EATING
De Niro Café.....................(see 23)
La Tinaja..............................22 B2
Open Plaza...........................23 C2
Sociedad Española................24 A3
Yo Helados...........................25 C2

DRINKING
Richmond Bar.......................26 C2

SHOPPING
Mercado Artesanal Permanente y
　Fábrica de Alfombras..........27 A4

TRANSPORT
Aerolíneas Argentinas............28 B2
Bus Terminal........................29 D4

OTHER
Localiza................................30 C2

Map labels: Plaza Virgen del Valle; Perú; Almagro; Rojas; Prado; Esquiú; San Martín; Chacabuco; Mota Botello; Mate de Luna; Zurita; Rioja; Buenos Aires; Av Virgen del Valle; Paseo General Navarro; Caseros; Ayacucho; Junín; Madrid; Sarmiento; Rivadavia; Salta; Tucumán; Vicario Segura; 9 de Julio; Av República; Los Regionales; Av Hipólito Yrigoyen; Av Güemes; Plaza 25 de Mayo; Plaza 25 de Agosto; Estación del Ferrocarril Belgrano; 25 de Mayo; To Autocamping Municipal (4km); To Airport (22km)

works along with those of Varela Lezama, Roberto Gray, Antonio Berni, Benito Quinquela Martín, Vicente Forte and others.

Festivals & Events

The **Fiesta de Nuestra Señora del Valle** takes place for two weeks after Easter. In an impressive manifestation of popular religion, hordes of pilgrims come from the interior and from other Andean provinces to honor the Virgen del Valle.

The **Fiesta Nacional del Poncho** is held in the last fortnight of July. A crafts and industrial fair accompanies this festival of folkloric music and dance celebrating the importance of the poncho in the province.

During **Día de la Virgen** (the city's patron saint's day) on December 8, pilgrims from throughout the country overrun Catamarca to pay homage to the Virgen del Valle.

Sleeping

BUDGET

The tourist office keeps a list of private residences offering inexpensive lodging; other than that, *residenciales* (short-stay accommodations) are probably your best bet.

Sol Hotel (☎ 430803; solhotel@hotmail.com; Salta 1142; s/d US$11/15) The Sol's bright, cheery rooms are the best value out of the cheapies near the terminal. Some are much better than others; ask to see a few.

Residencial Tucumán (☎ 422209; Tucumán 1040; s/d US$7/10; ☒) This well-run, immaculately presented *residencial* has spotless rooms, is excellent value and is about a one-minute walk from the bus terminal.

Residencial Avenida (☎ 422139; Av Güemes 754; s/d US$5/7) The Avenida offers good-value (for the price) rooms *really* close to the bus terminal. Singles have shared bathrooms, doubles private ones. The central courtyard is a good place to soak up the sun.

Autocamping Municipal (RP 4; sites per tent/person US$2/1; ☒) Five kilometers west of town, in the Sierra de Ambato foothills, this is a pleasant spot by the Río El Tala. It has two shortcomings: as the city's major recreation site, with two swimming pools, it's loud and crowded on weekends and holidays (forget about sleeping); and it has fierce mosquitoes. Bathrooms are clean and there is electricity. To get here, take bus No 10 from Convento de San Francisco, on Esquiú, or from the bus terminal on Vicario Segura. The *confitería* has friendly staff and basic food, but it's cheaper to buy provisions in town.

THE AUTHOR'S CHOICE

Hotel Casino Catamarca (☎ 432928; www .hotelcasinocatamarca.com in Spanish; César Carman s/n; s/d US$17/21; ☒ ☒) With the most character of all of Catamarca's hotels, this one is a real bargain. Rooms are spacious, and the ones at the rear overlook a well-kept garden area. One thing, though – the place can get noisy on weekends when they host parties.

MIDRANGE

Hotel Suma Huasi (☎ 435699; hotelescatamarca@hot mail.com; Sarmiento 541; s/d US$13/22; P ☒) The best value of the hotels in the center, the Suma Huasi offers decent-sized rooms with firm beds and a seemingly endless supply of hot water in the showers.

Hotel Colonial (☎ 423502; Av República 802; s/d US$10/13) An attractively decorated colonial-style converted house. Rooms are spacious and spotless. Try to get one facing the rear for a bit more peace and quiet.

Hotel Ancasti (☎ 435951; hotelancasti@cedeconet .com.ar; Sarmiento 520; s/d US$26/35) The Ancasti has a certain fading charm. It's an attractive place overall, with good views of the mountains and supermodern bathrooms.

Hotel Arenales (☎ 430307; www.hotel-arenales.com .ar in Spanish; Sarmiento 542; s/d US$22/28; ☒) A lot more humble than its neighbors, the Arenales is nonetheless excellent value, with some good views and comfortable, if slightly fraying, rooms.

Hotel Pucará (☎ 430698; Caseros 501; s/d US$13/18) The over-the-top mix of '70s kitsch and imitation Ming-dynasty vases may well appeal to some. Rooms are comfortable and quiet.

Hotel Inti Huasi (☎ 435705; Av República 299; s/d US$17/24; ☒) This hotel has a good feel to it. Rooms are unrenovated, but tidy and comfortable.

TOP END

Amerian Catamarca Park (☎ 425444; www.amerian .com in Spanish; Av República 347; s/d US$40/50; P ☒ ☒ ☒) The only place even approaching a five-star hotel in town, the Amerian has spotless, modern rooms and all the usual top-end mod cons. Rooms at the front have great mountain views.

Eating

Open Plaza (☎ 404718; Av República 580; mains US$2-6; ☒ breakfast, lunch & dinner) Electric neon red-and-blue lighting gives this funky place a night-club feel, which is probably where most of its patrons are from in the wee hours. The food is simple and filling, and they also have a good range of cocktails.

La Tinaja (☎ 435853; Sarmiento 533; mains US$5) La Tinaja has low prices and sometimes live music. Handy if you're staying in the center.

De Niro Café (Av República 590; mains US$6-12; ☒ breakfast, lunch & dinner) Next to Open Plaza, this place has a larger menu, including

ALFREDO MAIQUEZ

Plaza San Martín (p78), Buenos Aires

KRZYSZTOF DYDYNSKI

Evita Perón's grave (p78), Recoleta
Cemetery, Buenos Aires

Bar 6 (p96), Palermo Viejo, Buenos Aires

KRZYSZTOF DYDYNSKI

Caminito, La Boca (p77), Buenos Aires

ALFREDO MAIQUEZ

Iguazú Falls (p189)

Students, Salta (p223)

Colonial architecture, Salta (p223)

pizzas and meat dishes, and is a good spot for coffee in the mornings.

Sociedad Española (☎ 431896; Av Virgen del Valle 725; meals US$3-7) The Spanish Society is always worth hunting down for traditional Spanish dishes, including seafood. It's a grand old place, worth the trek for some fine dining

Yo Helados (cnr Av República & Rivadavia; ice cream US$1-3; ☼ 9:30am-11pm) This chain store serves good ice cream.

The bus terminal has an upstairs food hall serving burgers, pizzas and other fast food, good for a meal while waiting for your next bus. There are also a couple of cafés here.

Drinking

Richmond Bar (☎ 423823; Av República 534) This mirrored-ceiling bar is a good place for a quiet drink; or if you like your entertainment livelier, things heat up on Saturday nights when there is tango from 11pm.

Shopping

Mercado Artesanal Permanente y Fábrica de Alfombras (Virgen del Valle 945; ☼ 8am-12:30pm & 4-8:30pm Mon-Fri, 9am-noon & 4:30-8pm Sat, 9am-noon Sun) For Catamarca's characteristic hand-tied rugs, visit this market. Besides rugs, the market sells ponchos, blankets, jewelry, red onyx sculptures, musical instruments, hand-spun sheep and llama wool, and basketry.

There's also a small, informal **crafts market** (Plazoleta 5 de Julio, Rivadavia) in the evening.

Catamarca is the place to buy walnuts, including rich but tasty *nueces confitadas* (sugared walnuts), olives, raisins and wines. Regional specialty shops are concentrated on Rivadavia, between Plaza 25 de Mayo and the Convento de San Francisco.

Getting There & Away

AIR

Aerolíneas Argentinas (☎ 424460; Sarmiento 589, 8th fl) flies daily except Sunday to Buenos Aires (US$100). For US$2, the Aerolíneas Servicios Diferenciales minibus goes to **Aeropuerto Felipe Varela** (☎ 430080, 435582; RP 33), 22km east of town.

BUS

The long-overdue facelift of Catamarca's privatized **bus terminal** (☎ 423415; Av Güemes 850) is now complete and is a vast improvement.

Following are sample destinations and fares around the country.

Destination	Cost (US$)	Duration (hr)
Andalgalá	5	5
Aimogasta	3	3
Belén	6	4
Buenos Aires	22	16
Córdoba	7	5
Jujuy	13	10
Londres	5	3½
Mendoza	13	10
Paraná	16	18
Pocitos	13	15
Posadas	28	18
Resistencia	20	24
Rosario	17	11
Salta	11	6
San Juan	10	8
Santa Rosa	19	16
Santiago del Estero	6	4½
Tinogasta	5	5
Tucumán	8.50	4

AROUND CATAMARCA

According to local legend, in 1619 or 1620 the image of the Virgen del Valle appeared in **Gruta de la Virgen del Valle**, 7km north of downtown Catamarca on RP 32. The present image is a replica of that in Catamarca's cathedral, and a protective structure shelters the grotto itself. Empresa Cotca's bus No 104 goes to the Gruta every 40 minutes.

The Sierra de Famatina, the province's highest mountain range, is visible from the road to picturesque **Villa Las Pirquitas**, near the dam of the same name, 29km north of Catamarca via RN 75. The foothills en route shelter small villages with hospitable people and interesting vernacular architecture.

Camping is possible at the basic *balneario* (river beach), where the shallows are too muddy for swimming. The very attractive **Hostería Municipal** (☎ 03833-492030; s/d US$6/10) is great value, with clean and comfortable rooms.

From Catamarca's bus terminal, Empresa Cotca's bus No 101 leaves hourly for the village.

ANDALGALÁ

☎ 03835

At the north end of the Sierra de Manchao, 200km from Catamarca via RN 75 and RP 46, Andalgalá is a possible stopover on the scenic route from Catamarca to Belén via the Cuesta de Chilca; RP 46 continues west

THE ANDEAN NORTHWEST

to the equally scenic Cuesta de Belén. Gutiérrez buses from Catamarca to Belén take this spectacular route.

Hotel Aquasol (☎ 422615; Carranza s/n; s/d US$12/17; ☒ ☒), three blocks uphill from the bus terminal, offers the most comfortable rooms in town. They are surprisingly spacious and modern, with small patios. **El Buffalo** (Nuñez del Prado s/n; meals US$2-4; ☼ breakfast, lunch & dinner) is the most pleasant of the plazaside eateries. It's light and airy and serves good pizza, *minutas* (short orders) and pasta.

BELÉN

☎ 03835 / pop 12,250 / elevation 1250m

What exactly happened to little Belén? Did it get a visit from 'queer eye for a straight town?' An otherwise nondescript little hamlet way out in the middle of nowhere, this place has some way-styling eating and sleeping options. It's also the self-appointed poncho capital of the country, and one of the best places for woven goods, particularly ponchos, in Argentina. There are many *teleras* (textile workshops) dotted around town, turning out their wares made from llama, sheep and vicuña wool.

Before the arrival of the Spaniards in the mid-16th century, the area around Belén was Calchaquí territory, on the periphery of the Inca empire. After the Incas fell, it became the *encomienda* of Pedro Ramírez Velasco, founder of La Rioja, but its history is intricately intertwined with nearby Londres, a Spanish settlement which shifted several times because of floods and Calchaquí resistance. More than a century passed before, in 1681, the priest José Bartolomé Olmos de Aguilera divided a land grant among veterans of the Calchaquí wars on the condition that they support evangelization in the area.

Orientation & Information

In the western highlands of Catamarca, Belén is 89km west of Andalgalá, 289km from the provincial capital and 180km southwest of Santa María. The **municipal tourist office** (☎ 461 304; ☼ 7am-1pm & 2-8pm) is in the bus terminal.

Sights & Activities

The neoclassical brick **Iglesia Nuestra Señora de Belén** dates from 1907 and faces Plaza Olmos y Aguilera. It is well shaded by pines and colossal pepper trees. The provincial **Museo Cóndor Huasi** (cnr Lavalle & Rivadavia; admission

US$0.30; ☼ 9am-noon & 4-7pm Mon-Sat, 9am-noon Sun) displays an impressive assortment of Diaguita artifacts.

On December 20, the town officially celebrates its founding, **Día de la Fundación**, but festivities begin at least a week earlier with a dance at the foot of the Cerro de la Virgen, three blocks west of the plaza. A steep 1900m trail leads to a 15m statue of the Virgin, side by side with a 4.5m image of the Christ child.

Sleeping & Eating

Hotel Belén (☎ 461501; www.belencat.com.ar in Spanish; cnr Belgrano & Cubas; s/d US$13/18; ☒ ☒ ☒) The most stylish hotel in northern Argentina? At these prices, definitely. Check the exposed rock bathrooms, with inlaid-tile mosaics on the floors and wall. The rooms are immaculate, spacious and quiet.

Hotel Samay (☎ 461320; Urquiza 349; s/d US$10/12) The basic rooms here come with TV, and are clean and comfortable, but by no means lavish.

On summer nights, restaurants near Plaza Olmos y Aguilera set up tables right on the plaza itself.

1900 (☎ 461100; Belgrano 391; mains US$2-4; ☼ breakfast, lunch & dinner) Another stylish addition to the whole Belén scene, this restaurant/bar features all the regular steak, pizza, pasta options with excellent service (did that waiter just dress my salad at the table?) and good-value set meals.

El Único (cnr General Roca & Sarmiento; mains US$2-6) This is the best *parrilla* in town. It features an attractive *quincho* (thatch-roof hut) and regional specialties such as *locro* are worth trying here.

There are several good ice creameries around the plaza.

Shopping

Cuna del Poncho (☎ 461091; Roca 144) The place to go for reasonably priced woven goods, as they sell direct. They also accept major credit cards and arrange shipping.

Getting There & Away

Belén's **bus terminal** (cnr Sarmiento & Rivadavia), one block south and one block west of the plaza, has both provincial and limited long-distance services. Destinations include Andalgalá (US$3, two hours), Catamarca (US$6, four hours), Chumbichá, Córdoba (US$12, 14 hours), La Rioja, Salta (US$10, 12½ hours), Santa María (US$5, five hours), Tinogasta and Tucumán (US$9, eight hours).

AROUND BELÉN

Only 15km southwest of Belén, sleepy **Londres** (population 1800) is the province's oldest Spanish settlement, dating from 1558, though it moved several times before returning here in 1612; the inhabitants fled again during the Calchaquí uprising of 1632. The **Festival Provincial de la Nuez** (Provincial Walnut Festival) takes place here the first fortnight of February, but more interesting are the nearby Inca ruins at Shinkal. Seven local buses daily go to Londres from Belén.

About 60km north of Belén via RN 40, the village of **Hualfín** features a colonial chapel beneath a small promontory whose 142-step staircase leads to a *mirador* with panoramic views of cultivated fields and the distant desert. Buses between Belén and Santa María stop here.

Around town, look for locally grown paprika often sprinkled on creamy slices of goat cheese.

LA RIOJA

☎ 03822 / pop 147,800 / elevation 500m

Arriving by bus in La Rioja, you're struck by two things: the gorgeous peaks of the Sierra de Velasco that surround the town, and the fact that the bus terminal is terribly run-down, in a terribly run-down part of town. Leave the terminal far behind and make your way to the center, where a couple of lovely plazas, some good restaurants and some interesting museums await. Summer temperatures can be searing – folks here take their siesta very seriously.

Juan Ramírez de Velasco founded Todos los Santos de la Nueva Rioja in 1591. Dominican, Jesuit and Franciscan missionaries helped 'pacify' the Diaguita Indians and paved the way for Spanish colonization of what Vásquez de Espinosa called 'a bit of Paradise.'

The city's appearance reflects the conflict and accommodation between colonizer and colonized: the architecture combines European designs with native techniques and local materials. Many early buildings were destroyed in the 1894 earthquake, but the city has been entirely rebuilt.

Orientation

At the base of the picturesque Sierra de Velasco, La Rioja is relatively small, with all points of interest and most hotels within easy walking distance of each other.

North–south streets change their names at Rivadavia, but east–west streets are continuous.

Information

INTERNET ACCESS

Cybermás (Rivadavia 763; ☯ 24hr; per hr US$0.30) Internet access.

MONEY

La Rioja has no money-exchange offices, and bank hours are limited, but some travel agencies may change money. There are also several banks with ATMs.

Banco de Galicia (Buenos Aires) Changes US dollars and does credit-card advances.

POST

Post office (Av JD Perón 258)

TELEPHONE

Locutorio (529 Pelagio Luna; per hr US$0.30; ☯ 7am-2am) Has Internet facilities; it's opposite Plaza 25 de Mayo.

TOURIST INFORMATION

ACA (☎ 425381; cnr Dalmacio Vélez Sársfield & Copiapó)

Municipal tourist office (☎ 427103; fax 426648; Av JD Perón 715; ☯ 8am-1pm & 3-9pm) Friendly, eager staff. Distributes a good city map and brochures of other provincial destinations. Hotel information includes only officially registered hotels, excluding many cheaper possibilities.

Provincial tourist office (☎ 428839; turismolarioja@ hotmail.com; cnr Av JD Perón & Urquiza; ☯ 8am-1pm & 4-9pm Mon-Fri) Helpful staff. On weekends, there's usually a *guardia* (watchman) on hand.

TRAVEL AGENCIES

Furlan Viajes (☎ 420895; furlanlr@arnet.com.ar; Rivadavia 479) Can help with most travel arrangements.

Sights

LANDMARK BUILDINGS

La Rioja is a major devotional center, so most landmarks are ecclesiastical. Built in 1623 by Diaguita Indians under the direction of Dominican friars, the **Convento de Santo Domingo** (cnr Pelagio Luna & Lamadrid) is Argentina's oldest convent. The date appears in the carved algarroba doorframe, also the work of Diaguita artists.

THE ANDEAN NORTHWEST

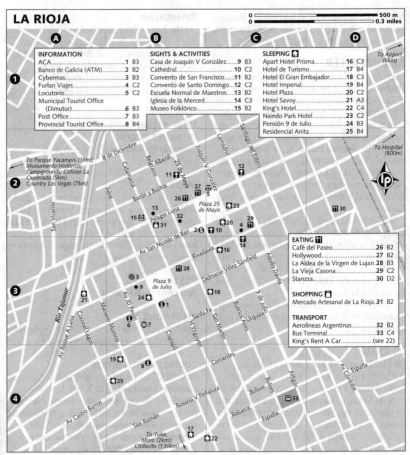

LA RIOJA

0 / 500 m
0 / 0.3 miles

INFORMATION
ACA...1 B3
Banco de Galicia (ATM)............2 B2
Cybermas.................................3 B3
Furlan Viajes............................4 C2
Locutorio..................................5 C2
Municipal Tourist Office
(Dimutur)...............................6 B3
Post Office................................7 B3
Provincial Tourist Office..........8 B4

SIGHTS & ACTIVITIES
Casa de Joaquín V González......9 B3
Cathedral.................................10 C2
Convento de San Francisco.....11 B2
Convento de Santo Domingo..12 C2
Escuela Normal de Maestros...13 B2
Iglesia de la Merced................14 C3
Museo Folklórico.....................15 B2

SLEEPING
Apart Hotel Prisma..................16 C3
Hotel de Turismo.....................17 B4
Hotel El Gran Embajador........18 C3
Hotel Imperial.........................19 B4
Hotel Plaza..............................20 C2
Hotel Savoy.............................21 A3
King's Hotel.............................22 C4
Naindo Park Hotel....................23 C2
Pensión 9 de Julio...................24 B3
Residencial Anita.....................25 B4

To Airport (6km)

To Hospital (800m)

To Parque Yacampis (3km);
Monumento Histórico;
Campgrounds; Coliseo La
Quebrada (5km)
Country Las Vegas (7km)

Plaza 25
de Mayo

Plaza 9
de Julio

EATING
Café del Paseo........................26 B2
Hollywood...............................27 B2
La Aldea de la Virgen de Lujan.28 B3
La Vieja Casona.......................29 C2
Stanzza...................................30 D2

SHOPPING
Mercado Artesanal de La Rioja.31 B2

TRANSPORT
Aerolíneas Argentinas.............32 B4
Bus Terminal...........................33 C4
King's Rent A Car..................(see 22)

To Yuka,
Moro (2km);
Chilecito (130km)

The **Convento de San Francisco** (cnr 25 de Mayo & Bazán y Bustos) houses the image of the Niño Alcalde, a Christ-child icon symbolically recognized as the city's mayor. Also here is the cell occupied in 1592 by San Francisco Solano, a priest known for educating native peoples and defending their rights.

The Byzantine 1899 **Cathedral** (cnr Av San Nicolás de Bari & 25 de Mayo) contains the image of patron saint Nicolás de Bari, an object of devotion for both *riojanos* (people who live in La Rioja) and the inhabitants of neighboring provinces. The **Iglesia de la Merced** (cnr Rivadavia & 9 de Julio) replaced a Mercedarian church destroyed by the 1894 earthquake.

One of Argentina's greatest educators, and founder of the Universidad de La Plata,

lived in the **Casa de Joaquín V González** (Rivadavia 952). The neoclassical **Escuela Normal de Maestros**, the teachers' school situated on Pelagio Luna between Catamarca and Belgrano, dates from 1884.

MUSEO FOLKLÓRICO

While this **museum** (☎ 428500; Pelagio Luna 811; admission US$0.50; ⊙ 9am-noon & 4-8pm Tue-Fri, 9am-noon Sun) credibly re-creates an authentic 19th-century house, with all the furnishings and objects necessary for everyday life, its thematic exhibits are even better. One hall displays ceramic reproductions representing mythological beings from local folklore, but it also contains particularly good Tinkunako materials (see Festivals & Events, p255), horse gear, an artisans workshop and even diet statistics on criollo (in colonial period, an American-born Spaniard, but the term is now used for any Latin American of European descent) food (*locro* and *humitas* are much healthier than fatty empanadas).

PARQUE YACAMPIS
On the western edge of town at the foot of the Sierra de Velasco, this once neatly landscaped park has become increasingly rundown, but still has panoramic views, a small zoo where some local fauna such as rheas run free, and a popular swimming pool.

Festivals & Events
Folkloric La Chaya, the local variant of Carnaval, attracts people from throughout the country. Its name, derived from a Quechua word meaning 'to get someone wet,' should give you an idea of what to expect.

Festival del Viñador, honoring local vintners, takes place at the beginning of the Villa Unión's March grape harvest. During the festival there is music, dancing and tasting of regional wines, most notably the artisanal *vino patero*, made by traditional foot stomping of the grapes. Villa Unión is west of La Rioja and approximately 260km by road.

Taking place at midday December 31, the religious ritual of **El Tinkunako** re-enacts the original ceremony of San Francisco Solano's 1593 mediation between the Diaguitas and the Spanish conquerors. To accept peace, the Diaguitas imposed two conditions: resignation of the Spanish *alcalde* (mayor) and his replacement by the Christ child.

Sleeping
BUDGET
La Rioja lacks a large tourist infrastructure, especially in budget hotels, but the tourist office maintains a list of private homes offering accommodations for about US$6 per person.

Pensión 9 de Julio (☎ 426955; cnr Copiapó & Dalmacio Vélez Sársfield; s/d US$7/10) Definitely the best budget deal in town, this place has clean and pleasant rooms. A shady, vine-covered patio overlooking the plaza is another bonus.

Residencial Anita (☎ 424836; Coronel Lagos 476; s/d US$25/35) The family-run Anita features comfortable-enough rooms in a quiet

neighborhood. The plant-filled patio is a bonus, and the playful pet dogs may appeal to some.

Hotel Imperial (☎ 422478; Mariano Moreno 345; s/d US$10/13; P ⊠) A newish place out in the middle of a residential area, the Imperial has reasonable comfort at decent prices.

Country Las Vegas (sites per person US$1.50) The best and closest campground is on RN 75, Km 8, west of town; to get there, catch city bus No 1 southbound on Perón.

MIDRANGE & TOP END
La Rioja's more expensive hotels are in hot competition; when things are quiet you'll get some good deals. Discounts are generally available if you pay cash and aren't afraid to bargain.

Hotel Plaza (☎ 425215; www.plazahotel-larioja.com .ar in Spanish; cnr 9 de Julio & Av San Nicolás de Bari; s/d US$28/33; P ⊠ ⊠) Some rooms here overlook the plaza, making them a good deal. Others open onto internal lightwells (not so attractive, but still good for ventilation). The place has a pleasant old-timey feel in the lobby and restaurant which vaguely follows through to the rooms.

King's Hotel (☎ 422122; Av Juan Facundo Quiroga 1070; s/d US$30/40; P ⊠ ⊠) Formerly the finest hotel in town, King's still has more atmosphere than the newcomers. The buffet breakfast is grand, and other amenities include sundeck and gymnasium.

Naindo Park Hotel (☎ 470700; www.naindopark hotel.com; San Nicolás de Bari 475; s/d US$28/33; P ⊠ ⊠) La Rioja's newest hotel is a bit incongruous in this fairly traditional city. All the five-star comforts are here, and rooms are spacious and modern.

Hotel El Gran Embajador (☎ 438580; www.gran hotelembajador.com.ar; San Martín 250; s/d US$12/17; P ⊠) This sunny little place is very tidy; the rooms upstairs are larger and sunnier and some have balconies. It's good value for money, and hugely popular as a result; reservations are advised.

Hotel de Turismo (☎ 422005; cnr Av Perón & Quiroga; s/d US$20/25; P ⊠ ⊠) Out by the bus terminal, the Turismo is a hulking old place that's still holding it together pretty well. Rooms have small balconies and the swimming pool/sun deck area is the place to be on a sunny day.

Hotel Savoy (☎ 426894; hotelsavoy@infovia.com.ar; San Nicolás de Bari 1100; s/d US$13/17; ⊠) On the

THE ANDEAN NORTHWEST

river, a short way out of town, this is a tranquil little hotel. Rooms are cool and a bit on the dark side, but spacious enough.

Apart Hotel Prisma (☎ 421567; cnr Rivadavia & Buenos Aires; s/d US$17/27) Heavy on the brown tilework and brass ornamentation, the 'apartments' here have a kitchenette which would serve for cooking up breakfast or snacks.

Eating

Regional dishes to look for include *locro*, juicy empanadas differing from the drier ones of the Pampas, *chivito asado* (barbecued goat), *humitas*, *quesillo* (a cheese specialty) and olives. Don't miss the local bread, baked in *hornos de barro* (adobe ovens). There is also a good selection of dried fruits, preserves and jams from figs, apples, peaches and pears. Don't hesitate to order house wines, which are invariably excellent.

Stanzza (☎ 430809; Dorrego 1641; dishes US$4-6) One of the best places to eat in town, this friendly neighborhood restaurant serves up imaginative seafood and Italian dishes in an intimate environment.

Café del Paseo (☎ 422069; cnr Pelagio Luna & 25 de Mayo; sandwiches US$1.50-3, pizzas US$3; ☒ breakfast, lunch & dinner) This is an appealing Spanish mission–style *confitería* with an outdoor area that's terrific for a spot of people-watching. Café del Paseo is where the new meets the old: the mobile-phone clique mingles with families and tables of older men chewing the fat over another slow-paced La Rioja day.

La Vieja Casona (☎ 425996; Rivadivia 427; mains US$3-6) Popular day and night, this is an excellent choice for regional specialties, as well as standard Argentine dishes like *parrillada* (mixed grill including steak). It's a large, open slate-floor restaurant with wonderful smells wafting from the busy kitchen.

Hollywood (cnr 25 de Mayo & Pelagio Luna; meals US$3-4; ☒ breakfast, lunch & dinner) This place could well be the perfect restaurant. There's outdoor or air-con seating, tasty Middle Eastern–styled tapas, a wide range of Argentine standards on the menu, and it stays open 'til the wee, wee hours for those post-midnight munchies.

La Aldea de la Virgen de Lujan (☎ 460305; Rivadavia 756, meals US$3-5; ☒ breakfast, lunch & dinner) Serving good-value breakfasts and a fairly predictable range of dinner options, lunch-time is the place to be at this spot, when they offer a good range of regional specialties.

Entertainment

If you're up for a late night, there are a number of discos where you can show the locals your latest moves. They all charge around US$3/1 for guys/girls, although there are often promotions where women get in for free. All open about 1am or 2am on weekends and pound away until the early morning.

Yuka (☎ 1567-6226; Av Félix de la Colina) Also has a restaurant where you can chow down on *lomitos* and pizzas.

Other recommendations:

Millennium (San Martín) Opposite the Colegio Nacional.

Moro (cnr Av Laprida & Buenos Aires)

Performers of the stature of Leon Gieco perform at **Coliseo La Quebrada** (Av San Francisco), 5.5km west of downtown; other events include theatrical performances.

Shopping

La Rioja has unique weavings that combine indigenous techniques and skill with Spanish designs and color combinations. The typical *mantas* (bedspreads) feature floral patterns over a solid background. Spanish influence is also visible in silverwork, including tableware, ornaments, religious objects and horse gear. La Rioja's pottery is entirely indigenous; artists utilize local clay to make distinctive pots, plates and flowerpots. *Riojano* wine has a national reputation; Saúl Menem, father of the ex-president, founded one of the major bodegas.

La Rioja crafts are exhibited and sold at **Mercado Artesanal de La Rioja** (Pelagio Luna 792; ☒ 8am-noon & 4-8pm Tue-Fri, 9am-noon Sat & Sun), as are other popular artworks at prices lower than most souvenir shops.

Getting There & Away

AIR

Aerolíneas Argentinas (☎ 426307; Belgrano 63) flies Monday to Saturday to Buenos Aires (US$90).

BUS

La Rioja is home to an ageing **bus terminal** (☎ 425453; cnr Artigas & España), though plans to build a new terminal have been around for a while.

Destination	Cost (US$)	Duration (hr)
Buenos Aires	20	22
Catamarca	4	2
Chilecito	3	3
Córdoba	8	6
Jujuy	8	8
Mendoza	16	8
Pagancillo	3	3½
Pocitos	17	14
Salta	18	14
San Juan	7	6
San Luis	9	12
Santiago del Estero	11	7
Tucumán	7	6

Getting Around

From Plaza 9 de Julio, bus No 3 goes to **Aeropuerto Vicente Almonacid** (☎ 425483), 7km east of town on RP 5. An airport cab costs around US$3. A taxi from the bus terminal to the city center costs about US$2.

King's Rent A Car (☎ 422122; cnr Av Juan Facundo Quiroga & Copiapó) is in the King's Hotel.

AROUND LA RIOJA

According to legend, San Francisco Solano converted many Diaguita Indians at the site of **Monumento Histórico Las Padercitas**, a Franciscan-built colonial adobe chapel now sheltered by a stone temple, 7km west of town on RN 75. On the second Sunday of August, pilgrims convene to pay homage to the saint. Bus Nos 1 and 3 go to the site.

Beyond Las Padercitas, RN 75 climbs and winds past attractive summer homes, bright red sandstone cliffs, lush vegetation and dark purple peaks whose cacti remind you that the area is semidesert.

Balneario Los Sauces, 15km from La Rioja at the dam, is a pleasant place for a leisurely picnic or outing.

From Balneario Los Sauces you can hike or drive up the dirt road to 1680m **Cerro de la Cruz**, which affords panoramic views of the Yacampis Valley and the village of Sanagasta. The top also has a ramp for hang gliding, a popular local activity. Sanagasta-bound buses can drop you off here.

CHILECITO

☎ 03825 / pop 42,250

The snowcapped peaks that surround Chilecito provide a marked contrast to this hot and barren little town, which is the province's second-largest city. In a scenic valley at the foot of the massive Nevado de Famatina (and Cerro Velazco), this is a quiet place, easy to get around on foot and is worth a day at the most. Wine tasting is a good way to while away a few hours as you wait for your next bus, and you can also check out the crumbling Che Guevara statue in the main square, one of the few such tributes to the famous Argentine in the whole country.

Information

MONEY
Banco de la Nación and Nuevo Banco de La Rioja (ATM) are on opposite corners of Plaza Sarmiento.

Banco Macro (Castro Barros, btwn 25 de Mayo & 9 de Julio) Has an ATM.

POST
Post office (cnr Joaquín V González & Av Pelagio Luna)

TELEPHONE
Locutorio (Joaquín V González) Near Castro y Bazán.

TOURIST INFORMATION
Provincial tourist office (☎ 422688; Castro y Bazán, btwn La Plata & Joaquín V González; ⓨ 8am-9pm) Has enthusiastic staff and good material. There is also a small booth on Plaza Sarmiento.

Sights

MUSEO MOLINO DE SAN FRANCISCO
Chilecito founder Don Domingo de Castro y Bazán owned this colonial flour mill, whose **museum** (J Ocampo 63; admission US$0.30; ⓨ 8am-1pm & 2:30-7:30pm Mon-Fri, 8am-12:30pm & 2:30-8pm Sat & Sun) houses an eclectic assemblage of archaeological tools, antique arms, early colonial documents, minerals, traditional wood and leather crafts, plus weavings and paintings. The building itself merits a visit, but the artifacts are a big plus.

SAMAY HUASI
Joaquín V González, founder of the prestigious Universidad Nacional de La Plata, used this building, 3km from Chilecito past La Puntilla, as his country retreat. Now belonging to the university, the building houses a natural sciences, archaeology and mineralogy **museum** (admission free; ⓨ 8am-1pm & 1:30-7:30pm Mon-Fri, 8am-noon & 2-6:30pm Sat & Sun) and a valuable collection of paintings by Argentine artists.

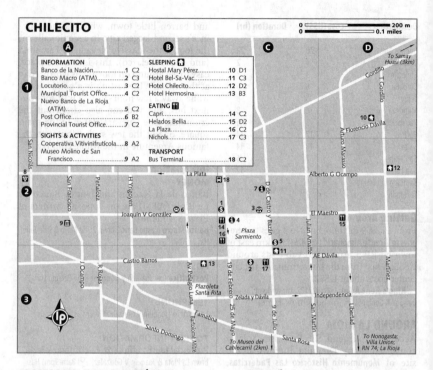

CHILECITO

INFORMATION			SLEEPING		
Banco de la Nación	1	C2	Hostal Mary Pérez	10	D1
Banco Macro (ATM)	2	C3	Hotel Bel-Sa-Vac	11	C3
Locutorio	3	C2	Hotel Chilecito	12	D2
Municipal Tourist Office	4	C2	Hotel Hermosina	13	B3
Nuevo Banco de La Rioja					
(ATM)	5	C2	EATING		
Post Office	6	B2	Capri	14	C2
Provincial Tourist Office	7	C2	Helados Bella	15	D2
			La Plaza	16	C2
SIGHTS & ACTIVITIES			Nichols	17	C3
Cooperativa Vitivinifrutícola	8	A2			
Museo Molino de San			TRANSPORT		
Francisco	9	A2	Bus Terminal	18	C2

COOPERATIVA VITIVINIFRUTÍCOLA

La Rioja is one of the best areas to taste the fruity white *torrontés*, though it's far from the only wine the province has to offer. One block north and five blocks west of Plaza Sarmiento is the province's largest **winery** (☎ 423150; La Plata 646). It's open to visitors for tours and tastings; call to arrange a tour. There's an excellent selection of wine, as well as dried fruit, for sale.

MUSEO DEL CABLECARRIL

From the southern approach to Chilecito, about 2km southwest of Plaza Sarmiento, Estación No 1 del Cablecarril was the initial stop on the nine-station trip to La Meji-cana. More than 260 towers sustained the 36km cable to its ultimate destination, 3510m higher than the town itself.

The cable-car line was constructed in 1903; the on-site **museum** (admission free, but a tip is appropriate; � 8am-8pm Mon-Fri) preserves the still-functional (though rarely used) wagons that, until 1935, carried men and supplies to the mine in a little less than four hours. A 39-step spiral staircase climbs to the platform, where

ore carts and even passenger carts now wait silently in line. Alongside the platform is a wooden crane, built of Sitka spruce in 1913.

Well-versed guides lead tours, in Spanish only, from the museum proper in the former mine offices, where there are mining artifacts, minerals and communications equipment, including an early mobile phone.

Sleeping

The tourist office keeps a list of private homes, which are the cheapest accommodations in town for about US$6 per person.

Hostal Mary Pérez (☎ 423156; hostal_mp@hotmail .com; Florencio Dávila 280; r per person US$10) A neat little *residencial* in the northeast of town that is more like a family-run hotel. Rooms come with TV and telephone. There's also a fully equipped apartment that sleeps six, costing US$10 per person, with discounts for groups of four or more.

Hotel Chilecito (☎ 422201; Timoteo Gordillo 101; s/d ACA members US$7/11, nonmembers US$10/16; Ⓟ Ⓧ Ⓡ) The biggest hotel in town is worth the money if you're going to be using the pool. Rooms are spacious, but showing signs of wear.

Hotel Hermosina (☎ 425421; Castro Barrios 178; s/d US$10/15; Ⓟ 🐾) The best deal in the center, the rooms here are clean and functional, if unexciting. Those at the front are well ventilated, but toward the rear they can get a bit stuffy.

Hotel Bel-Sa-Vac (☎ 422977; helsavar@hotmail.com; cnr 9 de Julio & AE Dávila; s/d US$10/13) Utterly forgettable (but reasonable) rooms right on the plaza. Rooms at the front have the views, but the ones toward the rear are much quieter.

Eating

The best places to eat are all located on the plaza 25 de Mayo.

Nichols (cnr 9 de Julio & Dávila; mains US$2-3; 🕑 breakfast, lunch & dinner) The best thing about this fairly ordinary bar/confitería is that they put tables out across the road under a shady part of the plaza – a perfect hangout for steamy days and balmy evenings.

Capri (cnr 19 de Febrero & Joaquín Gonzalez; mains US$2-3.50; 🕑 breakfast, lunch & dinner) With a bit more class than the rest, Capri is a good place to stop by for a quick sandwich or pizza. They often have specials of the day, so it's worth asking.

La Plaza (☎ 422696; 25 de Mayo 58; mains US$3-4; 🕑 breakfast, lunch & dinner) Right on the plaza (as the name may suggest), this modern café serves the usual range of steaks, pizzas and pastas, with all-you-can-eat specials on Wednesday and Sunday. The US$3 set lunches are a bargain.

Helados Bellia (cnr El Maestro & Libertad) is good for fine ice cream.

Getting There & Away

There is a **bus terminal** (cnr La Plata & 19 de Febrero). Some bus companies running minibuses in the area have separate offices around the plaza. La Riojana on El Maestro and Inter Rioja on Castro Barros, opposite Plaza Sarmiento, go to La Rioja regularly every day. Maxi Bus at Zelada y Dávila goes to La Rioja about four times daily for US$10 roundtrip.

Transporte Ariel (☎ 422161) has minibuses that leave from the bus terminal for Nonogasta (US$0.50) and Sañogasta (US$1).

There are regular services from the terminal to Buenos Aires (US$38, 25 hours), Córdoba (US$14, six hours), Rosario, Villa Unión, San Juan (US$14, seven hours), Patquía, Mendoza (US$15, nine hours) and La Rioja (US$3, three hours).

AROUND CHILECITO

Only the roaring water of the *acequias* (irrigation ditches) disrupts the peaceful, unpaved streets of **Nonogasta**, birthplace of educator Joaquín V González. In a prosperous agricultural valley 16km south of Chilecito, this small town features charming adobe architecture (including González's house and a 17th-century church), polite, friendly people, and good wines from Bodegas Nicarí. Transporte Ariel makes the run between Chilecito and Nonogasta regularly, leaving from the plaza in Nanogasta.

With 800 turns, **Cuesta de Miranda** – a mountainous stretch of RN 40 through the Sierra de Sañogasta, 56km west of Chilecito – is one of the most spectacular roads in Argentina's northern Andes and one of the province's major scenic attractions. Although not paved, the surface is smooth and wide enough for safety; still, sounding the horn before the innumerable blind turns is a good idea. At the highest point, 2020m above sea level, there's a vista from which the Río Miranda looks like a frozen silver ribbon below.

PARQUE NACIONAL TALAMPAYA

Riojanos like to compare Talampaya, a 215,000-hectare national park southwest of Chilecito, to the USA's Grand Canyon. A better comparison would be southern Utah's arid canyon country, since only a trickle of permanent surface water winds through what, in the Quechua language, translates as the 'Dry River of the Tala.' This is a fitting description for this desert of scorching days, chilly nights, infrequent but torrential summer rains and gusty spring winds.

Talampaya's upgrade in recent years from provincial to national park status means it should attract more attention; visits are likely to increase and visitor services to improve, but for the moment both are limited.

Visitors may not use their own vehicles on park roads; only contracted guides with pickup trucks offer tours of sandy canyons where aboriginal petroglyphs and mortars adorn streambed sites. Nesting condors scatter from cliffside nests as vehicles invade their otherwise undisturbed habitat. On the usual two-hour tour from the park's headquarters, vehicles pass the dunes of **El Playón**, leading to the **Puerta de Talampaya** (Gate of Talampaya) entrance to the canyon.

Back on the road, the vehicles enter the red sandstone canyon, whose eastern wall reveals a conspicuous fault. The next major stops are the **Chimenea del Eco**, an extraordinary echo chamber where your voice seems to come back louder than your original call, and a nature trail to the **Bosquecillo** (Little Forest), a representative sample of native vegetation. On the return the major point is **El Cañón de los Farallones** (Canyon of Cliffs) where, besides condors and turkey vultures, you may see eagles and other birds of prey 150m above the canyon floor.

Longer four-hour excursions are possible to Los Pizarrones, as well as other sites such as Los Cajones, Ciudad Perdida and Los Chañares.

Two-hour excursions in the park cost US$23 for up to eight people; proceeds go directly to guides. Three-hour trips cost US$40 for up to eight people and six-hour trips are US$50. These trips can be organized inside the park. If you can, sit in front with the guide one way, and in the back of the truck the other way.

Orientation & Information

Talampaya is 141km southwest of Chilecito via a combination of RN 40's scenic Cuesta de Miranda route, RP 18 and RP 26. Via RP 26, it is 55km south of Villa Unión and 58km north of Los Baldecitos, the turnoff for San Juan's Parque Provincial Ischigualasto.

From the junction with RP 26, a paved eastbound lateral leads 14km to the Puerta de Talampaya entrance, where there's a **confitería** (☎ 03825-470397) serving simple meals and cold drinks. It is also a visitor center; a ranger is usually on duty to collect the US$1 admission. There are some good dinosaur illustrations depicting the early Triassic, 250 million years ago.

There is also a **park office** (☎ 470356) in Villa Unión.

Sleeping

There are no accommodations in the park itself, though it's possible to camp informally at the *confitería,* which has toilets but no showers.

Pagancillo, just 29km north of the park, is probably the best place for basic accommodations in the area. If you stay here it may be possible to get a lift into the park with the ranger. There are five *casas de familia* in Pagancillo; these accommodations cost about US$6/8 per single/double. Readers have reported good things about **Hospedaje Pagancillo** (☎ 03825-47039; per person US$8; dinner US$4). The facilities are basic but spotless and it's run by a friendly family.

Getting There & Away

Travelers without their own cars can take the Transportes Rápido bus from La Rioja to Pagancillo, 29km from Talampaya, where most of the park personnel reside; from there the rangers will help you get to the park, where it is necessary to pay for the excursions.

Córdoba & the Central Sierras

Smack in the center, Córdoba is the geographical heart of Argentina. Spend a little time here, and you'll find yourself believing it's the spiritual heart as well. That's because the people, *córdobeses*, are just so damn friendly. Whether you're chillin' in the plaza of the provincial capital, shopping in its Mercado Norte, or tossing back lagers on the sunny patio of a German microbrewery in the mountains, the interactions you'll have here will make you feel at home.

Córdoba has yet to hit it big with foreign tourists, that spectacle-hungry bunch with Andean peaks and Patagonian glaciers on the mind. Which means you won't find a hotel in the province with two-tier pricing, and you'll rarely feel someone's out to make a buck on you (Hey, leather jacket, amigo?). What you will find is amiable folks in the city with the country's most exquisitely preserved colonial architecture, majestic Jesuit missions in little mountain towns, and gentle mountain ranges. Be sure to visit the Jesuit mission of Alta Gracia, one of five provincial missions declared Unesco World Heritage sites. Head to La Cumbre for paragliding over the beautiful Río Pinto, and visit Villa General Belgrano, a tree-filled village straight out of the German Alps. Spend a day hiking outside the resort village of La Cumbrecita, and when you're finished with life in the trees, return to Córdoba for a wild night on Calle Rondeau.

Neighboring San Luis province sees even fewer foreign tourists, and its spectacular Parque Nacional Sierras de las Quijadas, similar to San Juan's more famous Ischigualasto (Valle de la Luna), is cheaper, far easier to reach and equally impressive.

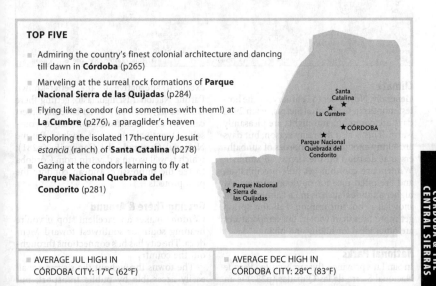

TOP FIVE

- Admiring the country's finest colonial architecture and dancing till dawn in **Córdoba** (p265)
- Marveling at the surreal rock formations of **Parque Nacional Sierra de las Quijadas** (p284)
- Flying like a condor (and sometimes with them!) at **La Cumbre** (p276), a paraglider's heaven
- Exploring the isolated 17th-century Jesuit *estancia* (ranch) of **Santa Catalina** (p278)
- Gazing at the condors learning to fly at **Parque Nacional Quebrada del Condorito** (p281)

Santa Catalina
La Cumbre
CÓRDOBA
Parque Nacional Quebrada del Condorito
Parque Nacional Sierra de las Quijadas

- AVERAGE JUL HIGH IN CÓRDOBA CITY: 17°C (62°F)
- AVERAGE DEC HIGH IN CÓRDOBA CITY: 28°C (83°F)

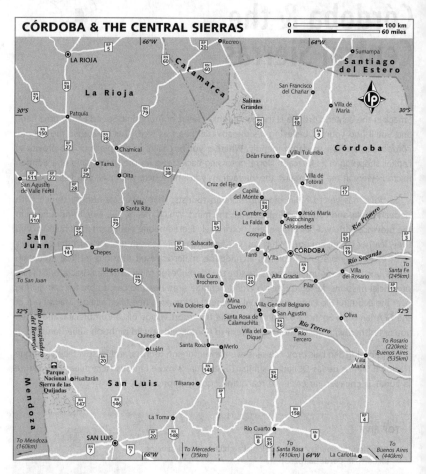

CÓRDOBA & THE CENTRAL SIERRAS

Climate

Generally, November to February are the hottest months in the Central Sierras, when 29°C days are common, and nights are pleasantly warm. This is also the rainy season, but days are sunny enough for the hordes of sunbathers that descend on the sierras all summer. Winters are cool but get little precipitation and are often nice for outdoor pursuits. At higher altitudes (such as in La Cumbre), light snowfall is not uncommon. Fall and spring get more rain than winter, but temperatures are often ideal for hiking and biking.

National Parks

In San Luis province, the rarely visited Parque Nacional Sierra de las Quijadas (p284) is an excellent alternative to the better-known Parque Nacional Ischigualasto: getting there is far easier, and you'll often have the desert canyons and rock formations all to yourself. Argentina's youngest park is Parque Nacional Quebrada del Condorito (p281), which is well worth a day trip from Córdoba to see the impressive Andean condors the park protects.

Getting There & Around

Córdoba makes an excellent stop if you're heading south or southwest toward Mendoza. The city has bus connections throughout the country.

The towns throughout the sierras are all easily accessible by public transport, but many tiny, remote towns and Jesuit *estancias* can only be reached with your own wheels. The sierras' dense network of roads, many well paved but others only gravel, make them good candidates for bicycle touring; Argentine drivers here seem a bit less ruthless than elsewhere in the country. A mountain bike is still the best choice.

CÓRDOBA

☎ 0351 / pop 1,300,000 / elevation 400m
With a total of seven universities, Córdoba is the educational center of Argentina, and its large student population gives the city a vibrancy unlike any other. You'll never run out of bars to hop or people to meet, and you'll find it difficult to leave once you slide into the scene. What's more, Córdoba boasts Argentina's best-preserved colonial architecture, from the breathtaking 17th-century Manzana Jesuítica (Jesuit Block) to underground Jesuit crypts, to the country's oldest university. Although this is Argentina's second-largest city, its downtown is easily explored on foot. The colonial center, the hip restaurants and bars of Nueva Córdoba, and the weekend crafts market – one of the best in the country – in Barrio Güemes are all within walking distance of each other.

ORIENTATION

Córdoba is 715km northwest of Buenos Aires and 330km south of Santiago del Estero via RN 9. Most colonial sites lie within a few blocks of Plaza San Martín, the city's urban nucleus. The commercial center is just northwest of the plaza, where the main pedestrian malls – 25 de Mayo and Rivera Indarte – intersect each other. Obispo Trejo, just west of the plaza, has the finest concentration of colonial buildings. Just south of downtown, Parque Sarmiento offers relief from the bustling, densely built downtown.

East–west streets change names at San Martín/Independencia and north–south streets change at Deán Funes/Rosario de Santa Fe.

INFORMATION
Internet Access
Cyber cafés are tucked into *locutorios* (telephone kiosks) throughout the center, and they're everywhere in Nueva Córdoba.

Stone (☎ 15-547-6458; Av Marcelo T de Alvear 370; per hr US$0.30; ⏰ 10am-dawn) One of the grooviest cyber joints in town. Pizzas, drinks and empanadas too.

Laundry
Trapitos (☎ 422-5877; Independencia 898; full service about US$1.70)

Medical Services
Emergency Hospital (☎ 421-0243; cnr Catamarca & Blvd Guzmán)

Money
Downtown, *cambios* (exchange houses) and ATMs are on Rivadavia just north of the plaza; both can also be found at the main bus terminal and airport.
Cambio Barujel (cnr Rivadavia & 25 de Mayo) High commissions.
Maguitur (☎ 421-6200; 25 de Mayo 122) Charges 3% on traveler's checks.

Post
Main post office (Av General Paz 201)

Tourist Information
ACA (Automóvil Club Argentino; ☎ 421-4636; cnr Av General Paz & Humberto Primo)
Casa Cabildo Tourist Information Office (☎ 428-5856; Independencia 30; ⏰ 8am-8pm) Provincial and municipal tourist boards together maintain their main information office here in the historic Casa Cabildo.
Provincial tourist office airport (☎ 434-8390; Aeropuerto Pajas Blancas; ⏰ 8am-8pm Mon-Fri); bus terminal (☎ 433-1980; ⏰ 8am-9pm).

Travel Agencies
Asatej (☎ 422-9453; www.asatej.com in Spanish; Av Vélez Sarsfield 361, Patio Olmos, Local 319) Third floor of Patio Olmos shopping center. Nonprofit student travel agency with a great staff. Open to all ages and nonstudents.

SIGHTS
There's plenty to see in Córdoba, so allow yourself at least a couple of days for wandering around. Most churches are open roughly from 9am to noon and from 5pm to 8pm. Museum opening hours change regularly depending on the season and the administration.

Centro
Downtown Córdoba is a treasure of colonial buildings and other historical monuments.

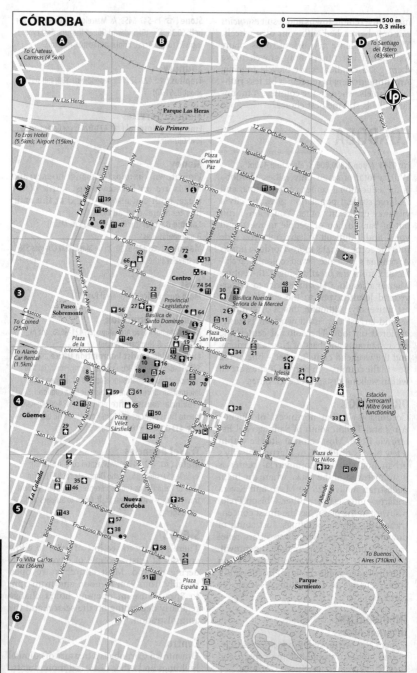

CÓRDOBA

0 _____ 500 m
0 _____ 0.3 miles

CÓRDOBA & THE
CENTRAL SIERRAS

INFORMATION
ACA..1 B2
Asatej..(see 65)
Cambio Barujel.................................2 C3
Casa Cabildo Tourist Information Office.3 B3
Emergency Hospital...........................4 D3
Hospital San Roque...........................5 C4
Maguitur..6 C3
Main Post Office................................7 B3
Provincial Tourist Office..................(see 69)
Stone...8 A4
Trapitos..9 B5

SIGHTS & ACTIVITIES
Cabildo..(see 3)
Capilla Doméstica............................10 B4
Casa del Obispo Mercadillo...............11 C3
Colegio Nacional de Monserrat...........12 B4
Cripta Jesuítica................................13 B3
Cripta Jesuítica................................14 B3
Iglesia Catedral................................15 B3
Iglesia de la Compañía de Jesús..........16 B4
Iglesia de Santa Teresa y Convento de
   Carmelitas Descalzas de San José....17 B4
Latitud Sur...................................(see 38)
Manzana Jesuítica............................18 B4
Museo de Arte Religioso Juan de
   Tejeda.......................................19 B4
Museo de la Ciudad.........................20 B4
Museo Histórico de la Universidad Nacional de
   Córdoba...................................(see 26)
Museo Histórico Provincial Marqués de
   Sobremonte...............................21 C3
Museo Iberoamericano de Artesanías..(see 38)
Museo Municipal de Bellas Artes Dr Genaro
   Pérez..22 B3

Museo Provincial de Bellas Artes Emilio
   Caraffa......................................23 B6
Palacio Ferreyra..............................24 B5
Parroquia Sagrado Corazón de Jesús de los
   Capuchinos...............................25 B5
Universidad Nacional de Córdoba........26 B4

SLEEPING 🏠
Córdoba Backpackers........................27 B3
Ducal Suites...................................28 C4
Hotel de la Cañada..........................29 A4
Hotel Garden..................................30 C3
Hotel Helvetia................................31 C4
Hotel Heydi....................................32 D5
Hotel Roma Termini.........................33 D4
Hotel Sussex...................................34 C4
Hotel Viena....................................35 A5
Hotel Viña de Italia..........................36 D4
Ritz Hotel.......................................37 C4
Tango Hostel...................................38 B5

EATING 🍴
Alcorta..39 A2
Alfonsina.......................................40 B4
Beto's..41 A4
Doña Anastasia...............................42 A4
El Arrabal.......................................43 A5
La Bodega del Bacalao.....................44 B4
La Mamma.....................................45 A2
La Nieta 'e la Pancha.......................46 A5
La Parrilla de Raul............................47 B2
La Perla...48 C3
La Vieja Esquina.............................49 B3
Las Tinajas.....................................50 B4
Lomitos 348...................................51 B6
Mandarina......................................52 B4

Mercado Norte................................53 C2
Verde Que te Quiero Verde...............54 B3

DRINKING 🍷
But Mitre.......................................55 A5
Cuernavaca.....................................56 B3
El Sha..57 B5
Good Bar..58 B5
María María....................................59 A4

ENTERTAINMENT 🎭
Cineclub Municipal Hugo del Carril......60 B4
Patio del Tango...........................(see 3)
Teatro del Libertador General San
   Martín.......................................61 B4

SHOPPING 🛍
Camping Shop.................................62 B3
Feria Artesanal...............................63 A5
La Emilia..64 B3
Patio Olmos Shopping Center............65 B4
Regionales La Fama..........................66 B3
Talabartería Crespo.........................67 B3

TRANSPORT
Aerolíneas Argentinas.......................68 A2
Austral.......................................(see 68)
Bus Terminal..................................69 D5
Europcar (Hotel Dora)......................70 B4
Lan Chile.......................................71 A2
Lloyd Aéreo Boliviano......................72 B3
Mercado Sud Minibus Terminal..........73 B4
Varig...74 B3

OTHER
Facultad de Lenguas.........................75 B4

IGLESIA CATEDRAL

Begun in 1577, the construction of Córdoba's **cathedral** (guided visit US$2; ☉ 9am-noon & 5-8pm) dragged on for over two centuries under several architects, including Jesuits and Franciscans, and though it lacks any sense of architectural unity, it's a beautiful structure. Crowned by a Romanesque dome, it overlooks Plaza San Martín, at Independencia and 27 de Abril. The lavish interior was painted by renowned *cordobés* (Córdoban) painter Emilio Caraffa. Guided visits leave hourly between 9am and 5pm from Psje Santa Catalina 61, the entry on the north side of the cathedral.

MANZANA JESUÍTICA

Córdoba's beautiful **Manzana Jesuítica** (Jesuit Block), like that of Buenos Aires, is also known as the Manzana de las Luces (Block of Enlightenment), and was initially associated with the influential Jesuit order.

Designed by the Flemish Padre Philippe Lemaire, the **Iglesia Compañía de Jesús** (admission free; cnr Obispo Trejo & Caseros) dates from 1645 but was not completed until 1671, with the successful execution of Lemaire's plan for a cedar roof in the form of an inverted ship's hull. Lemaire was once, unsurprisingly, a boat builder. Inside, its baroque altarpiece

is carved Paraguayan cedar from Misiones province. The **Capilla Doméstica** (Domestic Chapel; guided visits per person US$1; ☉ 10am, 11am, 5pm & 6pm), completed in 1644, sits directly behind the church on Caseros. Its ornate ceiling was made with cowhide stretched over a skeleton of thick taguaro cane and painted with pigments composed partially of boiled bones. Guided visits (the only way in) leave from inside the Universidad Nacional de Córdoba.

In 1613 Fray Fernando de Trejo y Sanabria founded the Seminario Convictorio de San Javier, which, after being elevated to university status in 1622, became the **Universidad Nacional de Córdoba** (☎ 433-2075; Obispo Trejo 242; ☉ 9am-1pm & 4-8pm). The university is the country's oldest and contains, among other national treasures, part of the Jesuits' Grand Library and the **Museo Histórico de la Universidad Nacional de Córdoba** (☎ 433-2075; guided visits per person US$1; ☉ 10am, 11am, 5pm & 6pm Tue-Sun). Guided visits are the only way to see the inside and are well worth taking. They let you to wander through the Colegio and peek into the classrooms while students run around.

Next door, the **Colegio Nacional de Monserrat** (Obispo Trejo 294) dates from 1782, though the college itself was founded in 1687 and transferred after the Jesuit expulsion. Though the interior cloisters are original, the exterior was considerably modified in 1927 by restoring architect Jaime Roca, who gave the building its present baroque flare.

In 2000, Unesco declared the Manzana Jesuítica a World Heritage site, along with five Jesuit *estancias* throughout the province.

MUSEO HISTÓRICO PROVINCIAL MARQUÉS DE SOBREMONTE

It's worth dropping into one of the county's most important **historical museums** (☎ 433-1661/71; Rosario de Santa Fe 218; admission US$0.30; ☼ 10am-5pm Tue-Thu, 8am-2pm Sat) if only to see the colonial house it occupies: an 18th-century home that once belonged to Rafael Núñez, the colonial governor of Córdoba and later Viceroyal of the Río de la Plata. It has 26 rooms, seven interior patios, meter-thick walls and an impressive wrought-iron balcony supported by carved wooden brackets.

CRIPTA JESUÍTICA

The Jesuits, at the beginning of the 18th century, built the **Cripta Jesuítica** (cnr Rivera Indarte & Av Colón; admission US$0.20; ☼ 9am-2pm Mon-Fri). It was originally designed as a novitiate and later converted to a crypt and crematorium. Abandoned after the Jesuit expulsion, it was demolished and buried around 1829 when the city, while expanding Av Colón, knocked the roof into the subterranean naves and built over the entire structure. It remained all but forgotten until Telecom, while laying underground telephone cable in 1989, accidentally ran into it. The city, with a new outlook on such treasures, exquisitely restored the crypt and uses it regularly for musical and theatrical performances and art exhibits. Entrances, which one might mistake for subway stairs, lie on either side of Av Colón in the middle of the Rivera Indarte pedestrian mall.

MUSEO MUNICIPAL DE BELLAS ARTES DR GENARO PÉREZ

This museum is prized for its collection of paintings from the 19th and 20th centuries. Works, including those by Emilio Caraffa, Lucio Fontana, Lino Spilimbergo, Antonio Berni and Antonio Seguí, chronologically display the history of the *cordobés* school of painting, at the front of which stands the museum's namesake, Genaro Pérez. The Palacio Garzón, an unusual turn-of-the-century building named for its original owner, houses the **museum** (☎ 433-1512; Av General Paz 33; admission

US$0.30; ☼ 9am-7pm Tue-Sun), which also has outstanding changing contemporary art exhibits.

PLAZA SAN MARTÍN & AROUND

Córdoba's lovely and lively central plaza dates from 1577. Its western side is dominated by the white arcade of the restored **Cabildo** (colonial town-council building), completed in 1785 and containing three interior patios, as well as basement cells. All are open to the public as part of the **Museo de la Ciudad** (☎ 433-1543; Independencia 30; admission free; ☼ 4-9pm Mon, 9am-1pm Tue-Sun).

The slightly hidden **Casa del Obispo Mercadillo** (Rosario de Santa Fe 39), on the plaza's northern side, is worth a look for its impressive colonial wrought-iron balcony.

Occupying nearly half a city block, the **Iglesia de Santa Teresa y Convento de Carmelitas Descalzas de San José** (cnr Caseros & Independencia; admission free; ☼ 6-8pm) was completed in 1628 and has functioned ever since as a closed-order convent for Carmelite nuns. Only the church itself is open to visitors. Once part of the convent, the **Museo de Arte Religioso Juan de Tejeda** (☎ 423-0175; Independencia 122; admission US$0.70; ☼ 9am-noon Wed-Sat), next door, exhibits religious artifacts, as well as paintings by *cordobés* masters.

Nueva Córdoba

Before the northwestern neighborhoods of Chateau Carreras and Cerro de las Rosas lured the city's elite to their peaceful hillsides, Nueva Córdoba was the neighborhood of the *cordobés* aristocracy. It's now popular with students, which explains the proliferation of brick high-rise apartment buildings. Still, a stroll past the stately old residences that line the wide Av Yrigoyen reveals the area's aristocratic past.

Nueva Córdoba's landmark building, the private **Palacio Ferreyra** (Av H Yrigoyen 551), stands nearly hidden behind a hedge-covered fence just before Plaza España at the southern end of Yrigoyen. It was built in 1900 and designed by Ernest Sanson in the Louis XVI style. On the way down Yrigoyen, swing a left on Obispo Oro to see the marvelous neo-Gothic **Parroquia Sagrado Corazón de Jesús de los Capuchinos** (cnr Buenos Aires & Obispo Oro; admission free), built between 1928 and 1934, whose glaring oddity is its missing steeple (omitted on purpose to symbolize human imperfection). Among the numerous sculptures that cover the church's facade are those of Atlases symbolically struggling to bare the spiritual weight of the religious figures above them (and sins and guilt of the rest of us).

One of the city's best contemporary art museums is the neoclassical **Museo Provincial de Bellas Artes Emilio Caraffa** (☎ 433-3414; Av H Yrigoyen 651; admission free; ⏰ 11am-7pm Tue-Sun). It stands ostentatiously on the eastern side of Plaza España. Architect Juan Kronfuss designed the building as a museum and it was inaugurated in 1916. Exhibits change monthly. South of the museum the city unfolds into its largest open-space area, the **Parque Sarmiento**, designed by Charles Thays, the architect who designed Mendoza's Parque General San Martín.

Güemes

Once a strictly working-class neighborhood, Güemes is now known for the eclectic **antique stores** and **artisan shops** that line the main drag of Belgrano, between Rodriguez and Laprida. Its weekend feria artisanal (p272), one of the country's best, teems with antique vendors, arts and crafts and a healthy dose of Córdoba's hippies. It's within the same block as the **Museo Iberoamericano de Artesanías** (☎ 433-4368; cnr Belgrano & Rodriguez; admission free; ⏰ 9am-8pm Tue-Sun), which houses beautiful crafts from throughout South America. A good way back to the city center is along **La Cañada**, an acacia-lined stone canal with arched bridges.

COURSES

Córdoba is an excellent place to study Spanish; in many ways, being a student is what Córdoba is all about. Lessons cost about US$10 per hour for one-on-one courses or US$80 to US$125 per week in small classes.
Coined (☎ 429-9402; www.coined.com.ar; Caseros 873)
Facultad de Lenguas (☎ 433-1073/5, ext 30; www.lenguas.unc.edu.ar; Av Vélez Sarsfield 187) Part of the Universidad Nacional de Córdoba.

TOURS

City tours (in Spanish US$2.70, in English US$5) Absorb Córdoba's rich history by taking one of the guided city tours that depart daily at 9:30am and 4:30pm from the Casa Cabildo (p265). Reserve a day in advance if you want a tour in English.
Latitud Sur (☎ 425-6023; www.latitudsurtrek.com.ar in Spanish; Fructuoso Rivera 70) Run by an enthusiastic young couple with boundless knowledge of both the sierras and the city, Latitud Sur offers mountain-bike, trekking, rock-climbing and horse-riding tours throughout the Sierras

de Córdoba, including day trips to Los Gigantes and Parque Nacional Quebrada del Condorito (p281). Prices range from US$18 to US$25, including transport, guide and lunch. Paragliding costs US$50 and skydiving US$94 (US$120 if you want it videotaped). It's an excellent operation, and you'll see things you wouldn't otherwise. City tours are outstanding, fun and only cost US$1.70 per person. English is spoken.

FESTIVALS & EVENTS

During the first three weeks of April, the city puts on a large **crafts market** (locally called 'FICO') at the city fairgrounds, on the town's north side near Chateau Carreras stadium. Bus No 31 from Plaza San Martín goes there. Córdoba celebrates the **founding of the city** on July 6. Mid-September's **Feria del Libro** is a regional book fair.

SLEEPING

Hotels on and around Plaza San Martín (Centro) make exploring the center a cinch, but you'll have to walk several blocks for dinner and nightlife. Hotels along La Cañada and in Nueva Córdoba, on the other hand, mean going out to dinner and hitting the bars is a simple matter of walking down the street. There are some good hotels located near the bus terminal, but some only rent rooms by the hour.

Centro

Córdoba Backpackers (☎ 422-0593; www.cordobabackpackers.com.ar; Deán Funes 285; 4-bed dm US$4/4.25, 6-bed dm US$3.50/3.75, d US$10/11.50, with shared bathroom US$9.50/10; 🖳) With a superb central location, comfortable common areas (including a cane-sided bar), TV room, spacious backyard, an airy kitchen, and a huge rooftop terrace with views of the basilica, Córdoba Backpackers is one prize hostel. You can pitch a tent in the back for US$2 per person. Breakfast is available for US$0.80 to US$1.25. Rates include free coffee and taxi service from the bus terminal.

Hotel Garden (☎ 421-4729; 25 de Mayo 35; s/d US$9/15.50) This attractive, clean hotel has an excellent location, a friendly staff, rooms with TVs and decent beds, and two covered interior patios. Rooms are on the small side, and one reader felt it was a bit dark, but it's a great deal regardless.

Hotel Sussex (☎ 422-9070/5; www.hotelsussexcba.com.ar; San Jerónimo 125; s/d US$22/28.50; P 🛒) In a sophisticated building just off the main plaza, the Sussex is one of Córdoba's oldest hotels, though its remodeled rooms have a worn 1960s feel. The 11th-floor breakfast room has stunning views over the plaza, and the rooftop pool is open during summer. Get a room with a view and you're stylin'.

Ducal Suites (☎ 570-8888; www.hotelducal.com.ar in Spanish; Corrientes 207; s/d US$30/34; P 🍴 📶) This is another modern beauty, where guests have access to a fabulous rooftop pool (it's clean, filtered and heated too!) with dozens of chaise longues around the deck. Spacious rooms have kitchenettes and ample bathrooms, but the TVs sure seem small.

Hotel Helvetia (☎ 421-7297; San Jerónimo 479; s/d US$7/8.50, with shared bathroom US$4/5) The Helvetia is beat up but it definitely has its own character. Large, windowless and rather dilapidated rooms have tall shuttered doors opening onto an empty interior patio. It's very basic but cheap and – thanks to the orange walls – even a little cheerful. There's an attached café.

Ritz Hotel (☎ 421-5031/2/3; San Jerónimo 495; s/d US$11.50/18.50; P) Step back into a dark and faded 1960s elegance at this 60-room hotel with its dimly lit lounge, wood-paneled walls and big leather sofas. Suited bellhops will lead you down wide, worn hallways to small but comfortable rooms.

Nueva Córdoba & La Cañada

Tango Hostel (☎ 425-6023; Fructuoso Rivera 70; www.latitudsurtrek.com.ar in Spanish; dm US$5, d with shared/private bathroom US$10/11) This immaculate and intimate new hostel boasts a fabulous staff, clean dorm rooms with only four to five beds in each, spotless bathrooms and lots of traveler information lying around. The well-equipped kitchen, comfy eating area and common room are all conducive to socializing, and the young owners know heaps about adventure tourism. Excellent.

Hotel Viena (☎ 460-0909; www.hotelviena.com.ar; Laprida 235; s US$17.50-18.50, d US$18.50-23; 🍴 📶) A professional staff runs around this tidy

---

THE AUTHOR'S CHOICE

La Nieta 'e La Pancha (☎ 468-1920; Belgrano 783; mains US$4-5, set lunch US$3) A wonderful staff prepares and serves a changing menu of delectable regional specialties, creative pastas and house recipes. Be sure to save room for dessert. Simply put, it's one of the best restaurants in town.

50-room hotel making sure everything is in order. The pricier rooms have deluxe mattresses and all have TV and telephone. There are lots of nooks for sitting in the lobby area, and there's a restaurant on the premises. It feels much smaller than it is. Good choice.

Hotel de la Cañada (☎ 421-4649; www.hoteldelacaniada.com.ar in Spanish; Av Marcelo T de Alvear 580; s/d US$31.50/40; P 🍴 📶 📠 📶) This stylish wood-and-brick construction near La Cañada is one of the city's swankiest hotels; its location is superb, and though it's large, it still feels personal. The huge rooms are immaculate, and perks include a swimming pool, sauna, gym, terrace bar and an army of friendly staff members. Great for a splurge.

Around the Bus Terminal

Hotel Heydi (☎ 421-8906; www.hotelheydi.com.ar in Spanish; Blvd Illia 615; s/d US$16/23; P 🍴) Near the bus terminal, this is the best of the bunch: a modern, immaculate place with a friendly, professional staff.

Hotel Viña de Italia (☎ 422-6589; www.hotelvinadeitalia.com.ar; San Jerónimo 611; s/d US$13.50/18.50; P 🍴) There's a bit of elegance left in this 150-room hotel, and the midsize rooms all include TV, telephone, air-con and heating. Light blue satiny couches grace the lobby downstairs, and there's a decent restaurant attached.

EATING

Mercado Norte (cnr Rivadavia & Oncativo; 🕐 closed Sun) Córdoba's indoor market has delicious and inexpensive food, such as pizza, empanadas and seafood; browsing the clean stalls selling every imaginable cut of meat, including whole *chivitos* (kid) and pigs, is a must.

La Mamma (☎ 421-2212; cnr Av Alcorta & Santa Rosa; pastas US$3-4, meats US$5-6) This is by far the city's best pasta; the *tríptico* (a plate of three pastas with three sauces) is sublime.

Beto's (☎ 424-6225; Blvd San Juan 450; mains US$3-6.50) Excellent *parrilla* (grill) with a superb *parrillada completa* (mixed grill) including eight cuts of meat and a full salad bar (US$6 to US$7).

La Vieja Esquina (☎ 424-7940; cnr Belgrano & Caseros; empanadas US$0.50; 🕐 closed Sun) Cozy little place serving excellent empanadas and other baked savories. The *locro* (spicy stew) is tempting but a little heavy on the oil. Great place.

Lomitos 348 (☎ 469-7975; Estrada 146; sandwiches US$1.50-2.50) It may look average when you step in, but 348 is known for serving the best *lomitos* (steak sandwiches) in the city.

Verde Que te Quiero Verde (☎ 421-8820; 9 de Julio 36; lunch US$2-3; ☻ lunch) Delicious vegetarian buffet that also serves set meals.

La Perla (☎ 421-4112; Av Olmos 265; mains US$2-4; ☻ noon-3:30pm & 8pm-12:30am) This popular down-home eatery, with a hilariously attentive staff, has huge lunch specials and filling Italian- and Spanish-influenced mains.

Alfonsina (☎ 427-2847; Duarte Quirós 66; pizzas US$2-4; ☻ 8am-dawn, closed 4-8pm Sat) Slip into this laid-back bar-cum-pizzeria for great atmosphere and outstanding pizzas. Decorations are as eclectic as the crowd, and folks sit for hours smoking and talking. Great place to try *mate*.

Doña Anastasia (☎ 424-1716; Blvd San Juan 325; mains US$5-7) Upscale restaurant with an excellent wine list and food and atmosphere to match. Seafood, steaks, chicken dishes and pastas make up the menu, and all are beautifully presented. Good for a romantic dinner for two.

La Parrilla de Raul (☎ 424-7865; Jujuy 278; mains US$2.50-3.50) Of Córdoba's many *parrillas*, this is probably the most atmospheric: it's small and dimly lit, and the walls are stacked with Argentine wines. *Parrillada* for two costs only US$3.50 to US$5, not including extras such as drinks or salad.

La Bodega del Bacalao (☎ 418-7288; Montevideo 86; mains US$4-6; ☻ dinner) Small, softly lit Bodega del Bacalao is as good at atmosphere as it is at Spanish food. Fair prices for top wines. Romantic.

Las Tinajas (☎ 411-4150; Blvd San Juan 32; lunch US$3.50 Mon-Fri, US$4-5 Sat & Sun, dinner US$4-5) The country's largest *tenedor libre* (all-you-can-eat restaurant) serves a mind-boggling array of international cuisine.

Alcorta (☎ 424-7452; Av Alcorta 330; mains US$5-6) This upmarket *parrilla*, esteemed for its grilled meats (many say they're the best in town), also serves delicious pasta and fish. Try the *mollejitas al sauvignan blanc* (sweetbreads in a white wine sauce).

El Arrabal (☎ 460-2990; www.elarrabal.com.ar in Spanish; Belgrano 899; mains US$3.50-6) El Arrabal serves imaginative regional and house specialties, but the real reason to come is the live tango every night at 11pm. Make a reservation.

LOVE BY THE HOUR

Every city in Argentina has *hoteles por hora* (hourly rate hotels), where people take their secret lovers for a romp in the good old proverbial hay. They vary from cheap, nondescript *residenciales* (cheap hotels) to deluxe love pads with black lights, wall-to-wall mirrors, nonstop sex-TV, Jacuzzis and room-service menus featuring every imaginable sex toy under the sun. These deluxe versions are a part of under-the-table Argentine culture that shouldn't be missed (provided you're traveling with a partner who's game, of course).

Córdoba boasts four deluxe *hoteles por hora* on the road to the airport, and if you haven't experienced one of these Argentine institutions, now's your chance. Although they're geared toward folks with cars, you can go in a taxi (trust us, we know). Here's a quick primer on how they work.

First, it's all about anonymity. As you drive into the hotel a big number flashes on a sign; that's your room number. Drive to the garage door with your number on it, pull in and close the garage door; if you're in a taxi, the driver will drop you in the garage and leave. Close the garage door and enter the room.

In five minutes the phone will ring, and the attendant will ask you if you'd like a complimentary beverage, which he or she then delivers through a tiny sliding door in the wall so no one sees anybody. When the attendant knocks on the door, you open it, take your drinks and pay for the room (US$16 for two hours is the going rate). After that, it's two hours of fun and games. Ten minutes before your time is up, the attendant will courteously ring again to tell you your time is up.

Of the four hotels on the airport road, the best is **Eros Hotel** (Camino al aeropuerto, Km 5.5; 2 hr US$16). It has en-suite Jacuzzis, bedside control panels, all the right TV channels and *all* the fun stuff. And it's impeccably clean.

A taxi costs about US$4 each way. If you take one, call a *remise* (telephone taxi) from your hotel and have the driver pick you up in two hours. They all know the drill – no pun intended.

Mandarina (☎ 426-4909; Obispo Trejo 171; mains US$3-7) Decent Chinese dishes and tasty pizzas and pastas are all cooked with flare at this cozy hideaway, and the mixed drinks are guaranteed to knock you out. Take a break from the meat and try one of the delicious salads.

DRINKING

Córdoba's drink of choice is Fernet (a strong, medicinal-tasting herbed liquor from Italy), almost always mixed with Coke. If you don't mind a rough morning, start in on the stuff.

The best place to barhop is Nueva Córdoba. Take a walk down Calle Rondeau between Avs H Yrigoyen and Chacabuco after midnight and choose from dozens of bars. The street is packed with people Thursday through Sunday night, and you can walk safely from bar to bar until dawn.

María María (Blvd San Juan 230) Across from Patio Olmos shopping center, this dark, cozy bar often gets excellent bands playing a variety of styles. It's a comfortable place, good for dancing or sitting around.

Cuernavaca (27 de Abril 354; ⏰ midnight-dawn Wed-Sat) Large, loud and fun, Cuernavaca is the place to go on Wednesday night, when it's so crowded you'll barely be able to move. For breathing room, stop by other nights.

El Sha (☎ 15-650-0908; Obispo Trejo 879; ⏰ closed Mon) Tiled arches, dim lighting, cozy booths, white beanbag chairs and electronica give this mosquelike bar a very chilled feel. Great for lounging.

But Mitre (www.butmitre.com; Av Marcelo T de Alvear 635) Extremely popular bar-cum-dance club on La Cañada. Check it out, especially on Thursday night.

THE AUTHOR'S CHOICE

Cineclub Municipal Hugo del Carril (☎ 433-2463; www.ccmunicipal.org.ar in Spanish; Blvd San Juan 49; admission US$0.50; box office ⏰ 9am-late) For a great night (or day) at the movies, pop into this municipal film house which screens everything from art flicks to Latin American award winners and local films. Shows start as early as 10am. Pick up a program. There's also live music and theatrical performances. For the price it simply can't be beat.

Good Bar (☎ 15-459-5771; cnr Buenos Aires & Larrañaga; ⏰ nightly) You'll recognize it by the surfboard stuck on the front of the building and the crowd inside warming up after midnight.

ENTERTAINMENT

On Friday nights, the city hosts the **Patio del Tango** (admission US$1, with dance lessons US$2) on the outdoor Patio Mayor of the historic Cabildo (weather permitting), kicking off with two-hour tango lessons. Times vary, so it's best to stop by the Casa Cabildo Tourist Information Office (p265).

La Voz del Interior, Córdoba's main newspaper, has a reasonably comprehensive entertainment section every Thursday with show times and the like.

Theater & Cinema

Teatro del Libertador General San Martín (☎ 433-2319; Av Vélez Sársfield 365; admission US$5-45; box office ⏰ 9am-9pm) It's well worth going to a performance here, if only to see the opulence of the country's most historic theater. The theater was completed in 1891, and the floor was designed to be mechanically raised and leveled to the stage, so seats could be removed, allowing for grand parties among the aristocracy of the early 1900s. Be discreet if you bring your camera.

SHOPPING

Antique stores line Calle Belgrano in Barrio Güemes, where there is also one of the country's best weekend **artisans' market** (cnr Rodríguez & Belgrano; ⏰ 5-10pm Sat & Sun). You'll find Argentine handicrafts at several stores downtown.

La Emilia (☎ 423-8402; Deán Funes 18) Though this shop has its share of shoddy souvenirs, there are still plenty of excellent regional crafts to choose from.

Regionales La Fama (☎ 422-8354; 9 de Julio 336; ⏰ closed Sun) This store deals in high-quality artisan knives, leather goods, alpaca woolens and other regional crafts.

Talabartería Crespo (☎ 421-5447; Obispo Trejo 141; ⏰ closed Sun) Leather goods made from *carpincho* (a large rodent that makes a beautifully spotted leather) are the specialty here. Sweaters, knives and *mate* paraphernalia grace the shelves as well.

Camping Shop (☎ 424-1264; Tucumán 127; ⏰ closed Sun) High-quality sleeping bags, packs, jackets, and trekking and camping equipment.

GETTING THERE & AWAY

Air

Córdoba's international airport, **Ingeniero Ambrosio Taravella** (☎ 475-0392), charges a US$18 departure tax on all international departures from here.

Aerolíneas Argentinas/Austral (☎ /fax 482-1025; Av Colón 520) has offices located downtown and flies several times daily to Buenos Aires (US$47 to US$148) and Mendoza (US$64 to US$69).

Southern Winds (☎ 0810-777-7979, 446-7866/7; Alcorta 192 at Colón) flies several times a day to Buenos Aires (US$42 to US$80) with connections throughout the country.

Lan Chile (☎ 0800-222-2424; Alcorta 206) flies daily to Santiago, Chile (US$100 to US$250, one way).

U-air (☎ 425-4190; www.uair.com in Spanish) was changing offices as we went to press, but call for tickets and location; it flies daily to Montevideo (about US$70 one way).

Lloyd Aéreo Boliviano (☎ 421-6458; Av Colón 166) flies twice a week to Santa Cruz de la Sierra, Bolivia (about US$270 one way).

Varig (☎ 482-0967; 9 de Julio 40, 2nd fl, Local 33) flies to Sao Paulo, Brazil (from US$370 one way).

Bus

Córdoba's **bus terminal** (NETOC; ☎ 423-4199, 423-0532; Blvd Perón 300) is about a 15-minute walk from downtown and has every service imaginable.

Sierras del Córdoba, Sierras de Calamuchita and Transportes La Cumbre all serve Córdoba's mountain hinterlands, including Villa General Belgrano (US$2.50, two hours) and Mina Clavero (US$3.50, three hours). Other nearby destinations in the sierras are easier and more quickly reached from the Mercado Sud minibus terminal (right). Minibus ticket offices in the main bus terminal are at booths 63 to 73 on the middle level.

Buses to Patagonia are invariably *coche cama* (sleepers), usually with breakfast and dinner.

There are several, and sometimes more than a dozen, daily departures to the destinations listed following. Check the **terminal tourist office** (☎ 433-1980) for the best deals, cheapest fares and highest services. The following prices are midseason and will fluctuate between companies and with the country's travel demands.

Destination	Cost (US$)	Duration (hr)
Bahía Blanca	21	12
Bariloche	25-37	22
Buenos Aires	11-22	10
Catamarca	10	5-6
Comodoro Rivadavia	30-40	25
Corrientes	20	12
Esquel	30	25
Formosa	22	15
Jujuy	17	12
La Rioja	8.50	7
Mar del Plata	36	16
Mendoza	10-12	10
Merlo	5	5½
Montevideo	32	15
Neuquén	25	15-16
Paraná	10	6
Puerto Iguazú	16-20	20
Puerto Madryn	38-48	18-20
Resistencia	20	11-12
Río Gallegos	40-55	36
Roque Sáenz Peña	20	14
Rosario	10	6
Salta	15	12
San Juan	10-15	8
San Luis	7	8
San Martín de los Andes	36-40	21
Santa Fe	10	5
Santiago del Estero	6	5
Tucumán	10-12	8

Several companies offer service to Chilean destinations including Santiago (US$20 to US$27, 15½ hours) and Val Paraíso (US$20 to US$27, 16 hours), though most involve changing buses in Mendoza.

Minibus

Frequent minibuses leave from **Mercado Sud Minibus Terminal** (Blvd Illia near Buenos Aires) for Villa Carlos Paz (US$1.50, one hour), Cosquín (US$2, 1¼ hours), La Falda (US$2.50, two hours), La Cumbre (US$3, 2½ hours), Capilla del Monte (US$3.20, three hours), Jesús María (US$1.30, one hour) and Alta Gracia (US$1, one hour). For La Cumbrecita you must go first to Villa General Belgrano (US$2.50, two hours); it's another US$3 and 1½ hours from there. There are also buses to Mina Clavero (US$4, 2¾ hours).

GETTING AROUND

The airport is 15km north of town via Av Monseñor Pablo Cabrera. From the main bus

CÓRDOBA & THE CENTRAL SIERRAS

terminal, the Empresa Ciudad de Córdoba bus marked 'Salsipuedes' goes to the airport. A taxi into town shouldn't cost you more than US$4.

Buses require *cospeles* (tokens), available for US$0.30 from nearly every kiosk in town.

A car is very useful for visiting some of the nearby Jesuit *estancias* that cannot be reached by bus. Economy cars cost about US$49 with 400km or US$57 with unlimited kilometers. Try the following:

Alamo (☎ 499-8436; Sheraton Hotel, Duarte Quirós 1300) Best prices we found.

Europcar (☎ 422-4867, 481-7683; Entre Ríos 70) Inside Hotel Dora.

THE CENTRAL SIERRAS

The Central Sierras tend to take a back seat, at least in the eyes of foreigners, to the dramatic scenery of the nearby Andes, but the area's small resort towns and outdoor opportunities are boundless. The beautifully situated towns of La Falda, La Cumbre and Capilla del Monte lie north of the capital along the RN 38 in the Valle de Punilla, and are great spots to simply kick back, hike or swim, especially in spring and fall when the crowds thin out. Southwest of the capital are the towns of Alta Gracia, with its Jesuit ruins, and Villa General Belgrano, an odd Germanesque resort. RN 20 is the southwestern route through the spectacular Altas Cumbres, traversing the southern mountains to the river-crossed town of Mina Clavero and down the western slopes of the Sierra de Comechingones to the mountain resort of Merlo, on the eastern edge of San Luis province.

The provincial tourist office in Córdoba provides thorough maps and slick brochures of the entire region.

VILLA CARLOS PAZ

☎ 03541 / pop 46,400 / elevation 600m

Only 36km west of Córdoba, on the shores of so-called Lago San Roque (in reality a large reservoir), Villa Carlos Paz is a minor-league, freshwater Mar del Plata. In summer, hordes of Argentines crowd its lakeshores, pack its dance floors and descend upon its disproportionate number of kitschy attractions, including a monstrous cuckoo clock. Foreigners generally find it less than appealing.

The **tourist office** (☎ 436430; San Martín-Yrigoyen intersection; ☽ 7am-11pm summer, 7am-9pm rest of year) distributes useful maps and guides to local services (which are plentiful).

Carlos Paz has some excellent hotels, but they're packed through the summer. **Hotel Ritz** (☎ 422126; http://usuarios.arnet.com.ar/hotelritz; Uruguay 38; r US$16) is a cheerful place (on an ugly street) with a retro interior and friendly owners.

Buses travel to Córdoba (US$1.50, one hour, every 15 minutes) from the **bus terminal** (San Martín 400). There are also regular departures to towns throughout Valle de Punilla and to Buenos Aires (from US$13.50, 11 hours).

COSQUÍN

☎ 03541 / pop 18,000 / elevation 720m

Cosquín, 26km north of Carlos Paz on the RN 38, is known for its **Festival Nacional del Folklore**, a nine-day national folk-music festival which has been held in the last week of January since 1961. The town gets packed for the festival, stays busy all summer and goes pleasantly dead the rest of the year. East of town, 1260m **Cerro Pan de Azúcar** offers good views of the sierras and, on a clear day, the city of Córdoba. The **municipal tourist office** (☎ 453701; San Martín 560; ☽ 8am-9pm Mon-Fri, 9am-6pm Sat & Sun) has a good map of the town.

Sleeping & Eating

Hotel Ideal (☎ 453043; Perón 1159; r US$7-14) Near the bus terminal, this owner-operated hotel is wonderfully friendly and reasonably comfortable. Rooms have TV and fan.

Petit Hotel (☎ 451311; A Sabattini 739; r low/high season US$10/16) Friendly, quiet hotel with an attractive patio and the requisite *parrilla* for *asados* (barbecues).

Paraíso de las Sierras (☎ 452190; San Martín 729; r US$29-60; ☒) A well-landscaped back patio, complete with pool and bar, makes this modern place very inviting. Rooms are spacious with satiny red bedspreads, TV and large bathrooms.

Pizzería Raffaelo (San Martín 730; mains US$3-4) Good pizzas, pastas and empanadas.

Parrilla Saint Jean (☎ 451059; San Martín 200; mains 2.50-7) Locals insist this is the best *parrilla* in town.

Getting There & Away

There are many daily departures north to La Falda (US$0.60, 45 minutes), La Cumbre

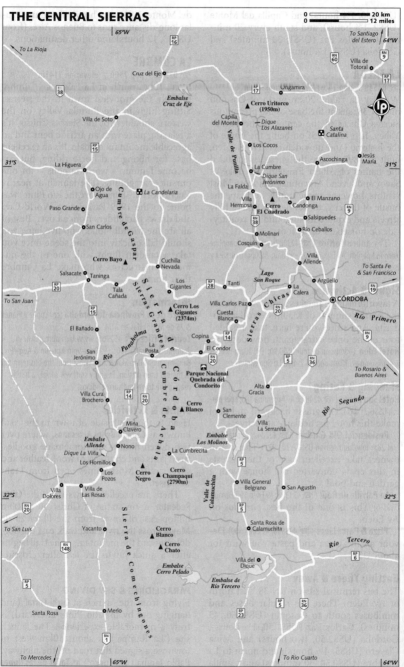

THE CENTRAL SIERRAS

0 — 20 km
0 — 12 miles

65°W

RP 16

To La Rioja

38

Cruz del Eje

To Santiago del Estero

RN 60

64°W

RN 9

Villa de Totoral

RP 17

Embalse Cruz de Eje

Capilla del Monte

Cerro Uritorco (1950m)

Ungamira

Villa de Soto

Dique Los Alazanes

Santa Catalina

RP 15

Los Cocos

Ascochinga

Jesús María

31°S

La Higuera

La Cumbre

Dique San Jerónimo

31°S

Ojo de Agua

La Candelaria

La Falda

El Manzano

Paso Grande

Villa Hermosa

Cerro El Cuadrado

Candonga

RN 9

San Carlos

RN 38

Salsipuedes

Molinari

Río Ceballos

Cerro Bayo

Cuchilla Nevada

Cosquín

Villa Allende

Salsacate

Taninga

Los Gigantes

RP 28

Tanti

Lago San Roque

To Santa Fe & San Francisco

RP 20

Tala Cañada

Sierras Grandes

La Calera

RN 19

CÓRDOBA

To San Juan

RP 15

Cerro Los Gigantes (2374m)

Villa Carlos Paz

Sierras Chicas

RN 20

El Bañado

Cuesta Blanca

Río Primero

RN 9

San Jerónimo

Río Panaholma

La Posta

Copina

RP 14

El Condor

RN 20

Villa Cura Brochero

RP 14

RN 20

Cumbre de Córdoba

Parque Nacional Quebrada del Condorito

Cerro Blanco

Alta Gracia

RP 5

RN 36

To Rosario & Buenos Aires

Mina Clavero

San Clemente

Río Segundo

Embalse Allende

Dique La Viña

Nono

Embalse Los Molinos

Villa La Serranita

Los Hornillos

La Cumbrecita

Villa Dolores

Los Pozos

Cerro Negro

Cerro Champaquí (2790m)

RP 5

Villa de Las Rosas

Villa General Belgrano

San Agustín

32°S

RN 20

Sierra de Comechingones

32°S

To San Luis

Yacanto

Cerro Blanco

Santa Rosa de Calamuchita

Río Tercero

RN 148

Cerro Chato

Villa del Dique

RP 6

Embalse Cerro Pelado

Embalse de Río Tercero

RP 5

Santa Rosa

Merlo

RP 5

RN 36

RN 1

To Mercedes

65°W

To Rio Cuarto

64°W

CÓRDOBA & THE CENTRAL SIERRAS

(US$1.50, 1¼ hours) and Capilla del Monte (US$2, 1¾ hours); and south every 20 minutes to Carlos Paz (US$1, 30 minutes) and Córdoba (US$2, 1¼ hours).

LA FALDA

☎ 03548 / pop 14,617 / elevation 934m

Woodsy La Falda, 20km north of Cosquín on RN 38, sits at the base of the precipitous Sierras Chicas in the center of the Punilla Valley. It prides itself on being the home of the historic (and now defunct) Hotel Eden, built in 1897, where the guest list included the names of Albert Einstein, the duke of Savoy and several Argentine presidents. Most visitors, however, come simply to escape the bustle of the city, to wander La Falda's hilly streets and explore its surrounding countryside on horseback or by foot.

The **tourist office** (☎ 423007; www.lafaldaonline .com in Spanish; Av España 50; ☒ 8am-8:30pm) is very helpful.

Sights & Activities

A favorite **hiking** trail takes about two hours to the nearby summit of 1350m Cerro La Banderita. And since you're here, take a guided tour of the once extravagant, now decaying **Hotel Eden** (admission by tour US$0.90; ☒ 10am-noon & 2-4pm summer, 10am-noon & 2-4pm Fri-Sun winter).

Sleeping & Eating

Hotel San Remo (☎ 424875; Av Argentina 105; r per person US$6-7; ☒) The grassy backyard and pool make this hotel particularly attractive.

Residencial Old Garden (☎ 422842; Capital Federal 28; r low/high season US$17/20; ☒) The live-in owners take excellent care of their guests in this cozy, converted old house with a garden and pool.

La Parrilla de Raúl (☎ 421128; Av Edén 1000; mains US$3-6) This is one of the best *parrillas* on Av Eden.

Pizza & Pasta Libre (☎ 425513; Av Eden 500) Devour all the pizza and pasta you want for about US$3.

Getting There & Away

The bus terminal sits on RN 38, just north of Av Eden. There are regular buses and minibuses south to Cosquín (US$0.60, 45 minutes), Carlos Paz (US$1.50, 1¼ hours), Córdoba (US$2.50, two hours) and Mina Clavero (US$5, 4½ hours); and north to La Cumbre (US$0.50, 30 minutes) and Capilla

del Monte (US$1, one hour). There are regular long-distance runs to Buenos Aires (from US$13, 12 hours) and other destinations.

LA CUMBRE

☎ 03548 / pop 7500 / elevation 1141m

Some 18km north of La Falda, La Cumbre is likely the grooviest town in the sierras. Sitting high in the Punilla Valley on the western shoulders of the Sierras Chicas, it's a relaxing place with an artistic bent and an agreeable mountain climate. It's an excellent base for hiking and horse riding, but has become famous – world famous – for one pursuit: paragliding. The launch at nearby Cuchi Corral, 380m above the Río Pinto, was home to the 1999 Paragliding World Cup and draws paragliders from all over. Best of all are the friendly folks who live here; you should fall quickly into the scene once you take a tandem flight with one of the numerous instructors who make La Cumbre their home.

Information

Banco de la Provincia de Córdoba (cnr Lopez y Planes & 25 de Mayo) Has an ATM.

Tourist office (☎ 452966; www.lacumbre.gov.ar in Spanish; Av Caraffa 300; ☒ 8am-9pm Apr-Jun & Aug-Nov, 8am-midnight Dec-Mar & Jul) Across from the bus terminal in the old train station. Friendly staff will supply a handy map of the town and surroundings.

Sights & Activities

Head to the south side of town to the road known as **Camino de los Artesanos**, where over two dozen homes sell homemade goodies, from jams and chutneys to wool, leather and silver crafts. Most homes open from 11am to sunset.

There are excellent views from the **Cristo Redentor**, a 7m statue of Christ on a 300m hilltop east of town; from the Plaza 25 de Mayo, cross the river and walk east on Córdoba toward the mountains – the trail begins after a quick jut to the left after crossing Cabrera.

PARAGLIDING & SKY DIVING

Flying from the launch at **Cuchi Corral** (and hanging out by the Río Pinto afterward) is truly a memorable experience. The launch site ('La Rampa') is about 10km west of town via a signed dirt road off the highway. Pablo Jaraba ('El Turco') at **Taller de las Nubes**

(☎ 15-570951; tallerdelasnubes@hotmail.com) and **Fechu** (☎ 15-574568) both offer tandem flights and lessons. Everyone charges about the same. Tandem flights cost US$33 for a half hour; full courses cost US$400.

At the **Aeroclub La Cumbre** (☎ 452544; Camino a los Troncos s/n), you can arrange everything from tandem flights to ultralights. Ask for Andy Hediger (former paragliding world champion) or Hernán Pitocco (number four in the world in paragliding acrobatics). You can also test your nerves parachuting with **Nicolás López** (☎ 452544; www.redbullaerobatix.com in Spanish).

HORSE RIDING & MOUNTAIN BIKING

Chachito Silva at **La Chacra** (☎ 451703; Pje Beiró s/n) and **Estancia El Viejo Piquete** (below) offer horseback excursions lasting from a few hours to multiple days. Prices run from about US$10 to US$17 for a half-day excursion and US$50 to US$57 for two days, including a full *asado* in the mountains.

Horacio Dorado (☎ 451575, 15-637451; Belgrano 449) rents quality mountain bikes (half/full day US$5/7) and offers guided rides, including transfers and food, for US$24 per person per day.

Sleeping

The proprietors of all the following places can arrange any activities available in La Cumbre.

Estancia El Viejo Piquete (☎ 15-635948; elviejo piquete@yahoo.com.ar; via Calle Mons Pablo Cabrera; d with full board US$57) For a relaxing stay in a divine location about 2.5km north of town, treat yourself to a night or two at this remote three-room *estancia* with fabulous views over the Valle de Punilla. There are only three rooms. Horse riding, hiking and other excursions are offered for guests and non-guests alike.

La Fonda (felipeobarrio@hotmail.com; Bartolomé Jaime; r per person US$12-15) Built in 1925, this Spanish-style house – which looks more like a castle – was recently reopened as a guest house. It lies 2km outside town on the road to Cruz Chica, and its gregarious owner alone will make your stay worthwhile.

Camping El Cristo (☎ 451893; Monseñor P Cabrera s/n; sites US$2) Below the Cristo Redentor east of town, La Cumbre's exceptional campgrounds are only a short tramp from the center.

> ### THE AUTHOR'S CHOICE
>
> **El Condor** (☎ 452870; el_condor_2001@yahoo .com.ar; Bartolomé Jaime 204; dm US$4; r with shared/private bathroom US$7/8.50) Thanks to its friendly owner and homey feel, this 1938 English-style home is easily the best deal in town. The house itself has a cozy living room and eight private rooms, some with private bathrooms and all with antique armoires and dressers. The small dorm area in back boasts a communal kitchen and an outdoor *parrilla*.

Eating & Drinking

El Pájaro Goloso (☎ 15-631885; Ruta 38, Km 67; mains US$3.50-5; ☽ 11am-midnight Dec-Mar & Jul; 11am-midnight Sat & Sun Apr-Jun & Aug-Nov) Located 5km south of town at the Aeroclub La Cumbre, El Pájaro Goloso serves up some of the best food in town, including a delicious Thai chicken curry, chicken dips with three sauces, and desserts to die for. Outside seating and views too.

Dream Bar (25 de Mayo 488, near Corrientes; pizzas US$1-1.50; ☽ 10am-late Dec-Mar & Jul, 4pm-late Thu-Sun rest of year) Join the paragliding crowd and the other friendly locals at this laid-back pizzeria-cum-bar where the music gets louder and the crowd gets friendlier as the night progresses.

La Casona del Toboso (☎ 451436; Belgrano 349; mains US$3-5) You're guaranteed to eat well at this local favorite with outdoor seating and a menu heavy on meats and pastas.

El Pungo (☎ 451378; www.elpungopub.com.ar in Spanish; Camino de los Artesanos s/n; cover US$3-5; ☽ noon-late Sat & Sun) This somewhat legendary watering hole attracts musicians from all over the country (Argentine folk musicians Charly Garcia and Fito Paez have both played here).

Getting There & Away

Buses depart regularly from La Cumbre's convenient **bus terminal** (General Paz near Caraffa), heading northward to Capilla del Monte (US$0.60, 30 minutes) or south to La Falda (US$0.50, 30 minutes), Cosquín (US$1.50, 1¼ hours), Villa Carlos Paz (US$1.85, 1½ hours) and Córdoba (US$3, 2½ hours). Minibuses are the fastest way to Córdoba. There is also direct service to Buenos Aires (US$12 to US$20, 12½ hours).

AROUND LA CUMBRE

Capilla Del Monte is an attractive town (elevation 979m) 18km north of La Cumbre on the RN 38. It not only attracts paragliders and outdoor enthusiasts to its surrounding countryside, but reputedly receives frequent visits from UFOs (*Ovnis*) as well, most frequently to the nearby 1979m-**Cerro Uritorco**, the highest peak in the Sierras Chicas. The 3km hike to the top affords spectacular views.

Capilla del Monte itself has plenty of restaurants and lodging, and there's a **tourist office** (☎ 03548-481903; Rivadavia 540). There is frequent bus service south to Córdoba (US$3.20, three hours), stopping at all towns on the RN 38, and long-distance service to Buenos Aires.

JESÚS MARÍA

☎ 03525 / pop 27,000

Jesús María, 48km north of Córdoba, is home to one of the finest Jesuit *estancias* in the province. It was built in 1618, and the Jesuits, after losing their operating capital to pirates off the Brazilian coast, sold wine they made here to support their university in colonial Córdoba. Set on superbly landscaped grounds, the church and convent now constitute the **Museo Jesuítico Nacional de Jesús María** (☎ 420126; admission US$0.60; ☺ 8am-7pm Mon-Fri, 10am-noon & 2-6pm Sat & Sun). The museum has good archaeological pieces from indigenous groups throughout Argentina, informative maps of the missionary trajectory and well-restored (though dubiously authentic) rooms.

Jesús María is also home to the annual **Fiesta Nacional de Doma y Folklore** (www.festivaljesusmaria.com in Spanish), a 10-day celebration of gaucho horsemanship and customs beginning the first weekend of January.

With limited accommodations and little else to do, Jesús María is best as a day trip from Córdoba. Frequent buses (US$1.30, one hour) leave Córdoba's Mercado Sud and main bus terminals (see p273) daily.

ESTANCIA SANTA CATALINA

☎ 03525

Some 20km northwest of Jesús María, the Jesuit *estancia* of **Santa Catalina** (☎ 421600; www.santacatalina.info; admission US$0.60-2; ☺ 10am-1pm & 2-6pm Tue-Sun winter, 10am-1pm & 3-7pm summer, closed Jan, Feb, Jul & Semana Santa) is one of the most beautiful of the Sierra's Unesco World Heritage sites. It's a quiet, tiny place, where the village store

occupies part of the *estancia*, and old-timers sit on the benches outside and watch the occasional gaucho ride past on a horse. It's like stepping back in time.

Santa Catalina is the only Unesco World Heritage *estancia* still under private ownership. Part of the family owns and operates **La Ranchería de Santa Catalina** (☎ 424467, 15-538957; www.la-rancheria.com.ar in Spanish; r per person US$17), a lovely restaurant, inn and crafts store in the *ranchería*. It has only two rooms, which occupy the former slave quarters and, while small, are carefully decorated in a ranch style and have the original stone walls.

A taxi out here from Jesús María costs about US$6.

ALTA GRACIA

☎ 03547 / pop 39,000 / elevation 550m

Only 35km southwest of Córdoba, the colonial mountain town of Alta Gracia makes an excellent day trip from the capital. The main attraction is the 17th-century Jesuit *estancia*, whose exquisite church, nighttime lighting, and lovely location between a tiny reservoir and the central plaza make it one of the most impressive of Córdoba's World Heritage sites. Revolutionary Che Guevara spent his adolescence in Alta Gracia and his former home is now a museum. Most visitors find a day enough and head back to Córdoba for the night.

The **tourist office** (☎ 428128; www.altagracia.gov.ar in Spanish; Reloj Público, cnr Av del Tajamar & Calle del Molino; ☺ 7am-10:30pm summer, 7am-7pm winter) occupies an office in the clock tower.

Sights & Activities

THE JESUIT ESTANCIA

From 1643 to 1762, Jesuit fathers built the **Iglesia Parroquial Nuestra Señora de la Merced** (west side of Plaza Manuel Solares; admission free) the *estancia's* most impressive building. Directly south of the church, the colonial Jesuit workshops of **El Obraje** (1643) are now a public school. Beside the church is the **Museo Histórico Nacional del Virrey Liniers** (☎ 421303; admission US$0.60, free Wed; ☺ 9am-8pm Tue-Fri, 9:30am-12:30pm & 5-8pm Sat, Sun & holidays), named after former resident Virrey Liniers, one of the last officials to occupy the post of Viceroy of the River Plate. On Wednesday and Friday, admission includes an informative guided tour.

Directly north of the museum, across Av Belgrano, the **Tajamar** (1659) is one of the city's several 17th-century dams, which together made up the complex system of field irrigation created by the Jesuits.

MUSEO CASA DE ERNESTO CHE GUEVARA

In the 1930s, the family of youthful Ernesto Guevara moved here because a doctor recommended the dry climate for his asthma (see the boxed text, below). Though Che lived in several houses, the family's primary residence was Villa Beatriz, which was recently purchased by the city and restored as the **museum** (☎ 428579; Avellaneda 501; admission US$0.60, Wed free; ☾ 9am-7pm, until 8pm summer). Its cozy interior is now adorned with a photographic display of Che's life, and a small selection of Che paraphernalia (including cigars, of course) is on sale.

Sleeping & Eating

Posada B&B (☎ 421811; www.posadabyb.com.ar in Spanish; Eduardo Madero 339; s/d US$6/12) You couldn't ask for a friendlier, more welcoming place to lay your head. This three-room B&B is immaculately kept, and the breakfasts of fresh bread and jams are all homemade. Two rooms share a bathroom and one room has its own bathroom.

Hostal Hispania (☎ 426555; Av Vélez Sársfield 57; s/d US$10/17; ☒) Located in a handsome turn-of-the-century wooden building, this place boasts spacious rooms which open onto a covered porch (complete with chaise longues) overlooking the large garden. Wooden wainscoting and floors add to the charm of the rooms here, and the owners are friendly.

La Fausta (Sarmiento 573; mains US$1-4; ☾ closed Mon) Small restaurant serving *comida criolla* (typical Argentine food), including *locro* and empanadas.

Trattoria Oro (☎ 425619; España 18; mains US$3-6) Varied menu and excellent service; opposite Plaza Manuel Solar.

THE LEGEND OF CHE GUEVARA

One of Cuba's greatest revolutionary heroes, in some ways even eclipsing Fidel Castro himself, was an Argentine. Ernesto Guevara, known by the common Argentine interjection 'che,' was born in the city of Rosario in 1928 and spent his first years in Buenos Aires. In 1932, after Guevara's doctor recommended a drier climate for his severe asthma, Guevara's parents moved to the mountain resort of Alta Gracia, where the young Guevara would spend his adolescence.

He later studied medicine in the capital and, in 1952, spent six months riding a motorcycle around South America, a journey that would steer Guevara's sights beyond middle-class Argentina to the plight of South America's poor. The journal he kept during his trip, now known as *The Motorcycle Diaries*, recently hit bookstore shelves around the world and inspired the movie of the same name, staring Mexico's Gael García Bernal.

After his journey, Guevara traveled to Central America and fatefully landed in Mexico, where he met Fidel Castro and other exiles. Together the small group would sail to Cuba on a rickety old yacht and begin the revolution that overthrew Cuban dictator Fulgencio Batista in 1959. Unable to resign himself to the bureaucratic task of building Cuban socialism, Guevara tried, unsuccessfully, to spread revolution in the Congo, Argentina and finally Bolivia, where he was killed in 1967.

Today Che is known less for his eloquent writings and speeches than for his striking black-and-white portrait as the beret-wearing rebel – an image gracing everything from T-shirts to CD covers – taken by photojournalist Alberto Korda in 1960. Although these commercialized versions of Che are hardly a poke at the belly of global capitalism, they have managed to irritate some: Korda sued Smirnoff in 2000 for using his famous photograph to sell vodka, and a 1998 Taco Bell ad, in which a talking, beret-wearing Chihuahua barks 'Viva Gorditas' to a cheering crowd, sparked furor in Miami's Cuban–American community.

In 1997, on the anniversary of Che's death, the Argentine government issued a postage stamp honoring Che's Argentine roots. You can take a look as the stamps, as well as other government-sponsored tributes from around the world, by visiting Alta Gracia's modest but lovely Museo Casa de Ernesto Che Guevara (see above), inaugurated June 14, 2001, on what would have been Che's 73rd birthday. If you're in Buenos Aires, take a peek inside the Museo Ernesto Che Guevara (p81), a funky garage-sale-like assortment of Che memorabilia.

Getting There & Away

Minibuses depart regularly for Córdoba (US$1, one hour) from in front of the clock tower near the main plaza. Córdoba-bound buses also leave from the **bus terminal** (Tacuarí at Perón) near the river. Buses to Villa General Belgrano stop every hour on RP 5, about 20 blocks along Av San Martín from the center.

VILLA GENERAL BELGRANO

☎ 03546 / pop 6000 / elevation 820m

Surrounded by evergreens high in the Valle de Calamuchita, Villa General Belgrano is Córdoba's cultural and gastronomical anomaly. The relaxed resort town deems itself the 'Pueblos de las Culturas' (Village of the Cultures) and flaunts its origins as a settlement of unrepatriated survivors from the German battleship Graf Spee, which sank near Montevideo during WWII.

Since 1964 the town has even celebrated its own **Oktoberfest** (elevated in 1972 to status of Fiesta Nacional de la Cerveza; National Beer Festival) during the first two weekends in October. Aside from its scenery, Villa General Belgrano is your one chance to fill up on scrumptious pastries, chocolate, *torta selva negra* (black forest cake), goulash and, at the local microbrewery, delicious German style-lagers.

The **tourist office** (☎ 461215; www.elsitiodelavilla .com/municipio in Spanish; Plaza José Hernández; ☻ 8am-8:30pm) is on the main strip.

Activities

To go horse riding, look for Sr Martinez, who sets up behind the bus terminal in summer and charges around US$3.50 an hour. Otherwise contact **Pituco Sanchez** (☎ 463142), who offers horse riding year-round at similar prices. **Rapisenda** (☎ 463740; Ojo de Agua 90) rents mountain bikes for about US$3.50 per hour.

Sleeping & Eating

In the December to March high season, hotel prices rise and rooms book quickly. Unless you book weeks before Oktoberfest, plan on hitting the festival as a day trip from Córdoba.

Albergue El Rincón (☎ 461323; rincon@calamuchita net.com.ar; dm US$4.50, r per person with private bathroom US$6, sites US$2.50) This beautiful Dutch-owned hostel, surrounded by forest, has excellent, spacious dorm rooms, outdoor and indoor

kitchens, a *parrilla* and its own biodynamic farm. Outstanding breakfasts cost US$1.50, and lunch and dinner US$2.50. It's a good 600m walk from behind the bus terminal to the entrance gate; follow the signs.

Bremen Hotel (☎ 461133; info@hotelbremen.com; RP 5, Km 741; s/d low season US$27/32, high season US$37/48) From its relaxing tearoom to the spacious bedrooms, this old hotel is truly exquisite.

Tirol D' Andrea Hotel (☎ 461166; cnr Ojo de Agua & San Martín; d US$37; ☻) Smack in the center of town, this is one of Belgrano's better-value hotels. Seven rooms have small balconies over the street, while another four overlook the small deck and pool area.

There are numerous restaurants along the main strip of Roca and San Martín.

Arte Bar (☎ 463522; Julio A Roca 88; mains US$2-5) Breaking the German mold that so defines General Belgrano, Arte Bar is a refreshing café serving tasty sandwiches for lunch and a changing menu for dinner. Live music starts at 10:30pm on Friday and Saturday.

Cervecería Viejo Munich (☎ 463122; San Martín 362; mains US$3.50-6) This oddly decorated microbrewery serves delicious goulash, spaetzle (dumplings) and, of course, beer.

Getting There & Away

The **bus terminal** (Av Vélez Sársfield) is uphill from San Martín, the main thoroughfare. Buses leave every hour for Córdoba (US$2.50, two hours), and daily for Buenos Aires (US$14, 11 hours).

LA CUMBRECITA

☎ 03546 / pop 600

You'll be hard pressed to find a more tranquil town in the Sierras than La Cumbrecita, a pedestrian-only village nestled into the pines, on a mountainside above the Valle de Calamuchita. There's not a lick of pavement, and dirt roads and trails wind through the village of alpine-style homes, restaurants and shops. Numerous trails meander into the mountains where big red spotted mushrooms grow in the rainy season. Visitors must park their cars in the dirt parking lot (US$1.50) before crossing the bridge over Río del Medio by foot.

The helpful **tourist office** (☎ 481088; www.la cumbrecita.gov.ar in Spanish; ☻ 8:30am-9pm summer, 10am-6pm winter) is on the left, right after you cross the bridge into town. There are even a few Internet cafés in the village.

Sights & Activities

The best reason to visit La Cumbrecita is to hike. Short trails are well marked and the tourist office offers a crude but useful map of the area. A 25-minute hike will take you to **La Cascada**, a waterfall tucked into the mountainside. **La Olla** is the closest swimming hole, surrounded by granite rocks (people jump when it's deep enough). **Cerro La Cumbrecita** (1400m) is the highest point in town, about a 20-minute walk from the bridge. Outside town, the highest mountain is the poetically named **Cerro Wank** (1715m); a hike to the top takes about 40 minutes.

For guided hikes further into the mountains, as well as horse riding (US$10 for three hours), trout fishing and mountain biking, contact **Cumbrecita Viajes** (☎ 481087, 15-475168; Las Truchas s/n), which has an office on the main road in town. The company can also take you trekking to the top of **Cerro Champaqui** (2790m), the highest peak in the sierras, for about US$20 per person.

Sleeping & Eating

La Cumbrecita has over 20 hotels and *cabañas* in the surrounding hills; the tourist office is a good resource. Make reservations in summer (January and February), during Semana Santa (Easter week) and during Villa General Belgrano's Oktoberfest (see opposite). Hardcore budget travelers will find few options.

La Campana (☎ 481062; r low/high season US$18.50/22) Cozy place with giant rooms and fully equipped kitchenettes.

Tilcara Hotel (☎ 481019; Calle Pública s/n; r per person incl breakfast & dinner US$18.50; P) La Cumbrecita's most economical hotel is clean, comfortable and friendly to boot.

Confitería Tante Liesbeth (☎ 481079; ☼ 4-7:30pm Thu-Sun summer, 4-7:30pm Sat & Sun winter) This is the village's most traditional teahouse, set creekside about a 10-minute walk from the bridge.

El Paseo (☎ 15-650395; mains US$2-4) Marvelous outdoor deck right above La Olla swimming hole. Great for afternoon beer.

Getting There & Away

From Villa General Belgrano, **Transportes Pajaro Blanco** (☎ 461709; Av San Martín 105), across from the Shell station on the way into town, has departures to La Cumbrecita (US$3 roundtrip, 1½ hours) at 7am, 10am, noon, 4pm and 6:50pm Monday through Friday,

and at 8am, 10am, noon, 4pm and 6:50pm on Saturdays and Sundays. There are no direct buses from Córdoba.

PARQUE NACIONAL QUEBRADA DEL CONDORITO

elevation 1900-2300m

Argentina's newest national park protects 37,000 hectares of stunning rocky grasslands across the Pampa de Achala in the Sierras Grandes. The area, particularly the *quebrada* (gorge) itself, is an extremely important condor nesting site and flight training ground for fledgling condors. If you have any desire to see an Andean condor, this is the place. A 9km, two- to three-hour hike from the park entrance at **La Pampilla** leads to the Balcón Norte (North Balcony), a cliff top over the gorge where you can view the massive birds circling on the thermals rising up the gorge. You can visit easily as a day trip from Córdoba or on your way to Mina Clavero.

Any bus from Córdoba to Mina Clavero will drop you at La Pampilla (US$4, about 1½ hours), where a trailhead leads to the gorge. To return to Córdoba (or on to Mina Clavero), flag a bus from the turnout. Latitud Sur (p269) offers recommended day tours to the park for US$22 per person.

For more information contact **Intendencia del PN Quebrada del Condorito** (☎ 03541-433371, 03541-15-621727; www.quebradacondorito.com.ar; Sabattini 33) in Villa Carlos Paz.

MINA CLAVERO

☎ 03544 / pop 8000 / elevation 915m

This popular resort gets busy in the summer but turns wonderfully quiet in the spring and fall. The limpid streams, rocky waterfalls, numerous swimming holes and idyllic mountain landscapes provide a relaxing escape for refugees from the faster-paced life of Córdoba and Buenos Aires. Hiking the rocky banks of the Río Mina Clavero only requires a short walk out of town. In high season the *balnearios* (swimming holes) are packed, and the main strip of town, San Martín, gets hopping with happy vacationers.

Mina Clavero is 170km southwest of Córdoba via RN 20, the splendid Nuevo Camino de las Altas Cumbres (Highway of the High Peaks). It sits at the confluence of Río de Los Sauces and Río Panaholma, in the Valle de Traslasierra.

The **tourist office** (☎ 470171; www.minaclavero .gov.ar in Spanish; Av San Martín 1464; ☺ 7am-midnight Dec-Mar, 9am-9pm Apr-Nov) has standard brochures and a useful map of town.

Sights & Activities

Mina Clavero's *balnearios* get mobbed in the summer, but are often empty the rest of the year. The magnificent, boulder-strewn gorges of the Río Mina Clavero are easily explored; simply walk east on Urquiza from San Martín and follow the signs about 1km uphill to **Nido de Agila**, the best swimming hole around, and carry on from there. Head west along the Río de Los Sauces and you'll hit **Los Elefantes**, a *balneario* named for its elephant-like rock formations. A 3km walk south along the river will take you to the village of **Villa Cura Brochero**, where you'll find more of the black pottery characteristic of this region.

Sleeping

Many accommodations close around the end of March, when the town almost rolls up the sidewalks.

La Casa de Pipa (☎ 470480; www.lacasadepipa.com in Spanish; Hernán Cortés at Colón; d/tr US$33/40; closed May & Jun; ⓟ ⓧ ⓡ) Treat yourself to a night or two at this meandering single-story inn. Ten comfortable rooms open onto a huge garden with a pool, *parrilla* and lots of shady lawn for afternoon siestas.

Residencial El Parral (☎ 470005; Av Intendente Vila 1430; r per person US$5; ☺ Oct-May; ⓟ) Run by a delightful older woman, this small *residencial* (cheap hotel) has plain rooms and a small backyard. It's no frills but it's comfortable, clean and the best price you'll find in town. It's one block uphill from San Martín.

Hotel Palace (☎ 470390; www.comprasvirtual.com /hotelpalace; Mitre 847; s/d US$12/23) The highlight of this 40-room French-owned hotel is the huge backyard that slopes to the riverside. Shade trees and lounge chairs make it tough to leave the grounds. Rooms are slightly worn, but the garden makes up for it.

Eating

Most of Mina Clavero's restaurants are along San Martín, south of the bridge.

La Parrilla de Nahuel (☎ 471052; San Martín 1309; mains US$3-6) Modest *parrilla* with big windows overlooking the Río Mina Clavero.

Rincón Suizo (☎ 470447; Champaqui 1200; ice creams US$2.50-4, mains US$4-7) This comfy teahouse on the river prides itself on its homemade ice creams, delicious Swiss food (including fondue, raclette and ratatouille) and *torta selva negra*, but the prices do verge on the extortionate.

Anastasia (☎ 471079; San Martín 1250; mains US$1.50-3.50; ☺ closed Mon) Cool bar-cum-restaurant with an outdoor patio and pizza, empanadas and coffee.

Getting There & Away

The **bus terminal** (Mitre 1191) is across the Río Mina Clavero from the town center. There are several daily buses to Córdoba (US$4, three hours) and at least three a day to Merlo (US$3, 2½ to three hours). Minibuses to Córdoba are faster (US$4, 2¾ hours). **TAC** (☎ 470420) has daily service to Buenos Aires (US$20, 13 hours). For destinations in San Juan and Mendoza, go to nearby Villa Dolores (US$1.25, one hour).

AROUND MINA CLAVERO
Museo Rocsen & Nono

Operated by Juan Santiago Bouchon, an anthropologist, curator and passionate collector who first came to Argentina in 1950 as cultural attaché to the French embassy, this eclectic **museum** (☎ 03544-498218; admission US$1.75; ☺ 9am-sunset) reveals just how strange the world really is. It contains more than 11,000 pieces including antique motorcycles, mounted butterflies, Esso gas pumps, human skulls, Buddha statues, film projectors, Catholic altars, 19th-century instruments of torture, a shrunken head and a 1200-year-old Peruvian mummy. It's truly a one-of-a-kind museum, and requires plenty of time to explore.

The museum is 5km outside the pastoral village of **Nono**, a one-time indigenous settlement 8km south of Mina Clavero. It's pretty relaxing to just hang out on the grassy plaza and wander around the village nodding to the folks sitting on benches outside their homes.

There are regular minibuses from Mina Clavero to Nono's main plaza, from where you'll have to take a taxi (about US$3 one way) or walk to the museum. If you do take a taxi, arrange for the driver to come back for you. A taxi from Mina Clavero to Nono costs US$3.

MERLO

☎ 02656 / pop 15,000 / elevation 890m

The climate continues to dry up as RN 20 slowly winds its way down into neighboring San Luis province. As it does, it passes the RP 5, which continues directly south to the town of Merlo, a growing resort known for its gentle microclimate (the local tourist industry buzzword) in a relatively dry area.

The **municipal tourist office** (☎ 476078; Coronel Mercau 605; ⏰ 8am-8pm) has maps and information on hotels and campgrounds.

Yana-Munay (☎ 475055; Av de los Césares 3261; r per person US$15; teahouse ⏰ 4pm to 1hr after sunset) is an outstanding teahouse in the hills with a couple of rooftop bedrooms and expansive views toward the west. Its hillside gardens are an exquisite spot for tea.

Merlo is 109km southwest of Mina Clavero, but actually tucked into the northeast corner of San Luis province. The **bus terminal** (RN 1 at Calle de las Ovejas) is about eight blocks south of the center. Buses go daily to Mina Clavero (US$3, 2½ to three hours), Villa Carlos Paz (US$4.50, five hours), Córdoba (US$5, 5½ hours), San Luis (US$4, three hours), Mendoza (US$10 to $14, 6½ hours), Buenos Aires (US$13 to US$22, 12 hours) and other major cities in central Argentina.

SAN LUIS & AROUND

San Luis province is popularly known as La Puerta de Cuyo (The Door to Cuyo). Cuyo describes the combined provinces of Mendoza, San Juan and San Luis (also see the boxed text, p288), but because of San Luis' greater proximity to Cordoba province, it's included instead in this chapter. Residents of San Luis province (*puntanos*) resolutely assert their singularity within Cuyo's regional identity.

Few foreigners explore this region, which makes the provincial highlight – Parque Nacional Sierra de las Quijadas – all the more enjoyable for those that do get out here.

SAN LUIS

☎ 02652 / pop 57,846 / elevation 700m

The streets are narrow, the bars are small and the people are friendly in little old San Luis (founded in 1594), capital of its namesake province. The only real reason to visit the city, however, is its proximity to nearby

Parque Nacional Sierra de las Quijadas, a smaller, yet in some ways, equally impressive version of the more famous Ischigualasto of neighboring San Juan province. The former is certainly easier to get to. The capital is also a convenient stopover if you're heading west to Mendoza from Merlo, or east toward Buenos Aires.

Orientation

On the north bank of the Río Chorrillos, San Luis is 260km from Mendoza via RN 7, 456km from Córdoba via RN 148 and 850km from Buenos Aires via either RN 7 or RN 8.

The commercial center is along the parallel streets of San Martín and Rivadavia between Plaza Pringles in the north and Plaza Independencia in the south.

Information

Several banks, mostly around Plaza Pringles, have ATMs.

ACA (☎ 423188; Av Illia 401)

La Web (cnr Rivadavia & Tomas Jofré; per hr US$0.50) There are countless other cybercafés downtown.

Post office (cnr Arturo Illia & San Martín)

Regional hospital (☎ 422627; Av República Oriental del Uruguay 150) On the eastward extension of Bolívar.

Tourist office (☎ 423957, 423479; www.turismoensan luis.gov.ar; intersection of Junín, San Martín & Av Arturo Illia; ⏰ 8am-8pm) The helpful staff can supply a good map of the town and its attractions.

Sights & Activities

The center of town is the beautiful tree-filled Plaza Pringles, anchored on its eastern side by San Luis' handsome 19th-century **cathedral** (Rivadavia). Provincial hardwoods such as algarrobo were used for the cathedral's windows and frames, and local white marble for its steps and columns.

On the north side of nearby Plaza Independencia is the provincial **Casa de Gobierno** (government house). On the south side of the plaza, the **Iglesia de Santo Domingo** (cnr 25 de Mayo & San Martín) and its convent date from the 1930s, but reproduce the Moorish style of the 17th-century building they replaced. Take a peak at the striking algarrobo doors of the attached **Archivo Histórico Provincial** around the corner on San Martín.

Dominican friars at the **mercado artesanal** (25 de Mayo at Rivadavia; ⏰ 8am-1pm Mon-Fri), next to Iglesia de Santo Domingo, sell gorgeous

CÓRDOBA & THE CENTRAL SIERRAS

handmade wool rugs as well as ceramics, onyx crafts and weavings from elsewhere in the province.

Also stroll over to the handsome former **train station** (1884–87) for a look at its green corrugated-metal roofs and decorative ironwork.

Sleeping & Eating

San Luis' better hotels cater to a business crowd, filling up quickly on weekdays and offering discounts on weekends.

Inca Hotel (☎ /fax 424923; www.inca-hotel.com.ar in Spanish; Bolívar 943; s/d US$11.75/16) This small hotel with a café downstairs is easily the best value in town. Rooms are spacious but plain with cable TV and decent bathrooms, and the staff is very attentive. Tours to Ischigualasto are arranged.

Hotel Mitre (☎ 424599; Mitre 1043; s/d US$6.75/10) Attended by the owner, this simple place has cramped, dark rooms and a small back patio. Worn out but clean.

Hotel Aiello (☎ 425609; www.hotelaiello.com; Av Illia 431; s/d US$18.75/23.50; P X ⬚ ⬚) San Luis' best hotel is well worth the price.

Traditional San Luis dishes include *locro*, *empanadas de horno* (baked empanadas) and *cazuela de gallina* (chicken soup); restaurants, however, are in short supply.

La Porteña (☎ 431722; Junín 696; pizza slices US$1.20-1.80) Delightful family restaurant where the waiters are all over 50 and the food is hearty and tasty.

Los Robles (☎ 436767; Av Colón 684; mains US$3-6) One of the town's best, this casually elegant restaurant serves good pastas and *parrillada* and tasty *chivito a la parrilla* (grilled kid).

There are numerous laid-back bars along Av Illia hopping with the town's youth. It's easy to walk along and take your pick.

Getting There & Around
AIR

The **San Luis airport** (☎ 422427/57) is only 3km outside the center; taxis cost around US$3.

Aerolíneas Argentinas (☎ 425671, 437981; Av Illia 472) flies twice daily to Buenos Aires (US$95) via San Rafael (US$71) except weekends, when there's one flight daily.

BUS & CAR

San Luis' **bus terminal** (☎ 424021; España, btwn San Martín & Rivadavia) is about six blocks north of the main plaza. There are daily depart-

ures to the destinations in the following table. For destinations such as Neuquén and Bariloche, you must head to Mendoza or San Rafael. Expreso Jocolí covers provincial destinations including Merlo (US$4, three hours).

Destination	Cost (US$)	Duration (hr)
Buenos Aires	14-22	11
Córdoba	7	6
Mar del Plata	27-35	18
Mendoza	7	4
Paraná	17	10½
Resistencia	27-34	20
Rosario	10-14	11
San Juan	6.50	4
San Rafael	7	4
Santa Fe	17	10

Located inside the Gran Hotel España, **Hertz** (☎ 15-549002; Av Illia 300) rents cars for about US$52 per day with 300km.

PARQUE NACIONAL SIERRA DE LAS QUIJADAS

Resembling San Juan's Parque Provincial Ischigualasto, this rarely visited **national park** (admission US$4) sets aside 150,000 hectares of red sandstone canyons and dry lake beds among the Sierra de las Quijadas, whose peaks reach 1200m at Cerro Portillo. Recent paleontological excavations by the Universidad Nacional de San Luis and New York's Museum of Natural History unearthed dinosaur tracks and fossils from the Lower Cretaceous, about 120 million years ago.

Despite the shortage of visitors here, access to the park is excellent: buses from San Luis to San Juan will drop visitors just beyond the village of Hualtarán, about 110km northwest of San Luis via RN 147 (the highway to San Juan). At this point, a 6km dirt road leads west to a viewpoint overlooking the **Potrero de la Aguada**, a scenic depression beneath the peaks of the sierra that collects the runoff from much of the park and is a prime wildlife area. It's sometimes possible to catch a lift from the junction, where the park rangers have a house, to the overlook.

Hiking possibilities are excellent in the park, but the complex canyons require a tremendous sense of direction or, preferably, the assistance of a local guide. Even

CHRIS BEALL

Lago Nahuel Huapi (p345), Bariloche, Lake District

MANFRED GOTTSCHALK

Puente del Inca (p301), Mendoza province

Nightlife, Córdoba (p272)

JOHN MAIER JR

Laguna Frías, Parque Nacional Nahuel Huapi (p345), Lake District

ALFREDO MAIQUEZ

Torres del Paine (p432), Patagonia

RICHARD I'ANS

TOM BOYDEN

Southern elephant seal (p365), Reserva
Faunística Península Valdés, Patagonia

Petrified forests at Monumento Natural Bosques
Petrificados (p383), Santa Cruz province

MANFRED GOTTSCH

experienced hikers should beware of summer rains and flash floods, which make the canyons extremely dangerous. Guides can be hired at the park entrance.

There's a shady **campground** (sites free), near the overlook, and a small store with groceries and drinks, including very welcome ice-cold beer.

Buses traveling from San Luis to San Juan will drop you at the park entrance and ranger station (US$3, 1½ hours), from where it's a 6km walk to Portrero de la Aguada, where you can hire guides (about US$5). To hire a guide, try to arrive before about 2:30pm, when they pack up and leave. Buses from San Juan to San Luis pass every hour or so, but they don't always stop. Hitchhiking back to San Luis is an alternative, though the wait can sometimes be long.

Mendoza & the Central Andes

A little mountain climbing, a day or two of wine tasting, a couple of sunny afternoons wandering the tree-lined avenues of one of Argentina's most beautiful provincial capitals – what more could you want? Welcome to *La Tierra de Sol y Buen Vino*, the Land of Sun and Good Wine, as *mendocinos* (inhabitants of Mendoza province) refer to their home.

Not only does Mendoza produce 70% of the country's wine (time to start drinkin'!), it's also home to some of the country's most exciting outdoor pursuits. Add neighboring San Juan province (which, by the way, is famous for its Syrah and white wines…gulp) to the picture, and you have some of the most eye-popping, jaw-dropping scenery in the country. From the highest peak in the Americas, to the windiest reservoir, to some of South America's best snow parks and driest powder, the central Andes means copious amounts of fun in the sun.

Head to southern Mendoza province for volcanic landscapes near Malargüe that are so utterly spectacular they're considered as internationally important as Perito Moreno and Iguazú Falls. You'll see why at Parque Provincial Payunia, which boasts the world's highest concentration of volcanic peaks. Be sure to also get your feet into neighboring San Juan province to explore the wildly eroded rock-scapes of Parque Provincial Ischigualasto or the painfully scenic Valle de Calingasta, where some of the Andes' highest peaks loom over the meandering Río Los Patos, and shimmering blankets of stars cover the nighttime skies.

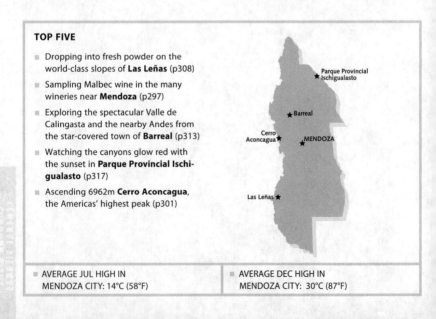

TOP FIVE

- Dropping into fresh powder on the world-class slopes of **Las Leñas** (p308)
- Sampling Malbec wine in the many wineries near **Mendoza** (p297)
- Exploring the spectacular Valle de Calingasta and the nearby Andes from the star-covered town of **Barreal** (p313)
- Watching the canyons glow red with the sunset in **Parque Provincial Ischigualasto** (p317)
- Ascending 6962m **Cerro Aconcagua**, the Americas' highest peak (p301)

Parque Provincial
★ Ischigualasto

★ Barreal

Cerro
Aconcagua ★   ★ MENDOZA

Las Leñas ★

- AVERAGE JUL HIGH IN MENDOZA CITY: 14°C (58°F)
- AVERAGE DEC HIGH IN MENDOZA CITY: 30°C (87°F)

MENDOZA & THE CENTRAL ANDES

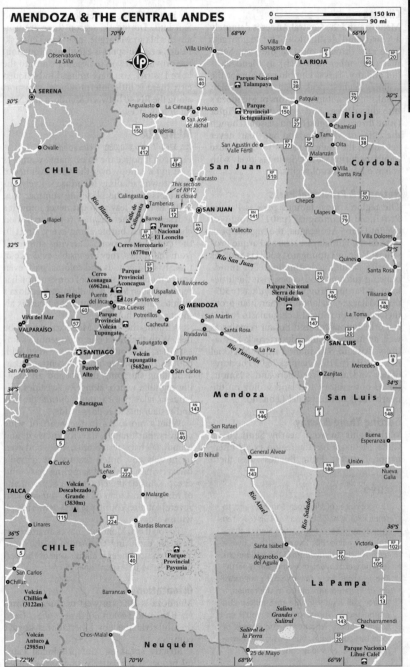

Climate

Mendoza and the Central Andes is definitely a year-round destination. The region gets little rain through most of the year. Summer (December to March) in Mendoza is hot and dry. This is climbing season for the region's highest peaks. Fall is spectacular, thanks to the autumnal colors of Mendoza's introduced trees and grape vines. Winter (June through August) is ski season. Though the cities of Mendoza and San Juan never get snow, the highest passes to Chile close regularly during winter. Spring is lovely with warm days and cool nights.

National & Provincial Parks

The region's most famous park is Parque Provincial Aconcagua (p301), home of 6962m Cerro Aconcagua, the highest peak outside the Himalayas. Nearby Parque Provincial Volcán Tupungato (p303) is another favorite climbing destination. For mind-blowing volcanic landscapes, visit the little-known Parque Provincial Payunia (p307) near Malargüe. Neighboring San Juan province Parque Provincial Ischigualasto (p317) is world famous for its dinosaur remains as well as its spectacular desert rock formations. Also in San Juan, Parque Nacional El Leoncito (p315) occupies 76,000 hectares of dry Andean pre-cordillera and is famous for its observatory and land sailing on the nearby flats of Pampa del Leoncito.

Getting There & Away

With flights to/from nearby Santiago de Chile, Mendoza has the region's only international airport. From Buenos Aires there

---

CUYO

The provinces of Mendoza, San Juan and, to some extent, neighboring San Luis (covered in the Cordoba & the Central Sierras chapter) are traditionally known as the Cuyo, a term which is derived from the indigenous Huarpe word *cuyum*, meaning 'sandy earth.' The Huarpes were the original practitioners of irrigated agriculture in the region, a legacy still highly visible throughout the region today. The term is one you'll encounter often, whether in the names of local bus companies, businesses and newspapers, or in everyday conversation.

---

are regular flights to Mendoza, San Juan and San Luis. During ski season there are usually flights to Malargüe, near Las Leñas ski resort. Bus transport is excellent throughout the province. If you're heading south to the Lake District, you have to head to Neuquén city; there is little interprovincial transport along the RN 40 between Mendoza and Neuquén provinces.

MENDOZA

☎ 0261 / pop 130,000 / elevation 703m

First you'll notice the trees: giant sycamores forming a canopy over the wide avenues of downtown, shading Mendoza's lively inhabitants from the blistering summer sun. With all those leaves, you'd never know it's a desert. But the *acequias* (open irrigation channels) that burble along every street in the city give it away. Carrying snowmelt from the Andes, they are visible evidence of the city's indigenous and colonial past, even where modern quake-proof construction has replaced fallen historic buildings. Mendoza's architecture, hidden behind the trees, is almost an afterthought.

Without the trees, Mendoza would be hell. With them, it's one of Argentina's finest cities, with outdoor cafés crowded with coffee-drinkers, five beautiful central plazas, a bustling shopping district and an exciting nightlife which, along Av Arístides Villanueva, takes place as much *outside* the bars and restaurants as it does inside.

What's more, it's in the heart of wine country. Fortunately, the city knows it, and Mendoza's bars, restaurants, stores and even its hostels and hotels feature the region's finest wines, making sampling easy and cheap. Outside the city, in the departments of Maipú and Lujan de Cuyo, you can visit several of the country's best wineries all within a day.

To top it off, Mendoza makes an excellent base for exploring the Andes to the west. When you consider it all, it's one of the best places to be in Argentina.

Orientation

Mendoza is 1050km west of Buenos Aires via RN 7 and 340km northwest of Santiago de Chile via the Los Libertadores border complex.

Strictly speaking, the provincial capital proper is a relatively small area with a population of only about 130,000, but the inclusion of the departments of Las Heras, Guaymallén and Godoy Cruz, along with nearby Maipú and Luján de Cuyo, swells the population of Gran Mendoza (Greater Mendoza) to nearly 900,000.

The city's five central plazas are arranged like the five-roll on a die, with Plaza Independencia in the middle and four smaller plazas lying two blocks from each of its corners. Be sure to see the beautifully tiled Plaza España.

Av San Martín is the main thoroughfare, crossing the city from north to south, and Av Las Heras is the principal commercial street.

A good place to orient yourself is the **Terraza Mirador** (free; 🕗 8am-8pm), which is the rooftop terrace at **City Hall** (9 de Julio 500), offering panoramic views of the city and the surrounding area.

Information
BOOKSTORES
Centro Internacional del Libro (☎ 420-1266; Lavalle 14) Small selection of classics and best-sellers in English.
Rubén Simoncini Libros (☎ 420-2988; San Juan 1108) One of many bookstores around the intersection of San Juan and Garibaldi; some English books in stock.
Yenny (☎ 423-5317; San Martín 1087) Some books in English.

IMMIGRATION
Immigration office (☎ 424-3512; San Martín 1859) In Godoy Cruz, south of the city center.

INTERNET ACCESS
Internet cafés are ubiquitous throughout the center, and all charge about US$0.30 per hour. There are several large ones along the Sarmiento *peatonal* (pedestrian street).
Telefónica (cnr Av Sarmiento & San Martín; per hr US$0.35) Serves coffee and has telephones too.

LAUNDRY
La Lavandería (☎ 429-4782; San Lorenzo 352; full service about US$2.75)
Laverap (☎ 423-9706; Av Colón 547; full service about US$2.75)

MEDICAL SERVICES
Hospital (☎ 420-0600, 420-0063; cnr José F Moreno & Alem)
Servicio Coordinado de Emergencia (☎ 428-0000) Call for ambulance.

MONEY
There are many ATMs downtown. The two following banks are architectural landmarks; Banco Mendoza is massive.
Banco de la Nación (cnr Necochea & 9 de Julio)
Banco Mendoza (cnr Gutiérrez & San Martín)
Cambio Santiago (Av San Martín 1199) Charges 2% commission on traveler's checks.

POST
Post office (Av San Martín at Colón)

TOURIST INFORMATION
ACA (Automóvil Club Argentina; ☎ 420-2900; cnr Av San Martín & Amigorena)
Municipal tourist offices (www.turismo.mendoza.gov.ar in Spanish) bus terminal (☎ 431-5000, 431-3001; 🕗 7am-11pm); City Hall (☎ 449-5185; fax 449-5186; 9 de Julio 500; 🕗 8:30am-1:30pm Mon-Fri); Garibaldi ☎ 420-1333; Garibaldi sidewalk, near Av San Martín; 🕗 9am-9pm) The head office is at City Hall but the Garibaldi office is best for most questions.
Provincial tourist office (☎ 420-2800; www.turismo .mendoza.gov.ar in Spanish; Av San Martín 1143; 🕗 8am-10pm Mon-Fri) Good maps, plenty of brochures.

TRAVEL AGENCIES
Asatej (☎ /fax 429-0029/30; mendoza@asatej.com.ar; Av Sarmiento 223) Recommended student and discount travel agency. Also representative of Argentina Rafting Expediciones, which is based in Potrerillos (p299).
Isc Viajes (☎ 425-9259; www.iscviajes.com; Av España 1016) Travel agent and Amex representative.

Sights
MUSEO FUNDACIONAL & AROUND
Mendoza's **Museo Fundacional** (☎ 425-6927; cnr Alberdi & Videla Castillo, Ciudad Vieja; admission US$1; 🕗 8am-8pm Mon-Sat, 3-10pm Sun) protects excavations of the colonial *cabildo* (town council), destroyed by an earthquake in 1861. At that time, the city's geographical focus shifted west and south to its present location. A series of small dioramas depicts Mendoza's history, working through all of human evolution as if the city of Mendoza were the climax (maybe it was).

Walk to the museum from downtown and you'll pass some bizarre sights near **Parque Bernardo O'Higgins**. First check out the **Acuario Municipal Mendoza** (Municipal Aquarium; ☎ 425-3824; cnr Ituzaingó & Buenos Aires; admission US$0.50; 🕗 9am-9pm, until 10pm summer). Nothing at this small underwater freak show seems to have changed since its inauguration in 1945 (except the

MENDOZA

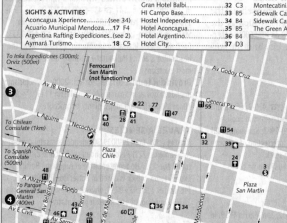

INFORMATION
ACA	1	C5
Asatej	2	C5
Banco de la Nación	3	C4
Bus Turístico	(see 10)	
Cambio Santiago	4	C4
Centro Internacional del Libro	5	D4
German Consulate	6	C5
Hospital	7	E5
Isc Viajes	8	C5
Italian Consulate	9	A3
Municipal Tourist Office	10	C5
Municipal Tourist Office	11	B6
Post Office	12	C6
Provincial Tourist Office	13	C5
Rubén Simoncini Libros	14	D5
Telefónica	15	C5
Terraza Mirador (City Hall)	(see 11)	
Yenny	16	C5

SIGHTS & ACTIVITIES
Aconcagua Xperience	(see 34)	
Acuario Municipal Mendoza	17	F4
Argentina Rafting Expediciones	(see 2)	
Aymará Turismo	18	C5

Betancourt Rafting	19	D4
Campo Base Travel & Adventure	20	C5
Centro Anaconda Serpentario	21	E4
Esquí Mendoza Competición	22	B3
Extreme	23	A5
Iglesia, Convento y Basílica de San Francisco	24	C4
Laverap	25	A6
Museo Histórico General San Martín	26	D3
Museo Municipal de Arte Moderno	27	B4
Museo Popular Callejero	28	B3
Ríos Andinos	29	A4
Southern Winds	30	C5

SLEEPING
B&B Plaza Italia	31	A5
Gran Hotel Balbi	32	C3
HI Campo Base	33	B5
Hostel Independencia	34	B4
Hotel Aconcagua	35	B5
Hotel Argentino	36	B4
Hotel City	37	D3

Hotel Crillón	38	A4
Hotel del Sol	39	C3
Hotel Petit	40	B3
Hotel Rincón Vasco	41	B3
Hotel Ritz	42	A4
Hotel Zamora	43	A4
Palace Hotel	44	C4
Park Hyatt Mendoza	45	B4
Winca's Hostel	46	A4

EATING
de Un Rincón de La Boca	47	B3
De una	48	A4
Facundo	49	A4
Helados Ferruccio Soppelsa	50	A4
La Barra	51	A4
La Mora	52	A5
La Tasca de Plaza España	53	C5
Mercado Central	54	C3
Montecatini	55	C3
Sidewalk Cafés	56	C5
Sidewalk Cafés	57	C5
The Green Apple	58	B6

To Inka Expediciones (300m);
Orviz (500m)

Ferrocarril San Martín (not functioning)

Av Godoy Cruz

Corrientes

Córdoba

Av JB Justo

Av Las Heras

Av General Paz

L Aguirre

Necochea

San Luis

To Chilean Consulate (1km)

N Avellaneda

Plaza Chile

Entre Ríos

To Spanish Consulate (500m)

Gutiérrez

Espejo

Plaza San Martín

Buenos Aires

A Álvarez
To Parque General San Martín (400m)

Av Belgrano

Pedro

25 de Mayo

Chile

Patricias Mendocinas

Av España

9 de Julio

Av San Martín

Lavalle

Av E Civit

Av Sarmiento

Plaza Independencia

Liniers

Rivadavia

Av Sarmiento (ped mall)

Catamarca

La Rioja

Salta

Garibaldi

Plaza Italia

Montevideo

Amigorena

Aristides Villanueva

San Lorenzo

Plaza España

Av LN Alem

To Cocina Poblana (200m);
Damajuana Hostel (300m);
El Palenque (300m);
3-90 (400m);
Por Acá (500m)

Av Mitre

P de la Reta

Plaza Pellegrini

Don Bosco

Zuloaga

Don Bosco

Pardo

To Israeli Consulate (1.5km);
Godoy Cruz, Gabriel
Cabrera Expediciones,
Immigration Office (6km)

Av Colón

Lombardo

San Martín

Av José Vicente Zapata

Vargas

Av Pedro Molina

Rondeau

To Cielito Lindo (1.5km)

To Soul Café (50m);
Tablao (300m)

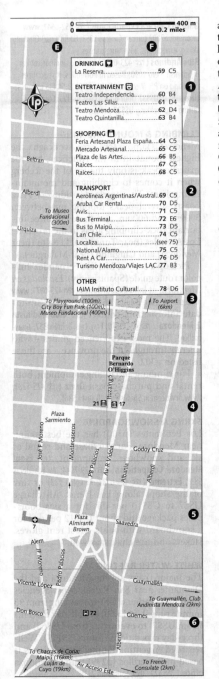

algae levels on the glass). But it's hard not to gaze in awe at the motionless, tongueless albino frogs (which really don't move) or the 'armored pig,' a very ugly fish from the Río Paraná. Skip the crocodile exhibit. Across the street, the **Centro Anaconda Serpentario** (☎ 425-1393; Ituzaingó 1420; adult/child under 12 US$1/0.30; ☼ 9:30am-1pm & 3:30-8pm) houses some 50 snakes (in equally small cages), including a giant yellow Burmese python. Continuing north through the park, check out the tiny Gaudiesque **playground** and the miniature **City Boy fun park**, which looks straight out of some backward carnival scene from the 1950s. Makes for a great day with the kids (or a trippy day with friends).

OTHER MUSEUMS
Underground at the Plaza Independencia, the **Museo Municipal de Arte Moderno** (☎ 425-7279; Plaza Independencia; admission US$1; ☼ 9am-1pm & 4-9pm Mon-Sat) is a relatively small but well-organized facility with rotating modern and contemporary art exhibits.

Across town, stroll down Av Las Heras to the **Museo Popular Callejero** (Av Las Heras, btwn 25 de Mayo & Perú; admission free; ☼ 24hr), an innovative sidewalk museum. It consists of a series of encased street-side dioramas with odd clay sculptures depicting changes in one of Mendoza's major avenues since its 1830 creation in a dry watercourse.

Northeast of the sidewalk museum, the **Museo Histórico General San Martín** (☎ 425-7947; Remedios Escalada de San Martín 1843; admission US$1; ☼ 9am-1pm Mon-Fri) honors José de San Martín, the general who liberated Argentina from the Spanish and whose name graces parks, squares and streets everywhere in Argentina; the Libertador is especially dear to Mendoza, where he resided with his family and recruited and trained his army to cross into Chile.

IGLESIA, CONVENTO & BASÍLICA DE SAN FRANCISCO
Many *mendocinos* consider the image at this **church** (Necochea 201; admission US$0.50; ☼ 9am-1pm Mon-Sat) of the Virgin of Cuyo, patron of San Martín's Ejército de los Andes (Army of the Andes), miraculous because it survived Mendoza's devastating 1968 earthquake. In the Virgin's semicircular chamber, visitors leave tributes to her and to San Martín. A mausoleum within the building holds the

remains of San Martín's daughter, son-in-law and granddaughter, which were repatriated from France in 1951.

PARQUE GENERAL SAN MARTÍN

Walking along the lakeshore and snoozing in the shade of the rose garden in this beautiful 420-hectare park is a great way of enjoying one of the city's highlights. Take Mitre/Civit out to the park and admire some of Mendoza's finest houses on the way. Pick up a park map at the **Centro de Información** (☎ 420-5052, ext 22; cnr Av Los Platanos & Av Libertador; ✆ 9am-5pm), just inside the impressive entry gates, shipped over from England and originally forged for the Turkish Sultan Hamid II. The park was designed by Charles Thays, who designed Parque Sarmiento in Córdoba, in 1897. Its famous **Cerro de la Gloria** has a monument to San Martín's Ejército de los Andes for their liberation of Argentina, Chile and Peru from the Spaniards. On clear days, views of the valley make the climb especially rewarding. In the park, several run-down **museums** focus on archaeology, mineralogy and natural history and are good to pass a few hours.

Bus No 110 ('Favorita') from around Plaza Independencia or Plaza España goes to the park. From the park entrance, open-air buses called *bateas* carry visitors to the summit of Cerro de la Gloria.

Activities

Once you've sucked down enough fine wine and tramped around the city a bit, get yourself into the Andes, Mendoza's other claim to fame, for some of the most spectacular mountain scenery you'll ever lay your eyes upon. Numerous agencies organize climbing and trekking expeditions, rafting trips, mule trips and cycling trips. For Aconcagua guides, see p302.

Aconcagua Xperience (☎ 423-1806; www.aconcagua -xperience.com.ar; Hostel Independencia, Av Mitre 1237) Trekking, logistics, guide and mule hire. Well regarded for trekking, climbing and Aconcagua.

Aymará Turismo (☎ 420-2064; 9 de Julio 1023) Mule trips, trekking, rafting.

Betancourt Rafting (☎ 429-9965; www.betancourt .com.ar; Lavalle 35, Local 8) Rafting, mountain biking, paragliding.

Campo Base Travel & Adventure (☎ 425-5511; www .cerroaconcagua.com in Spanish; Av Sarmiento 231) Offers all adventures imaginable from trekking to paragliding to more conventional day trips.

Gabriel Cabrera Expediciones (☎ 452-0641; www .aconcagua2002.com.ar; Caseros 1053, Godoy Cruz) Climbing, skiing, expeditions, adventure courses.

Ríos Andinos (☎ 423-6970; www.riosandinos.com.ar in Spanish; Perú 1090) Based in Potrerillos, it specializes in rafting on Río Mendoza. Rafting US$13.50 (35 minutes, class I–II) to US$37 (four hours, class III–IV). Combined rafting and trekking US$37 per day.

CLIMBING & MOUNTAINEERING

Mendoza is famous for Cerro Aconcagua, the highest mountain in the Americas, but the majestic peak is only the tip of the iceberg when it comes to climbing and mountaineering here. The nearby Cordón del Plata boasts several peaks topping out between 5000m and 6000m, and there are three important rock-climbing areas in the province: Los Arenales (near Tunuyán), El Salto (near Mendoza) and Chigüido (near Malargüe).

Pick up a copy of Maricio Fernandez' full-color route guide (Spanish only), *Escaladas en Mendoza*, at **Inka Expediciones** (☎ 425-0871; www .inka.com.ar; Juan B Justo 345, Mendoza). For up-to-date information, contact the **Club Andinista 2 Mendoza** (☎ 431-9870; Fray Luis Beltrán 357, Guaymallén). The most experienced guides – who operate throughout the province – are those listed on p302.

For climbing and hiking equipment, both rental and purchase, visit **Orviz** (☎ 425-1281; www.orviz.com in Spanish; Av JB Justo 536).

SKIING & SNOWBOARDING

Los Penitentes (p300) has the best skiing near Mendoza. For purchase and rental of ski and snowboard equipment, try **Esquí Mendoza Competición** (☎ 429-7944; Av Las Heras 583), **Extreme** (☎ 429-0733; Av Colón 733) or any of the shops along Las Heras. All charge US$7 to US$10 per day for a skis-boots-poles package and about US$12 per day for a snowboard with boots. Most rent gloves, jackets and tire chains, as well.

WHITE-WATER RAFTING

The major rivers are the Mendoza and the Diamante, near San Rafael. Most agencies mentioned earlier offer trips ranging from 35 minute runs (US$13.50) or half-day descents (from US$7) to overnight (from US$63) and three-day expeditions (from US$117). Well-regarded Argentina Rafting Expediciones is based in Potrerillos (p299) with a Mendoza **office** (☎ 429-0029, Sarmiento 223).

Courses

IAIM Instituto Intercultural (☎ 429-0269; www.in
tercultural.com.ar in Spanish; www.spanishcourses.com.ar;
Rondeau 277) offers Spanish-language instruction for foreigners.

Tours

Bus Turístico (Tourist Bus; ☎ 420-1333) Get a route map
of the city's Bus Turístico from the Garibaldi municipal tourist
office and take in Mendoza's sights from a red double-decker.
Good for 24 hours, the ticket allows you to board and re-
board at any of several fixed stops throughout the city. The
circuit begins at the corner of Garibaldi and Av San Martín,
near the municipal tourist office, and goes as far as the summit of Cerro de la Gloria.

Turismo Mendoza/Viajes LAC (☎ /fax 429-2013;
lacviajes@yahoo.com.ar; Av Las Heras 543) Several conventional travel agencies, such as this one, organize trips in and
around town. Among the possibilities are half-day tours of
the city (US$7); tours of the wineries and Dique Cipoletti
(US$8.50); or full-day tours to Villavicencio (US$10), or the
alta montaña (high cordillera) around Potrerillos, Vallecitos
and Uspallata (US$18.50).

Festivals & Events

Mendoza's biggest annual event, the **Fiesta
Nacional de la Vendimia** (National Wine Harvest
Festival), lasts about a week, from late February to early March. It features a parade on
Av San Martín with floats from each department of the province, numerous concerts
and folkloric events, and it all culminates in
the coronation of the festival's queen in the
Parque General San Martín amphitheater.

Sleeping

BUDGET

Mendoza has abundant accommodations
in all categories. For March's Fiesta de la
Vendimia, reservations are highly advisable.
All the hostels mentioned here have weekly
asados (Argentine barbeques), which are
generally great fun.

Winca's Hostel (☎ 425-3804; www.wincashostel
.com.ar; Av Sarmiento 717; dm/d US$6/16.50; ✗ ✗ 🖳)
This is one impressive hostel, with spacious
rooms, real mattresses, a handsome kitchen
and a giant backyard. Its warm orange paint
job adds to the cheer, and everything is kept
immaculately clean. Bike rentals are available,
and plenty of cultural activities are on offer.

Damajuana Hostel (☎ 425-5858; www.damajuana
hostel.com.ar in Spanish; Arístides Villanueva 282; dm US$7-
7.50, d US$22; 🖳 🖳) Damajuana's unbeatable
location on Arístides Villanueva means some

THE AUTHOR'S CHOICE

Hostel Independencia (☎ 423-1806; www
.hostelindependencia.com.ar; Av Mitre 1237; d
US$4.50, d/tr with bathroom US$7/7.75; 🖳) This
excellent 60-bed hostel occupies a historic
mansion with an ornate interior of wain-
scoting, hardwood floors, arched entryways
and an excellent common area. There's a
huge back patio and spacious rooms with
four to 10 beds in each. The wine bar tops
it all off.

of the city's best bars and restaurants are just
outside the front door. The building itself is
a beautiful converted house with a stylish,
comfy common area opening on to a huge
backyard, complete with swimming pool.

HI Campo Base (☎ 429-0707; www.campo-base.com
.ar in Spanish; Mitre 946; dm members/nonmembers
US$3.50/4, d per person US$4/5; 🖳) This lively hostel just off the main plaza is popular with
climbers; perks include bike rentals, communal *asados*, organized tours and lots of talk.
Some rooms have cozy bunks and lockers,
others are basic.

Hotel Petit (☎ 423-2099; fax 425-0682, Perú 1459;
s/d US$12/15; 🖳) Although everything – from
the elevator to the bathrooms – are, indeed,
petite, this is excellent value and warmly
comfortable. The lobby makes you want to
sit around and talk to old ladies. English
spoken.

Hotel Zamora (☎ 425-5537; www.hotelzamora.net
firms.com in Spanish; Perú 1156; s/d US$10/15) Hotel
Zamora is rightfully popular for its atmospheric Spanish-colonial architecture and
colorful tile work. Rooms, however, are
small and simple, with saggy beds, but if you
choose carefully (avoid the annex rooms
across the street) they are great deals.

MIDRANGE

B&B Plaza Italia (☎ 423-4219; www.mechitito.cjb.net;
Montevideo 685; d/tr US$28/37; 🅿 ✗) This six-room
B&B is hard to beat when it comes to friendliness and good breakfasts. The house is lovely,
the owners (who speak English) are divine,
and the living room is just right for reading.
It's like being at home.

Palace Hotel (☎ 423-4200; Av Las Heras 70; s/d
US$17/27; 🅿 ✗) Old-time hotel with little
character (unlike the staff), but definitely
good value.

Hotel Ritz (☎ 423-5155; hotelritz@pabloariosto.com; Perú 1008; s/d US$28/35; P ⊠ 🖵) As one traveler remarked, the decor, with its brown fake-silk bedspreads, gold-frame mirrors and orange sinks and toilets, looks straight out of an *I Love Lucy* episode. But it's a great deal. Tables are out on the sidewalk, and the bathrooms are big.

Hotel del Sol (☎ 438-0218; hoteles@ciudad.com.ar; Av Las Heras 212; s/d US$15/22; P) On busy Las Heras, this 28-room hotel, in a well-preserved old building, offers fair-size rooms with ample bathrooms and small, stark lounge areas on each floor. Good deal.

Hotel City (☎ 425-1343; cityhotelmendoza@yahoo .com; General Paz 95; s/d US$10/16; P ⊠) The price here includes TV, bathroom and air-con, but rooms have little character. It's on a lively street and the entryway is far from appealing, but it's fine for a couple of nights' sleep.

Hotel Rincón Vasco (☎ 423-3033; Av Las Heras 590; s/d US$13/18; P ⊠) In a good location on the busy, restaurant-strewn Av Las Heras, this slightly worn hotel is good value, especially if you get a balcony (and don't mind the street noise).

Hotel Crillón (☎ 429-8494; www.hcrillon.com.ar; Perú 1065; s/d US$30/38; P ⊠ 🏊) This is a modern, unpretentious place with carpeted rooms, firm beds, good bathrooms (complete with towel-warmers) and a great swimming pool across the street.

Grand Hotel Balbi (☎ 423-3500; balbistarhotel@arnet .com.ar; Av Las Heras 340; s/d US$32/40; ⊠ 🏊) Another hotel locked in time (1947 to be exact), the three-star Balbi has a good swimming pool and giant lobby. Sparse hallways lead you to spotless rooms (that smell of air-freshener), with wooden bed frames and outdated air-conditioners. But it's comfortable and classy.

Hotel Argentino (☎ 405-6300; Espejo 455; www .argentino-hotel.com in Spanish; s/d US$43/50; P ⊠ 🖵)

THE AUTHOR'S CHOICE

La Barra (☎ 15-654-1950; Belgrano 1086; meats US$4-8) Skip the slow service and mediocre food of the *parrillas* along Sarmiento and head straight for La Barra, where the owner personally tends the grill, cooking his meats with two types of wood (one for flavor, one for heat), while his partner tends to the blissed-out diners in front. The *matambre de cerdo* (pork) is truly sublime.

One of two hotels on the Plaza Independencia, the newly remodeled Argentino has small but immaculate rooms, decor that looks like it's straight out of an Ikea catalog, and a back patio with a miniature pool.

TOP END

Hotel Aconcagua (☎ 420-4455; www.hotelaconcagua .com; San Lorenzo 545; d US$53-70; P ⊠ 🖵 🏊) Four-star Hotel Aconcagua has it all, with manicurists and hairstylists on premises, a sauna and pool and some multilingual staff. It's the second biggest in town, built in 1978 for the soccer World Cup.

Park Hyatt Mendoza (☎ 441-1234; www.mendoza .park.hyatt.com; Chile 1124; r US$97-212; ste from US$300; P ⊠ 🖵 ⊠ 🏊) Facing Plaza Independencia, Mendoza's only five-star hotel is a real beauty, and walk-in rates can be surprisingly affordable (from the splurge perspective), considering the quality and comfort of the ultrachic rooms.

Eating

Some of Mendoza's best restaurants, often with outdoor seating and lively young crowds, are along Av Arístides Villanueva, the western extension of Av Colón. West of Plaza Independencia, Av Sarmiento is lined with the city's most traditional, albeit touristy, *parrillas* (grills), while east of the plaza along the Sarmiento *peatonal*, you'll find numerous sidewalk cafés with outdoor seating. The Sarmiento cafés are required visiting for coffee.

Mercado Central (cnr Av Las Heras & Patricias Mendocinas; ☯ 8am-1pm & 4-7pm Mon-Sat, restaurants open all day) The central market, where a variety of stalls offer inexpensive pizza, empanadas, sandwiches and specialty grocery items, is likely the best budget choice. The exceptional value and great atmosphere make it one of Mendoza's highlights.

El Palenque (☎ 15-454-8023; Arístides Villanueva 287; mains US$3-5; ☯ closed Sun) Don't miss this superb, extremely popular restaurant styled after an old-time *pulpería* (tavern), where the house wine is served in traditional *pinguinos* (white ceramic penguin-shaped pitchers). The food and appetizers are outstanding, and the outside tables are always full and fun.

La Tasca de Plaza España (☎ 423-3466; Montevideo 117; meals US$4-6) With excellent Mediterranean and Spanish tapas (mostly seafood), great wines, intimate atmosphere, good art and friendly service, La Tasca is one of Mendoza's best.

Tablao (☎ 424-5544; San Juan 165; lomitos US$3) Do not deny yourself the culinary joy of devouring one of Mendoza's best *lomitos* (steak sandwiches), served here on *pan casero* (homemade bread). It's an institution.

Cocina Poblana (☎ 15-511-3949; Arístides Villanueva 217; dishes US$1-2; ☻ closed Sun) The very tasty, inexpensive Middle Eastern food (hummus, falafel, dolmas) comes as a welcome break from all that steak.

Cielito Lindo (☎ 424-4383; cnr Hipolito Irigoyen & Av España; mains US$4; ☻ dinner Tue-Sun) Good Mexican food, great fajitas. Well worth the US$2 cab ride from the center. Margaritas and microbrews too.

La Mora (☎ 438-1044; Perú 928; mains US$3.50-5; ☻ dinner Mon-Sat) Small restaurant with imaginative international fare consisting mostly of tasty kabobs and a delicious mixed *bruscetta* platter for an appetizer.

3-90 (☎ 429-1112; Arístides Villanueva 463; mains US$3-4) Extremely popular pasta joint with a friendly staff and a very long list of cheap hit-and-miss pasta dishes. Good value.

Facundo (☎ 420-2866; Av Sarmiento 641; mains US$3-5.50) Highly regarded *parrilla* with a massive 600g *bife de chorizo* (sirloin) on the menu. Plenty of other dishes to choose from.

Montecatini (☎ 425-2111; General Paz 370; mains US$4-6) For over 40 years Montecatini has been dishing out some of the city's finest pasta, handmade by the same chefs for nearly as long. The dated but classic *Godfather* atmosphere and side-street location add to the appeal.

de un Rincón de La Boca (☎ 425-6848; Av Las Heras 485; pies US$1-3) Many argue this is the best pizza in town (it's the crust). Both this and a branch in the Mercado Central sell slices (US$0.25 to US$0.75).

De una (☎ 423-2849; cnr Av Belgrano & A Alvarez; sandwiches US$2.50, pizzas US$1.50-4; ☻ closed lunch Sun) Superb sandwiches, great pizzas, good prices and outdoor seating.

Green Apple (☎ 429-9444; Av Colón 458; buffet US$3.50) Small vegetarian buffet with fair selection of average dishes.

Helados Ferruccio Soppelsa (☎ 422-9000; cnr Av Emilio Civit & Av Belgrano; ice cream US$1-3) Soppelsa has been scooping up what's arguably the city's best ice cream since 1927. Don't miss it (or the retro *Jetson*-like decor).

THE AUTHOR'S CHOICE

Teatro Las Sillas (☎ 429-7742; teatrolassillas@ yahoo.com; San Juan 1436; admission US$0.75-5) Housed in the Centro Catalan, this theater space is a must on Friday nights at midnight, when US$0.75 gets you in to the *milonga* (dance) where couples tango until dawn; it's the real thing. There's theater and live music on Thursday nights and events throughout the week.

Drinking

For a great night on the town, walk down Av Arístides Villanueva, where it's bar after bar; in summer, entire blocks fill with tables and people enjoying the night.

Por Acá (☎ 420-0346; Arístides Villanueva 557) Purple and yellow outside and polka-dotted upstairs, this bar-cum-lounge gets packed after 2am, and by the end of the night, dancing on the tables is not uncommon. Good retro dance music.

BU (☎ 15-510-7722; Arístides Villanueva 215) Electronic music and chill-out tunes accompany grilled plates at this very popular bar.

La Reserva (☎ 420-3531; Rivadavia 32) This small, predominantly gay bar has some great entertainment, including flamenco, drag shows, electronica DJ's and theater, always followed by dancing until the wee hours; the fun kicks in after midnight. The crowd is mixed.

Entertainment

Check the tourist offices or museums for a copy of *La Guía,* a monthly publication with comprehensive entertainment listings. *Los Andes,* the daily rag, also has a good entertainment section.

DANCE CLUBS

Finding a dance floor generally means abandoning downtown for one of two areas: the northwest suburb of **El Challao**, or **Chacras de Coria**, along the RP 82 in the southern outskirts. The former is reached by bus No 115 from Sarmiento. Chacras de Coria is reached from the stop on La Rioja by bus No 10, *interno* (internal route number) 19, or from the corner of 25 de Mayo and Rivadavia by bus No 10, *interno* 15. In both cases simply asking the driver for *los boliches* (the nightclubs) is enough to find the right stop. The nightclubs are all right next to each other, and you can walk along to take your pick from the ever-changing array.

THEATER & LIVE MUSIC

Soul Café (☎ 425-7489; San Juan 456; admission US$1-3) Grab a table and enjoy everything from live *rock en español* (Spanish-language rock) to jazz and theater. Shows start after 10pm.

The main theaters in town are **Teatro Quintanilla** (☎ 423-2310; Plaza Independencia), alongside the Museo Municipal de Arte Moderno; the nearby **Teatro Independencia** (☎ 438-0644; cnr Espejo & Chile); and **Teatro Mendoza** (☎ 429-7279; San Juan 1427).

Shopping

Av Las Heras is lined with souvenir shops, leather shops, chocolate stores and all sorts of places to pick up cheap Argentine trinkets. Items made of *carpincho* (spotted tan suede made from a large rodent) are uniquely Argentine and sold in many of the stores.

Plaza de las Artes (Plaza Independencia; 5-11pm Fri-Sun) Outdoor crafts market in the Plaza Independencia.

Feria Artesanal Plaza España (Plaza España; 5-10pm Fri-Sun) Crafts fair in Plaza España with mediocre-quality goods.

Raices (☎ 425-4118; España 1092) High-quality weavings, *mates*, jewelry and more. There is another location on Av Sarmiento 162.

Mercado Artesanal (☎ 420-4239; Av San Martín 1143; closed Sun) This cooperative offers provincial handicrafts, including vertical-loom weavings (Huarpe-style) from northwest Mendoza, horizontal looms (Araucanian-style) from the south, woven baskets from Lagunas del Rosario, and lots of braided, untanned leather horse gear. The Mercado Artesenal is located below the provincial tourist office.

Getting There & Away

AIR

Aerolíneas Argentinas/Austral (☎ 420-4185; Av Sarmiento 82) share offices; Aerolíneas flies several times daily to Buenos Aires (US$97 to US$107).

Lan Chile (☎ 425-7900; Rivadavia 135) flies twice daily to Santiago de Chile (US$100 to US$190), the only international flights from Mendoza.

Southern Winds (☎ 429-3200, 429-7077; España 943) flies twice Monday through Friday and once Saturday and Sunday to Buenos Aires (US$72 to US$100) with connections through the country.

BUS

Mendoza is a major transport hub from which you can get just about anywhere in the country. There are daily departures from Mendoza's **bus terminal** (☎ 431-5000, 431-3001; cnr Av Gobernador Videla & Av Acceso Este, Guaymallén) to the destinations in the following table, and sometimes upwards of 10 to 20 per day to major cities. Prices reflect midseason fares.

Domestic

Several companies send buses daily to Uspallata (US$2.50, two hours) and Los Penitentes (US$3.50, four hours), the latter for Aconcagua.

In ski season, several companies go directly to Las Leñas (about US$7, 6½ hours); Mendoza Viajes leaves from Av Sarmiento and 9 de Julio, rather than the terminal.

A number of companies offer morning service to the Difunta Correa Shrine (p312; US$6 roundtrip, departs 7:30am) in San Juan province; it's three hours each way and the bus waits three hours before returning.

Destination	Cost (US$)	Duration (hr)
Bahía Blanca	22	16
Bariloche	31	20
Barreal	5.50	4
Buenos Aires	14-25	13-17
Catamarca	15	10
Comodoro Rivadavia	49	30
Córdoba	10-12	10
Jujuy	27-34	20
Malargüe	7	6-7
Mar del Plata	37	19
Neuquén	16-25	10-12
Puerto Iguazú	50-65	36
Puerto Madryn	37-47	23-24
Resistencia	28	24
Río Gallegos	69	41
Rosario	13-20	12
Salta	23-34	18
San Agustín del Valle Fértil	10	6
San Juan	3.50-6	2½
San Luis	7	3½
San Martín de los Andes	25	19-20
San Rafael	3.50	3
Santa Fe	20	14
Tucumán	18-26	14
Zapala	10	9½

International

Numerous companies cross the Andes every day via RN 7 (the Paso de Los Libertadores) to Santiago de Chile (US$10, seven hours), Viña del Mar (US$10, seven hours) and Valparaíso (US$10, eight hours). The pass sometimes closes in winter due to bad weather; be prepared to wait (sometimes days) if weather gets extreme.

Several carriers have connections to Lima, Perú (US$100, 60 to 70 hours), via Santiago, and there are at least two weekly departures to Montevideo, Uruguay (from US$40, 22 hours), some with onward connections to Punta del Este and Brazil.

Getting Around

TO/FROM THE AIRPORT

Plumerillo International Airport (☎ 448-2603) is 6km north of downtown on RN 40. Bus No 68 ('Aeropuerto') from Calle Salta goes straight to the terminal.

BUS

Mendoza's **bus terminal** (☎ 431-5000, 431-3001; cnr Av Gobernador Videla & Av Acceso Este, Guaymallén) is really just across the street from downtown. After arriving, walk under the Videla underpass (it's lined with merchandise stalls) and you'll be heading toward the center, about 15 minutes away. Otherwise, the 'Villa Nueva' trolley (actually a bus) connects the terminal with downtown.

Local buses cost US$0.25 – more for longer distances such as the trip to the airport – and require a magnetic Mendobus card, which can be bought at most kiosks in denominations of AR$2 (US$0.65) and AR$5 (US$1.65). Most *lineas* (bus lines) also have *internos* (internal route numbers) posted in the window; for example, *linea* 200 might post *interno* 204 or 206; watch for both numbers. *Internos* indicate more precisely where the bus will take you.

CAR

Rental-car agencies are at the airport and along Primitivo de la Reta.

Aruba Car Rental (☎ 423-4071; Primitivo de la Reta 936, Local 5)

Avis (☎ 447-0150; Primitivo de la Reta 914)

Localiza (☎ 429-6800; Primitivo de la Reta 936, Local 4)

National/Alamo (☎ 429-3111; Primitivo de la Reta 928)

Rent A Car (☎ 425-2959; Primitivo de la Reta 915)

AROUND MENDOZA

Sites in this section are Mendoza's closest major attractions, but you could easily visit Puenta del Inca and Las Cuevas (near the Chilean border; see p303) in a day.

Wineries

Thanks to a complex and very old system of river-fed aqueducts, land that was once a desert now supports 70% of the country's wine production (see the boxed text, p298). Mendoza province is wine country, and many wineries near the capital offer tours and tasting. Countless tourist agencies offer day tours, hitting two or more wineries in a precisely planned day, but it's also easy enough to visit on your own. Hiring a *remise* (telephone taxi) is also feasible. All winery tours and tastings are free, though some push hard for sales at the end, and you never taste the *good* stuff without paying. Malbec, of course, is the definitive Argentine wine.

With a full day, it's easy to hop on buses and hit several of the area's most appealing wineries in the outskirts of neighboring Maipú, only 16km away. Another option is the area of Luján de Cuyo, 19km south of Mendoza, which also has many important wineries. Buses to Maipú leave from La Rioja, between Garibaldi and Catamarca in downtown Mendoza; buses to wineries in Luján de Cuyo leave from Mendoza's bus terminal.

Mendoza's tourist office on Garibaldi near Av San Martín provides a basic but helpful map of the area and its wineries. Also look for the useful three-map set *Wine Map: Wine and Tasting Tours* (Wine Map, 2004–05).

Bodega Escorihuela (☎ 0261-424-2744; escorihuela adm@simza.com.ar; cnr Belgrano & Pte Alvear, Godoy Cruz; ⏱ tours 9:30am, 10:30am & 11:30am, 12:30pm, 2:30pm & 3:30pm), founded in 1884, is one of the country's oldest wineries. It has an art gallery, a restaurant and a famous barrel from Nancy, France, with an impressive sculpture of Dionysus. Take bus 'T' from Mendoza's Av Sarmiento at Av San Martín.

Bodega La Rural (Museo del Vino; ☎ 0261-497-2013; Montecaseros 2625, Coquimbito, Maipú; ⏱ 9:30am-5:30pm Mon-Fri with tours every half hr, 10am-1pm Sat & Sun with tours every hr) is the maker of the esteemed Rutini and Felipe Rutini wines, and should be top on your list if only for its outstanding **wine museum**, the biggest in South America. Tours are offered in English. From the stop on La Rioja in Mendoza, take bus No 173.

FINER & FINER ARGENTINE WINE   Chris Moss

Wine making goes back over 500 years in Argentina, to when the first Spanish colonists planted grapes in several regions of the interior. The Jesuits planted their own vineyards in the north, developing the criolla grape. It wasn't until the 19th-century immigration boom that French, Italian and Spanish settlers began to take enology seriously, bringing in their countries' best grapes to grow vines in western Argentina, where the rain shadow of the Andes provided an ideal setting for industrial viticulture. The opening of the rail line from Buenos Aires to Mendoza in 1884 meant wine could travel to the wealthy capital and compete with the imported bottles kept in patricians' cellars.

But for all the French mansions in Buenos Aires, the wines never rivaled European ones. Up until a mere decade ago, the most famous thing about *vino argentino* was that it never left the country. The second most famous thing was that – according to critics and merchants – this was just as well, since the vast majority of wines produced by Argentine wineries were too low grade for export. As a result, the natives were welcome – and encouraged – to drink every last drop.

This they certainly did. Though Argentina has been the world's fifth-largest wine producer for some time, the domestic market traditionally drank almost every drop of the stuff. In the 1960s annual consumption stood as high as 25L per capita, compared with around 10L at present. That said, any good *asado* (barbecue) is still incomplete without a bottle of *vino fino* (a decent varietal or a blend) or, at the low end, a *vino comun* (table wine) in a flagon with a blast of soda to smooth its rough edges. Recently, as beer has gained in popularity in Argentina, the big vineyards have had to market themselves internationally, necessitating better wine-making technology and a better product. On the whole, the response from international wine competitions, critics and consumers has been favorable, and Argentine wines are now a common sight worldwide.

Still, there are compelling reasons to indulge in a drop or three of Argentine wine while here and check out the local wine scene. One, you get to visit Argentina's wine mecca, Mendoza, with its hundreds of charming vineyards producing almost three-quarters of the country's total wine crop. Here irrigation techniques first introduced by the native Huarpe Indians are still used to water the desertlike landscape. The upscale ambitions of big, high-tech vineyards like Etchart, Norton, Catena and La Agricola are gradually rubbing off on smaller producers, and all are keen to show off their wares. Whether you are visiting a major establishment or a small operation, if you're lucky the owners – and many wineries are still family-owned and run – will be around to show you their grand old oak barrels and latest international-standard metallic vats.

Another reason for wine-inspired travel is that while only a few dozen big-brand labels are exported, the choice of labels within Argentina is vast, and some exceptional wines are available only at their source or in the big city bistros. The vineyards often do wine tasting at the end of brief tours, and chances are they'll spoil you. Finally, and crucially, wine – like other legal vices – is pretty cheap in Argentina, even when the quaffing is of a high quality.

Argentine wines are made from grapes of European origin, and the familiar Cabernet, Chardonnay and Syrah varieties abound. The hot climate in Mendoza favors reds, and Argentine Malbecs, rightly famed in international wine circles, can be outstanding. For fans of white, *torrontés*, a Spanish grape unpopular outside Argentina, produces some of the best bottles. For a few pesos, wines produced by Graffigna, Santa Julia and San Telmo are ultrareliable; for a bottle from the south, Río Negro's Patagonia is very good. If you want to splurge, try Catena or Weinert wines, and the local bubbly from Moet & Chandon is a relatively economical way to look rich.

Corkage can double the prices in bars and restaurants so check the menu offerings.

Bodega Viña El Cerno (☎ 0261-481-1567; Moreno 631, Coquimbito, Maipú; ◷ tours 9am-5pm Mon-Fri, or with reservations Sat & Sun), built in 1864, is a romantically small winery surrounded by vineyards. It's well worth a visit. From the stop on La Rioja, take bus No 170.

Bodega Giol (☎ 0261-497-6777; Ozamis 1040, Maipú; ◷ tours 9am-7pm Mon-Sat, 11am-2pm Sun) is known

for its turn-of-the-century brick facade and the magnificent barrel won by the winery in France in 1910. From the La Rioja stop, take bus No 174.

Luigi Bosca (☎ 0261-498-0437; San Martín 2044, Luján de Cuyo; guided visits at 10:30am Mon-Sat), which also produces Finca La Linda, is one of Mendoza's premier wineries. If you're into wine, don't miss it. Call beforehand to reserve a space for the 10:30am visit. Take bus number 380 from Mendoza's bus terminal.

The modern **Bodegas Chandon** (☎ 0261-490-9900; RN 40, Km 29, Luján de Cuyo; ☉ 9:30am-12:30pm & 2-5pm Mon-Fri, 9:30am-12:30pm Sun Feb, Mar & Jul, 9:30am-12:30pm & 2-3:30pm Mon-Fri rest of year) is popular with tour groups and known for its sparkling wines (champagne). Tours are available in English. Take bus No 380 (US$0.75, one hour) from platform 53 in Mendoza's bus terminal.

Catena Zapata (☎ 0261-490-0214; Calle Cobos 5519, Agrelo, Luján de Cuyo; visits/tours by appointment 10am-6pm Mon-Sat) is Argentina's most esteemed winery; its pioneering owner, Nicolas Catena, is often likened to California's Robert Mondavi. Tours are fairly mundane, but tasting – if you put down the cash – can be educational indeed. Get there by taxi (cheaper if you bus to Luján and grab one from there).

Cacheuta

☎ 02624 / elevation 1237m

About 40km west of Mendoza in the department of Luján de Cuyo, Cacheuta is renowned for its medicinal thermal waters and agreeable microclimate. There is lodging at the lovely **Hotel Termas Cacheuta** (☎ 490152/3; RP 82, Km 38; s/d with full board Sun-Thu US$51/86, Fri & Sat US$70/117; ☒), where prices include a swimming pool, hot tubs, massage and mountain bikes, in addition to optional recreation programs. Nonguests may use the baths for US$3.50 per person.

Campers can pitch a tent at **Camping Termas de Cacheuta** (☎ 482082; RN 7, Km 39; per person US$5).

Expreso Uspallata (in Mendoza ☎ 0261-438-1092) runs daily buses to Cacheuta for US$5 round-trip. The price includes entrance to the pools (not the spa). Otherwise it's US$1 one way.

Potrerillos

☎ 02624 / elevation 1351m

Set above the newly built Potrerillos reservoir in beautiful Andean precordillera, Potrerillos is one of Mendoza's white-water meccas, usually visited during a day's rafting trip from the capital.

Located about 1km uphill from the ACA campground, **Argentina Rafting Expediciones** (☎ 482037; www.argentinarafting.com in Spanish; Ruta Parilago; day trips with transfer from Mendoza US$17-43) offers rafting and kayaking on the Río Mendoza. Trips range from a 5km, one-hour

Class II float to a 50km, five-hour Class III–IV descent over two days (US$82). Set up trips at the office in Mendoza or at the base here in Potrerillos. Mendoza also has an **office** (☎ 0261-429-0029; Sarmiento 223).

Camping del ACA (☎ 482013; RN 7, Km 50; sites members/nonmembers US$3.50/4, extra tent US$1) offers shady sites near the reservoir just below the new town.

The tourist office situated at the entrance to town has a list of *cabañas* (cabins) along the wooded road to El Salto.

For delicious traditional cooking, don't miss friendly **El Futre** (☎ 482006; www.elfutrecocina bar.com.ar in Spanish; Ruta Parilago s/n; mains US$3.50), at the same location as Argentina Rafting.

Villavicencio

☎ 0261 / elevation 1800m

If you've ordered mineral water from any restaurant or café in Argentina, odds are you've ended up with a bottle of Villavicencio on your table. These springs are the source, and their spectacular mountain setting once hosted the prestigious thermal baths resort of the **Gran Hotel de Villavicencio** (admission free; grounds ☉ 8am-8pm). Popular with the Argentine elite during the middle of the 20th century, the resort has been closed for more than a decade; promises have floated around for years that it would 'soon' reopen (Grupo Danone has made the latest for 2006, but don't count on it).

Panoramic views from the hair-raising winding turns leading to Villavicencio make the journey an attraction in itself. There is free camping alongside the attractive **Hostería Villavicencio** (☎ 424-6482; meals US$2.50-4.75), which has no accommodations but serves light meals, coffee and beer.

Expreso Jocolí, in Mendoza, runs buses from the terminal to Villavicencio (51km northwest of Mendoza on RP 52) on Wednesday, Saturday and Sunday.

USPALLATA

☎ 02624 / pop 3000 / elevation 1751m

About 105km west of Mendoza, the crossroads town of Uspallata is a leafy island of álamos (poplars) in an otherwise desolate but delightful valley between the precordillera and some of the Andes' highest peaks. The town is slightly chaotic at the main intersection but delightfully mellow elsewhere. The polychrome mountains surrounding the town so resemble highland central Asia that director Jean-Jacques Annaud used it as the location for the epic film *Seven Years in Tibet*, starring Brad Pitt. For travelers, it's an excellent base for exploring the surrounding mountains.

There's a post office and a Banco de la Nacion, which has an ATM. The unequipped **tourist office** (☎ 420410; RN 7 s/n; ☼ 9am-8pm) is across from the YPF station.

Sights & Activities
A kilometer north of the highway junction in Uspallata, a signed lateral leads to ruins and a museum at the **Museo Las Bóvedas** (admission US$0.35; ☼ 10am-7pm Tue-Sun), a smelting site since pre-Columbian times. On view are unintentionally comical dioramas of battles that took place during General Gregorio de Las Heras' campaign across the Andes in support of San Martín. The museum itself is a dud, but the structure (resembling two giant white breasts) is well worth seeing.

Fototravesías 4x4 (☎ 420185; www.fototravesias 4x4.com in Spanish; day trips per person US$12-17), near the main intersection, offers exciting 4x4 tours in the surrounding mountains. The owner is a photographer (it's located in the photography shop), and is especially sensitive to getting good shots.

Next door, **Minimarket La Terminal** (☎ 0261-15-416-0714; RP 52 s/n; bike rental per hr US$1.50) rents mountain bikes.

Sleeping & Eating
In summer high season (when climbers from around the world descend on the area), reservations are wise.

Hostería Los Cóndores (☎ 420002; www.hostallos condores.com.ar in Spanish; Las Heras s/n; s US$16-21, d US$26-35) Close to the junction, this hotel has spacious, carpeted rooms with huge bathrooms and an on-site restaurant. Higher prices include half-board.

Hotel Viena (☎ 420046; Av Las Heras 240; s/d US$10/14) This warmly recommended hotel, east of the highway junction, has simple, comfortable rooms with bathroom.

Hostel Uspallata (in Mendoza ☎ 0261-429-3220; www.hosteluspallata.com; RN 7 s/n; dm US$7.50) Friendly hostel 5km east of town with plain but comfortable rooms, a Ping-Pong table and a café. There's good hiking from the hostel, and free pick up from the bus terminal.

Gran Hotel Uspallata (☎ /fax 420003/66/67; reser vas@atahoteleria.com.ar; RN 7, Km 1149; ste s/d US$26/33; standard d US$31, with shared bathroom US$11; ☒) Though it looks a bit shopworn since its Peronist glory days, this resort hotel, about 1km west of the junction, offers an interesting taste of old-school Argentine tourism – pretend it's 1950 and you're rich. The hallways are large, almost daunting, there's a bowling alley, and the rooms come complete with pink chenille bedspreads.

Parrilla San Cayetano (☎ 420149) Behind the YPF station, this *parrilla* is a convenient stop offering decent food for travelers en route to and from Chile.

Getting There & Away
Expreso Uspallata (☎ 420045) runs several buses daily to and from Mendoza (US$3.50, 2½ hours). Buses continue to Las Cuevas (from Uspallata US$2.50, two hours), near the Chilean border, and stop en route at Los Penitentes, Puente del Inca and the turnoff to Laguna Los Horcones for Parque Provincial Aconcagua. They can be flagged from all of these locations on their return to Uspallata from Las Cuevas.

Andesmar has daily morning departures to Santiago (US$8.50, six hours) and Valparaiso (US$8.50, seven hours) in Chile.

All buses leave from the Expreso Uspallata office in the little strip mall near the junction.

LOS PENITENTES
☎ 02624
So-named because the pinnacles resemble a line of monks, **Los Penitentes** (☎ 420229; www .lospenitentes.com in Spanish) has both excellent scenery and snowcover (when it snows). It's 165km west of Mendoza via RN 7, and offers downhill and cross-country skiing at an altitude of 2580m. Lifts and accommodations are modern, and the vertical drop on some of its 21 runs is more than 700m. Services include a ski school, equipment rentals (skis US$8.50 per day, snowboards US$12) and several restaurants and cafeterias. For transportation details, see above.

In high ski season (July and August) and during peak climbing season (December through March), make reservations up to a month in advance for all of the following:

Hostel Los Penitentes (in Mendoza ☎ 0261-429-0707; www.penitentes.com.ar; per person US$7) This cozy converted cabin, owned by Mendoza's HI Campo Base, accommodates 20 people in extremely close quarters, and has a kitchen, wood-burning stove and three shared bathrooms. It's all good fun with the right crowd. Lunch and dinners are available for US$2.50 to US$3.50 each.

Hostería Los Penitentes (in Mendoza ☎ 0261-438-0222, 429-3014; d in ski season with half-board US$33) This modest *hostería* (lodging house) with plain, comfortable rooms has a restaurant and bar and offers full board with ski passes (US$447 per week with full board and unlimited skiing).

Hotel & Hostería Ayelén (in Mendoza ☎ 0261-427-1123; www.ayelen.net; d hostería/hotel US$22/30) Four-star resort hotel with comfortable accommodations in the main hotel and cheaper rooms in the *hostería* alongside. The lobby and restaurant are great, but the wallpaper in the rooms could use a change.

PUENTE DEL INCA
☎ 0264

One of Argentina's most striking natural wonders, this stone bridge over the Río de las Cuevas glows a dazzling orange from the sediment deposited by the warm sulfuric waters. The brick ruins of an old spa, built as part of a resort and later destroyed by flood, sit beneath the bridge, slowly yielding their form to the sulfuric buildup from the thermal water that trickles over, around and through it; it makes for an unforgettable dip.

Puente del Inca, 2720m above sea level and 177km from Mendoza, sits between Parque Provincial Aconcagua and Parque Provincial Volcán Tupungato. It enjoys a spectacular setting, and whether or not you climb, it's a good base for exploring the area. Trekkers and climbers can head north to the base of Aconcagua, south to the pinnacles of Los Penitentes (see the previous section), or even further south to 6650m Tupungato (p303).

About 1km before Puente del Inca (directly across from Los Puquios), the small **Cementario Andinista** is a cemetery for climbers who died on Aconcagua. It's well worth a peek and drives home the dangers of climbing these great mountains.

In summer, free camping is possible at the nearby mini ski resort of **Los Puquios** (☎ 420 190; www.lospuquios.com.ar). There are two accommodations options at Puente del Inca:

Refugio La Vieja Estación (in Mendoza ☎ 0261-452-1103; www.refugioinca@yahoo.com; dm US$5-6; meals US$2.75) is a rustic hostel in Puente del Inca's old wooden train station, built in the late 1800s. It's popular with climbers during peak season but can be wonderfully quiet other times of the year. It will probably relocate across the highway in 2006 or 2007 with the completion of the Trasandino Railway.

Hostería Puente del Inca (☎ 420266; RN 7, Km 175; s/d US$27/34, with half-board US$32/40) has comfortable rooms and a huge restaurant (with an overpowering smell of budget air-freshener) serving US$5 set meals. It's the most comfortable in the area and fills up fast in climbing season.

For transportation details, see opposite.

PARQUE PROVINCIAL ACONCAGUA
North of RN 7, nearly hugging the Chilean border, Parque Provincial Aconcagua protects 71,000 hectares of the wild high country surrounding the western hemisphere's highest summit, 6962m Cerro Aconcagua. Passing motorists (and those who can time their buses correctly) can stop to enjoy the view of the peak from **Laguna Los Horcones**, a 2km walk from the parking lot just north of the highway.

There's a ranger available 8am to 9pm weekdays, 8am to 8pm Saturday. There are also rangers at the junction to Plaza Francia, about 5km north of Los Horcones; at Plaza de Mulas on the main route to the peak; at Refugio Las Leñas, on the Polish Glacier Route up the Río de las Vacas to the east; and at Plaza Argentina, the last major camping area along the Polish Glacier Route.

Only highly experienced climbers should consider climbing Aconcagua without the relative safety of an organized tour.

Cerro Aconcagua
Often called the 'roof of the Americas,' the volcanic summit of Aconcagua covers a base of uplifted marine sediments. The origin of the name is unclear; one possibility is the Quechua term Ackon-Cahuac, meaning 'stone sentinel,' while another is the Mapuche phrase Acon-Hue, signifying 'that which comes from the other side.'

Italian-Swiss climber Mathias Zurbriggen made the first recorded ascent in 1897. Since then, the peak has become a favorite destination for climbers from around the world, even though it is technically less challenging than other nearby peaks. In 1985 the Club Andinista Mendoza's discovery of an Incan mummy at 5300m on the mountain's southwest face proved that the high peaks were a pre-Columbian funerary site.

Reaching the summit requires a commitment of at least 13 to 15 days, including acclimatization time; some climbers prefer the longer but more scenic, less crowded and more technical Polish route.

Potential climbers should acquire RJ Secor's climbing guide *Aconcagua* (Seattle, The Mountaineers, 1999). The web page www.aconcagua.com.ar is also helpful.

Nonclimbers can trek to **base camps** and **refugios** (rustic shelters) beneath the permanent snow line. On the Northwest Route there is also the rather luxurious and expensive **Hotel Refugio Plaza de Mulas** (in Mendoza ☎ 0261-421-4330; www.refugioplazademulas.com.ar; r per person US$27-40, with full board US$60-72, dm with/ without full board US$50/17; �☀ Nov-Mar), the highest hotel in the world.

PERMITS

From December to March, permits are obligatory for both trekking and climbing in Parque Provincial Aconcagua; park rangers at Laguna Horcones will not permit visitors to proceed up the Quebrada de los Horcones without one. Fees vary according to the complex park-use seasons. Permits cost US$30/50 for trekkers (three/seven days), and US$300 for climbers (20 days) during high season, from December 15 through January 31; US$20/40 for trekkers and US$200 for climbers during midseason, from December 1 to December 14 and February 1 through February 20; and US$20/30 (trekking) and US$100 (climbing) in low season, from November 15 through November 30 and February 21 through March 15. Argentine nationals pay half price at all times.

Organized tours rarely, if ever, include the park entrance fee. Fees must be paid in Argentine pesos or US dollars only, and you must bring your original passport with you when you pay the fee. The permit start-date takes effect when you enter the park.

The three-day trekking permit can be purchased directly at Horcones ranger station, but hikers with the three-day permit are not allowed above 4200m. All other permits are available only in Mendoza at

the **Dirección de Recursos Naturales & Renovables** (☎ 0261-425-2090, sales ☎ 0261-425-2031; Edificio Cuba, Las Tipas at Los Robles; ☀ 8am-6pm Mon-Fri, 9am-1pm Sat & Sun Nov 15-Mar 15), at the entrance to Parque San Martín. There is regularly talk of moving this, so check with the tourist office in Mendoza beforehand.

ROUTES

There are three main routes up Cerro Aconcagua. The most popular one, approached by a 40km trail from Los Horcones, is the **Ruta Noroeste** (Northwest Route) from Plaza de Mulas, 4230m above sea level. The **Pared Sur** (South Face), approached from the base camp at Plaza Francia via a 36km trail from Los Horcones, is a demanding technical climb.

From Punta de Vacas, 15km southeast of Puente del Inca, the longer but more scenic **Ruta Glaciar de los Polacos** (Polish Glacier Route) first ascends the Río de las Vacas to the base camp at Plaza Argentina, a distance of 76km. Wiktor Ostrowski and others pioneered this route in 1934. Climbers on this route must carry ropes, screws and ice axes, in addition to the usual tent, warm sleeping bag and clothing, and plastic boots. This route is more expensive because it requires the use of mules for a longer period.

MULES

The cost of renting cargo mules, which can carry about 60kg each, has gone through the roof: the standard fee among outfitters is US$120 for the first mule from Puente del Inca to Plaza de Mulas, though two mules cost only US$160. A party of three should pay about US$240 to get their gear to the Polish Glacier Route base camp and back.

For mules, contact Rudy Parra at Aconcagua Trek or Fernando Grajales, following. If you're going up on an organized tour, the mule situation is, of course, covered.

TOURS

Many of the adventure-travel agencies in and around Mendoza arrange excursions into the high mountains (see p292). It is also possible to arrange trips with overseas operators.

The following are the area's most established and experienced operators:
Daniel Alessio Expediciones (www.alessio.com.ar)
Located in Mendoza, contact online.

Fernando Grajales (☎ /fax 0261-428-3157, 15-500-7718; www.grajales.net) Contact by telephone in Mendoza. Fernando operates from Hostería Puente del Inca (p301) from December to March.

Inka Expediciones (☎ 0261-425-0871; www.inka.com.ar, www.aconcagua.cc; Juan B Justo 345, Mendoza) Fixed and tailor-made expeditions. Airport to airport costs US$1800-2000.

Rudy Parra's Aconcagua Trek (in Mendoza ☎ /fax 0261-431-7003; www.rudyparra.com; aconcagua@rudyparra.com) Contact Rudy by telephone. Rudy operates at nearby Los Puquios (p301) from December to March.

Several guides from the Asociación de Guías de Montaña lead two-week trips to Aconcagua, including **Alejandro Randis** (☎ 0261-496-3461) and **Daniel Pizarro** (☎ 0261-423-0698).

All guides and organized trips are best set up online or by telephone at *least* a month in advance. Everything – guides, mules, hotels etc – must be booked far in advance during peak climbing months.

Getting There & Away

The two park entrances – Punta de Vacas and Laguna Los Horcones – are directly off RN 7 and are well signed. The Los Horcones turnoff is only 4km past Puente del Inca. If you're part of an organized tour, transport will be provided. To get here by bus, take an early morning Expreso Uspallata bus (see p300) from Mendoza. Buses bound for Chile will stop at Puente del Inca, but often fill up with passengers going all the way through.

From Los Horcones, you can walk back along the RN 7 to Puente del Inca or time your buses and catch a Mendoza-bound bus back down.

LAS CUEVAS & CRISTO REDENTOR

Pounded by chilly but exhilarating winds, situated nearly 4000m above sea level on the Argentine–Chilean border, the rugged high Andes make a fitting backdrop for Cristo Redentor, the famous monument erected after a territorial dispute between the two countries was settled in 1902. The view is a must-see either with a tour or by private car (a tunnel has replaced the hairpin road to the top as the border crossing into Chile), but the first autumn snowfall closes the route. You can hike the 8km up to El Cristo via trails if you don't have a car.

In the nearby settlement of Las Cuevas, 10km east of the Chilean border and 15km from Puente del Inca, **Arco de Las Cuevas** (☎ 0261-426-5273; mains US$3.50; dm US$8.50) has extremely basic bunks and only two bathrooms (which everyone in the restaurant uses as well). The restaurant, however, serves what one traveler called the 'best lentil soup ever' (hunger and cold make mighty good sauces).

Parque Provincial Volcán Tupungato

Tupungato (6650m) is an impressive volcano, partly covered by snowfields and glaciers, and serious climbers consider the mountain a far more challenging, interesting and technical climb than Aconcagua. The main approach is from the town of **Tunuyán**, 82km south of Mendoza via RN 40, where the **tourist office** (☎ 02622-488097, 02622-422193; República de Siria & Alem) can provide info. Many of the outfitters who arrange Aconcagua treks can also deal with Tupungato (see opposite).

SAN RAFAEL

☎ 02627 / pop 98,000 / elevation 690m

Majestic old sycamores line the streets of downtown San Rafael, and the open irrigation channels that water them trace the city's clean, tiled sidewalks. But what you'll really notice are the bicycles. No other city in Argentina has this number of peddlers, who cycle everywhere, giving a relaxed flow to life in San Rafael.

There is nothing to do in town (part of its allure) except wander its shady streets and plazas or while the day away in a café. There are, however, several esteemed wineries nearby that are well worth a visit. The city has also become a popular base for exploring (or driving through) the nearby Cañon de Atuel, and for scenic rafting on the Río Atuel.

Orientation

San Rafael is located 230km southeast of the city of Mendoza via RN 40 and RN 143, and 189km northeast of Malargüe via RN 40. Most areas of interest in town are northwest of the Av H Yrigoyen–Av San Martín intersection.

Information

Banco de Galicia (Av H Yrigoyen 28) Several banks along Yrigoyen have ATMs, including Banco de Galicia.

Cambio Santiago (Almafuerte 64) Charges 2.5% on traveler's checks.

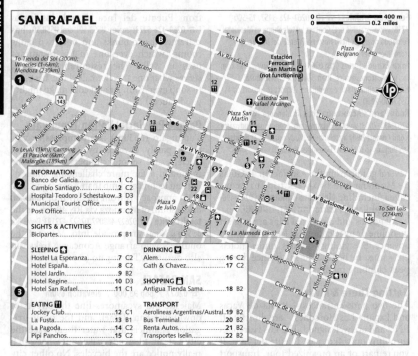

SAN RAFAEL

Hospital Teodoro J Schestakow (☎ 424490; Emilio Civit 151)

Leufú (☎ /fax 428164; Cabildo 1483) There are numerous agencies offering standard local excursions to Valle Grande and nearby wineries. Leufú does rafting, mountain biking and other activities.

Municipal tourist office (☎ 424217; www.sanrafael -tour.com; Av H Yrigoyen 745; ☽ 8am-8pm) Helpful staff and useful brochures and maps.

Post office (cnr San Lorenzo & Barcala)

Sights & Activities

San Rafael is flat (hence the bikes), and when in Rome…get a bike. Try **Bicipartes** (☎ 430260; Chile 445; per half-day/day US$3.50/5; ☽ 8am-1pm & 4-9pm Mon-Sat).

There are three wineries within walking or cycling distance of town offering free tours and tasting. Head west on RN 143, which has a welcome bike path (really!) along its side. The modern and highly regarded **Bianchi Champañera** (☎ 435600; www .vbianchi.com; cnr Ruta 143 & Calle Valentín Bianchi; ☽ 9am-12:30pm & 2-5pm) is the furthest west, but still only 6km away. Tours are friendly, offering visitors a glimpse into the making

of sparkling wine (champagne), and English is spoken. Unfortunately you have to sit through a short video before the tour. If you're cycling, make this your last stop for the free glass of champagne before the peddle back.

Only about 4km out, **Fincas Andinas** (Salafia; ☎ 430095; www.fincasandinas.com.ar; Yrigoyen 5800; ☽ guided visits every half hour 9:30am-4pm Mon-Fri) makes excellent champagne as well as Malbec and Cabernet.

Suter (☎ 421076; www.sutersa.com.ar in Spanish; Yrigoyen 2850; ☽ 9am-7pm Mon-Sat) is a rather unromantic, modern affair, but a worthwhile stop for some discounted wine. For US$25 you can set up a half-day tour, visiting the vineyards with an agronomist, tasting specialty wines and eating a big lunch in the vineyard.

Sleeping

Hotel Jardín (☎ /fax 434621; consultas@jardinhotel.com; Av H Yrigoyen 283; s/d US$14/22) The immaculate Jardín has excellent service, firm beds and pleasantly decorated rooms with TV, telephone, desks and even hairdryers. Rooms open onto a faux-Italian open-air interior, and coffee is free and waiting in the breakfast area.

Hotel España (☎ 424055; hotelespanasrl@volsinectis.com.ar; Av San Martín 270; s US$10-15, d US$18-$23) It may not scream 'Spain,' but the mod 1960s-ish Spanish style interior is definitely unique. The cheaper rooms in the 'colonial' sector open onto a delightful patio area, making them more attractive (and a better deal) than the spacious rooms in the pricier 'celeste' sector.

Hostel La Esperanza (☎ 427978; Avellaneda 263; dm/s/d US$5.50/8/13) The lobby and breakfast area here are wonderfully comfortable, but the rooms are pretty dilapidated. Good deal if you're on a budget. Kitchen privileges US$1 extra.

Hotel Regine (☎ 421470; www.hotelregine.com.ar; Independencia 623; r US$30; P ⓧ) Though it's several blocks from the center (not a big deal in quiet San Rafael), the big swimming pool, expansive grassy backyard with plenty of lawn chairs, and its quiet location make the Regine very relaxing.

Hotel San Rafael (☎ 430125; Day 30; s/d US$27/37; P) This five-story, three-star hotel is a comfortable place located near the plaza, and rooms on the upper floors have good light and pretty views. Wooden headboards and flowered bedspreads make for the usual hotel-room feel.

Camping El Parador (☎ 427983; Isla Río Diamante; sites US$5) Located six kilometers south of downtown.

Eating

La Alameda (☎ 434850; Av Pedro Vargas 1961; all-you-can-eat parrilla US$5.50; ⓧ dinner Tue-Sat, lunch Sun) It's well worth the US$1.50 cab ride out to this family-run restaurant, where the mixed all-you-can-eat *parrilla* is as good as the service is friendly.

Jockey Club (☎ 422336; Belgrano 330; lunch & dinner US$4.50) One of the town's classier, old-school restaurants, Jockey Club offers the standard main courses accompanied by an all-you-can-eat salad bar.

La Fusta (☎ 429726; Av H Yrigoyen 538; full dinner US$5.50) Brightly lit and very popular, La Fusta serves a variety of meat and chicken dishes with rich but tasty sauces (including plum, gorgonzola and pepper-cream). The US$5.50 includes your choice of a main dish, salad and dessert bars.

THE AUTHOR'S CHOICE

Alem (☎ 15-539654; cnr Alem & Av Bartolomé Mitre; ⓧ 10pm-late Wed-Sat) Do your best to drop into this bar for the long list of cocktails and what's likely to be the most stylishly designed interior you'll find in all of Mendoza province. It's hard to believe it's San Rafael.

Tienda del Sol (☎ 425022; Av H Yrigoyen 1663; sandwiches US$2.50-3) Stylish sandwich shop (try the Tienda del Sol with chicken and blue cheese) with outdoor tables and massive, creative hot sandwiches.

La Pagoda (☎ 433868; Av Bartolomé Mitre 216; tenedor libre US$2.75) This is an all-you-can-eat joint with the usual smattering of salad, chicken and Chinese dishes on offer. Quality: mediocre.

Pipi Panchos (Chile near Pellegrini; sandwiches US$1.50-2) This minimarket with three outdoor tables is *the* spot to go for cheap *lomitos* (steak sandwiches).

Drinking

Gath & Chavez (☎ 434960; Av San Martín 98) San Rafael's most attractive café, with sidewalk tables, is an excellent hangout, day or night.

Shopping

There are numerous crafts stores found around town, all of which stock the usual souvenirs. For something a bit more authentic, pick up a pair of *bombachas* (commonly worn gaucho-influenced pants with button-cuff bottoms) for about US$8 at friendly **Antigua Tienda Sama** (☎ 15-553111; Godoy Cruz 123); they're subtle enough to wear anywhere.

Getting There & Around

Aerolíneas Argentinas/Austral (☎ 438808; Av H Yrigoyen 395) flies daily except Sunday to/from Buenos Aires (from US$100).

San Rafael's **bus terminal** (Coronel Suárez, btwn Avellaneda & Almafuerte) is conveniently located downtown.

Transportes Iselín (☎ 435998; Suarez 255) goes to Valle Grande/Cañon del Atuel (p306). Buses leave from the front of the office.

Patagonian destinations require a transfer in either Neuquén or Bariloche. There are regular daily departures to the following destinations:

Destination	Cost (US$)	Duration (hr)
Bariloche	27	14-15
Buenos Aires	25-32	13
Córdoba	14	12
El Nihuil	1.50	1½
Las Leñas	5	3
Mar del Plata	25	16
Malargüe	4	3
Mendoza	3.50	3
Neuquén	14	8
Rosario	15	12
San Juan	8.50	6
San Luis	7	4

Renta Autos (☎ 424623; rentaautos@infovia.com.ar; 25 de Mayo 380) offers the best deals on car rentals in town.

AROUND SAN RAFAEL

South of San Rafael along the Río Atuel, RP 173 passes through a multicolored ravine that locals compare to Arizona's Grand Canyon, though much of **Cañon del Atuel** has been submerged by four hydroelectric dams. Nevertheless, there is white-water rafting on its lower reaches, and several operators at the tourist complex of **Valle Grande** do short but scenic floats down the river, and other trips.

There are numerous places to stay in Valle Grande itself, which is a long stretch of *cabañas,* campgrounds and tour operators set up along the road. Most of them cater to large groups and are rather unpleasant, but the small **Cabañas Balcón del Atuel** (☎ 02627-426265; www.elbaqueano.org/balcondelatuel in Spanish; Ruta 173, Km 24; d US$27, cabaña for 6 US$40) has three comfortable *cabañas* and one double (all with kitchens), with a lovely grassy area over the river – a great spot to while away a day or two in the sun, especially in off-season.

Ruta 173 leads past the dam at Valle Grande, through the scenic Cañon del Atuel to the podunk village of **El Nihuil**, 79km from San Rafael.

Numerous San Rafael tour companies run day trips to Valle Grande, starting at US$12. For bus service to Valle Grande, Transportes Iselín leaves from in front of its office in San Rafael (see p305; US$1.50, 45 minutes). Buses to Nihuil take the alternate Ruta 144, which doesn't go through the canyon.

MALARGÜE

☎ 02627 / pop 23,000 / elevation 1400m

In the dry precordillera of the Andes, 189km southwest of San Rafael via paved RP 144 and RN 40, Malargüe draws visitors not so much for the town – it's not a particularly attractive place – but for outdoor pursuits in the spectacular volcanic mountains around it, which are geologically distinct from the Andes. For skiers, it's a cheaper alternative to the luxury hotels of nearby Las Leñas ski resort, which offers a 50% discount on lift tickets to anyone staying in Malargüe (hotels provide vouchers). Two fauna reserves, Payén and Laguna Llancancelo, are close by, and caving is possible at Caverna de las Brujas and Pozo de las Animas. The nearby Parque Provincial Payunia is a 450,000-hectare reserve with the highest concentration of volcanic cones in the world.

Information

Banco de la Nación (cnr San Martín & Inalicán) One of several banks downtown with ATMs.

Post office (cnr Adolfo Puebla & Saturnino Torres)

Tourist office (☎ 471659; www.malargue.gov.ar; RN40, Parque del Ayer; 🕑 8am-11pm) Helpful tourist office with facilities at the northern end of town, directly on the highway.

Tours & Activities

Several companies offer excellent 4WD and horse-riding excursions, and if you don't have a car, these are generally the best way to get into the surrounding mountains (see opposite). Possible day trips include Caverna de las Brujas (US$17 per person, which includes US$3.50 park entrance fee and obligatory guide), Los Molles (US$10), and the marvelous Laguna Llancancelo (US$12). One of the most exciting drives you might ever undertake is the 12-hour 4x4 tour through Parque Provincial Payunia (US$33); be sure your tour stops at all the sites; those that combine the visit with Laguna Llancancelo only visit half the sites in Payunia.

Amulén (Turismo Creativo; ☎ 470019; www.turismo-creativo.com in Spanish; San Martín 554) offers half-day horseback or hiking trips to the spectacular **Volcán Malacara** (US$20), which you should do your best to see. The company also offers a two-day trip through Parque Provincial Payunia complete with an *asado* under the stars.

Huarpes del Sol (☎ 15-557878; www.huarpesdelsol.com.ar in Spanish; San Martín 85) and **Receptivo**

Malargüe (☎ 471524; www.receptivomalargue.com.ar in Spanish; Batallón Nueva Creación 234) have both received excellent reports for their trips; the latter offers a wide array of adventure trips. The owner of **Karen Travel** (☎ /fax 470342; www .karentravel.com.ar; San Martín 54) speaks English and the company trips have received rave reviews.

Sleeping & Eating

Malargüe has abundant, reasonably priced accommodations. Prices quoted here are for ski season (June 15 through to September 15) and drop by up to 40% the rest of the year. Get a discount voucher from your hotel if you plan to ski at Las Leñas. Singles are nonexistent during ski season, when you'll likely be charged for however many beds are in the room.

Hotel de Turismo (☎ 471042; Av San Martín 224; s/d US$13/17) Rooms here are plain but comfortable and spacious, with TV and telephone; the upstairs rooms are the best. Good value.

Hotel Bambi (☎ /fax 471237; Av San Martín 410; s/d US$19/27) Friendly hotel with clean but faded rooms with basic bathrooms. It's the most comfortable place downtown.

Corre Caminos (☎ 471534; www.correcaminos; Telles Meneses 897; dm US$7; 🖳) Five blocks east of the clock tower, Corre Caminos' best feature (aside from its helpful owner) is the comfy new mattresses on all the bunks. It's a converted house with a big backyard.

Hostel Nord Patagonia (☎ 472276; www.nord patagonia.com; Fray Inalican 52 este; dm US$7.75; 🖳) Friendly hostel in a small converted house with fireplace and big wooden tables in a little common room.

Hostería La Posta (☎ 472079; San Martín 646; d US$17) The communal bathrooms are a bit shabby, and the rooms are only decent, but it's cheap. All rooms have bunks so they can cram 'em in during ski season.

Camping Municipal Malargüe (☎ 470691; Alfonso Capdevila s/n; sites US$1.75; 🌣 year-round) At the north end of town, 300m west of Av San Martín, this is the closest place to camp.

Doña María (☎ 471655; San Martín 156; mains US$2.75-3.50) Great empanadas, pastas and pizza, and good atmosphere to boot.

La Posta (☎ 471306; Av Roca 374; mains US$2-4) Malargüe's most established restaurant serves local specialties such as *chivito* (barbecued goat) and trout, but is best for pastas, pizzas and sandwiches.

Getting There & Around

There are flights to and from Buenos Aires in ski season only, leaving from the **Malargüe airport** (☎ 470098) at the south end of town. The Aerolíneas/Austral representative is **Karen Travel** (☎ 470342; Av San Martín 54).

There's a **bus terminal** (cnr Av General Roca & Aldao). There are several direct buses to Mendoza daily (US$7, seven hours), plus others requiring a change in San Rafael (US$4, three hours).

There is daily service in summer from Malargüe across the 2500m Paso Pehuenche and down the spectacular canyon of the Río Maule to Talca, Chile.

For transportation to Los Molles and Las Leñas ski resorts, contact any of the travel agencies listed under Tours opposite. They offer a roundtrip shuttle service, including ski rentals, from US$7 to US$10 per person.

Autotransportes Malargüe leaves from Plaza San Martín, at Torres, for Las Leñas (US$5 roundtrip) at 8:30am (arriving at 9:30am), and returns to Malargüe at 6pm.

AROUND MALARGÜE
☎ 02627

Geologically distinct from the Andean mountains to the west, the volcanically formed landscapes surrounding Malargüe are some of the most mind-altering in Argentina and have only recently begun to receive tourist attention. Visiting the following places is tough without your own transportation, though Malargüe's excellent travel agencies arrange excursions to all of them.

Just over 200km south of Malargüe, the spectacular **Parque Provincial Payunia** is a 450,000-hectare reserve with a higher concentration of volcanic cones (over 800 of them) than anywhere else in the world. The scenery is breathtaking and shouldn't be missed. The 12-hour 4X4 tours offered by most of the agencies in Malargüe (opposite) are well worth taking.

Lying within its namesake fauna reserve about 60km southeast of Malargüe, **Laguna Llancancelo** is a high mountain lake visited by more than 100 species of birds, including flamingos.

Caverna de Las Brujas is a magical limestone cave on Cerro Moncol, 72km south of Malargüe and 8km north of Bardas Blancas along RN 40. Its name means 'Cave of the Witches.'

Single 1100m lifts carry skiers up the relatively gentle slopes at **Los Molles**, a small, quiet ski resort along RP 222, 55km northwest of Malargüe. The thermal baths (US$3) set in old ruins make for a memorable dip. You can stay at the comfortable A-frame **Hotel Lahuen-Co** (☎ 499700; per person with half-board US$12); prices include two dips in the nearby thermal baths.

LAS LEÑAS
☎ 02627

Designed primarily to attract wealthy foreigners, **Las Leñas** (information office ☎ 471100; www.laslenas.com; ☉ mid-Jun–late Sep) is Argentina's most self-consciously prestigious ski resort, but despite the glitter it's not totally out of the question for budget travelers. Since its opening in 1983, it has attracted an international clientele who spend their days on the slopes and nights partying until the sun comes up. Because of the dry climate, Las Leñas has incredibly dry powder.

Las Leñas is 445km south of Mendoza, 200km southwest of San Rafael and only 70km from Malargüe, all via RN 40 and RP 222.

Its 33 runs cover 3300 hectares; the area has a base altitude of 2200m, but slopes reach 3430m for a maximum drop of 1230m.

Outside the ski season, Las Leñas is also attempting to attract summer visitors who enjoy weeklong packages offering activities such as mountain biking, horse riding and hiking.

Lift Tickets & Rentals
Prices for lift tickets vary considerably throughout the ski season. Children's tickets are discounted about 30%. One-day tickets range from US$28 in low season to US$42 in high season (half-day tickets US$18 to US$32). There are corresponding rates for three-day, four-day, one-week, two-week and season passes. Anyone lodging in Malargüe receives 50% off lift tickets (make sure you get a voucher from your hotel).

Lifts run 9am to 5pm daily. Rental equipment is readily available and will set you back about US$20 per day for skis and US$35 to US$40 per day for snowboards.

Sleeping & Eating
Las Leñas has a small village with three luxury hotels and a group of 'apart hotels,' all under the same management. They are generally booked as part of a weeklong package, which includes lodging, unlimited skiing and two meals per day. Despite the country's economic troubles, rates for foreigners staying in Las Leñas have changed little. All booking is done online at www.laslenas.com or centrally through **Ski Leñas** (in Buenos Aires ☎ 011-4819-6000/60; ventas@laslenas.com; Cerrito 1186, 8th fl).

Hotel Piscis (weekly adult package rates per person US$912-2435; ☒) The most extravagant of Las Leña's lodging is the five-star, 99-room Hotel Piscis. This prestigious hotel has wood-burning stoves, a gymnasium, sauna, an indoor swimming pool, the elegant Las Cuatro Estaciones restaurant, a bar, a casino and shops. Rates depend on time of the season, and are based on double occupancy.

Hotel Aries (US$750-1490) Aries is a four-star hotel with a sauna, gym facilities, a restaurant and luxuriously comfortable rooms.

Hotel Escorpio (US$730-1820) This 47-room hotel is nominally three stars, but still topnotch, with an excellent restaurant.

Apart Hotel Gemenis (weekly per person US$360-1365) and **Apart Hotel Delphos** (weekly per person US$360-1365) offer similar packages without meals but do have well-equipped kitchenettes, and guests can use the facilities at Hotel Piscis.

There are also small apartments with two to six beds and shared bathrooms, equipped for travelers to cook for themselves. Budget travelers can stay more economically at Los Molles, 20km down the road, or at Malargüe, 70km away.

Restaurants in the village run the comestible gamut, from cafés, sandwich shops and pizzerias to upscale hotel dining rooms. The finest restaurant of all is Las Cuatro Estaciones, in the Hotel Piscis.

Getting There & Away
In season, there are charter flights from Buenos Aires to Malargüe for about US$325 roundtrip, including transfers to and from Las Leñas.

There is bus service operating in season from Mendoza (p296), San Rafael (p305) and Malargüe (p307).

SAN JUAN
☎ 0264 / pop 119,000 / elevation 650m

With tall sycamores shading its streets, polished tile sidewalks to rival those found in

Mendoza and a brutal summer heat that inspires long afternoon siestas, San Juan is a cordial provincial capital with an enticingly unexplored feel. Most come here en route to Parque Provincial Ischigualasto (p317).

In 1944 a massive earthquake destroyed the city center, and Juan Perón's subsequent relief efforts are what first made him a national figure. Completely rebuilt since then, the downtown sparkles from the efforts of full-time custodians who sweep the sidewalks, and water and patrol the parks and plazas, shooing people off the manicured lawns.

The city goes dead in summer, especially on Sundays, when all of San Juan heads to the nearby shores of Dique Ullum for relief from the sun.

Orientation

San Juan is 170km north of Mendoza via RN 40 and 1140km from Buenos Aires. Like most Argentine cities, San Juan's grid pattern makes orientation very easy; the addition of cardinal points – *norte* (north), *sur* (south), *este* (east) and *oeste* (west) – to street addresses helps even more. East–west Av San Martín and north–south Calle Mendoza divide the city into these quadrants. The functional center of town is south of Av San Martín, often referred to as Av Libertador.

Information

ACA (☎ 422-3781; 9 de Julio 802)
Banco de San Juan (cnr Rivadavia & Entre Rios) Has ATM.
Cambio Santiago (General Acha 52 Sur) Money exchange.
Cyber Neo (cnr Mitre & Entre Ríos; per hr US$0.30) One of countless Internet cafés in San Juan.
Hospital Rawson (☎ 422-2272; cnr General Paz & Estados Unidos)
Laverap (Rivadavia 498 Oeste; full laundry service about US$1.50)
Mario Agüero Turismo (☎ 422-3652; General Acha 17 Norte) Offers organized tours including Parque Provincial Ischigualasto.
Post office (Av Ignacio de la Roza 259 Este)
Provincial tourist office (☎ 422-2431, 421-0004; www.turismo.sanjuan.gov.ar in Spanish; Sarmiento 24 Sur; ☼ 7am-8pm Mon-Fri, 9am-8pm Sat & Sun) Has a good map of the city and its surroundings plus useful information and brochures on the rest of the province, particularly Parque Provincial Ischigualasto.
Saitur Saul Saidel (☎ 422-2700; saitur@saulsaidel.com; José Ignacio de la Roza 112 Este) Offers city tours and day trips to Ischigualasto and elsewhere.

THEY CALL THE WIND EL ZONDA

While traveling through San Juan, especially in fall and winter, you may become acquainted – through hearsay if not through experience – with one of the region's meteorological marvels: *el zonda*. Much like the Chinook of the Rockies or the foehn of the European Alps, the zonda is a dry, warm wind that can raise a cold day's temperatures from freezing to nearly 20°C (68°F). The zonda originates with storms in the Pacific that blow eastward, hit the Andes, dump their moisture and come whipping down the eastern slopes, picking up heat as they go. The wind, which varies from mild to howling, can last several days; *sanjuaninos* (people from San Juan) can step outside and tell you when it will end – and that it will be cold when it does. It's a regular occurrence, giving the region – and the *sanjuaninos* – severe seasonal schizophrenia, especially in winter.

Sights & Activities

Museum hours change often, so check with the tourist office for updated information.

The **Casa de Sarmiento** (☎ 422-4603; Sarmiento 21 Sur; admission US$0.50; ☼ 9am-1pm, plus 3-8pm Tue-Fri & Sun summer) is named for Domingo Faustino Sarmiento, whose prolific writing as a politician, diplomat, educator and journalist made him a public figure both within and beyond Argentina. Sarmiento's *Recuerdos de Provincia* recounted his childhood in this house and his memories of his mother, Doña Paula Albarracín, who paid for part of the house's construction by weaving cloth in a loom under the fig tree that still stands in the front patio. The house is now a museum.

The most interesting specimen at the **Museo de Ciencias Naturales** (Museum of Natural Sciences; ☎ 421-6774; admission free; ☼ 9:30am-1:30pm) is the skeleton of the dinosaur Herrerasaurus from Ischigualasto, though there are plenty of provincial minerals, fossils and other exhibits to mull over. The museum is next to the old train station on Av España at Maipú.

Museo de Vino Santiago Graffigna (☎ 421-4227; museografigna@adsw.com; Colón 1342 Norte; ☼ 9am-1pm Thu & Fri, 9am-2am Sat, 10am-8pm Sun; wine bar 9am-2am Fri & Sat) is a new wine museum well worth a visit. It also has a wine bar where you can taste many of San Juan's best wines.

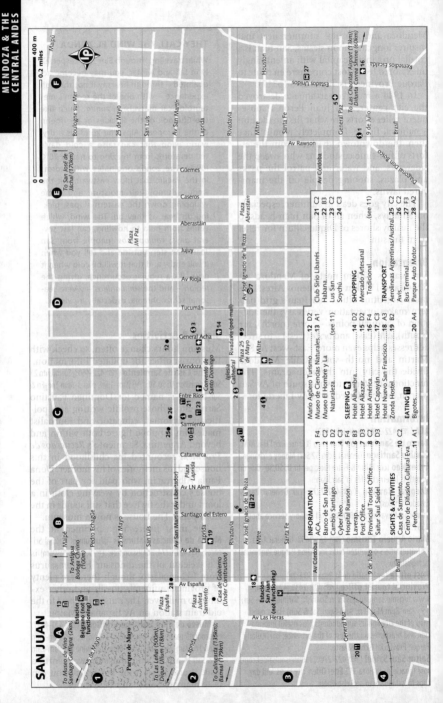

SAN JUAN

0 — 400 m
0 — 0.2 miles

INFORMATION
ACA.....................................1 F4
Banco de San Juan..............2 C2
Cambio Santiago..................3 D2
Cyber Neo.............................4 C3
Hospital Rawson...................5 F4
Laverap.................................6 B3
Post Office............................7 D3
Provincial Tourist Office.......8 C2
Saltur Saul Saidel.................9 D3

SIGHTS & ACTIVITIES
Casa de Sarmiento..............10 C2
Centro de Difusión Cultural Eva
   Perón................................11 A1

Mario Agüero Turismo.........12 D2
Museo de Ciencias Naturales.....13 A1
Museo El Hombre y La
   Naturaleza........................(see 11)

SLEEPING
Hotel Alhambra....................14 D2
Hotel Alkazar.......................15 D2
Hotel América......................16 F4
Hotel Capayán.....................17 C3
Hotel Nuevo San Francisco......18 A3
Zonda Hostel.......................19 B2

EATING
Bigotes...............................20 A4

Club Sirio Libanés................21 C2
Habana................................22 B3
Lus San................................23 C2
Soychú................................24 C3

SHOPPING
Mercado Artesanal
   Tradicional........................(see 11)

TRANSPORT
Aerolíneas Argentinas/Austral..25 C2
Avis.....................................26 C2
Bus Terminal........................27 F3
Parque Auto Motor...............28 A2

To try some samples of the region's famed *blanco sanjuanino* (San Juan white wine) and champagne, visit **Antigua Bodega Chirino** (☎ 421-4327; Salta 782 Norte; ☺ 8:30am-12:30pm & 4:30-8:30pm Mon-Sat).

At Av España and 25 de Mayo, the now-defunct Estación Belgrano (train station) has been recycled into the **Centro de Difusión Cultural Eva Perón**, a cultural center that includes the new anthropological museum, **Museo El Hombre y La Naturaleza** (admission US$0.30; ☺ 9am-noon & 5-9pm).

Sleeping

Zonda Hostel (☎ 420-1009; www.zondahostel.com.ar; Laprida 572 Oeste; dm US$5.75; P) New hostel in a lovingly converted house with a big backyard, Ping-Pong table, 16 beds and friendly young owners who know San Juan province intimately and are full of information on mountain climbing and other outdoor activities. One room has a great balcony over the street.

Hotel Nuevo San Francisco (☎ 427-2821; www .nuevo-sanfrancisco.com.ar in Spanish; Av España 284 Sur; s/d US$13/15.50; P ✹) One of the best in town, this welcoming, immaculate hotel has crisp, well-lit rooms with big TVs, white tile floors and a helpful staff.

Hotel Alhambra (☎ 421-4780; General Acha 180 Sur; s/d US$12/20; P ✹) Both the rooms and bathrooms are small, but it's spotless and charming, and little touches like leather chairs and gold ashtray stands in the hallways give it a kitschy appeal; upstairs rooms are best. Good value.

Hotel América (☎ 421-4514; www.hotel-america.com .ar; 9 de Julio 1052 Este; s US$13-16, d US$18-22; P ✹) This is excellent value in a drab location. It conveniently offers excursions through an on-site tour operator and is a popular place with a good restaurant.

Hotel Capayán (☎/fax 421-4222; hcapayan@infovia .com.ar; Mitre 31 Este; s/d US$15/22; P ✹) Popular with the business crowd, Capayán boasts a stylish basement bar and lounge and an excellent location on the central plaza. Unfortunately, the tiny rooms are a bit of a let down. But the bathrooms are big. Fair deal.

Hotel Alkazar (☎ 421-4965; www.alkazarhotel.com .ar in Spanish; Laprida 82 Este; s/d US$40/47; P ✹ ▢) Services at this five-star hotel include a spa, sauna and on-site masseuse, and the spacious rooms, stylishly designed decades ago, are still up to snuff.

Eating

Most restaurants are right downtown, but many of the city's hippest eateries are on Av Libertador San Martín, west España.

Lus San (☎ 422-6702; Laprida near Sarmiento; dozen empanadas US$2.50) Superb takeaway empanadas, as well as lasagna, roast chicken and more.

Club Sirio Libanés (☎ 422-3841; Entre Ríos 33 Sur; full meal US$3-5) This classy old-school establishment serves dishes with a Middle Eastern flare. The *pollo deshuesado en salsa de ajillo* (boned chicken in garlic sauce) is especially good.

Las Leñas (☎ 423-2100; Av San Martín 1670 Oeste; mains US$3-7) This oversized *quincho* (thatched-roof construction) serves excellent meat and monstrous portions of pasta, and gets festive on weekends.

Bigotes (☎ 422-6665; Las Heras 641 Sur; tenedor libre US$3.50) Classic all-you-can-eat *parrilla* with tie-clad male waiters running around with plates of meat and piles of French fries.

Habana (☎ 422-3483; Av Ignacio de la Roza 436 Oeste; ice cream US$1) Orgasmically delicious ice cream.

Shopping

The **Mercado Artesanal Tradicional** (Traditional Artisans Market; Centro de Difusión Cultural Eva Perón) is an excellent local handicrafts market including ponchos and the brightly colored *mantas* (shawls) of Jáchal.

Getting There & Away

AIR

Aerolíneas Argentinas/Austral (☎ 421-4158; Av San Martín 215 Oeste) flies twice daily to Buenos Aires (US$100) except Sunday (once only).

BUS

From San Juan's **bus terminal** (☎ 422-1604; Estados Unidos 492 Sur) there are international services to Santiago (US$12, 10 hours), Viña del Mar and Valparaíso, Chile, but they require a change of bus in Mendoza.

THE AUTHOR'S CHOICE

Soychú (☎ 422-1939; Av José Ignacio de la Roza 223 Oeste; tenedor libre US$2.50; ☺ noon-4pm & 9pm-midnight Mon-Sat, lunch only Sun) Kick the meat for a day and enjoy Soychú's *outstanding* vegetarian buffet. Arrive early for the best selection. Fresh juices too.

Except in summer, when there may be direct buses, service to Patagonian destinations south of Neuquén requires a change of bus in Mendoza, though through-tickets can be purchased in San Juan.

Various companies serve the following destinations daily.

Destination	Cost (US$)	Duration (hr)
Buenos Aires	22	14
Catamarca	9	8
Córdoba	10-15	8
Jujuy	15	18
La Rioja	7	6
Mendoza	4	2½
Neuquén	20	15½
Rosario	17	14
Salta	14	17
San Agustín de Valle Fértil	5	4½
San José de Jáchal	3.50	3
San Luis	7	4
San Rafael	8.50	6
Tucumán	12	13

Getting Around

Las Chacritas Airport (☎ 425-4133) is located 13km southeast of town on RN 20. A taxi or *remise* costs US$10 to US$14. For car rental, try **Avis** (☎ 422-4622, 15-504-3333; Av San Martín 163 Oeste) or **Parque Auto Motor** (☎ 422-6018; cnr Av San Martín & Av España); prices average US$64 per day with unlimited kilometers.

AROUND SAN JUAN
Wineries

One of South America's most curious wineries, **Cavas de Zonda** (☎ 494-5144; Zonda; ⊙ 9am-noon & 4-6pm) is in a cave about 16km west of San Juan, via the RP 12, near the town of Zonda. This champagne maker boasts having the only wine cellar in South America whose 'roof is a mountain' and, true or not, its temperatures are perfect for cellaring its excellent sparkling wines. And hey…it's a darn good marketing tool. Bus No 23 leaves the San Juan bus terminal from platform 20 six times daily.

Ten kilometers south of San Juan on the RN 40, **Anahata** (☎ 422-5807; Huerta Orgánica Anahata, Calle 11 s/n, 300m east of RN 40) makes some of the country's only organic champagne and other wine. Bus No 24 leaves the terminal seven times daily and will stop at the winery entrance.

Dique Ullum

Only 18km west of San Juan, this 3200-hectare reservoir is a center for nautical sports: swimming, fishing, kayaking, water-skiing and windsurfing (though no rental equipment is available). *Balnearios* (beach clubs) line its shores, and hanging out for a day in the sun is part of being in San Juan. At night, many of the *balnearios* function as dance clubs. Bus No 23 from Av Salta or No 29 from the San Juan bus terminal via Av Córdoba both go hourly to the dam outlet.

Difunta Correa Shrine

At Vallecito, about 60km southeast of San Juan, the shrine of the Difunta Correa, a popular saint, is one of the most fascinating cultural phenomenons in all of Argentina (see the boxed text, p314), and visiting the shrine is a mandatory stop if you're in the area.

Empresa Vallecito goes daily from San Juan to the shrine (US$2.75 roundtrip, 1¼ hours each way) at 8:30am and 4pm Monday through Saturday, and waits about an hour and 15 minutes before returning. On Sunday there are roundtrip buses at 8am, 10:30am, 11:45am, 3:30pm, 4:15pm and 7pm. Any other eastbound bus heading toward La Rioja or Córdoba will drop passengers at the entrance. There are also departures from Mendoza (see p296).

VALLE DE CALINGASTA

The Calingasta Valley is a vast smear of scenic butter cradled between the Andes and the rumpled, multicolored precordillera, and is one of the most beautiful regions in both San Juan and Mendoza provinces.

At the time of writing, it was possible to drive to Calingasta via the spectacular cliff-side RP 12, but plans exist to close this with the completion of two new reservoirs. Most maps will show the old road, but drivers will have to take RP 5 north to Talacasto, RP 436 west and the new RP 414 which meets up with upper RP 12 to Calingasta.

Calingasta

☎ 02648 / pop 2000 / elevation 1430m

Calingasta is a small agricultural town shaded by álamos on the shores of Río Los Patos. There's little to do, though a visit to the 17th-century adobe chapel **Capilla de Nuestra Señora**

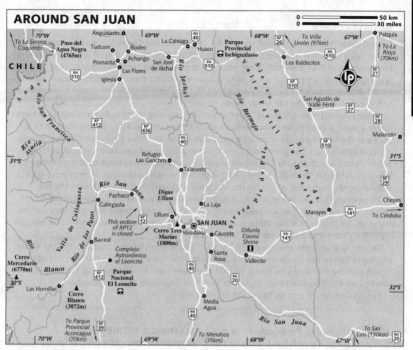

AROUND SAN JUAN

---

del Carmen makes for a nice stop on the way to Barreal. If driving, be sure to stop at **Cerro El Alcazar**, a towering wall of eroded mustard-colored rock protruding dramatically from the ochre mountains around it. It's about 15km south of town and some 500m east of the road (look for the signed dirt road).

The folks at Calingasta's **tourist information office** (RP 12), at the entrance to town from San Juan, are helpful for sights and lodging in the area.

If you wish to spend the night, lay your head at the modest **Hotel Calingasta** (☎ 421220, 421033; s/d US$6/12); you will also find a municipal campground.

Barreal

☎ 02648 / pop 1800 / elevation 1650m

Barreal's divine location makes it one of the most beautifully situated towns you'll likely ever come across. Sauces (weeping willows), álamos and eucalyptus trees drape lazily over the dirt roads that meander through town, and views of the Cordillera de Ansilta – a stretch of the Andes with seven majestic peaks ranging from 5130m

to 5885m – are simply astonishing. Wandering along Barreal's back roads is an exercise in dreamy laziness.

Presidente Roca is the main drag through town, a continuation of RP 412 that leads from Calingasta to Barreal and on to Parque Nacional Leoncito. Only a few streets have names; businesses listed without them simply require asking directions.

INFORMATION

Banco de la Nación (Presidente Roca s/n) Has an ATM.

IWS Comunicaciones (San Martín s/n; per hr US$0.75) Internet access. Slow.

Tourist office (☎ 441066; municipalidadecalingasta@ hotmail.com; Presidente Roca s/n; ☾ 9am-1:30pm & 3-8pm) Located inside the *municipalidad* (town hall); offers list of excursion operators and accommodations.

SIGHTS & ACTIVITIES

Wander down to the **Río Los Patos** and take in the sweeping views of the valley and the **Cordillera de Ansilta**, whose highest peak, **Ansilta**, tops out at 5885m. To the south, **Aconcagua** and **Tupungato** are both visible, as is the peak of **Cerro Mercedario** (6770m).

DIFUNTA CORREA

Legend has it that during the civil wars of the 1840s, Deolinda Correa followed the movements of her sickly conscript husband's battalion on foot through the deserts of San Juan, carrying food, water and their baby son in her arms. When her meager supplies ran out, thirst, hunger and exhaustion killed her. But when passing muleteers found them, the infant was still nursing at the dead woman's breast. Commemorating this apparent miracle, her shrine at Vallecito is widely believed to be the site of her death.

Difunta literally means 'defunct,' and Correa is her surname. Technically she is not a saint but rather a 'soul,' a dead person who performs miracles and intercedes for people; the child's survival was the first of a series of miracles attributed to her. Since the 1940s, her shrine, originally a simple hilltop cross, has grown into a small village with its own gas station, school, post office, police station and church. At 17 chapels or exhibit rooms, devotees leave gifts in exchange for supernatural favors. In addition, there are two hotels, several restaurants, a commercial gallery with souvenir shops, and offices for the nonprofit organization that administers the site.

Interestingly, truckers are especially devoted. From La Quiaca, on the Bolivian border, to Ushuaia in Tierra del Fuego, you will see roadside shrines with images of the Difunta Correa and the unmistakable bottles of water left to quench her thirst. At some sites there appear to be enough parts lying around to build a car from scratch!

Despite lack of government support and the Catholic Church's open antagonism, the shrine of Difunta Correa has grown as belief in her miraculous powers has become more widespread. People visit the shrine all year round, but at Easter, May 1 and Christmas, up to 200,000 pilgrims descend on Vallecito. Weekends are busier and more interesting than weekdays.

For information on getting to the shrine, see p312.

At the south end of Presidente Roca is a sort of triangular roundabout. Follow the road east (away from the Andes) until it leads into the hills; you'll see a small shrine and you can **hike** into the foothills for more stunning views.

Rafting is excellent – more for the scenery than for the rapids themselves – and most trips start 50km upriver at **Las Hornillas**. Las Hornillas (site of two *refugios* and a military outpost) also provides **climbing** access to the Cordón de la Rameda, which boasts five peaks over 6000m, including Mercedario. Climbing here is more technical than Aconcagua and many mountaineers prefer the area.

Barreal is best known for **carrovelismo** (land sailing), which people practice with a passion out on the gusty, cracked lake bed at Pampa El Leoncito, 20km from town and adjacent to the national park.

Ramon Ossa, a Barreal native, is a highly recommended mountain guide and excursion operator who knows the cordillera intimately; contact him at **Cabañas Doña Pipa** (☎ 441004; www.fortunaviajes.com.ar in Spanish). For access to the *refugio* at Las Hornillas, climbing information, guide services and **mountain bike** rental, visit **Maxi** at Cabañas Kummel (right).

SLEEPING & EATING

Cabañas Kummel (☎ 441206, in San Juan 0264-15-670-8273; Presidente Roca s/n near Hipolito Yrigoyen; cabaña for up to 6 US$20) Simple but delightful little *cabañas* with kitchens, grass outside and plenty of shade trees.

Posada San Eduardo (☎ 441046; posadasaneduardo@hotmail.com; cnr San Martín & Los Enamorados; s US$17-20, d US$27-33) This handsome adobe inn offers refreshing rooms with whitewashed walls and natural poplar bed frames and chairs. Some have fireplaces and all open onto an interior courtyard.

La Querencia (in San Juan ☎ 0264-15-436-4699; http://laquerenciaposada.tripod.com in Spanish; d US$25-32) La Querencia's main draw is its unimpeded views of the Andes. It's a stylized adobe-esque structure with zero trees to block the view, which also gives the place a desolate, unsheltered feel. The owners are fabulous and the breakfasts here are delicious.

Hotel de Turismol Barreal (☎ 441104; s/d US$30/60) Definitely a has-been, this is an attractive hotel from the outside, but the inside is a bit dreary. Still, it's far better than tolerable.

Restaurant Isidoro (☎ 441031; Presidente Roca s/n; mains US$2.75) Best eats in town.

Parque Nacional El Leoncito

Just south of Barreal, the 76,000-hectare Parque Nacional El Leoncito occupies a former *estancia* (ranch) typical of the Andean precordillera, though it's drier than the valley north of Barreal. Lately, its primary attraction is the Pampa de Leoncito where a dry lake bed makes for superb land sailing. The high, dry and wide-open valley rarely sees a cloud, also making for superb stargazing. Hence, the park is home to two important observatories: **Observatorio El Leoncito** (☎ 02648-441088; ☽ guided visits 10:15am, 11:15am, 3:15pm, 4:15pm & 5:15pm) and **Observatorio Cesco** (☎ 02648-441087; ☽ guided visits 10am, noon, 4pm & 6pm). Night visits must be scheduled ahead of time by contacting **Monica Grosso** (in San Juan ☎ 0264-421-3653).

Getting There & Away

For door to door service from San Juan to Calingasta (US$5, three hours) and Barreal (US$5, 3½ hours) contact **Remis Jose Luis** (in Barreal ☎ 02648-441095, in San Juan ☎ 0264-434-2317).

From the San Juan Bus terminal, El Triunfo goes daily to Calingasta (US$4.75, 3½ hours) and Barreal (US$5.50, four hours) at 8pm, with additional service at 8am on Monday and Friday. There is no bus service to Parque Nacional El Leoncito.

SAN JOSÉ DE JÁCHAL

☎ 02647 / pop 9700

Founded in 1751, surrounded by vineyards and olive groves, Jáchal is a charming village with a mix of older adobes and contemporary brick houses. *Jachalleros* (the local residents) are renowned for their fidelity to indigenous and gaucho crafts traditions; in fact, Jáchal's reputation as the Cuna de la Tradición (Cradle of Tradition) is celebrated during November's **Fiesta de la Tradición**. Except during festival season, however, finding these crafts isn't easy.

Across from the main plaza, the **Iglesia San José**, a national monument, houses the **Cristo Negro** (Black Christ), or Señor de la Agonía (Lord of Agony), a grisly leather image with articulated head and limbs, brought from Potosí in colonial times.

Of Jáchal's two identically priced hotels, **Hotel Plaza** (☎ 420256; San Juan near Sarmiento; s/d US$9/12, with shared bathroom US$6/9.50) is the best. The lobby and breakfast area is airy (complete with a constantly chirping caged bird)

THE AUTHOR'S CHOICE

El Alemán (☎ 441193; www.andentours.com.ar in Spanish; Calle Belgrano s/n; s/d US$12/20; mains US$2.50-4.50) Owned by a German-Argentine couple, this excellent restaurant serves the best food in the area and there's one very lovely apartment for rent. Breakfasts are superb and Jerome microbrew from Potrerillos is sold.

and the rooms have enough kitschy decor to keep them cheerful.

Next door, **Café Liberte** (San Juan near Sarmiento; mains US$1.50-2.50; ☽ dinner) serves delicious *lomitos* and decent pizzas.

There are several daily buses to San Juan (US$3.50, three hours) and Mendoza (US$16) from Jáchal's **bus terminal** (cnr San Juan & Obispo Zapata).

AROUND SAN JOSÉ DE JÁCHAL

An overnight trip up RN 40 north of San Juan allows visitors to pass through a beautiful landscape that is rich with folkloric traditions and rarely seen by foreigners. East of Jáchal, RN 40 climbs the precipitous **Cuesta de Huaco**, with a view of Los Cauquenes dam, before arriving at the sleepy village of **Huaco**, whose 200-year-old Viejo Molino (Old Mill) justifies the trip. There is no public transport from San Juan out this route.

Backtracking to RN 150 and heading westward, you pass through the town of Rodeo and into the department of Iglesia, home of the pre-cordillera thermal baths of Pismanta. RN 150 continues west to Chile via the lung-busting 4765m **Paso de Agua Negra** (open summer only). South of Pismanta, RP 436 returns to RN 40 and San Juan.

Rodeo

☎ 0264 / elevation 2010m

Rodeo is a small, ramshackle town with picturesque adobe houses typical of the region. There are several *cabañas* and *hosterías* in town, and Pismanta is only about 20km away. Rodeo has recently become famous – world famous – for **windsurfing**. The town is only 3km away from one of the best windsurfing sites on the planet: **Dique Cuesta del Viento**, where between mid-October and early May, wind speeds reach 120km per hour nearly every afternoon, drawing surfers from around the globe. Even if you don't take to the wind, it's worth spending a day or two wandering around Rodeo and hanging out on the beach absorbing the spectacular views and watching the insanity of airborne windsurfers.

Inside the town hall, the **tourist office** (municipalidad_iglesia@yahoo.com.ar; ☯ 8am-8pm) provides a list of places to stay and information on local attractions.

On Playa Lamaral, on the shore of the reservoir, HI affiliate **Rancho Lamaral** (in San Juan ☎ 422-5566, 15-671-8819; rancholamaral@arnet.com.ar; dm HI members/nonmembers US$4/5) offers simple dorm beds in an refurbished adobe house, and offers windsurfing classes (three/five days US$40/67) and rents all equipment. Nearby, the bar and shop **Puerto de Palos** (www.puertodepalos.net) also rents equipment and offers classes.

GETTING THERE & AWAY

From San Juan's bus terminal, UTE goes daily to Rodeo (US$3.50, two hours) at 8am, 2:30pm and 7:15pm. Valle del Sol leaves San Juan at 3pm Monday to Friday, at 7:30am Saturday and 7pm Sunday, but takes a longer route via Iglesia/Pismanta (US$4, 3½ hours).

Pismanta
☎ 02647

Part of the **Hotel Termas de Pismanta** (☎ 497 091/02; www.pismantahotel.com.ar in Spanish; s/d with full board US$30/50, with half-board s US$20-27, d US$34-41; 🏊), these 42°C thermal baths, set in a totally desolate landscape, are a good place to cleanse the well-traveled body. The hotel itself is comfortable but shows the wear of its 50-odd years; in fact, the whole place feels caught in a time warp. Nonguests pay US$4 to use the facilities.

If the complex is too pricey for a night, try **Hospedaje La Olla** (☎ 497003; r per person US$4.50, with full board US$12.50), a basic place with lots of character (and animal skins).

Iglesia SRL minibuses leave the San Juan bus terminal four times a week, and take RP 436 to Jáchal, stopping at Iglesia and Pismanta.

SAN AGUSTÍN DE VALLE FÉRTIL
☎ 02646 / pop 3000

If you're hankering for the hair-raising bus rides so generously offered in other South American countries, you can at least get a taste of them on the hairpin, cliffside turns on the way up to San Agustín. The town itself is a convenient base for exploring nearby Parque Provincial Ischigualasto, and accommodations are cheap and basic.

Founded in 1788, San Agustín de Valle Fértil is a cheerful village where people sit on the sidewalks on summer evenings greeting passersby. On weekends they drag out the *parrillas* to sell grilled chicken or beef. There are as many bicycles as automobiles, and even the usually aggressive Argentine motorist appears to appreciate the relaxed pace here.

Orientation

San Agustín lies among the Sierra Pampeanas, gentle sedimentary mountains cut by impressive canyons, 247km northeast of San Juan via RN 141 and RP 510, which continues to Ischigualasto and La Rioja. San Agustín is small enough that locals pay little attention to street names, so ask directions.

Information

Cámara de Turismo is a private tourist office that maintains an office in the bus terminal.

Municipal tourist office (General Acha; ☯ 7am-1pm & 5-10pm Mon-Fri, 8am-1pm Sat) Directly across from the plaza. Is exceptionally helpful with general information, and they can also help arrange car or mule excursions into the mountain canyons and backcountry.

Post office (cnr Laprida & Mendoza)

Sleeping & Eating

Hostería & Cabañas Valle Fértil (☎ 420015/16; www.alkazarhotel.com.ar in Spanish; s/d in hostería US$25/29, 4-person cabañas US$40) This place has the wraps on lodging in town with a well-sited *hostería* above the reservoir and fully equipped *cabañas* nearby. The *hostería* also has a good restaurant (mains US$3 to US$5) serving food from 6am to 11pm. Both are reached from Rivadavia on the way to the river.

The *hostería* also owns the town's best campground, **Camping Valle Fértil** (Rivadavia s/n; sites US$4) It's shaded by a monotone cover of eucalyptus trees, and gets very crowded during long weekends and holidays, but it's quiet enough off-season and midweek.

At **Pensión Doña Zoila** (☎ 420147; Mendoza s/n; s/d US$5/9) the rooms are boxlike and as basic as they come, but Doña Zoila takes excellent care of her guests. It's half a block off the plaza.

There are several other basic hotels and a few simple restaurants around town.

Getting There & Away

From San Agustín's **bus terminal** (Mitre, btwn Entre Ríos & Mendoza) daily buses head to San Juan (US$5, 4½ hours). Monday and Friday buses to La Rioja (US$4) can drop off passengers at the Ischigualasto turnoff.

Ask at the tourist office to arrange a tour to Parque Provincial Ischigualasto (about US$10).

PARQUE PROVINCIAL ISCHIGUALASTO

Also known fittingly as **Valle de la Luna** (Valley of the Moon; admission US$3.50), this spectacular provincial park is a step – or drive, as the case may be – into a world of surreal rock formations, dinosaur remains and glowing red sunsets. The park, named for an early Paleo-Indian culture, is in some ways comparable to North American national parks like Bryce Canyon or Zion, except that here, time and water have exposed a wealth of fossils (some 180 million years old from the Triassic period).

The park's museum displays a variety of fossils, including the carnivorous dinosaur Herrerasaurus (not unlike Tyrannosaurus rex), the Eoraptor lunensis (the oldest-known predatory dinosaur) and good dioramas of the park's paleoenvironments.

The 63,000-hectare park is a desert valley between two sedimentary mountain ranges, the Cerros Colorados in the east and Cerro Los Rastros in the west. Over millennia, at every meander in the canyon, the waters of the nearly dry Río Ischigualasto have carved distinctive shapes in the malleable red sandstone, monochrome clay and volcanic ash. Predictably, some of these forms have acquired popular names, including **Cancha de Bochas** (The Ball Court), **El Submarino** (The Submarine) and **El Gusano** (The

Worm) among others. The desert flora of algarrobo trees, shrubs and cacti complement the eerie landforms.

From the visitor center, isolated 1748m **Cerro Morado** is a three- to four-hour walk, gaining nearly 800m in elevation and yielding outstanding views of the surrounding area. Take plenty of drinking water and high-energy snacks.

Tours

If you have no private vehicle, an organized tour is the only feasible way to visit the park. These are easily organized in San Agustín (opposite), where you will surely be greeted by offers upon arrival. Otherwise ask the tourist office there about hiring a car and driver. Tour rates are about US$23 per person from San Juan (through any travel agency in town), or about US$3.50 per person from San Agustín. Tours from San Juan generally depart at 5am and return well after dark.

Sleeping & Eating

Camping is permitted at the visitor center, which also has a *confitería* (café) with simple meals (breakfast and lunch) and cold drinks; dried fruits and bottled olives from the province are also available. There are toilets and showers, but because water must be trucked in, don't count on them. There is no shade.

Getting There & Away

Ischigualasto is about 80km north of San Agustín via RP 510 and a paved lateral to the northwest. Given its size and isolation, the only practical way to visit the park is by private vehicle or organized tour. If you drive out on your own, after you arrive at the visitor center and pay the US$3.50 entrance fee, one of the rangers (who work on tips) will accompany your vehicle on a two- to three-hour, 45km circuit through the park. Note that the park roads are unpaved and some can be impassable after a rain, necessitating an abbreviated trip.

The Lake District

One of Argentina's most beloved travel destinations, the Lake District is visited each year by thousands who come to ski, hike, climb, fish, swim and otherwise enjoy the spectacular mountain scenery and hundreds of chilly, glacially formed lakes that give the region its name. An ideal way to explore this area, where national parks are the main attraction, is with a backpack, tent and campstove, allowing you to ditch the crowds and have the trees – not to mention a lake – to yourself. The region is also known for its scenic passes and lake crossings to Chile, which shares the Andean peaks and Valdivian forests with its Argentine companion.

The city of Neuquén, the region's northernmost transport hub, is home to some of the world's most important paleontological sites and worth a visit if you're at all interested in dinosaurs. Bariloche is the region's urban nucleus, and its unrivaled setting on the southeastern shore of Lago Nahuel Huapi brings a mixed bag of high-rise hotels, summer crowds, excellent restaurants and affordable accommodations. It's a superb base for exploring Parque Nacional Nahuel Huapi or hitting Cerro Catedral's scenic slopes in winter. Bariloche is the chief transport hub for destinations in southern Patagonia and Chile, and a short ride from laid-back El Bolsón.

The unpretentious fishing town of Junín de los Andes and the fashionable, tree-filled resort San Martín de los Andes both make excellent bases for exploring the spectacular Parque Nacional Lanín whose araucaria (monkey puzzle or pehuén) trees, snowcapped volcanoes and glistening mountain lakes make it one of the country's best hiking and trekking destinations.

TOP FIVE

- Feeling on top of world after a two-day hike up **Volcán Lanín**, Parque Nacional Lanín (p331)

- Carving up the slopes of **Cerro Catedral** (p346) in July

- Taking in the views along the spectacular lake-studded **Siete Lagos Route** (RN 234; p329)

- Kissing the world goodbye and hitting the early-autumn backcountry of **Parque Nacional Nahuel Huapi** (p345)

- Sleeping in mountain *refugios* outside **El Bolsón** (p348) and returning to town for strawberry waffles at the crafts fair

★ Volcán Lanín

★ Siete Lagos Route

★ Parque Nacional Nahuel Huapi

★ Cerro Catedral

★ El Bolsón

■ AVERAGE JUL HIGH IN BARILOCHE: 6°C (42°F)   ■ AVERAGE DEC HIGH IN BARILOCHE: 19°C (66°F)

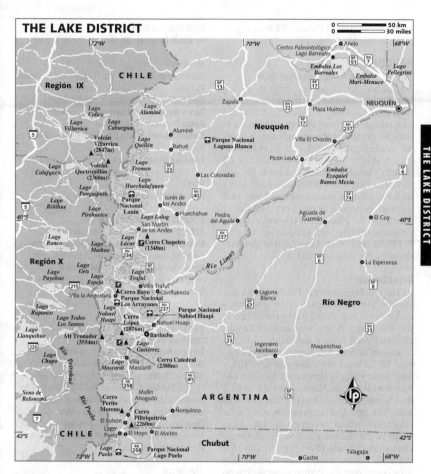

THE LAKE DISTRICT

Climate

Except for central and eastern Neuquén province (around Neuquén and Zapala), much of the Lake District is snowy and cold from June to August or September. The most scenic mountain roads (including the Seven Lakes Route) close regularly at this time, and the highest passes may not open until October. Fall sees warmish days and cold nights, while turning leaves and fewer tourists make it one of the best times to visit. Wildflowers make spring hiking beautiful. Summer days are generally quite warm, with cool nights.

National Parks

The spectacular but often crowded Parque Nacional Nahuel Huapi (p345) is the corner-stone of the Lake District's parks. Bordering it to the north, Parque Nacional Lanín (p331) gets fewer trail trampers and has equally spectacular sights, including Volcán Lanín and humbling pehuén (monkey puzzle) forests. The tiny Parque Nacional Arrayanes (p335) is worth a day trip from Villa La Angostura to check out its beautiful cinnamon-colored arrayán trees. See p49 for more on Argentina's parks.

Getting There & Away

The region's two primary ground transport hubs are Neuquén and Bariloche, where buses arrive from throughout the country. The main airports are in these cities, plus San Martín de los Andes, while smaller ones are in Zapala and El Bolsón. All have flights to/from Buenos Aires.

NEUQUÉN

☎ 0299 / pop 200,000 / elevation 265m

For the traveler, Neuquén is both the diving board into Patagonia and the gateway to the Argentine Lake District. More than a tourist destination, however, the city is the administrative center for the region's agricultural, oil, mining, and hydroelectric power industries. Industry bigwigs and businessfolk fill the city's hotels as much as tourists do, and travelers, after a few hours' diversion along its busy, modern streets, will probably find themselves itching to move on. And that is easy to do, for Neuquén is the area's principal transport hub, with good connections to Bariloche and other Lake District destinations, to the far south and to Chile.

Orientation

At the confluence of the Río Neuquén and the Río Limay, Neuquén is the province's easternmost city. Paved highways go east to the Río Negro valley, west toward Zapala, and southwest toward Bariloche.

Known as Félix San Martín in town, east–west RN 22 is the main thoroughfare, lying a few blocks south of downtown. Do not confuse it with Av San Martín (sans the 'Félix'), the obligatory homage to Argentina's national icon. The principal north–south street is Av Argentina, which becomes Av Olascoaga south of the old train station. Street names change on each side of Av Argentina and the old train station; most of the old rail yard now constitutes the Parque Central. Several diagonal streets bisect the conventional grid.

Information

CONSULATES & IMMIGRATION

Chilean consulate (☎ 442-2727; La Rioja 241)
Immigration office (☎ 442-2061; Santiago del Estero 466)

INTERNET ACCESS

Telecentro (Av Argentina at Ministro González; per hr US$0.50; ◷ 24hr)
Telecentro del Comahue (Av Argentina 147; per hr US$0.60)

LAUNDRY

Lavisec (Roca 137; wash US$0.50, dry US$1, service fee per load US$0.75) Full service or DIY.

MEDICAL SERVICES

Regional hospital (☎ 443-1474; Buenos Aires 421)

MONEY

Several banks along Av Argentina, between Parque Central and Roca, have ATMs. Zanellato (below) is an Amex representative.
Banca Nazionale del Lavoro (Av Argentina)
Banco Provincia (Av Argentina)
Cambio Olano (cnr Juan B Justo & H Yrigoyen) Money exchange.
Cambio Pullman (Ministro Alcorta 144) Money exchange.

POST

Post office (Rivadavia & Santa Fe)

TOURIST INFORMATION

ACA (☎ 442-2325; diagonal 25 de Mayo at Rivadavia)
Municipal Tourist Office kiosk (median strip of Av Argentina, btwn Carlos H Rodríguez & Juan B Alberdi)
Provincial tourist office (☎ 442-4089; www .neuquentur.gov.ar; Félix San Martín 182; ◷ 7am-9:30pm) Great maps and brochures.

TRAVEL AGENCIES

Neuquén's dozens of travel agencies are almost all near downtown.
Turismo Neuquén (☎ 448-0864; receptivo_tnqn@ speedy.com.ar; cnr Perito Moreno & Río Negro, Paseo del Sol, Local 37) Offers guided visits to paleontology sites of Lago Los Barreales, Plaza Huincul and Villa El Chocón. Prices are about US$25 per person (minimum two), including the taxi fare; cheaper if you have your own vehicle.
Zanellato (☎ 443-0105; claudia@zanellatoviajes.com.ar; Av Independencia 366) Amex representative; reliable for airline tickets and the like.

Sleeping

Neuquén's hotels are many but less than good value at the lower end of the spectrum; even midrange hotels rarely include breakfast.

Residencial Belgrano (☎ 448-0612, 442-4311; Rivadavia 283; s/d with breakfast US$9.50/15) The Belgrano is excellent value with tiny but cheerful rooms and a prime location near several cafés. If minor flaws like broken toothbrush holders, cracked bathroom tiles and trickling toilets don't bother you, it's a great place.

Hotel El Prado (☎/fax 448-6000; hotelelprado@ hotmail.com; Perito Moreno 484; s US$20-32, d US$30-43; Ⓟ ⚇ 🖳) Though not the priciest of Neuquén's hotels, the modern and immaculate El Prado is certainly one of its finest. The room price includes TV, phone and sauna use, and there's wireless Internet in the lobby.

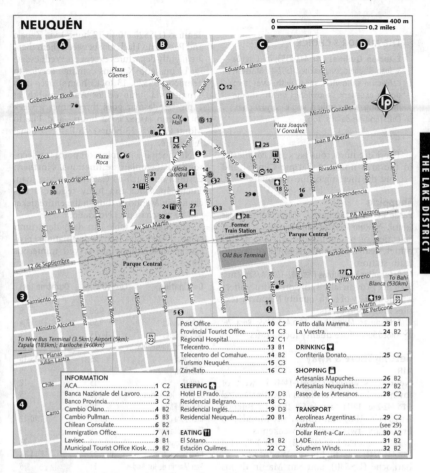

NEUQUÉN

0 _____ 400 m
0 _____ 0.2 miles

INFORMATION	
ACA	1 C2
Banca Nazionale del Lavoro	2 C2
Banco Provincia	3 C2
Cambio Olano	4 B2
Cambio Pullman	5 B3
Chilean Consulate	6 B2
Immigration Office	7 A1
Lavisec	8 B1
Municipal Tourist Office Kiosk	9 B2
Post Office	10 C2
Provincial Tourist Office	11 C3
Regional Hospital	12 C1
Telecentro	13 B1
Telecentro del Comahue	14 B2
Turismo Neuquén	15 C3
Zanellato	16 C2

SLEEPING	
Hotel El Prado	17 D3
Residencial Belgrano	18 D3
Residencial Inglés	19 D3
Residencial Neuquén	20 B1

EATING	
El Sótano	21 B2
Estación Quilmes	22 C2
Fatto dalla Mamma	23 B1
La Vuestra	24 B2

DRINKING	
Confitería Donato	25 C2

SHOPPING	
Artesanías Mapuches	26 B2
Artesanías Neuquinas	27 B2
Paseo de los Artesanos	28 C2

TRANSPORT	
Aerolíneas Argentinas	29 C2
Austral	(see 29)
Dollar Rent-a-Car	30 A2
LADE	31 B1
Southern Winds	32 B2

Cheaper rooms are darker and smaller and open onto an interior patio. The mattresses are all great.

Residencial Inglés (☎ 442-2252; Félix San Martín 534; s/d US$7/12) This is a plain, friendly place, and, though the price is right, the location is less than desirable (for sake of convenience). Rooms are small with lots of faded browns and yellows.

Residencial Neuquén (☎ 442-2403; Roca 109; s/d with breakfast US$15/20; ⬜) Offers small rooms, but they're clean, and the management is friendly; rooms facing the street are noisy.

Eating & Drinking

The many *confiterías* (cafés) along Av Argentina are all pleasant spots for breakfast and morning coffee.

El Sótano (Brown near Carlos H Rodríguez; mains US$2.75-4) Delicious homemade pastas and good wines grace the menu of this inviting, popular restaurant.

La Vuestra (☎ 442-8888; H Yrigoyen 90; mains US$2-3; set lunch US$2-3; ✆ closed Sun) Friendly little hangout with tasty pizzas and empanadas. Good lunch specials and plenty of mixed drinks.

Fatto dalla Mamma (☎ 442-5291; 9 de Julio 56; mains US$1.25-1.50) Both the house decor and the pastas are great at what's probably Neuquén's best pasta restaurant.

Confitería Donato (☎ 442-6950; Juan B Alberdi & Santa Fe; ✆ 7am-3am Sun-Thu, 7am-5am Fri & Sat) Classy, old-fashioned and dimly lit, this bar has tango on Thursdays and live bands on Saturdays; shows start late.

THE AUTHOR'S CHOICE

Estación Quilmes (☎ 443-2353; cnr Córdoba & Juan B Alberdi; sandwiches US$2-4) Modern café-cum-sandwich shop with over two dozen excellent sandwiches on the menu, including tasty grilled vegie sandwiches. Outstanding salads, too.

There are numerous bars and *confiterías* in the area north of Parque Central and around the meeting of the diagonals.

Shopping

Paseo de los Artesanos (Av Independencia, Parque Central; ☺ 10am-9pm Wed-Sun) Neuquén's largest selection of regional handicrafts is at this outlet, near Buenos Aires, north of the old train station.

Artesanías Neuquinas (☎ 442-3806; Av San Martín 57) This provincially sponsored store offers a wide variety of high-quality Mapuche textiles and wood crafts.

Artesanías Mapuches (☎ 443-2155; Roca 76; ☺ closed Sun) More quality local crafts.

Getting There & Away

AIR

Neuquén's **airport** (☎ 443-1444) is west of town on RN 22. **Aerolíneas Argentina/Austral** (☎ 442-2409/10/11; Santa Fe 52) flies to Buenos Aires (US$100) four times daily Monday to Friday and twice daily on weekends.

LADE city center (☎ 443-1153; Brown 163); airport (☎ 444-0244) has flights on Wednesdays to Bariloche (US$30), and San Martín de los Andes (Chapelco airport, US$30).

Southern Winds (☎ 442-0124; neuquenapt@sw .com.ar; Av San Martín 107) flies to Buenos Aires (US$70 to US$100, one-way) with connections throughout the country.

BUS

Neuquén is a major hub for provincial, national and international bus services. At time of writing, Neuquén was about to inaugurate its new **bus terminal** (Planas Teodoro s/n), located about 3.5km west of the Parque Central. The **old bus terminal** (☎ 442-4903; Bartolomé Mitre 147) – in case something mysteriously delays the opening of the new one – was next to the old train station in the Parque Central.

Several carriers offer service to Chile: **Expreso Caraza** (☎ 448-3779) and Igi-Llaima go to

Temuco (US$20, 10 to 12 hours) via Zapala and Paso Pino Hachado; between them there are nightly departures except on Wednesday. Igi-Llaima and Nar Bus combine service to Temuco (US$20, 13 to 15 hours) over Paso Tromen via Junín de los Andes nightly at 11pm. Andesmar goes three times a week to Osorno (US$25, 12 hours) and Puerto Montt (US$25, 13 hours) via Paso Cardenal A Samoré.

Neuquén is a jumping-off point for deep-south, Patagonian destinations. Northern destinations such as Catamarca, San Juan, Tucumán, Salta and Jujuy require a bus change in Mendoza, though the entire ticket can be purchased in Neuquén.

The following table lists daily departures to nearly all long-distance destinations; provincial destinations are served numerous times daily.

Destination	Cost (US$)	Duration (hr)
Aluminé	9.50	6
Bahía Blanca	9.50	7½
Buenos Aires	17-75	17
Comodoro Rivadavia	25	15-17
Córdoba	25	15-16
El Bolsón	14	9
Esquel	15	10
Junín de los Andes	9.50	5
Mar del Plata	19	14
Mendoza	16-25	10-12
Puerto Madryn	15	10
Río Gallegos	50	28
Rosario	22	14-18
San Martín de los Andes	11	6
San Rafael	14	8
Viedma	12	8
Villa La Angostura	13	8
Zapala	5	3

Getting Around

Neuquén is a good province to explore by automobile, but foreigners should be aware that RN 22, both east along the Río Negro valley and west toward Zapala, is a rough road with heavy truck traffic. On that note, try **Dollar Rent-a-Car** (☎ 442-0875, 15-580-0577; Carlos H Rodríguez), the only rental downtown.

ZAPALA

☎ 02942 / pop 35,800 / elevation 1200m

Windy, dusty and economically depressed, Zapala is little more than an ordinary desert

BIG, BIG BONES

In 1989, a local Neuquenian named Guillermo Heredia discovered a dinosaur bone on his property 7km east of the town of Plaza Huincul. Paleontologists investigated the site and later unearthed a dozen bones belonging to what they named *Argentinosaurus huinculensis* – the largest known dinosaur in the world. The gargantuan herbivore, dating from the mid-Cretaceous period, measured an incredible 40m long and 18m high.

The sheer size of the *Argentinosaurus huinculensis* is difficult to fathom, which is why stopping to gawk at the replica skeleton at Plaza Huincul's **Museo Municipal Carmen Funes** (☎ 0299-496-5486; museocarmenfunes@copelnet.com.ar; Córdoba 55; admission US$0.65; ☺ 8am-7:30pm Mon-Fri, 9am-8:30pm Sat & Sun) is a humbling lesson in size.

Along with Parque Provincial Ischigualasto (p317) in San Juan province, Neuquén is one of the earth's dinosaur hotspots. Here, three important paleontology sites – Plaza Huincul, Villa El Chocón and Centro Paleontológico Lago Barreales – lie within a couple hours' drive from Neuquén city and will delight anyone even slightly interested in dinosaurs.

About 80km southwest of Neuquén city, Villa El Chocón boasts the remains of the 100-million-year-old, 14m, eight-ton, meat-eating *Giganotosaurus Carolinii*, the world's largest known carnivore. Discovered in 1993 by fossil hunter Rubén Carolini, the dinosaur is even bigger than North America's better known *Tyrannosaurus rex*. El Chocón is also home to giant dinosaur footprints along the shore of Ezequiel Ramos Mexía reservoir. (One local confessed how families used to fire up *asados* – barbecues – in the footprints before they knew what they were!)

For true dino-freaks, the best place to satiate the hunger for bones is the **Centro Paleontológico Lago Barreales** (Costa Dinosaurio; ☎ 0299-15-404-8614; www.proyectodino.com.ar in Spanish; RP 51, Km 65; museum admission US$1; ☺ 9am-sunset), located 90km northwest of Neuquén. Here you can actually work – as in get your hands dirty digging – on-site with paleontologists in one of the world's only fully-functioning dinosaur excavation sites *open to the public*. You can visit the museum and take a guided tour of the site in about 1½ hours, but the real pleasure comes from the unique opportunity offered by sticking around. Prices (which help fund research) are US$30 for one day, US$140 for two days/one night, or about US$350 for five days/four nights. Under the supervision of renowned paleontologist and project director Jorge Calvo, you'll spend your days dusting off Cretaceous-period bones and picking at fossils, and your nights in the silence of the desert. As Calvo says, "when you set to work picking at the soft rock, uncovering fossilized leafs and bones that are 90 million years old, you forget about the rest of the world – some people even forget to eat."

Getting There & Away

From Neuquén, **Cooperativa El Petroleo** (☎ 448-7585) runs regular buses to Plaza Huincul (US$3, 1¾ hours). All buses between Neuquén and Zapala stop here. There are also regular buses to Villa El Chocón from Neuquén. Centro Paleontológico Lago Barreales is a bit more difficult to reach; contact the site for driving directions or possible transportation options (there are no buses to the site). If you drive, take RP 51, not RN 7.

mining town. The main excuse for rolling through town is to visit the nearby Parque Nacional Laguna Blanca (p324). Most people exploring the undeveloped northern reaches of the Lake District eventually pass through Zapala. Beyond its friendly inhabitants, however, the town itself won't hold the average traveler for long.

Zapala's main street is Av San Martín, which is an exit off the roundabout junction of RN 22 (which heads east to Neuquén and north to Las Lajas) and RN 40 (heading southwest to Junín de los Andes and north to Chos Malal).

Information

Banco de la Provincia del Neuquén (Cháneton 460) Bank and ATM.

Laguna Blanca National Park office (☎ 431982; lagunablanca@zapala.com.ar; Av Ejercito Argentino 260; ☺ 8am-3pm Mon-Fri) For information on Parque Nacional Laguna Blanca.

Tourist office (☎ 15-669847; www.zapaladigital.com.ar in Spanish; RN 22, Km 1398; ☺ 7am-9pm) Enthusiastically

THE LAKE DISTRICT

helpful tourist office. Located on highway, 2km west of town center.

Sleeping & Eating

Zapala has very limited accommodations.

Hotel Pehuén (☎ 423135; Etcheluz & Elena de la Vega; s/d with bathroom US$9.50/16, parking US$1; P) This is the best deal in town, conveniently near the bus terminal, with clean rooms, an attractive (classy, even) lobby and a good restaurant below.

Hotel Hue Melén (☎ 422344; hotelhuemelen@ hotmail.com; Almirante Brown 929; s/d US$16/27; P ✗) This three-star old-timer offers stark but spacious rooms and a 10% discount for cash payment.

El Chancho Rengo (☎ 422795; Av San Martín & Etcheluz) It's likely half the town saunters in here for an espresso each day. Outdoor tables and good coffee and sandwiches make it great for a light bite.

Getting There & Away

LADE (☎ 15-579506; Uriburu 397) flies Thursday to Neuquén (US$25) and Bariloche (US$60).

The **bus terminal** (Etcheluz & Uriburu) is about four blocks from Av San Martín, the main drag. Westbound buses from Neuquén en route to Junín de los Andes, San Martín de los Andes and Temuco, Chile, pass through Zapala. Most services to Buenos Aires (US$55, 16 hours) require changing buses in Neuquén (US$5, three hours), the nearest major hub. There are several daily buses to San Martín de los Andes (US$9, 3½ hours).

There is daily service to Laguna Blanca (US$5, ½ hour) and Aluminé (US$5, three to 3½ hours).

AROUND ZAPALA
Parque Nacional Laguna Blanca

At 1275m above sea level and surrounded by striking volcanic deserts, Laguna Blanca is only 10m deep, an interior drainage lake that formed when lava flows dammed two small streams. Only 30km southwest of Zapala, the lake is too alkaline for fish but hosts many bird species, including coots, ducks, grebes, upland geese, gulls and even a few flamingos. The 11,250-hectare park primarily protects the habitat of the black-necked swan, a permanent resident.

Starting 10km south of Zapala, paved and well-marked RP 46 leads directly through the park toward the Andean town of Alu-

miné; for transport details, see left. If you don't have your own transport, contact **Francisco Romero** (☎ 02942-423111), a local guide in Zapala who will take you out for the day.

There is a small improved campground with windbreaks, but bring all your own food; though there's a visitor center, there's no place to eat.

ALUMINÉ

☎ 02942 / pop 4000 / elevation 400m

Time seems to have stopped for Aluminé, and although it's an important tourist destination, it is less visited than destinations to the south. The town itself has a very local flair, with the main plaza alive with families and children on weekends. Most of the buildings are whitewashed brick, faded with time, and the streets are nearly all dirt, all a relief from the chalet-lined streets of San Martín and Bariloche. Situated 103km north of Junín de los Andes via RP 23, it's a popular fly-fishing destination and offers access to the less-visited northern sector of Parque Nacional Lanín. The Río Aluminé also offers excellent white-water rafting and kayaking.

Information

Banco del Provincia del Neuquén (cnr Conrado Villegas & Torcuato Mordarelli) Bank and ATM.

Nex Sur (☎ 496027; Av RIM 26 848; per hr before 6pm US$0.65, after 6pm US$1) Internet access; uphill from plaza.

Tourist office (☎ 496001; intendencia@alumine.com.ar; Christian Joubert, Plaza San Martín; ⏰ 8am-8pm mid-Mar–Nov, 9am-9pm Dec–mid-Mar)

Sights & Activities

The nearby Mapuche communities of Aigo and Salazar, on the 26km rolling dirt road to **Lago Ruca Choroi** (in Parque Nacional Lanín) sell traditional weavings, araucaria pine nuts, and, in summer time, *comidas típicas* (traditional dishes).

For rafting on the Río Aluminé (best in November), contact **Aluminé Rafting** (☎ 496322; aluminerafting@alumine.com.ar; Conrado Villegas 610). The tourist office keeps a list of available **fishing** guides and sells licenses (US$10/50 per day/ week).

Sleeping & Eating

The three *hosterías* in town are all pretty modest. High season coincides with the November through April fishing season.

Hostería Aluminé (☎ 496347; hosteriaaalumine@hotmail.com; Christian Joubert 312; s/d with bathroom US$14/19, with shared bathroom US$11/15) Comfortable old hotel facing the main plaza with large, somewhat drab but totally satisfactory rooms. Best in town. The attached **restaurant** (meals US$3-5) serves good food, especially the mixed pasta dish with *salsa de piñon y hongos* (pine nut and mushroom sauce).

Nid Car (☎ 496131; C Joubert & Benigar; s/d US$8.50/15) Run-of-the-mill hotel but definitely fine for a couple of nights. Cheapest in town.

La Chocolatería (☎ 496009; Av RIM 26 500; mains US$2-4; ☻ closed Mon) This is an excellent little restaurant/bar/chocolate shop serving goulash with spaetzle, pizzas, *pan montañés* (home-baked bread stuffed with vegies and meat) and more.

Getting There & Away
Aluminé Viajes and Albus go daily to/from Neuquén (US$9.50, six hours), Zapala (US$5, three to 3½ hours) and Junín de los Andes (US$6, three hours).

JUNÍN DE LOS ANDES
☎ 02972 / pop 18,000 / elevation 800m
The barren mountains surrounding Junín de los Andes are strikingly different from those of the similarly named San Martín de los Andes, only 41km south. By the traditional definition of 'beautiful mountain resort,' Junín is admittedly less attractive than its prestigious, leafy neighbor – but for that, it's also cheaper and can serve as a better base for exploring Parque Nacional Lanín. Attracting fly-fishing enthusiasts from just about everywhere, Junín deems itself the trout capital of Neuquén province and, to drive the point home, uses trout-shaped street signs.

Orientation
Paved RN 234 (known as Blvd Juan Manuel de Rosas in town) is the main thoroughfare, leading south to San Martín de los Andes and 116km northeast to Zapala via RN 40. North of town, graveled RP 23 heads to the fishing resort of Aluminé, while several secondary roads branch westward to Parque Nacional Lanín.

The city center is between the highway and the river. Do not confuse Av San Martín, which runs on the west side of Plaza San Martín, with Félix San Martín, two blocks further west.

Information
Banco de la Provincia de Neuquén (Av San Martín, btwn Suárez & Lamadrid) Opposite the plaza.
bits (Suárez 445 btwn Padre Milanesio & Don Bosco; per hr US$1) Internet access.
Club Andino Junín de los Andes (☎ 491637; Padre Milanesio 568, Local 12) In the Paseo Artesanal; provides information on the Volcán Tromen climb and other excursions within the national park.
Laverap Pehuén (Ponte 340) Laundry services.
Locutorio (Padre Milanesio 540) Opposite the plaza. It's easiest to make local or long-distance calls from this office.
Park office (☎ 491160; Padre Milanesio at Coronel Suárez; ☻ 9am-8:30pm Mon-Fri, 2:30-8:30pm Sat & Sun) Next to the tourist office. Has information on Parque Nacional Lanín.
Post office (Suárez & Don Bosco)
Tourist office (☎ 491160, 492575; www.junindelosandes .gov.ar in Spanish; Padre Milanesio 596 at Coronel Suárez, Plaza San Martín; ☻ 8am-11pm Nov-Feb, 8am-9pm Mar-Oct) Enthusiastically helpful staff. Fishing permits and list of licensed fishing guides available.

Sights & Activities
Junín's surroundings are more appealing than the town itself, but the private **Museo Moisés Roca Jalil** (Coronel Suárez & San Martín; admission free; ☻ 10am-noon Mon, Wed & Fri) boasts more than 400 Mapuche weavings and archaeological pieces well worth seeing.

West of town, near the end of Av Antártida Argentina, a wide dirt path called the **Vía Cristi** winds its way up the small Cerro de la Cruz (to get there, follow the cross) with impressive sculptures, bas-reliefs and mosaics vividly depicting the Conquest of the Desert, Mapuche legends, Christian themes and indigenous history.

The area around Junín is prime trout-fishing country, and the Río Aluminé, north of Junín, is an especially choice area. Catch-and-release is obligatory. For detailed information and equipment, visit the **Fly Shop** (☎ 491548; Illeras 448, Río Dorado Lodge), located west of the RN 234 (Blvd Juan Manuel de Rosas) at the northwest edge of town. Fishing licenses (inquire at the tourist office) cost US$67 for the season, US$50 per week or US$7 per day.

EXCURSIONS TO PARQUE NACIONAL LANÍN
In summer, buses leave the terminal several times a day for destinations within Parque Nacional Lanín (see p331), allowing you to hit the trails and camp in some beautiful

areas. The buses run three 'circuits' and charge US$3.50 for the return trip.

Lago Huechulafquen & Puerto Canoa (via RN 61)

From Puerto Canoa, on the north shore of the lake, there are three worthwhile hikes, including a 1½-hour roundtrip walk to the Cascada del Saltillo and a seven-hour roundtrip hike to **Cara Sur de Lanín** (south face of Volcán Lanín). For the latter, park rangers require you set out by 11am. Ranger stations are at both the entrance to Huechulafquen and at Puerto Canoa. From Puerto Canoa, the boat **Jose Julian** (☎ 421038, 429539) offers boat trips on the lake. Buses depart Junín's terminal twice in the morning (usually around 8am and 11am) and once in the afternoon (around 4pm). Be sure to catch the last bus back unless you plan to camp.

Circuito Tromen (via RN 23 & RN 60)

Buses depart twice daily to Lago Tromen, from where there is a 1½-hour roundtrip walk along the river, passing a fine araucaria forest and a lookout with fabulous views of the lake. Another 45-minute walk takes you to the base of **Volcán Lanín's Cara Norte** (north face). This is one departure point for the two- to three-day ascent of Lanín. Park rangers inspect equipment and test any climbers who plan to go without a guide. To hire a guide, contact the tourist office in Junín. This is the access point for the CAJA *refugio* and two military-owned *refugios*. Lago Tromen can also be reached by taking any bus that goes to Chile and getting off at Tromen.

Circuito Curruhué (via RP 62)

Buses depart once or twice daily for Lago Curruhué and Lago Epulafquen; near the

---

THE AUTHOR'S CHOICE

Hostería Chimehuín (☎ 491132; www.inter patagonia.com/hosteriachimehuin in Spanish; Coronel Suárez & 25 de Mayo; s US$8.50-17, d US$17-25) On lush grounds near the river, this long-established fishing *hostería* offers rooms in its old main lodge or in a modern sector outside; all are subtle, comfortable and exceptional value, whether you fish or not. Rooms in the newer sector have giant windows facing the river.

---

latter is a trailhead leads to the **Termas de Lahuen-Có** (also called Epulafquen), about one hour's walking time from the head. The springs are fairly undeveloped and there's a campsite. You can also hike to the crater of Volcán Achen Niyeu.

Festivals & Events

Every year, Junín celebrates its own lively **Carnaval del Pehuén** with parades, costumes, live music and the usual water balloons.

In January, the **Feria y Exposición Ganadera** displays the best of local cattle, horses, sheep, poultry and rabbits. There are also exhibitions of horsemanship, as well as local crafts exhibits, but this is the *estanciero's* (*estancia* owner's) show – the peons and the people get their chance at mid-February's **Festival del Puestero**, where the name of the game is music, food and fun, rather than livestock trading.

In early August, the Mapuche celebrate their crafts skills in the **Semana de Artesanía Aborígen**.

Sleeping

High season coincides with fishing season (November through April); during low season, prices are lower than those quoted here.

Posada Pehuén (☎ 491569; posadapehuen@jde andes.com.ar; Coronel Suárez 560; s/d US$10/15; 🖳) Attentive owners Eduardo and Rosi run this cozy little place in their attractive home and will help arrange all types of excursions. Rooms are cheerful with antler lamps adding a country flair. It's located between the plaza and the river.

Hostería Milla Piuke (☎ 492378, 492426; milla piuke@fronteradigital.net.ar; s/d US$25/29) Immaculate *hostería* five blocks south of downtown on Blvd Juan Manuel de Rosas (RN 234) with high, wood ceilings, large rooms, tiled floors, huge bathrooms, great beds and a bright breakfast area. Downside: it's a 10-minute walk to the center and it faces the highway.

Residencial El Cedro (☎ 492044, 15-601952; La-madrid 409; s/d US$8.50/17) Just off the plaza, this small, friendly place has decent, straightforward rooms and a breakfast area resembling a budget café.

Camping La Isla (☎ 491461; sites per person US$2, showers US$1.50) This municipal campground sits on the pleasant banks of the Río Chimehuín, three blocks east of the plaza. It has the standard facilities.

Eating

Junín has fairly mediocre restaurants, though local specialties like trout, wild boar or venison may be available.

Ruca Hueney (☎ 491113; Padre Milanesio 641; mains US$3-5) Ruca Hueney, Junín's oldest restaurant, is reliable and has the most extensive menu in town. Portions are large; service is abrupt.

La Aldea del Pescador (☎ 15-410610; Necochea 35; mains US$3.50-6) Great old place in a little house facing the highway, across from the YPF station. Delicious cheap *parrilla*, traditional plates and pastas. Worth the walk.

Roble Bar (☎ 491124; Ponte 331) Junín's main pizzeria offers baked empanadas and sandwiches as well.

Rotisería Tandil (Coronel Suárez 431) Excellent take-out empanadas.

Getting There & Away
Air
Junín and San Martín de los Andes share Chapelco airport, which lies midway between the two towns (see p331).

BUS
The **bus terminal** (☎ 492038; Olavarría & Félix San Martín) is only three blocks from the main plaza. Ko-Ko has service to Bariloche (US$16, four to six hours) via both the paved Rinconada route and the dusty but far more scenic Siete Lagos alternative. El Petróleo goes Tuesday to Aluminé (US$6, three hours). To Mendoza you must change buses in Neuquén. Empresa San Martín crosses the Andes to Temuco, Chile (US$12, six hours), via Paso Tromen (also known as Mamuil Malal). There are daily services to the following destinations:

Destination	Cost (US$)	Duration (hr)
Bahía Blanca	20	14
Buenos Aires	29-35	23
Córdoba	37	23
Neuquén	9.50	5
San Martín de los Andes	2	1
Zapala	7.50	4

SAN MARTÍN DE LOS ANDES

☎ 02972 / pop 26,000 / elevation 645m

Situated on a small bay on the eastern end of Lago Lácar, relaxed San Martín de los Andes is a fashionable and relatively costly mountain resort, drawing visitors (hordes of them in summer) to its quiet tree-lined streets and attractive lakeside beaches. The town retains much of the charm and architectural unity that once attracted people to Bariloche, and folks sit along the waterfront in summer sipping *mate* and chatting in the sun. It's pleasant just walking around the town, especially in the off-season.

San Martín's principal outlying attractions are Cerro Chapelco ski resort and Parque Nacional Lanín; it is also the northern jumping-off point for the scenically neck-straining Siete Lagos route, which runs south to Villa La Angostura and Bariloche.

Orientation
Nestled in striking mountain scenery, San Martín de los Andes straddles RN 234, which passes through town southbound to Villa La Angostura and Lago Nahuel Huapi. Northbound RN 234 heads to Zapala via Junín de los Andes. Almost everything in San Martín de los Andes is within walking distance of the *centro cívico* (civic center), and the shady lakefront park and pier are a delightful place to spend an afternoon. Av San Martín is the main commercial street, running north from the lakefront toward the highway to Junín.

Information
BOOKSTORES
Patalibro (☎ 421532; patalibro@yahoo.com.ar; Av San Martín 866) Good selection of books on Patagonia in Spanish; some Lonely Planet titles and novels in English. Carries the excellent *Sendas Y Bosques* park trail maps (US$2.50).

INTERNET ACCESS
Athos (☎ 429855; Av San Martín 808; per hr US$1) Internet access in kiosk, upstairs.

LAUNDRY
Laverap (☎ 428820; Capitán Drury 880; full service about US$3)

MEDICAL SERVICES
Ramón Carrillo Hospital (☎ 427211; Coronel Rohde & Av San Martín)

MONEY
Andina Internacional (☎ 427871; Capitán Drury 876) Money exchange.
Banco de la Nación (Av San Martín 687) Has an ATM.

POST
Post office (Roca & Coronel Pérez)

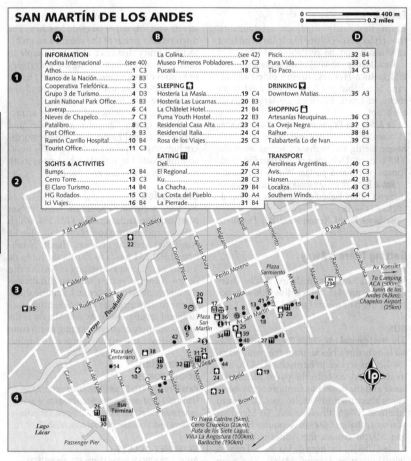

SAN MARTÍN DE LOS ANDES

INFORMATION	
Andina Internacional ....(see 40)	
Athos...**1** C3	
Banco de la Nación..........................**2** B3	
Cooperativa Telefónica..................**3** C3	
Grupo 3 de Turismo........................**4** D3	
Lanín National Park Office............**5** B3	
Laverap..**6** C4	
Nieves de Chapelco........................**7** C3	
Patalibro...**8** C3	
Post Office.......................................**9** B3	
Ramón Carrillo Hospital...............**10** B4	
Tourist Office................................**11** C3	
SIGHTS & ACTIVITIES	
Bumps...**12** B4	
Cerro Torre.....................................**13** C3	
El Claro Turismo.............................**14** B4	
HG Rodados....................................**15** C3	
Ici Viajes...**16** B4	

La Colina.............................(see 42)	
Museo Primeros Pobladores....**17** C3	
Pucará..**18** C3	
SLEEPING	
Hostería La Masía..........................**19** C4	
Hostería Las Lucarnas...................**20** B3	
La Châtelet Hotel...........................**21** B4	
Puma Youth Hostel........................**22** B3	
Residencial Casa Alta....................**23** C4	
Residencial Italia............................**24** C4	
Rosa de los Viajes..........................**25** C3	
EATING	
Deli..**26** A4	
El Regional.....................................**27** C3	
Ku..**28** C3	
La Chacha.......................................**29** C3	
La Costa del Pueblo......................**30** A4	
La Pierrade.....................................**31** B4	

Piscis...**32** B4	
Pura Vida..**33** C4	
Tio Paco..**34** C3	
DRINKING	
Downtown Matias..........................**35** A3	
SHOPPING	
Artesanías Neuquinas....................**36** C3	
La Oveja Negra...............................**37** C3	
Raihue...**38** B4	
Talabartería Lo de Ivan.................**39** C3	
TRANSPORT	
Aerolíneas Argentinas....................**40** C3	
Avis..**41** C3	
Hansen...**42** B3	
Localiza...**43** C3	
Southern Winds..............................**44** C4	

TELEPHONE
Cooperativa Telefónica (Capitán Drury 761)

TOURIST INFORMATION
Lanín National Park office (Intendencia del Parque Nacional Lanín; ☎ 427233; www.parquenacionallanin.gov.ar in Spanish; Emilio Frey 749; ⏰ 8am-2pm Mon-Fri) The office provides limited maps as well as brochures.

Nieves de Chapelco (☎ 429845, 427845; Av San Martín at Elordi) Provides information and sells lift tickets for the Cerro Chapelco ski resort.

Tourist office (☎ 425500, 427347; www.smandes .gov.ar; cnr Av San Martín & Rosas; ⏰ 8am-9pm, until 10pm Dec-Mar) Provides surprisingly candid information on hotels and restaurants, plus excellent brochures and maps.

TRAVEL AGENCIES
The agencies listed opposite, as well as many others along Av San Martín, Belgrano and Elordi, offer standard services as well as excursions.

Grupo 3 de Turismo (☎ 428453; San Martín 1141, Local 1) The Amex representative.

Sights
MUSEO PRIMEROS POBLADORES
Regional archaeological and ethnographic items such as arrowheads, spear points, pottery and musical instruments are the focus of the **Museo Primeros Pobladores** (admission US$1; ⏰ 2-7pm Mon-Fri), located two doors north of the tourist office, on Rosas near Av Roca.

RUTA DE LOS SIETE LAGOS

From San Martín, RP 234 follows an eminently scenic but rough, narrow and dusty route past numerous alpine lakes to Villa La Angostura. It's known as the Ruta de los Siete Lagos (Seven Lakes Route) and its spectacular scenery has made the drive famous. Tours from San Martín, Villa La Angostura and Bariloche regularly do this route, but there's also a scheduled bus service (p331).

Activities

Mountain biking is an excellent way to explore the surrounding area and a good way to travel the Siete Lagos road. Rent bikes at **HG Rodados** (☎ 427345; Av San Martín 1061) or **Ici Viajes** (☎ 427800; www.7lagos.com/iciviajes; Villegas 459). Both charge about US$5 per day.

For rafting on the Río Meliquina, south of San Martín, or the Río Hua Hum to the west, contact **Ici Viajes** (above), **El Claro Turismo** (☎ 428876, 425876; www.elclaroturismo.com.ar; Diaz 751) or **Pucará** (☎ 427218; Av San Martín 941). They all charge about US$25 for the all-day trip, including transfers. The river is spectacular and suitable for kids.

There are also excellent opportunities for trekking and climbing in Parque Nacional Lanín. Horacio Peloso, who is known by his nickname 'El Oso,' is a highly regarded mountain guide who arranges trips and rents equipment for climbing Lanín; contact him at **Cerro Torre** (☎ 429162; cerrotorre@smandes.com.ar; Av San Martín 960). He charges about US$127 per person, including equipment, plus another US$7 or so for transport. Otherwise contact Pucará.

Skiing and snowboarding at nearby Cerro Chapelco attract enthusiastic winter crowds (see p331). In San Martín, rental equipment is available at **Bumps** (☎ 428491; Villegas 459) and **La Colina** (☎ 427414; Av San Martín 532). Skis rent for US$8 to US$11 per day and snowboards for US$10 to US$13. You can also rent equipment on the mountain.

San Martín's several travel agencies offer full-day tours to a number of outlying sights.

Festivals & Events

San Martín celebrates its founding on February 4 with speeches, parades and other festivities; the **parade** itself is an entertainingly incongruous mix of military folks, firefighters, gauchos, polo players and foxhunters.

Sleeping

As a tourist center, San Martín is loaded with accommodations, but they're relatively costly in all categories, especially in summer high season (January to March) and peak ski season (mid-July and August) when reservations are a must. Quality, however, is mostly high. In low season, prices can drop by 40%.

BUDGET

Puma Youth Hostel (☎ 422443; puma@smandes.com.ar; A Fosbery 535; dm US$8, plus one-off sheet-rental fee US$0.65, d US$22) This is a pleasant, well-kept HI-affiliated hostel with a helpful young owner and dorm rooms with three to six beds in each; all have their own bathroom. There are three double rooms and a sparse but functional communal kitchen. Transfers to Cerro Chapelco are available.

Residencial Italia (☎ 427590; Coronel Pérez 977; s/d US$12/23, 3-person apt US$34) The friendly owner lives downstairs and rents out four immaculate, quiet rooms above. Beds are nice and firm and the place feels happily like grandma's house.

Camping ACA (☎ 427332; Av Koessler 2640; sites per person US$3, 2-person minimum fee) Spacious campground on the eastern outskirts of town. Avoid sites near the highway, however.

Playa Catritre (☎ 426986; RN 234, Km 5 sur; sites per person US$2-2.75, 2-person minimum fee) Playa Catritre is a pleasant site about 4km south of San Martín, but get a lakeside site rather than one that's smack in the middle of the parking area. Very popular with weekending families. All services plus a small store.

MIDRANGE

Rosa de los Viajes (☎ /fax 427320; Av San Martín 821; s/d US$27/33 ☑ closed Oct-Dec, May & Jun) The immaculate rooms are a bit sparse, but the hotel is central, comfortable and very welcoming. The breakfast area has a formal feel, and the hallways are wide and empty. But the rooms are good.

Residencial Casa Alta (☎ 427456; casaalta@sm andes.com.ar; Obeid 659; s/d US$17/20) This homey, family-operated place has three cozy rooms, wisely booked in advance. Besides Spanish, owner Pepe Guitiérrez speaks German, French, Portuguese, English and *lunfardo* (street slang).

Hostería Las Lucarnas (☎ 427085; fax 427985; Coronel Pérez 632; s/d US$27/33, US$13/20 low season; ☑ closed Oct-Dec, May & Jun) This tasteful stone

THE LAKE DISTRICT

THE AUTHOR'S CHOICE

Hostería La Masía (☎ /fax 427688; www .hosterialamasia.com.ar in Spanish; Obeid 811; s & d US$45-50; **P**) With cozy reading nooks, an intimate bar and breakfast area, a paddleball court and comfortable midsize rooms with luxurious bathrooms, this is easily one of San Martín's best. Fireplaces warm the lobby, and the owners are usually around to make sure everyone feels at home. Superb.

and wood structure has simple, welcoming rooms; try for a spot upstairs.

TOP END

La Châtelet Hotel (☎ 428294/96; www.hotellecha telet.com.ar; Villegas 960; d US$84, ste US$97; **P** **🖳** **🐾**) Very classy, very intimate chalet-style hotel with a comfortable lobby area, video library, and tasteful, homey rooms. Wooden slanted ceilings and squishy furniture add to the appeal.

Eating & Drinking

Ku (☎ 427039; Av San Martín 1053; mains US$6-7) Delightfully warm and welcoming *parrilla*. The chefs put unique spins on the usual dishes: sweet-and-sour venison, mustard-smoked sirloin, and grilled jabalí (wild boar) are just a few of the many delicious dishes.

La Pierrade (☎ 421421; cnr Mariano Moreno & Villegas; set price US$9.50) Here, you cook your food to your liking at the table over a heated stone. Chef up everything from *ciervo* (venison) and *lomo* (sirloin) to peppers, eggplant and zucchini. It's all you can eat (or cook) and lots of fun.

El Regional (☎ 425326; Villegas 953; mains US$3-4) The specialty here is on tap: El Bolsón's microbrewed beer. There are eight varieties, from blonde to bock. Also *tablas* (plates) of smoked regional food (pate, cheese, jabalí) and other regional specialties.

THE AUTHOR'S CHOICE

Pura Vida (☎ 429302; Villegas 745; mains US$2-3; ☽ closed lunch Sun) The delicious, fresh vegetarian dishes here are a godsend after all those meat menus and canned-salad bars. Chicken and fish items are available as well. Great soups.

La Chacha (☎ 429376; cnr Rivadavia & Av San Martín) Not as intimate as Ku, but perennially popular for delicious *parrillada*.

Deli (☎ 428631; cnr Villegas & Costanera MA Camino; mains US$1.50-4) Cheapest place on the lakeside with outdoor seating and reliable food. Good for afternoon beer and French fries. Very popular.

La Costa del Pueblo (☎ 429289; Av Costanera MA Camino near Obeid; mains US$3-5) Delicious trout, pasta and *parrilla*, great lakeside location and comfortable atmosphere.

Piscis (☎ 427601; Villegas 598) Primarily serving *parrillada*, Piscis is one of San Martín's favorite restaurants, slightly on the pricey side and mobbed in the evening. Excellent.

Tio Paco (☎ 427920; cnr Av San Martín & Capitán Drury; mains US$2.50-4) Great little bar-café with a full menu and a long list of mixed drinks, including coffee drinks (with booze), wine and cocktails. Pool table upstairs and a deck overlooking the main drag. Drinks cost US$1 to US$3.

Downtown Matias (☎ 421699; E Calderón s/n; ☽ 9pm-late Thu-Sat low season, nightly in summer) Irish 'pub' that's all the rage. Great views over the lake. If you're walking, head west on E Calderón and be ready for the *steep* climb up the road.

Shopping

Many local shops sell regional products and handicrafts.

Artesanías Neuquinas (☎ 428396; Rosas 790) Mapuche cooperative with high-quality weavings and wood crafts on offer.

La Oveja Negra (☎ 427248; Av San Martín 1045) Mapuche textiles.

Talabartería Lo de Ivan (☎ 420737; Capitán Drury 814) Specializes in gaucho regalia.

Raihue (☎ 423160; Av San Martín 436) Artisan knives, sweaters, leather, purses and ponchos.

Getting There & Away

AIR

Flights to Buenos Aires cost about US$87 if booked well in advance. **Aerolíneas Argentinas** (☎ 427003/04; Capitán Drury 876) is usually priciest, and flies daily except Wednesday. **Southern Winds** (☎ 424566/67; chapelco@sw.com.ar; Coronel Perez 904) flies on Thursday, Saturday and Sunday.

LADE (☎ 427672; office inside bus terminal) flies Wednesday to Zapala (US$20), Neuquén (US$20) and Bariloche (US$14), and Thursday to Buenos Aires (US$100).

BOAT

Plumas Verdes (☎ 428427, 427380) sails from the **passenger pier** (Muelle de Pasajeros; Costanera MA Camino) on the Av Costanera as far as Paso Hua Hum on the Chilean border, daily at 10am. The boat does not stop, however, to let passengers off at the border. The departure time changes annually; call the ferry company or check with the tourist office. The fare is US$60 plus US$4 national park fee.

BUS

The **bus terminal** (☎ 427044; Villegas & Juez del Valle) is a block south of the highway and 3½ blocks southwest of Plaza San Martín.

On Tuesdays, Thursdays and Saturdays at 6am, Igi-Llaima takes RP 60 over Paso Tromen (also known as Mamuil Malal) to Temuco, Chile (US$12, six hours), passing the majestic Volcán Lanín en route; sit on the left for views. Empresa San Martín goes on Tuesday, Thursday and Saturday at the same hour. There is no Sunday service.

El Petróleo takes RP 48 over Paso Hua Hum to Chile daily at 12:30pm. At Puerto Pirehueico (US$2.50, two hours) on its namesake lake the bus is ferried across to Puerto Fuy (US$12), from where there are onward buses toward Valdivia. From San Martín, there is direct service in summer via RN 231 over Paso Cardenal A Samoré (Puyehue) to Osorno and Puerto Montt.

If you're heading to Villa Traful or Bariloche, Transportes Ko-Ko regularly takes the scenic Siete Lagos route (RN 234) instead of the longer but smoother Rinconada route. To Aluminé (US$5.50, three hours), El Petróleo leaves on Tuesday only, at 8am.

There are frequent daily departures to the destinations listed in the following table.

Destination	Cost (US$)	Duration (hr)
Bahía Blanca	24	15-16
Bariloche	8	4½
Buenos Aires	35-47	20-23
Córdoba	36-40	21
Junín de los Andes	2	1
Mendoza	10	9½
Neuquén	11	6
San Rafael	27	14-15
Viedma	24	18
Villa La Angostura	2	2½
Villa Traful	4	2½
Zapala	9	4

Getting Around

Chapelco airport (☎ 428388; RN 234) is midway between San Martín and Junín. **Al Sur** (☎ 422 903) runs shuttles between San Martín and the airport; call for hotel pickup.

Transport options slim down during low season. In summer, Transportes Airen goes twice daily to Puerto Canoas on Lago Huechulafquen (US$3) and will stop at campgrounds en route. Albus goes to the beach at Playa Catritre (US$0.50) several times daily, while Transportes Ko-Ko runs four buses daily to Lago Lolog (US$1) in summer only.

Of the following car rental agencies, Hansen had the best prices on our visit (US$32 per day as opposed to around US$44 for the rest).

Avis (☎ 427704; Av San Martín 998)
Hansen (☎ 427997; Av San Martín 532)
Localiza (☎ 428876; Villegas 977)

AROUND SAN MARTÍN DE LOS ANDES
Cerro Chapelco

Only 20km southeast of San Martín, **Cerro Chapelco** (☎ 02972-427157) is one of Argentina's principal winter-sports centers, with runs for beginners and experts, and a maximum elevation of 1920m. The **Fiesta Nacional del Montañés**, the annual ski festival, is held the first half of August.

Lift-ticket prices vary, depending on when you go; full-day passes run from US$16 to US$29 for adults, US$13 to US$23 for children. The slopes are open from mid-June to early October. The low season is mid-June to early July and from August 28 to mid-October; high season is around the last two weeks of July.

The resort has a downtown information center (p328) that also sells lift tickets. Rental equipment is available on site as well as in town (p329).

Transportes Ko-Ko runs two buses each day (three in summer; US$3.50 return) to the park from San Martín's bus terminal. Travel agencies in San Martín also offer packages with shuttle service, or shuttle service alone (US$4 to US$6); they pick you up at your hotel.

PARQUE NACIONAL LANÍN

Dominating the view in all directions along the Chilean border, the snowcapped cone of 3776m Volcán Lanín is the centerpiece of Parque Nacional Lanín, which extends 150km

PARQUE NACIONAL LANÍN

0 _____ 40 km
0 _____ 20 miles

72°00'W · 71°30'W

Lago Colico · Lago Caburgua · Parque Nacional Huerquehue · Lago Norquinco

Lago Villarrica · Pucón · Lago Rucachoroi

Lago Quillén

Volcán Villarrica (2847m) · Parque Nacional Villarrica · Lago Tromen · 39°30'S

Lago Calafquen · Volcán Lanín (3776m) · Paso Tromen (Mamuil Malal) (1207m)

Piedra Mala · Puerto Canoa · RP 60

Lago Paimún · RP 61

Lago Paso Carirriñe Epulafquen · Lago Huechulafquen (1123m)

Lago Curruhué

Choshuenco · Lago Pirehueico · Volcán Choshuenco (2415m) · Parque Nacional Lanín · RP 62 · Junín de los Andes

40°00'S · Paso Hua Hum (659m) · Lago Lolog · 40°00'S

CHILE · RP 48 · Lago Lácar · San Martín de los Andes

Lago Maihue · Cerro Chapelco (1340m)

RN 234

Lago Huishué · Lago Villarino · Lago Falkner

40°30'S · Lago Gris · Lago Espejo · Lago Trafúl · 40°30'S

Parque Nacional Puyehue · RP 64 · To Bariloche

215 · Parque Nacional Nahuel Huapi · Villa Trafúl

72°00'W · 71°30'W

from Parque Nacional Nahuel Huapi in the south to Lago Ñorquinco in the north.

Protecting 379,000 hectares of native Patagonian forest, the Lanín park is home to many of the same species that characterize more southerly Patagonian forests, such as the southern beeches – lenga, ñire and coihue. More botanically unique to the area, however, are the extensive stands of the broadleaf, deciduous southern beech, raulí, and the curious pehuén, or monkey puzzle tree (Araucaria araucana), a pine-like conifer whose nuts have long been a dietary staple for the Pehuenches and Mapuches. Note that only indigenous people may gather piñones (pine nuts) from the pehuenes.

In addition to the views of Volcán Lanín and the unusual forests, the park also has recreational attractions in the numerous finger-shaped lakes carved by Pleistocene glaciers. Excellent campsites are abundant.

The towns of San Martín de los Andes, Junín de los Andes and Aluminé are the best starting points for exploring Lanín, its glacial lakes and the backcountry.

Information

The Lanín National Park office (p328) in San Martín produces brochures on camping, hiking and climbing in various parts of the park. These brochures are also distributed in the area's tourist offices. Scattered throughout the park proper are several ranger stations, but they usually lack printed materials. The Parque Nacional Lanín website (www.parquenacionallanin.gov.ar in Spanish) is full of useful information.

Lago Lácar & Lago Lolog

From San Martín, at the east end of the lake, there is bus service on RP 48, which runs along Lago Lácar to the Chilean border at Paso Hua Hum. You can get off the bus anywhere along the lake or get off at Hua Hum and hike to Cascada Chachín; bus drivers know the stop. From the highway, it's 3km down a dirt road and then another 20 minutes' walk along a trail to the waterfall. It's a great spot for a picnic.

Fifteen kilometers north of San Martín de los Andes, Lago Lolog offers good fishing in a largely undeveloped area. You'll find pleasant camping at **Camping Puerto Arturo** (free). Transportes Ko-Ko runs four buses daily, in summer only, to Lago Lolog from San Martín; the bus costs US$2.

Lago Huechulafquen

The park's largest lake is also one of its most central and accessible areas. Despite limited public transport, it can be reached from San Martín and – more easily – Junín de los Andes. RP 61 climbs from a junction just north of Junín, west to Huechulafquen and the smaller Lago Paimún, offering outstanding views of Volcán Lanín and access to trailheads of several excellent hikes.

From the ranger station at **Puerto Canoa**, a good trail climbs to a viewpoint on Lanín's shoulder, where it's possible to hike across to Paso Tromen or continue climbing to either of two *refugios*: the **RIM refugio** belongs to the army's Regimiento de Infantería de Montaña, while the **CAJA refugio** belongs to the Club Andino Junín de los Andes (p325). Both are fairly rustic but well kept and can be bases for attempts on the summit (for more detail, including information about permits and equipment, see right). The initial segment follows an abandoned road, but after about 40 minutes it becomes a pleasant woodsy trail along the **Arroyo Rucu Leufu**, an attractive mountain stream. Halfway to the *refugio* is an extensive **pehuén forest**, the southernmost in the park, which makes the walk worthwhile if you lack time for the entire route. The route to RIM's *refugio*, about 2450m above sea level, takes about seven hours one-way, while the trail to CAJA's *refugio* takes a bit longer.

Another good backcountry hike circles **Lago Paimún**. This requires about two days from Puerto Canoa; you return to the north side of the lake by crossing a cable platform strung across the narrows between Huechulafquen and Paimún. A shorter alternative hike goes from the very attractive campground at **Piedra Mala** to **Cascada El Saltillo**, a nearby forest waterfall. If your car lacks 4WD, leave it at the logjam 'bridge' that crosses the creek and walk to Piedra Mala – the road, passable by any ordinary vehicle to this point, quickly worsens after a harsh winter. Horses are available for rent at Piedra Mala. Transportes KoKo runs buses to Piedra Mala daily in summer from the San Martín bus terminal (p331).

Campsites are abundant along the highway; travelers camping in the free sites in the narrow area between the lakes and the highway must dig a latrine and remove their own trash. If you camp at the organized sites (which, though not luxurious, are maintained), you'll support Mapuche concessionaires who at least derive some income from lands that were theirs before the state usurped them a century ago. Good sites include **Camping Raquithue** (per person US$3), **Camping Piedra Mala** (per person US$2-3) and **Bahía Cañicul** (with/without electricity US$4/3).

Noncampers should treat themselves to a stay at **Hostería Refugio Pescador** (Puerto Canoa ☎ 02972-490210, Junín de los Andes ☎ 02972-491132; r per person with full board US$59) or the three-star **Hostería Paimún** (☎ 02972-491211; adelvalle@jandes .com.ar; s/d with full board US$70/90); both cater to fishing parties.

Lago Tromen

This northern approach to **Volcán Lanín**, which straddles the Argentine-Chilean border, is also the shortest and usually the earliest in the season to open for hikers and climbers. Before climbing Lanín, ask permission at the Lanín National Park office in San Martín (p328) or, if necessary, of the Gendarmería (border guards) in Junín. It's obligatory to show equipment, including plastic tools, crampons, ice axe and clothing – including sunglasses, sunblock, gloves, hats and padded jackets.

From the trailhead at the Argentine border station, it's five to seven hours to the **CAJA refugio** (capacity 14 people), at 2600m on the Camino de Mulas route; above that point, snow equipment is necessary. There's a shorter but steeper route along the ridge known as the Espina del Pescado, where it's possible to stay at the **RIM refugio** (capacity 20 people), at 2450m. Trekkers can cross the Sierra Mamuil Malal to Lago Huechulafquen via Arroyo Rucu Leufu.

Horacio Peloso at Cerro Torre in San Martín (p329) is an excellent guide for climbing Lanín. The hike usually takes two days: you leave early the first and stay at the RIM *refugio*, rise before dawn the following day, hike to the summit and walk down. If you want to go up in winter, he can set you up with guides to hike up and board or ski down (for experienced snowheads only).

Lago Quillén

Situated in the park's densest pehuén forests, this isolated lake is accessible by dirt road from Rahué, 17km south of Aluminé, and has many good **campsites**. Other nearby lakes include **Lago Rucachoroi**, directly west of Aluminé, and **Lago Ñorquinco** on the park's northern border. There are Mapuche reservations at Rucachoroi and Quillén.

Getting There & Away

Although the park is close to San Martín and Junín, public transport is minimal; see p330 and p325 for details. With some patience, hitching is feasible in high season. Buses over the Hua Hum and Tromen passes, from San Martín and Junín to Chile, will carry passengers to intermediate destinations but they are often full.

THE LAKE DISTRICT

VILLA TRAFUL

☎ 02944 / elevation 720m

A pinprick on the south shore of Lago Traful, Villa Traful offers excellent opportunities for camping, hiking and fishing in a relatively undeveloped area of Parque Nacional Nahuel Huapi. It's a tranquil, tiny resort village, 80km north of Bariloche via unpaved RP 65. It's right on the lakeshore with fabulous views over the water from the little pier. Continuing east of Traful along the Río Traful to RN 237, you roll through spectacular countryside (most of it owned by Ted Turner, hence the fences) with wild, towering rock formations very distinct from the areas to the south.

The **tourist office** (☎ 479099; www.interpatagonia .com/traful; ☺ daily summer, Sat-Wed only winter) is on the eastern side of the village.

Guides can easily be hired through the tourist office for horseback riding and hiking in the surrounding mountains. Everything books quickly during fishing season (November to April) and in January and February.

There are only a few places to stay unless you rent a *cabaña* (the tourist office has a complete listing). Across the road from the lake, **Hostería Villa Traful** (☎ 479005/06; per person US$12, cabañas US$50-54) is the oldest in the village and has four small, slightly drab but comfortable rooms and nine *cabañas* (with kitchen, TV and *parrilla*).

There are a couple of **restaurants** tucked into the trees and a general store to buy groceries.

Albus has daily services to San Martín de los Andes (US$4, 2½ hours) and Bariloche.

VILLA LA ANGOSTURA

☎ 02944 / pop 12,000 / elevation 850m

On the northwestern shore of Lago Nahuel Huapi, Villa La Angostura is a tranquil resort of attractive cabins and small *hosterías*

THE AUTHOR'S CHOICE

Albergue & Camping Vulcanche (☎ 479 028; dm US$5, with sheets US$6, d with bathroom US$15, camping per person US$1.50-3) In a beautiful wooded area on the eastern edge of the village, Vulcanche is a lovely HI facility with cozy common areas and plenty of open space outside.

---

tucked sporadically into the lakeside evergreens – well, most of it is anyway. The village consists of two distinct areas: El Cruce, which is the commercial center along the highway, and La Villa, nestled against the lakeshore, 3km to the south. Though La Villa is more residential, it still has hotels, shops, services and, unlike El Cruce, lake access. Despite rapid growth, this densely forested resort does not dominate its surroundings, so that, except along the highway, visitors are hardly aware of being in a town.

Villa La Angostura's most accessible natural asset is Parque Nacional Los Arrayanes, a small peninsula dangling some 12km into the lake from La Villa's edge. Nearby Cerro Bayo is a small but popular winter-sports center.

Orientation

Villa La Angostura is near the junction of RN 231 from Bariloche and RN 234 to San Martín de los Andes (100km). The junction gives the commercial strip of town the name of **El Cruce** (The Crossroads). Through town, RN 231 is known as Av Arrayanes and Av Siete (Seven) Lagos. **La Villa** is a 3km walk toward the lake on Blvd Nahuel Huapi.

La Villa and its surrounds are easily seen on foot, but if you're venturing further out, taxis are the only means of getting to the trailheads. They leave from the local terminal on Av Siete Lagos, just north of Los Arrayanes.

Information

Banco de la Provincia (Calle Las Frambuesas btwn Cerro Belvedere & Nahuel Huapi, El Cruce) Has an ATM.
HoraCero (☎ 495055; Av Arrayanes 45, El Cruce; Internet per hr US$1) Pizzeria with Internet in back.
Park administration office (☎ 494152; Nahuel Huapi, La Villa)
Post office (El Cruce)
Tourist office (☎ 494124; www.villalaangostura.gov.ar in Spanish; Av Siete Lagos 93, El Cruce; ☺ 8:30am-9pm)

Sights & Activities

Trekking, horseback riding and guided mountain bike rides are all offered by several outfitters in town, and the tourist office provides information on all. Mountain biking is a great way to explore the surrounding area; for rentals, try **Free Bikes** (☎ 495047; La Villa Blvd Nahuel Huapi 2150; El Cruce Topa Topa 102; full day US$5). For horseback riding (half-day to multi-day trips), contact Tero Bogani at **Cabalgatas Correntoso** (☎ 15-562085; www.cabalgata correntoso.com.ar), who brings the gaucho side of things to his trips. For sailboat rides around the lake (which can be rippin' on a windy day), contact captain **Jorge Rovella** (☎ 494834, 15-554153; velaaventura@yahoo.com.ar); a three-hour trip costs about US$50 for up to four people.

La Angostura's **Museo Histórico Regional** (Nahuel Huapi & El Calafate; admission free; ⌚ 11am-5pm Tue-Sat), on the road to La Villa, is worth popping into for a spot of Mapuche history, historical town photographs and old climbing relics.

PARQUE NACIONAL LOS ARRAYANES

This inconspicuous, overlooked park (admission US$4; pay at the national park office in La Villa), encompassing the entire Quetrihué peninsula, protects remaining stands of the cinnamon-barked arrayán, a member of the myrtle family. In Mapudungun, language of the Mapuche, the peninsula's name means 'place of the arrayanes.'

The park headquarters are at the southern end of the peninsula, near the largest concentration of arrayanes, in an area known as **El Bosque**. It's a three-hour, 12km hike from La Villa to the tip of the peninsula, on an excellent **interpretive nature trail**; brochures are available in the tourist office at El Cruce. You can also hike out and get the ferry back from the point (p336), or vice versa. There are two small lakes along the trail. Regulations require hikers to leave the park by 4pm in winter and around 6pm to 7pm in summer.

From the park's northern entrance at La Villa, a very steep 20-minute hike leads to two **panoramic overlooks** of Lago Nahuel Huapi.

CERRO BELVEDERE

A 4km **hiking trail** starts from Av Siete Lagos, northwest of the tourist office, and leads to an **overlook** with good views of Lago Correntoso, Nahuel Huapi and the surrounding mountains. It then continues another 3km to the 1992m summit. After visiting the overlook, retrace your steps to a nearby junction that leads to **Cascada Inayacal**, a 50m waterfall.

CENTRO DE SKI CERRO BAYO

From June to September, lifts carry skiers from the 1050m base up to 1700m at this relatively inexpensive **winter resort** (☎ 494189;

THE AUTHOR'S CHOICE

Hostería Las Balsas (☎ 494308; www.las balsas.com; d US$250; Ⓟ ⓧ) If you want to splurge on a place on Lago Nahuel Huapi, make this the one. Set on the small Las Balsas bay south of El Cruce, this 10-room *hostería* boasts stunning views and giant bay windows in a sublimely comfortable living room that make it hard to leave the building. Rates include use of the Jacuzzi, pool and gym. Not a detail is skipped. Take a taxi or call for pickup. Reservations essential in high season.

---

www.cerrobayoweb.com in Spanish; full-day pass US$13-23), 9km southeast of El Cruce via RP 66. All facilities, including rental equipment (US$6 to US$16), are available on site.

Sleeping

Except for camping and Angostura's one hostel, accommodations tend to be pricey; in summer, single rooms are almost impossible to find – expect to pay for two people. The following prices are for high season.

Hostel La Angostura (☎ 494843; www.hostella angostura.com.ar in Spanish; Barbagelata 157, El Cruce; dm US$6.50-7.50, d US$20) Along with great atmosphere, this friendly hostel boasts Ping-Pong, a pool table, pinball, darts and *meta-gol* (foosball) out in the front room. Big, comfy chairs grace the open TV area, and the rooms are small but immaculate. Each room has four to six beds and its own bathroom, and there's one double room.

Residencial Río Bonito (☎ 494110; riobonito@ ciudad.com.ar; Topa Topa 260, El Cruce; d US$15-19, s off-season only US$36) Owner friendliness way outshines the office-style carpeting, and the cleanliness kicks it into the great-value range. Though rooms are plain, there's something cheerful about the place. Great choice.

Hotel Angostura (☎ 494224, 494880; www.hotel angostura.com; Blvd Nahuel Huapi s/n, La Villa; d US$33-50, bungalows US$54-117) Built in the 1930s, this lovely hotel boasts fabulous views over the lake and has an excellent restaurant. The stairs and floors creak like mad, adding to the old-fashioned feel. Rooms are small and dated, but very cozy.

Camping Cullumche (☎ 494160; Blvd Quetrihué s/n; sites per person US$2.50-3) Well-signed from Blvd Nahuel Huapi, this secluded but large lakeside campground can get very busy in summer, but when it's quiet, it's lovely.

Also try **Camping Correntoso** (☎ 494829; Lago Correntoso; per person US$2), north of town. There are free sites along Lago Nahuel Huapi, too.

Eating

There are several restaurants and *confiterías* in El Cruce along Los Arrayanes and its cross-streets.

La Buena Vida (☎ 495200; Av Arrayanes 167, El Cruce; mains US$4-7; ☉ breakfast, lunch & dinner) Try La Buena Vida for breakfast and early-morning *churros*, or reasonably priced burgers and pastas. Delicious.

Parrilla Las Varas (☎ 494740; Av Arrayanes 235, El Cruce; parrilla US$3-5, mains US$3-6; ☉ closed Tue) Small local favorite for grilled meats and local game. Huge *bife de chorizo* and delectable venison brochettes.

La Encantada (☎ 495515; Cerro Belvedere 69, El Cruce; pizza US$4-6) Angostura's best pizza, cooked in a wood-burning stove.

Tinto Bistro (☎ 494924; Nahuel Huapi 34, El Cruce; mains US$6-8.50) Besides the fact that the food (regional cuisine prepared with European flair) is excellent, the owner, Martín Zorreguieta, is the brother of Máxima, princess of the Netherlands. Feast on that.

Gran Nevada (☎ 494512; Av Arrayanes 104, El Cruce; mains US$2-4) Very popular for cheap, whopping pasta dishes, pizzas, sandwiches and the usual grilled meats.

Getting There & Away

Villa La Angostura's **bus terminal** (junction of Av Siete Lagos & Av Arrayanes, El Cruce) is across the street from the tourist office in El Cruce. Some buses stop in El Cruce on runs between Bariloche and San Martín de los Andes.

For Chile, **Andesmar** (☎ 495217) and Via Bariloche go over Paso Cardenal Samoré to Osorno (US$14, three hours) and on to Puerto Montt (US$14, four to 4½ hours).

There are numerous daily departures to Bariloche (US$3, two hours) and two daily departures to Neuquén (US$16, seven to nine hours). Albus and Turismo Algorrobo go several times daily to San Martín de los Andes (US$2, 2½ hours) by the scenic Siete Lagos route.

Getting Around

Transportes 15 de Mayo runs hourly buses from the terminal to La Villa, up Av Siete

Lagos to Lago Correntoso, and south down Av Arrayanes to Puerto Manzano on Lago Nahuel Huapi. From July through September, and December through March, 15 de Mayo runs six or seven daily buses to the ski resort at Cerro Bayo.

Two companies run daily ferries from the dock (next to Hotel Angostura in La Villa) to the tip of Quetrihué peninsula, Parque Nacional Los Arrayanes (US$9.50 return, US$7 one-way, plus US$0.65 entry to pier, plus US$4 national park entrance), meaning you can hike the peninsula and take the boat back (or vice versa). Purchase tickets at the dock before hiking out, to secure a space on the return. Check with the tourist office for ever-changing ferry times. The ride takes 45 minutes.

BARILOCHE

☎ 02944 / pop 93,200 / elevation 770m
Once a tranquil and prestigious resort for the Argentine elite, Bariloche (formally San Carlos de Bariloche) has become, for better or worse, the Lake District's principal destination. It offers unrivaled resources for independent trekkers and climbers preparing to take to the backcountry of Parque Nacional Nahuel Huapi, as well as countless travel operators for those seeking climbing guides, fishing guides, horse rentals, rafting companies and rental equipment. The urban center of the Argentine Lake District, the city is also an important transportation hub for those heading into southern Patagonia or west to Chile.

Bariloche's proximity to the region's best ski resort makes it ground zero for the country's snow-heads and, for Argentine secondary students, it's the destination for the graduation bash. It is also the chocolate capital of Argentina, and the only thing that approaches the amount of storefront window space dedicated to fresh chocolate is the infinite number of peculiar gnomes of all sizes and demeanors sold in nearly every shop downtown.

Officially founded in 1902, the city really began to attract visitors after the southern branch of the Ferrocarril Roca train line arrived in 1934 and architect Ezequiel Bustillo adapted Central European styles into a tasteful urban plan. Bariloche is now known for its alpine architecture, which is given a

Patagonian twist through the use of local hardwoods and unique stone construction, as seen in the buildings of Bustillo's civic center.

The flip side of Bariloche's gain in popularity is uncontrolled growth: in the last two decades, the town has suffered as its quaint neighborhoods have given way to high-rise apartments and time-shares. The silver lining is that many accommodations have remained reasonably priced.

Orientation

Bariloche is 460km southwest of Neuquén via RN 237. Entering the town from the east, RN 237 becomes the Av 12 de Octubre (also called Costanera), continuing westward to the lakeside resort of Llao Llao. Southbound Calle Onelli becomes RN 258 to El Bolsón, on the border of Chubut province.

The principal commercial area is along Av Bartolomé Mitre. Do not confuse VA O'Connor (also known as Vicealmirante O'Connor or Eduardo O'Connor) with similarly named John O'Connor, which cross each other near the lakefront. Similarly, Perito Moreno and Ruiz Moreno intersect near Diagonal Capraro, at the east end of the downtown area.

Information

CONSULATES & IMMIGRATION
Chilean consulate (☎ 423050; Av Juan Manuel de Rosas 180)
Immigration office (☎ 423043; Libertad 191)

INTERNET ACCESS
El Refugio (Av Bartolomé Mitre 106, 1st fl; per hr US$0.65) Upstairs; fast connection.

LAUNDRY
Laverap Rolando (☎ 432-628; btwn Av Bartolomé Mitre & Perito Moreno; full service US$2-3); Quaglia (btwn Perito Moreno & Elflein; full service US$2-3)

MEDICAL SERVICES
Hospital (☎ 426100; Perito Moreno 601) *Long* waits, no charge.
Sanatorio San Carlos (☎ 429000/01/02, emergency ☎ 430000; Av Bustillo, Km 1; consultations US$10) Excellent medical clinic.

MONEY
Banks with ATMs are ubiquitous in the downtown area.

Cambio Sudamérica (Av Bartolomé Mitre 63) Change foreign cash and traveler's checks here.

POST
Post office (Perito Moreno 175)

TOURIST INFORMATION
ACA (☎ 423001; Av 12 de Octubre 785)
Club Andino Bariloche (☎ 424531; www.active patagonia.com.ar, www.clubandino.com.ar in Spanish; 20 de Febrero 30; ⊙ 9am-1pm & 4-8:30pm Dec-Mar, Mon-Fri only Apr-Nov) Best source of hiking information on Nahuel Huapi. For park details, see p345.
Municipal tourist office (☎ 423022, 423122; www .barilochepatagonia.info; Centro Cívico; ⊙ 8am-9pm) It has many giveaways, including useful maps and the blatantly commercial but still useful *Guía Busch*, updated annually and loaded with basic tourist information about Bariloche and its surroundings.
Nahuel Huapi national park office (Intendencia del Parque Nacional Nahuel Huapi; ☎ 423111; San Martín 24; ⊙ 8am-4pm Mon-Fri, 9am-3pm Sat & Sun)
Provincial tourist office (☎ 423188/89; secturrn@ bariloche.com.ar; cnr Av 12 de Octubre & Emilio Frey) Has information on the province, including an excellent provincial map and useful brochures in English and Spanish.

TRAVEL AGENCIES
Hiver Turismo (☎ 423792; Av Bartolomé Mitre 387) One of numerous agencies along Av Bartolomé Mitre and immediate cross-streets. Amex representative.

Sights

A stroll through Bariloche's Centro Cívico, with its beautiful log-and-stone buildings designed by architect Ezequiel Bustillo, is a must. Besides, posing for a photo with one of the barrel-toting Saint Bernards makes for a classic Argentine snapshot (if you feel like getting touristy), and views over the lake are superb. The buildings house the municipal tourist office and one of the country's best museums, the **Museo de la Patagonia** (☎ 422309; Centro Cívico; admission US$1; ⊙ 10am-12:30pm & 2-7pm Tue-Fri, 10am-1pm Mon & Sat). The last is filled with archaeological and ethnographic materials, lifelike stuffed animals and enlightening historical evaluations on such topics as Mapuche resistance to the Conquista del Desierto.

Activities

Bariloche and the Nahuel Huapi region are one of Argentina's major outdoor recreation areas, and numerous operators offer a variety of activities, particularly horseback riding,

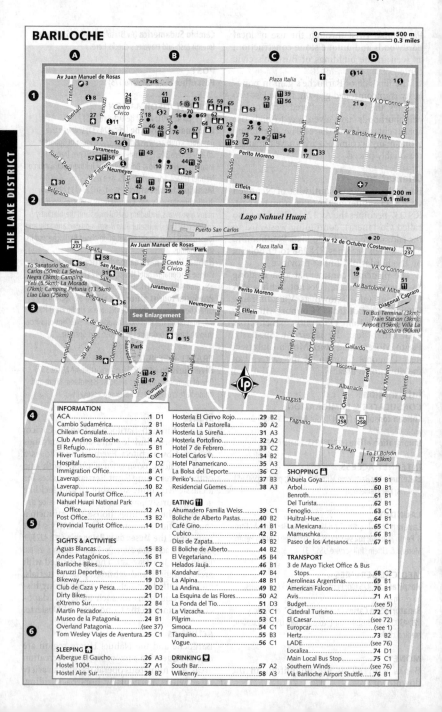

BARILOCHE

Lago Nahuel Huapi

INFORMATION
ACA	1 D1
Cambio Sudamérica	2 B1
Chilean Consulate	3 A1
Club Andino Bariloche	4 A2
El Refugio	5 B1
Hiver Turismo	6 C1
Hospital	7 D2
Immigration Office	8 A1
Laverap	9 C1
Laverap	10 B2
Municipal Tourist Office	11 A1
Nahuel Huapi National Park Office	12 A1
Post Office	13 B2
Provincial Tourist Office	14 D1

SIGHTS & ACTIVITIES
Aguas Blancas	15 B3
Andes Patagónicos	16 B1
Bariloche Bikes	17 C2
Baruzzi Deportes	18 B1
Bikeway	19 D3
Club de Caza y Pesca	20 D2
Dirty Bikes	21 D1
eXtremo Sur	22 B4
Martín Pescador	23 C1
Museo de la Patagonia	24 B1
Overland Patagonia	(see 37)
Tom Wesley Viajes de Aventura	25 C1

SLEEPING
Albergue El Gaucho	26 A3
Hostel 1004	27 A1
Hostel Aire Sur	28 B2
Hostería El Ciervo Rojo	29 B2
Hostería La Pastorella	30 A2
Hostería La Sureña	31 A3
Hostería Portofino	32 A3
Hotel 7 de Febrero	33 C2
Hotel Carlos V	34 B2
Hotel Panamericano	35 A3
La Bolsa del Deporte	36 C2
Periko's	37 B3
Residencial Güemes	38 A3

EATING
Ahumadero Familia Weiss	39 C1
Boliche de Alberto Pastas	40 B2
Café Gino	41 B1
Cubico	42 B2
Días de Zapata	43 B2
El Boliche de Alberto	44 B2
El Vegetariano	45 B4
Helados Jauja	46 B1
Kandahar	47 B4
La Alpina	48 B1
La Andina	49 B2
La Esquina de las Flores	50 A2
La Fonda del Tío	51 D3
La Vizcacha	52 C1
Pilgrim	53 C1
Simoca	54 C1
Tarquino	55 B3
Vogue	56 C1

DRINKING
South Bar	57 A2
Wilkenny	58 A3

SHOPPING
Abuela Goya	59 B1
Arbol	60 B1
Benroth	61 B1
Del Turista	62 B1
Fenoglio	63 C1
Huitral-Hue	64 B1
La Mexicana	65 C1
Mamuschka	66 B1
Paseo de los Artesanos	67 B1

TRANSPORT
3 de Mayo Ticket Office & Bus Stops	68 C2
Aerolíneas Argentinas	69 B1
American Falcon	70 B1
Avis	71 A1
Budget	(see 5)
Catedral Turismo	72 C1
El Caesar	(see 72)
Europcar	(see 1)
Hertz	73 B2
LADE	(see 76)
Localiza	74 D1
Main Local Bus Stop	75 C1
Southern Winds	(see 76)
Via Bariloche Airport Shuttle	76 B1

THE LAKE DISTRICT

mountain biking and white-water rafting. The following all have excellent reputations:

Andes Patagónicos (☎ 431777, 435561; www.andes patagonicos.com in Spanish; Av Bartolomé Mitre 125, Local 5) Agency offering all activities; representative for Tren Patagonico (p344). Offers tours down RN 40 October through April.

Overland Patagonia (☎ 461564; www.overland patagonia.com; Morales 555) Numerous trips throughout Patagonia. Also ski transfers for US$3.50 from any hotel in town. Owner of Periko's (p340).

Tom Wesley Viajes de Aventura (☎ /fax 435040; Av Bartolomé Mitre 385) Riding, mountain biking; long in the business. Also at Av Bustillo, Km 15.5.

MOUNTAINEERING & TREKKING

The national park office distributes a brochure with a simple map, adequate for initial planning, that rates hikes as easy, medium or difficult and suggests possible loops. Many of these hikes are detailed in Lonely Planet's *Trekking in the Patagonian Andes,* by Clem Lindenmayer.

The Club Andino Bariloche (p337) provides loads of information, and issues obligatory permits for trekking in Parque Nacional Nahuel Huapi. For US$3, their *Mapa General de la Guía de Sendas y Picadas* is cartographically mediocre, but has good trail descriptions and is indispensable for planning. They sell three additional trekking maps, all of which include mountain bike trails.

SKIING

Nahuel Huapi's ski resort, **Cerro Catedral** (☎ 423776), was once South America's trendiest, and has been superseded only by Las Leñas (near Mendoza) and resorts in Chile. Las Leñas has far superior snow (dry powder), but it lacks Catedral's strong point: views. There's nothing like looking over the shimmering lakes of Nahuel Huapi from its snowy slopes. What's more, you have a town to return to (unlike Las Leñas) and better prices.

If you need lessons, stop into the ski schools at Cerro Catedral or the Club Andino Bariloche (p337). For rental equipment, try Baruzzi Deportes or Martín Pescador (right). Equipment is also available on site. In addition to downhill skiing, there are also cross-country opportunities.

MOUNTAIN BIKING

Bicycles are ideal for the Circuito Chico (though this 60km loop demands endurance) and other trips near Bariloche; most roads are paved, the gravel roads are good, and Argentine drivers are less ruthless, slowing and even stopping for the scenery. Mountainbike rental, usually including gloves and helmet, costs US$5 to US$7 per day at a number of places. Try **Hostel Aire Sur** (p340), **Bariloche Bikes** (☎ 424657; Perito Moreno 520; ☺ closed Sun), **Bikeway** (☎ 424202; VA O'Connor 867) or **Dirty Bikes** (☎ 425616; VA O'Connor 681).

FISHING

Fly-fishing draws visitors from around the world to Argentina's accessible Andean-Patagonian parks, from Lago Puelo and Los Alerces in the south to Lanín in the north.

On larger lakes, such as Nahuel Huapi, trolling is the preferred method, while flyfishing is the rule on most rivers. The season runs mid-November to mid-April. For more information, contact the **Club de Caza y Pesca** (Hunting & Fishing Club; ☎ 422785; Costanera 12 de Octubre & Onelli). For rental equipment and guide hire, try **Baruzzi Deportes** (☎ 424922, 428 374; Urquiza 250) or **Martín Pescador** (☎ 422275; Rolando 257). Both offer guided fishing trips for about US$200 per day for one or two people (price is the same either way and includes all equipment, lunch, transport and guide). Fishing licenses are required and available at these shops.

HORSEBACK RIDING

Most travel agencies along Av Bartolomé Mitre offer horseback riding trips. For something special, contact the amiable Carol Jones at **Cabalgatas Carol Jones** (☎ 426508; www.caroljones .com.ar), who offers full-day horseback riding from her family *estancia* outside of town for US$35 per person. The price includes transport to/from town and an excellent *asado* outside. She also offer multi-day pack trips by horse for US$90 per person per day. Carol speaks English. All trips require a minimum of two people.

RAFTING & KAYAKING

Rafting and kayaking on the Río Limay and the Río Manso have become increasingly popular in recent years. The best time to be on the rivers is November through February, though you can raft October through Easter.

In business since 1991, **eXtremo Sur** (☎ 427 301, 524365; www.extremosur.com in Spanish; Morales 765) offers several trips on the Río Manso: the Manso Inferior (class II to III, US$37 per person) is suitable for all ages; the Manso a la Frontera (class III to IV, US$50 per person, ages 14 and up) is a fun and beautiful stretch of the river before the Chilean border. He also offers a three-day Expedición Río Manso (class III to IV, US$260 to US$317), where you camp riverside at excellent facilities. For the last, *asados* and all food and drink are included in the price.

Aguas Blancas (☎ 432799, 15-601155; www.aguas blancas.com.ar; Morales 564) also has an excellent reputation and offers similar trips. Located inside Albergue Patagonia Andina.

PARAGLIDING
The mountains around Bariloche make for spectacular paragliding. If you wish to take to the sky, it will cost you US$33 to US$44 for a tandem flight with, among others, **Luis Rosenkjer** (☎ 427588, 15-568388) or **Parapente Bariloche** (☎ 15-552403; Cerro Otto base).

Tours
Countless tourist agencies along and near Av Bartolomé Mitre, such as Catedral Turismo (p343), run minibus tours to the national park and as far south as El Bolsón. Prices range from US$5 for a half-day trip along the Circuito Chico to US$57 to San Martín de los Andes via the scenic Siete Lagos road.

Overland Patagonia (p339) offers a series of well-received camping tours; they range from the four-day Safari Siete Lagos (US$170 plus US$30 for food kitty) to the 18-day Safari del Fin del Mundo (US$1300 plus US$160 for food), which goes all the way to Tierra del Fuego. Its local tours always offer a little more kick (like hikes) than those offered by most agencies.

Festivals & Events
For ten days in August, Bariloche holds its **Fiesta Nacional de la Nieve** (National Snow Festival). In January and February, the **Festival de Música de Verano** (Summer Music Festival) puts on several different events, including the **Festival de Música de Cámara** (Chamber Music Festival), the **Festival de Bronces** (Brass Festival) and the **Festival de Música Antigua** (Ancient Music Festival). May 3 is the **Fiesta Nacional de la Rosa Mosqueta**, celebrating the fruit of the wild shrub used in many regional delicacies.

Sleeping
From camping and private houses to five-star hotels, Bariloche's abundant accommodations make it possible to find good value even in high season, when reservations are a good idea. Prices peak during ski season (July and August), drop slightly during high season (January and February) and are lowest the rest of the year. The following are high season prices.

HOSTELS & CAMPGROUNDS
Bariloche has numerous excellent hostels; all of the hostels listed here arrange excursions in Nahuel Huapi and offer weekend *asados*.

Albergue El Gaucho (☎ 522464; www.hostelel gaucho.com.ar; Belgrano 209; dm US$4.50-5.50, d with bathroom US$12; ✗ ▯) Immaculate hostel with two kitchens and two common rooms and plenty of space. Most rooms have only four beds, and there are three double rooms. The interior is slightly plain, but the rooms are comfortable.

Hostel 1004 (☎ 432228; www.lamoradahostel.com; San Martín 127, 10th fl, Bariloche Center bldg; dm US$5.50, d per person US$7) Occupying the 10th-floor penthouse of the tallest building in Bariloche, 1004 boasts *spectacular* views over Lago Nahuel Huapi from the giant living room, complete with sofas, fireplace and big wooden tables. Most of the rooms have the same views and none have more than four beds. The vibe is very mellow, and there are two communal kitchens. There's no sign; enter the Bariloche Center, take the elevator to the 10th floor, and look for room 1004.

Periko's (☎ 522326; www.perikos.com; Morales 555; dm low/high season US$5.50/6, d year-round US$15; ▯) Proof that lots can be done with little space and a bit of imagination, this cozy hostel boasts 36 beds in rooms with three to six beds each. The four doubles all have private bathrooms and the communal kitchen is huge. The owner rents bikes and operates tours throughout Patagonia (he owns Overland Patagonia, p339).

Hostel Aire Sur (☎ 522135; www.barilocheairesur .com.ar in Spanish; Elflein 158; dm US$4.50-5.50, d with shared bathroom US$12) Small, friendly, comfortable hostel with a backyard, Ping-Pong table, laundry facilities and a big kitchen.

La Bolsa del Deporte (☎ 423529; Palacios 405; dm US$3.50-5.75, d with bathroom US$14) Perks here include a climbing wall, Ping-Pong and partying. The bunks are all made of Patagonian Cypress (like the kitchen, the walls outside, and just about everything else), and the building is a work of art. Slightly cramped but friendly.

La Selva Negra (☎ 441013; Av Bustillo, Km 2.9; sites US$7) Located 3km west of town on the road to Llao Llao, this is the nearest organized camping area. It has good facilities, and you can step outside your tent to pick apples in the fall.

Other sites between Bariloche and Llao Llao include **Camping Yeti** (☎ 442073; Av Bustillo, Km 5.6; sites US$6) and **Camping Petunia** (☎ 461969; Av Bustillo, Km 13.5; sites US$6).

HOTELS & HOSTERÍAS

Hostería La Pastorella (☎ 424656; www.lodgebariloche.com/pastorella in Spanish; Belgrano 127; s low/ski/summer season US$18/37/28, d US$27/50/40; 🖳) This three-star 13-room *hostería* gives cozy a new meaning. Rooms are carpeted and have excellent beds, and the bathrooms (complete with tubs) are big. The highlight: an upstairs sauna where you can melt away that skiing chill. The comfy common room boasts a fully stocked bar. Excellent choice.

Hostería Portofino (☎ 422795; Morales 435; s/d US$10/15) The rooms here are small but spotless, with pastel-colored wallpaper and tidy bathrooms. The rooms downstairs open onto a hallway with windows overlooking a tiny interior patio. Rooms upstairs are more spacious. The breakfast room is large and bright, and the owners are lovely.

Hotel 7 de Febrero (☎ 422244; Perito Moreno 534; s/d US$12/20) Though conventional, this modest hotel is excellent value if you get an upper room with a view. Rooms all have TV and unattractive but clean office-style carpet. For the price and centrality, it's tough to beat.

Residencial Güemes (☎ 424785; Güemes 715; d low/high season US$13/17) In the quiet neighborhood of Barrio Belgrano, this owner-operated *residencial* is perfect for those seeking silence. The 10 rooms are small but immaculate with a sort of faded, '70s plainness. The huge common area with fireplace makes up for their lack of spaciousness.

Hotel Carlos V (☎ 425474, 430817; www.carlosvpatagonia.com.ar; Morales 420; s low/high season US$22/44, d US$29/57) Several readers have recommended this three-star hotel with a comfy lobby area and spacious, spotless, modern rooms with

THE LAKE DISTRICT

THE AUTHOR'S CHOICE

La Morada (☎ 442349; www.lamoradahostel.com; Cerro Otto, Km 5; dm US$6, d per person with shared/private bathroom US$7/8.50; 🖳) Set high above Bariloche on the slopes of Cerro Otto (about /km from town), La Morada is the perfect place to chill out and take in the views – which are no less than mind-altering. Dorm rooms have four beds in each, all have great views, and the common area is as welcoming as they come. Arrange for free transport at Hostel 1004 (see opposite), and shop for food before heading out. Superb.

TV and telephone. Prices include a buffet breakfast.

Hostería La Sureña (☎ 422013; www.advance.com.ar/usuarios/hosteria in Spanish; San Martín 432; s/d US$13/24) The small rooms are slightly less appealing than the building's attractive chalet style and comfy lobby-cum-breakfast area might prepare you for, but they're still very hospitable. Little touches like gold light fixtures make it all very welcoming.

Hostería El Ciervo Rojo (☎ 435241; www.elciervorojo.com in Spanish; Elflein 115; s/d US$20/27) Book in advance if you'd like to shack up at this pleasant, attractively restored *hostería*. Upstairs rooms are superior to those downstairs. The lobby is excellent.

Hotel Panamericano (☎ /fax 425846/50; www.panamericanobariloche.com; San Martín 536; r US$145-181, ste US$235-303; P ⊠ 🖳) Taking up nearly three city blocks with over-street bridges connecting the different sectors, the Panamericano is Bariloche's most luxurious hotel. It boasts a 10th-floor swimming pool with an attached health spa and Bariloche's only casino. Rooms are everything you'd hope for in a five-star hotel.

Eating

Bariloche has some of Argentina's best food, and it would take several wallet-breaking, belt-bursting and intestinally challenging weeks to sample all of the worthwhile restaurants. Regional specialties, including cordero (lamb, cooked over an open flame), jabalí (wild boar), ciervo (venison) and trucha (trout), are especially worth trying. Note that most formal restaurants (where reservations are advisable on weekends)

THE AUTHOR'S CHOICE

La Fonda del Tio (☎ 435011; Av Bartolome Mitre 1130; mains US$2-4, set lunch US$2.50) You won't find student crowds or primped ski bunnies at this modest local favorite, which whips out massive portions of hearty food for a very local crowd. A must if you're on a budget or feeling tired of the tourist scene.

---

collect a *cubierto* (cover charge) for bread and cutlery.

Tarquino (☎ 421601; 24 de Septiembre & Saavedra; mains US$4-6) Built entirely of Patagonian cypress, this esteemed restaurant resembles a hobbit house with its wood stairway, carved wooden doorway, fireplace and troll-like architecture. The Small menu is almost entirely *parrillada* (including a delicious cordero), though a pasta and a trout dish grace the menu as well. One of Bariloche's best.

El Boliche de Alberto (☎ 431433; Villegas 347; mains US$4-7) It's worth dining at this esteemed *parrilla* simply to see the astonished look on tourists' faces when a slab of beef the size of a football lands on the table; it's the US$10 *bife de chorizo* (the US$6 portion is plenty). Service is abrupt, but the meat is an experience.

Boliche de Alberto Pastas (☎ 431084; Elflein 163; mains US$4-7) Alberto does pastas as good as his beef, and he follows suit with huge portions.

Vogue (☎ 431343; Palacios 156; mains US$3-5) This popular, homespun little eatery serves up delicious pizzas (US$3.50 to US$7), calzones for two (US$4 to US$7), creative salads (US$2.50 to US$3.50), good empanadas (US$0.50) and straightforward but tasty pastas.

Cubico (☎ 15-522260; Elflein 47; mains US$4-7; ❤ from 6pm) Minimalism blends with snobbishness at this chic restaurant and bar with a menu of Patagonian dishes prepared with a Mediterranean flair. Live music on weekend nights. Popular; reader recommended.

La Andina (☎ 423017; Elflein 95; mains US$2-3) This delightfully friendly eatery, where the owner seems to know everyone, serves cheap pastas and pizzas, savory empanadas and a filling US$2 plate of the day.

Ahumadero Familia Weiss (☎ 435789; cnr Palacios & VA O'Connor; mains US$3-6) Specializing in smoked game and fish (as well as architectural extremism), Familia Weiss is a local favorite with live music on weekend nights.

El Vegetariano (☎ 421820; 20 de Febrero 730; 3-course set lunches & dinners US$3.50, mains US$2.50-4) This cozy vegetarian restaurant serves sublime set lunches and dinners, including tea.

La Esquina de las Flores (20 de Febrero 313; ❤ closed Sun) Excellent vegetarian restaurant and natural-foods market.

Kandahar (☎ 424702; 20 de Febrero 698; mains US$4-8) Another excellent choice for gourmet local specialties and intimate atmosphere. Salmon and trout dishes, cordero and other local meats. Spot it by the ski sign out front.

Simoca (☎ 426467; Palacios 264; mains US$2-3) If you can't make it to Tucumán for a bowl of *locro* (a hearty maize and tripe stew), you can get a delicious serving here for US$3. The empanadas (US$0.50 each) are truly divine (and according to everyone, the best in town).

Días de Zapata (☎ 423128; Morales 362; mains US$3-7) The owners are from Mexico's Distrito Federal, so it's not surprising they turn out good Mexican food, including three varieties of knockout fajitas.

Pilgrim (☎ 421686; Palacios 167; mains US$2.50-4) This self-proclaimed 'Celtic pub' serves Irish mains, Spanish tapas and a smattering of regional dishes. The local microbrews and imported ales are particularly appealing. Try the Cervezería Blest brews.

La Vizcacha (☎ 422109; Rolando 279; mains US$3-7) This excellent *parrilla* offers pleasant atmosphere and outstanding service.

La Alpina (☎ 425693; Perito Moreno 98; mains US$10-15; ❤ 10am-midnight) Very homey and good for coffee, tea, sweets and, surprisingly, *mate*, which is seldom found on restaurant menus.

Helados Jauja (Perito Moreno 14; ice cream US$0.50-1) Ask anyone in town who serves the best ice cream in Bariloche and they'll reply with one word: 'Jauja.' Many say it's the best in the country.

Café Gino (☎ 423446; Av Bartolomé Mitre 86; light meals US$1-2; ❤ closed Sun) Long-standing café, good for sandwiches and coffee. Cheap, small and totally unpretentious.

Drinking

Wilkenny (☎ 424444; San Martín 435; ❤ restaurant 11am-1am, bar until 6am) Bariloche's latest bar craze gets packed on weekends though it's open nightly with live music on Tuesday and Thursday nights. Get there early if you want to snag one of the comfy wooden booths (and bring your best pickup line).

Pilgrim (☎ 421686; Palacios 167) This pub (opposite) is a good place to knock back a few beers in a friendly atmosphere. Try the Cervezería Blest brews on tap.

South Bar (cnr Juramento & 20 de Febrero) Mellow local pub where you can actually have a conversation while you drink your beer. Darts too.

Shopping
CHOCOLATE
Bariloche is renowned for its chocolates, and dozens of stores downtown, from national chains to mom-and-pop shops, sell chocolates of every style imaginable. Quality of course varies, so don't get sick on the cheap stuff.

Mamuschka (☎ 423294; Av Bartolomé Mitre 216) Quite simply, the best chocolate in town. Don't skip it. Seriously.

Benroth (☎ 424491; Mitre 150) In our humble opinion, the best one after Mamuschka. Definitely try it.

La Mexicana (☎ 422505; Mitre 288) Bariloche's first chocolate store, started by the Ritter family in 1948, still produces delicious chocolates and fine *dulces* (jams). It's still owned by the same family, though the chocolate is no longer imported from Mexico (as it was when 'Oma' started the business), but from Ecuador and Brazil.

Abuela Goya (☎ 433861; Av Bartolomé Mitre 248) Another of Bariloche's longtime chocolate makers. Still small and still worth trying.

The next two listings are Bariloche institutions, and, while their giant stores are fun for the eyes, the chocolates are generally disappointing. But try for yourself.

Del Turista (☎ 420082; Av Bartolomé Mitre 239) This is a virtual supermarket of chocolate and a good place for ice cream, if you can take, as one reader put it, the 'weirdo 1970s yellow-brown a la Brady Bunch decor.'

Fenoglio (☎ 423119; Av Bartolomé Mitre & Rolando) Spot it by the giant *duendes* (gnomes) outside the door.

CLOTHING & CRAFTS
Arbol (☎ 423032; Av Bartolomé Mitre 263; ☼ closed Sun) For the latest in high Patagonian fashion (we

kid you not), drop by this Bariloche original, which produces beautifully designed fleeces, woolens, hats and jackets, as well as ceramics and decorative pieces. It has some beautiful clothing, especially for women.

Huitral-Hue (☎ 426760; Villegas 250; ☼ closed Sun) Good selection of traditional ponchos, textiles and wool sweaters.

Paseo de los Artesanos (Villegas & Perito Moreno) Local craftspeople display wares of wool, wood, leather, silver and other media here.

Getting There & Away
AIR
Aerolíneas Argentinas (☎ 422425; Av Bartolomé Mitre 185) has flights to Buenos Aires (US$200) twice daily Monday through Wednesday and three times daily the rest of the week. In high season there are direct weekly flights to Córdoba and El Calafate and possibly Ushuaia.

LADE (☎ 423562; Quaglia 238/242, Via Firenze center) flies at least once a week to Mar del Plata (US$100 to US$130), Neuquén (US$47), San Martín de los Andes (US$20), Zapala (US$30), El Bolsón (US$20), Esquel (US$30), Comodoro Rivadavia (US$56), Puerto Madryn (US$50) and Buenos Aires (US$100).

October to April, **Southern Winds** (☎ 423704; Quaglia 238/242, Via Firenze center) flies Sunday to El Calafate (US$140) and daily to Buenos Aires with connections throughout the country.

American Falcon (☎ 542944; Av Bartolomé Mitre 159) also flies weekly to Buenos Aires and offers similar (sometimes better) fares.

BOAT
Catedral Turismo (☎ 427143/44, 425444; catturventas@speedy.com.ar; www.crucedelagos.cl; Palacios 263) is the representative for the Cruce de Lagos, the scenic bus and boat combination traveling over the Andes to Puerto Montt, Chile (US$150, 12 hours). From Bariloche the journey begins around 9am (departure times vary) with a shuttle from Catedral's office to Puerto Pañuelo near Hotel Llao Llao. The passenger ferry from Puerto Pañuelo leaves immediately after the shuttle arrives, so if you want to have tea at Llao Llao, get there ahead of time on your own (but make sure you bought your ticket in advance). Service is daily in the summer and weekdays the rest of the year. In winter (mid-April to September), the trip takes two days, and passengers are required

THE LAKE DISTRICT

to stay the night in Peulla, Chile, where the only hotel will cost you an additional US$150 to US$179. You may be able to stay at Hotel Puerto Blest (www.hotelpuertoblest .com.ar in Spanish), which, at US$105, is a bit cheaper; ask about this option at Catedral Turismo. If you just visit Puerto Blest (boats leave from Puerto Pañuelo) and are not overnighting as part of the two-day lake crossing, the hotel charges US$42; essentially the price is higher for those who are taking the full lake-crossing.

Fruits and vegetables are not allowed into Chile. Bicycles are allowed on the boats, but not on the buses, so cyclists will have to ride the stretches between Bariloche and Pañuelo (25km), Puerto Blest and Puerto Alegre (15km), Puerto Frías and Peulla (27km), and Petrohué and Puerto Montt (76km); the tourist office may have info about alternative transport between Petrohué and Puerto Montt for cyclists hoping to avoid the ride.

It is no longer possible to purchase segments of the trip (except that between Puerto Pañuelo and Puerto Blest; US$23), but if you're cycling, Catedral Turismo will cut your rate slightly since you won't be riding the buses. Though the trip rarely sells out, it's best to book it at least a day or two in advance.

BUS

Bariloche's **bus terminal** (☎ 426999) and train station are located across the Río Ñireco on RN 237. Shop around for the best deals, since fares vary and there are frequent promotions. During high season, it's wise to buy tickets at least a day in advance. The bus terminal tourist office is helpful.

The principal route to Chile is over the Cardenal A Samoré (Puyehue) pass to Osorno (US$12, 4½ hours) and Puerto Montt (US$14, six to eight hours), which has onward connections to northern and southern Chilean destinations. Several companies make the run.

For northern destinations such as San Juan, La Rioja, Catamarca, Tucumán, Jujuy and Salta you must go to Mendoza. Buses to northeastern destinations usually connect through Buenos Aires, though you could also head to Rosario where there are frequent services northeast.

To San Martín de los Andes and Junín de los Andes, Albus, KoKo and **Turismo Algar-**

robal (☎ 427698) take the scenic (though often chokingly dusty) Siete Lagos route (RN 234; see p329), rather than the longer, paved La Rinconada (RN 40) route.

There are daily departures to the destinations in the following table. Regional destinations are served several times a day.

Destination	Cost (US$)	Duration (hr)
Bahía Blanca	32	12-14
Buenos Aires	27-35	20-23
Comodoro Rivadavia	24	14
Córdoba	25-37	22
El Bolsón	4	2
Esquel	6	4
Junín de los Andes	6	4
Mar del Plata	44	18-20
Mendoza	27	19
Neuquén	9-10	6
Puerto Madryn	27	14-18
Río Gallegos	30-37	28
Rosario	43	23-24
San Martín de los Andes	8	4½
San Rafael	25	17
Trelew	28	13-19
Viedma	20	16
Villa La Angostura	3	2

TRAIN

The **Tren Patagonico** (www.trenpatagonico.com.ar in Spanish) leaves the **train station** (RN 237), across the Río Ñireco next to the bus terminal. Departures for Viedma (16 hours) are Thursday and Sunday at 6pm; fares are US$9.50 *turista*, US$20 Pullman and US$37 *camarote* (1st-class sleeper). Departure times change frequently so it's best to check with the tourist office beforehand. Tickets can also be purchased at Andes Patagonico (p339).

Getting Around
TO/FROM THE AIRPORT

Bariloche's **airport** (☎ 422767) is 15km east of town via RN 237 and RP 80. **Via Bariloche** (☎ 429012; Quaglia 238/242, Via Firenze center) shuttles connect the airport with town (US$1.75, 15 minutes). Buses leave every hour to the airport, starting at 9:30am, from in front of the airline offices at Quaglia 242. A *remise* (taxi) costs about US$10.

BUS

At the main local bus stop, on Perito Moreno between Rolando and Palacios, Codao del Sur and Ómnibus 3 de Mayo run hourly buses to Cerro Catedral for US$0.80 one-way. Codao uses Av de los Pioneros, while 3 de Mayo takes Av Bustillo. Some bus fares are cheaper when bought inside the **3 de Mayo ticket office** (☎ 425648; Perito Moreno 480), where you can also pick up handy *horarios* (schedules) for all destinations.

From 6am to midnight, municipal bus No 20 leaves the main bus stop every 20 minutes for the attractive lakeside settlements of Llao Llao and Puerto Pañuelo (US$1, 40 minutes). Bus No 10 goes to Colonia Suiza (US$1, 50 minutes) 14 times daily. During summer, three of these, at 8:05am, noon and 5:40pm, continue to Puerto Pañuelo, allowing you to do most of the Circuito Chico (p346) using inexpensive public transport. Departure times from Puerto Pañuelo back to Bariloche via Colonia Suiza are 9:40am, 1:40pm and 6:40pm. You can also walk any section and flag down buses en route.

Ómnibus 3 de Mayo buses No 50 and 51 go to Lago Gutiérrez (US$2) every 30 minutes, while in summer the company's 'Línea Mascardi' goes to Villa Mascardi/Los Rápidos (US$1.75) three times daily. Ómnibus 3 de Mayo's 'Línea El Manso' goes twice Friday to Río Villegas and El Manso (US$3), on the southwestern border of Parque Nacional Nahuel Huapi.

Buses No 70, 71 and 83 stop at the main bus stop, connecting downtown with the bus terminal (US$0.35).

CAR

Bariloche is loaded with the standard car-rental agencies and is one of the cheapest places to rent in the country. Approximate prices following are for economy cars, and pricier options are available.

Avis (☎ 431648; San Martín 130) US$41 per day with 200km.

Budget (☎ 422482; budget.rentacar@bariloche.com.ar; Av Bartolomé Mitre 106, 1st fl) US$35 per day with 200km.

Catedral Rent-a-Car (☎ 441488, 15-633607; www .autoscatedral.com.ar in Spanish) US$29 per day with 150km; call for car.

El Caesar (☎ 426561, 15-551400; www.rentacarelcesar .com.ar in Spanish; Palacios 236) US$45 per day with 200km; located inside Catedral Turismo (p343).

Europcar (☎ 422611, 423000; Av 12 de Octubre 785) At ACA (p337).

Hertz (☎ 423457; Quaglia 352) US$41 per day with 200km.

Localiza (☎ 435374; cnr Emilio Frey & VA O'Connor) US$48 per day with 300km.

HITCHHIKING

It's easy to hitch along Av Bustillo as far as Km 8, after which traffic thins out and catching a lift means waiting longer. In summer, it's usually not to difficult to get around the Circuito Chico by thumb.

TAXI

A taxi from the bus terminal to the center of town costs around US$1.75. Taxis within town generally don't go over the US$1 mark.

PARQUE NACIONAL NAHUEL HUAPI
☎ 02944

One of Argentina's most visited national parks, Nahuel Huapi occupies 750,000 hectares in mountainous southwestern Neuquén and western Río Negro provinces. The park's centerpiece is Lago Nahuel Huapi, a glacial remnant over 100km long that covers more than 500 sq km. The lake is the source of the Río Limay, a major tributary of the Río Negro. To the west, a ridge of high peaks separates Argentina from Chile; the tallest is 3554m Monte Tronador, an extinct volcano that still lives up to its name (meaning 'Thunderer') when blocks of ice tumble from its glaciers. During the summer months, wildflowers blanket the alpine meadows.

Nahuel Huapi was created to preserve local flora and fauna, including its Andean-Patagonian forests and rare animals. Tree species are much the same as those found in Parque Nacional Los Alerces (p398), while the important animal species include the huemul (Andean deer) and the miniature deer known as pudú. Most visitors are unlikely to see either of these, but several species of introduced deer are common, as are native birds. Native and introduced fish species offer excellent sport.

A good source of information about the park is the national park office in Bariloche (see p337).

Books

For trekking maps and information about hiking in the region, see Lonely Planet's *Trekking in the Patagonian Andes,* by Clem Lindenmayer or, if you read Spanish, the locally published *Las Montañas de Bariloche,* by Toncek Arko and Raúl Izaguirre.

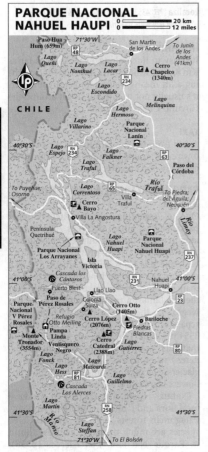

Circuito Chico

One of the area's most popular and scenic driving excursions, the Circuito Chico begins on Av Bustillo, on Bariloche's outskirts, and continues to the tranquil resort of **Llao Llao**, named for the 'Indian bread' fungus from the coihue tree. At **Cerro Campanario** (Av Bustillo, Km 18), the **Aerosilla Campanario** (☎ 427274) lifts passengers to a panoramic view of Lago Nahuel Huapi for US$5.

Llao Llao's **Puerto Pañuelo** is the point of departure for the boat and bus excursion across the Andes to Chile, as well as to Parque Nacional Los Arrayanes on Península Quetrihué, though you can visit Los Arrayanes more easily and cheaply from Villa La Angostura (p334).

Even if you don't plan to spend a night in the state-built **Hotel Llao Llao** (☎ 448530; fax 445781; d from US$320, d with lake views from US$423, studios US$498, cabañas US$650), Argentina's most famous hotel, take a stroll around the grounds. From Llao Llao you can double back to **Colonia Suiza**, named for its early Swiss colonists. A modest *confitería* has excellent pastries, and there are several campgrounds.

The road passes the trailhead to 2076m **Cerro López**, a three-hour climb, before returning to Bariloche. At the top of Cerro López it's possible to spend the night at Club Andino Bariloche's **Refugio López** (in Bariloche for reservations ☎ 442484, 15-580321; dm about US$3; ☒ mid-Dec–mid-Apr), where meals are also available.

Although travel agencies offer the Circuito Chico as a tour (US$13 through most agencies in Bariloche), it's easily done on public transportation or, if you're up for a 60km pedal, by bicycle (p339).

Cerro Otto

Cerro Otto (altitude 1405m) is an 8km hike on a gravel road west from Bariloche. There's enough traffic that hitching is feasible, and it's also a steep and tiring but rewarding bicycle route. The **Teleférico Cerro Otto** (☎ 441035; Av de Los Pioneros, Km 5) carries adult passengers to the summit for US$5, children for US$3.50; a free bus leaves from the corner of Av Bartolomé Mitre and Villegas or Perito Moreno and Independencia to the base of the mountain. Bring food and drink – prices at the summit *confitería* are truly extortionate.

Piedras Blancas (☎ 425720, ext 1708; Cerro Otto, Km 6) is the nearest ski area to Bariloche, and a popular area for summertime hiking.

There's a trail from Piedras Blancas to Club Andino's **Refugio Berghof** (☎ 522985, 15-559354), at an elevation of 1240m; make reservations, since there are only 20 beds. Meals are available here. The *refugio* also contains the **Museo de Montaña Otto Meiling** (guided visit US$1.50), named for a pioneering climber.

Cerro Catedral

This 2388m peak, 20km southwest of Bariloche, is the area's most important snow-sport center, open from mid-June to mid-October. Several chairlifts and the **Aerosilla Cerro Bellavista** (US$16) carry passengers up to 2000m, where there's a restaurant/*confitería* offering excellent panoramas.

There is a good mix of easy, intermediate and advanced skiing runs, with steep advanced runs at the top and some tree runs near the base. Lift lines can develop at this very popular resort, but the capacity is substantial enough that waits are not excessive.

The rates for lift passes vary from low to mid to high season, starting at US$16 and going up to US$27 per day for adults, US$12 to US$22 for children. One-week passes cost US$85 to US$147 for adults, and US$68 to US$119 for children. Basic rental equipment is cheap, but quality gear is more expensive. There are several on-site ski schools.

The Aerosilla Lynch also takes passengers up the mountain (adults US$9, children US$6) during summer, from 10am to 5pm daily except Monday. Several trekking trails begin near the top of the lift: one relatively easy four-hour walk goes to Club Andino's **Refugio Emilio Frey** (☎ 525248, 15-557718), where 40 beds and simple meals are available. This *refugio* itself is exposed, but there are sheltered tent sites in what is also Argentina's prime **rock-climbing** area.

Hostería Knapp (☎ 460021; www.hosteria-knapp .com.ar in Spanish; per person US$25) is at the base of the lifts. Alternatively you can stay in Bariloche; public transport from there is excellent, consisting of hourly buses from downtown with Ómnibus 3 de Mayo (p344).

Monte Tronador & Pampa Linda

Traveling via Lago Mascardi, it's a full-day trip up a dusty, single-lane dirt road to Pampa Linda to visit the **Ventisquero Negro** (Black Glacier) and the base of Tronador (3554m).

The area around Tronador resembles, in some ways, California's Yosemite Valley – you have to set your sights above the hotels, *confiterías* and parking lots to focus on the dozens of waterfalls that plunge over the flanks of the extinct volcanoes.

From Pampa Linda – the starting point for several excellent hikes – hikers can approach the snow-line Club Andino **Refugio Otto Meiling** (☎ 15-505123, 15-601701; dm US$5; meals US$5-8.50, kitchen use US$2.50) on foot (about four to six hours' hiking time) and continue to Laguna Frías via the **Paso de las Nubes**; it's a five- to seven-hour walk to an elevation of 2000m. It's also possible to complete the trip in the opposite direction by taking Cerro Catedral's ferry from Puerto Pañuelo

to Puerto Blest, and then hiking up the Río Frías to Paso de las Nubes before descending to Pampa Linda via the Río Alerce. The *refugio* itself prepares delicious meals and is well-stocked with good wine and beer. You can hire a guide at the *refugio* to take you on a number of excursions, which range from a three-hour hike to a nearby glacier to the multi-day ascent of Cumbre Argentina on Tronador.

Climbers intending to scale Tronador should anticipate a three- to four-day technical climb requiring experience on rock, snow and ice. Hostería Pampa Linda (below) arranges horseback riding in the area.

The road to Pampa Linda passes **Los Rápidos**, after which it becomes extremely narrow. Traffic is therefore allowed up to Pampa Linda until 2pm. At 4pm cars are allowed to leave Pampa Linda for the return. For US$5 each way, the Club Andino Bariloche has summer transport (end of November to April) to Pampa Linda daily at 8:30am and 10am, returning around 5pm, with **Expreso Meiling** (☎ 529875). Buses depart from in front of the Club Andino, and the 90km ride takes about 2½ hours. Park entry fees (US$4) must be paid en route at the ranger station at Villa Mascardi (the bus stops so you can do this).

Sleeping

In addition to those campgrounds in the immediate Bariloche area, there are sites at Lago Gutiérrez, Lago Mascardi, Lago Guillelmo, Lago Los Moscos, Lago Roca and Pampa Linda. *Refugios* charge US$2 to US$5 per night, about US$0.65 for day use, and sometimes about US$1 extra for kitchen privileges. *Refugios* are open from December to the end of April.

Within the park are a number of hotels tending to the luxurious, though there is also the moderately priced **Hostería Pampa Linda** (☎ 490517; www.tronador.com in Spanish; s/d US$28/42, with half-pension US$35/56). For a real treat, stay at the secluded **Hotel Tronador** (☎ 441062; www .hotel-tronador.com; s/d US$52/61; Nov–mid-Apr), at the northwest end of Lago Mascardi on the Pampa Linda road.

Getting There & Around

See p344 for transport information from Bariloche. For road conditions in and around the national parks, call **Parque Nacional Estado de Rutas** (☎ 105) toll-free from any telephone.

EL BOLSÓN

☎ 02944 / pop 20,000 / elevation 300m

The 42nd parallel defines the border between Río Negro and Chubut provinces and lends its name, Grado 42, to the mountains and fertile valley that surround El Bolsón, a laid-back little town synonymous with the pony-tailed back-to-nature folks who began to flock here in the 1970s. Since then, El Bolsón became the first town in Argentina to declare itself a 'non-nuclear zone' and an 'ecological municipality.' The town welcomes backpackers, who often find it a relief from Bariloche's commercialism and find themselves stuffing their bellies with natural and vegetarian foods and the excellent beer, sweets, jams and honey made from the local harvest.

Rows of poplars lend a Mediterranean appearance to the local *chacras* (farms), most of which are devoted to hops (El Bolsón produces nearly three-quarters of the country's hops) and fruits.

Motorists should note that El Bolsón is the northernmost spot to purchase gasoline at Patagonian discount prices.

Orientation

Near the southwestern border of Río Negro province, El Bolsón lies in a basin surrounded by high mountains, dominated by the longitudinal ridges of Cerro Piltriquitrón to the east and the Cordón Nevado along the Chilean border to the west. On the east bank of the Río Quemquemtreu, it is roughly midway between Bariloche and Esquel, each about 130km via RN 258 from Bolsón.

From the south, RN 258 enters town as Av Belgrano and becomes north–south Av San Martín through town. The principal landmark is the ovoid Plaza Pagano. Most services are nearby.

Information

ACA (☎ 492260; cnr Belgrano & Av San Martín) Automobile club.

Banco de la Nación (Av San Martín & Pellegrini) Has an ATM.

Club Andino Piltriquitrón (☎ 492600; Sarmiento, btwn Roca & Feliciano; ⏱ Dec-Mar only) Visitors interested in exploring the surrounding mountains can contact this office. Occasionally open 6pm to 8pm off season.

La Burbuja (☎ 15-639241; Paso 425; wash & dry US$2.50; ⏱ closed Sun) Laundry service.

Patagonia Adventure (☎ 492513; Pablo Hube 418) Travel agency.

Post office (Av San Martín 2806)

Rancho Net (Av San Martín at Av Belgrano; per hr US$0.65) Internet access.

Tourist office (☎ 492604, 455336; www.bolsonturistico .com.ar in Spanish; Av San Martín & Roca; ⏱ 9am-9pm, summer until 10pm) At the north end of Plaza Pagano. It has a good town map and brochures, plus thorough information on accommodations, food, tours and services. Maps of the surrounding area are crude but helpful. Superb staff.

Sights
FERIA ARTESANAL

Tuesday, Thursday and Saturday, local craftspeople sell their wares along the south end of Plaza Pagano from 10:00am to 4pm. The market boasts over 320 registered (and countless unregistered) artists, who make and sell everything from sculpted wooden cutting boards and handcrafted *mate* gourds to jewelry, flutes and marionettes. With numerous food vendors, it's also an excellent opportunity to sample local delicacies. On sunny Sundays the *feria* operates about half-tilt.

Tours

Grado 42 (☎ 493124; www.grado42.com in Spanish; Belgrano 406) offers extensive trekking, mountain biking and other tours around El Bolsón, as does **Maputur** (☎ 491440; Perito Moreno 2331).

Both also offer rafting on the Río Manso. Trips on the Manso Inferior (class II to III) cost US$24 per person (including lunch); on the Manso a la Frontera (class II to IV) trips cost US$40 (including lunch and dinner).

Festivals & Events

Local beer gets headlines during the **Festival Nacional del Lúpulo** (National Hops Festival), which takes place during four days in mid-February. El Bolsón also hosts a weekend **jazz festival** (www.elbolsonjazz.com.ar in Spanish) in December; dates vary.

Sleeping
BUDGET

Budget travelers are more than welcome in El Bolsón, where reasonable prices are the rule rather than the exception. The tourist office maintains a list of private houses that offer lodging.

Hostería Steiner (☎ 492224; Av San Martín 670; r with shared bathroom US$3.50-4, s/d with bathroom US$7/12) On the southern outskirts of town, Hostería Steiner sits on a beautiful, tree-filled lot with an expansive lawn and plenty of flowers. The newer rooms are motel-style with views of the garden, while those in the main building are more traditional. Breakfast and dinner are available.

Casa del Viajero Agustin Porro (☎ 493092; aporro@ elbolson.com.ar; www.lacasadelviajero.com; Libertad y Las Flores, Barrio Usina; per person US$4) For a taste of real El Bolsón, stay with amiable Agustin Porro, who has a tiny, rustic wooden house on his plot of land near the river, about eight blocks from town. The place is shared, hostel-style, and is definitely simple, but it's very homey. Call Agustin and he'll pick you up.

Albergue El Pueblito (☎ 493560; pueblito@hostels .org.ar; dm HI members/nonmembers US$4/3.50, d US$12/ 10) This HI affiliate, about 4km north of town in Barrio Luján, is a friendly facility with beds for 40 people and places to camp as well.

Residencial Salinas (☎ 492396; Roca 641; r per person with shared bathroom US$4-5) Small, basic, friendly and very central. The upstairs room is welcoming (but cold in winter). There's a communal stove and washbasin, and a small backyard.

Hotel Amancay (☎ /fax 492222; amancay@red42 .com.ar; Av San Martín 3217; s/d with bathroom US$15/22) This recently remodeled hotel is clean, comfy and conventional and definitely feels classy for El Bolsón.

Residencial Valle Nuevo (☎ 492087; 25 de Mayo 2329; d US$17) The rooms here do the trick, and some have kitchens.

Hotel Cordillera (☎ /fax 492235; cordillerahotel@ elbolson.com; Av San Martín 3210; s/d US$20/30) This three-star property is the biggest in town, with spacious rooms and good views from the upper floor.

Camping Refugio Patagónico (☎ 15-635463; Islas Malvinas s/n; sites per person US$1.75, d high season US$4) On the southeast end of Islas Malvinas, this pleasant campground is only a skip from town. Shade is minimal, but the apple trees and a nearby mountain make it a lovely spot. Showers are included.

Camping La Chacra (☎ 492111; per person US$2) Off Av Belgrano on the eastern edge of town, this campground is grassy and partially shaded.

Eating

El Bolsón's restaurants lack Bariloche's variety, but food is consistently good value and often outstanding, thanks to fresh, local ingredients and careful preparation. Trucha arco iris (rainbow trout) is the local specialty.

THE AUTHOR'S CHOICE

La Posada de Hamelin (☎ 492030; gcap ece@elbolson.com; Granollers 2179; s/d US$18/25) This handsome *hostería* has only four rooms, each of them delightfully cozy and with a private bathroom, big windows, and heaps of nooks and crannies. White stone walls, lots of wood, arched doorways, and a tiny breakfast area make for truly homey atmosphere. English and German spoken.

The Feria Artesanal (opposite) is by far the best, most economical place to eat. Goodies here include fresh fruit, Belgian waffles with berries and cream, huge empanadas for US$0.50, sandwiches, frittatas, *milanesa de soja* (soy patties), locally brewed beer and regional desserts.

Calabaza (☎ 492910; Av San Martín 2518; mains US$2-9; ☽ breakfast, lunch & dinner) Breakfast at Calabaza, which starts around US$0.50, is particularly delicious, though they do a good *plato del día* (daily special). There are vegetarian options, as well as trout, empanadas, pizza and regional *tablas* sampler plates for two (US$7 to US$9).

La Tosca (☎ 493669; light meals US$2-3) Behind the tourist office at Roca and Moreno, La Tosca offers typical café fare in a pleasant atmosphere – outside tables, too.

Cerro Lindo (☎ 492899; Av San Martín 2524; mains US$5-7) Serves some of El Bolsón's best traditional Patagonian fare – such as cordero (lamb), conejo (rabbit), ciervo (venison) and trucha (trout) – as well as large, tasty pizzas. Good music, reasonable prices and excellent service.

La Cocina (☎ 491453; Sarmiento 2434; mains US$2-3) Locals recommend this *parrilla* for cheap and tasty home cooking.

Las Brasas (☎ 492923; Sarmiento & Hube; US$2-4) Las Brasas is a superb choice for beef, with excellent service.

La Salteñita (☎ 493749; 25 de Mayo 2367; meals US$1-2) For spicy northern empanadas, try this cheap rotisserie.

Verde Menta (☎ 493576; Av San Martín 2137) This health-food store stocks a reasonable selection of whole foods, grains, dried fruits and herbs.

Cervecería El Bolsón (☎ 492595; RN 258, Km 123.9; mains US$2-4) The local brewery, 2km south of town just past the service station, has nine house brews on tap which will help chase down a variety of meals, including trout, pizza and sandwiches.

Jauja (☎ 492448; Av San Martín 2867; mains US$3-5) Jauja's ingredients are first-rate, the preparation is excellent, the decor appealing, and the service agreeable. Its extensive menu includes pasta with tasty sauces, pizza, fish, vegetarian plates, homemade bread and locally brewed beer. Save room to gorge yourself on the astoundingly good homemade ice cream (US$1 to US$2) next door at Helardería Jauja, one of Argentina's very best.

Shopping

El Bolsón is a craft hunter's paradise. Besides the twice-weekly **Feria Artesanal**, there are several other outlets for local arts and crafts.

Centro Artesanal Cumey Antú (☎ 15-412614; Av San Martín 2020) This outlet sells high-quality Mapuche clothing and weavings.

Central Artesanal Brillante Sol (☎ 15-412614; San Martín 1920) Cooperative of 25 Mapuche women who spin and weave their woolen textiles on wooden looms in back and sell the products in front.

Monte Viejo (☎ 491735; Pablo Hube at Av San Martín) High quality ceramics, wood crafts, silver, knives and Mapuche textiles.

Centro Artesanal El Bolsón (☎ 491150; Av San Martín 1059) Artist cooperative with a huge variety of high quality crafts.

Cabaña Micó (☎ 492691; Isla Malvinas 2753) For fresh fruit and homemade jams and preserves, visit these berry plantations.

Entertainment

Morena Café/Bristó (☎ 455353; Av San Martín & Pablo Hube) Friendly café-cum-bar which sometimes has live music.

Bar 442 (☎ 492313; Perito Moreno & Dorrego) This venue doubles as a disco on Friday nights and often has live music on Saturday nights.

Oveja Negra (Av San Martín 1997) Laid-back pub with friendly atmosphere.

Centro Cultural Eduardo Galeano (☎ 491503; cnr Dorrego & Onelli; admission varies) Small performance space featuring local (and sometimes international) theater, music and dance. Stop by for a program or ask around town.

Getting There & Away

AIR

LADE (☎ 492206; Perito Moreno at Plaza Pagano) flies Thursday to Bariloche (US$15), Buenos Aires

(US$100) and San Martín de los Andes (US$20); and Tuesday to Comodoro Rivadavia (US$30) and Esquel (US$15). All flights leave from El Bolsón's small **airport** (☎ 492066) at the north end of Av San Martín.

BUS

El Bolsón has no central bus terminal, but most companies are on or near Av San Martín.

Andesmar (☎ 492178; Belgrano & Perito Moreno) goes to Bariloche (US$4, two hours) and Esquel (US$2.75, two to three hours), and to points north of there, usually with a change in Neuquén (US$14, nine hours).

Via Bariloche/El Valle (☎ 455554; Roca 357) goes several times a day to Bariloche and Esquel and at least once a day to Buenos Aires. Transportes Esquel, at the same address, goes to Esquel on Tuesday and Friday at 8:30am.

TAC, represented by **Grado 42** (☎ 493124; Belgrano 406), goes to Bariloche and Neuquén; the company sells tickets to Mendoza, Córdoba and other northern destinations, though you'll have to change buses in Neuquén.

Don Otto (☎ 493910; cnr Belgrano & Güemes) goes to Bariloche and Comodoro Rivadavia, with connections in Esquel for Trelew and Puerto Madryn. **Transportes Nehuén** (☎ 491831; Sarmiento, near Roca) goes to El Maitén, Bariloche and Los Alerces.

Getting Around

BUS

Local bus service to nearby sights is extensive during the busy summer months, but sporadic in fall and winter, when you'll have to hire a taxi or take a tour. The tourist office provides up-to-date information. A bus ride in town costs US$0.35.

Transportes Nehuén (☎ 491831; Sarmiento, near Roca) has summer buses to many local destinations.

La Golondrina (☎ 492557) goes to Cascada Mallín Ahogado, leaving from the south end of Plaza Pagano; and to Lago Puelo, leaving from the corner of Av San Martín and Dorrego.

TAXI

Taxis (remises) are a reasonable mode of transport to nearby trailheads and campgrounds. Companies include **Radio Taxi Glaciar** (☎ 492892), **Patagonia** (☎ 493907) and **Suremiss** (☎ 492895); call for rides.

AROUND EL BOLSÓN

The outskirts of El Bolsón offer numerous ridges, waterfalls and forests for hikers to explore. If you give yourself plenty of time, and pack food and water, some of the following places can be reached by foot from town, though buses and *remises* to trailheads are reasonable. Mountain biking is an excellent way to get out on your own; for rentals try **La Rueda** (☎ 492465; Sarmiento 2972; half/full day US$7/10), in El Bolsón.

Cabeza del Indio

On a ridge-top 8km west of town, this metamorphic rock resembles a toothless hippie as much as it does a stereotypical profile of a 'noble savage,' from which the name 'Indian Head' was derived. The 7km trail up to the rock is reached by walking west on Azcuénaga from town. Part of it traverses a narrow ledge that offers the best views of the formation itself, but by climbing from an earlier junction you can obtain better views of the Río Azul and, in the distance to the south, Parque Nacional Lago Puelo.

Cascada Mallín Ahogado

This small waterfall, on the Arroyo del Medio, is 10km north of town, west of RN 258. Beyond the falls, a gravel road leads to Club Andino Piltriquitrón's **Refugio Perito Moreno** (☎ 493912; per night US$3, sleeping bag rental US$2, meals additional US$2.75), a great base for several outstanding hikes. The *refugio* has capacity for 80 people.

From the *refugio*, it's 2½ hours to the 2206m summit of **Cerro Perito Moreno** (☎ 493 912; lift pass US$3.50, ski rental US$5, snowboard rental US$10). In winter, there's skiing here at the Centro de Deportes Invernales Perito Moreno, where the base elevation is 1000m. The T-bar lifts reach 1450m.

Cascada Escondida

Downstream from the Cascada Mallín Ahogado, this waterfall is 8km from El Bolsón. There is a footpath beyond the bridge across the river at the west end of Av Pueyrredón.

Cerro Piltriquitrón

Dominating the landscape east of Bolsón, the 2260m summit of this granitic ridge yields panoramic views westward across the valley of the Río Azul to the Andean crest along the Chilean border. After driving or walking to the 1000m level (the 11km trip from El Bolsón costs about US$7 by taxi), another hour's steep, dusty walk leads through the impressive **Bosque Tallado** (Sculpture Forest) to the Club Andino's **Refugio Piltriquitrón** (☎ 492024; dm US$2.50, kitchen use US$0.50). Beds here are outstanding value, but bring your own sleeping bag. Moderately priced meals are available.

From the *refugio*, a steep footpath climbs along the rusted tow bar, then levels off and circles east around the peak before climbing precipitously up loose scree to the summit, marked by a brightly painted cement block. On a clear day, the tiring two-hour climb (conspicuously marked by paint blazes) rewards the hiker with views south beyond Lago Puelo, northwest to Monte Tronador and, beyond the border, the snow-topped cone of Volcán Osorno in Chile. Water is abundant along most of the summit route, but hikers should carry a canteen and bring lunch to enjoy at the top.

Cerro Lindo

Southwest of Bolsón, a trail from Camping Río Azul (a small campground reached by a secondary road from El Bolsón) goes to **Refugio Cerro Lindo** (☎ 492763; dm US$2.75), where you can get a decent bed; meals are extra. It's about four hours to the *refugio*, from which the trail continues to the 2150m summit.

El Hoyo

Just across the provincial border in Chubut, this town's microclimate makes it the local 'fresh fruit capital.' Nearby Lago Epuyén has good camping and hiking. For transport details, see opposite.

Parque Nacional Lago Puelo

In Chubut province, only 15km south of El Bolsón, this windy, azure lake is suitable for swimming, fishing, boating, hiking and camping. There are regular buses from El Bolsón in summer, but there's reduced service on Sunday and off-season, when you may have to hitch.

There are both free and fee campsites at the park entrance, including **Camping Lago Puelo** (☎ 499186; per person US$1.75).

The Argentine navy maintains a trailer close to the dock, where the launch **Juana de Arco** (☎ 493415) takes passengers across the lake to Argentina's Pacific Ocean outlet at the Chilean border (US$10, three hours).

From there it's possible to continue by foot or horseback to the Chilean town of Puelo on the Seno de Reloncaví, with connections to Puerto Montt. This walk takes roughly three days; for details on guided trips, contact Grado 42 (p348) in El Bolsón.

For US$12, the launches also take passengers to El Turbio, at the south end of the lake, where there's a campground.

EL MAITÉN
☎ 02945 / pop 3000

In open-range country on the upper reaches of the Río Chubut, about 70km southeast of El Bolsón, this small, dusty town is the end of the line for La Trochita, the old narrow-gauge steam train running between Esquel and El Maitén. It's also home to the workshops for La Trochita and a graveyard of antique steam locomotives and other railroad hardware – a train aficionado's dream.

Every February, the **Fiesta Provincial del Trencito** commemorates the railroad that put El Maitén on the map and keeps it there; it now doubles as the **Fiesta Nacional del Tren a Vapor** (National Steam Train Festival). Drawing people from all over the province and the country, it features riding and horse-taming competitions, live music and superb produce and pastries, including homemade jams and jellies.

El Maitén has a helpful **tourist office** (☎ 495 150; turismai@ar.inter.net).

Camping Municipal (per person US$1.75), directly on the river, gets crowded and noisy during the festival. **Hostería La Vasconia** (per person US$10) is on the plaza across from the train station.

Getting There & Away

Transportes Jacobsen buses connect El Maitén with Esquel at 8am Monday, Tuesday, Friday and Saturday. There's also regular minibus service to and from El Bolsón with Transportes Nehuén.

Train schedules change regularly for **La Trochita** (☎ 495190; www.latrochita.org.ar), so contact El Bolsón's tourist office (p348), Grado 42 in El Bolsón (p348), the train offices in either El Maitén or Esquel, or the tourist office in Esquel. At time of writing, it went only once a month to/from Esquel. Rest assured, you can still ride the rails every Wednesday and Saturday at 3pm and 5pm when La Trochita spins its 2½-hour **Paseo Turístico** (US$8.50, seniors US$7, children under six free), which departs and finishes in El Maitén. In low season, it runs only on Saturday at 2pm.

Patagonia

Exploring southern Patagonia in 1878, Lady Florence Dixie wrote, 'Without doubt there are wild countries more favoured by Nature in many ways. But nowhere else are you so completely alone. Nowhere else is there an area of 10,000 square miles which you may gallop over, and where…you are safe from the persecutions of fevers, friends…telegrams, letters and every other nuisance you are elsewhere liable to be exposed to.'

Although its name evokes jagged mountains, roaring rivers and crashing glaciers, Patagonia's salient feature is its endless expanse of nothingness. For now, RN 40, which parallels the Andes, remains an epic unpaved adventure, passing the country's most inaccessible parts, the awesome jagged Fitz Roy peaks, and some archaeological gems. Along the eastern seaboard, RN 3 is also a long haul, accessing Welsh settlements, Península Valdés marine reserve and petrified forests. A few forlorn roads connect the two highways, creating a graph of quirky towns, *estancias* and isolated outposts that might be the most Patagonic of all. Ask locals why they love Patagonia and most mention the sky: sunrises and sunsets cast endless streaks of amber and red, and night skies drip with stars. Ask visitors and they're likely to say it's the people.

This chapter covers the region from its political start at the mouth of Río Negro, continuing through Chubut and Santa Cruz provinces south to the Strait of Magellan. Chilean Patagonia's Punta Arenas, Puerto Natales and Parque Nacional Torres del Paine are also included.

PATAGONIA

TOP FIVE

- Witnessing icebergs calve off **Glaciar Perito Moreno** (p410), one of the world's most dynamic glaciers

- Trekking around Chile's **Parque Nacional Torres del Paine** (p432), one of South America's most spectacular parks

- Hiking in the stunning **Fitz Roy Range** (p405) near El Chaltén in the northern sector of Parque Nacional Los Glaciares

- Listening to cavorting southern right whales at the **Reserva Faunística Península Valdés** (p365)

- Feasting on fresh lamb chops while soaking up gaucho stories of life on the land at an **estancia** (p389) near Río Gallegos

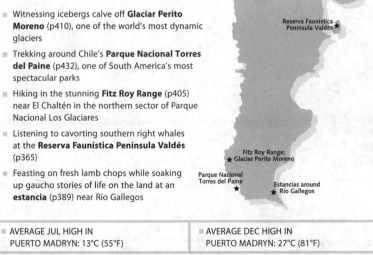

Reserva Faunística Península Valdés ★

Fitz Roy Range; ★ Glaciar Perito Moreno

Parque Nacional Torres del Paine ★

Estancias around ★ Río Gallegos

- AVERAGE JUL HIGH IN PUERTO MADRYN: 13°C (55°F)

- AVERAGE DEC HIGH IN PUERTO MADRYN: 27°C (81°F)

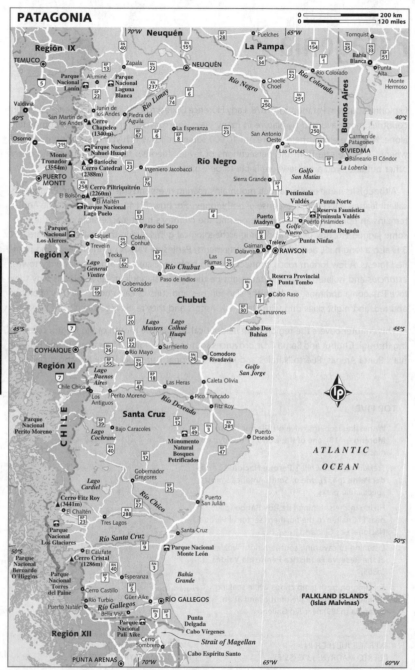

PATAGONIA

Climate

Argentine Patagonia lies in the rain shadow of the Chilean Andes, which block most Pacific storms. After storms drop precipitation on the seaward Andean slopes, powerful dry westerlies gust incessantly across the arid Patagonian plains. Because of oceanic influence where the South American continent tapers toward the south, the region's climate is generally temperate, but winter temperatures often drop well below freezing.

National Parks & Reserves

Patagonia is home to an embarrassment of national park riches: newly inaugurated coastal Monte León (p385); uniquely forested Los Alerces (p398); little-known Perito Moreno (p404); dazzling Los Glaciares (p405); the crowning Chilean gem of Torres del Paine (p432); Paleolithic Pali Aike (p427); and Chile's far-flung Bernardo O'Higgins (p432). It'd be a real shame to leave the region without visiting at least a couple of these natural wonders, not to mention the several world-class natural reserves like the Península Valdés (p365). To plan an itinerary that takes in some of the best of the parks, see the Southern National Parks Circuit (p25).

Getting There & Around

Patagonia is synonymous with unmaintained gravel roads, missing transport links and interminable bus rides. Fortunately, an ever-expanding network of charter and scheduled flights is emerging to connect all the highlights, at least in summer. Before skimping on your transportation budget, bear in mind that the region comprises a third of the world's eighth largest country. If you're bussing it along the eastern seaboard, note that schedules are based on the demands of Buenos Aires, with arrivals and departures frequently occurring in the dead of night. For transport with tour operators along the RN 40, see p392 and p478.

COASTAL PATAGONIA (ALONG RN 3)

Argentina's coastal RN 3 traverses some of Patagonia's most monotonous landscape, from Carmen de Patagones south to Río Gallegos. Stretches from one town to the next can be long and boring, but there are several worthwhile stops, especially for history and wildlife buffs. The Península Valdés, accessed via Puerto Madryn, is world-renowned for its sheltered bays where right whales frolic. Reserva Provincial Punta Tombo harbors one of South America's largest Magellanic penguin colonies and the Río Deseado estuary attracts an exceptional variety of seabirds. The region's history of settlement is apparent in Welsh-influenced towns like Gaiman, and Magellan's encounter with the Tehuelche at Puerto San Julián possibly inspired the name Patagonia (p357).

CARMEN DE PATAGONES

☎ 02920 / pop 18,000

Patagonia's historic gateway is the southernmost city in Buenos Aires province, 950km south of the capital via RN 3. The well-preserved buildings and steep cobblestone streets speak to its historic founding in 1779, when Francisco de Viedma founded both the town of Viedma and a fort along this northern shore of the river. The region's first colonists hailed from the Spanish county of Maragatería in León (to this day, townspeople are still called *maragatos*) and fashioned their first dwellings in the side of the hills. 'Patagones' claim to fame came in 1827, when its smaller and less-equipped forces repelled superior invaders during the war with Brazil.

Information

Banco de la Nación (Paraguay 2) 24-hour ATM.
Municipal tourist office (☎ 461777, ext 253; info patagones@infovia.com.ar; Bynon 186; ⊙ 7am-9pm Mon-Fri, plus 10am-1pm & 6-9pm Sat & Sun Dec-Feb)
Post office (Paraguay 38)
Telefónica (cnr Olivera 9 & Comodoro Rivadavia 365) Locutorio & Internet access.

Sights

The tourist office distributes brochures (in Spanish only) describing historic sites around Carmen de Patagones. Begin at **Plaza 7 de Marzo**; its original name, Plaza del Carmen, was changed after the 1827 victory over the Brazilians. Salesians built the **Templo Parroquial Nuestra Señora del Carmen** in 1883; its image of the Virgin, dating from 1780, is southern Argentina's oldest. On the altar are two of the original seven Brazilian flags captured in 1827. Just west of the church, the **Torre del**

PATAGONIA

CARMEN DE PATAGONES & VIEDMA

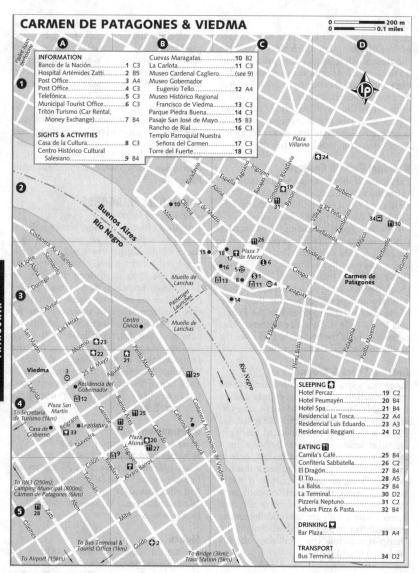

INFORMATION
Banco de la Nación.....................1 C3
Hospital Artémides Zatti...........2 B5
Post Office...................................3 A4
Post Office...................................4 C3
Telefónica...................................5 C3
Municipal Tourist Office.............6 C3
Tritón Turismo (Car Rental,
  Money Exchange).....................7 B4

SIGHTS & ACTIVITIES
Casa de la Cultura.......................8 C3
Centro Histórico Cultural
  Salesiano..................................9 B4

Cuevas Maragatas....................10 B2
La Carlota.................................11 C3
Museo Cardenal Cagliero......(see 9)
Museo Gobernador
  Eugenio Tello.........................12 A4
Museo Histórico Regional
  Francisco de Viedma.............13 C3
Parque Piedra Buena...............14 C3
Pasaje San José de Mayo.........15 B3
Rancho de Rial.........................16 C3
Templo Parroquial Nuestra
  Señora del Carmen.................17 C3
Torre del Fuerte.......................18 C3

SLEEPING
Hotel Percaz..................................19 C2
Hotel Peumayén............................20 B4
Hotel Spa......................................21 B4
Residencial La Tosca......................22 A4
Residencial Luis Eduardo..............23 A3
Residencial Reggiani......................24 D2

EATING
Camila's Café................................25 B4
Confitería Sabbatella.....................26 C2
El Dragón......................................27 B4
El Tio..28 A5
La Balsa...29 B4
La Terminal....................................30 D2
Pizzería Neptuno...........................31 C2
Sahara Pizza & Pasta.....................32 B4

DRINKING
Bar Plaza......................................33 A4

TRANSPORT
Bus Terminal.................................34 D2

Fuerte is the last vestige of the 1780 fort that once occupied the entire block.

Below the Torre, twin cannons from forts that guarded the Patagonian frontier flank the 1960s **Pasaje San José de Mayo** staircase that leads to the riverside. At the base of the steps, the 1820 **Rancho de Rial** (Mitre 94), is an adobe that belonged to the town's first elected mayor. Three blocks west, the **Cuevas Maragatas** (Maragatas Caves; Rivadavia s/n), excavated in the riverbank, sheltered the first Spanish families who arrived in 1779. Back at the base of the stairs, the early-19th-century **Casa de la Cultura** (Mitre 27) was the site of a *tahona* (flour mill). Across the street, **La Carlota** (Bynon & Mitre) is a former private residence (c 1800) decorated

LAND OF BIG FEET

The origin of Patagonia's name is obscure, but one theory asserts that it derives from the region's native inhabitants, encountered by Magellan's crew as they wintered in 1520 at Puerto San Julián, in the present-day province of Santa Cruz. According to this explanation, the Tehuelche Indians, tall of stature and wearing moccasins that made their feet appear exceptionally large, may have led Magellan to apply the name after the Spanish word *pata*, meaning paw or foot. On encountering the Tehuelche, Antonio Pigafetta, an Italian nobleman on Magellan's crew, remarked that one of them:

was so tall we reached only to his waist, and he was well proportioned...He was dressed in the skins of animals skillfully sewn together...His feet were shod with the same kind of skins, which covered his feet in the manner of shoes...The captain-general (Magellan) called these people Patagoni.

Another theory speculates that Magellan may have adopted the term 'Patagón,' the name of a fictional monster from a Spanish romance of the period, and applied it to the Tehuelche. Whatever the case, planting your own *patas* in Patagonia will be keeping true, at least in letters, to the name.

with typical 19th-century furnishings; ask about guided tours at the museum.

Parque Piedra Buena has a bust of the naval officer and Patagonian hero Luis Piedrabuena. A block west is the **Museo Histórico Regional Francisco de Viedma** (☎ 462729; admission US$0.50; ⏰ 10am–noon & 2:30–4:30pm Mon-Fri, 5-7pm Sat), housing an impressive collection of artifacts from Argentina's southern frontier, including details on the town's former black slave population. Along the river are recreational *balnearios*, popular spots for swimming and picnics in summer.

Sleeping & Eating

Accommodations options are better in Viedma, but if you stay there, it's worth a trip across the river to check out the bars and restaurants near the waterfront in Carmen de Patagones' converted historic buildings that come and go frequently.

Hotel Percaz (☎ 464104; cnr Comodoro Rivadavia & Irigoyen; s/d US$9/14; P) Percaz has clean, carpeted, no-frills rooms with awkwardly designed private bathrooms. Rooms without TV are slightly cheaper. Cash only.

Residencial Reggiani (☎ 461384; Bynon 422; s/d US$7/10; P) In a rambling 20-room home, Reggiani is notable for its location and friendliness of its owner. Rooms are dark and musty but heated. TVs are available. Rooms with shared bathroom are a bit cheaper.

La Terminal (cnr Barbieri & Bertorello; mains US$2-6) This may be one of the few times to seek out a bus terminal when you are starving. It's popular and one of the better full-menu restaurants.

Confitería Sabbatella (Comodoro Rivadavia 218; mains US$1-5; ⏰ to 2am) Sabbatella is a good, old-fashioned place for a shot of coffee or to shoot some pool.

Pizzería Neptuno (Comodoro Rivadavia 310; mains US$1-5) Inside an old building, fishing nets drape high above diners. The menu is basic – tortillas, pizzas, chicken dishes etc – but consistently good.

Getting There & Around

Bus, train and plane connections are more frequent in Viedma; from Patagones' **bus terminal** (☎ 462666; cnr Barbieri & Méjico) there's plenty of service to Bahía Blanca and Buenos Aires. Train tickets can also be purchased at the bus terminal.

Two bridges connect Carmen with Viedma, one for trains, the other for vehicles. The *balsa* (ferry) crosses the river to Viedma (US$0.25) every few minutes.

VIEDMA

☎ 02920 / pop 80,000

Río Negro's unexciting provincial capital, 960km from Buenos Aires and 275km south of Bahía Blanca, plays second fiddle to picturesque Patagones, but it's a compact practical base, with more bus connections and traveler services. In 1779, with his men dying of fever and lack of water at Península Valdés,

PATAGONIA

Francisco de Viedma put ashore to found the city. In 1879, it became the residence of the governor of Patagonia and the political locus of the country's enormous southern territory. A century later, the radical Alfonsín administration proposed moving the federal capital here from Buenos Aires.

Information

ATMs and Internet cafés are in the center along Buenos Aires.

Hospital Artémides Zatti (☎ 107, 422333; Rivadavia 351)

Post office (cnr 25 de Mayo & San Martín)

Secretaría de Turismo (☎ 422150; www.rionegrotur .com.ar; Caseros 1425; ☎ 9am-8pm) Located 15 blocks southwest of the plaza, with brochures for the entire province.

Tourist office (☎ 427171; ☺ 9am-8pm) At the bus terminal. It has lodging and transport details.

Tritón Turismo (☎ 431131; www.tritonturismo.com.ar in Spanish; Namuncurá 78) Changes traveler's checks, rents cars and runs tours.

Sights & Activities

In addition to exhibits on European settlement, the **Museo Gobernador Eugenio Tello** (San Martín 263; admission free; ☺ 9am-4:30pm Mon-Fri) has Tehuelche tools, artifacts, deformed skulls and skeletons.

The Salesian **Museo Cardenal Cagliero** (☎ 424 190; Rivadavia 34; admission free; ☺ 7am-1:30pm Mon-Fri) features some amazing ceiling paintings and a neat fish vertebrae cane (check out the cardinal's office). It is housed in the **Centro Histórico Cultural Salesiano**, the former Vicariato de la Patagonia, a massive 1890 brick structure on the corner of Colón.

The tourist office and Tritón Turismo organize tours of nearby attractions. Ask individual launch operators at the pier about kayak rentals and river cruises.

Festivals & Events

In mid-January, the weeklong **Regata del Río Negro** (www.regatadelrionegro.com.ar) includes the world's longest kayak race, which begins in Neuquén and ends in Viedma after 500km.

Sleeping

Hotel Spa (☎ 430459; piturburu@impsat1.com.ar; 25 de Mayo 174; s/d US$13/16; P ☒) Good-value rates for new rooms include use of hot and dry saunas. A small gym and indoor pool can be used for US$2 each and showers are available to nonguests for US$3.

Hotel Peumayén (☎ 425222/234; www.hoyviedma .com.ar/hotelpeumayen in Spanish; Buenos Aires 334; s/d US$13/17; P ☒) The older, business-focused Peumayén boasts friendly, professional service. Ask for a room on the 4th floor or overlooking the plaza. Rates may drop slightly on weekends.

Residencial La Tosca (☎ 428508; residencialtosca@ hotmail.com; Alsina 349; s/d US$13/20) The simple rooms have TV and private bathrooms and the staff is helpful. The next-door gym hosts basketball matches, so some evenings can be a bit noisy.

Residencial Luis Eduardo (☎ 420669; Sarmiento 366; s/d US$10/14) Rooms here come with satin bedcovers, gaudy tiles and small bathrooms, although some have bathtubs.

Camping Municipal (☎ 421341; per person US$1.50; ☺ Nov-Mar) This bleak, partially shaded riverside campground, 10 blocks west of RN 3 (a US$1 taxi ride), has hot showers and is easily reached via Comarca bus from downtown. Beware: mosquitoes in summer.

Eating & Drinking

Camila's Café (cnr Saavedra & Buenos Aires; snacks US$1-3; ☺ breakfast, lunch & dinner) The best bet for a quick breakfast, coffee, beer, wine or sandwiches.

Sahara Pizza & Pasta (☎ 421530; Saavedra 336; mains US$3-8) Locals mob this flashy pizzeria in the evening for fine noodles and pies.

La Balsa (☎ 431974; Costanero Av Villarino; mains US$4-9) With attentive service and views over the river, 'The Raft' is the best choice for local wines and a more formal meal.

El Tío (cnr Av Zatti & Colón; mains US$3-9; ☺ closed Mon) Charmed with tradition, this fun eatery serves up the usual *parrilla*, pizza and *rotisería* fare with avuncular flair.

El Dragón (Buenos Aires 366; lunch US$6, dinner US$7) The good buffet spread keeps this place busy. The vegetables are fresh and the Chinese dishes palatable; drinks aren't cheap, though.

Bar Plaza (☎ 428842; cnr Belgrano & Tucumán; ☎ closed Sun) Bustling with government pros quibbling about the economy over coffee and a smoke, this is the place to probe Viedma's soul. Sometimes there's live blues and tango on weekend evenings.

Getting There & Around

AIR

Aeropuerto Gobernador Castello (VDM; ☎ 422001) is 15km southwest of town on RP 51; a taxi costs US$4. **Aerolíneas Argentinas** (☎ 423033) flies three times a week to Buenos Aires (US$80 to US$156). **LADE** (☎ 424420) lands here en route to Trelew (US$38), Mar del Plata (US$42), Comodoro Rivadavia (US$46) and Buenos Aires (US$59).

BOAT

From the pier at the foot of 25 de Mayo, a ferry (US$0.25) frequently connects Viedma and Carmen de Patagones from 6:30am until 10pm.

BUS

Viedma's **bus terminal** (☎ 426850) is 13 blocks southwest of the plaza, a 20-minute walk or US$1 taxi from the center.

To Puerto Madryn, **Don Otto** (☎ 425952) and **El Cóndor** (☎ 423714) offer the best service. To Bariloche, **3 de Mayo** (☎ 425839) goes via Ruta 23, while **El Valle** (☎ 427501) takes longer via Ruta 22 and Ruta 6.

To get to Balneario El Cóndor (US$1) and La Lobería (US$1.50), **Ceferino** (☎ 426691) leaves from Plaza Alsina six times daily in summer.

Destination	Cost (US$)	Duration (hr)
Bahía Blanca	5	4
Bariloche	18	14-15
Buenos Aires	22-25	13
Comodoro Rivadavia	21	10-13
Las Grutas	4	2½
Puerto Madryn	10	5-6
Trelew	15	8

TRAIN

From the station on the southeast outskirts of town, **Sefepa** (☎ 422130; www.trenpatagonico.com.ar in Spanish) runs trains to Bariloche (economy/1st-class/Pullman/bed US$10/13/23/40, 17 hours) twice a week; children five to 12 pay half. Check the website for the current schedule, which changes often. It's one of Argentina's last long-distance trains, and includes dining and cinema cars.

COASTAL RÍO NEGRO

Río Negro's 400km of Atlantic coastline teems with activity in the summer, but shuts down off-season. Coined La Ruta de los Acantilados (Route of the Cliffs), this stretch of coastline's beauty resides in its majestic rock faces, some 20m high. Wave action against the ancient cliff faces (three to 13 million years old) has revealed a treasure trove of fossils.

At **Balneario El Cóndor**, a resort 31km southeast of Viedma at the mouth of the Río Negro, a large breeding colony of burrowing parrots makes its home in the cliff faces, but the main draw is the century-old lighthouse, Patagonia's oldest. Lodging includes **Hospedaje Río de los Sauces** (☎ 02920-497193; per person US$10) and the RV-friendly **Camping Ina Lauquen** (☎ 02920-497218; per person US$1).

La Lobería (Reserva Faunística de Punta Bermeja) is 60km from Viedma via RP 1, on the north coast of Golfo San Matías. Peak numbers of the permanent southern sea lion colony can be seen during the spring mating season, when fights between males are common as they come ashore to establish harems of up to 10 females each. From December onward, the females give birth. The observation balcony, directly above the mating beaches, is safe and unobtrusive. Buses from Viedma pass within 3km of colony.

At the northwest edge of Golfo San Matías, 179km west of Viedma along RN 3, the crowded resort of **Las Grutas** (The Grottos; www.balneariolasgrutas.com in Spanish) owes its name to its eroded sea caves. Thanks to an exceptional tidal range, the beaches can expand for hundreds of meters or shrink to just a few. The **tourist office** (☎ 02934-497470; Galería Antares, Primera Bajada) has tide schedules. Buses leave hourly to San Antonio Oeste, 16km northeast, with more lodging.

Besides free meals for bus drivers, **Sierra Grande**, 125km south of Las Grutas, only has one thing going for it: gasoline at subsidized *precios patagónicos* (Patagonian prices). Given that, most everyone fills up their tank, grabs a quick snack and carries on.

PUERTO MADRYN

☎ 02965 / pop 74,000

Nestled in a protected cove on the Golfo Nuevo, fast-growing Puerto Madryn is best known as a gateway to the wildlife sanctuary of Península Valdés. Its active beach lures *porteños* (residents of Buenos Aires) looking to escape big-city chaos, while tourists flock here to catch glimpses of the town's biggest attraction: visiting right whales. Madryn's campus of the Universidad de la Patagonia is known for its marine

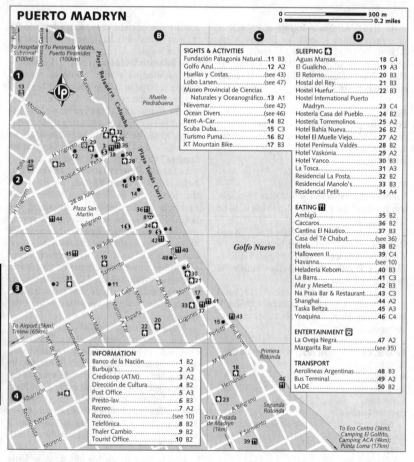

PUERTO MADRYN

SIGHTS & ACTIVITIES
Fundación Patagonia Natural...**11** B3	
Golfo Azul...............................**12** A2	
Huellas y Costas...................(see 43)	
Lobo Larsen..........................(see 47)	
Museo Provincial de Ciencias	
Naturales y Oceanográfico...**13** A1	
Nievemar...............................(see 42)	
Ocean Divers.........................(see 46)	
Rent-A-Car............................**14** B2	
Scuba Duba...........................**15** C3	
Turismo Puma.......................**16** B2	
XT Mountain Bike..................**17** B3	

SLEEPING
Aguas Mansas........................**18** C4	
El Gualicho............................**19** A3	
El Retorno.............................**20** B3	
Hostal del Rey.......................**21** B3	
Hostal Huefrar.......................**22** B3	
Hostel International Puerto	
Madryn..............................**23** C4	
Hostería Casa del Pueblo........**24** B2	
Hostería Torremolinos............**25** A2	
Hotel Bahía Nueva.................**26** B2	
Hotel El Muelle Viejo..............**27** A2	
Hotel Península Valdés...........**28** B2	
Hotel Vaskonia......................**29** A3	
Hotel Yanco..........................**30** B3	
La Tosca...............................**31** A3	
Residencial La Posta...............**32** B3	
Residencial Manolo's..............**33** B3	
Residencial Petit....................**34** A4	

EATING
Ambigú.................................**35** B2	
Caccaros...............................**36** B2	
Cantina El Náutico..................**37** B3	
Casa del Té Chabut................(see 36)	
Estela...................................**38** B2	
Halloween II..........................**39** C4	
Havanna................................(see 10)	
Heladería Kebom...................**40** B2	
La Barra................................**41** C3	
Mar y Meseta........................**42** B3	
Na Praia Bar & Restaurant......**43** C3	
Shanghai...............................**44** A2	
Taska Beltza..........................**45** A3	
Yoaquina..............................**46** C4	

ENTERTAINMENT
La Oveja Negra......................**47** A2	
Margarita Bar........................(see 35)	

TRANSPORT
Aerolíneas Argentinas.............**48** B3	
Bus Terminal.........................**49** A2	
LADE....................................**50** B2	

INFORMATION
Banco de la Nación.................**1** B2	
Burbuja's...............................**2** A3	
Credicoop (ATM)....................**3** A2	
Dirección de Cultura...............**4** B2	
Post Office............................**5** A3	
Presto-lav.............................**6** B3	
Recreo..................................**7** A2	
Recreo..................................(see 10)	
Telefónica.............................**8** B2	
Thaler Cambio.......................**9** B2	
Tourist Office........................**10** B2	

Golfo Nuevo

biology department, and ecological centers promote conservation and education. On the flip side, Madryn is the second-largest fishing port in the country and is home to Aluar, Argentina's first aluminum plant, built in 1974.

Founded by Welsh settlers in 1886, the town takes its name from Love Parry, Baron of Madryn. A couple of statues along the *costanera* (beach road) pay tribute to the Welsh: one to the role women have played, and the other, at the south end of town, to the Tehuelche, to whom the Welsh were much indebted for their survival.

Orientation

Puerto Madryn is just east of RN 3, 1371km south of Buenos Aires, 439km north of Comodoro Rivadavia and 65km north of Trelew. Activity concentrates along the *costanera* and two main parallel avenues, Roca and 25 de Mayo. Blvd Brown is the main drag alongside the beaches to the south.

Information

BOOKSTORES

Recreo (cnr 28 de Julio & Av Roca) Stocks a good selection of regional books, maps and a few English-language novels and guidebooks. There is another branch on the corner of 25 de Mayo and RS Peña.

INTERNET ACCESS & TELEPHONE

Call centers and Internet cafés abound in the center.

Telefónica (cnr Av Roca & 9 de Julio; ☺ 8am-midnight) Big call center with Internet.

LAUNDRY & SHOWERS

Burbuja's (☎ 472217; G Maíz 440; ☺ closed Sun) Full or self-service.

Dirección de Cultura (Av Roca 444) Showers (US$0.50) available downstairs.

Presto-lav (☎ 451526; Blvd Brown 605) Pick up and delivery available.

MEDICAL SERVICES

Hospital Subzonal (☎ 107, 451999; R Gómez 383)

MONEY

Some travel agencies accept traveler's checks as payment for tours.

Banco de la Nación (9 de Julio 117) ATM, changes traveler's checks.

Thaler Cambio (☎ 455858; Av Roca 493; ☺ 9:30am-1pm & 6-8pm Mon-Fri, 10am-1pm & 7-9pm Sat & Sun) Poorer rates for traveler's checks.

POST

Post office (cnr Belgrano & G Maíz)

TOURIST INFORMATION

Tourist Office (☎ 453504, 456067; www.madryn.gov.ar /turismo in Spanish; Av Roca 223; ☺ 7am-10pm Dec-Feb, reduced off-season) Helpful and efficient staff, and there's usually an English or French speaker on duty. Useful tips from travelers can be found in the *libro de reclamos* (complaint book). There's another helpful desk at the bus station.

Sights

ECOCENTRO

A celebration of the area's marine treasures, **Ecocentro** (☎ 457470; www.ecocentro.org.ar in Spanish; J Verne 3784; adult/concession US$5/3; ☺ 10am-7pm Tue-Sun) is not to be missed. Any trip to Valdés will be enhanced by a few hours at this masterpiece of interactive displays that gracefully combine artistic sensitivity with years of scientific research. Exhibits explore the unique marine ecosystem, the breeding habits of right whales, dolphin sounds, stories of southern elephant seal harems, a touch-friendly tide pool full of activity and much more. An English-language guidebook of the exhibits is available at the front desk.

Equally impressive is the building itself, from which whales may be spotted. A three-story tower acts as a library, with the top story, all glass and comfy couches, a great place to read, write or contemplate the fragile ocean community.

It's an enjoyable 40-minute walk or 15-minute bike ride along the *costanera*. Shuttles

run three times daily from the tourist office on Av Roca, or catch a Linea 2 bus to the last stop (La Universidad) and walk 1km.

MUSEO PROVINCIAL DE CIENCIAS NATURALES Y OCEANOGRÁFICO

Where else can one feel up strands of seaweed or ogle a preserved octopus, all within the grandeur of a catalog-ordered 1917 Victorian? At this **museum** (☎ 451139; cnr D García & Menéndez; admission US$1; ☺ 9am-1pm & 3-7pm Mon-Fri, 3-7pm Sat & Sun) in the Chalet Pujol, a *caracol* staircase leads into nine small rooms of marine and land mammal exhibits and preserved specimens, plus collections of Welsh wares. The explanations are in Spanish and are geared to youth science classes, but it's visually informative and creatively presented. Twist up to the cupola for panoramic views of the port.

FUNDACIÓN PATAGONIA NATURAL

This well-run nongovernmental **organization** (☎ 451920; www.patagonianatural.org in Spanish; MA Zar 760) monitors environmental issues in Patagonia. In a converted house, volunteers diligently nurse injured birds and marine mammals back to health. The friendly office staff is happy to answer questions about the region's coastal areas.

Activities

DIVING

Madryn and the Península Valdés are fast becoming Argentina's diving capitals. **Lobo Larsen** (☎ 15-516314, 15-681004; www.lobolarsen.com; Yrigoyen 144) and **Scuba Duba** (☎ 452699; scubadub@infovia .com.ar; Blvd Brown 893) are both quality PADI-affiliated operators. Night dives are offered at **Golfo Azul** (☎ 471649; www.pinosub.com in Spanish; Yrigoyen 200), which also runs a three-day, two-night diving trip aboard a catamaran. Most of the *balnearios* also offer diving, including **Ocean Divers** (☎ 472569, 15-660865; www.oceandivers .com.ar in Spanish; Balneario Yoaquina). Single-/two-tank dives around wrecks and sea lions cost around US$30/35.

WINDSURFING & KAYAKING

A hut next to **NaPraia Bar & Restaurant** (☎ 455 633; www.napraia.com.ar in Spanish; Blvd Brown 860) offers lessons and rents out regular and wide boards and kayaks by the hour. South of Muelle Piedrabuena, **Playa Tomás Curti** is a popular windsurfing spot.

BIKING & HIKING

XT Mountain Bike (☎ 472232; Av Roca 742) rents well-maintained beach cruisers and mountain bikes (US$5 to US$7 a day). NaPraia charges a bit less for older bikes. Several other outfits along Av Roca advertise rentals and guided tours; inspect the mechanics before heading out on a long ride. Also based at NaPraia, **Huellas y Costas** (☎ 15-680515; www.huellas ycostas.com; Blvd Brown 860) runs guided coastal hiking, mountain biking, kayaking and camping adventures.

Tours

Full-day tours to Península Valdés cost around US$30 (plus admission and whale-watching fees). The quality varies widely, depending on the vehicle, flexibility of the tour and foreign-language capability of guides. Distances are long, meaning that most of the 12 hours is spent en route. Reserve at least a day in advance; talk to other travelers and visit a handful of operators before booking.

Those most interested in wildlife should bring binoculars and may find it more enjoyable to stay overnight in Puerto Pirámides (p366). Tours to Punta Tombo (p373) from Puerto Madryn cost about the same as those offered from Trelew (p368), but they require a couple of hours extra driving time and thus less time with the penguins.

Recommended tour companies:

Cuyun-Co (☎ 451845; www.cuyunco.com; Av Roca 165) Flexible and personal tours.

Nievemar (☎ 455544; www.nievemartours.com.ar in Spanish; Av Roca 493) Amex representative; worth checking out.

Turismo Puma (☎ 471482; www.turismopuma.com in Spanish; 28 de Julio 46) Small groups, nature walks and excursions incorporating whale watching.

Sleeping

The tourist office posts a comprehensive list of prices, including nearby *estancias* (ranches) and apartments for rent (from US$10 per day per person). Rates at budget places don't generally include breakfast, and midrange places often insist that solo travelers pay for a double room in high season. High-season rates (given here) apply from mid-October through March, when non-Argentines may be quoted rates in dollars rather than pesos.

BUDGET

All hostels have kitchens and offer pickup from the bus station, but most are a short, flat walk away.

El Gualicho (☎ 454163; www.elgualicho.com.ar in Spanish; MA Zar 480; dm US$6-8, d US$28; P ☐) This popular, new convivial HI hostel has clean dorms, comfortable living spaces, a spacious kitchen, bike rentals and a grassy yard. Some doubles share a bathroom.

El Retorno (☎ 456044; www.elretornohostel.com.ar; Mitre 798; dm US$6-7, d with bathroom US$17-20) Completely refurbished, El Retorno is kept spotless and guests are lovingly attended to like stepchildren. The spacious dorms have lockers and some have en suite bathrooms. Extras include a nice upstairs solarium, barbecue area, laundry, bike rental and table tennis.

La Tosca (☎ 456133; www.latoscahostel.com; Sarmiento 437; dm US$5-6, d US$15-18) Recently built, this welcoming hostel has dorm rooms with good mattresses and private bathrooms lining an outdoor hall. There's a garden, and one of the young owners, a nutritionist, cooks delicious meals.

Hotel Yanco (☎ 471581; hotelyanco@hotmail.com; Av Roca 626; dm/s/d US$6.35/12.50/17.50) The backpacker crowd is tolerated here, even though it cramps Yanco's subdued style. Decent, budget rooms are shared with whomever else shows up – which is often nobody. Rooms facing Av Roca are noisy; whales have been spotted from the ones facing the ocean.

Residencial Petit (☎ 451460; hotelpetit@arnet.com .ar; MT de Alvear 845; s/d US$12/17; P) If you want to check on your car from the window, this motel-style place is handy – but inconvenient if walking. Management is attentive and the 18 rooms have cable TV. It's often full of European tour groups.

Hotel Vaskonia (☎ 472581; buce23@infovia.com.ar; 25 de Mayo 43; s/d US$10/14) Adequate rooms are a bit fusty and cramped, but the beds are comfortable and tidy – that is, if you can sleep through the thumping from nearby discos. Downsides: there's no breakfast or kitchen access.

From downtown, city bus No 2 goes within 0.5km of the southern campgrounds; get off at the last stop, called 'La Universidad.'

Camping El Golfito (☎ 454544; www.elgolfito .ultraguia.com.ar in Spanish; Camino a Punta Loma; sites per person US$1.50, cars US$3) Partially forested and with direct beach access, this is the best year-round bet, especially with the option of a hostel bed (bring your own linens). Camping rates include tent, car and showers.

Camping ACA (☎ 452952; Camino al Indio; members/nonmembers US$5/6; ✹ closed May-Aug) Large trees offer shelter from the incessant wind at this family-friendly, 800-site facility. Prices are for up to four people in gravel sites with car, trailer and tent. There's no cooking facilities, but there's a limited selection of snacks and sometimes prepared meals.

MIDRANGE & TOP END

Hostería Torremolinos (☎ 453215; www.patagonia torremolinos.com; MA Zar 64; s/d US$30/40; P 🖳) This intimate, owner-run retreat is the perfect choice for couples. The seven impeccable, well-furnished rooms feature queen-size beds, bathtubs and cable TV. Pale wood and cream interiors keep the place feeling cool, and Internet access is included. Reservations recommended.

Hostería Casa del Pueblo (☎ 472500; Av Roca 475; s/d US$23/30; P) This quaint, nicely refurbished older home fronting the *costanera* only has five rooms, a couple with ocean views. Yes, there's lots of traffic, but the thick walls keep things quiet and you can't beat the location.

Hotel Bahía Nueva (☎ 450045/145; www.bahia nueva.com.ar; Av Roca 67; s/d US$35/45; P 🖳) Bahía Nueva does a stellar job of mixing casual comfort with top-end services. The 40 cozy rooms are well groomed, but only a few have ocean views. There's a living room and library full of regional interest books, a bar with billiards and a TV (mostly to view movies and documentaries), plus plenty of tour information. The breakfast buffet earns high marks for fresh regional pastries. Non-Argentines booking ahead may be quoted higher rates.

Hotel Península Valdés (☎ 471292; www.hotel peninsula.com.ar; Av Roca 155; s/d US$59/66; P 🐾) The high-rise Valdés caters to tour groups with hands-on service, a spa, massage and beauty parlor and ocean views – request a room above tree line. All of the ample rooms have individual heating/air-con, piped-in music and cable TV.

Hostel International Puerto Madryn (☎ 474 426; http://usuarios.advance.com.ar/hi-pm; 25 de Mayo 1136; s & d US$20, 6-person apt US$35; ✹ closed May-Sep; P) On spacious grounds in a quiet residential neighborhood, this ex-hostel has converted to large private rooms. Some bathrooms are outside of the rooms, but there's shared kitchen access and they'll pick you up if you call from the bus station.

Residencial Manolo's (☎ 472390; manolos@speedy .com.ar; Av Roca 763; s US$15, d US$20-27, apt US$33-40) Set back from a busy road, the English-speaking Manolo's has a family atmosphere, a small shared kitchen, five good rooms with large bathrooms and an apartment suitable for up to five sleepy heads.

La Posada de Madryn (☎ 474087; www.la-posada .com.ar; Mathews 2951; s/d US$35/40; P 🖳) Situated a couple of blocks from the ocean in a residential barrio, the modern Posada is inconvenient to town, but offers tranquillity and rolling green lawns where songbirds compete with the echoes of tour groups. Catch a cab from the center for US$2.50.

Aguas Mansas (☎ 473103; www.aguasmansas.com; J Hernández 51; s/d US$27/30; P 🐾) Closer to the beach than other top-dime spots, here you'll find a smart, well-run place that is a comfortable, if small and old fashioned, getaway from the nearby beach scene.

Hotel El Muelle Viejo (☎ 471284; www.muelleviejo .com; Yrigoyen 38; d/q US$17/24; P) Crisp white linen curtains and bedspreads accent plump beds and pale wood furniture, and the 21 rooms have bathtubs and cable TV. In high season, they require a three-night stay for reservations and don't offer single rates.

Hostal del Rey (☎ 471156; www.cadenarayentray .com.ar; Blvd Brown 681; s/d US$25/32) The King is right on the beach, but it's part of a local chain and is rather dull in both service and structure. The 36 rooms are good quality, but have cramped all-in-one bathrooms.

Residencial La Posta (☎ 472422; residencialla posta@infovia.com.ar; Av Roca 33; s/d US$17/20) La Posta enjoys a good location but gets mixed reviews. Some find the basic rooms clean, quiet and spacious. Others gripe about the lack of real matrimonial beds, skimpy breakfast and inconsistent attention from the family that runs the place. Prices seem to be negotiable.

Eating

Taska Beltza (☎ 15-668085; 9 de Julio 345; mains US$4-9; ✹ closed Mon, dinner only Tue) Chef Negro spins delicately prepared dishes in this old Basque Center. From robust pasta to tender steamed fish, each meal is expertly seasoned, if a bit skimpy. Try the homemade banana ice cream drizzled with dark chocolate sauce and *dulce de leche* (creamy caramel, Argentina's national sweet). Reservations advised.

PATAGONIA

Mar y Meseta (☎ 458740; Av Roca 485; mains US$3-9) Clever, fresh seafood dishes, such as the catch-of-the-day in honey, prawns in champagne and rabbit with chocolate, are served outside on the wood deck or in the artsy orange bistro-style dining room.

Ambigú (☎ 472451; cnr Av Roca & RS Peña; mains US$2-8) The competition is stiff, but many consider this local institution's pizzas to be the best in town. In a renovated historic bank building, it has a sports bar feel and extensive wine list.

Caccaros (☎ 453767; Av Roca 385; set lunch US$3, mains US$3-8) With a small bar, patio seating and a subtle nautical theme, this casual bistro entertains a steady crowd with fresh shellfish appetizers, grilled meats, sandwiches, a decent wine list, Bob Marley on the stereo and solid café fare.

Estela (☎ 451573; RS Peña 27; parrilla US$2-8, pastas US$2-4; ✹ closed Mon) Estela dishes out popular *parrilla*, pasta and a good dose of hearty conversation in an intimate setting.

La Barra (☎ 454279; Blvd Brown 779; mains US$3-9) Sushi, *parrilla*, creative stone-baked, thin-crust pizzas and heaping salad bowls keep this casual, colorful place packed and boisterous until 2am.

NaPraia Bar & Restaurant (☎ 473715; Blvd Brown 860; breakfast US$2-5; ✹ breakfast, lunch & dinner) A more informal choice for beachside eating, this one offers power breakfasts and crunchy salads, and morphs into a lively bar in the evening.

Cantina El Náutico (☎ 471404; Av Roca 790; set lunch with wine US$4, mains US$3-7) Photos of Argentine celebs attest to the popularity of this touristy seafood house. Check what's in season, then sauce it up with a lemony creamy *salsa maitre d'hotel*. Meals are reasonable, but drinks are expensive.

Yoaquina (☎ 456058; Blvd Brown 1050; mains US$5-8; ✹ lunch & dinner year-round, breakfast high season only) Dark wood and a pompous waitstaff clashes with the casual beachside scene, but the breezy patio makes this a nice place for breakfast, coffee or an after-dinner drink. There's a decent set-lunch menu, but you'll do better elsewhere for seafood dinner.

Casa del Té Chubut (☎ 451311; Av Roca 369; tea service US$5) Just like Gaiman, but with a beach view, this local English-speaking institution is known for *alfajores* (cookie-type sandwiches) and tasty *torta galesa* (Welsh black cake).

There's also à la carte café fare like *licuados* (blended fruit drinks) and sandwiches.

Also recommended:

Havanna (☎ 473373; cnr Roca & 28 de Julio; snacks US$1-3) Smart, smoky café open early to late, with sugarbomb *alfajores* and specialty coffees.

Halloween II (☎ 450909; Av Roca 1355; mains US$1-7) The best takeaway pizza and empanadas in town.

Heladería Kebom (Av Roca 540; US$1-2) Popular ice creamery with a kids' playground.

Entertainment

Bars and dance clubs come and go with the marine life, so ask what's hip for the moment.

La Oveja Negra (Yrigoyen 144) Burlap sacks, revolutionary posters and occasional live rock and folk music are the fare at this fun bar, which also serves hearty pub grub.

Margarita Bar (cnr Av Roca & RS Peña) A very trendy place with brick walls, gentle lighting and suave Latin music.

Getting There & Away

Due to limited connections, it pays to book in advance here, especially if you are heading for the Andes. Though Puerto Madryn has its own modern airport, most commercial flights still arrive in Trelew (p371), 65km south.

AIR

LADE (☎ 435740; Av Roca 119) puddle jumps once or twice each week to Bahía Blanca (US$38), Comodoro Rivadavia (US$43), Esquel (US$45), El Bolsón (US$45), Bariloche (US$45), Mar del Plata (US$51), El Calafate (US$94), Río Gallegos (US$96) and Buenos Aires (US$65).

Aerolíneas Argentinas (☎ 451998; Av Roca 427) doesn't have any flights here – they all land in Trelew – but it does have a ticketing representative.

Upstart **American Falcon** (☎ 0810-222-3252; www.americanfalcon.com.ar in Spanish) plans to offer several roundtrips a week to Buenos Aires (US$89), with possible connections to El Calafate and Ushuaia.

BUS

Puerto Madryn's full-service **bus terminal** (☎ 451789; Doctor Avila btwn Independencia & Necochea), behind the historic 1889 Estación del Ferrocarril Patagónico, has an ATM and a helpful tourist information desk.

Bus companies include: **Andesmar/Central Argentino** (☎ 473764), **Don Otto** (☎ 451675), **28 de Julio** (☎ 472056), **Mar y Valle** (☎ 472056), **Que Bus** (☎ 455805), **Ruta Patagonia** (☎ 454572), **TAC** (☎ 474938) and **TUS** (☎ 451962).

Destination	Cost (US$)	Duration (hr)
Bariloche	27-30	14-15
Buenos Aires	32-40	18-20
Comodoro Rivadavia	10	6-8
Córdoba	25-30	18
Esquel	14-18	7-9
Mendoza	38-40	23-24
Neuquén	16	12
Puerto Pirámides	3.50	1½
Río Gallegos	24-25	15-20
Trelew	2	1
Viedma	10	5-6

Getting Around

Renting a bicycle (p361) is the perfect way to get around town and explore some of the nearby natural attractions.

TO/FROM THE AIRPORT

Aeropuerto El Tehuelche (PMY; ☎ 456774) is 5km west of town, at the junction with RN 3. Southbound 28 de Julio buses from Puerto Madryn to Trelew, which run hourly Monday through Saturday between 6am and 10pm, will stop at Trelew's airport on request.

Flamenco Tour (☎ 455505) runs a door-to-door shuttle service (US$2) to Madryn's airport, while **Eben-Ezer** (☎ 472474) runs a service (US$4.50) to Trelew's airport.

CAR

Before renting a car to visit Península Valdés, consider that a roundtrip is a little over 300km. A group of three or four sharing expenses can make a rental or *remise* (and possibly a freelance guide) a relatively reasonable and more flexible alternative to bus tours – if you don't have to pay for extra kilometers.

Rental rates vary, depending on the mileage allowance and age and condition of the vehicle. **Sigma Rent-a-Car** (☎ 15-699465; www.sigmarentacar.com) has vehicles from US$60 per day including insurance and 400km. There are many agencies offering similar deals along or near Av Roca. Note to northbound motorists: the last place with cheap gas is 139km north in Sierra Grande.

AROUND PUERTO MADRYN

Home to a permanent sea lion and cormorant rookery, the **Reserva Faunística Punta Loma** (admission US$3.50) is 17km southwest of Puerto Madryn via a good but winding gravel road. The overlook is about 15m from the animals, which are best seen during low tides. Many travel agencies organize two-hour tours (US$13.50) according to the tide schedules; otherwise, check tide tables and hire a car or taxi, or make the trek via bicycle.

Twenty kilometers north of Puerto Madryn via RP 1 is **Playa Flecha** observatory, a recommended whale-watching spot.

RESERVA FAUNÍSTICA PENÍNSULA VALDÉS

Península Valdés is one of South America's finest wildlife reserves, attracting more than 80,000 visitors per year. With a total area of 3600 sq km and more than 400km of coastline, it's home to sea lions, elephant seals, guanacos, rheas, Magellanic penguins and numerous seabirds. The peninsula's biggest attraction – literally and figuratively – is the endangered *ballena franca austral* (southern right whale). The warmer, more enclosed waters along the Golfo Nuevo, Golfo San José and the coastline near Caleta Valdés from Punta Norte to Punte Hércules are prime breeding zones between June and mid-December. In 1999, the peninsula was named a Unesco World Heritage site. (For details on the region's wildlife, see p374.)

Sheep *estancias* occupy most of the peninsula's interior, which includes one of the world's lowest continental depressions, the salt flats of Salina Grande and Salina Chica, 42m below sea level. At the turn of the 20th century, Puerto Pirámides, the peninsula's only village, was the shipping port for the salt extracted from Salina Grande.

About 17km north of Puerto Madryn, paved RP 2 branches off RN 3 across the Istmo Carlos Ameghino to the entrance of the **reserve** (admission US$12; valid for 2 days). The **Centro de Interpretación** (☉ 8am-8pm), 22km beyond the entrance, focuses on natural history, displays a full right whale skeleton and has material on the peninsula's colonization, from the area's first Spanish settlement at Fuerte San José to later mineral exploration. Don't miss the stunning panoramic view from the observation tower.

PATAGONIA

Puerto Pirámides

☎ 02965 / pop 250, whales 400-600

What was once a sleepy salt-exporting port is now a relaxed village. The only place in the area with a variety of food and lodging, it's the preferred base for whale-watching trips and exploring the peninsula. In summer, weekends can get ridiculously crowded, but off-season and weekdays Pirámides regains its serenity.

A small **tourist office** (☎ 495084; www.puerto piramides.gov.ar in Spanish) is at the end of the first road down to the beach. Av de las Ballenas is the main drag, with the most lodging options. There's no bank (but Internet and an ATM are supposedly on the way), so change money in Puerto Madryn. Tourist activities are clustered around the sandy half-moon beach. For visitors without cars, there's a sea lion colony less than 5km from town, with magnificent sunsets and good views across the Golfo Nuevo toward Puerto Madryn.

ACTIVITIES

Whale-watching excursions (US$15 to US$30, children under 12 half-price), which offer close-up glimpses of spyhopping, breaching and tailing cetaceans, can be arranged in Puerto Madryn or Puerto Pirámides. Recommended outfitters include **Peke Sosa** (☎ 495010; www.pekesosa.com.ar in Spanish; 2nd bajada al mar) and **Hydrosport** (☎ 495065; www.hydrosport .com.ar; 1st bajada al mar), which runs sunset tours and has naturalists and submarine audio systems on board.

When deciding which tour to join, ask other travelers and check what kind of boat will be used: smaller, Zodiac-style inflatable rafts are a better choice than the larger bulldozer variety. By law, outfitters are not allowed within 100m of whales without cutting the motor, nor allowed to pursue them. Outside of whale-watching season (June to December), boat trips aren't worthwhile unless you adore sea lions and shorebirds.

Other emerging adventure options, including **diving**, **snorkeling**, **mountain biking**, **kayaking** and **horse riding**, can be arranged in Puerto Madryn or via local outfitters. Alternatively, check out the **sandboarding** hill at the end of the second road down to the beach.

SLEEPING

If you're interested in watching wildlife, it's worth staying overnight, instead of trying to see everything in a daylong mad dash from Puerto Madryn. Watch for signs advertising rooms, cabins and apartments for rent along the main drag.

Budget

Casa de Tía Alicia (☎ 495046; Av de las Ballenas s/n; per person US$7) This old tin house exudes *buena onda* (good vibes). The rooms have windows

---

THE LITTLE PRINCE

From an apartment in Manhattan in 1941, a French pilot and writer, in exile from the battlefields in Europe, scripted what would become one of the most read children's fables, *The Little Prince*. Antoine St-Exupéry, then 40 years old, had spent the previous 20 years flying – in the Sahara, the Pyrenees, Egypt and Patagonia, where he was director of Aeropostal Argentina from 1929 to 1931. Intertwined in the lines of *The Little Prince* and Asteroid B612 are images of Patagonia that stayed with him while flying over the barren landscape and braving the incessant winds.

It has become popular legend that the shape of Isla de los Pájaros, off the coast of Península Valdés, inspired the elephant-eating boa constrictor (or hat, as you may see it), while the perfectly conical volcanoes on the asteroid owe their shape to the volcanoes St-Exupéry flew over en route to Punta Arenas, Chile. The author's illustrations show the little prince on the peaks of mountains, unquestionably those in the Fitz Roy Range (one such peak now bears his name). And, possibly, meeting two young daughters of a French immigrant after an emergency landing in Concordia, near Buenos Aires, helped mold the character of the prince.

St-Exupéry never witnessed the influence his mythical royal character would have; in 1944, just after the first publication of *The Little Prince*, St-Exupéry disappeared during a flight to join French forces-in-exile stationed in Algiers.

St-Exupéry's years in Patagonia also figure in two critically acclaimed novels, *Night Flight* and *Wind, Sand and Stars*, both worthwhile reads on long Patagonia trips. Or simply watch the miles go by and, every now and then, as the little prince requested, try to draw a sheep.

and share two bathrooms. Ask about their private tours. If it's full, try nearby **Hospedaje El Medano** (☎ 495032; d US$12).

Refugio de Luna (☎ 495083; Av de las Ballenas s/n; dm/d US$7/27, 3-person apt with hot tub US$50) The attractive, but crunched, guest cabin is perched above the house with excellent views, while rooms in the main house are spacious and inviting. Breakfast, including homemade wholemeal bread, is US$2 extra and afternoon tea may be available to nonguests.

Camping Municipal (☎ 495084; per person US$1.50) Down the road behind the gas station, with clean toilets, a store, hot pay showers and sheltered gravel sites. When things get crowded in summer finding a corner can be difficult. Whatever you do, avoid camping on the beach: high tide is really high and has washed sleeping logs away.

Midrange

Estancia del Sol (☎ 495007; Av de las Ballenas s/n; s/d US$20/26) The earnest owners do their best to make for a pleasant stay in the modest rooms. It's popular with students and families, and has a decent eatery serving homemade scones for breakfast and decent meals at midday.

Motel ACA (☎ 495004; Av Roca s/n; r US$29; **P**) The 16 noisy beachfront motel rooms have heating and cable TV. The attached restaurant has good views and serves fresh seafood.

Top End

Paradise (☎ 495030; www.hosteriaparadise.com.ar; 2nd bajada al mar; s/d US$100/120; **P** 🖳) Offers topnotch, attractive brick-walled rooms, two with stellar views and Jacuzzi tubs. More informal cabins are good options for groups and families. The downstairs restaurant-bar is among the best in town. Outside of the whale-watching season, rates are 50% lower.

Posada Austral (☎ 495006; www.patagoniafranca .com; 1st bajada al mar; garden/oceanview r with half-pension US$133/174; **P** 🖳) By far the nicest hotel in town, this new three-star retreat caters to tour groups with well-appointed suites, an abundant buffet breakfast and good meals in the oceanfront restaurant, which is open to nonguests.

EATING & DRINKING

There are several restaurants by the water, down the first street to the right as you enter town. Note that water here is desalinated,

thus it's best for those with sensitive guts to stick to the bottled stuff. If self-catering, it's best to bring your groceries from Puerto Madryn.

Mammadeus (☎ 495050; Av de las Ballenas s/n; mains US$4-10) Fresh shellfish is the ticket – the hearty fish stew is a taste bonanza. Good tunes keep the place mellow and the staff keeps it friendly. On summer nights the bar stays open 24/7 and the joint goes disco.

Quimey Quipan (☎ 458609; 1st bajada al mar; mains US$2-8; ☽ breakfast, lunch & dinner) Two side-by-side locations dish breakfast, towering sandwiches and cheap set seafood menus. The bar is popular and there's a decent wine list.

Pub Paradise (☎ 495030; Av de las Ballenas s/n; mains US$2-15) Synonymous with Pirámides, Paradise is the town's hangout and popular tour-group stop. Enjoy the buzz of activity with a cold beer, sandwich or pizza while watching the sunset spin the bluffs gold.

La Estación (☎ 495047; Av de las Ballenas s/n; mains US$2-7) Opposite the YPF gas station, this bar and eatery has a nice deck and cheery atmosphere.

GETTING THERE & AROUND

During summer, Mar y Valle buses travel from Puerto Madryn to Puerto Pirámides (US$3.50, 1½ hours) at 9am and 6pm, with limited service in the off-season. Bus tours from Puerto Madryn may allow passengers to get off at Puerto Pirámides.

Around Puerto Pirámides

If you're driving around the peninsula, take it easy. Roads are *ripio* (gravel) and washboard, with sandy spots that send wheels spinning. If you're in a rental car, make sure you get all the details on the insurance policy. Hitching here is nearly impossible and bike travel long and unnervingly windy.

ISLA DE LOS PÁJAROS

In Golfo San José, 800m north of the isthmus, this bird sanctuary is off-limits to humans, but visible through a powerful telescope; it contains a replica of a chapel built at Fuerte San José. See opposite to find out how this small island figures in Antoine de St-Exupéry's *The Little Prince*.

PUNTA DELGADA

In the peninsula's southeast corner, 76km southeast of Puerto Pirámides, sea lions and, in spring, a huge colony of elephant seals are visible from the cliffs. The lighthouse complex is now the luxury **Faro Punta Delgada Hotel** (☎ 02965-406304, 15-406304; www .puntadelgada.com; half-/full board d US$184/215, mains US$5-20), with a good restaurant serving *haute estancia* fare and often taken over by tour groups. Free guided naturalist walks down to the beach leave frequently in high season.

PUNTA CANTOR & CALETA VALDÉS

In spring, elephant seals haul themselves onto the long gravel spit at this sheltered bay, 43km north of Punta Delgada. In September, females give birth to pups, while males fight it out to impress the females, all of which makes for fantastic photo ops from the trails that wind down the hill. Guanaco sometimes stroll along the beach. The decent self-service restaurant **Parador La Elvira** (☎ 15-406183; www.laelvira.com.ar; snacks US$1-3) has a salad bar, coffee, drinks and rest rooms. A few kilometers north of the roadhouse, there's a sizable colony of burrowing Magellanic penguins.

PUNTA NORTE

Rarely visited by tour groups (mainly for reasons of time and distance), Punta Norte has an enormous mixed colony of sea lions and elephant seals. But the real thrill is the orcas; from mid-February through mid-April these 'killer whales' come here to feast on the unsuspecting colonies of sea lions. Chances are you won't see a high-tide attack in all its gory glory, but the grace of the orcas is reason enough to venture here. There's a small but good museum focusing on marine mammals, with details on the Tehuelche and the area's sealing history.

TRELEW

☎ 02965 / pop 108,000

Strolling Trelew's streets, you might hear elders exchanging news in Welsh or see a tutor conducting classes to keep the antique language alive. A few historic buildings preserve a sense of heritage, but nowadays it's the region's commercial center and convenient base for visiting the Welsh villages of Gaiman and Dolavon.

Founded in 1886 as a railway junction to unite the Río Chubut valley with the Golfo Nuevo, Trelew (tre-*ley*-ooh) owes its easily mispronounced name to the Welsh contraction of *tre* (town) and *lew* (after Lewis Jones, who promoted railway expansion). During the following 30 years, the railway reached Gaiman, the Welsh built their Salón San David, and Spanish and Italian immigrants settled in the area. In 1956, the federal government promoted Patagonian industrial development and Trelew's population skyrocketed.

Orientation

Trelew is 65km south of Puerto Madryn via RN 3. The center of town surrounds Plaza Independencia, with most services on Calles 25 de Mayo and San Martín, and along Av Fontana. East–west streets change names on either side of Av Fontana. Between the main north–south streets are semi-pedestrian passageways.

Information

There are scores of banks downtown with ATMs and several *locutorios* with Internet around the plaza.

ACA (Automóvil Club Argentina; ☎ 435197; cnr Av Fontana & San Martín)

Marva Lavadero Sarmiento (Sarmiento 363) Self- and auto-service laundry and dry cleaners.

Post office (cnr 25 de Mayo & Mitre)

Tourist office (☎ 426819; www.trelewpatagonia.gov.ar; Mitre 387; ⏲ 8am-9pm) Helpful and well-stocked, with some English-speaking staff and brochures.

Sights

The tourist office sometimes has an informative walking-tour brochure, in Spanish and English, describing most of the city's historic buildings.

MUSEO PALEONTOLÓGICO EGIDIO FERUGLIO

The pride of Trelew, this well-organized and attractive natural history **museum** (☎ 420 012; Av Fontana 140; admission US$2; ⏲ 10am-8pm) has realistic dinosaur exhibits and fossils of plant and marine life. Nature sounds and a video accent the informative plaques; however, if you can't read the Spanish explanations, the experience falls short. The collection includes local dinosaurs, such as the tehuelchesaurus, patagosaurus and titanosaurus. Feruglio was an Italian paleontologist who came to Argentina in 1925 as a petroleum geologist for YPF.

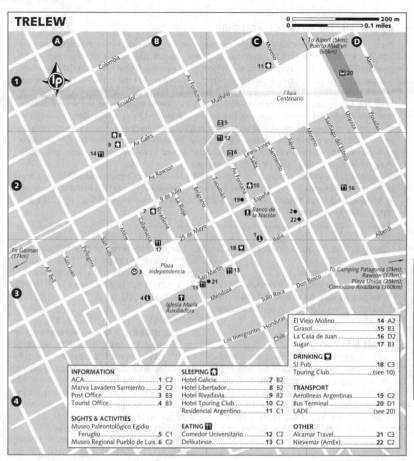

TRELEW

INFORMATION	
ACA	**1** C2
Marva Lavadero Sarmiento	**2** C2
Post Office	**3** B3
Tourist Office	**4** B3

SIGHTS & ACTIVITIES
Museo Paleontológico Egidio	
Feruglio	**5** C1
Museo Regional Pueblo de Luis	**6** C2

SLEEPING	
Hotel Galicia	**7** B2
Hotel Libertador	**8** B2
Hotel Rivadavia	**9** B2
Hotel Touring Club	**10** C2
Residencial Argentino	**11** C1

EATING
Comedor Universitario	**12** C2
Delikatesse	**13** C3

El Viejo Molino	**14** A2
Girasol	**15** B3
La Casa de Juan	**16** D2
Sugar	**17** B3

DRINKING
SJ Pub	**18** C3
Touring Club	(see 10)

TRANSPORT
Aerolíneas Argentinas	**19** C2
Bus Terminal	**20** D1
LADE	(see 20)

OTHER
Alcamar Travel	**21** C3
Nievemar (AmEx)	**22** C2

The museum sponsors group tours to **Geoparque Paleontológico Bryn Gwyn**, in the badlands along the Río Chubut (25km from Trelew, or 8km south of Gaiman via RP 5). The three-hour guided visits are a walk through time, along a well-designed nature trail past a wealth of exposed fossils dating as far back as the Tertiary, some 40 million years ago.

MUSEO REGIONAL PUEBLO DE LUIS

In the former railway station, this **museum** (☎ 424062; cnr Av Fontana & 9 de Julio; admission US$1; ⏰ 7am-1pm & 3-9pm Mon-Fri) displays historical photographs, clothing and period furnishings, but lacks explanations. The train stopped running in 1961, but the antique steam engine and other machinery outside are worth a stop.

Tours

Several travel agencies run excursions to Reserva Provincial Punta Tombo (around US$30, plus US$7 admission), some passing by Puerto Rawson on the way back to see *toninas overas* (Commerson's dolphins) when conditions are agreeable. The actual time at Punta Tombo is only about 1½ hours. Full-day trips to Península Valdés are on offer, but going to Puerto Madryn (p362) first is a better bet: there are more options, prices are similar and there's less driving time. Note that distances to all these sites are very long and more time is spent

ROCKY TRIP: THE WELSH IN PATAGONIA

Welsh nationalists, frustrated with English domination, sought a land where they could exercise sufficient political autonomy to retain their language, religion and cultural identity. Deciding on desolate Patagonia, they appealed to the Argentine government, which, after initial misgivings due partly to the British presence in the Falklands, granted land in the lower Río Chubut valley.

Misfortune and disillusion plagued the 153 first arrivals from the brig *Mimosa* in the winter of 1865. The Patagonian desert bore no resemblance to their verdant homeland, and several children died in a storm that turned a two-day coastal voyage into a 17-day ordeal. Only a handful of the immigrants were farmers in well-watered Wales, yet their livelihood was to be agriculture in arid Chubut. After near starvation in the early years, the colonists engineered suitable irrigation systems with the help of Tehuelche living in the area, and increased their harvests, permitting the gradual absorption of more Welsh immigrants.

Eventually, the Welsh occupied the entire lower Chubut valley and founded the towns and teahouses of Rawson, Trelew, Puerto Madryn and Gaiman. *Rocky Trip: The Route of the Welsh in Patagonia*, by Jorge Miglioli and Sergio Sepiurka, is an impressive, well-illustrated, bilingual history of this migration.

in transit than at the attractions; take water and snacks.

Local agencies worth checking out include Amex-representative **Nievemar** (☎ 434 114; www.nievemartours.com.ar in Spanish; Italia 98), which accepts traveler's checks, and **Alcamar Travel** (☎ 421448; San Martín 146).

Festivals & Events

On July 28, **Gwyl y Glaniad** celebrates the landing of the first Welsh by taking tea in one of the many chapels. The **Eisteddfod de Chubut** (☎ 430156), a Welsh literary and musical festival, has been held here since 1875 and continues, in late October, every year. On October 20, the **Aniversario de la Ciudad** commemorates the city's founding in 1886.

Sleeping

There's a much better selection of accommodations in Puerto Madryn (p362).

BUDGET

Hotel Rivadavia (☎ 434472; www.cpatagonia.com/rivadavia in Spanish; Rivadavia 55; s/d US$9/15, shared bathroom US$5.35/10; P) Up on a hill, owner-run Rivadavia offers right-size firm mattresses, but the cramped bathroom setup means showers get seats wet. The best, brightest rooms are upstairs. Breakfast (US$1) is served in the TV-oriented lobby.

Residencial Argentino (☎ 436134; Moreno 93; s/d US$7/11) Near the bus terminal, this impersonal stone maze offers decent rooms with private bathrooms amid kitsch murals. Breakfast (US$1) and TV (US$1.65) are extra.

Camping Patagonia (☎ 428968; 7km out RN 7 off route to Rawson; per person US$1.35) A clean and green campground with a sundries shop, electricity and hot showers, but limited public transport.

MIDRANGE

Hotel Libertador (☎ 420220; www.hotellibertadortw .com; Rivadavia 31; s/d/ste US$26/32/39; P X 💻) Comfortable standard rooms are softly decorated with flowing curtains and indirect light. All bathrooms have large tubs, and superior VIP rooms are more spacious. Breakfast in the good restaurant (opposite) is buffet-style and parking is free. There's a 5% discount for cash.

Hotel Touring Club (☎ 433997/98; htouring@ speedy.com.ar; Av Fontana 260; s/d US$14/20; P 💻) In the quest for historic allure, this place is a jackpot. The 30 rooms are small but adequate, with quaint old touches and modern conveniences like BBC. The common quarters are gloriously old fashioned, but the real star here is breakfast in the downstairs *confitería* (opposite).

Hotel Galicia (☎ 433802; www.hotel-galicia.com.ar; 9 de Julio 214; s/d US$20/30; P) Galicia has cozy rooms with luxury style, good bathrooms and friendly staff. Older singles are available for US$15, but they're cramped, thin-walled and lack ventilation.

Eating

El Viejo Molino (☎ 428019; Av Gales 250; set menu US$6, mains US$3-10; 🕙 closed Mon) In a restored 1914 brick flour mill, this smart, attractive place is busiest on weekend nights. Enjoy a wood-fired *parrilla* – of beef, chicken or even vegies – or a variety of pastas or fish. An extensive wine list adds to the pleasure.

Libertador (☎ 420220; mains US$4-9) Fresh meat and produce, homemade pastas and a traditional menu make the restaurant of this hotel (opposite) worth the short but steep walk.

La Casa de Juan (☎ 421534; Moreno 360; mains US$2-7; ☽ closed Mon) Besides 39 choices of toppings, the best pizzeria in town also offers an assortment of pastas, all served inside a cozy, creaky old house.

Sugar (☎ 435978; 25 de Mayo 247; mains US$2-6) Facing the plaza, Sugar is a popular, if stark, place for snacks and drinks. Service is pleasant and the quality meals include an assortment of salads and set menus.

Delikatesse (☎ 430716; cnr Belgrano & San Martín; mains US$8-12) Popular and brightly lit, this pizzeria offers empanadas, typical, family-friendly meals and large but bland pasta dishes, all topped off with oft-times pretentious service.

Girasol (☎ 437280; San Martín 188; buffet US$4) Scarf all you want for lunch or dinner, including *parrilla*, at this popular *tenedor libre* (all-you-can-eat restaurant). Drinks are overpriced.

Comedor Universitario (cnr 9 de Julio & Av Fontana; meals US$1.75; ☽ lunch 12:30-2:30pm daily, dinner 9-10:30pm Mon-Sat) Line up with university students for the cheapest meal in town. The set menus (ranging from burgers and lentils to polenta) include juice and a small dessert.

Drinking

Touring Club (☎ 433997/98; Av Fontana 240; snacks US$1-3; ☽ 6:30am-2am) The lore at this historic hostelry's *confitería* will inspire anyone to sidle up to the bar and fire up a heated conversation. The amicable owner, shuffling waiters, historic photos, pressed tin ceiling and vintage liquor bottles crowding the 1920s barback all add to the allure.

SJ Pub (☎ 423474; San Martín 57) Up front is a nondescript ice-cream parlor, but out back is an inviting dark-wood watering hole with cans of Guinness and Kilkenny and a friendly staff.

Getting There & Away

AIR
Aerolíneas Argentinas (☎ 420210; 25 de Mayo 33) flies direct daily to Buenos Aires (US$171)

and several times a week to Esquel (US$145), Bariloche (US$232), Ushuaia (US$302) and El Calafate (US$320).

LADE (☎ 435740), based at the bus terminal, flies a couple of times a week to Comodoro Rivadavia (US$47), Buenos Aires (US$71) and other northern Patagonian destinations. Airport tax is US$2.

BUS
Trelew's full-service **bus terminal** (☎ 420121) is six blocks northeast of downtown. **28 de Julio** (☎ 432429) goes to Gaiman (US$0.80) 18 times a day between 7am and 11pm (reduced weekend service), most continuing to Dolavon (US$1.65). Buses to Rawson (US$0.65) leave every 15 minutes.

28 de Julio and **Mar y Valle** (☎ 432429) run hourly buses to Puerto Madryn (US$2, one hour). Mar y Valle goes to Puerto Pirámides (US$5, 2½ hours) Thursday and Sunday morning, with additional service in summer. **El Ñandú** (☎ 427499) goes to Camarones (US$11, three hours) at 8am Monday, Wednesday and Friday.

Long-distance bus companies include **El Cóndor** (☎ 431675), **Que Bus** (☎ 422760), **Andesmar** (☎ 433535), **TAC** (☎ 431452), **TUS** (☎ 421343) and **Don Otto** (☎ 429496).

Of several departures daily for Buenos Aires, Don Otto has the most comfortable and most direct service. Only Don Otto goes to Mar del Plata, while TAC goes to La Plata. TAC and Andesmar service the most towns. For Comodoro Rivadavia there are a few daily departures with TAC, Don Otto or Andesmar, all of which also continue on to San Julián and Río Gallegos.

Destination	Cost (US$)	Duration (hr)
Bahía Blanca	15	12
Bariloche	31	13
Buenos Aires	23-33	18-21
Caleta Olivia	14	6
Comodoro Rivadavia	10-16	5-6
Córdoba	23	19
Esquel	11-14	8-9
La Plata	23	19
Mar del Plata	33	17-21
Mendoza	38	24
Neuquén	18	10
Puerto Madryn	2	1
Río Gallegos	20-24	14-17
Viedma	15	8

PATAGONIA

Getting Around

Trelew's **airport** (TRE; ☎ 428021) is 5km north of town off RN 3. Taxis charge US$3 to downtown, US$8 to Gaiman and US$22 to Puerto Madryn.

Car rental agencies at the airport include **Avis** (☎ 434634) and **Localiza** (☎ 430070).

AROUND TRELEW

Rawson, 17km east of Trelew, is Chubut's provincial capital, but nearby **Playa Unión**, the region's principal playground, has the capital attraction: *toninas overas* (Commerson's dolphins; see p374). Playa Unión is a long stretch of white-sand beach with blocks of summer homes. Dolphin tours (US$15, 1½ hours) depart **Puerto Rawson** from April to December. For reservations, contact **Toninas Adventure** (☎ 483472, 15-666542).

Empresas Rawson and 28 de Julio buses depart from Trelew for Rawson (US$0.65) frequently Monday to Friday and every 20 to 30 minutes on weekends. Get off either at Rawson's plaza or bus station and hop on a green 'Bahía' bus, which heads to Puerto Rawson before turning around.

GAIMAN

☎ 02965 / pop 5750

Teahouses, dinosaur fossils, Welsh-speaking *abuelos* (grandparents), seaweed and stocking factories, and a park of recycled soda bottles: Gaiman is, to say the least, random.

Tehuelche once wintered in this river valley, thus the name Gaiman, meaning Stony Point or Arrow Point. The Welsh constructed their first house here in 1874 and peacefully coexisted with the Tehuelche. Later immigrant groups of *criollos*, Germans and Anglos joined the Welsh and continued cultivation of fruit, vegetables and fodder in the lower Río Chubut valley. Today, about a third of the residents claim Welsh ancestry and teahouses try to hold on to the afternoon tradition, increasingly diluted by overbaked tourism.

Gaiman is 17km west of Trelew via RN 25. The town's touristy center is little more than a crisscross of streets snuggled between barren hills and the Río Chubut. Av Eugenio Tello is the main road, connecting the main town entrance to leafy Plaza Roca. Most of the teahouses and historic sites are within four blocks of the plaza. Across the river is the more industrial and residential zone.

Information

There's an ATM on the plaza at Banco del Chubut and *locutorios* and Internet along the main drag.

Post office (cnr Evans & Yrigoyen) Just north of the river bridge.

Tourist office (Casa de Informes; ☎ 491571; www .gaiman.gov.ar; cnr Rivadavia & Belgrano; ☒ 9am-9pm Mon-Sat, 2-8pm Sun) Ask here for a map and guided tours of historic houses.

Sights

Architecturally distinctive churches and chapels dot the town. **Primera Casa** (cnr Tello & Evans; admission US$0.50; ☒ by request at tourist office) is the first house, built in 1874 by David Roberts. Dating from 1906, the **Colegio Camwy** (cnr Jones & Rivadavia) is considered the first secondary school in Patagonia.

The old railway station houses the **Museo Histórico Regional Gales** (☎ 491007; cnr Sarmiento & 28 de Julio; admission US$0.35; ☒ 3-7pm Tue-Sun), a fine small museum with an intriguing collection of pioneer photographs.

The **Museo Antropológico** (cnr Bouchard & Jones; admission US$0.35; ☒ 9am-1pm & 2-8pm Mon-Fri, 2-8pm Sat & Sun) is a humble homage to the indigenous groups' cultures and history. Nearby is the 300m **Túnel del Ferrocarril**, a brick tunnel through which the first trains to Dolavon passed in 1914.

Located at the western entrance to town is **Parque El Desafío** (www.eldesafiogaiman.com.ar in Spanish; Av Brown 52; admission US$1.65, under 10 free; ☒ dawn-dusk), the masterpiece park of folk art junque created by eccentric octogenarian Joaquín Alonso, the 'Dalí of Recycling.' Soda-can flowers, bottle-bottom bulbs and walkways of cable and piping lead to installments of whimsy, the explanations wittingly mocking of today's values. El Desafío gained Guinness World Record status in 1998 as Earth's largest 'recycled' park, with over 50,000 repurposed wine and beer bottles. Right on the riverbank, parts of it are sometimes flooded, but that doesn't stop Alonso from continuing. More impressive than the park itself is insatiable Joaquín, whose wisdom and humor are found on the plaques that pepper the park. As one proclaims, '*Si quieres vivir mejor, mezcla a tu sensatez unos gramos de locura*' ('If you want to live better, mix up your sensibility with a few grams of craziness').

Sleeping

Hostería Gwesty Tywi (☎ 491292; http://usuarios
.advance.com.ar/gwestywi; Jones 342; s/d US$13.50/20;
P 🖳) Run by a friendly Argentine-Welsh
couple, this B&B is an immaculate, comfortable home away from home, with meals
available from a typical Celtic-style tavern
up the street.

Dyffryn Wyrdd (☎ 491777; www.dwhosteria.com.ar
in Spanish; Tello 103; s/d US$9/15; P) Another good
homey choice with modern rooms and a
pleasant, inviting atmosphere.

Camping Nain (☎ 491048; Chacra 227, Bryn Gwyn;
per person US$1) Not very central and only open
in summer, but the campground has electricity and hot showers. Ask at the tourist
office about other options.

Eating

*Tarten afal, tarten gwstard, cacen ffrwythau,
spwnj jam* and *bara brith* and a bottomless
pot of tea – mouth watering yet? For those
splurging on afternoon tea, keep in mind
that busloads of tourists may descend, taint-
ing the experience: look for places without
the buses in front, or wait until they depart.
Whatever you do, eat a light lunch! Teahouses open around 3pm.

Ty Nain (☎ 491126; Yrigoyen 283; tea US$6; 🕑 closed
May) For pure aesthetic, Ty Nain wins. Ivy-
covered whitewashed walls lead inside the
cozy 1890 home. Afterwards, check out the
small museum of authentic Welsh artifacts.

Ty Cymraeg (☎ 491010; Matthews 74; tea US$6)
Some consider Cymraeg to have the most
authentic tea service, in the most authentic
of riverside houses. What's not original is
the view of the factory across the way.

Breuddwyd (☎ 491133; Yrigoyen 320; snacks US$1-
4, tea US$5) Run by the great-granddaughter
of the founder of Gaiman's first teahouse,
this modern café will make sure you leave
with a full belly. Ask about rooms for rent
upstairs.

The younger crowd gravitates toward
Tabern Las Pub (☎ 15-665097; cnr Tello & 9 de Julio;
mains US$3-6) for pizza, beer, caffeine and basic
meals. At the other end of the spectrum,
El Ángel (☎ 491460; Rivadavia 241; mains US$5-10)
serves stylish seasonal dinners in a romantic setting by reservation only.

Getting There & Away

During the week, 28 de Julio buses depart for
Trelew frequently from Plaza Roca; weekend
services are fewer. Most buses to Dolavon use
the highway, but some take the much longer
gravel 'valley' route. *Remise* service is cheaper
in Gaiman than in Trelew; the trip to Trelew
costs US$4 for up to four passengers.

AROUND GAIMAN

Welsh for 'river meadow,' untouristed **Dolavon** (population 2500), 19km west of Gaiman
via paved RN 25, remains about as authentic
a historic Welsh agricultural town as can
be. Wooden waterwheels line the irrigation
canal, framed by swaying poplars. The historic center is full of brick buildings, including the 1880 **Molino Harinero** (☎ 492290;
romanogi@infovia.com.ar; Maipú 61; guided tour per person US$1, meals US$2-6; 🕑 call owner Romano Giallantini)
with still-functioning machinery and a café-
restaurant serving handmade breads and
pastas with local wines and cheeses.

RESERVA PROVINCIAL PUNTA TOMBO

Continental South America's largest penguin nesting ground, **Punta Tombo** (admission US$7; 🕑 dawn-dusk Aug-Apr) has a colony of
over a half-million Magellanic penguins,
and attracts many birds, most notably king
and rock cormorants, giant petrels, kelp
gulls, flightless steamer ducks and black
oystercatchers.

Trelew-based agencies run day-long tours
(around US$30, not including entrance fee),
but may cancel if bad weather makes the unpaved roads impassable. If possible, come in
the early morning to beat the crowds. Most
nesting areas in the 200-hectare reserve are
fenced off: respect the limits and remember
that penguins can inflict serious bites. Punta
Tombo is 110km south of Trelew (180km
south of Puerto Madryn) via well-maintained
gravel RP 1, and a short southeast lateral.

There's a bar and *confitería* on-site, but
it's best to bring a picnic lunch. Motorists
can proceed south to Camarones (below)
via scenic but desolate Cabo Raso.

CAMARONES & CABO DOS BAHÍAS

☎ 02965 / pop 1000

The only time sleepy Camarones, the closest
town to the Cabo Dos Bahías nature reserve,
comes to life is in early February for the **Fiesta
Nacional del Salmón** (National Salmon Festival).
Spanish explorer Don Simón de Alcazaba
y Sotomayor anchored here around 1545,
naming it part of his attempted Provincia de

PATAGONIA

PATAGONIA WILDLIFE

A whole cast of wild characters hangs out along the rugged coast of Southern Argentina. Jackass penguins, dolphins, killer whales, sea lions and elephant seals – to name just a few – are some of the big-name stars that draw wildlife spectators to these lonely Atlantic shores. Read on for a profile of some of the region's top celebrities.

Magellanic Penguin

When: August to April, peak season December through February
Where: Península Valdés, Punta Tombo, Cabo Dos Bahías, Seno Otway (Chile)
What: *Sphenicus magellanicus;* in Spanish *pingüino magellánico*

Also known as the jackass penguin for its characteristic braying sound, the Magellanic penguin is black to brown in shading and has two black-and-white bars going across the upper chest. They average 45cm in height and weigh about 3.15kg. Winters are spent at sea, but males arrive on land in late August, followed by territorial fights in September as burrows and nests are prepared. In October, females lay their eggs. Come mid-November, when eggs are hatched, the males and females take turns caring for and feeding the chicks with regurgitated squid and small fish. In December, it's a madhouse of hungry demanding chicks, adults coming in and out of the sea with food, and predatory birds trying to pick out the weaklings. Come January, chicks start to molt and take their first steps into the sea, and by February, it's a traffic jam at the beach as chicks take to the sea. By March, juveniles start their migration north, followed in April by the adults.

Penguins are awkward on land, but in the water they are swift and graceful, reaching speeds of up to 8km per hour. They are also naturally curious, though if approached too quickly they scamper into their burrows or toboggan back into the water. They will bite if you get too close. The least disruptive way to observe them is to sit near the burrows and wait for them to come to you.

Over a million pairs of these penguins exist, but their populations are threatened by human activity and oil spills.

Southern Right Whale

When: June to mid-December, peak season September and October
Where: Golfo Nuevo and the Golfo San José, Península Valdés
What: *Eubalaena australis;* in Spanish *ballena franca austral*

Averaging nearly 12m in length and weighing more than 30 tons, southern right whales enter the shallow waters of Península Valdés in the spring to breed and bear young. Females, which are larger than males, will copulate a year after giving birth, and may pick out the best male partner by fending off the pack of males trailing her for hours to see which one can sustain. For the past three decades, researchers have been able to track individual whales by noting the pattern of callosities, made white against the black skin by clusters of parasites, found on the whale's body and head. Right whales don't have teeth, but trap krill and plankton with fringed plates (baleen) that hang from the upper jaw. The slow-moving right whale was a favorite target of whalers because, unlike other species, it remained floating on the surface after being killed; after more than half a century of legal protection, South Atlantic right whale populations are now slowly recovering.

Killer Whale

When: June to mid-December, peak season September and October
Where: Península Valdés
What: *Ornicus orca;* in Spanish *orca*

These large dolphins, black with white underbellies, live in pods consisting of one male, a cluster of females and the young. Upon maturity, the males leave the pod to create their own. Males, which can reach more than 9m in length and weigh as much as 6000kg, live an average of 30 years, while the females, substantially smaller at 7m and about 4000kg, live about 50 years, calving approximately every 10 years. The ominous dorsal fin can reach nearly 2m high. They prey on fish, penguins, dolphins and seals, and will hunt in groups to prey upon larger whales. At Punta Norte near Península Valdés they hunt sea lions and elephant seals by almost beaching themselves and waiting for the waters to wash a few unfortunates their way. In the 1970s, groups concerned with the livelihood of the sea lions requested the whales be shot, to either kill or scare them away, before they decimated the sea lion colonies. Fortunately, this reaction was short lived and made clear the inevitability of the food chain.

Southern Sea Lion

When: year-round
Where: widely distributed along Patagonia coasts
What: *Otaria flavescens;* in Spanish *lobo marino*

Aggressive southern sea lions feed largely on squid and the occasional penguin – no matter how tempting, don't approach them too closely for photo ops. The bull has a thick neck and large head with longer hair around the neck, creating the appearance of a lion's mane. An adult male can weigh 300kg and measure 2m, while the females weigh around 200kg. Bulls fight to control their harems and breed with up to 10 females per season. Females give birth once each season, with less than a week before being ready for mating again. Unlike the elephant seal, pups nurse only from their mothers.

Southern Elephant Seal

When: year-round; births and mating between September and November
Where: widely distributed along Patagonia coasts; Península Valdés, Punta Norte and
             Caleta Valdés
What: *Mirounga leonina;* in Spanish *elefante marino*

Elephant seals take their common name from the male's enormous proboscis, which does indeed resemble an elephant's trunk. Bulls (males) reach nearly 7m in length and can weigh over 3500kg, but the females are substantially smaller. They spend most of the year at sea, and have been observed diving to a depth of 1500m and stay submerged for over an hour in search of squid and other marine life. (The average dive depth and duration are 1000m and 23 minutes.)

Península Valdés has the only breeding colony of southern elephant seals on the South American continent. The bull elephant comes ashore in late winter or early spring, breeding after the already pregnant females arrive and give birth. Dominant males known as 'beachmasters' control harems of up to 100 females but must constantly fight off challenges from bachelor males. Females give birth to a pup once a year, each pregnancy lasting 11 months of that year. For 19 days after the birth the female nurses the pup, during which time she will lose close to 40% of her body weight, while the pup's increases by 300%. Pups will sometimes nurse from other females. After the 19 days, the mother becomes available for breeding again.

Commerson's Dolphin

When: year-round; breeding season November to February
Where: Puerto San Julián, Playa Unión, Puerto Deseado
What: *Cephalorhynchus commersonii;* in Spanish *tonina overa*

Outgoing and acrobatic, the Commerson's dolphin is a favorite along shallow areas of coastal Patagonia. Adults are quite small, about 1.5m in length, and brilliantly patterned in black and white with a rounded dorsal fin. Young mammals are gray, brown and black; the brown slowly disappears and the gray fades to striking white. In small groups, they play around the sides of boats, breaching frequently and sometimes bowriding. The Commerson's dolphins eat shrimp, squid and bottom-dwelling fish. In Argentina, they are illegally captured to use as crab bait.

Nueva León. When the wool industry took off, Camarones became the area's main port for wool and sheepskins. After Comodoro finished its massive port, Camarones was all but deserted. Local wool is very fine, a fact that didn't go unnoticed by justice of the peace Don Mario Tomás Perón, who operated the area's largest *estancia*, Porvenir, on which his son Juan would romp about.

Thirty rough kilometers southeast of Camarones, the isolated **Cabo Dos Bahías** (admission US$5; year-round) rookery attracts far fewer visitors than Punta Tombo, making it a worthwhile alternative. You'll be rewarded with orcas and up-close interaction with a huge colony of nesting penguins in spring and summer, whales in winter and a large concentration of guanacos and rheas. Seabirds, sea lions, foxes and fur seals are year-round residents.

Sleeping & Eating

Hotel Kau I Keu Kenk (0297-496-3004; cnr Sarmiento & Roca; s/d US$15/25, shared bathroom US$10/15) Rooms in the newer wing have heat, views and better bathrooms. The *menú del día* is US$6. Lunch is all-you-can-eat seafood appetizers, fish entrees and *parrilla*.

At the waterfront port, **Camping Camarones** (San Martín; per person/vehicle US$1/1) is somewhat shaded but rather small. Bathrooms have hot showers and there's electricity. At Cabo Dos Bahías, pitch a tent for free at the **Club Náutico** or on any of the beaches en route.

Getting There & Away

On RN 3, from a gas station junction 180km south of Trelew, paved RP 30 leads 72km to Camarones. Ñandú buses return to Trelew (US$11, three hours) three times a week. For transport to Cabo Dos Bahías (around US$15 per person), chat with Don Roberto at Hotel Kau I Keu Kenk.

COMODORO RIVADAVIA

0297 / pop 160,000

Surrounded by low hills of drilling rigs, oil tanks and wind-energy farms, hardworking Comodoro (as it's commonly known) has little in its favor. But, as a relatively modern gateway to other nearby attractions and the eastern end of the Corredor Biocéanico highway that leads to Coyhaique, Chile, it has good traveler services, mostly on the principal commercial streets Av San Martín

and Rivadavia. If you get stuck here, a climb up 212m to the mirador atop Cerro Chenque, smack dab in the middle of the city with views to Golfo San Jorge, or a visit to the state-of-the-art petroleum museum, are enjoyable time-killing excursions.

Founded in 1901, Comodoro was once a transport hub for ranching from nearby Sarmiento. But the town struck it rich in 1907 when workers drilling for water struck black gold instead. Near the country's first major oil gusher, Comodoro became a state pet, gaining a large port, airport and paved roads, and today is a powerhouse in the now privatized oil industry. Looking around, you wouldn't know that the recession hit hard here in 2001 – this boomtown has a flashy new casino and is high-rolling again.

Information

Locutorios abound around downtown.

ACA (446-0876; cnr Dorrego & Alvear) Maps and road info.

Banco de la Nación (cnr Av San Martín & Güemes) Most of Comodoro's banks and ATMs, including this one, are along Avs San Martín or Rivadavia.

Centro Internet Comodoro (Av San Martín 536) Stays open late.

Hospital Regional (107, 444-2287; Av Hipólito Yrigoyen 950)

Laverap (Av Rivadavia 287)

Post office (cnr Av San Martín & Moreno)

Thaler Cambio (Av San Martín 272) Changes traveler's checks.

Tourist office (446-2376; www.comodoro.gov.ar /turismo in Spanish; Av Rivadavia 430; 8am-3pm Mon-Sat) Friendly, well stocked and well organized. Desk at bus terminal open 7am to 10pm.

Sights

MUSEO NACIONAL DEL PETRÓLEO

Built by the former state oil agency YPF, but now managed by the Universidad Nacional de Patagonia, the national **petroleum museum** (455-9558; San Lorenzo 250; admission US$1.50, concession US$0.80; 9am-6pm Tue-Fri, 2-6pm Sat & Sun) boasts guided tours and gushing exhibits on the region's natural and cultural history, oil technology and social and historical aspects of petroleum development. Historical photos merit special mention, but there are also fascinating, detailed models of tankers, refineries, and the entire zone of exploitation.

The museum is in the suburb of General Mosconi, 3km north of downtown. Take a

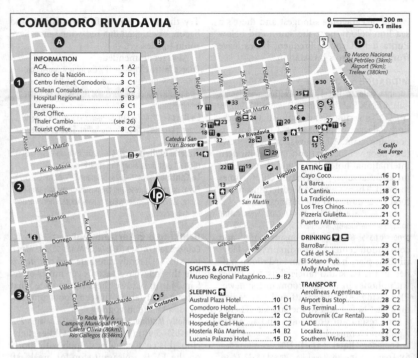

COMODORO RIVADAVIA

0 ———— 200 m
0 ———— 0.1 miles

INFORMATION
ACA....................................1 A2
Banco de la Nación.............2 D1
Centro Internet Comodoro....3 C1
Chilean Consulate................4 C2
Hospital Regional................5 B3
Laverap...............................6 C1
Post Office..........................7 D1
Thaler Cambio.................(see 26)
Tourist Office......................8 C2

SIGHTS & ACTIVITIES
Museo Regional Patagónico.....9 B2

SLEEPING
Austral Plaza Hotel..............10 D1
Comodoro Hotel..................11 C1
Hospedaje Belgrano.............12 C2
Hospedaje Cari-Hue............13 C2
Hostería Rúa Marina............14 B2
Lucania Palazzo Hotel..........15 D2

EATING
Cayo Coco...........................16 D1
La Barca..............................17 B1
La Cantina...........................18 C1
La Tradición.........................19 C1
Los Tres Chinos....................20 C1
Pizzería Giulietta..................21 C1
Puerto Mitre........................22 C2

DRINKING
BarroBar..............................23 C1
Café del Sol.........................24 C1
El Sótano Pub......................25 C1
Molly Malone......................26 C1

TRANSPORT
Aerolíneas Argentinas...........27 D1
Airport Bus Stop..................28 C2
Bus Terminal.......................29 C2
Dubrovnik (Car Rental)........30 D1
LADE..................................31 C2
Localiza..............................32 C2
Southern Winds...................33 C1

To Museo Nacional
del Petróleo (3km);
Airport (9km);
Trelew (380km)

Golfo
San Jorge

Catedral San
Juan Bosco

Plaza
San Martín

To Rada Tilly &
Camping Municipal (15km);
Caleta Olivia (80km);
Río Gallegos (834km)

PATAGONIA

remise from downtown (US$2) or bus No 7 Laprida or No 8 Palazzo bus (10 minutes).

MUSEO REGIONAL PATAGÓNICO

Decaying natural history specimens at this **museum** (☎ 477-7101; cnr Av Rivadavia & Chacabuco; admission free; ☀ 10am-6pm Mon-Fri, 3-7pm Sat & Sun) nearly overshadow the small yet entertaining archaeological and historical items, including some good pottery and spear points and materials on early South African Boer immigrants.

Tours

Several agencies arrange trips to Bosque Petrificado Sarmiento (p379) and Cueva de las Manos (p403). **Mónica Jury** and **Pedro Mangini** (☎ 446-5337; www.ruta-40.com in Spanish) speak English, German and Italian and organize well-informed, personalized 4x4 trips around Patagonia.

Sleeping

Catering mainly to business travelers and long-term laborers, lodging here fits two categories: the ritzy and the run-down (and often full). However, there are a few serviceable spots.

BUDGET

Hostería Rúa Marina (☎ 446-8777; Belgrano 738; s/d US$13/22, old section US$9/19) Most rooms don't have windows, but have ceiling fans – try for No 18 or 20. The welcoming staff, central location and hydromassage tubs in the new rooms make Rúa Marina a long-running favorite.

Hospedaje Cari-Hue (☎ 447-2946; Belgrano 563; s/d US$10/17) It's central, albeit noisy, with gnomes in the garden patio and a quirky owner. Breakfast and cheaper rooms with shared bathroom are available.

Hospedaje Belgrano (☎ 447-8439; Belgrano 546; s/d US$7.50/11, with shared bathroom US$5/8) Just like grandma's house, with homey, basic, old-fashioned rooms, nice hallways and a cat and dog.

Camping Municipal (☎ 445-2918; Rada Tilly; per person/tent US$1/1) At the windy beach resort of Rada Tilly, 15km south of Comodoro, this campground has evenly distributed sites with windbreaking shrubs. The wide beach is one of Patagonia's longest and there's a sea lion colony near the south end below Punta del Marqués. Frequent buses leave from Comodoro's bus station.

MIDRANGE & TOP END

Lucania Palazzo Hotel (☎ 449-9300; www.lucania -palazzo.com in Spanish; Moreno 676; s/d/ste US$75/85/98; P 💻) Towering over downtown, the sparkling Palazzo is proof that Comodoro is booming again. All rooms sport ocean views (but poor ventilation) and tasteful modern international hotel decor, and there are six presidential suites – just in case OPEC comes to town. There's a haute Mediterranean seafood restaurant and full business center.

Austral Plaza Hotel (☎ 447-2200; www.austral hotel.com.ar in Spanish; Moreno 725; s/d US$34-39/42, superior s/d US$55-68/75; P 💻) Business hotel and convention center extraordinaire, this labyrinthine place has boxy standard rooms hidden in the back and fancier business suites with phones in the bathroom in the newer Plaza wing. Attentive staff and a sweeping breakfast buffet add to the sparkle. There's a slick restaurant downstairs and access to a golf and tennis club.

Comodoro Hotel (☎ 447-2300; www.comodoro hotel.com.ar in Spanish; 9 de Julio 770; s/d US$32/37, superior US$40/47; P 💻) Drab standard rooms in this business-ready high-rise have plump beds and bidets, while the superior ones are more attractive, remodeled with larger bathrooms. Rates include a buffet breakfast and Internet.

Eating

The oil boom has bankrolled a taste for fine dining. If you're hankering for stylish cuisine, pick up the free *Sabores del Sur* restaurant directory, published by Chubut's hotel association.

Los Tres Chinos (☎ 444-1168; Av Rivadavia 341; buffet US$4-4.50) Always crowded, Los Tres Chinos' spread features some 40 items (including vegie options) as well as *parrilla*. Drinks here can be expensive.

Cayo Coco (☎ 447-3033; Av Rivadavia 102; mains US$4-9) Kitty-corner to La Anónima supermarket (which has cheap takeout), Cayo Coco wood-fires up an imaginative variety of pizzas and calzones.

La Tradición (☎ 446-5800; Mitre 675; mains US$4-12; ☎ closed Sun) A popular, top-quality *parrilla* with a variety of expertly prepared dishes.

Try the tenderloin with ham, cheese and bacon, or chicken in a red-wine sauce. Save room for dessert.

Also recommended:

Puerto Mitre (☎ 447-6175; cnr Mitre & Ameghino; mains US$5-10) Clever decorations and stylish service are hardly noticed once the beers and cheesy pizza with fresh toppings arrive.

La Barca (☎ 447-3710; Belgrano 935; mains US$3-9) Order à la carte or head for the buffet. Seafood is the specialty.

Pizzería Giulietta (☎ 446-1201; Belgrano 851; mains US$3-7) Best pizza along this stretch.

La Cantina (☎ 446-0023; Belgrano 845; mains US$3-7) Pizzas drip with cheese and the pastas come with ample sauce, although neither wins culinary kudos. Check window for daily specials.

Drinking & Entertainment

Café del Sol (☎ 440-0034; Av San Martín 502; breakfast & snacks US$1-4) Trendy café-bars and *confiterías* like this one have taken over much of Av San Martín. Cruise the strip and see what catches your fancy – it seems pool and *rock en español* are in vogue.

Molly Malone (☎ 447-8333; Av San Martín 292; mains US$1-5) Run by the Golden Oldies rugby club, this cozy corner café/pub with sports on the TV is a pleasant stop for breakfast, set lunch, *cafécito* (quick coffee) and newspaper, or a Quilmes in the evening.

BarroBar (☎ 444-5155; Av San Martín 626) A trendy yuppie bar with creative art and live theater, salsa and tango.

El Sótano Pub (Av San Martín 239) Hidden in a basement, this lively pub serves up pool and a good variety of live music on weekends.

Getting There & Away

The Corredor Biocéanico – RN 26, RP 20 and RP 55 – is a straight highway link to Coyhaique, Chile and its Pacific port, Puerto Chacabuco. Developers are promoting this commercial transport route as an alternative to the Panama Canal, since there's a year-round pass and it's the continent's shortest distance between ports on both oceans. Paved RN 26, RP 20 and RN 40 lead to Esquel and Bariloche.

AIR

Aerolíneas Argentinas (☎ 444-0050; Av Rivadavia 156) flies a couple of times daily to Buenos Aires (US$198) and a couple of times a week to Neuquén (US$229). **Southern Winds**

(☎ 447-7200; Mitre 943) flies almost daily to Río Gallegos (US$58) and Buenos Aires (US$96), with possible future connections to El Calafate.

Comodoro is the hub for **LADE** (☎ 447-0585; Av Rivadavia 360), which wings it at least once a week to Bariloche (US$42 to US$55), El Calafate (US$55), Esquel (US$23 to US$30), Puerto Madryn (US$47), Río Gallegos (US$37 to US$48), Trelew (US$47), Ushuaia (US$77), Viedma (US$50) and points in between. Schedules and routes change as often as the winds; airport tax is US$2.

BUS

All buses plying RN 3 stop at the **bus terminal** (☎ 446-7305; Pellegrini 730) – don't miss the kitsch relief maps of Chabut and handy bus schedule chart above the tourist office.

Andesmar (☎ 446-8894) departs twice daily, at 5:30am and 2:30pm, for points north including Trelew, Rawson, Puerto Madryn and San Antonio Oeste, then heads inland toward Córdoba. **TAC** (☎ 444-3376) follows the same route through Patagonia, leaving at 8:30am, but continues to Bahía Blanca, La Plata and Buenos Aires. For points south, TAC departs at 8:30pm for Caleta Olivia, Puerto San Julián and Río Gallegos.

Etap (☎ 447-4841) runs to Sarmiento three times daily, to Esquel once daily, to Río Mayo once daily, Coyhaique three times weekly at 1am and to Río Senguer four times weekly.

For Los Antiguos and connections to Chile Chico, **La Unión** (☎ 446-2822) and **Sportsman** (☎ 444-2988) have two buses daily, stopping in Perito Moreno. For other Chilean destinations, **Turíbus** (☎ 446-0058) goes to Coyhaique (US$23) Wednesday and Saturday at 8am.

Destination	Cost (US$)	Duration (hr)
Bahía Blanca	25-29	15
Bariloche	22	14
Buenos Aires	30-37	24
Caleta Olivia	3	1
Esquel	13-15	8-9
Los Antiguos	12-15	6
Puerto Deseado	10	4-5
Puerto Madryn	10	6-8
Río Gallegos	14	9-11
Trelew	10-16	5-6
Viedma	21	10-13

Getting Around

Aeropuerto General Mosconi (CRD; ☎ 454-8190) is 9km north of town. The No 8 'Directo Palazzo' bus (US$0.50) goes there directly from outside the downtown bus terminal.

Expreso Rada Tilly links Comodoro's terminal to the nearby beach resort (US$0.60) every 20 minutes weekdays, every 30 minutes on weekends.

Rental cars are available from **Avis** (☎ 454-8483; at airport) and **Localiza** (☎ 446-3526; Av Rivadavia 535). **Dubrovnik** (☎ 444-1844; www.rentacardubrovnik .com; Moreno 941) rents 4WD vehicles (US$100 to US$150 a day with 150km free).

SARMIENTO

☎ 0297 / pop 8300

After 148km of oil derricks and desert drudgery west from Comodoro along RN 26 and RP 20, tree-green Sarmiento, with Lago Musters and Lago Colué Huapi nearby, is an inviting stop, and the gateway to the petrified forests, 30km south. Considered Argentina's southernmost irrigated town, it's been an agricultural center since its founding in 1897. Unfortunately, the industry has come at a cost: Colué Huapi, of great concern to area ecologists, is a puddle of its former self.

There's a helpful **tourist office** (☎ 489-8220; turismo@coopsar.com.ar; cnr Infanteria 25 & Pietrobelli) with a good map of town and the region.

Facing the plaza, the **Museo Regional Desiderio Torres** (Coronel 355; admission free; ☺ 10am-1pm & 5-8pm Mon-Sat, 10am-5pm Sun) has surprisingly good archaeological and paleontology displays, plus indigenous artifacts, with an emphasis on weavings. Just before the entrance to town is **Granja San José** (☎ 489-3733), a hydroponics farm that sells exquisite jams.

Room and board is available in a 1930s homestead at the recommended **Chacra Labrador** (☎ 489-3329, 15-509-3537; agna@coopsar.com.ar; www.agrotourpatagonia.itgo.com; s/d US$22/33), where the attentive Dutch- and English-speaking owners Annelies and Nicholás grow cherries, feed nonguests and organize excursions to nearby attractions. It's 10km east of Sarmiento, 1km before the Río Senguer bridge – call for pickup from town.

Etap buses run daily to Sarmiento (US$5) from Comodoro Rivadavia and Esquel.

BOSQUE PETRIFICADO SARMIENTO

These petrified **forests** (admission US$5; ☺ dawn-dusk), 30km southeast of Sarmiento, are much more easily accessed than the Monumento Natural Bosques Petrificados further south. A trail leads through a beautifully quiet and ghostly area that has the appearance of a lumberyard gone mad; 'wood' chips cover the ground and huge petrified logs are scattered about. Unlike the petrified forest in Santa Cruz, the trunks here are not of original fallen trees, but were brought from the mountainous regions by strong river currents about 65 million years ago. The most impressive area of the park has a handful of large trunks set against the red and orange striated bluffs.

Tour buses usually leave by 5pm. Try to stay through sunset, when the striped bluffs of Cerro Abigarrado and the multi-hued hills turn brilliantly vivid. Rangers guide tours and, as you leave the park, if they are suspicious, will ask you to empty your pockets to expose any stolen pieces. A 'box of shame' shows what some have tried to sneak out. It's possible to arrange a car and driver (around US$25) in Sarmiento for the 1½-hour roundtrip.

CALETA OLIVIA
☎ 0297 / pop 37,000

On coastal RN 3, the breezy oil- and fish-processing port Caleta Olivia has little to recommend it. It is, however, a convenient place to change buses to more inspiring locales, such as the petrified forests, Puerto Deseado or Los Antiguos. The port was built in 1901 as part of a plan to run the telegraph along the coast, and was named after the only woman on board that first ship.

Discovery of oil in 1944 turned the face of industry from wood and sheep transport to petroleum, as evidenced by the ghostlike 10m-high Monumento al Obrero Petrolero dominating the downtown traffic circle. Colloquially called 'El Gorosito,' the muscular oil worker looks north, symbolizing the link between this area's industry and Argentina's oil-poor northern reaches.

Orientation
Entering town from the north, RN 3 becomes Av Jorge Newbery, then Av San Martín (the main thoroughfare), continuing after the traffic circle along southeast diagonal Av Eva Perón. The southwest diagonal, Av Independencia, the center of the casino and teenage action, becomes RP 12. Most streets run

diagonal to San Martín, except in the northeast quadrant. The port and pebbly beach are four blocks east of the traffic circle.

Information
Banks along San Martín have ATMs but don't change traveler's checks. *Locutorios* and some of Southern Cone's biggest Internet cafés also line San Martín.

Post office (25 de Mayo at Yrigoyen)

Tourist office (☎ 485-0988; caletaolivia@santacruz.gov .ar; cnr San Martín & Güemes; ☉ 7am-10pm) Enthusiastic, near the monument, with a map of town.

Sleeping & Eating
For what accommodations offer, rates are steep, and breakfast an additional cost. Av Independencia has lots of bars, cafés and ice-cream shops.

Hotel Robert (☎ 485-1452; hrobert@mcolivia.com .ar; San Martín 2151; s US$18-40, d US$27-50; P) Sterile rooms and tasteless meals taint Robert's two-to three-star status, but it's the best hostelry in town. Breakfast (available to nonguests) is US$2 and there's a 10% cash discount.

Posada Don David (☎ 857-7661; Yrigoyen 2385; s/d with shared bathroom US$10/13) Basic rooms line a tight corridor and the bathrooms need work, but overall, well-run Don David is clean and pleasant. Recommended meals (US$2 to US$5; closed Sunday) at the popular, casual eatery start with a crisp salad, followed by homemade pasta or *parrilla*.

Residencial Las Vegas (☎ 485-1177; Yrigoyen 2094; r per person with private bathroom US$10) The owners are kind, but won't be winning any Martha Stewart awards. Ceilings are high and the back rooms are quiet, but there's no TV and, except for fans, precious little ventilation.

Hotel Capri (☎ 485-1132; Hernández 1145; s/d with private bathroom US$7/10; P) For the better half of a century, the fun-loving owners have offered basic rooms (upstairs are best) off a central hallway.

Camping Municipal (☎ 485-0999, ext 476; cnr Brown & Guttero; 1/2 people US$1/1.50, with car US$1.50/2) In an exposed gravel lot near the busy beach, the campground lacks privacy but has 24-hour security, hot showers and barbecue pits.

El Puerto (☎ 485-1313; Independencia 1060; set meals US$5.50, mains US$3-8) The linens are crisp and bleach-white and the formal seafood meals are spendy, but if you're looking for a power lunch, it's the best bet in town.

Variedades Pizzería (☎ 485-6555; Independencia 52; lunch US$3.50, mains US$2-6) Of the family-friendly eateries along the main drag, this bright place is the least smoky and most cheery. Besides pizza and empanadas, there's a good set lunch, beer, wine and thick slices of vegetable pie.

Getting There & Away

The **bus terminal** (cnr Bequin & Tierra del Fuego) is 3km northwest of downtown (less than US$1 by *remise*). The main north–south carriers leave for Comodoro Rivadavia (US$3, one hour) hourly from 7am to 11pm, with less service on Sunday, and for Río Gallegos (US$11 to US$13, seven to 10 hours) four times daily between 8:30pm and 2am, passing Puerto San Julián. Sportsman and La Unión serve Puerto Deseado (US$7.50, 3½ hours), Perito Moreno (US$9, four hours) and Los Antiguos (US$11, five hours) in the early morning and late afternoon.

PUERTO DESEADO

☎ 0297 / pop 12,000

Some 125km southeast of the RN 3 junction, RN 281 weaves through valleys of warbled pink rock, past packs of guanaco, ending at the serene and attractive deep-sea fishing town of Puerto Deseado. The glacial pace and historic buildings, plus the submerged estuary of Ría Deseado (p383), brimming with seabirds and marine wildlife, make this a worthwhile detour.

After a destructive storm in 1520, Hernando de Magallanes stayed in the estuary's sheltered waters to repair the fleet, naming the area 'Río de los Trabajos.' In 1586, English privateer Cavendish explored the estuary and named it after his ship *Desire*, the name that stuck. Fleets from around the world descended on the port for whaling and seal hunting, compelling the Spanish crown to send a squadron of colonists, under the command of Antonio de Viedma. A harsh winter didn't bode well for them, however, and more than 30 died of scurvy. Those who survived moved inland to form the short-lived colony of Floridablanca. In 1834, Darwin surveyed the estuary, as did Perito Moreno in 1876.

Orientation

Puerto Deseado is two hours southeast of the RN 3 junction at Fitz Roy via dead-end RN 281. The center of activity is the axis formed by the main drags, San Martín and Almirante Brown.

Information

Banks, ATMs, *locutorios* and Internet are all found along San Martín.

Banco de la Nación (San Martín)

Darwin Expediciones (☎ 15-624-7554; www.darwin -expeditions.com; España 2601) Tours of Reserva Natural Ría Deseado (p383).

Ecowash (☎ 487-0490; Piedra Buena 859; ✛ closed Sun) Full-service laundry.

Los Vikingos (☎ 487-0020, 15-624-5141/4283; Estrada 1275) Tours include Reserva Natural Ría Deseado (p383) and Monumento Natural Bosques Petrificados (p383).

Post office (San Martín 1075)

Ría Deseado Tourist Office (☎ 487-0220; www .puertodeseado.gov.ar; San Martín 1525; ✛ 10am-1pm & 5-8pm Mon-Fri) There's another English-speaking desk at the bus station.

Transporte Fede (☎ 15-624-4878; Gregores 1142) For visits to Monumento Natural Bosques Petrificados (p383).

Vagón Histórico Tourist Office (cnr San Martín & A Brown; ✛ 9am-9pm)

Sights & Activities

Puerto Deseado's historical monuments testify to the town's better days as the terminus of the Ferrocarril Patagónico, a cargo and passenger route that hauled wool and lead from Chilean mines from Pico Truncado and Las Heras, 280km northwest. Pick up a *Guía Historica* walking tour map (in Spanish only) from either tourist office.

The imposing English-designed **Estación del Ferrocarril Patagónico** (✛ 4-7pm Mon-Fri; admission by donation), off Av Oneto, was the coastal terminus for the line, built by Yugoslav stonecutters in 1908. In the center of town, the restored 1898 **Vagón Histórico** (cnr San Martín & Almirante Brown) is locally known as the car from which rebel leader Facón Grande prepared the 'Patagonia Rebellion.' (In 1979, the car was going to be sold for scrap, but the townspeople blocked the roads to keep the car in its rightful spot.) A few blocks west is the attractive **Sociedad Española** (San Martín 1176), c 1915.

The **Museo Regional Mario Brozoski** (☎ 487-0673; cnr Colón & Belgrano; admission free; ✛ 10am-5pm Mon-Fri) displays relics of the English corvette *Swift*, sunk off the coast of Deseado in 1776, located in 1982, and from which divers continue to recover artifacts.

PUERTO DESEADO

0   500 m
0   0.3 miles

INFORMATION
Banco de la Nación..................1 C2
Ecowash................................2 D2
Los Vikingos..........................3 B2
Post Office.............................4 C2
Ría Deseada Tourist Office.......5 B2
Vagón Histórico
  Tourist Office.......................6 C2

SIGHTS & ACTIVITIES
Club Naútico.........................7 B3
Museo Regional Mario Brozoski..8 C3
Sociedad Española..................9 C2

SLEEPING
Camping La Costanera..........10 D3
Hotel Los Acantilados...........11 A2

Residencial Los Olmos............12 D2
Residencial Sur.....................13 B2

EATING
Don Pipo.............................14 B1
El Pingüino..........................15 D2
El Refugio del Marino.............16 B2
Kokomo...............................17 B2

DRINKING
Perico's..............................18 C2
Quinto Elemento..................19 D2

ENTERTAINMENT
Jackaroe Boliche...................20 C2

TRANSPORT
Estación del Ferrocarril
  Patagónico..........................21 D2

To Darwin Expediciones (500m);
Camping Cañadón Giménez
(4km); RN 3 (127km);
Coleta Olivia (214km)

To Bus
Terminal
(150m)

Ría Deseada

In summer, the **Club Naútico** rents windsurfing boards and kayaks. Inquire at the pier about sport fishing possibilities.

Sleeping

Ask the tourist office about (relatively) nearby *estancias*.

Hotel Los Acantilados (☎ 487-2167; www.pdeseado.com.ar/acantour in Spanish; cnr Pueyrredón & España; s/d US$17/25, with ocean view US$22/35, ste US$55; P) Perched atop a pink-stone bluff overlooking the port, superior rooms have great views, as does the attractive dining room. Added perks are congenial owners and TV lounge with fireplace. The breakfast buffet is bland but bountiful. It's often full of tour groups, so book ahead.

Residencial Los Olmos (☎ 487-0077; Gregores 849; s/d US$12/16; P) Tidy and friendly, this well-run place is the best budget option, with TV, heat and private bathrooms in all 17 rooms.

Residencial Sur (☎ 487-0522; Ameghino 1640; s/d with shared bathroom US$12/20; P) Large and well run, Sur is often busy with traveling workers – fishing crews, mainly. Rooms are basic, bathrooms are sparkling and breakfast is included. Other meals and a few rooms with private bathroom may be available.

Camping La Costanera (☎ 15-625-2890; Av Costanera; per person & tent US$1.50, trailer bunks per person US$4) Rates at this year-round waterfront campground vary by site. It has good toilets and showers, but incessant winds can be a nuisance and some campsites are stony.

Camping Cañadón Giménez (☎ 15-624-8602; Ruta 281; sites US$2-5) Four kilometers northwest of town, but only 50m from the Ría Deseado, this year-round campground is protected by forest and high rocky walls. Prices depend on number of people and whether the site has a fire pit and picnic table. Basic provisions are available, as are showers and hot water.

Eating

El Pingüino (☎ 487-2105; Piedra Buena 958; mains US$3-6; ☽ closed Sun) Locals rave about this place, and rightly so. It serves the best meals in town. Enjoy fresh catches with tasty sauces, or any pasta dish, in a warm, animated dining room. There's a set menu and good wine list, but service lags when there's only one waiter to assist the gregarious owner.

Kokomo (☎ 487-2134; cnr Sarmiento & San Martín; mains US$2-6; ◷ noon-1am Wed-Mon) The patio overlooking the plaza is a nice spot to enjoy wood-fired oven pizzas. It also delivers. The adjacent ice-cream shop is superb.

El Refugio del Marino (☎ 15-621-5290; Pueyrredón 224; tapas US$1-5; ◷ to 2am) Sailors and fishermen, most hailing from Spain, congregate at this friendly, stylish bar to throw back tapas and glasses of cheap *tinto* (red wine). Come in for the set lunch to swap tall tales with the boys.

Don Pipo (cnr Don Bosco & Rivadavia; mains US$2-5) Not big on aesthetics, popular Pipo feeds starving sailors with quantities of pasta and decent *parrilla*.

Drinking & Entertainment

Late-night drinking and dancing spots include **Perico's** (San Martín 1294), the pub **Quinto Elemento** (cnr Don Bosco & 12 de Octubre) and the swanky disco **Jackaroe Boliche** (Mariano Moreno 663), in an unfortunate building.

Getting There & Away

LADE (☎ 487-2674), at the bus terminal, provides cheap thrills by flying at least once a week to San Julián (US$13), Comodoro Rivadavia (US$16), Río Gallegos (US$30) and Buenos Aires (US$97).

The **bus terminal** (Sargento Cabral 1302) is on the northeast side of town, nine long blocks and slightly uphill from San Martín and Oneto. Taxis to/from the center should cost no more than US$1.

There are six departures daily to Caleta Olivia (US$7.50, 3½ hours). Three buses continue to Comodoro Rivadavia (US$10, five hours). Leaving on the 1pm bus (which doesn't run Sunday) allows for the quickest connection to Perito Moreno and Los Antiguos. One bus leaves nightly at 7:30pm for Río Gallegos (US$18, 12 hours).

If you're thinking of getting off at godforsaken Fitz Roy (where locals claim the only thing to see is the wind!) to continue on to Comodoro or Río Gallegos, think again: buses arrive at a demonic hour and the only place to crash is the campground behind Multirubro La Illusion.

RESERVA NATURAL RÍA DESEADO

Considered one of South America's most important marine preserves, Ría Deseado is the unique result of a river abandoning its bed, allowing the Atlantic waters to invade 40km inland and create a perfect shelter for marine life. Several islands and other sites provide nesting habitat for seabirds, including Magellanic penguins, petrels, oystercatchers, herons, terns and five species of cormorants. Isla Chaffers is the main spot for the penguins, while Banco Cormorán offers protection to rock cormorants and the strikingly beautiful gray cormorant. Isla de los Pingüinos has nesting rockhoppers and breeding elephant seals. Commerson's dolphins, sea lions, guanacos and ñandús (ostrichlike rhea) can also be seen while touring the estuary.

Darwin Expediciones (p381) runs circuits that take in viewing of Commerson's dolphins, Isla Chaffers, Banco Cormorán and a walk to a penguin colony (US$15, 2½ hours). A longer tour takes in all of the above plus another 15km of the estuary (US$25, five hours). There's a four- to five-person minimum and tours leave depending on tides, usually early morning or midafternoon. Los Vikingos (p381) has bilingual guides and organizes overland trips. The best time to visit the reserve is December to April.

MONUMENTO NATURAL BOSQUES PETRIFICADOS

During Jurassic times, 150 million years ago, this area enjoyed a humid, temperate climate with flourishing forests, but intense volcanic activity buried them in ash. Erosion later exposed the mineralized *Proaraucaria* trees (ancestors of the modern *Araucaria*, unique to the southern hemisphere), up to 3m in diameter and 35m in length. Today, the 15,000-hectare **Petrified Forest Natural Monument** (admission free; ◷ 9am-9pm year-round) has a small visitor center, English-language brochure and short interpretive trail, leading from park headquarters, to the largest concentration of petrified trees. Until its legal protection in 1954, the area was plundered for some of its finest specimens; please don't perpetuate this unsavory tradition.

Other parts of the scenic desert park also merit exploration, but consult with park rangers before heading toward the peak of Madre e Hija. Bring water; there's none at the site.

The park is 157km southwest of Caleta Olivia, accessed from the good gravel RP 49, leading 50km west from a turnoff at

PATAGONIA

Km 2074 on RN 3. There's no public transport directly to the park. Buses from Caleta Olivia will drop you at the junction, but you may wait several hours for a lift into the park. Los Vikingos (p381) runs tours from Puerto Deseado, or try Transporte Fede (p381).

There's basic **camping**, as well as provisions, at **La Paloma**, 20km before the park headquarters. Camping in the park is strictly prohibited.

PUERTO SAN JULIÁN
☎ 02962 / pop 6000

One of Patagonia's more historically intriguing coastal towns, sleepy San Julián, 350km south of Caleta Olivia, can claim to be the place where the name 'Patagonia' came to be (see p357), and where the likes of Magellan, Viedma, Drake and Darwin all stopped. Today, it's a decent pitstop and the place to see Commerson's dolphins.

The late-19th-century wool boom brought permanent settlement, thanks to pioneering Scots. From the early 1900s until the decline of wool prices during the past two decades, the British-owned San Julián Sheep Farming Company was the region's primary economic force. Currently, mining and seafood processing are the major industries.

Information
Banco de la Nación (cnr Mitre & Belgrano) ATM on San Martín.

Dirección de Turismo (☎ 454396; www.sanjulian.gov.ar in Spanish; Magallanes s/n; ☼ 7am-9pm Mon-Fri, 5-9pm Sat & Sun) There's also a high-season kiosk at San Martín 500.

Post office (cnr San Martín & Belgrano)

Telephone (cnr San Martín & Rivadavia) *Locutorio* with Internet.

Sights & Activities
In a classic Magellanic house, the **Museo Regional y de Arte Marino** (cnr Vieytes & Rivadavia; admission free; ☼ 9am-1pm & 4-9pm Mon-Fri, 10am-1pm & 4-9pm Sat & Sun) features archaeological artifacts and historical materials, as well as contemporary fine art. Well-informed guides, some of whom speak English, put the many objects and photographs in intriguing historical context.

Two-hour boat trips around Bahía San Julián (US$10 per person), visiting penguin and imperial cormorant rookeries at Banco Cormorán and Banco Justicia, are run by

Expediciones Pinocho (☎ 452856; cnr Mitre & 9 de Julio). From December to March, there's a good chance you'll see the Commerson's dolphin (p374).

Sleeping & Eating
Hotel Bahía (☎ 454028; San Martín 1075; s/d US$22/29; **P**) The newest and nicest place in town, the Bahía has modern, comfortable rooms and professional service.

Posada Kau Yenu (☎ 452431; cnr San Martín & Calafate; s/d US$12/17; **P**) Helpful owner Don Ernesto fills his cozy home with good spirits and affection. Service is personal and the breakfast breads are homemade.

Residencial Sada (☎ 452013; San Martín 1112; s/d US$12/19; **P**) Breakfast is included at this good bet with warm, clean rooms, TV and large bathrooms. From the bus terminal, turn left and walk four blocks.

Hostería Municipal (☎ 452300; 25 de Mayo 917; s/d US$13/20; **P**) The zigzag corridor design means all rooms have bay views. It's welcoming and professionally run, and the rooms are quiet, clean, have TV and shipshape bathrooms.

Hotel Álamo (☎ 454092; RN 3; s/d US$9/12; **P**) Next to the EG3 gas station (no sign, inquire inside) and the RN 3 junction, Alamo is a small, adequate place with a good restaurant and private bathrooms.

Autocamping Municipal (☎ 452806; Magallanes 650; per person/car US$1/1.65) On the waterfront at the north end of Vélez Sarsfield, this full-service campground has hot showers, laundry and windbreaks.

El Muelle Viejo (☎ 453009; cnr 9 de Julio & Mitre; pastas US$4-9) Gaze over the bay at the Club Naútico while enjoying well-prepared fresh catch, breadsticks and Roquefort butter.

La Rural (☎ 454066; Ameghino 811) A good, old-fashioned spot near the museum for seafood or *parrilla*.

Casa Lara (San Martín 400; mains US$2-5) Mingle over a drink or quick meal in the late evening hours, surrounded by nostalgic locals, gingham and lace, in a 1901 building.

Getting There & Away
AIR
LADE (☎ 452137), located at the bus terminal, soars at least once each week for Puerto Deseado (US$12), Río Gallegos (US$19), Comodoro Rivadavia (US$24) and Buenos Aires (US$102).

BUS

Most RN 3 buses visit San Julián's **bus terminal** (☎ 452082; San Martín 1552) at insane hours. The best bets are Don Otto, which has service at 6:20am, and Andesmar, with early morning and late evening departures. TAC has the most comfortable buses. Fares to Caleta Olivia and Comodoro Rivadavia or Río Gallegos range between US$6 and US$10.

Slightly more expensive door-to-door service options are **Sur Servicio** (☎ 454044; San Martín 1380) to Comodoro Rivadavia and **Gold Tour** (☎ 452265; San Martín 1075) to Río Gallegos. **Transporte Cerro San Lorenzo** (☎ 452403; Berutti 970) serves Gobernador Gregores (US$9) on Tuesday and Saturday at 7am and Thursday and Sunday at 1pm.

ESTANCIA LA MARÍA

Some 150km northwest of Puerto San Julián amid the Patagonia steppe, Estancia La María has 84 caves with excellently preserved rock paintings dating back 12,600 years. Three different cultures, all before the Tehuelche, adorned these geologic corners in what is today probably Patagonia's most important discovery of *arte rupestre* (cave paintings). The only way to see these treasures is by guided tour with the *estancia* owners.

This is also a great choice for those looking for a night on an *estancia*. La María is accessed via RP 25 and RP 77. Contact the kind owners **Pepa and Fernando Behm** (in San Julián ☎ 02962-452233, 15-449827; Saavedra 1168; d with private/shared bathroom US$20/10, per tent incl hot shower US$5; ☑ Oct-May) for reservations and transport options. Breakfast is available (US$2), as is the recommended *asado* (barbecue; US$17).

PARQUE NACIONAL MONTE LEÓN

Inaugurated in 2004, Argentina's first coastal national park protects over 60,000 hectares of striking headlands, archetypal Patagonian steppe and 40km of dramatic coastline. These impressive landscapes, formerly an *estancia,* are home to abundant Magellanic penguins, sea lions, guanacos and unusual geographic features like **La Olla** (a huge cave-like structure eroded by the ocean). Perhaps its most interesting attraction is **Isla Monte León**, a high offshore sea stack heavily mined for guano between 1933 and 1960. Now being recolonized by cormorants, Dominican gulls, skuas and other seabirds, the island is accessible at low tide, when it's also possible to walk in La Olla – the tidal range is great and the water returns fast.

The park's entrance is 30km south of Comandante Luis Piedrabuena or 205km north of Río Gallegos, directly off RN 3. A visitor center is in the works near the charming **Hostería Monte León** (in Buenos Aires ☎ 011-4621-4784, in Ushuaia ☎ 02901-43-1851; www.monteleon-patagonia.com; full pension s/d US$130/210; ☑ Nov-Apr), which occupies the *estancia's* former *casco* (big house). Contact Monte León about organized excursions and for details about full room and board in a vintage farmhouse at nearby **Estancia Dor-Aike**.

RÍO GALLEGOS

☎ 02966 / pop 100,000

Most travelers quickly transfer through this fast-growing provincial capital, en route to El Calafate, southern Chile or Tierra del Fuego. The largest town south of Comodoro Rivadavia, it has an intriguing assortment of restored historic buildings and museums that make for an enjoyable short stay.

As the wool industry boomed in the early 1900s, the region attracted Brits and Chileans seeking more land and fortune. Less than 20% of the original population was native Argentine. When coal was discovered 230km away in Río Turbio, the narrow-gauge railway delivered the deposits to the port. Gallegos' economy now revolves around nearby oilfields, while coal deposits are shipped to oceangoing vessels at Punta Loyola. Home to a large military base, Río Gallegos played an active role during the Falkland/Malvinas War (p424); there are several memorials to the battles around town.

Information

IMMIGRATION

Immigration office (☎ 420205; Urquiza 144; ☑ 9am-3pm Mon-Fri)

INTERNET ACCESS

There are several other *cibers* along Av Roca with relatively slow access.

J@vaCyberCafé (☎ 422775; Av Roca 923; ☑ until 3 or 4am; snacks US$1-3) After checking email, enjoy breakfast, sandwiches or a beer while flipping through an English-language magazine.

LAUNDRY

Aike Lavar (☎ 420759; Corrientes 277) Full-service laundry.

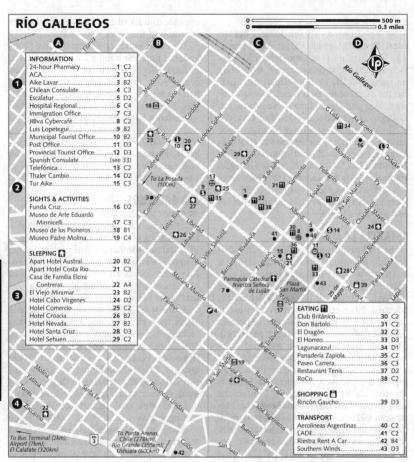

RÍO GALLEGOS

INFORMATION	
24-hour Pharmacy	1 C2
ACA	2 D2
Aike Lavar	3 B2
Chilean Consulate	4 C3
Escalatur	5 D2
Hospital Regional	6 C4
Immigration Office	7 C3
J@va Cybercafé	8 C2
Luis Lopetegui	9 B2
Municipal Tourist Office	10 B2
Post Office	11 D3
Provincial Tourist Office	12 D3
Spanish Consulate	(see 33)
Telefónica	13 D2
Thaler Cambio	14 D2
Tur Aike	15 C3

SIGHTS & ACTIVITIES	
Funda Cruz	16 D2
Museo de Arte Eduardo Minicelli	17 C3
Museo de los Pioneros	18 B1
Museo Padre Molina	19 C4

SLEEPING	
Apart Hotel Austral	20 B2
Apart Hotel Costa Río	21 C3
Casa de Familia Elcira Contreras	22 A4
El Viejo Miramar	23 B2
Hotel Cabo Vírgenes	24 D2
Hotel Comercio	25 B2
Hotel Croacia	26 B2
Hotel Nevada	27 B2
Hotel Santa Cruz	28 D3
Hotel Sehuen	29 C2

EATING	
Club Británico	30 C2
Don Bartolo	31 C2
El Dragón	32 C2
El Horreo	33 D3
Lagunacazul	34 D1
Panadería Zapiola	35 C2
Paseo Carrera	36 C3
Restaurant Tenis	37 D2
RoCo	38 C2

SHOPPING	
Rincón Gaucho	39 D3

TRANSPORT	
Aerolíneas Argentinas	40 C2
LADE	41 C2
Riestra Rent A Car	42 B4
Southern Winds	43 D3

To La Posada (100m)

To Bus Terminal (2km);
Airport (7km);
El Calafate (320km)

To Punta Arenas,
Chile (278km);
Río Grande (355km);
Ushuaia (600km)

MEDICAL SERVICES
24-hour pharmacy (cnr Av Roca & 9 de Julio)
Hospital Regional (☎ 107, 420025; J Ingenieros 98)

MONEY
Several banks on Av Roca have ATMs.
Luis Lopetegui (Zapiola 469; ☺ 9:30am-noon & 3-7:30pm Mon-Fri, 9am-1pm Sat) Deals in US dollars and Chilean pesos.
Thaler Cambio (Av San Martín 484; ☺ 10am-3pm Mon-Fri, 10am-1pm Sat) Changes traveler's checks.

POST
Post office (Av Roca 893)

TELEPHONE
Telefónica (Av Roca 1328) One of several late-night *locutorios* on Av Roca with Internet.

TOURIST INFORMATION
ACA (☎ 420477; Orkeke 10)
Municipal tourist office (☎ 436917/20; www.rio gallegos.gov.ar; cnr Av Roca & Córdoba; ☺ 9am-3pm Mon-Fri) Desks at airport and bus terminal keep longer hours.
Provincial tourist office (☎ 422702; www.santacruz .gov.ar in Spanish; Av Roca 863; ☺ 9am-7pm Mon-Fri, 10am-1pm & 5-8pm Sat & Sun) Most helpful, with maps, bilingual staff and detailed info.

TRAVEL AGENCIES
Escalatur (☎ 420001; escalatur@speedy.com.ar; cnr Alberdi & Av San Martín) Trips to El Calafate and Cabo Vírgines (US$20 per person).
Tur Aike (☎ 422436; turaiketurismo@ciudad.com.ar; Zapiola 63) Helpful for airline bookings.

PATAGONIA

Sights

At the Complejo Cultural Provincial, the **Museo Padre Molina** (☎ 423290; Ramón y Cajal 51; admission free; ☼ 9am-8pm) has temporary modern art exhibitions, plus informative displays on geology, dinosaurs, Tehuelche ethnology (with excellent photographs) and local history. There's also a handicrafts center selling high-quality knitted sweaters and woven shawls.

Opposite Plaza San Martín, the **Museo de Arte Eduardo Minnicelli** (Maipú 13; admission free; ☼ 8am-6pm Tue-Fri, 3-7pm Sat & Sun) houses paintings by Santa Cruz artists.

In a typical prefabricated 1890s metal-clad house shipped from England, the **Museo de los Pioneros** (☎ 437763; cnr Elcano & Alberdi; admission free; ☼ 10am-8pm) has good displays on early immigrant life. **Funda Cruz** (G Lista 60) is another attractive, imported, prefabricated wooden house. Once a customs office, it now hosts cultural activities as well as a *salón de té.*

Sleeping

Since hotels cater mainly to business travelers, good-value budget accommodations are scarce.

BUDGET

La Posada (☎ 436445; Ameghino 331; r US$17) One of the more attractive older places in town, this inn fills up fast with out-of-towners waiting for medical appointments. The rooms are cool, carpeted and clean and all surround a sunny internal garden. Meals are served in the ranch-style dining area.

Hotel Cabo Vírgenes (☎ 422134/41; paulo_lunzevich@arnet.com.ar; C Rivadavia 252; s/d US$13/19; **P**) A couple of blocks from the river, this welcoming option offers professional service and a 10% ACA discount. The hallways are narrow and the rooms cramped (except for a few larger family rooms), but all are quiet.

Hotel Nevada (☎ 425990; Zapiola 480; s US$9-12, d US$14-17; **P** 🖳) The funky curtains and jungle of plants in the lobby lend a certain mustiness, but the small rooms are clean and the beds firm. Consider the pricier rooms – shared bathrooms are few and cramped.

Casa de Familia Elcira Contreras (☎ 429856; Zuccarino 431; dm US$6) You'll feel right at home at this clean, congenial place with large shared bathrooms and kitchen access. It's a 15-minute walk from the bus station (no sign; cross RN3; taxi US$0.75).

MIDRANGE & TOP END

Hotel Sehuen (☎ 425683; www.hotelsehuen.unlugar.com in Spanish; Rawson 160; s US$16-20, d US$22-26; **P**) Bright and airy, modern Sehuen is an all-round good-value and business-traveler favorite. Everything is spotless and rates vary according to room size.

Apart Hotel Austral (☎ 435588; www.apartaustral.com in Spanish; Av Roca 1505; s US$19-23, d US$28; **P** 🖳) The newest, most modern place in town has cheerful, well-furnished mini-apartments with basic kitchens.

Hotel Croacia (☎ 422997; Urquiza 431; s/d US$23/28) Formally a Yugoslav community center, the 20-room Croacia is run by a conscientious couple who provide top-quality service. Rooms are quiet with good-size bathrooms. An abundant breakfast is an extra US$1.50.

El Viejo Miramar (☎ 430401; Av Roca 1630; s/d US$14/24; **P**) Adjacent to the Esso station, this attractive, personable place has comfortable, if somewhat dark rooms. The amicable owner includes breakfast and opens his kitchen for guests to boil water.

Hotel Santa Cruz (☎ 420601/2; htlscruz@infovia.com.ar; cnr Av Roca & C Rivadavia; s/d US$20/27, superior US$35/48; **P**) This three-star business favorite has inviting rooms with tiny bathrooms and firm beds. Superior rooms occupy a modern wing, while older rooms are in the 'traditional' wing. Opt for the rooms along the internal patio. US$5 gets you time in the sauna.

Hotel Comercio (☎ 422458; hotelcomercio@infomacionrgl.com.ar; Av Roca 1302; s/d US$30/43; **P** 🖳) The three-star Comercio caters to your inner businessman with modern, renovated rooms and large bathrooms. Extras include a breezy bar and plush sofas in the lobby. Rooms fronting the street can be noisy. There's a 10% cash discount.

Apart Hotel Costa Río (☎ 423027; Av San Martín 673; s/d US$45/60; **P** 🖳) Looking dated at 14 years young, the chintzy feel of the glimmering gold front door says it all. There are 51 family-friendly kitchenettes apartments, plus four suites with full kitchens; all are quiet and spacious. Rates include breakfast and sauna and cash payment nets a 15% discount.

Eating & Drinking

RoCo (☎ 420203; Av Roca 1157; mains US$3-10; ☼ closed Sun dinner & Mon lunch) Attentive service and an extensive menu, including a good array of

---

THE AUTHOR'S CHOICE

Lagunacazul (☎ 444114; cnr G Lista & Sarmiento; mains US$5-8) Here's the best reason to spend the night in Río Gallegos. Exquisite seasonal preparations of fresh local seafood are the focal point of the refined Magellanic lunch and dinner at this stylishly rustic Patagonic *comedor* (cafeteria). Vibrant modern art, down-tempo beats and artisanal touches, such as blown-glass napkin rings, round out the stimulating sensual experience. For a special evening, reserve the romantic private dining room and don't miss the upstairs handicrafts shop after dessert.

---

salads, pasta, seafood and *parrilla*, and a full wine list, make RoCo the most popular formal diner in town.

El Horreo (☎ 426462; Av Roca 862; mains US$5-12) In the historic Sociedad Española building, this is *the* place to dine and be seen, with a pleasant upstairs bar, good salads and an emphasis on Spanish cuisine.

Don Bartolo (☎ 427297; Sarmiento 124; pizzas US$3-7, parrilla for 2 US$13) Serious *parrilla* and stone-oven pizzas with fresh toppings are the highlights here. Create-your-own salads are good veg options.

Paseo Carrera (☎ 427289; Av Roca 1012; mains US$1-4) In the cinema lobby, this popular, informal café-bar serves good coffee, homemade pastas and daily pizza, as well as beer specials.

Restaurant Tenis (☎ 422507; Avellaneda 25; set lunch US$3.35) The set lunches at the town's tennis club (served adjacent to Argentina's first indoor court) are simple, filling and homemade.

El Dragón (☎ 428578; 9 de Julio 27; buffet US$5) Under extreme lights, the Chinese *tenedor libre* offers a varied, if heavy, spread. There is plenty to choose from for lunch and dinner, including *parrilla*.

Club Británico (☎ 425223; Av Roca 935; mains US$5-9) Mainly a formal restaurant with passable fare, this wannabe gents bar is best appreciated over a wee dram of after-dinner whisky.

Panadería Zapiola (cnr Rawson & Zapiola; snacks US$1-2; ⌚ 24hr) Take a number to take away mouthwatering empanadas and pastries from this sweet-smelling corner bakery.

Shopping

Rincón Gaucho (☎ 420669; Av Roca 619) *Epa!* Everything for aspiring well-outfitted gauchos is here, from knives and chaps to *mate* paraphernalia. There's plenty for the *gauchitas*, too. The owner enthusiastically explains the purposes and customs of every stylish hat.

Getting There & Away

AIR

Airport tax is US$2. Inquire locally to see if upstart airlines **All Boarders** ('All-B'; ☎ 431666; www.allbordersair.com) or **Via Patagonia** are flying to Río Grande, Ushuaia or Calafate.

Aerolíneas Argentinas (☎ 422020/21; Av San Martín 545) flies daily to Buenos Aires (US$212 to US$414), sometimes via Ushuaia (US$193). **Southern Winds** (☎ 437171/72; Errázuriz 26) flies to Comodoro (US$54) and Buenos Aires (US$100). **LADE** (☎ 422316; Fagnano 53/57) flies several times a week to Río Grande (US$19 to US$27), El Calafate (US$32), Comodoro Rivadavia (US$36 to US$49), Ushuaia (US$44) and Buenos Aires (US$92).

BUS

Río Gallegos' **bus terminal** (☎ 442159; cnr RN 3 & Av Eva Perón) is 3km southwest of the center. Companies include **El Pingüino** (☎ 442169), **Líder** (☎ 442160), **Bus Sur** (☎ 442687), **Andesmar** (☎ 442195), **Sportman** (☎ 442595) and **TAC** (☎ 442 042). Buses to Chile include **Ghisoni** (☎ 442687), **Pacheco** (☎ 442765) and **Tecni-Austral** (☎ 442427). **Taqsa** (☎ 442194; Estrada 71) beelines straight from the airport to Puerto Natales and El Calafate.

Destination	Cost (US$)	Duration (hr)
Buenos Aires	53	36-40
Caleta Olivia	11-13	7-10
Comodoro Rivadavia	14	9-11
El Calafate	10	4-5
El Chaltén	25	9
Esquel	29-32	19
Los Antiguos	22	12
Puerto Madryn	24-25	15-20
Puerto Natales (Chile)	8-10	5-7
Punta Arenas (Chile)	7-10	5-6
Río Grande	18	7-8
Río Turbio	10	5
San Julián	8	4½
Trelew	20-24	14-17
Ushuaia	25-27	12-14

Getting Around

It's easy to share metered taxis (US$1 to US$3) between downtown, the bus terminal and **Stand International Airport** (RGL; ☎ 442340), 7km northwest of town. From Av Roca, buses marked 'B' or 'terminal' link the center and the bus station (US$0.35).

Car rental is expensive due to the poor conditions of the roads to most places of interest. Despite exchange rates, rental deals are often better in Punta Arenas, Chile (p426). For local rentals, try **Riestra Rent A Car** (☎ 421321; Av San Martín 1504).

ESTANCIAS AROUND RÍO GALLEGOS

Visiting a working *estancia* affords an intimate glimpse into the unique Patagonian lifestyle. These are not luxury hotels, but homes that have been converted into comfortable lodgings. Meals are often shared with the owners, and participation in the daily work life is encouraged. Booking ahead is essential, since most places are open only in summer and fill up fast. For *estancias* in Santa Cruz province, contact the provincial tourist office (p385) or see www.estanciasdesantacruz.com.

Estancia Güer Aike (in Río Gallegos ☎ 02966-423895, in Buenos Aires ☎ 011-4394-3486; full pension per person US$150; ☉ Oct-Apr) is at the junction of northbound RN 3 and westbound RP 5, 35km west of Río Gallegos. Its small lodge, Truchaike, enjoys 12km of private river frontage and is a world-famous trout fishing destination. The ranch can be visited for lunch or dinner (US$20), but call in advance.

Estancia Monte Dinero (☎ 02966-426900; www .montedinero.com.ar in Spanish; RP 1, 120km south of Río Gallegos; day trip US$20, per person with breakfast/full pension US$45/95; ☉ Oct-Apr) has been run by the same English-speaking family for five generations. A museum displays an intriguing assortment of goods salvaged from the wreckage of the ship that sunk soon after the Greenshoes sailed here from Ireland in 1886. Intricate handpainted doors, billiards and well-appointed rooms help maintain a comfortable, old-world environment. Dudes are shown the typical *estancia* gigs – dog demos, shearing etc – and can also take trips to **Cabo de Vírgenes**, where Magellanic penguins nest September through March. Travel agencies in Río Gallegos offer day trips starting in mid-November, usually making a quick stop at the *estancia's casco*.

INLAND PATAGONIA (ALONG RN 40)

Paralleling the awe-inspiring Andean range, north of Bariloche down to the Chilean border near Puerto Natales then jigging east to the Atlantic coast, the mythic RN 40 (La Ruta Cuarenta) is the uttermost of Southern Cone road trips. Mile after mile of mostly gravel road provides access to Argentina's prized possessions – Los Glaciares and Perito Moreno national parks, rock art at Cueva de las Manos, the oasis of Los Antiguos and some of the continent's most renowned fishing lakes.

Paving is proceeding apace, but navigating RN 40 still has its hardships: public transport is limited to a few summer-only tourist shuttle services, and driving still requires plenty of preparation and patience.

This section picks up RN 40 in Esquel, from where it continues paved until south of Gobernador Costa. From there on down, it's *ripio* most of the way, with certain sections, mainly near population centers, paved. Hit the road before President Kirschner finishes his term in 2007, when the provincial government is aiming to have most of the highway tamed under asphalt.

ESQUEL

☎ 02945 / pop 36,000 / elevation 570m

Set in western Chubut's dramatic, hikable foothills, Esquel mainly attracts visitors with its proximity to Parque Nacional Los Alerces and other Andean recreation areas. Most people zip through en route to Bariloche or Chile, but it's an easy-going and exceedingly friendly base camp for abundant adventure activities – the perfect place to chill out for a few days after hard traveling on RN 40.

Founded at the turn of the 20th century, Esquel is the region's main livestock and commercial center. It's also the historic southern end of the line for La Trochita (p394), the narrow-gauge steam train that now runs as far north as El Maitén. The town takes its name from a Mapuche term meaning either 'bog' or 'place of the thistles.'

Orientation

RN 259 zigzags through town to the RN 40 junction, which heads north to El Bolsón and

PATAGONIA

southeast to Comodoro Rivadavia. South of town, RN 259 passes a junction for Parque Nacional Los Alerces en route to Trevelin.

Information

INTERNET ACCESS
Cyber Club (Av Alvear 961) Two floors of online madness.

LAUNDRY
Laverap (Mitre 543) Self- or full service.

MEDICAL SERVICES
Hospital Zonal (☎ 107, 451074; 25 de Mayo 150)

MONEY
Banco de la Nación (Av Alvear at General Roca) ATM and changes traveler's checks.
Banco del Chubut (Av Alvear 1131) Has ATM.

POST
Post office (cnr Avs Fontana & Av Alvear)

TOURIST INFORMATION
ACA (☎ 452383; cnr 25 de Mayo & Av Ameghino) Inside YPF gas station, sells fishing licenses.
Tourist office (☎ 451927; www.esquel.gov.ar in Spanish; Av Alvear 1220; ◷ 7am-11pm) Well organized, helpful and multilingual.

Sights & Activities

Most attractions, notably Parque Nacional Los Alerces, are near Esquel rather than in it. The **Museo de Culturas Originarias Patagónicas** (☎ 451929; Belgrano 330; donation US$0.50; ◷ 8:30am-1pm & 2:30-8pm Mon-Fri, 9am-noon & 5-8pm Sat, 5-8pm Sun) has a modest collection of Mapuche artifacts.

The Roca train station is now a free **train museum** (p394); even travelers arriving by bus or air should try to witness the arrival or departure of **La Trochita**.

Esquel's nearby lakes and rivers offer some excellent **fishing** from November through April. Licenses (day/week US$10/50) can be purchased at most gas stations, including the **YPF gas station** (cnr 25 de Mayo & Av Ameghino) that houses the ACA.

Mountain biking is also popular. Rent bikes (per half-day/day US$3.35/5) at **Tierra** (☎ 454 366; cnr Rivadavia & General Roca), where the friendly staff can hook you up with a guide or trail details.

Full-day **whitewater rafting** trips on the Río Corcovado (Class II to IV) are run by **Expediciones Patagonia Aventura** (EPA; ☎ 454366,

15-684085; www.epaadventure.com.ar in Spanish; cnr Rivadavia & General Roca), which offers a host of other recommended outdoor excursions.

For **skiing** information, see the La Hoya section (p395).

Tours

Numerous travel agencies, including **Esquel Tours** (☎ 452832; esqueltours@ar.inter.net; Pellegrini 881), sell tickets for the Circuito Lacustre boat excursion in Parque Nacional Los Alerces (p398); buying a ticket in Esquel assures a place on the often-crowded trip. Full-day excursions, including the lake cruise, cost US$23 when sailing from Puerto Chucao, US$30 from Puerto Limonao, including transfers to and from the park.

There are also full-day trips to El Bolsón/ Lago Puelo and Corcovado/Carrenleufú (US$27). Half-day trips include La Hoya winter-sports complex; the nearby Welsh settlement of Trevelin and the Futaleufú hydroelectric complex (US$13); and the narrow-gauge railway excursion to Nahuel Pan (US$15).

Festivals & Events

February's weeklong **Semana de Esquel** celebrates the city's 1906 founding. The **Fiesta Nacional de Esquí** (National Skiing Festival) takes place in mid-September at La Hoya.

Sleeping

BUDGET
Casa del Pueblo (El Batxoky; ☎ 450581; www.epaadventure.com.ar in Spanish; San Martín 661; dm HI member/nonmember US$4.35/5.35; ✗) Run by the friendly folks at EPA/Tierra, this activity-oriented HI hostel has the lowdown on adventure options. There's a shared kitchen, cable TV in the comfy living room, grassy backyard shaded by a cherry tree, laundry room, mountain bike rentals and plans for private rooms.

Residencial El Cisne (☎ 452256; Chacabuco 778; s/d US$7/10) A good, strictly run deal: nine modern, comfortable, quiet rooms in two buildings. The rooms are spotless with TVs and there are laundry facilities to boot. Ring at No 777 if there's no answer at No 778.

Residencial Ski (☎ 451646; San Martín 961; s/d US$10/14; ℗) A clean, friendly place with 32 decent, no-nonsense, carpeted rooms with cable TV. Breakfast is US$1.25.

Hotel Argentino (☎ 452237; 25 de Mayo 862; per person with private/shared bathroom US$7/5) This some-

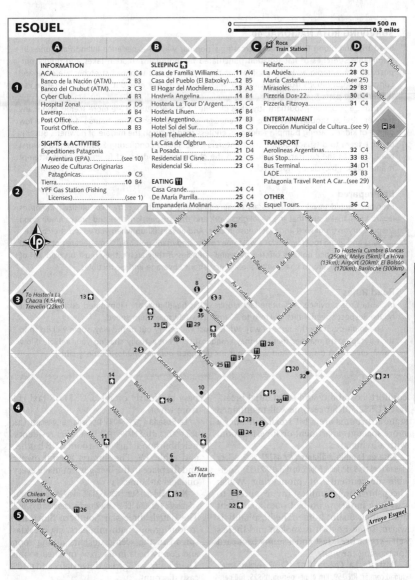

ESQUEL

0   500 m
0   0.3 miles

INFORMATION	
ACA...1	C4
Banco de la Nación (ATM).........2	B3
Banco del Chubut (ATM)...........3	C3
Cyber Club.................................4	B3
Hospital Zonal...........................5	D5
Laverap.....................................6	B4
Post Office.................................7	C3
Tourist Office............................8	B3

SIGHTS & ACTIVITIES	
Expeditiones Patagonia	
Aventura (EPA)................(see 10)	
Museo de Culturas Originarias	
Patagónicas..........................9	C5
Tierra.......................................10	B4
YPF Gas Station (Fishing	
Licenses).........................(see 1)	

SLEEPING	
Casa de Familia Williams..........11	A4
Casa del Pueblo (El Batxoky)....12	B5
El Hogar del Mochilero............13	A3
Hostería Angelina....................14	B1
Hostería La Tour D'Argent.......15	C4
Hostería Lihuen......................16	B4
Hotel Argentino.......................17	B3
Hotel Sol del Sur......................18	B3
Hotel Tehuelche.......................19	B4
La Casa de Olgbrun..................20	C4
La Posada.................................21	D4
Residencial El Cisne..................22	C5
Residencial Ski.........................23	C4

EATING	
Casa Grande............................24	C4
De María Parrilla......................25	C4
Empanadería Molinari..............26	A5

Helarte....................................27	C3
La Abuela.................................28	C3
María Castaña....................(see 25)	
Mirasoles..................................29	B3
Pizzería Dos-22........................30	C4
Pizzería Fitzroya......................31	C4

ENTERTAINMENT	
Dirección Municipal de Cultura..(see 9)	

TRANSPORT	
Aerolíneas Argentinas..............32	C4
Bus Stop...................................33	B3
Bus Terminal............................34	D1
LADE..35	B3
Patagonia Travel Rent A Car..(see 29)	

OTHER	
Esquel Tours............................36	C2

To Hostería Cumbre Blancas
(250m); Melys (5km); La Hoya
(13km); Airport (20km); El Bolsón
(170km); Bariloche (300km)

To Hostería La
Chacra (4.5km);
Trevelin (22km)

Plaza
San Martín

PATAGONIA

---

times rowdy hostel-cum-hotel has a popular bar (p394) and unique old rooms, each with their own bathroom. Get one at the back for the best chance at shut eye.

El Hogar del Mochilero (☎ 452166; General Roca 1028; dm US$2.65, camping per person US$1.65) Besides renting beds in the huge 30-bunk room (bring a sleep sack), this friendly crash pad

allows camping in the tree-shaded backyard; kitchen, free firewood and hot showers available. If Carlos isn't around, check the house across the street.

MIDRANGE
Hostería Angelina (☎ 452763; Av Alvear 758; s/d US$20/27; P) Angelina draws praise for its

SURVIVING RUTA NACIONAL 40

Road tripping along RN 40 is an increasingly popular way to experience inland Patagonia. Interminable stretches of flat isolation punctuated by mountains, hidden lakes and quirky outposts attract intrepid adventurers. Most of the mythic route's unpaved stretches are wide and compacted. Conditions from December to March are generally fine, but heavy precipitation can render some parts inaccessible.

Truth be told, many southern stretches of Chile's Carretera Austral are more scenic. And many travelers feel as though they have seen enough of RN 40 after several hours – let alone a few days – of kidney-jarring bumping along an endless road through the middle of nowhere. But this doesn't seem to dissuade gung-ho adventurers dead set on conquering South America's worst road. Quite to the contrary: just to add to the challenge, hundreds of foolhardy souls attempt it annually on bicycle or motorcycle.

Be Prepared

Everyone should travel with necessary repair equipment. If renting, carry two full-size *neumáticos* (spare tires), make sure that the headlights work and that suspension, tires and brakes are in good shape. Carry extra gas, oil and water, just in case. And always fill up when you've got the chance.

Glass and flying rocks are never a welcome combo and many potential damages are not covered under the insurance policies offered by rental agencies; if they aren't, they must be paid out of your pocket. Be sure to check with the agency about coverage and deductibles.

Road Rules

In Santa Cruz province, Argentine law requires that headlights are illuminated during daylight hours. Respect speed limits: 65km/h to 80km/h is a safe maximum speed.

Sheep *always* have the right of way. While most will scurry out of the way, some will do so in such a haphazard manner that you may wonder if they are actually chasing your vehicle. Slow down, give them distance. And watch out for unsigned *guardaganados* (cattle guards).

comfort, hospitality and substantial breakfasts (US$2.50). Since some well-maintained standard rooms are a bit small, consider a more spacious apartment or superior room with a living area.

Casa de Familia Williams (☎ 452872; guinguiw@ ciudad.com.ar; 9 de Julio 606/620; d/q US$23/33) Sociable descendents of pioneering Welsh sheep-breeding families invite guests to stay in a modern two-bedroom apartment above their quaint home. The hospitality is warm, some English is spoken and there's self-service breakfast and a sunny backyard for passing the *mate*.

Hostería La Chacra (☎ 452802; rinilachacra@ ciudad.com.ar; RN 259, Km 4; per person US$25, full pension US$70; P ☒ ⬜) Owner Rini Griffiths, who sings in Esquel's Welsh chorus, is a real joy and caters to all whims with a custom mix of homemade Argentine, Welsh and American food. Her 1970s country home has five ample rooms and hosts a steady stream of fisherfolk who appreciate the hearty meals and casual ambience. Buses

pass by hourly or it's a US$1.65 taxi ride from town.

La Posada (☎ 454095; laposada@art.inter.net; Chacabuco 905; s/d US$14/19; P) In a quiet residential neighborhood, this four-room B&B has heat and cable TV. The library, helpful owners and fireplace in the living room make everyone feel at home.

Hotel Sol del Sur (☎ 452189; www.hsoldelsur.com.ar in Spanish; 9 de Julio 1086; s/d with buffet breakfast US$20/30) The dated, three-star Southern Sun caters to tour groups with minibars, big breakfast spread in the scenic upstairs dining room and comfy beds in its cozy, updated rooms. There's a travel agency downstairs and a 10% cash discount.

Hostería Lihuen (☎ 452589; San Martín 822; s/d US$22/33) Though the rooms are undistinguished, it's well located near the leafy Plaza San Martín. Bigger rooms are good for groups of four.

Hostería La Tour D'Argent (☎ 454612; www.latour dargent.com.ar in Spanish; San Martín 1063; s/d US$30/46) This is a nondescript place, appealing for

Driving Etiquette

Signal 'howdy' to oncoming drivers by flashing your headlights or raising an index finger with your hand on the steering wheel. Unwritten rule: stop to help anyone stranded on the side of the road. There's no 'roadside assistance' here and mobile phones are useless in the mountains and along most west–east stretches. Along windy roads, toot your horn before barreling through blind curves.

When another car approaches, slow down and move to the side of the road to avoid stones flying out from under the wheels. Flash your headlights to signal a desire to pass. The car in front should slow down to let you by. If you're being overtaken, move over and slow down until the cloud of dust has settled. For maximum security, consider adding a windshield screen for protection. Another recommendation is to cover headlights with transparent, industrial-strength tape to minimize the cracking should a stone hit. If you need to stop, don't slam on the brakes, an act that will send the car skidding along the road. Instead, slow down and use the clutch to lower the speeds until you can safely park it on the side the road.

Letting Someone Else Deal with It

A group of travel agencies (www.corredorpatagonico.com in Spanish) coordinates two-day mini-van transport along RN 40 from El Calafate to Bariloche, via El Chaltén, Perito Moreno and Los Antiguos. Service is regular from mid-October to early April, depending on demand and road conditions. Some departures may include a stop at Cueva de las Manos (p403) en route.

Chaltén Travel (in El Calafate ☎ 02902-492212/480, in Buenos Aires ☎ 011-4326-7282; www.chaltentravel.com in Spanish; Libertador 1177, El Calafate) runs northbound shuttles on odd-numbered days at 8am from El Calafate and El Chaltén to Perito Moreno and Los Antiguos (US$55, minimum 13 hours), transferring to another minivan for the paved portion of RN 40 to Bariloche (US$95 total) the next morning. It's possible to hop on and off along the route, but space on the next shuttle is neither reservable nor guaranteed.

See p478 for more agencies offering transport along RN 40.

PATAGONIA

its friendliness rather than its humdrum character.

TOP END

Hostería Cumbres Blancas (☎ 455100; www.cumbresblancas.com.ar in Spanish; Av Ameghino 1683; s/d US$60/80; P 🖫) Esquel's fanciest modern inn features 20 warm, well-appointed rooms and luxurious suites. There's wireless Internet throughout the complex, which includes a sauna, health club, fly casting pond and putting green.

La Casa de Olgbrun (☎ 450536; www.patagoniaexpress.com/olgbrun.htm in Spanish; San Martín 1137; 4-/6-person r US$50/70) Above the artisan shop of the same name, this attractive inn has just four rooms, each with an iron cooker, refrigerator and a well-equipped kitchen. They're all restful and tastefully decorated. Off-season rates are 50% less.

Hotel Tehuelche (☎ 452420/1; www.cadenarayentray.com.ar in Spanish; cnr 9 de Julio & Belgrano; s/d US$37/52; P) The business-friendly Tehuelche has 55 rooms and a young, helpful English-speaking staff. Rooms are comfy and have large bathrooms; the best are on the upper levels away from the street.

Eating

Melys (☎ 452677; Miguens 346) Everybody and their auntie seems to be opening a teahouse in Esquel. North of town opposite the prison, Melys is recommended by locals as the most traditional.

Mirasoles (☎ 15-687664; Av Alvear 1069; dinner US$5-10) This elegant, upscale spot cooks up creative, healthy dishes like tabbouleh salad, stuffed squash and soy *milanesas* (breaded steak).

Casa Grande (☎ 452370; General Roca 441; mains US$2-5) Regional specialties like jabalí (wild boar) and fresh trout are all oven-baked at this casual fine dining spot in a creaky old house with burlwood chandeliers. Portions are generous and there are plenty of vegie options.

La Abuela (☎ 451704; Rivadavia 1109; set lunch US$3, dinner US$2-4) This friendly mom-and-pop can't be beat for cheap, palatable specials; you get your choice of meat or a sandwich, plus salad, potato and a quarter carafe of passable house wine.

De María Parrilla (☎ 452503; Rivadavia 1024; full parrilla US$5) De María has lamb, pork and goat in addition to the usual beef; there's a salad bar on weekends and a decent daily special menu.

Empanadería Molinari (☎ 454687; Molinari 633; dozen empanadas US$3.35) Friendly owners Belcha and Jorge bake mouthwatering takeaway empanadas daily, including vegie options. Wait for a few minutes and they'll heat them up to snack on the spot.

Worthwhile pizzerias here (mains US$2 to US$6) include **Pizzería Fitzroya** (☎ 450512; Rivadavia 1050) and **Pizzería Dos-22** (☎ 454995; cnr Av Ameghino & Sarmiento).

Also recommended:

María Castaña (cnr 25 de Mayo & Rivadavia; snacks US$1-3) Good for breakfast and drinks; bring cigars and loaf in the overstuffed chairs.

Helarte (cnr Rivadavia & Sarmiento; scoops US$1-2) *Super-bueno* ice cream.

Entertainment

Dirección Municipal de Cultura (☎ 451929; Belgrano 330) Sponsors regular music, cinema, theater and dance events.

Hotel Argentino (p390) For something a bit more lowbrow, try this friendly Wild West saloon where the disco can get lively on weekends.

Getting There & Around

AIR

Esquel's **airport** (ESQ; ☎ 451676) is 20km east of town off RN 40. **Gales al Sur** (☎ 455757), at the airport and bus terminal, runs door-to-door shuttles (US$2.35). Taxis cost around US$7.

Aerolíneas Argentinas (☎ 453614; Av Fontana 406) flies to Bariloche (US$102) and Buenos Aires (from US$137) several times a week.

LADE (☎ 452124; Av Alvear 1085) flies several times weekly to Bariloche (US$28), Como-

---

LA TROCHITA: THE OLD PATAGONIAN EXPRESS

Clearly an anachronism in the jet age, Ferrocarril Roca's *La Trochita*, Argentina's famous narrow-gauge steam train, averages less than 30km/h on its meandering weekly journey between Esquel and El Maitén – if it runs at speed. Despite the precarious economics of its operations, the project has survived even the most concerted efforts to shut it down. In its current incarnation, subsidized by the city of Esquel and the governments of Río Negro and Chubut, La Trochita – which Paul Theroux facetiously called *The Old Patagonian Express* – it provides both a tourist attraction and a service for local citizens.

Like many other state projects, completion of the line seemed an interminable process. In 1906, the federal government authorized the southern branch of the Roca line, between Puerto San Antonio on the Atlantic coast and Lago Nahuel Huapi. In 1922, Ferrocarriles del Estado began work on the narrow-gauge section; it didn't reach the halfway point of Ñorquinco until 1939. In 1941 the line made it to the workshops at El Maitén, and in 1945 it reached the end of the line at Esquel.

Since then, the line has suffered some of the oddest mishaps in railroad history. Three times within a decade, in the late 1950s and early 1960s, the train was derailed by high winds, and ice has caused other derailments. In 1979, a collision with a cow derailed the train at Km 243 south of El Maitén; the engine driver was the appropriately named Señor Bovino.

In full operation until 1993, La Trochita's 402km route between Esquel and Ingeniero Jacobacci was probably the world's longest-remaining steam-train line, with half-a-dozen stations and another nine *apeaderos* (whistle-stops); the Belgian Baldwin and German Henschel engines refilled their 4000L water tanks at strategically placed *parajes* (pumps) every 40km to 45km. Most of the passenger cars, heated by wood stoves, date from 1922, as do the freight cars.

The only regular passenger service aboard La Trochita is the infrequent nine-hour ride between Esquel (see opposite) and El Maitén (p352). A much more frequent option during the summer is the Tren Turístico service from Esquel's station (now a museum) to Nahuel Pan, the first station down the line, 20km east. For a small additional charge, you can organize with one of the Esquel travel agencies (p390) to return by minibus. Train schedules vary widely depending on the season; you can verify the current timetable online.

doro Rivadavia (US$22 to US$29) and Buenos Aires (US$100); and at least once to El Maitén (US$7), El Bolsón (US$8), Puerto Madryn (US$50), Río Gallegos (US$54) and El Calafate (US$113).

BUS

Esquel's full-service **bus terminal** (☎ 451566; cnr Av Alvear & Brun) is an easy walk from the center.

Transportes Jacobsen (☎ 453528) goes Monday and Friday at 8am and 5:30pm to Futaleufú, Chile (US$3.35, two hours), and hourly to Trevelin (US$0.65, 30 minutes), stopping near the corner of Av Alvear and 25 de Mayo on the way out of town. They go to El Maitén (US$4.35, two hours) at 1:30pm Tuesday, Thursday and Saturday, returning at 4pm.

In summer, **Transportes Esquel** (☎ 453529) goes through Parque Nacional Los Alerces (US$2 to US$6) to Lago Puelo daily at 8am and 2pm, plus a 7:30pm service that goes only as far as Lago Verde; the first service combines with lake excursions and service is reduced off-season.

There are daily departures to the following destinations:

Destination	Cost (US$)	Duration (hr)
Bariloche	5-7	4
Buenos Aires	68	30
Comodoro Rivadavia	13-15	8-9
El Bolsón	3-4	2½
Neuquén	15-20	10
Puerto Madryn	14-18	7-9
Río Gallegos	29-32	19
Trelew	11-14	8-9

TRAIN

The narrow-gauge steam train La Trochita (also known by the Spanish diminutive El Trencito; see opposite) departs from the diminutive **Roca train station** (☎ 451403; www.latrochita.org.ar; cnr Roggero & Urquiza; ⏰ 8am-2pm Mon-Sat). There's a frequent 45-minute tourist-oriented service (popular with groups, book ahead) to Nahuel Pan (US$8.35, under six free) and infrequent passenger service to the railroad workshops at El Maitén (US$33, nine hours). For the timeless *Old Patagonian Express* feeling, it's best to catch a bus to El Maitén (p352) for the less touristy excursion to Desvio Thomae. Confirm schedules online or via the tourist office.

CAR

Compact rental rates start around US$25 a day, including 100km and insurance. Try **Patagonia Travel Rent A Car** (☎ 455811, 15-692174; patagoniatravelrentacar@ciudad.com.ar; Av Alvear 1041), which has a good range of vehicles.

AROUND ESQUEL
La Hoya

Only 13km north of Esquel, with a base elevation of 1350m, the winter-sports area of **La Hoya** (☎ 453018; full-day lift pass high/low season US$11/7) is a family-friendly favorite of Argentines and Chileans. It's cheaper and less crowded than Bariloche, but experienced skiers consider it pretty tame. The season lasts from June until October, with the National Ski Festival the second week of September. Summer activity options include hiking, riding the chairlift and horse riding.

Equipment can be rented on site or at sport shops in Esquel, including Tierra (p390). Buses to La Hoya from Esquel's terminal cost US$4 per person; a taxi costs US$8, a better deal for a group and a lot faster.

Cholila & Leleque

Bruce Chatwin's travel classic *In Patagonia* recounts Butch Cassidy and the Sundance Kid's ranching efforts near this picturesque riverside farming community outside the northeast entrance to Parque Nacional Los Alerces. A few years ago, US authors Anne Meadows and Daniel Buck located the bandits' homestead, just off RP 71 at Km 21 near the turnoff to the Casa de Piedra teahouse, 8km north of Cholila (see p396). Cholila's enthusiastic **Casa de Informes** (☎ 02945-498040/131; RP 71 at RP 15) has a helpful regional map and will gladly point you in the right direction.

Transportes Esquel buses from Esquel to El Bolsón pass close enough for a fleeting glimpse of the cabin on the west side of the highway, but visitors with their own vehicle or time to spare can stop for a look at the overlapping log construction, typical of North America but unusual in this region. The rapidly deteriorating structures, which are reached by the first gate to the right, are looked after by the Sepúlveda family. Close any gates you open and ask permission from the caretaker before looking around or taking photographs.

Afterwards, you can follow the signs for 1km to the Calderón family's **Casa de Piedra**

(☎ 02945-498056; RP 71, Km 20), which offers tea, sweets and preserves, as well as information. The hospitable Calderóns, of Spanish-Welsh-English-French-Basque-Mapuche descent, let rooms for around US$15 per person with breakfast, from December to April. Call ahead to let them know you are coming.

To return to Esquel, if driving, you can follow unpaved RP 71 north for 20km to the pavement at the first crossroads, and continue 116km on paved RN 40 back to Esquel, passing the new **Museo Leleque** (in Buenos Aires ☎ 011-4326-5156; www.benetton.com/patagonia; RN 40, Km 1440; ☎ 11am-5pm Thu-Tue Mar-Dec, until 7pm

---

BUTCH & SUNDANCE'S PATAGONIAN REFUGE *Daniel Buck & Anne Meadows*

The only standing relic of Butch Cassidy and the Sundance Kid's South American adventure are the rough-hewn log ranch buildings by the Río Blanco in Chubut's Cholila Valley. Aladín Sepúlveda, a bibulous shepherd, was in residence when we first visited in 1985. His father had come over the Andes from Chile and begun leasing the property in the early 1900s. It had been Aladín's only home.

The ranch's link to outlaw history was little known in the 1980s, except to locals, because hardly anyone associated Butch and Sundance with Patagonia. The Paul Newman and Robert Redford movie that had transformed the American bandits into international icons had ignored their Argentine episode altogether. But by the time Aladín died in 1999, well into his 70s, he was enjoying a second career entertaining increasing numbers of visitors with colorful tales of the outlaws' life in Cholila.

Butch and Sundance – and Sundance's chum, Ethel Place – arrived in the Cholila Valley in 1901, at a time when Argentina was attracting immigrants from all over the world, and its government was eager to settle some of them in the sparsely populated southern territories. Appealing reports of homesteading opportunities in the region were appearing in US newspapers. One story, on the extension of the Southern Railway from Bahía Blanca west to Neuquén, rhapsodized that the 'Valley of the Río Negro is one of the most beautiful and fertile territories in the republic,' and that further south was 'a land of wild apples and wild strawberries, of hill and dale, of beautiful scenery, of pastoral and mineral wealth.' Best of all, the government was handing out land for free.

By all accounts, Butch and Sundance had every intention of giving up their delinquent ways and settling permanently in Cholila. They bought livestock, filed land petitions and built a ranch. In 1902, Butch wrote to a friend in Utah that 'the country is first class,' that 'it can't be beat for' stock raising and that he 'had never seen finer grass country.' He said they had '300 cattle, 1500 sheep, and 28 good saddle horses,' and would soon be sending cattle over the Andes to a slaughterhouse in Chile. Another hint of what their life was like comes from Primo Capraro, a Bariloche architect who spent a night with the trio in 1904 at their ranch, nestled in a grove of willow trees. He later recalled: 'The house was simply furnished and exhibited a certain painstaking tidiness, a geometric arrangement of things, pictures with cane frames, wallpaper made of clippings from American magazines, and many beautiful weapons and lassos. The men were tall, slender, laconic, and nervous, with intense gazes. The lady, who was reading, was well-dressed.'

Their neighbors, some of whose descendants still live in the valley, were from Chile, Wales, England, Ireland, Scotland and Texas. One of the Texans had even been a sheriff back home, but among expatriate settlers, amity was the rule. When the territorial governor came through on an inspection tour, Butch and Sundance hosted a party. The governor danced with Ethel while Sundance played his guitar.

Their idyll was smashed in early 1905, when they were wrongly suspected of a bank robbery in Río Gallegos and forced to flee. A few months later, as a departing thumb-in-the-eye, they held up a bank in Villa Mercedes, near Mendoza. Ethel returned to the United States and vanished, while Butch and Sundance migrated to Chile and Bolivia. In November 1908, after a couple of years working in a mine camp, they robbed another mine's payroll and died in a shootout with a Bolivian military patrol.

Anne Meadows is the author of *Digging Up Butch and Sundance* (University of Nebraska Press, 2003). See http://ourworld.compuserve.com/homepages/danne for further reading suggestions.

Jan & Feb), which has many Mapuche artifacts and narrates the history of the region from the perspective of the Benetton family.

TREVELIN
☎ 02945 / pop 6400 / elevation 735m

An easy day trip from Esquel, historic Trevelin (treh-veh-lehn), from the Welsh for town (tre) and mill (velin), is the only community in interior Chubut that retains any notable Welsh character. If Esquel epitomizes laid-back, Trevelin is downright sleepy. It's worth spending a night or two if you're keen to explore the surrounding countryside.

Orientation
Just 22km south of Esquel via paved RN 259, Trevelin's urban plan is unusual for an Argentine city: at the north end of town, eight streets radiate like the spokes of a wheel from Plaza Coronel Fontana. The principal thoroughfare, Av San Martín, is the southward extension of RN 259, which forks west 50km to the Chilean border and Futaleufú, 12km beyond.

Information
Banco del Chubut (cnr San Martín & Brown) Just south of plaza, with an ATM.
Gales al Sur (☎ 480427; Patagonia 186) Esquel buses stop at this travel agency, which arranges tours.
Post office (San Martín) Just south of the plaza.
Telefónica (cnr San Martín & El Malacara) Locutorio, next to Gales al Sur. Open late, with dial-up Internet.
Tourist office (☎ 480120; www.trevelin.org in Spanish; Plaza Fontana; ✆ 8am-9pm) Helpful, with a free town map and English-speaking staff.

Sights & Activities
The **Museo Regional Molino Viejo** (☎ 480189; cnr 25 de Mayo & Molino Viejo; admission US$0.65; ✆ 11am-8:30pm Dec-Mar, 11am-6:30pm Apr-Nov) occupies the restored remains of a 1922 grain mill and is stuffed with interesting historic artifacts. It's a couple of blocks east of the plaza, at the end of 25 de Mayo.

Two blocks northeast of Plaza Coronel Fontana, the monument **Tumba de Malacara** (☎ 480108; admission US$1; ✆ 10am-8pm) holds the carcass of a horse whose bravery enabled its Welsh rider, John Evans, to escape a re-taliatory raid by Araucanians who had been attacked by the Argentine army during the Conquista del Desierto. His granddaughter gives an animated talk in Spanish. There's

---

THE AUTHOR'S CHOICE

Casaverde Hostal (☎ 480091, 15-691535; www.casaverdehostel.com.ar; Los Alerces s/n; dm with/without HI card US$5.35/6, s/d with private bathroom US$16/19, 6-person cabin US$50; 🅿 🖳) Relax after a few days' hard traveling along RN 40 at this convivial, rustic log-timbered HI hostel. The spacious rooms, inviting common areas and views of the surrounding mountains are wonderful. Spanish and fly-fishing lessons tempt many to extend their stay. The optional breakfast includes bottomless mugs of real coffee, homemade bread and jams. Bibi, Charly and family await atop a hill just outside of town, a 10-minute walk from the plaza off Av Fontana.

also the **Cartief Taid**, a museum replica of Evans' home.

Festivals & Events
Every Sunday in summer, and on alternate Sundays the rest of the year, there's an **artisans' market** in Plaza Coronel Fontana. On March 19, the **Aniversario de Trevelin** celebrates the founding of the city. The **Eisteddfod**, a lively Welsh festival, takes place in late October.

Sleeping
Residencial Pezzi (☎ 480146; hpezzi@intramed.com.ar; Sarmiento 353; per person with private bathroom US$9) Reservations are advised at this pleasant, family-run hotel with a large garden.

Cabañas Oregon (☎ 480408; contreraso@ciudad.com.ar; cnr San Marín & JM Thomas; 2-person cabin low/high season US$15/25; 🅿) These pleasant, rustic log cabins with kitchen, TV and private bathroom are scattered around an apple orchard on the south side of town.

Küiméy Ruca Cabañas (☎ 480008/438; Fortín Refugio 57; 3-person cabin US$20) Off the central plaza above the recommended pizzeria of the same name, these are comfortable, well-equipped cabins with kitchens.

Refugio Wilson (☎ 480427; wilson@galesalsur.com.ar; office at Patagonia 185; campsite/cot US$1.65/3; 🅿) This rustic refugio is 7km west of town on Cerro La Monja, just below timberline in the Cordón Situación. It's got a bar, small store and is a good trekking, mountain biking and horse riding basecamp. Ring ahead to arrange a ride.

Eating

Just as visitors to Trelew flock to Gaiman, so visitors to Esquel head to Trevelin for Welsh tea. Off-season, confirm teahouse hours before heading out from Esquel. For a savory snack, look for the guy on the south side of the plaza selling grilled *choripán* sausage sandwiches (US$0.80) starting in the late afternoon.

Nain Maggie (☎ 480232; Perito Moreno 179; tea service US$5) Trevelin's oldest teahouse occupies a modern building but maintains high traditional standards. Along with a bottomless pot, it offers outstanding sweets, traditional Welsh black cake and scones hot from the oven. One serving of grandma's treats is plenty for two.

Las Mutisias (☎ 480165; San Martín 170; tea service US$4) The only other teahouse where everything is reliably homemade.

Getting There & Away

Frequent daily buses to Esquel (US$0.80, 30 minutes) stop on RN 259 in front of Gales al Sur. There are three weekly buses to Futaleufú (US$1.50, one hour), just across the Argentine/Chilean border (open 8am to 8pm or 9pm), and five weekly to Carrenleufú (US$3, two hours), another border crossing.

PARQUE NACIONAL LOS ALERCES

☎ 02945

Resembling California's giant sequoia, the alerce (Patagonian cypress) flourishes in southern Patagonia's temperate forests. Individual specimens of this beautiful, long-lived tree can reach over 4m in diameter and exceed 60m in height. Like the giant sequoia, it has suffered overexploitation because of its valuable timber. West of Esquel, this 263,000-hectare park protects some of the largest remaining alerce forests.

Environment & Climate

Hugging the eastern slope of the Andes, the peaks of Parque Nacional Los Alerces don't exceed 2300m, and their receding alpine glaciers are less impressive than the continental ice fields of Parque Nacional Los Glaciares. They have left, however, a series of nearly pristine lakes and streams that offer attractive vistas and excellent fishing.

Because the Andes are relatively low here, westerly storms deposit nearly 3m of rain annually. The park's eastern sector, though, is much drier. Winter temperatures average 2°C, but can be much colder. The summer mean high reaches 24°C, but evenings are usually cool.

Plants & Animals

While its wild backcountry supports some wildlife (including seldom-seen huemuls, or Andean deer), Los Alerces exists primarily to preserve botanical riches. Besides the alerce, other important coniferous evergreens and deciduous broadleaf trees characterize the dense Valdivian forest, with its almost impenetrable undergrowth of chusquea, a solid bamboo. Conifers include another species of cypress and the aromatic Chilean incense cedar.

The genus *Nothofagus* ('false beech,' but commonly known as 'southern beech'), to which most of the larger broadleaf tree species in the park belong, abides only in the southern hemisphere. Unique local species include ñire, coihue and lenga. Another interesting species is the arrayán, whose foliage and peeling cinnamon-colored bark bear resemblance to the madrone *Arbutus menziesii* of the western US coastal states and British Columbia.

Information

During the high season (Christmas to Semana Santa) foreigners are charged a US$4 admission fee, which may increase to US$10 in 2005.

Intendencia & Museo y Centro del Interpretación (☎ 471015/20; ☷ 8am-9pm in summer, 9am-4pm rest of year) In Villa Futalaufquen, rangers staff this natural history museum and have details about hiking, camping, rules and regulations and guided excursions.

Activities

As well as sailing and hiking, the travel agencies in Esquel offer fishing, canoeing, mountain biking, snorkeling and horseriding excursions.

SAILING

Traditionally, **Circuito Lacustre** is Los Alerces' most popular excursion and involves sailing from Puerto Limonao up Lago Futalaufquen through the narrow channel of the Río Arrayanes to Lago Verde. Low water levels now make it necessary to hike the short distance between Puerto Mermoud, at the north end

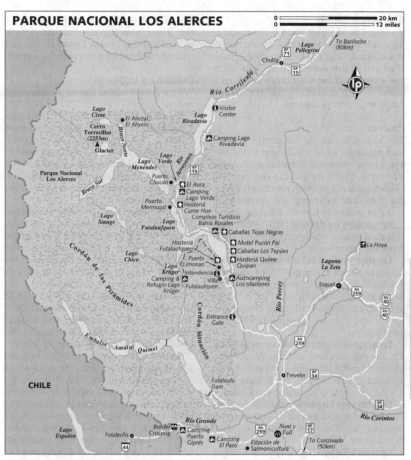

PARQUE NACIONAL LOS ALERCES

of Lago Futalaufquen, and Puerto Chucao on Lago Menéndez.

Launches from Puerto Chucao handle the second segment of the trip (US$20; 1½ hours) to the nature trail **El Alerzal**, the most accessible stand of alerces. From Puerto Limonao, the excursion costs US$30. Departures are at 10am from Limonao and noon from Chucao, returning to Chucao at 5pm and to Limonao at 7pm; in summer, purchase tickets in Esquel to assure a seat.

The launch remains docked over an hour at El Alerzal trailhead, sufficient for a unhurried hike around the loop trail that also passes **Lago Cisne** and an attractive waterfall to end up at 4000-year-old **El Abuelo** (The Grandfather).

HIKING

Unfortunately, because of fire hazard, authorities don't allow backcountry camping at El Alerzal or in other parts of the park's *zona intangible* (off-limits zone). Most longer hikes require registration with park rangers.

For day hiking, there are several interpretive trails located near **Lago Futalaufquen**. The only trekking option is the 25km trail from **Puerto Limonao** along the south shore of Futalaufquen to **Refugio Lago Krüger** (p400), which can be done in a long day, or alternatively can be broken up by camping at **Playa Blanca**. Boat excursions from Puerto Limonao to Lago Krüger cost US$15 per person.

Sleeping & Eating

En route to the park, watch for roadside signs advertising ideal picnic goods: home-made bread, delicious Chubut cheese, fresh fruit and Welsh sweets. In the Villa, there are a couple of basic grocery stores and a summer-only restaurant, but it's best to bring your own provisions.

CAMPING

Los Alerces has several full-service, drive-in campgrounds, all of which have hot show-ers, grocery stores and restaurants on-site or nearby. There are free (no services) and semi-organized campsites near most of these fee sites. The following are organized in order of proximity to Villa Futalaufquen.

Autocamping Los Maitenes (☎ 471006; per person US$2.35) A grassy, shady campground 200m from the Intendencia.

Complejo Turístico Bahía Rosales (☎ 471044; camping per person US$2-3, refugio d US$28, 4-person cabin from US$60) This sprawling complex is at the north end of Futalaufquen, 15km from the Intendencia. It has it all, from camping to cabins and *refugios*, plus plenty of sporty possibilities.

Camping Lago Verde (☎ 454421; per person US$3-5) On the eastern shore of its namesake lake, this campground is 35km northwest of Villa Futalaufquen. Besides nearby El Aura lodge, it's the only option on this tranquil lake.

Camping Lago Rivadavia (☎ 454381; per person US$3.35) At Lago Rivadavia's south end, this tranquil lakefront campground is 42km north of the Villa.

Camping & Refugio Lago Krüger (☎ 471015/20, ext 23; www.lagokruger.com; camping/full-pension per

---

THE AUTHOR'S CHOICE

Hostería Futalaufquen (☎ 471008/9; www .brazosur.com; for reservations Av Alvear 442, Es-quel; with breakfast & dinner d US$187-198, 4-5 person apt US$264-379; P) This very dignified, tasteful country inn is 4.5km north of the Villa at the end of the road on the quieter western shore. It's the park's most appeal-ing lakefront lodging, with only nine rooms and three log cabins (without kitchens). If you've come all this way, it's worth paying a bit more for the lake view. The teahouse and superb but expensive restaurant La-huan are open to the public.

---

person US$3/60) Accessible by the 25km trail that leaves from Hostería Futalaufquen, or by launch from Puerto Limonao, this is a relatively isolated lakefront *refugio* complex.

CABAÑAS & HOSTERÍAS

With a group, cabins can be an affordable option.

El Aura (in Buenos Aires ☎ 011-4312-7415; www .hosteriaselaura.com; d US$260, all-inclusive per person US$360-500; P) Lago Verde's only accom-modations option is this brand-new 'wilder-ness resort' and fishing getaway, 35km north of the Villa. The thoughtfully designed com-plex includes a gourmet restaurant and four stylish bungalows.

Hostería Cume Hue (☎ 450503; www.cumehue .com.ar; half/full pension per person US$34/40; P) This homey, fishing-friendly inn, 27km north of the Villa, attracts a fanatic angling crowd with 1970s rooms that share bathrooms be-tween two rooms. A couple of rooms with private bathroom cost a bit more.

Cabañas Los Tepúes (☎ 451869, 15-684917; lostepues@hotmail.com; 2-/4-/8-person cabins US$27/33/67; P) These spacious cabins are 8km north of the Villa on the eastern side of Lago Futa-laufquen, on a hill overlooking the lake.

Hostería Quime Quipan (☎ 471021; www.cpata gonia.com/quimequipan in Spanish; per person half-pension US$80, cabin without meals from US$75; ☒ Nov-Apr; P) At the south end of the lake, 5.5km from the Villa. Rooms are comfortable, if dated and utilitarian, with lakeview rooms worth the US$7 more. It also has a six-person cabin with a kitchen. The charming restaurant, which is a popular après-fishing pitstop, serves good meals to nonguests.

Getting There & Away

For information on getting to/from the park, see p395.

GOBERNADOR COSTA

☎ 02945 / pop 2000

Along the humdrum stretch between Esquel and Río Mayo, at the intersection with RP 20 for Sarmiento and Comodoro Rivadavia, this cattle town has some decent travelers' ser-vices. Some 20km west of town, RP 19 leads to **Lago General Vintter** and several smaller blue-ribbon lakes near the Chilean border; camping is possible along the shores.

In town, **Camping Municipal** (per person US$1) has electricity and hot water. The similar

Residencial El Jair (☎ 491012; cnr San Martín & Sarmiento) and **Mi Refugio** (☎ 491087; Av Roca) both charge under US$10 for rooms with private bathroom.

Several buses a week stop here between Comodoro Rivadavia and Bariloche. To reach Río Mayo, most buses skip this portion of bumpy (and entirely boring) RN 40 by taking RP 20 south, paralleling Río Senguer to the Río Mayo cutoff.

RÍO MAYO

☎ 02903 / pop 3500, sheep 800,000

Only soldiers and waylaid gauchos spend more than a few hours at this dusty gas-up pitstop, 200km south of Gobernador Costa, 135km north of Perito Moreno and 274km west of Comodoro Rivadavia. The **Casa de Cultura** (☎ 420400; Ejército Argentino s/n; ☼ 9am-noon & 3-6pm) houses a tourist office and **Banco del Chubut** (cnr Yrigoyen & Argentina) has an ATM. January's **Festival Nacional de la Esquila** features merino wool quality competitions, plus – drum roll, please – the dramatic crowning of the National Sheepshearing Queen.

Lodging ranges from the riverside **Camping Municipal** (☎ 420400; Av E Argentino s/n; per vehicle US$5) to **Hotel San Martín** (☎ 420066; San Martín 400; per person with shared bathroom US$5) to **Hotel Akatá** (☎ 420054; San Martín 640; per person US$8) or the most upscale **El Viejo Kavadonga** (☎ 420020; San Martín 573). The hotels all have reasonable restaurants.

There are daily early morning services from the **bus terminal** (☎ 420264; cnr Fontana & Irigoyen) to Comodoro Rivadavia (US$12, four hours) and Coyhaique, Chile (US$13), plus a less frequent service to Esquel (US$13, seven hours). The only regularly scheduled services on the rugged stretch of RN 40 to Perito Moreno are summer-only backpacker shuttles (p402).

PERITO MORENO

☎ 02963 / pop 3500

Not to be confused with the eponymous national park or the Perito Moreno Glacier further south in Los Glaciares national park, this uninspiring agricultural settlement is a brief stopover en route to the more inviting Andean oasis of Los Antiguos. Its primary appeal is as a jumping-off point for Cueva de las Manos and Parque Nacional Perito Moreno. The main drag, San Martín, leads north to RP 43 and south to RN 40; it's

128km south to Bajo Caracoles and 135km north to Río Mayo.

The town's historic moment of glory came in 1898, when explorer Perito Moreno challenged Chile's theory of '*divortum aquarum continental*' border definition (basically, that the headwaters of a Pacific-flowing river should be in Chilean territory) by rerouting the Río Fénix, which flows through town, to Atlantic-bound Río Deseado. The river and the area stayed in Argentina, and the town took his name.

Information

Banco de la Nación (cnr San Martín & Perito Moreno)
Banco de Santa Cruz (San Martín & Rivadavia) Has an ATM.
CTC (Perito Moreno 1032) Cheap Internet access.
Hospital Distrital (☎ 107, 432040; Colón 1237)
Post office (cnr JD Perón & Belgrano)
Telefónica (cnr San Martín & Saavedra)
Tourist office (☎ 432732; turismompm@tierraaustral .com.ar; San Martín 1065; ☼ 7am-11:30pm Mon-Fri & 8am-3pm Sat & Sun) There is also a desk at the bus terminal.

Tours

GuanaCondor Tours (☎ 432303; jarinauta@santacruz .com.ar; Perito Moreno 1087) runs tours to Cueva de las Manos, accessing the park via either Estancia Los Toldos (US$27 per person, difficult hike) or Bajo Caracoles (US$33). The owner, Harry Nauta, is bilingual and the drive down – in a sturdy, noisy but reliable 1985 Soviet army van *Olga* – is half the fun.

Sleeping & Eating

There are a couple of well-stocked *panaderías* (bakeries) and grocery stores along San Martín.

Hotel Americano (☎ 432074; San Martín 1327; s/d/tr US$10/15/20; ℗) Small and attended by a kind family, rooms are tidy and all have TVs, but some lack windows. Try for a newer room. Breakfast is US$1.65 extra and the restaurant up front serves good meals.

Posada el Caminante (☎ 432204; Rivadavia 937; s/d US$12/17; ℗) Señora Ethiel Pessolano makes guests feel at home with her knack for good chat. The four spacious rooms, accessed from the quiet living area, have comfy beds, heat and private bathrooms. An abundant breakfast (US$1.65 extra) is worthwhile, especially during fruit season.

Hotel Belgrano (☎ 432019; San Martín 1001; s/d US$10/17) Most folks end up here when

Chaltén Travel shuttles stop here in the middle of the night. Some off-street rooms lack windows, while others have cable TV for the same price. Bathrooms are clean and the downstairs restaurant serves good coffee and hearty meals.

Hotel Santa Cruz (☎ 432133; Belgrano 1565; s/d US$8/10; **P**) Boxy cell-block rooms are across a gravel driveway and the unkempt bathrooms in a dark corner behind the main house, but locals maintain this is one of the better budget options for women. The bar, Patagonically kitsch, is worth a visit for the vintage foosball table, to play some pool or enjoy a stiff drink with the local eccentrics.

Camping Municipal (Laguna de los Cisnes, off Mariano Moreno; sites per person US$1.35, plus per car or tent US$0.65, 6-person cabañas per person US$3.35) On the south side of town, this is your cheapest option. It's shaded by breezy poplars and has hot showers (US$0.65) in heated bathrooms. The *cabañas*, while private, are cramped.

Getting There & Away

Taxis (US$1) provide the only transport between town and the bus station at the north end, other than a flat 15-minute walk. After the new international airport (PMQ) opens in mid-2005, **LADE** (☎ 432055; San Martín 1059) should resume flights to El Calafate, Río Gallegos, Río Grande and Ushuaia.

Buses leave daily at 11am and 10pm for Los Antiguos (US$3, one hour); and at 7am and 4pm for Comodoro Rivadavia (US$10, five hours) via Caleta Olivia (US$9, four hours). Daily services to El Calafate go via RN 3. November to April, Chaltén Travel heads south to El Chaltén/El Calafate (US$43, up to 15 hours) on even-numbered days. **Condor Patagonico** (☎ 02944-525488) continues north to Bariloche (US$50) in connection with shuttles coming from the south. For more details, see p412.

LOS ANTIGUOS
☎ 02963 / pop 2500

Picturesque rows of Lombardy poplars provide windbreaks for the irrigated farms of Los Antiguos, a pleasant stopover near the Chilean border on the south shore of Lago Buenos Aires. Before the arrival of Europeans, Tehuelche frequented this 'banana belt' in their old age – the town's name is a near-literal translation of a Tehuelche name 'I-Keu-khon,' meaning Place of the Elders.

Volcán Hudson's 1991 eruption covered the town in ash, but farms have successfully bounced back. The surrounding fields yield an abundant harvest: raspberries, strawberries, cherries, apples, apricots, pears, peaches and plums. The **Fiesta de la Cereza** (Cherry Festival), featuring rodeos and live music, celebrates its favorite crop during the second weekend of January. In summer, **Lago Buenos Aires**, South America's second biggest lake, is warm enough for swimming. **Río Jeinemeni** is a favored spot for trout and salmon fishing.

Orientation

Los Antiguos occupies the delta formed by Río Los Antiguos and Río Jeinemeni, which constitutes the border with Chile. Most services are on or near east–west Av 11 de Julio, which heads west to the Chilean frontier at Chile Chico, the region's most convenient border crossing. Perito Moreno and RN 40 are 60km to the east.

Information

Banco de Santa Cruz (11 de Julio 531) 24-hour ATM.
Ciber Patagonia (cnr Patagonia Argentina & Fierro) Open late for Internet.
Locutorio (Alameda 436) Also has Internet.
Post office (Gregores 19)
Tourist information office (☎ 491261; www.los antiguos.gov.ar in Spanish; 11 de Julio 446; ☺ 8am-8pm) Helpful, with a map of town and farms selling fresh produce.

Sleeping & Eating

Albergue Padilla (☎ 491140; San Martín 44; per person US$7.35, d with bathroom US$20; **P**) Look no further when your Ruta 40 shuttle lands here after dark. The modern rooms are warm and comfortable, with plenty of hot water and a shared kitchen. Ask about visiting the family's farm for an afternoon of cherry picking. They sell RN 40 shuttle tickets and have the latest Chilean border crossing and ferry details.

Hostería Antigua Patagonia (☎ 491038; www.antiguapatagonia.com.ar in Spanish; Ruta 43 Acceso Este; s/d US$33/44; **P**) For a bit of lakeside luxury, this place is three-star plush, equipped with sauna, gym, bikes and billiards. Rooms, each with a lake view, are attractively appointed with oversize beds and rustic furniture. Meals feature a fresh bounty of salmon, lamb and local produce. It's 2km east of town, off the road to Perito Moreno.

Hotel Argentino (☎ 491132; 11 de Julio 850; s/d US$13/22; P) Rooms all have private bathroom and TV, but it's the outstanding breakfast (US$1.50) and hearty set lunches and dinners (US$3) that keep the regular crowd of farmers, gauchos and businessmen smiling.

Camping Municipal (☎ 491265; RN 43; per person US$1, cabins US$7) On the lakeshore 1.5km east of town, sites here are protected from the wind. Hot showers are available in the evening.

Getting There & Away

Sportman (☎ 491175; Patagonia Argentina 428) runs buses to Perito Moreno (US$3, one hour), Caleta Olivia (US$11, five hours) and Comodoro Rivadavia (US$12 to US$15, six hours) at 4:30pm daily. Less reliable **La Unión** (☎ 491078; cnr 11 de Julio & San Martín) buses head east around 3:30pm.

Transportes Padilla (☎ 491140; San Martín 44) crosses the border (8am to 9pm or 10pm daily, often closed noon to 2pm) to Chile Chico (US$3) several times daily.

The *Barcaza El Pilchero* ferry (☎ 00-56-67-411864) supposedly crosses Lago Buenos Aires daily from Chile Chico to Puerto Ibañez (US$4, vehicle US$35, three to six hours, weather depending). Alternatively, it's possible to continue overland around the lake's southern shore to Carretera Austral and Coyhaique.

ESTANCIA TELKEN & CAÑADON ARROYO DEL FEO

One of the best stops along this stretch of RN 40, **Estancia Telken** ☎ 02963-432079, in Buenos Aires ☎ 011-4797-7216/1950; jarinauta@santacruz.com.ar; RN 40, 25km south of Perito Moreno; s US$39-94, d US$56-144; camping per 2 people US$10; ☼ year-round) is a welcoming place to rest up and enjoy the countryside. Settlers founded the *estancia* in 1915, which, despite a growing dependency on tourism, remains a working sheep and horse ranch run by the charming Coco and Petti Nauta. Coco's family hails from Dutch settlers, while Petti descends from a New Zealand clan and has many fascinating stories of yesteryear. Delicious, abundant meals are served family-style, and English and Dutch are spoken.

Hiking possibilities are endless, including a worthwhile meander along a creek bed up to the **Meseta de Lago Buenos Aires**. Or, ask Petti to take you to **Cueva de Piedra**, a small cave snuggled in a silent valley of guanacos, eagles and the occasional armadillo. Guided horse riding is also available.

About 25km south of Telken is the turn-off to the private **Cañadon Arroyo del Feo**, a deep red-rock river canyon that narrows into steep ravines. A 6km walk, which involves fording the swift stream several times, leads to **Cueva Grande del Feo** (also known as Cueva Altamirante), with well-preserved rock art, approximately 7000 years old.

Harry Nauta, Coco and Petti's son who runs GuanaCondor in Perito Moreno (p401) organizes trips to the *arroyo* (creek), stopping for a quick break at Telken.

CUEVA DE LAS MANOS

Provincial laterals off RN 40 are rough but scenic along the Río de las Pinturas, where the rock art of **Cueva de las Manos** (Cave of the Hands; admission US$5; ☼ dawn-dusk) graces the most notable of several archaeological sites, proclaimed a Unesco World Heritage site in 1999. Dating from about 7370 BC, these polychrome rock paintings cover recesses in the near vertical walls with imprints of human hands as well as drawings of guanacos and, from a later period, more-abstract designs. Of the some 800 images, more than 90% are of left hands; one has six fingers.

There are two points of access, a more direct route via Bajo Caracoles, 46km away on the south side of the river, and another from Hostería Cueva de las Manos, on the north side, via a footbridge. Guides in Perito Moreno organize day-long trips, usually around US$30 per person. There's an information center and a basic **confitería** at the reception house near the southern entrance, but it's best to bring your own food.

Hostería Cueva de las Manos (☎ 02963-432839/856, in Buenos Aires ☎ 011-4901-0436; d per person with breakfast US$30, dm US$10; ☼ Nov-Apr) is a short distance off RN 40 at Estancia Los Toldos, 60km south of Perito Moreno. It has four carpeted rooms with private bathroom, restaurant and room service.

Estancia Casa de Piedra (☎ 02963-432-1990; off RN 40; camping per tent US$2, s/d US$7/10), 76km south of Perito Moreno, has basic rooms and allows camping; showers are US$2.

BAJO CARACOLES

Not much has changed since Bruce Chatwin described this tiny, remote hamlet as 'a crossroads of insignificant importance

PATAGONIA

with roads leading all directions apparently to nowhere' in *In Patagonia* in 1975, but it does have the only reliable gas pump between Perito Moreno (128km north) and Tres Lagos (409km south).

Besides a house selling pickles and homemade bread, there's the new **Servicios Generales Ruta 40 Hostel** where the friendly family allows camping and asks US$7 per firm dorm bed. The only other place to crash is **Hotel Bajo Caracoles** (☎ 02963-490100; d with/without bathroom US$17/25), which has expensive provisions, the only private telephone in town and lures bus drivers with legendary *asado* (barbecue).

Heading south, RN 40 takes a turn for the worse: it's 100km to **Las Horquetas**, a blip on the radar screen where RN 40 and RPs 27 and 37 intersect. From here it's another 128km southeast via RP 27 to Gobernador Gregores.

PARQUE NACIONAL PERITO MORENO

Beneath the Sierra Colorada, a painter's palette of sedimentary peaks, guanacos graze peacefully alongside aquamarine lakes in this gem of the Argentine park system, which is not to be confused with Parque Nacional Los Glaciares further south, home to the famous Perito Moreno Glacier. Honoring the park system's founder, this remote but increasingly popular park encompasses 115,000 hectares along the Chilean border, 310km southwest of the town of Perito Moreno.

Besides guanacos, there are also pumas, foxes, wildcats, chinchillas, huemul (Andean deer) and many birds, including condors, rheas, flamingos, black-necked swans, cauquén (upland geese) and caranchos (crested caracaras). Predecessors of the Tehuelche left evidence of their presence with rock paintings in caves at Lago Burmeister. Beyond the park boundary, glacier-topped summits such as 3700m Cerro San Lorenzo tower over the landscape.

As precipitation increases toward the west, the Patagonian steppe grasslands along the park's eastern border become sub-Antarctic forests of southern beech, lenga and coihue. Because the base altitude exceeds 900m, weather can be severe. Summer is usually comfortable, but warm clothing and proper gear are imperative in any season. The water is pure but you must bring all food and supplies.

Information

Visitors must register at the park's information center, on the eastern boundary; it's stocked with informative maps and brochures. Rangers offer a variety of guided hikes; they can also be contacted via the national parks office in Gobernador Gregores (p400), where it may be possible to arrange a ride.

Sights & Activities

Consult park rangers for backpacking options and guided walks to the pictographs at **Casa de Piedra** on Lago Burmeister, and to **Playa de los Amonites** on Lago Belgrano, where there are fossils. From Estancia La Oriental, it's a 2½-hour hike to the summit of 1434m **Cerro León**. From the peak, where guanacos can be spotted, there's a dazzling panorama. Immediately east of the summit, the volcanic outcrop of **Cerro de los Cóndores** is a nesting site for the Andes' totem species. Puma have also been spotted here.

Sleeping

There are free campgrounds at the information center (barren and exposed, no fire allowed); at Lago Burmeister, 16km from the information center (more scenic, and well sheltered among dense lenga forest, fire allowed); and at El Rincón, 15km away (no fires). None have showers, but there are pit toilets.

Estancia La Oriental (☎ 02962-452196, in Buenos Aires ☎ 011-4343-2366/9568; gesino@fibertel.com.ar; per person US$50-60, site US$7.50; ⊗ Oct-Mar; ⊛) At the foot of Cerro León, at the end of the road on the north shore of Lago Belgrano, La Oriental is a popular group-tour stop and the ideal base camp for exploring the park's varied backcountry. Colonies of condors and horse-riding trips add to its Patagonic appeal. Meals are well praised.

Getting There & Away

Public transport options change often; check with tourist offices in Perito Moreno, Los Antiguos and El Calafate for updates. Hitching is possible from the RN 40 highway junction, at least in summer, but the park is so large that getting to trailheads presents difficulties. From April to November, the road becomes impassable at times. If you're driving, carry spare gas and tires.

GOBERNADOR GREGORES

☎ 02962 / pop 3000

Gobernador Gregores, 60km east on RP 25, is the nearest town to Parque Nacional Perito Moreno, which is still 200km west. It's a good place to stock up on supplies, and arranging transport here is easier and cheaper than in the town of Perito Moreno. There's a **tourist office** (☎ 491398; San Martín 409; ☻ 8am-8pm Mon-Fri) and **national parks administration office** (☎ 491477; San Martín 882).

Seventy kilometers west of town via RP 29, the waters of **Lago Cardiel** are well loved by anglers for blue-ribbon salmon and rainbow trout fishing. From the junction to the lake it's another 116km to **Tres Lagos**, where a jovial couple run a 24-hour YPF station, then another 123km southwest to El Chaltén.

Summer-only **Camping Nuestra Señora del Valle** (cnr Roca & Chile; sites US$1.50) has showers, hot water and barbecue pits. For beds and meals, try **Cañadón León** (☎ 491082; Roca 397; per person US$10) or **Hotel San Francisco** (☎ 491039; San Martín 463; s/d US$15/25).

LADE (☎ 491008; Colón 544) motors a couple of times a week to San Julián (US$16), Puerto Deseado (US$20), Río Gallegos (US$22), Comodoro Rivadavia (US$24) and Buenos Aires (US$101).

Cerro San Lorenzo (cnr San Martín & Alberdi) buses leave for San Julián (US$9) several times a week at 6pm, while **El Pulgarcito** (San Martín 704) and **El Pegaso** (Pejkovic 520) both go to Río Gallegos.

EL CHALTÉN & PARQUE NACIONAL LOS GLACIARES (NORTH)

☎ 02962

Parque Nacional Los Glaciares is divided into geographically separate northern and southern sectors. El Calafate (p412) is the gateway town for the southern sector of the park. The northern half of the park takes in the Fitz Roy Range, indisputably one of the most majestic mountain areas of the Andes and now a famous spot for trekking and mountaineering.

At the entrance to the northern sector, the village of **El Chaltén** was slapped together in 1985 to claim the land before Chile could. It's Argentina's youngest town, with a winter population of a few hundred that swells in the summer, when thousands of outdoor nuts from all corners of the world turn up to explore the range. Services catering to peakbaggers continue to evolve rapidly: the trick will be if the town can retain its quirky frontier feel after the paving of RP 23 is complete. Cerro Fitz Roy's Tehuelche name, for which the town is now named, has been translated as 'peak of fire' or 'smoking mountain,' an apt description of the cloud-enshrouded summit, which the Tehuelche may have considered a volcano. Perito Moreno (p401) and Carlos Moyano later named it after the *Beagle's* Capitan FitzRoy, who navigated Darwin's expedition up the Río Santa Cruz in 1834, coming within 50km of the cordillera.

Capilla de las Escaladores, in El Chaltén, a simple chapel of Austrian design, memorializes the many climbers who have lost their lives to the precarious peaks since 1953.

Information

Newspapers, cell phones and money exchange have yet to hit El Chaltén, but there's now mercurial satellite Internet, a gas station, long-distance call centers – and land set aside for an ATM, bus terminal and mobile phone antennae. There's even a cemetery plotted out…but nobody's been buried there yet. Credit cards are virtually useless, but traveler's checks, euros and US dollars are widely accepted; ask around to find out who's changing money. Surf www.elchalten .com for a good overview of town.

Chaltén Travel (☎ 493005/92; cnr Güemes & Lago del Desierto) Books airline tickets and offers weather-dependent Internet service for US$4 an hour.

Municipal tourist office (☎ 493011; Güemes 21; ☻ 8am-8pm) Along with the hostels, this friendly office is the best source of nonpark information.

Park ranger office (☎ 493004/24; admission free, but donations welcome; ☻ 8am-7pm) Daytime buses all stop for a short bilingual orientation at this new visitor center, just before the bridge over the Río Fitz Roy. Park rangers distribute a map and town directory and do a good job of explaining the park's ecological issues. Rangers can answer questions about the area's hikes, and issue climbing permits. They also post a lodging list.

Puesto Sanitario (☎ 493033; Agostini btwn McLeod & Güemes) Provides basic health services.

Viento Oeste (☎ 493021/200; San Martín 898) En route to Camping Madsen, this shop sells books, maps and souvenirs and rents a wide range of camping equipment, as do several other sundries shops around town.

Zafarrancho Behind Rancho Grande Hostel (p408), this bar-café has Internet and screens movies.

PATAGONIA

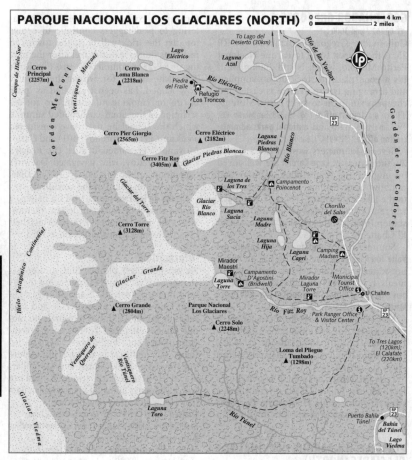

PARQUE NACIONAL LOS GLACIARES (NORTH)

Hiking

For more information on hiking, read Lonely Planet's *Trekking in the Patagonian Andes*.

LAGUNA TORRE

If the weather is good (ie little wind) and the skies are clear, make this hike (three hours one way) a priority, since the peak of Cerro Torre is the most difficult to see on normal blustery days. The trail is accessed from El Chaltén, either from behind Hostería Los Ñires or from the artisans' market north of the town. After a gentle initial climb, it's a fairly level walk through tranquil beech forests and along the Río Fitz Roy until a final steep climb up the lateral moraine left by the receding Glaciar del Torre. The **Mirador**

Laguna Torre offers a breathtaking view of the majestic spire of 3128m Cerro Torre rising out of the valley in the background. Look for the 'mushroom' of snow and ice that caps the peak. This precarious formation is the final obstacle for hard-core climbers, who often spend weeks waiting for decent weather.

The trail then meets up with the route passing Lagunas Madre and Hija, a moderate, somewhat muddy trail linking to Campamento Poincenot. Another 20 minutes further is Laguna Torre, where you will see some stunning views of the principal southern peaks of the Fitz Roy Range. **Campamento D'Agostini** (also called Campamento Bridwell), the base camp for climbers of Cerro Torre, is at the lake. Follow the trail along the lake's north side for about an hour to **Mirador Maestri** (no camping).

LAGUNA DE LOS TRES
This hike to a high alpine tarn is a bit more strenuous (four hours one way). The trail starts from the yellow-roofed pack station at **Camping Madsen**. After about an hour, there's a signed lateral to excellent free backcountry **campsites** at Laguna Capri. The main trail continues gently through wind-swept forests and past small lakes, meeting up with the trail from Lagunas Madre and Hija. Carry-ing on through windworn ñire forest (a small, deciduous southern beech species) and along boggy terrain leads to **Río Blanco** (three hours) and the woodsy, mice-plagued **Campamento Poincenot**. Across the river, the trail splits at Río Blanco to head to Río Eléctrico. Stay left to reach a climbers' base camp. From here the trail zigzags steeply up the tarn to the eerily still glacial **Laguna de Los Tres** and an extraordinary close view of 3405m Cerro Fitz Roy. Clouds ever huddle in the rocky crevasses, whipping up with a change in wind. Be prepared for high, potentially hazardous winds and allow time for contemplation and recovery. Scurry down 200m to the left of the lookout for an exceptional view of the emerald green **Laguna Sucia**.

PIEDRA DEL FRAILE
At Campamento Poincenot, the trail swings west to Laguna de los Tres or northeast along Río Blanco to Valle Eléctrico and Piedra del Fraile (eight hours from town; five hours from the Río Blanco turnoff). The trail leads to **Glaciar Piedras Blancas** (four hours), the last part of which is a scramble over massive granite boulders to a turquoise lake with dozens of floating icebergs and constant avalanches on the glacier's face. The trail then passes through pastures and branches left upvalley along **Río Eléctrico**, enclosed by sheer cliffs, before reaching the private **Refugio Los Troncos** (site US$3). The campground has a sundries shop and excellent services and the owners have information on recommended nearby trails. Rather than backtrack to Río Blanco and the Laguna de los Tres trail, it's possible to head east, hopping over streams to RP 23, the route back to El Chaltén. You'll pass **Chorillo del Salto**, shortly before reaching Camping Madsen.

Buses to Lago del Desierto (below) drop hikers at the Río Eléctrico bridge (US$7).

LOMA DEL PLIEGUE TUMBADO
Heading southwest from the park ranger's office, this trail (four to five hours one way) skirts the eastern face of Loma del Pliegue Tumbado going toward Río Túnel, then cuts west and heads to Laguna Toro. It offers the best views of the Torres and Fitz Roy. In fact, it's the only hike that allows views of both sections at once. The hike is rather gentle, but be prepared for strong winds and carry extra water.

LAGO DEL DESIERTO & BEYOND
Some 37km north of El Chaltén is Lago del Desierto, near the Chilean border, a nice day-trip option when it's raining and there's no chance of catching a glimpse of the Fitz. A 500m trail leads to an overlook that often has fine views of the lake, surrounding mountains and glaciers.

Minibus service to Lago del Desierto leaves El Chaltén from the Rancho Grande Hostel at 11am and returns at 4:30pm (US$10 roundtrip). Other similar services depart El Chaltén between 7:30 and 9am to coincide with boat tours of Lago del Desierto and return from the south end of the lake from the inviting restaurant **Hostería El Pilar** (☎ 493002; www.hosteriaelpilar.com.ar) around noon and 3pm.

The alternative to the boat tour is a five-hour walking track between the south end and the north end of the lake. From the lake's north end, it's increasingly popular to walk or bicycle to the Chilean border post, with hundreds of travelers now using the crossing each year. It's particularly popular with cyclists traveling on to the Chilean frontier outpost Candelaria Mansilla (where a family offers meals, camping and basic farmhouse accommodations; bring Chilean pesos from Calafate, if possible) via cargo boat from the southernmost outpost of Villa O'Higgins, in Chile's Aisén region. If you leave El Chaltén first thing in the morning, it's possible to cross the Chilean border and reach Candelaria Mansilla in one long day.

The boat from Candelaria Mansilla to Villa O'Higgins (US$10 to US$20, five hours) leaves according to the whims of the mercurial Capitan Pirincho. The **municipalidad** (☎ 56-7721-1849) in Villa O'Higgins may be

PATAGONIA

able to help with further information and sleeping options. In El Chaltén, Albergue Patagonia (right) and the tourist office can supply current details on this ever-evolving adventure option.

Ice Climbing & Trekking

Several companies offer ice climbing courses and ice treks, some including sleds pulled by Siberian huskies. **Fitzroy Expediciones** (☎ 493017; www.fitzroyexpediciones.com.ar; Güemes s/n, El Chaltén) runs glacier trekking excursions from Campamento D'Agostini (Bridwell). The trek usually begins at 9:30am, starting with a 1½ hour walk to Glaciar Grande, then three hours on the glacier, returning to the campground around 5pm. Some groups head out the same day from El Chaltén, which makes for a very arduous trip; it's recommended to make reservations in town, but to head to Bridwell yourself and camp there the night prior. Bring extra food and water. Fitzroy Expediciones also arrange multiday guided hikes over the **Hielo Patagónico Continental** (Continental Ice Field). This route, catering to serious trekkers, involves technical climbing, including use of crampons and some strenuous river crossings. Rates range from US$50 to US$150 per day.

Horse Riding

Horses can be used to trot around town and to carry equipment with a guide (prices negotiable), but are not allowed unguided on national park trails. From El Chaltén, guided rides to Laguna Torre and Río Blanco cost anywhere from US$25 to US$50 per horse, depending on group size. Outfitters include **Rodolfo Guerra** (☎ 493020; opposite Camping Madsen) and **El Relincho** (☎ 493007, in El Calafate ☎ 491961; San Martín s/n, El Chaltén).

Lake Cruises

Contact **Viedma Discovery** (☎ 493103/110; www .elchalten.com/viedmadiscovery; Güemes s/n, El Chaltén) about tourist launches from the teahouse at Puerto Bahía Túnel on the north shore of Lago Viedma; the trip takes in impressive views of Viedma Glacier, grinding from Cerro Fitz Roy. A five-hour excursion costs US$20, plus US$7 for roundtrip transport.

Sleeping

In El Chaltén, demand often outpaces availability; book ahead, especially if you are arriving in the middle of the night. Or, bring a bombproof tent – there's always space in the campgrounds. There are several new high-end places under construction, such as the imposing **Cerros del Chaltén** (☎ 0800-333-7282; www.loscerrosdelchalten.com) resort that lords over the center of town – an outstanding example of why Chaltén could use a wee bit of zoning. Except for the backcountry campgrounds, all the following sleeping options are located in El Chaltén.

Camping

Free backcountry campgrounds are very basic, with one pit toilet; bury human waste as far from water sources as possible. Some sites have dead wood with which to create windbreaks. Fires are prohibited. Water is pure as glacial melt; make sure all cleaning is done downstream from the campground. Pack out all trash.

Campamento Confluencia (El Chaltén; sites free) Across from the park ranger office and visitor center, and with no amenities.

Campamento Madsen (El Chaltén; sites free) Windy and exposed, at the end north of San Martín along the banks of Río de las Vueltas, with a few trees and plenty of spots to access water. Showers (US$1) and laundry service (US$4 per load) are available for all campers at Rancho Grande Hostel (opposite) between 8am and 4pm.

Camping El Refugio (☎ 493221; San Martín s/n; showers/sites/dm US$1.35/3.35/8) An exposed but private campground, with hot showers, sparse firewood (fires ok) and a basic *albergue* (hostel).

El Relincho (☎ 493007; San Martín s/n; sites US$4) This is another private campground, similarly wind-whipped.

Albergue del Lago (☎ 493010; Lago del Desierto 135; sites per person US$3.35, dm US$8) The partyhearty crowd seems to end up camping outside this hostel, which has a shared kitchen and funky showers.

BUDGET
Seven *albergues* offer dorm beds, but they fill up fast in summer. Unless otherwise noted, thin walls, cramped dorms and insufficient shared facilities are the norm.

Albergue Patagonia (☎ 493019; patagoniahostel@ yahoo.com.ar; San Martín 493; per person HI members/nonmembers US$7/8; ⊗ Sep-May; 🅟 🚫) Unwind in the cozy loft that's full of books, videos and old *National Geographic* magazines. There's a small shared kitchen, lockers and heating in each room. Breakfast is served next door at Fuegia Bistro for an extra charge. The friendly owners speak Dutch and English, rent mountain bikes and are exceptionally helpful.

Rancho Grande Hostel (☎ 493092; www.hostels patagonia.com; San Martín 724; HI members/nonmembers US$7/8, meals US$2-6; P ✗) This spacious, if soulless, facility on the north end of town packs in the backpackers, especially those dumped here by buses in the middle of the night. Clean four-bed rooms are prepped with plenty of blankets and bathrooms have several showers. The shared kitchen is tiny, and the common dining area has lots of light, but both are often crowded with nonguests. The café prepares decent meals, including vegie options, as well as good cakes and class-A coffees.

Cabañas Arco Iris (☎ 493116; Halvorsen s/n; dm US$8, cabins US$30-55) Colorful cabins in this small complex all have towels, fridges and private bathrooms. Dorm share bare-bones facilities and there's a decent restaurant/bar up front.

Condor de Los Andes (☎ 493101; www.condor delosandes.com; cnr Río las Vueltas & Halvorsen; dm US$8.50) The young owners cultivate a 'party' atmosphere with a healthy dose of rock music at this basic but welcoming and well-heated place.

MIDRANGE

La Base Hospedaje (☎ 493031; labase@elchaltenpata gonia.com.ar; cnr Lago del Desierto & Hensen; s/d/tr US$30/37/45) Across the street from Los Ñires (below), the Base is good value, with six private rooms, two shared kitchen facilities, self-service breakfast and exceptional views. The owners, Eduardo and Marcela, have an impressive multilingual video collection, to be enjoyed in a loft lounge, and run a small sundries kiosk.

Nothofagus B&B (☎ 493087; www.elchalten.com /nothofagus; cnr Hensen & Riquelme; s/d/tr US$32/40/50, with shared bathroom US$22/25/37; ☾ Sep-Apr; P ✗) Attended by well-traveled Eva and Gerardo, this new nonsmoking chalet-style retreat has a varied choice of nice carpeted rooms, some with great views, homemade bread at breakfast and other meals by request.

Hostería Los Ñires (☎ 493009; www.elchalten.com /losnires; cnr Lago del Desierto & Hensen; s/d US$27/33;

THE AUTHOR'S CHOICE

Ruca Mahuida (☎ 493018; Lionnel Terray 104; mains US$5-13; ✗) Kudos to Ruca's chef Pablo Randazzo for his creative cuisine: vegetarian risottos, wild game and delicate surf-and-turf fare bathed in aromatic sauces. It's casual and cozy, with views of the massif and sheepskins on the benches.

 ☾ Oct-Apr; P) One of Chaltén's original hostels has expanded and upgraded to private rooms. The best rooms are upstairs (a few with Fitz views), while the original rooms downstairs cost a bit less. The setting is secluded and the rooms are comfortable, with good bathrooms and bedding. Some showers are elbow-bumpingly small.

Posada Poincenot (☎ 493022; www.chaltentravel .com; San Martín 615; s/d/tr/q US$27/33/38/43; P) Adjacent to Rancho Grande, Poincenot is a small, serene affair with kind, conscientious owners. The larger rooms are a good choice for families; all have private bathroom.

TOP END

Posada Lunajuim (☎ 493047; www.elchalten.com/luna juim; Trevisan s/n; s/d/tr US$85/100/125; P) Reader-recommended, with larger rooms for the same price in newer wing. The owners are charming, and Bibi's B&W photographs grace the walls. The bedding and furnishings are top quality, and the lounge/dining room, with a library and fireplace, provides a warm spot to pass a rainy day.

Hostería El Puma (☎ 493095; www.elchalten.com /elpuma; Lionnel Terray 212; s/d/tr US$95/110/125; P) This quaint and comfortable eight-room lodge provides high standards of luxury for those who desire intimacy without overt pretensions. There's attentive service, a good breakfast and a nice reading lounge with a fireplace.

Fitz Roy Inn (☎ 493062; www.elchalten.com/fitzroy inn in Spanish; San Martín 520; s/d US$78/82; P) Most guests of this inn arrive from Calafate as part of a Cal Tur package, including half-pension. Nondescript, with narrow beds and mediocre service, it's merely passable for those not on a group tour.

Eating

Groceries, especially fruits and vegies, are limited and expensive. Bring what you can

THE AUTHOR'S CHOICE

El Bodegón Cervecería (☎ 493109; San Martín; snacks & drinks US$2-4) Brewmistress Blanca and her *simpatico* English-speaking staff keep this rustic, atmospheric micro-brew pub hopping from the moment hikers retreat from the hills until late. Grab a bowl of popcorn and a guitar or journal to doodle in, then savor a stein of unfiltered blond pilsner or turbid bock. After a windy day on the trail, it's doesn't get much better than this.

from El Calafate. All the following options are in El Chaltén.

Fuegia Bistro (☎ 493019; San Martín 493; breakfast US$2-4, dinner US$5-8; ✓ breakfast, lunch & dinner; ✗) Dutch chef Esther delivers savory entrees in a cozy atmosphere. All entrees include side dishes – try the lamb stew. There are always a couple of vegie options and the wine list is very reasonable.

Patagonicus (☎ 493025; cnr Güemes & Madsen; mains US$3-7) Tall windows let the light stream over bulky wood tables and through the comfortable bar. Pizza choices run the gamut, all well accompanied by a variety of salads and wine. The cakes and coffee are tasty, too.

Las Lengas (☎ 493023/044/227; cnr Güemes & Viedma; lunch US$3, mains US$2-5) Open year-round for hearty homemade set lunches, lentil soup and *puchero* (thick vegie-based stew), it's popular with vitamin-starved climbers looking to refuel after extended stints at altitude.

Also recommended:

Josh Aike (☎ 493008; Lago del Desierto 104; snacks US$1-5) Irresistible chocolate factory with loads of climbing history on the walls, serving everything from spirit-spiked hot cocoa to wine and fondue.

La Casita (☎ 493042; San Martín s/n; mains US$3-7) Popular pastas; crowded and smoky.

El Súper (☎ 493039; cnr Lago del Desierto & Güemes) Best-stocked market for basic provisions.

Domo Blanco (☎ 493036; Güemes s/n; scoops US$1-2) Homemade ice cream.

Getting There & Away

El Chaltén is located 220km from El Calafate. After the paving of RN 40 and RP 23 is finished, journey times listed here should be cut in half.

For El Calafate (US$15, five hours), Chaltén Travel (p405) departs daily in summer

at 6:30am and 6pm from Rancho Grande; and Cal Tur leaves from Fitz Roy Inn at 6pm daily. Service is less frequent off-season.

Transportes Lago del Desierto (☎ 493044; cnr Güemes & Viedma) runs minivans several times a week to coastal destinations on RN 3, including Parque Nacional Monte León (US$28, eight hours) and Río Gallegos (US$30, 10 hours).

Chaltén Travel heads north via RN 40 to Perito Moreno, Los Antiguos (up to 15 hours, both US$64) and Bariloche (US$115, two days) on even-numbered days at 8am.

PARQUE NACIONAL LOS GLACIARES (SOUTH)

The centerpiece of the southern sector of **Parque Nacional Los Glaciares** (admission US$10) is, without a doubt, breathtaking **Glaciar Perito Moreno** (Perito Moreno Glacier, often referred to locally as the Glaciar Moreno or Moreno Glacier), one of Earth's most dynamic and accessible ice fields. A low gap in the Andes allows moisture-laden Pacific storms to drop their loads east of the divide, where they accumulate as snow. Over millennia, under tremendous weight, this snow has recrystallized into ice and flowed slowly eastward. The 1600-sq-km trough of Lago Argentino, the country's largest single body of water, is unmistakable evidence that glaciers were once far more extensive than today.

Sixteen times between 1917 and 2004, as the 60m-high glacier has advanced, it has dammed the Brazo Rico (Rico Arm) of Lago Argentino, causing the water to rise. Several times, the melting ice below has been unable to support the weight of the water behind it and the dam has collapsed in an explosion of water and ice. To be present when this spectacular cataclysm occurs is unforgettable.

Visiting the Moreno Glacier is no less an auditory than visual experience, as huge icebergs on the glacier's face calve and collapse into the **Canal de los Témpanos** (Iceberg Channel). From a series of catwalks and vantage points on the Península de Magallanes visitors can see, hear and photograph the glacier safely as these enormous chunks crash into the water. The glacier changes appearance as the day progresses (sun hits the face of the glacier in the morning).

The main gateway town to the park's southern sector, El Calafate (p412), is 80km west of the glacier by road.

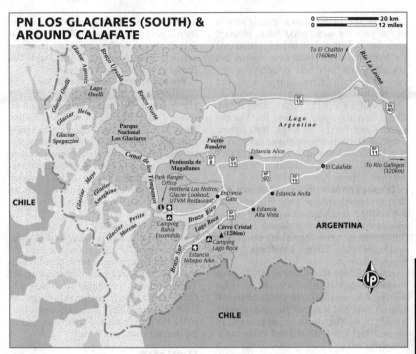

PN LOS GLACIARES (SOUTH) & AROUND CALAFATE

Activities

Boat trips allow one to sense the magnitude of the Moreno Glacier, even though the boats keep a distance. **Hielo y Aventura** (☎ 02902-492094/205; www.hieloyaventura.com; Av Libertador 935, El Calafate) runs Safari Nautico (US$25, including transport from El Calafate), a one-hour tour of Brazo Rico, Lago Argentino and the south side of Canal de los Témpanos. Catamarans crammed with up to 130 passengers leave hourly between 11:30am and 3:30pm from Puerto Bajo de las Sombras. Hielo y Aventura also offers **minitrekking** (US$70, plus US$13 for transport) on the Moreno Glacier, a five-hour affair involving a quick boat ride from Puerto Bajo de las Sombras, a walk through lenga forests, a quick chat on glaciology and then a 1½-hour ice walk using crampons. Children under eight are not allowed; reserve ahead and bring your own food.

To see the glacier's main north face, **René Fernandez Campbell** (☎ 02902-492340; www.glaciar essur.com.ar; Libertador 867, El Calafate) operates 320-passenger boats (US$7) from below the UTVM restaurant near the main look-

out, every hour on the half-hour between 10:30am and 4:30pm.

GLACIAR UPSALA & ONELLI

Upsala Glacier – 595 sq km huge, 60km long and some 4km wide in parts – is larger than the Moreno Glacier, but less spectacular. On an extension of the Brazo Norte (North Arm) of Lago Argentino, it's accessible by launch from Puerto Bandera, 45km west of Calafate by RP 11 and RP 8. René Fernandez Campbell (left) and **Upsala Explorer** (☎ 02902-491034; www.upsalaexplorer.com.ar; 9 de Julio 69, El Calafate) run boat tours (US$90 to US$126) to Upsala and more expensive tours to Onelli and Spegazzini glaciers. If icebergs are cooperating, boats may allow passengers to disembark at Bahía Onelli to walk half a kilometer to iceberg-choked **Lago Onelli** where the Onelli and Agassiz glaciers merge. Meals are expensive, but you can bring your own picnic.

LAGO ROCA

Mountain forest and lake blend together in the south arm of Lago Argentino to create a serene escape. In this most southerly section of the park are some good hikes, pleasant camping and *estancia* accommodations. At La Jerónima, **Cerro Cristal** is a rugged but rewarding 3½-hour hike beginning at the education camp (not a campground), just before the Camping Lago Roca entrance, 55km southwest of El Calafate along RP 15. On a clear day, you can see the Moreno Glacier and Torres del Paine. **Leutz Turismo** (☎ 02902-492316; leutzturismo@cotecal.com.ar; 25 de Mayo 43, El Calafate) runs day trips (US$23 plus meals) to Lago Roca, including a tour of Estancia Nibepo Aike.

Camping Lago Roca (☎ 02902-499500; www.losgla ciares.com/campinglagoroca; per person US$3, trailers with beds d US$15) A few kilometers past the education camp, this is a well-sheltered, attractive, full-service spot offering fishing equipment and horse riding. There's a **confitería** that offers hot showers.

Estancia Nibepo Aike (☎ 02966-492858/9; www .nibepoaike.com.ar; RP 15, Km 60; s/d US$55/75; ☺ Oct-Apr) Nibepo Aike overlooks the southern arm of Lago Argentino, 5km past the campground on RP 15. It offers the usual assortment of *estancia* highlights, but the real attraction is simply to relax.

Sleeping & Eating

Camping near the glacier offers the chance to see its changing colors in different degrees of daylight. At the lookout, the year-round **UTVM** (☎ 02902-499400; snacks US$1-7, lunch US$4-6) restaurant offers sandwiches, coffee and desserts, and a set lunch for which reservations are advised.

Camping Bahía Escondida (reservations ☎ 491 002; per person US$2) Just over 72km west of El Calafate and only 7km from the Moreno Glacier, this woodsy, drive-in campground has well-maintained sites. Those near the store

and showers are clustered close together, but there's plenty of quiet and elbow room further down the washed-out road. There are excellent views, hot water, a small store and fire pits. Expect crowds in summer.

Hostería Estancia Helsingfors (in Buenos Aires ☎ 011-4315-1222; www.helsingfors.com.ar; s/d US$165/ 325; ☺ Oct-Apr) On Lago Viedma's southern shore, 170km from El Chaltén and 180km from El Calafate, Helsingfors was established by Finnish pioneers. Its spectacular setting, personalized service and access to some of the park's gems make it a highly regarded luxury destination. Rates represent a two-day, one-night stay, with transfers, an excursion and gourmet meals.

Getting There & Away

The Moreno Glacier is 80km west of Calafate via paved RP 11, passing through the breathtaking scenery around Lago Argentino. Bus tours are frequent in summer; see Tours opposite, or simply stroll down El Calafate's Av Libertador. Buses to the glacier leave Calafate (US$13 to US$15 roundtrip) in the early morning and afternoon, returning around noon and 7pm.

EL CALAFATE
☎ 02902 / pop 8000
El Calafate, 320km northwest of Río Gallegos, and 32km west of RP 5's junction with northbound RN 40, is one of a few places that claims its livelihood from a single tourist attraction, the spectacular Glaciar Perito Moreno, some 80km away in Parque Nacional Los Glaciares. Calafate continues to expand rapidly as accessibility to the park improves.

The center of town, formally known as 'Av del Libertador General San Martín' but typically abbreviated 'Av Libertador,' is prettily lit, tree-lined and stuffed with souvenir shops, restaurants and showy weekend vacationers. Beyond the main drag, pretensions melt away quickly; horses replace Porsches along muddy roads leading to ad-hoc developments that show few signs of any planning.

Some visitors complain about Calafate's costly services and in-your-face tourism, but hey, it's a gateway to the crashing icebergs and the transport hub for the Fitz Roy Range in the national park's northern sector. January and February are the most

---

THE AUTHOR'S CHOICE

Hostería Los Notros (☎ 499510, reservations ☎ 4814-3934; www.losnotros.com; all-inclusive 2-night packages per person from US$930) The only formal lodging near the Moreno Glacier, Los Notros is blessed with spectacular views throughout the property. The stylish rooms are outfitted in luscious fabrics and comforts and package rates include guided excursions and gourmet meals.

GLACIOLOGY 101

Rivers of ice, creators of contour and subjects of awe. Glaciers are, well, very cool places. And for those who didn't pack their geology textbooks, here's a summary for you to study and impress your friends.

The heart of the glacier, so to speak, is the accumulation area, on which snow falls, and as the weight increases, compacts to ice. This extra weight forces the glacier to move downhill. As it surges along, the melted ice on the bottom mixes with rock and soil, grinding it up and creating a kind of lubricant that helps the glacier keep pushing along. All that movement in turn causes cracks and deformities in the ice, called crevasses. At the same time, debris of the crushed rock is forced to the sides of the glacier, creating moraines. Where the glacier melts is called the ablation area. When there's more accumulation than melting at the ablation area, the glacier advances; but when there's more melting or evaporation, the glacier recedes.

What makes a glacier blue? Areas of the glacier that are not compacted have air bubbles into which the long wavelengths of white light are absorbed, thus we see simply white. In the areas where the ice becomes more compact, due to the weight on the top pushing ice particles together, blue light (short wavelengths) is still transmitted. The more compact the ice, the longer the path the light has to travel and the bluer the ice appears. Where the glacier melts and calves into lakes, it dumps with it 'glacial flour' comprised of the ground-up rock, giving the water a milky, grayish color. This same sediment remains unsettled in some lakes and diffracts the sun's light, creating the stunning turquoise, pale-mint and azure colors that speckle these otherworldly glacial regions.

popular, thus most costly, months to visit. A new winter tourism push may eventually create a year-round visitor season.

Information

LAUNDRY
El Lavadero (☎ 492182; 25 de Mayo 43) US$3 per load.

MEDICAL SERVICES
Hospital Municipal Dr José Formenti (☎ 107, 491001; Av Roca 1487)

MONEY
The most reliable ATM is at the airport.
Banco Santa Cruz (Av Libertador 1285) Changes traveler's checks but ATM is often out of cash.
Thaler Cambio (Av Libertador 1242) Usurious rates for traveler's checks, but open weekends.

POST
Post office (Av Libertador 1133)

TELEPHONE & INTERNET ACCESS
Cooperativa Telefónica (CTC; cnr Espora & Moyano)
Cooperativa Telefónica (CTC; Av Libertador near Perito Moreno)
Telefónica (Libertad 996) Call center with slow Internet access.

TOURIST INFORMATION
ACA (☎ 449-1004; cnr 1 de Mayo & Av Roca)

Municipal tourist office (☎ 491090/466; www.el calafate.gov.ar in Spanish; ☽ 8am-10pm) At the bus terminal; some English-speaking staff.
Parques Nacional Los Glaciares office (☎ 491005/ 755; Av Libertador 1302; ☽ 8am-7pm Mon-Fri, 10am-8pm Sat & Sun) Brochures and a decent map of Parque Nacional Los Glaciares.

TRAVEL AGENCIES
Most agents deal exclusively with nearby excursions and are unhelpful for other areas.
Tiempo Libre (☎ 491207; tiempolibre@cotecal.com.ar; 25 de Mayo 43) Books flights.

Sights & Activities
The **Museo de El Calafate** (Av Libertador 575; admission free; ☽ 8am-7pm Mon-Fri, 10am-4pm Sat & Sun) has displays of arrowheads, natural history and early photographs. Alongside the lakeshore, north of town, **Laguna Nimez** (admission US$0.65; ☽ 9am-9pm) is prime bird-watching habitat. For a workout, hike up **Cerro Calafate** (850m) from behind Hostel del Glaciar Pioneros.

Tours
Some 40 travel agencies arrange excursions to the Moreno Glacier and other local attractions. Tour prices (US$18 to US$25 per person) don't include the park entrance fee. Ask agents and other travelers about

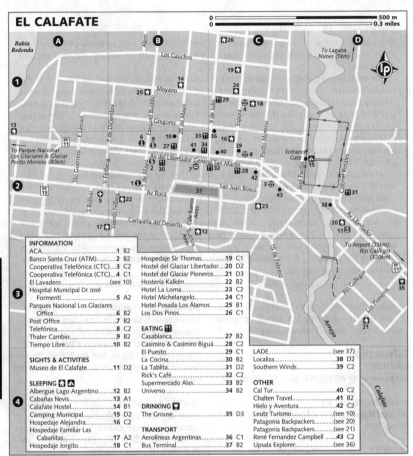

EL CALAFATE

INFORMATION	
ACA...**1** B2	
Banco Santa Cruz (ATM)..........**2** B2	
Cooperativa Telefónica (CTC)...**3** C2	
Cooperativa Telefónica (CTC)...**4** C1	
El Lavadero.............................(see 10)	
Hospital Municipal Dr José	
Formenti...............................**5** A2	
Parques Nacional Los Glaciares	
Office...................................**6** B2	
Post Office................................**7** B2	
Telefónica................................**8** C2	
Thaler Cambio..........................**9** B2	
Tiempo Libre..........................**10** B2	

SIGHTS & ACTIVITIES	
Museo de El Calafate..............**11** D2	

SLEEPING	
Albergue Lago Argentino........**12** B2	
Cabañas Nevis........................**13** A1	
Calafate Hostel.......................**14** B1	
Camping Municipal..................**15** D2	
Hospedaje Alejandra...............**16** C2	
Hospedaje Familiar Las	
Cabañitas............................**17** A2	
Hospedaje Jorgito...................**18** C1	

Hospedaje Sir Thomas.............**19** C1	
Hostel del Glaciar Libertador...**20** D2	
Hostel del Glaciar Pioneros.....**21** D3	
Hostería Kalkén......................**22** B2	
Hotel La Loma........................**23** C2	
Hotel Michelangelo................**24** C1	
Hotel Posada Los Álamos.........**25** B1	
Los Dos Pinos.........................**26** C1	

EATING	
Casablanca..............................**27** B2	
Casimiro & Casimiro Biguá.......**28** C2	
El Puesto.................................**29** C1	
La Cocina................................**30** B2	
La Tablita...............................**31** D2	
Rick's Café..............................**32** C2	
Supermercado Alas..................**33** B2	
Universo.................................**34** B2	

DRINKING	
The Grouse.............................**35** D3	

TRANSPORT	
Aerolíneas Argentinas.............**36** C1	
Bus Terminal...........................**37** B2	

LADE......................................(see 37)	
Localiza..................................**38** D2	
Southern Winds......................**39** C2	

OTHER	
Cal Tur...................................**40** C2	
Chalten Travel........................**41** B2	
Hielo y Aventura....................**42** C2	
Leutz Turismo.....................(see 10)	
Patagonia Backpackers.........(see 20)	
Patagonia Backpackers.........(see 21)	
René Fernandez Campbell **43** C2	
Upsala Explorer...................(see 36)	

---

added benefits, like extra stops, boat trips, binoculars or multilingual guides. Sharing a taxi (from US$50 roundtrip with up to four hours waiting at the glacier) can be a good, more flexible alternative.

Cal Tur (☎ 491368; Av Libertador 1080) Specializes in El Chaltén tours and lodging packages.

Chaltén Travel (☎ 492212/480; www.chaltentravel.com in Spanish; Av Libertador 1174) Recommended tours to the glacier, stopping for wildlife viewing; binoculars provided; also specializes in RN 40 trips.

Patagonia Backpackers (☎ 491243, 492243; www .glaciar.com) Operates out of both branches of Hostel del Glaciar (right) and organizes recommended 'alternative' and full-moon trips to the glacier (US$25) and guided trekking, camping and ice-hiking combos in El Chaltén.

Sleeping

Rates and availability fluctuate widely by season; peak season is January and February, but it can extend from early November to April. In general, rates are relatively poor value compared with the rest of Argentina.

BUDGET

Most hostels offer pickup from the bus terminal.

Hostel del Glaciar Libertador (☎ 491792; www .glaciar.com; Av Libertador 587; dm US$8-10, s US$37-73, d US$45-81; 🖳) HI members get significant discounts on the modern hotel-style private rooms at this brand-new, purpose-built HI hostel, the newer sister of Hostel del Glaciar Pioneros. The facilities are top-notch, the powerful heating is radiant and the friendly, energetic staff have loads of travel tips in several languages.

Hostel del Glaciar Pioneros (☎ 491243; www .glaciar.com; Los Pioneros 251; dm US$7-8, s/d US$30/33; 🖥) An easy 10-minute walk from town, this sociable hostel is always active with packers. Common rooms are comfortable, the kitchen and dorms a tad small, and there's a good pub-restaurant. The multilingual staff provides good info and organizes popular excursions.

Calafate Hostel (☎ 492450/2; www.hostelspata gonia.com; G Moyano 1226; dm US$8-12, r US$23-33; 🖥) This log cabin on steroids has ample common spaces, a wraparound terrace, a well-equipped kitchen, lively bar, considerate English-speaking staff and fun trips to the glacier and Fitz Roy.

Los Dos Pinos (☎ 491271/632; www.losglaciares .com/losdospinos; 9 de Julio 358; sites US$2.50, dm US$4-6, r with shared/private bathroom US$18/36) The quieter Los Dos Pinos lodging labyrinth has a crowded full-service campground, poorly insulated dorms with clean bathrooms and kitchen facilities. Rooms with shared bathroom are a better deal.

Hospedaje Alejandra (☎ 491328; Espora 60; s/d US$11/14) There's seven small but pleasant rooms with shared bathroom, plus one apartment, all accessed via the sprightly owner's living room. The downsides: there's no breakfast and you may need to request hot water.

Hospedaje Jorgito (☎ 491323; Moyano 943; sites/r per person US$2.50/8) Family-run Jorgito has a shared kitchen and warm, practical lodging surrounded by a bounty of flowers. The backyard orchard provides the most central in-town camping.

Camping Municipal (☎ 492622; J Pantín; per person US$2) Woodsy, well-used sites straddle the creek just north of the bridge into town. There's separate areas for auto and tent campers, good toilets, hot showers, potable water and firewood for sale.

MIDRANGE
The tourist office has a complete list of *cabañas* and apart-hotels, which are the best deals for groups and families.

Hospedaje Familiar Las Cabañitas (☎ 491118; lascabanitas@cotecal.com.ar; Valentin Feilberg 218; s/d US$30/45) Storybook A-frames with loft beds, gardens overflowing with English lavender

and charming owners with an eye for the romantic make these cabins a good option. Breakfast isn't included, but there's tea and coffee service, as well as kitchen use.

Cabañas Nevis (☎ 493180; www.cabanasnevis .com.ar; Av Libertador 1696; cabins US$45-60; 🅿) Just beyond the center en route to the glacier, these cute, two-story A-frame cabins near the bay hold up to eight people. The complex occupies a nice grassy lot, all have kitchenettes and cable TV and English is spoken.

Hospedaje Sir Thomas (☎ 492220; www.cotecal .com.ar/hospedajesirthomas in Spanish; Espora 257; s/d US$23/40; 🅿) Friendly Sir Thomas offers 10 bright, modern and woodsy (if a bit sterile) rooms, all with private bathroom and individual heating.

Hotel La Loma (☎ 491016; www.lalomahotel.com; Av Roca 849; r US$40-90; 🅿 🏊) In a quiet upper quarter of town, ranch-style La Loma has ample gardens and the only indoor pool in town. Rooms are decorated with old furniture, while the reception and cozy dining area brim with an open fire, plenty of books and creaky wooden floors. The only drawback of the cheaper rooms is the all-in-one bathrooms. Breakfast includes fresh homemade breads.

TOP END
International-class, five-star chains like Kempinski and Sheraton are poised to up the luxury ante in 2005.

Hotel Posada Los Álamos (☎ 491144; www.posada losalamos.com; Moyano 1355; s/d/ste US$175/188/283; 🅿 🖥) Calafate's original resort trills in luxury: plush rooms, overstuffed sofas, spectacular gardens, tennis courts, putting greens, the superb La Posta restaurant and lavish buffet breakfast are enough to almost forget about seeing that glacier – but some find the walls a bit thin for a four-star getaway.

Hostería Kalkén (☎ 491073/687; www.losglaciares .com/kalken; Valentin Feilberg 119; s/d US$70/85; 🅿) Helpful staff, a quiet central location and comfortable rooms make this cheaper top-end place a restful option. Breakfast here is excellent.

Hotel Michelangelo (☎ 491045; www.hotelguia .com/hoteles/michelangelo in Spanish; Moyano 1020; s/d US$54/72; 🅿) This intimate tour-group favorite has solid 'glacial' walls bedecked in historic photos. There's a good restaurant, buffet breakfast and excellent multilingual service. Rooms facing the back interior patio are more peaceful than those facing the street.

Eating

For a quick snack, there are several good ice-cream and chocolate shops along Av Libertador.

La Tablita (☎ 491065; Coronel Rosales 24; mains US$3-7) Considered the town's best *parrilla*, popular La Tablita piles on the meat, and has chicken and cheese options, garlic parsley French fries and an extensive wine list.

Rick's Café (☎ 492148; Av Libertador 1091; buffet US$5-7, mains US$3-5) While buffets in touristy towns all too often suffer dried-out dingy food, Rick's does it right with consistently good varieties.

El Puesto (☎ 491260; cnr G Moyano & 9 de Julio; mains US$3-8) In one of the town's oldest houses (c 1949), this is a cozy place for good wood-fired pizzas, pastas and grilled meats.

Universo (☎ 491009; Av Libertador 1108; mains US$2-5) Well regarded by locals and tourists alike, the pastas and pizzas are the best fare, dished out in an informal family-style dining room. Vegie options are mainly spinach.

Casablanca (☎ 491402; Av Libertador 1202; mains US$2-5) There's good music and rather slow service here, plus filling burgers and over-priced coffee drinks.

La Cocina (☎ 491758; Av Libertador 1245; mains US$3-8) A recommended rustic place for salads and well-prepared pasta.

Supermercado Alas (☎ 491249; 9 de Julio 59) Stock up here on picnic goods and trekking fare: fresh produce, dried soups, breads and deli items.

THE AUTHOR'S CHOICE

Casimiro & Casimiro Biguá (☎ 492590; Av Libertador 963; mains US$5-10) The ambience is warm and the staff is wonderful at this casual yet refined grill and *vinoteca* (wine bar). With an impressive list of 180 Argentine wines to choose from, it's no wonder Argentine President Nestor Kirchner often drops by to sample the Italian and Patagonian cuisine; his weekend house is around the corner, behind Posada Los Álamos. The original location is more intimate, but there's an equally inviting new spin-off a couple doors down specializing in *asado* and *parrilla*.

Drinking

The Grouse (☎ 491281; Av Libertador 351; drinks US$1-4) This vaguely Celtic-themed pub/nightclub aims to appeal to all whims, with thumping techno, generous mixed drinks and draught cans of Guinness.

Getting There & Away

AIR

Inaugurated in late 2000, the modern **Aeropuerto El Calafate** (ECA; ☎ 491220/30) is 23km east of town off RP 11; the departure tax is US$18.

Aerolíneas Argentinas (☎ 492814/16; 9 de Julio 57) flies every day to Bariloche (US$155 to US$297), Ushuaia (US$100 to US$269), Trelew (US$105 to US$280) and both Aeroparque and Ezeiza in Buenos Aires (US$105 to US$210).

Southern Winds (☎ 491498; Espora 35) goes a couple of times a week to Buenos Aires (US$98) and Bariloche (US$147) – sit on the left-hand side for the best views – and may start serving Ushuaia in 2005.

LADE (☎ 491262; at bus terminal) flies a few times a week to Río Gallegos (US$32), Comodoro Rivadavia (US$56), Ushuaia (US$77), Esquel (US$96), Puerto Madryn (US$103), Buenos Aires (US$92) and other smaller regional airports.

Chilean **Aerovías DAP** (☎ 491143; www.dap.cl) serves Puerto Natales on weekdays (US$50, 30 minutes) from mid-November until mid-March.

BUS

Calafate's hilltop **bus terminal** (Av Roca s/n) is easily reached by a pedestrian staircase from the corner of Av Libertador and 9 de Julio. Book ahead in high season, as outbound seats can be in short supply.

For El Chaltén (US$15, five hours), several companies share passengers and leave daily at 7:30am, 8am and 6:30pm, stopping midway at Estancia La Leona for coffee and tasty pies.

For Puerto Natales (US$15, five to eight hours), **Bus Sur** (☎ 491842) and **Zaahj** (☎ 491631) depart daily around 8am and 6:30pm, crossing the border at Cerro Castillo, where it may be possible to connect to Torres del Paine. **Bus Sur** (☎ 491444) goes daily at 8:30am via Río Turbio.

For Río Gallegos (US$10, five hours), buses go daily at 9am. **Freddy** (☎ 452671) offers connections to Bariloche and Ushuaia that require leaving in the middle of the night and a change of buses in Río Gallegos.

From mid-October to April, **Chaltén Travel** (p413) runs shuttles north along RN 40 to Perito Moreno and Los Antiguos (US$64), departing on even-numbered days at 8am, to connect with onward service to Bariloche the next morning. The same service leaves from El Chaltén.

Getting Around

Aerobus (☎ 491588) provides door-to-door airport shuttle service for US$3; taxis charge around US$8. There are several car rental agencies at the airport, including **Localiza** (☎ 491398, 15-622565).

AROUND CALAFATE

From El Calafate, paved RN 40 cuts southeast across the infinite vastness of the steppe for 95km, where it jogs south at **El Cerrito** and turns to gravel. Staying on paved RP 5 means a slow-going, five-hour, 224km bore of a trip southeast to **Río Gallegos**. Halfway along RP 5 at Km 146 is the utilitarian **Hotel La Esperanza** (☎ 02902-499200; per person US$7), a gas station and restaurant with quick, friendly service. From here, paved RP 7 connects back to RN 40 for the Chilean border crossing at Cerro Castillo–Cancha Carrera, Parque Nacional Torres del Paine and Puerto Natales.

CHILEAN PATAGONIA

Anyone venturing to Argentina's southern highlights will most likely also make a jaunt into Chile to enjoy the Andes' other wild side. Chilean Patagonia, a rugged, mountainous region sculpted by westerly winds, consists of the Aisén and Magallanes regions, separated by the southern continental ice field. This section covers Punta Arenas, Puerto Natales and spectacular Parque Nacional Torres del Paine. For in-depth coverage of Chile, pick up Lonely Planet's *Chile & Easter Island*.

Most nationals of countries with which Chile has diplomatic relations don't need a visa to enter the country. Upon entering, customs officials issue you a tourist card, valid for 90 days and renewable for another 90; authorities take it seriously, so guard it closely to avoid the hassle of replacing it.

If arriving by air, US citizens must pay a one-time reciprocal entry fee of US$100, valid for the life of the passport; Canadians pay US$55 and Australians US$34.

Chile is more expensive than Argentina, and US cash is not as widely accepted.

PUNTA ARENAS

☎ 61 / pop 125,000

The most convenient base for transport options around the remote Magallanes region, 'Sandy Point' is an attractive mixture of elaborate mansions dating from the wool boom of the late 19th and early 20th centuries and good traveler's services. Nothing sums the vibe up better than hanging out in the basement bar of the ornate Club de la Unión, where Antarctic explorers, geologists, Torres del Paine trekkers and cruiseship softies commune, all thrilled to be in such a spectacular corner of the world.

Founded in 1848 as a penal settlement and military garrison, Punta Arenas proved to be conveniently situated for ships headed to Alta California during the gold rush. During its early years, the economy depended on wild animal products and it didn't take off until the last quarter of the 19th century, after the territorial governor authorized the purchase of 300 pure-bred sheep from the Falkland Islands. This successful experiment encouraged others to invest in sheep and, by the turn of the century, nearly two million animals grazed the territory.

Information
BOOKSTORES
World's End (☎ 213117; Plaza Muñoz Gamero 1011) Maps, photo books, souvenirs and Lonely Planet guides in English and Spanish.

INTERNET ACCESS
Broadband has yet to arrive, so most places are stuck with relatively slow satellite Internet service. Many backpacker hostels have access, as do most telephone call centers. Rates average US$1 to US$1.50 an hour.
E-Green Internet (Fagnano 565-A)
GonFish (Croacia 1028) Punta's original *ciber* offers notebook hookups, a multilingual book exchange and expert help with all digital needs, including photo downloads.

LAUNDRY
Hostels do laundry for a bit less than *lavanderías*, which charge around US$6 per load.

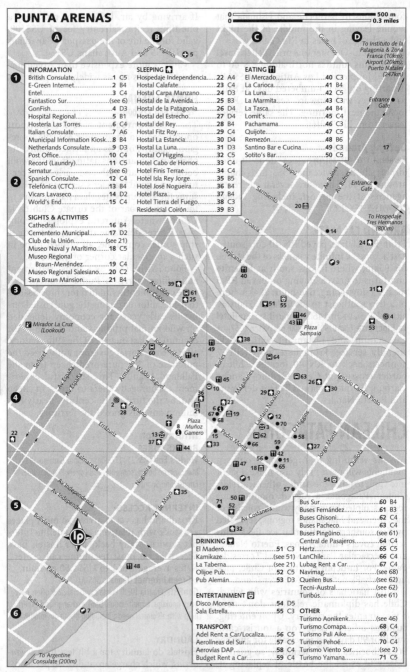

PUNTA ARENAS

| 0 | 500 m |
| 0 | 0.3 miles |

INFORMATION
British Consulate	**1**	C5
E-Green Internet	**2**	B4
Entel	**3**	C4
Fantastico Sur	(see 6)
GonFish	**4**	D3
Hospital Regional	**5**	B1
Hostería Las Torres	**6**	C4
Italian Consulate	**7**	A6
Municipal Information Kiosk	**8**	B4
Netherlands Consulate	**9**	D3
Post Office	**10**	C4
Record (Laundry)	**11**	C5
Sernatur	(see 6)
Spanish Consulate	**12**	C4
Telefónica (CTC)	**13**	B4
Vicars Lavaseco	**14**	D2
World's End	**15**	C5

SIGHTS & ACTIVITIES
Cathedral	**16**	B4
Cementerio Municipal	**17**	D2
Club de la Unión	(see 21)
Museo Naval y Marítimo	**18**	C5
Museo Regional Braun-Menéndez	**19**	C4
Museo Regional Salesiano	**20**	C2
Sara Braun Mansion	**21**	B4

SLEEPING
Hospedaje Independencia	**22**	A4
Hostal Calafate	**23**	C4
Hostal Carpa Manzano	**24**	D3
Hostal de la Avenida	**25**	B3
Hostal de la Patagonia	**26**	D4
Hostal del Estrecho	**27**	D4
Hostal del Rey	**28**	B4
Hostal Fitz Roy	**29**	C4
Hostal La Estancia	**30**	D4
Hostal La Luna	**31**	D3
Hostal O'Higgins	**32**	C5
Hotel Cabo de Hornos	**33**	C4
Hotel Finis Terrae	**34**	C4
Hotel Isla Rey Jorge	**35**	B5
Hotel José Nogueira	**36**	B4
Hotel Plaza	**37**	B4
Hotel Tierra del Fuego	**38**	C3
Residencial Coirón	**39**	B3

EATING
El Mercado	**40**	C3
La Carioca	**41**	B4
La Luna	**42**	C5
La Marmita	**43**	C3
La Tasca	**44**	B4
Lomit's	**45**	C4
Pachamama	**46**	C3
Quijote	**47**	C5
Remezón	**48**	B6
Santino Bar e Cucina	**49**	C5
Sotito's Bar	**50**	C5

DRINKING
El Madero	**51**	C3
Kamikaze	(see 51)
La Taberna	(see 21)
Olijoe Pub	**52**	C5
Pub Alemán	**53**	D3

ENTERTAINMENT
| Disco Morena | **54** | D5 |
| Sala Estrella | **55** | C3 |

TRANSPORT
Adel Rent a Car/Localiza	**56**	C5
Aerolíneas del Sur	**57**	C3
Aerovías DAP	**58**	C4
Budget Rent a Car	**59**	C4
Bus Sur	**60**	B4
Buses Fernández	**61**	B3
Buses Ghisoni	**62**	C4
Buses Pacheco	**63**	C4
Buses Pingüino	(see 61)
Central de Pasajeros	**64**	C4
Hertz	**65**	C5
LanChile	**66**	C4
Lubag Rent a Car	**67**	C4
Navimag	(see 68)
Queilen Bus	(see 62)
Tecni-Austral	(see 62)
Turibús	(see 61)

OTHER
Turismo Aonikenk	(see 46)
Turismo Comapa	**68**	C4
Turismo Pali Aike	**69**	C5
Turismo Pehoé	**70**	C4
Turismo Viento Sur	(see 2)
Turismo Yamana	**71**	C5

To Instituto de la Patagonia & Zona Franca (10km); Airport (20km); Puerto Natales (247km)

Entrance Gate

Entrance Gate

To Hospedaje Tres Hermanos (800km)

Mirador La Cruz (Lookout)

Plaza Sampaio

Plaza Muñoz Gamero

To Argentine Consulate (200m)

PATAGONIA

Record (☎ 243607; O'Higgins 969)
Vicars Lavaseco (☎ 241526; Sarmiento 726)

MEDICAL SERVICES
Sernatur has a list of recommended doctors.
Hospital Regional (☎ 205000; cnr Arauco & Angamos)

MONEY
Travel agencies in the center along Roca and
Lautaro Navarro change cash and traveler's
checks. All are open weekdays and Satur-
day, with a few open on Sunday morning.
Many hotels and restaurants accept US
dollars at a fair exchange rate. Banks with
ATMs dot the city center.

POST
Post office (Bories 911)

TELEPHONE
Entel (Lautaro Navarro 957)
Telefónica/CTC (Nogueira 1116)

TOURIST INFORMATION
Municipal Information Kiosk (☎ 200610; www.punta
arenas.cl in Spanish; ☉ 8am-8pm Mon-Sat) South side of
the plaza.
Sernatur (☎ 225385; www.sernatur.cl; Magallanes 960;
☉ 8:15am-8pm Mon-Fri in summer, 8:15am-6pm Mon-Thu,
8:15am-5pm Fri rest of year) Just off the main plaza in an
interior courtyard, the national tourist office has friendly,
well-informed, multilingual staffers.

Sights & Activities
PLAZA MUÑOZ GAMERO
Landscaped with exotic conifers, spruced
up in late 2004 and surrounded by opulent
mansions, this central plaza is the heart of
Punta Arenas. Note the monument commemorating the 400th anniversary of Magellan's voyage, donated by wool baron José
Menéndez in 1920. Facing the plaza's north
side is the **Club de la Unión** (☎ 241489; admission
US$2; ☉ 10:30am-1pm & 5-8:30pm Tue-Fri, 10:30am-1pm
& 8-10pm Sat, 11am-2pm Sun), the former **Sara Braun
mansion**, some rooms of which are open to
public visits. Just east is the former Sociedad Menéndez Behety, which now houses
the offices of Turismo Comapa (p420). To
the west is the **cathedral**.

MUSEO REGIONAL BRAUN-MENÉNDEZ
Also known as the Palacio Mauricio Braun,
this opulent mansion testifies to the wealth
and power of pioneer sheep farmers in the

late 19th century. One of Mauricio Braun's
sons donated the house to the state against
other family members' wishes. The well-
maintained interior is divided into one part
regional historical museum (booklets with
English descriptions are available) and the
other half displays the original exquisite
French nouveau family furnishings, from
the intricate wooden inlay floors to Chinese
vases.

The **museum** (☎ 244216; Magallanes 949; admission
US$1.75, Sun free; ☉ 10:30am-5pm Mon-Sat, 10:30am-2pm
Sun in summer, to 2pm daily in winter) is most easily
accessed from Magallanes. There's a café
downstairs in what used to be the servants'
quarters.

CEMENTERIO MUNICIPAL
In death as in life, Punta Arenas' first families flaunted their wealth – wool baron José
Menéndez's extravagant tomb is, according
to Bruce Chatwin, a scale replica of Rome's
Vittorio Emanuele monument. But the
headstones among the topiary cypresses in
the walled **municipal cemetery** (main entrance at
Av Bulnes 949; ☉ 7:30am-8pm) also tell the stories
of Anglo, German, Scandinavian and Yugoslav immigrants. There's also a monument
to the Selk'nam (Onas) and a map posted
inside the main entrance gate.

The cemetery is an easy 15-minute stroll
northeast of the plaza, or catch any taxi
colectivo (shared cab with specific route)
from in front of the Museo Regional Braun-
Menéndez on Magallanes.

MUSEO NAVAL Y MARÍTIMO
Punta Arenas' naval and maritime **museum**
(☎ 205479; Pedro Montt 981; admission US$1; ☉ 9:30am-
12:30pm & 3-6pm Tue-Sat) has varied exhibits
on model ships, naval history, the unpre-
cedented visit of 27 US warships to Punta
Arenas in 1908, and a fine account of the
Chilean mission that rescued British explorer
Sir Ernest Shackleton's crew from Antarctica. The most imaginative display is a ship's
replica, complete with bridge, maps, charts
and radio room.

MUSEO REGIONAL SALESIANO
Especially influential in settling the region,
the Salesian order collected outstanding
ethnographic artifacts, but their **museum**
(☎ 221001; Av Bulnes 336; admission US$3; ☉ 10am-
6pm Tue-Sun) takes a self-serving view of the

PATAGONIA

Christian intervention, portraying missionaries as peacemakers between Indians and settlers. The best materials are on indigenous groups and the mountaineer priest Alberto de Agostini.

INSTITUTO DE LA PATAGONIA

Part of the Universidad de Magallanes, the Patagonian Institute's **Museo del Recuerdo** (☎ 207056; Av Bulnes 01890; admission US$1.75; ◷ 8:30am-11am & 2:30-6pm Mon-Fri) features a collection of antique farm and industrial machinery, a typical pioneer house and shearing shed and a wooden-wheeled shepherds' trailer. The library has a display of historical maps and a series of historical and scientific publications. Any taxi *colectivo* to the *zona franca* (duty-free zone) will drop you across the street.

Tours

Tours to the pingüinera (p426) at Seno Otway (65km north) start around US$10, plus US$5 admission, leaving at 4pm daily October through March. Tours to Puerto Hambre and the restored wooden Fuerte Bulnes cost US$14, plus US$2 admission, leaving at 10am. It's possible to do both tours in one day; however, sharing a rental car and going at opposite times affords a chance to actually see the sites rather than the strings of tour groups. Most lodgings will help arrange tours – if they don't run their own operation. Torres del Paine tours are abundant from Punta Arenas, but the distance makes for a very long day; it's best to head to Puerto Natales (p427) and organize transport from there.

Five-hour tours on the *Barcaza Melinka* land for an hour at the thriving Magellanic penguin colonies on **Isla Magdalena** (adult/child US$30/15). They depart the port on Tuesday, Thursday and Saturday, December through February. Book tickets through **Turismo Comapa** (☎ 200200; www.comapa.com; Magallanes 990) and bring a picnic – snacks on the ferry aren't that exciting.

Recommended agencies:

Fantastico Sur (☎ 61-710050; www.lostorres.com; Magallanes 960)

Turismo Aonikenk (☎ 228332; www.aonikenk.com; Magallanes 619) English-, German- and French-speaking guides.

Turismo Pali Aike (☎ 223301; www.turismopaliaike.com; Lautaro Navarro 1129)

Turismo Pehoé (☎ 244506; www.pehoe.com; José Menéndez 918)

Turismo Viento Sur (☎ 226930; www.vientosur.com; Fagnano 585)

Turismo Yamana (☎ 710567; www.yamana.cl; Errázuriz 932) Kayaking trips on Magellan Strait.

Sleeping

BUDGET

Hospedaje Tres Hermanos (☎ 225450; residencialtreshnos@yahoo.com; Angamos 1218; per person with shared/private bathroom US$7/10; ℗) Quiet, comfortable rooms in this rambling old family-run house include breakfast and kitchen use. It's friendly and excellent value.

Hostal O'Higgins (☎ 227999; O'Higgins 1205; per person US$10, d US$26; ℗) In what used to be dormitories for the teams that play at the adjacent gym, excellently located O'Higgins is spotlessly clean with large, locker room–style bathrooms, hot showers and a large shared kitchen. Recommended doubles with private bathroom are out back by the tranquil waterfront.

Hostal La Luna (☎ 221764; hostalluna@hotmail.com; O'Higgins 424; per person without/with bathroom US$10/12; ▣) Snuggle in full-size beds under heavy goosedown comforters at this old house with spacious rooms. Light streams through the kitchen and living room, which are open to guests, as are laundry facilities. It's a small home (only six rooms, the best downstairs), which keeps the place intimate.

Hostal Fitz Roy (☎ 240430; hostalfitzroy@hotmail.com; Lautaro Navarro 850; per person with shared bathroom US$9-13, 4-person apt US$34; ℗ ▣) Run by an experienced Torres del Paine guide, staying here feels more like being a guest in somebody's home. Continental breakfasts are ample, common spaces comfortable and the ambience inviting. All rooms have phones and TV, making them popular with Antarctica researchers awaiting word of flights.

Hostal La Estancia (☎ 249130; carmenalecl@yahoo.com; O'Higgins 765; dm US$9.50, s US$22, d US$27-33; ▣) Run by a friendly young couple, the Estancia has attractive upstairs rooms, decent beds and rock-hard pillows. A filling breakfast is included, as is a full entertainment center with English-language TV.

Hostal del Rey (☎ 223924; www.chileaustral.com/hdelrey; Fagnano 589; dm US$10, 2-/4-person apt US$30/60; ℗) Tiny corridors lead to sweet dorms with down comforter–covered beds. The best bets here are the downstairs apartments with full kitchens, hot water and TV.

Hospedaje Independencia (☎ 227572; Av Independencia 374; cabins US$16-23, r with shared bathroom US$8, basic dm US$6, camping per person US$3) Run by a young couple, the casual Independencia has good-size dorm rooms, kitchen use and camping in the somewhat muddy front yard, plus a couple of private heated cabins across town. No breakfast is served.

Residencial Coirón (☎ 226449; Armando Sanhueza 730; per person US$10) Opposite the Fernández bus terminal, owner-attended Coirón is funky but handy, with sunny upstairs singles and breakfast included.

MIDRANGE

Rates at midrange establishments include breakfast but don't reflect the additional 18% IVA charge, which foreigners in Chile aren't required to pay if paying with US cash, traveler's checks or credit card. In the off-season (mid-April to mid-October), rates can drop by up to 40%.

Hotel Plaza (☎ 241300; www.chileaustral.com /hplaza; Nogueira 1116; s/d US$72/87; 🖳) Staying at the Plaza, located in a converted mansion, brings to light the opulence of the city's history. Cozy, carpeted rooms with high ceilings, some with great views of the plaza and most with bathtubs, make this a worthwhile three-star choice in the heart of the town. Many famous Everest climbers have rested their weary feet here.

Hostal Calafate (☎ 241281; www.calafate.cl in Spanish; Magallanes 922; s/d US$38/54, with shared bathroom US$26/38; P 🖳) In the heart of downtown, the laid-back Calafate boasts long hallways, large rooms with TV, free parking, friendly youthful staff and a popular Internet café in the lobby. The only drawback is the street noise.

Hostal del Estrecho (☎ 241011; www.chileanpata gonia.com/estrecho in Spanish; José Menéndez 1048; s/d US$47/60, with shared bathroom US$20/33; P) Whether with a group or on your own, Estrecho's kindly owners will put you up in huge carpeted rooms full of bunk beds. The included buffet breakfast is served in the cozy dining area, as is the set lunch.

Hostal Carpa Manzano (☎ 242296; Lautaro Navarro 336; s/d US$45/56; P) In a quiet residential neighborhood near the cemetery, this oh-so-relaxing spot has 10 pleasant rooms, most of which overlook a side path festooned with

flowers. All rooms come with private bathroom and cable TV.

Hostal de la Avenida (☎ 247532; Av Colón 534; s/d US$42/59; P) Around the corner from the Fernández bus terminal, the Avenida is a solid option with seven pleasant, slightly dark rooms. Unfortunately they impose a credit card surcharge and don't recognize the IVA discount.

Hostal de la Patagonia (☎ 249970; www.ecotour patagonia.com; O'Higgins 730; s/d US$40/50) Rooms are perfectly adequate at this quiet, boxy, but conscientiously run spot.

TOP END

Hotel José Nogueira (☎ 248840; www.hotelnogueira .com; Bories 959; s/d US$149/179, ste US$255-298; P 🖳) If Hotel Cabo de Hornos (following) is the king, this hotel, in part of the Sara Braun mansion, is surely the queen. Rooms have modern amenities but retain period furnishings; the lobby is wired for wi-fi. A highlight is sipping a cocktail or dining on seasonal regional cuisine beneath what may be the world's most southerly grape arbor in the atmospheric restaurant, formerly a winter garden.

Hotel Cabo de Hornos (☎ 242134; www.hotelcabo dehornos.cl; Plaza Muñoz Gamero 1025; s US$99-117, d/ste US$130/242; P ⊠ 🖳) The king of business-friendly hotels has 100 solid rooms with pleasant decor and good views. There's a sauna and business center, and the professional staff is quick to help. The bar is cozy but costly.

Hotel Isla Rey Jorge (☎ 248220; www.hotelislarey jorge.com; 21 de Mayo 1243; s/d/ste US$119/146/199; P 🖳) With wi-fi Internet, this chic, modern hotel features traditional English style in its 25 attractive rooms and relaxing common spaces. Its good maritime-themed pub and restaurant, and location close to the port, make it popular with cruise passengers.

Hotel Finis Terrae (☎ 228200; www.hotelfinis terrae.com; Av Colón 766; s/d US$140/160, ste US$216-260; ⊠ 🖳) Sunny standard rooms are a good deal, with attractive furnishings and courteous staff. The 6th-floor restaurant and lounge has spectacular views of town and the Strait of Magellan.

Hotel Tierra del Fuego (☎ 226200; www.punta arenas.com; Av Colón 716; s/d US$89/98; P) Rather drab in design and decor, the Tierra del Fuego at least has modern amenities, some nice views and an attractive bar that stays pretty active. It's often full with tour groups but the smoky café-pub and restaurant are popular with locals.

Eating

Centolla (king crab) season is July to November. Erizos (sea urchins) are available November to July. If heading to Torres del Paine, stock up on groceries and trail mixes here beforehand.

Remezón (☎ 241029; 21 de Mayo 1469; US$6-12) Remezón's chef impresses with delicately prepared and supremely delicious dishes, such as oysters and clams au gratin, fresh crab with lemon, and salmon smoked with black tea. Equally imaginative are the baked sierra crab *canelones* (stuffed pasta tubes). Service is unpretentious and welcoming; they are quick to pour a pisco sour to get you going.

Sotito's Bar (☎ 243565; O'Higgins 1138; mains US$8-24; ☺ lunch only Sun) One of the city's more long-lasting formal affairs and catering heavily to tourists. Salmon with mixed seafood sauce will put you back only US$10, but servings of fresh crab are dearer.

Santino Bar e Cucina (☎ 220511; Av Colón 657; mains US$3-9) Hip Santino is most popular as a bar, but it serves oversized savory crepes and tasty pizzas, plus plates of seafood with an assortment of sauces.

Quijote (☎ 241225; Lautaro Navarro 1087; mains US$4-9) Recommended for consistently good meals and service, Quijote fills up at lunchtime with the business folk enjoying US$5 fixed-price lunches. It's also a good bet for breakfast, cake or a quick espresso.

El Mercado (☎ 247415; Mejicana 617; mains US$4-10; ☺ 24hr) This local institution heaps on an assortment of seafood specials, from scallops stewed in garlicky sauce, to baked

---

THE AUTHOR'S CHOICE

La Marmita (☎ 222056; Plaza Sampaio 678; set lunch US$4.35, mains US$5-7) A jovial husband-and-wife team infuse typical Magellanic dishes with a unique twist, employing fresh local ingredients, and their sweet kids as helpers. Inside the colorful old wooden house, the ambience is warmed by upbeat music and a wood-burning stove. Delicate preparations, like the fresh fish stew that arrives in a heavy cast-iron pot, all feature a personal touch. *Buen provecho,* indeed.

---

creamed centolla (crab) to mussels *à la parmesana*. There's a full bar, English menu and cheaper sandwiches.

Lomit's (☎ 243399; José Menéndez 722; mains US$2-5; ☺ 10am-2:30am) Despite the slow service, Lomit's attracts packs of locals and travelers, probably because it's open when other places are closed for the night. Made-to-order burgers and sandwiches are generous and tasty. Saddle up to the bar for faster service.

La Carioca (☎ 224809; José Menéndez 600; mains US$4-7) Praised for pizzas, sandwiches and cold lager beer, plus a daily lunch special.

Also recommended:

La Luna (☎ 228555; O'Higgins 974; mains US$5-10) A wide variety of fresh seafood and pastas.

La Tasca (☎ 242807; Plaza Muñoz Gamero 771; mains US$7-15) In the stylish Casa España, with good views, set lunch weekdays and fresh seafood for dinner.

Pachamama (☎ 226171; Magallanes 619-A) Bulk trail-mix munchies and organic products.

Drinking

La Taberna (☎ 241317; Sara Braun Mansion; ☺ 7pm-2am, until 3am weekends) In the dark, low-ceiling basement of the mansion, this tavern is the place to huddle in a booth and swap tales of Andean and Antarctic adventures. The environment is tops, but the mixed drinks could be better.

Pub Alemán (cnr Croatia & O'Higgins) Stop by this atmospheric, restored castlelike place for a stiff drink and dose of English or German conversation. There's live jazz piano some Friday or Saturday nights.

El Madero (Bories 655) Madero gets packed with the pre-disco crowds bustling about from table to table and saucing up on stiff drinks. Afterwards, head downstairs to **Kamikaze** (☎ 248744; cover US$5 with a free drink), tripped out with South Pacific flares and tiki torches, which hosts the occasional live rock act. To find the building, look for the wrecked plane on the roof.

Olijoe Pub (☎ 223728; Errázuriz 970; ☺ 6pm-2am) Faux-historic Olijoe has an upscale feel but relaxing ambience – a good place for a snack (pizzas, burgers and sandwiches) or a quiet drink. Try the house special Glaciar, a potent mix of pisco, horchata, milk and curuçao.

Entertainment

Disco Morena (☎ 245832; José Menéndez 1173) Cavernous venue, in the forlorn waterfront area, keeps on thumping long after the rest of the city has turned in for the night.

Sala Estrella (Mejicana 777; tickets US$2) Head to this aging theater for movies.

Shopping

Zona Franca (Zofri; ⊗ closed Sun) The duty-free zone is a large, polished conglomeration of shops that is worth checking out if you're looking for film, electronics, computer accessories or camera equipment. *Colectivos* shuttle back and forth from downtown along Av Bulnes throughout the day.

Getting There & Away

The tourist offices distribute a useful brochure which details all forms of transport available.

AIR

LanChile (☎ 241100, 600-526-2000; www.lan.com; Lautaro Navarro 999) flies several times daily to Santiago (US$152 one way) with a stop in Puerto Montt (US$105 one way), and Saturday to the Falkland Islands/Islas Malvinas (US$580 roundtrip).

Newcomer **Aerolíneas del Sur** (in Santiago ☎ 02-210-9000; Pedro Montt 969) announced plans to offer direct, nonstop flights twice daily between Santiago and Punta Arenas, with an initial published advance-purchase fare of US$180. **Sky Airline** (in Santiago ☎ 600-600-2828, 02-353-3169; www.skyairline.cl) began flying daily in December 2004 between Santiago and Punta Arenas, with a stop either in Puerto Montt or Concepción.

Aerovías DAP (☎ 223340, airport ☎ 213776; www.dap.cl; O'Higgins 891) flies to Porvenir (US$23) and back twice daily except Sunday from November to March; to Puerto Williams (US$64) several times a week; to Ushuaia (US$100) on Tuesday and Friday at 9am; and in summer to Río Grande (US$90) on a charter-only basis. Luggage is limited to 10kg per person.

DAP also does three-hour excursion flights over Cabo de Hornos (Cape Horn; US$300) on Sunday, possibly stopping in Puerto Williams en route. DAP also flies monthly to Chile's Teniente Marsh air base in Antarctica to tour Base Frei (one-/two-day US$1875/2600); weather depending, the schedule permits one or two nights in Antarctica before returning to Punta Arenas.

BOAT

The *Barcaza Melinka*, operated by **Transbordadora Austral Broom** (☎ 218100; www.tabsa.cl in Spanish; Av Bulnes 05075), sails to Porvenir, Tierra del Fuego (US$6.50, 2½ to four hours) from the Tres Puentes ferry terminal north of town; catch taxi *colectivos* in front of Museo Regional Braun-Menéndez. Boats usually depart in the early morning and return in the late afternoon; schedules and travel time depend on the mercurial weather. Make reservations to ferry your vehicle (US$40) by calling the office.

A faster way to get to Tierra del Fuego (US$2, 20 minutes) is the Punta Delgada–Bahía Azul ('Cruce Primera Angostura') crossing, northeast of Punta Arenas. Broom ferries sail every 90 minutes between 8:30am and 10pm. Call ahead for vehicle reservations (US$18).

Broom is also the agent for ferries from Tres Puentes to Puerto Williams (p455), on Isla Navarino, which sail three or four times per month, Wednesday only, returning Saturday, both at 7pm (reclining seat/bunk US$120/150 including meals, 34 to 38 hours) – trust us, the extra $30 for a bunk is worthwhile.

September through May, **Cruceros Australis** (in Santiago ☎ 02-442-3110; www.australis.com) runs breathtakingly scenic four- to seven-day luxury cruises aboard the 130-passenger *MV Mare Australis* and brand-new *MV Via Australis*, from Punta Arenas through the Cordillera de Darwin, Parque Nacional Alberto de Agostini, the Beagle Channel, and Puerto Williams, Ushuaia (Argentina), and back. Rates start from US$681 per person, double occupancy in low season (October and April) and reach US$4160 for a high-season single (mid-December through February). Most passengers only sail one leg. Departures from Ushuaia include a possibility of disembarking at Cape Horn. Turismo Comapa (p420) handles local bookings.

Navimag (☎ 200200; www.navimag.com; Magallanes 990), which runs ferries from Puerto Natales to Puerto Montt via the spectacular Chilean fjords, is also represented by Comapa. For fare and schedules, see p431.

BUS

Plans for a central terminal are in the works; for the time being buses depart from company offices, most within a block or two of

PATAGONIA

THE FALKLAND ISLANDS/ISLAS MALVINAS

☎ 500 / permanent nonmilitary pop 2500, sheep 700,000

The sheep boom in Tierra del Fuego and Patagonia owes its origins to a cluster of islands 500km to the east in the South Atlantic Ocean. These islands, the Islas Malvinas (to the Argentines) or Falkland Islands (to the British) were explored, but never fully captured either country's interest. Very little transpired on the islands until the mid-19th-century wool boom in Europe, when the Falkland Islands Company (FIC) became the islands' largest landholder. The population, mostly stranded gauchos and mariners, grew rapidly with the arrival of English and Scottish immigrants. In an unusual exchange, in 1853 the South American Missionary Society began transporting Yahgan Indians from Tierra del Fuego to Keppel Island to catechize them.

Argentina has laid claim to the islands since 1833, but it wasn't until 1982 that Argentine president Leopoldo Galtieri, then drowning in economic chaos and allegations of corruption, decided that reclaiming the islands would unite his country behind him. However, English Prime Minister Margaret Thatcher (who was also suffering in the polls) didn't hesitate for a moment in striking back, thoroughly humiliating Argentina in what became known as the Falkland Islands War. A severe blow to Argentina's nationalist pride, the ill-fated war succeeded in severing all diplomatic ties between the two nations.

On July 14, 1999, a joint statement issued by the British, Falkland Islands and Argentine governments promised closer cooperation on areas of economic mutual interest. In August 2001, British Prime Minister Tony Blair visited Argentina in an effort to further improve ties between the countries. Nevertheless, relations with Argentina remain distinctly cool, with most South American trade going via Chile.

Besides being an unusually polemic piece of property, what about the Falklands will intrigue the intrepid traveler? Bays, inlets, estuaries and beaches create a tortuous, attractive coastline that is home to abundant wildlife. Striated and crested caracaras, cormorants, oystercatchers, snowy sheathbills and a plethora of penguins – Magellanic, rockhopper, macaroni, gentoo and king – share top billing with elephant seals, sea lions, fur seals, five dolphin species and killer whales.

Stanley (population 1600), the islands' capital on East Falkland, is an assemblage of brightly painted metal-clad houses and a good place to throw down a few pints and listen to island lore. 'Camp' – as the rest of the islands is known as – is home to settlements that began as company towns (hamlets where coastal shipping could collect wool) and now provide rustic backcountry lodging and a chance to experience pristine nature and wildlife.

Planning

The best time to visit is from October to March, when migratory birds (including penguins) and marine mammals return to the beaches and headlands. The first cruise ships to South Georgia and Antarctica turn up in early November and the last ones depart around the end of March. Fun events to plan a trip around include the annual sports meetings featuring horse racing, bull riding and sheepdog trials, which take place in Stanley between Christmas and New Year's, and on East and West Falkland at the end of the shearing season, usually in late February. Summer never gets truly hot (maximum high is 24°C or 75°F), but high winds can chill the air. For details, pick up Lonely Planet's *Falklands & South Georgia Island* guide.

Information

Stanley's **Jetty Visitors Centre** (☎ 22281; jettycentre@horizon.co.fk), at the public jetty on Ross Rd, distributes excellent brochures about things to do in and around Stanley. The *Visitor Accommodation Guide* lists lodgings and places that allow camping around the Islands. Another helpful source of information is **Falkland Islands Tourism** (☎ 22215; www.tourism.org.fk). In the UK, contact **Falkland House** (☎ 020-7222-2542; www.falklandislands.com; 14 Broadway, Westminster, London SW1H 0BH).

Visas & Documents

Visitors from Britain and Commonwealth countries, the EU, North America, Mercosur countries and Chile don't need visas. If coming from another country, check with the British Consulate. All nationalities must carry a valid passport, an onward ticket, proof of sufficient funds (credit cards are fine) and pre-arranged accommodations. In practice, arrivals who don't have pre-booked accommodations are held in the arrivals area while rooms are found.

Money

There's no ATM on the Falklands and only one bank in Stanley, so bring plenty of cash. Pound sterling and US dollars in cash or traveler's checks are readily accepted, but the exchange rate for US currency is low. There's no need to change money to FK£, which are not accepted off the islands. In peak season, expect to spend US$70 to US$100 per day, not including airfare, within the islands, less if camping or staying in self-catering cottages.

Getting There & Away

From South America, **LanChile** (www.lan.com) flies to Mt Pleasant International Airport (MPA; near Stanley) every Saturday from Santiago, Chile, via Puerto Montt, Punta Arenas and – one Saturday each month – Río Gallegos, Argentina. Roundtrip fares are US$760 from Santiago, US$580 from Punta Arenas. Book a week in advance to save US$40 to US$80.

From RAF Brize Norton (www.raf.mod.uk/rafbrizenorton), in Oxfordshire, England, there are regular Royal Airforce flights to Mt Pleasant (18 hours, including a two-hour refueling stop on tiny Ascension Island in the South Atlantic). One-way fares are 30-day apex/standard UK£790/1280. Travelers continuing on to Chile can purchase one-way tickets for half the fare. Contact the Travel Coordinator at Falkland House in London, or in Stanley, the **Falkland Islands Company** (FIC; ☎ 27600; www.the-falkland-islands-co.com), on Crozier Place.

Getting Around

From Stanley, **Figas** (☎ 27219; figas.fig@horizon.co.fk) serves outlying destinations in eight-seater aircraft. Travel within the Falklands costs around FK£1 per minute.

Island Shipping (☎ 22345/6; www.shipping.horizon.co.fk) carries a few passengers on its freighter MV *Tamar* while delivering wool and supplies to outlying settlements. Berths are limited; day trips cost FK£20, overnights cost FK£25 per day, including meals.

Several Stanley operators run day trips to East Falkland settlements, including **Discovery Tours** (☎ 21027; www.discoveryfalklands.com), **Ten Acre Tours** (☎ 21155; www.tenacrestours.horizon .co.fk) and **South Atlantic Marine Services** (☎ 21145; www.falklands-underwater.com).

Falkland Frontiers/Hebe Tours (☎ 21561; www.tourism.org.fk/pages/hebe-tours.htm) conducts fishing and wildlife tours. **Seaview** (☎ 22669; www.tourism.org.fk/pages/seaview.htm) arranges visits to Kidney Island, with its colonies of sea lions and rockhopper penguins.

Trekking and camping are feasible; however, there are no designated trails and getting lost is not unheard of. Always seek permission before entering private land.

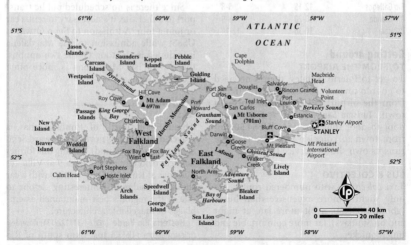

Av Colón. Buy tickets at least a couple of hours (if not a day or two during summer) in advance. The **Central de Pasajeros** (☎ 245811; cnr Magallanes & Av Colón) is the closest thing to a central booking office.

For Ushuaia, Ghisoni continues direct, but travelers report Pacheco stops too long in Río Grande – minivans to Ushuaia leave throughout the day and may cost slightly less (depending on exchange rates) than a through ticket.

Companies and daily destinations include the following:

Buses Fernández/Pingüino (☎ 221429/812; www .busesfernandez.com; Armando Sanhueza 745) Puerto Natales, Torres del Paine, Río Gallegos.

Buses Ghisoni/Queilen (☎ 222714; Lautaro Navarro 975) Río Gallegos, Río Grande, Ushuaia, Coyhaique, Puerto Montt.

Buses Pacheco (☎ 225527; www.busespacheco.com; Av Colón 900) Puerto Natales, Puerto Montt, Río Grande, Río Gallegos, Ushuaia.

Bus Sur (☎ 227145; www.bus-sur.cl; José Menéndez 565) El Calafate, Puerto Natales, Río Gallegos, Río Turbio, Ushuaia, Coyhaique, Puerto Montt.

Tecni-Austral (☎ 222078; Lautaro Navarro 975) Río Grande.

Turíbus (☎ 227970; www.busescruzdelsur.cl in Spanish; Armando Sanhueza 745) Puerto Montt, Osorno, Chiloé.

Destination	Cost ($US)	Duration (hr)
Coyhaique	45-50	20-22
Puerto Montt	50-59	30-36
Puerto Natales	5-7	3-4
Río Gallegos	12-15	5-8
Río Grande	18-20	8-9
Ushuaia	30-36	12-14

Getting Around

TO/FROM THE AIRPORT

To get to Puerto Natales, there's no need to go into town since buses depart directly from the airport (PUQ), 21km north of town. **Turismo Sandy Point** (☎ 222241) runs door-to-door shuttle service (US$4.50) to/ from town to coincide with flights. DAP runs its own shuttle service (US$2).

BUS & COLECTIVO

Taxi *colectivos,* with numbered routes, are only slightly more expensive than buses (about US$0.50, a bit more late at night and on Sundays), far more comfortable and much quicker.

CAR

Renting cars in Chile to cross the border into Argentina is prohibitively expensive due to international insurance requirements. If heading for El Calafate, it's cheaper to rent in Argentina. Cars are, however, cheap and easy to buy further north and are a good option for exploring Torres del Paine.

Punta Arenas has Chilean Patagonia's most economical rates, and locally owned agencies tend to provide better service. Recommended **Adel Rent a Car/Localiza** (☎ 235 471/2, 09-882-7569; www.adelrentacar.cl; Pedro Montt 962) provides attentive service, competitive rates, airport pickup and good travel tips. Other choices include **Budget** (☎ 225983; O'Higgins 964), **Hertz** (☎ 248742; O'Higgins 987) and **Lubag** (☎ 242023; Magallanes 970).

AROUND PUNTA ARENAS
Penguin Colonies

There are two substantial Magellanic penguin colonies near Punta Arenas: easier to reach is **Seno Otway** (Otway Sound) with about 6000 breeding pairs, about an hour northwest of the city, while the larger (50,000 breeding pairs) and more interesting **Monumento Natural Los Pingüinos** is accessible only by boat to Isla Magdalena in the Strait of Magellan (p420). Neither are as impressive as the larger penguin colonies in Argentina or the Falkland Islands. Tours to Seno Otway usually leave in the afternoon; however, visiting in the morning is best for photography because the birds are mostly backlit in the afternoon.

Since there is no scheduled public transport to either site, it's necessary to rent a car or join a tour. Admission to Seno Otway is US$5, while admission to Isla Magdalena is included in the tour. Of the two options, the trip to Isla Magdalena is more often recommended.

Río Verde
☎ 61

About 50km north of Punta Arenas, a graveled lateral leads northwest toward Seno Skyring (Skyring Sound), passing this former *estancia* before rejoining Ruta 9 at Villa Tehuelches at Km 100. Only visitors with a car should consider this interesting detour to one of the region's best-maintained assemblages of Magellanic architecture.

Hostería Río Verde (☎ 61-311122/131; rioverde@ chileaustral.com; r US$30) Just 6km south of Río

Verde proper and 90km from Punta Arenas, this hotel is best known for its meat-lovers Sunday lunches (US$12), with large portions of lamb, pork or seafood. An enormous fireplace and views over Isla Riesgo make it a welcoming place, and the rooms are comfortable.

Río Rubens

Roughly midway between Villa Tehuelches and Puerto Natales on blustery, paved Ruta 9, Río Rubens is a fine trout-fishing area and, for travelers with their own transport, an ideal spot to break the 250km journey from Punta Arenas. The hearty meals and pleasant free riverside camping make it popular with cyclists.

Hotel Río Rubens (☎ 09-640-1583; www.hotelrio rubens.cl in Spanish; Km 183; s/d/cabins US$20/30/75; **P**) This is a comfy, welcoming old country-style inn and, at these rates, it's a bargain. The restaurant serves outstanding meals, including lamb and seafood.

Estancia San Gregorio

☎ 61

Some 125km northeast of Punta Arenas, straddling Ruta 255 to Río Gallegos, this once enormous (36,000 hectares) *estancia* is now more a ghost town of faded yellow corrugated iron, but it is maintained by a few people and the large shearing shed is still used. The skeletal remains of beached ships are a memory of the days when a narrow-gauge railroad delivered goods to Punta Arenas.

Hotel El Tehuelche (☎ 227532, 198-3006; sergios cabini@hotmail.com; Ruta 255, Km 104; s/d US$29/49; **P**) About 30km northeast of San Gregorio, at the junction for the Punta Delgada ferry to Chilean Tierra del Fuego, this *hostería* was the *casco* for the British-owned Estancia Kimiri Aike until 1968. High ceilings, fading floral wallpaper, warm yellow bathrooms with clawfoot tubs and antique furnishings, plus gas fireplaces in some of the rooms, make this a comfortable and entertaining stopover. Downstairs, the restaurant serves sandwiches and meals either in the main room or, when sunny, in the large sunroom.

Parque Nacional Pali Aike

Along the Argentine border, west of the Monte Aymond border crossing to Río Gal-

legos, this 5030-hectare park is an area of volcanic steppe where, in the 1930s, Junius Bird's excavations at 17m-deep **Pali Aike Cave** yielded the first Paleo-Indian artifacts associated with extinct New World fauna such as the milodón and the native horse *Onohippidium*.

The **park** (admission US$2) has several hiking trails, including a 1700m path through the rugged lava beds of the **Escorial del Diablo** to the impressive **Crater Morada del Diablo**; wear sturdy shoes or your feet could be shredded. There's also a 9km trail from Cueva Pali Aike to **Laguna Ana**, where there's another shorter trail to a site on the main road, 5km from the park entrance.

Parque Nacional Pali Aike is 200km northeast of Punta Arenas via Ch 9, Ch 255 and a graveled secondary road from Coooperativa Villa O'Higgins, 11km north of Estancia Kimiri Aike. There's also an access road from the Chilean border post at Monte Aymond. There is no public transport, but Punta Arenas travel agencies offer full-day tours from US$65 for up to four people.

PUERTO NATALES

☎ 61 / pop 21,000

On the shores of Seno Última Esperanza (Last Hope Sound), 250km northwest of Punta Arenas via Ruta 9, Puerto Natales is the southern terminus of the spectacular ferry trip through the northern Chilean fjords. When the Navimag ferry arrives, disgorging sea-weary backpackers, the town comes alive. Once dependent on sheep and fishing, it's now base camp for trekkers heading to Parque Nacional Torres del Paine (p432) and has frequent transport to El Calafate, Argentina (p412).

Information

BOOKSTORES
World's End (☎ 414725; Blanco Encalada 226-A) Tip-of-the-world souvenirs, books and Torres trekking maps.

LAUNDRY
Servilaundry (☎ 412869; Bulnes 513) Most hostels also offer service.

MEDICAL SERVICES
Hospital (☎ 411533; cnr O'Higgins & Pinto)
Redfarma (Arturo Prat 158) Buy motion sickness pills (Bonamina or Mareamin) here before Navimag trips. They are also sold on board.

MONEY

Most banks in town have ATMs. Agents along Blanco Encalada change traveler's checks.

Stop Cambios (Baquedano 386) Changes cash and traveler's checks.

POST

Post office (Eberhard 429)

TELEPHONE & INTERNET ACCESS

Internet is widespread but slow throughout town.

Telefónica/CTC (Blanco Encalada 298)

TOURIST INFORMATION

The best bilingual portal for the region is www.torresdelpaine.cl.

Municipal Tourist Office (☎ 411263; Bulnes 285; ⏰ 8:30am-12:30pm & 2:30-6pm Tue-Sun) In the Museo Histórico, with attentive staff and region-wide lodgings listings.

Sernatur (☎ 412125; infonatales@sernatur.cl; Costanera P Montt 19; ⏰ 9am-7pm) Not as helpful as the municipal tourist office.

TRAVEL AGENCIES

Most travel agencies ply similar services: park tours, maps and equipment rental. The following have some bilingual staff:

Antares Patagonia (☎ 414611; www.antarespatagonia.com; Barros Arana 111) Specializes in trekking in El Calafate, El Chaltén and Torres del Paine. Can help facilitate climbing permits.

Baqueano Zamora (☎ 413953; www.baqueanozamora.com in Spanish; Baquedano 534)

Big Foot (☎ 414276/611; www.bigfootpatagonia.com; Bories 206) Popular glacier hikes, climbing, kayaking and mountaineering trips, plus ice- and rock-climbing seminars.

Fortaleza Expediciones (☎ 410595; www.fortalezapatagonia.cl; Arturo Prat 234) Knowledgeable; rents camping gear.

THE AUTHOR'S CHOICE

Hostal Dos Lagunas (☎ 415733; doslagunas@hotmail.com; Baros Arana 104; per person US$14) Managed by the very kind, gentle and attentive Alejandro, Andrea and family, this intimate home away from home has large, warm rooms, good showers and laundry service, filling breakfasts and loads of spot-on, multilingual travel tips. Reserve ahead.

Knudsen Tour (☎ 414747; knudsentour@yahoo.com; Blanco Encalada 284) Well regarded, with trips to Calafate, Torres del Paine and alternative routes along Seno Último Esperanza.

Path@gone/Andescape/Onas (☎ 413290/1; www.pathagone.com; Eberhard 595) The central point for reserving *refugios*, campsites and transport to Torres del Paine. Also runs a decent hostel.

Turismo Comapa (☎ 414300; www.comapa.com; Bulnes 533) Navimag ferry and airline bookings.

Sleeping

Prices at nonbudget establishments don't reflect the additional 19% IVA, which foreigners are not required to pay if paying with US dollars or credit cards. In the off-season, many places drop prices by as much as 40%. Reserve ahead if you are arriving on the ferry.

BUDGET

For a small town, Puerto Natales is chock full of places to stay, keeping prices reasonable. Most places rent equipment and can help arrange transport, and most rates include a basic breakfast.

Erratic Rock Hostel (☎ 411472; www.erraticrock.com; Baquedano 719; dm/s/d US$10/14/28; 🖳) A full-on, clean and cozy trekkers' and climbers' hostel, with good breakfast. Internet is free, staff are multilingual. They'll stow your pack and rent you serious climbing gear.

Patagonia Aventura (☎ 411028; Tomás Rogers 179; dm US$7) Run by some mellow guys and featuring hip decor, Patagonia Adventure has a great kitchen, home-baked bread, trip advice and rental trekking gear.

Niko's Residencial (☎ 412810; residencialnikos@hotmail.com; Ramírez 669; r with shared/private bathroom US$7/11) Readers recommend personally attended Niko's for the quiet rooms, separate travelers kitchen and family-style dinner (US$5). Bring your own towel and toilet paper and you'll be sittin' pretty. They organize winter trips to Torres del Paine.

Also recommended:

Backpacker's Magallania (☎ 414950; Tomás Rogers 255; dm US$5) Bring a sleeping bag. Dorms fill up fast at this friendly, whimsically decorated place. Kitchen privileges, but no breakfast.

Residencial Bernardita (☎ 411162; O'Higgins 765; dm US$10) Quiet rooms, breakfast and kitchen use. Rooms in the back annex are more private than those in the main house.

Los Inmigrantes (☎ 413482; Pinto 480; dm US$7) A good choice for serious hikers who need rental gear

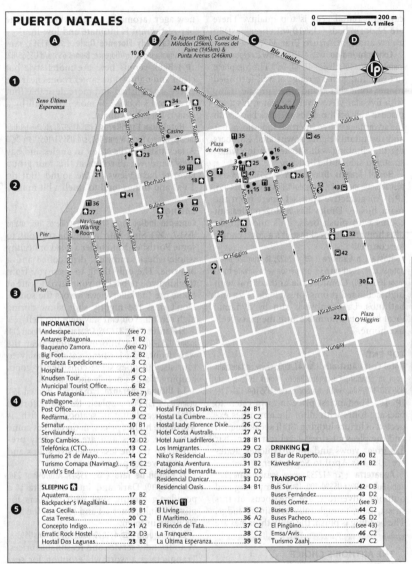

PUERTO NATALES

To Airport (8km), Cueva del
Milodón (25km), Torres del
Paine (145km) &
Punta Arenas (246km)

Seno Última
Esperanza

Río Natales

Stadium

Plaza
de Armas

Casino

Plaza
O'Higgins

PATAGONIA

and want the inside scoop. Shared kitchen, but no breakfast.

Residencial Danicar (☎ 412170; O'Higgins 707; dm US$6.50; ✗) Family-run and strictly nonsmoking with good dorm beds.

Casa Teresa (☎ 410472; Esmeralda 483; dm US$7) Basic dorm beds, good breakfast and kind owners, but no kitchen access.

MIDRANGE
Casa Cecilia (☎ 411797; redcecilia@entelchile.net; Tomás Rogers 60; s/d US$30/35, without bathroom US$12/22; ✗) Impeccably clean and with hearty home-made bread for morning toast, Cecilia is well loved. The kitchen is small and rooms are crowded, but showers are good, the multilingual owners are helpful and the

camping rental gear is top quality. There are 22 dorm beds (US$10 with breakfast) in a new annex at Arturo Prat 367.

Concepto Indigo (☎ 413609; www.conceptoindigo.com; Ladrilleros 105; r US$23-47; 🖳 ✖) The hip place in town, Indigo has a range of well-furnished rooms, some shared and others private, many with five-star views over the water. It's a fab place to kick off the shoes and kick back, with the advantage of free Internet, slideshows, bar and restaurant (right) downstairs. Climbers dig the climbing wall situated on the wind-sheltered side of the building.

Hostal Francis Drake (☎ 411553; www.chileaustral.com/francisdrake; Bernardo Phillipi 383; s/d US$44/55; P) An attractive spot set apart from the main bustle, Drake has a dozen pleasant rooms with plush beds, TVs and phones, plus homemade breakfast; it's a good choice for couples.

Hostal La Cumbre (☎ 412422; la_cumbrechile@hotmail.com; Eberhard 533; per person with private bathroom US$17-20) Comfortable and central with high-ceilinged rooms, plush beds, TVs and bathtubs, La Cumbre is run by dynamic local women who make sure the place feels like home.

TOP END

Hotel Costa Australis (☎ 412000; www.costaustralis.com in Spanish; Costanero Pedro Montt 262; s/d/ste US$130/147/306, with harbor view US$164/181/318; P 🖳) The fanciest place in town caters to package tours with all of the amenities expected of luxury lodging. Staff speak English and the pleasant street-level restaurant-bar has great views and plush couches. Rates are 50% less April to September.

Aquaterra (☎ 412239; www.aquaterrapatagonia.com; Bulnes 299; r US$80-100; P) Pampering and outdoor adventure are the focus at this smart, new, thoughtfully appointed lodge. The bedding is plush, the body therapies are

---

THE AUTHOR'S CHOICE

El Living (Arturo Prat 156; snacks US$2-5) Cosmo lounge living, straight out of London. Proper tea, filter coffee, fresh-squeezed juices, shakes and cakes, gringo veg food, comfy chairs, multilingual mags and baked bean sandwiches. What better way to treat yourself after a wind-blown trek? If they had a bathtub, we'd move in.

---

new agey (aromatherapy, reiki etc) and the bar-restaurant is intimate and low-lit.

Hostal Lady Florence Dixie (☎ 411158; www.chileanpatagonia.com/florence; Bulnes 655; s/d US$66/82; P) Back rooms here are motel-style but clean and light, while larger rooms near the street are polished and more desirable (but cost US$15 to US$20 more). It's run by a smart, friendly woman.

Hotel Juan Ladrilleros (☎ 415978; afv@entelchile.net; Costanero Pedro Montt 161; s/d US$93/105; P ✖) A lackluster 1970s study in angles and bay view windows, all rooms at this tour group favorite have views of the sound (but no TVs) and things tend to smell a bit musty.

Eating

Concepto Indigo (☎ 413609; Ladrilleros 105; mains US$3-7; ✖) Sink into a couch, trip out to some Portishead and order a salad or healthy whole-wheat sandwich, drip coffee and a brownie. The only thing to keep you from thinking you're back in your favorite café at home are the killer views across the sound. Don't miss the nightly slide show during high season. You can stay here too (left).

El Marítimo (☎ 414995; Costanero Pedro Montt 214; mains US$5-10) An informal eatery near the waterfront, El Marítimo caters heavily to tourists, but does serve consistently good, heaping platters of fish and seafood.

La Última Esperanza (☎ 411391; Eberhard 354; mains US$5-15) For a splash, this more formal affair, specializing in seafood and fish, is worth the higher prices; main entrees come with side dishes and are exquisitely prepared. Or try the less expensive soups and a few powerful pisco sours.

El Rincón de Tata (☎ 413845; Arturo Prat 236; mains US$4-10) Dark and intimate, Tata is a popular gathering spot with travelers for mixed drinks, Internet and some of the better pizza in town.

La Tranquera (☎ 411039; Bulnes 579; mains US$3-8) With friendly service and reasonable prices, Tranquera is a worthwhile option for seasonal meat like rabbit, as well as soup, draft beer and fish plates.

Drinking

El Bar de Ruperto (☎ 410863; cnr Bulnes & Magallanes) Ruperto has chess, dominoes, board games, live DJs and Internet access, all of which get mighty interesting after a few oversized drinks.

Kaweshkar (Eberhard 161) They boast that they aren't in Lonely Planet – we hope this review won't shatter their street cred. The music is trendy, the DJs are live, the munchies are creative and the lounge scene is chill, yo.

Getting There & Away

AIR
Aerovías DAP (www.dap.cl) flies a seven-seater to El Calafate, Argentina (US$50, one hour) at 9am weekdays from the small airfield (PNT), a few kilometers north of town on the road to Torres del Paine. The closest LanChile office is in Punta Arenas (p423).

BOAT
A highlight of many people's Patagonian sojourn is the four-day, three-night northbound voyage through Chile's spectacular fjords aboard Navimag's MV *Magallanes* car and passenger ferry.

To confirm when the ferries are due, contact **Turismo Comapa** (p428) a couple of days before the estimated arrival date. The *Magallanes* leaves Natales early Friday and stops in Puerto Edén (or the advancing Glaciar Pía XI on southbound sailings) en route to Puerto Montt. Boats usually arrive in the morning of the same day and depart either later that day or on the following day, but schedules vary according to weather conditions and tides. Disembarking passengers must stay on board while cargo is transported; those embarking have to spend the night on board.

High season is November to March, midseason is October and April; and low season is May to September. Most folks end up in dorm-style, 22-bed berths but often wish they had sprung for a private cabin. Fares, which vary according to view, cabin size and private or shared bathroom, include all meals (including veg options if requested while booking, but bring water, snacks and drinks anyway) and interpretive talks.

Per-person fares range from US$200 for a bunk berth in low season to US$290 for a quadruple A cabin in midseason to US$1690 for a single AAA cabin in high season; students/seniors receive a 10% to 15% discount. Check online (www.navimag.com) for current schedules and rates.

BUS
Puerto Natales has no central bus terminal, though several companies stop at the junc-

tion of Valdivia and Baquedano. Book at least a day ahead, especially for early morning departures, in high season. Services are greatly reduced in the off-season.

To Torres del Paine, most companies shuttle back and forth two to three times daily; Buses Gomez and JB are your best bets, leaving between 7am and 8am and around 2:30pm. If you miss the morning buses, you'll have to pay again for the afternoon one. Note that if you're heading to Pehoé in the off-season, you need to take the morning bus to meet the catamaran (US$12.50 one way, US$20 roundtrip; two hours). Returns from the Administración leave at 1:30pm and 6:15pm. These schedules are in constant flux, so double-check them before heading out.

For El Calafate, note that taking the very long day tour to the Moreno Glacier and staying in El Calafate after the tour is slightly cheaper than going by regular bus, spending the night and then paying for the price of a tour the next day.

Companies and destinations include the following:

Bus Sur (☎ 411325; www.bus-sur.cl in Spanish; Baquedano 558) Punta Arenas, Torres del Paine, Coyhaique, Puerto Montt, El Calafate, Río Gallegos, Río Turbio, Ushuaia.

Buses Fernández/Pingüino (☎ 411111; www.buses fernandez.com; Ramírez 399) Torres del Paine, Punta Arenas, Río Gallegos.

Buses Gomez (☎ 411971; www.busesgomez.com in Spanish; Arturo Prat 234) Torres del Paine.

Buses JB (☎ 412824; Arturo Prat 258) Torres del Paine.

Buses Pacheco (☎ 414513; www.busespacheco.com; Baquedano 244) Punta Arenas.

Turismo Zaahj (☎ 412260/355; www.turismozaahj .co.cl in Spanish; Arturo Prat 236/70) Torres del Paine, El Calafate.

Destination	Cost (US$)	Duration (hr)
El Calafate	20–30	5–7
Punta Arenas	5–7	3–4
Río Gallegos	12	4–7
Torres del Paine	5–6	3–4
Ushuaia	42	12–14

Getting Around
Car rental is expensive and availability is limited; you'll get better rates in Punta Arenas or Argentina.

Try **Emsa/Avis** (☎ 241182; Bulnes 632). **World's End** (Blanco Encalada 226-A) rents bikes.

PATAGONIA

CUEVA DEL MILODÓN

Just 25km northwest of Puerto Natales, Hermann Eberhard discovered the remains of an enormous ground sloth in the 1890s. Nearly 4m high, the herbivorous milodón ate the succulent leaves of small trees and branches, but became extinct in the late Pleistocene. The 30m-high cave contains a tacky plastic life-size replica of the animal. It's worth a stop, whether to appreciate the cave itself or take an easy walk up to a lookout point.

Admission is US$5/2.50 in high/low season; camping (no fires) and picnicking are possible. Torres del Paine buses pass the entrance, which is 8km from the cave proper. Infrequent tours from Puerto Natales cost around US$5; alternatively, you can hitch or share a taxi (which will cost about US$20 roundtrip with one-hour wait). Outside of high season, bus services are infrequent.

PARQUE NACIONAL BERNARDO O'HIGGINS

The southern reaches of Chile's largest national park are due west of Puerto Natales. The park abuts Parque Nacional Torres del Paine and extends north along the Argentine border as far as Parque Nacional Laguna San Rafael.

Turismo 21 de Mayo (☎ 411978; www.turismo 21demayo.cl in Spanish; Eberhard 560) runs full-day boat excursions to Glaciar Serrano in the otherwise inaccessible park. Leaving around 8:30am (coffee and cookies provided) the boat passes Glaciar Balmaceda, then goes to the jetty at Puerto Toro. A 20-minute walk along a footpath leads to the base of Glaciar Serrano where visitors can dawdle about for 1½ hours before heading back on the boat to return via the same route to Puerto Natales. En route, passengers will catch glimpses of numerous glaciers and waterfalls, cormorants and occasional Andean condors. Whether the trip justifies the cost of US$60 is debatable; if the weather is bad, the boat will turn around and a percentage of the cost will be refunded. Path@gone (p428) sells a similar tour on the boat *Galicia*.

Possibly a more interesting alternative, and great way to access Torres del Paine, is to take the boat to Glaciar Serrano and then hop on a Zodiac, which will take passengers to lunch at Estancia Balmaceda (US$15) and continue up Río Serrano, ar-

riving at the southern border of the park by 5pm to meet the last bus back to town. The same tour can be done leaving the park, but may require camping near Río Serrano to catch the Zodiac at 9am. The trip costs US$90 at Turismo 21 de Mayo or Onas (p428).

PARQUE NACIONAL TORRES DEL PAINE

Soaring almost vertically more than 2000m above the Patagonian steppe, the Torres del Paine (Towers of Paine) are spectacular granite pillars that dominate the landscape of what may be South America's finest **national park** (admission high/low season US$17/8.50).

Before its creation in 1959, the park was part of a large sheep *estancia*, and it's still recovering from nearly a century of overexploitation of its pastures, forests and wildlife. Part of Unesco's Biosphere Reserve system since 1978, it shelters flocks of ñandú (ostrichlike rhea), Andean condors, flamingos and many other species.

The park's outstanding conservation success has undoubtedly been the guanaco (*Lama guanicoe*), which grazes the open steppes where its main natural enemy, the puma, cannot approach undetected. After more than a decade of effective protection from poachers, the large and growing herds of guanacos barely flinch when humans or vehicles approach.

For hikers and trekkers, this 181,000-hectare park is an unequaled destination, with a well-developed trail network and *refugios* and campgrounds at strategic spots. The weather is changeable (some say you get four seasons in a day here), with the strong westerlies that typify Patagonia. There's no such thing as bad weather, just poor preparation. Good foul-weather gear is essential; a warm synthetic sleeping bag and wind-resistant tent are imperative for those undertaking the Paine circuit and recommended for those doing the extremely popular 'W,' named for the rough approximation to the letter that it traces out on the map.

Guided day trips from Puerto Natales are possible, but permit only a bus-window glimpse of what the park has to offer. Instead, plan to spend anywhere from three to seven days to enjoy the hiking and other activities.

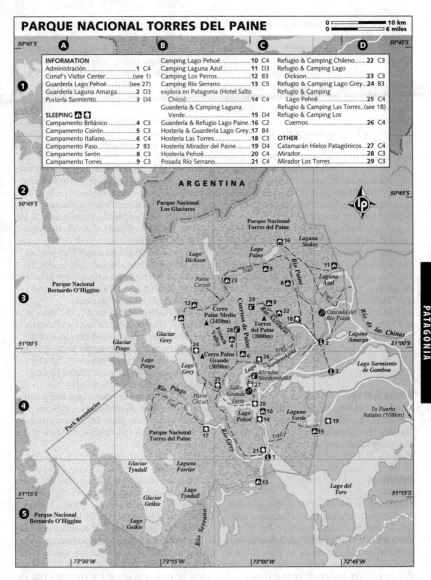

PARQUE NACIONAL TORRES DEL PAINE

0 — 10 km
0 — 6 miles

INFORMATION
Administración..............................1 C4
Conaf's Visitor Center................(see 1)
Guardería Lago Pehoé..............(see 27)
Guardería Laguna Amarga..........2 D3
Portería Sarmiento......................3 D4

SLEEPING
Campamento Británico..................4 C3
Campamento Coirón......................5 C3
Campamento Italiano....................6 C4
Campamento Paso.........................7 B3
Campamento Serón.......................8 C3
Campamento Torres......................9 C3

Camping Lago Pehoé....................10 C4
Camping Laguna Azul...................11 D3
Camping Los Perros.....................12 B3
Camping Río Serrano...................13 C5
explora en Patagonia (Hotel Salto
Chico).......................................14 C4
Guardería & Camping Laguna
Verde.......................................15 D4
Guardería & Refugio Lago Paine..16 C2
Hostería & Guardería Lago Grey..17 B4
Hostería Las Torres.....................18 C3
Hostería Mirador del Paine.........19 D4
Hostería Pehoé............................20 C4
Posada Río Serrano.....................21 C4

Refugio & Camping Chileno.......22 C3
Refugio & Camping Lago
Dickson....................................23 C3
Refugio & Camping Lago Grey..24 B3
Refugio & Camping
Lago Pehoé..............................25 C4
Refugio & Camping Las Torres..(see 18)
Refugio & Camping Los
Cuernos...................................26 C4

OTHER
Catamarán Hielos Patagónicos...27 C4
Mirador......................................28 C4
Mirador Los Torres.....................29 C3

PATAGONIA

Orientation & Information

The park is 112km north of Puerto Natales via a good but sometimes bumpy gravel road that passes Villa Cerro Castillo, where there's a seasonal border crossing to Argentina at Cancha Carrera. The road continues 38km north, where there's a junction to the park's little-visited southern Laguna Verde sector.

Three kilometers north of this junction the highway forks west along the north shore of Lago Sarmiento to the **Portería Sarmiento**, the park's main entrance where entrance fees are collected. It's another 37km to the **Administración** (park headquarters), where the **Conaf visitor center** features a good exhibit on local ecology, plus videos that provide a good overview of the park's attractions.

A new road is being built from Puerto Natales to the Administración. It currently ends at the Río Serrano, but once the new bridge opens it will open up a shorter, more direct southern approach to the park; this alternative route is certain to alter transport options.

If you're visiting during the high season (especially January and February), plan your trip as far in advance as possible if you want to stay in a *refugio*. Campsites are usually available on short notice, but now that nearly 200,000 people visit annually, Conaf may regulate the flow of people into the most popular parts of the park.

Visiting during the winter season (from around May to mid-September) has the upsides of little wind and no crowds, but the downsides of unpredictable weather and heavy snowfall, reduced services and restriction to travel on low-level routes. The shoulder seasons of early December and March are some of the best times for trekking.

A wildfire started by an over-turned camping stove burned more than 15,500 hectares (7% of the entire park) in late February 2005.

Books & Maps

The best trekking maps, by JLM and Luis Bertea Rojas, are easily found in Puerto Natales. For detailed trekking and camping suggestions and maps, consult Lonely Planet's *Trekking in the Patagonian Andes*.

Activities

HIKING

To circuit or to 'W,' that is the question. And the answer lies in one's time and stamina. Doing the circuit (basically the 'W' plus the backside of the park) takes five to eight days, while the 'W' takes at least three to four. If you're not driving, figure another day or two for transport connections.

Most trekkers start both routes from Laguna Amarga, although it's also possible to hike from park headquarters or take the catamaran to Pehoé and start from there. The treks are not without difficulty and hikers have suffered serious injuries and even died. For this reason Conaf frowns upon solo trekkers, but how they can regulate is dubious (if alone, buddy-up with someone when registering). It is, however, always prudent to hike with others, if only to make sure that someone knows where you are or can help should the weather turn or the vicious winds toss you off the trail (it happens).

The 'W'

Most people trek the 'W' right to left (east to west), starting at Laguna Amarga, but going the other way provides better views of the Cuernos.

Refugio Las Torres to Mirador Las Torres Four hours one way, this relatively easy hike goes up Río Ascencio to a treeless tarn beneath the eastern face of the Torres del Paine proper. The last hour is a knee-popping scramble up boulders. There are camping and *refugios* at Las Torres and Chileno, with wild camping at Campamento Torres, for a stunning sunrise hike.

Refugio Las Torres to Los Cuernos Seven hours one way, hikers should keep to the lower trail (the upper trail, which is not marked on maps, is not recommended – many get lost). There's camping and a *refugio*. Winds are fierce along this section during the high season.

To Valle Frances Five hours one way from Cuernos or Pehoé, this hike is considered the most beautiful stretch – in good weather – between 3050m Paine Grande to the west and the lower but still spectacular Cuernos del Paine (Horns of Paine) to the east, with glaciers hugging the trail. There's camping at Italiano, and at Británico, for those energetic enough to lug everything that far.

Refugio Lago Pehoé to Refugio Lago Grey Four hours one way from Pehoé, this hike follows a relatively easy trail with a few bits of challenging downhill scampers. The glacier lookout is another half-hour. There are camping and *refugios* at both ends.

The Circuit

Doing the whole loop takes in the 'W,' as described above, plus the backside between Refugio Grey and Refugio Las Torres. There are no *refugios* along this stretch and camping is very basic. You'll need foul-weather camping and trekking gear, as mud (sometimes knee-deep), snow and wind are inevitable. While the popularity of the 'W' means you'll see lots of people along the way, that's not the case along the backside. Trekking alone is inadvisable (and restricted by Conaf). Make friends with others before heading out.

Refugio Lago Grey to Campamento Paso Four hours from Guardas to Paso, about two hours going the opposite way; hikers might want to go left to right (west to east), which means ascending the pass rather than slipping downhill.

Campamento Paso to Perros Approximately four hours, this route has plenty of mud and sometimes snow. What appears to be a campsite right after crossing the pass, isn't. Keep going until you see a shack.

Campamento Perros to Dickson Around 4½ hours, it's relatively easy but a windy stretch.

Campamento Dickson to Seron Six hours, as the trail wraps around Lago Paine, winds can get fierce and the trails vague; stay along the trail furthest away from lake. It's possible to break trek at Campamento Coiron.

Campamento Seron to Laguna Amarga Four to five hours, you can end the trek with a chill-out night and a decent meal at Refugio Las Torres, which comes much recommended.

Day Hikes

A four-hour hike leading to **Lago Paine**, whose northern shore is accessible only from Laguna Azul, offers considerable solitude and breathtaking scenery. There's a rustic Refugio Lago Paine at the lake en route.

For a shorter day hike, walk from Guardería Lago Pehoé, on the main park highway, to **Salto Grande**, a powerful waterfall between Lago Nordenskjöld and Lago Pehoé. Another easy hour's walk leads to **Mirador Nordenskjöld**, an overlook with superb views of the lake and cordillera.

GLACIER TREKKING & KAYAKING

Big Foot (p428) is the only outfitter authorized to lead day-long ice hikes on Glaciar Grey (US$75), which involve a long hike, rappelling on to the glacier, walking on the glacier with crampons and harnesses, chances to view ice caves, and ice climbing before heading back. Three-day kayaking trips along Río Serrano and visiting Glaciar Balmaceda cost US$500. A one-day kayak along the Fjord Eberhardt costs US$120.

HORSE RIDING

In the saddle is one of the best ways to experience the park. Due to property divisions, horses cannot cross from western sections (Lago Grey, Pehoé, Río Serrano) to the eastern part managed by Hostería Las Torres/Fantastico Sur and vice versa. (Basically, Refugio Los Cuernos is the cut-off.) **Baqueano Zamora** (p428) runs half-day excursions to Lago Pingo, Laguna Amarga, Lago Paine and Lago Azul for around US$55, including a country-style lunch. Hostería Las Torres (p436) controls the eastern area

and charges US$69 per full day, with snack included.

Sleeping & Eating

Book ahead. Arriving at the park without reservations, especially in the high season, means you may be stuck without a place to stay, either in the *refugios* or in the organized campsites – there's always space at the free campgrounds. Most travel agencies can call in reservations, but to be sure, deal directly with the main concessions – Path@gone/Andescape (p428) in Puerto Natales and Fantastico Sur (p420) in Punta Arenas. The latter manages Torres, Chileno and Los Cuernos and Seron *refugios* and campgrounds; the former manages Grey, Dickson and Los Perros.

Readers have reported that some *refugios* may require photo ID (ie a passport) upon check-in – ask about this while booking to avoid having to pay twice for a reservation. Once checked in, staff can radio ahead to confirm your next reservation. Patience is also of importance. Campsite and *refugio* staff do their best to deal with the intense flow of trekkers, but can't meet everyone's expectations. Given the rates, however, you would think that they could hire some extra hands.

CAMPING

Campgrounds at the *refugios* – Las Torres, Chileno, Cuernos, Pehoé and Grey – all charge around US$6 per campsite, including overtaxed hot showers. *Refugios* rent decent equipment: tent US$11 per night, sleeping bag US$6, mat/mattress US$3 and stove US$5; but in high season it's prudent to bring your own gear in case the *refugios* run out. They also have hot showers and small stores with expensive pastas, soup packets and butane gas. All other sites (opposite) are administered by Conaf; they are free and very basic (rain shelters and pit toilets). Rodents have become a problem at many campgrounds; hang food from trees to avoid packs and tents being chewed through. Campsites at Británico are used mainly by climbers, but provide welcome remoteness and spectacular views.

REFUGIOS

The eight *refugios* listed under the hiking descriptions have individual rooms with

PATAGONIA

four to eight bunk beds, kitchen privileges (during specific hours and for lodgers only), meals and hot showers. A bed costs US$17 to US$30 (full pension US$42 to US$50), sleeping bag rental US$6 and meals US$6 to US$12. Should the *refugio* be full, the staff should be able to provide all necessary camping equipment. Most *refugios* close by the end of April. Refugio Pehoé is the only one that stays open year-round. If still open to the public, Conaf-controlled Refugio Lago Toro, near the Administración, costs US$6 in one large dorm room, with kitchen and hot showers (US$1).

HOTELS & HOSTERÍAS

Hostería Las Torres (☎ 710050; www.lastorres.com; Magallanes 960, Punta Arenas; high/low season s US$131-179/79-98, d US$149-197/89-119; **P**) Constantly expanding, Las Torres is tucked away 7km west of Guardería Laguna Amarga. The wings of the hotel are all connected, separated by spacious living rooms, while the rooms are warm and attractively decorated. Buffet meals (dinner US$30) are elaborate, artistic affairs. The spa has a sauna, Jacuzzi and many revitalizing treatments. Reserve ahead to arrange a free transfer from Laguna Amarga.

Hostería Lago Grey (☎ 225986; www.austrohoteles.cl; Lautaro Navarro 1061, Punta Arenas; s/d/tr US$173/199/228; **P**) Although at the outlet of iceberg-dotted Lago Grey, the crowded rooms at this year-round retreat are cut off from the views by thick windbreaking trees, but the café (lunch or dinner US$25) overlooks the grandeur. Zodiac boat tours are available on the lake, but not on to the glacier.

Hostería Pehoé (☎ 244506, in Punta Arenas ☎ 248 888; www.pehoe.com; s/d US$160/175, superior with lake view US$195/215; **P**) On a small island in the lake of the same name, the inn is linked to the mainland by a long footbridge. It enjoys panoramic five-star views of the Cuernos del Paine and Cerro Paine Grande, but the dated rooms are merely standard. The restaurant and bar are open to the public, but service can be slow.

Hostería Mirador del Payne (☎ 226930; www.miradordelpayne.com; Fagnano 585, Punta Arenas; s/d/tr US$132/152/173; **P**) This comfortable inn at the working Estancia El Lazo in the park's seldom-seen southern Laguna Verde sector comes recommended by readers for serenity, spectacular views and fabulous service – but not for ease of park access. Activities include bird-watching, horse riding and sport fishing. Call to arrange a ride from the road junction.

Posada Río Serrano (☎ 412911, in Puerto Natales ☎ 413953; www.baqueanozamora.com; dm US$25, d with/without bathroom US$90/66; **P**) Restored but still rustic, this genteel and rambling 19th-century ranch house has 13 rooms, a restaurant (dinner US$15), bar and cozy living room focused on the fireplace. It's a popular base camp for horse riding and fishing trips to nearby lakes and rivers.

Getting There & Away

For details of transport to the park, see p431. Hitching from Puerto Natales is possible, but competition is heavy. Note that reaching El Calafate from the park in the same day requires joining a tour or careful advance planning, since there is no direct service and most buses aren't timed with making that connection in mind. You can

---

THE AUTHOR'S CHOICE

explora en Patagonia (in Santiago ☎ 02-206-6060; www.explora.com; per person double-occupancy 4 nights US$1560-2688; 8 nights US$2740-4778; **P** 🖥 🛳) Part of the innovative explora group's refined adventure travel concept, Hotel Salto Chico is the park's most sophisticated lodging option, perched above the eponymous waterfall at the outlet of Lago Pehoé. The rates also include airport transfers, full gourmet board paired with fine house wines, and a wide variety of exhilarating excursions led by the young, affable bilingual guides. The interiors of the graceful building effortlessly interweave landscape hues into the fabrics and intricately simple details. Behind the lodge (beware of the winds), a spa complete with heated lap pool, sauna, massage rooms and open-air Jacuzzi await. The real strength is the absolutely magnificent views across the turbid lake of the entire Paine massif from most of the property, the majority of the rooms…even some of the bathtubs.

try getting off in Cerro Castillo and waiting for a onward ride to Argentina, but the most reliable option is to first return to Puerto Natales.

Getting Around

Buses drop off and pick up passengers at Laguna Amarga, the Hielos Patagónicos catamaran launch at Pudeto and at park headquarters, coordinating with the catama-

ran schedule, which leaves Pudeto for Pehoé (one way/roundtrip US$17/30 per person) at 9:30am, noon and 6pm December to mid-March, noon and 6pm in late March and November and at noon only in September, October and April. Another launch plies Lago Grey between Hostería Lago Grey and Refugio Lago Grey (US$30 one way, 1½ to two hours), a couple of times a day; contact the *hostería* (opposite) for the schedule.

PATAGONIA

Tierra del Fuego

Ever since the 16th-century voyages of Magellan and the 19th-century explorations of FitzRoy and Darwin aboard the *Beagle*, and even to the present, this 'uttermost part of the earth' has fascinated intrepid travelers. From the barren plains of the north, to virgin lenga forests draped in 'old man's beard,' and glaciers descending nearly to the ocean, the archipelago never ceases to enthrall those who gravitate here to explore its mystery. The Yahgan Indians stoked the fires that inspired Europeans to give this region its name, now famous throughout the world.

The region comprises one large island, Isla Grande de Tierra del Fuego, and many smaller ones, most of them uninhabited. The Strait of Magellan separates the islands from the South American mainland. This chapter covers both Argentine and Chilean sections of the territory, including Chilean Isla Navarino.

If you are wondering what it feels like to be at the end of the world, look no further.

TOP FIVE

- Enjoying the utmost views from Glaciar Martial and visiting lakes and mountains near **Ushuaia** (p445)

- Trekking around the true end of the world on Isla Navarino outside **Puerto Williams** (p455)

- Lending a hand with the sheepshearing at working *estancias* (ranches) like **Estancia Viamonte** (p443), near Río Grande

- Stopping to fill up the *mate* thermos and purchase the best baked goods on the island in **Tolhuin** (p444), near Lago Fagnano

- Admiring the impressive bone collections at Museo Acatushún at **Estancia Harberton** (p455)

- AVERAGE JUL HIGH IN USHUAIA: 4°C (39°F)   - AVERAGE DEC HIGH IN USHUAIA: 13°C (56°F)

TIERRA DEL FUEGO

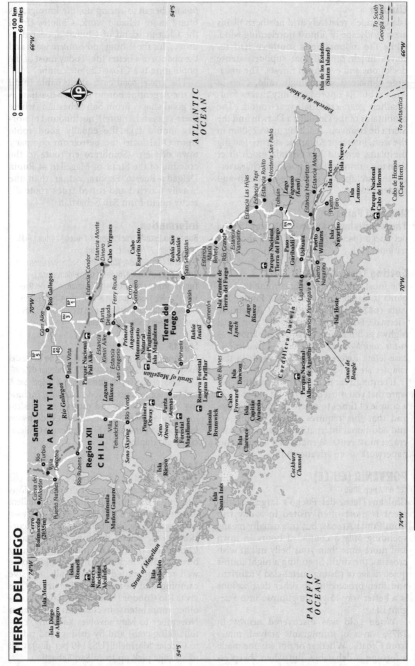

Climate

Isla Grande's relatively arid northern plains are a landscape of almost unrelenting wind, while the mountainous southern half receives much rainfall that supports dense deciduous and evergreen forests. The maritime climate is surprisingly mild, even in winter, but its unpredictability makes foul-weather gear essential year-round. The mountains of the Cordillera Darwin and the Sierra de Beauvoir, reaching up to 2500m in the west, intercept Antarctic storms, leaving the plains around Río Grande much drier than the storm-battered bogs that characterize the archipelago's remote southern and western zones.

National Parks

The island is home to Parque Nacional Tierra del Fuego (p454), Argentina's first shoreline national park.

Getting There & Around

The most common overland route to Patagonia is via the ferry crossing at Punta Delgada (p423). Unlike the rest of Argentina, Tierra del Fuego has no designated provincial highways, but has secondary roads known as *rutas complementarias,* modified by a lowercase letter. References to such roads in this chapter are 'RC-a,' for example.

If renting a car in mainland Argentina, beware that you must cross in and out of Chile a couple of times to reach Tierra del Fuego, and that this requires special documents and additional international insurance coverage; most rental agencies can arrange this paperwork given advance notice.

PORVENIR (CHILE)

☎ 61 / pop 5000

Chilean Tierra del Fuego's largest settlement is most often visited in a day trip from Punta Arenas, but this usually means spending only a couple of hours in town and more time than your belly might wish crossing the strait. Spending a night in this quiet village of rusting, metal-clad Victorians and then proceeding to other destinations is a better way to gain a glimpse into Fuegian life.

When gold was discovered nearby in 1879, waves of immigrants arrived, many from Croatia. Whether or not anyone made a fortune is debatable. But when sheep *es-*

tancias began to spring up, the immigrants found more reliable work. Chilotes (from the Chilean island of Chiloé) appeared in droves, for the fishing and *estancia* work and the chance of a better life. Today most of the population is a Croat-Chilote combo.

The gravel road east, along Bahía Inútil to the Argentine border at San Sebastián, is in good shape. From San Sebastián (where there's gas and a motel), northbound motorists should take the equally good route from Onaisín to the petroleum company town of Cerro Sombrero en route to the crossing of the Strait of Magellan at Punta Delgada–Puerto Espora, rather than the heavily traveled and rutted truck route directly north from San Sebastián.

Information

Banco de Estado (cnr Philippi & Croacia) 24-hour ATM.
CTC (Philippi 277) Next to the bank.
Hospital (☎ 580034; Wood, btwn Señoret & Guerrero)
Post office (Phillipi 176) Faces the verdant plaza.
Tourist office (☎ 580094/8; Zavattaro 402; ☼ 9am-5pm Mon-Fri, 11am-5pm Sat & Sun) Information is also available at the handicrafts shop on the *costanera* (seaside road) between Phillipi and Schythe.

Sights

On the plaza, the intriguing **Museo de Tierra del Fuego** (☎ 580094/8; Zavattaro 402; admission US$0.80; ☼ 9am-5pm Mon-Fri, 10:30am-1:30pm & 3-5pm Sat & Sun) has some unexpected materials, including Selk'nam skulls and mummies, musical instruments used by the mission Indians on Isla Dawson and an exhibit on early Chilean cinematography.

Tours

The tourist office can arrange tours of old gold-panning sites, horse-riding excursions and other ways to enjoy the area. **Cordillera Darwin Expediciones** (☎ 580747, 09-640-7204; www.cordilleradarwin.com; Señoret 512) organizes excursions to see Peale's dolphins around Bahía Chilote in a traditional Chilote-style fishing boat (US$85, including meals), plus some well-recommended longer, all-inclusive camping and horseback-riding trips. One visits Río Condor (US$130 per day) and another, more intense five-day adventure from November to May involves kayaking, centolla (king crab) and fly-fishing, and riding to Glaciar Marinelli (US$140 per day). Call to arrange pick up from San Sebastián.

Sleeping & Eating

Hotel España (☎ 580160; Croacia 698; s/d US$20/35, with shared bathroom US$9/11) Older rooms are darker and share bathrooms, while ample rooms in the new wing have goods beds, large windows, cropped harbor views and TV on request.

Hotel Rosas (☎ 580088; Philippi 296; s/d US$27/36) All the rooms are clean and have heat and cable TV, the owner Alberto knows heaps about the region, and the restaurant serves up some great seafood. Lunch, with drinks, costs about US$7.

Hostería Los Flamencos (☎ 580049; Merino s/n; s/d US$33/45; **P**) Overlooking the harbor, Flamencos is neglected but still the fanciest hotel in town. The manager, however, is charming and does what he can to make your stay more inviting.

Residencial Colón (☎ 581157; Riobó 198; per person with shared bathroom US$7; **P**) The rooms are basic and have treacherous heating facilities, but this place, a block east of the plaza, is the best low-budget option. A filling lunch costs US$3.50.

Hotel Central (☎ 580077; Philippi 298; s/d US$27/35) The rooms are small and cozy but not all have heat. Rates are discounted after the first night.

El Chispa (☎ 580054; Señoret 202; mains US$3-6; r per person US$10) In a century-old aquamarine firehouse, El Chispa's friendly family serves up good-value breakfasts and fresh seafood. There are several basic rooms with shared bathroom upstairs. It's a couple of blocks uphill from the water.

Club Croata (☎ 580053; Señoret 542; mains US$4-8) A more formal experience, this social club filled with sports trophies serves rich fish dishes accompanied by classical music. There's an inviting bar in back and the owner will happily fill you in on Croatian influence in the region.

Restaurant Puerto Montt (☎ 580207; Croacia 1169; mains US$3-6) When boats are in the harbor, this rough and tumble joint is where the fishing crews feast on huge portions. It's the perfect place to capture Porvenir's personality.

Getting There & Around

Aerovías DAP (☎ 580089; www.dap.cl; Señoret near Gamero) flies to Punta Arenas (US$23) twice daily except Sunday.

Transbordadora Broom (☎ 580089; www.tabsa.cl) operates the car-passenger ferry *Melinka* to Punta Arenas (US$7/45 per person/vehicle, 2½ to four hours) Tuesday through Saturday at 2pm, Sundays and holidays at 5pm.

The bus to the ferry terminal (US$1), 5km away, departs from the waterfront kiosk an hour before the ferry's departure. Taxis charge at least four times as much.

For the airport, 6km north of town, DAP runs a door-to-door shuttle (US$1.75) and taxis charge US$4.50.

RÍO GRANDE
☎ 02964 / pop 58,000

The longest that most travelers stay in windswept Río Grande is a few hours, before hopping a bus to Ushuaia, 230km southwest. That is, of course, unless they've come to fish. Exclusive fly-in lodges on *estancias* around Río Grande lure the likes of Hollywood heavy hitters and former US presidents with some of the world's best blue-ribbon angling for colossal sea-run trout. The only hint of this fame, however, is the monster trout sculpture at the entrance to town.

In 1886 the villainous gold seeker Julius Popper stumbled across the mouth of Río Grande, home to Selk'nam (or Ona). As wool baron José Menéndez's sheep stations developed (see p443), a makeshift service town grew. The Salesian order, under the guidance of Monseñor Fagnano, set up a mission in 1893 in an attempt to 'protect' the Selk'nam from the growing development.

Río Grande continued to grow as a petroleum service center, and its duty-free status, created in an attempt to spur on town development, has brought in electronics manufacturing plants and plenty of wholesale appliance stores. The military played an important role here in the Falkland/Malvinas War; many memorials around town pay tribute to the fallen soldiers.

Information

Most visitor services are along Avs San Martín and Belgrano.

Banco de la Nación (cnr San Martín & 9 de Julio) ATM; several others nearby.

Don Pepe (cnr 9 de Julio & Rosales; ☎ 24hr) Supermarket with a burger grill, *locutorio* (telephone office) and Internet access.

El Lavadero (Moreno 221) Laundry.

Farmacia Central (cnr San Martín & Piedrabuena; ☎ 24hr)

Instituto Fueguino de Turismo (Infuetur; ☎ 424326; www.tierradelfuego.org.ar; Espora 533; ⏱ 9am-9pm) South side of the plaza.

Mariani Travel (☎ 426010; Rosales 281) Books flights and represents nearby *estancias* (see opposite).

Municipal tourist kiosk (☎ 431324; rg-turismo@ netcombbs.com.ar; on plaza; ⏱ 9am-8pm) Helpful, with maps, *estancia* brochures and fishing details.

Post office (Rivadavia, btwn Moyano & Alberdi)

Thaler Cambio (☎ 421154; Rosales 259) Changes traveler's checks.

Sights

In a restored *galpón* (sheepshearing shed), the **Museo de la Ciudad** (☎ 430414; Alberdi 555; admission free; ⏱ 9am-5pm Mon-Fri, 3-7pm Sat) has impressive exhibits, from logging to military displays, postal communications to cartography, indigenous artifacts to yet another milodón.

Ten kilometers north of town on RN 3, the 1893 Misión Salesiano houses a **Museo Histórico y Natural Monseñor Fagnano** (☎ 421642; adult/child US$0.65/0.35; ⏱ 9:30am-noon & 3-7pm Tue-Sun), containing geological and natural-history exhibits and a wealth of ethnographic artifacts. When the mission's work of protecting the Selk'nam dissolved (basically, there were no more living), the mission was converted into an agrotechnical school, now considered the region's best. Fresh Salesian cheeses and produce may be purchased in the tearoom and there's often al fresco *parrilla* on Sunday afternoon. Horseback rides may be available and students (female students were not admitted until 1997) conduct informal tours of the greenhouses and dairy farms. Take *colectivo* (local bus) Línea B, which runs downtown every hour from San Martín.

Sleeping

Since most travelers overnighting are here either to fish or do business, lodging tends to be overpriced, not to mention sparse. A number of places do cater to the budget-conscious, but most are not recommendable; those that are fill up fast. High-end places discount 10% for cash payments.

Hotel Argentino (☎ 422546; hotelargentino@yahoo .com; San Martín 64; dm US$7.35, s/d US$10/17) The real draw here is the friendly ambience – a mix of locals and travelers kicking back in chummy common areas. The basic dorm rooms are off the main house, with hot showers, a shared kitchen, breakfast and luggage storage on offer.

Hotel Villa (☎ 424998; San Martín 281; s/d/ste US$33/38/66; P 🖴) Opposite Casino Status, this newly refurbished place has a popular restaurant and a dozen polished, spacious rooms outfitted with down duvets and all the mod cons.

Hotel Federico Ibarra (☎ 430071, 430883; www .federicoibarrahotel.com.ar in Spanish; Rosales 357; s/d/ste US$33/40/66; 🖴) Well-maintained rooms with views of the plaza are pleasant, but can be noisy at this business-friendly favorite. Rooms without the view are equally large, well appointed and much quieter. If anything, the central heating is too strong.

Apart Hotel Keyuk'n (☎ 424435; aparthotelkeyukn@ speedy.com.ar; Colón 630; s/d/q US$30/34/47; P) Spacious, fully equipped apartments make this one of the best deals for groups or families. Each two-floor unit has a kitchen, large bathroom, living and dining room, cable TV, plus comfortable beds with lots of extra bedding.

Hotel Isla del Mar (☎ 422883; isladelmar@arnet .com.ar; Güemes 963; s/d US$24/27; P 🖴) Facing the bay, the bright-pink Isla del Mar has some decent rooms – ask for one upstairs – with large bathrooms and worn-out furniture. The staff are quite helpful.

Posada de los Sauces (☎ 432895; www.posadade lossauces.com.ar; Elcano 839; s/d standard US$42/52, deluxe US$54/67, ste US$100; P 🖴) Catering mostly to high-end anglers, Los Sauces has the sturdy, woodsy feel of an upmarket fishing lodge. Deluxe rooms come with Jacuzzi bath. The upstairs bar-restaurant, outfitted in dark wood and forest green, is just waiting for cigar smoke and tall tales to fill the air; good seafood and sensibly priced drinks speed the exaggeration along.

Eating

La Rueda (☎ 433982; Islas Malvinas 998; mains US$2-7) On the north edge of town off RN 3 (US$1 taxi), 'the Wheel' is an outstanding mix of excellent food and precise service. Home-made pasta dishes, big enough to feed two, are served bubbling hot in platters that can be reheated (try the *sorrentinos* (large ravi-olis). *Parrilla* and fish mains are equally fill-ing and include a self-serve salad bar full of fresh fixings. Wines are equally good value. There's a new 'express' branch in the center at Moreno and 9 de Julio.

La Nueva Piamontesa (☎ 424366; Belgrano 601; mains US$2-6; ⏱ 24hr) Country store gone wild, this fantastic, well-stocked deli has *parrilla*, pizza, pasta and sandwiches for take-out, delivery or in-store dining.

Epa!!! (☎ 425334; Rosales 445; mains US$1-6) The hippest spot in town is part curvaceous bar, part *Jetson*-esque café, with deep pleather booths, a popular set lunch, hot and cold sandwiches and a laundry list of cocktails

La Nueva Colonial (☎ 425353; cnr Lasserre & Belgrano; mains US$4-9) Effusive owner-chef Cesar, who has no qualms about sitting down with guests in his sauce-spattered apron while still in a sweat, cooks up much-praised pasta and fish dishes in a cozy log cabin. Some find the gruff gregariousness a fun distraction; others consider it an imposition.

Ibarra Hotel (☎ 430071; Rosales 357; mains US$1-4) Facing the plaza, this popular hotel *confitería* (café) is a pleasant, sunny spot to enjoy coffee or a light meal.

Café Sonora (☎ 423102; Moreno 705; mains US$3-8) Beneath Woodstock and The Doors posters, the order here is bready pizza. It's a comfortable, clean place to watch a soccer match or nurse a coffee.

Getting There & Around

The **airport** (RGA; ☎ 420699) is off RN 3, a short cab ride from town. **Aerolíneas Argentinas** (☎ 424467; San Martín 607) flies direct daily to Buenos Aires (US$290). **Líneas Aéreas del Estado** (LADE; ☎ 422968; Lasserre 445) flies a couple of times weekly to Río Gallegos (US$20 to US$26), Comodoro Rivadavia (US$46 to US$62) and Buenos Aires (US$102). Inquire locally to see if upstart airlines **All Borders** ('All-B'; www.allbordersair.com) or **Via Patagonia** (www.viapatagonia.com) are flying to Río Gallegos, Ushuaia or Calafate.

At the time of writing, there was no central bus terminal, but plans for one were in the works. **Tecni-Austral** (☎ 426953, 430610; Moyano 516) goes to Ushuaia (US$8, three hours) daily except Sunday at 6pm, with a stop in Tolhuin (US$4, one hour); to Punta Arenas (US$18, seven to nine hours) on Monday, Wednesday and Friday at 10am; and to Río Gallegos (US$18, seven to eight hours) weekdays at 9:30am. **Buses Pacheco** (☎ 425611; 25 de Mayo 712) goes to Punta Arenas (US$18, seven to nine hours) Tuesday, Thursday and Saturday at 10:30am.

A better option to Ushuaia and Tolhuin are the door-to-door minivan services (US$8.35) run by **Lider** (☎ 420003, 424-2000; Moreno 635) and **Transportes Montiel** (☎ 420997, 421366; 25 de Mayo

712) several times daily. Call to reserve a seat; tickets must be paid for in person.

ESTANCIAS AROUND RÍO GRANDE

Wool baron José Menéndez' first *estancia* – La Primera Argentina, now known as **Estancia José Menéndez**, 20km southwest of town via RN 3 and RC-b – covered 160,000 hectares, with over 140,000 head of sheep. His second bite into this land, of which he was most proud, was La Segunda Argentina, totaling 150,000 hectares. Later renamed **Estancia María Behety** (in Buenos Aires ☎ 011-4331-5061; www.maribety .com.ar in Spanish) after his wife, it's still a working ranch and features the world's largest shearing shed, 17km west of town via RC-c. They mainly cater to tour groups and elite anglers, with a deluxe 12-person fly-fishing lodge overlooking the Río Grande. Contact Mariani Travel (opposite) for package details.

Several of the area's smaller *estancias* have opened to small-scale tourism, offering a unique chance to learn about the area's history and enjoy its magic; reserve as far in advance as possible.

The sons of early settler Thomas Bridges (see Estancia Harberton, p455) established **Estancia Viamonte** (☎ 02964-430861, 15-616813; www .estanciaviamonte.com; s/d with breakfast & dinner US$100/ 165, full board per person US$150; ☺ Oct-Apr & by arrangement) in 1902 at the request of the Selk'nam. The *estancia* is alongside RN 3, 45km south of Río Grande, on the northern end of the Lucas Bridges Trail, which eventually leads to Harberton, near Ushuaia. The Goodalls, descendents of the Bridges, now run it as a working ranch, with 22,000 head of sheep on 40,000 hectares, and continue the family tradition of offering guests refuge with warm, unpretentious hospitality and hearty meals. From well-appointed rooms in the Sea View house, you can listen to the crashing of the waves across RN 3. Guided activity possibilities include horseback riding, hiking and fly-fishing the Río Ewan. Advance reservations are greatly appreciated and highly recommended.

Enjoying an excellent locale, **Estancia Las Hijas** (☎ 02901-434617; daniels@netcombbs.com.ar) has plans to open to tourism. If you are planning to hop from one *estancia* to the other, this would be good choice right before the RC-a junction.

Begun by the first rural doctor in Tierra del Fuego, the working, 10,000-hectare

Basque-Provençal-style **Estancia Tepi** (☎ 02964-427245, 15-504-2020; www.estanciatepi.com.ar in Spanish; RC-a, Km 5; day trip/B&B/full pension/deluxe per person US$20/30/100/120; ☻ Dec-Mar) has thermal baths, horseback rides, treks and tours. It's 80km from Río Grande and 150km from Ushuaia.

Estancia Rolito (☎ 02901-437351, 02901-432419; www.tierradelfuego.org.ar/rolito in Spanish; RC-a, Km 14; r per person with half-/full pension US$60/80), in a forest of ñire and lenga, is small, comfortable, very Argentine and very inviting. The owners make sure everyone stays content with meals of homemade bread, garden vegies and heaping plates of Fueguino lamb. Day trips from Ushuaia (25 de Mayo 34 at Turismo de Campo) stop by for lunch or dinner and guided horseback riding. Rolito is 100km from Río Grande and 150km from Ushuaia.

TOLHUIN & LAGO FAGNANO

Tolhuin (population 2000), a quiet but fast-growing frontier town of small plazas and sheltering evergreens, fronts the eastern shore of Lago Fagnano, also known as Lago Kami. Named for the Selk'nam word meaning 'like a heart,' Tolhuin is practically the heart of Tierra del Fuego: 132km south of Río Grande and 104km northeast of Ushuaia via an increasingly paved road that's scheduled for completion in 2006. Most travelers tend to skip right over it, but if you are looking for a unique and tranquil spot, Tolhuin is well worth checking out.

However long your stay, you will probably end up in what is undeniably the heart of town, **Panadería La Unión** (☎ 02901-492202; www.panaderialaunion.com.ar in Spanish; Jeujepen 450; ☎ 24hr). Buses stop here for a quick break, and everyone scurries inside to purchase bags of first-rate pastries and fill up their thermoses with hot water. There's also a *locutorio*, lots of magazines and even a webcam of Lago Fagnano, a huge glacial trough that's a popular spot for boating and fishing.

Sleeping & Eating

Modern lakeside cabin complexes like **Cabañas Khami** (☎ 15-611243, 15-566045; www.cabanias

---

FISH ARE JUMPIN'

Rivers teem with trout, anglers strain under the pull of immense catches, and tales of the one that got away drown out the soccer match on TV: it's fishing season in Tierra del Fuego. Famous the world over, the desolate stretch of the island around Río Grande attracts Hollywood stars, heads of state and former US presidents, all in search of the perfect day of angling. Usually they are in luck.

In 1933 pioneer John Goodall stocked the rivers around Río Grande with brown, rainbow and brook trout. Similar to the success of the region's sheep stations, the sport-fishing industry took off as the fish populated the rivers. The brown trout, originally from Europe, ventured out to sea, returning to these rivers to spawn. Over the decades they have continued this back-and-forth migration, creating one of the world's best sea-run trout-fishing areas; some specimens from this region weigh in at 15kg. Rainbow trout from the western US are nearly as impressive, with individual fish reaching 9kg.

Most fishing excursions are organized through outside agents, mostly in the USA. 'Public' fishing rivers, on which trips can be organized, include the Fuego, Menéndez, Candelaria, Ewan and MacLennan. Many of the more elite angling trips are lodged in *estancias*, which have exclusive use of some of the best rivers.

Flies Rubber legs and wooly buggers

License fees Up to US$40 per day or US$200 per season, depending on where you fish

Limit One fish per person per day

Methods Spinning and fly casting; no night fishing

Season November 1 to April 15, with catch-and-release restrictions from April 1 to April 15

License 1 is valid for fishing throughout the province, except in the national park. Contact **Asociación Caza y Pesca** (☎ 02901-423168; cazapescaush@infovia.com.ar; Maipú 822) in Ushuaia, or **Club de Pesca John Goodall** (☎ 02964-424324; Ricardo Rojas 606) in Río Grande.

License 2 is valid for fishing in the national park and in Patagonia areas. Contact the National Parks office in Ushuaia (see p447).

khami.com.ar; 6-person cabin US$110) are springing up here as fast as Argentine urbanites can flee the city and as quickly as local sawyers can chop wood. You might find rental details at the *panadería* or nascent **tourist office** (www.tierradelfuego.org.ar/tolhuin) behind the gas station, but your best bet is Ushuaia's main tourist office (p447).

Hostería Kaikén (☎ 02964-492208) With views of the lake, 1960s-style Hostería Kaikén was undergoing extensive renovation at the time of writing and will likely to be worth checking out.

About 10km north of town are a couple of camping possibilities, both with bathrooms, hot showers and fire pits: the more desirable **Camping Hain del Lago Khami** (☎ 02901-1560-3606; robertoberbel@hotmail.com; camping per person US$1, refugios for 3/5 people US$8.50/17) and nearby **Camping Centro de Empleados de Comercio** (per person US$1.65).

Within walking distance of the *panadería* are Pizzería La Amistad, the inviting Posada de los Ramírez and a *parrilla* firing up loads of lamb.

Getting There & Away

Buses and minivans passing along RN 3, which are often full in high season, all stop at the *panadería* en route to Ushuaia or Río Grande (US$4.50).

USHUAIA

☎ 02901/ pop 58,000

Set between the Beagle Channel and jagged glacial peaks rising from sea level to nearly 1500m, Ushuaia boasts a dramatic location that few places can match. But one is tempted to say Ushuaia boasts a little too much of its 'World's End' status: yes, it is the southernmost city in the world, but the relentless marketing of this superlative runs the risk of overpowering the very remoteness it aims to promote. As the most important gateway to Antarctica, port for cruising yachts and coveted destination for belt-notching travelers, Ushuaia caters well to the growing numbers of tourists, offering myriad activities in and around town, and enjoys a national park for a neighbor. For those seeking adventure, first-rate hiking and skiing opportunities await just minutes from town.

In 1870 the British-based South American Missionary Society made Ushuaia its first permanent Fuegian outpost, but only artifacts, shell mounds, Thomas Bridges' famous dictionary of the Yahgan language and memories remain of the Yahgan people who once flourished here.

Between 1884 and 1947, Argentina incarcerated many of its most notorious criminals and political prisoners here and on remote Isla de los Estados (Staten Island). In 1906 the military prison was moved to Ushuaia and, in 1911, it was combined with the Carcel de Reincidentes, which had incarcerated civilian recidivists since 1896.

Since 1950 the town has been an important naval base. Industries such as electronics assembly, with higher wages and other perks, encouraged people to settle here, which in turn resulted in a jumble of housing developments advancing in the few directions the mad geography allows.

Orientation

Paralleling the Beagle Channel, Maipú becomes Malvinas Argentinas west of the cemetery, then turns into RN 3, continuing 12km to Parque Nacional Tierra del Fuego. To the east, public access ends at Yaganes, which heads north to meet RN 3 going north toward Lago Fagnano. Most visitor services are on or within a couple blocks of San Martín, a block inland from the waterfront.

Information

BOOKSTORES

Boutique del Libro (☎ 432117; 25 de Mayo 62) Comprehensive, multilingual selection of literature, guidebooks and pictorials.

IMMIGRATION

Immigration (☎ 422334; Beauvoir 1536; ☻ 9am-noon Mon-Fri)

LAUNDRY

Most lodgings offer laundry service.
Los Tres Ángeles (☎ 422687; Juan M Rosas 139; per load US$1.65).
Qüalis (☎ 432578; Deloquí 368)

MEDICAL SERVICES

Hospital Regional (☎ 107, 423200; cnr Maipú & 12 de Octubre)

MONEY

Several banks on Maipú and San Martín have ATMs.

TIERRA DEL FUEGO

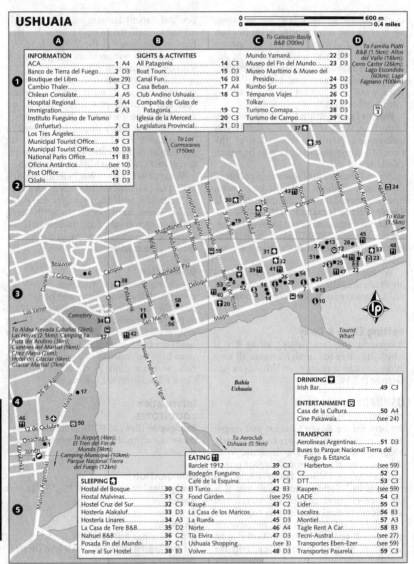

USHUAIA

INFORMATION		
ACA	1	A4
Banco de Tierra del Fuego	2	D3
Boutique del Libro	(see 29)	
Cambio Thaler	3	C3
Chilean Consulate	4	A5
Hospital Regional	5	A4
Immigration	6	A3
Instituto Fueguino de Turismo (Infuetur)	7	C3
Los Tres Ángeles	8	C3
Municipal Tourist Office	9	C3
Municipal Tourist Office	10	D3
National Parks Office	11	B3
Oficina Antártica	(see 10)	
Post Office	12	D3
Qüalis	13	D3

SIGHTS & ACTIVITIES		
All Patagonia	14	C3
Boat Tours	15	D3
Canal Fun	16	D3
Casa Beban	17	A4
Club Andino Ushuaia	18	C3
Compañía de Guías de Patagonia	19	C2
Iglesia de la Merced	20	C3
Legislatura Provincial	21	D3

Mundo Yamaná	22	D3
Museo del Fin del Mundo	23	D3
Museo Marítimo & Museo del Presidio	24	D2
Rumbo Sur	25	D3
Témpanos Viajes	26	C3
Tolkar	27	D3
Turismo Comapa	28	D3
Turismo de Campo	29	C3

SLEEPING		
Hostal del Bosque	30	C2
Hostal Malvinas	31	C3
Hostel Cruz del Sur	32	C3
Hostería Alakaluf	33	D3
Hostería Linares	34	A3
La Casa de Tere B&B	35	D2
Nahuel B&B	36	C2
Posada Fin del Mundo	37	C1
Torre al Sur Hostel	38	B3

EATING		
Barcleit 1912	39	C3
Bodegón Fueguino	40	C3
Café de la Esquina	41	C3
El Turco	42	B3
Food Garden	(see 25)	
Kaupé	43	C2
La Casa de los Maricos	44	D3
La Rueda	45	D3
Norte	46	A4
Tía Elvira	47	D3
Ushuaia Shopping	(see 3)	
Volver	48	D3

DRINKING		
Irish Bar	49	C3

ENTERTAINMENT		
Casa de la Cultura	50	A4
Cine Pakawaia	(see 24)	

TRANSPORT		
Aerolíneas Argentinas	51	D3
Buses to Parque Nacional Tierra del Fuego & Estancia Harberton	(see 59)	
C2	52	C3
DTT	53	C3
Kaupen	(see 59)	
LADE	54	C3
Lider	55	C3
Localiza	56	B3
Montiel	57	A3
Tagle Rent A Car	58	B3
Tecni-Austral	(see 27)	
Transportes Eben-Ezer	(see 59)	
Transportes Pasarela	59	C3

Banco de Tierra del Fuego (San Martín 396) Best rates for traveler's checks.

Cambio Thaler (San Martín 778; ☒ 10am-1pm & 5-8pm Mon-Fri, 10am-1pm Sat) Convenience equals slightly poorer exchange rates.

POST
Post office (cnr San Martín & Godoy)

TELEPHONE & INTERNET ACCESS
Relatively slow Internet access (around US$1 per hour) is available at call centers along San Martín.

TOURIST INFORMATION
ACA (☎ 421121; cnr Malvinas Argentinas & Onachaga)
Instituto Fueguino de Turismo (Infuetur; ☎ 421423;

www.tierradelfuego.org.ar; Maipú 505; 🕒 8am-9pm Mon-Fri, 9am-8pm Sat & Sun) On ground floor of Hotel Albatros.
Municipal tourist office (🕾 432000, airport 🕾 423 970, on Tierra del Fuego 🕾 0800-333-1476; www.e-ushuaia .com in Spanish; San Martín 674; 🕒 8am-9pm Mon-Fri, 9am-8pm Sat & Sun) Very helpful, with a message board and multilingual brochures, as well as good lodging, activities and transport info and English- and French-speaking staff. Also at the airport and pier.
National Parks office (Administración de Parques Nacionales; 🕾 421315; San Martín 1395; 🕒 9am-4pm Mon-Fri)

Sights

MUSEO MARÍTIMO & MUSEO DEL PRESIDIO
When convicts were moved from Staten Island to Ushuaia in 1906 they began building the national prison, which was finished in 1920. The spokelike halls of single cells were designed to house 380, but in the prison's most active period held up to 800. Closed as a jail in 1947, it now houses the **Museo Marítimo & Museo del Presidio** (🕾 437481; www.ushuaia.org; cnr Yaganes & G Paz; admission US$5; 🕒 9am-8pm). It's a fine port of call on a blustery day. Halls showing penal life are intriguing, but mainly because of the informative plaques, which are only in Spanish. Two of the more illustrious inmates were author Ricardo Rojasand and Russian anarchist Simón Radowitzky.

On the upper floor of one hall is a display on Antarctic exploration. Perhaps the most worthwhile part of the museum is the exhibit containing incredibly detailed scale models of famous ships, spanning 500 years and providing a unique glimpse into the region's history. Informative pamphlets in English about this exhibit are available at reception. In the courtyard are the remains of the world's narrowest gauge freight train, which transported prisoners between town and work stations.

MUNDO YAMANÁ
More an experience than museum, the **Mundo Yamaná** (🕾 422874; Rivadavia 56; admission US$1.65; 🕒 10am-8pm) is an exploration of the Fueguinos' attempts to bring the Yamaná culture to life. Some of the expertly detailed dioramas (details in English and Spanish) are based on accessible bays and inlets of the national park; coming here before hiking in the park (p454) adds a new level of awareness.

MUSEO DEL FIN DEL MUNDO
Built in 1903 for the territorial governor Manuel Fernández Valdés, this building was a branch of the Banco de la Nación up until 1978 when it was transformed into the **Museo del Fin del Mundo** (🕾 421863; cnr Maipú & Rivadavia; admission US$3.35; 🕒 9am-8pm). Exhibits on Fuegian natural history, stuffed birdlife, aboriginal life and the early penal colonies, and replicas of an early general store and bank, are of moderate interest.

HISTORIC BUILDINGS
The tourist office distributes a free city-tour map with information on many of the historic houses around town. At Maipú 465, **Legislatura Provincial** (Provincial Legislature; 1894) was the governor's official residence. The century-old **Iglesia de la Merced** (San Martín & Don Bosco), was built with convict labor. **Casa Beban** (cnr Maipú & Pluschow; admission free; 🕒 10am-8pm Mon-Fri, 4-8pm Sat & Sun) was built in 1911 using parts ordered from Sweden. Today the house hosts local art exhibits.

Activities

HIKING & TREKKING
Hiking possibilities should not be limited to the national park (p454); the entire mountain range behind Ushuaia, with its lakes and rivers, is a hiker's high. However, many trails are poorly marked or not marked at all; some hikers who have easily scurried uphill have gotten lost trying to find the trail back.

The **Club Andino Ushuaia** (🕾 422335; Juana Fadul 50; 🕒 10am-12:30pm & 2-9:30pm Mon-Fri, 10am-2pm Sat) sells a map (US$5) and bilingual trekking, mountaineering and mountain-biking guidebook (US$12) with rough maps and plenty of trail description. The club occasionally organizes hikes and can recommend hiking guides. Unguided trekkers are strongly encouraged to register with the Club or the tourist office (left) before heading out – and check in after a safe return. In an emergency, contact the **Civil Guard** (🕾 103, 22108).

Compañía de Guías de Patagonia (p449) organizes treks and is often recommended as a reliable information source.

Cerro Martial & Glaciar Martial
A good hike from downtown leads up to Glaciar Martial, where you can enjoy views of Ushuaia and the Beagle Channel; in fact, the views are possibly more impressive than the actual glacier. Catch a taxi up the hill for under US$2, or if up for an all-day hike, follow San Martín west and keep ascending

YAMANÁ & SELK'NAM RITUALS

As Charles Darwin saw it, the Yamaná (or Yahgan) of the Beagle Channel – naked except for a loincloth and sealskin cape, paddling about in canoes with all their most important possessions, including bows, dogs and even fire – were 'subhuman beings…without spiritual life.'

Perhaps, had old Chuck spent more time on land rather than concocting his theories aboard ship, he might have noticed that the Yamaná had a rich system of spiritual beliefs. They believed in a Supreme Being, Watauinewa, and had shamans who talked to spirits who the Yamaná believed controlled the weather and the hunt. Darwin might have seen that during the Kina ceremony, in which boys are initiated to adulthood, the men dressed themselves as gods, painting their bodies with black carbon and the region's white and red clays, holding tall masks and dancing to represent the different spirits: Kina-Miami, the guardian; Tulema-Yaka, the tutor; Hani-Yaka, the energy giver.

North of the island's mountain range, another group held a similar ritual. The Selk'nam (or Ona to the Yamaná and, later, to the Europeans) believed in a Supreme Being, Temankel, and also believed that women once controlled the lands, keeping the men subordinate with clever sorcery. According to the story, the men learned of this ploy and decided the only way to gain control would be to kill all of the women except the youngest, and play the same game of fear.

Thus the Hain ceremony was created, held within and around a conical tent that women were not allowed to approach, under penalty of death. Men painted their bodies using the same black carbon and red white clays mixed with guanaco fat, and they created masks from the bark of trees. Boys went through the initiation process, learning about the different spirits and interpreting the symbolism as each zigzagged, striped or dotted body danced and leapt into the air, all the while instilling fear in the women and small children watching from afar. Spirits included Matan, the magic dancer and spirit of happiness; Kulan, the terrible vixen who descends from the sky, selects her man and then kidnaps him to make love to her; and Koshmenk, Kulan's jealous husband.

---

as it zigzags (there are many hiker shortcuts) to the ski run 7km northwest of town. At this point either take the **Aerosilla** (US$3.35; ☻ 10am-4pm) chairlift or walk another two hours to make a full day of it. The weather is changeable, so take warm, dry clothing and sturdy footwear. Minivans leave from the corner of Maipú and 25 de Mayo every half hour from 10am to 6:30pm (US$3.50 roundtrip).

BOATING

Popular half-day boat trips around the Beagle Channel – with destinations such as the sea-lion colony at Isla de los Lobos, and Isla de Pájaros, with its extensive cormorant colonies – leave in the morning and afternoon from the tourist pier on Maipú between Lasserre and Roca.

Tres Marías Excursiones (☎ 421897; www.tresmarias exc.com; Tourist Wharf) charges around US$30 for a four-hour morning or afternoon excursion on the Beagle Channel with a maximum of 10 passengers; they are the only outfitter with permission to land on Isla 'H' in the Isla Bridges natural reserve, which has shell mounds and a rock-cormorant colony.

Alternatively, try a more expensive catamaran trip or the historic 70-passenger **Barracuda** (☎ 437606), which chugs to the Faro Les Eclaireurs lighthouse and Isla de los Lobos (US$17, three hours).

SKIING

Ski resorts string the nearby mountains – all accessed from RN 3 – with both downhill and cross-country options. The season runs from June to September, although only July is really busy. Ushuaia's biggest ski event is the annual **Marcha Blanca**, a symbolic recreation of San Martín's historic August 17 crossing of the Andes.

The largest resort is **Cerro Castor** (☎ 15-605 604/6; www.cerrocastor.com in Spanish; full-day lift tickets US$18-26), 27km from Ushuaia, with 15 slopes spanning 400 hectares. Rentals are available for skis, boards, blades and cross-country skis. There's a good restaurant at the base and a nice place to chill and have afternoon tea at the summit.

Another large area, **Altos del Valle** (☎ 422234; gatocuruchet@hotmail.com), 19km from Ushuaia, is known for breeding Siberian and Alaskan huskies. In addition to downhill skiing, it has good cross-country and snowshoeing areas, with full rentals and full-moon trips.

For a quick swoosh near town, Club Andino (p447) runs cross-country and downhill slopes only 3km and 5km away. **Centro de Deportes Invernales Glaciar Martial** (☎ 421423, 423340) is 7km northwest of town, with rental equipment and downhill runs well suited for beginners.

Transportes Pasarela and Alvarez buses run shuttles (US$5) from the corner of 25 de Mayo and Maipú to the ski centers along RN 3 three times daily. Each center also provides its own transport from downtown Ushuaia.

Tours

At last count, 27 agencies were vying for a slice of the tourist pie. The key is to line up activities with agencies that know how to have fun. Luckily, most agencies are noncompetitive, so they'll refer you to another agency that will better fit your desires. Most 'nonconventional' (ie trekking, horseback riding, canoeing, mountain biking, 4WD backroading and, in winter, dog sledding) excursions visit Parque Nacional Tierra del Fuego or Lago Fagnano. We hope that the irony of selling trips to watch invasive, non-native beavers as 'ecotourism' outings isn't lost only upon us. The following recommendations barely skim the tip of the iceberg of what's available:

All Patagonia (☎ 430622; www.allpatagonia.com; Juana Fadul 60) Amex rep offering more conventional and luxurious trips.

Canal Fun (☎ 437395; www.canalfun.com; Rivadavia 82) Run by hip young guys, which adds a good level of thrill and amusement to their trips (US$40 to US$80). Popular options include paddling inflatable kayaks though the park, kayaking on Lago Roca, off-roading around Lago Fagnano and a day-long multisport outing around Estancia Harberton.

Compañía de Guías de Patagonia (☎ 437753, 15-618426; www.companiadeguias.com.ar; Campos 795) Organizes full-day treks with climbing and ice-hiking (US$47) and two-day high-mountain treks to Cerro Alvear (US$117) with glacier camping.

Rumbo Sur (☎ 421139; www.rumbosur.com.ar; San Martín 350) Ushuaia's longest-running agency specializes in more conventional activities.

Témpanos Viajes (☎ 436020; www.ushuaiaoutdoors .com.ar in Spanish; San Martín 626) Offers both sedentary and more active excursions.

Tolkar (☎ 431408/12; www.tolkarturismo.com.ar; Roca 157) Another helpful, popular all-round agency, affiliated with Tecni-Austral buses.

Turismo de Campo (☎ 437451; www.turismodecampo .com in Spanish; 25 de Mayo 64) Organizes light trekking, Beagle Channel sailing trips and visits to Estancia Rolito near Río Grande. Also sells a wide variety of nine- to 12-night Antarctica passages.

Turismo Comapa (☎ 430727; www.comapa.com; San Martín 245) Confirm Navimag and Cruceros Australis passages here.

Sleeping

In the summer high season, especially January and February, demand is high and you shouldn't arrive without reservations. It can also be difficult to find a bed in early March, when everything is booked for the Fin del Mundo Marathon. In winter, many of the places that stay open drop their rates a bit. The municipal tourist office (p447) posts a list of available accommodations outside after closing time.

BUDGET

Hostels in Ushuaia are replicating like horny mosquitoes. All have kitchens and most offer Internet access. Rates typically drop 25% in the low season (April to October).

Hostel Cruz del Sur (☎ 423110; www.xdelsur.com .ar; Deloquí 636; dm US$7; 🖳) Cozy four- to six-bed dorms (with heaters, thin mattresses and bedding, some rooms with a view) can get noisy, and when filled to capacity, the bathrooms are taxed to the max. But the welcoming hosts do a fine job of rounding up groups to explore nearby areas. Kitchens are well stocked, there's a pleasant library and tea or coffee is always available.

Torre al Sur Hostel (☎ 430745; www.torrealsur .com.ar; Gobernador Paz 1437; dm HI member/nonmember US$6/6.65; 🖳) Perched high on a hill, this colorful HI hostel has some fabulous views to complement the caring management and usual services. Don't expect privacy: the small, maze-like dorm rooms can be noisy. The crowning glory is the wraparound-window tower room, with grand vistas.

Los Comoranes (☎ 423459; www.loscormoranes.com; Kamshen 788; dm with/without HI card US$6.65/7.35; 🖳) Ten minutes' walk north of the center, this purpose-built HI hostel has good six-bed dorms, with radiant heating, facing outdoor hallways. Rates include an hour of Internet and an incoming transfer.

ANTARCTICA: THE ICE

Once the lone continent barely touched by humans, Antarctica is now firmly established (for better or for worse) as a trendy tourist destination.

A total of 27,537 tourists (37.7% from the USA, 16.8% from Germany, 12.9% from the UK and 7.5% from Australia), plus 16,200 staff and crew, landed, cruised around or flew over the ice during the 2003–04 season – more than triple the number of visitors in 1992–93. Of these embarkations, a vast majority left from Ushuaia. By contrast, Antarctica's summer and overwintering populations are only 5000 and 1200 respectively.

So long as you've got two or three weeks to spare, hopping on board a ship to Antarctica is not at all out of the question. Tour companies charge anywhere from US$3000 to US$68,000, although some ships now allow walk-ons, which can cost as little as US$2500 to US$5000.

Some voyages take in the Falkland Islands and South Georgia (human population 10 to 20, estimated penguin population two to three million!); others go just to the Antarctic Peninsula, while others focus on retracing historic expeditions. The season runs mid-November to mid-March. Friendly and informative **Oficina Antártica** (☎ 423340; antartida@tierradelfuego.org.ar; ☼ 9am-5pm Mon-Fri, Sat & Sun if there are boats), on Ushuaia's tourist pier, keeps a list of departures and arrivals. They can also direct would-be last-minute passengers to travel agencies that handle bookings.

A small but growing handful of visitors reach Antarctica aboard private vessels. All are sailboats (although obviously equipped with auxiliary engines), and some have even wintered in sheltered anchorages such as Yankee Harbor at Greenwich Island or near Palmer station on the Antarctic Peninsula. In three decades of Antarctic cruising, there have been about 200 yacht voyages to 'the Ice.' For some reason, this type of travel particularly seems to appeal to the French.

International Association of Antarctica Tour Operators (IAATO; ☎ 970-704-1047; www.iaato.org) members that abide by its strict guidelines for responsible travel include the following:

Adventure Associates (☎ 61-2-9389-7466; www.adventureassociates.com) Offers trips to a number of parts of Antarctica on several different ships.

Antarctic Logistics & Expeditions (☎ 801-266-4876/4982; www.antarctic-logistics.com) The only private company offering flights to Antarctica's interior.

AntarcticaXXI (☎ 56-61-228-783; www.antarcticaxxi.com) The only air-cruise combo: fly from Punta Arenas to Chile's Frei station on King George Island, then transfer to the 46-passenger ship *Grigoriy Mikheev* for several days of cruising the South Shetlands and peninsula region.

Camping La Pista del Andino (☎ 435890; www .lapistadelandino.com.ar in Spanish; Alem 2873; per person US$2.65; ☼ Oct-Apr) Located at the Club Andino's ski area, this pleasant campground is a steep 3km uphill trek. It offers grassy or forest sites with views. There are cooking facilities, good common areas and bikes for rent. It also has a bar-restaurant with good atmosphere, but could use more showers and toilets. Call for free pick up from the airport/town center (taxis to the center of town cost US$1.25).

Camping Municipal, 10km west of town on RN 3, is en route to Parque Nacional Tierra del Fuego. This free campground has an attractive setting but minimal facilities.

MIDRANGE

Enough bed and breakfasts – often with shared bathroom – have sprung up that Ushuaia now has a B&B association. There's no central contact, but the tourist office can provide a complete list. They cost a bit more than hostels, but less than most hotels, and offer a much more intimate, amiable atmosphere.

Galeazzi-Basily B&B (☎ 423213; www.geocities.com /galeazzibasily; Valdéz 323; s/d US$17/24, 4-person cabin US$70; P ⌨) One of the joys of travel is meeting people who bring out the best in an area, and this well-traveled family does just that. For lucky lodgers, the hospitality is huge (and good breakfast and kitchen use is included). Two double rooms share a bathroom, and English, French, Italian and Portuguese are spoken. In the backyard, there are two fully equipped kitchenette cabins, plus another large alpine-style house sleeping six is available in December and January. Book ahead.

Familia Piatti B&B (☎ 437104, 15-613485; www .interpatagonia.com/familiapiatti in Spanish; Bosque del Faldeo 812, Bosque del Faldeo; s/d/tr US$33/40/50; P ⌨) Hidden in a wooded neighborhood, this family-

Aurora Expeditions (☎ 61-2-9252-1033, in Australia ☎ 1800-637-688; www.auroraexpeditions.com.au) Offers scuba diving, sea kayaking, mountain climbing and camping and operates the 54-passenger *Polar Pioneer* and the 46-passenger *Akademik Shokalskiy*.

Clipper Cruise Line (☎ 314-952-6700, in USA ☎ 800-325-0010; www.clippercruise.com) Recommended voyages, some including South Georgia and the Falkland Islands, traveling aboard the 122-passenger *Clipper Adventurer*.

Heritage Expeditions (☎ 64-3-365-3500, in NZ ☎ 0800-262-8873, in Australia ☎ 1800-143-585; www .heritage-expeditions.com) Antarctic tourism's only family-run business operates the 48-passenger *Spirit of Enderby* to New Zealand's sub-Antarctic islands, Macquarie Island and the Ross Sea region. It also offers scuba diving and carries a helicopter on Antarctic voyages.

Lindblad Expeditions (☎ 212-765-7740, in USA ☎ 800-397-3348; www.expeditions.com) The 110-passenger *Endeavour* offers kayaking and carries a remotely operated vehicle that delivers underwater video footage to the ship's lounge.

Mountain Travel-Sobek (☎ 510-594-6000, in USA ☎ 888-687-6235; www.mtsobek.com) Sells several trips and offers kayaking.

Peregrine Expeditions (☎ 61-3-9663-8611; www.peregrine.net.au) Adventure-oriented trips are offered aboard the 110-passenger *Akademik Ioffe* and 110-passenger *Akademik Sergey Vavilov*, including camping and kayaking.

Quark Expeditions (☎ 203-656-0499, in USA ☎ 800-356-5699, in UK ☎ 44-1494-464-080; www.quark expeditions.com) Offers a variety of trips to the peninsula and Ross Sea region aboard the powerful Russian-flagged, helicopter-equipped, 108-passenger icebreaker *Kapitan Khlebnikov*.

WildWings/WildOceans Travel (☎ 44-117-9658-333; www.wildwings.co.uk) Operates bird- and wildlife-focused tours.

Zegrahm Expeditions (☎ 206-285-4000, in USA ☎ 800-628-8747; www.zeco.com) Offers high-end cruises on several different vessels.

GAP Adventures (☎ 800-465-5600; www.gap.ca) is a newcomer to polar latitudes – and not yet an IAATO member – but is reader-recommended for its good food, reasonably priced trips and well-equipped ships.

Lonely Planet's newly revised *Antarctica* guidebook by Jeff Rubin has details on many possible voyages plus comprehensive background information on the great frozen continent.

---

friendly B&B has a couple of very comfortable carpeted rooms outfitted with down duvets and native lengua wood furniture, plus a great deck on which to relax. Hiking trails nearby lead up the mountains. The friendly owners are multilingual (English, Italian and Portuguese) and can arrange transport and guided excursions. Reserve ahead to arrange a free incoming transfer.

Nahuel B&B (☎ 423068; byb_nahuel@yahoo.com .ar; 25 de Mayo 440; s/d with shared bathroom US$23/30; Ⓟ 🖳) You get your own keys and come and go as you please at this family home a short walk uphill from the center. A couple of the rooms have great views and there is some English spoken. There's laundry service and tea and coffee are always available.

La Casa de Tere B&B (☎ 422312, 435913; www.la casadetere.com.ar; Rivadavia 620; s/d/tr with shared bathroom US$20/25/37; Ⓟ) With only three rooms, guests receive plenty of personal attention

from the helpful owner. It's brand new, breakfast is notable, there's kitchen use and great views from the tidy rooms. There's also cable TV and a fireplace in the living room. It's a short but steep walk uphill from the center.

Hostal Malvinas (☎ 422626; www.hostalmalvinas .com; Deloquí 615; s/d US$37/43) Recently redecorated Malvinas offers pleasant carpeted rooms (no TVs), some with great harbor views and all with good bathrooms, firm beds and clunky gas heaters. Hot drinks and pastries are available all day long downstairs in the breakfast nook.

Hostería Alakaluf (☎ 436705; www.alakalufhos teria.com.ar; San Martín 146; s/d US$33/50; 🖳) Family-owned and operated Alakaluf allows kitchen use and sports rooms with harbor and mountain views. It's a good deal given the heart-of-town location and thus fills up fast. They also offer transportation services.

TIERRA DEL FUEGO

Posada Fin del Mundo (☎ 434847, 437345; www
.posadafindelmundo.com.ar; cnr Rivadavia & Valdéz; s/d/tr
US$50/55/75; ⓟ) The worldly owners make all
feel welcome in their ever-evolving home.
The eight rooms are on the small side but
beds are long, breakfast is generous and the
attractive living room, library and dining
area are inviting. It's on a quiet street, a
good four-block walk uphill out of town.

Aldea Nevada Cabañas (☎ 422851/68; www.aldea
nevada.com.ar; Martial 1430; 2-4/6 people US$65/80,
3-night minimum; ⓟ) In a lenga forest 2.5km
uphill from town, 10 modern but rustic log
cabins line up, each one expertly designed
with kitchen, wood stoves, plenty of space
and lots of charm.

Hostal del Bosque (☎ 430777; www.hostaldel
bosque.com.ar; Magallanes 709; s/d US$64/82; ⓟ) A
good choice, del Bosque's mini-apartments
have kitchenettes, tables and sofas, but no
fans – smelly food not allowed. Its hillside
location affords some good views but non-
Argentines may incur a steep *turista* (gringo)
surcharge of upwards of US$30 per night.

Hostería Linares (☎ 423594; www.hosterialinares
.com.ar; Deloquí 1522; s/d/ste US$34/50/60; ⓟ ▢)
Fragile trinkets and antiques lend an air
of formality to this inn, but the 10 rooms
are warm and comfortable and some have
spectacular views. Taking breakfast while
watching the sunrise color the harbor is the
winning ticket here.

TOP END

Consult the tourist office for a complete list
of fully-equipped *cabañas*.

Las Hayas (☎ 430710/8; www.lashayas.com.ar; Martial 1650; s & d US$199, ste US$257-379; ⓟ ▢ ▨)
When Nelson Mandela is honeymooning
or Mercosur presidents are in town, they
stay at Ushuaia's only five-star resort, dramatically perched 3km above town. There's a
wide variety of top-notch rooms, and the
stunning Beagle Channel views continue
seamlessly from the meeting facilities and
gourmet restaurant to the health club and
nine-hole golf course.

Cumbres del Martial (☎ 424779; www.cumbresdel
martial.com.ar in Spanish; Martial, Km 5; r/ste US$150/250;
ⓟ ▢) These stylish, modern, fully equipped,
family-friendly cabins are nestled at the base
of the Martial glacier, with a homey dining
room and balconies overlooking the forest.
To top it all off, the delicious breakfast treats
are homemade.

Hotel del Glaciar (☎ 430640; www.hoteldelglaciar
.com; Martial 2355; d/tr/ste with bay view US$179/229/
269, glacier view US$159/215/239; ⓟ ▢) Catering
mostly to the convention crowd, with oversized foyers, fireplaces and bars, Glaciar has
tip-top service and cushy rooms with ample
windows.

Eating

Bodegón Fueguino (☎ 431972; San Martín 859; mains
US$5-8) A historic 100-year-old Fuegian home
creates the ideal backdrop for casual *comidas
típicas* like lamb prepared more ways than
you ever dreamed of – think orange-honey
sauce. The casual, intimate ambience makes
it popular with locals for *picadas* (hors
d'oeuvres) shared over a glass of wine or
artesian beer. An early dinner crowd chows
down on fresh grilled fish, salad and lots of
vegie options.

Kaupé (☎ 422704; Roca 470; mains US$8-12) Chef
Ernesto Vivian's creations, served in a romantic home with great views, are sublime
reminders that haute cuisine extends to
even the most southerly reaches. Try the
parchment-baked sea bass with julienned
leeks, or chicken Bengali in a buttery curry
sauce. Or just come in the evening to enjoy
some of Argentina's best wines while taking
in a brilliant view. Reservations advised.

Chez Manu (☎ 432253; Martial 2135; mains US$8-
16) Chef Emmanuel accents regional cuisine
with a French touch. Try salmon *en brioche*
with a leek fondue or a mixed plate of cold
fruits de mer. The three-course set lunch is
the best deal. It's 2km from town heading
toward the glacier.

Volver (☎ 423977; Maipú 37; meals US$5-12) The
best waterfront seafood option (especially for
crab soup), snug Volver is also worth a visit
for its history. Built by the second chief of the
prison (and later police chief), the building
housed several prisoners after the Ushuaia
prison closed. Later, Rafaela Ishton, the last
pure Ona, moved in, remaining until 1985.
Newspapers that were used as wallpaper and
insulation remain, and every nook holds
some historic knickknack.

Café de la Esquina (☎ 423676; San Martín 605; mains
US$2-6; ☽ breakfast, lunch & dinner) The best place to
scope out the newest flock of tourists in town,
'the Corner' is wall-to-wall, floor-to-ceiling
windows. There's a bar and the kitchen whips
up good breakfasts and some knockout cakes
and sandwiches.

TIERRA DEL FUEGO

Tía Elvira (☎ 424725; Maipú 349; mains US$3-12) Waterfront Elvira enjoys a stellar reputation for seafood preparations at lunch and dinner. Before eating, take a gander at the small museum lining the entrance hall.

La Casa de los Mariscos (☎ 421928; San Martín 232; mains US$3-11) Small, simple and open late, gingham-dressed La Casa prepares some mighty fine seafood and fish, such as *trucha fuegina* (trout bathed in a creamy sauce with calamari).

La Rueda (☎ 436540; San Martín 193; a la carte US$3-7, lunch & dinner buffet US$6.50) Of the *parrillas* along this strip, this one if most often recommended. Ordering a drink is mandatory with the buffet, which includes dessert.

Food Garden (☎ 424808; San Martín 318; mains US$2-6; ☽ breakfast, lunch & dinner) A comfortable spot with an English-language menu and good informal fare such as sandwiches, salads, large breakfasts and draft beer. Upstairs is a predisco bar bordering on glitzy camp.

El Turco (☎ 424711; San Martín 1440; mains US$2-6) Fast, attentive service, large portions and a hint of elegance make 'The Turk' a local favorite. Pizzas, *minutas* (snacks), fish and pasta are all well prepared.

Ushuaia Shopping (☎ 436868; San Martín 788; set lunch US$4, dinner US$3-10) Hidden in this bustling shopping arcade is one of the better choices for good-quality meals. The set lunch includes three courses and coffee.

Also recommended:

Norte (cnr 12 de Octubre & Karukinka; meals US$3/kg) The cafeteria at this huge supermarket dishes out quantity-over-quality dollops of pastas, soups, salads and rotisserie chicken.

Barcleit 1912 (☎ 433015; Juana Fadul 148; mains US$3-7) Rickety historic home famous for its generous food handouts during the pioneering days continues the tradition with a hearty US$2.50 set lunch.

Drinking & Entertainment

Irish Bar (cnr 9 de Julio & Deloqui) It's a looong way from Dublin, but locals recommend this bar for an evening of pints, lively banter and occasional live music.

Küar (☎ 437396; P Moreno 2232) Gringos gather after excursions at waterfront Küar for microbrewed ale and porter, pub grub and endless Beagle Channel views.

First-run movies are shown at **Cine Pakawaia** (☎ 436500; cnr Yaganes & Gobernador Paz; tickets US$2), the Presidio's fully restored hangar-style theater. Hidden behind a gym, the **Casa**

de la Cultura (☎ 422417; cnr Malvinas Argentinas & 12 de Octubre) hosts occasional live music shows.

Getting There & Away

AIR

The airport departure tax is US$20. **Aerolíneas Argentinas** (☎ 421218; Roca 116) jets several times daily to Buenos Aires (US$166 to US$305), sometimes stopping in Río Gallegos (US$100 to US$165) or El Calafate (US$100 to US$250). If you can score a seat on the less-than-daily flights, **LADE** (☎ 421123; San Martín 542) can't be beat to Buenos Aires (US$113), Comodoro Rivadavia (US$77), El Calafate (US$77) and Río Gallegos (US$43).

Chilean airline **Aerovías DAP** (www.dap.cl) flies Monday and Friday at 10:30am to Punta Arenas (US$100), and has two-hour charter-only overflights of Cabo de Hornos (US$260) via Puerto Williams.

Aeroclub Ushuaia (☎ 421717, 421892; www.aero clubushuaia.org.ar) offers scenic flightseeing tours (US$35 to US$100 per person) and flights to Puerto Williams, Chile (US$80 to US$100 per person), on a charter basis.

BOAT

Charter boats anchored in Ushuaia's harbor may take passengers to Puerto Williams (US$60 to US$80) the next time they are heading out. Travel agencies such as Témpanos Viajes (p449) link travelers with yachts for an extra fee.

Around 20 private yachts charter trips to Cabo de Hornos, Antarctica and, less often, South Georgia Island. These trips must be organized well in advance; the most popular weeklong charter, rounding Cape Horn, costs upwards of US$1200 per person. A recommended charter is the reformed racing yacht **Fernande** (☎ 15-561080; www.fernandexp.com), captained by Pascal Grinberg. His three decades of sailing ensure skill and safety at the helm, while the on-deck ambience is mellow and unpretentious.

From September through May, Cruceros Australis (p423) runs luxurious four- to seven-day sightseeing cruises to Punta Arenas and back, catering mostly to mature travelers. Saturday departures from Ushuaia include the possibility of disembarking at Cape Horn. The cruise visits many otherwise inaccessible glaciers, but time alone or hiking opportunities are limited; focus is more on nature talks and group

TIERRA DEL FUEGO

excursions. Turismo Comapa (p449) handles local bookings.

BUS

Book outgoing bus tickets with as much anticipation as possible; many readers have complained about getting stuck here in high season. Other common complaints include confusion and long waits at the ferry and numerous border crossings.

Tecni-Austral (☎ 431408/12; Roca 157) buses for Río Grande (US$8, 3½ hours) leave from the travel agency Tolkar daily except Sunday at 6am, stopping in Tolhuin (US$4.35, two hours) en route. There's onward connecting service on Monday, Wednesday and Friday to Punta Arenas and weekdays to Río Gallegos (both US$27, 12 to 14 hours).

Lider (☎ 436421; Gobernador Paz 921) and **Montiel** (☎ 421366; San Martín 547) run door-to-door minivans to Río Grande (US$8.35) six to eight times daily.

On Maipú at the foot of 25 de Mayo, **Transportes Pasarela** (☎ 433712) run shuttles to Lago Esmeralda (US$3), Lago Escondido (US$5) and Lago Fagnano (US$7), leaving around 10am and returning at 2pm and 6:30pm. If planning to stay overnight, ask to pay just one way (more likely if there are many people traveling) and arrange for pick up. Transportes Eben-Ezer and Kaupen offer similar service and leave from nearby.

For transport to Parque Nacional Tierra del Fuego, see opposite.

Getting Around

Taxis to/from the modern airport (USH), 4km southwest of downtown on the peninsula across from the waterfront, cost US$2 to US$3, and there's local bus service along Av Maipú. **DTT** (San Martín 1258) rents bikes for US$12 per day. Taxis can be chartered for around US$10 per hour.

Including insurance, rental rates for compact cars start around US$25 to US$35 per day with minimal mileage allowances. The best rates are with **C2** (☎ 436388; San Martín 845). Also try **Tagle Rent A Car** (☎ 433084; San Martín 1199) and **Localiza** (☎ 430739; San Martín 1222). Some places may not charge for drop off in other parts of Argentine Tierra del Fuego.

PARQUE NACIONAL TIERRA DEL FUEGO

West of Ushuaia by 12km, the beautiful **Tierra del Fuego National Park** (via RN 3; admission US$4),

Argentina's first coastal national park, extends 63,000 hectares from the Beagle Channel in the south to beyond Lago Fagnano/Kami in the north. However, only a couple of thousand hectares along the southern edge of the park are open to the public, with a miniscule system of short, easy trails that are designed more for day-tripping families than backpacking trekkers. The rest of the park is protected as a *reserva estricta* (strictly off-limits zone). Despite this, a few scenic hikes along the bays and rivers, or through dense native forests of evergreen coihue, canelo and deciduous lenga, are worthwhile. For truly spectacular color, come in the fall when hillsides of ñire burst out in red.

Plenty of birdlife graces the park, especially along the coastal zone. Keep an eye out for condors, albatross, cormorants, gulls, terns, oystercatchers, grebes, kelp geese and the comical, flightless, orange-billed steamer ducks. Common invasive beasties include the European rabbit and the North American beaver, both of which are wreaking ecological havoc. Gray and red foxes, enjoying the abundance of rabbits, may also be seen.

Hiking

Just 3km from the entrance gate, the **Senda Pampa Alta** (5km) heads up a hill, passing a beaver dam along the way. Views from the top are impressive. A quick 300m further leads to a *senda* (trail) paralleling the Río Pipo and some waterfalls. A more popular saunter is along the **Senda Costera** (6.5km), accessed from the end of the Bahía Ensenada road. This trail meanders along the bay, once home to Yamaná. Keep an eye out for shell middens, now covered in grass. The trail ends at the road, which leads 1.2km further to the **Senda Hito XXIV** (5km), a level trail through lenga forest along the northern shore of Lago Roca; this trail terminates at an unimposing Argentine–Chilean border marker. **Senda Cerro Guanaco** (8km) starts at the same trailhead, but climbs up a 970m hill to reach a great viewpoint.

After running 3242km from Buenos Aires, RN 3 takes its southern bow at gorgeous Bahía Lapataia. **Mirador Lapataia** (1km), connecting with **Senda Del Turbal** (2km), winds through lenga forest to access this highway terminus. Other walks in this section include the self-guided nature trail **Senda Laguna Negra** (950m), through peat bogs, and the **Senda**

Castorera (800m), along which beaver dams, and possibly beavers themselves, can be spotted in the ponds.

Sleeping & Eating

Campgrounds are the only lodging in the park. Most are free, lack services, and get crowded, which means sites can and do get filthy. Camping Ensenada is 16km from the entrance and nearest the Costera trail; Camping Río Pipo is 6km from the entrance and easily accessed by either the road to Cañadon del Toro or by the Pampa Alta trail. Camping Las Bandurrias, Camping Laguna Verde and Camping Los Cauquenes are on the islands in Río Lapataia.

The only fee-based campground, 9km from the entrance, is **Camping Lago Roca** (per person with shower US$3). It's also the only one that has hot showers, a good *confitería* and a tiny (expensive) grocery. However, there's plenty of room in the park to rough it at wild sites. Note that water at Lago Roca is not potable; boil it before using.

Getting There & Away

Buses leave from the corner of Maipú and 25 de Mayo in Ushuaia several times daily from 9am to 6pm, returning approximately every two hours between 8am to 8pm. Depending on your destination, a roundtrip fare runs US$6 to US$8, and you need not return the same day. Taxi fares shared between groups can be the same price as bus tickets.

The most touristy – and possibly the slowest – way to get to the park is via **El Tren del Fin de Mundo** (☎ 431600; www.trendelfindemundo.com .ar; one way/roundtrip US$16/17), which departs from the Estación del Fin de Mundo, 8km west of Ushuaia, three or four times daily in summer and once or twice in winter. Nontrain aficionados prefer to take the ride one way and return via minibus.

Hitching to the park is feasible, but many cars will already be packed.

ESTANCIA HARBERTON

Historic **Estancia Harberton** (☎ 422742; www.estanciaharberton.com; admission US$5; ◷ 10am-7pm Oct 15-Apr 15) was founded in 1886 by Thomas Bridges and family. It was Tierra del Fuego's first *estancia* and thus contains the island's oldest house. Bridges' son Lucas made the location famous in his memoir of life among the Yahgan, *The Uttermost Part of the Earth*.

It's now owned and run by the Goodalls, direct descendents of the Bridges.

Harberton is a working station, although only a few thousand sheep remain on 20,000 hectares. The location is splendid and the history alluring. A one-hour **guided tour** takes in the family cemetery and a garden where foliage names are given in Yahgan, Selk'nam and Spanish. There's also tea service (US$4), complete lunch (US$10), optional excursions to the Reserva Yecapasela penguin colony and a replica of a Yahgan dwelling.

Worth the trip is the impressive **Museo Acatushún** (www.acatushun.com; admission US$1.65), created by Natalie Prosser Goodall, a North American biologist who married into the family. Emphasizing the region's marine mammals, the museum has thousands of mammal and bird specimens inventoried; among the rarest specimens is a Hector's beaked whale. Much of this vast inventory was found at Bahía San Sebastián, north of Río Grande, where an up to 11km difference between high and low tide leaves animals stranded.

With advance permission, free primitive camping is allowed at Río Lasifashaj, Río Varela and Río Cambaceres. Lodging is offered in the 1950 Shepards' house and remodeled 1901 Cook house for US$60 to US$80 per person per day with breakfast, or an extra US$30 for full board.

Harberton is 85km east of Ushuaia via RN 3 and rough RC-j, a 1½ to 2-hour drive one way. Shuttles leave from the base of 25 de Mayo at Av Maipú in Ushuaia at 9am, returning around 3pm (US$15 roundtrip). Daylong catamaran tours organized by agencies in Ushuaia cost around US$45.

PUERTO WILLIAMS (CHILE)

☎ 61 / pop 2250

Somewhere along the way, the Chilean settlement of Puerto Williams got overlooked in all of Ushuaia's 'end of the world' hype. But anyone who visits this outpost will soon know which place can truly lay claim to the title. On Isla Navarino, across the Beagle Channel from Argentine Tierra del Fuego, the sleepy naval settlement isn't much to look at: sterile gray military barracks, prefabricated shiplap houses with white picket fences and makeshift corrugated iron dwellings, with horses grazing in yards along gravel streets.

The village centers around a freshly sodded green roundabout and a concrete slab plaza called the Centro Comercial. But above, below and beyond Puerto Williams is some of the Southern Cone's most breathtaking scenery. Within minutes of town you can be deep in lenga and ñire forests festooned with old man's beard. Trails lead past beaver dams, bunkers and army trenches as they climb steeply up into the mountains and deeper into forests. It's the easygoing townspeople that make this one of the most endearing places in Tierra del Fuego.

Mid-19th-century missionaries and then fortune-seekers during the 1890s gold rush established a permanent European presence here. Nowadays it's an official port of entry for yachts bound for Cape Horn and Antarctica.

Information

Near the main roundabout, the Centro Comercial has the post office, Internet (US$2.50 an hour), DAP airline's representative and a couple of call centers. Money exchange (US cash only, US$100 minimum) and Visa advances are possible at Banco de Chile, where the ATM is only accessible from 10am to 2pm. Most shops accept US dollars at decent rates.

Friendly Wolf at **Turismo SIM** (☎ 621150/062; www.simltd.com; Austral 74) has details about the rampant sailing, trekking and expedition possibilities south of the 54th parallel, including Cape Horn, the Cordillera Darwin, Isla Navarino, the South Georgia Islands and the Antarctic Peninsula. The **municipalidad** (☎ 621011; www.municipalidadcabode hornos.cl in Spanish; O'Higgins 165) runs a rarely staffed tourist **info kiosk** (☎ 621012) at the roundabout.

Sights & Activities

Near the entrance to the military quarters is the original bow of the *Yelcho*, which rescued Ernest Shackleton's Antarctic expedition from Elephant Island in 1916.

The free **Museo Martín Gusinde** (☎ 621043; cnr Araguay & Gusinde; donation requested; ⏱ 9am-1pm & 2:30-7pm Mon-Fri, 2:30-6:30pm Sat & Sun), honoring the German priest and ethnographer who worked among the Yahgans from 1918 to 1923, focuses on ethnography and natural history.

A 15-minute walk east of town along the waterfront in the settlement of Villa Ukika, **Kipa-Akar** (House of Woman) is a crafts shop

housed in a Yamaná dwelling that features traditional construction and handicraft demonstrations; it's open mostly when boats are in port.

Omora (www.omora.org), which is Latin America's southernmost ethnobotanical park, has trails showing regional foliage described in Yamaná, Latin and Spanish. Take the road to the right of the Virgin altar 4km (an hour) toward Puerto Navarino. Donations help advocate for the creation of a Cape Horn Biosphere Reserve.

A superb lookout point (four hours roundtrip), **Cerro Bandera** can be reached via the beginning of the Dientes Circuit. The trail ascends steeply through the mossy forest to sparse alpine terrain and great vistas. For details on trekking possibilities, refer to Lonely Planet's *Trekking in the Patagonian Andes*.

Many local lodgings can arrange tours of the island. For yacht tours to Antarctica and around the Beagle Channel, as well as trekking, climbing and riding expeditions, contact Turismo SIM.

Sleeping

Families sometimes rent out rooms; check with the *municipalidad*. About 3km east of town, the new **Hotel Lakutaia** (www.lakutaia.cl; d around US$100) is scheduled to open in 2005; contact Aerovías DAP (opposite) for details.

Hostal Coirón (☎ 621227; www.simltd.com; Maragano 168; dm US$14) Catering to backpackers, the central Coirón's convivial atmosphere makes it the top choice for swapping globetrekking tales. Three small dorms share a bathroom while the communal kitchen and a large table promote group meals.

Restaurant & Lodging Patagonia (☎ 621075, 621294; pedroortiz@chilesat.net; Yelcho 230; per person with shared bathroom/full pension US$13/23, apt per person with bathroom/full pension US$18/28; ⌨) The salty owner of the Club Naval de Yates Micalvi bar (see the boxed text, opposite) rents out rooms and will cook up a menagerie of wild game (beaver, goose, octopus etc) on request.

Residencial Pusaki (☎ 621020; Piloto Pardo 242; r with shared bathroom US$12) Owners Tano, Pati and sons offer clean, warm rooms in cozy family surroundings.

Eating

Of the few supermarkets, Simon & Simon is the best, with fresher vegies, fast food and great pastries.

Restaurant Cabo de Hornos (☎ 621067, 621232; Maragano 146; mains US$3-8) With views overlooking town, this is the place to try local wild game: beaver, crab, goose, guanaco and rabbit, plus organic salmon, lamb and more traditional Magellanic meats.

Diente de Navarino (☎ 621074; Centro Comercial; mains US$5) The huge 'fisherman's lunch' and beers with dinner will fill you up fast at this rowdy bar-cum-eatery.

Drinking

Throw back a few beers and handfuls of peanuts at **Pingüino Pub** (Centro Commercial) before heading to **Disco Extasis** (Piloto Pardo) on a Friday or Saturday night.

Getting There & Away

Aerovías DAP (☎ 621051; www.dap.cl; Plaza de Ancla s/n) flies to Punta Arenas (US$64) daily except Sunday. DAP flights to Antarctica may make a brief stopover here.

Transborda Broom (www.tabsa.cl) ferries depart Saturdays at 7pm for Punta Arenas (reclining seat/bunk US$120/150 including

---

THE AUTHOR'S CHOICE

Club Naval de Yates Micalvi (drinks US$2-5, sandwiches US$5) Officers down stiff drinks and crab sandwiches at Tierra del Fuego's most atmospheric watering hole, inside a beached 1925 cargo boat at the harbor. Sailors and Antarctic explorers from around the world also hold forth amid souvenirs of former adventurers, vying to outdo one another's tales, which grow louder and grander as the night progresses.

---

meals, 34 to 38 hours); the bunk is worth the extra dollars since passenger berths are small and the reclining Pullman seats not as comfortable as one might wish on such a long trip.

Regular connections between Puerto Williams and Ushuaia, in Argentine Tierra del Fuego, may resume at some point. For the latest scoop, chat up the staff at Club Naval de Yates Micalvi (see the boxed text, above) or Turismo SIM (opposite).

Directory

CONTENTS

ACCOMMODATIONS

Accommodations in Argentina range from campgrounds to five-star luxury hotels, with excellent options in all categories. At the more tourist-oriented hotels, the staff usually speaks a smattering of English, though at more provincial accommodations you'll need to learn the Spanish basics.

All but the cheapest hotels have private bathrooms, and most hotels include breakfast – usually *medialunas* (croissants) and weak coffee or tea – in the price. Generally, assume both are included as you flip through listings in this book. Many hotels provide temporary luggage storage for travelers with late afternoon or evening flights or bus trips.

Some hotels, particularly pricier hotels in tourist hotspots such as Patagonia, operate on a two-tier price system, charging foreigners more than nationals.

For long-term rentals in the capital, see p91. Note that you can extend a stay at practically any hotel in any city for a discounted price. Make sure to negotiate this *before* you begin your stay.

Prices

Throughout this book, accommodations are generally categorized by price: budget (up to US$15 per double), midrange (up to $50 per double), and top end (over US$50 per double). Even in Buenos Aires you can land outstanding accommodations for under US$50, and throughout the country, US$20 will buy you a comfortable double room. Hostels outside Buenos Aires rarely charge more than US$6 per bed, usually around US$4 to US$5.

Accommodations prices in this book, to the best of our knowledge, all include tax and are high-season rates. Budget and midrange hotels almost always include taxes when quoting their prices. If you're inquiring on your own into a top-end hotel, however, be sure to ask; pricier hotels often quote fares before tax – a whopping 21%! High season is generally July and August (except in Patagonia), Semana Santa (Easter week) and January and February. Outside these times, prices can drop upwards of 40% from the rates quoted in this book.

Camping & Refugios

Camping can be one of the most splendid ways to experience Argentina, particularly the Lake District and Patagonia, where there are countless outstanding campgrounds. Nearly every Argentine city or town has fairly centralized municipal campgrounds, where you can pitch a tent for under US$3 per night and sometimes for free; these are hit-and-miss, sometimes delightfully woodsy, sometimes crowded and ugly. Free sites are often excellent, especially in the Lake District, though they lack facilities.

Private sites usually have excellent facilities: hot showers, toilets, laundry, a barbecue for grilling, a restaurant or *confitería* (café), a grocery store, and sometimes even a swimming pool. Personal possessions are generally secure, since attendants keep a watchful eye on the grounds, but don't leave anything lying around unnecessarily.

For comfort, invest in a good, dome-style tent with a rain-fly before coming to South America, where camping equipment is costlier and often inferior. A three-season sleeping bag should be adequate for almost any weather. A good petrol- or kerosene-burning stove is also a good idea, since white gas *(bencina)* is expensive and available only at chemical-supply shops or hardware stores. Bring mosquito repellent, since many campgrounds are near rivers or lakes.

There are, of course, opportunities for more rugged camping in the national parks and the backcountry. Some parks have *refugios,* basic shelters for hikers in the high country that are usually free, have some sort of cooking facilities and are filled with saggy but welcome bunks.

Estancias

An increasingly popular way of passing an Argentine vacation is to stay at an *estancia* (ranch, often called *fincas* in the northwest). Especially common in the area around Buenos Aires and throughout Patagonia, they can be an amazing way to spend some time in remote areas. In the Lake District and Patagonia, they're often geared toward fishers. Costs per day at the more established *estancias* can exceed US$100, including room, board and some activities. Tourist offices generally offer complete listings.

Hospedajes, Pensiones & Residenciales

These are Argentina's cheapest accommodations, and the differences among them are sometimes ambiguous; all may even be called hotels. Rooms and furnishings are modest and usually clean, and there are often a few rooms with shared bathrooms (if you're after something even cheaper).

An *hospedaje* is usually a large family home with a few extra bedrooms (the bathroom is shared). Similarly, a *pensión* offers short-term accommodations in a family home but may also have permanent lodgers. Meals may be available.

PRACTICALITIES

- Argentina uses the metric system for weights and measures.

- Electrical current is 220 volts, 50 cycles, and there are two types of electric plugs: either with two rounded prongs or with three angled flat prongs. Adapters from one to the other are available.

- Buenos Aires' two leading daily newspapers, available throughout Argentina, are *Clarín* and *La Nación.* The outstanding English-language daily *Buenos Aires Herald* covers Argentina and the world from an international perspective and is available in most of the large cities. Also see p71.

- In Buenos Aires, tune into FM 92.7 for 24-hour tango or FM 92.3 for Argentine *folklore* (folk music).

- In Argentine addresses, the word *'local'* refers to a suite or office. If an address has 's/n,' short for *sin numero* (without number), the address has no street number.

Residenciales figure more commonly in tourist-office lists. In general, they occupy buildings designed for short-stay accommodations, although some (known euphemistically as *albergues transitorios*) cater to clientele who intend only *very* short stays of two hours maximum. Prostitutes occasionally use them, but so do young Argentine couples with no other indoor alternative.

Hostels

Hostels are sprouting up throughout Argentina like grass in the Pampas, and nearly every town with tourist appeal has one. Most are excellent places to stay, where you can meet and hang out with fellow travelers, get great travel advice and enjoy one of the fun *asados* (traditional Argentine barbecues) that are practically de rigueur. All have common kitchens and living spaces, as well as shared bathrooms, and many have at least one private double. What's more, most hostels are run by an enthusiastic, conscientious staff with its finger on the pulse of Argentine travel, meaning few establishments in all of Argentina are as helpful in finding out the best places to visit. But remember that Argentines are night owls and hostellers tend to follow suit, so earplugs can be handy indeed.

Card-carrying HI members will save a nominal US$0.30 to US$1.50 on a bed at HI facilities. Most hostels, however, are private.

There are some excellent online resources, including **Argentina Hostelling International** (www.hostels.org.ar), **Hostel World** (www.hostelworld .com) and **Argentina Top Hostels** (www.hostelsar.com .ar). All three allow you to book online.

Hotels

Proper hotels vary from utilitarian one-star accommodations to five-star luxury. However, many one-star places are better value than three- and four-star lodgings. In general, hotels provide a room with private bathroom, often a telephone, and usually a TV. Normally they have a *confitería* or restaurant and almost always include breakfast in the price. In the top categories you will have room and laundry service, a swimming pool and perhaps a gym, a bar, shopping galleries and other luxuries.

Rentals & Homestays

House and apartment rentals can save you money if you're staying in one place for an extended period. In resort locations, such as Mar del Plata or Bariloche, you can lodge several people for the price of one by seeking an apartment and cooking your own meals. Check tourist offices or newspapers for listings.

During the tourist season, mostly in the interior, families rent rooms to visitors. Often these are excellent bargains, permitting access to cooking and laundry facilities and hot showers, as well as encouraging contact with Argentines. Tourist offices in most smaller towns, but even in cities as large as Salta and Mendoza, maintain lists of such accommodations.

ACTIVITIES

Argentina has a cornucopia of outdoor activities, offering everything from trekking in the Lake District and Patagonia, mountaineering in Mendoza and San Juan, to snow sports, cycling and fishing.

Cycling

Cycling has become a popular activity, and geared-out Argentine cyclists are a common site on the road. Both road and mountain bikes are common, but the latter are indispensable for riding on bad roads in remote areas. The best areas for relatively scenic spins are Mendoza and the Lake District (especially the Siete Lagos route; p329), though desolate Patagonian gravel roads attract hardy mountain bikers willing to put up with the often insanely strong winds. Many towns and cities, especially those catering to the tourist trade, have places where you can rent bicycles, though quality is often dubious.

There are many good road routes for bicycling, especially around the Lake District and in the Andean Northwest; the highway from Tucumán to Tafí del Valle, the direct road from Salta to Jujuy, and the Quebrada de Cafayate would be exceptionally beautiful rides on generally good surfaces.

For more information, see p477.

Fishing

Patagonia and the Lake District together constitute one of the world's premier fly-fishing destinations, where introduced trout species (brown, brook, lake and rainbow) and landlocked Atlantic salmon reach massive sizes in cold rivers surrounded by spectacular scenery. Native species, which should *always* be thrown back, are generally smaller and include perca (perch), puyen, Patagonian pejerrey, and the rare peladilla. Fishing is almost always mandatory catch and release. In the Lake District, Junín de los Andes (p325) is the self-proclaimed trout capital of Argentina; lining up a guide there to take you to Parque Nacional Lanín's superb trout streams is easy. Nearby Aluminé (p324) sits on the banks of the Río Aluminé, one of the country's most highly regarded trout streams. Bariloche (p339) is another excellent base. Further south, Parque Nacional Los Alerces (p398) has outstanding lakes and rivers, and there's even superb fishing as far south as Tierra del Fuego.

In subtropical Northeast Argentina (p150), the wide Río Paraná attracts spin fishers and trollers (heaven forbid) from around the world, who pull in massive river species such as sábalo, surubí and dorado.

Fishing licenses are required everywhere and are available at tackle shops, the local *club de caza y pesca* (hunting and fishing club) and sometimes at tourist offices and

YPF (gas) stations. For most of the country, prices are US$7 per day, US$50 per week and US$67 for the season. Trolling fees cost extra. In Tierra del Fuego, prices are higher. You must pay the regular fees mentioned here, plus an additional fee for preferential zones. The priciest of these zones are the Río Grande and Río Menendez areas, which cost foreigners an additional US$33 per day, US$67 for one to two weeks and US$133 for the season.

In the Lake District and Patagonia, the season runs November to mid-April, while in the northeast the season runs February to October.

The **Asociación de Guías Profesionales de Pesca del Parque Nacional Nahuel Huapi y Patagonia Norte** (www.guiaspatagonicos.com.ar in Spanish) maintains a list of licensed guides for northern Patagonia and the Lake District.

Hiking & Trekking

Argentina's vast open spaces offer plenty of wilderness walks. The most scenic areas – with plenty of water and vegetation – are the southern Andean national parks along the Chilean border, from Parque Nacional Lanín (p331) at the northern tip of the Lake District, to Parque Nacional Los Glaciares (p410) toward the south. Tierra del Fuego (p438) also offers some superb hiking. The high Andean reaches west of Mendoza (p288) are better for climbing high peaks, but there's some great trekking in the area as well. The northern Andes around the Quebrada de Humahuaca (p219) are also good, and the gentle Central Sierras (p274) offers something off the beaten track.

See Lonely Planet's *Trekking in the Patagonian Andes* for more information on southern Andean walks.

Mountaineering

The Andes are a mountain climber's dream, especially in San Juan and Mendoza provinces, where the highest peaks are found. While the most famous climb is Aconcagua (p301), the highest peak in the Americas, there are plenty of others in the Andes – many of them more interesting and far more technical. Near Barreal in San Juan province (p313), the Cordón de la Rameda boasts five peaks over 6000m high, including the mammoth Cerro Mercedario which tops out at 6770m. The region is less congested than

Aconcagua, offers more technical climbs and is preferred by many climbers. Also near here is the majestic Cordillera de Ansilta (p313), with seven peaks scraping the sky at altitudes between 5130m and 5885m.

The magnificent Fitz Roy Range (p405), in southern Patagonia, is another popular area, as are the mountains of Parque Nacional Nahuel Huapi (p345), around Bariloche.

Skiing

Although surprisingly little-known to outsiders, Argentine skiing can be outstanding. Most locations offer super powder, good cover and plenty of sunny days. Many resorts have large ski schools with instructors from all over the world, so even language is not a problem. At some of the older resorts equipment can be a little antiquated, but in general the quality of skiing more than compensates.

There are three main areas where skiers can indulge themselves: the Mendoza region, featuring Las Leñas (which has the best snow and longest runs in the country; p308) and Los Molles near Malargüe (p308); the Lakes District, including Cerro Catedral near Bariloche (which has the best views in the country; see p346) and Chapelco near San Martín de los Andes (p331); and the world's most southerly commercial skiing near Ushuaia in Tierra del Fuego (see p448). The ski season generally runs mid-June to mid-October.

White-Water Rafting & Kayaking

This increasingly popular activity takes place on the rivers that descend from the Andean divide, from San Luis and Mendoza on south. The main possibilities are the Río Mendoza and Río Diamante in the Mendoza region (see p292), the Río Hua Hum and Río Meliquina near San Martín de los Andes (see p329), and the Río Limay and Río Manso near Bariloche (see p339). Some of these, most notably the Limay, are gentle Class II floats, but most of the rest are Class III-plus white water.

Wind Sports

Paragliding is popular in Argentina and it's a great place to take tandem flights or instruction. Why? Firstly because it's so affordable here (a 30-minute tandem flight will set you back about US$35) and secondly because there are some outstanding places to do it. Many agencies in Bariloche (p340) offer paragliding, and views are superb. Perhaps the best place of all, however, is La Cumbre (p276), in Cordoba's Central Sierras.

Dique Cuesta del Viento (literally 'slope of the wind reservoir'; p315), near Rodeo in San Juan province, is one of the world's best windsurfing and kite-surfing destinations. Its consistent and extremely powerful wind blows every afternoon from October to early May, attracting folks from around the world. Nearby, in Parque Nacional El Leoncito (p315), the Pampa del Leoncito has become the epicenter of *carrovelismo* (land sailing), where people zip across the dry lake bed beneath Andean peaks in sail cars. If you're interested, head to Barreal (p313).

BUSINESS HOURS

Traditionally, business hours in Argentina commence by 8am and break at midday siesta (rest) for three or even four hours, during which people return home for lunch and a brief nap. After siesta, shops reopen until 8pm or 9pm. This schedule is still common in the provinces, but government offices and many businesses in Buenos Aires have adopted a more conventional 8am to 5pm schedule in the interests of 'greater efficiency.' For typical business hours of specific types of businesses, see inside the front cover.

CHILDREN

Argentina is extremely child-friendly in terms of safety, health, people's attitudes and family-oriented activities, although there are regional differences. Numerous plazas and public parks, many with playgrounds, are safe and popular gathering spots for families.

Argentines are very helpful on public transport. Often someone will give up a seat for a parent and child, but if that does not occur, an older person may offer to put the child on his or her lap. This is also a country where people frequently touch each other, so your children may be patted on the head or gently caressed.

Basic restaurants provide a wide selection of food suitable for children (vegetables, pasta, meat, chicken, fish), but adult portions are normally so large that small children rarely need a separate order. Waiters are accustomed to providing extra plates and cutlery for children, though some places may add a small additional charge. Argentina's high-quality ice cream is a special treat.

Breast-feeding in public is not uncommon, though many women are discreet and cover themselves. Poorly maintained public bathrooms may be a concern for some parents. Always carry toilet paper and wet wipes. While a woman may take a young boy into the ladies' room, it would be socially unacceptable for a man to take a girl of any age into the men's room.

CLIMATE CHARTS

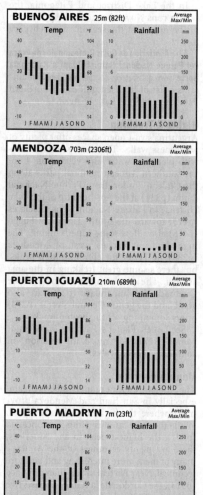

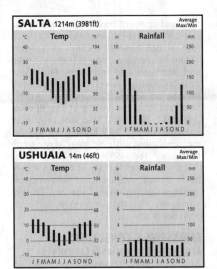

COURSES

Most opportunities for Spanish-language instruction are in Buenos Aires (see p83), though cities such as Mendoza (p293) and Córdoba (p269) are also excellent places to kick-start or hone your Spanish. Córdoba is a city of students, meaning you'll feel right at home going to school, and you'll find plenty of opportunities to set up exchanges with local students.

Small-group instruction or individual tutoring offer the best opportunities for improving language skills, and are affordable options. Ten hours a week of private instruction averages US$70 to US$90 while 20 hours a week will set you back US$125 to US$200. Hourly rates average US$7 to US$10.

CUSTOMS

Argentine officials are generally courteous and reasonable toward tourists. If you cross the border frequently and carry an inordinate amount of electronic equipment (such as cameras or laptop computers), however, you should have a typed list of equipment and serial numbers (get it stamped by authorities while going into the country). A pile of the appropriate purchase receipts might also help.

Depending on where you have been, officials focus on different things. Travelers southbound from the central Andean countries may be searched for drugs, while those

from bordering countries will have fruits and vegetables confiscated. Carrying drugs will pretty much get you into trouble no matter which country you're coming from.

DANGERS & ANNOYANCES

Tell your neighbor Ethel you're off to Argentina, and her eyes get big and, 'Gosh, is it safe down there?' It is. Most people leave Argentina without ever feeling they were in a sketchy situation. The country's flailing economy, however, has put street crime (pickpocketing, bag-snatching and armed robbery) on the rise, especially in Buenos Aires (see p72), but Argentina is still the safest country for travel in South America. This isn't to say you should skip down the street drunk with your money belt strapped to your forehead, but, with a little common sense, you can visit Argentina's big cities as safely as you could London, Paris or New York. In the small towns of the provinces you'd have to *search* for a crook to rob you.

Bus terminals are always full of families both traveling and saying goodbyes, but always keep an eagle eye on your bags. This is especially true in Buenos Aires' Retiro station, where travelers have turned around to find their bags gone.

Kidnappings in Buenos Aires have lately received a lot of press, but these are *rarely* aimed at foreigners. The country's economic downturn has also prompted scattered riots and daily protests in Buenos Aires, so it's wise to be aware of current political events. But generally these have little effect on tourists other than blocking traffic.

Being a pedestrian (which assumes the presence of cars) in Argentina is a different story. Many Argentine drivers jump the gun when the traffic signal is about to change to green, drive extremely fast and change lanes unpredictably. Even though pedestrians at corners and crosswalks have legal right of way (ha!), very few drivers respect this and will hardly slow down when you are crossing. Be especially careful of buses, which can be reckless and, because of their large size, particularly painful.

The police and military have a reputation for being corrupt or irresponsible, but, while a foreign visitor may experience petty harassment (usually to procure payment of a bribe), both are generally helpful and courteous to tourists. If you feel you're being patted down for a bribe, you can respond by tactfully paying up (see p468), or asking the officer to accompany you to the police station to take care of it. The latter may lead the officer to drop it, or lead you in the labyrinthine bureaucracy of the Argentine police system.

Many Argentines are heavy smokers. Prepare yourself to be exposed to tobacco smoke in restaurants, bars, cafés, stores, offices and on the streets. A few restaurants have no-smoking areas. Smoking is prohibited on buses and all domestic flights.

DISABLED TRAVELERS

Travelers with disabilities will find things somewhat difficult. Those in wheelchairs in particular will quickly realize that many cities' narrow, busy and uneven sidewalks are difficult to negotiate. Crossing streets is also a problem, since not every corner has ramps and Argentine drivers don't have much patience for slower pedestrians, disabled or not. Nevertheless, Argentines with disabilities do get around, and in Buenos Aires there exists a few buses described as *piso bajo*, which lower to provide wheelchair lifts.

Most hotels do not have wheelchair-accessible rooms (at least as they're known in other parts of the world), meaning doors are narrow and there is little space to move around inside the room. Bathrooms at midrange and budget hotels are notoriously small, making it difficult for anyone to get around in. For truly accessible rooms, you'll have better luck in pricier hotels.

In Buenos Aires, **Movidisc** (☎ 011-4328-6921; www.movidisc-web.com.ar in Spanish; Av Roque Sáenz Peña 868, 3rd fl) offers private transport and day tours in vans fully equipped for wheelchair users. If you're taking a tour with another agency, Movidisc can provide transport alone, provided you ask your tour company to arrange it with Movidisc.

Also check out the following organizations online, all of which offer countless links to other resources.

accesible.com (www.accesible.com)
Access-able Travel Source (www.access-able.com)
Mobility International (www.miusa.org)
National Information Communication Awareness Network (www.nican.com.au)

DISCOUNT CARDS

The International Student Identity Card (ISIC), available for US$11 through the student and discount travel agency **Asatej** (Map pp64-7; ☎ 011-4114-7500; www.asatej.net; Florida 835, Room 320, 3rd fl, Buenos Aires), can help travelers obtain discounts on public transportation and admissions to museums. Often any official-looking university identification may be an acceptable substitute. An HI card, available for US$14 at the **HI office** (Map pp64-7; ☎ 011-4511-8712; www.hostels.org.ar; Florida 835, Room 319, 3rd fl, Buenos Aires), will get you small discounts on your stay at any HI facility (see p459).

Travelers over the age of 60 can sometimes obtain senior-citizen discounts on museum admissions and the like. Usually a passport with date of birth is sufficient evidence of age.

EMBASSIES & CONSULATES
Argentine Embassies & Consulates

Argentina has diplomatic representation throughout Latin America, North America, Western Europe and Australia.

Australia ACT (☎ 02-6273 9111; www.argentina.org.au; John McEwen House, Level 2/7 National Cct, ACT 2600); Sydney (☎ 02-9262 2933; 44 Market St, Level 20, NSW 2000)

Bolivia La Paz (☎ 02-241-7737; Calle Aspiazu 497, Casilla 64, La Paz)

Brazil Foz do Iguaçu (☎ 045-574-2969; Travessa Eduardo Bianchi 26); Rio de Janeiro (☎ 021-2553-1646/1459/1568; Praia de Botafogo 228, SL 201); São Paulo (☎ 011-3897-9522; www.embarg.org.br; Paulista 2313, sobreloja)

Canada Montreal (☎ 514-842-6582; www.consargenmtl.com; 2000 Peel St, Suite 600, Quebec H3A 2W5); Ottawa (☎ 613-236-2351; www.argentina-canada.net; 90 Sparks St, Suite 910, Ontario K1P 5B4)

Chile Puerto Montt (☎ 65-253996; cpmon@entelchile.net; Av Pedro Montt 160); Punta Arenas (☎ 61-261912; congen ecaren@yahoo.com.ar; 21 de Mayo 1878); Santiago (☎ 02-582-2500; www.embargentina.cl; Calle Miraflores 285)

France Paris (☎ 01 45 53 33 00; 6 rue Cimarosa, 75116 Paris)

Germany Berlin (☎ 030-226689; Kleiststrasse 23-26, 4 Stock, 10787); Bonn (☎ 0228-228010; Robert-Koch-Str 104, 53127)

Ireland Dublin (☎ 01-269 1546; 15 Ailesbury Dr, Ballsbridge)

Netherlands The Hague (☎ 70-365 48 36; Javastraat 20, An Den Haag)

New Zealand Wellington (☎ 04-472 8330; www.arg.org.nz; Level 14/142 Lambton Quay, PO Box 5430 Wellington)

Paraguay Asunción (☎ 021-212320; www.embajada-argentina.org.py; cnr España & Boquerón); Encarnación (☎ 071-201066; cenca@itacom.com.py; Artigas 960)

UK London (☎ 020-584 6494; www.argentine-embassy
-uk.org; 65 Brook St, London W1K 4AH)

Uruguay Montevideo (☎ 02-902-8166; emb-uruguay
.mrecic.gov.ar/index1.html; Cuareim 1470); Punta del Este
(☎ 042-441632; Calle 25 544; ☽ 15 Dec-15 Mar)

USA Chicago (☎ 312-819-2610/04; hrgcchic@aol.com; 205
N Michigan Ave, Suite 4209, IL 60601); Houston (☎ 713-871-
8935; chous_ar@hotmail.com; 3050 Post Oak Blvd, Suite
1625, TX 77056); Los Angeles (☎ 213-954-9155; www.con
suladoargentino-losangeles.org; 5055 Wilshire Blvd, Suite
210, CA 90036); Miami (☎ 305-373-1889/7794; www.con
suladoargentinoenmiami.org; 800 Brickell Ave, Penthouse 1,
FL 33131); New York (☎ 212-603-0400/03; www.congen
argentinany.com; 12 W 56th St, NY 10019); Washington, DC
(☎ 202-238-6460/6400; www.embajadaargentinaeeuu
.org; 1600 New Hampshire Av, 20009)

Embassies & Consulates in Argentina

Following is a list of embassies and consul-
ates in Buenos Aires. Some countries have
both an embassy and a consulate here, but
only the most central location is listed. Diplomatic offices in other Argentine cities are
listed after their respective name.

Australia Buenos Aires (Map pp68-9; ☎ 011-4779-3500;
Villanueva 1400, Palermo)

Bolivia Buenos Aires (Map pp64-7; ☎ 011-4381-0539;
Av Belgrano 1670, 1st fl, Montserrat); Jujuy (Map p214;
☎ 0388-424-0501; Independencia 1098; ☽ 9am-1pm
Mon-Fri); La Quiaca (☎ 0388-422 283; C Rep Arabe
Siria 531; ☽ 7am-6:30pm Mon-Fri); Salta (Map p224;
☎ 0387-421-1040; Mariano Boedo 34, Salta; ☽ 9am-2pm
Mon-Fri); Tucumán (off Map p240; ☎ 0381-425-2224; Av
Aconquila 1117)

Brazil Buenos Aires (Map pp64-7; ☎ 011-4515-6500,
011-4394-5264; Carlos Pellegrini 1363, 5th fl, Retiro); Paso
de los Libres (☎ 03772-425411; Plaza Independencia at
Mitre 842); Puerto Iguazú (Map p194; ☎ 03757-421348;
Córdoba 264)

Canada Buenos Aires (Map pp68-9; ☎ 011-4808-1000;
Tagle 2828, Palermo)

Chile Buenos Aires (Map pp64-7; ☎ 011-4394-6582;
San Martín 439, 9th fl, San Nicolás); Bariloche (Map p338;
☎ 02944-423050; Av Juan Manuel de Rosas 180); Esquel
(Map p391; ☎ 02945-451189; Molinari 754); Jujuy (off
Map p214; ☎ 0388-424-0905; Pacarú 50, Los Perales;
☽ call for appointment); Mendoza (off Map pp290-1;
☎ 0261-425-4844; Paso de los Andes 1147); Neuquén
(Map p321; ☎ 0299-442-2727; La Rioja 241); Río Gallegos
(Map p386; ☎ 02966-422364; Mariano Moreno 148); Salta
(Map p224; ☎ 0387-431-1857; Santiago del Estero 965;
☽ 8am-1pm Mon-Fri); Ushuaia (Map p446; ☎ 02901-
430909; Jainén 50) The Ushuaia branch is southwest of town.

France Buenos Aires (Map pp64-7; ☎ 011-4312-2409;
Santa Fe 846, 4th fl, Retiro); Mendoza (off Map pp290-1;

☎ 0261-423-1542; Av Houssay 790); Salta (Map p224;
☎ 0387-431-4726; Santa Fe 156; ☽ 8:30-9:30pm
Mon & Wed); Tucumán (Map p240; ☎ 0381-421-8202;
Crisóstomo Álvarez 471; ☽ 6:30pm Mon & Fri only,
appointment necessary)

Germany Buenos Aires (Map pp68-9; ☎ 011-4778-2500;
Villanueva 1055, Palermo); Mendoza (Map pp290-1;
☎ 0261-429-6539; Montevideo 127, 1st fl, No 6); Posadas
(Map p185; ☎ 03752-435508; Junín 1811, 1st fl; ☽ 8am-
noon Mon-Fri); Salta (Map p224; ☎ 0387-421-6525; Urquiza
409; ☽ 9-11am Mon, Wed & Fri); Tucumán (off Map p240;
☎ 0381-424-2730; 9 de Julio 1042; ☽ 4-8pm Mon & Wed)

Israel Buenos Aires (Map pp64-7; ☎ 011-4338-2500;
Av de Mayo 701, 10th fl, Montserrat); Mendoza (off Map
pp290-1; ☎ 0261-428-2140; Lamadrid 738)

Italy Buenos Aires (Map pp64-7; ☎ 011-4816-6132;
Marcelo T de Alvear 1125, Retiro); Mendoza (Map pp290-1;
☎ 0261-423-1640; Necochea 712); Salta (Map p224;
☎ 0387-431-4455; Santiago del Estero 497); Tucumán
(Map p240; ☎ 0381-422-3830; fax 0381-431-0423; San
Martín 623, 5th fl; ☽ 9:30am-5pm Tue)

Japan Buenos Aires (Map pp64-7; ☎ 011-4318-8200;
Bouchard 547, 17th fl, Microcentro)

Netherlands Buenos Aires (☎ 011-4338-0050; Olga
Cossenttini 831, 3rd fl, Edificio Porteño II, Puerto Madero)

Paraguay Buenos Aires (Map pp64-7; ☎ 011-4815-
9801; Viamonte 1851, Balvanera); Corrientes (☎ 03783-
426576; Córdoba 969); Posadas (Map p185; ☎ 03752-
423858; San Lorenzo 179)

Peru Buenos Aires (Map pp64-7; ☎ 011-4334-0970;
Florida 165, Galería Güemes, 2nd fl) Enter from Bartolome
Mitre.

Spain Buenos Aires (Map pp64-7; ☎ 011-4811-0070;
Guido 1760, Recoleta); Mendoza (off Map pp290-1;
☎ 0261-420-2252; Agustín Alvarez 455); Río Gallegos
(Casa España; Map p386; ☎ 02966-422131; Av Roca 866);
Tucumán (off Map p240; ☎ 0381-435-3042; Mate de Luna
4107; ☽ 9am-noon Mon, Tue, Thu & Fri)

UK Buenos Aires (Map pp64-7; ☎ 011-4808-2000; Dr Luis
Agote 2412, Palermo)

Uruguay Buenos Aires (Map pp64-7; ☎ 011-4807-3032;
Av Las Heras 1915, Recoleta); Colón (☎ 03447-421999; San
Martín 417; ☽ 8am-2pm Mon-Fri) Concordia (Map p180;
☎ 0345-421-0380; Pellegrini 709); Gualeguaychú (Map
p175; ☎ 03446-426168; Rivadavia 510)

USA Buenos Aires (Map pp68-9; ☎ 011-5777-4533;
Colombia 4300, Palermo)

Consulates in Neighboring Countries

Argentina Foz do Iguaçu, Brazil (Map p197; ☎ 574-
2969; Travessa Eduardo Bianchi 26; ☽ 9:30am-2pm
Mon-Fri); Punta Arenas, Chile (Map p418; ☎ 261532,
261912; 21 de Mayo 1878); Villazón, Bolivia (☎ 0591-
2597; cnr Av República Argentina & Calle Río, Villazón;
☽ 9am-1pm Mon-Fri)

Italy Punta Arenas, Chile (Map p418; ☎ 221596; 21 de Mayo 1569)

Netherlands Punta Arenas, Chile (Map p418; ☎ 248100; Magallanes 435)

Spain Punta Arenas, Chile (Map p418; ☎ 213563, 239977; Ibañez 05730)

UK Punta Arenas, Chile (Map p418; ☎ 239880; reesking@tie.cl; Catarata del Niágara 01325 cnr Av Roca) Also at Antartida 21 travel agency.

FESTIVALS & EVENTS

Argentina is less prone to wild festivals than other South American countries, but there are several fiestas well worth catching if you're around when they're on. For a list of national public holidays, see opposite.

January
Festival Nacional del Folklore In the Central Sierras near Córdoba, the town of Cosquín hosts the National Festival of Folk Music (p274) during the last week of January.

February/March
Buenos Aires Tango (www.festivaldetango.com.ar) During the last week of February and first week of March, Buenos Aires celebrates its native dance with masterful performances shown at different venues all over the city.

Carnaval Though the pre-Lenten festival is not as rockin' in Argentina as it is in Brazil, the celebration is rowdy in the northeast, especially in the cities of Gualeguaychú (p175) and Corrientes (p168). Dates vary around the end of February and beginning of March.

Fiesta Nacional de la Vendimia (www.vendimia .mendoza.gov.ar in Spanish) Mendoza's National Wine Harvest Festival (p293) kicks off with parades, folkloric events and a royal coronation – all in honor of Mendoza's intoxicating beverage. Takes place in Mendoza city around the end of February/beginning of March.

May
Día de Virgen of Luján (May 8) Large numbers of believers arrive in Luján (p120) to honor the Virgin Mary; other large pilgrimages to Luján take place in early October and on December 8.

October
Fiesta Nacional de la Cerveza/Oktoberfest (http://elsitiodelavilla.com/oktoberfest in Spanish) Join the swillers and oompa bands at the National Beer Festival, Villa General Belgrano's Oktoberfest (p280) in the Central Sierras. Takes place in the first two weeks of October.

Eisteddfod This lively Welsh festival, featuring plentiful grub and choral singing, takes place in late October in Trelew (p370) and Trevelin (p397).

November
Día de la Tradición (November 10) The Day of Traditional Culture festival kicks off with a salute to the gaucho and is especially significant in San Antonio de Areco (p124), the most gaucho of towns. Also important in San José de Jáchal (p315).

FOOD

For a mouthwatering idea of all the food you can eat while traveling in Argentina, see p52. In the Eating sections in this book, our favorites are always listed first. In larger cities such as Buenos Aires, sections are organized by neighborhood. Generally, you can eat extremely well on little money. In a budget restaurant, expect to pay less than US$2 for a filling meal. You can eat well in midrange restaurants and pay less than US$8, including wine or beer, while a top-end restaurant will set you back US$20 or so including a great bottle of wine, appetizer, dessert and a (hopefully) delicious main course. We price restaurants by 'mains' or 'meals;' the former refers to the price of a main course, the latter to that of a full meal.

GAY & LESBIAN TRAVELERS

Argentina is a strongly Catholic country, but there active gay and lesbian scenes in Buenos Aires. Argentine men are more physically demonstrative than their North American and European counterparts, so behaviors such as kissing on the cheek in greeting or a vigorous embrace are innocuous even to those who express unease with homosexuals. Lesbians walking hand in hand should attract little attention, since heterosexual Argentine women frequently do so, but this would be very conspicuous behavior for males. When in doubt, it's best to be discreet.

For gay-oriented activities in Buenos Aires, check out the **Gay Guide** (Buenos Aires ☎ 011-4833-1332; www.thegayguide.com.ar). **Pride Travel** (Map pp64-7; ☎ 011-5218-6556; www.pride-travel.com; Paraguay 523, Room 2E) is a gay-oriented travel agency in the capital which helps arrange short- or long-term stays in Buenos Aires. For much more on what's gay in Buenos Aires, see the boxed text on p85. Also check out the following websites:

Gayscape (www.gayscape.com) Loads of links on the Argentina page.

Global Gayz.com (www.globalgayz.com) Has a South America section full of news, tips and links about gay travel in the region, with a small section on Argentina.

International Lesbian and Gay Association (ILGA; www.ilga.org) Click 'Countries' and find the Argentina page for excellent news and information. Also links to international lesbian, gay and transgender organizations.

Mundo Gay (www.mundogay.com in Spanish) Excellent online publication out of Buenos Aires; don't miss the M@g@zine.

HOLIDAYS

Government offices and businesses are closed on the numerous public holidays. If the holiday falls on a midweek day or weekend day, it's often bumped to the nearest Monday. Public transport options are also more limited and fill up fast. The following list does not include provincial holidays, which may vary considerably. For Argentina's best festivals and events, see opposite.

New Year's Day January 1.

Semana Santa (Easter week) March/April, dates vary; most businesses close on Good Friday; major travel week.

Día de las Malvinas April 2; Commemorates the day in 1829 that Argentina claimed military rule over the Islas Malvinas (Falkland Islands).

Labor Day May 1.

Revolución de Mayo May 25; commemorates the 1810 revolution against Spain.

Día de la Bandera (Flag Day) June 20.

Independence Day July 9.

Día de San Martín August 17; marks the anniversary of José de San Martín's death (1778–1850).

Día de la Raza (Columbus Day) October 12.

Día de la Concepción Inmaculada December 8; religious holiday that celebrates the immaculate conception of the Virgin Mary.

Christmas Day December 25.

INSURANCE

In addition to health insurance (p482) and car insurance (p479), a policy that protects baggage and valuables, like cameras and camcorders, is a good idea. Keep your insurance records separate from other possessions in case you have to make a claim.

INTERNET ACCESS

The Internet has struck it big in Argentina, and you'll find at least one Internet café in even the smallest towns. In cities, they seem to occupy every other building, with even the smallest *locutorios* (telephone centers) having a few computers. Rates average US$0.35 per hour in most cities, while in smaller towns where competition is slimmer, they can reach US$1.50 per hour.

Some Spanish keyboards can be a little tricky, especially when trying to find the '@' symbol (or *'arroba'* in Spanish). You can ask the attendant *'¿Cómo se hace arroba?'* If that doesn't work, try holding down the Alt key and typing 64 on the number pad with Number Lock on.

Traveling with a laptop is another great way to stay in touch with life back home, but unless you know what you're doing, it's fraught with potential problems. Remember, the power-supply voltage in Argentina may vary from that at home, though many laptops now have their own internal converters. Otherwise, the best investment is a universal AC adapter for your appliance. Be sure you buy one that's rated for electronics, *not* the standard ones for hairdryers and the like sold at most luggage stores.

Also, your PC-card modem may or may not work once you leave your home country, and you won't know for sure until you try. The safest option is to buy a reputable 'global' modem before you leave home, or to buy a local PC-card modem. The telephone socket in Argentina will probably be different from home, so ensure that you have at least a US RJ-11 telephone adapter that works with your modem. You can almost always find an adapter that will convert from RJ-11 to the local variety. For more info on traveling with a laptop, see www.teleadapt.com.

LEGAL MATTERS

Argentina presently enjoys civilian government, but the police and military both have a reputation for corruption and abuse of power. However, as a tourist it is very unlikely you will ever experience this if you obey the law. Police, however, can demand identification at any moment and for whatever reason. Always carry your documents and always be courteous and cooperative.

The legal drinking age is 18. Though it's not uncommon to see folks drinking beer on the street or in plazas, it's technically illegal to do so. Marijuana is illegal in Argentina and can land you in jail. Cocaine and other substances that are illegal in the US and most European countries are also illegal here. Though constitutionally a person is innocent until proven guilty, people are regularly held for years without a trial. If arrested, you have the constitutional right to a lawyer, a telephone call and to remain silent.

TWO-TIER PRICING

With the devaluation of the peso in 2000, Argentina became a highly affordable destination practically overnight. With the subsequent upswing in tourism, however, the good ol' annoying two-tier pricing system emerged: businesses in certain areas (mostly in Buenos Aires, but also in Patagonia, and parts of the Lake District and the Andean northwest) charge Argentines one price, and foreigners a higher price, regardless of whether they're banking euros, pounds or dollars. While you won't find this everywhere, you will encounter it at museums in Buenos Aires, national parks, the national airline (Aerolíneas Argentinas) and upscale hotels throughout the country.

No Argentine in their right mind would offer a *coima* (bribe) to a police officer. The police do not accept them. However, things are often taken care of on the spot (ahem!) by asking '*¿Con cuanto podemos arreglar este malentendido?*' ('How much to fix up this misunderstanding?') or '*¿Como podemos arreglar esto mas rápido?*' ('What can we do to expedite this situation?').

MAPS

Tourist offices throughout the country will give you free city maps that are good enough for tooling around town.

With offices in nearly every Argentine city, the Automóvil Club Argentino (ACA) publishes regularly updated maps of provinces and cities. Members of foreign automobile clubs can purchase them with a significant 40% discount, bringing the average total to about US$3.

International Travel Maps (www.itmb.com) publishes fairly useful Buenos Aires and Argentina maps.

Geography nerds will adore the topographic maps available from the **Instituto Geográfico Militar** (Cabildo 381, Palermo, Buenos Aires; ☻ 8am-1pm Mon-Fri). Go to Subte Ministro Carranza, or take bus No 152 to get there. These maps are difficult to obtain outside the capital.

MONEY

Carrying cash and an ATM card is the way to go in Argentina.

All prices in this book are given in US dollars (US$) unless otherwise indicated. The Argentine unit of currency is the peso ($). See the inside front cover for exchange rates. Also see p18 for information on costs.

Since 2001, when the Argentine government devalued the peso amid an economic crisis that rocked the nation, the peso has been hovering steadily at about three to the US dollar, though visitors should keep an eye on current economic events.

ATMs

Cajeros automáticos (ATMs) are found in nearly every city and town in Argentina and can also be used for cash advances on major credit cards. They're the best way to get money, and nearly all have instructions in English. Almost all ATMs use Cirrus, Plus or Link systems.

Cash

Paper money comes in denominations of two, five, 10, 20, 50 and 100 pesos. One peso equals 100 *centavos*; coins come in denominations of one (rare), five, 10, 25 and 50 *centavos,* and one peso.

At present, US dollars are accepted by many tourist-oriented businesses, but you should always carry some pesos.

Counterfeiting, of both local and US bills, has become a problem in recent years, and merchants are very careful when accepting large denominations. You should be too; look for a clear watermark or running thread on the largest bills.

Credit Cards

The most widely accepted credit cards are Visa and MasterCard, though American Express and a few others are also valid in many establishments. Before you leave home, warn your credit card company that you'll be using it abroad.

Some businesses add a *recargo* (surcharge) of 5% to 10% toward credit-card purchases. Also, the actual amount you'll eventually pay depends upon the exchange rate not at the time of sale, but when the purchase is posted to an overseas account, sometimes weeks later.

If you use a credit card to pay for restaurant bills, be aware that tips can't usually be added to the bill. Some lower-end hotels and private tour companies will not accept credit cards. Holders of MasterCard and Visa can get cash advances at Argentine banks and most ATMs.

Moneychangers

US dollars are by far the preferred foreign currency, although Chilean and Uruguayan pesos can be readily exchanged at the borders. Cash dollars and euros can be changed at *cambios* (exchange houses) in most larger cities, but other currencies can be difficult to change outside Buenos Aires.

Taxes & Refunds

Under limited circumstances, foreign visitors may obtain refunds of the *impuesto al valor agregado* (IVA; value-added tax) on purchases of Argentine products upon their departure from the country. A 'Tax Free' (in English) window decal identifies merchants participating in this program. Hang on to your invoice and you can obtain refunds in Buenos Aires at Ezeiza, Aeroparque Jorge Newbery and the Buquebus terminal at Darsena Norte.

Tipping & Bargaining

In restaurants, it is customary to tip about 10% of the bill, but in times of economic distress Argentines frequently overlook the custom. In general, waiters are poorly paid, so if you can afford to eat out, you can afford to tip. Even a small *propina* (tip) will be appreciated, but note that restaurant tips can't be added to a credit card bill.

Taxi drivers don't expect tips, but it's customary to round up to the nearest peso if the difference isn't much.

Unlike many other South American countries, bargaining is generally not the norm in Argentina.

Traveler's Checks

Very high commissions are levied on traveler's checks, which are difficult to cash anywhere and specifically *not* recommended. Stores will *not* accept traveler's checks, and outside Buenos Aires it's even harder to change them.

PHOTOGRAPHY

Film in Argentina is comparable to that in Western countries, both in quality and price. But it's far cheaper to develop film here than it is in Europe or the US. Devel-

oping quality is generally high, so do it before you leave for home and save yourself a bundle. Developing 36 midsize color prints costs about US$7.

Print developing is widely available in the country. For slide developing, you'll have fewer choices except in Buenos Aires.

Lonely Planet's *Travel Photography* is easy to carry and is excellent for honing your photography skills.

POST

Correo Argentino, the privatized postal service, has become more reliable over the years but mail still occasionally gets waylaid. International letters and postcards under 20g cost US$1.35; a letter over 20g costs US$3.20. Certified letters to the US cost US$4.45 for up to 100g, and US$4.75 to the rest of the world. For essential overseas mail, send it *certificado* (certified).

You can receive mail via *poste restante* or *lista de correos*, both equivalent to general delivery, at any Argentine post office. Instruct your correspondents to address letters clearly (capitalizing your last name) and to indicate a date until which the post office should hold them; otherwise, the mail will be returned or destroyed. Charges are US$1.50 per letter. To receive mail in Buenos Aires have your letter sent like this:

Sarah SMITH (last name in capitals)
Lista de Correos
Correo Central
Sarmiento 189
(1003) Capital Federal
Argentina

Argentine domestic couriers, such as Andreani and OCA, and international couriers, like DHL and Federal Express, are still more dependable than the post office. The last two have offices only in the largest cities, while the former two usually serve as their connections to the interior of the country.

SHOPPING

As Argentine food is famous for beef, so Argentine clothing is famous for leather. In Buenos Aires, many downtown shops cater to the tourist trade in leather jackets, handbags and shoes. Quality and prices can vary greatly, so shop around before buying, but overall all are a great deal. Shopkeepers are aggressive but sometimes open to bargaining.

DIRECTORY

Argentines are very fashion-conscious, with the latest styles displayed along Florida and Santa Fe in Buenos Aires and on the main shopping streets in cities throughout the country. The best shopping area for the fashion-minded is Palermo Viejo (p104) in Buenos Aires, where countless boutique shops sell beautiful clothing, shoes and designer items. Pick up a free Palermo maps (available at most hotels) that lists most of the best stores and briefly describes their wares.

Bariloche is especially well known for woolen goods. Jewelry is another quality Argentine product, made frequently with 18-karat gold. In Buenos Aires, try the jewelry shops on Libertad, south of Corrientes.

Mate paraphernalia make good souvenirs. Gourds and *bombillas* (metal straws with filters for drinking *mate*) range from simple and inexpensive aluminum, to elaborate and expensive gold and silver. In the province of Salta, the distinctive *ponchos de Güemes* are a memorable choice.

In artisans' *ferias,* found throughout the country, the variety of handicrafts is extensive; the best of these is the weekend *feria* (fair) in Córdoba (p272).

Argentines are well-read and interested in both national and world literature, and Buenos Aires has a good selection of general- and special-interest bookstores. Since the end of the military dictatorship, the capital has re-established itself as a publishing center; April's Feria del Libro (book fair; p85) is South America's largest, with over 600 exhibitors drawing over a million visitors.

Foreign-language books tend to be very expensive, but there's a good selection (including this and other Lonely Planet guides) at Buenos Aires' better bookstores and, occasionally, those in the interior.

Many places add a surcharge to credit card purchases; ask before you pay.

SOLO TRAVELERS

Traveling alone can be one of the most rewarding experiences in life. You're far more likely to meet locals and fellow travelers – which is really what travel's all about – without the shell of companionship. Mind you, it can get lonely at times, and it's certainly nice to have a mate to watch your bags for you, or your back when you're snapping photos, but these benefits are often outweighed by the joy of meeting locals. Argentines are quick to invite solo travelers to an *asado* or elsewhere, and even quicker to strike up conversation. What's more, with Argentina's abundance of new hostels, you can easily hook up with other travelers when you're feeling lonely.

Traveling alone as a woman, unfortunately, inherently entails more risk than traveling as a man. But countless women travel alone safely in Argentina every day; it's one of the safest countries in South America to do so. For more information for women travelers, see p472.

TELEPHONE & FAX

Two companies, Telecom and Telefónica, split the city's telephone services. For emergencies dial ☎ 107, police ☎ 101, fire ☎ 100. Directory Assistance is ☎ 110.

The easiest way to make a local phone call is to find a *locutorio,* which has private cabins where you make your calls and then pay all at once at the register. There is a *locutorio* practically on every other block; they cost about the same as street phones, are much quieter and you won't run out of coins. Most *locutorios* are supplied with phone books.

To use street phones, you'll pay with regular coins or *tarjetas telefónicas* (magnetic phone cards available at many kiosks). You'll only be able to speak for a limited time before you get cut off, so carry enough credit.

International collect calls or calls by credit card are not necessarily cheaper than calling from long-distance telephone offices. Long-distance offices are usually busy during evenings and weekends, when overseas calls are cheaper. Prices for Europe are about US$0.45 per minute, depending on the time of day; calling the USA costs US$0.25 to US$0.30. Australia costs more.

Faxes are widely used in Argentina and available at most *locutorios* and Internet cafés. Costs are the price of the call plus about US$0.50 per page.

MOBILE PHONES

It's now possible to use a tri-band GSM world cell phone in Argentina. Other systems in use are CDMA and TDMA. This is a fast-changing field so check the current situation before you travel; take a look at www.kropla.com or do an Internet search on GSM cell phones for the myriad of products on the market. In Buenos Aires and other larger cities, you can buy cell phones that use SIM chips for about US$65. Cell-phone rentals are available in Buenos Aires for around US$12 per week, including 50 minutes of local calls; some five-star hotels offer free cell-phone use.

PHONE CODES

When dialing abroad from Argentina, you must first dial '00,' followed by the country code. The *característica* (area code) for Buenos Aires is ☎ 011, and all telephone numbers in the Greater Buenos Aires area have eight digits. Area codes vary wildly throughout the provinces; those of larger cities have four digits (always beginning with a '0'), followed by a seven digit telephone number. Smaller towns have six-digit telephone numbers and five-digit area codes (again, always beginning with a zero). Basically, when calling from outside an area code, you're always going to dial 11 numbers.

Cell-phone numbers are preceded by '15,' which you must dial unless calling from another cell phone. Toll-free numbers begin with ☎ 0800 or ☎ 0810.

PHONECARDS

Telephone calling cards such as Argentina Global and Hable Mas are sold at nearly all kiosks and make domestic and international calls far cheaper (for US$3.50 you can talk to the US for nearly 45 minutes). However, they must be used from a fixed line such as a home or hotel telephone (provided you can dial outside the hotel). They cannot be used at most pay phones. Some *locutorios* allow you to use them, and although they levy a surcharge, the call is still far cheaper than dialing direct. When purchasing one, tell the clerk the country you will call so they give you the right card.

TIME

Argentina is three hours behind GMT and does not observe daylight saving time. When it's noon in Argentina, it's 10am in New York, 7am in San Francisco, 3pm in London and 1pm the next day in Sydney (add one hour to these times during daylight saving). Argentina tells time by the 24-hour clock ('military time'). See also p505.

TOILETS

Public toilets in Argentina are better than in most of South America, but there are cer-

---

COUNTRY CODES

To call a number in Argentina from another country, dial your international access code, then the country code for Argentina (☎ 54), then the area code (without the zero) and number.

To call a telephone number in Chile from another country, the country code is ☎ 56. The country code for Uruguay is ☎ 598; for Brazil the code is ☎ 55 and for Bolivia ☎ 591.

---

tainly exceptions. For the truly squeamish, the better restaurants and cafés are good alternatives. Large shopping malls often have public bathrooms. Always carry your own toilet paper, since it often runs out in public restrooms, and don't expect luxuries like soap, hot water and paper towels either.

TOURIST INFORMATION

Argentina's national tourist board is the **Secretaría Nacional de Turismo** (www.turismo.gov.ar). Almost every city or town has a tourist office, usually on or near the main plaza or at the bus terminal. Each Argentine province also has its own representation in Buenos Aires; most, though not all, of these are well organized, often offering a computerized database of tourist information, and are well worth a visit before heading for the provinces.

The offices listed here are all provincial tourist offices located in Buenos Aires (area code ☎ 011).

Buenos Aires (☎ 4373-2508; Av Callao 235)
Catamarca (☎ 4374-6891; Córdoba 2080)
Chaco (☎ 4372-5209; Av Callao 322)
Chubut (☎ 200-666-2904, 4382-2009; Sarmiento 1172)
Córdoba (☎ 4371-1688, 4373-4277; Av Callao 332)
Corrientes (☎ 4394-7418; San Martín 333, 4th fl)
Entre Ríos (☎ 4328-2284; Suipacha 844)
Formosa (☎ 4381-7048; Hipólito Yrigoyen 1429)
Jujuy (☎ 4393-6096; Av Santa Fe 967)
La Pampa (☎ 4326-0511; Suipacha 346)
La Rioja (☎ 4815-1929; Av Callao 745)
Mendoza (☎ 4371-7301, 4371-0835; Av Callao 445)
Misiones (☎ 4322-0686; Av Santa Fe 989)
Neuquén (☎ 4343-2324/95, ext 1004/5; Maipú 48)
Río Negro (☎ 4371-5599, 4371-7273; Tucumán 1916)
Salta (☎ 4326-1314; Diagonal Norte/Roque Sáenz Peña 933)
San Juan (☎ 4382-9241; Sarmiento 1251)
San Luis (☎ 4822-0426; Av Libertador 356, 15th fl, B)

Santa Cruz (☎ 4325-3098; Suipacha 1120)
Santa Fe (☎ 4375-4569; Montevideo 373, 2nd fl)
Santiago del Estero (☎ 4326-3733; Florida 274)
Tierra del Fuego (☎ 4325-1809; Av Sarmiento 745)
Tucumán (☎ 4322-0010, ext 124; Suipacha 140)

VISAS

Nationals of the USA, Canada, most Western European countries, Australia and New Zealand do not need visas to visit Argentina. In theory, upon arrival all nonvisa visitors must obtain a free tourist card, good for 90 days and renewable for 90 more. In practice, immigration officials issue these only at major border crossings, such as airports and on the ferries and hydrofoils between Buenos Aires and Uruguay. Although you should not toss your card away, losing it is no major catastrophe; at most exit points, immigration officials will provide immediate replacement for free.

Dependent children traveling without *both* parents theoretically need a notarized document certifying that both parents agree to the child's travel. Parents may also wish to bring a copy of the custody form; however, there's a good chance they won't be asked for either document.

Very short visits to neighboring countries usually do not require visas. Despite what a travel agency might say, you probably don't need a Brazilian visa to cross from the Argentine town of Puerto Iguazú to Foz do Iguaçu and/or Ciudad del Este, Paraguay, if you return the same day, although you should bring your passport. The same is true at the Bolivian border town of Villazón, near La Quiaca, and the Paraguayan crossing at Encarnación, near Posadas. Remember, though, that the information here can change quickly.

Visa Extensions

For a 90-day extension in Buenos Aires, visit the **immigration office** (Map pp64-7; Dirección Nacional de Migraciones; ☎ 011-4317-0200; Antártida Argentina 1355). Set aside some time, money and patience, as this US$100 process can be bureaucratic and time-consuming.

Another option if you're staying more than three months is to cross into Colonia or Montevideo (both in Uruguay) for a day or two before your visa expires, then return

with a new 90-day visa. However, this only works if you don't need a visa to enter Uruguay; Australians do.

WOMEN TRAVELERS

Being a woman in Argentina is a challenge, especially if you are young, traveling alone and/or come with an inflexible liberal attitude. In some ways Argentina is a safer place for a woman than Europe, the USA and most other Latin American countries, but dealing with this machismo culture can be a real pain in the ass.

Some males brimming with testosterone feel the need to comment on a woman's attractiveness. This often happens when the woman is alone and walking by on the street; it occasionally happens to two or more women walking together, but never to a heterosexual couple. Verbal comments include crude language, hisses, whistles and *piropos* (flirtatious comments), which many Argentine males consider an art of complimenting a woman. *Piropos* are often vulgar, although some can be creative and even eloquent. (One cited in the *Buenos Aires Herald* was 'Oh God, the sky is parting and angels are falling.') Much as you may want to kick them where it counts, the best thing to do is completely ignore the comments. After all, many *porteñas* (women from Buenos Aires) do enjoy getting these 'compliments,' and most men don't necessarily mean to be insulting; they're just doing what males in their culture are taught to do.

On the plus side of machismo, expect men to hold a door open for you and always let you enter first, including getting on buses; this gives you a better chance at grabbing an empty seat, so get in there quick.

WORK

Argentina is *very* short on jobs – many locals are unemployed or underemployed – and foreign travelers shouldn't expect to find any work other than teaching English. Working out of an institute, native English-speakers (certified or not) can earn about US$5 to US$7 per hour. You should take into account slow periods like January and February, when many locals leave town on vacation. Most teachers work 'illegally,' heading over to Uruguay every three months for a new visa.

Transportation

CONTENTS

GETTING THERE & AWAY

ENTERING THE COUNTRY

Entering Argentina is straightforward; immigration officials at airports are generally quick to the point and waste few words, while those at border crossings may take a little more time scrutinizing your passport before stamping it. When entering by air, you officially must have a return ticket, though this is rarely asked for.

Anyone entering the country is required to have a valid passport. Once you're in the country, police can still demand identification at any moment. It's a good idea to carry at least a copy of your passport around town at all times. For information on visa requirements, see opposite.

AIR

Argentina has flights linked up with North America, the UK, Europe, Australia, New Zealand and South Africa, and from all South American countries except the Guianas. Alternatively, you can fly to a neighboring country, such as Chile or Brazil, and continue overland to Argentina.

Airports & Airlines

Aerolíneas Argentinas, the national carrier, enjoys a good reputation for its international flights. Southern Winds operates flights between Santiago, Chile, and Mendoza and Córdoba. Nearly all other international flights arrive at Buenos Aires' **Aeropuerto Internacional Ministro Pistarini** (Ezeiza; ☎ 5480-6111), which is about a 45-minute bus or cab ride out of town. Airports in several provincial capitals and tourist destinations are earmarked as 'international': this usually means they receive flights from neighboring countries. Basic information on most Argentine airports can be found online at www.aa2000.com.ar. Airports include the following:

Bariloche (code BRC; ☎ 02944-422767)
Córdoba (code COR; ☎ 0351-475-0392)
Jujuy (code JUJ; ☎ 0388-491-1102)
Mendoza (code MDZ; ☎ 0261-448-2603)
Puerto Iguazú (code IGR; ☎ 03757-420595)
Río Gallegos (code RGL; ☎ 0296-442340/4)
Rosario (code ROS; ☎ 0341-451-2997)
Salta (code SLA; ☎ 0387-424-2904)
Tucumán (code TUC; ☎ 0381-426-4906)
Ushuaia (code USH; ☎ 0291-424422)

AIRLINES FLYING TO & FROM ARGENTINA

The following airlines fly to and from Argentina and are listed with their telephone numbers and addresses in Buenos Aires (area code ☎ 011) when possible.
Aerolíneas Argentinas (code ARG; Map pp64-7; ☎ 0810-222-86527; www.aerolineas.com; Perú 2; hub Ezeiza, Buenos Aires). Also at Map pp64-7; Av Leandro N Alem 1134.

THINGS CHANGE...

The information in this chapter is particularly vulnerable to change. Check directly with the airline or a travel agent to make sure you understand how a fare (and ticket you may buy) works and be aware of the security requirements for international travel. Shop carefully. The details given in this chapter should be regarded as pointers and are not a substitute for your own careful, up-to-date research.

Air Canada (code ACA; Map pp64–7; ☎ 4393-9045; www.aircanada.ca; Av Córdoba 656; hub Toronto)

Air France (code AFR; Map pp64–7; ☎ 4317-4700; www.airfrance.fr; Paraguay 610, 14th fl; hub Charles De Gaulle, Paris)

Alitalia (code AZA; Map pp64–7; ☎ 4310-9970; www.alitalia.com; Av Santa Fe 887; hubs Malpensa, Milan & Fiumicino, Rome)

American Airlines (code AAL; Map pp64–7; ☎ 4318-1111; www.aa.com; Av Santa Fe 881)

American Falcon (code AFB; Map pp64–7; ☎ 0810-222-3252; www.americanfalcon.com.ar; Santa Fe 963; hub Buenos Aires)

Avianca (code AVA; Map pp64–7; ☎ 4394-5990; www.avianca.com; Carlos Pellegrini 1163, 4th fl)

British Airways (code BA; Map pp64–7; ☎ 4320-6600; www.britishairways.com; Carlos Pellegrini 1163; hub Heathrow, London)

KLM (code KLM; Map pp64–7; ☎ 4326-8422; www.klm.com; Suipacha 268, 9th fl)

LanChile (code LAN; Map pp64–7; ☎ 4378-2222; www.lanchile.com; Cerrito 866; hub Santiago, Chile)

Líneas Aéreas del Estado (LADE) (code LDE; Map pp64–7; ☎ 5129-9001; www.lade.com.ar; Perú 714; hub Buenos Aires)

Lloyd Aéreo Boliviano (code LAB; Map pp64–7; ☎ 4323-1900; www.labairlines.com; Carlos Pellegrini 141; hub La Paz, Bolivia)

Pluna (code PUA; Map pp64–7; ☎ 4329-9211; www.pluna.com.uy; Florida 1; hub Montevideo)

Qantas Airways (code QFA; Map pp64–7; ☎ 4514-4730; www.qantas.com.au; Av Córdoba 673, 14th fl; hub Sydney)

Southern Winds (code SWD; Map pp64–7; ☎ 4515-8600; www.sw.com.ar; Av Santa Fe 784; hub Aeroparque Jorge Newberry, Buenos Aires)

Swiss International Air (code SWR; Map pp64–7; ☎ 4319-0000; www.swiss.com; Santa Fe 846, 1st fl)

Transportes Aéreos de Mercosur (code TAM; Map pp64–7; ☎ 0810-333-3333; www.tam.com.py; Cerrito 1026; hub Asunción, Paraguay)

United Airlines (code UAL; Map pp64–7; ☎ 0810-777-8648; www.united.com.ar; Av Eduardo Madero 900, 1st fl)

Varig (code VRG; Map pp64–7; ☎ 4329-9211; www.varig.com.br; Córdoba 972, 4th fl)

DEPARTURE TAX

Departure taxes on international flights out of Argentina are generally *not* included in the price of your ticket. Make sure you ask. If the departure tax is not included, you must pay it in Argentine pesos ($54) or US dollars (US$18) after check-in and have the tax sticker placed on your ticket.

Tickets

From almost everywhere, South America is a relatively costly destination, but discount fares can reduce the bite considerably. Contacting a travel agency that specializes in Latin American destinations can turn up the cheapest fares.

INTERCONTINENTAL (RTW) TICKETS

Some of the best deals for travelers visiting many countries on different continents are Round-the-World (RTW) tickets. Itineraries from the USA, Europe or Australia usually include five or six stopovers (including Buenos Aires). Fares can vary widely, but to get an idea, check out **Airtreks** (www.airtreks.com). Similar 'Circle Pacific' fares allow excursions between Australasia and South America. These types of tickets are certain to have restrictions, so check the fine print carefully.

Australia & New Zealand

Qantas (www.qantas.com.au) flies to Buenos Aires from Sydney with a stop in Auckland; it also flies from Sydney to Tahiti twice a week to connect with the **LanChile** (www.lanchile.com) Tahiti–Easter Island–Santiago service, which has connections to Buenos Aires – a tempting flight if you want to see Easter Island or Tahiti. **Air New Zealand** (www.airnz.co.nz) does the same from Auckland.

Yet another way to get to Buenos Aires is to travel via the USA (Los Angeles, Dallas or Miami) with either **American Airlines** (www.aa.com) or **United Airlines** (www.united.com).

For tickets in Australia, try **STA Travel** (☎ 1300 733 035; www.statravel.com.au) or **Flight Centre** (☎ 133 133; www.flightcentre.com.au). For strictly online bookings, try www.travel.com.au.

Both **Flight Centre** (☎ 0800 243 544; www.flightcentre.co.nz) and **STA Travel** (☎ 0508 782 872; www.statravel.co.nz) have branches throughout New Zealand. Online, try www.travel.co.nz.

Canada

Air Canada operates the only nonstop flight from Canada to Buenos Aires, which leaves from Toronto. Airlines such as American and Continental make connections in New York, Miami and Los Angeles. **Travel Cuts** (☎ 800-667-2887; www.travelcuts.com) is Canada's student travel agency. For online bookings you can try **Expedia** (www.expedia.ca) and **Travelocity** (www.travelocity.ca).

Continental Europe

The following travel agencies are good possibilities for bargain fares from Continental Europe.

France

Anyway (☎ 0892 893 892; www.anyway.fr)
Lastminute (☎ 0892 705 000; www.lastminute.fr)
Nouvelles Frontières (☎ 0825 000 747; www .nouvelles-frontieres.fr)
OTU Voyages (www.otu.fr) This agency specializes in student and youth travelers.

Germany

Expedia (www.expedia.de)
Just Travel (☎ 089 747 3330; www.justtravel.de)
STA Travel (☎ 01805 456 422; www.statravel.de) For travelers under the age of 26.

Italy

CTS Viaggi (☎ 06 462 0431; www.cts.it) Specializes in student and youth travel.

Netherlands

Airfair (☎ 020 620 5121; www.airfair.nl)

Spain

Barcelo Viajes (☎ 902 116 226; www.barceloviajes.com)

South America

Buenos Aires is well connected to most other capital cities in Latin America. Prices range from a cheap US$60 one-way hop to/from Montevideo, Uruguay, to a $400 flight to/from La Paz, Bolivia or Quito, Ecuador.

UK & Ireland

Direct services to Buenos Aires are available with **Aerolíneas Argentinas** (in London ☎ 020-7494 1001) and many other airlines. Varig has connections via Rio de Janeiro and São Paulo.

An excellent place to start your inquiries is **Journey Latin America** (☎ 020-8747 3108; www .journeylatinamerica.co.uk). In Ireland try **Holidays Online** (www.holidaysonline.ie). Other recommended travel agencies:

Bridge the World (☎ 0870 444 7474; www.b-t-w.co.uk)
Flightbookers (☎ 0870 010 7000; www.ebookers.com)
Flight Centre (☎ 0870 890 8099; flightcentre.co.uk)
North-South Travel (☎ 01245 608 291; www.north southtravel.co.uk) Donates part of its profit to projects in the developing world.
Quest Travel (☎ 0870 442 3542; www.questtravel.com)
STA Travel (☎ 0870 160 0599; www.statravel.co.uk) For travelers under the age of 26.

Trailfinders (www.trailfinders.co.uk)
Travel Bag (☎ 0870 890 1456; www.travelbag.co.uk)

USA

The principal gateways are Miami, Dallas, New York and Los Angeles. **Aerolíneas Argentinas** (☎ 800-333-0276) and numerous other airlines fly to Buenos Aires.

Latin American travel specialist **eXito Travel** (☎ 800-655-4053; www.exitotravel.com) offers some of the cheapest fares around as well as personal service (such as flight changes from abroad, travel recommendations and more) from an impressively well-informed staff.

The largest student travel agency in the US is **STA Travel** (☎ 800-777-0112; www.statravel.com).

For online bookings, try the following:
Cheap Tickets (www.cheaptickets.com)
Expedia (www.expedia.com)
Lowestfare.com (www.lowestfare.com)
Orbitz (www.orbitz.com)
Travelocity (www.travelocity.com)

LAND

Bicycle

There is no extra charge for entering Argentina by land with a bicycle.

Border Crossings

There are numerous border crossings from neighboring Chile, Bolivia, Paraguay, Brazil and Uruguay; the following lists are only the principal crossings. Generally, border formalities are straightforward as long as all your documents are in order. For info on necessary visas and documents, see p472.

BOLIVIA

The following are options:
La Quiaca to Villazón Many buses go from Jujuy and Salta to La Quiaca, where you must walk or take a taxi across the Bolivian border.
Aguas Blancas to Bermejo From Orán, reached by bus from Salta or Jujuy, take a bus to Aguas Blancas and then Bermejo, where you can catch a bus to Tarija.
Pocitos to Yacuiba Buses from Jujuy or Salta go to Tartagal and then on to the Bolivian border at Pocitos/Yacuiba, where there are trains to Santa Cruz.

BRAZIL

The most common crossing is from Puerto Iguazú (p193) to Foz do Iguaçu (p196). Check both cities for more information on the peculiarities of this border crossing, especially if you're crossing the border into Brazil only to see the other side of Iguazú Falls. For specifics, see the boxed text on p198.

There are also border crossings from Paso de los Libres (Argentina; p182) to Uruguaiana (Brazil), and from Santo Tomé (Argentina; p183) to São Borja (Brazil).

CHILE

Except in far southern Patagonia, every land crossing between Argentina and Chile involves crossing the Andes. Due to weather, some high-altitude passes close in winter. There are numerous crossings into Chile; the following are the most commonly used.

Salta to San Pedro de Atacama Twelve-hour bus ride through the altiplano with stunningly beautiful scenery.

Mendoza to Santiago The most popular crossing between the two countries, passing 6960m Aconcagua en route.

Bariloche to Puerto Montt The famous 12-hour bus-boat combination is a wallet-busting US$150. Make advance bookings in summer. Takes two days in winter. See p343.

Los Antiguos to Chile Chico Those entering from Chile can access the rugged Ruta 40 from here and head down to El Chaltén and El Calafate. Best in summer, when there's actually transport available.

El Calafate to Puerto Natales & Parque Nacional Torres del Paine Probably the most beaten route down here, heading from the Perito Moreno Glacier (near El Calafate) to Parque Nacional Torres del Paine (near Puerto Natales). Several buses per day in summer; one to two daily in the off-season.

Ushuaia to Punta Arenas Daily buses in summer, fewer in winter, on this 12- to 18-hour trip (depending on weather conditions), which includes a ferry crossing at either Porvenir or Punta Delgada/Primera Angostura.

URUGUAY & PARAGUAY

There are two direct border crossings between Argentina and Paraguay: Clorinda (p208) to Asunción, and Posadas (p184) to Encarnación.

Border crossings from Argentine cities to Uruguayan cities include Gualeguaychú (p174) to Fray Bentos, Colón (p178) to Paysandú, and Concordia (p180) to Salto. All involve crossing bridges. Buses from Buenos Aires to Montevideo and other waterfront cities, however, are slower and less convenient than the ferries (or ferry-bus combinations) across the Río de la Plata (see right).

Bus

Travelers can bus to Argentina from most bordering countries. Buses are usually comfortable, modern and fairly clean. Crossing over does not involve too many hassles; just make sure that you have any proper visas (p472) beforehand.

RIVER

There are several river crossings between Uruguay and Buenos Aires that involve ferry or hydrofoil, and often require combinations with buses.

Buenos Aires to Montevideo High-speed ferries carry passengers from downtown Buenos Aires to the Uruguayan capital in only 2½ hours. See p113.

Buenos Aires to Colonia Daily ferries (2½ hours) and hydrofoils (45 minutes) to Colonia, with direct bus connections to Montevideo (three hours more). See p111.

Buenos Aires to Piriápolis In summer, a three-hour ferry ride connects the resort town of Piriápolis with the Argentine capital at least once a day.

Tigre to Carmelo Regular passenger launches speed from the Buenos Aires suburb of Tigre to Carmelo (services also go to Montevideo and Colonia from Tigre). See p110.

SEA

Arriving in Argentina by sea is uncommon indeed, although Chilean company **Navimag** (www.navimag.com) operates the famous ferry from Puerto Montt, Chile (near Bariloche), down the length of Chilean Patagonia to Puerto Natales, Chile, near Parque Nacional Torres del Paine (due west of Río Gallegos).

GETTING AROUND

AIR
Airlines in Argentina

The national carrier is **Aerolíneas Argentinas/Austral** (☎ 0810-222-86527; www.aerolineas.com), though it's not necessarily better than its competitors. In fact, **Southern Winds** (☎ 011-4515-8600; www.sw.com.ar) serves nearly as many destinations and is usually cheaper for foreigners because, unlike Aerolíneas Argentinas, it doesn't charge foreigners more than nationals. **Líneas Aéreas del Estado** (LADE; ☎ 011-5129-9001; www.lade.com.ar), the air force's passenger service, has some of the least expensive air tickets and makes Patagonian destinations its specialty. **American Falcon** (☎ 0810-222-3252; www.americanfalcon.com.ar) is the country's newest airline. Between these airlines, nearly every major city is linked to Buenos Aires.

Nearly all domestic flights (except for LADE's hops around Patagonia) have connections only through **Aeroparque Jorge New-**

bery (☎ 011-5480-6111; www.aa2000.com.ar), a short distance from downtown Buenos Aires. Southern Winds has a few short-haul flights linking some provincial destinations without passing through the capital.

Flying with certain airlines on certain flights can be financially comparable or even cheaper than covering the same distance by bus, but demand is heavy and flights, especially to Patagonian destinations in summer, are often booked well in advance.

Air Passes

If you're planning to travel around the country only by air, consider Aerolíneas Argentinas' 'Visit Argentina' pass. It's available for purchase only *outside* Argentina, but it will save you a considerable amount of money *if* you're flying to Argentina with Aerolíneas Argentinas. If you're flying with another airline, the savings are less. Check out pass details at www.aerolineas.com.

BICYCLE

If you dig cycling your way around a country, Argentina has some good potential. It will also save you some dough: partnered with camping, cycling can cut the costs of your trip fourfold. And of course you'll see more details and meet more curious locals.

Racing bicycles are suitable for some paved roads, but these byways are often narrow; a *todo terreno* (mountain bike) is safer and more convenient, allowing you to use the unpaved shoulder and the very extensive network of graveled roads throughout the country. Argentine bicycles are improving in quality but are still not equal to their counterparts in Europe or the USA.

There are two major drawbacks to long-distance bicycling in Argentina. One is the wind, which in Patagonia can slow your progress to a crawl. The other is Argentine motorists: on many of the country's straight, narrow, two-lane highways, they can be a serious hazard to bicyclists. Make yourself as visible as possible, and wear a helmet. Of course you'll need to bring an adequate repair kit and extra parts (and the mental know-how to use them), some good directions (unpaved roads on maps can be unreliable) and enough food and water till the next town. In Patagonia, a windbreaker and warm clothing are essential. Don't expect much traffic on some back roads.

For ideas on where you might want to ride, see p460.

Hire

Reasonable bicycle rentals (mostly mountain bikes) are available in many popular tourist destinations, such as Mendoza, Bariloche and other towns throughout the Lake District and Córdoba's Central Sierras. Prices are affordable, setting renters back no more than US$7 per day.

Purchase

Many towns have bike shops, but high-quality bikes are expensive and repair parts can be hard to come by. If you do decide to buy while you're here, you're best off doing so in Buenos Aires. Selection in other major cities – even Córdoba and Mendoza – is pretty slim.

BOAT

Opportunities for boat or river travel in and around Argentina are very limited, though there are regular international services to/from Uruguay (see opposite) and to/from Chile via the Lake District (see p343).

Although the journey is in Chile, a classic route south along the Patagonian Andes is the Navimag boat trip (see opposite).

Otherwise, if you must be on the water, head to the Buenos Aires suburb of Tigre (p110), where there are numerous boat excursions around the delta of the Río de la Plata.

BUS

If you're doing any serious traveling around Argentina, you'll become very familiar with the country's excellent bus network, which reaches almost everywhere. Buses are fast, surprisingly comfortable and can be a rather luxurious experience. It's the way most Argentines get around. Larger luggage is stowed in the hold below, security is good and attendants always tag your bags (and should be tipped). If you have a long way to go – say Buenos Aires to Mendoza – overnight buses are the way to go, saving you a night's accommodations – and the day for fun.

Hundreds of bus companies serve different regions but a few bigger lines really dominate the long-haul business:

Andesmar (www.andesmar.com in Spanish) Serves the entire country.

Chevallier (www.nuevachevallier.com in Spanish) Serves the entire country.

El Rápido International (www.elrapidoint.com.ar in Spanish) Buenos Aires, Mendoza, Córdoba, Rosario. International service to Santiago and Viña del Mar, Chile, and Lima, Peru.

Via Bariloche (www.viabariloche.com.ar) Serves most destinations in La Pampa province, the Lake District and Patagonia.

Most cities and towns have a central bus terminal where each company has its own ticket window. Some companies post fares and schedules prominently, and the ticket price and departure time is always on the ticket you buy. Expect (Argentine) fast-food stalls, kiosks and newspaper vendors inside or near almost every terminal. There are generally few hotel touts or other traveler-hassling types at terminals.

Classes

This is where it gets fun. Better bus lines such as Chevallier and Andesmar (not to mention dozens of others) have modern Mercedes or Volvo coaches with spacious, cushy leather seats, large windows, air-conditioning, toilets, TVs and sometimes even an attendant serving coffee and snacks. Spend a little money and you'll be playing bingo for wine as you roll across the Pampas (no kidding!).

On overnight trips it's well worth the extra US$5 to US$7 to go *coche cama* (sleeper class), though the cheaper *coche semi-cama* (semisleeper) is definitely manageable. In

---

PATAGONIA

The famed RN 40 (La Ruta Cuarenta; p392), south of Gobernador Costa, is infrequently traveled, rough and blessed with zero public transport – almost. Recently, several businesses have sprung up offering transport (really they're just microbus tours) along this route. Based in Bariloche at Periko's hostel (p340), **Overland Patagonia** (www.over landpatagonia.com) offers one of the cheapest trips down to El Calafate: US$267 for the four-day trip. **Corredor Patagónico** (www .corredorpatagonico.com) stretches it to six days and charges US$720. Both offer variations of the trip with various levels of extras that kick up or drop the price. None of these services operate outside the fair-weather period of November through March.

---

coche cama, seats are wider, recline almost flat and are far more comfortable. If you want to lay totally flat, you can go *ejecutivo* (executive), which is available on a few popular runs such as Buenos Aires–Córdoba or Buenos Aires–Rosario. If pinching pesos, *común* (common) is the cheapest class. For trips under about five hours, there's usually no choice and buses are *común* or beat-up *semi-cama,* which are both usually just fine.

Costs

Bus fares vary widely depending on season, class and company, and can cost anywhere from about US$1 to US$2 per hour on *común* or *semi-cama,* to US$3 to US$5 for *coche cama.* Prices given in the Getting There & Away sections throughout this book are approximate and are mid- to high-season fares, generally in *semi-cama.* Patagonia runs tend to be the most expensive. Credit cards are generally not accepted. Following are sample fares from Buenos Aires.

Destination	Cost ($US)
Bariloche	40
Comodoro Rivadavia	39
Córdoba	12-18
Mar del Plata	15
Mendoza	15-35
Puerto Iguazú	32
Puerto Madryn	39
Rosario	10

Reservations

Often you don't need to buy bus tickets ahead of time unless you're traveling on a Friday between major cities, when overnight *coche cama* services sell out fast. During holiday stretches such as late December, January, July and August, tickets sell quickly, so you're best off buying yours ahead of time. As soon as you arrive somewhere, especially if it's a town with limited services, find out which companies go to your next destination and when, and plan your trip out around that.

Seasons

In the Lake District and northern Patagonia, bus services are outstanding during summer (November through March), when there are many microbus routes to campgrounds, along lake circuits, to trail heads and to other destinations popular with tourists. Outside summer, however, these services stop, and getting around becomes much more difficult.

CAR & MOTORCYCLE

Because Argentina is so large, many parts are accessible only by private vehicle, despite the country's extensive public transport system. This is especially true in Patagonia, where distances are great and buses can be infrequent. Besides, with your own wheels, you can stop for photo ops or bathroom breaks at the side of the road whenever you want.

Although motorbikes have become fashionable among some Argentines, they are very expensive, and there appears to be no motorcycle-rental agencies in Argentina.

Automobile Associations

If driving in Argentina, whether your own car or a rental, it's worthwhile being a member – you may *already* be – of the **Automóvil Club Argentino** (ACA; Map pp64-7; ☎ 011-4802-6061; www.aca.org.ar in Spanish; Av del Libertador 1850, Palermo, Buenos Aires), which has offices, service stations and garages throughout the country, offering free road service and towing in and around major destinations. ACA recognizes members of most overseas auto clubs, such as the American Automobile Association (AAA) and grants them privileges, including road service and discounts on maps and accommodations. Bring your card. Otherwise ACA membership costs about US$30 a month.

Bring Your Own Vehicle

Chile is probably the best country on the continent for shipping a vehicle from overseas, though Argentina is feasible. Getting the vehicle out of customs typically involves routine paperwork. If the car is more than a few days in customs, however, storage charges can add up quickly. To find a reliable shipper, check the yellow pages of your local phone directory under Automobile Transporters.

Driver's License & Documents

You must have an International Driving Permit to supplement your national or state driver's license. If you are stopped, police will inspect your automobile registration and insurance and tax documents, all of which must be up to date. Except in Buenos Aires, security problems are few.

Drivers of Argentine vehicles must carry their title document (*tarjeta verde* or 'green

card'); if it's a rental, make sure it's in the glove box. For foreign vehicles, customs permission is the acceptable substitute. Liability insurance is obligatory, and police often ask to see proof of insurance at checkpoints.

Fuel & Spare Parts

Nafta (gas) costs US$0.57/0.64 per liter for normal/super (US$2.16/2.43 per US gallon). However, in Patagonia (where much of Argentina's oil fields are) it's nearly half that. *Estaciones de servicio* (gas stations) are fairly common (especially YPFs), but outside the cities keep an eye on your gas gauge, and off the beaten track in Patagonia it's a good idea to carry extra fuel. Tolls on privatized highways cost on average US$0.67 per 100km.

Hire

Renting a car in Argentina, if you can cough up the cash, is well worth it because it allows you the freedom to go and stop wherever you please and to visit those backcountry places that buses don't. The best deals are almost always with the locally owned agencies (when you can find them) rather than the ever-present international ones. To rent a car, you must be at least 21 years of age and have a valid driver's license and a credit card. To drive you must have an international driving permit, but renters rarely ask for this.

The cheapest and smallest vehicles cost anywhere from US$30 per day with 150km included to US$60 per day with 200km. The cheapest place to rent a car (due to all the competition) is Bariloche; if you're heading down to Patagonia or plan to drive for a while, this is a good place to rent, though rental prices in Patagonia have dropped considerably (provided you're not renting a 4WD). Although unlimited-kilometer deals do exist, they are much more expensive. Reserving a car with one of the major international agencies in your home country sometimes gets you lower rates.

Insurance

Liability insurance is obligatory in Argentina, and police ask to see proof of insurance at checkpoints. Fortunately, coverage is reasonably priced. Insuring a US$20,000 car with basic liability insurance costs about US$80 per month. The cost is lower, of course, if you have an old rust bucket. If you plan on taking the car to neighboring countries, make sure it

ROAD DISTANCES (KM)

	Buenos Aires	Córdoba	Mendoza	Neuquén	Resistencia	Salta	Ushuaia
Buenos Aires	---						
Córdoba	715	---					
Mendoza	1050	670	---				
Neuquén	1158	1137	855	---			
Resistencia	1023	875	1587	2012	---		
Salta	1510	897	1227	2082	780	---	
Ushuaia	3171	3228	3393	2353	3983	4125	---

will remain covered (you'll have to pay extra). Among reputable insurers in Argentina are **Mapfre** (www.mapfre.com.ar in Spanish) and the **ACA** (www.aca.org.ar in Spanish).

Purchase

If you are spending several months in Argentina, purchasing a car is an alternative worth exploring. If you resell the car at the end of your stay, it may turn out even more economical. On the other hand, any used car can be a risk, especially on Patagonia's rugged back roads.

If you purchase a car, you must deal with the exasperating Argentine bureaucracy. You must have the title (*tarjeta verde*), and license tax payments must be up to date. As a foreigner, you may find it useful to carry a notarized document authorizing your use of the car, since the bureaucracy moves too slowly to change the title easily. Argentines themselves rarely change the title over because of the expense involved.

As a foreigner you may own a vehicle in Argentina but, in theory at least, you may not take it out of the country even with a notarized authorization. Do not expect to find a dependable used car for less than about US$3000. Prices will be higher for a *gasolero* (a vehicle that uses cheaper diesel fuel).

Road Rules & Hazards

Anyone considering driving in Argentina should know that Argentine drivers are aggressive and commonly ignore speed limits, road signs and even traffic signals. That said, once you're out of the city, driving is a joy.

Though most Argentine highways have a speed limit of 80km/h, and some have been raised to 100km/h or more, hardly anybody pays attention to these or any other regulations. During the Pampas harvest season, pay particular attention to slow-moving farm machinery, which, though not a hazard in its own right, brings out the worst in impatient Argentine motorists. Night driving is not recommended; in many regions animals hang out on the road for warmth, and plowing into an Argentine cow is not fun.

Have on hand some emergency reflectors (*balizas*), and a 1kg fire extinguisher. Headrests are required for the driver and passengers, and seatbelts are now obligatory (though few people wear them). Motorcycle helmets are also obligatory, although this law is rarely enforced.

You won't often see police patrolling the highways, but you will meet them at major intersections and roadside checkpoints where they conduct meticulous document and equipment checks. Equipment violations can carry heavy fines, but such checks are more commonly pretexts for graft. For instance, if the police ask to check your turn signals (which almost no Argentine bothers to use), brake lights or hand brake, it may well be a warning of corruption in progress. The police may claim that you must pay the fine at a local bank, which may not be open until the following day, or if it's on a weekend, until Monday. If you are uncertain about your rights, state in a very matter-of-fact manner your intention to contact your embassy or consulate, or feign such complete ignorance of Spanish that you're more trouble than the police think it's worth. It may be possible to pay the fine on the spot (wink, wink). Ask, '*¿Puedo pagar la multa ahora?*' ('Can I pay the fine right now?').

HITCHHIKING

Hitchhiking is never entirely safe in any country in the world. Travelers who decide to hitch should understand that they are taking a small but potentially serious risk. People who do choose to hitch will be safer if they travel in pairs and let someone know where they are planning to go.

Along with Chile, Argentina is probably the best country for hitching in all of South America. The major drawback is that Argentine vehicles are often stuffed full with families and children, but truckers will frequently pick up backpackers. At the *servicentros* (gas stations) at the outskirts of large Argentine cities, where truckers gas up their vehicles, it's often easy to solicit a ride.

Women can and do hitchhike alone, but should exercise caution and especially avoid getting into a car with more than one man. In Patagonia, where distances are great and vehicles few, hitchers should expect long waits and carry warm, windproof clothing.

There are a few routes along which hitching is undesirable. RN 40, from El Calafate to Perito Moreno and Río Mayo, is a challenge to your patience, and the lack of services along the way is a serious drawback. Up north, the scenic route from Tucumán to Cafayate is difficult past Tafí del Valle. Throughout the Lake District, hitching is common, especially out in the country where locals regularly get around by thumbing it.

LOCAL TRANSPORTATION
Bus

Local Argentine buses *(colectivos)* are notorious for charging along the *avenidas,* spewing clouds of black smoke while traveling at breakneck speeds. Riding on one is a good way to see the cities and get around, providing you can sort out the often complex bus systems. Buses are clearly numbered and usually carry a placard indicating their final destination. Since many identically numbered buses

serve slightly different routes (especially in bigger cities), pay attention to these placards. To ask 'Does this bus go to (the beach)?' say '*¿Va este colectivo a (la playa)?*'

Most city buses operate on coins; you pay as you board. In some cities, such as Mendoza, you must buy prepaid bus cards or – in the case of Córdoba – *cospeles* (tokens). In both cases, they can be bought at any kiosk.

Subway

Buenos Aires is the only Argentine city with a subway system (known as Subte), and it's the quickest way of getting around the city center. For details, see p109.

Taxi & Remise

The people of Buenos Aires make frequent use of taxis, which are digitally metered and cheap. Outside Buenos Aires, meters are common but not universal, and it may be necessary to agree upon a fare in advance. Drivers are generally polite and honest, but there are exceptions; be sure the meter is set at zero, and be sure it's on. It is customary to round up the fare as a tip.

Where public transportation can be scarce, it's possible to hire a cab with a driver for the day to visit places off the beaten track. If you bargain, this can actually be cheaper than a rental car, but negotiate the fee in advance.

Remises are radio taxis without meters that generally offer fixed fares within a given zone. They are an increasingly popular form of transportation and are usually cheaper than taxis. They don't cruise the city in search of fares, as taxis do, but hotels and restaurants will phone them for you if you ask.

TRAIN

Despite major reductions in long-distance train service, rail lines continue to serve most of the Buenos Aires suburbs and some surrounding provinces. During the holiday periods like Christmas or national holidays, buy tickets in advance. Train fares tend to be lower than comparable bus fares, but trains are slower and there are much fewer departure times and destinations.

Train buffs will want to take the narrow-gauge La Trochita (see the boxed text, p394), which runs from Esquel to El Maitén. Another legendary ride is the Tren a las Nubes (Train to the Clouds; p230), which leaves Salta on most Saturdays, March to November.

Health
Dr David Goldberg

CONTENTS

Medically speaking, there are two South Americas: tropical South America, which includes most of the continent except for the southernmost portion, and temperate South America, which includes Chile, Uruguay, southern Argentina and the Falkland Islands. The diseases found in tropical South America are comparable to those found in tropical areas in Africa and Asia. Particularly important are mosquito-borne infections, including malaria, yellow fever and dengue fever, which are not a significant concern in temperate regions.

Prevention is the key to staying healthy in Argentina. Travelers who receive the recommended vaccines and follow common-sense precautions usually come away with nothing more than a little diarrhea.

BEFORE YOU GO

Bring medication in its original, clearly labeled container. A signed, dated letter from your physician describing your medical conditions and medications, including generic names, is also a good idea. If carrying syringes or needles, be sure to have a physician's letter documenting their medical necessity.

INSURANCE

If your health insurance doesn't cover you for medical expenses abroad, consider getting extra insurance. Find out in advance if your insurance plan will make payments directly to providers or reimburse you later for overseas health expenditures. (In many countries doctors expect payment in cash.)

MEDICAL CHECKLIST

- acetaminophen (Tylenol) or aspirin
- adhesive or paper tape
- antibacterial ointment (eg Bactroban; for cuts and abrasions)
- antibiotics
- antidiarrheal drugs (eg loperamide)
- antihistamines (for hay fever and allergic reactions)
- anti-inflammatory drugs (eg ibuprofen)
- bandages, gauze, gauze rolls
- DEET-containing insect repellent for the skin
- iodine tablets (for water purification)
- oral rehydration salts
- permethrin-containing insect spray for clothing, tents and bed nets
- pocket knife
- scissors, safety pins, tweezers
- steroid cream or cortisone (for poison ivy and other allergic rashes)
- sunblock
- syringes and sterile needles
- thermometer

INTERNET RESOURCES

There is a wealth of travel health advice on the Internet. For further info, the **Lonely Planet website** (www.lonelyplanet.com) is a good place to start. The **World Health Organization** (www.who.int/ith) publishes a superb book called *International Travel and Health,* which is revised annually and is available online at no cost. Another website of general interest is **MD Travel Health** (www.mdtravelhealth.com), which provides complete travel-health recommendations for every country and is updated daily.

It's usually a good idea to consult your government's travel health website before departure, if one is available:

Australia www.smartraveller.gov.au
Canada www.hc-sc.gc.ca/english/index.html

UK www.doh.gov.uk/traveladvice
US www.cdc.gov/travel

FURTHER READING

For further information, see Lonely Planet's *Healthy Travel Central & South America*. If you're traveling with children, Lonely Planet's *Travel with Children* may be useful. The *ABC of Healthy Travel*, by E Walker et al, is another valuable resource.

IN TRANSIT

DEEP VEIN THROMBOSIS (DVT)

Blood clots may form in the legs (deep vein thrombosis or DVT) during plane flights, chiefly because of prolonged immobility. The longer the flight, the greater the risk. Though most blood clots are reabsorbed uneventfully, some may break off and travel through the blood vessels to the lungs, where they could cause life-threatening complications.

The chief symptom of DVT is swelling or pain of the foot, ankle or calf, usually – but not always – on just one side. When a blood clot travels to the lungs, it may cause chest pain and difficulty breathing. Travelers with any of these symptoms should immediately seek medical attention.

To prevent the development of DVT on long flights, you should walk about the cabin, perform isometric contractions of the leg muscles (ie flex the leg muscles while sitting), drink plenty of fluids and avoid alcohol and tobacco.

JET LAG & MOTION SICKNESS

Jet lag is common when crossing more than five time zones, resulting in insomnia, fatigue, malaise or nausea. To avoid jet lag try drinking plenty of (nonalcoholic) fluids and eating light meals. Upon arrival, get exposure to natural sunlight and readjust your schedule (for meals, sleep etc) as soon as possible.

Antihistamines such as dimenhydrinate (Dramamine) and meclizine (Antivert, Bonine) are usually the first choice for treating motion sickness. Their main side effect is drowsiness. An herbal alternative is ginger, which works like a charm for some people.

HEALTH

RECOMMENDED VACCINATIONS

Since most vaccines don't produce immunity until at least two weeks after they're given, visit a physician four to eight weeks before departure. No vaccines are required for Argentina, but a number are recommended.

Vaccine	Recommended For	Dosage	Side Effects
chickenpox	travelers who've never had chickenpox	2 doses 1 month apart	fever; mild case of chickenpox
hepatitis A	all travelers	1 dose before trip; booster 6-12 months later	soreness at injection site; headaches; body aches
hepatitis B	long-term travelers in close contact with the local population	3 doses over 6-month period	soreness at injection site; low-grade fever
measles	travelers who have never had measles or completed a vaccination course	1 dose	fever; rash; joint pains; allergic reactions
rabies	travelers who may have contact with animals and may not have access to medical care	3 doses over 3-4 week period	soreness at injection site; headaches; body aches
tetanus-diphtheria	all travelers who haven't had booster within 10 years	1 dose lasts 10 years	soreness at injection site
typhoid	all travelers	4 capsules by mouth, 1 taken every other day	abdominal pain; nausea; rash
yellow fever	travelers to the northeastern forest areas	1 dose lasts 10 years	headaches; body aches; severe reactions are rare

IN ARGENTINA

AVAILABILITY & COST OF HEALTH CARE

Good medical care is available in Buenos Aires but may be variable elsewhere, especially in rural areas. Most doctors and hospitals expect payment in cash, regardless of whether you have travel health insurance.

The US Embassy website at http://usembassy.state.gov/posts/ar1/wwwhdoctors.html has an extensive list of physicians, dentists, hospitals and emergency services. If you're pregnant, be sure to check this site before departure to find the name of one or two obstetricians in the area you'll be visiting.

If you develop a life-threatening medical problem, you'll probably want to be evacuated to a country with state-of-the-art medical care. (For an ambulance, call ☎ 107.) Since this may cost thousands of dollars, be sure you have insurance to cover this before you depart. You can find a list of medical evacuation and travel-insurance companies on the US State Department website at www.travel.state.gov/medical.html.

Most pharmacies in Argentina are well supplied. Many medications that require a prescription in the USA and Canada are available over the counter, though they may be relatively expensive. If you're taking any medication on a regular basis, be sure you know its generic (scientific) name, since many pharmaceuticals go under different names in Argentina.

INFECTIOUS DISEASES

Dengue Fever

Dengue fever is a viral infection found throughout South America. In Argentina, dengue occurs in Salta province in the northwestern part of the country. Dengue is transmitted by Aedes mosquitoes, which prefer to bite during the daytime and are usually found close to human habitations, often indoors. They breed primarily in artificial water containers, such as jars, barrels, cans, cisterns, metal drums, plastic containers and discarded tires. As a result, dengue is especially common in densely populated, urban environments.

Dengue usually causes flu-like symptoms, including fever, muscle aches, joint pains, headaches, nausea and vomiting, often followed by a rash. The body aches may be quite uncomfortable, but most cases resolve uneventfully in a few days. Severe cases usually occur in children under the age of 15 who are experiencing their second dengue infection.

There is no treatment for dengue fever except to take analgesics such as acetaminophen/paracetamol (Tylenol) and drink plenty of fluids. Severe cases may require hospitalization for intravenous fluids and supportive care. There is no vaccine. The cornerstone of prevention is insect protection measures (see p487).

Hepatitis A

Hepatitis A is the second most common travel-related infection (after traveler's diarrhea). It's a viral infection of the liver that is usually acquired by ingestion of contaminated water, food or ice, though it may also be acquired by direct contact with infected persons. The illness occurs throughout the world, but the incidence is higher in developing nations. Symptoms may include fever, malaise, jaundice, nausea, vomiting and abdominal pain. Most cases resolve without complications, though hepatitis A occasionally causes severe liver damage. There is no treatment.

The vaccine for hepatitis A is extremely safe and highly effective. If you get a booster six to 12 months later, it lasts for at least 10 years. You really should get it before you go to Argentina. The safety of the hepatitis A vaccine has not been established for pregnant women or children under two years; instead, they should be given a gammaglobulin injection.

Hepatitis B

Like hepatitis A, hepatitis B is a liver infection that occurs worldwide but is more common in developing nations. Unlike hepatitis A, the disease is usually acquired by sexual contact or by exposure to infected blood, generally through blood transfusions or contaminated needles. The vaccine is recommended only for long-term travelers (on the road more than six months) who expect to live in rural areas or have close physical contact with the local population. Additionally, the vaccine is recommended for anyone who anticipates sexual contact with the local inhabitants or a possible need for medical, dental or other treatments while abroad, especially if a need for transfusions or injections is expected.

The hepatitis B vaccine is safe and highly effective. However, a total of three injections are necessary to establish full immunity. Several countries added the hepatitis B vaccine to the list of routine childhood immunizations in the 1980s, so many young adults are already protected.

Malaria

Malaria occurs in every South American country except Chile, Uruguay and the Falkland Islands. It's transmitted by mosquito bites, usually between dusk and dawn. The main symptom is high spiking fevers, which may be accompanied by chills, sweats, headache, body aches, weakness, vomiting or diarrhea. Severe cases may involve the central nervous system and lead to seizures, confusion, coma and death.

For Argentina, taking malaria pills is strongly recommended for travel to rural areas along the borders with Bolivia (lowlands of Salta and Jujuy provinces) and Paraguay (lowlands of Misiones and Corrientes provinces). There is a choice of three malaria pills, all of which work about equally well. Mefloquine (Lariam) is taken once weekly in a dosage of 250mg, starting one to two weeks before arrival and continuing through the trip and for four weeks after return. The problem is that a certain percentage of people (the number is controversial) develop neuropsychiatric side effects, which may range from mild to severe. Atovaquone/proguanil (Malarone) is a newly approved combination pill taken once daily with food starting two days before arrival and continuing through the trip and for seven days after departure. Side effects are typically mild. Doxycycline is a third alternative, but may cause an exaggerated sunburn reaction.

In general, Malarone seems to cause fewer side effects than mefloquine and is becoming more popular. The chief disadvantage is that it has to be taken daily. For longer trips, it's probably worth trying mefloquine; for shorter trips, Malarone will be the drug of choice for most people.

Protecting yourself against mosquito bites is just as important as taking malaria pills (for recommendations see p487), since none of the pills are 100% effective.

If you do not have access to medical care while traveling, you should bring along additional pills for emergency self-treatment, which you should take if you can't reach a doctor and you develop symptoms that suggest malaria, such as high spiking fevers. One option is to take four tablets of Malarone once daily for three days. However, Malarone should not be used for treatment if you're already taking it for prevention. An alternative is to take 650mg quinine three times daily and 100mg doxycycline twice daily for one week. If you start self-medication, see a doctor at the earliest possible opportunity.

If you develop a fever after returning home, see a physician, as malaria symptoms may not occur for months.

Rabies

Rabies is a viral infection of the brain and spinal cord that is almost always fatal. The rabies virus is carried in the saliva of infected animals and is typically transmitted through an animal bite, though contamination of any break in the skin with infected saliva may result in rabies. Rabies occurs in all South American countries.

The rabies vaccine is safe, but a full series requires three injections and is quite expensive. Those at high risk for rabies, such as animal handlers and spelunkers (cave explorers), should certainly get the vaccine. In addition, those at lower risk for animal bites should consider asking for the vaccine if they might be traveling to remote areas and might not have access to appropriate medical care if needed. The treatment for a possibly rabid bite consists of the rabies vaccine with rabies immune globulin. It's effective, but must be given promptly. Most travelers don't need rabies vaccine.

All animal bites and scratches must be promptly and thoroughly cleansed with large amounts of soap and water and local health authorities contacted to determine whether or not further treatment is necessary. Also see p487.

Typhoid Fever

Typhoid fever is caused by ingestion of food or water contaminated by a species of salmonella known as *Salmonella typhi*. Fever occurs in virtually all cases. Other symptoms may include headache, malaise,

HEALTH

muscle aches, dizziness, loss of appetite, nausea and abdominal pain. Either diarrhea or constipation may occur. Possible complications include intestinal perforation, intestinal bleeding, confusion, delirium or (rarely) coma.

Unless you expect to take all your meals in major hotels and restaurants, a typhoid vaccine is a good idea. It's usually given orally, but is also available as an injection. Neither vaccine is approved for use in children under two years.

The drug of choice for typhoid fever is usually a quinolone antibiotic such as ciprofloxacin (Cipro) or levofloxacin (Levaquin), which many travelers carry for treatment of traveler's diarrhea. However, if you self-treat for typhoid fever, you may also need to self-treat for malaria, since the symptoms of the two diseases may be indistinguishable.

Yellow Fever

Yellow fever is a life-threatening viral infection transmitted by mosquitoes in forested areas. The illness begins with flu-like symptoms, which may include fever, chills, headache, muscle aches, backache, loss of appetite, nausea and vomiting. These symptoms usually subside in a few days, but one person in six enters a second, toxic phase characterized by recurrent fever, vomiting, listlessness, jaundice, kidney failure and hemorrhage, leading to death in up to half of the cases. There is no treatment except for supportive care.

The yellow fever vaccine is strongly recommended for all travelers greater than nine months of age who visit the northeastern forest areas near the border with Brazil and Paraguay. For an up-to-date map showing the distribution of yellow fever in Argentina, go to the Center for Disease Control (CDC) website at www.cdc.gov/travel/diseases/maps/yellowfever_map2.htm.

The yellow fever vaccine is given only in approved yellow fever vaccination centers, which provide validated International Certificates of Vaccination (yellow booklets). The vaccine should be given at least 10 days before any potential exposure to yellow fever and remains effective for approximately 10 years. Reactions to the vaccine are generally mild and may include headaches, muscle aches, low-grade fevers, or discomfort at the injection site. Severe, life-threatening reactions have been described but are extremely rare. In general, the risk of becoming ill from the vaccine is far less than the risk of becoming ill from yellow fever, and you're strongly encouraged to get the vaccine.

Taking measures to protect yourself from mosquito bites (opposite) is an essential part of preventing yellow fever.

Other Infections

Argentine hemorrhagic fever occurs in the Pampas, chiefly from March through October. The disease is acquired by inhalation of dust contaminated with rodent excreta or by direct rodent contact.

Brucellosis is an infection of domestic and wild animals that may be transmitted to humans through direct animal contact or by consumption of unpasteurized dairy products from infected animals. Symptoms may include fever, malaise, depression, loss of appetite, headache, muscle aches and back pain. Complications may include arthritis, hepatitis, meningitis and endocarditis (heart-valve infection).

Chagas' disease is a parasitic infection that is transmitted by triatomine insects (reduviid bugs), which inhabit crevices in the walls and roofs of substandard housing in South and Central America. In Argentina, Chagas' disease occurs north of latitude 44 degrees 45'. Transmission is greatest during late spring (November and December). The triatomine insect lays its feces on human skin as it bites, usually at night. A person becomes infected when he or she unknowingly rubs the feces into the bite wound or any other open sore. Chagas' disease is extremely rare in travelers. However, if you sleep in a poorly constructed house, especially one made of mud, adobe or thatch, you should be sure to protect yourself with a bed net and a good insecticide.

Cholera is extremely rare in Argentina. A cholera vaccine is not recommended.

Hantavirus pulmonary syndrome is a rapidly progressive, life-threatening infection acquired through exposure to the excretions of wild rodents. Most cases occur in those who live in rodent-infested dwellings in rural areas. In Argentina, hantavirus infections are reported from the north-central and southwestern parts of the country.

HIV/AIDS has been reported from all South American countries. Be sure to use condoms for all sexual encounters.

Leishmaniasis occurs in the mountains and jungles of all South American countries except for Chile, Uruguay and the Falkland Islands. The infection is transmitted by sandflies, which are about one-third the size of mosquitoes. In Argentina, most cases occur in the northeastern part of the country and are limited to the skin, causing slowly growing ulcers over exposed parts of the body. A more severe type of Leishmaniasis disseminates to the bone marrow, liver and spleen. The disease may be particularly severe in those with HIV. There is no vaccine. To protect yourself from sandflies, follow the same precautions as for mosquitoes (see right), except that netting must be finer mesh (at least 18 holes per 2.54cm or to the linear inch).

Louse-borne typhus occurs in mountain areas, and murine typhus, which is transmitted by rat fleas, occurs in warmer rural and jungle areas in the north.

Tick-borne relapsing fever, which may be transmitted by either ticks or lice, is caused by bacteria that are closely related to those which cause Lyme disease and syphilis. In Argentina, tick-borne relapsing fever occurs in the northern part of the country. The illness is characterized by periods of fever, chills, headaches, body aches, muscle aches and cough, alternating with periods when the fever subsides and the person feels relatively well. To minimize the risk of relapsing fever, follow tick precautions (see p488) and practice good personal hygiene at all times.

TRAVELER'S DIARRHEA

To prevent diarrhea, avoid tap water unless it has been boiled, filtered or chemically disinfected (with iodine); only eat fresh fruits or vegetables if cooked or peeled; be wary of dairy products that might contain unpasteurized milk; and be highly selective when eating food from street vendors.

If you develop diarrhea, be sure to drink plenty of fluids, preferably an oral rehydration solution containing lots of salt and sugar. A few loose stools don't require treatment but if you start having more than four or five stools a day, you should start taking an antibiotic (usually a quinolone drug) and an antidiarrheal agent (such as loperamide). If diarrhea is bloody, persists for more than 72 hours or is accompanied by fever, shaking chills or severe abdominal pain you should seek medical attention.

ENVIRONMENTAL HAZARDS
Animal Bites

Do not attempt to pet, handle or feed any animal, with the exception of domestic animals known to be free of any infectious disease. Most animal injuries are directly related to a person's attempt to touch or feed the animal.

Any bite or scratch by a mammal, including bats, should be promptly and thoroughly cleansed with large amounts of soap and water, followed by application of an antiseptic such as iodine or alcohol. The local health authorities should be contacted immediately for possible post-exposure rabies treatment, whether or not you've been immunized against rabies. It may also be advisable to start an antibiotic, since wounds caused by animal bites and scratches frequently become infected. One of the newer quinolones, such as levofloxacin (Levaquin), which many travelers carry in case of diarrhea, would be an appropriate choice.

Snakes and leeches are a hazard in some areas of South America. In the event of a bite from a venomous snake, place the victim at rest, keep the bitten area immobilized, and move the victim immediately to the nearest medical facility. Avoid tourniquets, which are no longer recommended.

Mosquito Bites

To prevent mosquito bites, wear long sleeves, long pants, hats and shoes (rather than sandals). Bring along a good insect repellent, preferably one containing DEET, which should be applied to exposed skin and clothing, but not to eyes, mouth, cuts, wounds or irritated skin. Products containing lower concentrations of DEET are as effective, but for shorter periods of time. In general, adults and children over 12 years should use preparations containing 25% to 35% DEET, which usually lasts about six hours. Children between two and 12 years of age should use preparations containing no more than 10% DEET, applied sparingly, which will usually last about three hours. Neurologic toxicity has been reported from DEET, especially in children, but appears to be extremely uncommon and generally related to overuse. DEET-containing compounds should not be used on children under the age of two.

Insect repellents containing certain botanical products, including oil of eucalyptus

HEALTH

TRADITIONAL MEDICINE

Some common traditional remedies:

problem	treatment
altitude sickness	gingko
jet lag	melatonin
mosquito-bite prevention	eucalyptus oil; soybean oil
motion sickness	ginger

and soybean oil, are effective but last only 1½ to two hours. DEET-containing repellents are preferable for areas where there is a high risk of malaria or yellow fever. Products based on citronella are not effective.

For additional protection, you can apply permethrin to clothing, shoes, tents and bed nets. Permethrin treatments are safe and remain effective for at least two weeks, even when items are laundered. Permethrin should not be applied directly to skin.

Don't sleep with the window open unless there is a screen. If sleeping outdoors or in accommodations that allows entry of mosquitoes, use a bed net, preferably treated with permethrin, with edges tucked in under the mattress. The mesh size should be less than 1.5mm. If the sleeping area is not otherwise protected, use a mosquito coil, which will fill the room with insecticide through the night. Repellent-impregnated wristbands are not effective.

Tick Bites

To protect yourself from tick bites, follow the same precautions as for mosquitoes, except that boots are preferable to shoes, with pants tucked in. Be sure to perform a thorough tick check at the end of each day. You'll generally need the assistance of a friend or mirror for a full examination. Ticks should be removed with tweezers, grasping them firmly by the head. Insect repellents based on botanical products, described above, have not been adequately studied for insects other than mosquitoes and cannot be recommended to prevent tick bites.

Water

Tap water is generally not safe to drink. Vigorous boiling for one minute is the most effective means of water purification. At

altitudes greater than 2000m, boil for three minutes.

Another option is to disinfect water with iodine. You can add 2% tincture of iodine to 1L of water (five drops to clear water, 10 drops to cloudy water) and let stand for 30 minutes. If the water is cold, longer times may be required. Or you can buy iodine pills such as Globaline, Potable-Aqua and Coghlan's, available at most pharmacies. Instructions are enclosed and should be carefully followed. The taste of iodinated water may be improved by adding vitamin C (ascorbic acid). Iodinated water should not be consumed for more than a few weeks. Pregnant women, those with a history of thyroid disease, and those allergic to iodine should not drink iodinated water.

A number of water filters are on the market. Those with smaller pores (reverse osmosis filters) provide the broadest protection, but they are relatively large and are readily plugged by debris. Those with somewhat larger pores (microstrainer filters) are ineffective against viruses, although they remove other organisms. Manufacturers' instructions must be carefully followed.

TRAVELING WITH CHILDREN

When traveling with young children, be particularly careful about what you allow them to eat and drink, because diarrhea can be especially dangerous in this age group and because the vaccines for hepatitis A and typhoid fever are not approved for use in children under two years.

In general, children under nine months should not be brought to northeastern forest areas near the border with Brazil and Paraguay, where yellow fever occurs, since the vaccine is not safe in this age group.

Chloroquine, which is the main drug used to prevent malaria, may be given to children, but insect repellents must be applied in lower concentrations.

WOMEN'S HEALTH

You can find an English-speaking obstetrician in Argentina by going to the US Embassy website at http://usembassy.state.gov/posts/ar1/wwwhdoctors.html. However, medical facilities will probably not be comparable to those in your home country. In general, it's safer to avoid travel to Argentina late in pregnancy.

Language

CONTENTS

Spanish (known as *castellano* in Argentina and the rest of South America) is the official language and it is spoken throughout the country.

A number of immigrant communities have retained their languages as a badge of identity. In central Patagonia, for instance, there are pockets of Welsh speakers, but despite a recent revival of the language in Argentina, it is in danger of disappearing. Welsh cultural traditions remain strong in these regions, however, even reaching into the tourist industry.

English is studied, spoken and understood by many Argentines (especially in the capital). Italian is the language of the largest immigrant group and also understood by some, as is French. German speakers are numerous enough to support a weekly *porteño* newspaper, *Argentinisches Tageblatt*.

Argentina has over a dozen indigenous tongues, though some are spoken by very few individuals. In the Andean Northwest, Quechua speakers are numerous, and most of these are also Spanish speakers. In the southern Andes, there are at least 40,000 Mapuche speakers. In northeastern Argentina, there are about 15,000 speakers of both Guaraní and Toba.

ARGENTINE SPANISH

In addition to their flamboyance, an Argentine's Italian-accented Spanish pronunciation and other language quirks readily identify them throughout Latin America and abroad. The most prominent peculiarities are the usage of the pronoun *vos* in place of *tú* for 'you,' (see El Voseo on p490) and the trait of pronouncing the letters **ll** and **y** as 'zh' (as in 'azure') rather than 'y' (as in English 'you') as in the rest of the Americas. Note that in American Spanish, the plural of the familiar *tú* or *vos* is *ustedes,* not *vosotros,* as in Spain.

There are many vocabulary differences between European and American Spanish, and among Spanish-speaking countries in the Americas. The speech of Buenos Aires, in particular, abounds with words and phrases from the colorful slang known as *lunfardo*. Although you shouldn't use *lunfardo* words unless you are supremely confident that you know their every implication (especially in formal situations), you should be aware of some of the more common everyday usages (see Lunfardo on p494). Argentines normally refer to the Spanish language as *castellano* rather than *español*.

Every visitor should make an effort to speak Spanish, whose basic elements are easily acquired. If possible, take a brief night course at your local university or community college before departure. Even if you can't speak very well, Argentines are gracious folk and will encourage your use of Spanish, so there is no need to feel self-conscious about vocabulary or pronunciation. There are many common cognates, so if you're stuck, try Hispanicizing an English word – it's unlikely you'll make a truly embarrassing error. Do not, however, admit to being *embarazada* unless you are in fact pregnant. (See Cognates & Condoms on p492 for other usages to avoid.)

PHRASEBOOKS & DICTIONARIES

Lonely Planet's *Latin American Spanish Phrasebook* is not only amusing but can also get you by in many adventurous situations. Another very useful language resource is

EL VOSEO

Spanish in the Río de la Plata region differs from that of Spain and the rest of the Americas, most notably in the informal of the word 'you.' Instead of *tuteo* (the use of *tú*), Argentines commonly speak with *voseo* (the use of *vos*), a relic from 16th-century Spanish requiring slightly different grammar. All verbs change in spelling, stress and pronunciation. Examples of -*ar*, -*er* and -*ir* verbs are given below – the pronoun *tú* is included for contrast. Imperative forms (commands) also differ, but negative imperatives are identical in both *tuteo* and *voseo*.

The Spanish phrases included in this book use the *vos* form. An Argentine inviting a foreigner to address him or her informally will say *Me podés tutear* (literally, 'You can call me *tú*') even though they'll use the *vos* forms in subsequent conversation.

Verb	Tuteo	Voseo
hablar (to speak): **You speak/Speak!**	*Tú hablas/¡Habla!*	*Vos hablás/¡Hablá!*
soñar (to dream): **You dream/Dream!**	*Tú sueñas/¡Sueña!*	*Vos soñás/¡Soñá!*
comer (to eat): **You eat/Eat!**	*Tú comes/¡Come!*	*Vos comés/¡Comé!*
poner (to put): **You put/Put!**	*Tú pones/¡Pon!*	*Vos ponés/¡Poné!*
admitir (to admit): **You admit/Admit!**	*Tú admites/¡Admite!*	*Vos admitís/¡Admití!*
venir (to come): **You come/Come!**	*Tú vienes/¡Ven!*	*Vos venís/¡Vení!*

the University of Chicago *Spanish-English, English-Spanish Dictionary*. Its small size, light weight and thorough entries make it perfect for travel.

PRONUNCIATION

Pronunciation of Spanish is not difficult. Many Spanish sounds are similar to their English counterparts, and the relationship between pronunciation and spelling is clear and consistent. Unless otherwise indicated, the English examples used below take standard American pronunciation.

Vowels & Diphthongs

a	as in 'father'
e	as in 'met'
i	as the 'i' in 'police'
o	as in British English 'hot'
u	as the 'u' in 'rude'
ai	as the 'ai' in 'aisle'
au	as the 'ow' in 'how'
ei	as the 'ei' in 'vein'
ia	as the 'ya' in 'yard'
ie	as the 'ye' in 'yes'
oi	as the 'oi' in 'coin'
ua	as the 'wa' in 'wash'
ue	as the 'we' in 'well'

Consonants

Spanish consonants are generally the same as in English, with the exceptions listed following. The consonants **ch**, **ll** and **ñ** are generally considered distinct letters, but in dictionaries **ch** and **ll** are now often listed alphabetically under **c** and **l** respectively. The letter **ñ** still has a separate entry after **n** in alphabetical listings.

b	similar to English 'b,' but softer; referred to as *b larga*
c	as in 'celery' before **e** and **i**; elsewhere as the 'k' in 'king'
ch	as in 'choose' before **a**, **o** and **u**; elsewhere as the 'k' in 'king'
d	as in 'dog'; between vowels and after **l** or **n**, it's closer to the 'th' in 'this'
g	as the 'ch' in the Scottish *loch* before **e** and **i** (*kh* in our pronunciation guides); elsewhere, as in 'go'
h	invariably silent
j	as the 'ch' in the Scottish *loch* (*kh* in our pronunciation guides)
ll	as the 'y' in 'yellow'
ñ	as the 'ni' in 'onion'
r	as in 'run,' but strongly rolled
rr	very strongly rolled
v	similar to English 'b,' but softer; referred to as *b corta*
x	usually pronounced as **j** above; as in 'taxi' in other instances
y	as the 'sh' in ship when used as a consonant
z	as the 's' in 'sun'

Word Stress

In general, words ending in vowels or the letters **n** or **s** are stressed on the second-last syllable, while those with other endings have stress on the last syllable. Thus *vaca* (cow) and *caballos* (horses) are both stressed on the next-to-last syllable, while *ciudad* (city) and *infeliz* (unhappy) are stressed on the last syllable.

Written accents generally indicate words that don't follow the rules above, eg *sótano* (basement), *América* and *porción* (portion).

GENDER & PLURALS
In Spanish, nouns are either masculine or feminine, and there are rules to help determine gender (there are of course some exceptions). Feminine nouns generally end with -**a** or with the groups -**ción**, -**sión** or -**dad**. Other endings typically signify a masculine noun. Endings for adjectives also change to agree with the gender of the noun they modify (masculine/feminine -**o**/-**a**). Where both masculine and feminine forms are included in this language guide, they are separated by a slash, with the masculine form first, eg *perdido/a* (lost).

If a noun or adjective ends in a vowel, the plural is formed by adding **s** to the end. If it ends in a consonant, the plural is formed by adding **es** to the end.

ACCOMMODATIONS
I'm looking for ... *Estoy buscando ...* e·stoy boos·kan·do ...
Where is ...?
¿Dónde hay ...? don·de ai ...
  a hotel *un hotel* oon o·tel
  a boarding *una* oo·na
  house *residencial* re·si·den·si·al
  a youth hostel *un albergue* oon al·ber·ge
     de juventud de khoo·ven·tood

Are there any rooms available?
¿Tienen habitaciones libres?
tye·nen a·bee·ta·syon·es lee·bres

I'd like a ... *Quisiera una* kee·sye·ra oo·na
room. *habitación ...* a·bee·ta·syon ...
  double *doble* do·ble
  single *individual* een·dee·vee·dwal
  twin *con dos camas* kon dos ka·mas

How much is it *¿Cuánto cuesta* kwan·to kwes·ta
per ...? *por ...?* por ...
  night *noche* no·che
  person *persona* per·so·na
  week *semana* se·ma·na

private/shared *baño privado/* ba·nyo pree·va·do/
bathroom *compartido* kom·par·tee·do

MAKING A RESERVATION
(for phone or written requests)
To ... *A ...*
From ... *De ...*
Date *Fecha*

I'd like to book ... *Quisiera reservar ...* (see the list under 'Accommodations' for bed and room options)
in the name of ... *en nombre de ...*
for the nights of ... *para las noches del ...*
credit card ... *... tarjeta de crédito*
  number *número de*
  expiry date *fecha de vencimiento de*

Please confirm ... *Puede confirmar ...*
  availability *la disponibilidad*
  price *el precio*

---

full board *pensión completa* pen·syon kom·ple·ta
too expensive *demasiado caro* de·ma·sya·do ka·ro
cheaper *más económico* mas e·ko·no·mee·ko
discount *descuento* des·kwen·to

Does it include breakfast?
¿Incluye el desayuno? een·kloo·she el de·sa·shoo·no
May I see the room?
¿Puedo ver la habitación? pwe·do ver la a·bee·ta·syon
I don't like it.
No me gusta. no me goos·ta
It's fine. I'll take it.
Está bien. La alquilo. es·ta byen la al·kee·lo
I'm leaving now.
Me voy ahora. me voy a·o·ra

CONVERSATION & ESSENTIALS
Hello. *Hola.* o·la
Good morning. *Buenos días.* bwe·nos dee·as
Good afternoon. *Buenas tardes.* bwe·nas tar·des
Good evening/ *Buenas noches.* bwe·nas no·ches
night.
Bye. *Chau.* chow
See you soon. *Hasta luego.* as·ta lwe·go
Yes. *Sí.* see
No. *No.* no
Please. *Por favor.* por fa·vor
Thank you. *Gracias.* gra·syas
Many thanks. *Muchas gracias.* moo·chas gra·syas
You're welcome. *De nada.* de na·da
Pardon me. *Perdón.* per·don

COGNATES & CONDOMS

False cognates are words that appear to be very similar but have different meanings in different languages. In some instances, these differences can lead to serious misunderstandings. The following is a list of some of these words in English with their Spanish cousins and their meaning in Spanish. Note that this list deals primarily with the Río de la Plata region, and usages may differ elsewhere in South America. Also, be careful with some words from Spain, like *coger*, which in Mexico and South America doesn't mean 'to get or catch' but 'to fuck.' It will take only one instance of being laughed at for claiming you need to fuck the bus before you quickly learn what to really say.

| English | | |
Spanish	Meaning in Spanish	
actual		
actual	current (at present)	
carpet		
carpeta	looseleaf notebook	
embarrassed		
embarazada	pregnant	
fabric		
fábrica	factory	
to introduce		
introducir	to introduce (eg an innovation)	
notorious		
notorio	well known, evident	
to present		
presentar	to introduce (a person)	
precise		
preciso	necessary	
preservative		
preservativo	condom	
sensible		
sensible	sensitive	
violation		
violación	rape	

Excuse me.   *Permiso.*   per·*mee*·so
(used when asking permission, eg to get by someone)
Forgive me.   *Disculpe.*   dees·*kool*·pe
(used when apologizing)

How are you?
¿Cómo está? (pol)   co·mo es·*ta*
¿Cómo estás? (inf)   co·mo es·*tas*
What's your name?
¿Cómo se llama? (pol)   ko·mo se sha·ma
¿Cómo te llamás? (inf)   ko·mo te sha·mas

My name is ...
Me llamo ...   me *sha*·mo ...
It's a pleasure to meet you.
Mucho gusto.   moo·cho *goos*·to
The pleasure is mine.
El gusto es mío.   el *goos*·to es *mee*·o
Where are you from?
¿De dónde es? (pol)   de *don*·de es
¿De dónde sos? (inf)   de *don*·de sos
I'm from ...
Soy de ...   soy de ...
Where are you staying?
¿Dónde estás alojado/a?   *don*·de es·*tas* a·lo·*kha*·do/a
May I take a photo?
¿Puedo tomar una foto?   *pwe*·do to·*mar* oo·na *fo*·to

DIRECTIONS
How do I get to ...?
¿Cómo puedo llegar a ...? ko·mo *pwe*·do she·*gar* a ...
Is it far?
¿Está lejos?   es·*ta* le·khos

SIGNS	
Entrada	Entrance
Salida	Exit
Información	Information
Abierto	Open
Cerrado	Closed
Prohibido	Prohibited
Comisaria	Police Station
Baños	Toilets
Hombres/Caballeros	Men/Gentlemen
Mujeres/Damas	Women/Ladies

Go straight ahead.
Siga derecho.   see·ga de·*re*·cho
Turn left.
Voltée a la izquierda.   vol·*te*·e a la ees·*kyer*·da
Turn right.
Voltée a la derecha.   vol·*te*·e a la de·*re*·cha
Can you show me (on the map)?
¿Me lo podría indicar   me lo po·*dree*·a een·dee·*kar*
(en el mapa)?   (en el *ma*·pa)

north	norte	nor·te
south	sur	soor
east	este	s·te
west	oeste	o·es·te
here	aquí	a·kee
there	allí	a·shee
avenue	avenida	a·ve·nee·da
block	cuadra	kwa·dra
street	calle	ka·she

EMERGENCIES

Help!	¡Socorro!	so·ko·ro
Go away!	¡Déjeme!	de·khe·me
Get lost!	¡Váyase!	va·sha·se

Call ...!	¡Llame a ...!	sha·me a ...
an ambulance	una ambulancia	oo·na am·boo·lan·sya
a doctor	un médico	oon me·dee·ko
the police	la policía	la po·lee·see·a

It's an emergency.
Es una emergencia.   es oo·na e·mer·khen·sya
Could you help me, please?
¿Me puede ayudar,   me pwe·de a·yoo·dar
por favor?   por fa·vor
I'm lost.
Estoy perdido/a. (m/f)   es·toy per·dee·do/a
Where are the toilets?
¿Dónde están los baños?   don·de es·tan los ba·nyos

HEALTH

I'm sick.
Estoy enfermo/a.   es·toy en·fer·mo/a
I need a doctor.
Necesito un médico.   ne·se·see·to oon me·dee·ko
Where's the hospital?
¿Dónde está el hospital?   don·de es·ta el os·pee·tal
I'm pregnant.
Estoy embarazada.   es·toy em·ba·ra·sa·da
I've been vaccinated.
Estoy vacunado/a.   es·toy va·koo·na·do/a

I'm allergic to ...	Soy alérgico/a a ...	soy a·ler·khee·ko/a a ...
antibiotics	los antibióticos	los an·tee·byo·tee·kos
nuts	las frutas secas	las froo·tas se·kas
penicillin	la penicilina	la pe·ni·see·lee·na

I'm ...	Soy ...	soy ...
asthmatic	asmático/a	as·ma·tee·ko/a
diabetic	diabético/a	dya·be·tee·ko/a
epileptic	epiléptico/a	e·pee·lep·tee·ko/a

I have ...	Tengo ...	ten·go ...
a cough	tos	tos
diarrhea	diarrea	dya·re·a
a headache	un dolor de cabeza	oon do·lor de ka·be·sa
nausea	náusea	now·se·a

LANGUAGE DIFFICULTIES

Do you speak (English)?
¿Habla/Hablás (inglés)? a·bla/a·blas (een·gles) (pol/inf)
Does anyone here speak English?
¿Hay alguien que hable ai al·gyen ke a·ble
inglés?   een·gles
I (don't) understand.
(No) Entiendo.   (no) en·tyen·do
How do you say ...?
¿Cómo se dice ...?   ko·mo se dee·se ...
What does ... mean?
¿Qué quiere decir ...?   ke kye·re de·seer ...

Could you please ...?	¿Puede ..., por favor?	pwe·de ... por fa·vor
repeat that	repetirlo	re·pe·teer·lo
speak more slowly	hablar más despacio	a·blar mas des·pa·syo
write it down	escribirlo	es·kree·beer·lo

NUMBERS

0	cero	ce·ro
1	uno/a	oo·no/a
2	dos	dos
3	tres	tres
4	cuatro	kwa·tro
5	cinco	seen·ko
6	seis	seys
7	siete	sye·te
8	ocho	o·cho
9	nueve	nwe·ve
10	diez	dyes
11	once	on·se
12	doce	do·se
13	trece	tre·se
14	catorce	ka·tor·se
15	quince	keen·se
16	dieciséis	dye·see·seys
17	diecisiete	dye·see·sye·te
18	dieciocho	dye·see·o·cho
19	diecinueve	dye·see·nwe·ve
20	veinte	vayn·te
21	veintiuno	vayn·tee·oo·no
30	treinta	trayn·ta
31	treinta y uno	trayn·tai oo·no
40	cuarenta	kwa·ren·ta
50	cincuenta	seen·kwen·ta
60	sesenta	se·sen·ta
70	setenta	se·ten·ta
80	ochenta	o·chen·ta
90	noventa	no·ven·ta
100	cien	syen
101	ciento uno	syen·to oo·no
200	doscientos	do·syen·tos
1000	mil	meel

LANGUAGE

SHOPPING & SERVICES

I'd like to buy ...
Quisiera comprar ...   kee·*sye*·ra kom·*prar* ...

I'm just looking.
Sólo estoy mirando.   so·lo es·*toy* mee·*ran*·do

May I look at it?
¿Puedo mirarlo?   pwe·do mee·*rar*·lo

How much is it?
¿Cuánto cuesta?   kwan·to kwes·ta

That's too expensive for me.
Es demasiado caro   es de·ma·*sya*·do *ka*·ro
para mí.   pa·ra mee

Could you lower the price?
¿Podría bajar un poco   po·*dree*·a ba·*khar* oon *po*·ko
el precio?   el *pre*·syo

I don't like it.
No me gusta.   no me *goos*·ta

I'll take it.
Lo llevo.   lo *ye*·vo

Do you accept ...?	¿Aceptan ...?	a·sep·tan ...
credit cards	tarjetas de crédito	tar·*khe*·tas de kre·dee·to
traveler's checks	cheques de viajero	che·kes de vya·*khe*·ro

less	menos	me·nos
more	más	mas
large	grande	gran·de
small	pequeño	pe·ke·nyo

I'm looking for (the) ...	Estoy buscando ...	es·toy boos·kan·do
ATM	el cajero automático	el ka·*khe*·ro ow·to·ma·tee·ko
bank	el banco	el ban·ko
bookstore	la librería	la lee·bre·*ree*·a
embassy	la embajada	la em·ba·*kha*·da
exchange office	la casa de cambio	la *ka*·sa de kam·byo
general store	la tienda	la tyen·da
laundry	la lavandería	la la·van·de·*ree*·a
market	el mercado	el mer·ka·do
pharmacy	la farmacia	la far·ma·sya
post office	los correos	los ko·re·os
supermarket	el supermercado	el soo·per·mer·ka·do
tourist office	la oficina de turismo	la o·fee·*see*·na de too·rees·mo

What time does it open/close?
¿A qué hora abre/cierra?   a ke o·ra a·bre/sye·ra

LUNFARDO

Below are are some of the spicier *lunfardo* (slang) terms that you may hear on your travels in Argentina.

boliche – disco or nightclub
boludo – jerk, asshole, idiot; often used in a friendly fashion, but a deep insult to a stranger
bondi – bus
buena onda – good vibes
carajo – asshole, prick, bloody hell
chabón/chabona – kid, guy/girl (term of endearment)
che – hey
fiaca – laziness
guita – money
macanudo – great, fabulous
mango – one peso
masa – a great, cool thing
mina – woman
morfar – eat
pendejo – idiot
piba/pibe – cool young guy/girl
piola – cool, clever
pucho – cigarette
re – very, as in *re interestante* (very interesting)

Some Lunfardo Phrases

¡Ponete las pilas! – Get on with it! (literally 'Put in the batteries!')
Diez puntos – OK, cool, fine (literally 'Ten points')
Me mataste – I don't know; I have no idea (literally 'You've killed me')
Le faltan un par de jugadores – He's not playing with a full deck (literally 'He's a couple of players short (of a team)')
Che boludo – the most *porteño* phrase on earth. Ask a friendly local youth to explain.

I want to change some money/traveler's cheques.
Quiero cambiar dinero/cheques de viajero.
kye·ro kam·*byar* dee·ne·ro/che·kes de vya·*khe*·ro

What's the exchange rate?
¿Cuál es el tipo de cambio?
kwal es el tee·po de kam·byo

I want to call ...
Quiero llamar a ...
kye·ro ya·*mar* a ...

Where's the local Internet cafe?
¿Dónde hay un cibercafé por acá?
don·de ai oon sy·ber·ka·*fay* por a·ka

I'd like to get Internet access.
Quisiera usar internet.
kee·*sye*·ra oo·*sar* in·tair·net

airmail	correo aéreo	ko·re·o a·e·re·o
letter	carta	kar·ta
registered mail	certificado	ser·tee·fee·ka·do
stamps	estampillas	es·tam·pee·shas

TIME & DATES

What time is it?	¿Qué hora es?	ke o·ra es
It's (one) o'clock.	Es la (una).	es la (oo·na)
It's (six) o'clock.	Son las (seis).	son las (seys)
midnight	medianoche	me·dya·no·che
noon	mediodía	me·dyo·dee·a
half past two	dos y media	dos ee me·dya

now	ahora	a·o·ra
today	hoy	oy
tonight	esta noche	es·ta no·che
tomorrow	mañana	ma·nya·na

Monday	lunes	loo·nes
Tuesday	martes	mar·tes
Wednesday	miércoles	myer·ko·les
Thursday	jueves	khwe·ves
Friday	viernes	vyer·nes
Saturday	sábado	sa·ba·do
Sunday	domingo	do·meen·go

January	enero	e·ne·ro
February	febrero	fe·bre·ro
March	marzo	mar·so
April	abril	a·breel
May	mayo	ma·sho
June	junio	khoo·nyo
July	julio	khoo·lyo
August	agosto	a·gos·to
September	septiembre	sep·tyem·bre
October	octubre	ok·too·bre
November	noviembre	no·vyem·bre
December	diciembre	dee·syem·bre

TRANSPORT
Public Transport

What time does	¿A qué hora ...	a ke o·ra ...
... leave/arrive?	sale/llega?	sa·le/she·ga
the bus	el autobus	el ow·to·boos
the plane	el avión	el a·vyon
the ship	el barco	el bar·ko

airport	el aeropuerto	el a·e·ro·pwer·to
bus station	la estación de autobuses	la es·ta·syon de ow·to·boo·ses
bus stop	la parada de autobuses	la pa·ra·da de ow·to·boo·ses
luggage check room	guardería equipaje	gwar·de·ree·a e·kee·pa·khe
ticket office	la boletería	la bo·le·te·ree·a

I'd like a ticket to ...
Quiero un boleto a ... kye·ro oon bo·le·to a ...
What's the fare to ...?
¿Cuánto cuesta hasta ...? kwan·to kwes·ta a·sta ...

student's (fare)	de estudiante	de es·too·dyan·te
1st class	primera clase	pree·me·ra kla·se
2nd class	segunda clase	se·goon·da kla·se
one-way	ida	ee·da
return	ida y vuelta	ee·da ee vwel·ta
taxi	taxi	tak·see

Private Transport

pickup (truck)	camioneta	ka·myo·ne·ta
truck	camión	ka·myon
hitchhike	hacer dedo	a·ser de·do

I'd like to hire	Quisiera	kee·sye·ra
a/an ...	alquilar ...	al·kee·lar ...
bicycle	una bicicleta	oo·na bee·see·kle·ta
car	un auto	oon ow·to
4WD	un todo terreno	oon to·do te·re·no
motorbike	una moto	oo·na mo·to

ROAD SIGNS

Acceso	Entrance
Estacionamiento	Parking
Ceda el Paso	Give Way
Despacio	Slow
Dirección Única	One-Way
Mantenga Su Derecha	Keep to the Right
No Adelantar	No Passing
Peaje	Toll
Peligro	Danger
Prohibido Estacionar	No Parking
Prohibido el Paso	No Entry
Stop	Stop
Salida de Autopista	Exit Freeway

Is this the road to ...?
¿Se va a ... por esta carretera? se va a ... por es·ta ka·re·te·ra
Where's a petrol station?
¿Dónde hay una gasolinera? don·de ai oo·na ga·so·lee·ne·ra
Please fill it up.
Lleno, por favor. she·no por fa·vor
I'd like (20) liters.
Quiero (veinte) litros. kye·ro (vayn·te) lee·tros

| diesel | diesel | dee·sel |
| gas/petrol | gasolina | ga·so·lee·na |

LANGUAGE

leaded (regular) *gasolina con* ga·so·*lee*·na kon
plomo *plo*·mo
unleaded *gasolina sin* ga·so·*lee*·na seen
plomo *plo*·mo

(How long) Can I park here?
¿(Por cuánto tiempo) (por *kwan*·to *tyem*·po)
Puedo estacionar aquí? *pwe*·do e·psta·syon·*ar* a·*kee*
Where do I pay?
¿Dónde se paga? *don*·de se *pa*·ga
I need a mechanic.
Necesito un ne·se·*see*·to oon
mecánico. me·*ka*·nee·ko
The car has broken down (in ...).
El auto se ha averiado el *ow*·to se a a·ve·*rya*·do
(en ...). (en ...)
The motorbike won't start.
No arranca la moto. no a·*ran*·ka la *mo*·to
I have a flat tyre.
Tengo un pinchazo. *ten*·go oon peen·*cha*·so
I've run out of petrol.
Me quedé sin gasolina. me ke·*de* seen ga·so·*lee*·na
I've had an accident.
Tuve un accidente. *too*·ve oon ak·see·*den*·te

TRAVEL WITH CHILDREN

Do you mind if I breast-feed here?
¿Le molesta que dé de pecho aquí?
le mo·*les*·ta ke de de *pe*·cho a·*kee*
Are children allowed?
¿Se admiten niños?
se ad·*mee*·ten *nee*·nyos

I need ...
Necesito ... ne·se·*see*·to ...
Do you have ...?
¿Hay ...? ai ...
a car baby seat
un asiento de seguridad para bebés
oon a·*syen*·to de se·goo·ree·*dad* pa·ra be·*bes*
a child-minding service
un servicio de cuidado de niños
oon ser·*vee*·syo de kwee·*da*·do de *nee*·nyos
a creche
una guardería
oo·na gwar·de·*ree*·a
(disposable) diapers/nappies
pañales (de usar y tirar)
pa·*nya*·les (de oo·*sar* ee tee·*rar*)
an (English-speaking) babysitter
una niñera (de habla inglesa)
oo·na nee·*nye*·ra (de *a*·bla een·*gle*·sa)
formula (infant milk powder)
leche en polvo
le·che en *pol*·vo
a highchair
una trona
oo·na *tro*·na
a potty
una pelela
oo·na pe·*le*·la
a stroller
un cochecito
oon ko·che·*see*·to

Also available from Lonely Planet:
Latin American Spanish Phrasebook

LANGUAGE

Glossary

For an explanation of food-related terms, see p52, for accommodation terms, p458, and for language in general, p489.

abuelos – grandparents

ACA – Automóvil Club Argentino, which provides maps, road service, insurance and other services, and operates hotels and campgrounds throughout the country

acequia – irrigation canal

aerosilla – chairlift

alcalde – mayor

alerce – large coniferous tree, resembling a California redwood, from which Argentina's Parque Nacional Los Alerces takes its name

apeadero – whistle-stop

arrayán – tree of the myrtle family, from which Argentina's Parque Nacional Los Arrayanes takes its name

arroyo – creek, stream

arte rupestre – cave paintings

asado – the famous Argentine barbecue

autopista – freeway or motorway

baliza – emergency reflector

balneario – any swimming or bathing area, including beach resorts, river beaches and swimming holes

balsa – ferry

bandoneón – an accordion-like instrument used in tango music

barra brava – fervent soccer fan; the Argentine equivalent of Britain's 'football hooligan'

bencina – white gas, used for camp stoves; also known as *nafta blanca*

bicho – any small creature, from insect to mammal; also used to refer to an ugly person

boleadoras – weighted, leather-covered balls attached to a length of thin rope, historically used as a hunting weapon by gauchos and some of Argentina's indigenous peoples; thrown at a guanaco or rhea's legs, they entangle the animal and bring it down

boliche – nightclub or disco

bombachas – a gaucho's baggy pants; can also mean women's underwear

bombilla – metal straw with filter for drinking *mate*

buena onda – good vibes

cabildo – colonial town council; also, the building that housed the council

cacerolazo – a form of street protest; it first occurred in December 2001 where people took to their balconies in Buenos Aires banging pots and pans *(cacerolas)* to show their discontent; the banging moved to the streets, then to cities throughout Argentina, and culminated in the resignation of President de la Rua

cajero automático – ATM

caldén – a tree characteristic of the Dry Pampas

camarote – 1st-class sleeper

cambio – money-exchange office; also *casa de cambio*

campo – the countryside; alternately, a field or paddock

característica – telephone area code

carnavalito – traditional folk dance

carpincho – capybara, a large (but cute) aquatic rodent that inhabits the Paraná and other subtropical rivers

carrovelismo – land sailing

cartelera – an office selling discount tickets

casa de cambio – money-exchange office, often shortened to *cambio*

casa de familia – family accommodations

casa de gobierno – literally 'government house,' a building now often converted to a museum, offices etc

castellano – the term used in much of South America for the Spanish language spoken throughout Latin America; literally refers to Castilian Spanish

catarata – waterfall

caudillo – in 19th-century Argentine politics, a provincial strongman whose power rested more on personal loyalty than political ideals or party affiliation

centro cívico – civic center

cerro – hill, mountain

certificado – certified mail

chacarera – traditional folk dance

chacra – small, independent farm

chamamé – folk music of Corrientes

chusquea – solid bamboo of the Valdivian rainforest in Patagonia

coche cama – sleeper class

coima – a bribe; one who solicits a bribe is a *coimero*

colectivo – local bus

combi – long-distance bus

comedor – basic cafeteria

común – common class

Conaf – Corporación Nacional Forestal, Chilean state agency in charge of forestry and conservation, including management of national parks like Torres del Paine

confitería – café serving light meals

conjunto – a musical band

Conquista del Desierto – Conquest of the Desert, a euphemism for General Julio Argentino Roca's late-19th-century war of extermination against the Mapuche of northern Patagonia

contrabajo – double bass
correo – post office
corriente – current
cospel – token used in public telephones
costanera – seaside, riverside or lakeside road or walkway
criollo – in colonial period, an American-born Spaniard, but now used for any Latin American of European descent; the term also describes the feral cattle and horses of the Pampas
cruce – crossroads
cuatrerismo – cattle rustling

desaparecidos (los) – the disappeared; the victims (estimated at up to 30,000) of Argentina's Dirty War who were never found
dique – a dam; the resultant reservoir is often used for recreational purposes; can also refer to a drydock
Dirty War – see *Guerra Sucia*
dorado – large river fish in the Paraná drainage, known among fishing enthusiasts as the 'Tiger of the Paraná' for its fighting spirit
duende – gnome

edificio – a building
ejecutivo – executive class
encomienda – colonial labor system, under which Indian communities were required to provide laborers for Spaniards *(encomenderos)*, and the Spaniards were to provide religious and language instruction; in practice, the system benefited Spaniards far more than native peoples
epa – an exclamation meaning 'Hey! Wow! Look out!'
ERP – Ejército Revolucionario del Pueblo, a revolutionary leftist group in the sugar-growing areas of Tucumán province in 1970s that modeled itself after the Cuban revolution; it was wiped out by the Argentine army during the Guerra Sucia
esquina – street corner
estación de servicio – gas station
estancia – extensive ranch for cattle or sheep, with an owner or manager *(estanciero)* and dependent resident labor force; many are now open to tourists for recreational activities such as riding, tennis and swimming, either for weekend escapes or extended stays
este – east

facón – a knife used by gauchos that is traditionally worn in the small of the back behind the belt
folklore – Argentine folk music
fútbol – soccer

gasolero – motor vehicle that uses diesel fuel, which is much cheaper than ordinary gasoline in Argentina
guardaganado – cattle guard (on a road or highway)
guardia – watchman

Guerra Sucia – the Dirty War of the 1970s, of the Argentine military against left-wing revolutionaries and anyone suspected of sympathizing with them; also referred to as the 'military period'
guitarrón – an oversized guitar used for playing bass lines

horario – schedule

ichu – bunch grass of the Andean altiplano
ida – one-way
ida y vuelta – roundtrip
iglesia – church
interno – internal bus-route number; also a telephone extension number
IVA – *impuesto de valor agregado*; value-added tax, often added to restaurant or hotel bills in Argentina

jejenes – annoying biting insects
jineteada – rodeo

libro de reclamos – complaint book
locutorio – private long-distance telephone office; usually offers fax and Internet services as well
lunfardo – street slang

manta – a shawl or bedspread
manzana – literally, 'apple'; also used to define one square block of a city
Maragatos – inhabitants of Carmen de Patagons
mate – tea made from *yerba mate* leaves; Argentina is the world's largest producer and consumer of *mate* and preparing and drinking the beverage is an important social ritual; the word also refers to the *mate* gourd the tea is prepared in
mazorca – political police of 19th-century Argentine dictator Juan Manuel de Rosas
mercado artesanal – handicraft market
meseta – interior steppe of eastern Patagonia
mestizo – a person of mixed Indian and Spanish descent
milonga – in tango, refers to a song, a dance or the dance salon itself
minutas – snacks or short orders
mirador – scenic viewpoint, usually on a hill but often in a building
monte – scrub forest; the term is often applied to any densely vegetated area
Montoneros – left-wing faction of the Peronist party that became an underground urban guerrilla movement in 1970s
municipalidad – city hall

nafta – gasoline or petrol
neumático – spare tire
norte – north

oeste – west
Ovnis – UFOs

parada – a bus stop
paraje – pump
parrilla – mixed grill; also *parrillada*
paseo – an outing, such as a walk in the park or downtown
pato – duck; also a gaucho sport where players on horseback wrestle for a ball encased in a leather harness with handles
peatonal – pedestrian mall, usually in the downtown area of major Argentine cities
pehuén – araucaria, or 'monkey puzzle' tree of southern Patagonia
peña – club that hosts informal folk-music gatherings
percha – perch, also means coathanger
picada – in rural areas, a trail, especially through dense woods or mountains; in the context of food, hors d'oeuvres or snacks
pingüinera – penguin colony
piqueteros – picketers
piropo – a flirtatious remark
piso – floor
porteño/a – inhabitant of Buenos Aires, a 'resident of the port'
precios patagónicos – Patagonian prices
precordillera – foothills of the Andes
primera – 1st class on a train
Proceso – short for El Proceso de Reorganización Nacional, a military euphemism for its brutal attempt to remake Argentina's political and economic culture between 1976 and 1983
propina – a tip, for example, in a restaurant or cinema
pucará – in the Andean Northwest, a pre-Columbian fortification, generally on high ground commanding an unobstructed view in several directions
pulpería – a country store or tavern
puna – Andean highlands, usually above 3000m
puntano – a native or resident of Argentina's San Luis province

quebracho – literally, 'axe-breaker'; tree common to the Chaco that is a natural source of tannin for the leather industry
quebrada – a canyon
quincho – thatch-roof hut, now often used to refer to a building at the back of a house used for parties

rambla – boardwalk
rancho – a rural house, generally of adobe, with a thatched roof
recargo – additional charge, usually 10%, that many Argentine businesses add to credit-card transactions
reducción – an Indian settlement created by Spanish missionaries during the colonial period; the most famous are the Jesuit missions in the triple-border area of Argentina, Paraguay and Brazil
refugio – a usually rustic shelter in a national park or remote area
remise – radio taxi without a meter that generally offer fixed fares within a given zone; also *remís*

riacho – stream
ripio – gravel
rotisería – take-out shop
rotonda – traffic circle, roundabout
RN – Ruta Nacional; a national highway
RP – Ruta Provincial; a provincial highway
ruta – highway

s/n –*sin número*, indicating a street address without a number
sábalo – popular river fish in the Paraná drainage
salar – salt lake or salt pan, usually in the high Andes or Argentine Patagonia
samba – traditional folk dance
semi-cama – semisleeper class
sendero – a trail in the woods
servicentro – gas station
siesta – lengthy afternoon break for lunch and, sometimes, a nap
Subte – the Buenos Aires subway system
sur – south
surubí – popular river fish frequently served in restaurants

tahona – flour mill
tapir – large hoofed mammal of subtropical forests in northern Argentina and Paraguay, a distant relative of the horse
tarjeta magnética – magnetic bus card
tarjeta telefónica – telephone card
tarjeta verde – 'green card'; title document for Argentine vehicles which drivers must carry
teleférico – gondola cable-car
telera – textile workshop
tenedor libre – all you can eat
todo terreno – mountain bike
tola – high-altitude shrubs in the altiplano of northwestern Argentina
torrontés – dry white wine from Cafayate
trapiche – sugar mill
turista – 2nd class on a train, usually not very comfortable

vicuña – wild relative of domestic llama and alpaca, found in Argentina's Andean northwest only at high altitudes
vinoteca – wine bar
vino tinto – red wine

yacaré – South American alligator, found in humid, subtropical areas
YPF – Yacimientos Fiscales Petrolíferos, Argentina's former national oil company
yungas – in northwestern Argentina, transitional subtropical lowland forest

zapateo – folkloric tap dance
zona franca – duty-free zone
zonda – a hot, dry wind descending from the Andes

Behind the Scenes

THIS BOOK

This 5th edition of *Argentina* was researched and written by Danny Palmerlee (coordinating author), Sandra Bao, Andrew Dean Nystrom and Lucas Vidgen. Danny, Sandra, Ben Greensfelder, Carolyn Hubbard and Alan Murphy wrote the previous edition. Also contributing to *Argentina* 5 were Thomas Kohnstamm (The Culture), Dereck Foster (Food & Drink), Dr David Goldberg (Health), Chris Moss ('Finer & Finer Argentine Wine' boxed text), and Daniel Buck and Anne Meadows ('Butch & Sundance's Patagonian Refuge' boxed text).

THANKS from the Authors

Danny Palmerlee First I have to thank La Diablo, Pimpollo and everyone else in La Cumbre who made my stay so wonderful. Isabel, where are you? I couldn't have done half of this if it weren't for the help and friendship of everyone in Córdoba: history buff Paula Bonelli, carting pro Germán González Castro, mamá Carina Martinetto, *cebador* Claudia Martinetto, hiking guide Ignacio Maciel, dance partner Marina Favalli and, of course, Nipicopolepe. In Mendoza, many thanks to Mercedes Viotti of Casa Italia for introducing me into the city's culinary wonders. In San Juan, Natacha and Juan of Zonda Hostel helped immensely. Also in San Juan, my deepest of thanks to Andrea Amin, Daniele Ares and Maria Jose Ares who so kindly dragged a total stranger to their *asado*.

On the home front, hugest of hugs to my star editor Suki Gear (you're the best, Suki!) and rockin' coauthors Andrew, Lucas and Sandra. Also thanks

to Ben G for comin' through with the tough stuff in the end.

To my parents for putting me up (and putting up with me) once again, I can't thank you enough. Most of all, to my partner in crime, Aimee Sabri, for her love, endless support and awesome dinners.

Sandra Bao Many people helped me on this guide, and I thank everyone profusely. My *porteño* godparents, Elsa and Norberto Mallarini, were always there for me and ready to stuff me with absolutely delicious homemade cooking; Andrew McGregor was a fab roommate and endlessly entertaining – see you at the movies, Wayward Son! Thea Morton was a great help and an even better dinner companion; Jorge Barchi knows more about the working details of BA than anyone I can think of; Roberto Frassinetti and Florencia Rodríguez are super people and outstanding tour guides; Josh Hinden is just a very cool dude; Lucas Markowiecki is in a class by himself.

Many thanks also to Sylvia Zapiola, Rachel Loftspring, Carlos Kaplan and Eduardo Tagliani for their help and opinions, and to the countless other *porteños* and expats I met who helped me out in their own way. Thanks to Suki Gear, for doing all the work back in Oakland. Special gratitude to my supportive parents, David and Fung, and to my brother, Daniel. And especially to my loving husband, Ben Greensfelder, without whose help I could not have finished this book.

Andrew Dean Nystrom Mil gracias a Pablo, la Federación Gaucha de Tierra del Fuego y toda la fa-

---

THE LONELY PLANET STORY

The story begins with a classic travel adventure: Tony and Maureen Wheeler's 1972 journey across Europe and Asia to Australia. There was no useful information about the overland trail then, so Tony and Maureen published the first Lonely Planet guidebook to meet a growing need.

From a kitchen table, Lonely Planet has grown to become the largest independent travel publisher in the world, with offices in Melbourne (Australia), Oakland (USA) and London (UK). Today Lonely Planet guidebooks cover the globe. There is an ever-growing list of books and information in a variety of media. Some things haven't changed. The main aim is still to make it possible for adventurous travelers to get out there – to explore and better understand the world.

At Lonely Planet we believe travelers can make a positive contribution to the countries they visit – if they respect their host communities and spend their money wisely. Every year 5% of company profit is donated to charities around the world.

milia Marquez en Río Grande; a la familia fuegina más típica de Romina para el asado barbaro; las familias Piatti y Galeazzi-Basily; Capitanes Narizón y Cabezón Smith desde el otro Culo del Mundo; Gustavo, Beto, Katu y el equipo de Canal Fun; Sandra Bao for the BA tips; Carolyn Hubbard for her previous research, kind advice and spot-on tips; María de Nahuel; John Simon, Carolina y familia de Estancia Viamonte; Nacho Cabana for the laughs; Samuel at UTVM for the mate; Nancy Pfeiffer and ATMS; Jose Rodriguez; Charly, Bibi y familia; Rodrigo Harding; Danny Feldman; Blanca, Manu y Ian – ¡keep walking!; Melina Paoloni; Gerson Reyes y la familia Adel; Carlos Gonzalez Macaya; Hernán Jofré; Olivier Potart; Raul Satori; la familia Padilla; Alejandro Javier Andres Cardenas Lobo y familia; Dan Buck and Anne Meadows; Armado Perez; Wolf Kloss; Guingui Williams and Michael Gough; Gonzalo Badiola y familia; Beth Rypins; Brian Ruszczyk and the entire H20 Patagonia team; Suki, Danny, Lucas and the entire LP crew; Joe, Dolores, mom, dad, Morgan and Gus for keeping the fire going at home; y finalmente, al Vírgen de Luján.

Lucas Vidgen Once again, my biggest thanks go to the people of Argentina, for creating a country that's so much fun to travel in, research and write about. Special mention should go to all the bus station staff for never asking why I wanted times and prices for 18 destinations and didn't end up buying a ticket to any of them.

To the staff in all the tourist offices, for their unending smiles and mountains of information, and especially to the woman in Cachi, who asked if I was Spanish – I'm still smiling about that one!

Thanks to América Hernández, Andrés Curci, Léon Ibarra, Isabel Guzmán, Peta Neylan, Alberto Mitre, Alejandro Fernández and Diego Alimena. To everyone I didn't get a chance to catch up with this time – in particular Andrew Starke, Aida Martinez and Teresa Armendariz – next time, I promise!

To my fellow authors, Danny, Sandra, Andrew and Molly – always a pleasure to get together and talk shop, even if it is only by email sometimes.

Lastly, big ups to Control Machete, Molotov and Juanes, for providing a (not very Argentinean) soundtrack to my trip.

CREDITS
Commissioning Editor Suki Gear
Coordinating Editor Sasha Baskett
Coordinating Cartographers Andrew Smith, David Connolly
Coordinating Layout Designer Katherine Marsh

Managing Editor Bruce Evans
Managing Cartographer Adrian Persoglia
Assisting Editors Julia Taylor, Charlotte Orr, Laura Gibb
Assisting Cartographers Laurie Mikkelson, Owen Eszeki, Jack Gavran
Color & Cover Designer Sonya Brooke
Project Manager Fabrice Rocher
Language Content Coordinator Quentin Frayne

Thanks to Jeff Campbell, Gus Balbontin, Jodie Martire, Glenn Beanland, Fiona Siseman, Laura Jane, Wayne Murphy, Kate McDonald, Adriana Mammarella and Sally Darmody.

THANKS from Lonely Planet
Many thanks to the following travelers who used the last edition and wrote to us with helpful hints, useful advice and interesting anecdotes.

A Beatriz Abad, Hugo Achugar, Alfons Adam, Jadwiga Adamczuk, Hayley Adams, Doug Adamson, Pat Adamson, Tamila Ahmadov, Volkan Akkurt, Tim Alcott, Erik Alcron, John Alexander, Dai Alford, Daniel Alford, Rune Alkstrand, Martin Allan, Bill Allen, Mariam Allen, Kim Allin, Spencer Allman, Ralph Alquero, Sogol Aminan, Dov Amir, Philip Amphlett, Mercedes Anchezar, Daniel Anderbring, Katrine Helsing Andersen, David & Molly Anderson, Debbie Anderson, Heidi Anderson, Matt Anderson, Pat Anderson, E B Andersson, Belinda Andrews, Miguel Angel Alonso, Guillermo Angel Peisina Lemos, Lois Angharad, Nico Anklam, Wally Apostolakis, Lilian Aquines, Karl Aragundi, Eltonio Aralijo Goncalves, Irene Arce, Judy Arday, Claudia Ardison, Gilles Arie, Wayne Arizmendi, Dudley Arnold, Robert Aronoff, Chris Ashton, Stefan Ast, Tessa Atkins, Ashu Atwal, Jörg Ausfelt, Jenny Auton, Elinor Awkin, Graham & Linda Ayers, Michael Ayling, Christie Ayral, Marfarida Azevedo **B** Carl M Ba, Margit Bachek, Karl Backhaus, John Backiel, Christine Badre, Bernard Badzioch, Erich Baechler, Juan Baiocchi, Bart Bakker, Joze Balas, Chris Ball, David Ballantyne, Philipp Balscheit, Claudia Balscheit, Mandy Baltar, Johannes Bang, Justin Bannister, Richard Barclay, Guy Barker, Arlen L Barn, Carolyn Barnato, Norris Barr, Craig Barrack, Richard Barragan, Kathy Barragan, Nick Barraud, Florence Barrere, Tim Barrett, Dom Barry, Alice Barton, Paul Bates, Mick Bauer, Christoph Baumgarten, Tobias Baumgartner, Jane Beamish, John Beaven, Andrzej Bednarski, Frans Beems, Anja Behrendt, Ben Beiske, Gabrielle & Hilbert Belksma-Rutten, Daphne Bell, Anne-Trine Benjaminsen, Cindy Benner, Matthew David Bennett, Max Berends, Miranda Berends, Alex Berger, Ingregerd Berghall, Soren Berghall, Aran Bergman, Megan Berkle, Tim & Trish Bermon, Fergal Bernard, Irene Bernhard, BJ Bernstein, Goran Berntsson, Joel Bertrand, Mariano Besio, John Beston, Mariana Beuermann, Roberta Bianchi, Loretta Biasutti, Sebastiaan Biehl, Renee Bikker, Iain Bird, Monique Birenbaum, Ueli Bischof, Simon Bishop, Gordon Bissar, Alastair Bisson, Caroline Black, Frances Black, Paul Black, Ray Black, Ray E Black, Colleen Blake, Roberto Blanc, Yaroslav

Blanter, Frank Blattner, Pascal Bleuel, Sandra Bleuel, Esther Bloem, Marisa Blumhagen, Michele Bocacci, Giorgio Boccia, Avi Bodha, Annette Bodier, Juergen Boehler, Andre Boessenkool, Paul Bol, Cristian Bolero Sutter, Olivier Bongard, Justin Boocock, Clelia Booman, Wilm-Jan Boon, Chris Booth, Andy Bornmann, Savannah Borsellino, Mireille Bos, Brenda Bosch, Marelie Bosch, Eric Boschmann, Marcel & Claudia Bot, Liliam Boti Llanes, Anthony Boult, Eddie Bowden, Patrick Bowes, Jeff Bowman, William Bradley, A Bregman, Francis Brekke, Gert-jan Bremer, Laura Breuning, Catherine Brew, Fran Brew, Chantal Briere, Jenny Brierley, Mark Briggs, Marianne Brito, Larissa Broger, Richard Brooks, Linda Broschofsky, Berne Broudy, Dawson Brown, Terry Brown, Jean-Yves Bruckert, Sabine Brueschweiler, Stephane Bryant, Nicky Buckingham, Quentin Buckingham, Peter Bugarski, Ian Bunton, Simon Burges, Paige Burgess, Rollo Burgess, Matthew Burke, Agi & Shanf Burra, Carlos Alberto Burset, Stephen Busack, Soeren Buschmann, Robert Bussewitz, Sandra & Diego Bustillo, Helen Butler, Pedro Butler, R Butler, Bente Buus, Jasper F Buxton **C** Jose Antonio Caballero, Charles Calderbank, Valerie Calderbank, Joshua D Callahan, Liz Callegari, Michele Callisaya, Emma Callow, Julie Cameron, Kerry Cameron, Veronica Caminos, Jose Candeias, Nadia Candolt, Stuart Candy, Laura Cangas, Janko Capel, Eric Carlson, Caroline Carlsson, Juan Carrera, Laura Carrizo, Roz Carter, Jens Cartsen Jackwerth, Jordi Carvallo, Florencia Casado, Debora Casarin, Anne Casement, Carmel Castellan, Ana Cristina Cavalcante Goncalves, Mike Cavendish, Julio Cesar Lovece, Deepak Chadha, Jukie & Antoine Chambaz, Mm Chan, Anthony Chant, Jenny Chantry, Brandyn Chapman, Matthias Chardon, Pierre Chaurette, Ginni Chave, Alejandro Chavez-Badiola, Matthew Chell, Andrew Chenoweth, Jeff Cheong, Kirsten Claiden-Yardley, Helene Clappaz, Lucy Claridge, Peter Clark, Claire Closmann, Alex Cloutier, Andrew Cockburn, Karen Cockburn, Magdalena Coelho, Milton Cogheil, Dale Coghlan, Kevin Coghlan, Niv Cohen, Helen Cole, Neil Cole, Phillip Colin, Pablo Collavino, Peter Collins, Shawn Collins, Simona Colombo, David Connor, Filippa Connor, Ravindra Conway, Chris Cook, Kit Cooper, Dan Coplan, Edward Corbett, Polly Corbishley, Aaron Corcoran, Leanne Corcoran, Arnaud Corin, Renae Cosgrove, Juan Costa Diez, Bryce Coulter, Bob Coyne, Nina Craig, Laura Creasey, Andrea Crenna, Paul Crovella, Louis Crowe, Pam Crowest, Brian Cuff, Frank Curry, Lauren Cuteliffe **D** Stephan D' Costa, María Aparecida da Costa Felipe, Erin Daldry, Phillip A Dale, Annika Dalén, Andrew Dalton, Alan Damson, Leonne Damson, Elisabethe Dank, John Dank, Robert D'Avanzo, Jane Davey, Phil & Ginny Davies, Natalia Daza, Kimberly de Berzunza, Hans de Bont, Annie de Elia, Michel de Groot, Julianne de Lange, Karen De Roeck, Lydia de Visser, Esther de Waal, Jodie Deignan, Christine Delley, Chris Demathieu, Markus Deml, Uta Dempwolff, Lia Dendraki, Alex DeNeui, Iglesias Denisse, Merel Dessens, Sebastian Detomaso, Damien Diament, Tomas Diaz Mathe, Ian C Dickinson, Natalie Dicks, Donald Dickson, Alison Dieguez, Rose Diekstra, Max Dietrich, Eckhard Dietz, Idshe ten Dijk, Armin Dirks, Martin Djuvfelt, Millie Dobson, Markus Doebele, Eva Dolne, Gabriela Domecq, Juan Pablo Dominguez, Chris Donovan, Robert Dormer, Christoph Dorn, Andreas Dorr, Sergio dos Santos, Niels Doun, Jacqueline Dowling, Joey Doyle, Paul Doyle, Catherine Dragotta, Jason Drautz, Jorg Droste, Christina du Rietz, Catherine Ducrest, Laurent Ducrest, Jan Dudeck, Murray Dulac, Tim Dun, Andrew Duncan, Phil Dunnington, Julio Duran, Alain & Margaret Duval, Denis Duysens, Nicole Dyer, Chris Dziadul **E** Manuel E, Yasmin Ebrahim, Sandy Edelsward, Roger Paul Edmonds, Kurt Egger, Noelle Ehrenkaufer, Michael Eiche, Patrick Ekerot, John Eklund, Reneko Elema, Peter Eliason, Dana Ellerbrock, Stephen Ellis, Klaus Elskamp, Philippa Eng, Mannie English, Sarah Eno, Donald C Erbe, Maren Erchinger, Susan Erk, Sara Esrick, Marie Eugelstad, William Evelyn, Ann Ez El Din **F** Bobby F, Jan Faassen, Bruce Faecher, Alexandre Fage-Moreel, Sze Fairman, Kristen Faith, Graciela Falivene, Seb Falk, Michael Feder, Judy Fennessy, Gazda Ferenc, Mauren Fergus, Antonia Fernandez, Juan-Pablo Fernández, Alexis Ferrand, Marcelo Ferrante, Andreas Fertin, Christina Fetterhoff, Hakon Fiebrig, Arthur Filho, Suki Finney, Claudio Fiore, Alistair Firth, Charlotte Firth, Paul Fish, Kimberly Fisher, Adrian Flash, Sam Fleischner, Doug Fleming, Elisabeth Folkunger, Luca Fontana, Montse Fontellas, Louise Forrest, Kent Foster, Claire Francis, Kay Freebern, Jonathan Freeman, Jay Freistadt, Marjolein Friele, Mark Fritz, Richard Fromer, Ingrid Fuchs, Johannes Fulcher, Rachel Fulcher, Dave Fuller, Lesly Furness, Sophie Fyfe **G** C Gabriel Alperovich, Tim Gage, Matthew Galbraith, Anna Galka, Tomasz Galka, Carlos Galvalizi, Cristian Miglioli Gamarra, Odile Garaffa, Fabian Garbolino, Andres Garcia, Ben Garrett, Sean Garrett, Patrick Garvey, Julia Gaylard, George Gayoso, Melanie Geppert, Eoin Gibbons, Andrew Gibson, Vital Gil, Christopher Gilbert, Juan Pablo Giometti, Katherine Glen, Frans Glissenaar, Ron Glynn, Monti Godfrey, Cecile Golden, Albert D Goldson, Nick Goldwater, Maria Gomez, Pamela Gómez, Agustin Gonzalez Soler, Oscar Gonzalez van Eijk, Lori Goodfellow, Jason Goodman, Jerry Gottlick, Natalie Gracia, Greco Graciela, Luca Graf, Kevin Graham, Robert Grant, Frank Graziano, Charles Green, Megan Green, Nicholas Green, Charles Greenwood, Maura Griffin, David P Grill, Lianne Groothoff, Wendy Gruber, Michael K Gschwind, Tora Gudmundsson, Tora & Anders Gudmundsson, Robson Guedes dos Santos, Flavio Guidotti, Wade Guthrie, Daniel Gutmann, Daniel Gutsell, Matthias Gutzeit, Pierre Guyot **H** Erich Haas, Shir Hadad, Patrick Hagans, Sonja Hagen, Andrea Hagenauer, Bethan Haines, Andrew Hall, Peter Haller, Tessa Hanevelt, Miguel Hanna, Matt Harding, Robert Harding, Remco Harms, Lynda Harpley, Deanna Harris, Samantha Harrison, Imke und Markus Hartig-Jansen, Anthony Harvey, Or Hasson, Gerlind Hauser, Natasha Haverty, Rhonda Hawkins, Simon Hawliczek, Susan Hayre, Peter Heath, Louie Hechanova, Michelle Hecht, Darlene Hector, Sven Hedinger, Sigrid Hegmann, Mike & Linda Hehir, Peter & Rosemarie Heinig, Cyndi Heller, Katrine Helsing Andersen, Chantal Henderson, Neil & Christine Hepburn, Peter Hertrampf, Eitan Hess, Julia Hewett, Dawn Hewitt, Michele Heymann, Kathryn Hiestand, Francesca Hilbron, Paula Hill, John Hinchcliffe, Naida Hindert, M Hinten, Rachel Hirschi, Rebecca Hoffman, Todd Holland, Roos Hollenberg, Trude Holmen, Andrew Holmes, Cynthia Holzapfel, Saskia Hoogerwerf, Leo Horochowski, Koosje van der Horst, Sarah Horton, Clarissa Horwood, Elizabeth Q Howard, Richard Howitt, Melanie Howlett, Jess Smergel Hrog, Amondine Huchette, Jock & Alan Hughes, Katrina Hughes, Stephanie Hughes, David Hulsenbek, Olga Humlová, Jason

Humphreys, David L Huntzinger, Maddie Hurford, Edgar Hutte, Carsten Hviid, Kirsten Hyde **I** Marco Ibarra, Cleide Pires Inácio, Silvia Infanzon, Andrena Irons, Peter Irvine, Nuria Ivorra **J** Bastiaan Jaarsma, Priscilla Jabur, Chloe Jacob, Gygax Jacqueline, Margarete Jager, Robert Jam Klop, Dave James, Ingo Janas, Danny Jannens, Leonie Janssen, Andy Jefferson, Karmen Jehovcan, Alden Jencks, Dorothea Jensen, Jim Jensen, Stephanie Jerosch, Ken Jewkes, Fabio Joffe, Bill Johnson, Carolyn Johnson, Luke Jones, Megan Jones, Wade Jones, Horst Jung, Manfred Jung **K** Dale Kabat, Markus Kaim, Tina Kames, Harry Kangassalo, C Karp, Roswitha Katscher, Yuval Katznelson, Yorgos Kechagioglou, Tom Keeley, Susan Keevil, Horst Kehler, Elisa Kelly, Mary Kelly, Miriam Kelly, Vera Kempe, Julia Kentnor, Ton Kersbergen, Nazruddin Khan, Rolando Kienitz, Paul K Kim, Justine Kirby, Claudia Klein-Hitpass, Josef Klimek, Andrea Kluska, James Knox, Helke Knuetter, Andreas D Koch, Gabi Koch, Steven Koenig, Konstanee Kogler, Stefan Kolb, Anatol Kolendo, Jo-ann Kolmes, Marika Konings, Jim Koppensteiner, Andreas Kornowski, Johanna Koskinen, Adam Kosminski, Michiel Kraak, Frank Krautter, Joanna Kreckler, Gitta Krukenberg, Rainer Krukenberg, Ann Krumboltz, Lars Kuipers, Jessica Kullander, Peter Kunkel **L** Robert la Franco, Kerstin Labatzke, Rene Labrecque, Edith Lackner, Claire Lalande, Peter Lambert, Erik Lampalzer, Donna Lancaster, Jerry Lang, David Langbroek, Christy Lanzl, Markku Larjavaara, Amber Larkin, Chris Larkin, Lise Larsen, Justin LaSala, T B Laursen, Mark Lavery, Karen Lawson, Dominiqu & Siobhan Le Meur, Ron Leach, Isabel Ledesma, Janice Ledwidge, Andrea Lee, Graeme Lee, Howard Lee, Zoe Leighton, Inga Lena, Marcel Lensvelt, Manfred Lenzen, Fabrice Lestideau, Vallann Lester, Kristin Letcher, Anna Levander, Milton Lever, Larry Lewis, Tim Lewis, Gil Liberman, Barbara Lich, Jonathan Lieberman, Ana & Wolfram Lietz, Sigrid Lievens, Frederico Lifsichtz, Henrik B Lindskoug, Manuel Lins, Bill Lira, Sol Lisdero, Beatrice Lits, Alfred Little, Patricia Lodge, Joachim Loeblein, Stefan Loibner, David Longman, Frederic Lopez, Juan Jose Lopez, Agnes Lorgnier, Antoine Lorgnier, Inge Lozano, Andrew Ludasi, Dirk Luebbers, Peter Luescher, A Lukosky, Walt Lukßcs, Francesco Lulli, Sophia Lund, Anita Lung, P D Lynam, Damian Lynch, Fiona Lynch **M** John Macdonald, Gregor Macek, Cyntia Machado, Ron Machado, Mary Mackenzie, Sebastian Madina, Bob Magnus, Marcella Magotti, Kimberly Mahony, Rene Mally, Richard Manasseh, Fabian Mannequin, Nadine Mannequin, Amaya Manzano, Pablo Manzano Baena, Alessandro Marco Lindenmann, Will Markle, Milena Marmora, Aaron Marriott, Elizabeth Marriott, June Marshall, Peter Marson, Darlene Martin, Santiago Martin, Trajan Martin, David Martinez, George Martinez, Daniel Masse, E Massrey, Fatimah Mateen, Mario Mathieu, Joyce Matthijssen, Maria Maxfield, Pamela Mazza, Richard McCaig, Anderson McCammont, AnneMarie McCarthy, Rick Mccharles, Matt Mccomb, Marilyn McDonald, Scott Mchardy, Mike McKay, Gary McKenzie, Adam McKissack, Colin McLaren, Jane McManus, Mark McNulty, Arnout Meester, Bjoern Mehlhorn, Brett Meier-Tomkins, B Meijer, Marieke Meijer, Martie Meijer, Hans Meister, Ulla Melchiorsen, Ivenise Aparecida Mendes, Gordon Merrick, David Merriman, David Meurer, Gail Meyer, Hamid Mezaib, Mariano Mezzatesta, Monica Middleton, Ross Middleton, James Millership, David Mills, Pete

Minor, Anna Mitchell, David Mitchell, Kjell Mittag, Jesper E Mogensen, Wilfred E Mole, Angel Daniel Molina, Daniel Molina, Ruth Molloy, Andrew Moody, Meredith Moon, Martin Moorcroft, Janie Moore, Amalia Moran, Jose Maria Moreno, Nancy W Morgan, Catherine Moroz, Dan Morris, Doug Morrison, Lars Mosbach, Fernando Moser, Maria Cristina Mossa, Ariel Motta, Fabiano Mouro Viera, Patrick Moyroud, Andreas Mueller, Gabriele Muller, Jennifer Murby, Franklin Murillo, Marco Murillo, Kieran Murphy, Lori Murphy, Nikki Murphy, Shannon Murphy, Christopher Mutlow, Tony Myers **N** Ingrid Naden, Jyoti Nanda, Kiran Nandra, Marco Natalino, John Naughton, Eleanor Nauman, Neal Neal, David Neidermeier, Michelle Nelder, Bruce Nesbitt, Marcia Nesbitt, Chris Neuhauser, Linn Nichels, Jan Nielsen, K Nielsen, Caroline Ninnes, Gustavo Nisivoccia, Eva Nordenskjold, Tegwen Northam, Alejandra Novillo, Petra Nowak, Michael Ny **O** Clare O'Brien, Kerry O'Brien, Roo O'Brien, Betty Odell, Nina Ödling, Arno Oehri, Nina Ogrin, Ole Olesen, Carlos Omar Campora, Philip Opher, Andreas Ort, Dave Orton, Bernadette O'Sullivan, Carsten Ottesen, Alice Owen, Ken Ow-Wing **P** Claudia Pace, Joe Pace, Astrid Padberg, Conny Padt, Joanna Page, Zsolt Palotas, Luciana Volcato Panzarini, Victorio Panzica, Julie Pappas, Spiras Pappas, Efrain Pardo, Alice Parham, Aristea Parissi, Nick Parker, Julia Parkin, Alexa Parliyan, Nisim Parliyan, Johnny Parsons, Michael Partington, Daniel Paz, Douglas Peacocke, Lucy Peile, Marzena Pejlak, Jonathan Penny, Fernanda Perez, Vito Perillo, Steve Perry, Beate Pesch, Don Peterson, Ginger Peterson, Jim Peterson, Walter Pfeiffer, Patricio Phelan, Jerson Philips, Heather Piepkorn, B Pierre, Julie Pike, Shai Pilosof, Stephanie Pinte, Fernanda Pirani, Jan Pisek, Will Pizzolato, Jaroslav Plainer, Mandy Planert, Susan Plant, Cameron Plewes, Janice Plewes, Anne Podt, Andreas Poethen, Eric Pohlman, Chantal Poiesz, Daniel Pokora, Tom Polk, Sergio Gustavo Pollastri, Claudia Ponikowski, Adrian Pope, Marieke Poppe, Elisabeth Post-Madden, James Power, Daniel Pozzi, Jean-Luc Praz, Chris Preager, Reinhard Prenzel, Trish Preston, David Price, Ian Prior, Julie Wood Prosperi, Tatiana Prowell, Laurence Prulho **Q** Mike Quick **R** Ramon Rabinovitch, Maggie Racklyeft, Soni Rajeev, Christa Randzio-Plath, Chris Raphael, Peggy Raphael, Sheikh Rasul, Gill Ratcliffe, Thomas Rau, Steven Reeves, Christian Reh, Ruth Rehwald, Chris Reicher, Malcolm Reid, VIncent Reidy, Sven Remijnsen, Anabella & Maurizio Ribanelli, Roberta Rice, Wilhelm Richard, Jonathan Richards, Mary Richards, Dean Richardson, Norman Richardson, Jana Richter, Veronique Rigaud, Fabbio Robbi, Scott Roberts, Catherine Robinson, Helen Robinson, Mike Robinson, Vanessa Rodd, Renaud Rodier, Cristiane Rodrigues Santos, Alfredo Rodriguez, Gonzalo Rodriguez, Ramiro Rodriguez, Antje Roeder, Julia Rogers, Andrea Rogge, Yael Roitman, Ingrid Rol, Sophia Rome, Jorge Romero, Albert Van de Rooy, Joachim Rose, Tim Rose, Gérard Rosilio, Adriana Rossini, Hans R. Roth, Jens Roth, Thomas Rothe, Catherine Rourke, Harald Roy, Andrew Ruben, Debra Ruben, Hansruedi Ruchti, Dan Ruff, Max Ruggier, Birgit Ruhfus, Michael Ruppert **S** Kathy Saad, Andrea Sadlo, Freddy Esteban Saieg, Rania Salameh, Valentina Salapura, Thomas Salvini, Claude Samuel, Stefan Samuelsson, Sofia San Martino, Claudio Sanchez, Al Sandine, Janet L Sanfilippo, Larissa Sanio, Jorge Santamaria, Anderson Santos, Roney Perez dos Santos, Carolina Sanz, Michael

J Saunders, Ross Savoy, April Schauer, Silke Schefold, Renate Schepen, Andre Scherphof, Iris Schick, Frank Schilbach, Sandra Schilling, German Schlatter, Beate Schmahl, Hauke Schmidke, Bernd Schmidt, Marike Schmidt, Katharina Schneider, Pia Schneider, Alison Schoemann, Marion Schosser, Toralf Schrinner, Andreas Schafer, Helga Schubert, W Schuurman, Marianne Scott, J E O Screen, Sebastian Sorge, Martin Sczendzina, Jonathan Sear, Diego J Seckbach, Meike Seele, Javier Segurotti, Christine Seichter, Lawrence Seifert, Joel Selanikio, Sybille Seliner, Gavin Sexton, Jerome Sgard, Owen Shaffer, Myra Shapiro, Alexander Sharman, Helen & Wolfe Sharp, Amy Shatzkin, Craig Shaw, Peter & Florence Shaw, Robert Shaw, Tersina Shieh, David Shotlander, Bogdan Siewierski, L Siffredi, Vahid Sigari-Majd, Stuart Sill, Heron Silva, Belinda Simmonds, Maxine Simmons, Carolina Simon, Terry Simon, Daniel Simons, Anthony Simpson, Gregg Simpson, Jean Sinclair, Anneke Sips, Nathan Skon, Veronika Skvarova, Jenny Slepian, Jeroen Slikker, Jess Smergel Hrog, Harold Smith, Pete Smith, Sally Smith, Steven Smith, Kaiyote Snow, TJ Snow, Charlotte Snowden, P Sobczuk, Pablo Soledad, Morten Solnordal, Erica Sonneveld, Nia Sopiwnik, Matias Soriano, Maurizio Spadari, Carlo Spagnolo, Tracy Sparkes, Murray Sparks, Kavitha Sreeharsha, John Stahle, Uh Stamm, Richard Stanaway, Lilian Starobinas, Lisa Starr, Heather Staveley, Yariv Steinberg, Juerg Steiner, Sibylle Steiner, Michael Steingress, Anja Stemmer, Paul Steng, Janig Stephens, Andrew Stephensen, Jerri Stephenson, Patrick Sterckx, Peter Sterni, Colin Steward, Don Stewart, Johannes Stigler, Patrick

Stobbs, Carmine Stoffo, Kristin Stokeng, Bill & Ann Stoughton, Fiédéric Stoven, Lena Strandberg, Will Stroll, Peter Struijs, Sandra Stuer, Adrian Stuerm, Alexander Sturm, Tony Sturm, Pavel Suchy, Kathie Sund, Mark Sund, Carl Swanson, Wilbert Sybesma, Jacob Sykes, Pete Syms, Eileen Synnott, Marc Szaleniec **T** Andreas Toelke, Ariola Tamay, Celeste Tarricone, Emanuela Tasinato, Cristina Taubenschlag, Will Taygan, Alexandra Tayler, Allison Taylor, Emily Taylor, Nana Taylor, Tom Taylor, Alison Teeman, Caroline ten Thije-Gerding, Christine Terashita, Angelika & Kurt Teuschl, Sabine Thielicke, John Thiels, Andreas Thiess, Liz Thomas, Michel Thomas, Rod Thomas, John Thomson, Mark Thornburg, Katrin Thuernau, Jacques & Beatriz Thuery, Denise Tibbey, Raquel Tibery, Aranea Tigelaar, Sally Tillett, Jos Tilmans, Bryan Tilson, Carl Tiska, Robert Tissing, A Toelle, Mari Tomine Lunden, Elizabeth Tompkin, Paul Toms, Diego Tonelli, Natalie Tornatore, Javier Travin, Heidi Tschanz, Mr Turfrault, Mark Turner, David Twine, Tom Tyler **U** Stefan Uhl, Laura Uittenbogaard, Lorena Uriarte **V** M Valitchek, Marcelo Vallejos, Zoltan Vamosi, Barbara van Amelsfort, Dave Van de Lindeloof, Reijco Van De Pol, Nancy Van de Putte, Maurits van den Boorn, Iris van den Ham, Christiaan van der Blij, Hans van der Veen, Jurgen van der Zwart, Dionne van Dijk, Stefan Alexander van Dijk, Hans van Dommele, Ingrid van Dommele, Natalie van Eckendonk, Martijn van Geelen, Fred van Geloof, Paul van Homelen, Regina Van Horne, Stan Van Loon, Christophe Van Overloop, Berry van Waes, Ingrid Van Wentlann, Steven Vanderhilst, María Varela, Robert Varga, Fernando Velazquez, Ann Vercouture, Janaína Vergara, Malin M Vestheim, Sebastian Villarreal, Thomas Villette, Brenda Villoria, Phil Vincent, Karina V M, Marion Vogel, Barbara Vorburger, Peer Voss, Elin Vrang, Jens Vrang **W** Eric Wagensonner, James Wainwright, Michael Walensky, Rory Walsh, Jeanie Wantz, J P Watney, Herb Watson, Robert Watson, Michael Watt, Carrie Wayne, Wilford Weeks, Frank Weidenmueller, John Weingarten, Alexander Weissmann, Amanda Wells, Jonas Wernli, Stephen G Wesley, Alex West, Linda White, Shelly White, Deborah Whitehill, Harry Whitehill, Corinne Whiting, David Wickham, John Wight, Stephanie Wildes, Hanna Wilhelm, Henrietta Wilkins, Wayne & Pat Williams, Russell Willis, Anne Wilshin, Sylvia Wilson, Godofredo Wimmer, Norbert Winkler, Simon Winterburn, Yvonne Withers, Jeff Woakes, Elias Wolfberg, Kim Wolfenden, Andrew Wolton, Nick Wood, Sophie Wood, Jennifer Worsham, Darren Wosol, John Wray, Neil Wray, Eoin Wrenn, Bernie Wright, Heather Wright, John M Wright, Lisa Wright, Sarah Wright, Mary Lee Wu, Martin Wunderlich, Prescott Wurlitzer **Y** Ariel Yablon, Maite Yael, Hagai Yanay, Darrin Yoder, Andrew Young, G Michael Yovino-Young **Z** Sylwia Zablocka, Dasa Zabric, Martina & Basil Zavoico, Dieter Zeiml, Paula Zimbrean, Roland Zimmerman, Phil Zirngast, Don Zobel, Vamosi Zoltan, Georg Schulze Zumkley

SEND US YOUR FEEDBACK

We love to hear from travelers – your comments keep us on our toes and help make our books better. Our well-traveled team reads every word on what you loved or loathed about this book. Although we cannot reply individually to postal submissions, we always guarantee that your feedback goes straight to the appropriate authors, in time for the next edition. Each person who sends us information is thanked in the next edition – and the most useful submissions are rewarded with a free book.

To send us your updates – and find out about Lonely Planet events, newsletters and travel news – visit our award-winning website: **www.lonelyplanet.com/feedback**.

Note: We may edit, reproduce and incorporate your comments in Lonely Planet products such as guidebooks, websites and digital products, so let us know if you don't want your comments reproduced or your name acknowledged. For a copy of our privacy policy visit www.lonelyplanet.com/privacy.

ACKNOWLEDGMENTS

Globe on back cover © Mountain High Maps 1993 Digital Wisdom, Inc.

Daniel Buck and Anne Meadows for the boxed text 'Butch & Sundance's Patagonian Refuge.'

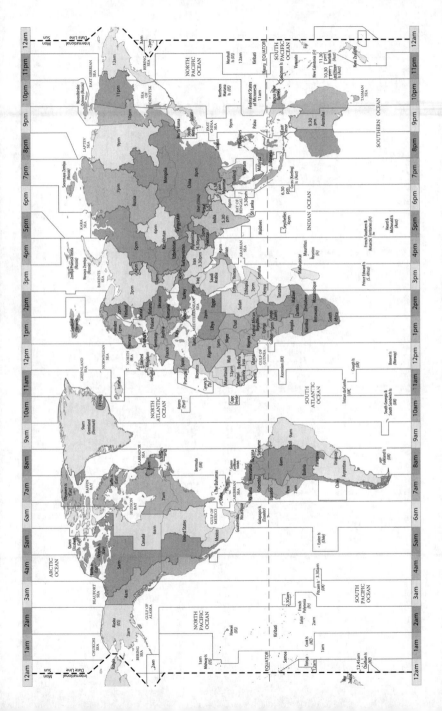

Index

Index

000 Map pages
000 Location of color photographs

INDEX

000 Map pages
000 Location of color photographs

000 Map pages
000 Location of color photographs

INDEX

MAP LEGEND

ROUTES

Tollway	One-Way Street
Freeway	Street Mall/Steps
Primary Road	Tunnel
Secondary Road	Walking Tour
Tertiary Road	Walking Tour Detour
Lane	Walking Trail
Track	Walking Path
Unsealed Road	Pedestrian Overpass

TRANSPORT

Ferry	Rail
Metro	Rail (Underground)
Monorail	Tram
Bus Route	Cable Car, Funicular

HYDROGRAPHY

River, Creek	Canal
Intermittent River	Water
Swamp	Lake (Dry)
Glacier	Lake (Salt)

BOUNDARIES

International	Regional, Suburb
State, Provincial	Cliff
Disputed	

AREA FEATURES

Airport	Land
Area of Interest	Mall
Beach, Desert	Market
Building	Park
Campus	Reservation
Cemetery, Christian	Rocks
Cemetery, Other	Sports
Forest	Urban

POPULATION

○ CAPITAL (NATIONAL)	◉ CAPITAL (STATE)
● Large City	● Medium City
● Small City	○ Town, Village

SYMBOLS

Sights/Activities

	Beach
	Castle, Fortress
	Christian
	Jewish
	Monument
	Museum, Gallery
	Pool
	Ruin
	Skiing
	Winery, Vineyard
	Zoo, Bird Sanctuary

Eating

	Eating

Drinking

	Drinking
	Café

Entertainment

	Entertainment

Shopping

	Shopping

Sleeping

	Sleeping
	Camping

Transport

	Airport, Airfield
	Border Crossing
	Bus Station
	General Transport

Other

	Other Site
	Parking Area

Information

	Bank, ATM
	Embassy/Consulate
	Hospital, Medical
	Information
	Internet Facilities
	Police Station
	Post Office, GPO
	Telephone

Geographic

	Lookout
	Mountain, Volcano
	National Park
	Pass
	River Flow
	Shelter, Hut
	Waterfall

LONELY PLANET OFFICES

Australia
Head Office
Locked Bag 1, Footscray, Victoria 3011
☎ 03 8379 8000, fax 03 8379 8111
talk2us@lonelyplanet.com.au

USA
150 Linden St, Oakland, CA 94607
☎ 510 893 8555, toll free 800 275 8555
fax 510 893 8572, info@lonelyplanet.com

UK
72–82 Rosebery Ave,
Clerkenwell, London EC1R 4RW
☎ 020 7841 9000, fax 020 7841 9001
go@lonelyplanet.co.uk

Published by Lonely Planet Publications Pty Ltd

ABN 36 005 607 983

© Lonely Planet 2005

© photographers as indicated 2005

Cover photographs: Gaucho Argentina, Michael Friang/Alamy (front); Perito Moreno Glacier, Wes Walker/Lonely Planet Images (back). Many of the images in this guide are available for licensing from Lonely Planet Images: www.lonelyplanetimages.com

All rights reserved. No part of this publication may be copied, stored in a retrieval system, or transmitted in any form by any means, electronic, mechanical, recording or otherwise, except brief extracts for the purpose of review, and no part of this publication may be sold or hired, without the written permission of the publisher.

Printed by SNP Security Printing Pte Ltd, Singapore

Lonely Planet and the Lonely Planet logo are trademarks of Lonely Planet and are registered in the US Patent and Trademark Office and in other countries.

Lonely Planet does not allow its name or logo to be appropriated by commercial establishments, such as retailers, restaurants or hotels. Please let us know of any misuses: www.lonelyplanet.com/ip

Although the authors and Lonely Planet have taken all reasonable care in preparing this book, we make no warranty about the accuracy or completeness of its content and, to the maximum extent permitted, disclaim all liability arising from its use.